enVision™ Algebra 1

Student Edition

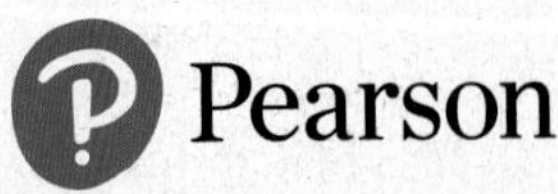

ISBN-13: 978-0-328-93157-6
ISBN-10: 0-328-93157-8

7 19

Contents in Brief

enVision™ Algebra 1

Reviewers & Consultants

Mathematicians

David Bressoud, Ph.D.
Professor Emeritus of Mathematics
Macalester College
St. Paul, MN

Karen Edwards, Ph.D.
Mathematics Lecturer
Harvard University
Cambridge, MA

Teacher Reviewers

Jennifer Barkey
K-12 Math Supervisor
Gateway School District
Monroeville, PA

Miesha Beck
Math Teacher/Department Chair
Blackfoot School District
Blackfoot, ID

Joseph Brandell, Ph.D.
West Bloomfield High School
West Bloomfield Public Schools
West Bloomfield, MI

Andrea Coles
Mathematics Teacher
Mountain View Middle School
Blackfoot, ID

Julie Johnson
Mathematics/CS teacher (9 - 12)
Williamsville Central Schools
Williamsville, NY

Tamar McPherson
Plum Sr HS/Math Teacher
Plum School District
Pittsburgh, PA

Melisa Rice
Math Department Chairperson
Shawnee Public Schools
Shawnee, OK

Erin Zitka
6-12 Math Coordinator
Forsyth County
Cumming, GA

Jeff Ziegler
Teacher
Pittsburgh City Schools
Pittsburgh, PA

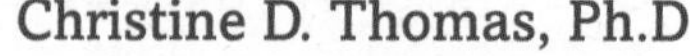

Authors

Dan Kennedy, Ph.D

- Classroom teacher and the Lupton Distinguished Professor of Mathematics at the Baylor School in Chattanooga, TN
- Co-author of textbooks Precalculus: Graphical, Numerical, Algebraic and Calculus: Graphical, Numerical, Algebraic, AP Edition
- Past chair of the College Board's AP Calculus Development Committee.
- Previous Tandy Technology Scholar and Presidential Award winner

Eric Milou, Ed.D

- Professor of Mathematics, Rowan University, Glassboro, NJ
- Member of the author team for Pearson's **enVision**math**2.0** 6-8
- Member of National Council of Teachers of Mathematics (NCTM) feedback/advisory team for the Common Core State Standards
- Author of *Teaching Mathematics to Middle School Students*

Christine D. Thomas, Ph.D

- Professor of Mathematics Education at Georgia State University, Atlanta, GA
- Past-President of the Association of Mathematics Teacher Educators (AMTE)
- Past NCTM Board of Directors Member
- Past member of the editorial panel of the NCTM journal *Mathematics Teacher*
- Past co-chair of the steering committee of the North American chapter of the International Group of the Psychology of Mathematics Education

Rose Mary Zbiek, Ph.D

- Professor of Mathematics Education, Pennsylvania State University, College Park, PA
- Series editor for the NCTM *Essential Understanding* project

Contributing Author

Al Cuoco, Ph.D

- Lead author of CME Project, a National Science Foundation (NSF)-funded high school curriculum
- Team member to revise the Conference Board of the Mathematical Sciences (CBMS) recommendations for teacher preparation and professional development
- Co-author of several books published by the Mathematical Association of America and the American Mathematical Society
- Consultant to the writers of the Common Core State Standards for Mathematics and the PARCC Content Frameworks for high school mathematics

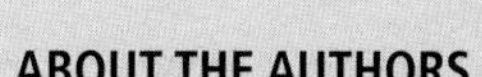

enVision™ Algebra 1 offers a carefully constructed lesson design to help you succeed in math.

Step 1 At the start of each lesson, you and your classmates will work together to come up with a solution strategy for the problem or task posed. After a class discussion, you'll be asked to reflect back on the processes and strategies you used in solving the problem.

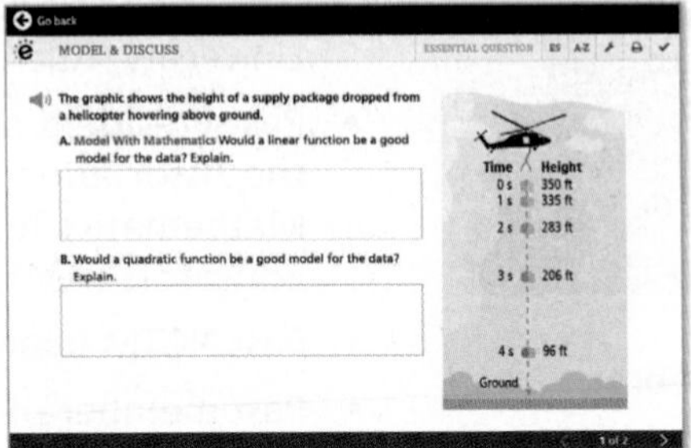
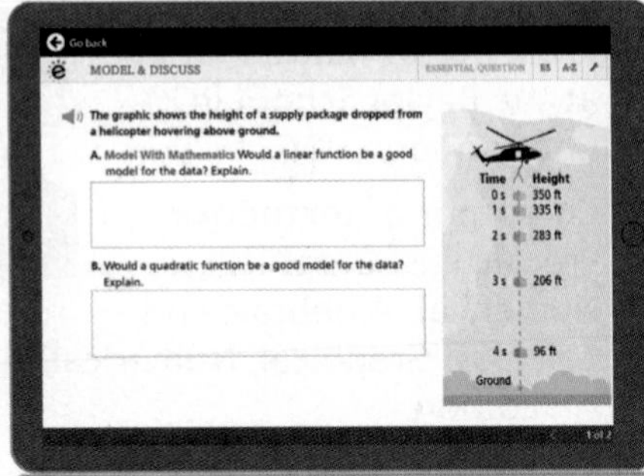

Step 2 Next, your teacher will guide you through new concepts and skills for the lesson.

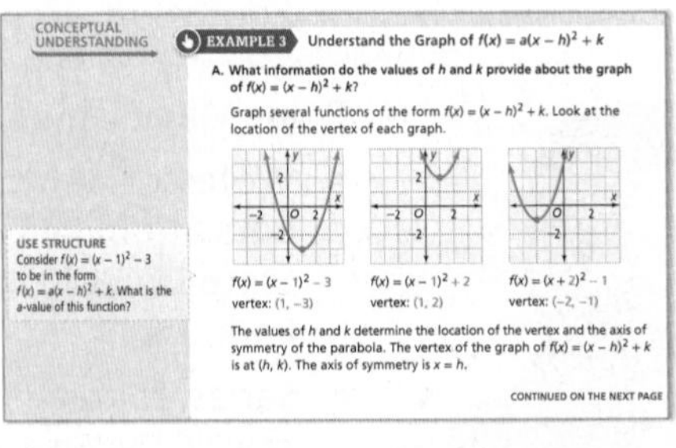
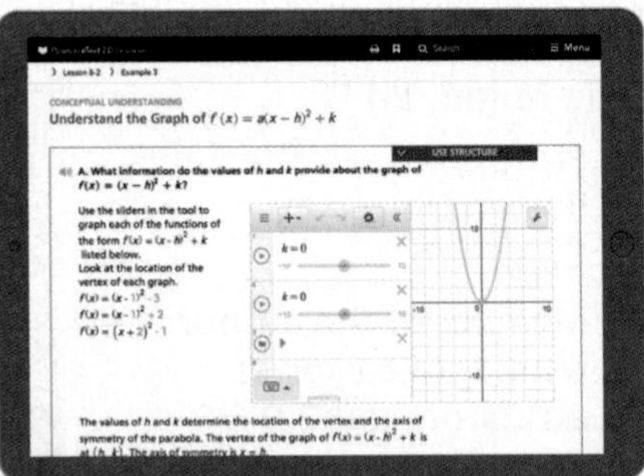

After each example, you work out a problem called the **Try It!** to solidify your understanding of these concepts.

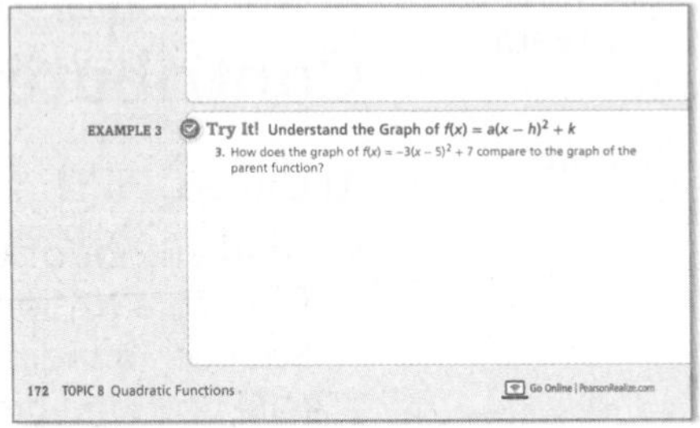
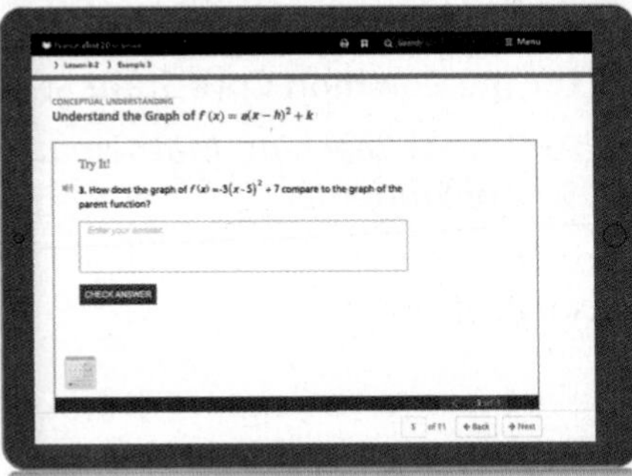

In addition, you will periodically answer **Habits of Mind** questions to refine your thinking and problem-solving skills.

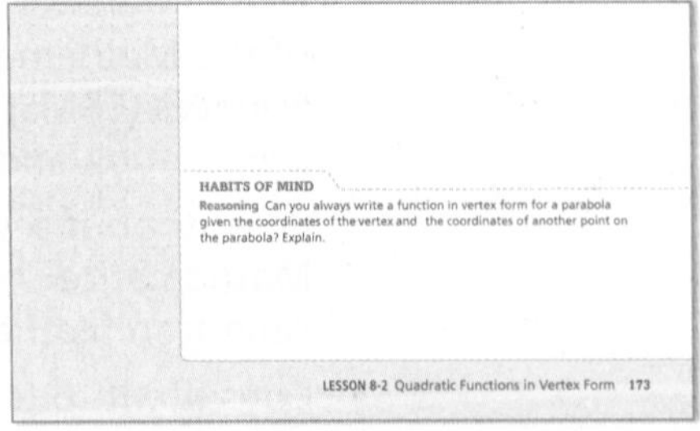
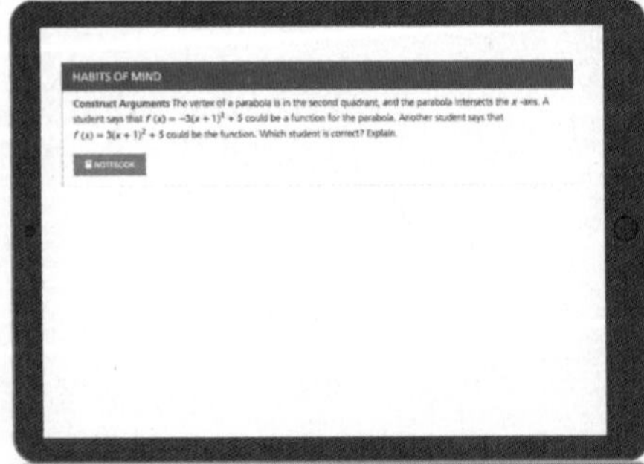

This part of the lesson concludes with a Lesson Check that helps you to know how well you are understanding the new content presented in the lesson. With the exercises in the **Do You Understand?** and **Do You Know How?**, you can gauge your understanding of the lesson concepts.

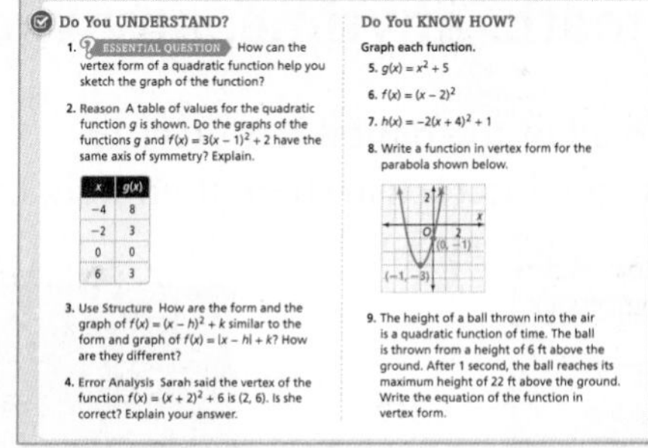

Do You UNDERSTAND?

1. ESSENTIAL QUESTION How can the vertex form of a quadratic function help you sketch the graph of the function?
2. Reason A table of values for the quadratic function g is shown. Do the graphs of the functions g and $f(x) = 3(x - 1)^2 + 2$ have the same axis of symmetry? Explain.

x	$g(x)$
−4	8
−2	3
0	0
6	3

3. Use Structure How are the form and the graph of $f(x) = (x - h)^2 + k$ similar to the form and graph of $f(x) = -(x - h) + k$? How are they different?
4. Error Analysis Sarah said the vertex of the function $f(x) = (x + 2)^2 + 6$ is (2, 6). Is she correct? Explain your answer.

Do You KNOW HOW?

Graph each function.

5. $g(x) = x^2 + 5$
6. $f(x) = (x - 2)^2$
7. $h(x) = -2(x + 4)^2 + 1$
8. Write a function in vertex form for the parabola shown below.
9. The height of a ball thrown into the air is a quadratic function of time. The ball is thrown from a height of 6 ft above the ground. After 1 second, the ball reaches its maximum height of 22 ft above the ground. Write the equation of the function in vertex form.

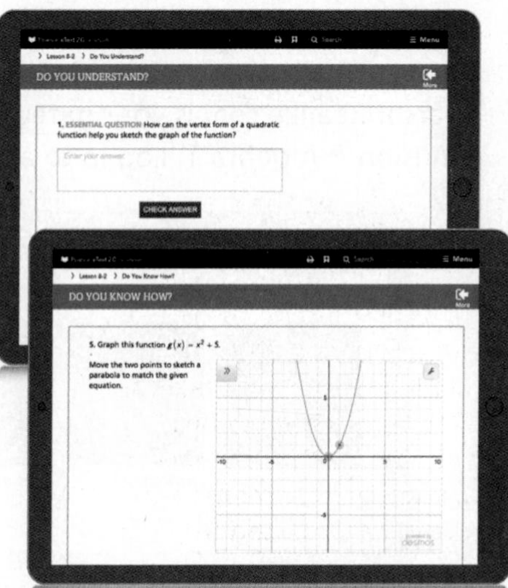

Step 3 In Step 3, you will find a balanced exercise set with **Understand** exercises that focus on conceptual understanding, **Practice** exercises that target procedural fluency, and **Apply** exercises for which you apply concept and skills to real-world situations. The **Assessment Practice** exercises offer practice for high stakes assessments. Your teacher may have you complete the assignment in print or online at PearsonRealize.com

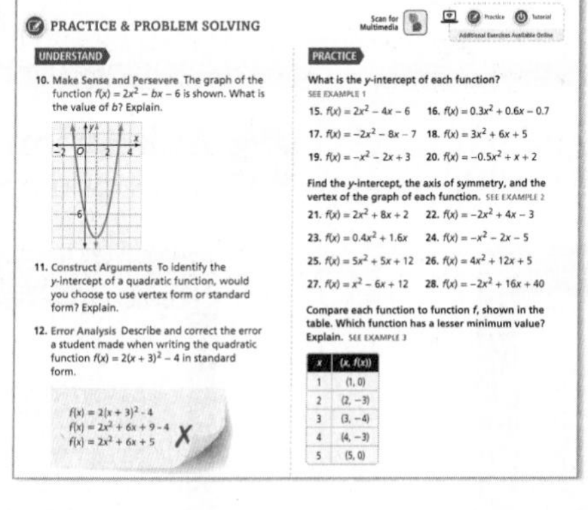

PRACTICE & PROBLEM SOLVING

UNDERSTAND

10. Make Sense and Persevere The graph of the function $f(x) = 2x^2 - bx - 6$ is shown. What is the value of b? Explain.
11. Construct Arguments To identify the y-intercept of a quadratic function, would you choose to use vertex form or standard form? Explain.
12. Error Analysis Describe and correct the error a student made when writing the quadratic function $f(x) = 2(x + 3)^2 - 4$ in standard form.

$f(x) = 2(x + 3)^2 - 4$
$f(x) = 2x^2 + 6x + 9 - 4$
$f(x) = 2x^2 + 6x + 5$

PRACTICE

What is the y-intercept of each function? SEE EXAMPLE 1

15. $f(x) = 2x^2 - 4x - 6$
16. $f(x) = 0.3x^2 + 0.6x - 0.7$
17. $f(x) = -2x^2 - 8x - 7$
18. $f(x) = 3x^2 + 6x + 5$
19. $f(x) = -x^2 - 2x + 3$
20. $f(x) = -0.5x^2 + x + 2$

Find the y-intercept, the axis of symmetry, and the vertex of the graph of each function. SEE EXAMPLE 2

21. $f(x) = 2x^2 + 8x + 2$
22. $f(x) = -2x^2 + 4x - 3$
23. $f(x) = 0.4x^2 + 1.6x$
24. $f(x) = -x^2 - 2x - 5$
25. $f(x) = 5x^2 + 5x + 12$
26. $f(x) = 4x^2 + 12x + 5$
27. $f(x) = x^2 - 6x + 12$
28. $f(x) = -2x^2 + 16x + 40$

Compare each function to function f, shown in the table. Which function has a lesser minimum value? Explain. SEE EXAMPLE 3

x	$(x, f(x))$
1	(1, 0)
2	(2, −3)
3	(3, −4)
4	(4, −3)
5	(5, 0)

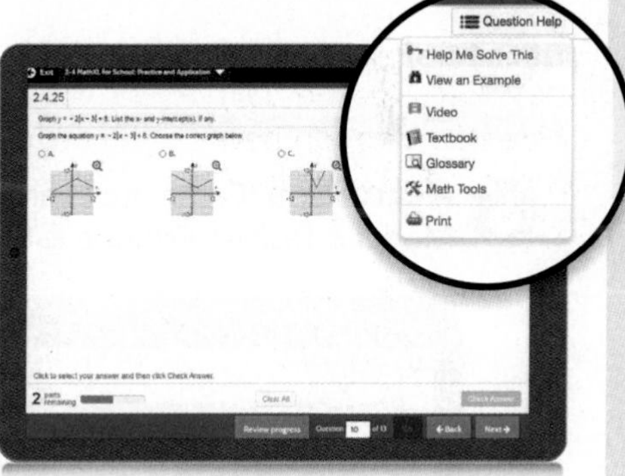

Step 4 Your teacher may have you take the Lesson Quiz after each lesson. You can take the quiz online or in print. To do your best on the quiz, review the lesson problems in that lesson.

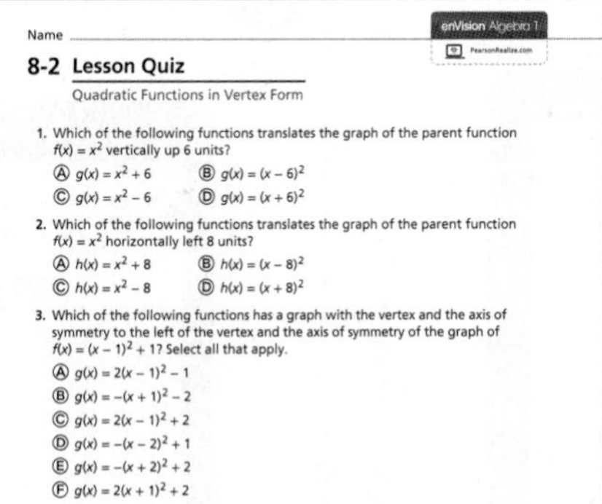

Name

enVision Algebra 1

8-2 Lesson Quiz

Quadratic Functions in Vertex Form

1. Which of the following functions translates the graph of the parent function $f(x) = x^2$ vertically up 6 units?
   Ⓐ $g(x) = x^2 + 6$ Ⓑ $g(x) = (x - 6)^2$
   Ⓒ $g(x) = x^2 - 6$ Ⓓ $g(x) = (x + 6)^2$
2. Which of the following functions translates the graph of the parent function $f(x) = x^2$ horizontally left 8 units?
   Ⓐ $h(x) = x^2 + 8$ Ⓑ $h(x) = (x - 8)^2$
   Ⓒ $h(x) = x^2 - 8$ Ⓓ $h(x) = (x + 8)^2$
3. Which of the following functions has a graph with the vertex and the axis of symmetry to the left of the vertex and the axis of symmetry of the graph of $f(x) = (x - 1)^2 + 1$? Select all that apply.
   Ⓐ $g(x) = 2(x - 1)^2 - 1$
   Ⓑ $g(x) = -(x + 1)^2 - 2$
   Ⓒ $g(x) = 2(x - 1)^2 + 2$
   Ⓓ $g(x) = -(x - 2)^2 + 1$
   Ⓔ $g(x) = -(x + 2)^2 + 2$
   Ⓕ $g(x) = 2(x + 1)^2 + 2$

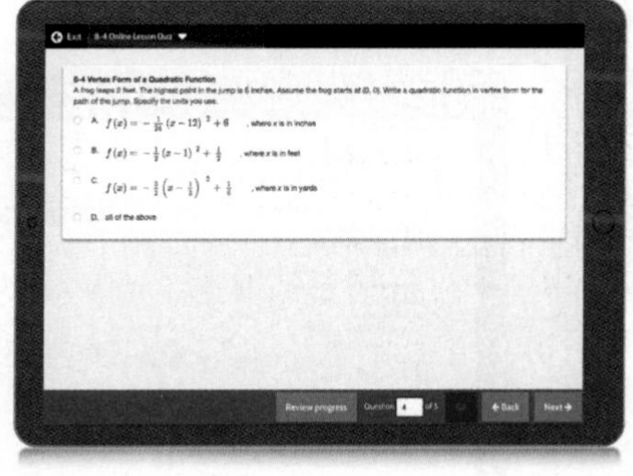

Digital Resources

Everything you need for math, anytime, anywhere.

PearsonRealize.com is your gateway to all of the digital resources for enVision™ Algebra 1. Log in to access your interactive student edition, called Realize Reader.

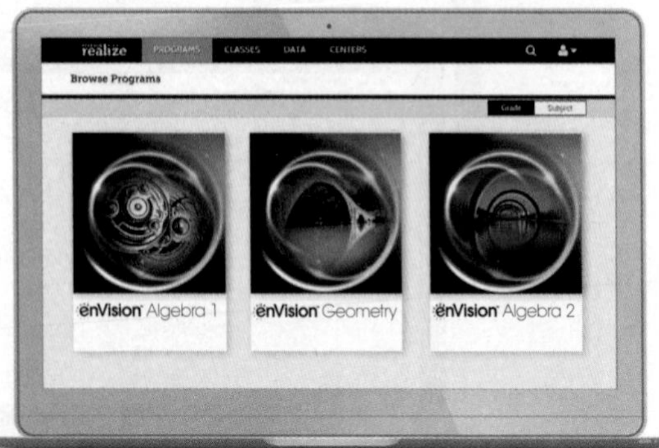

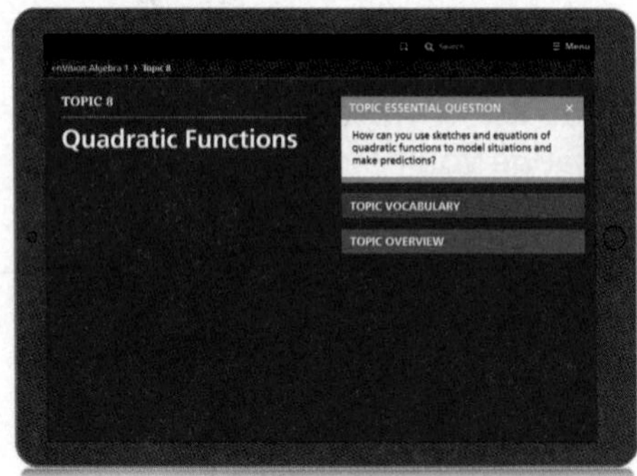

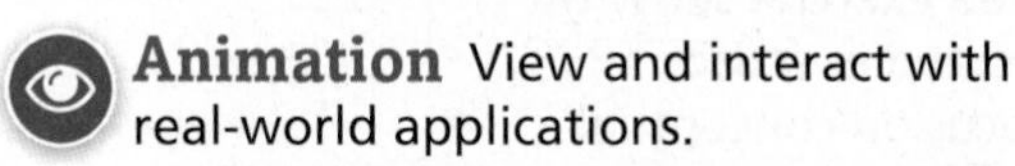

In PearsonRealize, you can:

Activities Complete Explore & Reason, Model & Discuss, Critique & Explain activities.

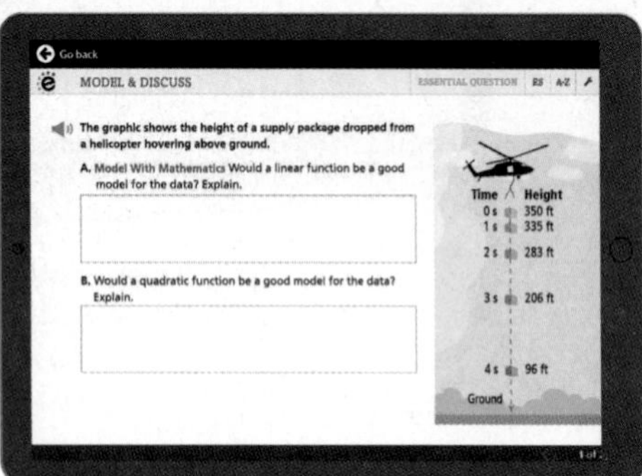

Activities Interact with Examples and Try Its.

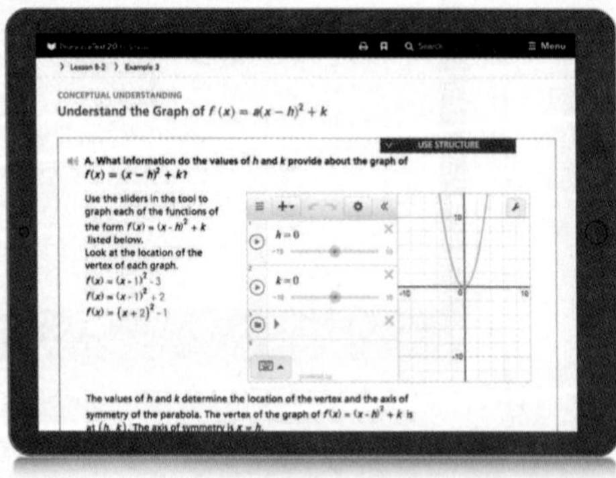

Animation View and interact with real-world applications.

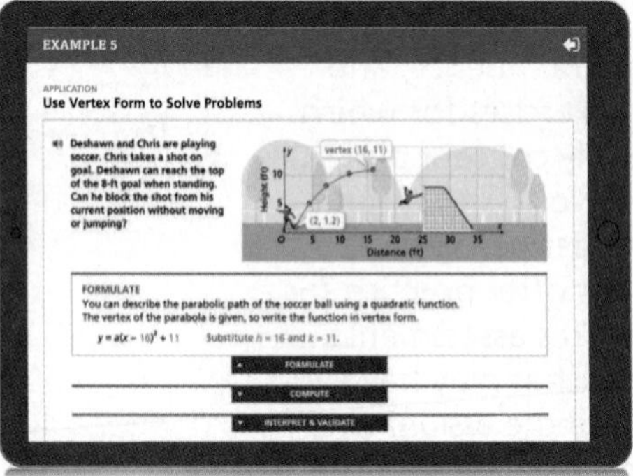

Practice Practice what you've learned.

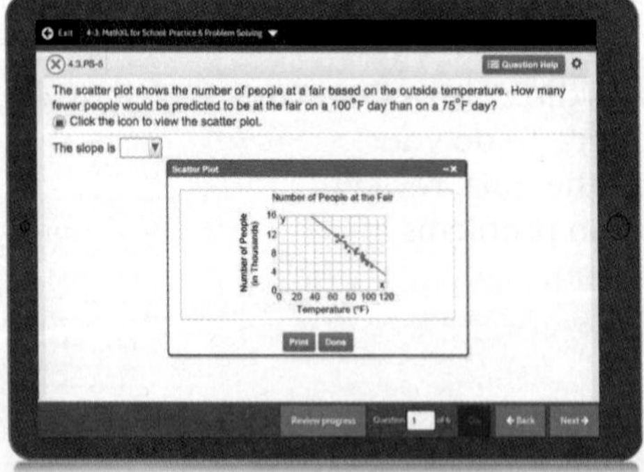

Videos Watch clips to support Mathematical Modeling in 3 Acts Lessons and enVision™ STEM Projects.

Assessment Show what you've learned.

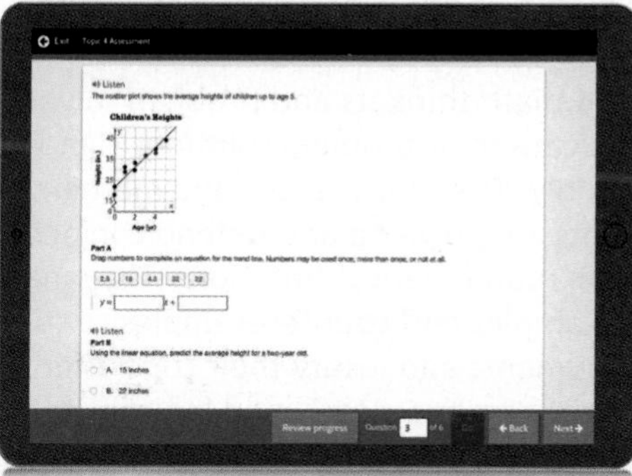

Tutorials Get help from Virtual Nerd, right when you need it.

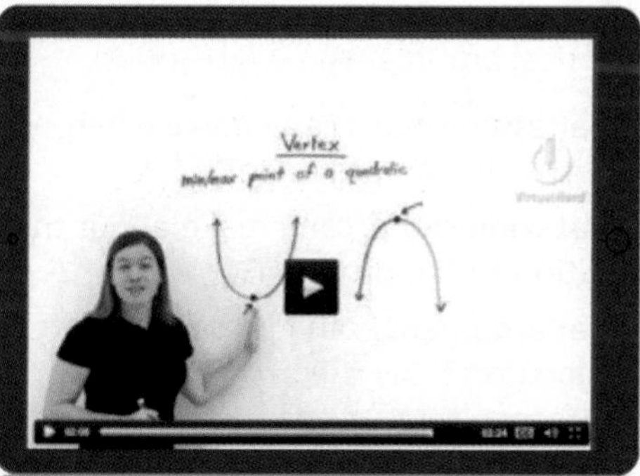

Concept Sumary Review key lesson content through multiple representations.

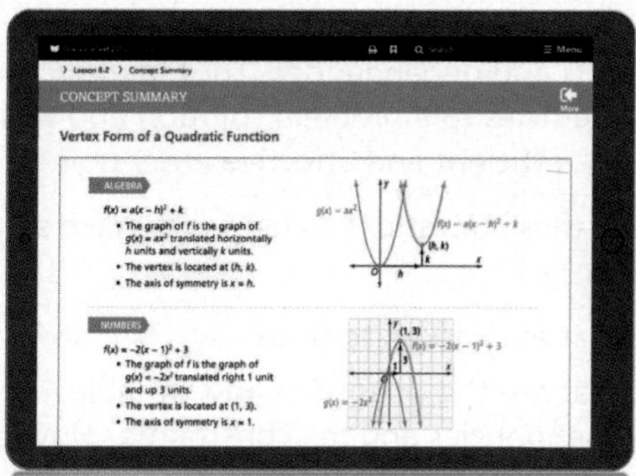

Glossary Read and listen to English and Spanish definitions.

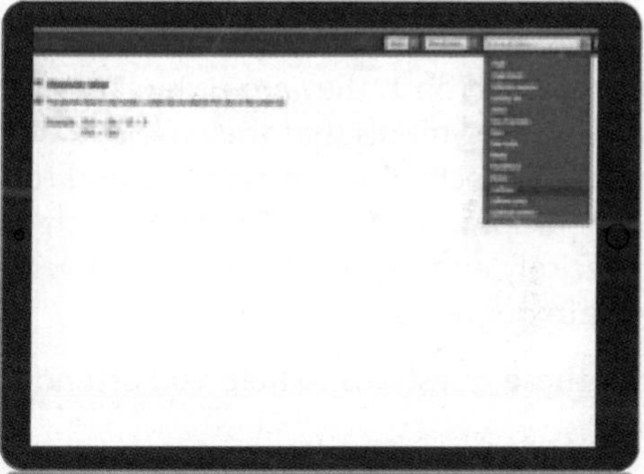

Math Tools Explore math with digital tools and manipulatives.

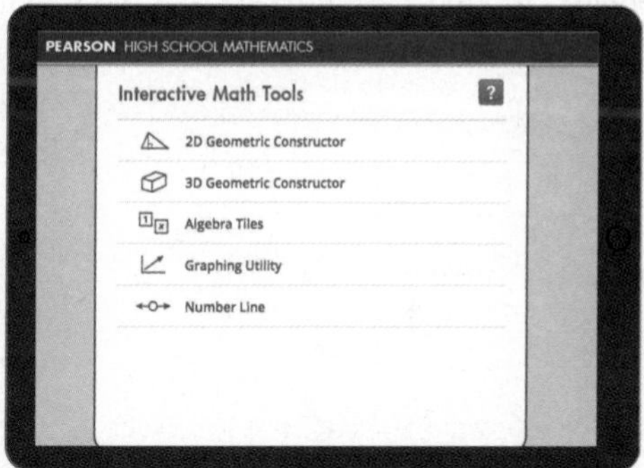

Mathematical Practices and Processes

Problem Solving

Make sense of problems and persevere in solving them.

Proficient math thinkers are able to read through a problem situation and can put together a workable solution path to solve the problem posed. They analyze the information provided and identify constraints and dependencies. They identify multiple entries to a problem solution and will choose an efficient and effective entry point.

Consider these questions to help you make sense of problems.

- What am I asked to find?
- What are the quantities and variables? The dependencies and the constraints? How do they relate?
- What are some possible strategies to solve the problem?

Attend to precision.

Proficient math thinkers communicate clearly and precisely the approach they are using. They identify the meaning of symbols that they use and always remember to specify units of measure and to label accurately graphical models. They use mathematical terms precisely and express their answers with the appropriate degree of accuracy.

Consider these questions to help you attend to precision.

- Have I stated the meaning of the variables and symbols I am using?
- Have I specified the units of measure I am using?
- Have I calculate accurately?

Reasoning and Communicating

Reason abstractly and quantitatively.

Proficient math thinkers make sense of quantities in problem situations. They represent a problem situation using symbols or equations and explain what the symbols or equation represent in relationship to a problem situation. As they model a situation symbolically or mathematically, they explain the meaning of the quantities.

Consider these questions to help you reason abstractly and quantitatively.

- How can I represent the problem using equations or formulas?
- What do the numbers, variables, and symbols in the equation or formula represent?

Construct viable arguments and critique the reasoning of others.

Proficient math thinkers and problem solvers communicate their problem solutions clearly and convincingly. They construct sound mathematical arguments and develop and defend conjectures to explain mathematical situations. They make use of examples and counterexamples to support their arguments and justify their conclusions. When asked, they respond clearly and logically to the positions and conclusions of others, and compare two arguments, identifying any flaws in logic or reasoning that the arguments may contain. They ask questions to clarify or improve the position of a classmate.

Consider these questions to help you construct mathematical arguments.

- What assumptions can I make when constructing an argument?
- What conjectures can I make about the solution to the problem?
- What arguments can I present to defend my conjectures?

Representing and Connecting

Model with mathematics.

Proficient math thinkers use mathematics to represent a problem situation and make connections between a real-world problem situation and mathematics. They see the applicability of mathematics to solve every-day problems and explain how geometry can be used to solve a carpentry problem or algebra to solve a proportional relationship problem. They define and map relationships among quantities in a problem, using appropriate tools. They analyze the relationships and draw conclusions about the solutions.

Consider these questions to help you model with mathematics.

- What representations can I use to show the relationship among quantities or variables?
- What assumptions can I make about the problem situation to simplify the problem?

Use appropriate tools strategically.

Proficient math thinkers strategize about which tools are more helpful to solve a problem situation. They consider all tools, from paper and pencil to protractors and rulers, to calculators and software applications. They articulate the appropriateness of different tools and recognize which would best serve the needs for a given problem. They are especially insightful about technological tools and use them in ways that deepen or extend their understanding of concepts. They also make use of mental tools, such as estimation, to determine the appropriateness of a solution.

Consider these questions to help you use appropriate tools.

- What tool can I use to help me solve the problem?
- How can technology help me solve the problem?

Seeing Patterns and Generalizing

Look for and make use of patterns.

Proficient math thinkers see mathematical patterns in the problems they are solving and generalize mathematics principles from these patterns. They see complicated expressions or equations as single objects composed of many parts.

Consider these questions to help you see structure.

- Can I see a pattern in the problem or solution strategy?
- How can I use the pattern I see to help me solve the problem?

Look for generalizations.

Proficient math thinkers notice when calculations are repeated and can uncover both general methods and shortcuts for solving similar problems.

Consider these questions to help you look for regularity in repeated reasoning.

- Do I notice any repeated calculations or steps?
- Are there general methods that I can use to solve the problem?
- What can I generalize from one problem to another?
- How reasonable are the results that I am getting?

Key Concepts in Algebra 1

Proficiency with key concepts and skills of Algebra I is often cited as a requisite for college- and career-readiness. These foundational concepts of algebraic thinking provide the gateway to advanced mathematics.

At the heart of **enVision™ Algebra 1** is the study of functions. Through the study of specific functions: notably linear, exponential, quadratic functions, you will be able to see the structure of functions, to make generalization about all functions, and to describe the uniqueness of specific functions. Within the study of functions, you will work with various types of real numbers, from rational and radicals, to irrational. You will apply properties of numbers and equality to carry out operations within different functions, all with the goal of seeing the applicability of mathematics to describe and model a wide range of natural or man-made events. The focus on transforming functions will help you build connections between the algebraic and graphical representations of functions.

Listed below are the key concepts that you will be studying in **enVision Algebra 1**.

Number and Quantities

- A monomial consists of a single term made up of a number, a variable, an exponent, or any combination thereof.
- A polynomial is made up of monomials.
- Polynomials can be added, subtracted, and multiplied.
- Polynomials form a system that is closed under the operations of addition, subtraction, and multiplication. This system is analogous to the integers.
- Polynomials can be factored to reveal zeros. The zeros can be used to construct a rough graph of the function defined by the polynomial.
- A rational exponent can be rewritten as a radical expression. A radical expression can be rewritten as a rational exponent.
- Properties of integer exponents can be applied when rewriting expressions with rational and radical exponents.
- Properties of rational and irrational numbers can explain sums and products of rational and irrational numbers.

Solving Equations and Inequalities

- Equations and inequalities in two or more variables represent relationships between quantities. They can be used to model real-world situations.
- Rearranging an equation, using the same reasoning as in solving equations, reveals key information about a quantity of interest.
- Each step in solving an equation can be explained and justified mathematically.
- Properties of real numbers and equality hold for all types of equations. These properties, along with properties of inequality, can be applied to solve any equation or inequality.
- Equations and inequalities in two or more variables can represent constraints of the context they represent.
- A system of equations can have no solutions, one solution, or infinitely many solutions.
- A system of inequalities has infinitely many solutions.
- The solutions to equations and inequalities in two or more variables can be graphed in a coordinate plane.
- The solutions to equations and inequalities in two or more variables can be interpreted as viable or non-viable in relationship to the context represented.
- The graph of an equation in two variables is the set of all its solutions plotted in the coordinate plane.
- The graph of the solution to a linear inequality in two variables is a half-plane on a coordinate plane.
- The graph of the solution to a system of linear inequalities in two variables is the intersection of the corresponding half-planes.
- A system of linear equations can be solved by graphing the system or through algebraic manipulation.
- Linear equations can be solved algebraically through substitution or elimination.

Key Concepts in Algebra 1

A Study of Functions

- A function describes a relationship between two quantities. A function consists of inputs, called the domain, and outputs, called the range.
- A function can be written using function notation.
- A function can be rewritten in different forms. Each form reveals different information about the context it models.
- A function can be evaluated for inputs in its domain.
- A function can be represented in different ways: algebraically, in a graph, in a table, or by a verbal description.
- A function has parameters that can be interpreted in terms of the context it models.
- The domain and range of a function may be restricted based on the contextual situation.
- Key features of the graph of a function reveal information about the relationship between the two quantities that the function models.
- A table of values of a function has key features that reveal information about the relationship between the two quantities that the function models.
- The properties of two (or more) functions of the same type can be compared even when the functions are represented in different ways (algebraically, graphically, numerically in tables, or by verbal descriptions).
- The average rate of change of a function can be estimated from a graph or calculated algebraically.
- The average rate of change of a function over a given interval reveals information about the relationship between the two quantities that the model represents.
- The domain of a function can be determined from its graph.
- Standard functions can be combined using arithmetic operations.
- The graph of a function reveals the type of the function. For example, the graph of these functions is easily recognizable: square root, cube root, and piecewise-defined functions, which include step functions and absolute value functions.
- Changing parameters of a function leads to transformations in the graph of the function.
- The graphs of functions can be transformed in similar and predictable ways.
- A function can be classified as even or odd. An even or odd function is recognizable from its graph or the algebraic expression that represents the function.
- A function can have an inverse function.

Linear Functions and Equations

- A linear function represents a situation in which one quantity changes at a constant rate per unit interval relative to another quantity.
- A linear function grows by equal differences over equal intervals.
- The graph of a linear function is a straight line that can show *x*- and *y*-intercepts.
- An arithmetic sequence is a type of linear function. It can be defined recursively or explicitly. It can be used to model a real-world situation.
- The domain of an arithmetic sequence is a subset of the integers.
- In a linear function, the slope represents the rate of change and the *y*-intercept represents a constant term. These parameters have meaning in the context of a situation or data set.
- Linear equations or functions can be used to represent and solve real-world and mathematical problems.
- A correlation coefficient represents the goodness of fit of a data set to a linear model.

Quadratic Functions and Equations

- A quadratic function or equation can be solved by inspection (e.g., for $x^2 = 49$), taking square roots, completing the square, using the quadratic formula, or by factoring.
- Factoring a quadratic expression reveals the zeros of the function it defines.
- Completing the square in a quadratic expression reveals the maximum or minimum value and the symmetry of the function it defines.
- The parameters of a quadratic function, *a*, *b*, *c*, reveal important information about the graph of the function.
- The graph of a quadratic function shows *x*- and *y*-intercepts, when appropriate, the vertex, intervals of increase and decrease, and the maxima, or minima.
- A system of equations can consist of a linear equation and a quadratic equation in two variables. The system can be solved graphically or algebraically.
- The method of completing the square can be used to transform any quadratic equation in *x* into an equation of the form $(x - p)^2 = q$ that has the same solutions.
- The quadratic formula can be derived from the equation $(x - p)^2 = q$.
- At times, the quadratic formula gives complex solutions in the form $a \pm bi$ for real numbers *a* and *b*.
- A quadratic equation can have two solutions, one solution, or no real solutions.
- The discriminant can be used to determine the number of solutions of a quadratic function.

Exponential Functions and Equations

- An exponential function grows by equal factors over equal intervals.
- An exponential function represents a situation in which a quantity grows or decays by a constant rate per unit interval relative to another.
- A geometric sequence is a type of exponential function. It can be defined recursively or explicitly. It can be used to model a real-world situation.
- The domain of a geometric sequence is a subset of the integers.
- The graph of an exponential function shows *x*- and *y*-intercepts, when appropriate, and end behavior.
- A quantity that increases exponentially eventually exceeds a quantity increasing linearly or quadratically.
- The parameters of an exponential function reveal important information about the context that the function represents.
- The properties of exponents can be used to interpret expressions for exponential functions.
- The properties of exponents can be used to transform expressions for exponential functions.

Statistics

- Data can be represented using a variety of displays. Some data can be plotted on the real number line to create dot plots, histograms, and box plots.
- The shape of the data distribution reveals key information about the center and spread of the data set. It can also reveal extreme outliers in the data set.
- Comparing the shapes of the data distribution for two different data sets reveals important information about the data sets.
- Two-way frequency tables can be used to summarize categorical data for two categories.
- The relative frequencies – joint, marginal, and conditional relative frequencies – of a data set can be interpreted to reveal possible associations or trends in the data.
- Data on two quantitative variables can be represented in a scatter plot. The scatter plot can show how the variables are related.
- A function can be fit to a data set. The function fitted to a data set can be used to solve problems in the context of the data. The function is often linear or exponential.
- The context of a data set may suggest the type of function that fits the data.
- The fit of a function to a data set can be informally assessed by plotting and analyzing residuals.
- Correlation suggests that the behavior of one variable is linked to the behavior of a second variable. Causation indicates that the behavior of one variable is caused by the behavior of a second variable.

TOPIC 1

Solving Equations and Inequalities

TOPIC 2

Linear Equations

TOPIC 3

Linear Functions

TOPIC 4

Systems of Linear Equations and Inequalities

TOPIC 5

Piecewise Functions

TOPIC 6

Exponents and Exponential Functions

TOPIC 7

Polynomials and Factoring

TOPIC 8

Quadratic Functions

TOPIC 9

Solving Quadratic Equations

TOPIC 10

Working With Functions

TOPIC 11

Statistics

TOPIC 1

Solving Equations and Inequalities

TOPIC ESSENTIAL QUESTION

What general strategies can you use to solve simple equations and inequalities?

Topic Overview

Topic Vocabulary

- compound inequality
- element of a set
- formula
- identity
- literal equation
- set
- subset

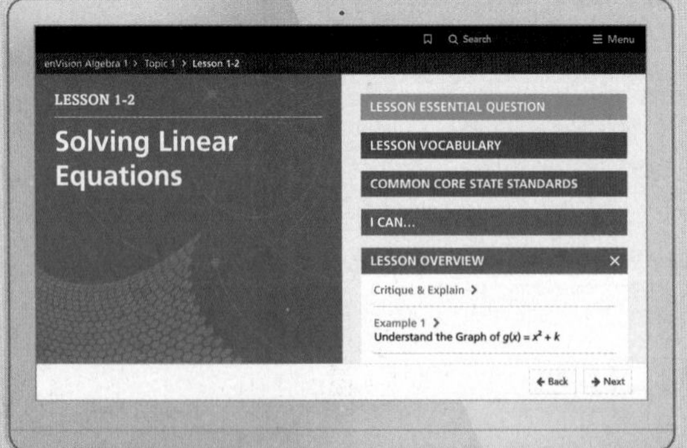

 Go online | **PearsonRealize.com**

Digital Experience

 **INTERACTIVE STUDENT EDITION** Access online or offline.

 **ACTIVITIES** Complete ***Explore & Reason, Model & Discuss***, and ***Critique & Explain*** activities. Interact with Examples and Try Its.

 **ANIMATION** View and interact with real-world applications.

 **PRACTICE** Practice what you've learned.

Collecting Cans

Many schools and community centers organize canned food drives and donate the food collected to area food pantries or homeless shelters.

A teacher may hold a contest for the student who collects the most cans. The teacher will track the number of cans each student brings in. Sometimes students have their own ways of keeping track. You'll see how some students kept track in the Mathematical Modeling in 3 Acts lesson.

TOPIC 1

VIDEOS Watch clips to support ***Mathematical Modeling in 3 Acts Lessons*** and **enVision™ *STEM Projects***.

CONCEPT SUMMARY Review key lesson content through multiple representations.

ASSESSMENT Show what you've learned.

GLOSSARY Read and listen to English and Spanish definitions.

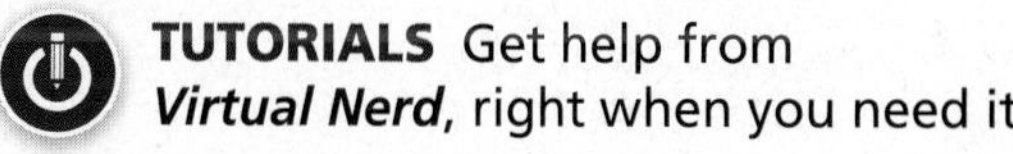

TUTORIALS Get help from ***Virtual Nerd***, right when you need it.

MATH TOOLS Explore math with digital tools and manipulatives.

Did You Know?

The average American teenager spends about 9 hours each day on a digital device.

- 90% of Americans own a cellphone
- 64% of Americans own a smartphone

In general, people keep their cellphones on and with them at all times.

1 GB ≈ 250 songs ≈ 435 photos ≈ 5 mins of HD video

How Teens Spend Their Screen Time

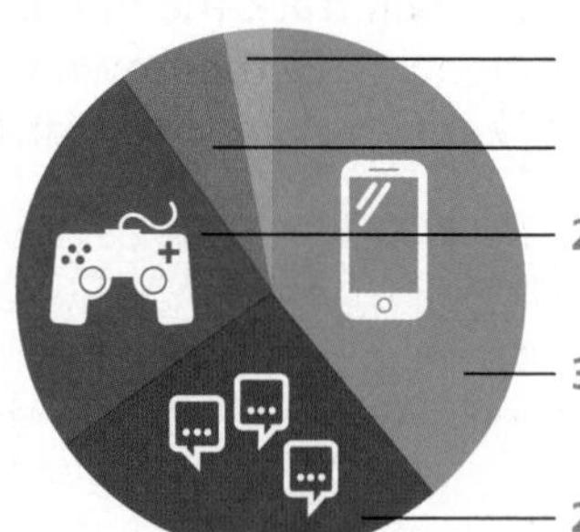

Your Task: Design a Smartphone

Smartphones are many things to many people. You and your classmates will decide what a new smartphone will be able to do, how you want it to look and feel, and how much storage it should have.

1-1 Operations on Real Numbers

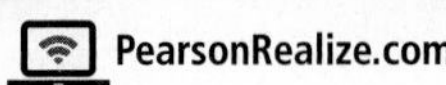

I CAN... reason about operations on real numbers.

VOCABULARY

- element of a set
- set
- subset

CRITIQUE & EXPLAIN

Cindy and Victor are playing a math game. The winner must get three in a row of the same type of real number and justify how the numbers are alike. Cindy said she won because she was able to get three rational numbers on a diagonal. Victor said he won with three positive numbers in a column.

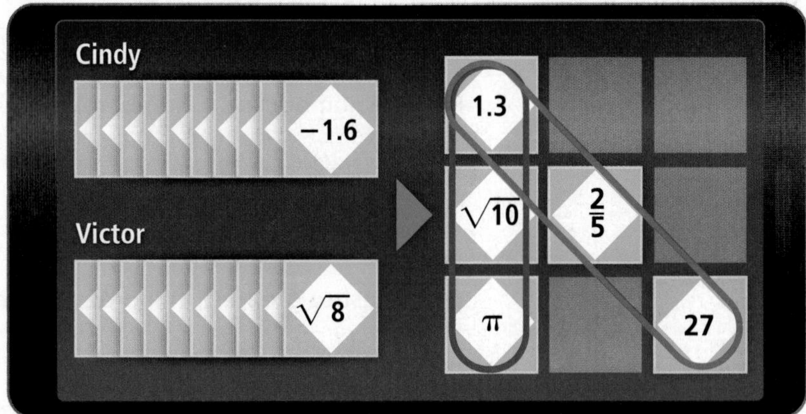

A. Can both players say they won for different reasons? Explain.

B. Reason Can you make other groups using the numbers shown that are all the same kind of real number? In how many ways can you do this?

ESSENTIAL QUESTION

How can you classify the results of operations on real numbers?

EXAMPLE 1 Understand Sets and Subsets

In the set of numbers from 1 to 10, which elements are in both the subset of even numbers, and the subset of multiples of 5?

A **set** is a collection of objects such as numbers. An **element of a set** is an object that is in the set. Write a set by listing the elements, enclosed in curly braces ("{" and "}").

Name of the set → $A = \{1, 2, 3, 4, 5, 6, 7, 8, 9, 10\}$ ← Elements of the set

MAKE SENSE AND PERSEVERE Write out each subset. Then see which elements are common to both.

Set B is a **subset** of set A if each element of B is also an element of A.

$B = \{2, 4, 6, 8, 10\}$ ← Elements of A that are even

$C = \{5, 10\}$ ← Elements of A that are multiples of 5

The number 10 is the only number that is an element of both subsets.

Try It! **1.** Which numbers in set A are elements in both the subset of odd numbers and the subset of multiples of 3?

APPLICATION

EXAMPLE 2 Compare and Order Real Numbers

Jim is playing a math game where he needs to put a set of three cards in numerical order. His cards show $\frac{40}{11}$, $\sqrt{\frac{324}{36}}$, and $\sqrt{10}$. Order the cards from least to greatest.

> **STUDY TIP**
> It is easier to compare and order real numbers when they are all in the same form. Rewrite real numbers to the equivalent decimal form so you can compare them easily.

Find the decimal equivalent for each number.

$\frac{40}{11} = 3.\overline{63}$ $\quad\sqrt{\frac{324}{36}} = \frac{18}{6} = 3$ $\quad\sqrt{10} \approx 3.2$

Plot the numbers on a number line.

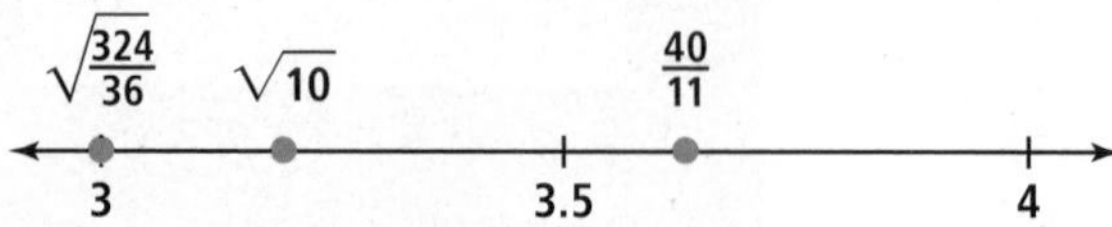

From least to greatest, the order of the cards is $\sqrt{\frac{324}{36}}$, $\sqrt{10}$, and $\frac{40}{11}$.

Try It! 2. Order each set of cards from least to greatest.

a. $0.25, \sqrt{\frac{1}{9}}, \frac{6}{25}$

b. $\sqrt{\frac{121}{25}}, 2.25, \sqrt{5}$

CONCEPTUAL UNDERSTANDING

EXAMPLE 3 Operations With Rational Numbers

A. Is the sum of two rational numbers always a rational number?

You can try several different cases of adding two rational numbers.

$\frac{1}{2} + \frac{1}{3} = \frac{5}{6}$ $\quad\frac{7}{8} + \frac{3}{4} = \frac{13}{8}$ $\quad\frac{11}{5} + \frac{1}{6} = \frac{71}{30}$

In each case, the sum is also rational. But you cannot try *every* pair of rational numbers since there are infinitely many of them. How can you know whether it is true for *all* rational numbers?

Use variables to represent any rational number.

a, b, c, and *d* are integers with $b \neq 0$, and $d \neq 0$.

$$\frac{a}{b} + \frac{c}{d} = \frac{ad}{bd} + \frac{bc}{bd}$$
$$= \frac{ad + bc}{bd}$$

Since $b \neq 0$ and $d \neq 0$, $bd \neq 0$ also.

Since $ad + bc$ and bd are integers, and $bd \neq 0$, the sum is rational.

B. Is the product of two rational numbers always a rational number?

Use the same strategy as in part A, using variables to represent any rational number.

a, b, c, and *d* are integers with $b \neq 0$, and $d \neq 0$.

$$\frac{a}{b} \bullet \frac{c}{d} = \frac{ac}{bd}$$

Since $b \neq 0$ and $d \neq 0$, $bd \neq 0$ also.

Since ac and bd are integers, and $bd \neq 0$, the product is rational.

Try It! 3. Is the quotient of two rational numbers always a rational number? Explain.

EXAMPLE 4 Operations With Rational and Irrational Numbers

A. Is the sum of a rational number and an irrational number rational or irrational?

If you could write the sum of an irrational and a rational number as a rational number, you could write the following equation.

irrational

rational $\frac{a}{b} + c = \frac{p}{q}$ rational

$$c = \frac{pb - aq}{bq}$$

In the rational numbers above, *a*, *b*, *p*, and *q* are integers, with $b \neq 0$ and $q \neq 0$. This means that

- $pb - aq$ is an integer and
- bq is an integer not equal to 0.

Therefore $\frac{pb - aq}{bq}$ is a rational number. But this is equal to *c*, an irrational number. Can a number be both rational and irrational? No, it cannot.

So what went wrong? The mistake was to assume that you could write the sum $\frac{a}{b} + c$ in the form $\frac{p}{q}$.

The sum of a rational number and an irrational number is always an irrational number.

B. Is the product of a rational number and an irrational number rational or irrational?

Write the product as a rational number.

irrational

rational $\frac{a}{b} \cdot c = \frac{p}{q}$ rational

$$c = \frac{bp}{aq}$$

COMMON ERROR

If you do not address the case where $a = 0$, you might conclude that the product of any rational number and any irrational number is irrational. But that is not true.

As in part A, *c* is both rational and irrational. So the assumption that you can write $\frac{a}{b} \cdot c$ as $\frac{p}{q}$ at all is wrong.

Also notice that in order to divide by *a* when calculating *c*, you have to assume that $a \neq 0$. What happens in the original equation if $a = 0$?

Then $\frac{a}{b} = 0$, and $\frac{a}{b} \cdot c = 0$ for *any* number *c*.

So the product of a rational number and an irrational number is always irrational, unless the rational number in the product is 0.

Try It! **4.** Is the difference of a rational number and an irrational number always irrational? Explain.

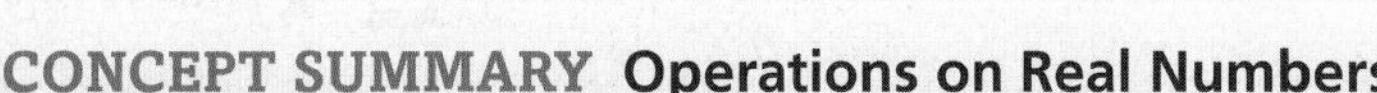

CONCEPT SUMMARY Operations on Real Numbers

WORDS

The sum of two rational numbers is always rational.

The product of two rational numbers is always rational.

The sum of a rational number and an irrational number is always irrational.

The product of a nonzero rational number and an irrational number is always irrational.

NUMBERS

Sums: $\frac{2}{9} + \frac{4}{6} = \frac{32}{36}$

Products: $\frac{2}{9} \cdot \frac{4}{6} = \frac{8}{54}$

Sums: $\sqrt{3} + \frac{1}{3} = \frac{3\sqrt{3} + 1}{3}$

Products: $\sqrt{3} \cdot \frac{1}{3} = \frac{\sqrt{3}}{3}$

ALGEBRA

Sums: $\frac{a}{b} + \frac{c}{d} = \frac{ad + cb}{bd}$

Products: $\frac{a}{b} \cdot \frac{c}{d} = \frac{ac}{bd}$

Sums: $\frac{a}{b} + c \neq \frac{p}{q}$, when c is irrational

Products: $\frac{a}{b} \cdot c \neq \frac{p}{q}$, when c is irrational

Do You UNDERSTAND?

1. ESSENTIAL QUESTION How can you classify the results of operations on real numbers?

2. **Communicate Precisely** Explain why the sum of a rational number and an irrational number is always irrational.

3. **Vocabulary** Are the rational numbers a *subset* of the *set* of all real numbers? Are the rational numbers a *subset* of the irrational numbers? Explain?

4. **Error Analysis** Jacinta says that the product of a rational number and an irrational number is always irrational. Explain her error.

5. **Reason** Let $D = \{-2, -1, 0, 1, 2\}$. Is D a subset of itself? Explain.

Do You KNOW HOW?

Determine whether set B is a subset of set A.

6. $A = \{0, 1, 2, 3, 4\}$
   $B = \{1, 2\}$

7. $A = \{2, 3, 5, 7, 11\}$
   $B = \{3, 5, 7, 9, 11\}$

Order each set of numbers from least to greatest.

8. $\sqrt{200}$, 14, $\frac{41}{3}$

9. $\frac{2}{3}$, $\sqrt{\frac{9}{16}}$, 0.6

10. The park shown is in the shape of a square. Is the perimeter rational or irrational?

Area = 24,200 yd²

? yd

PRACTICE & PROBLEM SOLVING

Scan for Multimedia

Practice Tutorial

Additional Exercises Available Online

UNDERSTAND

11. Reason Identify each solution as rational or irrational.

a. $\frac{4}{7} + \frac{-1}{3}$ **b.** $\sqrt{4} \cdot \frac{2}{5}$

12. Higher Order Thinking Is the product of two irrational numbers always an irrational number? Explain.

13. Error Analysis Describe and correct the error a student made when ordering numbers from least to greatest.

$\sqrt{144}, \frac{234}{3}, 68.12$

$\sqrt{144} = 72$

$\frac{234}{3} = 78$

$68.12, \sqrt{144}, \frac{234}{3}$ ✗

14. Mathematical Connections The bulletin board is in the shape of a square. Find two rational numbers that are within $\frac{1}{8}$ in. of the actual side length.

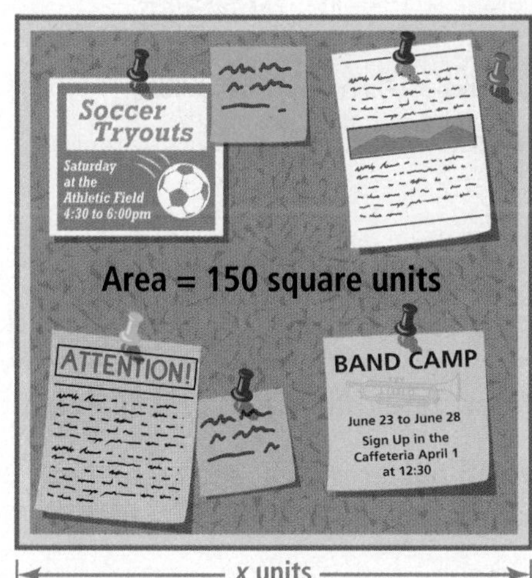

15. Construct Arguments Tell whether each statement is *always true, sometimes true,* or *never true*. Explain.

a. An integer is a whole number.

b. A natural number is a rational number.

c. An irrational number is an integer.

PRACTICE

List all subsets of the real numbers from the list below that each number belongs to. SEE EXAMPLE 1

- real numbers
- irrational numbers
- rational numbers
- integers
- whole numbers

16. 10.5 **17.** $\frac{4}{7}$

18. 6 **19.** 0

20. $\sqrt{2}$ **21.** –29

Order the numbers shown from least to greatest. SEE EXAMPLE 2

22. $3.5, \frac{10}{3}, \sqrt{14}$ **23.** $\frac{1}{3}, 0.1\overline{6}, \sqrt{\frac{1}{4}}$

Match each number to the letter that represents its position on the number line. SEE EXAMPLE 2

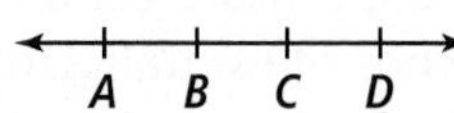

24. $-\sqrt{120}$

25. $-\sqrt{\frac{400}{4}}$

26. $-\frac{23}{2}$

27. –11.75

Determine whether each sum, difference, product, or quotient represents a rational number or an irrational number. Explain how you know without simplifying. SEE EXAMPLES 3 AND 4

28. $\frac{6}{23} - \frac{\sqrt{2}}{2}$

29. $\frac{6}{23} - \frac{15}{127}$

30. $\frac{6}{23} \div \frac{15}{127}$

31. $\frac{6}{23} \div \frac{\sqrt{2}}{2}$

32. Is the difference of two rational numbers always a rational number? Explain. SEE EXAMPLE 3

33. Is the quotient of a rational number and an irrational number always irrational? Explain. SEE EXAMPLE 4

Practice Tutorial

Mixed Review Available Online

PRACTICE & PROBLEM SOLVING

APPLY

34. Make Sense and Persevere Adam wraps the top edge of the gift box shown with gold ribbon.

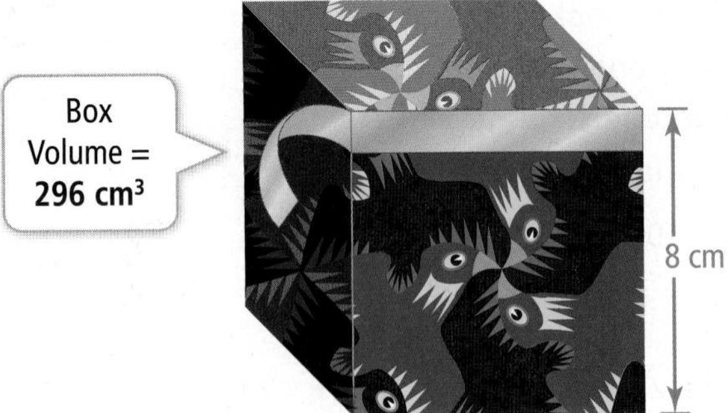

The top and bottom edges of the box are square. If Adam has $24\frac{1}{4}$ in. of gold ribbon, does he have enough to decorate the top of the box?

35. Reason In statistics, *continuous data* can have values equal to any real number, such as the average temperature for an area or the number of inches of rainfall. Other sets of data are *discrete*. Examples of discrete data are the number of students in a school district, the number of home runs hit by a baseball team in a season, and the number of letters handled by the post office each month. Which subset of the real numbers is the best one to use to describe discrete data?

36. Make Sense and Persevere Helena builds a shed in her backyard. There is a larger section for large tools, like her lawn mower, and a smaller section for small tools. Each section has a square floor. What is the length of the entire shed? What type of number is the length? List as many types of numbers for the length as you can.

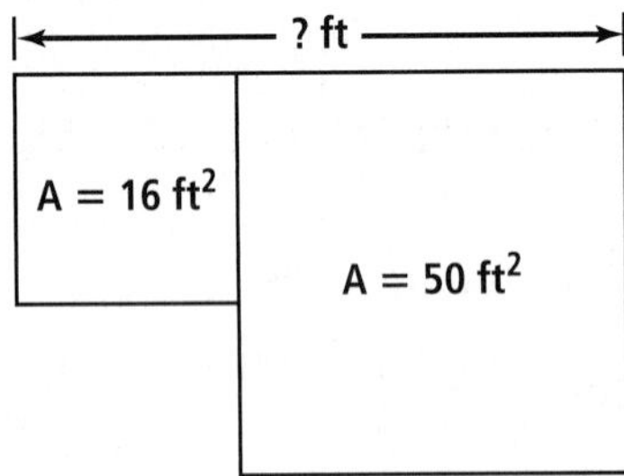

ASSESSMENT PRACTICE

37. Is 0.62473 a member of the set? For each set of real numbers, select *Yes* or *No*.

	Yes	No
natural numbers	❑	❑
whole numbers	❑	❑
integers	❑	❑
rational numbers	❑	❑
irrational numbers	❑	❑
real numbers	❑	❑

38. SAT/ACT What is the square root of $\sqrt{\frac{144}{256}}$?

Ⓐ $\frac{2}{3}$ Ⓑ $\frac{3}{4}$ Ⓒ $\frac{3}{16}$ Ⓓ $\frac{9}{4}$ Ⓔ $\frac{9}{16}$

39. Performance Task A basketball coach is considering three players for Most Valuable Player (MVP). The table shows the proportion of shots each player made of the shots they attempted.

Player	Free Throws	Field Goals (2 pts)	3-Point Shots
Martin	71%	49.5%	32%
Corey	$\frac{4}{5}$	$\frac{9}{20}$	$\frac{1}{3}$
Kimberly	0.857	0.448	0.338

Part A For a technical foul, the team can pick any player they want to shoot the free throw. Which player should the team pick? Explain.

Part B Which player is most successful with their field goal shots? Explain.

Part C Rank the players by the percentage of the 3-point shots each made.

Part D If all the players attempted the same number of shots, which player would you choose as the MVP? Justify your answer.

1-2 Solving Linear Equations

PearsonRealize.com

I CAN… create and solve linear equations with one variable.

MODEL & DISCUSS

Joshua is going kayaking with a group during one of his vacation days. In his vacation planning, he budgeted $50 for a kayak rental.

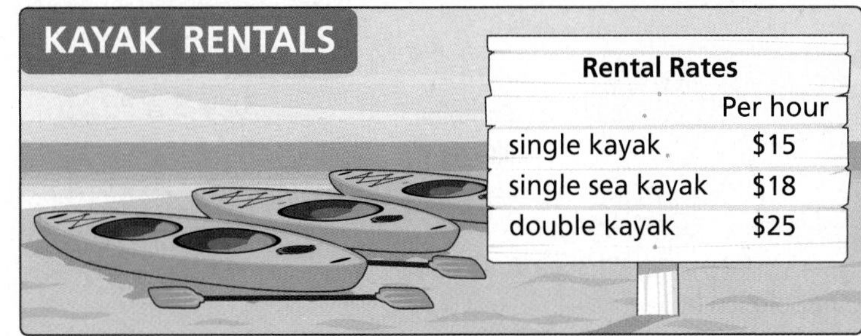

A. How can Joshua determine the number of hours he can rent a kayak for himself? Describe two different options.

B. Joshua found out that there is a $25 nonrefundable equipment fee in addition to the hourly rates. How does this requirement change the mathematics of the situation?

C. **Look for Relationships** How do the processes you used for parts A and B differ? How are they the same?

ESSENTIAL QUESTION

How do you create equations and use them to solve problems?

CONCEPTUAL UNDERSTANDING

EXAMPLE 1 Solve Linear Equations

What is the value of x in the equation $\frac{2(x+4)}{3} - 8 = 32$?

VOCABULARY
Remember, a *variable* is an unknown quantity, or a quantity that can vary. An *equation* is a mathematical statement with two expressions set equal to each other. A *solution of an equation* is a value for the variable that makes the equation a true statement.

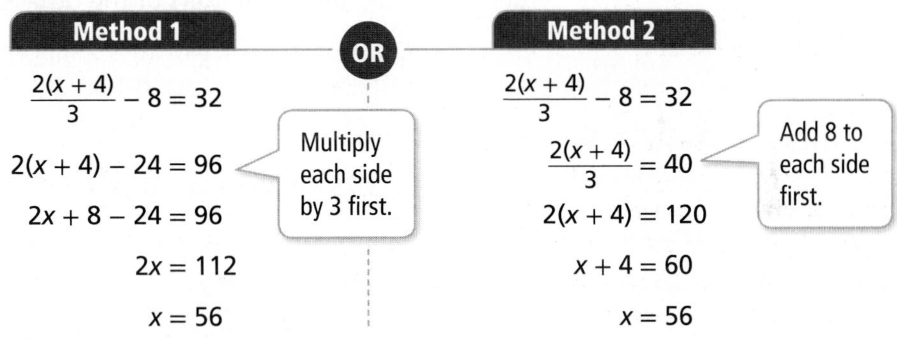

Method 1

Multiply each side by 3 first.

$$\frac{2(x+4)}{3} - 8 = 32$$
$$2(x+4) - 24 = 96$$
$$2x + 8 - 24 = 96$$
$$2x = 112$$
$$x = 56$$

OR

Method 2

Add 8 to each side first.

$$\frac{2(x+4)}{3} - 8 = 32$$
$$\frac{2(x+4)}{3} = 40$$
$$2(x+4) = 120$$
$$x + 4 = 60$$
$$x = 56$$

Each solving method yields the same solution. Is one method better than the other?

Look at how the expression on the left side of the original equation is built up from x.

$$x \rightarrow x+4 \rightarrow 2(x+4) \rightarrow \frac{2(x+4)}{3} \rightarrow \frac{2(x+4)}{3} - 8$$

Notice how Method 2 applies these steps in reverse to isolate x. This is often a good strategy and can lead to simpler solution methods.

Try It! **1.** Solve the equation $4 + \frac{3x-1}{2} = 9$. Explain the reasons why you chose your solution method.

EXAMPLE 2 Solve Consecutive Integer Problems

The sum of three consecutive integers is 132. What are the three integers?

Write an equation to model the problem. Then solve.

$$x + (x + 1) + (x + 2) = 132$$

The three integers are consecutive, so each is 1 greater than the previous.

Combine like terms.

$$3x + 3 = 132$$

$$3x + 3 - 3 = 132 - 3$$

$$\frac{3x}{3} = \frac{129}{3}$$

$$x = 43$$

STUDY TIP
You can check the solution by substituting the value in the original equation.

The first of the three consecutive numbers is 43.
The three consecutive numbers whose sum is 132 are 43, 44, 45.

Try It! 2. The sum of three consecutive odd integers is 57. What are the three integers?

APPLICATION

EXAMPLE 3 Use Linear Equations to Solve Mixture Problems

A lab technician needs 25 liters of a solution that is 15% acid for a certain experiment, but she has only a solution that is 10% acid and a solution that is 30% acid. How many liters of the 10% and the 30% solutions should she mix to get what she needs?

Formulate Write an equation relating the number of liters of acid in each solution. Represent the total number of liters of one solution with a variable, like x. Then the total number of liters of the other solution must be $25 - x$.

25 L of 15% solution = x L of 10% solution + $(25 - x)$ L of 30% solution

$$(0.15)(25) = 0.10x + 0.30(25 - x)$$

Compute

$$3.75 = 0.1x + 7.5 - 0.3x$$

$$3.75 - 7.5 = 0.1x - 0.3x + 7.5 - 7.5$$

Subtract 7.5 from each side

$$-3.75 = -0.2x$$

$$3.75 = 0.2x$$

$$\frac{3.75}{0.2} = \frac{0.2x}{0.2}$$

Divide each side by 0.2.

$$18.75 = x$$

Interpret Since x represents the number of liters of the 10% acid solution, the lab technician should use 18.75 liters of the 10% solution. Since $25 - x$ represents the number of liters of the 30% acid solution, she should use 25 – 18.75, or 6.25 liters of the 30% solution.

Try It! 3. If the lab technician needs 30 liters of a 25% acid solution, how many liters of the 10% and the 30% acid solutions should she mix to get what she needs?

APPLICATION

EXAMPLE 4 Use Linear Equations to Solve Problems

Four friends use an online coupon to get discounts on concert tickets. They spent $312 for the four tickets. What was the price of one ticket without the discount?

Your online order is complete.

Your order details are shown below for your reference.

ORDER # 328
Sec B, Row 10, Seats 13-16

	Quantity	Price
Tickets	4	?
Discount	$15.00	4 x $15.00
Order Total		**$312**

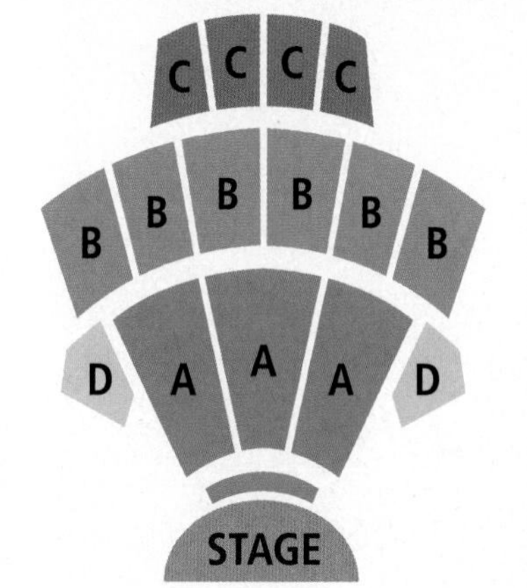

Step 1 Write an equation to represent the problem situation.

Let p represent the original ticket price.

4 • original ticket price minus $15 = $312

$$4(p - 15) = 312$$

COMMON ERROR
Subtract 15 from the price of each ticket, not from the total cost of four undiscounted tickets.

Step 2 Solve the equation.

$$4(p - 15) = 312$$
$$\frac{4(p - 15)}{4} = \frac{312}{4}$$
$$p - 15 = 78$$
$$p - 15 + 15 = 78 + 15$$
$$p = 93$$

The ticket price without the discount was $93.

Try It! **4.** The same four friends buy tickets for two shows on consecutive nights. They use a coupon for $5 off each ticket. They pay a total of $416 for 8 tickets. Write and solve an equation to find the original price of the tickets.

APPLICATION

EXAMPLE 5 Solve Work and Time Problems

LaTanya will walk her bike from her house to the bike shop, which is 1.5 mi from her house, to get the bike fixed. She expects to wait 30 min for the repair. Then she will ride her bike home. Can she be home in one hour?

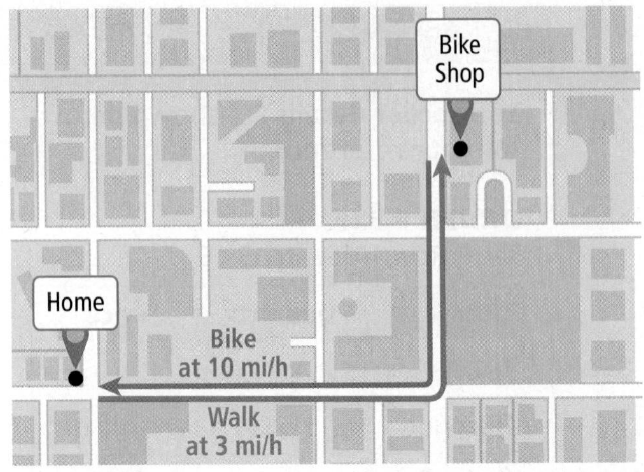

Step 1 Write an equation to represent the situation.

Time walking + Time at the shop + Time biking = Total time

$$\frac{1.5 \text{ miles}}{3 \text{ miles per hour}} + \frac{1}{2}\text{ hour} + \frac{1.5 \text{ miles}}{10 \text{ miles per hour}} = t$$

The equation $\frac{1.5}{3} + \frac{1}{2} + \frac{1.5}{10} = t$ represents the situation.

MAKE SENSE AND PERSEVERE
Look for relationships between the distance traveled and the rate when you write the equation.

Step 2 Solve for t.

$$\frac{1.5}{3} + \frac{1}{2} + \frac{1.5}{10} = t$$

$$(30)\frac{1.5}{3} + (30)\frac{1}{2} + (30)\frac{1.5}{10} = 30t$$

Multiply each side by the least common denominator.

$$15 + 15 + 4.5 = 30t$$

$$\frac{34.5}{30} = \frac{30t}{30}$$

$$1.15 = t$$

It will take LaTanya 1.15 h, or 1 h 9 min to get home after leaving to get her bike repaired. She will need more than 1 h.

Try It! 5. LaTanya leaves her house at 12:30 P.M. and bikes at 12 mi/h to Marta's house. She stays at Marta's house for 90 min. Both girls walk back to LaTanya's house along the same route at 2.5 mi/h. They arrive at LaTanya's house at 3:30 P.M. How far is Marta's house from LaTanya's house?

CONCEPT SUMMARY Create and Solve Linear Equations

Use the following information about Kelsey's visit to the flower shop.

- Kelsey bought some roses and tulips.
- She bought twice as many tulips as roses.
- Roses cost \$5 each.
- Tulips cost \$2 each.
- Kelsey spent \$36 total.

How many of each kind of flower did Kelsey buy?

WORDS Write an equation to represent the situation.

Cost of Roses + Cost of Tulips = Total Cost

(Cost of One Rose)(Number of Roses) + (Cost of One Tulip)(Number of Tulips) = Total Cost

ALGEBRA $\$5 \cdot x + \$2 \cdot 2x = \$36$

$$5x + 4x = 36$$

$$9x = 36$$

$$x = 4$$

Kelsey bought 4 roses and 8 tulips.

Do You UNDERSTAND?

1. **ESSENTIAL QUESTION** How do you create equations and use them to solve problems?
2. **Reason** What is a first step to solving for x in the equation $9x - 7 = 10$? How would you check your solution?
3. **Use Structure** For an equation with fractions, why is it helpful to multiply both sides of the equation by the LCD?
4. **Error Analysis** Venetta knows that 1 mi $\approx$ 1.6 km. To convert 5 mi/h to km/h, she multiplies 5 mi/h by $\frac{1 \text{ mi}}{1.6 \text{ km}}$. What error does Venetta make?

Do You KNOW HOW?

Solve each equation.

5. $4b + 14 = 22$
6. $-6k - 3 = 39$
7. $15 - 2(3 - 2x) = 46$
8. $\frac{2}{3}y - \frac{2}{5} = 5$
9. Terrence walks at a pace of 2 mi/h to the theater and watches a movie for 2 h and 15 min. He rides back home, taking the same route, on the bus that travels at a rate of 40 mi/h. The entire trip takes 3.5 h. How far along this route is Terrence's house from the theater? Explain.

PRACTICE & PROBLEM SOLVING

Scan for Multimedia

Practice | Tutorial

Additional Exercises Available Online

UNDERSTAND

10. **Use Structure** What could be a first step to solving the equation $3x + -0.5(x + 3) + 4 = 14$? Explain.

11. **Make Sense and Persevere** The sum of four consecutive integers is –18. What is the greatest of these integers?

12. **Error Analysis** Describe and correct the error a student made when solving the equation $4 = -2(x - 3)$. What is the correct solution?

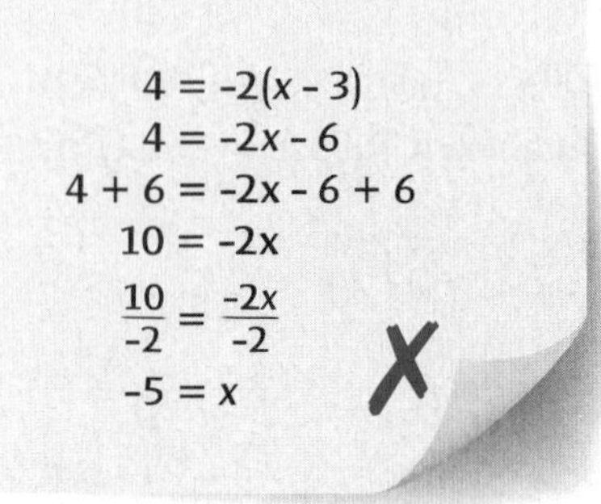

13. **Communicate Precisely** Parker ran on a treadmill at a constant speed for the length of time shown. How many miles did Parker run? Explain.

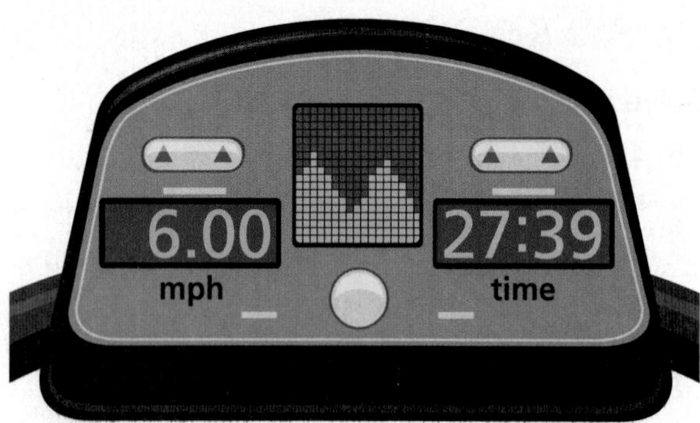

14. **Reason** The Division Property of Equality says that for every real number a, b, and c, if $a = b$ and $c \neq 0$, then $\frac{a}{c} = \frac{b}{c}$. Why does the property state that $c \neq 0$?

15. **Higher Order Thinking** Tonya's first step in solving the equation $\frac{1}{2}(2y + 4) = -6$ is to use the Distributive Property on the left side of the equation. Deon's first step is to multiply each side by 2. Which of these methods will result in an equivalent equation? Explain.

PRACTICE

Solve each equation. SEE EXAMPLES 1 AND 2

16. $-4x + 3x = 2$

17. $7 = 5y - 13 - y$

18. $7m - 4 - 9m - 36 = 0$

19. $-2 = -5t + 10 + 2t$

Solve each equation. SEE EXAMPLES 3 AND 4

20. $2(2x + 1) = 26$

21. $-2(2z + 1) = 26$

22. $92 = -4(2r - 5)$

23. $10(5 - n) - 1 = 29$

24. $-(7 - 2x) + 7 = -7$

25. $200 = 16(6t - 3)$

Solve each equation. SEE EXAMPLE 5

26. $\frac{1}{2}x + 2 = 1$

27. $\frac{3}{2}x - \frac{2}{3}x = 2$

28. $\frac{1}{5}(k - 3) = \frac{3}{4}$

29. $\frac{7}{60} = \frac{5}{24}w + \frac{11}{12}$

30. $\frac{3m}{4} - \frac{m}{12} = \frac{7}{8}$

31. $1{,}290 = \frac{h}{10} + \frac{h}{5}$

Solve each equation.

32. $0.1r - 1 = 0.65$

33. $1.2n + 0.68 = 5$

34. $0.025(q + 2) = 2.81$

35. $-0.07p - 0.6 = 5$

36. $1.037x + 0.02x + 25 = 30.285$

37. $-0.85t - 0.85t - 3.9 = -8.15$

38. A bee flies at 20 feet per second directly to a flowerbed from its hive. The bee stays at the flowerbed for 15 minutes, then flies directly back to the hive at 12 feet per second. It is away from the hive for a total of 20 minutes. SEE EXAMPLE 5

    a. What equation can you use to find the distance of the flowerbed from the hive?

    b. How far is the flowerbed from the hive?

PRACTICE & PROBLEM SOLVING

APPLY

39. Reason A fastpitch softball player signs a six-year contract. Her agent expects that she will earn \$1,000,000 over the next six years. If the agent is right, how many bonus payments, on average, should the pitcher expect each year? Explain.

40. Make Sense and Persevere There are nine water bottles in Devin's refrigerator. He adds three full boxes of water bottles to the refrigerator. Then he adds two more boxes that each have 1 fewer bottle than a full box. When he is done, there are 67 bottles in the refrigerator. Write and solve an equation to find the number of bottles in a full box.

41. Construct Arguments Yuson used her calculator to solve the equation $\frac{4}{5}x - 8 = 3$. She entered the following on her screen and got an incorrect answer. How could she use parentheses to find the correct answer? Explain. What is the correct answer?

42. Communicate Precisely A scientist makes an acid solution by adding drops of acid to 1.2 L of water. The final volume of the acid solution is 1.202 L. Assuming the volume of each drop is 0.05 mL, how many drops were added to the water? About what percent of the solution is acid? Round to the nearest hundredth of a percent.

ASSESSMENT PRACTICE

43. Anna bought 8 tetras and 2 rainbow fish for her aquarium. The rainbow fish cost \$6 more than the tetras. She paid a total of \$37. Which of the following are true? Select all that apply.

Ⓐ The cost of 4 tetras is the same as the cost of a rainbow fish.

Ⓑ One rainbow fish plus 5 tetras cost \$21.

Ⓒ An equation to find the cost r, in dollars, of a rainbow fish is $8r + 2(r + 6) = 37$

Ⓓ Reducing the number of rainbow fish by 1 would result in a total cost of \$28.50.

Ⓔ An equation to find the cost t, in dollars, of a tetra t is $8t + 2t + 6 = 37$.

44. SAT/ACT What is the solution of $1{,}200 - 5(3x + 30) = 600$?

Ⓐ 30 Ⓑ 50 Ⓒ 150 Ⓓ 200 Ⓔ 250

45. Performance Task A mason will lay rows of bricks to build a wall. The mason will spread $\frac{3}{8}$ inch of mortar on top of all but the last row of bricks. The finished wall will be $1\frac{1}{8}$ inch less than 4 feet high.

Part A The mason wants to lay the bricks so that the shortest edge of each brick is vertical. How many rows of bricks are needed? Show your work.

Part B Suppose the mason decides to lay bricks so that the 3-inch edge is vertical. If the mason lays the same number of rows of bricks that were used for the wall described in Part A, how high will this wall be?

Activity | Assess

1-3 Solving Equations With a Variable on Both Sides

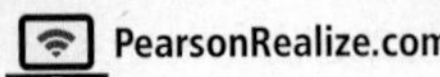

PearsonRealize.com

I CAN… write and solve equations with a variable on both sides to solve problems.

VOCABULARY

- identity

EXPLORE & REASON

Some friends want to see a movie that is showing at two different theaters in town. They plan to share three tubs of popcorn during the movie.

	Theater A	Theater B
Ticket Price	\$14.50	\$13.00
Popcorn	\$5.75	\$6.75

A. **Construct Arguments** Which movie theater should the friends choose? Explain.

B. For what situation would the total cost at each theater be exactly the same? Explain.

C. There are different methods to solving this problem. Which do you think is the best? Why?

ESSENTIAL QUESTION

How do you create equations with a variable on both sides and use them to solve problems?

EXAMPLE 1 Solving Equations With a Variable on Both Sides

A. What is the value of *x* in the equation shown?

$$3x - 10 + 4x = -2(x - 4) + 9$$

Distribute the –2.

Combine like terms.

$$7x - 10 = -2x + 8 + 9$$

$$7x + 2x = 8 + 9 + 10$$

Collect like terms on the same side of the equation.

$$9x = 27$$

$$\frac{9x}{9} = \frac{27}{9}$$

$$x = 3$$

STUDY TIP

It does not matter if you add 10 to each side first or add $2x$ to each side first. Either order will result in the same equation, $9x = 27$.

B. What is the value of *n* in the equation shown?

$$\frac{1}{2}(n - 4) - 7 = -2n + 6$$

$$\frac{1}{2}(n - 4) = -2n + 13$$

Multiply each side by 2 to eliminate the fraction.

$$n - 4 = -4n + 26$$

$$n + 4n = 26 + 4$$

Collect like terms on the same side of the equation.

$$5n = 30$$

$$n = 6$$

Try It! **1.** Solve each equation.

a. $100(z - 0.2) = -10(5z + 0.8)$ **b.** $\frac{5}{8}(16d + 24) = 6(d - 1) + 1$

CONCEPTUAL UNDERSTANDING

EXAMPLE 2 Understand Equations With Infinitely Many or No Solutions

A. What is the value of x in $4x + 6 = 2(2x + 3)$?

Use algebra tiles to represent and solve $4x + 6 = 2(2x + 3)$.

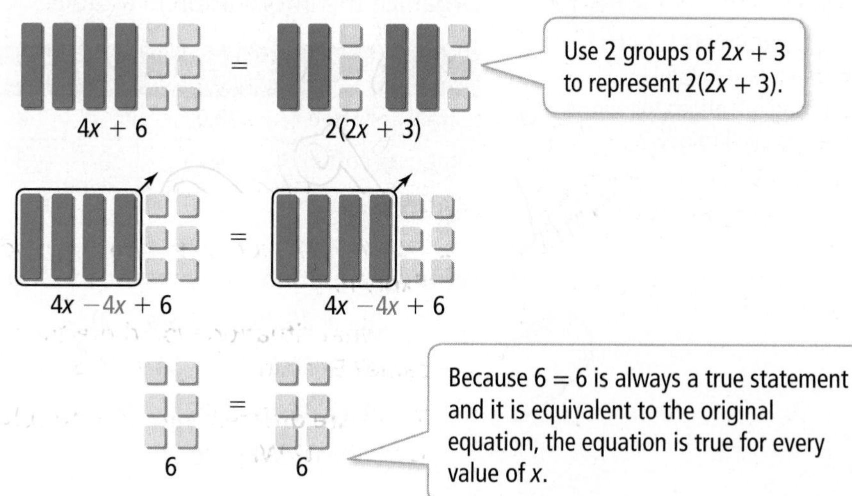

VOCABULARY
Since this equation is true for all values of the variable, it is sometimes referred to as having *infinitely many solutions.*

The equation $4x + 6 = 2(2x + 3)$ is true for all values of x.

An equation that is true for all values of the variables is an **identity**.

B. What is the value of x in $6x - 5 = 2(3x + 4)$?

Solve for x.

$$6x - 5 = 2(3x + 4)$$
$$6x - 5 = 6x + 8$$
$$6x - 6x - 5 = 6x - 6x + 8$$
$$-5 = 8$$

Maintain the equality by subtracting $6x$ from each side.

STUDY TIP
Recall that you can assign a value to the variable in an equation to check whether the equation is true.

There is no value of x that makes the equation true. Therefore, the equation has no solution.

Try It! **2.** Solve each equation. Is the equation an identity? Explain.

a. $t - 27 = -(27 - t)$

b. $16(4 - 3m) = 96\left(-\frac{m}{2} + 1\right)$

APPLICATION

EXAMPLE 3 Solve Mixture Problems

Arabica coffee costs \$28 per pound and Robusta coffee costs \$8.75 per pound. How many pounds of Arabica coffee must you mix with 3 pounds of Robusta coffee to make a blend that costs \$15.50 per pound?

Organize the information in a table.

USE APPROPRIATE TOOLS
How are tables helpful in organizing quantities to represent situations algebraically?

	Price (\$/lb)	·	Amount (lb)	=	Total cost (\$)
Arabica coffee	28.00		a		$28a$
Robusta coffee	8.75		3		26.25
Coffee blend	15.50		$a + 3$		$15.5(a + 3)$

Write an equation to represent the situation.

$$28a + 26.25 = 15.5(a + 3)$$
$$28a + 26.25 = 15.5a + 46.5$$
$$28a - 15.5a = 46.5 - 26.25$$
$$12.5a = 20.25$$
$$a = 1.62$$

You must mix 1.62 pounds of Arabica coffee with 3 pounds of Robusta coffee to make a blend that costs \$15.50 per pound.

Try It! 3. How many pounds of Arabica coffee should you mix with 5 pounds of Robusta coffee to make a coffee blend that costs \$12.00 per pound?

APPLICATION

EXAMPLE 4 Use Equations to Solve Problems

Cameron pays \$0.95 per song with his current music service. A new music download service charges \$0.89 per song with a \$12 joining fee. Should Cameron switch to the new service?

Music Downloads
Current Plan
\$0.95 per song
New Plan
\$12.00
TO JOIN
\$0.89 per song

Formulate Write an equation to represent when the cost for any number of songs, s, is the same for both services.

New music service = Cameron's current music service

$$0.89s + 12 = 0.95s$$

Compute Solve the equation to find the number of songs at which the cost for each option will be the same.

$$0.89s - 0.89s + 12 = 0.95s - 0.89s$$
$$12 = 0.06s$$
$$\frac{12}{0.06} = \frac{0.06s}{0.06}$$
$$200 = s$$

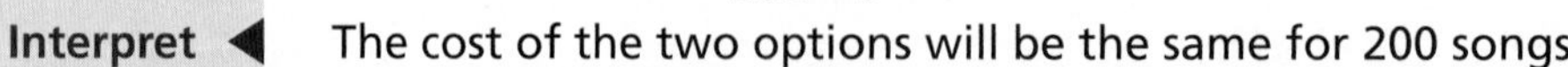

Interpret The cost of the two options will be the same for 200 songs.

If Cameron plans to purchase more than 200 songs, he should switch to the new service because it will cost less than his current service.

CONTINUED ON THE NEXT PAGE

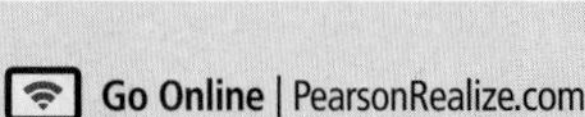

EXAMPLE 4 CONTINUED

 **Try It!** 4. Cameron's friend tells him of another service that has a \$15 joining fee but charges \$0.80 per song. At what number of songs does this new service become a less expensive option than Cameron's current service?

 CONCEPT SUMMARY Solve Equations with a Variable on Both Sides

Linear equations can be used to solve mathematical and real-world problems.

WORDS You can use properties of equality to solve an equation with variables on both sides. Equations can have one solution, infinitely many solutions, or no solution.

NUMBERS

$$3x - 6 = 3(x - 2)$$
$$3x - 6 = 3x - 6$$
$$3x - 3x - 6 = 3x - 3x - 6$$
$$-6 = -6$$

The equation is true for all values of x. It is an identity. It has infinitely many solutions.

$$3x - 2 = 3x - 6$$
$$3x - 3x - 2 = 3x - 3x + 6$$
$$-2 = 6$$

The equation is not true for any value of x. It has no solutions.

 Do You UNDERSTAND?

1. ESSENTIAL QUESTION How do you create equations with a variable on both sides and use them to solve problems?

2. **Vocabulary** Why does it make sense to describe an equation that has infinitely many solutions as an *identity*?

3. **Error Analysis** Isabel says that the equation $x - 2 = -(x - 2)$ has no solution because a number can never be equal to its opposite. Explain the error Isabel made.

4. **Look For Relationships** You are solving an equation with a variable on each side. Does the side on which you choose to isolate the variable affect the solution? Why might you choose one side over the other?

Do You KNOW HOW?

Solve each equation.

5. $5(2x + 6) = 8x + 48$

6. $-3(8 + 3h) = 5h + 4$

7. $2(y - 6) = 3(y - 4) - y$

8. $8x - 4 = 2(4x - 4)$

9. For how many games is the total cost of bowling equal for the two bowling establishments?

Family Bowling

Cost (dollars)		
	Game	4.00
	Shoes	1.00

Knight Owl Bowling

Cost (dollars)		
	Game	3.75
	Shoes	2.00

PRACTICE & PROBLEM SOLVING

Scan for Multimedia

Practice | Tutorial

Additional Exercises Available Online

UNDERSTAND

10. **Reason** Do only equations with variables on both sides ever have no solution? Or can an equation with the variable on one side have no solution? Justify your answer.

11. **Generalize** How do you know whether an equation is an identity? How many solutions does an identity have? Explain.

12. **Error Analysis** Describe and correct any error a student may have made when solving the equation $0.15(y - 0.2) = 2 - 0.5(1 - y)$.

$$
\begin{aligned}
0.15(y - 0.2) &= 2 - 0.5(1 - y) \\
0.15y - 0.3 &= 2 - 0.5 + 0.5y \\
0.15y - 0.3 &= 1.5 + 0.5y \\
(100)(0.15y - 0.3) &= 100(1.5 + 0.5y) \\
15y - 30 &= 150 + 50y \\
15y - 30 - 15y - 150 &= 150 + 50y \\
&\quad - 15y - 150 \\
-180 &= 35y \\
-\frac{180}{35} &= y
\end{aligned}
$$

13. **Reason** When Nicky tried to solve an equation using properties of equality, she ended up with the equation $-3 = -3$. What equation might she have tried to solve? What is the solution of the equation?

14. **Mathematical Connections** The triangle shown is isosceles. Find the length of each side and the perimeter.

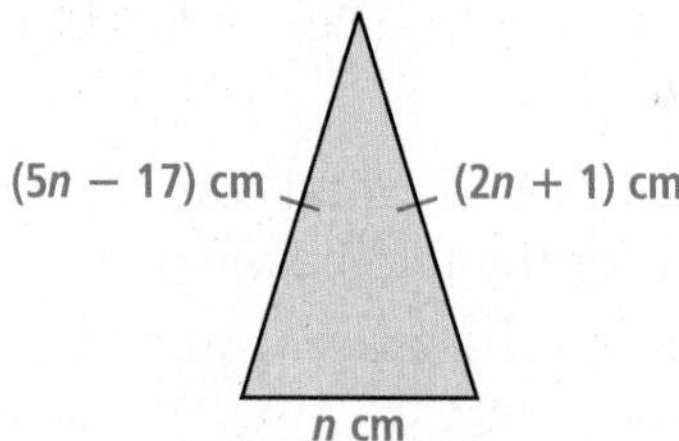

15. **Higher Order Thinking** The equation shown has a missing value.

$$-2(2x - \blacksquare) + 1 = 17 - 4x$$

a. For what missing value is the equation an identity?

b. For what missing value(s), if any, does the equation have exactly one solution?

c. For what missing value(s), if any, does the equation have no solution?

PRACTICE

Solve each equation. SEE EXAMPLES 1–3

16. $5x - 4 = 4x$
17. $7x = 8x + 12$
18. $27 - 3x = 3x + 27$
19. $34 - 2x = 7x$
20. $5r - 7 = 2r + 14$
21. $-x = 7x - 56$
22. $5(n - 7) = 2(n + 14)$
23. $6w - 33 = 3(4w - 5)$
24. $3(x - 2) = 9x$
25. $6(x + 5) = 3x$
26. $\frac{4x + 6}{2} = \frac{3x - 15}{3}$
27. $\frac{q + 1}{2} = \frac{q - 1}{3}$
28. $2c + 3 = 2c + 3$
29. $12b + 9 = 12b + 11$
30. $x - 27 = -(27 - x)$
31. $4(x + 9) = x + 9$
32. $16(4 - 3m) = 96\left(-\frac{m}{2} + 1\right)$
33. $6y - 8 = 2(3y - 4)$
34. $5(5t + 1) = 25t - 7$
35. $-3k + 4 = -2 - 6k$
36. $\frac{1}{4}(2(x - 1) + 10) = x$
37. $\frac{6x + 8}{2} - 4 = 3x$
38. $3y = \frac{8 - 12y}{4} + 2$
39. $0.25t = 0.25 - t$
40. $0.625(x + 10) - 10 = 0$

Solve each problem. SEE EXAMPLE 4

41. Tavon has a \$50 gift card that loses \$2 for each 30-day period it is not used. He has a \$40 card that loses \$1.50 for each 30-day period it is not used.

a. Write and solve an equation for the number of 30-day periods until the value of the gift cards will be equal.

b. What will the value of each card be when they have equal value?

42. A cereal box manufacturer changes the size of the box to increase the amount of cereal it contains. The equations $12 + 7.6n$ and $6 + 8n$, where n is the number of smaller boxes, are both representative of the amount of cereal that the new larger box contains. How many smaller boxes equal the same amount of cereal in the larger box?

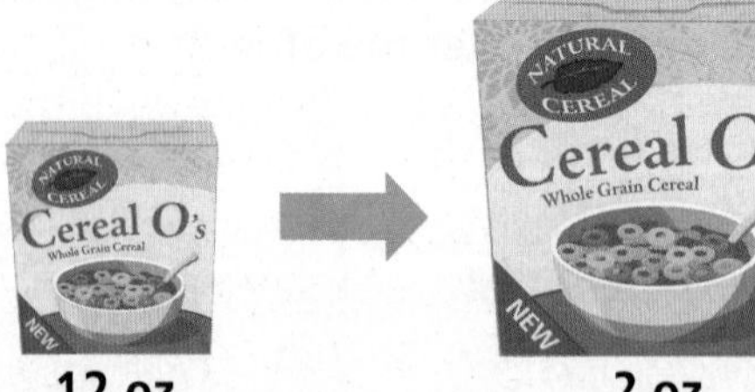

PRACTICE & PROBLEM SOLVING

Practice Tutorial

Mixed Review Available Online

APPLY

43. Model With Mathematics Arthur wants to buy an item that costs p dollars before tax. Using a 6% sales tax rate, write two different expressions that represent the price of the item after tax. Show that the two expressions are equal.

44. Model With Mathematics Two window washers start at the heights shown. One is rising, the other is descending. How long does it take for the two window washers to reach the same height? Explain.

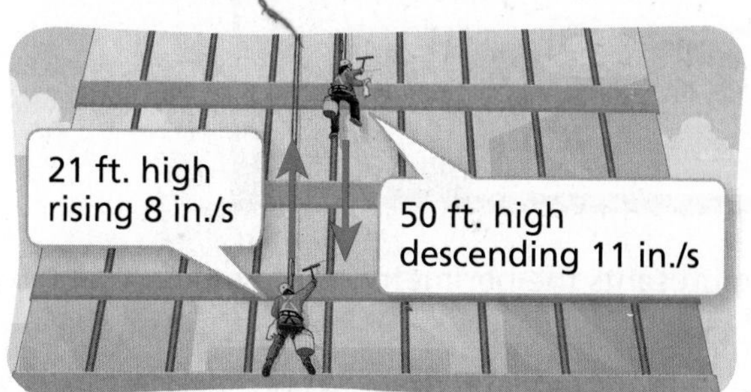

45. Construct Arguments Jamie will choose between two catering companies for an upcoming party. Company A charges a set-up fee of \$500 plus \$25 for each guest. Company B charges a set-up fee of \$200 plus \$30 per guest.

a. Write expressions that you can use to determine the amount each company charges for g guests.

b. Jamie learns that the \$500 set-up fee for Company A includes payment for 20 guests. The \$25 per guest charge is for every guest over the first 20. If there will be 50 guests, which company will cost the least? Explain.

46. Construct Arguments A two-year prepaid membership at Gym A costs \$250 for the first year plus \$19 per month for the second year. A two-year prepaid membership at Gym B costs \$195 for the first year plus \$24 per month for the second year. Leah says the cost for both gym memberships will be the same after the 11th month of the second year. Do you agree? Explain.

47. Model With Mathematics A red balloon is 40 feet above the ground and rising at 2 ft/s. At the same time, a blue balloon is at 60 feet above the ground and descending at 3 ft/s. What will the height of the balloons be when they are the same height above the ground?

ASSESSMENT PRACTICE

48. Which equations have no solution? Select all that apply.

Ⓐ $x - 9 = 2(x - 3) + 12$

Ⓑ $5(-2x + 7) + 3 = -10x + 38$

Ⓒ $\frac{1}{2}(6x - 4) = 3(x - 2)$

Ⓓ $0.01x + 0.001 = \frac{1}{100}(x + 10)$

Ⓔ $3(x + 2) + 1 = x + 2(4 + x)$

49. SAT/ACT Which equation is an identity?

Ⓐ $\frac{9x}{15} + 27 = \frac{9x}{15} + \frac{27}{15}$

Ⓑ $3\left(\frac{x}{2} + 16\right) - 16 = \frac{3}{2}x$

Ⓒ $-4(3 - 2x) = -12 - 8x$

Ⓓ $-5\left(\frac{x}{15} - 16\right) - 30 = 50 - \frac{1}{3}x$

Ⓔ $36\left(\frac{3}{4}x - 2\right) + 72 = -72 + 27x$

50. Performance Task Benito and Tyler are painting opposite sides of the same fence. Tyler has already painted $19\frac{1}{2}$ feet of his side of the fence when Benito starts painting.

Part A How long will it take for the two sides of the fence to have an equal number of feet painted? How many feet will be painted on Benito's side of the fence when the two sides have an equal number of feet painted?

Part B Tyler claims that because he started painting first, he will finish painting his side of the fence before Benito finishes painting his side. Is this true? Explain.

Part C The painter who finishes first gets to rest while the other painter finishes. How long will the painter who finishes first get to rest? Explain.

1-4 Literal Equations and Formulas

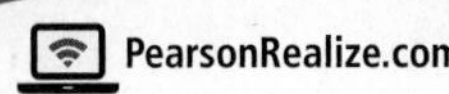

I CAN... rewrite and use literal equations to solve problems.

VOCABULARY

- formula
- literal equation

MODEL & DISCUSS

Nora drew a nonsquare rectangle. Then she drew the length of each side from end to end to make a line segment to represent the perimeter.

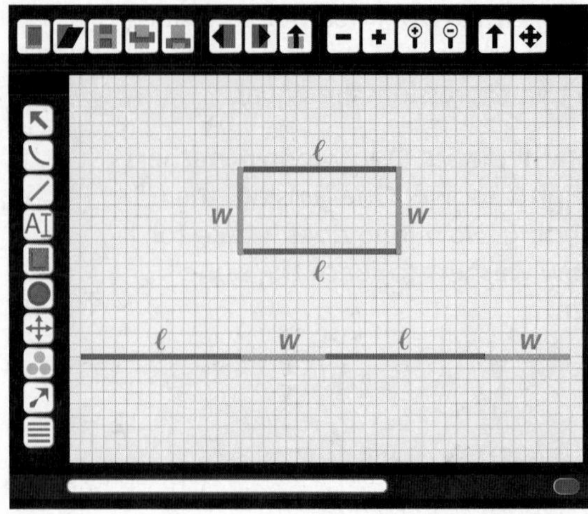

A. Write an equation that represents the perimeter of the model shown.

B. Rearrange the order of the sides so you can represent the perimeter with a different equation. Is this equation equivalent to your first equation?

C. Use Structure How many different ways can you express the relationship in parts A and B? Are any of them more useful than others?

ESSENTIAL QUESTION How is rewriting literal equations useful when solving problems?

CONCEPTUAL UNDERSTANDING

EXAMPLE 1 Rewrite Literal Equations

Janet wants to calculate the time it takes to earn a certain amount of interest on a principal amount in an investment with simple interest. What equation can she use?

A **formula** is an equation that states a relationship between one quantity and one or more other quantities. Use the simple interest formula, $I = prt$, and solve for t. The formula $I = prt$ is a **literal equation** because letters represent both variables and known constants.

I = interest
p = principle
r = interest rate
t = time

> **VOCABULARY**
> One definition of *literal* is *of, relating to, or expressed in letters*. A literal equation is an equation expressed in letters, or variables.

$$I = prt$$

$$\frac{I}{pr} = \frac{prt}{pr}$$

$$\frac{I}{pr} = t$$

You use properties of equality to solve literal equations for a variable just as you do linear equations.

When she writes the equation this way, she can use what she knows (I, p, and r) to calculate what she needs (t).

Try It! **1.** What equation can Janet use to calculate the principal amount?

EXAMPLE 2 Use Literal Equations to Solve Problems

In a half hour, Sarah is meeting her friends at the lake, 6 mi from her house. At what average speed must she ride her bike to get there on time?

Step 1 Solve the distance formula for r.

$$d = rt$$

Remember, distance = rate • time.

$$\frac{d}{t} = r$$

Step 2 Find the average speed, or rate, at which Sarah must ride her bike to be on time.

$$\frac{d}{t} = r$$

$$\frac{6}{0.5} = r$$

Substitute 6 for d and 0.5 for t.

$$12 = r$$

Sarah needs to ride her bike at an average speed of 12 mi/h to get to the lake on time.

REASON
How is the structure of the literal equation related to units for rate?

Try It! 2. Sarah is going to the store 2.5 mi away. She has only 15 min to get there before they close. At what average speed must she ride to get to the store before they close?

EXAMPLE 3 Rewrite a Formula

A worker at a framing store is making a rectangular frame. He knows that the perimeter of the frame is 144 in. and the length is 40 in. How can he determine the width of the frame?

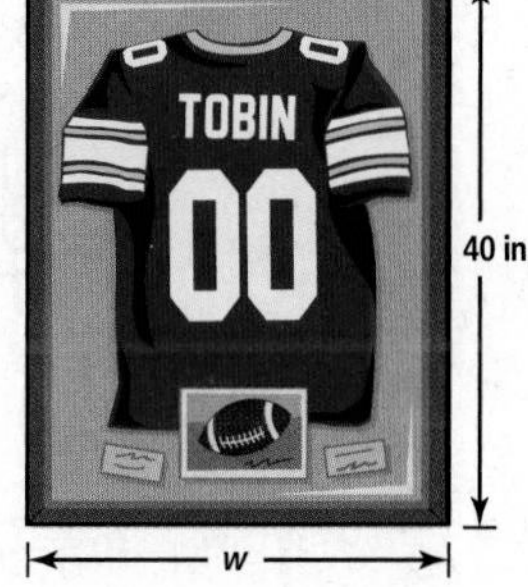

Step 1 Rewrite the perimeter formula $P = 2\ell + 2w$ in terms of w.

$$P - 2\ell = 2\ell + 2w - 2\ell$$

$$\frac{P - 2\ell}{2} = \frac{2w}{2}$$

$$\frac{P - 2\ell}{2} = w$$

The perimeter formula in terms of w is $w = \frac{P - 2\ell}{2}$.

Step 2 Use the literal equation to solve for w when P is 144 and ℓ is 40.

$$w = \frac{P - 2\ell}{2}$$

$$w = \frac{144 - 2(40)}{2}$$

$$w = \frac{144 - 80}{2} = 32$$

The width of the frame is 32 in.

COMMON ERROR
Do not divide just 2ℓ by 2 on the left side. Divide the entire expression $P - 2\ell$ by 2. The entire left side of the equation is one expression and must be divided by 2.

Try It! 3. Write the formula for the area of a triangle, $A = \frac{1}{2}bh$ in terms of h. Find the height of a triangle when $A = 18$ in.^{2} and $b = 9$ in.

APPLICATION

EXAMPLE 4 Apply Formulas

According to Teo's bread recipe, he should bake the bread at 190°C for 30 minutes. His oven measures temperature in °F. To what temperature in °F should he set his oven?

Formulate ◀ Rewrite the formula to find the Fahrenheit temperature that is equal to 190°C.

Compute ◀ **Step 1** Solve for F.

$$C = \frac{5}{9}(F - 32)$$

$$\frac{9}{5} \cdot C = \frac{9}{5} \cdot \frac{5}{9}(F - 32)$$

Dividing by a fraction is the same as multiplying by its reciprocal.

$$\frac{9}{5}C = F - 32$$

$$\frac{9}{5}C + 32 = F - 32 + 32$$

$$\frac{9}{5}C + 32 = F$$

Step 2 Use the formula for F to find the Fahrenheit temperature equivalent to 190°C.

$$\frac{9}{5}C + 32 = F$$

$$\frac{9}{5}(190) + 32 = 374$$

Interpret ◀ Teo should set the oven to 374°F.

Try It! **4.** The high temperature on a given winter day is 5°F. What is the temperature in °C?

CONCEPT SUMMARY Literal Equations and Formulas

WORDS Literal equations can use letters for both constants and variables. A formula is a kind of literal equation where one quantity is related to one or more other quantities.

To solve for a particular variable in a literal equation, you rewrite the equation, isolating the variable.

ALGEBRA The volume of a rectangular prism is given by the following formula.

$$V = \ell wh$$

To find a formula for h, the height of the prism, solve for h.

$$V = \ell hw$$

$$\frac{V}{\ell w} = \frac{\ell hw}{\ell w}$$ Divide each side by ℓw.

$$\frac{V}{\ell w} = h$$

$$h = \frac{V}{\ell w}$$

Do You UNDERSTAND?

1. **ESSENTIAL QUESTION** How is rewriting literal equations useful when solving problems?

2. **Communicate Precisely** How is solving $2x + c = d$ similar to solving $2x + 1 = 9$ for x? How are they different? How can you use $2x + c = d$ to solve $2x + 1 = 9$?

3. **Vocabulary** Explain how literal equations and formulas are related.

4. **Error Analysis** Dyani began solving the equation $g = \frac{x-1}{k}$ for x by adding 1 to each side. Explain Dyani's error. Then describe how to solve for x.

Do You KNOW HOW?

Solve each literal equation for the given variable.

5. $y = x + 12$; x

6. $n = \frac{4}{5}(m + 7)$; m

7. Use your equation from Exercise 6 to find m when $n = 40$.

8. William got scores of q_1, q_2, and q_3 on three quizzes.

   a. Write a formula for the average x of all three quizzes.

   b. William got an 85 and an 88 on the first two quizzes. What formula can William use to determine the score he needs on the third quiz to get an average of 90? What score does he need?

PRACTICE & PROBLEM SOLVING

Scan for Multimedia

Practice Tutorial

Additional Exercises Available Online

UNDERSTAND

9. **Mathematical Connections** Some two-step equations can be written in the form $ax + b = c$, where a, b, and c are constants and x is the variable.

   a. Write the equation $ax + b = c$ in terms of x.

   b. Use the formula to solve $3x + 7 = 19$ and $\frac{1}{2}x - 1 = 5$.

10. **Make Sense and Persevere** The flag of the Bahamas includes an equilateral triangle. The perimeter of the triangle is $P = 3s$, where s is the side length. Solve for s. Use your formula to find the dimensions of the flag in feet and the area in square feet when the perimeter of the triangle is 126 inches.

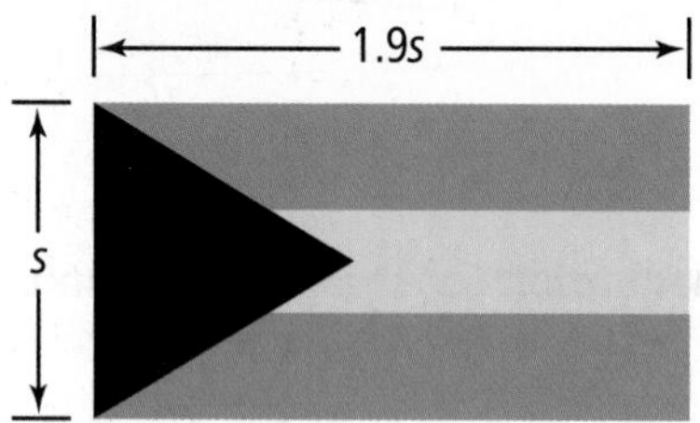

11. **Error Analysis** Describe and correct the error a student made when solving $kx + 3x = 4$ for x.

$$kx + 3x = 4$$
$$kx + 3x - 3x = 4 - 3x$$
$$kx = 4 - 3x$$
$$\frac{kx}{k} = \frac{4 - 3x}{k}$$
$$x = \frac{4 - 3x}{k} \quad ✗$$

12. **Higher Order Thinking** Given the equation $ax + b = c$, solve for x. Describe each statement as *always*, *sometimes*, or *never* true. Explain your answer.

   a. If a, b, c, are whole numbers, x is a whole number.

   b. If a, b, c, are integers, x is an integer.

   c. If a, b, c, are rational numbers, x is a rational number.

PRACTICE

Solve each equation for the indicated variable.
SEE EXAMPLES 1 AND 2

13. $\frac{b}{c} = a$; c

14. $k = a - y$; y

15. $dfg = h$; f

16. $w = \frac{x}{a - b}$; x

17. $2x + 3y = 12$; y

18. $2n = 4x + 2y$; n

19. $abc = \frac{1}{2}$; b

20. $y = \frac{3}{5u} + 5$; u

21. $8(x - a) = 2(2a - x)$; x

22. $12(m + 3x) = 18(x - 3m)$; m

23. $V = \frac{1}{3}\pi r^2 h$; h

24. $V = \frac{1}{3}\pi r^2(h - 1)$; h

25. $y(a - b) = c(y + a)$; y

26. $x = \frac{3(y - b)}{m}$; y

27. $F = -\frac{Gm}{r^2}$; G

28. Use the area formula $A = \ell w$ to write a formula for the length ℓ of the baking sheet shown.
SEE EXAMPLE 3

29. You can determine the approximate temperature in degrees Fahrenheit by counting the number of times a cricket chirps in one minute. Then multiply that by 7, divide by 30, and add 40. SEE EXAMPLE 4

   a. Write a formula for estimating the temperature based on the number of cricket chirps.

   b. Write a new formula for the number of chirps you would expect in one minute at a given Fahrenheit temperature.

   c. Use the formula to find the number of chirps in one minute when the temperature is 89°F.

PRACTICE & PROBLEM SOLVING

APPLY

30. Model With Mathematics Water boils at different temperatures at different elevations. The boiling temperature of water is 212°F at sea level (0 ft) but drops about 1.72°F for every 1,000 feet of elevation. Write a formula for the boiling point at a given elevation. Then solve the formula for the elevation when the boiling point for water is 190°F.

31. Reason In the National Hockey League, the goalie may not play the puck outside the isosceles trapezoid behind the net. The formula for the area of a trapezoid is $A = \frac{1}{2}(b_1 + b_2)h$.

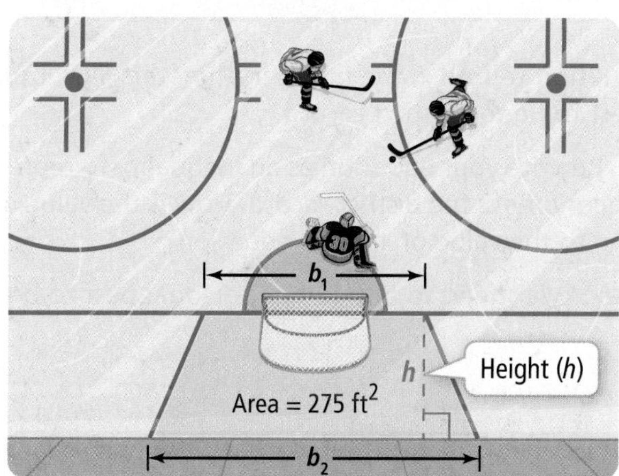

a. Solve the formula for either base, b_1 or b_2.

b. Use the formula to find the length of the base next to the goal given that the height of the trapezoid is 11 ft and the base farthest from the goal is 28 ft.

c. How can you find the distance d of each side of the base that extends from the goal given that the goal is 6 ft long? What is the distance?

32. Use Appropriate Tools The formula for cell D2 is shown in the spreadsheet. Use the data shown in row 3 to write a formula for cell A3.

= A2*B2*C2

	A	B	C	D
1	length	width	height	volume
2	3	4	5	60
3	■	10	12	600
4	6	12	13	936

ASSESSMENT PRACTICE

33. Given the proportion $\frac{a}{b} = \frac{c}{d}$, solve for c.

34. SAT/ACT The formula for the area of a sector of a circle is $A = \frac{\pi r^2 s}{360}$. Which formula shows s expressed in terms of the other variables?

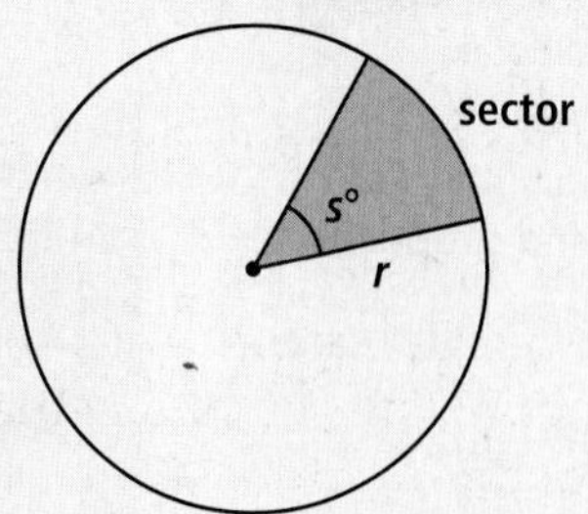

Ⓐ $s = \frac{\pi r^2 A}{360}$

Ⓑ $s = \frac{360}{\pi r^2 A}$

Ⓒ $s = 360\pi r^2 A$

Ⓓ $s = \frac{360A}{\pi r^2}$

Ⓔ $s = \frac{A}{360\pi r^2}$

35. Performance Task A manufacturer can save money by making a can that maximizes volume and minimizes the amount of metal used. For a can with radius r and height h, this goal is reached when $2\pi r^3 = \pi r^2 h$.

Part A Solve the equation for h. How is the height related to the radius for a can that meets the manufacturer's goal?

Part B The area of a label for a can is $A = 2\pi rh$. Use your result from Part A to write a formula giving the area of a label for a can that meets the manufacturer's goals.

1-5 Solving Inequalities in One Variable

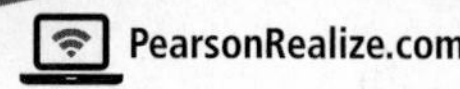

I CAN… solve and graph inequalities.

MODEL & DISCUSS

Skyler competes in the high jump event at her school. She hopes to tie or break some records at the next meet.

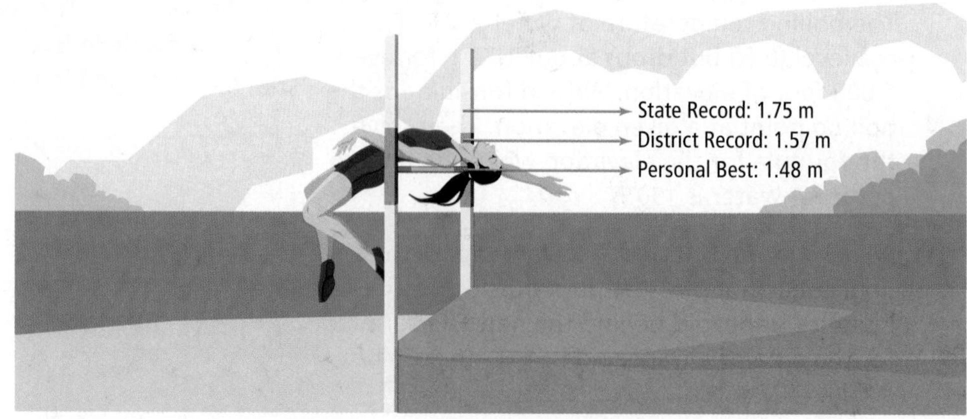

A. Write and solve an equation to find x, the number of meters Skyler must add to her personal best to tie the district record.

B. Look for Relationships Rewrite your equation as an inequality to represent the situation where Skyler *breaks* the district record. How is the value of x in the inequality related to the value of x in the equation?

C. How many meters does Skyler need to add to her personal best to break the state record?

ESSENTIAL QUESTION

How are the solutions of an inequality different from the solutions of an equation?

EXAMPLE 1 Solve Inequalities

Solve $-4(3x - 1) + 6x \geq 16$ and graph the solution.

$$-4(3x - 1) + 6x \geq 16$$

$$-12x + 4 + 6x \geq 16$$

$$-12x + 4 - 4 + 6x \geq 16 - 4$$

Apply the properties of inequalities to solve for x.

$$-12x + 6x \geq 12$$

$$-6x \geq 12$$

$$\frac{-6x}{-6} \leq \frac{12}{-6}$$

Remember that the direction of the inequality symbol is reversed when both sides of the inequality are multiplied or divided by negative values.

$$x \leq -2$$

Graph the solution.

STUDY TIP
Recall that when you graph the solution of an inequality on a number line, you use an open circle if the inequality symbol is $<$ or $>$, and a closed circle if the inequality symbol is $\leq$ or $\geq$.

Try It! 1. Solve each inequality and graph the solution.

a. $-3(2x + 2) < 10$

b. $2(4 - 2x) > 1$

EXAMPLE 2 Solve an Inequality With Variables on Both Sides

Solve $3.5x + 19 \geq 1.5x - 7$. Then graph the solution.

Solve the inequality.

$$3.5x + 19 \geq 1.5x - 7$$

$$3.5x - 1.5x + 19 - 19 \geq 1.5x - 1.5x - 7 - 19$$

Collect like terms on the same side of the inequality.

$$2x \geq -26$$

$$x \geq -13$$

Graph the solution.

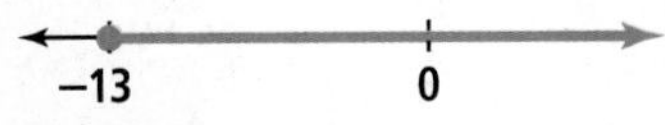

Try It! **2.** Solve $2x - 5 < 5x - 22$. Then graph the solution.

CONCEPTUAL UNDERSTANDING

EXAMPLE 3 Understand Inequalities With Infinitely Many or No Solutions

A. Solve $-3(2x - 5) > -6x + 9$.

$$-3(2x - 5) > -6x + 9$$

$$-6x + 15 > -6x + 9$$

$$-6x + 6x + 15 > -6x + 6x + 9$$

$$15 > 9$$

The original inequality is equivalent to $15 > 9$, a true statement. What does this mean?

Using the same steps above, you can show that the inequality is true for any value of x. So all real numbers are solutions of the inequality.

B. Solve $4x - 5 < 2(2x - 3)$.

$$4x - 5 < 2(2x - 3)$$

$$4x - 5 < 4x - 6$$

$$4x - 4x - 5 < 4x - 4x - 6$$

$$-5 < -6$$

LOOK FOR RELATIONSHIPS Consider the definition of the solution to an inequality. What would the graph of an inequality with no solution look like?

Since the inequality results in a false statement ($-5 < -6$), any value of x you substitute in the original inequality will also result in a false statement.

This inequality has no solution.

Try It! **3.** Solve each inequality.

a. $-2(4x - 2) < -8x + 4$ **b.** $-6x - 5 < -3(2x + 1)$

APPLICATION

EXAMPLE 4 Use Inequalities to Solve Problems

Derek wants to order some roses online. For what number of roses is it less expensive to order from Florist A? From Florist B?

Florist A:
$4.75 per blue rose plus $40 delivery charge.

Florist B:
$5.15 per red rose plus $25 delivery charge.

Formulate ◀ Write an inequality to compare the total cost of x roses from each florist.

The cost of x roses at Florist A is less than the cost of x roses at Florist B.

$$4.75x + 40 \quad < \quad 5.15x + 25$$

Set up the inequality to find the number of roses it would take for Florist A to be less expensive.

Compute ◀ Solve for x.

$$4.75x + 40 < 5.15x + 25$$

$$4.75x - 4.75x + 40 < 5.15x - 4.75x + 25$$

$$40 - 25 < 0.4x + 25 - 25$$

$$\frac{15}{0.4} < \frac{0.4x}{0.4}$$

$$37.5 < x$$

Interpret ◀ The solution is all real numbers greater than 37.5. However, the number of roses must be a whole number.

If Derek plans to buy 38 or more roses, then Florist A is less expensive.
If Derek plans to buy 37 or fewer roses, then Florist B is less expensive.

Try It! **4.** If Florist B increases the cost per rose to $5.20, for what number of roses is it less expensive to order from Florist A? From Florist B?

CONCEPT SUMMARY Solving Inequalities in One Variable

WORDS To solve inequalities, use the Properties of Inequalities to isolate the variable.

The solution of an inequality is the set of all real numbers that makes the inequality true. Some inequalities are true for all real numbers (like $x + 3 < x + 7$), but others have no solutions (like $x + 7 < x + 3$).

ALGEBRA

$$-5(2x - 3) \leq 34$$

$$-10x + 15 \leq 34$$

$$-10x + 15 - 15 \leq 34 - 15$$

$$-10x \leq 19$$

$$\frac{-10x}{-10} \geq \frac{19}{-10}$$

Reverse the inequality when multiplying or dividing by a negative number.

$$x \geq -1.9$$

Do You UNDERSTAND?

1. ESSENTIAL QUESTION How are the solutions of an inequality different from the solutions of an equation?

2. **Reason** How is dividing each side of $x > 0$ by a negative value different from dividing each side by a positive value?

3. **Vocabulary** Give an example of two inequalities that are equivalent inequalities. Explain your reasoning.

4. **Error Analysis** Rachel multiplied each side of $x \geq 2$ by 3. She wrote the result as $3x \leq 6$. Explain the error Rachel made.

Do You KNOW HOW?

Solve each inequality and graph the solution.

5. $\frac{1}{2}x < 6$

6. $-4x \geq 20$

7. $8 \leq -4(x - 1)$

8. $3x - 2 > 4 - 3x$

9. Lourdes plans to jog at least 1.5 miles. Write and solve an inequality to find x, the number of hours Lourdes will have to jog.

PRACTICE & PROBLEM SOLVING

Scan for Multimedia

Practice | Tutorial

Additional Exercises Available Online

UNDERSTAND

10. Construct Arguments Let a, b, and c be real numbers, $c \neq 0$. Show that each of the following statements is true.

a. If $a > b$ and $c < 0$, then $ca < cb$.

b. If $a > b$ and $c < 0$, then $\frac{a}{c} < \frac{b}{c}$.

11. Use Structure For each of the graphs below, write an inequality that the graph represents. Explain your reasoning.

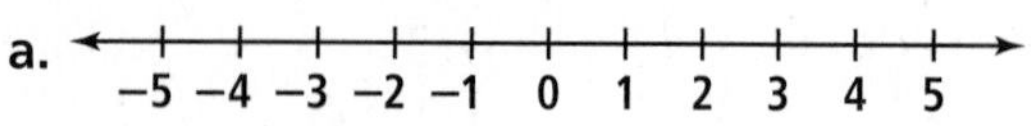

12. Construct Arguments Describe and correct the error a student made when solving the inequality shown.

$3x - 1 > 5$

$3x - 1 + 1 > 5 + 1$ Add 1 to each side.

$3x > 6$ Simplify.

$\frac{3x}{3} < \frac{6}{3}$ Divide each side by 3.

$x < 2$ Simplify.

13. Mathematical Connections Jake's solution to the equation $-4(2x - 3) = 36$ is shown.

$$-4(2x - 3) = 36$$
$$-8x + 12 = 36$$
$$-8x + 12 - 12 = 36 - 12$$
$$-8x = 24$$
$$\frac{-8x}{-8} = \frac{24}{-8}$$
$$x = -3$$

How is the solution to $-4(2x - 3) > 36$ similar to and different from the solution shown?

14. Higher Order Thinking Suppose each side of the inequality $a - b < 0$ is multiplied by c.

a. If $c < 0$ and $c(a - b) > 0$, write an inequality to represent the relationship between a and b.

b. If $c < 0$, is $c(a - b)$ always greater than 0? Explain your reasoning.

PRACTICE

Solve each inequality and graph the solution. SEE EXAMPLES 1 AND 4

15. $x + 9 > 15$

16. $-\frac{1}{5}x > -10$

17. $5x + 15 \leq -10$

18. $-0.3x < 6$

19. $6x \geq -0.3$

20. $-3x > 15$

21. $\frac{1}{4}x > \frac{1}{2}$

22. $x - 8.4 \leq 2.3$

23. $2.1x \geq 6.3$

24. $-2.1x + 2.1 < 6.3$

25. $-\frac{3}{8}x - 20 + 2x > 6$

26. $\frac{2}{3}x + 14 - 3x > -7$

27. $0.5x - 4 - 2x \leq 2$

28. $4x + 1 + 2x \geq 5$

Match each inequality to the graph that represents its solution. Explain your reasoning. SEE EXAMPLE 1

29. $-2(3x - 1) > 20$

30. $2(1 - 3x) < 20$

31. $-2(1 - 3x) > 16$

32. $2(3x - 1) < 16$

A.
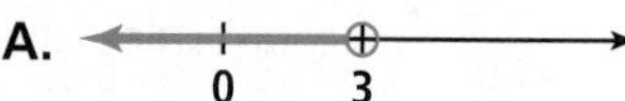

B.
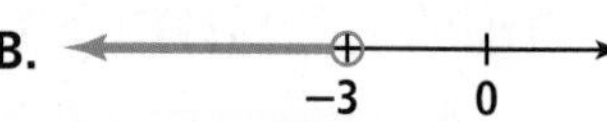

C.

D.
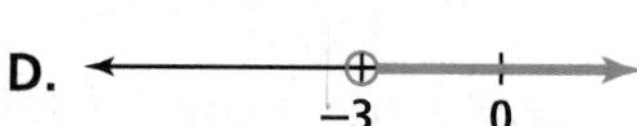

Solve each inequality. SEE EXAMPLE 2

33. $2x + 5 < 3x + 4$

34. $2(7x - 2) > 9x + 6$

Solve each inequality and tell whether it has infinitely many or no solutions. SEE EXAMPLE 3

35. $\frac{3}{4}x + \frac{3}{4} - \frac{1}{2}x \geq -1$

36. $\frac{1}{4}x + 3 - \frac{7}{8}x < -2$

37. $-5(2x + 1) < 24$

38. $4(3 -2x) \geq -4$

39. $7.2x + 6 \leq 2.4x$

40. $-2x - 5 \geq 3x - 25$

41. $2x + 12 > 2(x + 6)$

42. $0.5x + 8 < 2x - 4$

A solution is graphed for each inequality below. Describe the changes that need to be made, if any, to each graph. SEE EXAMPLE 3

43. $3x - 24 \leq -2(2x - 30)$

44. $-2(x - 5) \geq -2x + 10$

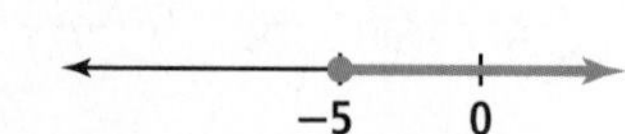

PRACTICE & PROBLEM SOLVING

APPLY

45. **Make Sense and Persevere** Luke and Aisha are traveling on the same road, in the same direction. Luke is driving at a rate of 50 mi/h, and Aisha is driving at a rate of 55 mi/h. Write and solve an inequality to find when Aisha will be ahead of Luke on the highway. Let x represent time in hours.

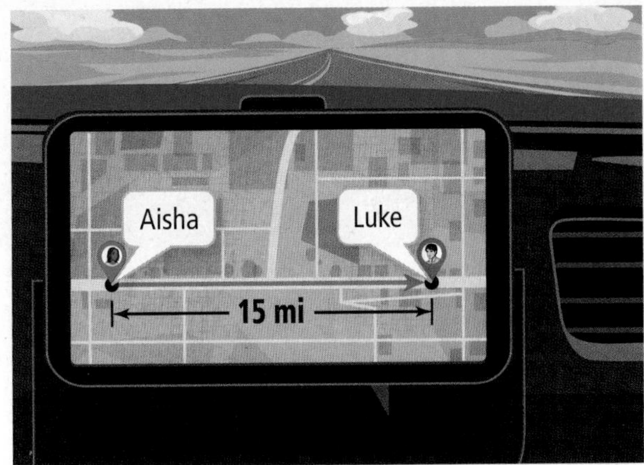

46. **Make Sense and Persevere** An office manager is selecting a water delivery service. Acme H_2O charges a \$15 fee and \$7.50 per 5-gallon jug. Best Water charges a \$24 fee and \$6.00 per 5-gallon jug. How many 5-gallon jugs will the office have to buy each month for the cost of Best Water to be less than that of Acme H_2O?

47. **Model With Mathematics** Charlie can spend up to \$8 on lunch. He wants to buy a tuna sandwich, a bottle of apple juice, and x pounds of potato salad. Write and solve an inequality to find the possible numbers of pounds of potato salad he can buy.

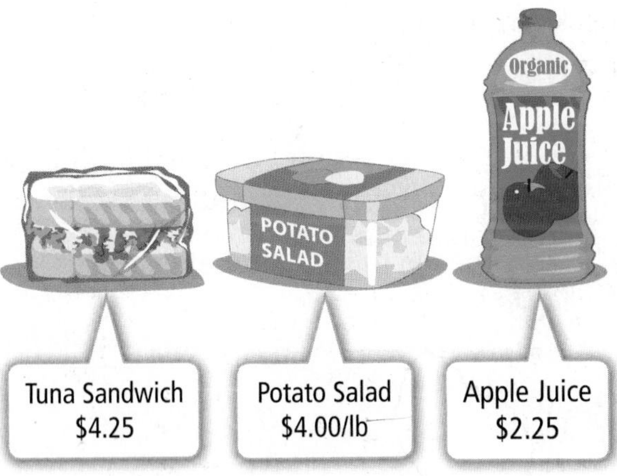

ASSESSMENT PRACTICE

48. Match each inequality with the equivalent inequality.

A. $-\frac{1}{2}x > -\frac{3}{2}$ I. $x < 3$

B. $\frac{1}{2}x > \frac{3}{2}$ II. $x > 3$

C. $\frac{3}{2}x > \frac{1}{2}$ III. $x > \frac{1}{3}$

D. $-\frac{3}{2}x > -\frac{1}{2}$ IV. $x < \frac{1}{3}$

49. **SAT/ACT** Which of the following is the solution of $0.125x + 1 - 0.25x < -3$?

Ⓐ $x < -0.5$
Ⓑ $x < 0.5$
Ⓒ $x > 0.5$
Ⓓ $x < 32$
Ⓔ $x > 32$

50. **Performance Task** Students have organized a three-day walkathon to raise money for charity. The average walking speeds of four participants are given in the table below.

Name	Walking Speed (mi/h)
Elijah	3.2
Aubrey	3
Mercedes	2.4
Steve	3.5

Part A Write and solve an inequality to determine how many hours it would take Steve to walk at least 21 mi on Day 1.

Part B At the beginning of Day 2, Mercedes is 2 mi ahead of Elijah. Write and solve an inequality to determine the hours x when Elijah will be behind Mercedes.

Part C At the beginning of Day 3, Elijah starts walking at the marker for Mile 42, and Aubrey starts walking at the marker for Mile 42.5. Write and solve an inequality to determine the hours when Elijah is ahead of Aubrey.

PearsonRealize.com

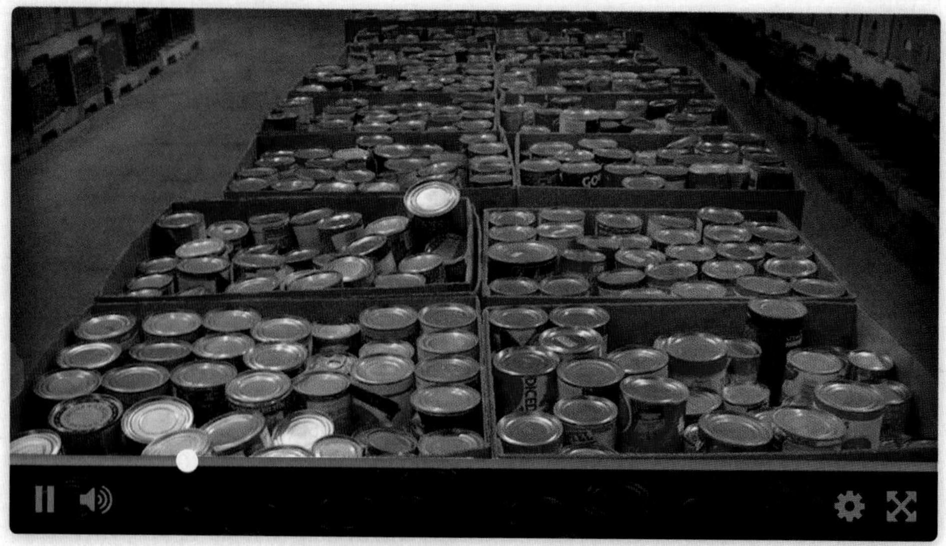

Collecting Cans

Many schools and community centers organize canned food drives and donate the food collected to area food pantries or homeless shelters.

A teacher may hold a contest for the student who collects the most cans. The teacher will track the number of cans each student brings in. Sometimes students have their own ways of keeping track. You'll see how some students kept track in the Mathematical Modeling in 3 Acts lesson.

Scan for Multimedia

ACT 1 Identify the Problem

1. What is the first question that comes to mind after watching the video?
2. Write down the main question you will answer about what you saw in the video.
3. Make an initial conjecture that answers this main question.
4. Explain how you arrived at your conjecture.
5. Write a number that you know is too small.
6. Write a number that you know is too large.

ACT 2 Develop a Model

7. Use the math that you have learned in this Topic to refine your conjecture.

ACT 3 Interpret the Results

8. Is your refined conjecture between the highs and lows you set up earlier?

Activity Assess

1-6 Compound Inequalities

PearsonRealize.com

I CAN… write and solve compound inequalities.

VOCABULARY

- compound inequality

EXPLORE & REASON

Hana has some blue paint. She wants to lighten the shade, so she mixes in 1 cup of white paint. The color is still too dark, so Hana keeps mixing in 1 cup of white paint at a time. After adding 4 cups, she decides the color is too light.

plus 4 c white paint

plus 1 c white paint

A. Explain in words how much paint Hana should have added initially to get the shade she wants.

B. **Model With Mathematics** Represent your answer to part A with one or more inequalities.

C. Hana decides that she likes the shades of blue that appear in between adding 1 cup and 4 cups of white paint. How can you represent the number of cups of white paint that yield the shades Hana prefers?

ESSENTIAL QUESTION

What are compound inequalities and how are their solutions represented?

CONCEPTUAL UNDERSTANDING

EXAMPLE 1 Understand Compound Inequalities

How can you use inequalities to describe the sets of numbers graphed below?

A. −3 0 2

The graph shows the solutions of two inequalities. The two inequalities form a *compound inequality*. A **compound inequality** is made up of two or more inequalities.

Write an inequality to represent the solutions shown in each part of the graph.

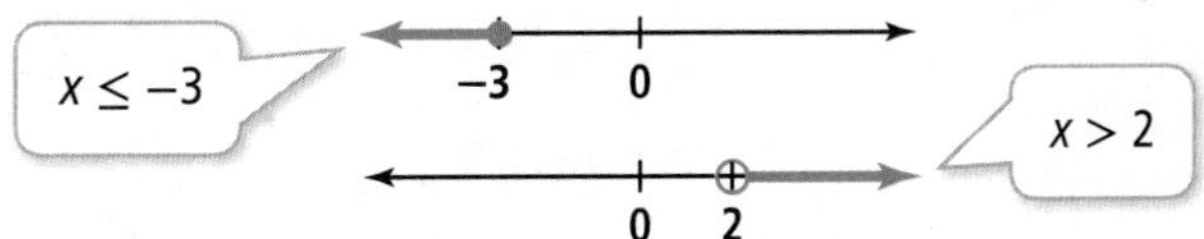

The compound inequality that describes the graph is $x \leq -3$ or $x > 2$.

MAKE SENSE AND PERSEVERE There is no number that can be less than −3 AND greater than 2. So it makes sense to use OR to write the compound inequality.

B.

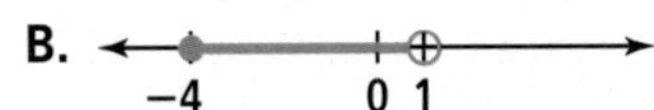

The solutions shown in the graph are greater than or equal to −4. They are also less than 1. Write two inequalities to represent this.

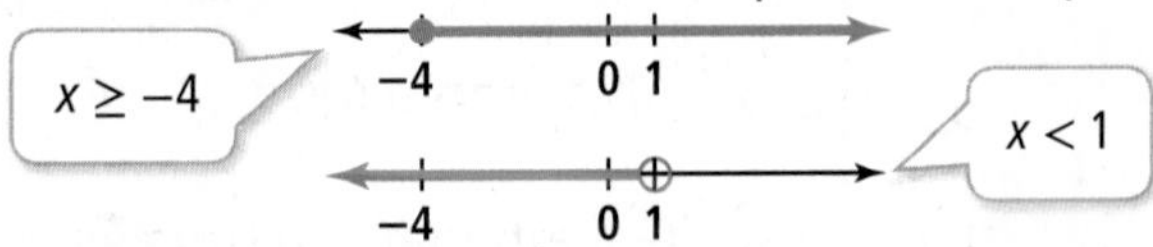

The compound inequality that describes the graph is $-4 \leq x$ and $x < 1$. You can also write this as $-4 \leq x < 1$.

Try It! **1.** Write a compound inequality for the graph.

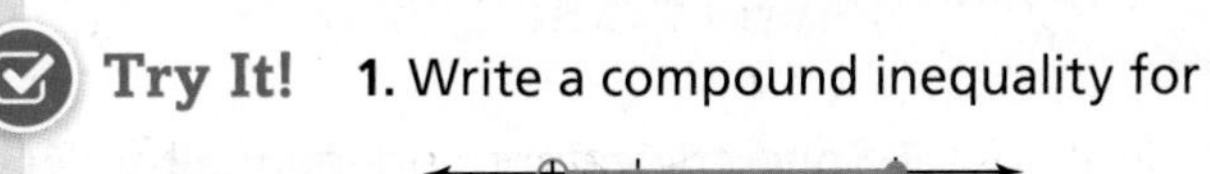

EXAMPLE 2 Solve a Compound Inequality Involving *Or*

Solve the compound inequality $5x - 7 < 13$ or $-4x + 3 > 11$. Graph the solution.

Solve each inequality.

$5x - 7 < 13$	or	$-4x + 3 > 11$
$5x - 7 + 7 < 13 + 7$		$-4x + 3 - 3 > 11 - 3$
$5x < 20$		$-4x > 8$
$\frac{5x}{5} < \frac{20}{5}$		$\frac{-4x}{-4} < \frac{8}{-4}$
$x < 4$		$x < -2$

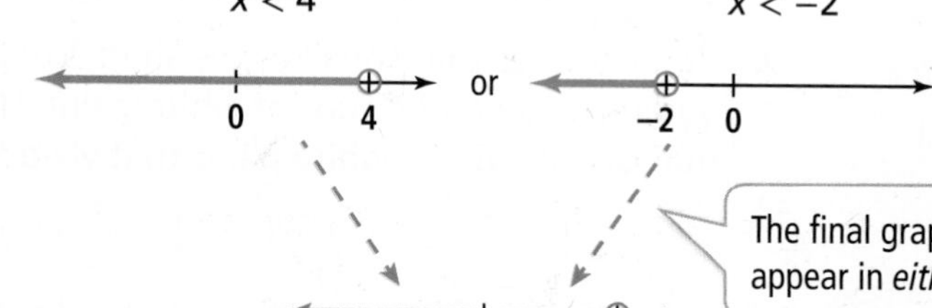

The final graph is all points that appear in *either* solution above.

COMMON ERROR
You may think that there should be two parts in the graph of the solutions. However, the solution to $x < -2$ is a subset of the solution to $x < 4$, so $x < 4$ is the complete solution.

The solution is $x < 4$, which is the set of all real numbers less than 4.

 **Try It!** 2. Solve the compound inequality $-3x + 2 > -7$ or $2(x - 2) \geq 6$. Graph the solution.

EXAMPLE 3 Solve a Compound Inequality Involving *And*

What is the solution of $-12 \leq 7x + 9 < 16$?

Solve each inequality.

$-12 \leq 7x + 9$	and	$7x + 9 < 16$
$-12 - 9 \leq 7x + 9 - 9$		$7x + 9 - 9 < 16 - 9$
$-21 \leq 7x$		$7x < 7$
$\frac{-21}{7} \leq \frac{7x}{7}$		$\frac{7x}{7} < \frac{7}{7}$
$-3 \leq x$		$x < 1$

−3 0 and 0 1

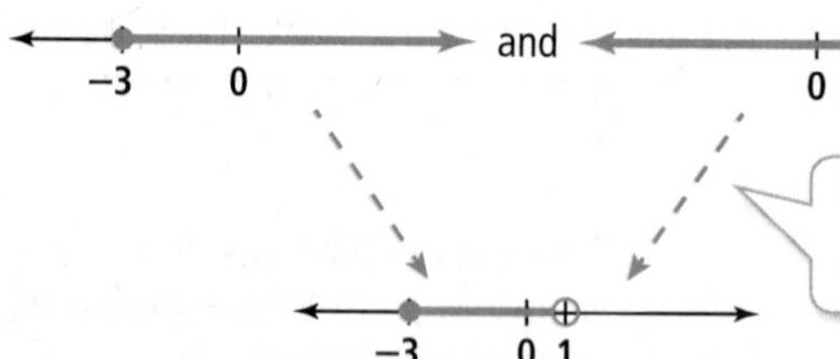

The final graph is all points that appear in *both* solutions above.

The solution is $x \geq -3$ and $x < 1$, or $-3 \leq x < 1$.

 **Try It!** 3. Solve the compound inequality $-2(x + 1) < 4$ and $4x + 1 \leq -3$. Graph the solution.

APPLICATION

EXAMPLE 4 Solve Problems Involving Compound Inequalities

Enrique plans a diet for his dog, River. River consumes between 510 and 540 Calories per day.

If River eats $1\frac{1}{2}$ servings of dog food each day, how many treats can she have?

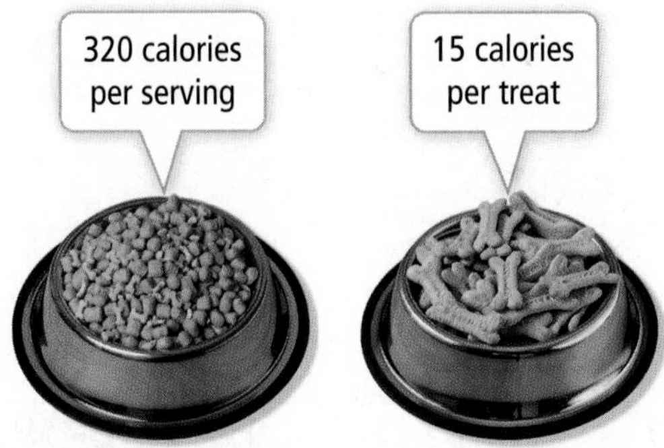

Formulate Model the situation with a compound inequality.

Let x represent the number of treats River can have each day.

Write an expression to represent River's total daily Calories.

$1\frac{1}{2}$ servings at 320 Cal. per serving plus x treats at 15 Cal. per treat

$$480 + 15x$$

Write a compound inequality for the number of dog treats each day.

at least 510 Calories at most 540 Calories

$$510 \leq 480 + 15x \leq 540$$

Compute Solve the compound inequality.

$$\begin{aligned} 510 &\leq 480 + 15x \leq 540 \\ 510 - 480 &\leq 480 + 15x - 480 \leq 540 - 480 \\ 30 &\leq 15x \leq 60 \\ \frac{30}{15} &\leq \frac{15x}{15} \leq \frac{60}{15} \\ 2 &\leq x \leq 4 \end{aligned}$$

The solution is $2 \leq x \leq 4$.

Interpret River can have at least 2 and at most 4 treats each day.

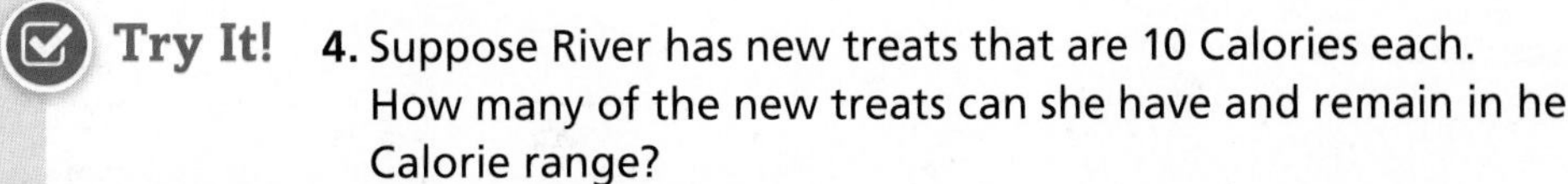

Try It! **4.** Suppose River has new treats that are 10 Calories each. How many of the new treats can she have and remain in her Calorie range?

CONCEPT SUMMARY Compound Inequalities

WORDS	The solution of a compound inequality involving or includes the solutions of one inequality as well as the solutions of the other inequality.	The solution of a compound inequality involving and includes only solutions of both inequalities where they coincide.
ALGEBRA	$x < a$ or $x > b$	$x > a$ and $x < b$ $a < x < b$
GRAPHS	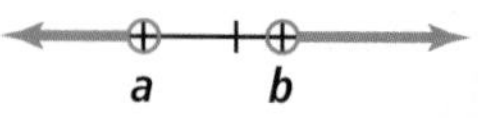 a b	a b

Do You UNDERSTAND?

1. **ESSENTIAL QUESTION** What are compound inequalities and how are their solutions represented?

2. **Look for Relationships** When $a < b$, how is the graph of $x > a$ and $x < b$ similar to the graph of $x > a$? How is it different?

3. **Vocabulary** A *compound* is defined as a *mixture*. Make a conjecture as to why the term *compound inequality* includes the word *compound*.

4. **Error Analysis** Kona graphed the compound inequality $x > 2$ or $x > 3$ by graphing $x > 3$. Explain Kona's error.

Do You KNOW HOW?

Write a compound inequality for each graph.

5. −4 −1 0

6. 0 2 8

Solve each compound inequality and graph the solution.

7. $4x - 1 > 3$ and $-2(3x - 4) \geq -16$

8. $2(4x + 3) \geq -10$ or $-5x - 15 > 5$

9. Nadeem plans to ride her bike between 12 mi and 15 mi. Write and solve an inequality to model how many hours Nadeem will be riding.

PRACTICE & PROBLEM SOLVING

Scan for Multimedia 

Additional Exercises Available Online

UNDERSTAND

10. **Look for Relationships** The compound inequality $x > a$ and $x > b$ is graphed below. How is the point labeled c related to a and b?

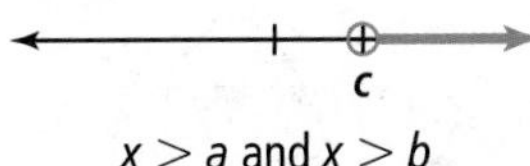

11. **Error Analysis** Describe and correct the error a student made graphing the compound inequality $x \geq 2$ and $x > 4$.

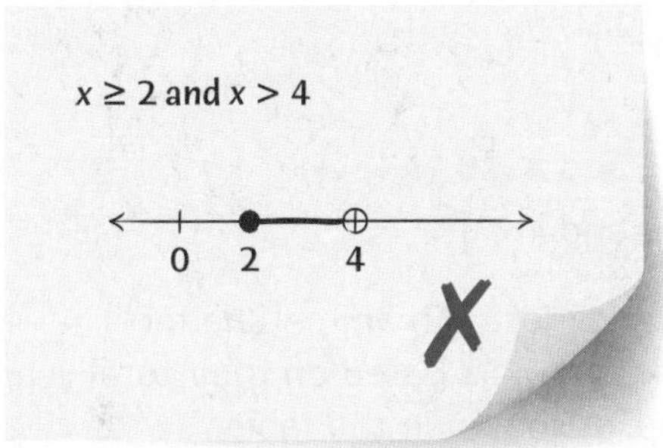

12. **Generalize** Suppose that $a < b$. Select from the symbols >, <, ≥, and ≤, as well as the words *and* and *or*, to complete the compound inequality below so that its solution is all real numbers.

x ▢ a ▢ x ▢ b

13. **Higher Order Thinking** Let a and b be real numbers.

a. If $a > b$, how is the graph of $x > a$ and $x > b$ different from the graph of $x > a$ or $x > b$?

b. If $a < b$, how is the graph of $x > a$ and $x > b$ different from the graph of $x > a$ or $x > b$?

c. If $a = b$, how is the graph of $x > a$ and $x > b$ different from the graph of $x > a$ or $x > b$?

14. **Mathematical Connections** Consider the solutions of the compound inequalities.

$4 < x < 8$ $\qquad$ $2 < x < 11$

Describe each solution as a set. Is one set a subset of the other? Explain your answer.

PRACTICE

Write a compound inequality for each graph. SEE EXAMPLE 1

15. −2 0 1

16. −5 −1 0

17. −0.5 0 0.25

18. −1.2 −0.4 0

Solve each compound inequality and graph the solution. SEE EXAMPLES 2 AND 3

19. $2x + 5 > -3$ and $4x + 7 < 15$

20. $2x - 5 > 3$ or $-4x + 7 < -25$

21. $2x - 5 > 3$ and $-4x + 7 < -25$

22. $-x + 1 > -2$ or $6(2x - 3) \geq -6$

23. $-x + 1 > -2$ and $6(2x - 3) \geq -6$

24. $-\frac{5}{8}x + 2 + \frac{3}{4}x > -1$ or $-3(x + 25) > 15$

The value for the area A of each figure is given. Write and solve a compound inequality for the value of x in each figure. SEE EXAMPLE 4

25. $35 \geq A \geq 25$ $\qquad$ **26.** $9 \leq A \leq 12$

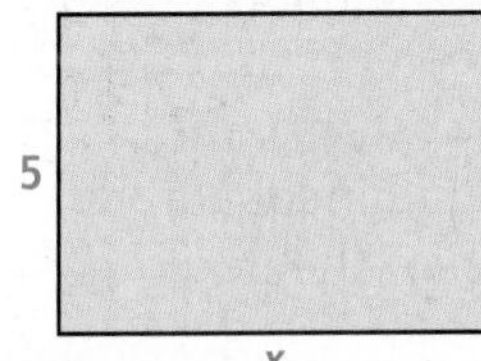

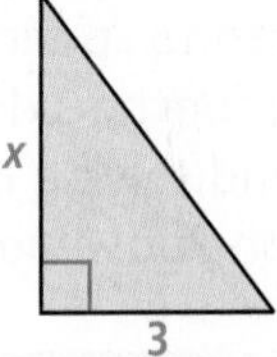

Write a compound inequality to represent each sentence below. SEE EXAMPLE 4

27. A quantity x is at least 10 and at most 20.

28. A quantity x is either less than 10 or greater than 20.

29. A quantity x is greater than 10 and less than 20.

APPLY

30. Reason Fatima plans to spend at least $15 and at most $20 on sketch pads and pencils. If she buys 2 sketch pads, how many pencils can she buy while staying in her price range?

31. Make Sense and Persevere A peanut company ships its product in a carton that weighs 20 oz when empty. Twenty bags of peanuts are shipped in each carton. The acceptable weight for one bag of peanuts is between 30.5 oz and 33.5 oz, inclusive. If a carton weighs too much or too little, it is opened for inspection. Write and solve a compound inequality to determine x, the weights of cartons that are opened for inspection.

32. Model With Mathematics Volunteers at an animal shelter are building a rectangular dog run so that one shorter side of the rectangle is formed by the shelter building as shown. They plan to spend between $100 and $200 on fencing for the sides at a cost of $2.50 per ft. Write and solve a compound inequality to model the possible length of the dog run.

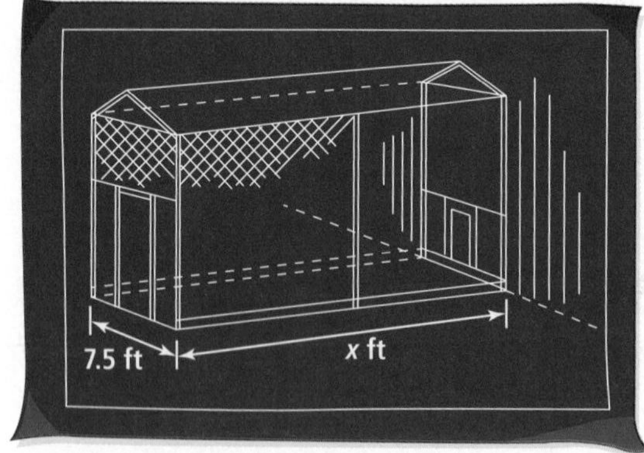

ASSESSMENT PRACTICE

33. Which of the following compound inequalities have the solution $x < 3$? Select all that apply.

Ⓐ $3x + 5 < 6$ or $-2x + 9 > 3$

Ⓑ $3x + 5 < 6$ and $-2x + 9 > 3$

Ⓒ $3x - 5 < 10$ and $-2x + 9 > 3$

Ⓓ $3x + 5 < 6$ or $-2x + 9 < 3$

Ⓔ $3x - 5 < 10$ or $-2x + 9 > 3$

34. SAT/ACT What is the solution of $0.2x - 4 - 2x < -0.4$ and $3x + 2.7 < 3$?

Ⓐ $x < -2$

Ⓑ $x < 0.1$

Ⓒ $x < 1$

Ⓓ $x > -2$ and $x < 0.1$

Ⓔ $x > -2$ and $x < 1$

35. Performance Task An animal shelter categorizes donors based on their total yearly donation, as shown in the table.

Donor Category	Total Yearly Donation
Bronze	< $100
Silver	≥ $100 and < $500
Gold	≥ $500 and < $1,000
Platinum	≥ $1,000

Part A Keenan donates the same amount each month. Write and solve a compound inequality for the monthly donation that will put him in the Gold category.

Part B Libby donated $50 during the first month of the year. If she makes three additional donations of equal amounts during the year, how much will she need to donate each time to be in the Silver category?

Part C Paula originally planned to donate $50 each month. After reviewing her budget, she decides that she must reduce her planned donation. By what amount can she reduce her original planned monthly donation of $50 so that she will be in the Silver category?

1-7 Absolute Value Equations and Inequalities

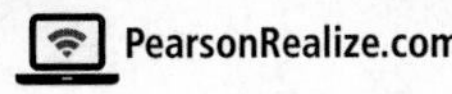

Activity Assess

I CAN… write and solve absolute value equations and inequalities.

MODEL & DISCUSS

Amelia is participating in a 60-mile spin-a-thon. Her spin bike keeps track of the simulated number of miles she travels. She plans to take a 15-minute break within 5 miles of riding 30 miles.

Spin-a-thon Schedule	
Event	**Time**
Start spinning	10:00 A.M.
Stop for break	■
Resume spinning	■

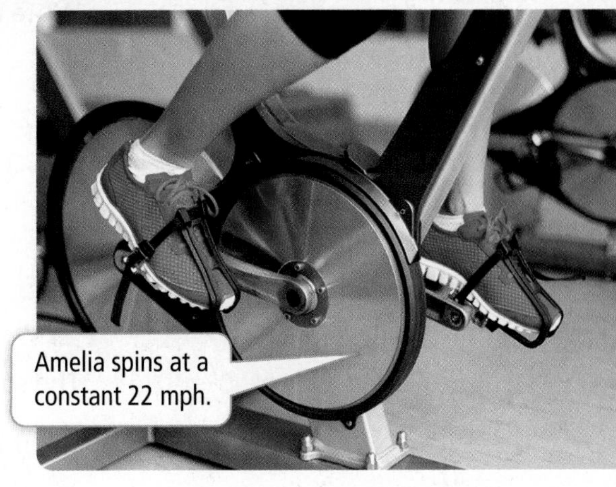

A. Write a compound inequality that models the number of miles Amelia spins before taking a break.

B. How is the number of miles Amelia spins before she takes a break related to the amount of time before she takes a break?

C. **Make Sense and Persevere** About how many hours will Amelia spin before she takes a break? Discuss how you could use your mathematical model to complete the spin-a-thon schedule.

ESSENTIAL QUESTION

Why does the solution for an absolute value equation or inequality typically result in a pair of equations or inequalities?

EXAMPLE 1 Understand Absolute Value Equations

A. What is the value of x in $7 = |x| + 2$?

Solve for x by isolating the absolute value expression on one side of the equation.

$$7 = |x| + 2$$
$$7 - 2 = |x| + 2 - 2$$
$$5 = |x|$$

Use the Subtraction Property of Equality.

STUDY TIP
The absolute value of a number is its distance from 0 on a number line.

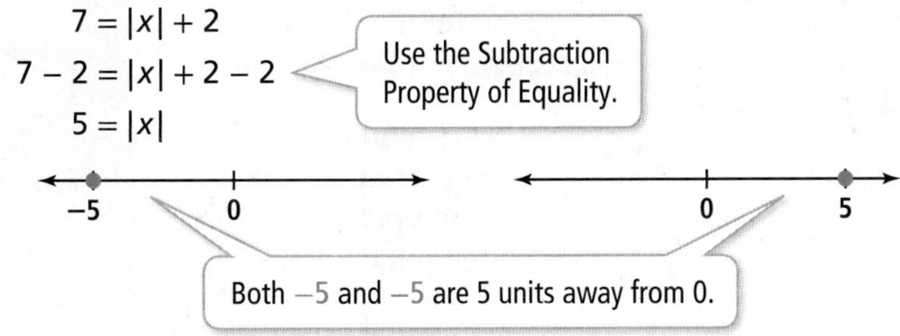

The solutions are $x = -5$ and $x = 5$.

Check the solutions.

$$7 \stackrel{?}{=} |-5| + 2 \qquad 7 \stackrel{?}{=} |5| + 2$$
$$\stackrel{?}{=} 5 + 2 \qquad \stackrel{?}{=} 5 + 2$$
$$= 7 ✓ \qquad = 7 ✓$$

CONTINUED ON THE NEXT PAGE

EXAMPLE 1 CONTINUED

USE STRUCTURE
When solving an absolute value equation in the form $|ax + b| = c$, use two different equations to find the solutions, $ax + b = c$ and $ax + b = -c$.

B. What is the value of x in $|2x - 3| = 1$?

Write and solve equations for the two possibilities:

$2x - 3$ is positive.

$$2x - 3 = 1$$
$$2x - 3 + 3 = 1 + 3$$
$$2x = 4$$
$$\frac{2x}{2} = \frac{4}{2}$$
$$x = 2$$

$2x - 3$ is negative.

$$2x - 3 = -1$$
$$2x - 3 + 3 = -1 + 3$$
$$2x = 2$$
$$\frac{2x}{2} = \frac{2}{2}$$
$$x = 1$$

The expression inside the absolute value symbol can be positive or negative. So the expression $2x - 3$ can be equal to 1 or -1.

The solutions are $x = 2$ and $x = 1$.

C. What is the value of x in $3|x + 6| + 8 = 5$?

Step 1 Isolate the absolute value expression.

$$3|x + 6| + 8 - 8 = 5 - 8$$
$$3|x + 6| = -3$$
$$\frac{3|x + 6|}{3} = \frac{-3}{3}$$

Step 2 Solve for x.

$$|x + 6| = -1$$

This equation has no solution.

The absolute value of a number is a distance and cannot be negative.

Try It! 1. Solve each equation.

a. $6 = |x| - 2$

b. $2|x + 5| = 4$

c. $|3x - 6| = 12$

EXAMPLE 2 Apply an Absolute Value Equation

STUDY TIP
You can use an absolute value equation to model a quantity "plus or minus" another quantity.

The cruising speed of Kennedy's boat is 25 mi/h. She plans to cruise at this speed for the distances shown in the diagram.

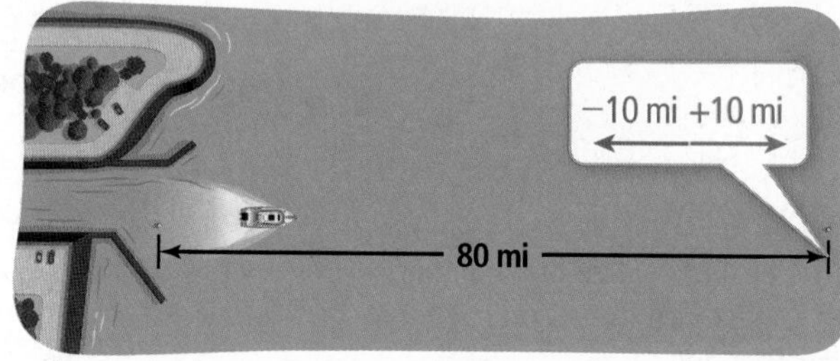

Not to scale

A. What equation models the number of hours x that Kennedy will travel?

$$|25x - 80| = 10$$

The distance Kennedy actually travels

10 miles from the 80-mile point

Final distance from the 80-mile point

CONTINUED ON THE NEXT PAGE

EXAMPLE 2 CONTINUED

B. What are the minimum number and maximum number of hours Kennedy will travel?

Write and solve equations for the two possibilities.

If Kennedy travels plus 10 miles, the absolute value expression is positive.

$$25x - 80 = 10$$
$$25x - 80 + 80 = 10 + 80$$
$$25x = 90$$
$$\frac{25x}{25} = \frac{90}{25}$$
$$x = 3.6$$

If Kennedy travels minus 10 miles, the absolute value expression is negative.

$$25x - 80 = -10$$
$$25x - 80 + 80 = -10 + 80$$
$$25x = 70$$
$$\frac{25x}{25} = \frac{70}{25}$$
$$x = 2.8$$

The solutions are $x = 3.6$ and $x = 2.8$.

Kennedy will travel at least 2.8 hours and at most 3.6 hours.

Try It! 2. What will be the minimum and maximum time that Kennedy will travel if she resets her cruising speed to 20 mi/h?

CONCEPTUAL UNDERSTANDING

EXAMPLE 3 Understand Absolute Value Inequalities

What are the solutions of an absolute value inequality?

COMMON ERROR
Remember to look at the > and < symbols when solving absolute value inequalities. Inequalities with absolute value have to be set up differently to solve if it is an "and" situation vs. an "or" situation.

Solve and graph two absolute value inequalities.

A.

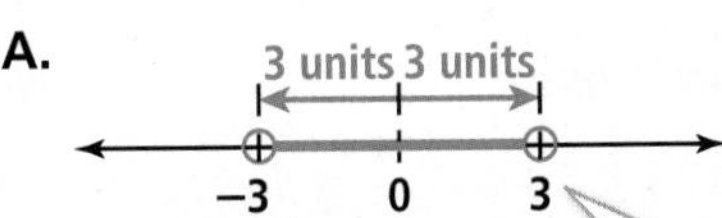

The distance between x and 0 must be less than 3, so the values 3 units to the right and 3 units to the left are solutions.

$|x| < 3$

$|x| < 3$ is equivalent to the compound inequality $x < 3$ *and* $x > -3$, which can also be written as $-3 < x < 3$.

B.

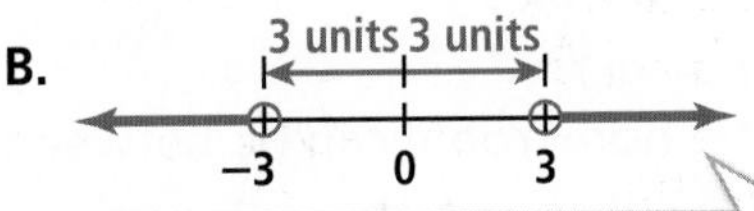

The distance between x and 0 must be greater than 3. So positive values of x must be greater than 3, and negative values of x must be less than −3.

$|x| > 3$

$|x| > 3$ is equivalent to the compound inequality $x < -3$ *or* $x > 3$.

Try It! 3. Solve and graph the solutions of each inequality.

a. $|x| > 15$

b. $|x| \leq 7$

APPLICATION

EXAMPLE 4 Write an Absolute Value Inequality

Members of the debate team are traveling to a tournament, where they will stay in a hotel for 4 nights. The total cost for each member must be within $20 of $175. Which of the hotels shown can they consider?

Hotel Room Costs*

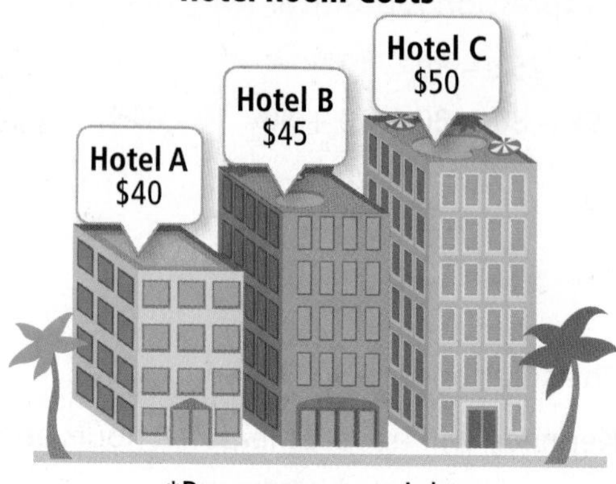

*Per person per night

Formulate Write an absolute value inequality to represent the situation.

Let x be the cost per night of a hotel room.

The difference between total cost and $175 is less than or equal to $20.

$$|4x - 175| \leq 20$$

Compute Solve the inequality to find the maximum and minimum hotel cost for each team member.

Maximum Cost	Minimum Cost
$4x - 175 \leq 20$	$4x - 175 \geq -20$
$4x - 175 + 175 \leq 20 + 175$	$4x - 175 + 175 \geq -20 + 175$
$4x \leq 195$	$4x \geq 155$
$\frac{4x}{4} \leq \frac{195}{4}$	$\frac{4x}{4} \geq \frac{155}{4}$
$x \leq 48.75$	$x \geq 38.75$

Interpret The cost of the hotel room can be between $38.75 and $48.75, inclusive.

The debate team can consider Hotel A or Hotel B.

Try It! **4.** If the debate team increased their limit to $200 plus or minus $20, would they be able to afford Hotel D at $55 per night? Explain.

CONCEPT SUMMARY Absolute Value Equations and Inequalities

WORDS

Absolute Value Equations

To solve an absolute value equation, isolate the absolute value expression. Then write two equations and solve.

Absolute Value Inequalities

If an inequality uses $<$ or $\leq$ and these symbols point to the variable in the solution, the solution uses "and". If an inequality uses $>$ or $\geq$ and these symbols point to the variable in the solution, the solution uses "or".

ALGEBRA

$$2|x - 17| = 18$$
$$|x - 17| = 9$$

$x - 17 = -9$ $\quad$ $x - 17 = 9$

$x = 8$ $\quad$ $x = 26$

$$|x| \leq 1$$
$$x \geq -1 \text{ and } x \leq 1$$

$$|x| > 2$$
$$x < -2 \text{ or } x > 2$$

DIAGRAMS

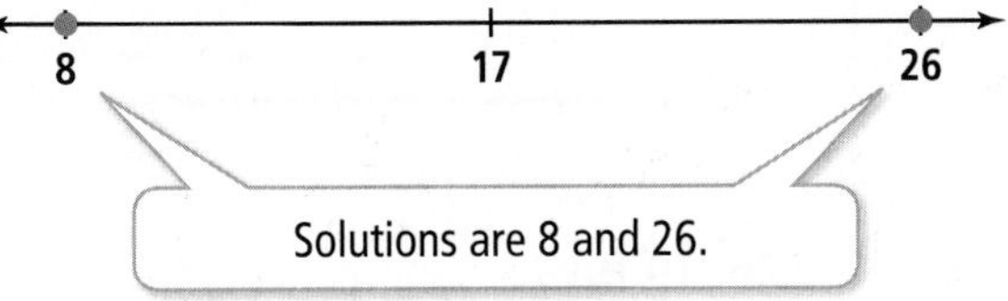

$|x| \leq 1$

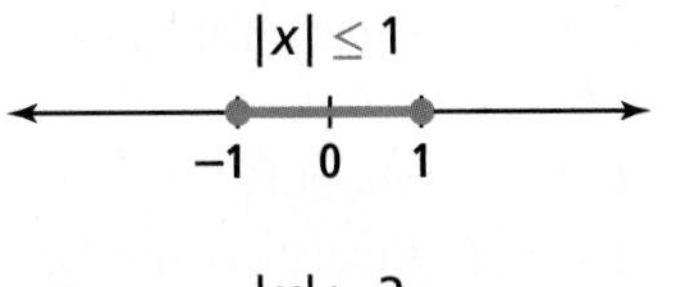

$|x| > 2$

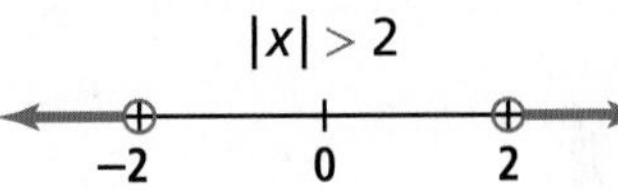

Do You UNDERSTAND?

1. ESSENTIAL QUESTION Why does the solution for an absolute value equation or inequality typically result in a pair of equations or inequalities?

2. **Reason** How is solving an absolute value equation similar to solving an equation that does not involve absolute value? How is it different?

3. **Vocabulary** Describe how you would explain to another student why the *absolute value* of a number cannot be negative.

4. **Error Analysis** Yumiko solved $|x| > 5$ by solving $x > -5$ and $x < 5$. Explain the error Yumiko made.

Do You KNOW HOW?

Solve each absolute value equation.

5. $5 = |x| + 3$

6. $|2x - 8| = 16$

Solve each absolute value inequality. Graph the solution.

7. $|3x - 6| \geq 9$

8. $|4x - 12| \leq 20$

9. On a road trip, Andrew plans to use his cruise control for 125 mi, plus or minus 20 mi. Write and solve an equation to find the minimum and maximum number of hours for Andrew's road trip.

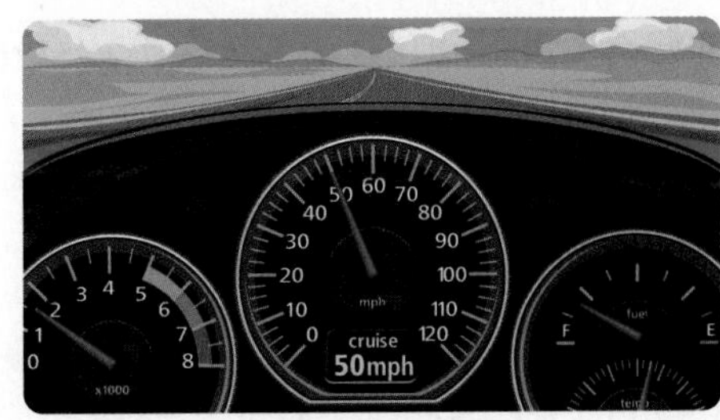

UNDERSTAND

10. **Make Sense and Persevere** Sasha is solving the absolute value equation $|2x| + 4 = 8$. What is the first step she should take?

11. **Use Structure** The absolute value inequality $5 \leq |x| - n$ is graphed below. What is the value of n?

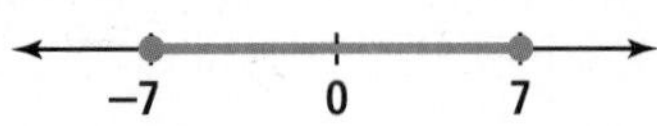

12. **Error Analysis** Describe and correct the error a student made when solving $2|x| < 16$.

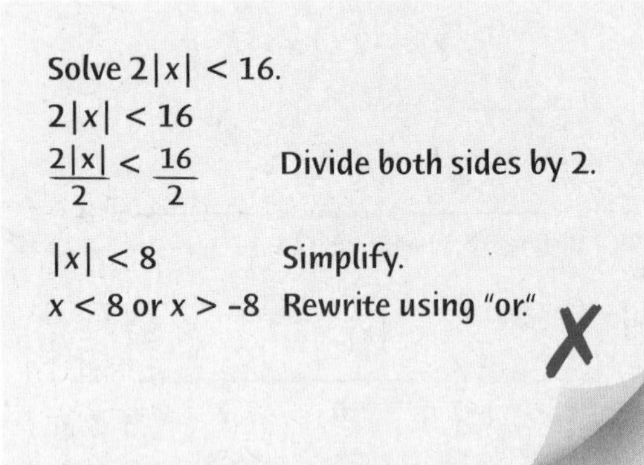
Solve $2|x| < 16$.
$2|x| < 16$
$\frac{2|x|}{2} < \frac{16}{2}$ Divide both sides by 2.
$|x| < 8$ Simplify.
$x < 8$ or $x > -8$ Rewrite using "or."
X

13. **Mathematical Connections** Jack wants to model a situation where the perimeter of the rectangle below is 6 ft plus or minus 1.5 ft.

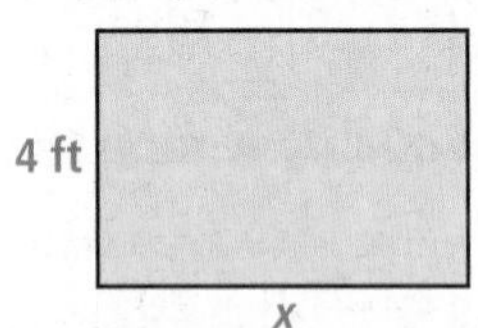

Because he is modeling a length "plus or minus" another length, he decides to use an absolute value equation for his model. Do you agree with his decision? Explain your reasoning.

14. **Higher Order Thinking** Let a, b, c, and x be real numbers.

a. How is solving $|ax| + b = c$ different from solving $|ax + b| = c$?

b. How is solving $|ax| + b \leq c$ different from solving $|ax + b| \geq c$?

PRACTICE

Solve each absolute value equation. SEE EXAMPLE 1

15. $2 = |x| - 1$
16. $|x| - 4 = 9$
17. $14 = |x| + 2$
18. $|x| + 4 = -9$
19. $|-2x + 8| = 20$
20. $|x - 4| = 9$
21. $2|x + 8| = 20$
22. $2|x - 8| = 20$
23. $5|x + 3| + 8 = 6$
24. $3|x - 2| - 8 = 7$

Write and solve an absolute value equation for the minimum and maximum times for an object moving at the given speed to travel the given distance. (Figures are not to scale.) SEE EXAMPLE 2

25. 5 mi/h

26. 10 ft/s

Solve each absolute value inequality. Graph the solution. SEE EXAMPLES 3 AND 4

27. $2 \leq |x| - 8$
28. $-2 > |x| - 8$
29. $|x| + 5 \geq 10$
30. $|x| + 2.4 < 3.6$
31. $|2x + 5| \geq 9$
32. $|2x - 5| < 9$
33. $-2|x + 4| \leq -6$
34. $-2|2x + 4| + 10 > -6$

Match each absolute value inequality to the graph that represents its solution. Explain your reasoning. SEE EXAMPLES 3 AND 4

35. $3|x| - 2 \leq 10$

A. 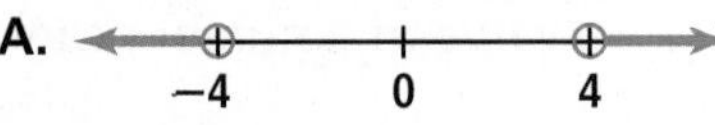

36. $2|x| - 1 < 7$

B. 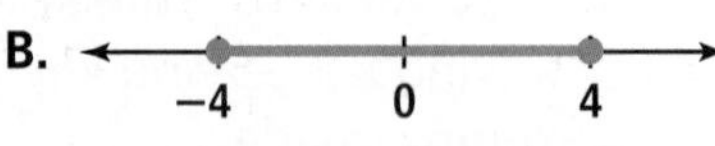

37. $3|2x| + 1 > 25$

C. 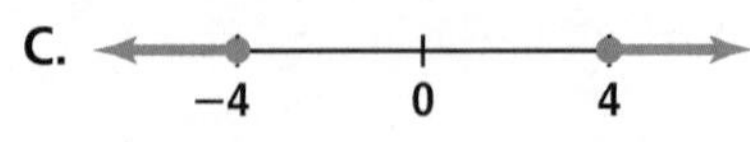

38. $2|4x| - 7 \geq 25$

D.
–4 0 4

PRACTICE & PROBLEM SOLVING

APPLY

39. Make Sense and Persevere A company manufactures cell phone cases. The length of a certain case must be within 0.25 mm of 125 mm, as shown (figure is not to scale). All cases with lengths outside of this range are removed from the inventory. How could you use an absolute value inequality to represent the lengths of all the cases that should be removed? Explain.

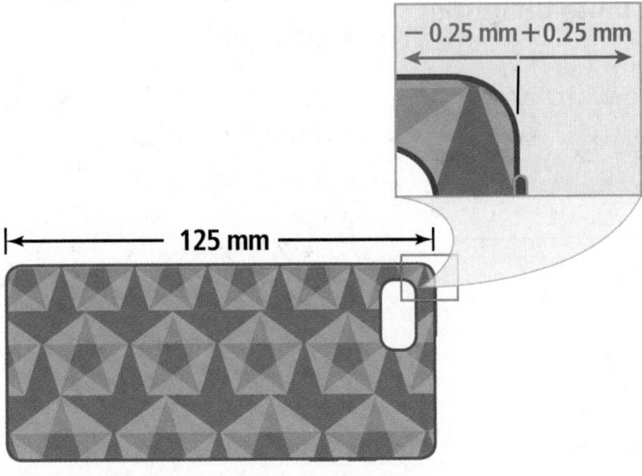

40. Construct Arguments Ashton is hosting a banquet. He plans to spend \$400, plus or minus \$50, at a cost of \$25 per guest. Solve $|25x - 400| = 50$ to find the maximum and minimum number of guests. If there can be up to 7 guests at each table, what is the minimum number of tables Ashton should reserve so that every guest has a seat?

41. Model With Mathematics Hugo is pumping regular gas into his truck. Write and solve an absolute value equation to represent how many gallons of gas will be pumped when the total is \$25 plus or minus \$0.50.

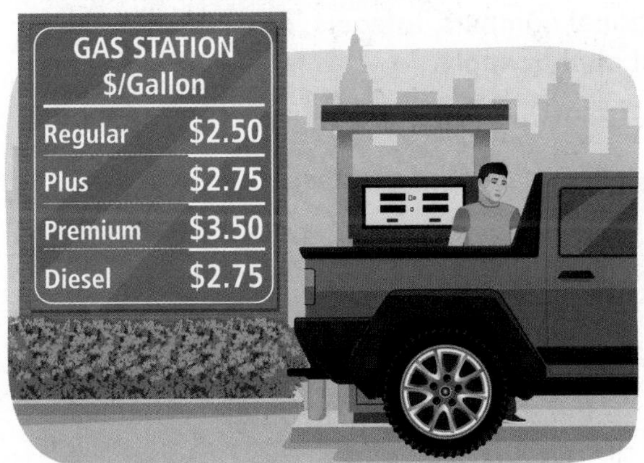

ASSESSMENT PRACTICE

42. Arrange steps in the solution to $2|x - 3| + 4 < 12$ in the correct order.

A. $-1 < x < 7$

B. $2|x - 3| + 4 < 12$

C. $2|x - 3| < 8$

D. $-4 < x - 3 < 4$

E. $|x - 3| < 4$

43. SAT/ACT What is the solution of $|4x - 6| = 2$?

Ⓐ $x = 1, x = 2$

Ⓑ $x = -1, x = 2$

Ⓒ $x = 1, x = -2$

Ⓓ $x = -1, x = -2$

Ⓔ $x = -2, x = 2$

44. Performance Task A road sign shows a vehicle's speed as the vehicle passes.

Part A The sign blinks for vehicles traveling within 5 mi/h of the speed limit. Write and solve an absolute value inequality to find the minimum and maximum speeds of an oncoming vehicle that will cause the sign to blink.

Part B Another sign blinks when it detects a vehicle traveling within 2 mi/h of a 35 mi/h speed limit. Write and solve an absolute value inequality to represent the speeds of the vehicles that cause the sign to blink.

Part C The sign is programmed to blink using absolute value inequalities of the form $|x - a| \le b$ and $|x - a| \ge b$. Which of these formulas is used to program the sign for cars traveling either 5 mi/h above or below the 20 mi/h speed limit? What are the values of a and b? Explain.

TOPIC 1

Topic Review

TOPIC ESSENTIAL QUESTION

1. What general strategies can you use to solve simple equations and inequalities?

Vocabulary Review

Choose the correct term to complete each sentence.

2. An equation rule for a relationship between two or more quantities is a(n) ________.
3. A combination of two or more inequalities using the word *and* or the word *or* is a(n) ________.
4. Any of the distinct objects of a set is called a(n) ________.
5. If each element of *B* is also an element of *A*, *B* is a(n) ________ of *A*.
6. A well-defined collection of elements is a(n) ________.
7. An equation where letters are used for constants and variables is a(n) ________.
8. An equation that is true for all values of the variable is a(n) ________.

- compound inequality
- element
- formula
- identity
- literal equation
- set
- subset

Concepts & Skills Review

LESSON 1-1 Operations on Real Numbers

Quick Review

Sums, differences, and products of rational numbers are rational. Quotients of rational numbers (when they are defined) are rational.

The sum and difference of a rational number and an irrational number are irrational. The product and quotient (when defined) of a rational number and an irrational number are irrational, *except* when the rational number is 0.

Example

Let *a*, *b*, *c*, and *d* be integers, with $b \neq 0$ and $d \neq 0$. Is the sum of $\frac{a}{b}$ and $\frac{c}{d}$ rational or irrational? Is their product rational or irrational?

$\frac{a}{b} + \frac{c}{d} = \frac{ad + bc}{bd}$ $\frac{a}{b} \cdot \frac{c}{d} = \frac{ac}{bd}$

The sum and product are both rational.

Practice & Problem Solving

9. Give an example of two irrational numbers whose product is rational.

For each number, determine whether it is an element of the real numbers, irrational numbers, rational numbers, integers, or whole numbers. List all that apply.

10. 13.9
11. $\sqrt{49}$
12. -48

Order from least to greatest.

13. $0.\overline{36}, \sqrt{15}, \sqrt{\frac{17}{3}}$
14. $\frac{29}{12}, 2.4, \sqrt{5.65}$

15. Make Sense and Persevere Taylor uses tape to mark a square play area in the basement for her daughter. The area measures 28 ft^2. Is the side length of the square rational or irrational? Explain.

LESSON 1-2 Solving Linear Equations

Quick Review

You can use properties of equality to solve linear equations. Use the Distributive Property and combine like terms, when needed.

Example

Solve $\frac{2}{3}(6x - 15) + 5x = 26$.

$\frac{2}{3}(6x - 15) + 5x = 26$

$4x - 10 + 5x = 26$ Distributive Property

$9x - 10 = 26$ Combine like terms.

$9x - 10 + 10 = 26 + 10$ Add 10 to each side.

$9x = 36$ Simplify.

$\frac{9x}{9} = \frac{36}{9}$ Divide each side by 9.

$x = 4$ Simplify.

Practice & Problem Solving

16. **Use Structure** What property would you use first to solve $\frac{1}{2}x - 6 = 10$? Explain.

Solve each equation.

17. $3(2x - 1) = 21$

18. $100 = 8(4t - 5)$

19. $\frac{5}{8} = \frac{3}{4}b - \frac{7}{12}$

20. $1.045s + 0.068 = 15.743$

21. **Model With Mathematics** The price for an adult movie ticket is $1\frac{1}{3}$ more than a movie ticket for a child. Ines takes her daughter to the movie, buys a box of popcorn for \$5.50, and spends \$26.50. Write and solve an equation to find the prices for each of their movie tickets.

LESSON 1-3 Solving Equations with a Variable on Both Sides

Quick Review

To solve equations with a variable on both sides, rewrite the equation so that all the variable terms are on one side of the equation and the constants are on the other. Then solve for the value of the variable.

Example

Solve $5x - 48 = -3x + 8$.

$5x - 48 = -3x + 8$

$5x - 48 + 3x = -3x + 8 + 3x$ Add $3x$ to each side.

$8x - 48 = 8$ Simplify.

$8x - 48 + 48 = 8 + 48$ Add 48 to each side.

$8x = 56$ Simplify.

$\frac{8x}{8} = \frac{56}{8}$ Divide each side by 8.

$x = 7$ Simplify.

Practice & Problem Solving

22. **Error Analysis** Describe and correct any errors a student may have made when solving the equation $0.6(y - 0.2) = 3 - 0.2(y - 1)$.

$$0.6(y - 0.2) = 3 - 0.2(y - 1)$$
$$0.6y - 0.12 = 3.2 - 0.2y$$
$$100(0.6y - 0.12) = 10(3.2 - 0.2y)$$
$$60y - 12 = 32 - 2y$$
$$60y - 12 + 12 + 2y = 32 + 12 - 2y + 2y$$
$$62y = 42$$
$$y = \frac{21}{31}$$

Solve each equation.

23. $21 - 4x = 4x + 21$

24. $6b - 27 = 3(5b - 2)$

25. $0.45(t + 8) = 0.6(t - 3)$

26. **Construct Arguments** Aaron can join a gym that charges \$19.99 per month, plus an annual \$12.80 fee, or he can pay \$21.59 per month. He thinks the second option is better because he plans to use the gym for 10 months. Is Aaron correct? Explain.

LESSON 1-4 Literal Equations and Formulas

Quick Review

You can use properties of equality to solve literal equations for a specific variable. You can use the rewritten equation as a formula to solve problems.

Example

Find the height of a cylinder with a volume of 1,650 cm³ and a radius of 6 cm.

Rewrite the formula for the volume of a cylinder in terms of h.

$$A = \pi r^2 h$$

$$\frac{A}{\pi r^2} = \frac{\pi r^2 h}{\pi r^2}$$

$$\frac{A}{\pi r^2} = h$$

Find the height of the cylinder. Use 3.14 for pi.

$$h = \frac{A}{\pi r^2}$$

$$h = \frac{1{,}650}{(3.14)(6)^2} = \frac{1{,}650}{(3.14)(36)} = \frac{1{,}650}{113.04} \approx 14.60$$

The height of the cylinder is about 14.60 cm.

Practice & Problem Solving

27. Error Analysis Describe and correct the error a student made when solving $a = \frac{3}{4}(b + 5)$ for b.

$$a = \frac{3}{4}(b + 5)$$

$$\frac{4}{3}a = \frac{3}{4}(b + 5)\frac{4}{3}$$

$$\frac{4}{3}a = b + 5$$

$$b = \frac{4}{3}a + 5$$

Solve each equation for the given variable.

28. $xy = k; y$

29. $a = \frac{2}{b} + 3c; c$

30. $6(2c + 3d) = 5(4c - 3d); d$

31. Model With Mathematics The formula for average acceleration is $a = \frac{V_f - V_i}{t}$, where V_f is the final velocity, V_i is the initial velocity, and t is the time in seconds. Rewrite the equation as a formula for the final velocity, V_f. What is the final velocity when a person accelerates at 2 ft/s² for 5 seconds after an initial velocity of 4 ft/s?

LESSON 1-5 Solving Inequalities in One Variable

Quick Review

The same strategies used for solving multistep equations can be used to solve multistep inequalities. When multiplying or dividing by a negative value, reverse the inequality symbol.

Example

Solve $-2(6x + 5) \leq 74$. Graph the solution.

$-2(6x + 5) \leq 74$

$-12x - 10 \leq 74$ .... Distributive Property

$-12x - 10 + 10 \leq 74 + 10$ .... Add 10 to each side.

$\frac{-12x}{-12} \geq \frac{84}{-12}$ .... Divide each side by −12.

$x \geq -7$ .... Simplify.

The solution is $x \geq -7$.

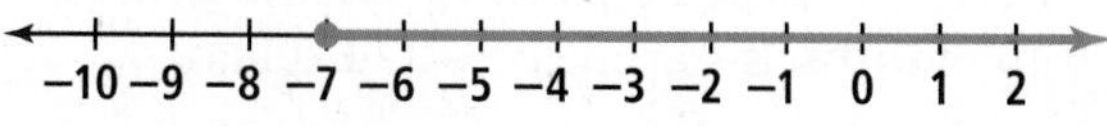

Practice & Problem Solving

32. Use Structure Write an inequality that represents the graph.

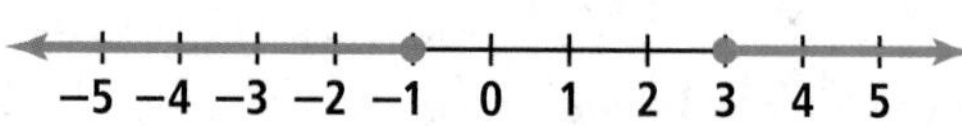

Solve each inequality and graph the solution.

33. $x + 8 > 11$

34. $4x + 3 \leq -6$

35. $2.4x - 9 < 1.8x + 6$

36. $3x - 8 \geq 4(x - 1.5)$

37. Make Sense and Persevere Neil and Yuki run a data entry service. Neil starts at 9:00 A.M. and can type 45 words per minute. Yuki arrives at 10:30 A.M. and can type 60 words per minute. Write and solve an inequality to find at what time Yuki will have typed more words than Neil. Let x represent the time in minutes.

LESSON 1-6 Compound Inequalities

Quick Review

When a compound inequality uses the word *and*, the solution must make both inequalities true. If a compound inequality uses the word *or*, the solution must make at least one of the inequalities true.

Example

Solve $-24 < 4x - 4 < 4$. Graph the solution.

Separate the inequality and solve each separately.

$-24 < 4x - 4$	$4x - 4 < 4$
$-24 + 4 < 4x - 4 + 4$	$4x - 4 + 4 < 4 + 4$
$-20 < 4x$	$4x < 8$
$-5 < x$	$x < 2$

The solution is $x > -5$ and $x < 2$, or $-5 < x < 2$.

Practice & Problem Solving

38. Construct Arguments Describe and correct the error a student made graphing the compound inequality $x > 3$ or $x < -1$.

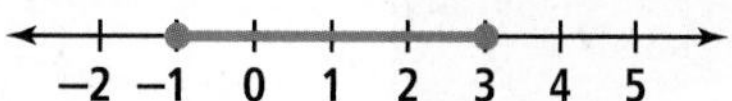

Solve each compound inequality and graph the solution.

39. $2x - 3 > 5$ or $3x - 1 < 8$

40. $x - 6 \leq 18$ and $3 - 2x \geq 11$

41. $\frac{1}{2}x - 5 > -3$ or $\frac{2}{3}x + 4 < 3$

42. $3(2x - 5) > 15$ and $4(2x - 1) > 10$

43. Model With Mathematics Lucy plans to spend between \$50 and \$65, inclusive, on packages of beads and packages of charms. If she buys 5 packages of beads at \$4.95 each, how many packages of charms at \$6.55 can Lucy buy while staying within her budget?

LESSON 1-7 Absolute Value Equations and Inequalities

Quick Review

When solving an equation or an inequality that contains an absolute value expression, you must consider both the positive and negative values of the absolute value expression.

Example

What is the value of x in $|4x + 7| < 43$?

Write and solve inequalities for the two cases.

$4x + 7$ is positive.	$4x + 7$ is negative.
$4x + 7 < 43$	$4x + 7 > -43$
$4x + 7 - 7 < 43 - 7$	$4x + 7 - 7 > -43 - 7$
$4x < 36$	$4x > -50$
$x < 9$	$x > -12.5$

The solution is $-12.5 < x < 9$.

Practice & Problem Solving

44. Make Sense and Persevere Thato is solving the absolute value equation $|3x| - 5 = 13$. What is the first step he should take?

Solve each absolute value equation or inequality.

45. $3 = |x| + 1$

46. $4|x - 5| = 24$

47. $3 > |x| - 6$

48. $|2x - 3| \leq 12$

49. Make Sense and Persevere A person's normal body temperature is 98.6°F. According to physicians, a person's body temperature should not be more than 0.5°F from the normal temperature. How could you use an absolute value inequality to represent the temperatures that fall outside of normal range? Explain.

TOPIC
2

Linear Equations

TOPIC ESSENTIAL QUESTION

Why is it useful to have different forms of linear equations?

Topic Overview

enVision™ STEM Project:
Design a Pitched Roof

2-1 Slope-Intercept Form

2-2 Point-Slope Form

2-3 Standard Form

Mathematical Modeling in 3 Acts:
How Tall is Tall?

2-4 Parallel and Perpendicular Lines

Topic Vocabulary

- parallel lines
- perpendicular lines
- point-slope form
- reciprocal
- slope-intercept form
- standard form of a linear equation
- *y*-intercept

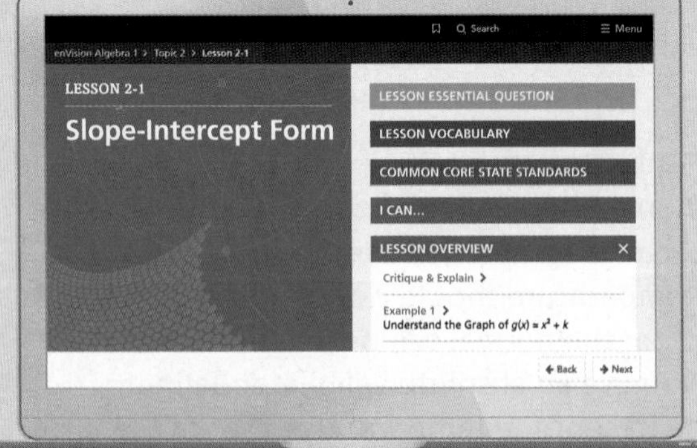

Go online | **PearsonRealize.com**

Digital Experience

INTERACTIVE STUDENT EDITION Access online or offline.

ACTIVITIES Complete ***Explore & Reason, Model & Discuss***, and ***Critique & Explain*** activities. Interact with Examples and Try Its.

ANIMATION View and interact with real-world applications.

PRACTICE Practice what you've learned.

MATHEMATICAL MODELING IN 3 ACTS

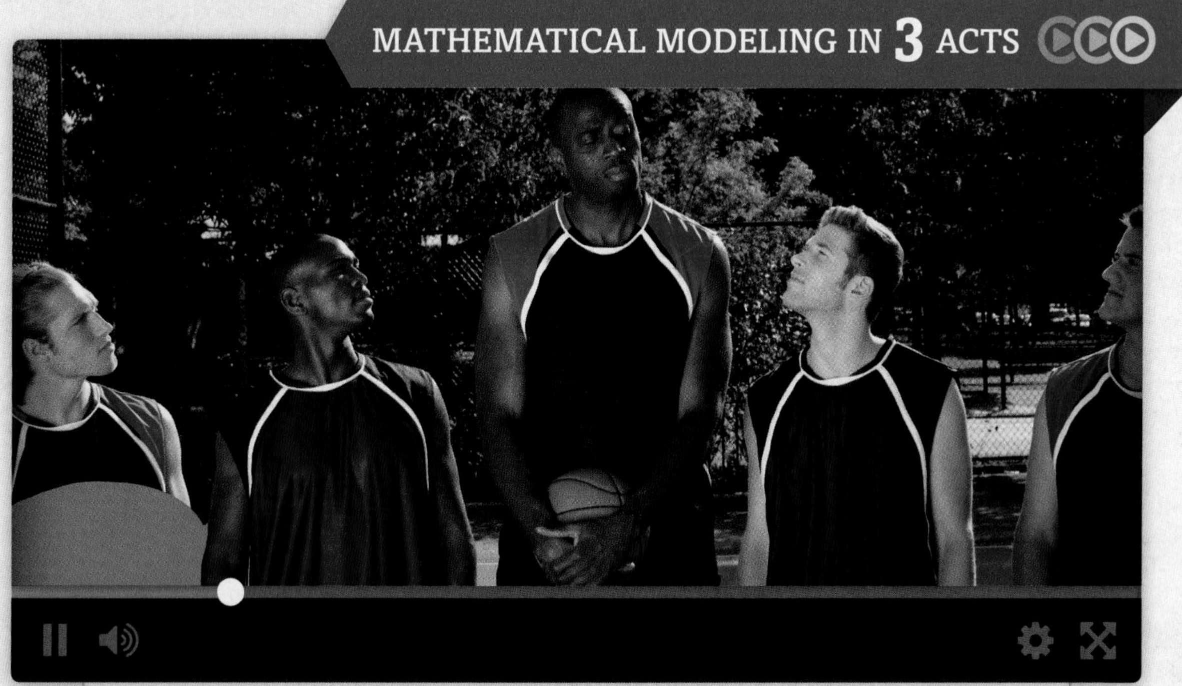

How Tall is Tall?

The world's tallest person in recorded history was Robert Wadlow. He was 8 feet 11.1 inches tall! Only 5% of the world population is 6 feet 3 inches or taller. What percent of the population would you guess is 7 feet or taller?

We usually use standard units, such as feet and inches or centimeters, to measure length or height. Did you ever wonder why? In the Mathematical Modeling in 3 Acts lesson you'll consider some interesting alternatives.

VIDEOS Watch clips to support ***Mathematical Modeling in 3 Acts Lessons*** and **enVision™ *STEM Projects.***

CONCEPT SUMMARY Review key lesson content through multiple representations.

ASSESSMENT Show what you've learned.

GLOSSARY Read and listen to English and Spanish definitions.

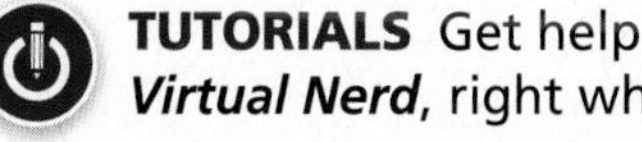

TUTORIALS Get help from ***Virtual Nerd***, right when you need it.

MATH TOOLS Explore math with digital tools and manipulatives.

Did You Know?

It takes 8 minutes 19 seconds for the sun's rays to travel 93 million miles to Earth. The amount of solar energy that hits Earth in 1 hour is enough to meet the energy demands of the world's population for 1 year.

In 2004, about 15,000 homes in the United States had solar panels. By the end of 2014, about 600,000 homes had solar panels.

Number of Solar Homes
(Increase over a 10-year period)

2004

2014

= 1,500 homes

What Is Roof Pitch?

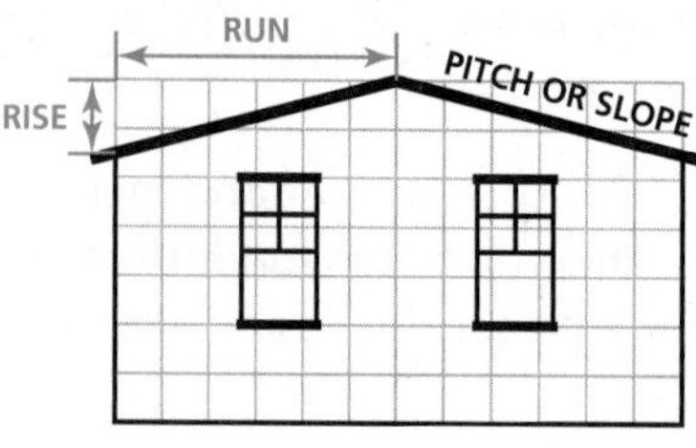

Roof pitch is closely related to slope. This roof's pitch is equivalent to 3 : 12, which means the roof rises (or falls) 3 inches for every horizontal foot.

The steepness, or pitch, of a roof affects many things, including the installation of solar panels and how much snow the roof can handle.

Solar panels are a collection of solar cells. Solar cells convert sunlight to electricity. The solar cells in a solar panel are arranged so that solar energy travels along a specific path.

Your Task: Design a Pitched Roof

You and your classmates will analyze roofs to determine their pitch. Then you will design a roof with a pitch that is appropriate for installing solar panels.

2-1 Slope-Intercept Form

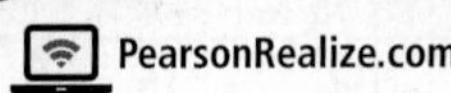
PearsonRealize.com

I CAN… write and graph linear equations using slope-intercept form.

VOCABULARY

- slope-intercept form
- *y*-intercept

MODEL & DISCUSS

Alani wants to buy a $360 bicycle. She is considering two payment options. The image shows Option A, which consists of making an initial down payment then smaller, equal-sized weekly payments. Option B consists of making 6 equal payments over 6 weeks.

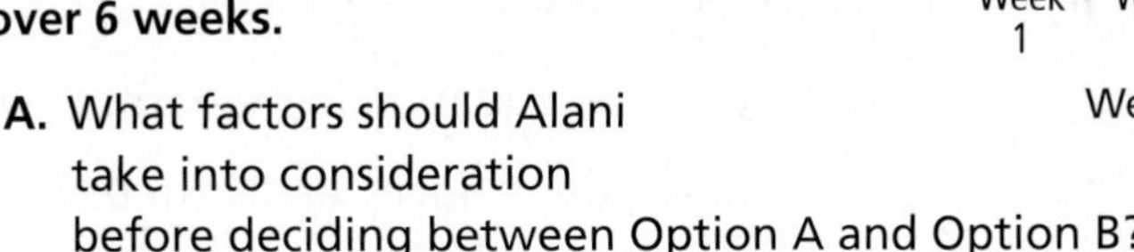

Weekly Bike Payments

A. What factors should Alani take into consideration before deciding between Option A and Option B?

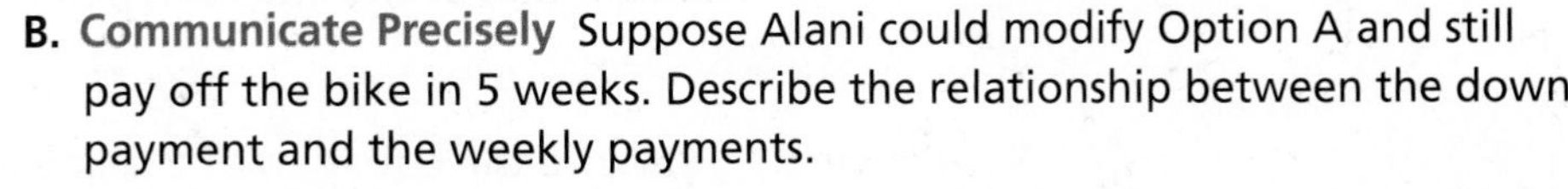

B. **Communicate Precisely** Suppose Alani could modify Option A and still pay off the bike in 5 weeks. Describe the relationship between the down payment and the weekly payments.

ESSENTIAL QUESTION

What information does the slope-intercept form of a linear equation reveal about a line?

EXAMPLE 1 Graph a Linear Equation

What is the graph of $y = \frac{4}{5}x + 2$?

The equation is in slope-intercept form. You can use the slope and *y*-intercept to graph the line.

$$y = \frac{4}{5}x + 2$$

Step 1 Identify the *y*-intercept in the equation.

The *y*-intercept is 2, so plot the point (0, 2).

Step 2 Use the slope to plot a second point.

$$m = \frac{4}{5} = \frac{\text{vertical change}}{\text{horizontal change}}$$

Start at (0, 2), move 4 units up and 5 units to the right to locate a second point. Plot the point (5, 6).

Step 3 Draw a line through the points.

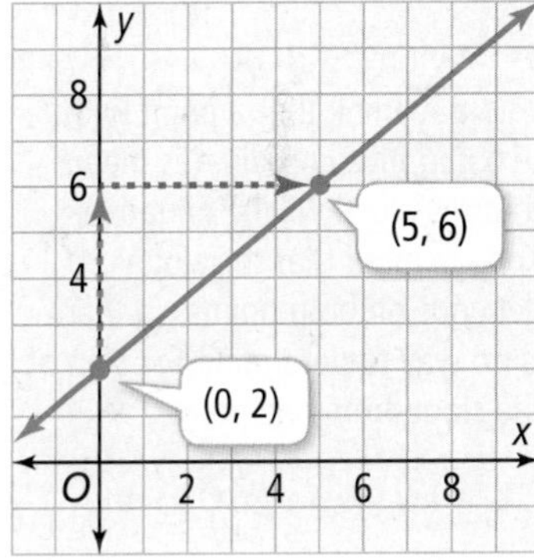

USE STRUCTURE
Think about the relationship between the value of the leading coefficient and the slope of the line.

Try It! 1. Sketch the graph of $y = -\frac{3}{4}x - 5$.

EXAMPLE 2 Write an Equation from a Graph

What is the equation of the line in slope-intercept form?

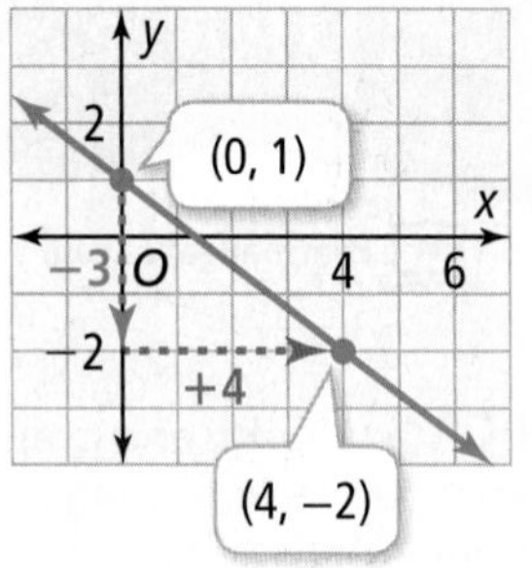

Step 1 Find the slope between two points on the line.

The line passes through (0, 1) and (4, −2).

$$\text{slope} = \frac{y_2 - y_1}{x_2 - x_1} = \frac{-3}{4}$$

STUDY TIP
If you can approximate the y-intercept by looking at the graph, you can use it as one of the two points for finding the slope.

Step 2 Find the y-intercept.

The line intersects the y-axis at (0, 1), so the y-intercept is 1.

Step 3 Write the equation in the form $y = mx + b$.

Substitute $-\frac{3}{4}$ for m and 1 for b.

The equation of the line in slope-intercept form is $y = -\frac{3}{4}x + 1$.

Try It! **2.** Write the equation of the line in slope-intercept form.

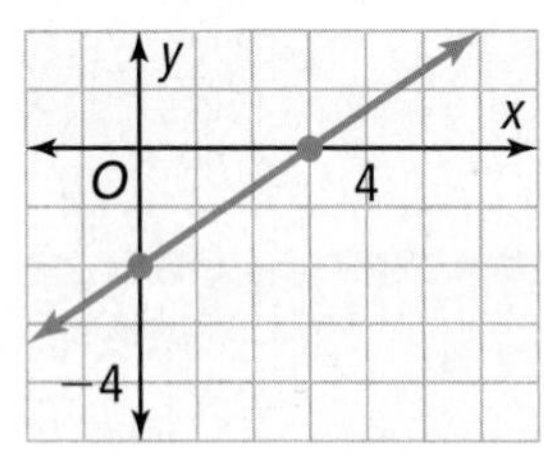

CONCEPTUAL UNDERSTANDING

EXAMPLE 3 Understand Slope-Intercept Form

How can you find an equation of a line that passes through two points if neither of them is the y-intercept?

Consider the line that passes through the points (−1, −2) and (3, 4).

Step 1 Find the slope of the line.

$$m = \frac{4 - (-2)}{3 - (-1)} = \frac{3}{2}$$

COMMON ERROR
You may think that a point with two negative coordinates means that the slope will be negative. Keep in mind that the slope depends on both points, so there is no way to determine the sign of the slope from one point.

Step 2 Use the slope and one point to find the y-intercept.

$4 = \frac{3}{2}(3) + b$ ········ Substitute $\frac{3}{2}$ for m and (3, 4) for (x, y) in $y = mx + b$.

$4 = \frac{9}{2} + b$ ········ Simplify.

$-\frac{1}{2} = b$ ········ Solve for b.

Step 3 Use the slope and the y-intercept to write the equation

$y = \frac{3}{2}x + \left(-\frac{1}{2}\right)$ ········ Substitute $\frac{3}{2}$ for m and $-\frac{1}{2}$ for b.

The equation in slope-intercept form of the line that passes through (−1, −2) and (3, 4) is $y = \frac{3}{2}x - \frac{1}{2}$.

Try It! **3.** Write the equation in slope-intercept form of the line that passes through the points (5, 4) and (−1, 6).

APPLICATION

EXAMPLE 4 Interpret Slope and y-Intercept

Allie received a gift card for her local coffee shop. Every time she goes to the shop, she gets a medium coffee. The graph shows the gift card balance at two points. How can Allie determine the number of medium coffees she can buy with the gift card if she does not know the original value of the card?

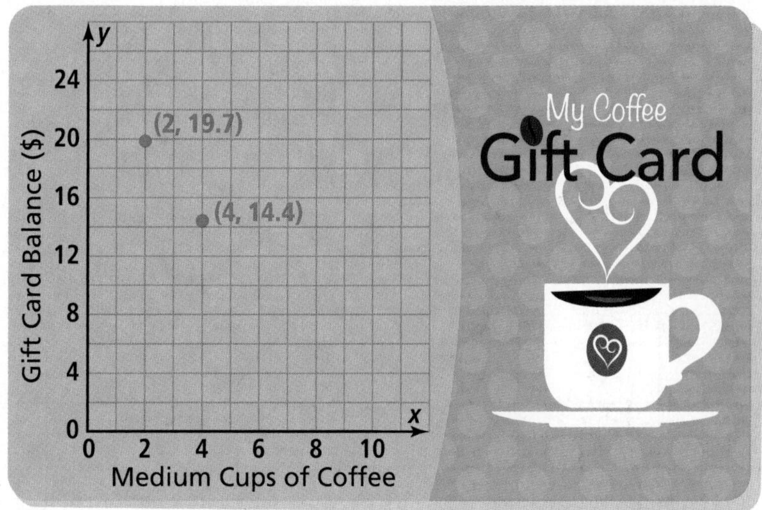

Step 1 Interpret the meaning of the two points.

(2, 19.7): After buying 2 coffees, Allie had \$19.70 left on the gift card.

(4, 14.4): After buying 4 coffees, Allie had \$14.40 left on the gift card.

Step 2 Find the slope. Then interpret the meaning of the slope.

Use the points (2, 19.7) and (4, 14.4).

$$m = \frac{19.7 - 14.4}{2 - 4}$$

$$= -2.65$$

The slope is −2.65, which means that the balance on the gift card decreases by \$2.65 each time Allie buys a medium coffee. The cost of a medium coffee is \$2.65.

Step 3 Use one point and the slope to find the *y*-intercept. Then interpret its meaning.

$$y = mx + b$$

$$19.7 = -2.65(2) + b$$

$$25 = b$$

The *y*-intercept is 25. It represents the original value of the gift card.

To determine the number of medium coffees she can buy with the gift card, Allie can divide \$25 by \$2.65. She can purchase 9 medium coffees with the gift card.

MODEL WITH MATHEMATICS
Does the line with slope −2.65 and *y*-intercept 25 model the situation for every value of *x*?

Try It! 4. Use information from Example 4 to write the equation in slope-intercept form. Find the *x*-intercept of the graph of the equation. What does the *x*-intercept mean in terms of the situation?

CONCEPT SUMMARY Slope-Intercept Form of a Linear Equation

WORDS The slope-intercept form of a linear equation is used when the slope and the y-intercept of a line are known.

ALGEBRA The slope-intercept form of a line is $y = mx + b$.

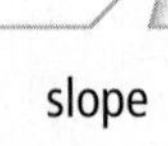

slope | y-intercept

NUMBERS $y = \frac{2}{3}x + 1$ | $y = -2x - 1$

GRAPH

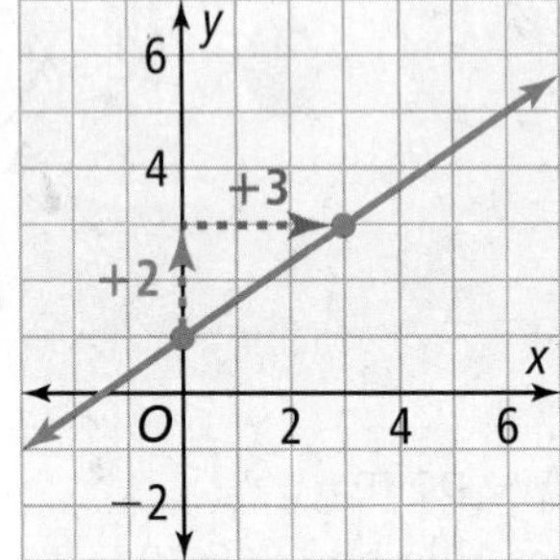

The line has a slope of $\frac{2}{3}$.
The y-intercept is 1.

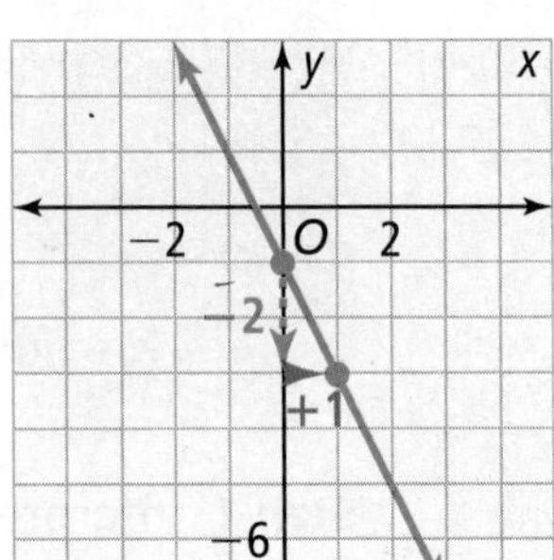

The line has a slope of −2.
The y-intercept is −1.

Do You UNDERSTAND?

1. **ESSENTIAL QUESTION** What information does the slope-intercept form of a linear equation reveal about a line?

2. **Communicate Precisely** How are the graphs of $y = 2x + 1$ and $y = -2x + 1$ similar? How are they different?

3. **Error Analysis** To graph $y = \frac{2}{3}x + 4$, Emaan plots one point at (0, 4) and a second point 2 units right and 3 units up at (2, 7). He then draws a line through (0, 4) and (2, 7). What error did Emaan make?

4. **Make Sense and Persevere** When writing the equation of a line in slope-intercept form, how can you determine the value of m in $y = mx + b$ if you know the coordinates of two points on the line?

Do You KNOW HOW?

Sketch the graph of each equation.

5. $y = 2x - 5$

6. $y = -\frac{3}{4}x + 2$

Identify the slope and y-intercept of the line for each equation.

7. $y = -5x - \frac{3}{4}$

8. $y = \frac{1}{4}x + 5$

Write the equation of each line in slope-intercept form.

9.

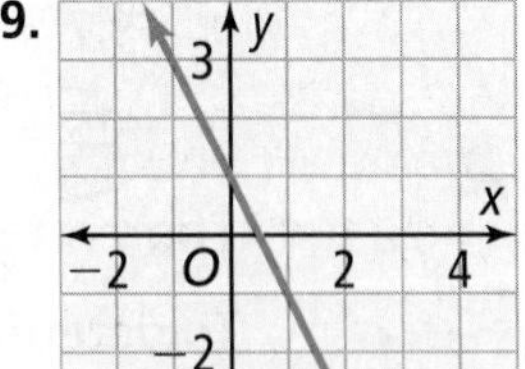

10.

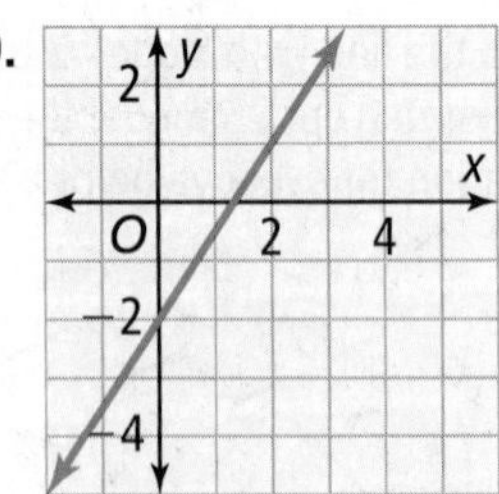

11. A line that passes through (3, 1) and (0, −3)

12. A line that passes through (−1, −5) and (4, −2)

PRACTICE & PROBLEM SOLVING

Scan for Multimedia

Additional Exercises Available Online

UNDERSTAND

13. Use Structure Aisha and Carolina each sketch a graph of the linear equation $y = -\frac{3}{4}x + 2$. Aisha uses the equation $y = \frac{-3}{4}x + 2$ to sketch the graph, and Carolina uses the equation $y = \frac{3}{-4}x + 2$.

a. Explain how this leads them to use different steps to construct their graphs.

b. Will the two graphs look the same? Explain.

14. Make Sense and Persevere Line g passes through the points $(-2.6, 1)$ and $(-1.4, 2.5)$, as shown. Find the equation of the line that passes through $(0, -b)$ and $(c, 0)$.

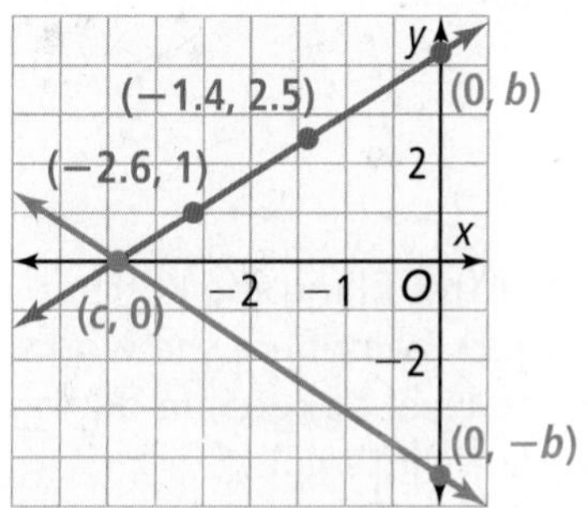

15. Error Analysis Describe and correct the error a student made when graphing the linear equation $y = -\frac{3}{4}x - 6$.

1. Plot the y-intercept at (0, 6).
2. Plot a second point 3 units down and 4 units right from (0, 6) at (4, 3).
3. Connect the points with a line.

✗

16. Mathematical Connections The points $A(0, 5)$, $B(4, 2)$ and $C(0, 2)$ form the vertices of a right triangle in the coordinate plane. What is the equation of the line that forms the hypotenuse?

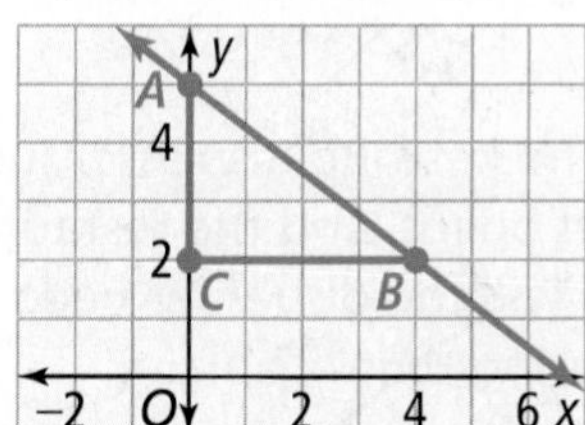

17. Higher Order Thinking The line $y = -0.5x + b$ passes through the points $(1, 5.5)$, $(3, p)$, $(4, 4)$, and $(7, n)$. Find b, n, and p.

PRACTICE

Sketch the graph of each equation. SEE EXAMPLE 1

18. $y = \frac{3}{8}x + 5$

19. $y = -\frac{1}{2}x + 3$

20. $y = -2x + 3$

21. $y = 3x - 6$

22. $y = -\frac{3}{5}x + 4$

23. $y = \frac{5}{2}x - \frac{1}{2}$

Write the equation of each line in slope-intercept form. SEE EXAMPLE 2

24.

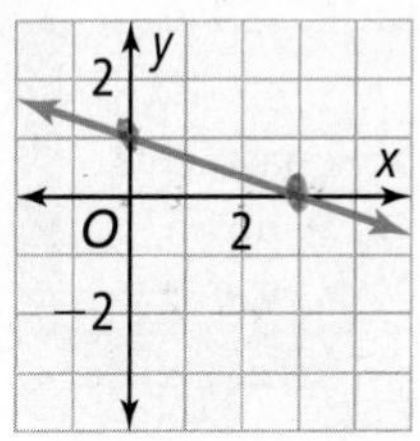

25.

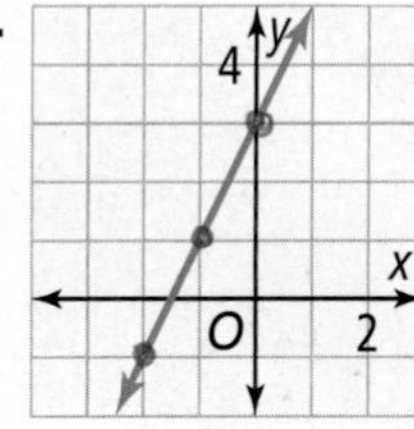

26.

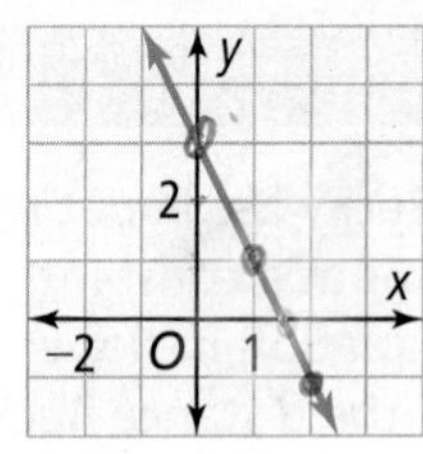

27.

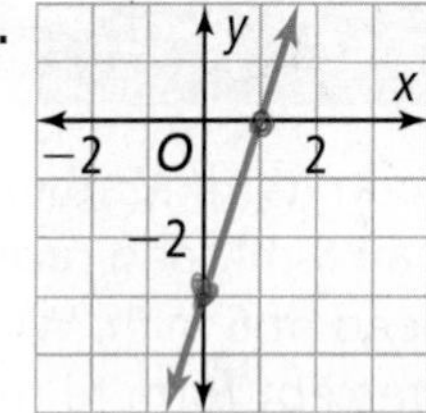

Write the equation of the line that passes through the given points. SEE EXAMPLE 3

28. (0, 1) and (2, 2)

29. (−2, −1) and (0, −5)

30. (4, 0) and (0, 2)

31. (−2, −6) and (1, 2)

32. $\left(\frac{3}{8}, 0\right)$ and $\left(\frac{5}{8}, \frac{1}{2}\right)$

33. (2, 1.5) and (0, 4.5)

34. Jordan will hike the trail shown at a rate of 4 mi/h. Write a linear equation to represent the distance Jordan still has to walk after x hours. What does the y-intercept of the equation represent? SEE EXAMPLE 4

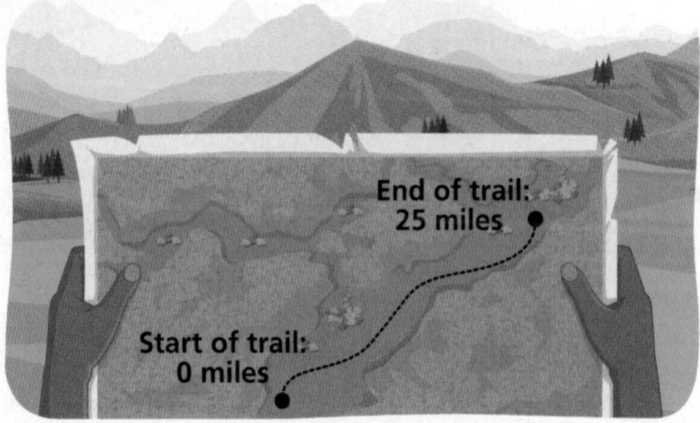

PRACTICE & PROBLEM SOLVING

APPLY

35. Make Sense and Persevere Naomi wants to buy a new computer for \$840. She is considering two payment plans that require weekly payments. Which plan will pay for the computer faster? Explain.

36. Model With Mathematics Becky is competing in an 8-mi road race. She runs at a constant speed of 6 mi/h. Write an equation in slope-intercept form to represent the distance Becky has left to run.

37. Construct Arguments Luis and Raul are riding their bicycles to the beach from their respective homes. Luis proposes that they leave their respective homes at the same time and plan to arrive at the beach at the same time. The diagram shows Luis's position at two points during his ride to the beach.

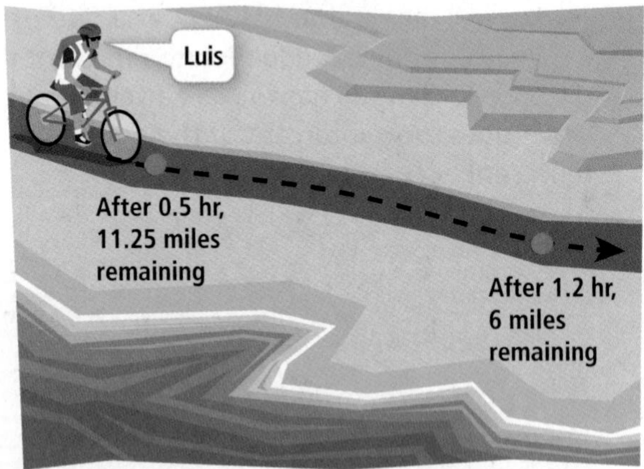

Write an equation in slope-intercept form to represent Luis's ride from his house to the beach. If Raul lives 5 miles closer to the beach than Luis, at what speed must Raul ride for the plan to work?

ASSESSMENT PRACTICE

38. Which of the following statements about the graph of $y = \frac{3}{4}x - 1$ are true? Select all that apply.

Ⓐ The slope of the line is -1.

Ⓑ The line intersects the point $\left(0, -\frac{3}{4}\right)$.

Ⓒ The line intersects the point (0, 1).

Ⓓ The *y*-intercept is -1.

Ⓔ The slope of the line is $\frac{3}{4}$.

Ⓕ The *y*-intercept is $\frac{3}{4}$.

39. SAT/ACT What is the equation of the line that has a slope of -3 and a *y*-intercept of 2?

Ⓐ $y = 2x - 3$

Ⓑ $y = 2x + 3$

Ⓒ $y = -3x + 2$

Ⓓ $y = -3x - 2$

Ⓔ $y = -3x - 3$

40. Performance Task After filling the ketchup dispenser at the snack bar where she works, Kelley measures the level of ketchup during the day at different hourly intervals.

Part A Assuming the ketchup is used at a constant rate, write a linear equation that can be used to determine the level of ketchup in the dispenser after *x* hours.

Part B How can you use the equation from Part A to find the level of ketchup when the dispenser is full?

Part C If Kelley fills the ketchup dispenser just before the restaurant opens, and the restaurant is open for 18 hours, will the dispenser need to be refilled before closing time? Explain.

2-2 Point-Slope Form

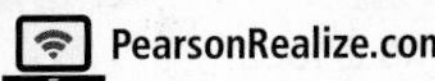

I CAN… write and graph linear equations in point-slope form.

VOCABULARY

- point-slope form

CRITIQUE & EXPLAIN

Paul and Seth know that one point on a line is (4, 2) and the slope of the line is −5. Each student derived an equation relating x and y.

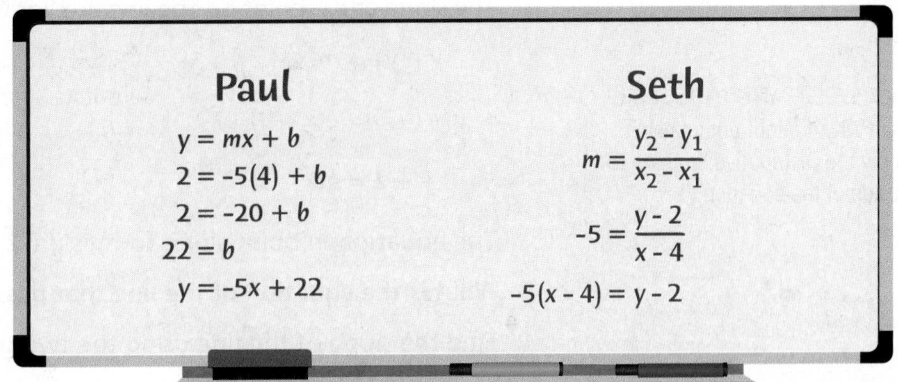

A. Do the two equations represent the same line? Construct a mathematical argument to support your answer.

B. Make Sense and Persevere Generate a table of values for each equation. How can you reconcile the tables with the equations?

ESSENTIAL QUESTION **What information does the point-slope form of a linear equation reveal about a line?**

CONCEPTUAL UNDERSTANDING

EXAMPLE 1 Understand Point-Slope Form of a Linear Equation

A. How can you write the equation of a line using any points on a line?

Use the slope formula to find the slope using a specific point (x_1, y_1) and any point (x, y).

$$m = \frac{y_2 - y_1}{x_2 - x_1}$$

$$m = \frac{y - y_1}{x - x_1}$$

Substitute x for x_2 and y for y_2.

$$m(x - x_1) = \frac{y - y_1}{x - x_1}(x - x_1)$$

Multiply both sides of the equation by $(x - x_1)$.

$$m(x - x_1) = y - y_1$$

$$y - y_1 = m(x - x_1)$$

You can write the equation of a line using any point, (x_1, y_1), and the slope, m, in **point-slope form**, $y - y_1 = m(x - x_1)$.

COMMUNICATE PRECISELY
What mathematical notation is important in this example?

B. Why is it helpful to have point-slope form in addition to slope-intercept form?

Using point-slope form allows you to write the equation of a line without knowing the y-intercept. You can use any two points on the line to write the equation.

Try It! 1. Describe the steps needed to find the y-intercept of the graph using point-slope form.

EXAMPLE 2 Write an Equation in Point-Slope Form

A. A line with a slope of $\frac{1}{2}$ passes through the point (3, –2). What form can you use to write the equation of the line? What is the equation in that form?

The slope and a point on the line are known, so use point-slope form.

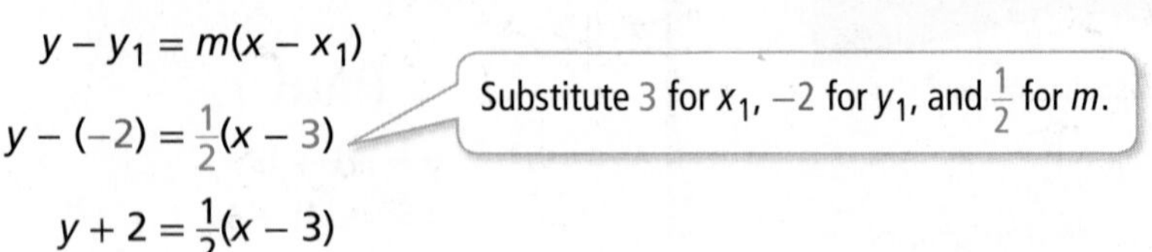

$$y - y_1 = m(x - x_1)$$

$$y - (-2) = \frac{1}{2}(x - 3)$$

Substitute 3 for x_1, −2 for y_1, and $\frac{1}{2}$ for m.

$$y + 2 = \frac{1}{2}(x - 3)$$

> **MAKE SENSE AND PERSEVERE**
> Explain why it might not be helpful to apply the Distributive Property to right side of the equation.

The equation in point-slope form is $y + 2 = \frac{1}{2}(x - 3)$.

B. What is the equation of the line that passes through (–4, 1) and (2, 3).

Find the slope of the line using the two given points.

$$m = \frac{y_2 - y_1}{x_2 - x_1}$$

$$= \frac{3 - 1}{2 - (-4)}$$

Substitute (2, 3) for (x_2, y_2) and (−4, 1) for (x_1, y_1).

$$= \frac{1}{3}$$

> **STUDY TIP**
> You can use either point as (x_1, y_1). You just need to be careful to substitute the x- and y-coordinates from the same point.

Use the slope and one point to write the equation.

$$y - y_1 = m(x - x_1)$$

$$y - 3 = \frac{1}{3}(x - 2)$$

Substitute 2 for x_1, 3 for y_1, and $\frac{1}{3}$ for m.

The equation in point-slope form is $y - 3 = \frac{1}{3}(x - 2)$.

Try It! 2. Write an equation of the line that passes through (2, –1) and (–3, 3).

EXAMPLE 3 Sketch the Graph of a Linear Equation in Point-Slope Form

What is the graph of $y - 3 = -\frac{2}{3}(x + 1)$?

Step 1 Identify a point on the line from the equation and plot it.

$$y - 3 = -\frac{2}{3}(x + 1)$$

$$y - 3 = -\frac{2}{3}(x - (-1))$$

The point is (−1, 3).

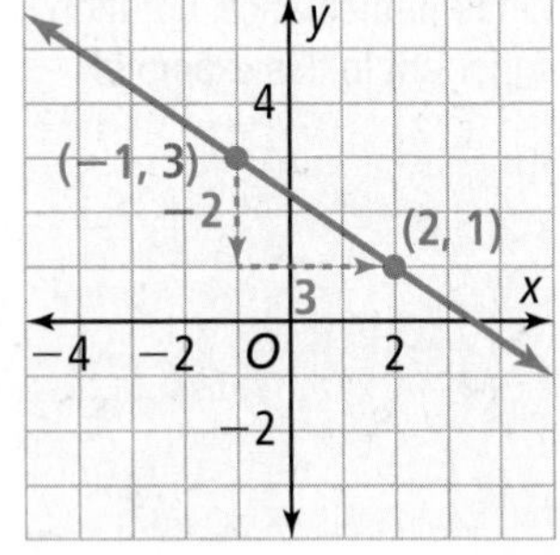

> **COMMON ERROR**
> You may think that the x-coordinate of the point is 1. Remember that point-slope form uses $x - x_1$ which in this case is $x - (-1)$.

Step 2 Use the slope to plot a second point.

$$m = \frac{-2}{3} = \frac{\text{vertical change}}{\text{horizontal change}}$$

Move 2 units down and 3 units right from the first point. Plot the point (2, 1).

Step 3 Sketch a line through the points.

 **Try It!** 3. Sketch the graph of $y + 2 = \frac{1}{2}(x - 3)$.

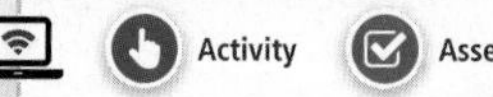

APPLICATION

EXAMPLE 4 Apply Linear Equations

An event facility has a banquet hall that can hold up to 250 people. The price for a party includes the cost of the room rental plus the cost of a meal for each guest. Marissa is planning an event for 75 people. She has budgeted \$1,200 for the party. Will it be enough?

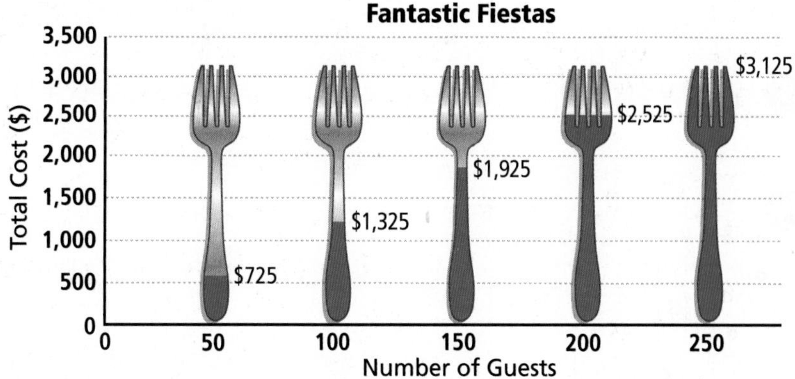

Formulate ◀ Determine which form of a linear equation is more useful.

The number of guests and the total costs represent different data points on a line. The point-slope form is more useful.

Compute ◀ The slope represents the cost of each meal. Use the two points (50, 725) and (100, 1,325) to find the slope.

$$m = \frac{y_2 - y_1}{x_2 - x_1}$$

$$= \frac{1{,}325 - 725}{100 - 50}$$ Substitute (50, 725) for (x_1, y_1) and (100, 1,325) for (x_2, y_2).

$$= 12$$

The slope is 12, so each meal costs \$12.

Use point-slope form to find the cost of the event for 75 guests.

$$y - y_1 = m(x - x_1)$$

$$y - 725 = 12(x - 50)$$ Substitute 50 for x_1, 725 for y_1, and 12 for m.

$$y - 725 = 12(75 - 50)$$ Substitute 75 for x.

$$y = 300 + 725$$ Simplify and solve for y.

$$y = 1{,}025$$

When $x = 75$, $y = 1{,}025$. The cost of the event for 75 guests is \$1,025.

Interpret ◀ Since Marissa budgeted \$1,200 for her event she will have enough money.

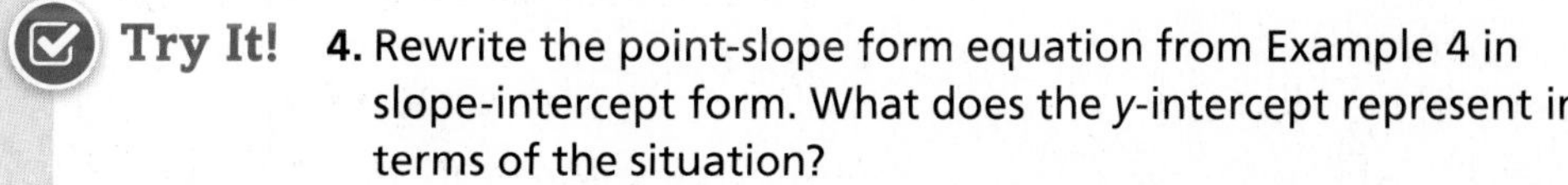

Try It! 4. Rewrite the point-slope form equation from Example 4 in slope-intercept form. What does the y-intercept represent in terms of the situation?

  Concept Summary  Assess

CONCEPT SUMMARY Point-Slope Form of a Linear Equation

WORDS The point-slope form of a linear equation is useful when you know the slope and at least one point on the line.

ALGEBRA $y - y_1 = m(x - x_1)$.

NUMBERS $y - 4 = \frac{3}{5}(x - 2)$ $y - 6 = -\frac{3}{4}(x + 5)$

GRAPH

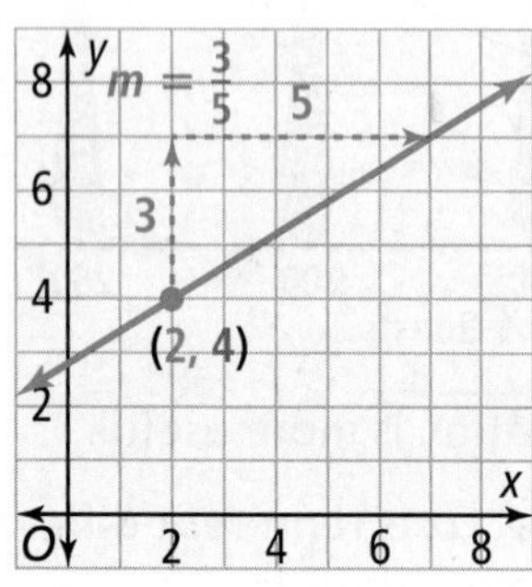

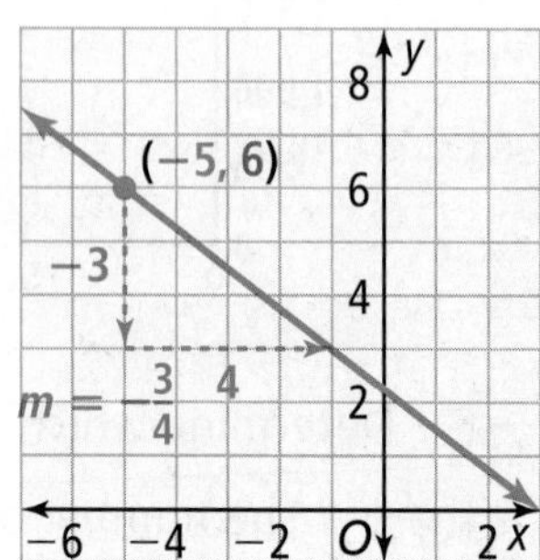

Do You UNDERSTAND?

1. ESSENTIAL QUESTION What information does the point-slope form of a linear equation reveal about a line?

2. **Use Structure** If you know a point on a line and the slope of the line, how can you find another point on the line?

3. **Error Analysis** Denzel identified (3, 2) as a point on the line $y - 2 = \frac{2}{3}(x + 3)$. What is the error that Denzel made?

4. **Generalize** You know the slope and one point on a line that is not the *y*-intercept. Why might you write the equation in point-slope form instead of slope-intercept form?

Do You KNOW HOW?

Write the equation of the line in point-slope form that passes through the given point with the given slope.

5. (1, 5); $m = -3$

6. (−4, 3); $m = 2$

Write an equation of the line in point-slope form that passes through the given points.

7. (4, 2) and (1, 6)

8. (−2, 8) and (7, −4)

9. Write the equation $y - 6 = -5(x + 1)$ in slope-intercept form.

10. Write the equation of the line in point-slope form.

a.

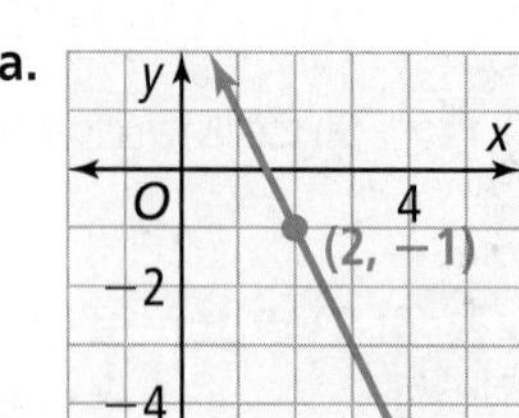

b.

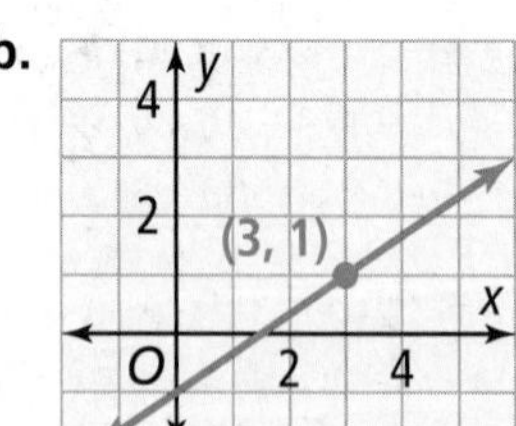

PRACTICE & PROBLEM SOLVING

Scan for Multimedia | Practice | Tutorial

Additional Exercises Available Online

UNDERSTAND

11. Use the graph of the line shown.

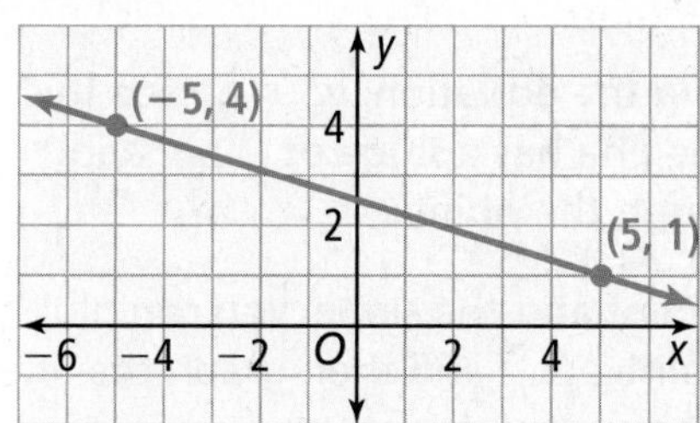

a. Write a point-slope form of the equation for the line shown.

b. Estimate the value of the y-intercept of the line.

c. **Construct Arguments** Use proportional reasoning to support your conjecture about the value of the y-intercept.

d. Rewrite the point-slope form of the equation in slope-intercept form to check your conjecture.

12. **Error Analysis** Describe and correct the error a student made when graphing $y + 5 = -\frac{3}{4}(x - 8)$.

1. Plot a point at (-5, 8).
2. Plot a point 3 units down and 4 units right from (-5, 8) at (-1, 5).
3. Connect the points with a line.

13. **Higher Order Thinking** In slope-intercept form $y = mx + b$, the y-intercept is located at $(0, b)$.

a. What equation do you get when you substitute $(0, b)$ for (x_1, y_1) in point-slope form $y - y_1 = m(x - x_1)$?

b. How are the slope-intercept and the point-slope forms related?

PRACTICE

Write the equation in point-slope form of the line that passes through the given point with the given slope. SEE EXAMPLES 1, 2, AND 3

14. $(3, 1)$; $m = 2$

15. $(2, -2)$; $m = -4$

16. $(2, -8)$; $m = -\frac{3}{4}$

17. $(-1, 4)$; $m = \frac{2}{3}$

18. $(-\frac{1}{2}, 2)$; $m = -1$

19. $(3.5, 7.5)$; $m = 1.5$

Write the equation of the line in point-slope form. SEE EXAMPLES 2 AND 3

20.

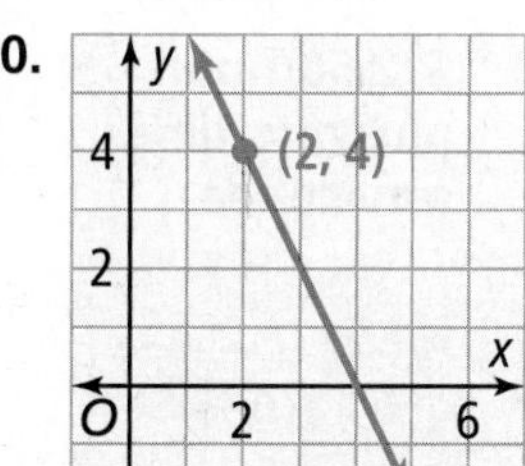

21.

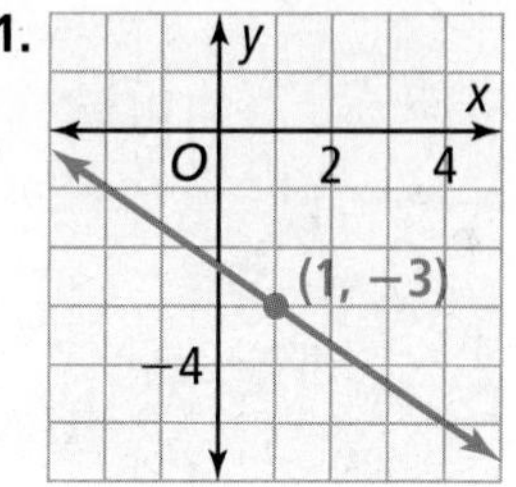

Write an equation of the line in point-slope form that passes through the given points. SEE EXAMPLE 2

22. $(2, 4)$ and $(3, 6)$

23. $(-1, -7)$ and $(2, -4)$

24. $(3, -5)$ and $(1, -8)$

25. $(-4, 12)$ and $(-7, -3)$

26. $(-4, -2)$ and $(1, 6)$

27. $(3, -\frac{1}{2})$ and $(1, \frac{3}{2})$

Sketch the graph of each equation. SEE EXAMPLE 3

28. $y + 2 = -3(x + 2)$

29. $y - 2 = 4(x - 1)$

30. $y + 1 = \frac{3}{2}(x - 1)$

31. $y - 3 = \frac{2}{5}(x + 1)$

32. $y - 1 = \frac{5}{4}(x + 2)$

33. $y + 5 = \frac{1}{2}(x + 3)$

Write an equation of the line in point-slope form that passes through the given points in each table. Then write each equation in slope-intercept form. SEE EXAMPLE 4

34.

x	y
15	100
20	115
25	130
30	145
35	160

35.

x	y
−4	−21
−2	−18
0	−15
2	−12
4	−9

PRACTICE & PROBLEM SOLVING

APPLY

36. Model With Mathematics Liam rented a pedal board for 5.5 hours and paid a total of $93.75. What is an equation in point-slope form that models the cost of renting a pedal board for x hours? How can Liam use the equation to find the one-time service charge?

37. Make Sense and Persevere Emery borrowed money from her brother to buy a new phone, and is paying off a fixed amount each week. After 2 weeks, she will owe $456, and after 5 weeks, she will owe $228.

a. What was the original amount Emery borrowed?

b. How much does she pay each week?

c. How useful are equations in point-slope and slope-intercept forms for answering each question?

38. Generalize The total price of a printing job at Incredible Invites includes the cost per invitation plus a one-time set-up fee.

25 invitations	50 invitations	75 invitations	100 invitations
$100	**$140**	**$180**	**$220**

Write equations in point-slope and slope-intercept forms to model the situation. What part of the equations represents the cost per invitation? Which form is easier to use to find information about the set-up fee? Explain.

ASSESSMENT PRACTICE

39. The line $y - 5 = \frac{9}{7}(x + 4)$ is graphed in the coordinate plane.

By inspecting the equation, you can see the graph of the line has a slope of ____ and passes through the point ____ .

Using the point and the slope, you can plot a second point ____ and then graph the line through the two points.

40. SAT/ACT A line with a slope of −2 passes through the point (3, −2). Which of the following is the equation of the line?

Ⓐ $y + 2 = -2(x - 3)$ Ⓑ $y - 2 = -2(x - 3)$

Ⓒ $y - 2 = -2(x + 3)$ Ⓓ $y + 2 = 2(x - 3)$

Ⓔ $y - 2 = 2(x + 3)$

41. Performance Task A railway system on a hillside moves passengers at a constant rate to an elevation of 50 m. The elevations of a train are given for 2 different locations.

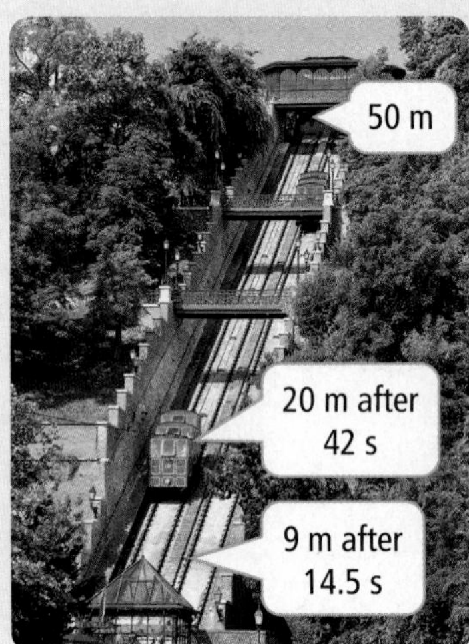

Part A Write an equation in point-slope form to represent the elevation of the train in terms of time. How can you use the equation to find the rate of increase in elevation of the train in meters per second?

Part B At what elevation does the train start initially? Write a linear equation in a form that gives the information as part of the equation. Explain your reasoning.

2-3 Standard Form

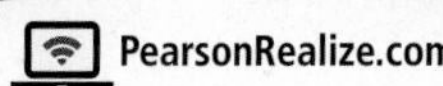

I CAN… write and graph linear equations in standard form.

VOCABULARY

- standard form of a linear equation

Activity Assess

EXPLORE & REASON

Jae makes a playlist of 24 songs for a party. Since he prefers country and rock music, he builds the playlist from those two types of songs.

Playlist

Country 1	Rock 14
Country 2	Country 15
Rock 3	Country 16
Rock 4	Rock 17
Country 5	Rock 18
Rock 6	Country 19
Country 7	Rock 20
Rock 8	Country 21
Rock 9	Rock 23
Country 10	Country 24
Rock 11	Country 25
Country 12	Country 26

A. Determine two different combinations of country and rock songs that Jae could use for his playlist.

B. Plot those combinations on graph paper. Extend a line through the points.

C. **Model With Mathematics** Can you use the line to find other meaningful points? Explain.

ESSENTIAL QUESTION **What information does the standard form of a linear equation reveal about a line?**

CONCEPTUAL UNDERSTANDING

EXAMPLE 1 Understand Standard Form of a Linear Equation

A. Hanna will spend \$150 on music festival tickets. Reserved seat tickets cost \$25 and general admission tickets cost \$10. How can you represent the situation with a linear equation?

Let x = cost of reserved seat tickets Let y = general admission tickets

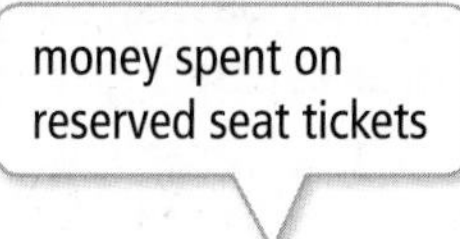

money spent on general admission tickets

total budget

$$25 \bullet x \quad + \quad 10 \bullet y \quad = 150$$

The equation, $25x + 10y = 150$ is in standard form. The **standard form of a linear equation** is $Ax + By = C$, where A, B, and C are integers, and A and B are not both equal to 0.

VOCABULARY
Remember, *integers* are rational numbers with no fractional or decimal part.

B. What information does the standard form give you that the slope-intercept form does not?

Compare equivalent slope-intercept and standard forms for the situation in Part A.

Slope-Intercept Form

$y = -2.5x + 15$

Hanna can buy 15 general admission tickets if she buys no reserved seat tickets.

When the equation is in slope-intercept form, you can determine the y-intercept by inspection. To find the x-intercept you still need to solve for $y = 0$.

AND

Standard Form

$25x + 10y = 150$

Hanna can spend \$150. This is the constraint.

When the equation is in standard form, you can determine the constraint by inspection.

REASON
What is the relationship between the sign of the slope and the quantities in the problems?

CONTINUED ON THE NEXT PAGE

Try It! **1.** Is it easier to find the x-intercept of the graph of the equations in Part B using slope-intercept or standard form? Explain.

EXAMPLE 2 Sketch the Graph of a Linear Equation in Standard Form

What is the graph of $3x - 2y = 9$?

To sketch a graph of a linear equation in standard form, find the x- and y-intercepts.

Step 1 Find the intercepts.

To find the x-intercept, substitute 0 for y and solve for x.

$$3x - 2y = 9$$
$$3x - 2(0) = 9$$
$$3x = 9$$
$$x = 3$$

The x-intercept is 3.

To find the y-intercept, substitute 0 for x and solve for y.

$$3x - 2y = 9$$
$$3(0) - 2y = 9$$
$$-2y = 9$$
$$y = -4.5$$

The y-intercept is -4.5.

Step 2 Sketch a graph of the line.

Plot the x-intercept at (3, 0).
Plot the y-intercept at (0, -4.5).

Sketch the line that passes through the intercepts.

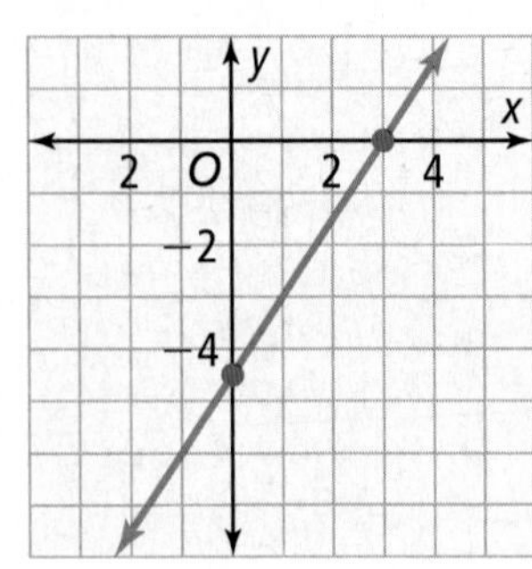

Try It! **2.** Sketch the graph of $4x + 5y = 10$.

EXAMPLE 3 Relate Standard Form to Horizontal and Vertical Lines

A. What does the graph of $Ax + By = C$ look like when $A = 0$?

Graph the line of $2y = 6$.

$$2y = 6$$
$$y = 3$$

The equation $y = 3$ does not include x, so x has no effect on the y-values. The value of y is 3 for every x-value, so the graph of $y = 3$ is a horizontal line.

In the coordinate plane, an equation in one variable means that the other variable has no effect on the equation or the graph.

When $A = 0$, the graph of $Ax + By = C$ is a horizontal line.

STUDY TIP
In a one-variable system, the graph of $y = 3$ is a point on a number line. In a two-variable system, the graph of $y = 3$ or $x = 3$ is a line on the coordinate plane.

CONTINUED ON THE NEXT PAGE

EXAMPLE 3 CONTINUED

B. What does the graph of $Ax + By = C$ look like when $B = 0$?

Graph the linear equation $3x = -6$.

$3x = -6$

$x = -2$

The value of x is -2, regardless of the value of y.

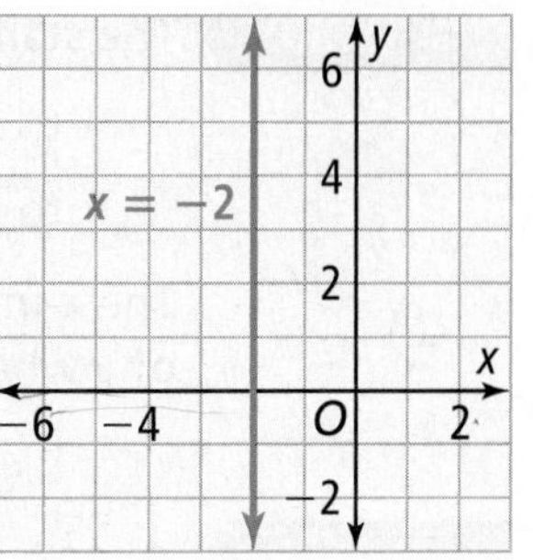

When $B = 0$, the graph of the $Ax + By = C$ is a vertical line.

USE APPROPRIATE TOOLS
Can you use slope-intercept or point-slope forms to generate equations for vertical and horizontal lines?

 **Try It!** **3.** Sketch the graph of each equation.

a. $3y = -18$ **b.** $4x = 12$

APPLICATION

EXAMPLE 4 Use the Standard Form of a Linear Equation

Tamira is making trail mix. She has $40 to spend on a mixture of almonds and cashews and wants about the same amount of almonds as cashews. How can she determine how many pounds of each kind of nut to buy?

Formulate Write and graph an equation to represent the situation.

price of almonds • x pounds + price of cashews • y pounds = $40

$8 \cdot x \quad + \quad 10 \cdot y \quad = 40$

Compute Find the x- and y-intercepts of $8x + 10y = 40$.

$8x + 10(0) = 40$ $\qquad$ $8(0) + 10y = 40$

$x = 5$ $\qquad$ $y = 4$

Graph the segment between the intercepts.

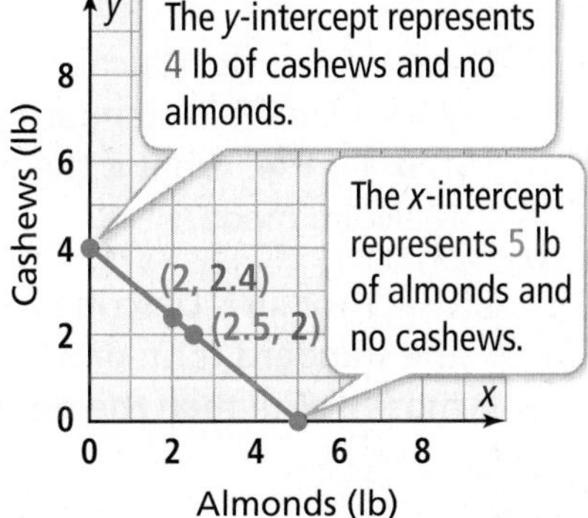

Interpret Tamira can use the graph of the equation to help her determine the amount of almonds and cashews to buy. Each point on the line represents a combination of almonds and cashews that costs a total of $40.

Tamira can buy 2 lb of almonds and 2.4 lb of cashews or 2.5 lb of almonds and 2 lb of cashews for $40.

 **Try It!** **4.** How does the equation change if Tamira has $60 to spend on a mixture of almonds and cashews? How many pounds of nuts can she buy if she buys only cashews? Only almonds? A mixture of both?

CONCEPT SUMMARY Standard Form of a Linear Equation

WORDS The standard form of a linear equation is useful

- to find the x- and y-intercepts easily.
- to write the equation of a vertical or horizontal line.

The x-intercept is the value of x when $y = 0$, and the y-intercept is the value of y when $x = 0$.

ALGEBRA $Ax + By = C$, where A, B, and C are integers, and A and B are not both equal to 0.

NUMBERS $2x - 3y = -3$

GRAPH

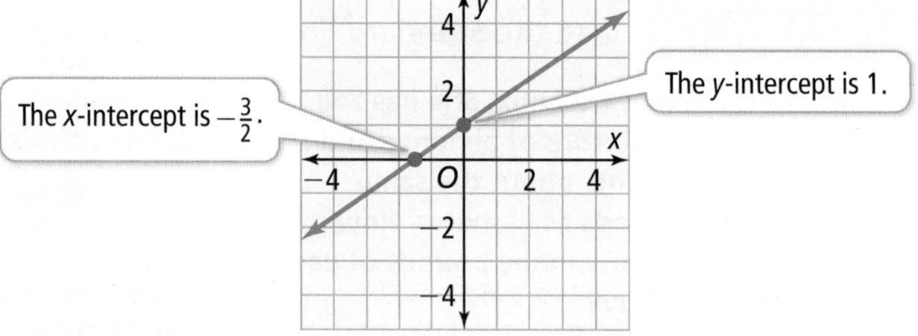

Do You UNDERSTAND?

1. **ESSENTIAL QUESTION** What information does the standard form of a linear equation reveal about a line?

2. **Communicate Precisely** How is the standard form of a linear equation similar to and different from the slope-intercept form?

3. **Error Analysis** Malcolm says that $y = -1.5x + 4$ in standard form is $1.5x + y = 4$. What is the error that Malcolm made?

4. **Use Structure** Describe a situation in which the standard form of a linear equation is more useful than the slope-intercept form.

Do You KNOW HOW?

Use the x- and y-intercepts to sketch a graph of each equation.

5. $x + 4y = 8$

6. $3x - 4y = 24$

7. $5x = 20$

8. $-3y = 9$

9. Deondra has \$12 to spend on a mixture of green and red grapes. What equation can she use to graph a line showing the different amounts of green and red grapes she can buy for \$12?

UNDERSTAND

10. **Use Structure** If $C = 24$, what values of A and B complete $Ax + By = C$ for each graph? Write the standard form for each equation.

a.

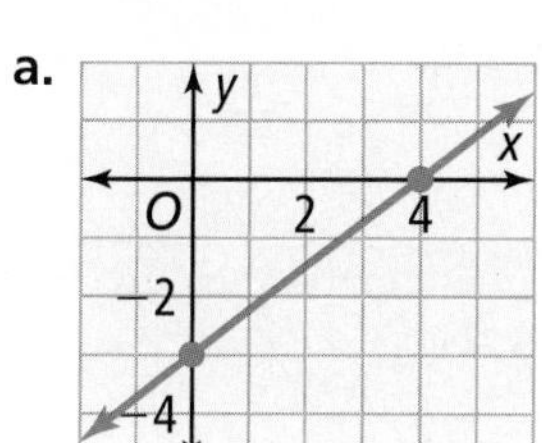

b.

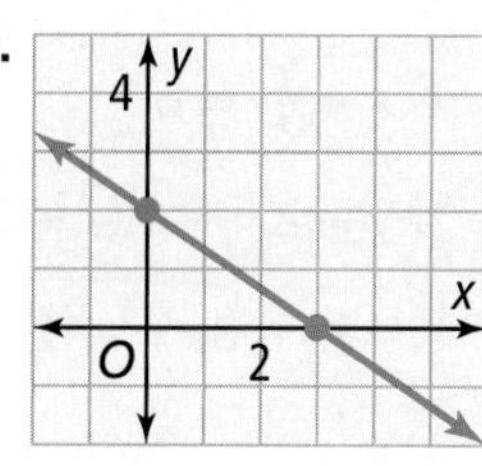

11. **Construct Arguments** Darren graphs the linear equations $y = -\frac{2}{5}x + 3$ and $2x + 5y = 15$. The graphs look identical so he believes that the equations represent the same line. What mathematical argument can he construct to show that the two forms are equivalent?

12. **Error Analysis** Describe and correct the error a student made finding the intercepts of the graph of the line $4x - 6y = 12$.

> 1. $4(0) - 6y = 12$
> 2. $6y = 12$, so $y = 2$; the y-intercept is 2.
> 3. $4x - 6(0) = 12$
> 4. $4x = 12$, so $x = 3$; the x-intercept is 3. ✗

13. **Mathematical Connections** Point A is one vertex of triangle ABC. Point B is the x-intercept of $6x - 4y = -12$ and point C is the y-intercept. What are points B and C? Sketch the triangle in the coordinate plane.

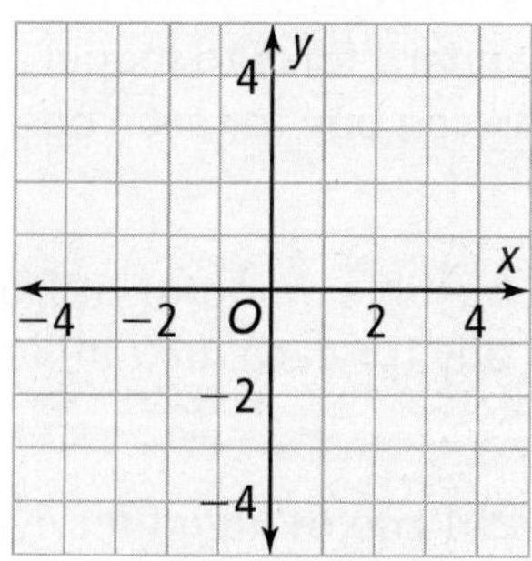

14. **Higher Order Thinking** Consider the line represented by the equation $5x + 2y = 10$. How is the slope of the line related to values of A, B, and C in standard form $Ax + By = C$?

PRACTICE

Identify the x- and y-intercepts of the graph of each equation. SEE EXAMPLES 1 AND 2

15. $2x + 5y = 10$
16. $3x - 4y = -24$
17. $10x + 5y = 120$
18. $2x - y = 8$

Sketch the graph of each equation. SEE EXAMPLE 2

19. $2x - 4y = 8$
20. $3x + 5y = 15$
21. $3x - 6y = -12$
22. $8x + 12y = -24$

Which line matches each equation? SEE EXAMPLE 2

23. $4x + 4y = -8$
24. $3x - 2y = -6$
25. $x + 2y = 2$
26. $3x - y = 3$

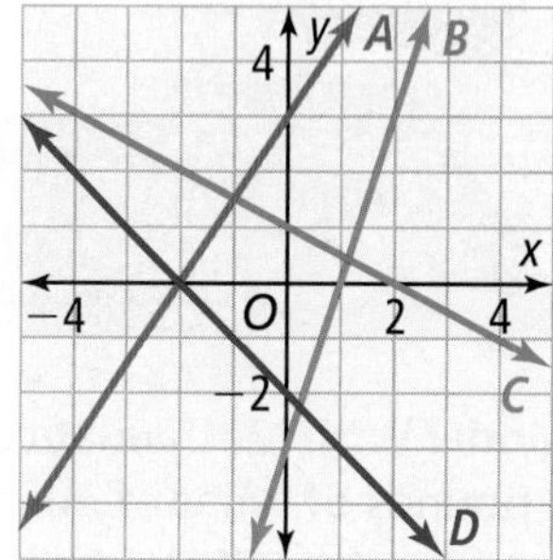

How is the graph of each equation related to standard form $Ax + By = C$? SEE EXAMPLE 3

27.

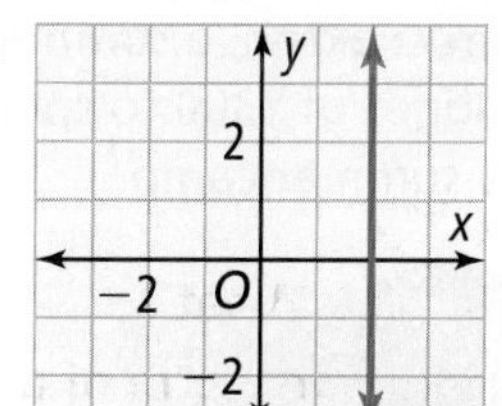

28.

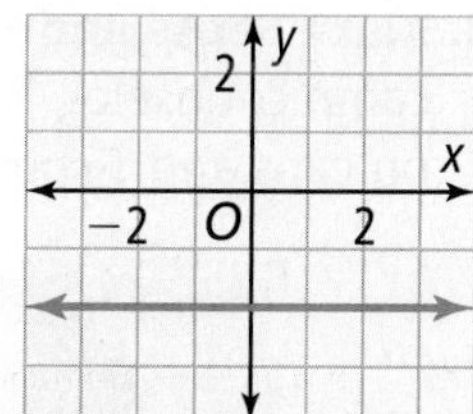

Sketch the graph of each equation. SEE EXAMPLE 3

29. $4x = 10$
30. $-6y = 3$
31. $3y = -15$
32. $-9x = -27$

Write each equation in standard form.

33. $y = 4x - 18$
34. $y = 2x + \frac{3}{7}$
35. $y = -\frac{1}{2}x - 10$
36. $y - 1 = \frac{2}{3}(x + 6)$

Write an equation in standard form of the line that passes through the given points.

37. (0, 2) and (8, 0)
38. (6, 0) and (0, 4)
39. (3, 0) and (0, −7)
40. (2, −3) and (2, 9)

PRACTICE & PROBLEM SOLVING

APPLY

41. Model With Mathematics Keisha is catering a luncheon. She has \$30 to spend on a mixture of Cheddar cheese and Swiss cheese. How many pounds of cheese can Keisha get if she buys only Cheddar cheese? Only Swiss cheese? A mixture of both cheeses? What linear equation in standard form can she use to model the situation?

42. Model With Mathematics Gregory can buy 4 pounds of wheat flour for \$8 and 5 pounds of rye flour for \$20. He has \$12 to spend on a flour mixture. What linear equation in standard form can Gregory use to model the situation?

43. Make Sense and Persevere Paxton, a summer camp counselor, has a budget of \$300 to spend on caps and T-shirts for a summer camp.

What equation can Paxton use to determine the number of caps and T-shirts he can order for \$300? If Paxton sketched a graph of the linear equation, would every point on the graph represent a possible solution? Explain.

ASSESSMENT PRACTICE

44. Which of the following equations has the same graph as $2x + 3y = 12$? Select all that apply.

Ⓐ $y = -\frac{2}{3}x + 4$

Ⓑ $x + \frac{3}{2}y = 6$

Ⓒ $y - 2 = -\frac{2}{3}(x - 3)$

Ⓓ $-2x - 3y = -12$

Ⓔ $y - 2 = -\frac{2}{3}x + 4$

45. SAT/ACT What is $\frac{3}{8}x + \frac{2}{3}y = 5$ written in standard form?

Ⓐ $y = -\frac{9}{16}x + \frac{15}{2}$

Ⓑ $y + \frac{3}{2} = -\frac{9}{16}(x - 16)$

Ⓒ $\frac{3}{8}x + \frac{2}{3}y = 5$

Ⓓ $3x + \frac{16}{3}y = 40$

Ⓔ $9x + 16y = 120$

46. Performance Task Fatima has a total of \$8 to spend to make fruit smoothies. She will use two types of fruit. The table shows the cost of each type of fruit per cup.

Fruit	Cost per cup (\$)
Mango	0.50
Pineapple	0.75
Strawberry	1.00

Part A What are the possible combinations of ingredients that Fatima can buy? Write a linear equation in standard form to model how many cups of fruit she can buy for each possible mixture.

Part B What are the possible amounts of fruit, in cups, that she can buy for each mixture in Part A?

Part C Fatima will add 1 cup of liquid for every cup of fruit to complete the smoothies. If she needs at least 24 cups of smoothies, which mixtures will allow her to make enough and still stay within her budget? Explain your reasoning.

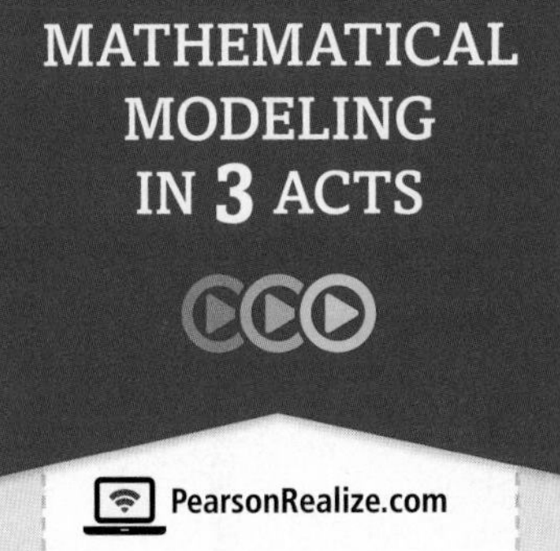

PearsonRealize.com

How Tall Is Tall?

The world's tallest person in recorded history was Robert Wadlow. He was 8 feet 11.1 inches tall! Only 5% of the world population is 6 feet 3 inches or taller. What percent of the population would you guess is 7 feet or taller?

We usually use standard units, such as feet and inches or centimeters, to measure length or height. Did you ever wonder why? In the Mathematical Modeling in 3 Acts lesson you'll consider some interesting alternatives.

ACT 1 Identify the Problem

1. What is the first question that comes to mind after watching the video?
2. Write down the main question you will answer about what you saw in the video.
3. Make an initial conjecture that answers this main question.
4. Explain how you arrived at your conjecture.
5. Write a number that you know is too small.
6. Write a number that you know is too large.
7. What information will be useful to know to answer the main question? How can you get it? How will you use that information?

ACT 2 Develop a Model

8. Use the math that you have learned in this Topic to refine your conjecture.

ACT 3 Interpret the Results

9. Is your refined conjecture between the highs and lows you set up earlier?
10. Did your refined conjecture match the actual answer exactly? If not, what might explain the difference?

Activity Assess

2-4 Parallel and Perpendicular Lines

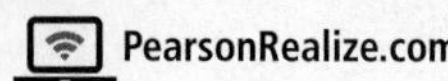

PearsonRealize.com

I CAN… write equations of parallel lines and perpendicular lines.

VOCABULARY

- parallel lines
- perpendicular lines
- reciprocal

EXPLORE & REASON

Graph these three equations using a graphing calculator.

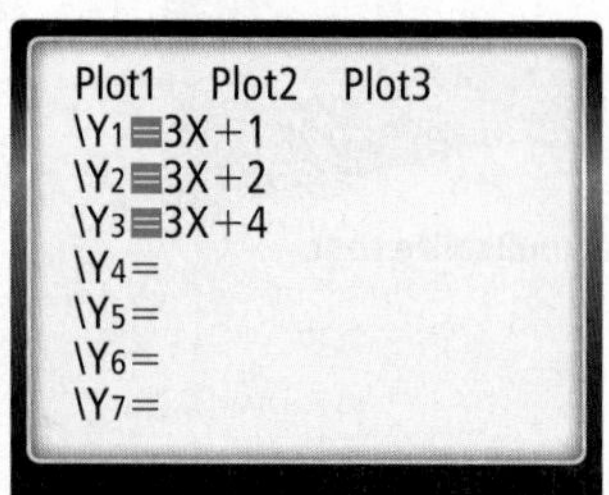

A. **Look for Relationships** Choose any two of the lines you graphed. How are they related to each other?

B. Does your answer to Part A hold for any two lines? Explain.

C. Write another set of three or more equations that have the same relationships as the first three equations.

ESSENTIAL QUESTION

How can the equations of lines help you identify whether the lines are parallel, perpendicular, or neither?

EXAMPLE 1 Write an Equation of a Line Parallel to a Given Line

What is the equation of the line in slope-intercept form that passes through the point (8, 9) and is parallel to the graph of $y = \frac{3}{4}x - 2$?

COMMUNICATE PRECISELY
Explain why it is necessary to use the term nonvertical when discussing slopes of parallel lines.

Parallel lines are lines in the same plane that never intersect. Nonvertical lines that are parallel have the same slope but different *y*-intercepts.

Step 1 Identify the slope of the given line.

$$y = \frac{3}{4}x - 2$$

The slope is $\frac{3}{4}$. The slope of a parallel line will be the same.

Step 2 Start with point-slope form. Use the given point and the slope of the parallel line.

$$y - y_1 = m(x - x_1)$$

$$y - 9 = \frac{3}{4}(x - 8)$$

$$y - 9 = \frac{3}{4}x - 6$$

Change point-slope form to slope-intercept form.

$$y = \frac{3}{4}x + 3$$

The equation of the line is $y = \frac{3}{4}x + 3$.

Try It! **1.** Write the equation of the line in slope-intercept form that passes through the point (–3, 5) and is parallel to $y = -\frac{2}{3}x$.

CONCEPTUAL UNDERSTANDING

EXAMPLE 2 Understand the Slopes of Perpendicular Lines

A. How can you create two perpendicular lines?

Perpendicular lines are lines that intersect to form right angles.

Draw two identical right triangles as shown.

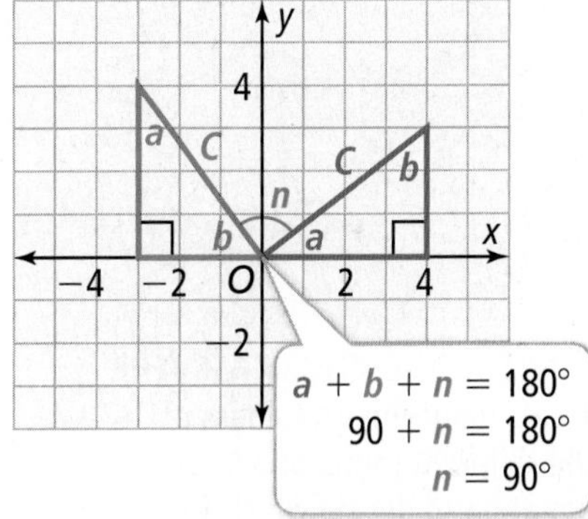

Because the angle sum for each triangle is 180° and the right angle is 90°, the sum of angles *a* and *b* in each triangle must be 90°. Angles *b*, *n*, and *a* form a straight angle of 180° at the origin, so *n* must equal 90°.

The hypotenuses (*C*) of the right triangles intersect at a right angle, so the lines that include them are perpendicular to each other.

B. How do the slopes of perpendicular lines compare?

Compute the slopes of lines ℓ and *p*.

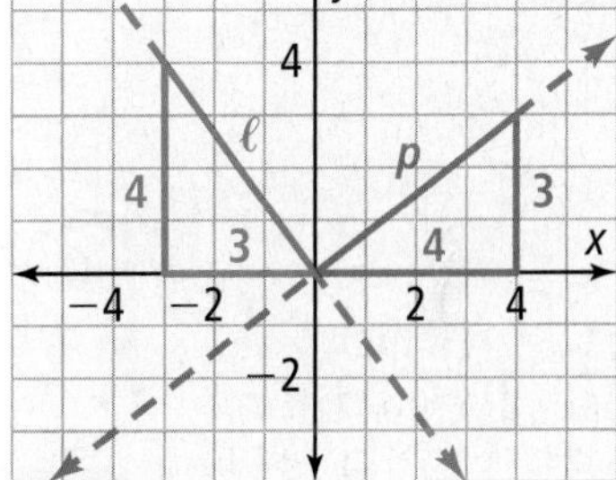

Line ℓ: $m = \frac{4-0}{-3-0} = -\frac{4}{3}$

Line *p*: $m = \frac{3-0}{4-0} = \frac{3}{4}$

The numbers $\frac{4}{3}$ and $\frac{3}{4}$ are reciprocals. The **reciprocal** of a number is 1 divided by that number. The reciprocal of *x* is $\frac{1}{x}$ when $x \neq 0$.

$$\text{Reciprocal of } \frac{3}{4} \text{ is } 1 \div \frac{3}{4} = 1 \cdot \frac{4}{3} = \frac{4}{3}.$$

VOCABULARY
Another way to state the definition is as follows: the product of reciprocals is 1.

$\frac{3}{4} \cdot \frac{4}{3} = 1$

So, the slopes of perpendicular lines are *opposite reciprocals*. Opposite reciprocals have a product of −1.

For example, $-\frac{4}{3} \cdot \frac{3}{4} = -\frac{12}{12} = -1$.

Try It! 2. Why does it make sense that the slopes of perpendicular lines have opposite signs?

EXAMPLE 3 Write an Equation of a Line Perpendicular to a Given Line

What is the equation of the line that passes through the point (1, 7) and is perpendicular to the graph of $y = -\frac{1}{4}x + 11$?

Step 1 Use the slope of the given line to determine the slope of the line that is perpendicular.

$y = -\frac{1}{4}x + 11$ — $m = -\frac{1}{4}$

The slope of a line perpendicular to the given line is the opposite reciprocal of $-\frac{1}{4}$. Use $\frac{4}{1}$, or 4, as the slope of the new line.

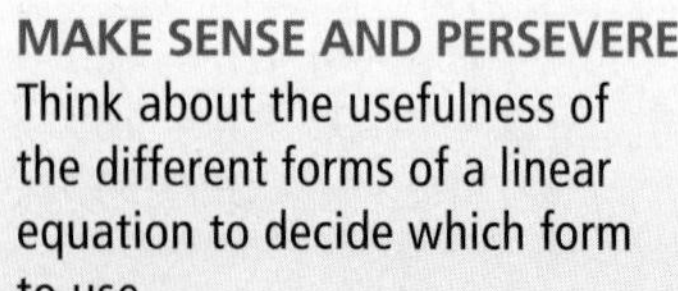

MAKE SENSE AND PERSEVERE
Think about the usefulness of the different forms of a linear equation to decide which form to use.

Step 2 Start with point-slope form. Use the given point and the slope of the perpendicular line.

$y - y_1 = m(x - x_1)$

$y - 7 = 4(x - 1)$ — Substitute 1 for x_1, 7 for y_1 and 4 for m.

The graph of $y - 7 = 4(x - 1)$ passes through the point (1, 7) and is perpendicular to the graph of $y = -\frac{1}{4}x + 11$.

Try It! **3.** Write the equation of the line that passes through the point (4, 5) and is perpendicular to the graph of $y = 2x - 3$.

EXAMPLE 4 Classify Lines

Are the graphs of the equations $3y = -4x + 6$ and $y = -\frac{3}{4}x - 5$ *parallel, perpendicular,* or *neither*?

Step 1 Identify the slope of each line.

Rewrite the equation of the line in slope-intercept form.

$$3y = -4x + 6 \qquad y = -\frac{3}{4}x - 5$$

$$\frac{3y}{3} = \frac{-4x + 6}{3}$$

$$y = -\frac{4}{3}x + 2 \qquad y = -\frac{3}{4}x - 5$$

The slopes of the lines are $-\frac{4}{3}$ and $-\frac{3}{4}$.

COMMON ERROR
You may confuse the slopes of perpendicular lines. The slopes of perpendicular lines are opposite reciprocals, not reciprocals.

Step 2 Compare the slopes of the lines.

The slopes of the lines, $-\frac{4}{3}$ and $-\frac{3}{4}$, are neither the same nor opposite reciprocals.

The graphs of the equations $3y = -4x + 6$ and $y = -\frac{3}{4}x - 5$ are neither parallel nor perpendicular.

Try It! **4.** Are the graphs of the equations *parallel, perpendicular,* or *neither*?

a. $y = 2x + 6$ and $y = \frac{1}{2}x + 3$

b. $y = -5x$ and $25x + 5y = 1$

APPLICATION

EXAMPLE 5 Solve a Real-World Problem

A landscaper plans to install two new paths in a park. The new Fountain Path will be perpendicular to the East Path and lead to the fountain. The new Picnic Path will be parallel to the Fountain Path and pass through the picnic area. What are the equations in point-slope form that represent the new paths?

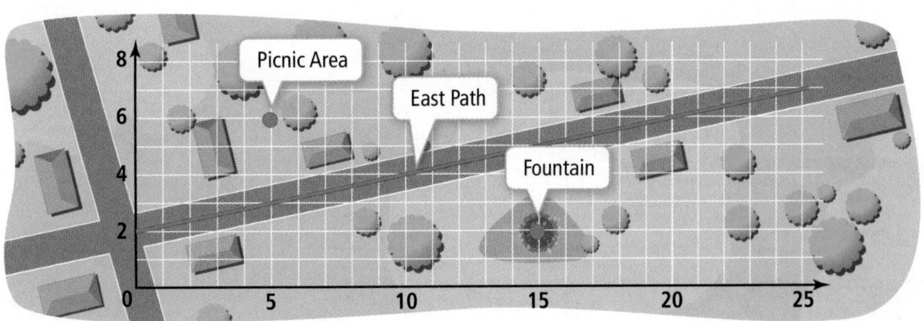

Formulate Find the slope of the line that represents the East Path. Then determine equations for the two new pathways.

The East Path passes through (0, 2) and (5, 3).

$$m = \frac{3 - 2}{5 - 0} = \frac{1}{5}$$

The slope of the line representing the East Path is $\frac{1}{5}$.

Compute Find an equation for the Fountain Path.

The slope is the opposite reciprocal of the slope of the East Path.

$y - 2 = -5(x - 15)$ The fountain is located at the point (15, 2).

Find the equation of the Picnic Path.

The slope is the same as the slope of the Fountain Path.

$y - 6 = -5(x - 5)$ The picnic area is located at the point (5, 6).

Interpret Equation of the line of the Fountain Path: $y - 2 = -5(x - 15)$

Equation of the line of the Picnic Path: $y - 6 = -5(x - 5)$

Try It! 5. The equation $y = 2x + 7$ represents the North Path on a map.

a. Find the equation for a path that passes through the point (6, 3) and is parallel to the North Path.

b. Find the equation for a path that passes through the same point but is perpendicular to North Path.

CONCEPT SUMMARY Parallel Lines and Perpendicular Lines

	Parallel Lines	Perpendicular Lines
WORDS	The graphs of two equations are parallel if the slopes are the same.	The graphs of two equations are perpendicular if the slopes are opposite reciprocals.
NUMBERS	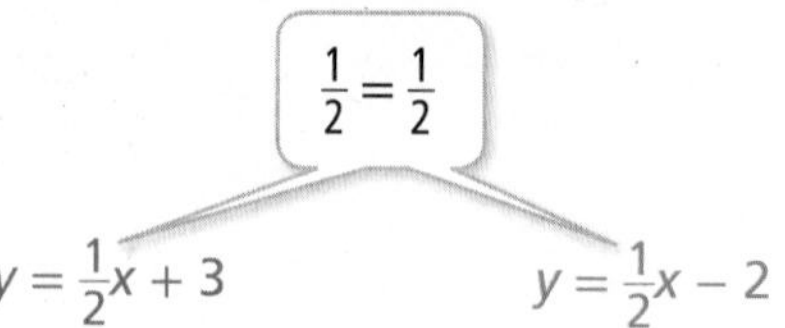 $y = \frac{1}{2}x + 3$ $y = \frac{1}{2}x - 2$	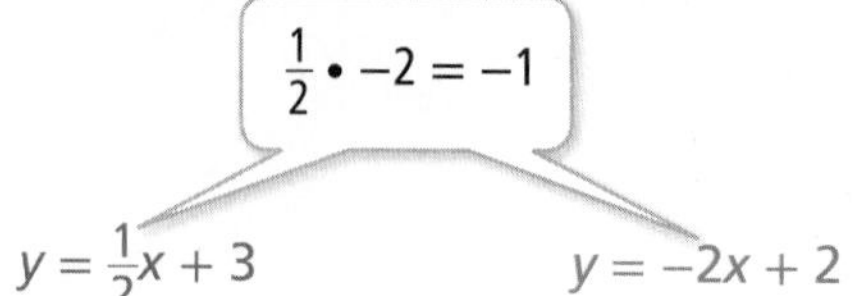 $y = \frac{1}{2}x + 3$ $y = -2x + 2$
GRAPHS	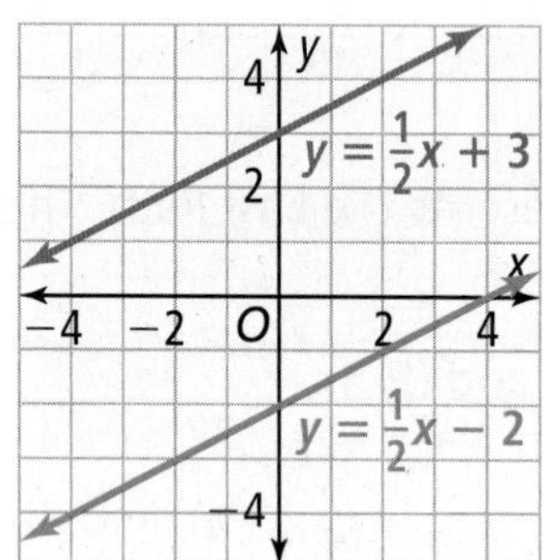	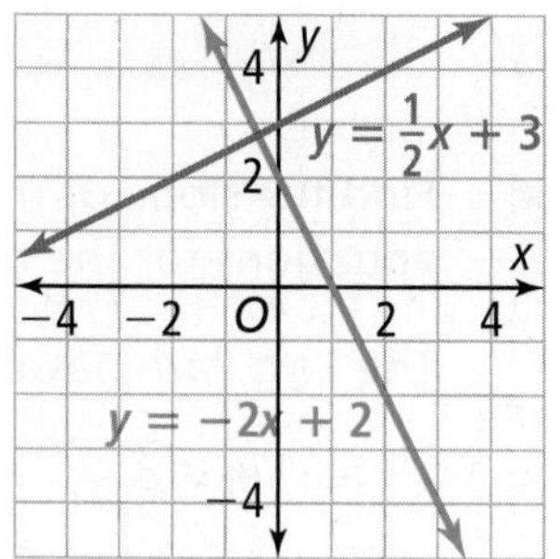

Do You UNDERSTAND?

1. ESSENTIAL QUESTION How can the equations of lines help you identify whether the lines are parallel, perpendicular, or neither?

2. **Error Analysis** Dwayne stated that the slope of the line perpendicular to $y = -2x$ is 2. Describe Dwayne's error.

3. **Vocabulary** Describe the difference between the slopes of two parallel lines and the slopes of two perpendicular lines.

4. **Use Structure** Is there one line that passes through the point (3, 5) that is parallel to the lines represented by $y = 2x - 4$ and $y = x - 4$? Explain.

Do You KNOW HOW?

The equation $y = -\frac{3}{4}x + 1$ represents a given a line.

5. Write the equation for the line that passes through (−4, 9) and is parallel to the given line.

6. Write the equation for the line that passes through (6, 6) and is perpendicular to the given line.

Are the graphs of the equations parallel, perpendicular, or neither?

7. $x - 3y = 6$ and $x - 3y = 9$

8. $y = 4x + 1$ and $y = -4x - 2$

9. What equation represents the road that passes through the point shown and is perpendicular to the road represented by the red line?

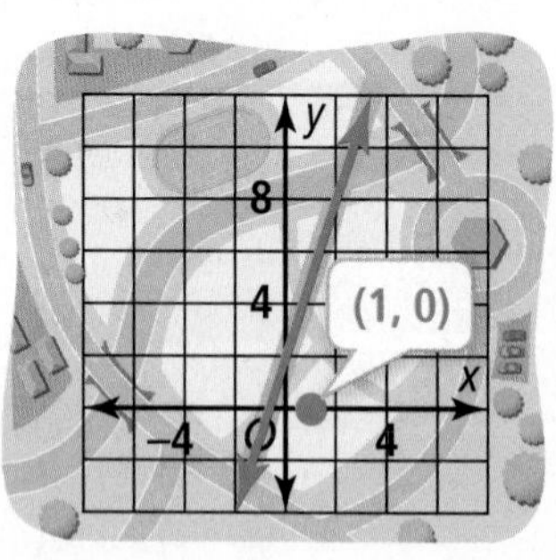

UNDERSTAND

10. **Use Structure** A line passes through points $A(n, 4)$ and $B(6, 8)$ and is parallel to $y = 2x - 5$. What is the value of n?

11. **Error Analysis** Describe and correct the error the student made when writing the equation of the line that passes through (−8, 5) and is perpendicular to $y = 4x + 2$.

$$y - 5 = \frac{1}{4}(x - (-8))$$
$$y - 5 = \frac{1}{4}x + 2$$
$$y - 5 + 5 = \frac{1}{4}x + 2 + 5$$
$$y = \frac{1}{4}x + 7 \quad ✗$$

12. **Reason** The graphs of $4x + 12y = 8$ and $y = mx + 5$ are perpendicular. What is the value of m?

13. **Mathematical Connections** Rectangles have four right angles and opposite sides that are parallel.
    a. Is the figure shown a rectangle? Explain.
    b. If not, how could the points change so it would be a rectangle?

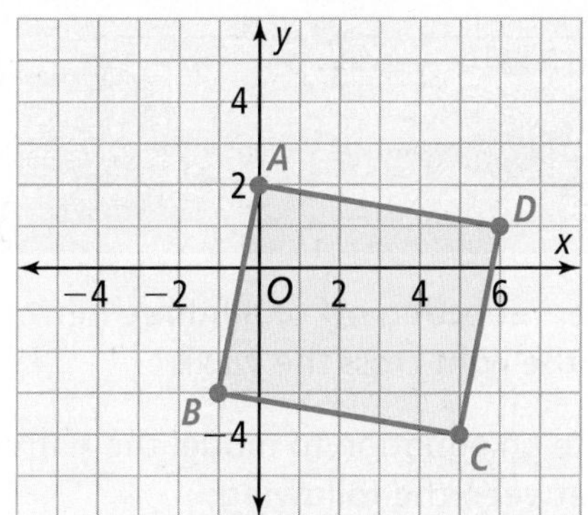

14. **Higher Order Thinking** Explain how you can determine whether the graphs of $5x - 3y = 2$ and $5x - 3y = 8$ are parallel without doing any calculations.

PRACTICE

Write the equation of the line that passes through the given point and is parallel to the given line. SEE EXAMPLE 1

15. $(5, -4)$; $y = \frac{1}{5}x - 4$
16. $(2, 7)$; $3x - y = 5$
17. $(-3, 2)$; $y = -4$
18. $(6, 4)$; $2x + 3y = 18$

19. Use the slopes of lines A and B to show that they are perpendicular to each other. SEE EXAMPLE 2

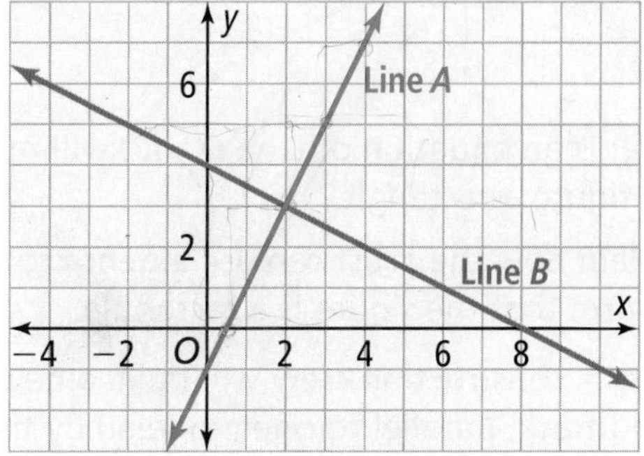

Write the equation of the line that passes through the given point and is perpendicular to the given line. SEE EXAMPLES 3 AND 5

20. $(-6, -3)$; $y = -\frac{2}{5}x$
21. $(0, 3)$; $3x - 4y = -8$
22. $(-2, 5)$; $x = 3$
23. $(4, 3)$; $4x - 5y = 30$

Are the graphs of each pair of equations parallel, perpendicular, or neither? SEE EXAMPLE 4

24. $y = 2x + 1$
    $2x - y = 3$
25. $y = \frac{1}{2}$
    $y = -3$
26. $x = 4$
    $y = 4$
27. $-2x + 5y = -4$
    $y = -\frac{5}{2}x + 6$

28. Copy and complete the table.

	Equation	Slope of a parallel line	Slope of a perpendicular line
a.	$y = \frac{1}{2}x + 6$		
b.	$x = -4.2$		
c.	$3x + 4y = 3$		
d.	$y = 3$		
e.	$y = x$		

PRACTICE & PROBLEM SOLVING

Practice | Tutorial

Mixed Review Available Online

APPLY

29. **Use Structure** An artist is drawing up plans for a mural. She wants to include a rectangle in her design.

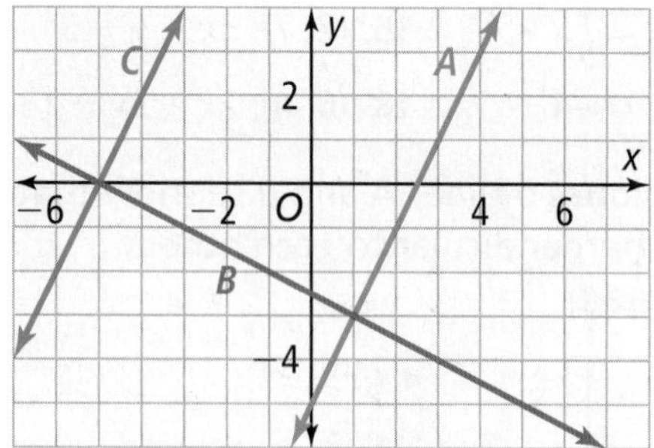

a. What is an equation of Line D that will make the figure a rectangle?

b. Explain how the artist can use algebra to confirm that the figure is a rectangle.

30. **Reason** A construction crew will build a new railroad track, parallel to one modeled by the line, which passes through the point (8, 5). What equation models the path of the new track?

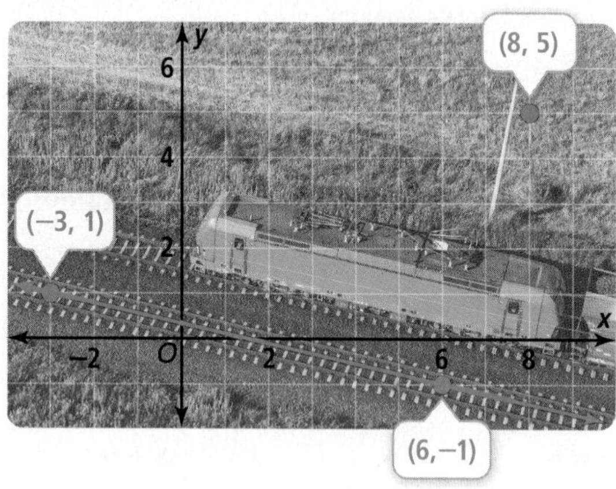

31. **Make Sense and Persevere** Elijah and Aubrey have summer jobs. Elijah deposits the same amount of money in his account every week. The equation $y = 125x + 72$ represents his bank balance any given week of the summer. Aubrey also deposits the same amount into her account every week. At the end of the third week she has \$398. At the end of the sixth week she has \$773.

a. Write an equation to represent Aubrey's bank balance any given week of the summer.

b. Would the graph of the equation for Aubrey's balance be parallel to the graph of Elijah's balance? Explain.

c. What do the parallel graphs mean in terms of the situation?

ASSESSMENT PRACTICE

32. Which of the following lines is perpendicular to $y = \frac{1}{4}x - 3$? Select all that apply.

Ⓐ $y = 4x$ Ⓑ $4x - y = -2$

Ⓒ $y = -4x + 6$ Ⓓ $8x - 2y = 3$

Ⓔ $y = 4x + 9$

33. **SAT/ACT** A line passing through $(6, a)$ and $(9, -4)$ is parallel to $2x - 3y = 6$. What is the value of a?

Ⓐ −6 Ⓑ −3

Ⓒ −2 Ⓓ 3

Ⓔ 6

34. **Performance Task** A video game is designed to model the path of a laser. A laser is placed at (2, −1) and is aimed at Mirror 1. Other mirrors are placed as shown. Each mirror is placed so the light will reflect at a 90° angle.

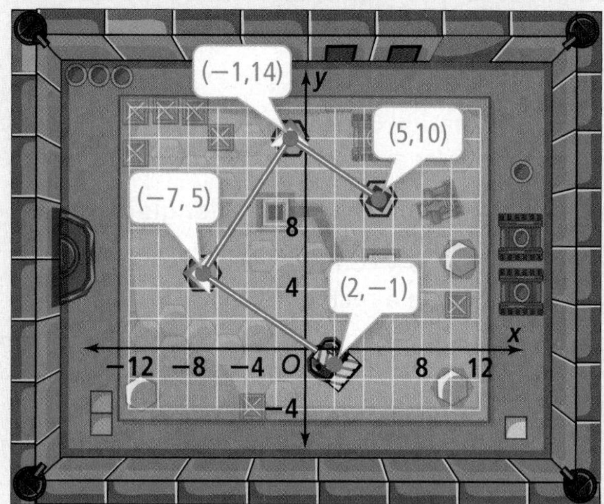

Part A After reflecting off of all three mirrors, where will the light cross the y-axis?

Part B Write an equation to model the path of the light between the following:

a. Laser and Mirror 1

b. Mirror 1 and Mirror 2

c. Mirror 2 and Mirror 3

d. Mirror 3 and y-axis

Part C Change the placement of the mirrors so that the laser light hits a target in Quadrant IV. Give the coordinates of the mirrors and the equations of lines that the path of the light would follow.

TOPIC 2

Topic Review

TOPIC ESSENTIAL QUESTION

1. Why is it useful to have different forms of linear equations?

Vocabulary Review

Choose the correct term to complete each sentence.

2. The slopes of two perpendicular lines are opposite ________.
3. The ________ of a linear equation is $Ax + By = C$, where A, B, and C are integers.
4. Nonvertical lines that are ________ have the same slope and different y-intercepts.
5. The ________ of a linear equation is $y = mx + b$.
6. You can write the equation of a line using any point (x_1, y_1) and the slope, m, in ________, $y - y_1 = m(x - x_1)$.

- parallel
- perpendicular
- point-slope form
- reciprocals
- slope-intercept form
- standard form
- y-intercept

Concepts & Skills Review

LESSON 2-1 Slope-Intercept Form

Quick Review

The **slope-intercept form** of a linear equation is $y = mx + b$, where m is the slope of the line and the y-intercept is b. The slope-intercept form is useful when the slope and the y-intercept of the line are known.

Example

Write the equation of the line in slope-intercept form that passes through (0, 4) and (2, 3).

$m = \frac{4-3}{0-2}$ ········ Use the slope formula.

$= -\frac{1}{2}$

$b = 4$ ········ The line intersects y-axis at (0, 4).

$y = mx + b$ ········ Write the equation in slope-intercept form.

$y = -\frac{1}{2}x + 4$ ········ Substitute $-\frac{1}{2}$ for m and 4 for b.

Practice & Problem Solving

Sketch the graph of each equation.

7. $y = 3x - 1$
8. $y = -1.5x + 3.5$

Write the equation of the line in slope-intercept form that passes through the given points.

9. (2, 0) and (4, 6)
10. (–1, 8) and (5, –2)

11. **Model With Mathematics** Ricardo wants to buy a new tablet computer that costs \$1,150. He will make a down payment of \$250 and will make monthly payments of \$50. Write an equation in slope-intercept form that Ricardo can use to determine how much he will owe after x months.

LESSON 2-2 Point-Slope Form

Quick Review

The **point-slope form** of a linear equation is $y - y_1 = m(x - x_1)$, where m is the slope and (x_1, y_1) is a specific point and (x, y) is any point on the line. The point-slope form is useful when you know the slope and a point that is not $(0, b)$.

Example

Write the equation of the line in point-slope form that passes through the points (2, 2) and (5, 1).

$m = \frac{y_2 - y_1}{x_2 - x_1}$ .... Find the slope of the line.

$= \frac{1 - 2}{5 - 2}$ .... Substitute (5, 1) for (x_2, y_2) and (2, 2) for (x_1, y_1).

$= -\frac{1}{3}$

$y - y_1 = m(x - x_1)$ .... Write the equation in point-slope form.

$y - 2 = -\frac{1}{3}(x - 2)$ .... Substitute $-\frac{1}{3}$ for m and (2, 2) for (x_1, y_1).

Practice & Problem Solving

Write the equation in point-slope form of the line that passes through the given point with the given slope.

12. (4, –2); $m = 0.5$

13. (–2, 5); $m = -3$

Write an equation in point-slope form of the line that passes through the given points.

14. (3, 1) and (–5, –2)

15. (1.5, 4) and (–2.5, 6)

16. Reason Jeffrey purchased a card for \$180 that gives him 20 visits to a new gym and includes a one-time fee for unlimited use of the sauna. After 5 visits, Jeff has \$123.75 left on the card, and after 11 visits, he has \$74.25 left on the card. Write an equation that Jeffrey can use to determine the cost of each visit and the fee for the sauna use.

LESSON 2-3 Standard Form

Quick Review

The **standard form** of a linear equation is $Ax + By = C$, where A, B, and C are integers. The standard form is useful for graphing vertical and horizontal lines, for finding the x- and y-intercepts, and for representing certain situations in terms of constraints.

Example

What are the x- and y-intercepts of the line $3x - 4y = 24$?

Substitute 0 for y and solve for x.

$3x - 4(0) = 24$

$x = 8$

Then substitute 0 for x and solve for y.

$3(0) - 4y = 24$

$y = -6$

The x-intercept is 8 and the y-intercept is –6.

Practice & Problem Solving

17. If $C = 15$, what values of A and B complete $Ax + By = C$ for the graph shown? Write the standard form of the equation.

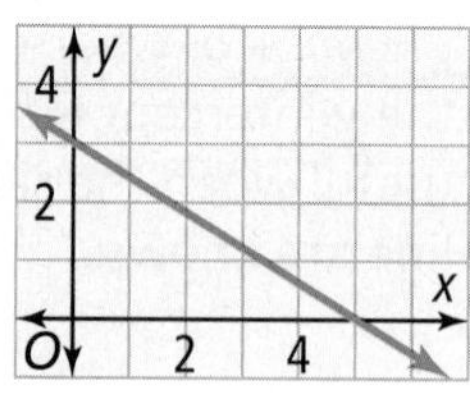

Write each equation in standard form.

18. $y = 4x - 5$

19. $y - 3 = 5(4 - x)$

Determine the x- and y-intercepts of each line.

20. $5x - 3y = 30$

21. $x + 3y = 24$

22. Model With Mathematics Jung-Soon has \$25 to spend on prizes for a game at the school fair. Lip balm costs \$1.25 each, and mini-notebooks cost \$1.50 each. Write a linear equation that can be used to determine how many of each prize she can buy.

LESSON 2-4 Parallel and Perpendicular Lines

Quick Review

Two nonvertical lines are **parallel** if they have the same slope, but different y-intercepts. Vertical lines are parallel if they have different x-intercepts. Two nonvertical lines are **perpendicular** if their slopes are opposite reciprocals. A vertical line and a horizontal line are perpendicular if they intersect and form right angles.

Example

Are the graphs of the equations $4y = 2x - 5$ and $y = -2x + 7$ parallel, perpendicular, or neither?

Determine the slope of each line.

$$4y = 2x - 5 \qquad y = -2x + 7$$

$$\frac{4y}{4} = \frac{2x - 5}{4}$$

$$y = \frac{1}{2}x - \frac{5}{4}$$

The slopes of the lines are $\frac{1}{2}$ and -2, so the graphs of the equations are perpendicular lines.

Practice & Problem Solving

23. The graphs of $3x + 9y = 15$ and $y = mx - 4$ are parallel lines. What is the value of m?

Write the equation for the line that passes through the given point and is parallel to the given line.

24. $(2, 1)$; $y = -3x + 8$

25. $(-3, -1)$; $x - 2y = 5$

Write the equation for the line that passes through the given point and is perpendicular to the given line.

26. $(1, 7)$; $x - 4y = 8$

27. $(-2, 6)$; $y = 0.5x - 3$

Are the graphs of the given pairs of equations parallel, perpendicular, or neither?

28. $y = \frac{1}{4}x - 8$
$2x + y = 5$

29. $3y + 2x = 9$
$y = -\frac{2}{3}x - 4$

TOPIC 3

Linear Functions

TOPIC ESSENTIAL QUESTION

How can linear functions be used to model situations and solve problems?

Topic Overview

Topic Vocabulary

- arithmetic sequence
- causation
- common difference
- continuous
- correlation coefficient
- discrete
- domain
- explicit formula
- extrapolation
- function
- function notation
- interpolation
- line of best fit
- linear function
- linear regression
- negative association
- negative correlation
- no association
- one-to-one
- positive association
- positive correlation
- range
- recursive formula
- relation
- residual
- sequence
- term of a sequence
- transformation
- translation
- trend line

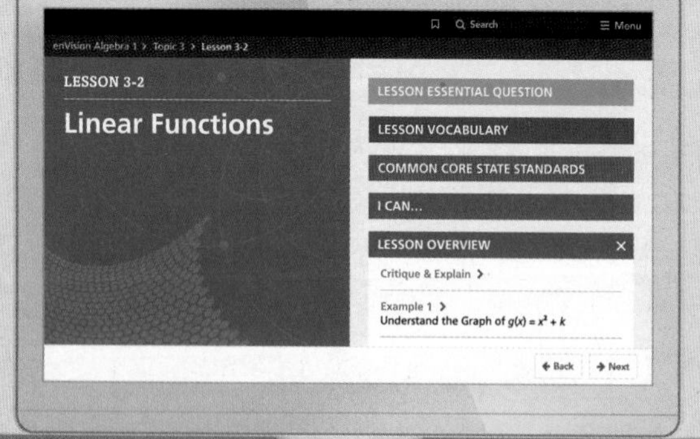

 Go online | **PearsonRealize.com**

Digital Experience

 **INTERACTIVE STUDENT EDITION** Access online or offline.

 **ACTIVITIES** Complete ***Explore & Reason, Model & Discuss***, and ***Critique & Explain*** activities. Interact with Examples and Try Its.

 **ANIMATION** View and interact with real-world applications.

 **PRACTICE** Practice what you've learned.

MATHEMATICAL MODELING IN 3 ACTS

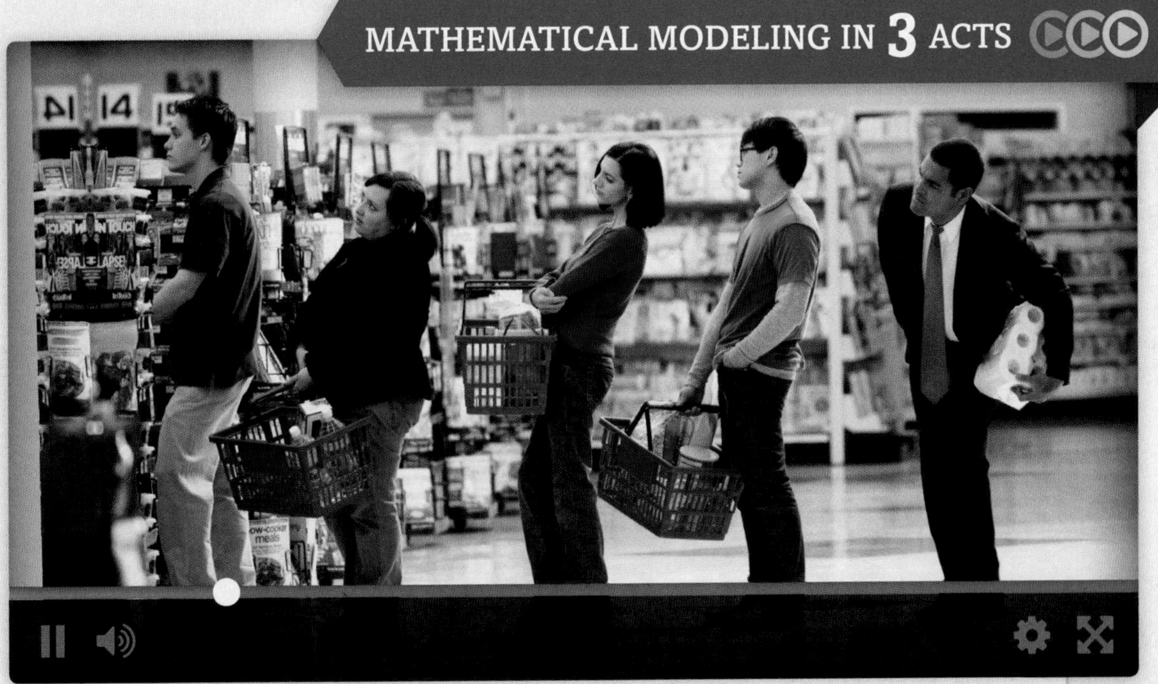

The Express Lane

Some supermarkets have self-checkout lanes. Customers scan their items themselves and then pay with either cash or credit when they have finished scanning all of the items. Some customers think these lanes are faster than the checkout lanes with cashiers, but others don't like having to bag all of their purchases themselves.

What's your strategy for picking a checkout lane at the grocery store? Think about this during the Mathematical Modeling in 3 Acts lesson.

TOPIC 3

VIDEOS Watch clips to support ***Mathematical Modeling in 3 Acts Lessons*** and **enVision™ *STEM Projects.***

CONCEPT SUMMARY Review key lesson content through multiple representations.

ASSESSMENT Show what you've learned.

GLOSSARY Read and listen to English and Spanish definitions.

TUTORIALS Get help from ***Virtual Nerd***, right when you need it.

MATH TOOLS Explore math with digital tools and manipulatives.

Did You Know?

Glass, aluminum, and other metals can be melted over and over again **without a loss in quality.** Paper can be recycled up to six times, with its quality decreasing each time.

Americans throw away **25,000,000 plastic bottles every hour.** If those bottles were recycled, they would offset the environmental impact of 625 round-trip flights between New York and London.

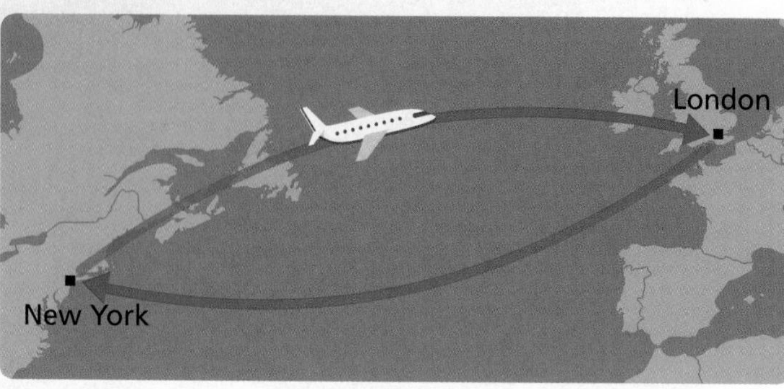

1 million recycled phones

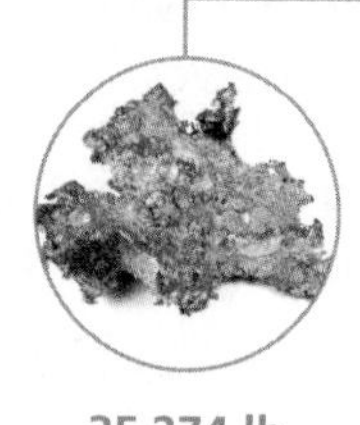

35,274 lb of copper

772 lb of silver

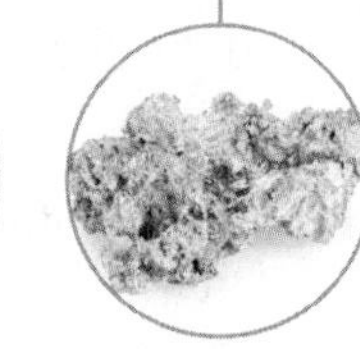

75 lb of gold

33 lb of palladium

How Recycling Offsets CO^2 Production

RECYCLE	SAVE
1 ton of plastic	1 ton of CO_2
1 ton of paper	3 tons of CO_2
1 ton of metal	3 tons of CO_2
3 tons of glass	1 ton of CO_2

Your Task: Planning a Recycling Drive

About 75% of the trash Americans generate is recyclable, but only about 30% gets recycled. You and your classmates will plan a recycling drive at your school to increase the amount of trash that gets recycled.

Activity Assess

3-1 Relations and Functions

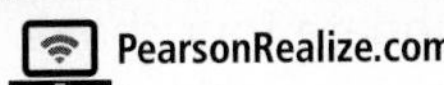
PearsonRealize.com

I CAN... determine whether a relation is a function.

VOCABULARY

- continuous
- discrete
- domain
- function
- one-to-one
- range
- relation

EXPLORE & REASON

The desks in a study hall are arranged in rows like the horizontal ones in the picture.

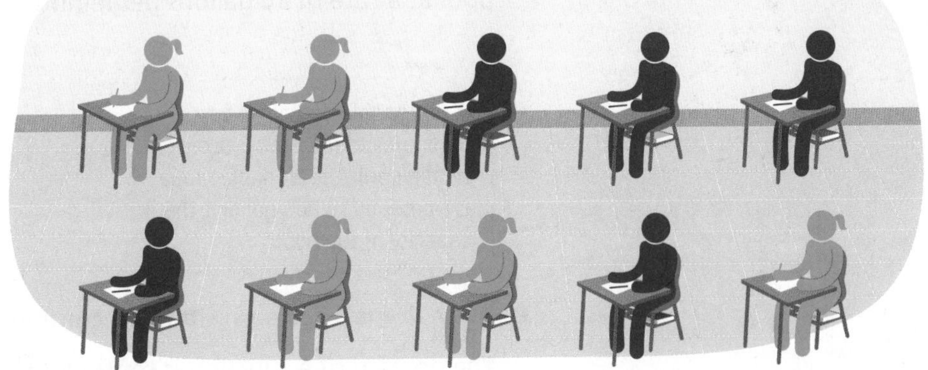

A. What is a reasonable number of rows for the study hall? What is a reasonable number of desks?

B. Look for Structure What number of rows would be impossible? What number of desks would be impossible? Explain.

C. What do your answers to Parts A and B reveal about what the graph of rows to desks looks like?

ESSENTIAL QUESTION

What is a function? Why is domain and range important in defining a function?

EXAMPLE 1 Recognize Domain and Range

What are the domain and the range of the function?

x	1	2	3	4	5
y	11	12	13	13	13

inputs

outputs

A **relation** is a set of ordered pairs. A **function** is a relation in which each input is assigned to exactly one output. The **domain** of a function is the set of inputs. The **range** of a function is the set of outputs. By convention, inputs are x-values and outputs are y-values.

The domain of this function is the set of x-values, {1, 2, 3, 4, 5}. The range is the set of y-values, {11, 12, 13}.

Try It! 1. Identify the domain and the range of each function.

a.

x	2	3	4	5	6
y	0	1	2	3	4

b.

x	−3	−1	1	3	4
y	1	3	−2	2	6

CONCEPTUAL UNDERSTANDING

EXAMPLE 2 Analyze Reasonable Domains and Ranges

A. A function can model each situation. What is a reasonable domain and range of each function?

A hose fills a 10,000-gallon swimming pool at a rate of 10 gallons per minute.

> A reasonable domain is from 0 minutes to the time it takes to fill the pool. A reasonable range is from 0 to 10,000 gallons, the capacity of the pool.

A restaurant needs to order chairs for its tables. One table can accommodate four chairs.

> A reasonable domain is from 0 tables to the number of tables needed. A reasonable range is multiples of 4 from 0 to 4 times the number of tables needed.

B. Is the domain for each situation continuous or discrete?

The domain of a function is **continuous** when it includes all real numbers. The graph of the function is a line or curve.

The domain of a function is **discrete** when it consists of just whole numbers or integers. The graph of the function is a series of data points.

Sketch a graph of each situation.

> The volume of water in the pool can be determined at any point in time, for any value of x.

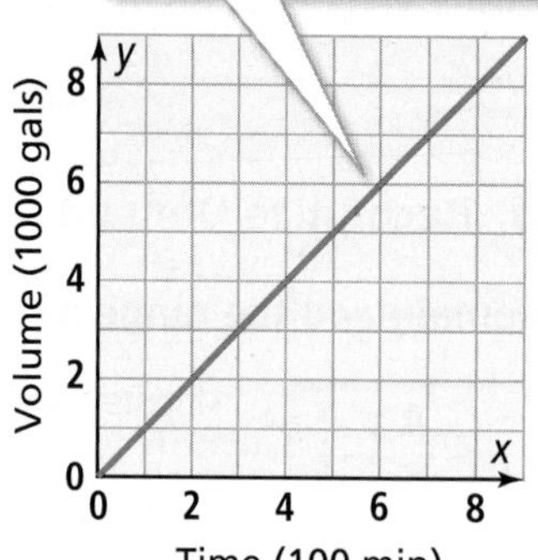

The domain is continuous.

> The number of tables and chairs must be whole numbers. There cannot be parts of tables or chairs.

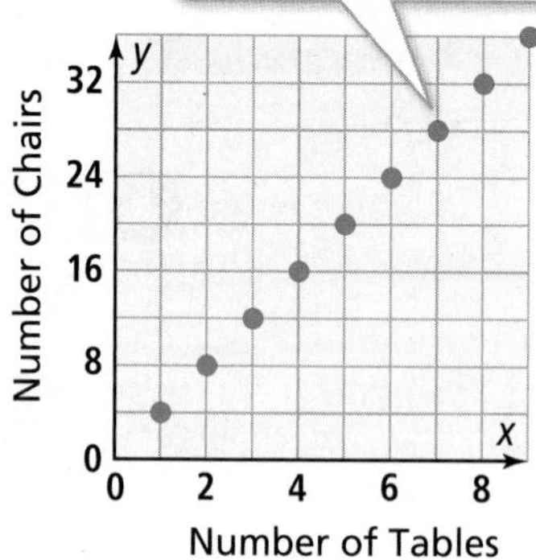

The domain is discrete.

MAKE SENSE AND PERSEVERE
What do the relationships in the two situations have in common?

 **Try It!** **2.** Analyze each situation. Identify a reasonable domain and range for each situation. Explain.

a. A bowler pays \$2.75 per game.

b. A car travels 25 miles using 1 gallon of gas.

EXAMPLE 3 Classify Relations and Functions

Is each relation a function? If so, is it one-to-one or not one-to-one?

A function is **one-to-one** if no two elements of the domain map to the same element in the range. When two or more elements of the domain map to the same element of the range, the function is **not one-to-one**.

A. {(1, 2), (5, 6), (7, −1), (8, 0)}

The relation is a function. Every element of the domain {1, 5, 7, 8} maps to exactly one element of the range {−1, 0, 2, 6}.

Since none of the range values are shared, the function is one-to-one.

COMMON ERROR
Two or more elements of the domain of a function can map to one element of the range, but two or more elements of the range, can not map to only one element of the domain.

B.

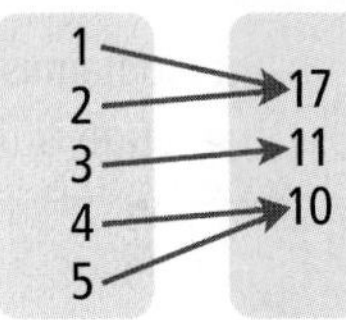

The relation is a function. Every element of the domain maps to exactly one element of the range.

Since more than one element in the domain maps to a single element in the range, the function is not one-to-one.

Try It! **3.** Is each relation a function? If so is it one-to-one or not one-to-one?

a.

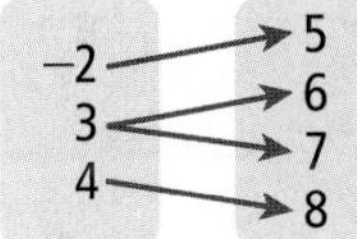

b.

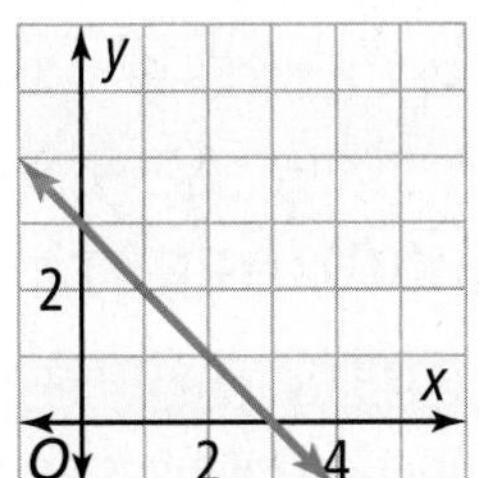

APPLICATION

EXAMPLE 4 Identify Constraints on the Domain

The diagram shows shipping charges as a function of the weight of several online orders. Based on the situation, what constraints, if any, are on the domain of the function?

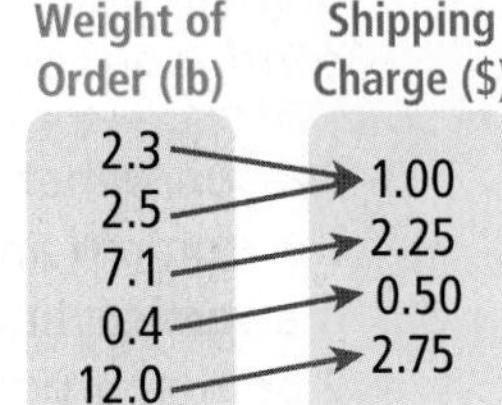

REASON
Think about the relationship between elements in the domain and the elements in the range.

An order must have a weight greater than zero, so the domain of the function is confined to values greater than 0.

Try It! **4.** Margaret has a monthly clothes budget of $50. She maps the amount of money she spends each month to the number of items of clothing she buys. What constraints are there on the domain?

CONCEPT SUMMARY Relations and Functions

WORDS A **relation** is any set of ordered pairs.

A relation is a **function** when each input, or element in the domain, has exactly one output, or element in the range.

TABLE

x	−5	−2	−1	2	4
y	0	4	−3	4	−1

Each element in the domain is associated with exactly one element in the range.

NUMBERS {(−5, 0), (−2, 4), (−1, −3), (2, 4), (4, −1)}

The domain is the set of x-values. The range is the set of y-values.

DIAGRAM

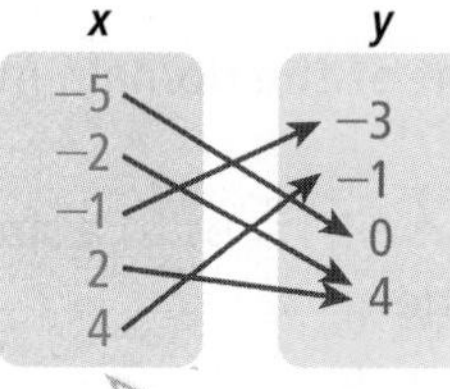

Each element in the domain is assigned one element in the range.

GRAPH

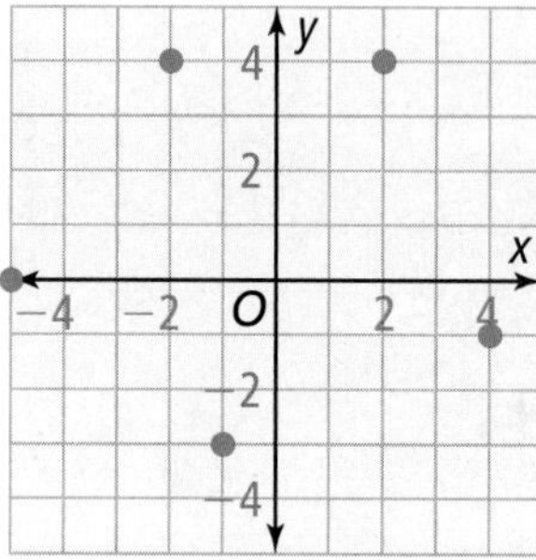

Do You UNDERSTAND?

1. ESSENTIAL QUESTION What is a function? Why is domain and range important when defining a function?

2. **Vocabulary** Maya is tracking the amount of rainfall during a storm. Describe the *domain* and *range* for this situation. Include *continuous* or *discrete* in your description.

3. **Reason** What can you conclude about the domain and the range of a function if a vertical line at $x = 5$ passes through 2 points? 1 point? No points? Explain.

4. **Error Analysis** Felipe states that every relation is a function, but not every function is a relation. Explain Felipe's error.

Do You KNOW HOW?

5. Use the graph to determine the domain and range of this relation. Is the relation a function?

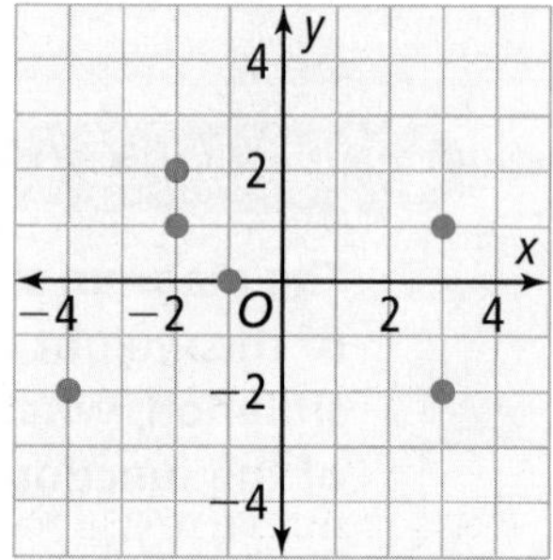

6. For the set of ordered pairs shown, identify the domain and range. Does the relation represent a function?

   {(1, 8), (5, 3), (7, 6), (2, 2), (8, 4), (3, 9), (5, 7)}

7. Each day Jacob records the number of laps and the distance he walks, in miles, on a track. Graph the relation and determine whether the distance that Jacob walks is a function of the number of laps.

   {(3, 0.75), (6, 1.5), (9, 2.25), (2, 0.5), (7, 1.75), (10, 2.5), (4, 1)}

PRACTICE & PROBLEM SOLVING

Scan for Multimedia

Additional Exercises Available Online

UNDERSTAND

8. **Use Structure** Identify the domain and range of each function.

a.

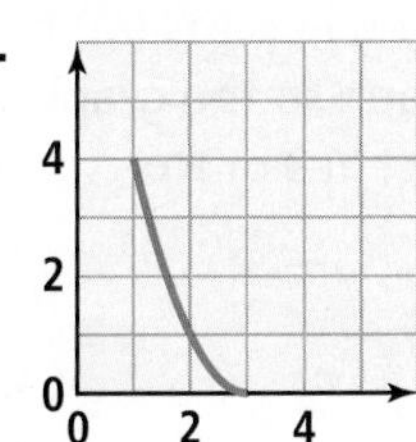

b.

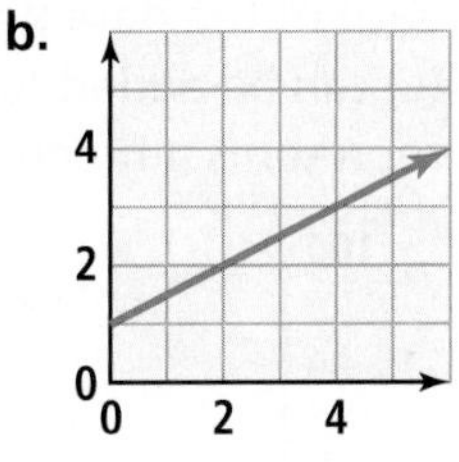

9. **Construct Arguments** If the domain of a relation is all whole numbers between 2.5 and 7.5, and the range contains 6 different values, can you determine whether the relation is a function? Explain your reasoning.

10. **Error Analysis** A student was asked to name all values of n that make the relation a function. Correct the error.

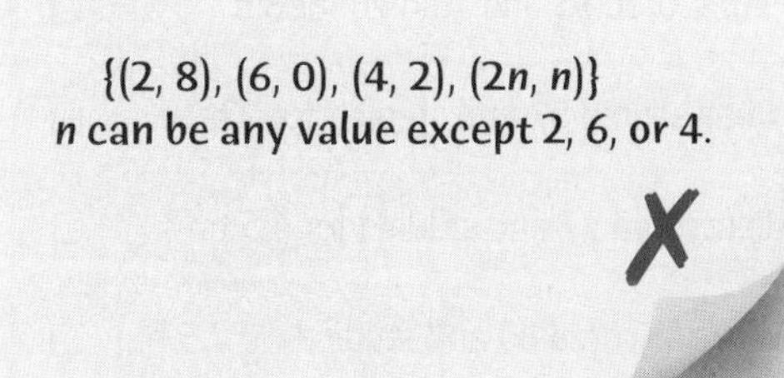

11. **Communicate Precisely** Describe two different representations that show a relation that is also a function. Explain.

12. **Higher Order Thinking** Relations mapping domain values to range values can be described as *one-to-one* or *not one-to-one*.

   a. If one x-value maps to many y-values (*one-to-many*), does the relation represent a function? If the x- and y-values are reversed, does the relation represent a function? Explain.

   b. If the relation is *not one-to-one*, does the relation represent a function? If the x- and y-values are reversed, does the relation represent a function? Explain.

   c. If the relation is *one-to-one*, does the relation represent a function? If the x- and y-values are reversed, does the relation represent a function? Explain.

PRACTICE

Identify the domain and range of each relation. Is the relation a function? Explain. SEE EXAMPLES 1 AND 3

13.

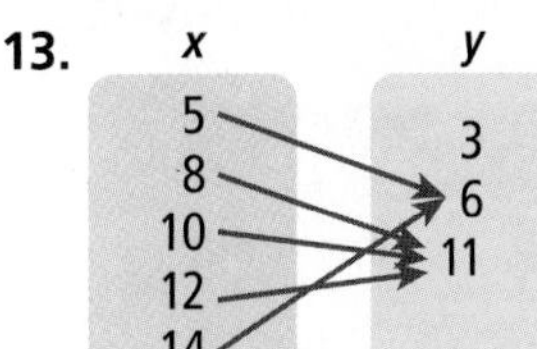

14.

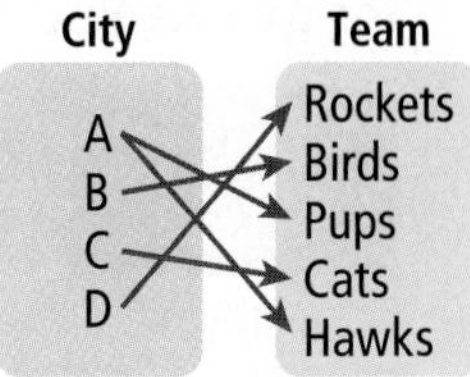

Analyze each situation. Identify a reasonable domain and range for each situation. SEE EXAMPLE 2

15. An airplane travels at 565 mph.

16. Tickets to a sporting event cost $125 each.

17. An average person consumes 2,000 Calories each day.

Determine whether each relation is a function. If yes, classify the function as one-to-one or not one-to-one. SEE EXAMPLE 3

18.

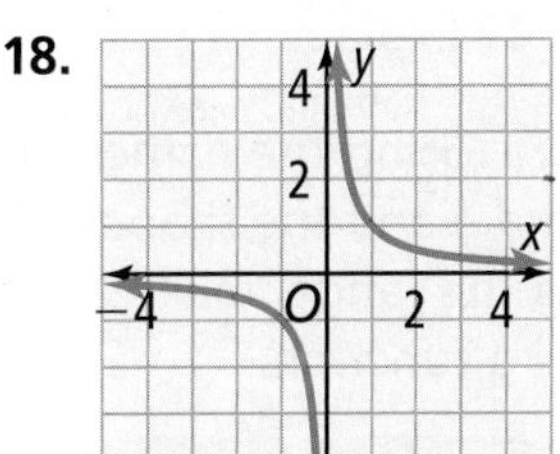

19.

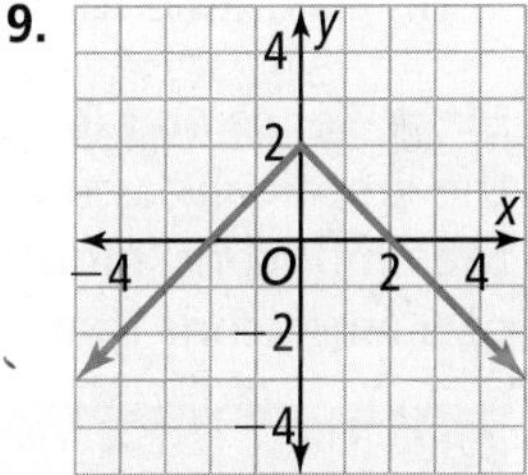

20.

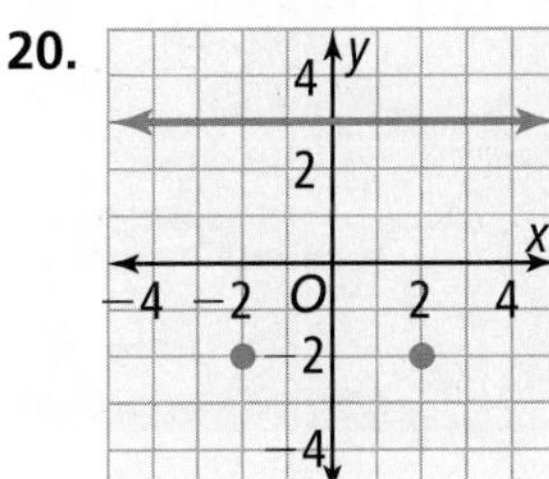

21.

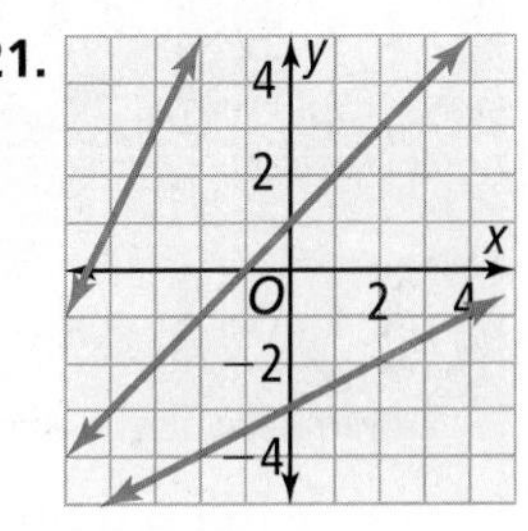

Identify any constraints on the domain. SEE EXAMPLE 4

22. Cameron earns an hourly wage at his job. He makes a table of the number of hours he works each week and the amount of money he earns.

23. Every day Isabel swims 10 to 20 laps in a 50-meter pool. She tracks the numbers of laps she swims and how long it takes her to complete the lap, in minutes.

PRACTICE & PROBLEM SOLVING

Practice | Tutorial

Mixed Review Available Online

APPLY

24. Model With Mathematics The table shows the number of minutes Drew spends in each class for two weeks.

Class	Week 1 Time (min)	Week 2 Time (min)
English	60	60
Math	90	60
History	45	45
Biology	45	45
Biology Lab	0	60

a. For Drew's week 1 classes, identify the domain and range. Is the relation a function? Explain.

b. For Drew's week 2 classes, identify the domain and range. Is the relation a function? Explain.

c. Is Drew's class time for week 2 a function of his class time for week 1? Explain.

25. Make Sense and Persevere Using the names of the emoticons as the domain and the shapes of the emoticons' mouths as the range, make a list of 5 emoticons that make a function.

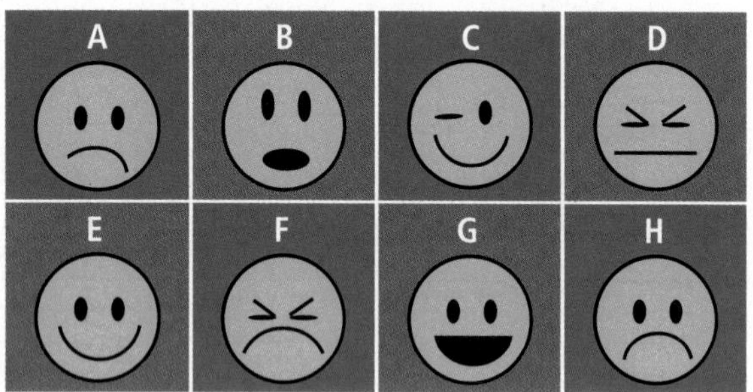

26. Reason After a train has traveled for $\frac{1}{2}$ hour, it increases its speed and travels at a constant rate for $1\frac{1}{2}$ hours.

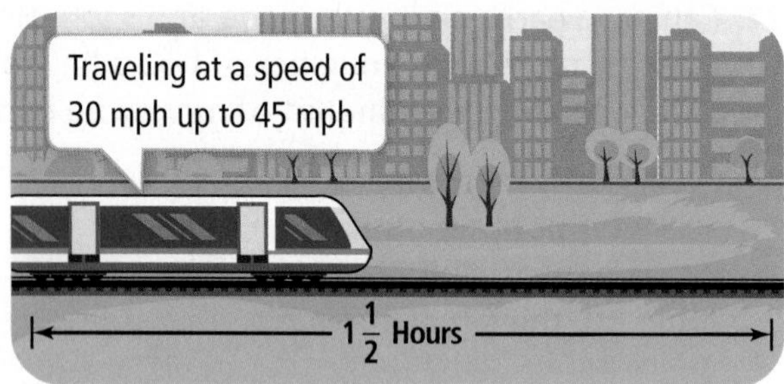

a. What is the domain? What is the range?

b. How can you represent the relationship between time traveled and speed?

c. Why did you choose this representation?

ASSESSMENT PRACTICE

27. The graph shows students' study times and their scores on a recent exam. Determine whether each of the data points given in parts (a) through (e) can be added to the graph so the graph still represents a function. Select **Yes** or **No**.

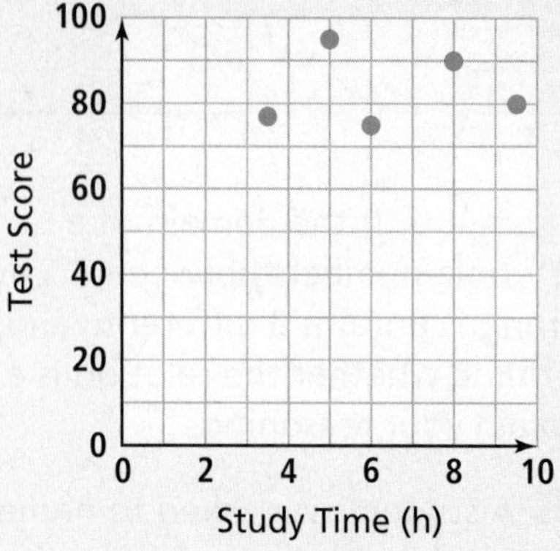

	Yes	No
a. Pilar scored 85 and studied for 8 h.	❑	❑
b. Naida scored 97 and studied for 9 h.	❑	❑
c. Alex scored 77 and studied for 4.5 h.	❑	❑
d. Damian scored 80 and studied for 7.5 h.	❑	❑
e. Dylan scored 90 and studied for 6 h.	❑	❑

28. SAT/ACT For a relation, where y is a function of x, and $y = 4$ when $x = 6$; which of the following does not represent another possible mapping in the relation?

Ⓐ $x = 3$ maps to $y = 2$

Ⓑ $x = 1$ maps to $y = 6$

Ⓒ $x = 0$ maps to $y = 0$

Ⓓ $x = 4$ maps to $y = 6$

Ⓔ $x = 6$ maps to $y = 2$

29. Performance Task City Tours rents bicycles for \$10 an hour with a maximum daily fee of \$100.

Part A Make a table that show the cost for renting a bicycle for 1, 3, 11, and 20 hours.

Part B Is cost a function of time? Explain.

Part C Is time a function of cost? Explain.

Activity Assess

3-2 Linear Functions

PearsonRealize.com

I CAN… identify, evaluate, graph, and write linear equations.

VOCABULARY

- function notation
- linear function

EXPLORE & REASON

The flowchart shows the steps of a math puzzle.

A. Try the puzzle with 6 different integers.

B. Record each number you try and the result.

C. Make a prediction about what the final number will be for any number. Explain.

D. **Use Structure** Would your prediction be true for all numbers? Explain.

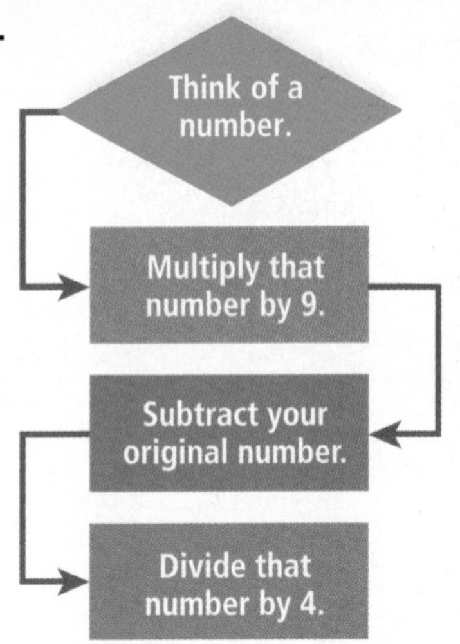

ESSENTIAL QUESTION How can you identify a linear function?

CONCEPTUAL UNDERSTANDING

EXAMPLE 1 Evaluate Functions in Function Notation

A. How can you represent a function rule?

Write the equation $y = 5x + 1$ using function notation.

Remember that a function is a rule that takes an input, or an element in the domain, and maps it to an output, or an element in the range.

Function notation is a method for writing variables as a function of other variables. The variable y, becomes a function of x, meaning the variable x is used to find the value of y. This helps distinguish between different functions. You can use the relationship between variables to solve problems and make predictions.

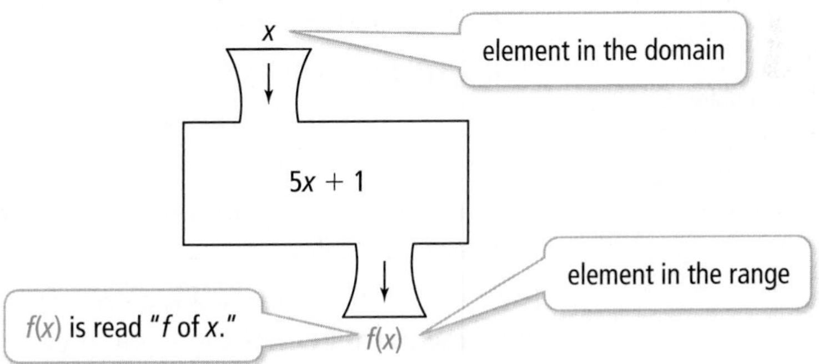

The function f is defined in function notation by $f(x) = 5x + 1$.

COMMUNICATE PRECISELY Function names are not restricted to f. What advantages are there to giving letter names to functions when modeling real-world situations?

COMMUNICATE PRECISELY $f(x)$ describes both the function that is being used, f, and the input value, x.

CONTINUED ON THE NEXT PAGE

EXAMPLE 1 CONTINUED

B. What is the value of $g(x) = 5x + 1$ when $x = 3$?

Evaluate $g(x) = 5x + 1$ for $x = 3$.

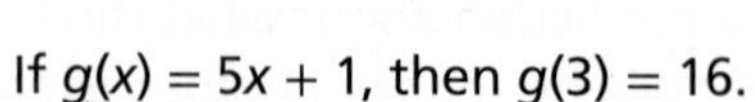

Substitute the input, 3, for every instance of x in the function.

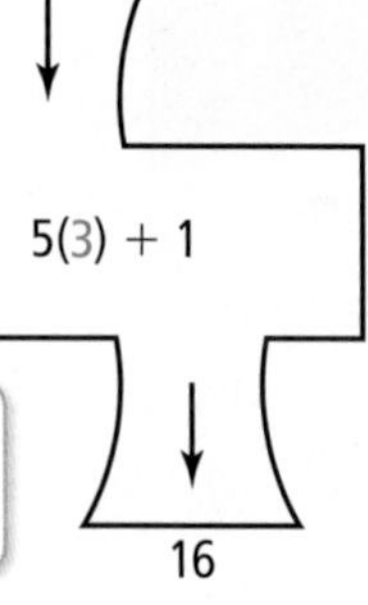

If $g(x) = 5x + 1$, then $g(3) = 16$.

Function notation can use letters other than f. Other commonly used letters are g and h.

Try It! **1. Evaluate each function for $x = 4$.**

a. $g(x) = -2x - 3$ **b.** $h(x) = 7x + 15$

EXAMPLE 2 Write a Linear Function Rule

The cost to make 4 bracelets is shown in the table.

How can you determine the cost to make any number of bracelets?

Step 1 Examine the relationship between the values in the table.

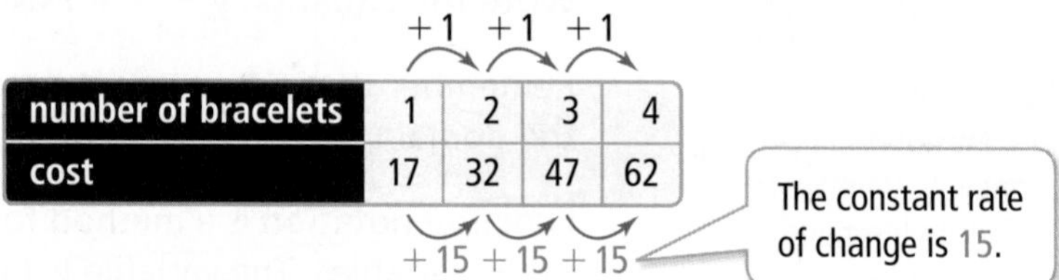

number of bracelets	1	2	3	4
cost	17	32	47	62

The constant rate of change is 15.

The relationship is linear.

Step 2 Write a function using slope-intercept form for the rule.

$f(x) = mx + b$

$f(x) = 15x + b$

Step 3 Find the value of b.

$17 = 15(1) + b$

$2 = b$

Substitute any ordered pair from the table.

You can use the function $f(x) = 15x + 2$ to determine the cost to make any number of bracelets.

The function $f(x) = 15x + 2$ is a linear function because the rule, $15x + 2$, is the same as the rule of the linear equation $y = 15x + 2$.

COMMON ERROR

You may think that the domain and range are all real numbers because the function $f(x) = 15x + 2$ has a domain and range of all real numbers. However, you need to consider the situation when determining the domain and range of a particular scenario.

Try It! **2.** Write a linear function for the data in each table using function notation.

a.

x	1	2	3	4
y	6.5	13	19.5	26

b.

x	1	2	3	4
y	1	4	7	10

APPLICATION

EXAMPLE 3 Analyze a Linear Function

A. Tamika records the outside temperature at 6:00 A.M. The outside temperature increases by 2°F every hour for the next 6 hours. If the temperature continues to increase at the same rate, what will the temperature be at 2:00 P.M.?

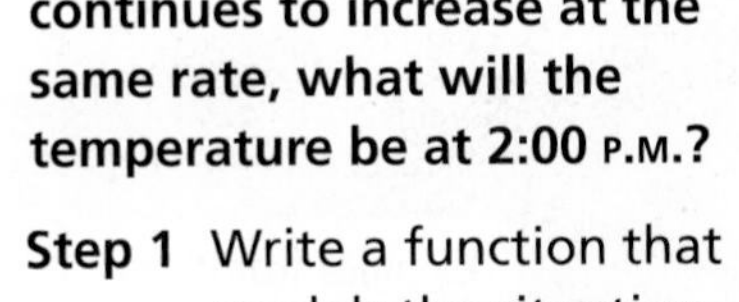

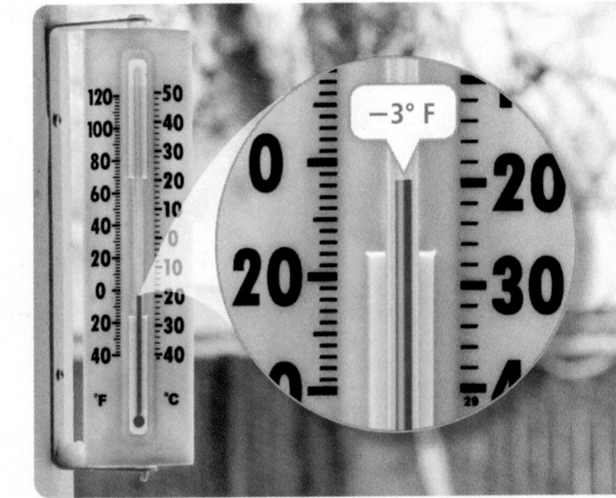

Step 1 Write a function that models the situation.

2°F increase each hour

$f(x) = 2x - 3$ — temperature at 6:00 A.M.

Step 2 Sketch a graph of the function.

The range of this function is the set of reasonable temperatures in °F greater than –3.

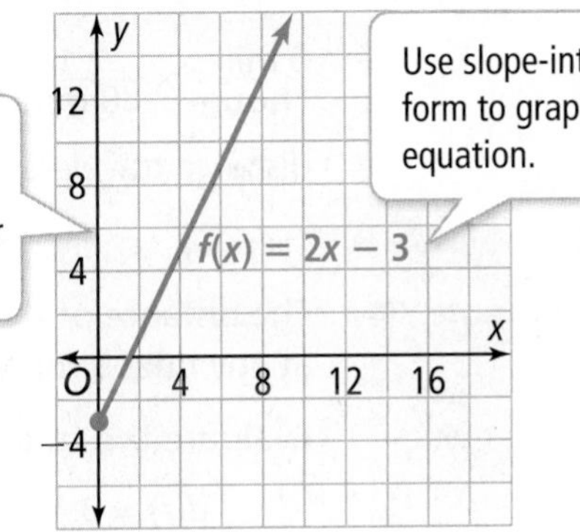

Use slope-intercept form to graph the equation.

Step 3: Find the value of y when $x = 8$.

$$y = 2(8) - 3$$
$$= 13$$

Assuming the temperature continues to increase at the same rate, the temperature at 2:00 p.m. will be 13°F.

The graph of $f(x) = 2x - 3$ is a line. A **linear function** is a function whose graph is a line.

MODEL WITH MATHEMATICS
What makes a function a good model over a given domain?

B. Does using a linear function realistically represent the temperature for the domain of $0 < x < 24$? Explain.

The graph of $f(x) = 2x - 3$ has a slope of 2, which represents the temperature rising 2°F each hour. However, when the sun sets it is unlikely that the temperature will continue to rise. The linear function is realistic for only a portion of the day.

Try It! 3. Sketch the graph of each function.

a. $f(x) = -x + 1$

b. $g(x) = 3x + 1$

EXAMPLE 4 Use Linear Functions to Solve Problems

A chairlift starts 0.5 mi above the base of a mountain and travels up the mountain at a constant speed. How far from the base of the mountain is the chairlift after 10 minutes?

Formulate Write a linear function to represent the distance the chairlift travels from the base of the mountain.

Let t = time in minutes.

$$\frac{6 \text{ miles}}{\text{hour}} \times \frac{1 \text{ hour}}{60 \text{ minutes}} = \frac{0.1 \text{ mile}}{\text{minute}}$$

The speed of the chairlift is in miles per hour, so convert the speed to miles per minute.

distance traveled = rate of the chairlift • time traveling + distance from the base

$$d(t) = 0.1 \cdot t + 0.5$$

Compute The distance of the chairlift from the base of the mountain at any time is represented by the linear function, $d(t) = 0.1t + 0.5$.

Evaluate the function for $t = 10$.

$$d(t) = 0.1(10) + 0.5$$
$$= 1 + 0.5$$
$$= 1.5$$

Interpret After 10 minutes, the chairlift will be 1.5 miles up the mountainside.

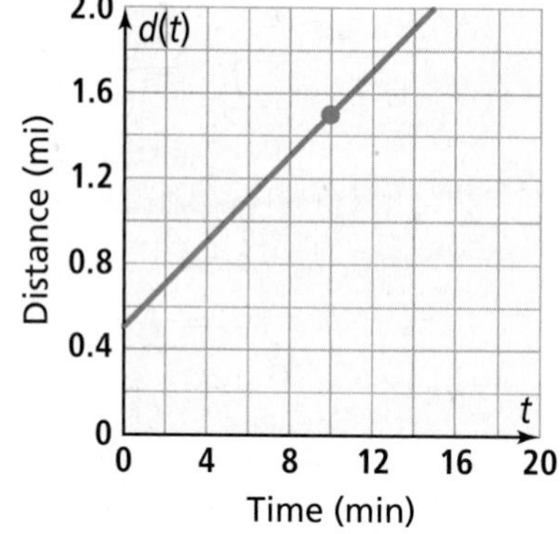

Try It! 4. In Example 4, how would the function, graph, and equation change if the speed is 4 mph? What is the effect on the domain?

CONCEPT SUMMARY Linear Function Representations

WORDS Linear functions are represented by words, rules, tables, or graphs. Function notation tells us the name of a function and the input variable.

ALGEBRA $f(x) = -2x + 1$

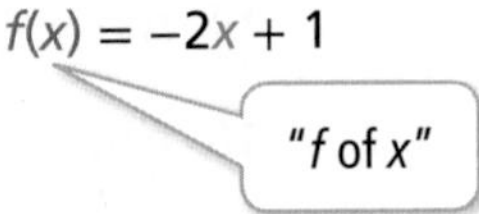

TABLE

x	−2	−1	0	1	2
$f(x)$	5	3	1	−1	−3

The table shows the domain and range of the function.

GRAPH The graph of the function $f(x) = -2x + 1$ is the graph of the linear equation $y = -2x + 1$.

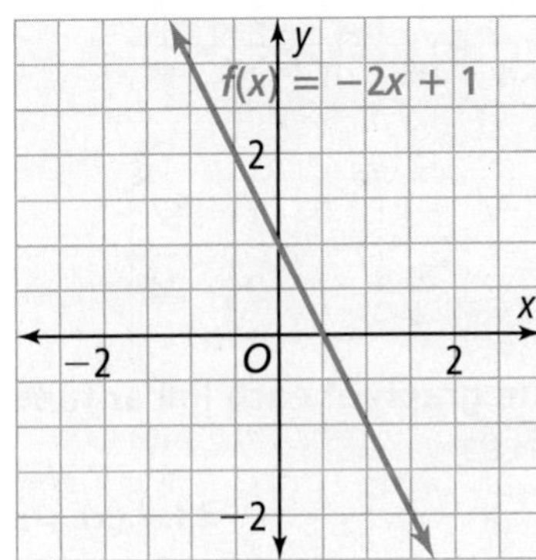

Do You UNDERSTAND?

1. **ESSENTIAL QUESTION** How can you identify a linear function?

2. **Communicate Precisely** Give a real-world example of a function that is linear and one that is not linear. Explain.

3. **Vocabulary** What is the difference between a *linear function* and a linear equation?

4. **Error Analysis** The cost of using a game facility is \$1 for every 12 minutes. Talisa writes the function for the cost per hour as $f(x) = 12x$. Explain Talisa's error.

Do You KNOW HOW?

Evaluate each function for $x = 2$ and $x = 6$.

5. $f(x) = 4x - 3$

6. $f(x) = -(x - 2)$

7. Sketch the graph of $f(x) = \frac{1}{2}x + 5$.

8. What function models the height of the periscope lens at time t? If the periscope reaches its maximum height after ascending for 22 seconds, what is the maximum height in feet?

PRACTICE & PROBLEM SOLVING

Scan for Multimedia

Practice | Tutorial

Additional Exercises Available Online

UNDERSTAND

9. **Use Structure** The two points on the graph are given by the function f.

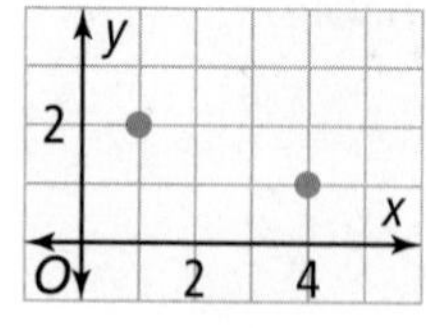

a. Use the two points to find the equation that represents the function f.

b. What is $f(6)$?

10. **Higher Order Thinking** Consider the functions $g(x) = 2x + 1$ and $h(x) = 2x + 2$ for the domain $0 < x < 5$.

a. Without evaluating or graphing the functions, how do the ranges compare?

b. Graph the two functions and describe each range over the given interval.

11. **Make Sense and Persevere** Customers at a deli can buy an unlimited amount of potato salad. The customer is not charged for the weight of the container.

a. The table shows the weight of the container with food and the cost. If 1 oz = 0.0625 lb, what is the price per pound of the potato salad? What is the weight of the container in pounds? What is the weight of the container and potato salad in pounds?

Weight (oz)	5	7	9	11	13
Cost ($)	■	1	2	3	4

b. If the store had not accounted for the weight of the container, how much would the customer be charged for the container? Is the cost of the container the same, or does it vary by how much potato salad is purchased? Explain.

12. **Error Analysis** Describe and correct the error a student made when finding the function rule for the data in the table.

x	1	2	3	4
y	10	19	28	37

When x increases by 1,
y increases by 9 each time.
When $x = 1$, $y = 10$.
So $y = 9x + 10$. ✗

PRACTICE

Find the value of $f(5)$ for each function.
EXAMPLE 1

13. $f(x) = 6 + 3x$

14. $f(x) = -2(x + 1)$

15. $f(a) = 3(a + 2) - 1$

16. $f(h) = -\frac{h}{10}$

17. $f(m) = 1 - 4\left(\frac{m}{2}\right)$

18. $f(m) = 2(m - 3)$

Write a linear function for the data in each table.
SEE EXAMPLE 2

19.

x	0	1	2	3	4
y	−1	4	9	14	19

20.

x	0	1	2	3	4
y	4	1.5	−1	−3.5	−6

21.

x	−2	−1	0	1	2
y	2	$\frac{1}{2}$	−1	$-2\frac{1}{2}$	−4

Sketch the graph of each linear function.
SEE EXAMPLE 3

22. $g(x) = x - 3$

23. $h(x) = 3 - x$

24. $f(x) = \frac{1}{2}(x - 1)$

25. $f(x) = 0.75(10 - x) + 1$

Use the graph for Exercises 26 and 27. SEE EXAMPLE 3

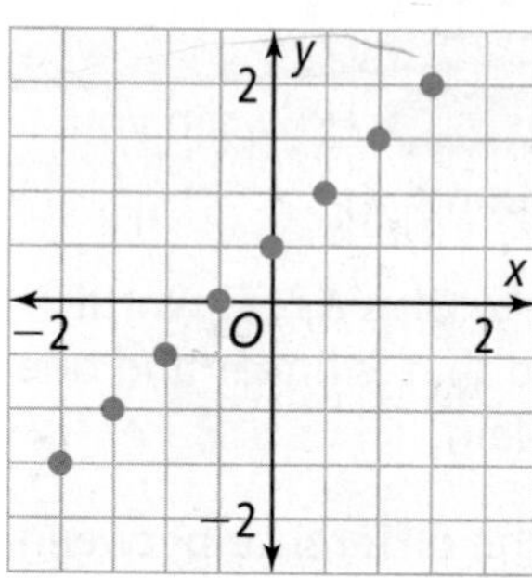

26. Is the function shown a linear function? Explain.

27. Describe the domain and range of the function.

28. Katrina buys a 64-ft roll of fencing to make a rectangular play area for her dogs. Use $2(l + w) = 64$ to write a function for the length, given the width. Graph the function. What is a reasonable domain for the situation? Explain. SEE EXAMPLE 4

PRACTICE & PROBLEM SOLVING

APPLY

29. Model With Mathematics A staff gauge measures the height of the water level in a river compared to the average water level. At one gauge the river is 1 ft below its average water level of 10 ft. It begins to rise by a constant rate of 1.5 ft per hour.

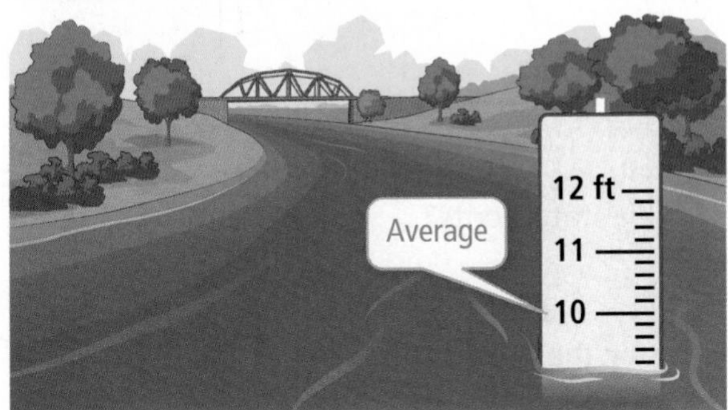

a. Graph the linear function to show the change in the water level over time.

b. Will the river reach a level of 7 ft above normal after 5 hours? Explain.

30. Use Structure Ramona's Garage charges the following labor rates. All customers are charged for at least 0.5 hr.

Ramona's Garage					
Hours	0.5	1	1.5	2	2.5
Labor	\$60	\$90	\$120	\$150	\$180

a. Write a linear function for the data in the table.

b. A repair job took 4 h and 15 min and required \$390 in parts. What is the total cost?

31. Reason A snack bar at an outdoor fair is open from 10 A.M. to 5:30 P.M. and has 465 bottles of water for sale. Sales average 1.3 bottles of water per minute.

a. Graph the number of bottles remaining each hour as a function of time in hours. Find the domain and range.

b. At this rate, what time would they run out of water? How many bottles of water are needed at the start of the next day? Explain.

ASSESSMENT PRACTICE

32. Consider the function $f(x) = 3(x - 1) - 0.4(9 - x)$. Match each expression with its equivalent value.

I. $f(2) + f(4)$	A. 3.4
II. $f(5)$	B. 3.6
III. $f(7) - f(6)$	C. 7.2
IV. $f(3)$	D. 10.4

33. SAT/ACT Determine a linear function from the data in the table. Which point is not part of the function?

x	$f(x)$
0	180
1	174
2	168
3	162
4	156

Ⓐ (12, 108)
Ⓑ (30, 0)
Ⓒ (−15, 270)
Ⓓ (21, 54)
Ⓔ (9, 120)

34. Performance Task Manuel calculates the business costs and profits to produce n hiking backpacks. Manuel's profit is his revenue minus expenses.

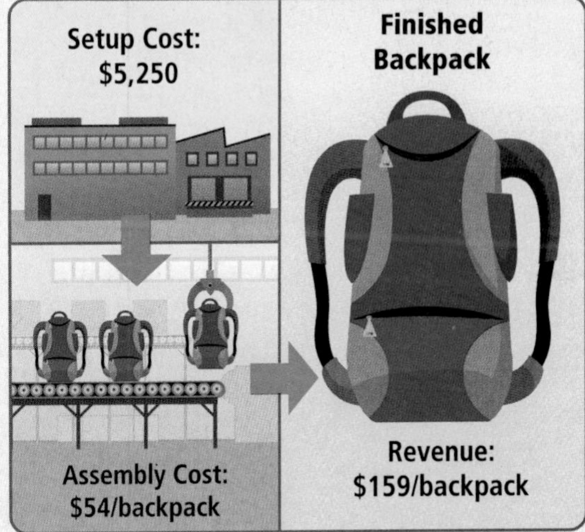

Part A Write a function to represent the profit Manuel makes selling n backpacks.

Part B Graph the profit function. What is a reasonable domain for this function for one year if his revenue is between \$4,000 and \$30,000? Is the function discrete or continuous? Explain.

Part C How much is his profit if he sells 43 backpacks? Explain.

3-3 Transforming Linear Functions

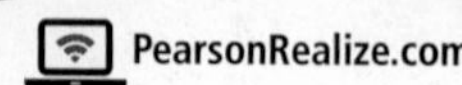

PearsonRealize.com

I CAN... transform linear functions.

VOCABULARY

- transformation
- translation

Activity Assess

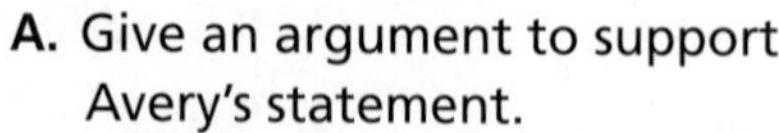

CRITIQUE & EXPLAIN

Avery states that the graph of *g* is the same as the graph of *f* with every point shifted vertically. Cindy states that the graph of *g* is the same as the graph of *f* with every point shifted horizontally.

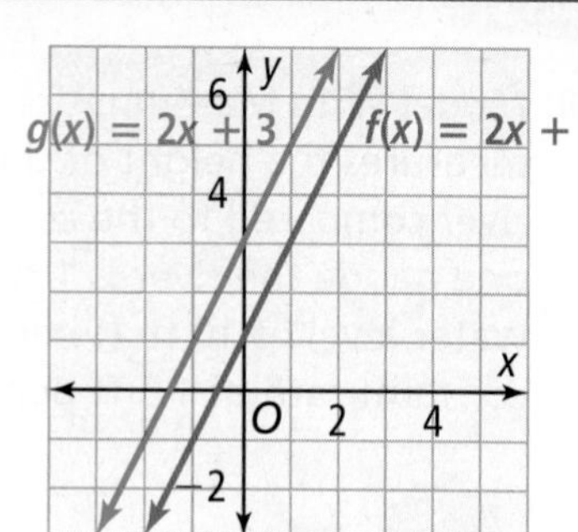

A. Give an argument to support Avery's statement.

B. Give an argument to support Cindy's statement.

C. **Look for Relationships** What do you know about linear equations that might support either of their statements?

ESSENTIAL QUESTION

How does modifying the input or the output of a linear function rule transform its graph?

APPLICATION

EXAMPLE 1 Vertical Translations of Linear Functions

The positions of 2 baby sea turtles making their way to the water after hatching from their eggs is recorded. They move at the same speed, with Byron starting 2 ft ahead of Frank's starting point.

A. What function represents each turtle's position as they make their way toward the shore?

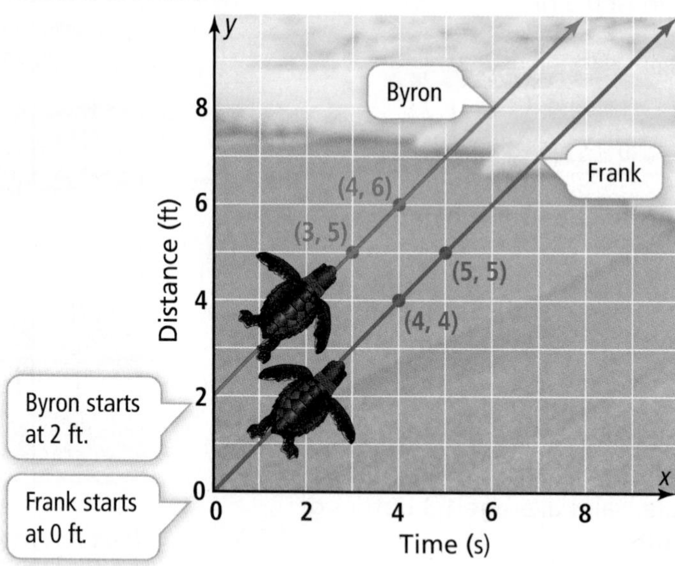

Find the speed of each turtle by finding the slope of each line.

Frank: $m = \frac{5-0}{5-0} = 1$ Byron: $m = \frac{6-2}{4-0} = 1$

Both turtles are moving at 1 ft/s.

The function $f(x) = x$ represents Frank's distance from his starting point, and $g(x) = x + 2$ represents Byron's distance from his starting point.

CONTINUED ON THE NEXT PAGE

EXAMPLE 1 CONTINUED

B. What happens to the graph of a function when you add a constant to its output?

Compare Byron's and Frank's graph.

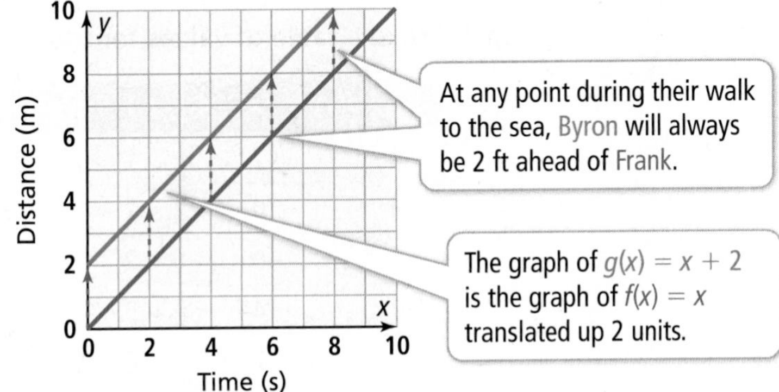

LOOK FOR RELATIONSHIPS
Look for relationships between the value of k and whether the vertical translation is up or down.

Adding a constant k to the output of a linear function *translates* the graph vertically by k units.

 **Try It!** **1.** Let $f(x) = -4x$.

a. How does the graph of $g(x) = -4x - 3$ compare with the graph of f?

b. How does the graph of $g(x) = -4x + 1.5$ compare with the graph of f?

DEFINITION

A **transformation** of a function f maps each point of its graph to a new location. One type of transformation is a *translation*. A **translation** shifts each point of the graph of a function the same distance. A translation may be horizontal or vertical.

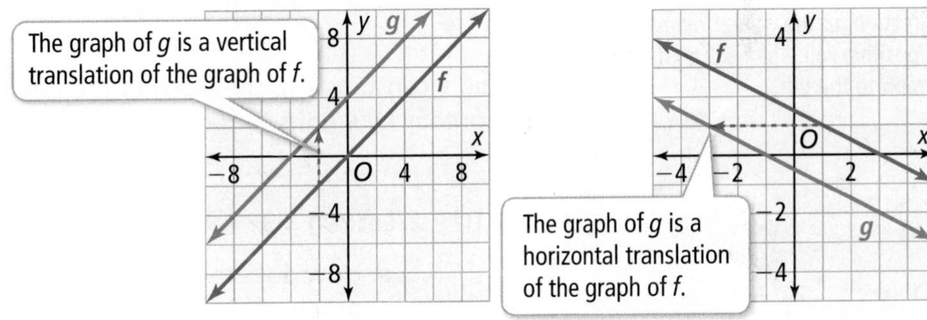

CONCEPTUAL UNDERSTANDING

EXAMPLE 2 Horizontal Translations of Linear Functions

How does adding a constant k to the input of a linear function affect its graph?

Consider the graphs of $f(x) = 2x - 4$ and $g(x) = 2(x + 5) - 4$.

Step 1 Make a table of values for $f(x) = 2x - 4$ and $g(x) = 2(x + 5) - 4$.

x	$f(x) = 2x - 4$	$x + 5$	$g(x) = 2(x + 5) - 4$
−4	−12	1	2(1) − 4 = −2
−3	−10	2	2(2) − 4 = 0
−2	−8	3	2(3) − 4 = 2
0	−4	5	2(5) − 4 = 6
1	−2	6	2(6) − 4 = 8
2	0	7	2(7) − 4 = 10
3	2	8	2(8) − 4 = 12

Step 2 Graph the functions $f(x) = 2x - 4$ and $g(x) = 2(x + 5) - 4$.

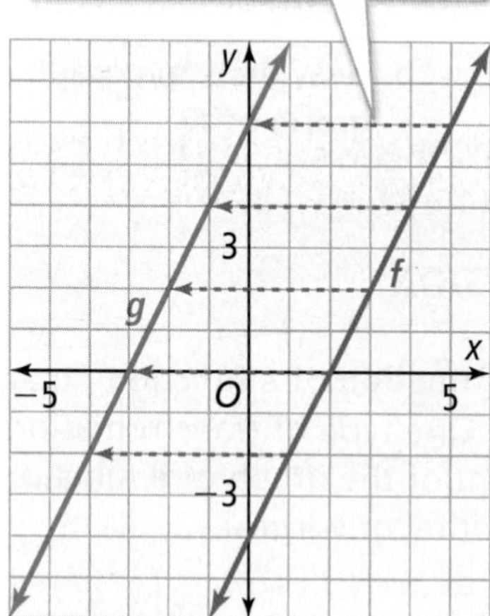

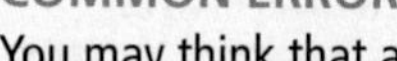

COMMON ERROR
You may think that a positive value of k in $g(x) = 2(x + k) - 4$ shifts the graph in a positive direction, to the right. However, a positive value of k shifts the graph to the left.

Adding a constant k to the input of the function translates the graph horizontally by k units.

Try It! **2.** Let $f(x) = 3x + 7$.

a. How does the graph of $g(x) = 3(x - 4) + 7$ compare with the graph of f?

b. How does the graph of $g(x) = 3(x + 9.5) + 7$ compare with the graph of f?

EXAMPLE 3 Stretches and Compressions of Linear Functions

A. How does multiplying the output of a linear function affect its graph?

Compare the graphs of $f(x) = x + 1$ and $g(x) = 4(x + 1)$.

x	$f(x) = x + 1$	$g(x) = 4(x + 1)$
−3	−2	−8
−2	−1	−4
−1	0	0
0	1	4
1	2	8

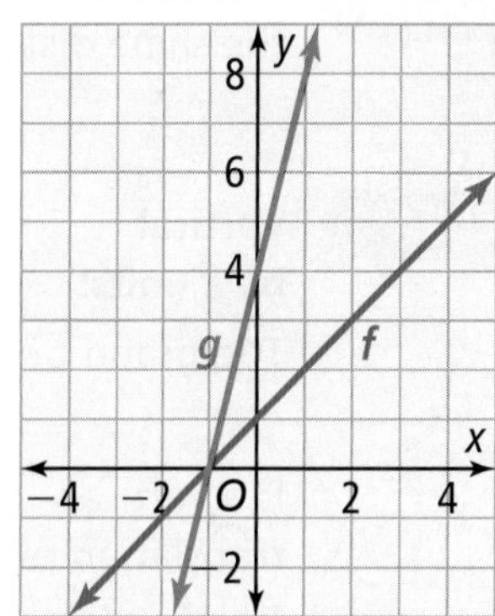

GENERALIZE
Is it always true that for a linear function *f*, the graphs of *f* and *kf* would have different *y*-intercepts?

The graph of *g* is vertical stretch of the graph of *f*, by a scale factor of 4. The slope and *y*-intercept are scaled by the same factor.

Multiplying the output of a linear function *f* by *k* scales its graph vertically. If $k > 1$, the transformed graph is a **vertical stretch**. If $0 < |k| < 1$ the transformed graph is a **vertical compression**.

B. How does multiplying the input of a linear function affect its graph?

Compare the graphs of $f(x) = x + 1$ and $g(x) = (3x) + 1$.

x	$f(x) = x + 1$	$g(x) = (3x) + 1$
0	1	1
1	2	4
2	3	7
3	4	10
6	7	19

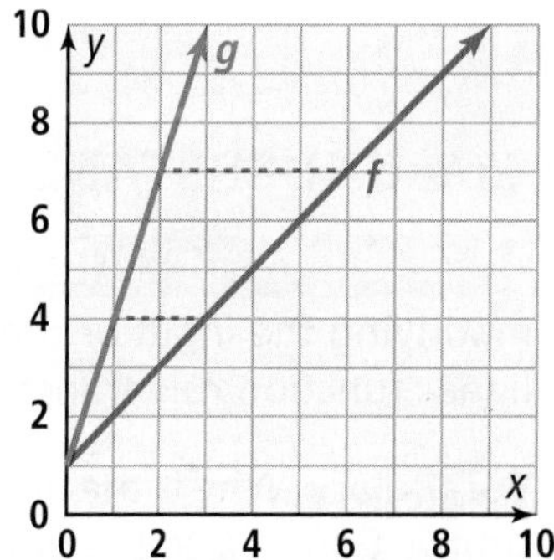

The graph of *g* is horizontal compression of the graph of *f*, by a scale factor of 3. The slope is changed by the same factor, but the *y*-intercept is unchanged.

Multiplying the input of a linear function *f* by *k* scales its graph horizontally. If $k > 1$, the transformed graph is a **horizontal compression**. If $0 < |k| < 1$ the transformed graph is a **horizontal stretch**.

Try It! 3. Let $f(x) = x - 2$.

a. How does the graph of $g(x) = 0.25(x - 2)$ compare with the graph of *f*?

b. How does the graph of $g(x) = 0.5x - 2$ compare with the graph of *f*?

CONCEPT SUMMARY Transformations of Linear Functions

	Translations		Stretches and Compressions	
WORDS	Translations shift each point of the graph the same distance horizontally or vertically.		Stretches and compressions scale the graph either horizontally or vertically.	
ALGEBRA	**Vertical by k units:** The graph of $g(x) = \left(\frac{1}{2}x - 2\right) + k$ is a vertical translation of $f(x) = \frac{1}{2}x - 2$.	**Horizontal by k units:** The graph of $g(x) = -2(x + k) + 2$ is a horizontal translation of $f(x) = -2x + 2$.	**Vertical by scale factor k:** The graph of $g(x) = k(-x + 2)$ is a stretch of $f(x) = -x + 2$ when $k > 1$.	**Horizontal by scale factor k:** The graph of $g(x) = k(-x) + 2$ is a compression of $f(x) = -x + 2$ when $k > 1$.
GRAPHS	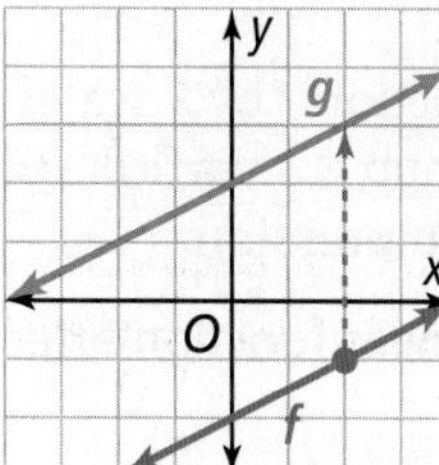	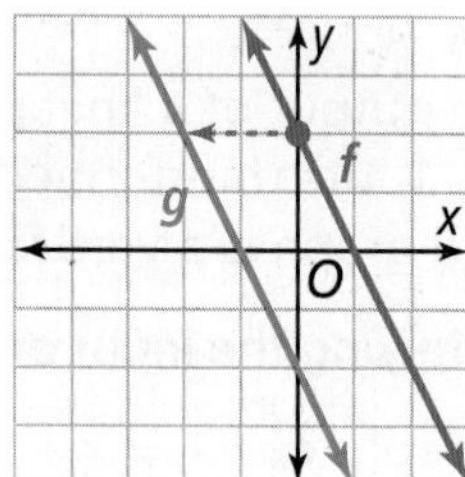	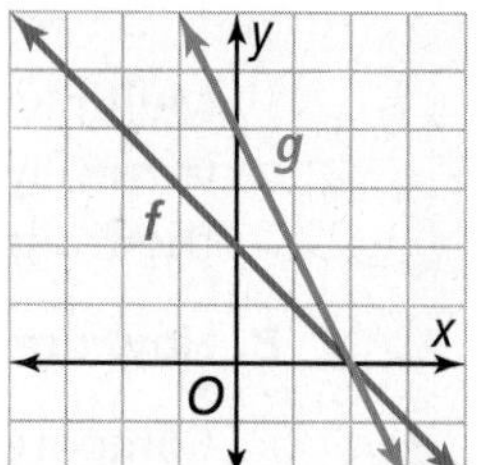	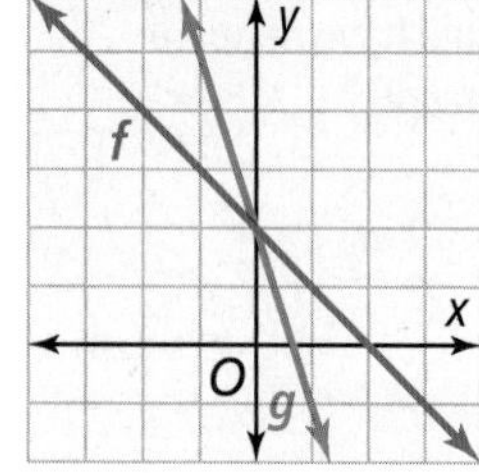

Do You UNDERSTAND?

1. ESSENTIAL QUESTION How does modifying the input or the output of a linear function rule transform its graph?

2. **Vocabulary** Why is the addition or subtraction of k to the output of a function considered a *translation*?

3. **Error Analysis** The addition or subtraction of a number to a linear function always moves the line up or down. Describe the error with this reasoning.

4. **Use Structure** Why does multiplying the input of a linear function change only the slope while multiplying the output changes both the slope and the y-intercept?

Do You KNOW HOW?

Given $f(x) = 4x + 1$, describe how the graph of g compares with the graph of f.

5. $g(x) = 4(x + 3) + 1$

6. $g(x) = (4x + 1) + 3$

Given $f(x) = x + 2$, describe how setting $k = 4$ affects the slope and y-intercept of the graph of g compared to the graph of f.

7. $g(x) = 4(x + 2)$

8. $g(x) = (4x) + 2$

9. The minimum wage for employees of a company is modeled by the function $f(x) = 7.25x$. The company decided to offer a signing bonus of \$75. How does adding this amount affect a graph of an employee's earnings?

Scan for Multimedia | Practice | Tutorial | Additional Exercises Available Online

UNDERSTAND

10. **Reason** Describe the transformation of the function $f(x) = \frac{1}{2}x - 2$ that makes the slope 2 and the y-intercept -8.

11. **Look for Relationships** Why do translations produce parallel lines?

12. **Error Analysis** A student graphs $f(x) = 3x - 2$. On the same grid they graph the function g which is a transformation of f made by subtracting 4 from the input of f. Describe and correct the error they made when graphing g.

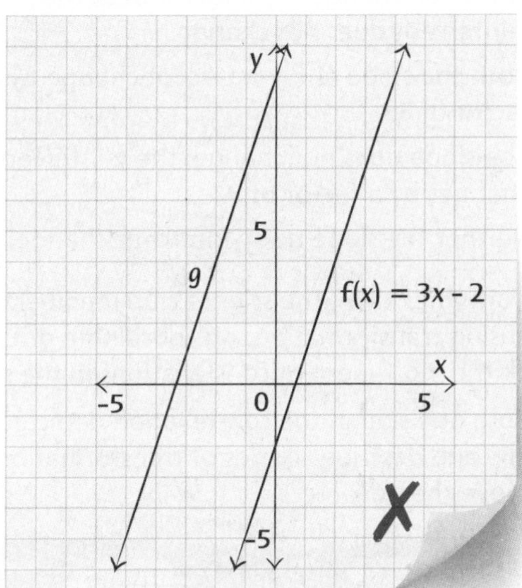

13. **Look for Relationships** Let $f(x) = \frac{1}{2}x - 3$. Suppose you subtract 6 from the input of f to create a new function g, then multiply the input of function g by 4 to create a function h. What equation represents h?

14. **Use Structure** Describe each transformation. Then write the equation of the transformed function.

$f(x) = 2x + 1$ $\qquad$ $g(x) = \frac{1}{3}x + 2$

	Transformation	Description	Function
a.	$f(x) - 5$		
b.	$g(x) + 4$		
c.	$3g(x)$		
d.	$\frac{1}{2}f(x)$		

PRACTICE

Given $f(x) = 3x + 5$, describe how the graph of g compares with the graph of f.
SEE EXAMPLES 1, 2, AND 3

15. $g(x) = (3x + 5) + 8$
16. $g(x) = (3x + 5) - 4$
17. $g(x) = 3(x + 10) + 5$
18. $g(x) = 3(x - 1) + 5$
19. $g(x) = 3(0.1x) + 5$
20. $g(x) = 5(3x + 5)$
21. $g(x) = 3(2x) + 5$
22. $g(x) = 8(3x + 5)$

Given $f(x) = 2x + 3$, describe how the value of k affects the slope and y-intercept of the graph of g compared to the graph of f. SEE EXAMPLE 3

23. $g(x) = 3(2x + 3)$
24. $g(x) = 2(0.5x) + 3$
25. $g(x) = \frac{1}{6}(2x + 3)$
26. $g(x) = 2\left(\frac{1}{8}\right)x + 3$
27. $g(x) = (2x + 3) - 3$
28. $g(x) = 2(x + 0.5) + 3$

Find the value of k for each function g. Then describe the graph of g as a transformation of the graph of f.

29.

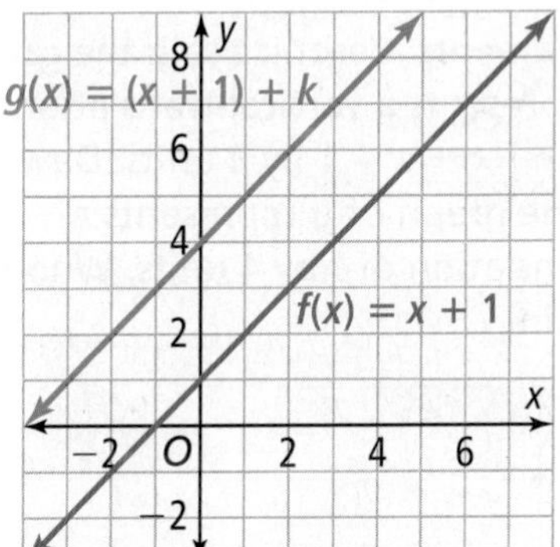

30.

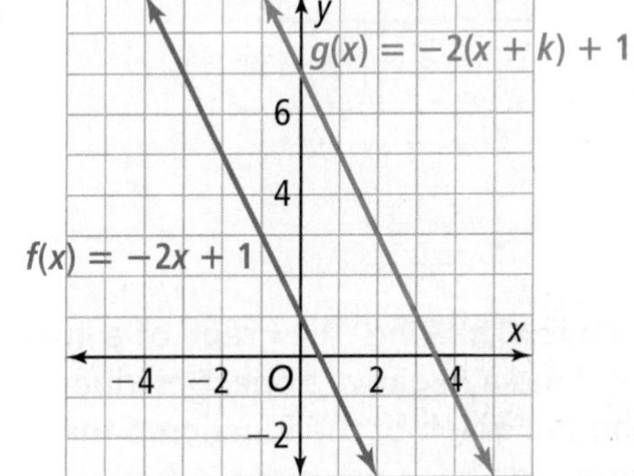

PRACTICE & PROBLEM SOLVING

Practice | Tutorial

Mixed Review Available Online

APPLY

31. Mathematical Connections The cost of renting a landscaping tractor is a \$100 security deposit plus the hourly rate.

a. The function f represents the cost of renting the tractor. The function g represents the cost if the hourly rate were doubled. Write each function.

b. How would the slope and y-intercept of the graph g compare to the slope and y-intercept of the graph of f?

32. Construct Arguments Veronica said the graph of g below represents a vertical translation of the function $f(x) = x + 1$ by 4 units. Dawn argued that the graph of g represents a horizontal translation of f by 4 units. Who is correct? Explain.

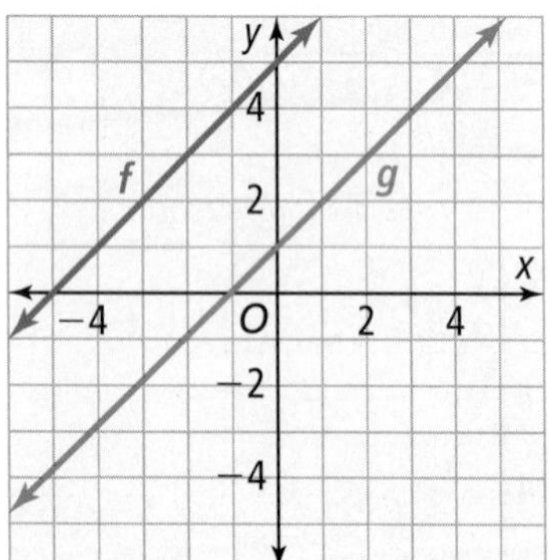

33. Higher Order Thinking The graph of a linear function f has a negative slope. Describe the effect on the graph of the function if the transformation has a value of $k < 0$.

a. adding k to the outputs of f

b. adding k to the inputs of f

c. multiplying the outputs of f by k

d. multiplying the inputs of f by k

ASSESSMENT PRACTICE

34. How is the graph of the function $g(x) = \frac{2}{5}x + 6$ transformed from the graph of the function $f(x) = \frac{2}{5}x$?

Ⓐ Moved up 6 units

Ⓑ Moved down 6 units

Ⓒ Moved left 6 units

Ⓓ Moved right 6 units

35. SAT/ACT Which of the following describes the differences between the graph of f and the graph of the output of f multiplied by 3?

Ⓐ The slope changes by a factor of 3; the y-intercept does not change.

Ⓑ Both the slope and y-intercept change by a factor of 3.

Ⓒ The slope does not change; the y-intercept changes by a factor of 3.

Ⓓ Neither the slope nor y-intercept change.

36. Performance Task The science club members are using transformations on coordinate grids to track the movement of constellations in the sky.

Choose one side of the constellation depicted below and describe a series of transformations to move the side.

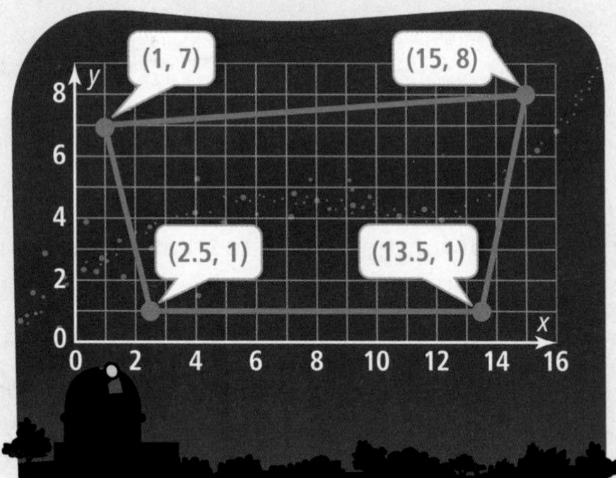

Copy and complete the table to record the motion.

Transformation	Function

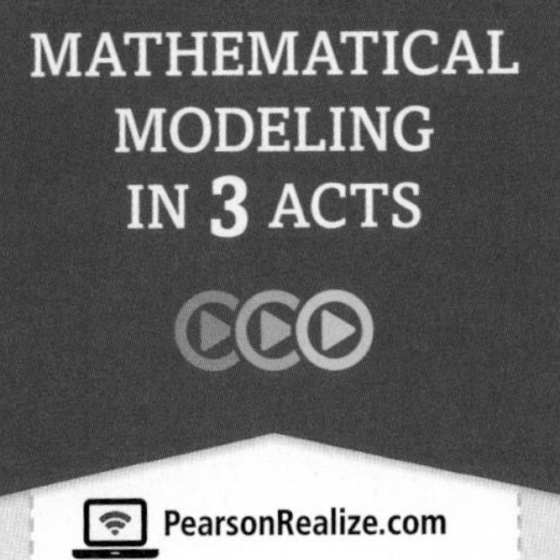

PearsonRealize.com

The Express Lane

Some supermarkets have self checkout lanes. Customers scan their items themselves and then pay with either cash or credit when they have finished scanning all of the items. Some customers think these lanes are faster than the checkout lanes with cashiers, but others don't like having to bag all of their purchases themselves.

What's your strategy for picking a checkout lane at the grocery store? Think about this during the Mathematical Modeling in 3 Acts lesson.

ACT 1 Identify the Problem

1. What is the first question that comes to mind after watching the video?
2. Write down the main question you will answer about what you saw in the video.
3. Make an initial conjecture that answers this main question.
4. Explain how you arrived at your conjecture.
5. What information will be useful to know to answer the main question? How can you get it? How will you use that information?

ACT 2 Develop a Model

6. Use the math that you have learned in this Topic to refine your conjecture.

ACT 3 Interpret the Results

7. Did your refined conjecture match the actual answer exactly? If not, what might explain the difference?

3-4 Arithmetic Sequences

PearsonRealize.com

I CAN... identify and describe arithmetic sequences.

VOCABULARY

- arithmetic sequence
- common difference
- explicit formula
- recursive formula
- sequence
- term of a sequence

EXPLORE & REASON

A fashion designer is designing a patterned fabric.

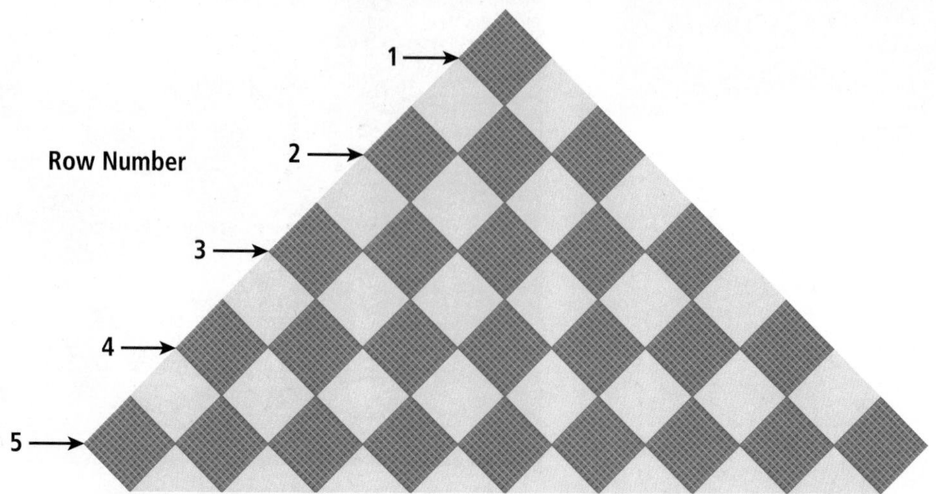

A. Copy and complete the table.

Row number	1	2	3	4	5
Number of Patterned Squares in the Row	1	■	5	■	■
Total Number of Patterned Squares	1	■	9	■	■

B. Use Structure What number patterns do you see in the rows of the table?

ESSENTIAL QUESTION How are arithmetic sequences related to linear functions?

CONCEPTUAL UNDERSTANDING

EXAMPLE 1 Connect Sequences and Functions

A. Is the ordered list 26, 39, 52, 65, 78 an arithmetic sequence?

A **sequence** is an ordered list of numbers that often forms a pattern. Each number is a **term of the sequence**. In an **arithmetic sequence**, the difference between any two consecutive terms is a constant called the **common difference**.

Find the differences between pairs of consecutive terms.

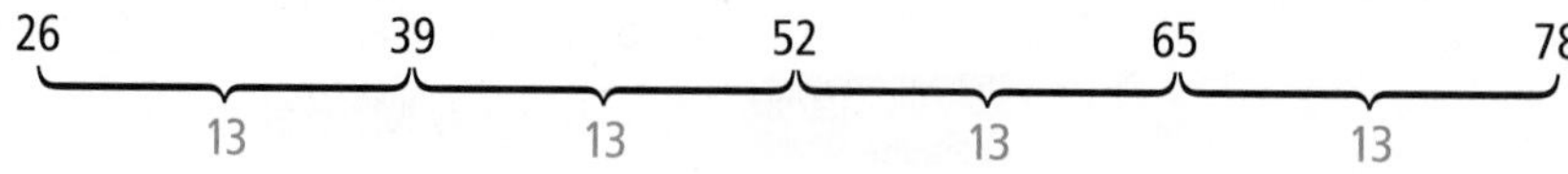

There is a common difference of 13, so this is an arithmetic sequence.

CONTINUED ON THE NEXT PAGE

STUDY TIP
A common difference must be the same, or common, between each pair of consecutive terms for the sequence to be an arithmetic sequence. A common difference can be any real number.

Activity Assess

EXAMPLE 1 CONTINUED

B. How are sequences related to functions?

You can think of a sequence as a function where the domain is restricted to the natural numbers and the range is the terms of the sequence.

REASON
Why are the values of n restricted?

For the sequence 26, 39, 52, 65, 78,

Let n = the term number in the sequence.

Let $A(n)$ = the value of the nth term of the sequence.

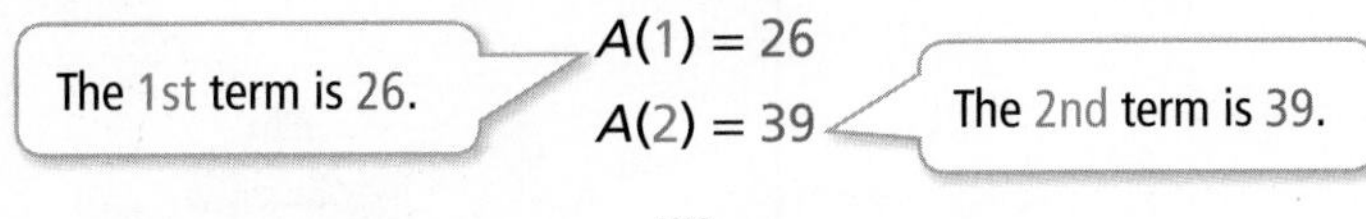

C. How do you represent sequences using subscript notation?

Subscript notation is commonly used to describe sequences.

$a_2 = 39$ The 2nd term is 39.

You can use either function or subscript notation to represent sequences.

Try It! 1. Is the domain of the function in Part B of Example 1 continuous or discrete? Explain.

DEFINITION

Recursive, in mathematics, means to repeat a process over and over again, using the output of each step as the next input. A recursive formula relates each term of a sequence to the previous term. It is composed of an initial value and a rule for generating the sequence.

The **recursive formula** for an arithmetic sequence is:

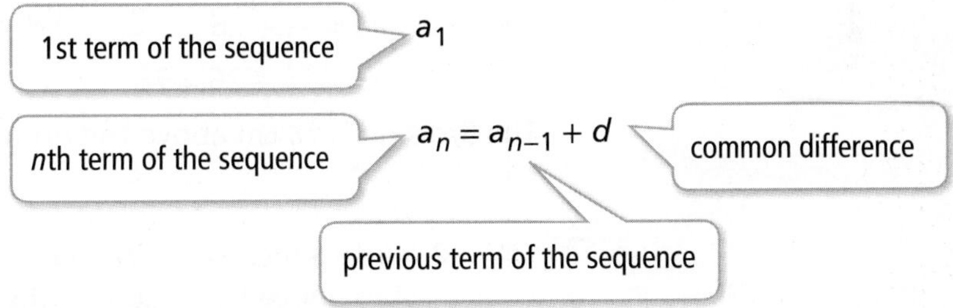

A recursive formula describes the pattern of a sequence and can be used to find the next term in a sequence.

Activity Assess

EXAMPLE 2 Apply the Recursive Formula

A. What is a recursive formula for the height above the ground of the *n*th step of the pyramid shown?

> **COMMON ERROR**
> Be careful not to assume that the first term and the common difference are the same in all arithmetic sequences. It is true for this sequence but not for all sequences.

Use the recursive formula.

$a_1 = 26$

$a_n = a_{n-1} + 26$ — Since each step is the same height, d is 26.

The formula $a_n = a_{n-1} + 26$ gives the height above the ground of the nth step with $a_1 = 26$.

B. Use the recursive formula to find the height above the ground of the 3rd step.

Find the height above the ground of the 2nd step.

$a_1 = 26$

$a_2 = a_1 + 26$ — Use a_1 to find a_2.

$a_2 = 26 + 26 = 52$

Find the height above the ground of the 3rd step.

$a_2 = 52$

$a_3 = a_2 + 26$ — Use a_2 to find a_3.

$a_3 = 52 + 26 = 78$

The 3rd step is 78 cm above the ground.

Try It! 2. Write a recursive formula to represent the total height of the nth stair above the ground if the height of each stair is 18 cm.

DEFINITION

An **explicit formula** expresses the nth term of a sequence in terms of n.

The explicit formula for an arithmetic sequence is:

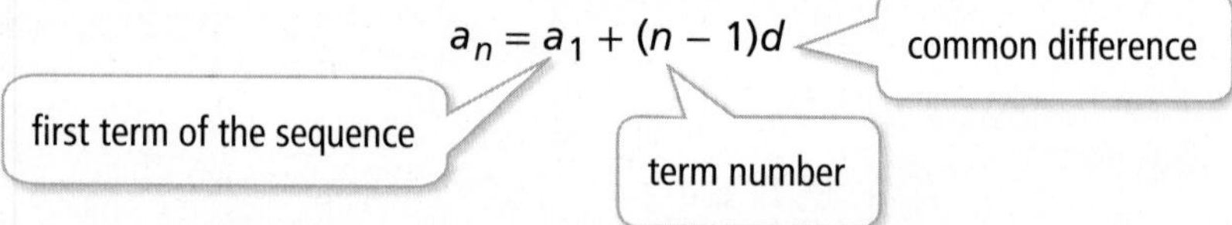

$$a_n = a_1 + (n - 1)d$$

APPLICATION

EXAMPLE 3 Apply the Explicit Formula

A. The cost of renting a bicycle is given in the table. How can you represent the rental cost using an explicit formula?

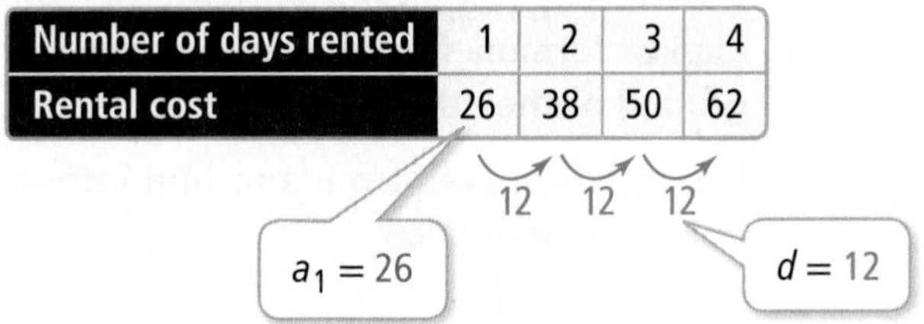

Number of days rented	1	2	3	4
Rental cost	26	38	50	62

To find the rental cost for n days, write an explicit formula for the nth term of the sequence.

Use the explicit formula.

$$a_n = 26 + (n - 1)12 \quad \text{Substitute 26 for } a_1 \text{ and 12 for } d.$$
$$= 26 + 12n - 12 \quad \text{Distributive Property}$$
$$= 14 + 12n \quad \text{Simplify.}$$

The explicit formula $a_n = 14 + 12n$ gives the rental cost for n days.

B. What is the cost of renting the bicycle for 10 days?

Use the explicit formula to find the 10th term in the sequence.

$$a_n = 14 + 12n$$
$$a_{10} = 14 + 12(10)$$
$$= 134$$

Substitute 10 for n.

The 10th term in sequence is 134. It costs $134 to rent the bicycle for 10 days.

C. How is the explicit formula of an arithmetic sequence related to a linear function?

The formula $a_n = 14 + 12n$ shows that the cost, a_n, is a function of the number of days, n, the bicycle is rented.

You can write this as a linear function, $f(x) = 12x + 14$, or as an equation in slope-intercept form, $y = 12x + 14$. The common difference, 12, corresponds to the slope of the graph.

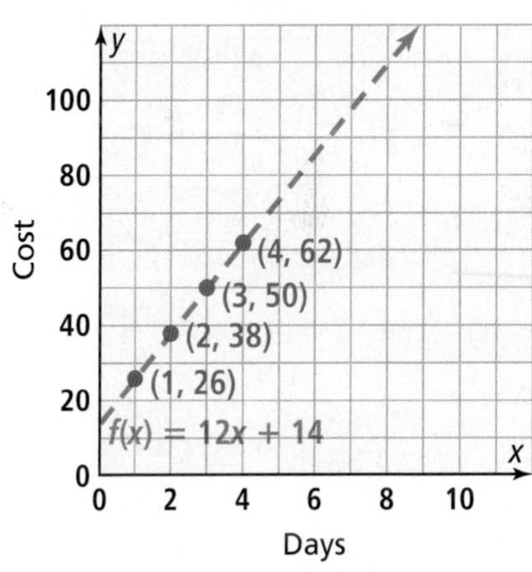

COMMON ERROR
You might think that the initial value of the sequence and the y-intercept of the graph of the equivalent linear function are the same, but they will not be the same if the initial value of the sequence is not zero.

Try It! 3. The cost to rent a bike is $28 for the first day plus $2 for each day after that. Write an explicit formula for the rental cost for n days. What is the cost of renting the bike for 8 days?

  Activity  Assess

EXAMPLE 4 Write an Explicit Formula From a Recursive Formula

The recursive formula for the height above the ground of the *n*th step of the stairs shown is $a_n = a_{n-1} + 4$ with $a_1 = 7$. What explicit formula finds the height above the ground of the *n*th step?

Use the recursive formula to find information about the sequence.

$a_1 = 7$

$a_n = a_{n-1} + 4$ — common difference

Write the explicit formula.

$a_n = a_1 + (n - 1)d$

$a_n = 7 + (n - 1)4$ .... Substitute 7 for a_1 and 4 for d.

The explicit formula $a_n = 7 + (n - 1)4$ can be used to find the height above the ground of the *n*th step.

Try It! **4.** Write an explicit formula for each arithmetic sequence.

a. $a_n = a_{n-1} - 3; a_1 = 10$ **b.** $a_n = a_{n-1} + 2.4; a_1 = -1$

EXAMPLE 5 Write a Recursive Formula From an Explicit Formula

The explicit formula for an arithmetic sequence is $a_n = 1 + \frac{1}{2}n$. What is the recursive formula for the sequence?

Step 1 Identify the common difference.

$a_n = 1 + \frac{1}{2}n$

$d = \frac{1}{2}$

Step 2 Find the first term of the sequence.

$a_n = 1 + \frac{1}{2}n$

$a_1 = 1 + \frac{1}{2}(1)$ .... Substitute 1 for n.

$a_1 = \frac{3}{2}$ .... Simplify.

Step 3 Write the recursive formula.

$a_n = a_{n-1} + d$

$a_n = a_{n-1} + \frac{1}{2}$ .... Substitute $\frac{1}{2}$ for d.

The recursive formula for the sequence is:

first term: $a_1 = \frac{3}{2}$; *n*th term: $a_n = a_{n-1} + \frac{1}{2}$

STUDY TIP
When writing a recursive formula for an arithmetic sequence, include the value of the first term, a_1.

Try It! **5.** Write a recursive formula for each explicit formula.

a. $a_n = 8 + 3n$ **b.** $a_n = 12 - 5n$

Concept Summary Assess

CONCEPT SUMMARY Arithmetic Sequences

WORDS An arithmetic sequence is a sequence of numbers that follows a pattern. The difference between two consecutive terms is a constant called the common difference.

FORMULAS

Recursive Formula

Used to describe a sequence and find the next few terms

$a_n = a_{n-1} + d$

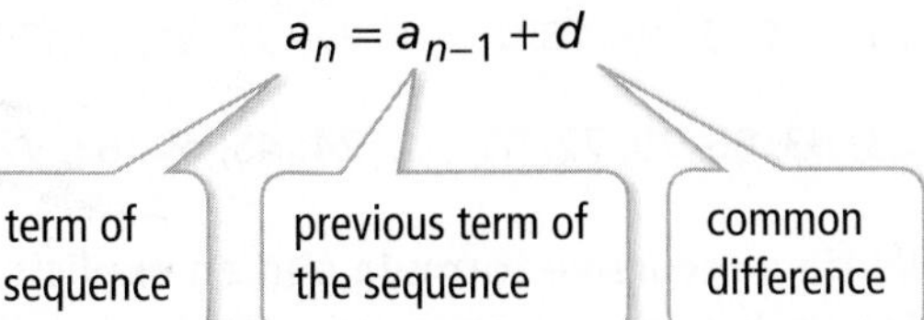

Explicit Formula

Used to find a specific term in the sequence

$a_n = a_1 + (n - 1)d$

nth term of the sequence

first term of the sequence

common difference

The first term of the sequence is a_1.

NUMBERS **1, 7, 13, 19, 25, . . .**

Use the recursive formula to describe the sequence and find the next two terms.

$a_n = a_{n-1} + 6$

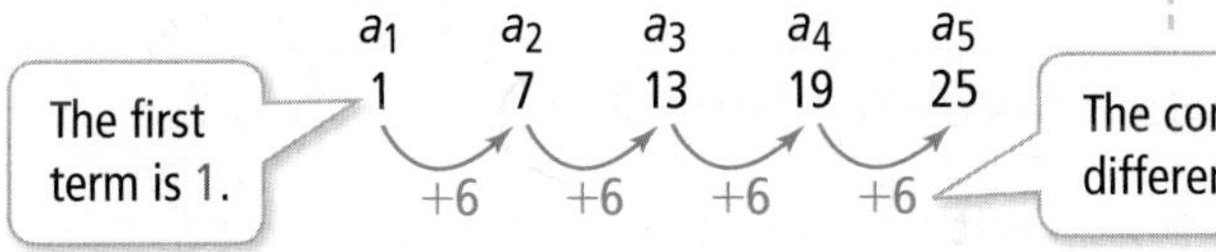

$a_6 = a_5 + 6$
$= 25 + 6$
$= 31$

$a_7 = a_6 + 6$
$= 31 + 6$
$= 37$

The next two terms are 31 and 37.

Use the explicit formula to find the 15th term in the sequence.

$a_n = 1 + (n - 1)6$

$a_{15} = 1 + (14)6$

$a_{15} = 85$

Do You UNDERSTAND?

1. **ESSENTIAL QUESTION** How are arithmetic sequences related to linear functions?

2. **Error Analysis** A student uses the explicit formula $a_n = 5 + 3(n - 1)$ for the sequence 3, 8, 13, 18, 23, ... to find the 12th term. Explain the error the student made.

3. **Vocabulary** When is a *recursive formula* more useful than an *explicit formula* for an arithmetic sequence?

4. **Communicate Precisely** Compare and contrast a recursive formula and an explicit formula for an arithmetic sequence.

Do You KNOW HOW?

Tell whether or not each sequence is an arithmetic sequence.

5. 15, 13, 11, 9, . . .

6. 4, 7, 10, 14, . . .

Write a recursive formula for each sequence.

7. 81, 85, 89, 93, 97, . . .

8. 47, 39, 31, 23, 15, . . .

9. An online store charges $5 to ship one box and $10 to ship two boxes. Write an explicit formula for an arithmetic sequence to represent the amount the online store charges to ship *n* boxes. Use the explicit formula to determine how much the online store charges when shipping 11 boxes.

UNDERSTAND

10. Make Sense and Persevere What can you tell about the terms of an arithmetic sequence when the common difference is negative?

11. Mathematical Connections How does the domain of an arithmetic sequence compare to the domain of a linear function? Explain.

12. Error Analysis Describe and correct the error a student made in identifying the common difference of the following sequence: 29, 22, 15, 8, 1, ...

> The common difference of the sequence is 7, since 29 - 22 = 7, 22 - 15 = 7, 15 - 8 = 7, and 8 - 1 = 7. ✗

13. Reason Given the common difference and the first term of an arithmetic sequence, which formula – the recursive or explicit formula – would be more useful to determine a_{500}? Explain. Would your answer change if you knew the value of term a_{499}? Explain.

14. Reason The graph of an arithmetic sequence is shown. Write a recursive formula for the arithmetic sequence if the y-value of each point is increased by 3.

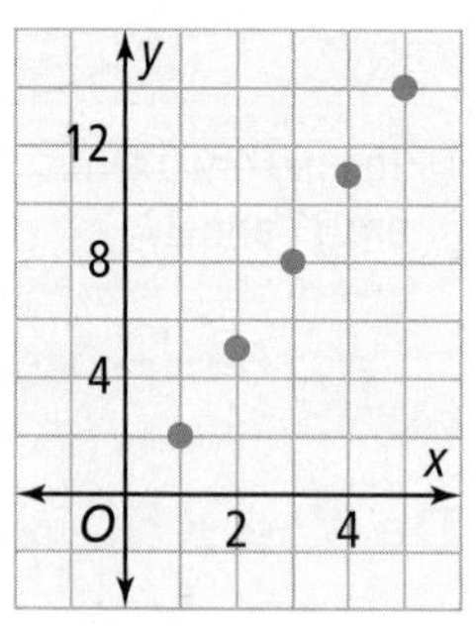

15. Use Structure Does an explicit formula for a sequence make sense assuming $n = 2.5$? Explain.

16. Higher Order Thinking Consider the following recursive formula which describes the Fibonacci sequence.

$a_1 = 1, a_2 = 1$

$a_{(n+1)} = a_n + a_{(n-1)}$

a. Find the first 6 terms of the sequence.

b. Is the Fibonacci sequence an arithmetic sequence? Explain.

PRACTICE

Tell whether or not each sequence is an arithmetic sequence. If it is, give the common difference, *d*. SEE EXAMPLE 1

17. 1, 15, 29, 43, 57, . . .

18. 77, 64, 51, 38, 25, . . .

19. 1, −2, 3, −4, 5, . . .

20. 3, 6, 9, 12, 15, . . .

21. 3, 6, 9, 15, 18, . . .

22. 37, 34, 31, 29, 26, . . .

23. 93, 86, 79, 72, 65, . . .

24. 45, 54, 63, 72, 81, . . .

Write a recursive formula and an explicit formula for each arithmetic sequence. SEE EXAMPLES 2 AND 3

25. 12, 19, 26, 33, 40, . . .

26. −4, 5, 14, 23, 32, . . .

27. 62, 57, 52, 47, 42, . . .

28. −15, −6, 3, 12, 21, . . .

29.

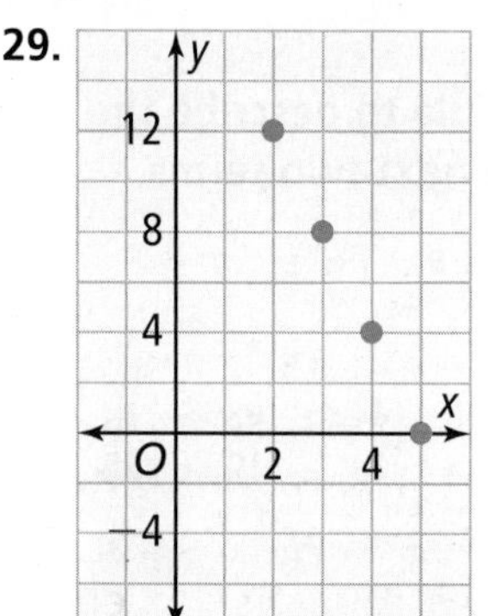

30.

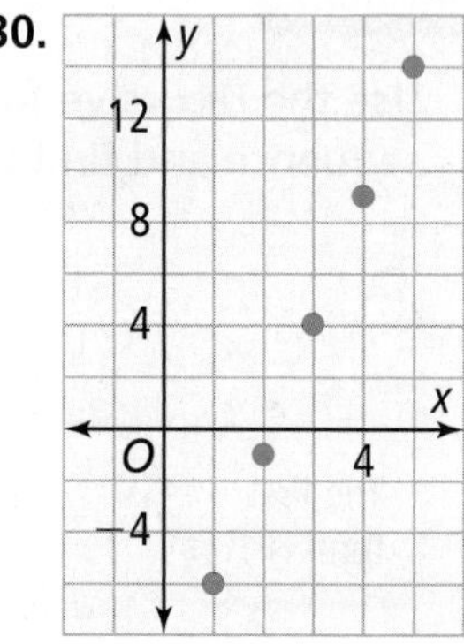

Write an explicit formula for each recursive formula. SEE EXAMPLE 4

31. $a_n = a_{n-1} + 15; a_1 = 8$

32. $a_n = a_{n-1} + 6; a_1 = 9$

33. $a_n = a_{n-1} - 2; a_1 = -1$

34. $a_n = a_{n-1} - 21; a_1 = 56$

35. $a_n = a_{n-1} + 1; a_1 = 12$

36. $a_n = a_{n-1} - 7; a_1 = -3$

Write a recursive formula for each explicit formula and find the first term of the sequence. SEE EXAMPLE 5

37. $a_n = 10 + 8n$

38. $a_n = 108 - n$

39. $a_n = -29 + 12n$

40. $a_n = 35 + 52n$

41. $a_n = \frac{7}{2} - 3n$

42. $a_n = 7 + \frac{1}{4}n$

PRACTICE & PROBLEM SOLVING

Mixed Review Available Online

APPLY

43. **Make Sense and Persevere** The lowest and leftmost note on a piano keyboard is an A. The next lowest A is seven white keys to the right. This pattern continues. Write an explicit formula for an arithmetic sequence to represent the position of each A key on the piano, counting from the left. If a piano has 52 white keys, in what position is the key that plays the highest A?

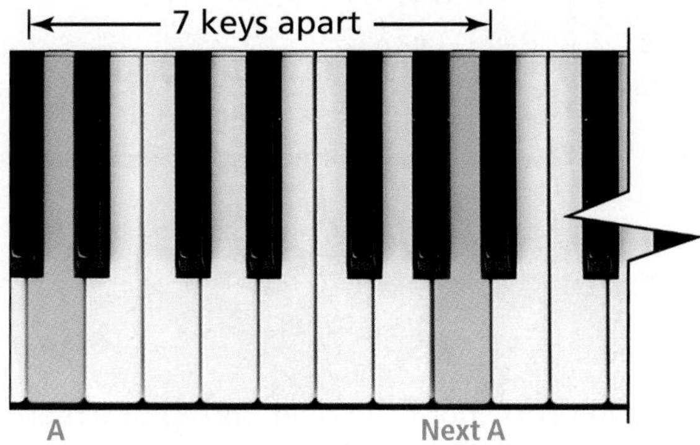

44. **Make Sense and Persevere** After the first raffle drawing, 497 tickets remain. After the second raffle drawing, 494 tickets remain. Assuming that the pattern continues, write an explicit formula for an arithmetic sequence to represent the number of raffle tickets that remain after each drawing. How many tickets remain in the bag after the seventh raffle drawing?

45. **Reason** In a video game, you must score 5,500 points to complete level 1. To move through each additional level, you must score an additional 3,250 points. What number would you use as a_1 when writing an arithmetic sequence to represent this situation? What would n represent? Write an explicit formula to represent this situation. Write a recursive formula to represent this situation.

ASSESSMENT PRACTICE

46. Fill in the blanks to complete the explicit formula that corresponds to the sequence shown.

14, 23, 32, 41, 50, . . .

a___ = __________ + __________ n

47. **SAT/ACT** Which sequence is an arithmetic sequence?

Ⓐ 1, 3, 5, 7, 11, . . .

Ⓑ 4, 6, 9, 13, 18, . . .

Ⓒ 8, 15, 22, 29, 36, . . .

Ⓓ 3, 6, 12, 24, 48, . . .

48. **Performance Task** A city sets up 14 rows of chairs for an outdoor concert. Each row has 2 more chairs than the row in front of it.

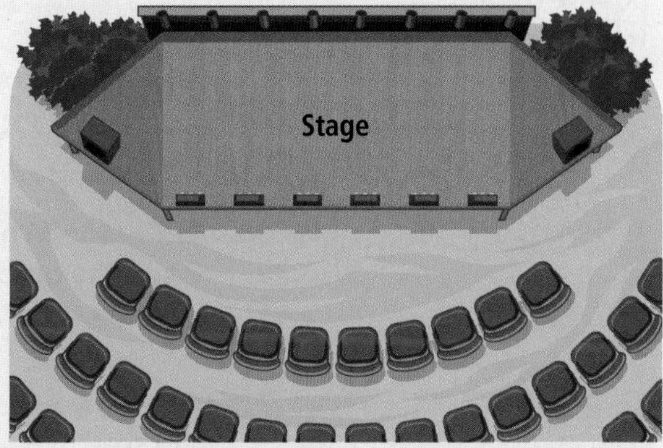

Part A Write a recursive formula to represent the number of chairs in the nth row.

Part B Write an explicit formula to represent the number of chairs in the nth row.

Part C Graph the sequence for the first 5 rows.

Part D What linear function represents the sequence? Which represents this situation best, this linear function or one of the formulas you wrote? Explain.

3-5 Scatter Plots and Lines of Fit

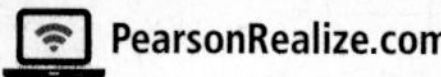

PearsonRealize.com

I CAN… use a scatter plot to describe the relationship between two data sets.

VOCABULARY
- negative association
- negative correlation
- no association
- positive association
- positive correlation
- trend line

MODEL & DISCUSS

Nicholas plotted data points to represent the relationship between screen size and cost of television sets. Everything about the televisions is the same, except for the screen size.

Screen (inches)	Cost ($)
40	300
42	350
43	400
48	480
50	500

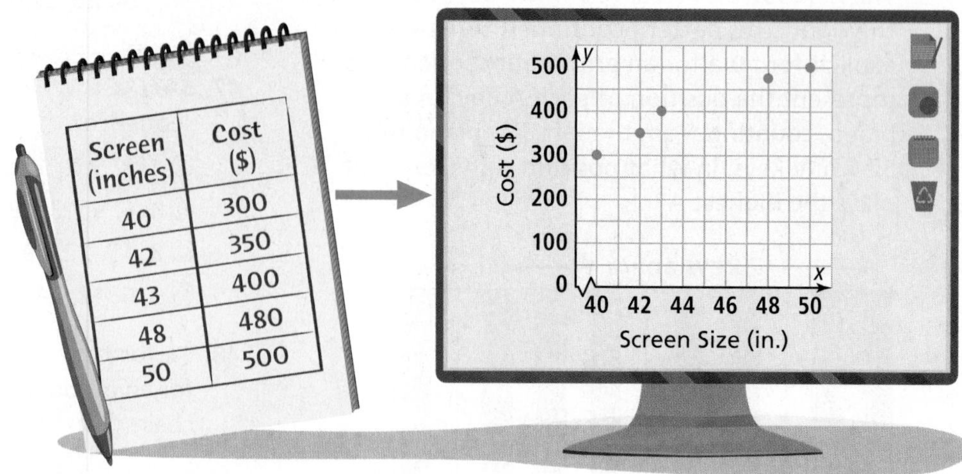

A. Describe any patterns you see.

B. What does this set of points tell you about the relationship of screen size and cost of the television?

C. **Reason** Where do you think the point for a 46-inch television would be on the graph? How about for a 60–inch TV? Explain.

ESSENTIAL QUESTION

How can you use a scatter plot to describe the relationship between two data sets?

CONCEPTUAL UNDERSTANDING

EXAMPLE 1 Understand Association

A. What is the relationship between the hours after sunrise, *x*, and the temperature, *y*, shown in the scatter plot?

Temperature After Sunrise

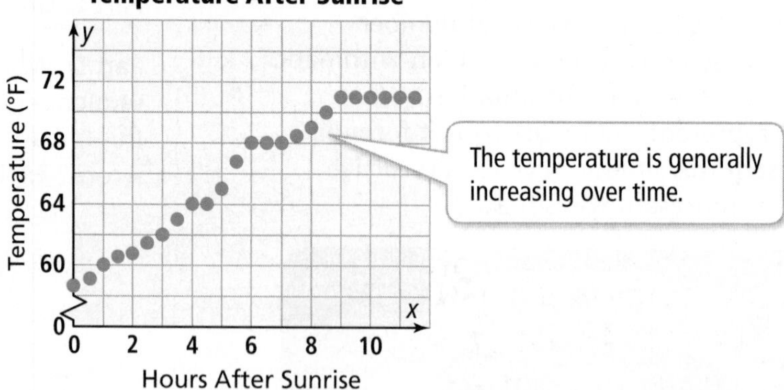

As the number of hours after sunrise increases, so does the temperature.

When *y*-values tend to increase as *x*-values increase, the two data sets have a **positive association**.

COMMON ERROR
You may think that since the points do not line up exactly, there is no relationship. However, when looking for an association, you are looking for a general trend.

CONTINUED ON THE NEXT PAGE

EXAMPLE 1 CONTINUED

B. What is the relationship between the hours after sunset, *x*, and the temperature, *y*, shown in the scatter plot?

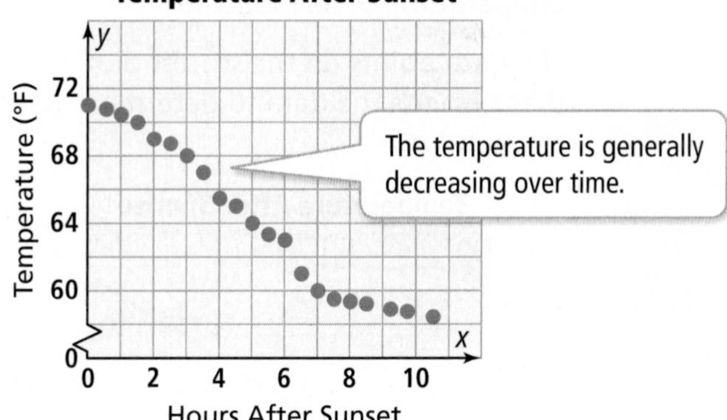

As the number of hours after sunset increases, the temperature decreases.

When *y*-values tend to decrease as *x*-values increase, the two data sets have a **negative association**.

COMMON ERROR
You may think that negative association means that there is no association between the data sets. However, the word "negative" describes the direction of the relationship.

C. What is the relationship between the hours after sunset, *x*, and the amount of rain, *y*, shown in the scatter plot?

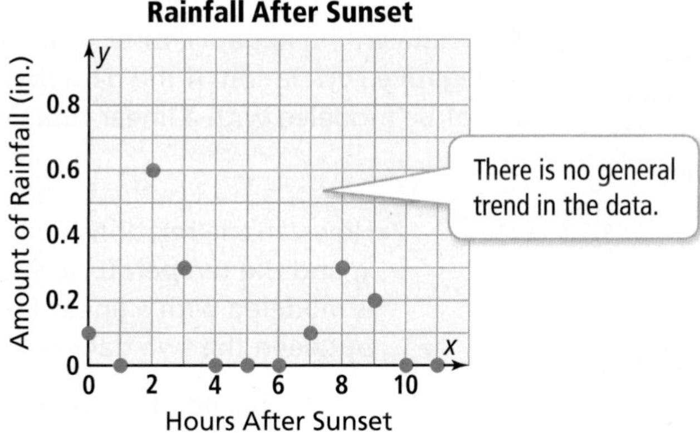

There is no relationship between the amount of rainfall and the number of hours after sunset.

When there is no general relationship between *x*-values and *y*-values, the two data sets have **no association**.

Try It! 1. Describe the type of association each scatter plot shows.

a.

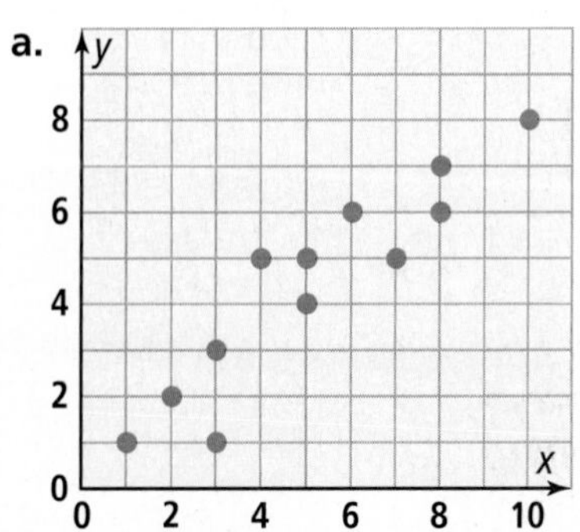

b.

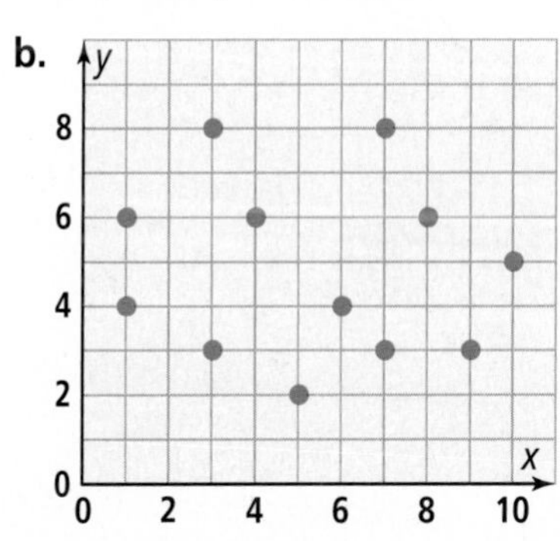

APPLICATION

EXAMPLE 2 Understand Correlation

How can the relationship between the hours after sunrise, x, and the temperature, y, be modeled?

The data points on the scatter plot approximate a line. Sketch a trend line that best fits the data to determine whether a linear function can model the relationship.

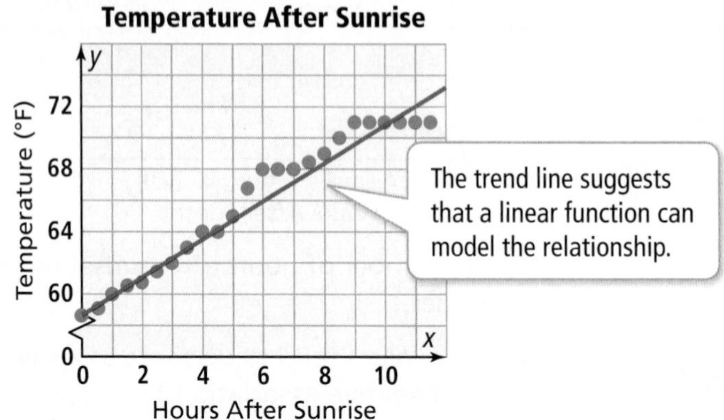

The scatter plot suggests a linear relationship. There is a **positive correlation** between hours after sunrise and the temperature.

When data with a negative association are modeled with a line, there is a **negative correlation**. If the data do not have an association, they can not be modeled with a linear function.

COMMON ERROR
You might think that negative correlation means that the data are not well correlated, but it refers only to the direction of the association.

Try It! 2. How can the relationship between the hours after sunset, x, and the temperature, y, be modeled? If the relationship is modeled with a linear function, describe the correlation between the two data sets.

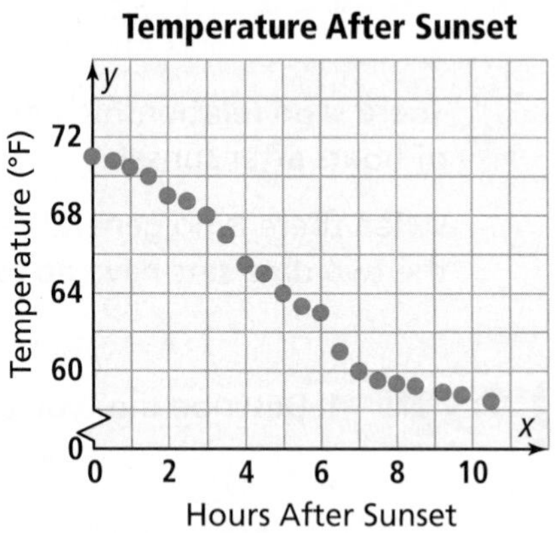

EXAMPLE 3 Write the Equation of a Trend Line

What trend line models the data in the scatterplot?

A **trend line** models the data in a scatter plot by showing the general direction of the data. A trend line fits the data as closely as possible.

COMMON ERROR
You may try to draw the trend line using existing data points. However, this does not always give you the best results.

Step 1 Sketch a trend line for the data.

A trend line approximates a balance of points above and below the line.

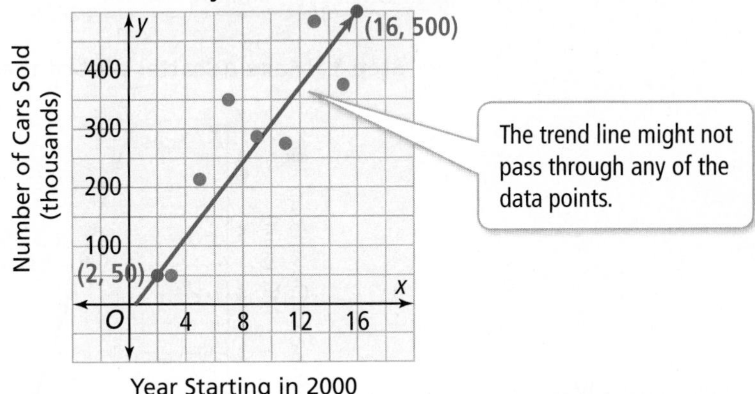

COMMUNICATE PRECISELY
Why do some trend lines stop at the x- or y-axis?

Step 2 Write the equation of this trend line.

Select two points on the trend line to find the slope.

$$m = \frac{500 - 50}{16 - 2} \approx 32.1$$

(2, 50) and (16, 500) are two points on the trend line.

Use the slope and one of the points to write the equation in slope-intercept form.

$$y - 50 = 32.1(x - 2)$$

$$y = 32.1x - 14.2$$

Use the point-slope formula.

The trend line that models the data is $y = 32.1x - 14.2$.

This trend line is one of many possible trend lines.

Try It! **3. a.** What trend line, in slope-intercept form, models the data from the Example 2 Try It?

b. Explain why there could be no data points on a trend line, yet the line models the data.

APPLICATION

EXAMPLE 4 Interpret Trend Lines

The table shows the amount of time required to download a 100-megabyte file for various Internet speeds. Assuming the trend continues, how long would it take to download the 100-megabyte file if the Internet speed is 75 kilobytes per second?

Internet Speed (kilobytes/s (KB/s))	35	40	45	50	55	60
Time to Download 100 Megabytes (min)	6.65	5.82	5.17	4.65	4.23	3.88

Step 1 Make a scatter plot of the data and sketch a trend line.

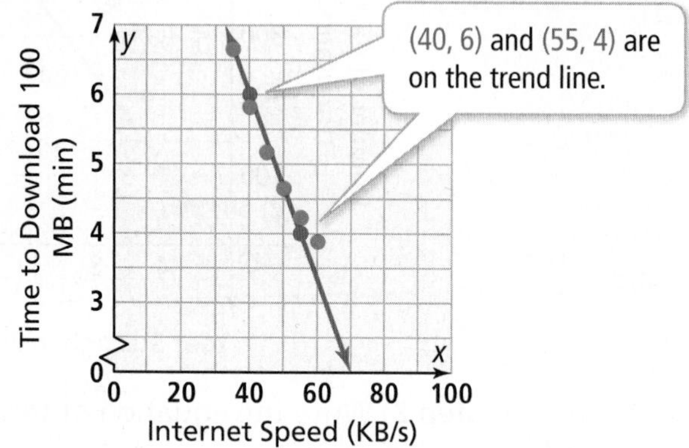

REASON
When a scatterplot has a break in the y-axis, can you visually interpret a trend line across the entire range?

Step 2 Find the equation of the trend line.

Select two points on the trend line to find the slope: (40, 6) and (55, 4)

$$m = \frac{6 - 4}{40 - 55} = \frac{2}{-15} \approx -0.13$$

Use the slope and one of the points to write the equation for the trend line.

$$y - 6 = -0.13(x - 40)$$
$$y = -0.13x + 11.2$$

Write the equation in slope-intercept form.

The equation of the trend line is $y = -0.13x + 11.2$.

Step 3 Use the equation of the linear model to find the y-value that corresponds to $x = 75$.

$$y = -0.13x + 11.2$$
$$= -0.13(75) + 11.2$$
$$= 1.45$$

Substitute 75 for x.

The download time would be 1.45 s.

Try It! **4.** What is the x-intercept of the trend line? Is that possible in a real-world situation? Explain.

CONCEPT SUMMARY Scatter Plots and Trend Lines

TABLE

Positive Association

x	1	2	3	4	5	6	7
y	2	3	3	4	6	7	7

Negative Association

x	1	2	2	4	5	6	6
y	7	7	5	4	3	3	1

GRAPHS

Positive Correlation

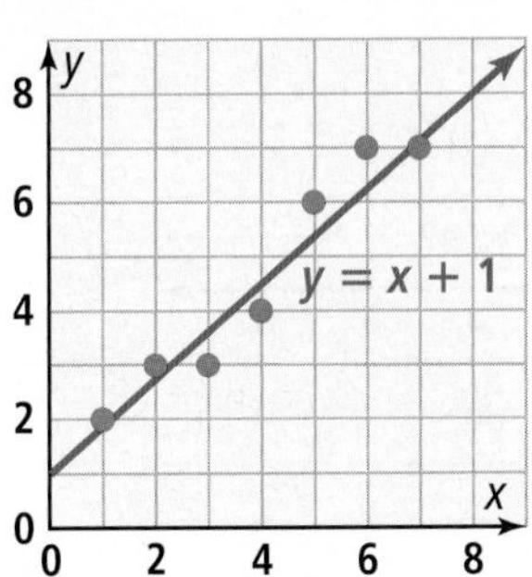

Negative Correlation

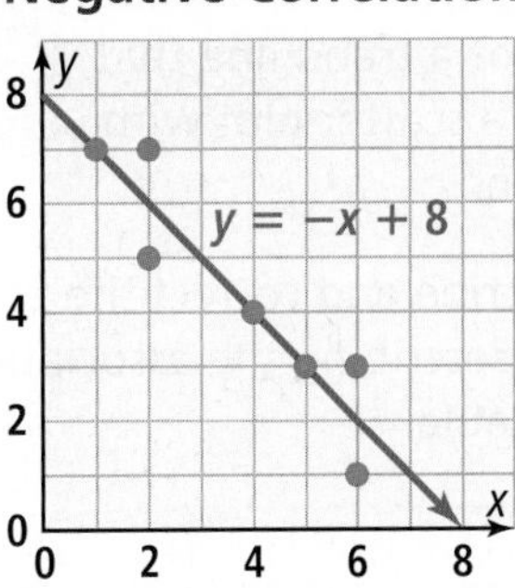

Do You UNDERSTAND?

1. **ESSENTIAL QUESTION** How can you use a scatter plot to describe the relationship between two data sets?

2. **Error Analysis** A student claims that if y-values are not increasing as x-values increase, then the data must show a negative association. Explain the error the student made.

3. **Vocabulary** In a scatter plot that shows a *positive association*, describe how y-values change as x-values increase.

4. **Make Sense and Persevere** Does a trend line need to pass through all the points in a scatter plot? Explain.

5. **Communicate Precisely** Describe how the point-slope formula is useful when writing the equation for a trend line.

Do You KNOW HOW?

Describe the type of association between x and y for each set of data. Explain.

6.

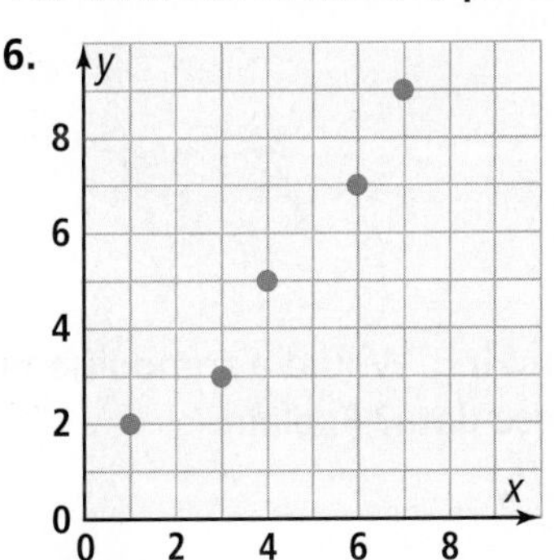

7.

x	4	6	7	9	10
y	9	7	5	3	3

8. The table shows the hours of studying, x, and a person's test score, y. What is the equation of a trend line that models the data? What does the slope of your trend line represent?

Hours of Studying	6	7	7	8	9
Test Score	77	80	83	87	92

UNDERSTAND

9. **Reason** Can you use any two of the given data points in a scatter plot to write an equation for a trend line? Explain.

10. **Look for Relationships** Describe the slope of a trend line that models the data in a scatter plot with positive correlation. Describe the slope of a trend line that models the data in a scatter plot with negative correlation.

11. **Error Analysis** Describe and correct the error a student made in describing the association of the data in the table.

x	19	18	17	17	15	13	11
y	3	6	7	8	10	11	12

The data in the table show positive association because y is increasing.

12. **Higher Order Thinking** Would a trend line be a good fit for these data? Explain.

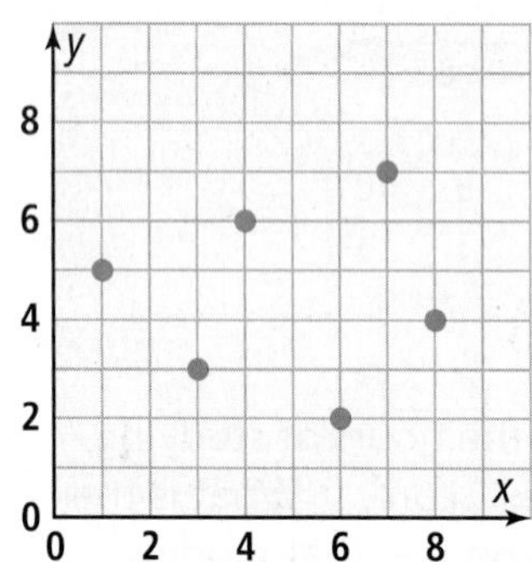

13. **Reason** Describe a set of data that has neither a positive nor a negative association, but that does have a valid trend line.

14. **Mathematical Connections** How could finding the y-intercept of a trend line for a data set help you determine the usefulness of the trend line as a model?

PRACTICE

Describe the type of association each scatter plot shows. SEE EXAMPLE 1

15.

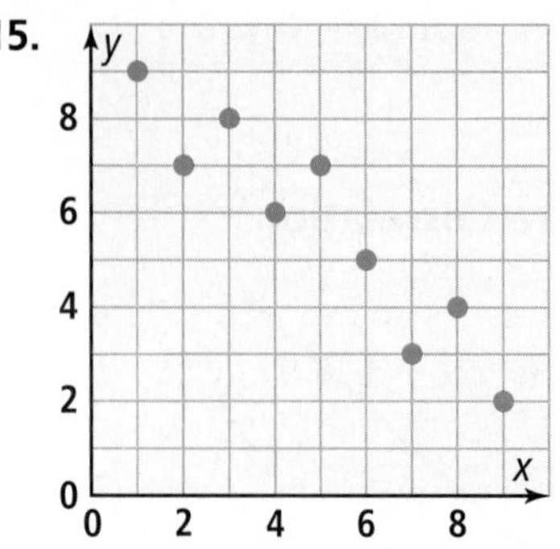

16.

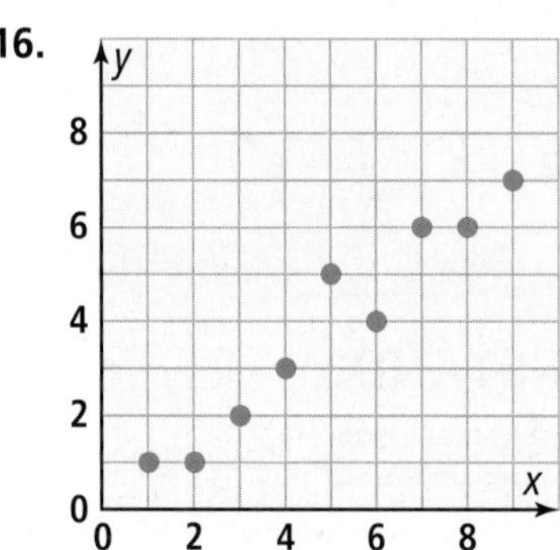

For each table, make a scatter plot of the data. Describe the type of association that the scatter plot shows. SEE EXAMPLE 2

17.

x	y
2	4
3	4
3	6
5	8
6	10

18.

x	y
1	9
2	7
5	3
6	2
6	1

19.

x	y
3	1
4	9
7	2
8	8
10	3

For each table, make a scatter plot of the data. Draw a trend line and write its equation.
SEE EXAMPLES 3 AND 4

20.

x	y
2	3
4	6
5	5
7	7
8	9
8	8

21.

x	y
3	9
5	8
5	6
6	5
6	6
8	3

22.

x	y
1	1
2	3
3	5
3	6
5	8
6	9

PRACTICE & PROBLEM SOLVING

Practice Tutorial

Mixed Review Available Online

APPLY

23. **Make Sense and Persevere** A student is tracking the growth of some plants. What type of association do you think the data would show? Explain.

Days Since Germination

24. **Model With Mathematics** When planting trees for reforestation purposes, different densities result in different numbers of trees per acre. The following table shows the recommended spacing in square feet and the corresponding trees per acre. What trend line models the data shown in the table? What do the slope and y-intercept of the trend line represent?

Spacing (ft^2), x	Trees per Acre, y
60	726
64	680
70	622
72	605
80	544
81	530
84	519
90	484
96	454
100	435

25. **Make Sense and Persevere** The table shows the maximum recommended viewing distances y, in feet, for an HDTV with screen size x, in inches. What trend line models the data shown in the table? What does the slope of the trend line represent?

x	40	43	50	55	60
y	8.3	9	10.4	11.5	12.5

ASSESSMENT PRACTICE

26. When two data sets have a negative association, the y-values tend to _____ when the x-values _____.

27. **SAT/ACT** Which equation could represent a possible trend line for the data in the scatter plot?

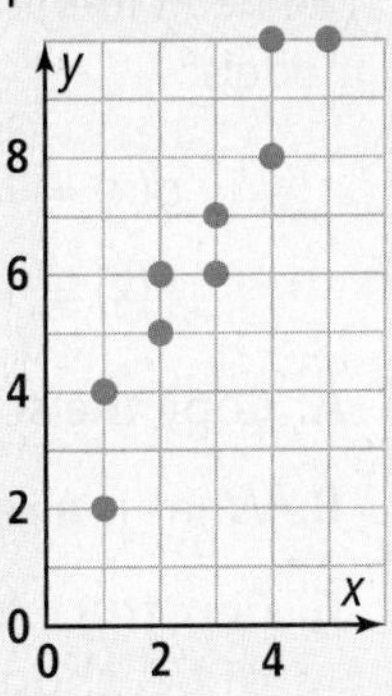

Ⓐ $y = -2x + 1$ Ⓑ $y = 2x + 1$

Ⓒ $y = -2x - 1$ Ⓓ $y = 2x - 1$

28. **Performance Task** A store records the price of kites in dollars, x, and the number of kites, y, sold at each price.

Kite Style	Price	Quantity
	$10.00	25
	$12.00	23
	$15.00	20
	$22.00	18
	$30.00	15

Part A Make a scatter plot of the data.

Part B What trend line models the data? What does the slope of the trend line represent?

Part C What factors other than price could influence the number of kites sold? Could you use any of these factors to make another scatter plot? Explain.

3-6 Analyzing Lines of Fit

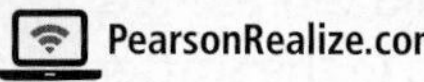

I CAN… find the line of best fit for a data set and evaluate its goodness of fit.

VOCABULARY

- causation
- correlation coefficient
- extrapolation
- interpolation
- line of best fit
- linear regression
- residual

Activity Assess

EXPLORE & REASON

The scatter plot shows the number of beachgoers each day for the first six days of July. The head lifeguard at the beach uses the data to determine the number of lifeguards to schedule based on the weather forecast.

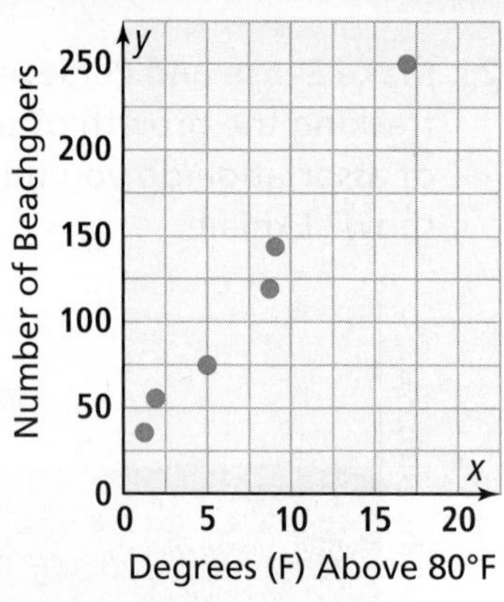

The head lifeguard compares two linear models:

$$g(x) = 13x + 25$$

$$h(x) = 12x + 30$$

A. Copy the scatter plot and graph the linear functions on the same grid.

B. What is a reasonable domain for each function? Explain.

C. **Construct Arguments** Which model is the better predictor of the number of beachgoers based on the temperature above 80°F? Defend your model.

ESSENTIAL QUESTION

How can you evaluate the goodness of fit of a line of best fit for a paired data set?

EXAMPLE 1 Find the Line of Best Fit

What is the equation of the line of best fit for the data in the table?

x	1	2	5	8	9	17
y	30	55	75	120	145	250

A **linear regression** is a method used to calculate the **line of best fit**. A line of best fit is the trend line that most closely matches the data.

Step 1 Enter the data into a graphing calculator.

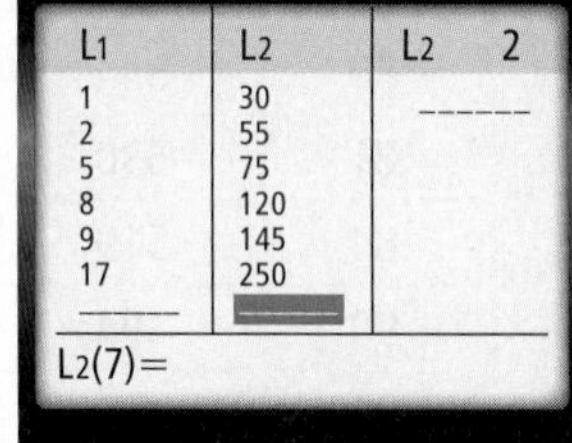

Step 2 Perform a linear regression.

Use the Linear Regression function. The values of a and b from the linear regression – the slope and the y-intercept – are displayed.

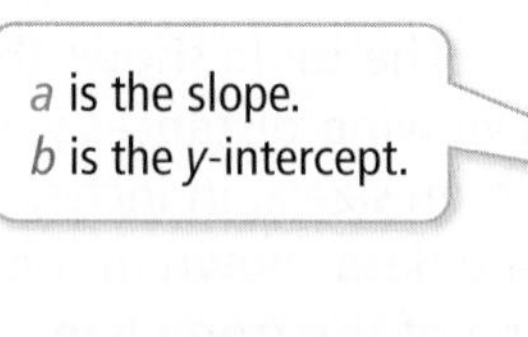

LinReg
y=ax+b
a=13.55882353
b=17.58823529
r^2=.9909817911
r=.9954806834

Step 3 Write the equation of the line of best fit. Substitute 13.56 for a and 17.59 for b.

$$y = 13.56x + 17.59$$

The equation for the line of best fit for the data is $y = 13.56x + 17.59$.

CONTINUED ON THE NEXT PAGE

 **Try It!** 1. Use the linear regression function to find the equation of the line of best fit for the data in the table.

x	1	2	4	5	7	8	9
y	5.4	6.1	8.1	8.5	10.3	10.9	11.5

CONCEPTUAL UNDERSTANDING

EXAMPLE 2 Understand Correlation Coefficients

What does the correlation coefficient reveal about the quantities in a bivariate data set?

When you perform a linear regression using technology, you are also given the correlation coefficient. The **correlation coefficient**, represented by *r*, is a number between −1 and 1 that indicates the direction and strength of the linear relationship between two quantitative variables in a **bivariate data set**, a set of data that uses two variables.

LinReg
y=ax+b
a=13.55882353
b=17.58823529
r^2=.9909817911
r=.9954806834

STUDY TIP
If your calculator is not showing the correlation coefficient, *r*, you may need to turn "Stat Diagnostics" ON in the MODE menu. On older calculators, you can choose "DiagnosticOn" from the CATALOG menu.

When the correlation coefficient is close to 1, there is a strong positive correlation between the two variables. That is, as the values of *x* increase, so do the values of *y*.

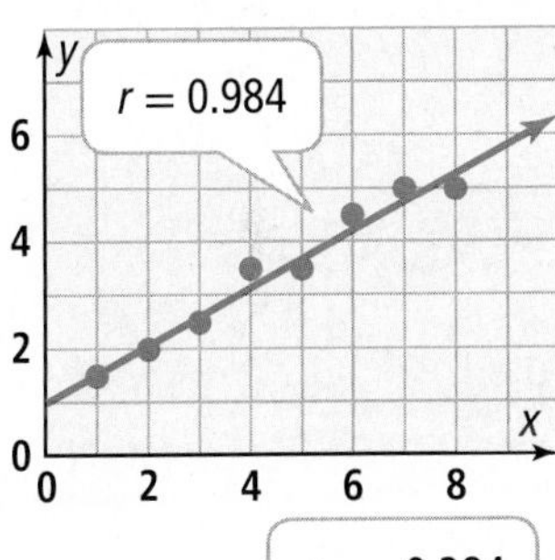

When the correlation coefficient is close to 0, there is a weak correlation between the two variables.

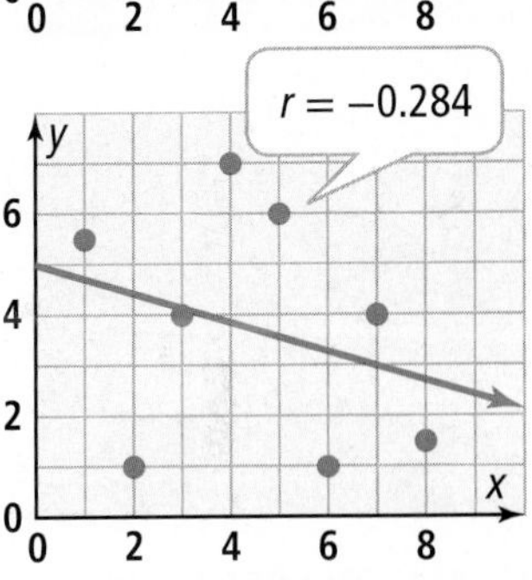

COMMON ERROR
You may think that a correlation coefficient of −1 indicates that there is no correlation. Instead, it tells you that there is a strong negative correlation.

When the correlation coefficient is close to −1, there is a strong negative correlation between the two variables.

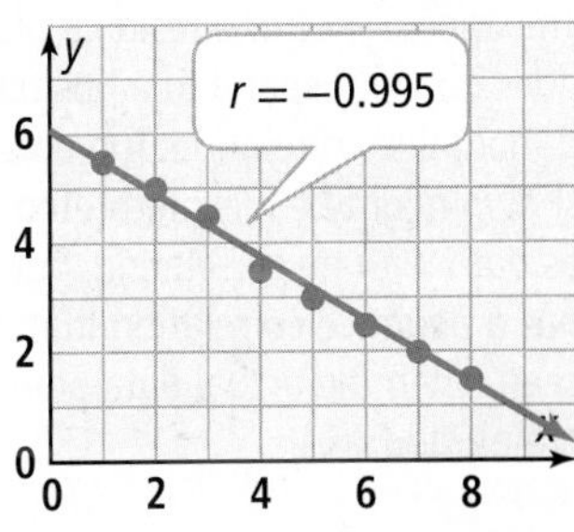

 **Try It!** 2. What does each correlation coefficient reveal about the data it describes?

a. $r = 0.1$ **b.** $r = -0.6$

CONCEPT Residuals

A **residual** is the difference between the y-value of a data point and the corresponding y-value from the line of best fit, or the predicted y-value.

residual = actual y-value − predicted y-value

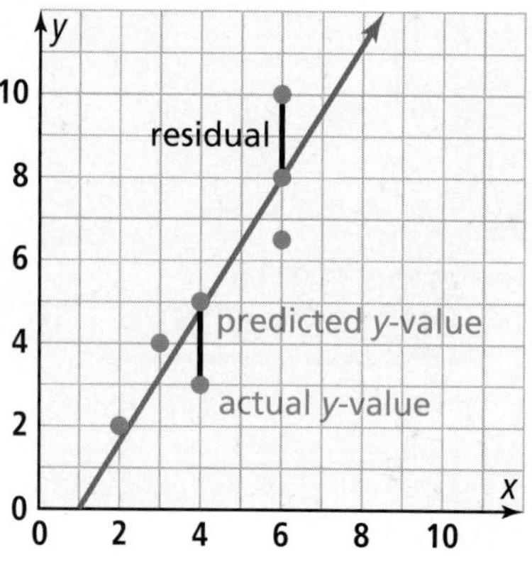

A residual plot shows how well a linear model fits the data set. If the residuals are randomly distributed on either side of the x-axis and clustered close to the x-axis, then the linear model is likely a good fit.

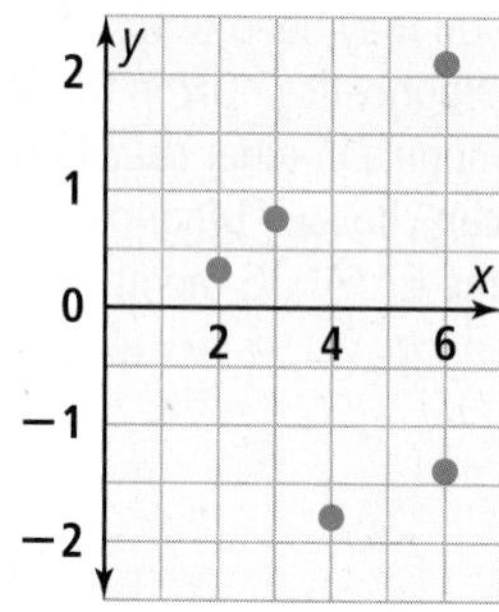

EXAMPLE 3 Interpret Residual Plots

Student enrollment at Blue Sky Flight School over 8 years is shown. The owner used linear regression to determine the line of best fit. The equation for the line of best fit is $y = -35x + 1208$. How well does this linear model fit the data?

Step 1 Evaluate the equation for each x-value to find the predicted y-values.

Step 2 Calculate the differences between the actual and predicted y-values for each x-value.

Step 3 Plot the residual for each x-value.

Blue Sky Flight School

Year (x)	Students (y)	Predicted value	Residual
0	1,235	1,208	27
1	1,178	1,173	5
2	1,115	1,138	−23
3	1,102	1,103	−1
4	1,020	1,068	−48
5	1,050	1,033	17
6	1,003	998	5
7	978	963	15

COMMON ERROR
The appearance of a residual plot does not correspond to a positive or negative correlation. The data shown might be misinterpreted as data with no correlation, but it has a negative correlation that is seen when the actual data points are plotted.

CONTINUED ON THE NEXT PAGE

EXAMPLE 3 CONTINUED

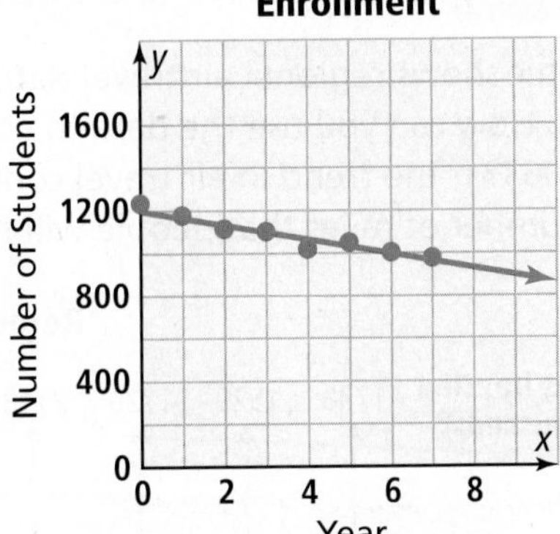

Residual Plot

The scatter plot with the line of best fit suggests that there is a negative correlation between years and enrollment.

The residual plot shows the residuals randomly distributed above and below the *x*-axis and somewhat clustered close to the *x*-axis. The linear model is likely a good fit for the data.

USE APPROPRIATE TOOLS
Why is it helpful to make a plot when analyzing residuals?

 **Try It!** 3. The owner of Horizon Flight School also created a scatter plot and calculated the line of best fit for her enrollment data shown in the table. The equation of the line of best fit is $y = 1.44x + 877$. Find the residuals and plot them to determine how well this linear model fits the data.

Year (x)	0	1	2	3	4	5	6	7
Students (y)	832	872	905	928	903	887	863	867

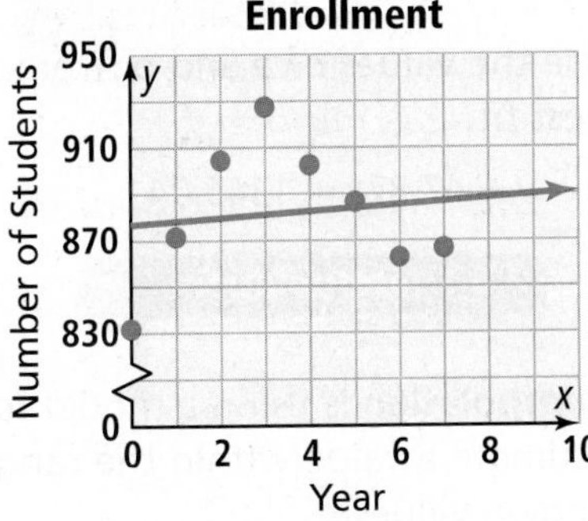

APPLICATION

EXAMPLE 4 Interpolate and Extrapolate Using Linear Models

The graphic shows regional air travel data recorded by a domestic airline company. How can you use the data to estimate the number of air miles people flew in 2003? If the trend in air travel continues, what is a reasonable estimate for the number of miles that people will fly in 2030?

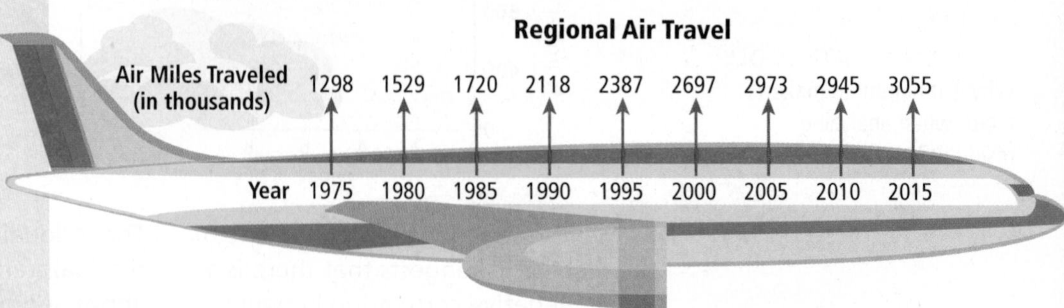

Formulate Plot the data points on a scatter plot. Using technology, perform a linear regression to determine the line of best fit for the data. For the *x*-values, use number of years since 1975.

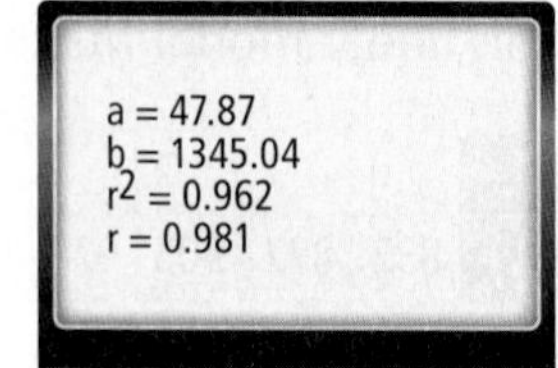

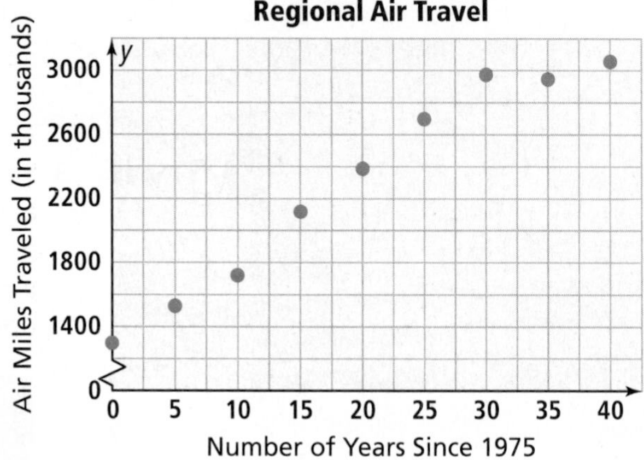

Compute Use the values of *a* and *b* (from the linear regression) to write the line of best fit.

$$y = 47.87x + 1345.04$$

Interpolation OR **Extrapolation**

Interpolation is using a model to estimate a value within the range of known values.

Interpolate to estimate the miles people flew in 2003, or 28 years after 1975.

$$y = 47.87(28) + 1345.04 = 2{,}685.4$$

Extrapolation is using a model to make a prediction about a value outside the range of known values.

Extrapolate to predict the miles that people will fly in 2030, 55 years after 1975.

$$y = 47.87(55) + 1345.04 = 3{,}977.89$$

Interpret The model predicts that people flew a total of 2,685 thousand air miles on the airline in 2003, and that people will fly a total of 3,978 thousand air miles in 2030. This prediction is not as reliable as the estimate for 2003 because the trend may not continue.

Try It! 4. Using the model from Example 4, estimate the number of miles people flew on the airline in 2012.

EXAMPLE 5 Correlation and Causation

COMMON ERROR
Be careful not to assume that if a correlation exists between two variables, that a change in one causes change in the other. The change could be caused entirely by a third, unknown variable.

A. A student found a positive correlation between the number of hours of sleep his classmates got before a test and their scores on the test. Can he conclude that he will do well on the test if he goes to bed early?

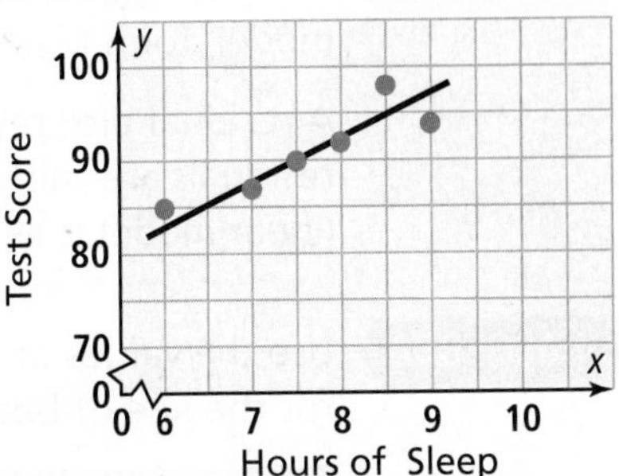

Causation describes a cause-and-effect relationship. A change in the one variable causes a change in the other variable.

To determine whether two variables have a causal relationship, you have to carry out an experiment that can control for other variables that might influence the relationship between the two target variables.

The student cannot conclude that he will do well if he goes to bed early. Other variables, like the time spent studying or proficiency with the content, could affect how well he does on the test.

B. A lifeguard notices that as the outside temperature rises, the number of people coming to the beach increases. Can she conclude that the change in temperature results in more people going to the beach?

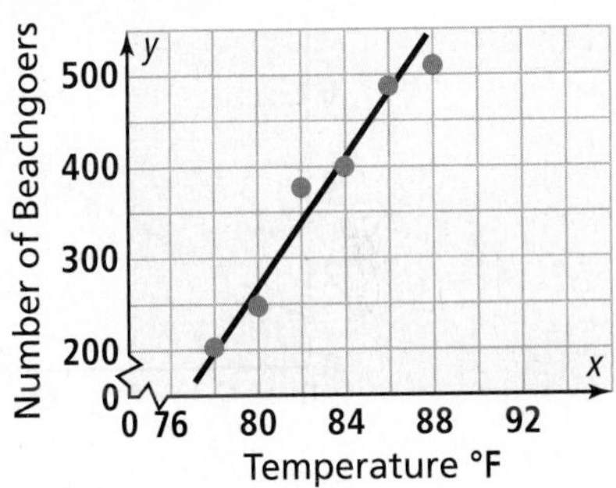

She did not carry out an experiment or control for other variables that might affect the relationship. These include weather forecast and time of year.

She cannot conclude that the only reason that more people come to the beach is the outside temperature.

Try It! 5. The number of cars in a number of cities shows a positive correlation to the population of the respective city. Can it be inferred that an increase of cars in a city leads to an increase in the population? Defend your response.

CONCEPT SUMMARY Linear Models, Lines of Best Fit, and Residuals

WORDS A linear regression is a method for finding the line of best fit, or a linear model, for a bivariate data set.

A residual plot reveals how well the linear model fits the data set. If the residuals are fairly symmetrical around and clustered close to the *x*-axis, the linear model is likely a good fit.

ALGEBRA Use the values of *a* and *b* from the linear regression to write the equation for the line of best fit. The equation is $y = 0.542x + 1$.

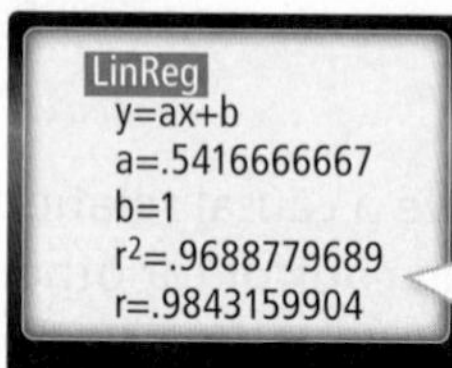

The correlation coefficient, *r*, describes the relationship between the two variables in a bivariate data set. It is a number between –1 and 1.

GRAPHS

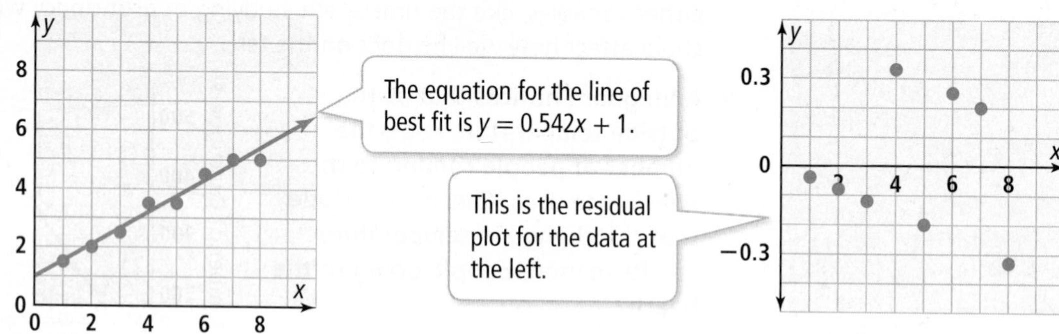

Do You UNDERSTAND?

1. **ESSENTIAL QUESTION** How can you evaluate the goodness of fit of a line of best fit for a paired data set?

2. **Vocabulary** Describe the difference between *interpolation* and *extrapolation*.

3. **Error Analysis** A student says that a correlation coefficient of –0.93 indicates that the two quantities of a data set have a weak correlation. Explain the error the student made.

4. **Look for Relationships** A student found a strong correlation between the age of people who run marathons and their marathon time. Can the student say that young people will run marathons faster than older people? Explain.

Do You KNOW HOW?

Use the table for Exercises 5 and 6.

x	10	20	30	40	50
y	7	11	14	20	22

5. Use technology to determine the equation of the line of best fit for the data.

6. Make a residual plot for the line of best fit and the data in the table. How well does the linear model fit the data?

7. The table shows the number of customers *y* at a store for *x* weeks after the store's grand opening. The equation for the line of best fit is $y = 7.77x + 38.8$. Assuming the trend continues, what is a reasonable prediction of the number of visitors to the store 7 weeks after its opening?

x	1	2	3	4	5	6
y	46	53	65	71	75	86

PRACTICE & PROBLEM SOLVING

Scan for Multimedia | Practice | Tutorial | Additional Exercises Available Online

UNDERSTAND

8. **Make Sense and Persevere** Two quantities of a data set have a strong positive correlation. Can the line of best fit for the data set have a correlation coefficient of 0.25? Explain.

9. **Error Analysis** Describe and correct the error a student made in determining the equation for the line of best fit for the data in the table.

x	3	6	9	12	15	18	21
y	4	17	28	40	55	67	72

Enter y data in L1 and x data in L2. Then perform a linear regression.
Line of best fit: $y = 0.25x + 1.83$

10. **Higher Order Thinking** Which is likely to be more accurate: an estimate through interpolation or a prediction through extrapolation? Explain.

11. **Generalize** Describe how the values of a and b in a linear model are related to the data being modeled.

12. **Look for Relationships** How can you use the graph of the line of best fit to make predictions about future behaviors of the quantities of the data set?

13. **Construct Arguments** Arthur and Tavon each calculated lines of best fit for their last five math tests. Based on the residual plots, Arthur states that his scores are more closely aligned to a linear model than Tavon's scores. Make a mathematical argument to support or refute Arthur's claim.

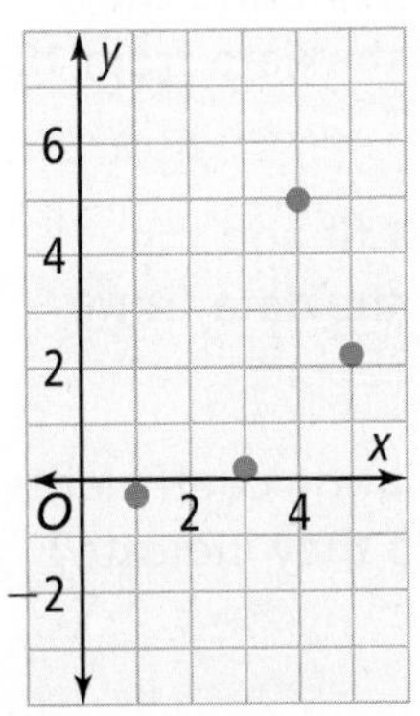

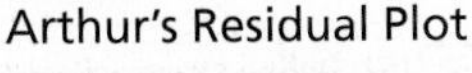

Arthur's Residual Plot

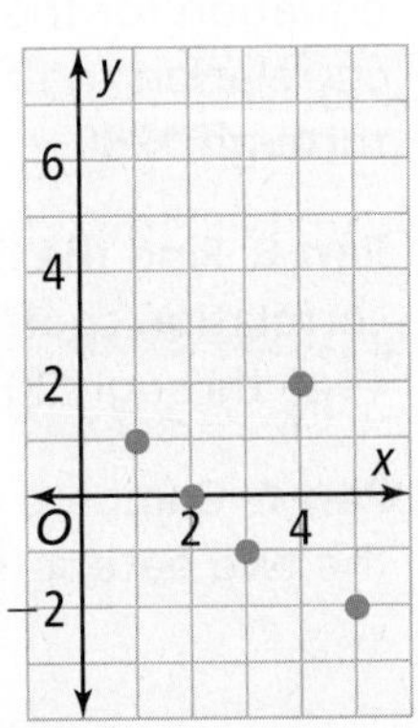

Tavon's Residual Plot

PRACTICE

Use technology to perform a linear regression to determine the equation for the line of best fit for the data. Estimate the value of y when $x = 19$. SEE EXAMPLES 1 AND 4

14.

x	y
12	35
14	39
16	41
18	44
20	48

15.

x	y
16	105
20	83
24	62
28	34
32	15

Describe the type of correlation indicated by each correlation coefficient. SEE EXAMPLE 2

16. $r = -0.89$

17. $r = 0.94$

18. $r = 0.23$

19. $r = -0.19$

Make a residual plot for each linear model and the data set it represents. How well does each model fit its data set? SEE EXAMPLE 3

20. $y = 0.14x + 12.8$

x	y
10	12
15	16
20	18
25	17
30	15

21. $y = -0.58x + 25.2$

x	y
10	19
15	17
20	14
25	10
30	8

Construct an argument for each scenario given. SEE EXAMPLE 5

22. The average monthly heating bills for houses in a neighborhood are positively correlated to the number of pets in the house. Can it be inferred that the number of pets in a household causes an increase in average monthly heating bills? Explain.

23. A person's level of education is positively correlated to the salary the person earns. Can it be inferred that a person with a doctorate degree will always earn more than a person with a bachelor's degree? Explain.

PRACTICE & PROBLEM SOLVING

APPLY

24. **Make Sense and Persevere** Temperatures at different times of day are shown. How can you describe the relationship between temperature and time? Would a linear model be a good fit for the data? Explain.

25. **Model With Mathematics** The table shows the number of miles people in the U.S. traveled by car annually from 1975 to 2015. The equation for the line of best fit is $y = 0.048x + 1.345$, where x is the number of years since 1975. What does the slope represent? Estimate the number of miles people in the U.S. traveled in 2007. What is a reasonable prediction for the number of miles people in the U.S. will travel in 2022?

Year	Vehicle-Miles Traveled in U.S. (in trillions)
1975	1.298
1980	1.529
1985	1.720
1990	2.118
1995	2.387
2000	2.697
2005	2.973
2010	2.945
2015	3.055

26. **Make Sense and Persevere** The table shows the file size y in megabytes of photos taken at different resolutions x in megapixels. The equation for the line of best fit is $y = 0.3x$. Use this equation to create a residual plot. What does the residual plot tell you about the data?

x	4	5	6	7	8	10	12
y	1.2	1.5	1.8	2.1	2.4	3.0	3.6

ASSESSMENT PRACTICE

27. Characterize the relationship of the two variables of different data sets represented by the correlation coefficients shown.

a. $r = -0.91$ **c.** $r = 0.87$

b. $r = 0.54$ **d.** $r = 0.07$

28. **SAT/ACT** Students who eat breakfast are more likely to do well in school. Which of the following can be inferred from this relationship?

Ⓐ The two events are causally related.

Ⓑ The more often a student eats breakfast, the better the student will do in school.

Ⓒ Without more evidence, it cannot be determined whether the correlation is causal.

Ⓓ Providing free breakfast to all students will close the achievement gap.

29. **Performance Task** Use the table to answer the questions.

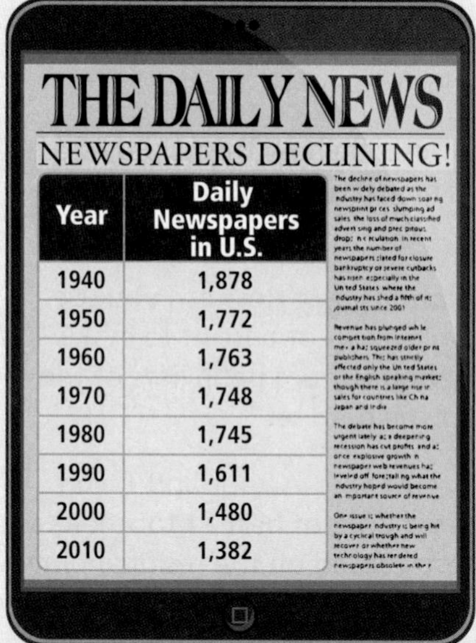
THE DAILY NEWS

NEWSPAPERS DECLINING!

Year	Daily Newspapers in U.S.
1940	1,878
1950	1,772
1960	1,763
1970	1,748
1980	1,745
1990	1,611
2000	1,480
2010	1,382

Part A Use technology to determine the equation for the line of best fit and the correlation coefficient for the data from 1940 through 1980.

Part B Find the line of best fit and the correlation coefficient for the data from 1940 through 2010.

Part C Compare the correlation coefficients of the two data sets. What do they indicate?

TOPIC 3

Topic Review

TOPIC ESSENTIAL QUESTION

1. How can linear functions be used to model situations and solve problems?

Vocabulary Review

Choose the correct term to complete each sentence.

2. When y tends to increase as x increases, the two data sets have a ________________.
3. A(n) ____________ is the difference between an actual and a predicted data value.
4. A(n) ____________ is an ordered list of numbers that often forms a pattern.
5. A trend line that most closely models the relationship between two variables displayed in a scatter plot is the ______________.
6. The ____________________ measures the strength and direction of the relationship between two variables in a linear model.

- arithmetic sequence
- correlation coefficient
- line of best fit
- linear regression
- positive association
- residual
- sequence
- term of a sequence
- trend line

Concepts & Skills Review

LESSON 3-1 Relations and Functions

Quick Review

A **function** is a relation in which every input, or element of the **domain**, is associated with exactly one output, or element of the **range**.

Example

Identify the domain and range of the ordered pairs in the table. Do the ordered pairs represent a function? Justify your response.

x	−2	0	3	5	9
y	−3.5	−1.5	1.5	3.5	7.5

The domain is {−2, 0, 3, 5, 9}. The range is {−3.5, −1.5, 1.5, 3.5, 7.5}.

Each element of the domain is associated with exactly one element of the range, so the ordered pairs represent a function.

Practice & Problem Solving

Identify the domain and range of each relation. Is the relation a function? Explain.

7. {(4, 1), (2, 3), (0, 4), (5, 3)}

8.

x	−1	−5	4	0	2
y	−5	−2	0	3	2

Reason **For 9 and 10, would a reasonable domain include all real numbers? Explain.**

9. A person drinks n ounces of a 20-ounce bottle of a sports drink.
10. A printer prints p pages at a rate of 25 pages per minute.

Construct Arguments **What constraints, if any, are there on the domain? Explain.**

11. An airplane ascends to a cruising altitude at the rate of 1,000 ft/min for m minutes.
12. The value of an automobile in d dollars decreases by about 10% each year.

LESSON 3-2 Linear Functions

Quick Review

A **linear function** is a function whose graph is a straight line. It represents a linear relationship between two variables. A linear function written in **function notation** is $f(x) = mx + b$ and $f(x)$ is read "f of x."

Example

A taxi company charges \$3.50 plus \$0.85 per mile. What linear function can be used to determine the cost of a taxi ride of x miles? How much would a 3.5-mile taxi ride cost?

Let d = distance of the taxi ride.

Cost of taxi ride = cost × distance + fee

$$f(d) = 0.85d + 3.5$$

Use the function to determine the cost of a 3.5-mile ride.

$$f(3.5) = (0.85)(3.5) + 3.5$$
$$= 6.475$$

The cost of a 3.5-mile taxi ride is \$6.48.

Practice and Problem Solving

Evaluate each function for the elements in the domain {–4, –2, 0, 2, 4}.

13. $f(x) = 2x - 1$

14. $f(t) = -3(t - 2)$

15. **Make Sense and Persevere** Melissa runs a graphic design business. She charges by the page, and has a setup fee. The table shows her earnings for the last few projects. What is her per-page rate, and what is her setup fee?

Cost (\$)	185	335	485	635
Page totals	2	4	6	8

16. **Use Structure** Tia's Computer Repair Shop charges the labor rates shown for computer repairs. What linear function can she use to determine the cost of a repair that takes 5.5 hours and includes \$180 in parts?

Hours	1	1.5	2	2.5
Labor (\$)	85	127.5	170	212.5

LESSON 3-3 Transforming Linear Functions

Quick Review

A **transformation** of a function f maps each point of its graph to a new location. A **translation** shifts each point of the graph of a function the same distance horizontally, vertically, or both. **Stretches** and **compressions** scale each point of a graph either horizontally or vertically.

Example

Let $f(x) = 2x - 1$. If $g(x) = (2x - 1) + 3$, how does the graph of g compare to the graph of f?

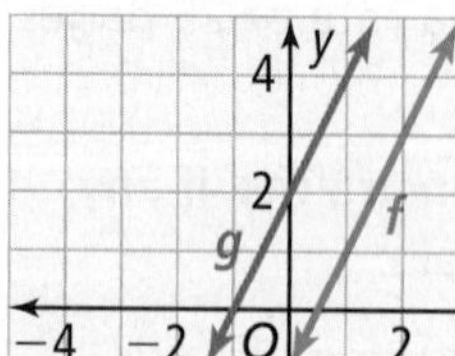

The graph of g is the translation of the graph of f three units up.

Practice & Problem Solving

Given the function $f(x) = x$, how does the addition or subtraction of a constant to the output affect the graph?

17. $f(x) = x - 2$

18. $f(x) = x + 5$

Given $f(x) = 4x - 5$, describe how the graph of g compares with the graph of f.

19. $g(x) = 4(x - 3) - 5$

20. $g(x) = 2(4x - 5)$

21. **Reason** Given $f(x) = -3x + 9$, how does multiplying the output of f by 2 affect the slope and y-intercept of the graph?

22. **Model With Mathematics** A hotel business center charges \$40 per hour to rent a computer plus a \$65 security deposit. The total rental charge is represented by $f(x) = 40x + 65$. How would the equation change if the business center increased the security deposit by \$15?

LESSON 3-4 Arithmetic Sequences

Quick Review

A **sequence** is an ordered list of numbers that often follows a pattern. Each number is a **term of the sequence**. In an **arithmetic sequence**, the difference between any two consecutive terms is a constant called the **common difference, *d*.**

The **recursive formula** is used to describe the sequence and find the next term in a sequence from a given term. The **explicit formula** is used to find a specific term of the sequence.

Example

What is the 12th term in the sequence shown?

−8, −5.5, −3, −0.5, 2.0,...

Determine the recursive formula to describe the sequence.

The common difference, *d*, is 2.5.

$$a_1 = -8$$

$$a_n = a_{n-1} + 2.5$$

Use the explicit formula to find the 12th term.

$$a_{12} = -8 + (12 - 1)2.5$$

$$a_{12} = 19.5$$

The 12th term of the sequence is 19.5.

Practice & Problem Solving

Tell whether each sequence is an arithmetic sequence. If it is, give the common difference. If it is not, explain why.

23. 48, 45, 41, 38, 34,...

24. −6, 5, 16, 27, 38,...

Write a recursive formula for each arithmetic sequence.

25. 2, 6, 10, 14, 18,...

26. −5, −8.5, −12, −15.5, −19,...

27. **Reason** A table of data of an arithmetic sequence is shown. Use the explicit formula for the arithmetic sequence to find the 15th term.

x	1	2	3	4	5
y	8	13	18	23	28

28. **Make Sense and Persevere** Gabriela is selling friendship bracelets for a school fundraiser. After the first day, she has 234 bracelets left. After the second day, she has 222 left. Assuming the sales pattern continues and it is an arithmetic sequence, how many bracelets will Gabriela have left to sell after the fifth day?

Quick Review

A paired data set (or a bivariate data set) has a **positive association** when y-values tend to increase as x-values increase and a **negative association** when y-values tend to decrease as x-values increase. When the relationship between the paired data can be modeled with a linear function, a **line of best fit** represents the relationship. The paired data are positively correlated if y-values increase as x-values increase and negatively correlated if y-values decrease as x-values increase.

Example

Yama takes a course to improve his typing speed. The scatter plot shows his progress over six weeks. What is the relationship between the number of weeks and Yama's typing speed?

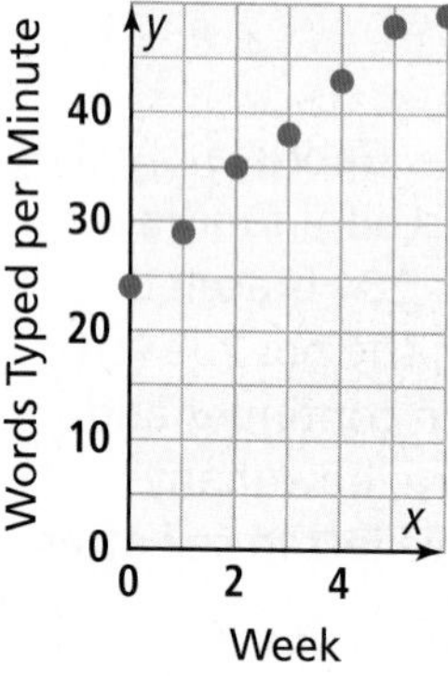

As the number of weeks of practice increases, so does the number of words typed per minute. The scatter plot shows a positive association that is approximately linear suggesting a positive correlation between weeks and words typed per minute.

Practice & Problem Solving

Describe the type of association each scatter plot shows.

29\.

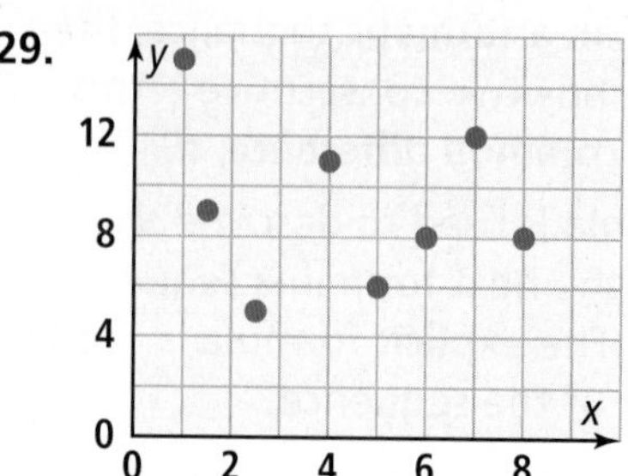

30\.

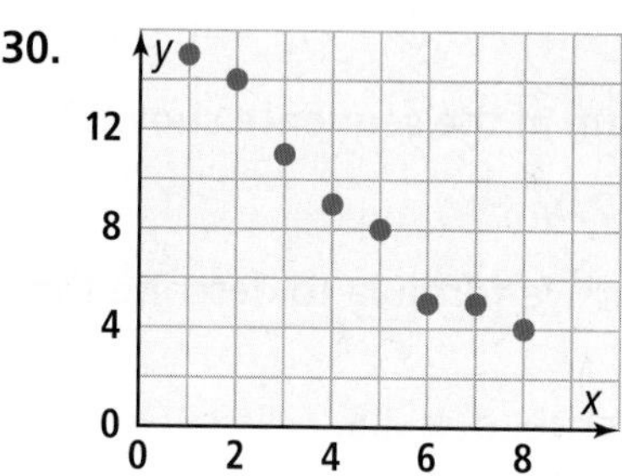

31\. **Reason** Where should the line of best fit be in relationship to the points plotted on a scatter plot?

Use Appropriate Tools **For each table, make a scatter plot of the data. If the data suggest a linear relationship, draw a trend line and write its equation.**

32\.

x	y
2	5
4	8
6	12
8	14
10	18

33\.

x	y
3	40
6	36
8	31
12	27
15	24

34\. **Model With Mathematics** The table shows the recommended distance of a light source y in feet, from the wall for different ceiling heights x in feet. What is the equation of the trend line that models the data shown in the table? What does the slope of the trend line represent?

x	8	9	10	11	12
y	20	27	33	40	48

Quick Review

Linear regression is a method used to calculate line of best fit. The **correlation coefficient** indicates the direction and strength of the linear relationship between two variables.
A **residual** reveals how well a linear model fits the data set. You can use the line of best fit to estimate a value within a range of known values **(interpolation)** or predict a value outside the range of known values **(extrapolation)**.

Example

The scatter plot shows the percentage of American adults with a high school diploma or higher from 1940 to 2010. Based on the residual plot below the scatter plot, how appropriate is the linear model for the data?

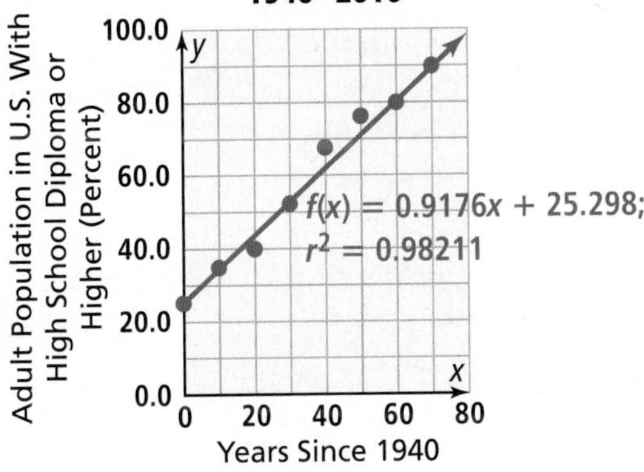

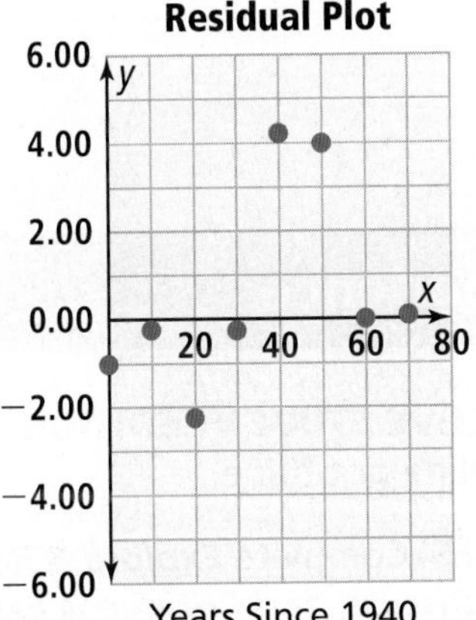

The residual plot shows the residuals distributed above and below the x-axis and clustered somewhat close to the x-axis. The linear model is likely a good fit for the data.

Practice & Problem Solving

Use technology to perform a linear regression to determine the equation for the line of best fit for the data. Estimate the value of y when $x = 25$.

35.

x	y
20	9
22	12
24	16
26	20
28	23

36.

x	y
6	85
12	81
18	75
24	69
30	63

37. Reason How are interpolation and extrapolation similar? How are they different?

38. Model With Mathematics The table shows the winning times for the 100-meter run in the Olympics since 1928. What is the equation of the line of best fit for the data? What do the slope and y-intercept represent? Estimate the winning time in 2010, and predict the winning time in 2020.

Year	Time (s)	Year	Time (s)
1928	10.80	1980	10.25
1932	10.30	1984	9.99
1936	10.30	1988	9.92
1948	10.30	1992	9.96
1952	10.40	1996	9.84
1956	10.50	2000	9.87
1960	10.20	2004	9.85
1964	10.00	2008	9.69
1968	9.95	2012	9.63
1972	10.14	2016	9.81
1976	10.06		

TOPIC

4

Systems of Linear Equations and Inequalities

? TOPIC ESSENTIAL QUESTION

How do you use systems of linear equations and inequalities to model situations and solve problems?

Topic Overview

Topic Vocabulary

- linear inequality in two variables
- solution of an inequality in two variables
- solution of a system of linear inequalities
- system of linear inequalities

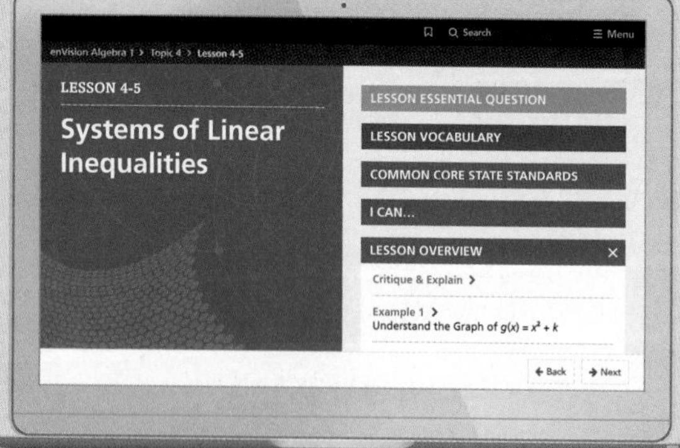

Go online | **PearsonRealize.com**

Digital Experience

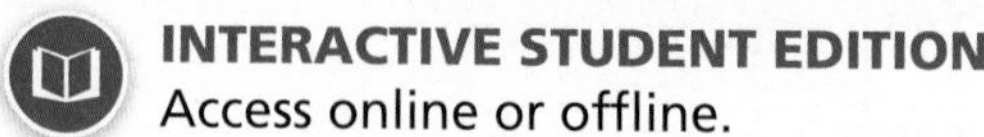

INTERACTIVE STUDENT EDITION Access online or offline.

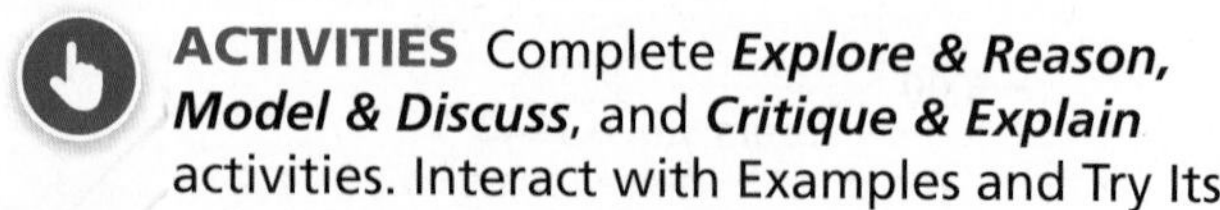

ACTIVITIES Complete ***Explore & Reason, Model & Discuss***, and ***Critique & Explain*** activities. Interact with Examples and Try Its.

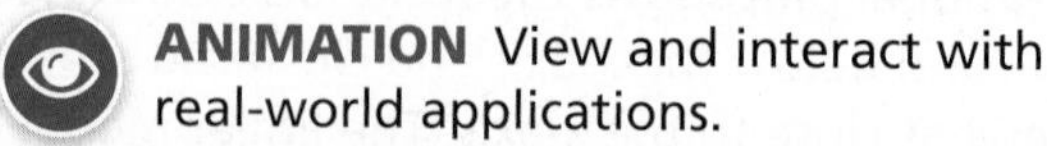

ANIMATION View and interact with real-world applications.

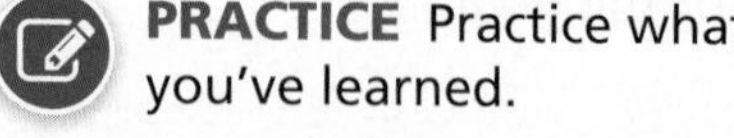

PRACTICE Practice what you've learned.

Get Up There!

Have you ever been to the top of a skyscraper? If so, you probably didn't take the stairs. You probably took an elevator. How long did it take you to get to the top? Did you take an express elevator?

Express elevators travel more quickly because they do not stop at every floor. How much more quickly can you get to the top in an express elevator? Think about this during the Mathematical Modeling in 3 Acts lesson.

TOPIC 4

VIDEOS Watch clips to support ***Mathematical Modeling in 3 Acts Lessons*** and **enVision™ *STEM Projects.***

CONCEPT SUMMARY Review key lesson content through multiple representations.

ASSESSMENT Show what you've learned.

GLOSSARY Read and listen to English and Spanish definitions.

TUTORIALS Get help from ***Virtual Nerd***, right when you need it.

MATH TOOLS Explore math with digital tools and manipulatives.

Video

Did You Know?

American farmers produce enough meat and grain for the United States plus extra to export to other countries. Farms use about 53.5 billion gallons of groundwater each day for irrigation.

Peak Water Demands	
Corn	July
Wheat	May and June
Soybeans	August

Corn is easier to grow than wheat and hardier in northern climates.

In 2012, soybeans became the biggest crop in the United States, with four times the acreage as in 1992. More soybeans are grown in the United States than in any other country.

1 bushel of wheat =

1 million individual kernels of wheat =

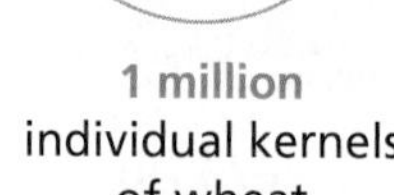

42 pounds of white flour =

60 pounds of whole-wheat flour =

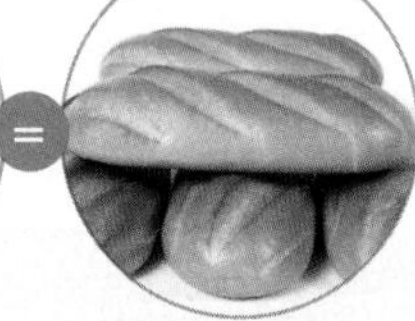

42 one and a half-pound loaves of white bread

Your Task: Growing Grain

You and your classmates will make decisions about growing crops on a farm. How much of each crop will you plant, and why?

4-1 Solving Systems of Equations by Graphing

PearsonRealize.com

I CAN… use graphs to find approximate solutions to systems of equations.

EXPLORE & REASON

Juan and Leo were supposed to meet and drive ATVs on a trail together. Juan is late so Leo started without him.

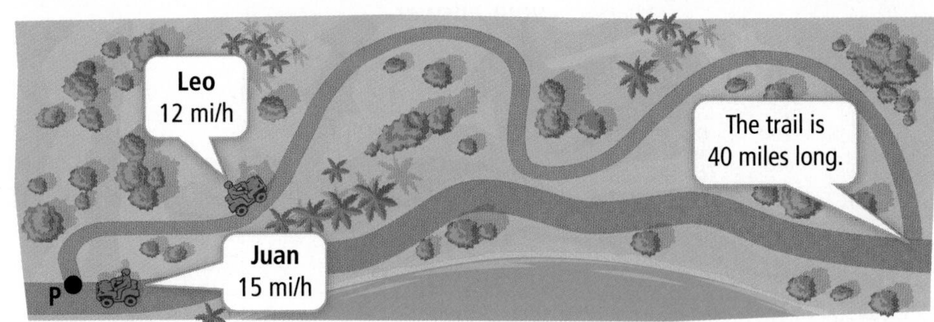

Not drawn to scale

A. Write an equation for Leo's distance from the starting point after riding for x hours. Write an equation for Juan's distance from the starting point if he starts h hours after Leo.

B. **Model With Mathematics** Suppose $h = 1$. How can you use graphs of the two equations to determine who finishes the trail first?

C. How much of a head start must Leo have to finish the trail at the same time as Juan?

ESSENTIAL QUESTION

How can you use a graph to illustrate the solution to a system of linear equations?

CONCEPTUAL UNDERSTANDING

EXAMPLE 1 Solve a System of Equations by Graphing

What is the solution of the system of equations? $y = -2x - 4$, $y = 0.5x + 6$

Use a graph to solve this system of equations.

Step 1 Graph both equations.

Step 2 Find the point of intersection. Since the point of intersection lies on both lines, it is a solution to both equations.

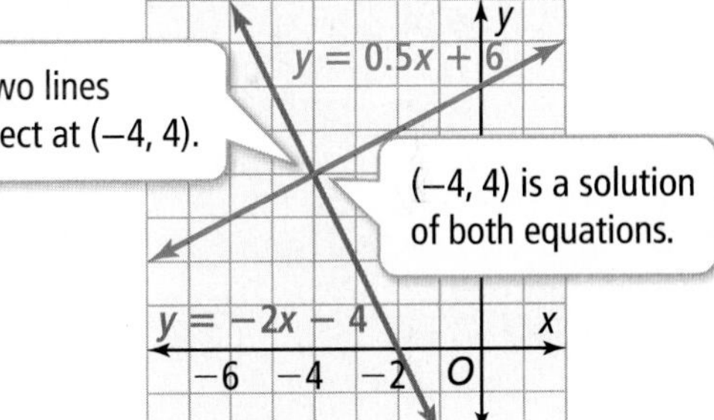

Step 3 Check that the solution works for both equations.

STUDY TIP
Substitute the x-coordinate for x and the y-coordinate for y.

$y = -2x - 4$	$y = 0.5x + 6$
$4 \stackrel{?}{=} -2(-4) - 4$	$4 \stackrel{?}{=} 0.5(-4) + 6$
$4 \stackrel{?}{=} 8 - 4$	$4 \stackrel{?}{=} -2 + 6$
$4 = 4$ ✓	$4 = 4$ ✓

Since there are no other points of intersection the system of equations has exactly one solution, $(-4, 4)$.

Try It! 1. Use a graph to solve each system of equations.

a. $y = \frac{1}{2}x - 2$
$y = 3x - 7$

b. $y = 2x + 10$
$y = -\frac{1}{4}x + 1$

EXAMPLE 2 Graph Systems of Equations With Infinitely Many Solutions or No Solution

What is the solution of each system of equations? Use a graph to explain your answer.

A. $15x + 5y = 25$
$y = 5 - 3x$

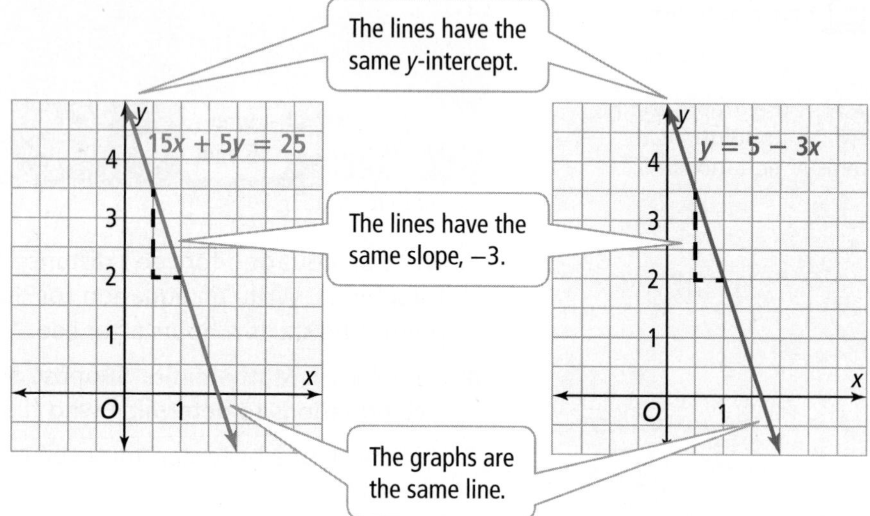

COMMON ERROR
You may think that the lines cannot be the same since the equations are different. However, if you write both equations in the same form, the equations will be identical.

All ordered pairs on the line are solutions of both equations, so all points on the line are solutions to the system of equations. There are infinitely many solutions to the system.

B. $y - 2x = 6$
$-4x + 2y = 8$

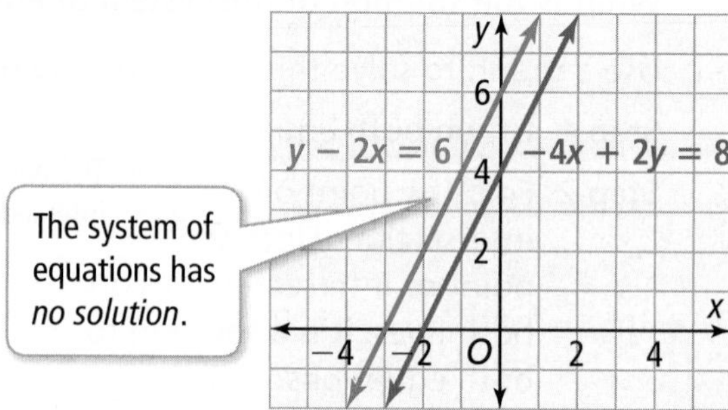

The lines are parallel, so there is no point of intersection. Therefore, there is no solution to this system of equations.

Try It! **2.** Use a graph to solve each system of equations.

a. $y = \frac{1}{2}x + 7$
$4x - 8y = 12$

b. $3x + 2y = 9$
$\frac{2}{3}y = 3 - x$

APPLICATION

EXAMPLE 3 Write a System of Equations

Monisha and Holly have 14 more days to finish reading the same novel for class. Monisha plans to read 9 pages each day, while Holly plans to read 20 pages each day. Assuming Holly and Monisha both maintain their reading plan, when will Holly catch up with Monisha? Who will finish reading the novel first?

Formulate Write a system of equations to represent Holly's and Monisha's reading paces.

Monisha: Total pages = 96 pages already read + 9 pages/day • x days

$$y = 96 + 9x$$

Holly: Total pages = 6 pages already read + 20 pages/day • x days

$$y = 6 + 20x$$

Compute Graph the system of equations. Find the point where the graphs intersect.

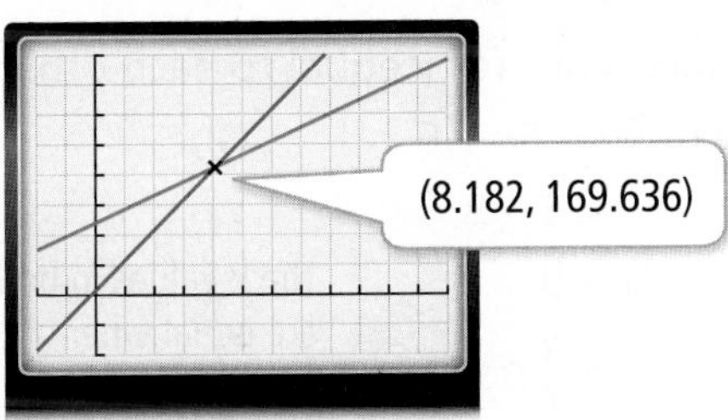

Interpret After a little more than 8 days of reading, Monisha will have read $96 + 9(8.182) \approx 170$ pages.

Holly will have read $6 + 20(8.182) \approx 170$ pages. So, Holly will catch up with Monisha in a little over 8 days.

Since the book is 220 pages long, and Holly is reading at a faster rate, she will finish reading the novel before Monisha.

Try It! 3. Suppose Monisha reads 10 pages each day instead.

a. How will that change the length of time it takes for Holly to catch up with Monisha?

b. Will Holly still finish the novel first? Explain.

EXAMPLE 4 Solve a System of Equations Approximately

What is the solution of the system of equations? $y = 2x - 3$, $y = -5x + 6$

Step 1 Use a graphing utility to graph both equations. Find the point of intersection.

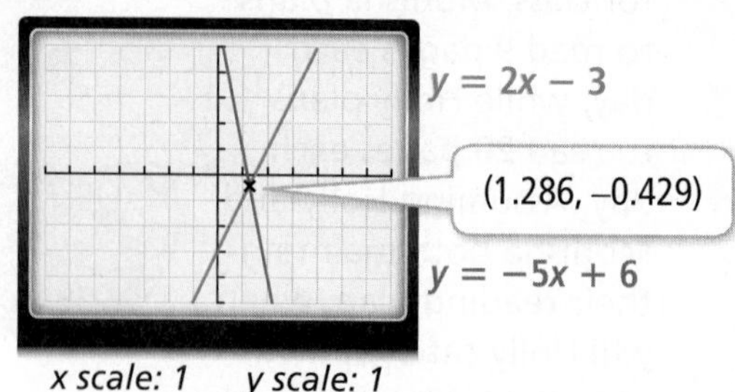

Step 2 Check the values of x and y in each equation to see if they satisfy both equations.

$$y = 2x - 3$$
$$-0.429 \stackrel{?}{=} 2(1.286) - 3$$
$$-0.429 \stackrel{?}{=} 2.572 - 3$$
$$-0.429 \neq -0.428$$

$$y = -5x + 6$$
$$-0.429 \stackrel{?}{=} -5(1.286) + 6$$
$$-0.429 \stackrel{?}{=} -6.43 + 6$$
$$-0.429 \neq -0.43$$

The solutions obtained by graphing are close to, but not equal to, the actual solutions.

REASON
What would happen if you substituted the exact solution into the system of equations?

The solution obtained by graphing, (1.286, –0.429) is correct to three decimal places, but it is not an exact solution. What is the exact solution? Consider which x-value gives you the same y-value in each equation.

Set the expressions for y equal to each other and solve for x.

$$2x - 3 = -5x + 6$$
$$2x + 5x = 6 + 3$$
$$7x = 9$$
$$x = \frac{9}{7}$$
$$= 1.\overline{285714}$$

The y-values in both equations are equal when $x = \frac{9}{7}$.

Now substitute for x in either equation to find y.

$$y = 2x - 3$$
$$= 2\left(\frac{9}{7}\right) - 3$$
$$= \frac{18}{7} - 3$$
$$= \frac{-3}{7}$$
$$= -0.\overline{428571}$$

$$y = -5x + 6$$
$$= -5\left(\frac{9}{7}\right) + 6$$
$$= \frac{-45}{7} + 6$$
$$= \frac{-3}{7}$$
$$= -0.\overline{428571}$$

The exact solution is $\left(\frac{9}{7}, -\frac{3}{7}\right)$. You will see more methods for finding exact solutions in later lessons.

Try It! 4. What solution do you obtain for the system of equations by graphing? What is the exact solution?

$y = 5x - 4$
$y = -6x + 14$

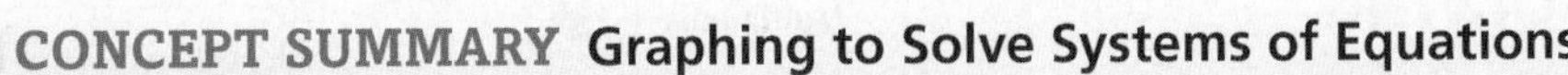

CONCEPT SUMMARY Graphing to Solve Systems of Equations

WORDS	A system of linear equations may have one solution . . .	. . . infinitely many solutions . . .	. . . or no solution.
ALGEBRA	$y = -x + 9$ $y = \frac{3}{5}x + 3$	$y = -x + 9$ $2y = -2x + 18$	$y = -x + 9$ $y = -x + 12$
GRAPHS	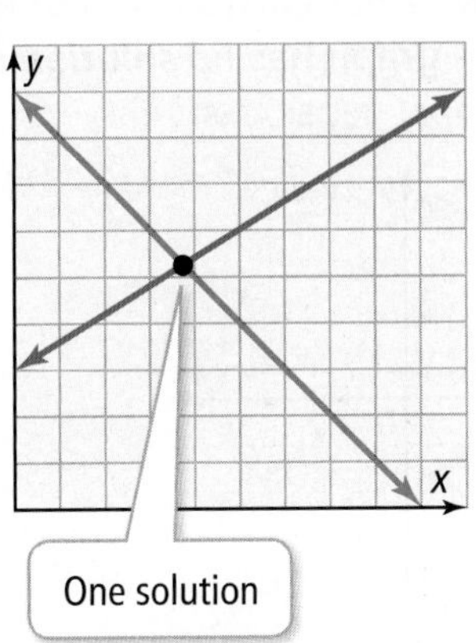	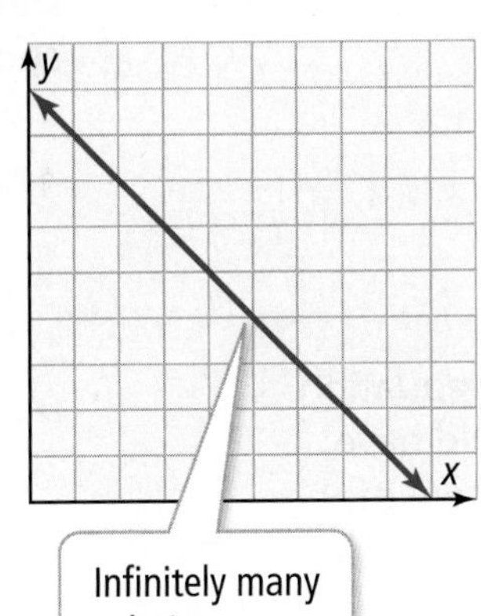	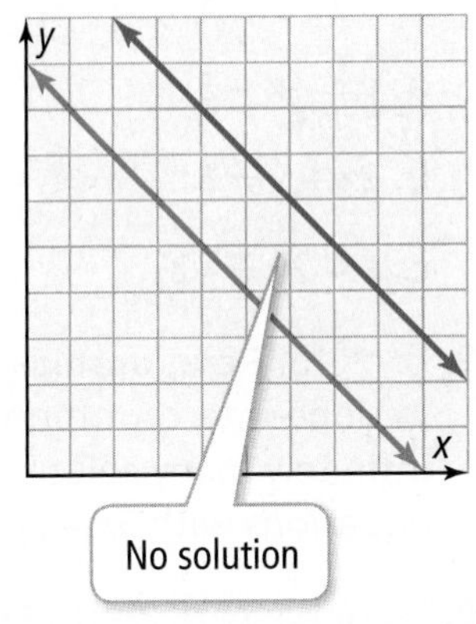

Do You UNDERSTAND?

1. **ESSENTIAL QUESTION** How can you use a graph to illustrate the solution to a system of linear equations?

2. **Model With Mathematics** How does the graph of a system of equations with one solution differ from the graph of a system of equations with infinitely many solutions or no solution?

3. **Reason** Why is the point of intersection for a system of equations considered its solution?

4. **Error Analysis** Reese states that the system of equations has no solution because the slopes are the same. Describe Reese's error.

$$y = -3x - 1$$
$$3x + y = -1$$

Do You KNOW HOW?

Solve each system of equations by graphing.

5. $y = 2x + 5$
   $y = -\frac{1}{2}x$

6. $y = -\frac{2}{3}x + 2$
   $2x + 3y = 6$

7. Juanita is painting her house. She can either buy Brand A paint and a paint roller tray or Brand B paint and a grid for the paint roller. For how many gallons of paint would the price for both options be the same? If Juanita needs 15 gallons of paint, which is the better option?

UNDERSTAND

8. Use Structure Describe the solution set for the system of equations that includes the equation of the line shown and each equation below.

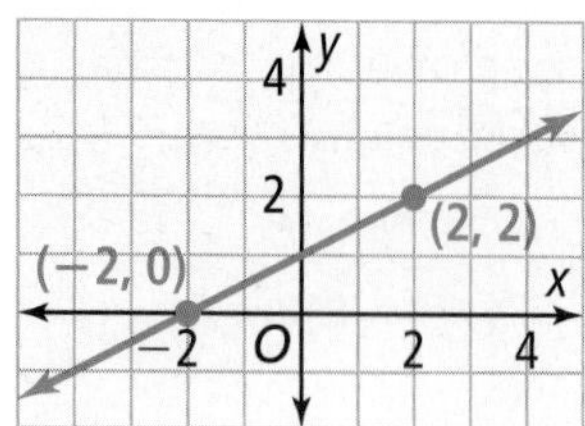

a. $y = \frac{1}{2}x - 3$

b. $2x + y = 6$

c. $x - 2y = -2$

9. Look for Relationships Write an equation in slope-intercept form that would have infinitely many solutions in a system of equations with $5x - 2y = 8$.

10. Communicate Precisely Copy and complete the table by writing the word *same* or *different* to show how the slope and *y*-intercept of each equation relate to the number of solutions in a system of two linear equations.

Number of solutions	Slopes	*y*-intercepts
One solution	■	■
Infinitely many solutions	■	■
No solution	■	■

11. Error Analysis Describe and correct the error a student made in finding the solution of the system of equations.

$y + 3x = 9$
$y = 3x + 9$

There are an infinite number of solutions since the coefficients of the variables and the constants are the same. ✗

12. Higher Order Thinking The solution of a system of equations is (3, 2). One of the equations in the system is $2x + 3y = 12$. Write an equation in slope-intercept form that could be the second equation in the system.

PRACTICE

Solve each system of equations by graphing. SEE EXAMPLE 1

13. $y = -2x - 2$
$y = 3x - 7$

14. $y = x$
$y = 2x$

15. $x + y = -5$
$y = \frac{1}{2}x - 2$

16. $3x + 2y = -3$
$2x - 3y = -15$

Determine whether each system of equations shown in the graph has *no solution* or *infinitely many solutions*. SEE EXAMPLE 2

17.

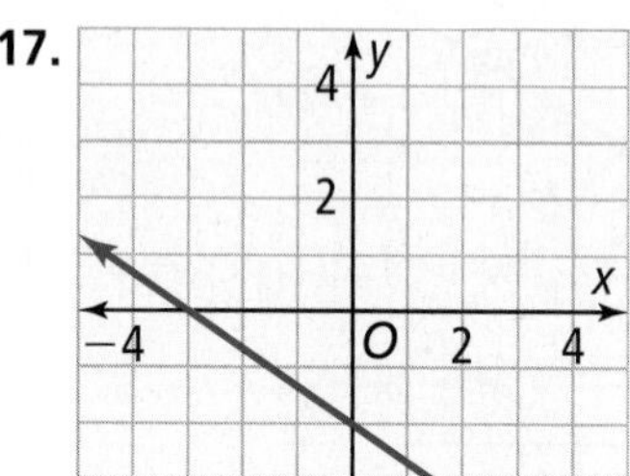

18.

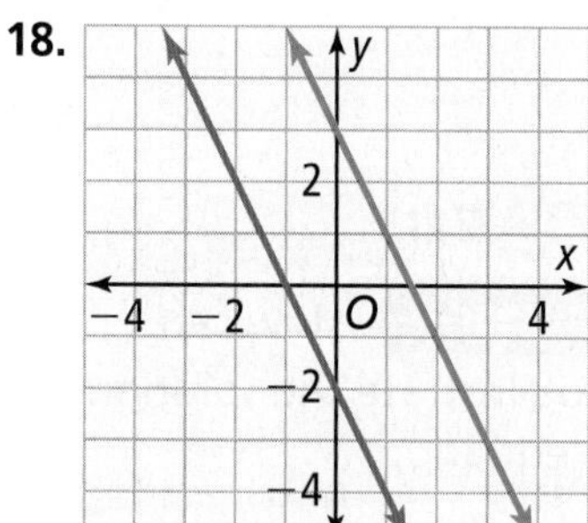

Write and solve a system of equations for the given situation. SEE EXAMPLE 3

19. Roshaun has saved \$150 and continues to add \$10 each week. Keegan starts with \$0 and saves \$25 each week.

a. In how many weeks will they have the same amount of money?

b. What amount of money will they each have saved?

Solve each system of equations by graphing. Round your answers to the thousandths, if necessary. SEE EXAMPLE 4

20. $y = 5x + 1$
$y = 2x + 6$

21. $y = -6x + 5$
$y = 4x + 3$

22. $y = 9x + 2$
$y = -3x - 4$

23. $y = \frac{1}{3}x + 9$
$y = -\frac{3}{4}x + 4$

PRACTICE & PROBLEM SOLVING

Practice | Tutorial

Mixed Review Available Online

APPLY

24. Use the graph to determine the solution for the system of equations.

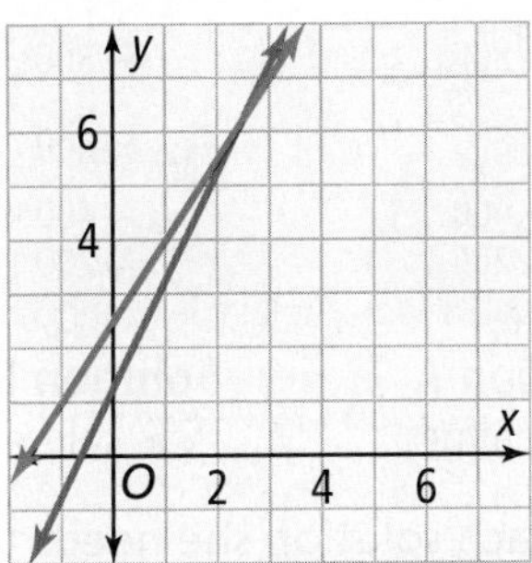

a. **Reason** How does the graph show that the solution of the system of equations has an x-value between 2 and 3?

b. What is the approximate solution of the system of equations?

25. Model With Mathematics Gabriela considers buying fleece jackets from Anastasia's Monograms or Monograms Unlimited. Anastasia's charges a one time design fee and a price per jacket. Monograms Unlimited only charges a price per jacket.

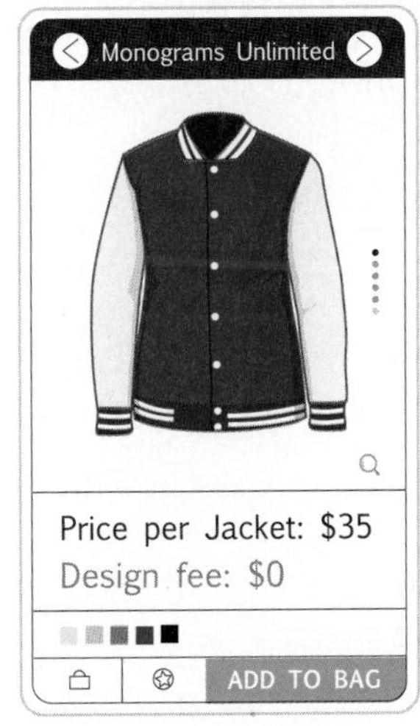

a. Write and solve a system of equations to represent the cost for a jacket from each company.

b. What does the solution mean?

c. Gabriela needs to buy 10 jackets. Which company should she choose? How does the graph help her decide? Explain.

26. Reason How do you know when the solution to a system of equations is a precise answer and when it is an approximate answer?

ASSESSMENT PRACTICE

27. Consider the system of equations.

$y = \frac{3}{4}x + 2$

$3x + 4y = 8$

The graph of the system of equations has _______ line(s) and the solution of the system is _______.

28. SAT/ACT Select which is the solution of the system of equations.

$y = -3x - 3$

$y = -0.5x + 2$

Ⓐ (0, 2) Ⓑ (−1, 0)

Ⓒ (−1, 2) Ⓓ (−2, 3)

29. Performance Task The lines that form the three sides of the triangle can be grouped into three different systems of two linear equations.

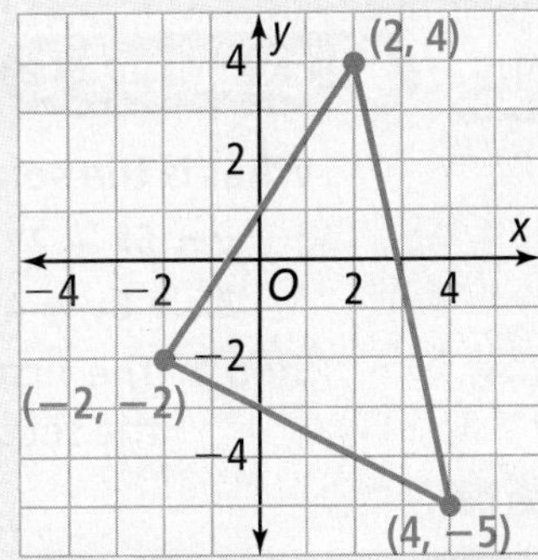

Part A Describe the system of equations that has each solution.

a. (2, 4)

b. (−2, −2)

c. (4, −5)

Part B Replace the solution (4, −5) to make an acute triangle. What are the coordinates of the new triangle?

Part C Describe the system of equations that will produce each of the new coordinates.

Activity Assess

4-2 Solving Systems of Equations by Substitution

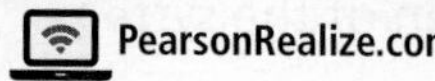
PearsonRealize.com

I CAN… solve a system of equations using the substitution method.

MODEL & DISCUSS

Rochelle is conducting an experiment on cells of Elodea, a kind of water plant. To induce plasmolysis at the correct rate, she needs to use an 8% saline solution, but she has only the solutions shown on hand.

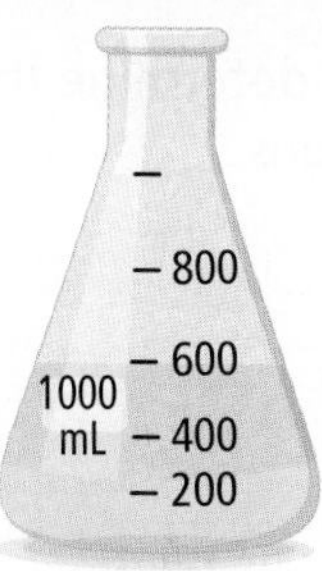

Solution A
10% saline

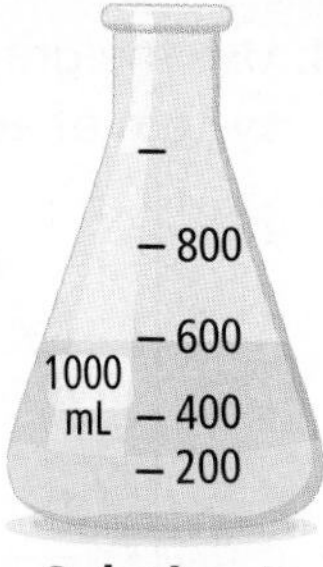

Solution B
5% saline

A. If Rochelle mixes the two solutions to get 1,000 mL of an 8% saline solution, which will she use more of? Explain.

B. How can Rochelle determine the amount of each solution she needs to make the 8% saline solution?

C. **Use Appropriate Tools** Are there any methods for solving this problem other than the one you used in part B? Explain.

ESSENTIAL QUESTION **How do you use substitution to solve a system of linear equations?**

CONCEPTUAL UNDERSTANDING

EXAMPLE 1 Solve Systems of Equations Using Substitution

What is the solution of the system of equations?

$$y = 6x + 7$$
$$3x - 8y = 4$$

Step 1 The first equation is already solved for y, so substitute $6x + 7$ for y in the second equation.

$$3x - 8y = 4$$
$$3x - 8(6x + 7) = 4$$

Substitute $6x + 7$ for y.

Step 2 Solve for x.

$$3x - 8(6x + 7) = 4$$
$$3x - 48x - 56 = 4$$
$$-45x - 56 = 4$$
$$-45x = 60$$
$$x = -\frac{4}{3}$$

Step 3 Substitute $-\frac{4}{3}$ for x in one of the equations and solve for y.

$$y = 6x + 7$$
$$y = 6\left(-\frac{4}{3}\right) + 7$$
$$y = -8 + 7$$
$$y = -1$$

This system of equations has exactly one solution, $\left(-\frac{4}{3}, -1\right)$.

COMMON ERROR
The value of the variable can be an expression, so be sure to use parentheses when substituting an expression for the value of a variable.

CONTINUED ON THE NEXT PAGE

EXAMPLE 1 CONTINUED

Step 4 Check by substituting the values into each of the original equations.

$$y = 6x + 7 \qquad 3x - 8y = 4$$

$$(-1) \stackrel{?}{=} 6\left(-\frac{4}{3}\right) + 7 \qquad 3\left(-\frac{4}{3}\right) - 8(-1) \stackrel{?}{=} 4$$

$$-1 \stackrel{?}{=} -8 + 7 \qquad -4 + 8 \stackrel{?}{=} 4$$

$$-1 = -1 \checkmark \qquad 4 = 4 \checkmark$$

Try It! 1. Use substitution to solve each system of equations.

a. $x = y + 6$
$x + y = 10$

b. $y = 2x - 1$
$2x + 3y = -7$

EXAMPLE 2 Compare Graphing and Substitution Methods

A vacation resort offers surfing lessons and parasailing. If a person takes a surfing lesson and goes parasailing, she will pay a total of \$175. On Friday, the resort collects a total of \$3,101 for activities. How much does each activity cost?

$x + y = 175 \qquad 20x + 16y = 3,101$

Let x be the price of a surfing lesson per person. Let y be the price of parasailing per person.

Method 1

Solve the system of equations by graphing.

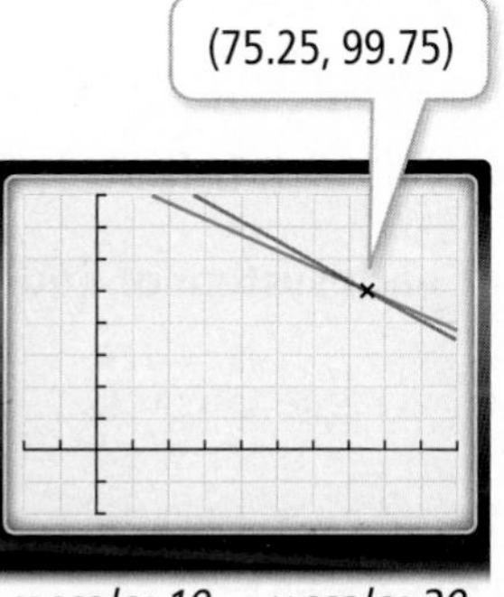

x scale: 10 y scale: 20

REASON
How could you show that (75, 100) is a good estimate for the solution of the system?

Check your answer.

$$x + y = 175$$
$$75.25 + 99.75 \stackrel{?}{=} 175$$
$$175 = 175 \checkmark$$

$$20x + 16y = 3,101$$
$$20(75.25) + 16(99.75) \stackrel{?}{=} 3,101$$
$$1,505 + 1,596 \stackrel{?}{=} 3,101$$
$$3,101 = 3,101 \checkmark$$

Surfing lessons cost \$75.25 and parasailing lessons cost \$99.75.

CONTINUED ON THE NEXT PAGE

EXAMPLE 2 CONTINUED

Method 2

Solve the system of equations by substitution.

Step 1 Solve one of the equations for either x or y.

$$x + y = 175$$
$$x + y - y = 175 - y$$
$$x = 175 - y$$

STUDY TIP
Remember that after solving one equation for a variable, you need to substitute the solution into the other equation in the system of equations.

Step 2 Substitute for x and solve for y.

$$20x + 16y = 3{,}101$$
$$20(175 - y) + 16y = 3{,}101$$
$$-4y = -399$$
$$y = 99.75$$

Substitute $175 - y$ for x.

Step 3 Substitute 99.75 for y in one of the equations and solve for x.

$$x + y = 175$$
$$x + 99.75 = 175$$
$$x = 75.25$$

Step 4 Check by substituting the values for x and y into each of the original equations.

$$x + y = 175$$
$$75.25 + 99.75 \stackrel{?}{=} 175$$
$$175 = 175 \checkmark$$

$$20x + 16y = 3{,}101$$
$$20(75.25) + 16(99.75) \stackrel{?}{=} 3{,}101$$
$$1{,}505 + 1{,}596 \stackrel{?}{=} 3{,}101$$
$$3{,}101 = 3{,}101 \checkmark$$

It costs \$75.25 to take a surfing lesson and \$99.75 to go parasailing.

Try It! 2. On Saturday, the vacation resort offers a discount on water sports. To take a surfing lesson and go parasailing costs \$130. That day, 25 people take surfing lessons, and 30 people go parasailing. A total of \$3,650 is collected. What is the discounted price of each activity?

EXAMPLE 3 Systems With Infinitely Many Solutions or No Solution

What is the solution of each system of equations?

A. $y = 3x + 1$
$6x - 2y = -2$

$$6x - 2y = -2$$
$$6x - 2(3x + 1) = -2$$
$$6x - 6x - 2 = -2$$
$$-2 = -2$$

Substitute $3x + 1$ for y and then simplify.

The statement $-2 = -2$ is an identity, so the system of equations has infinitely many solutions. Both equations represent the same line. All points on the line are solutions to the system of equations.

CONTINUED ON THE NEXT PAGE

EXAMPLE 3 CONTINUED

B. $5x - y = -4$
$y = 5x - 4$

$$5x - y = -4$$
$$5x - (5x - 4) = -4$$
$$5x - 5x + 4 = -4$$
$$4 = -4$$

Substitute $5x - 4$ for y and then simplify.

The statement $4 = -4$ is false, so the system of equations has no solution.

REASON
When the result of solving a system of equations is a false statement, there are no values of x and y that satisfy both equations.

Try It! **3.** Solve each system of equations.

a. $x + y = -4$
$y = -x + 5$

b. $y = -2x + 5$
$2x + y = 5$

APPLICATION

EXAMPLE 4 Model Using Systems of Equations

Nate starts a lawn-mowing business. In his business he has expenses and revenue. Nate's expenses are the cost of the lawn mower and gas, and his revenue is \$25 per lawn. At what point will Nate's revenue exceed his expenses?

Formulate Write a system of linear equations to model Nate's expenses and revenue.

In both equations, let y represent the dollar amount, either of expenses or revenue. Let x represent the number of lawns Nate mows.

Nate's expenses: $y = 2x + 200$

Nate's revenue: $y = 25x$

Nate has an initial expense of \$200 and then an additional expense of \$2 per lawn.

Compute Substitute for y in one of the equations.

$$y = 2x + 200$$
$$25x = 2x + 200$$
$$23x = 200$$
$$x \approx 8.7$$

Interpret Since x is the number of lawns Nate mows, he needs to mow 8.7 lawns before his expenses and revenue are equal. However, Nate is hired to mow whole lawns and not partial lawns, so he will need to mow 9 lawns.

Nate will need to mow 9 lawns before his revenue exceeds his expenses.

Try It! **4.** Funtime Amusement Park charges \$12.50 for admission and then \$0.75 per ride. River's Edge Park charges \$18.50 for admission and then \$0.50 per ride. For what number of rides is the cost the same at both parks?

  Concept Summary Assess

CONCEPT SUMMARY Solve by Graphing and by Substitution

GRAPHING

$x + y = 5.5$

$8x - 4y = 3.5$

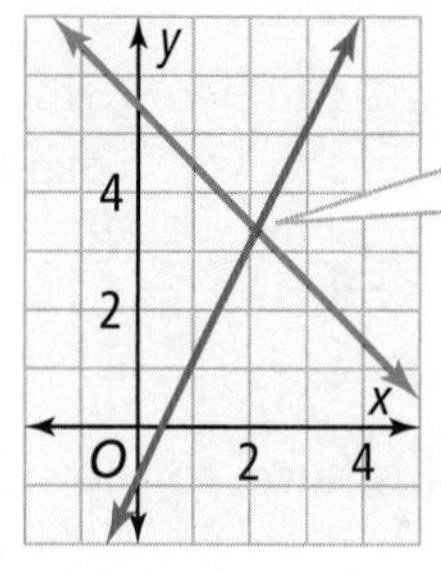

The point of intersection is about (2.1, 3.4).

SUBSTITUTION

$x + y = 5.5$

$8x - 4y = 3.5$

Solve for one variable.

$x + y = 5.5$

$x = 5.5 - y$

Substitute for *x*.

$8x - 4y = 3.5$

$8(5.5 - y) - 4y = 3.5$

$44 - 8y - 4y = 3.5$

$-12y = -40.5$

$y = 3.375$

Substitute for *y*.

$x + y = 5.5$

$x + 3.375 = 5.5$

$x = 2.125$

Do You UNDERSTAND?

1. ESSENTIAL QUESTION How do you use substitution to solve a system of linear equations?

2. **Use Appropriate Tools** When is using a graph to solve a system of equations more useful than the substitution method?

3. **Error Analysis** Simon solves a system of equations, in *x* and *y*, by substitution and gets an answer of 5 = 5. He states that the solution to the system is all of the points (*x*, *y*) where *x* and *y* are real numbers. Describe Simon's error.

4. **Use Structure** When solving a system of equations using substitution, how can you determine whether the system has one solution, no solution, or infinitely many solutions?

Do You KNOW HOW?

Use substitution to solve each system of equations.

5. $y = 6 - x$
   $4x - 3y = -4$

6. $x = -y + 3$
   $3x - 2y = -1$

7. $-3x - y = 7$
   $x + 2y = 6$

8. $6x - 3y = -6$
   $y = 2x + 2$

9. A sports store sells a total of 70 soccer balls in one month and collects a total of $2,400. Write and solve a system of equations to determine how many of each type of soccer ball were sold.

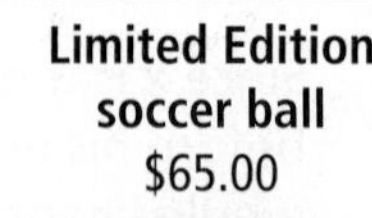

Limited Edition soccer ball $65.00

Pro NSL soccer ball $15.00

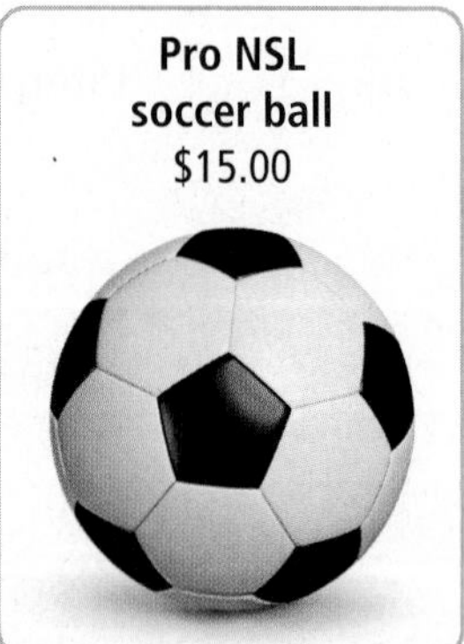

UNDERSTAND

10. **Use Structure** When given a system of equations in slope-intercept form, which is the most efficient method to solve: graphing or substitution? Explain.

11. **Look for Relationships** After solving a system of equations using substitution, you end up with the equation $3 = 2$. What is true about the slope and y-intercepts of the lines in the system of equations?

12. **Error Analysis** Describe and correct the error a student made in finding the number of solutions of the system of equations.
$x - 2y = -4$
$5x - 3y = 1$

$x = 2y - 4$
$5x - 3y = 1$
$2y - 4 - 2y = -4$
$-4 = -4$
Infinitely many solutions 

13. **Use Structure** When using substitution to solve systems of equations that have no solution or infinitely many solutions, the variables are the same on both sides. How is the solution determined by the constants in the equations?

14. **Model With Mathematics** The perimeter of a rectangle is 124 cm. The length is six more than three times the width. What are the dimensions of the rectangle?

15. **Mathematical Connections** Two angles are complementary. One angle is six more than twice the other. What is the measure of each angle?

16. **Higher Order Thinking** One equation in a system of equations is $5x - 2y = -4$.

    a. Write the second equation in the system of equations that would produce a graph with parallel lines.

    b. Write the second equation in the system of equations that would produce a graph with one line.

PRACTICE

Use substitution to solve each system of equations.
SEE EXAMPLE 1

17. $y = 2x - 4$
    $3x - 2y = 1$

18. $y = 3x - 8$
    $y = 13 - 4x$

19. $y = 2x - 7$
    $9x + y = 15$

20. $y = -\frac{1}{2}x$
    $2x + 2y = 5$

21. $x = 3y - 4$
    $2x - 3y = -2$

22. $x + 2y = -10$
    $y = -\frac{1}{2}x + 2$

Consider the system of equations. SEE EXAMPLE 2
$x + y = 5$
$2x - y = -2$

23. Solve the system of equations by graphing.

24. Solve the system of equations using the substitution method.

25. Which method do you prefer in this instance? Explain.

Identify whether each system of equations has infinitely many solutions or no solution.
SEE EXAMPLE 3

26. $4x + 8y = -8$
    $x = -2y + 1$

27. $2x - 3y = 6$
    $y = \frac{2}{3}x - 2$

28. $2x + 2y = 6$
    $4x + 4y = 4$

29. $2x + 5y = -5$
    $y = -\frac{2}{5}x - 1$

Write and solve a system of equations for the situation. SEE EXAMPLE 4

30. At a hot air balloon festival, Mohamed's balloon is at an altitude of 40 m and rises 10 m/min. Dana's balloon is at an altitude of 165 m and descends 15 m/min.

    a. In how many minutes will both balloons be at the same altitude?

    b. What will be the altitude?

31. Richard and Teo have a combined age of 31. Richard is 4 years older than twice Teo's age. How old are Richard and Teo?

PRACTICE & PROBLEM SOLVING

APPLY

32. Reason The sum of two numbers is 4. The larger number is 12 more than three times the smaller number. What are the numbers?

33. Use Structure In a basketball game, the Bulldogs make a total of 21 shots. Some of the shots are 2-point shots while others are 3-point shots. The Bulldogs score a total of 50 points. How many 2-point and 3-point shots did they make?

34. Make Sense and Persevere Stay Fit gym charges a membership fee of \$75. They offer karate classes for an additional fee.

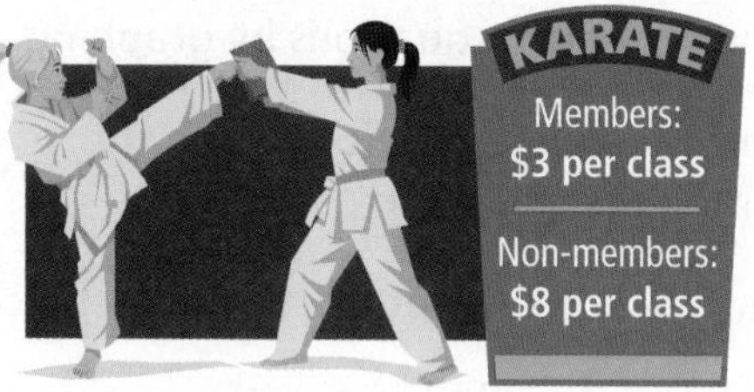

a. How many classes could members and non-members take before they pay the same amount?

b. How much would they pay?

35. Model With Mathematics Abby uses two social media sites. She has 52 more followers on Site A than on Site B. How many followers does she have on each site?

ASSESSMENT PRACTICE

36. What are the *x*- and *y*-coordinates of the solution for the system of equations?

$x = -y + 4$

$2x + 3y = 4$

x-coordinate = ______

y-coordinate = ______

37. SAT/ACT Describe the solution of the system of equations.

$2x - 5y = -5$

$y = \frac{2}{5}x - 2$

Ⓐ No solution

Ⓑ Infinitely many solutions

Ⓒ (10, 5)

Ⓓ (5, 3)

38. Performance Task Each side of a triangle lies along a line in a coordinate plane. The three lines that contain these sides are represented by the given equations.

Equation 1: $x - 2y = -4$

Equation 2: $2x + y = -3$

Equation 3: $7x - 4y = 12$

Part A Write three systems of equations that can be used to determine the vertices of the triangle.

Part B What are the coordinates of the vertices?

Part C Is this a right triangle? Explain.

4-3 Solving Systems of Equations by Elimination

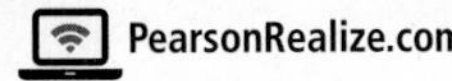

I CAN… solve systems of linear equations using the elimination method.

CRITIQUE & EXPLAIN

Sadie and Micah used different methods to solve the system of equations.

$$y = 2x + 3$$
$$4x - y = 5$$

Sadie's work

$4x - (2x + 3) = 5$
$4x - 2x - 3 = 5$
$2x - 3 = 5$
$2x = 8$
$x = 4$
$y = 2(4) + 3 = 11$
The solution is (4, 11).

Micah's work

$y = 2x + 3$ and $y = 4x - 5$
$2x + 3 = 4x - 5$
$8 = 2x$
$x = 4$
$y = 2(4) + 3$
$y = 11$
The solution is (4, 11).

A. In what ways are Sadie's and Micah's approaches similar? In what ways are they different?

B. Are both Sadie's and Micah's approaches valid solution methods? Explain.

C. Reason Which method of solving systems of equations do you prefer when solving, Sadie's method, or Micah's method? Explain.

ESSENTIAL QUESTION

Why does the elimination method work when solving a system of equations?

EXAMPLE 1 Solve a System of Equations by Adding

What is the solution to the system of equations?

$$x + y = 7$$
$$2x - y = 2$$

You can add equations to get a new equation that is easier to solve.

Match like terms.

$$\begin{array}{r} x + y = 7 \\ +\ 2x - y = 2 \\ \hline 3x + 0 = 9 \end{array}$$

Write the sums of like terms below.

This method works because of the Addition Property of Equality.

$$x + y = 7$$
$$x + y + (2x - y) = 7 + 2$$
$$(x + 2x) + (y - y) = 7 + 2$$
$$3x + 0 = 9$$

Since $2x - y$ and 2 are equal, you can add $2x - y$ to the left side and 2 to the right side.

COMMON ERROR
You may think that you need to add the same expression to each side of the equation. However, since $2x - y = 2$, adding one of the expressions to each side of the equation is still adding an equivalent value to each side of the equation.

Look carefully at the last two steps. They are the same as adding like terms in the original system of equations.

$$\begin{array}{r} x + y = 7 \\ +\ 2x - y = 2 \\ \hline 3x + 0 = 9 \end{array}$$

$$(x + 2x) + (y - y) = 7 + 2$$
$$3x + 0 = 9$$

CONTINUED ON THE NEXT PAGE

EXAMPLE 1 CONTINUED

So $3x = 9$, or $x = 3$. Now substitute 3 for x in either of the two equations in the system of equations.

$$x + y = 7$$
$$3 + y = 7$$
$$y = 4$$

The solution to the system of equations is (3, 4).

Try It! **1.** Solve each system of equations.

a. $2x - 4y = 2$
$-x + 4y = 3$

b. $2x + 3y = 1$
$-2x + 2y = -6$

CONCEPTUAL UNDERSTANDING

EXAMPLE 2 Understand Equivalent Systems of Equations

What is the solution to the system of equations?

$$\mathbf{x + 3y = 7}$$
$$\mathbf{2x + 2y = 6}$$

Before adding equations, multiply each side of one of the equations by a constant that makes either the x or y terms opposites.

$x + 3y = 7$ Multiply by −2. $-2(x + 3y) = -2 \cdot 7$

$2x + 2y = 6$ $\qquad 2x + 2y = 6$

MAKE SENSE AND PERSEVERE
The two equations have the same solution because of the Multiplication Property of Equality.

The result is an *equivalent system* that has the same solution as the original system. This is because the first equation has the same solution after multiplying each side by the same nonzero value.

Now solve by adding the equations.

$$\begin{array}{r} -2x - 6y = -14 \\ +\ 2x + 2y = 6 \\ \hline 0 - 4y = -8 \end{array}$$

Distribute the −2 on each side before adding.

So $-4y = -8$, or $y = 2$. Now substitute 2 for y in either of the two equations in the system.

$$x + 3y = 7$$
$$x + 3(2) = 7$$
$$x = 1$$

The solution to the system is (1, 2).

Try It! **2.** Solve each system of equations.

a. $x + 2y = 4$
$2x - 5y = -1$

b. $2x + y = 2$
$x - 2y = -5$

APPLICATION

EXAMPLE 3 Apply Elimination

A florist is making regular bouquets and mini bouquets. The florist has 118 roses and 226 peonies to use in the bouquets. How many of each type of bouquet can the florist make?

Formulate ◀ Let x be the number of regular bouquets and y be the number of mini bouquets.

Roses: $5x + 3y = 118$

Peonies: $11x + 5y = 226$

Compute ◀ Multiply each equation by constants to eliminate one variable.

$$\begin{aligned} 5x + 3y &= 118 \quad \text{Multiply by 5.} \quad & 25x + 15y &= 590 \\ 11x + 5y &= 226 \quad \text{Multiply by } -3. \quad & -33x - 15y &= -678 \\ & & \hline -8x + 0 &= -88 \\ & & x &= 11 \end{aligned}$$

There are many ways to do this. In this case, 15 is the LCM of 3 and 5.

Add the equations to eliminate y.

Solve for y.

$$\begin{aligned} 5(11) + 3y &= 118 \\ 55 + 3y &= 118 \\ 3y &= 63 \\ y &= 21 \end{aligned}$$

Substitute 11 for x and solve for y.

The solution is (11, 21).

Interpret ◀ The florist has enough roses and peonies to make 11 regular and 21 mini bouquets.

 **Try It!** **3.** Before the florist has a chance to finish the bouquets, a large order is placed. After the order, only 85 roses and 163 peonies remain. How many regular bouquets and mini bouquets can the florist make now?

EXAMPLE 4 Choose a Method of Solving

What is the solution of the system of equations?

A. $y = x + 13$

$2x + 7y = 10$

Since the first equation is already solved for one of the variables, you can easily substitute $x + 13$ for y.

$$2x + 7(x + 13) = 10$$
$$9x + 91 = 10$$
$$9x = -81$$
$$x = -9$$

$$y = -9 + 13$$
$$y = 4$$

The solution is (–9, 4).

B. $8x - 2y = -8$

$5x - 4y = 17$

The coefficient of y in the second equation is an integer multiple of the coefficient of y in the first equation. This makes it easy to eliminate the y variable.

STUDY TIP
Since the coefficients of the y-terms have the same sign, multiply by a negative number.

$8x - 2y = -8$ Multiply by −2. $-16x + 4y = 16$

$5x - 4y = 17$ $\quad 5x - 4y = 17$

$-11x + 0 = 33$ Add the equations.

$x = -3$ Solve for x.

Now solve for y.

$$5(-3) - 4y = 17$$
$$-15 - 4y = 17$$
$$-4y = 32$$
$$y = -8$$

To use the substitution method, you would have to solve for one of the variables first. Because of the structure of the equations, elimination is an easier method.

The solution is (–3, –8).

Try It! **4.** What is the solution of each system of equations? Explain your choice of solution method.

a. $6x + 12y = -6$
$3x - 2y = -27$

b. $3x - 2y = 38$
$x = 6 - y$

CONCEPT SUMMARY Elimination vs. Substitution

	Substitution	Elimination
WORDS	When one equation is already solved for one variable, or if it is easy to solve for one variable, use substitution.	When you can multiply one or both equations by a constant to get like coefficients that are opposite, use elimination.
ALGEBRA	$3x + y = 8$ $x = 2y - 2$ $3(2y - 2) + y = 8$ $6y - 6 + y = 8$ $7y = 14$ $y = 2$ $x = 2(2) - 2$ $= 2$	$3x - 7y = 16$ Multiply by 5. $15x - 35y = 80$ $5x - 4y = 19$ Multiply by -3. $-15x + 12y = -57$ $0 - 23y = 23$ $y = -1$ $3x - 7(-1) = 16$ $3x = 9$ $x = 3$

Do You UNDERSTAND?

1. ESSENTIAL QUESTION Why does the elimination method work when solving a system of equations?

2. **Error Analysis** Esteban tries to solve the following system.

   $7x - 4y = -12$

   $x - 2y = 4$

   His first step is to multiply the second equation by 3.

   $7x - 4y = -12$

   $3x - 6y = 12$

   Then he adds the equations to eliminate a term. What is Esteban's error?

3. **Construct Arguments** How can you determine whether two systems of equations are equivalent?

4. **Mathematical Connections** The sum of 5 times the width of a rectangle and twice its length is 26 units. The difference of 15 times the width and three times the length is 6 units. Write and solve a system of equations to find the length and width of the rectangle.

Do You KNOW HOW?

Solve each system of equations.

5. $4x - 2y = -2$
   $3x + 2y = -12$

6. $3x + 2y = 4$
   $3x + 6y = -24$

7. $4x - 3y = -9$
   $3x + 2y = -11$

8. $x - 3y = -4$
   $2x - 6y = 6$

9. Ella is a landscape photographer. One weekend at her gallery she sells a total of 52 prints for a total of $2,975. How many of each size print did Ella sell?

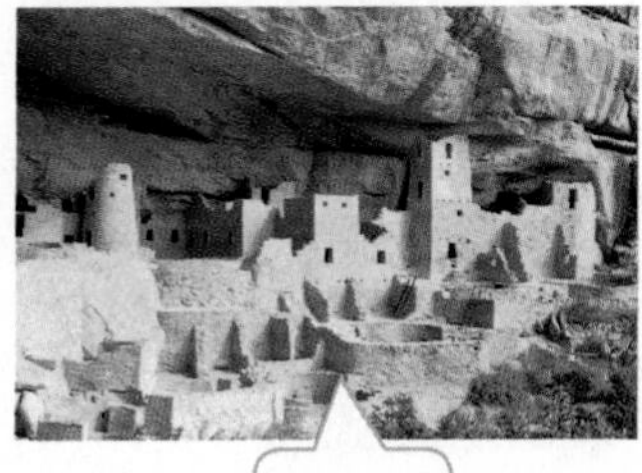

PRACTICE & PROBLEM SOLVING

Scan for Multimedia | Practice | Tutorial | Additional Exercises Available Online

UNDERSTAND

10. **Use Structure** How does the structure of a system of equations help you choose which solution method to use?

11. **Generalize** Consider the system of equations.

    $Ax + By = C$

    $Px + Qy = R$

    If the system has infinitely many solutions, how are the coefficients A, B, C, P, Q, and R related? If the system has no solution, how are the coefficients related?

12. **Use Appropriate Tools** Write and solve a system of equations for the graph shown.

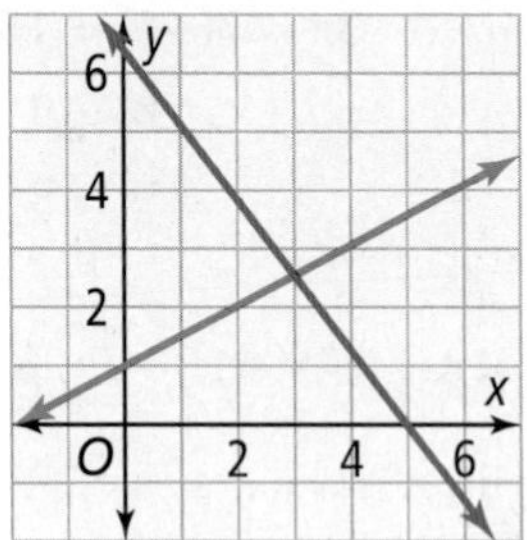

13. **Error Analysis** Describe and correct the error a student made in finding the solution to the system of equations.

    $2x - y = -1$

    $x - y = -4$

$2x - y = -1$
$-1(x - y) = -4$

$2x - y = -1$
$-x + y = -4$
$x = -5$

$2(-5) - y = -1$
$-10 - y = -1$
$-y = 9$

The solution is $(-5, -9)$.

14. **Use Structure** Explain the advantages of using substitution to solve the system of equations instead of elimination.

    $x = 6 + y$

    $48 = 2x + 2y$

PRACTICE

Solve each system of equations. SEE EXAMPLES 1 AND 3

15. $x - y = 4$
    $2x + y = 5$

16. $x - 2y = -2$
    $3x + 2y = 30$

17. $3x + 2y = 8$
    $x + 4y = -4$

18. $x - 2y = 1$
    $2x + 3y = -12$

19. $7x - 4y = -12$
    $x - 2y = 4$

20. $5x + 6y = -6$
    $7x - 3y = -54$

21. $2x + 5y = -20$
    $3x - 2y = -11$

22. $4x - 3y = 17$
    $2x - 5y = 5$

Is each pair of systems of equations equivalent? Explain. SEE EXAMPLE 2

23. $3x - 9y = 5$, $6x + 2y = 18$ $6x - 9y = 10$, $6x + 2y = 18$

24. $4y + 2x = -7$, $2y - 6x = 8$ $4y + 2x = -7$, $4y - 12x = 16$

25. $5x + 3y = 19$, $2x + 4y = 20$ $10x + 6y = 38$, $10x + 20y = 100$

Write and solve a system of equations to model each situation. SEE EXAMPLE 3

26. Two pizzas and four sandwiches cost \$62. Four pizzas and ten sandwiches cost \$140. How much does each pizza and sandwich cost?

27. At a clothing store, 3 shirts and 8 hats cost \$65. The cost for 2 shirts and 2 hats is \$30. How much does each shirt and hat cost?

Solve each system. Explain your choice of solution method. SEE EXAMPLE 4

28. $6x - 5y = -1$
    $6x + 4y = -10$

29. $8x - 4y = -4$
    $x = y - 4$

30. $5x - 2y = -6$
    $3x - 4y = -26$

31. $2x - 3y = 14$
    $5x + 4y = 12$

PRACTICE & PROBLEM SOLVING

APPLY

32. Construct Arguments DeShawn and Chris are solving the following system of equations.

$x - 4y = -8$

$3x + 4y = 0$

DeShawn says that the first step should be to add the two equations to eliminate y. Chris says that the first step should be to multiply the first equation by -3 so you can eliminate the x-terms.

Who is correct? Explain.

33. Generalize Describe a system of equations where each solution method would be the most efficient to use.

a. Graphing

b. Substitution

c. Elimination

34. Model With Mathematics Two groups of friends go to a baseball game. Each group plans to share the snacks shown. What is the price of one drink and one pretzel?

35. Higher Order Thinking Determine the value of n that makes a system of equations with a solution that has a y-value of 2.

$5x + 6y = 32$

$2x + ny = 18$

36. A group of 30 students from the senior class charters a bus to an amusement park. The total amount they spend on the bus and admission to the park for each student is $1,770.

A group of 50 students from the junior class also go to the amusement park, but they require two buses. If the group from the junior class spent $3,190 in total, how much does it cost to charter one bus?

ASSESSMENT PRACTICE

37. Solve the system of equations using elimination. Complete the solution of the system of equations.

$4x + 3y = 6$

$2x - 5y = 16$

$x =$ ________ and $y =$ ________

38. SAT/ACT A rental company can set up 3 small tents and 1 large tent in 115 min. They can set up 2 small tents and 2 large tents in 130 min. How much time is required to set up a small tent?

Ⓐ 15 min

Ⓑ 25 min

Ⓒ 35 min

Ⓓ 40 min

39. Performance Task At Concessions Unlimited, four granola bars and three drinks cost $12.50. Two granola bars and five drinks cost $15.00.

At Snacks To Go, three granola bars and three drinks cost $10.50. Four granola bars and two drinks cost $10.00.

Part A Write a system of equations for each concession stand that models the price of its items.

Part B Solve each system of equations. What do the solutions represent?

Part C You decide to open a new concessions stand and sell granola bars and drinks. Determine a price for each item that differ from the prices at Snacks To Go. Then write a system of equations to model the prices at your snack bar.

4-4 Linear Inequalities in Two Variables

PearsonRealize.com

I CAN… graph solutions to linear inequalities in two variables.

VOCABULARY

- linear inequality in two variables
- solution of a linear inequality in two variables

MODEL & DISCUSS

A flatbed trailer carrying a load can have a maximum total height of 13 feet, 6 inches. The photograph shows the height of the trailer before a load is placed on top. What are the possible heights of loads that could be carried on the trailer?

A. What type of model could represent this situation? Explain.

B. Will the type of model you chose show all the possible heights of the loads without going over the maximum height? Explain.

C. Reason Interpret the solutions of the model. How many solutions are there? Explain.

ESSENTIAL QUESTION

How does the graph of a linear inequality in two variables help you identify the solutions of the inequality?

CONCEPTUAL UNDERSTANDING

EXAMPLE 1 Understand an Inequality in Two Variables

STUDY TIP
You used substitution to test whether an ordered pair is a solution of an equation. You can do the same to test whether an ordered pair is a solution of an inequality.

A. What is the solution of the inequality $y \leq x - 1$?

The inequality $y \leq x - 1$ is an example of a **linear inequality in two variables**. It has the same form as a linear equation but uses an inequality symbol. The **solution of a linear inequality in two variables** is all ordered pairs (x, y) that make the inequality true.

You can plot these ordered pairs on a coordinate plane to understand the solution of the inequality.

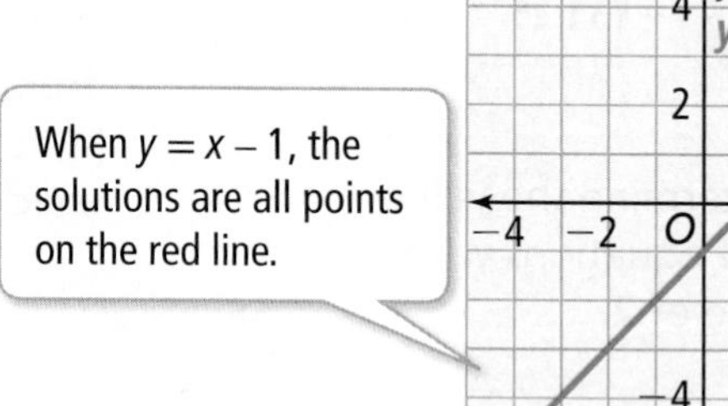

Now imagine drawing the blue ray for *every* x-value.

The solution of the inequality is all points on the line (called a *boundary line*) and in the shaded region.

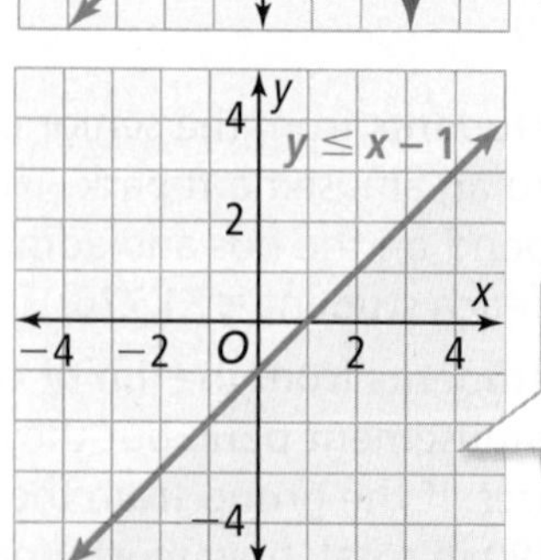

CONTINUED ON THE NEXT PAGE

EXAMPLE 1 CONTINUED

B. What is the solution of the inequality $y > x - 1$?

The process for finding the solution of $y > x - 1$ is similar to finding the solution of $y \leq x - 1$. For each x, find all values of y that are greater than $x - 1$.

COMMON ERROR
You may think that the graph of any line is solid, but for inequalities it is only a solid line when the inequality symbol is $\geq$ or $\leq$.

Since the inequality uses *greater than*, shade *above* the line.

The boundary line is a dashed line to indicate that points on it are *not* part of the solution.

The solution of the inequality is all points in the shaded region.

Try It! **1.** Describe the graph of the solutions of each inequality.

a. $y < -3x + 5$ **b.** $y \geq -3x + 5$

APPLICATION

EXAMPLE 2 Rewrite an Inequality to Graph It

The Science Club sells T-shirts and key chains to raise money. How many T-shirts and key chains could they sell to meet or exceed their goal?

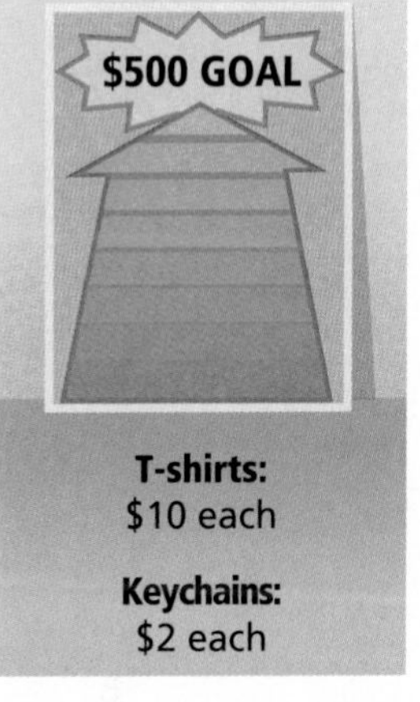

Formulate Let x represent the number of T-shirts sold and y represent the number of key chains sold. The total amount of money they make must equal or exceed $500.

$$10x + 2y \geq 500$$

Compute Solve the inequality for y.

$$10x + 2y \geq 500$$
$$2y \geq -10x + 500$$
$$y \geq -5x + 250$$

Graph the inequality.

Draw a solid line since the inequality is greater than or equal to.

Shade above the line since the slope-intercept form of the inequality uses $\geq$.

Interpret Any point in the shaded region or on the boundary line is a solution of the inequality. However, since it is not possible to sell a negative number of T-shirts or key chains, you must exclude negative values for each.

Try It! **2.** Will the Science Club meet their goal if they sell 30 T-shirts and 90 key chains? Explain in terms of the graph of the inequality.

EXAMPLE 3 Write an Inequality From a Graph

What inequality does the graph represent?

Determine the equation of the boundary line.

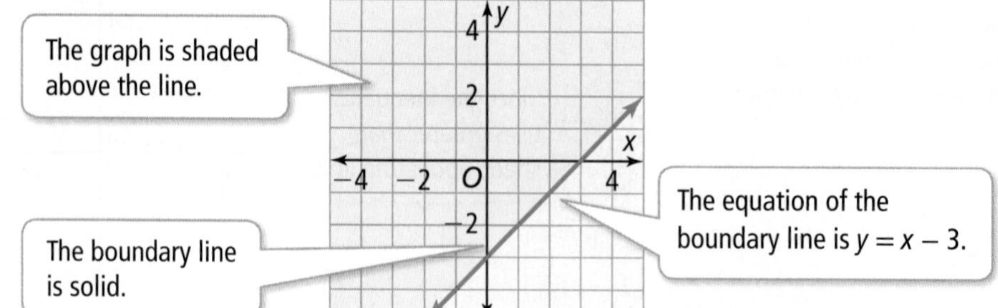

LOOK FOR RELATIONSHIPS
The graph gives you information about the inequality. What does the solid line tell you about the inequality?

The graph is shaded above the boundary line and the boundary line is solid, so the inequality symbol is $\geq$.

The inequality shown by the graph is $y \geq x - 3$.

Try It! **3.** What inequality does each graph represent?

a.

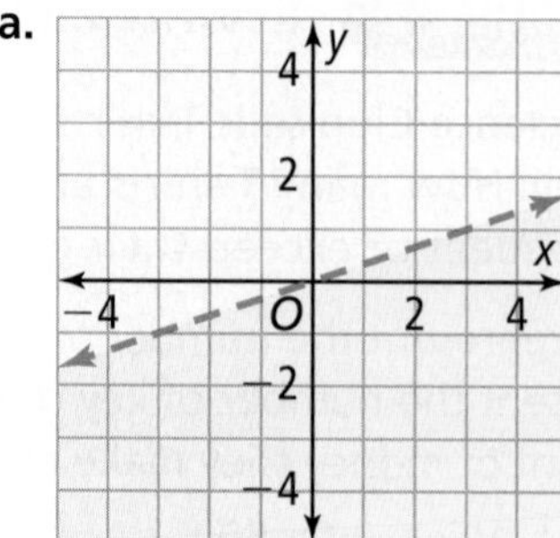

b.

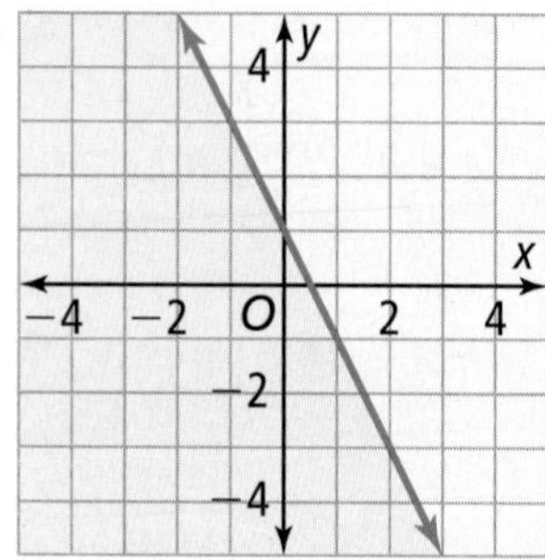

EXAMPLE 4 Inequalities in One Variable in the Coordinate Plane

What is the graph of the inequality in the coordinate plane?

A. $x \geq 3$?

You have graphed the solution of a one-variable inequality on a number line.

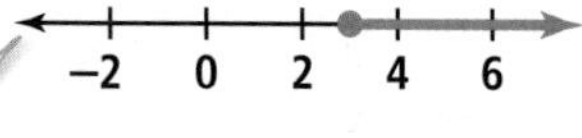

solution of $x \geq 3$ on a number line

You can write $x \geq 3$ as $x + 0 \cdot y \geq 3$. The inequality is true for all y, whenever $x \geq 3$.

Imagine stacking copies of the solution on the number line on top of each other, one for each y-value. The combined solutions graphed on the number line make up the shaded region on the coordinate plane.

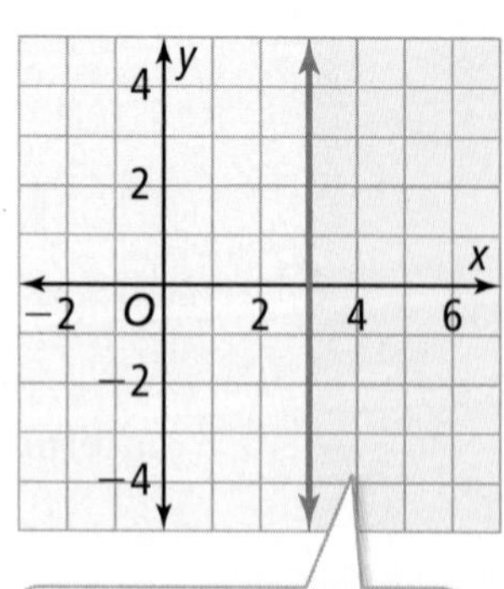

solution of $x \geq 3$ on a coordinate plane

CONTINUED ON THE NEXT PAGE

EXAMPLE 4 CONTINUED

B. $y < 2$?

You can graph the solution of the inequality on a vertical number line.

solution of $y < 2$ on a vertical number line

Notice that the solution on the number line matches the shaded area for any vertical line on the coordinate grid. This is because x can be any number, and the inequality will still be $y < 2$.

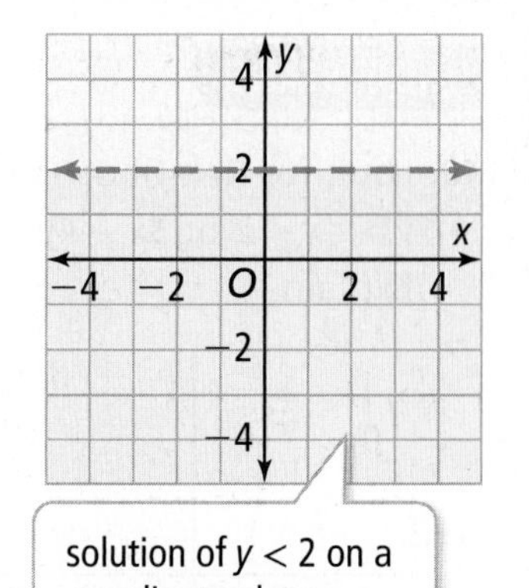

solution of $y < 2$ on a coordinate plane

LOOK FOR RELATIONSHIPS
How are the open circle and the dashed line similar?

Try It! **4.** Graph each inequality in the coordinate plane.

a. $y > -2$ **b.** $x \leq 1$

CONCEPT SUMMARY Linear Inequalities in Two Variables

ALGEBRA

$y \geq -\frac{3}{5}x + 1$

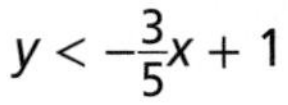

$y < -\frac{3}{5}x + 1$

GRAPH

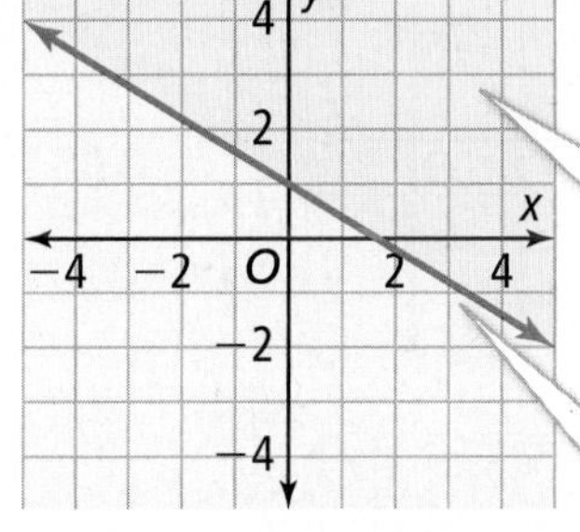

Solutions are points in the shaded region.

Solutions are also points on the solid line.

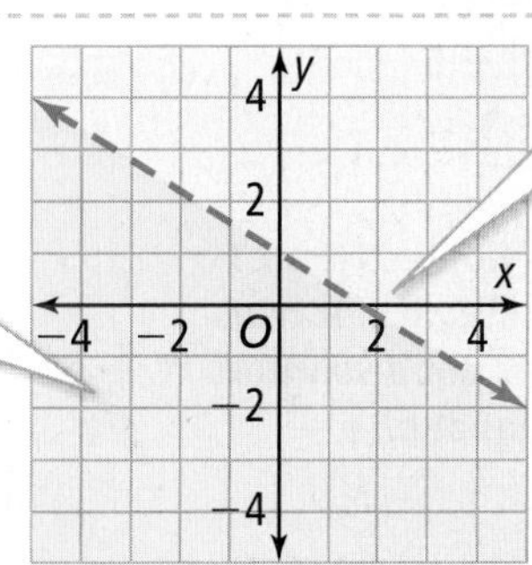

No solutions are on the dashed line.

Do You UNDERSTAND?

1. **ESSENTIAL QUESTION** How does the graph of a linear inequality in two variables help you identify the solutions of the inequality?

2. **Communicate Precisely** How many solutions does a linear inequality in two variables have?

3. **Vocabulary** In what form do you write one of the *solutions of an inequality in two variables*?

4. **Error Analysis** A student claims that the inequality $y < 1$ cannot be graphed on a coordinate grid since it has only one variable. Explain the error the student made.

Do You KNOW HOW?

Tell whether each ordered pair is a solution of the inequality $y > x + 1$.

5. (0, 1)
6. (3, 5)

Graph each inequality in the coordinate plane.

7. $y \geq 2x$
8. $y < x - 2$

9. What inequality is shown by the graph?

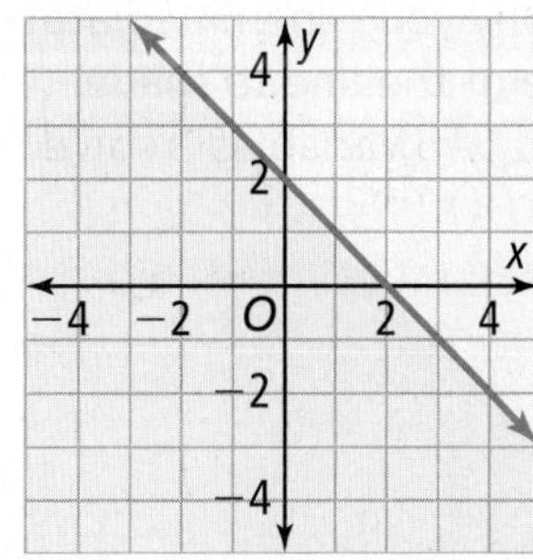

PRACTICE & PROBLEM SOLVING

UNDERSTAND

10. **Look for Relationships** Which inequality, $y > \frac{3}{4}x - 2$ or $3x - 4y < 8$, is shown by the graph? Explain.

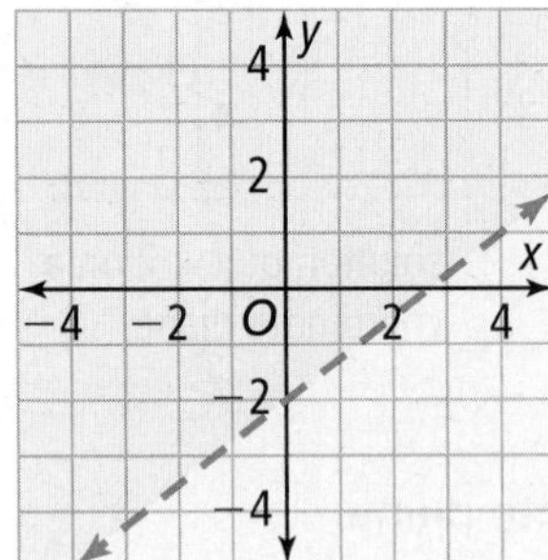

11. **Error Analysis** Describe and correct the error a student made in determining whether the ordered pair (1, 1) is a solution of the inequality $y \le -4x + 5$.

> $y \le -4x + 5$
> $1 \le -4(1) + 5$
> $1 \le -4 + 5$
> $1 \le 1$
> Since 1 is not less than 1, the inequality is not true. So, (1, 1) is not a solution of the inequality. ✗

12. **Higher Order Thinking** What is the graph of the inequality $x < y + 3$? How is this graph different from the graph of the inequality $y < x + 3$?

13. **Reason** Write an inequality in two variables for which (3, 7) and (−2, 3) are solutions.

14. **Mathematical Connections** Compare the graph of a linear inequality $x < 4$ on a number line with its graph on a coordinate plane. How are they similar?

15. **Generalize** Explain why you can immediately determine which side of the line to shade when an inequality in two variables is solved for y.

PRACTICE

Graph each inequality in the coordinate plane.

SEE EXAMPLES 1, 2 AND 4

16. $y \ge -2x + 3$
17. $y < x - 6$
18. $y \le \frac{2}{3}x - 1$
19. $y > x - 2$
20. $y < -0.5x + 2$
21. $y \ge 1.5x - 4$
22. $2x > 12$
23. $-2y \le 6$

What inequality is shown by each graph?

SEE EXAMPLE 3

24.

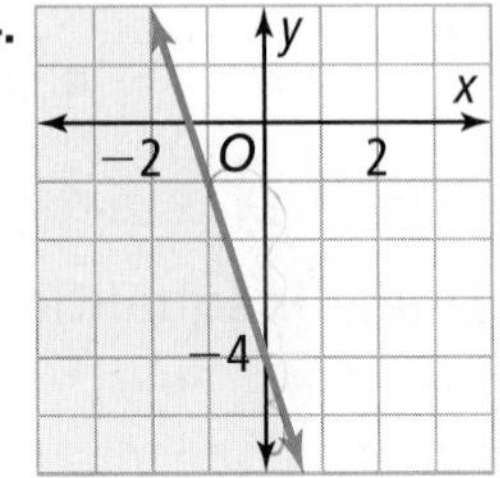

25.

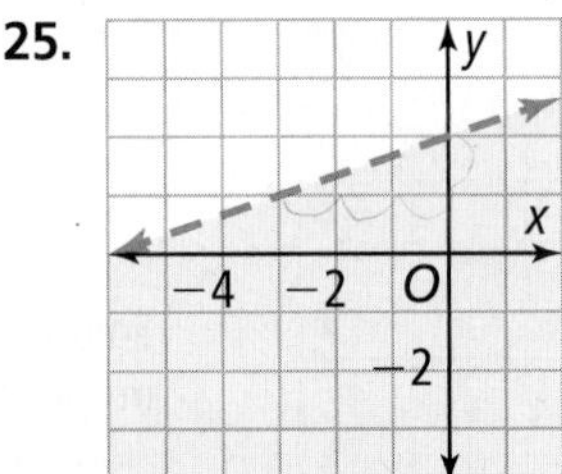

26.

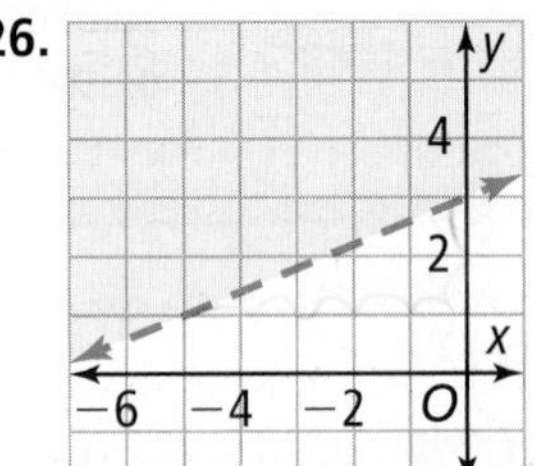

27.

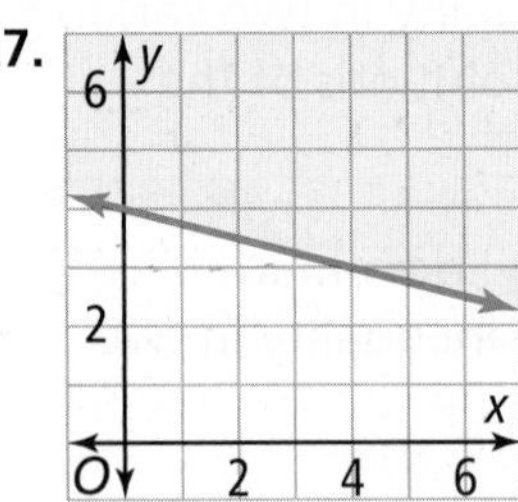

PRACTICE & PROBLEM SOLVING

APPLY

28. Make Sense and Persevere A school has \$600 to buy molecular sets for students to build models.

a. Write and graph an inequality that represents the number of each type of molecular set the school can buy.

b. Suppose the school decides to buy 20 of the large kits. How many of the small kits can the school now afford?

29. Model With Mathematics A freight elevator can hold a maximum weight of 2,500 pounds. A 180-pound person has a load of boxes to deliver. Some of the boxes weigh 25 pounds each and some weigh 60 pounds each.

a. Write and graph an inequality that represents the number of boxes the elevator can hold in one trip if the person is not in the elevator.

b. Write and graph an inequality that represents the number of boxes the elevator can hold in one trip if the person rides in the elevator.

c. Compare the graphs of the two inequalities.

30. Make Sense and Persevere A soccer team holds a banquet at the end of the season. The team needs to seat at least 100 people and plans to use two different-sized tables. A small table can seat 6 people, and a large table can seat 8 people. Write a linear inequality that represents the numbers of each size table the team needs. Graph the inequality. If the school has 5 small tables and 9 large tables, will this be enough for the banquet?

ASSESSMENT PRACTICE

31. Choose *Yes* or *No* to tell whether each ordered pair is a solution of the inequality $y > 7x - 3$.

	Yes	No
a. (2, 15)	❑	❑
b. (−3, −15)	❑	❑
c. (0, −3)	❑	❑
d. (1, 5)	❑	❑

32. SAT/ACT What inequality is shown by the graph?

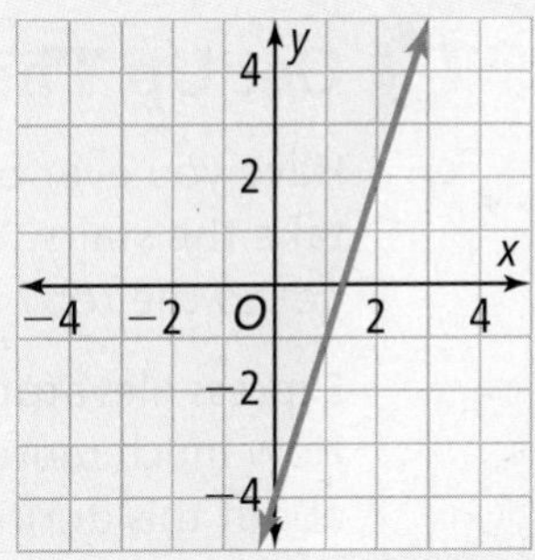

Ⓐ $y > 3x - 4$

Ⓑ $y > 4x - 3$

Ⓒ $y \geq 3x - 4$

Ⓓ $y \geq 4x - 3$

33. Performance Task A phone has a certain amount of storage space remaining. The average photo uses 3.6 MB of space and the average song uses 4 MB of space.

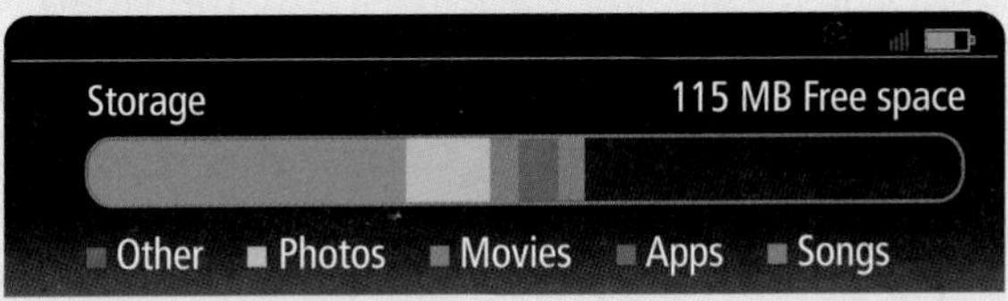

Part A Write a linear inequality to represent how many additional photos x and songs y the phone can store.

Part B Graph the inequality. Describe how the number of photos that are stored affects the number of songs that can be stored.

Part C Does the graph make sense outside of the first quadrant? Explain.

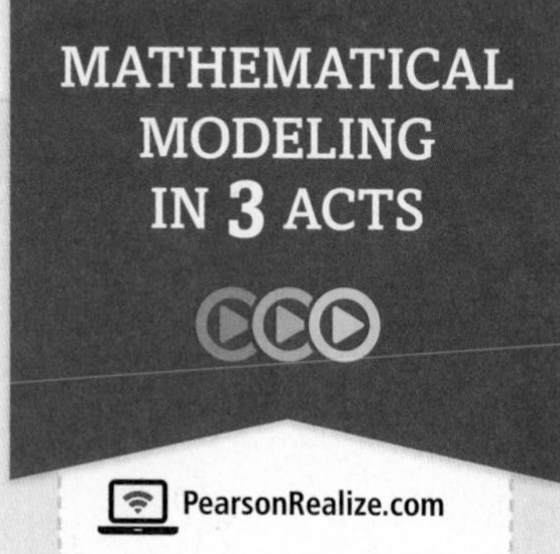

PearsonRealize.com

Get Up There!

Have you ever been to the top of a skyscraper? If so, you probably didn't take the stairs. You probably took an elevator. How long did it take you to get to the top? Did you take an express elevator?

Express elevators travel more quickly because they do not stop at every floor. How much more quickly can you get to the top in an express elevator? Think about this during the Mathematical Modeling in 3 Acts lesson.

ACT 1 Identify the Problem

1. What is the first question that comes to mind after watching the video?
2. Write down the main question you will answer about what you saw in the video.
3. Make an initial conjecture that answers this main question.
4. Explain how you arrived at your conjecture.
5. What information will be useful to know to answer the main question? How can you get it? How will you use that information?

ACT 2 Develop a Model

6. Use the math that you have learned in this Topic to refine your conjecture.

ACT 3 Interpret the Results

7. Did your refined conjecture match the actual answer exactly? If not, what might explain the difference?

Activity Assess

4-5 Systems of Linear Inequalities

PearsonRealize.com

I CAN… graph and solve a system of linear inequalities.

VOCABULARY

- solution of a system of linear inequalities
- system of linear inequalities

EXPLORE & REASON

The graph shows the equations $y = x - 1$ and $y = -2x + 4$.

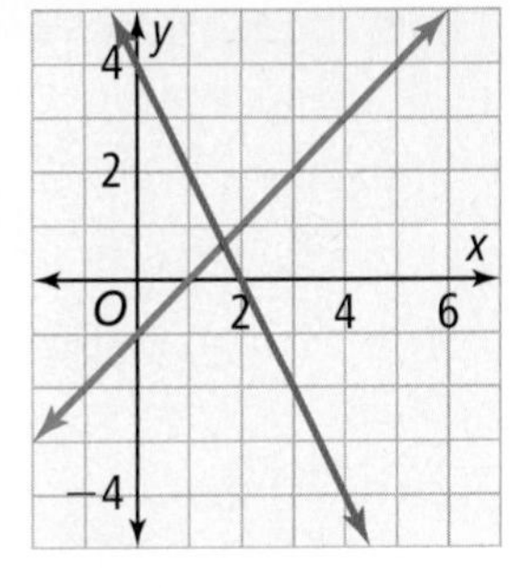

A. Choose some points above and below the line $y = x - 1$. Which of them are solutions to $y > x - 1$? Which are solutions to $y < x - 1$?

B. Choose some points above and below the line $y = -2x + 4$. Which of them are solutions to $y > -2x + 4$? Which are solutions to $y < -2x + 4$?

C. Look for Relationships The two lines divide the plane into four regions. How can you describe each region in terms of the inequalities in parts A and B?

ESSENTIAL QUESTION

How is the graph of a system of linear inequalities related to the solutions of the system of inequalities?

CONCEPTUAL UNDERSTANDING

EXAMPLE 1 Graph a System of Inequalities

What are the solutions to the system of linear inequalities?

A. $y > x - 2$
$y \leq -x + 1$

A **system of linear inequalities** is made up of two or more linear inequalities. **Solutions of a system of linear inequalities** are ordered pairs that make *all* of the inequalities true.

Look at the solutions of each inequality separately.

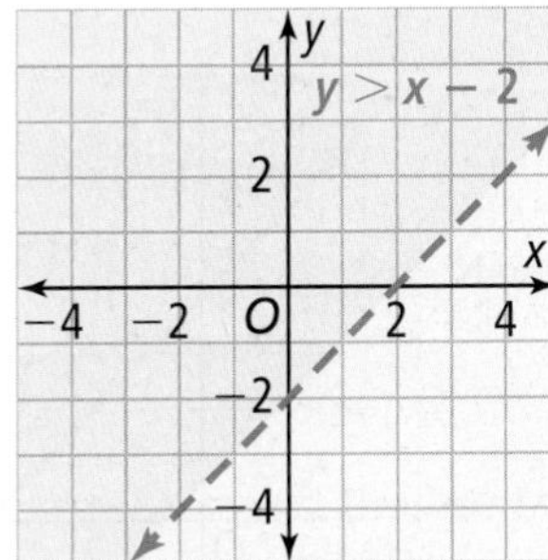

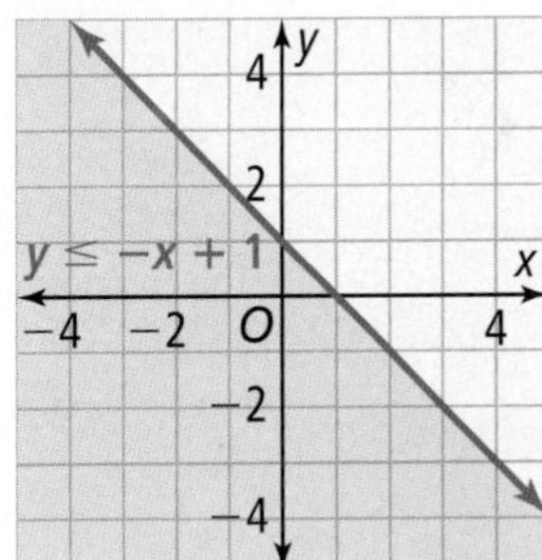

Now find points that are solutions to *both* inequalities.

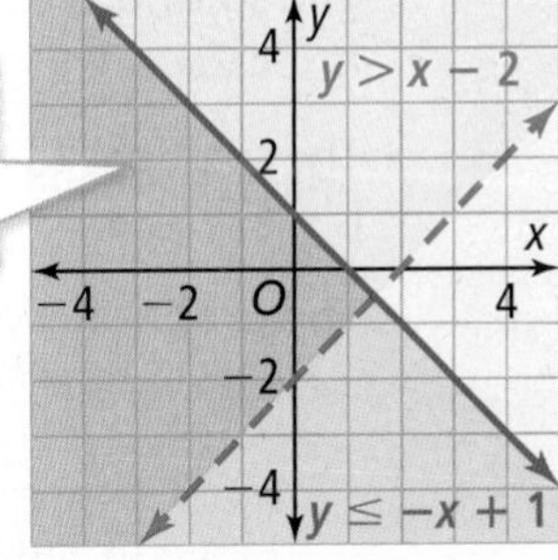

COMMON ERROR
Points on the solid boundary line for $y \leq -x + 1$ are solutions of the system only when they are also in the region representing the solutions to $y > x - 2$.

The solutions of the system of linear inequalities are the ordered pairs where the regions overlap.

CONTINUED ON THE NEXT PAGE

EXAMPLE 1 CONTINUED

B. $y \geq -x + 2$
$y < -x - 2$

Graph each inequality.

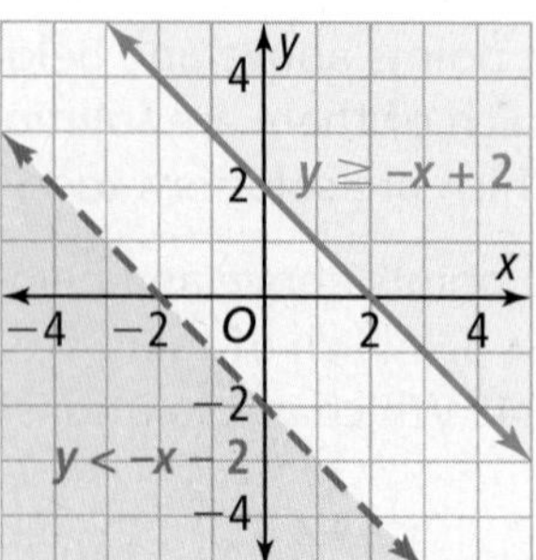

Since the slopes of the boundary lines are equal and their *y*-intercepts are different, they are parallel, and do not intersect.

The graphs do not overlap, so there is no solution to this system of inequalities.

Try It! **1.** Graph each system of inequalities.

a. $y < 2x$
$y > -3$

b. $y \geq -2x + 1$
$y > x + 2$

EXAMPLE 2 Write a System of Inequalities From a Graph

USE STRUCTURE
What information can you determine from the graphs of the lines? What information can you determine from the shaded region of the graph?

What system of inequalities is shown by the graph?

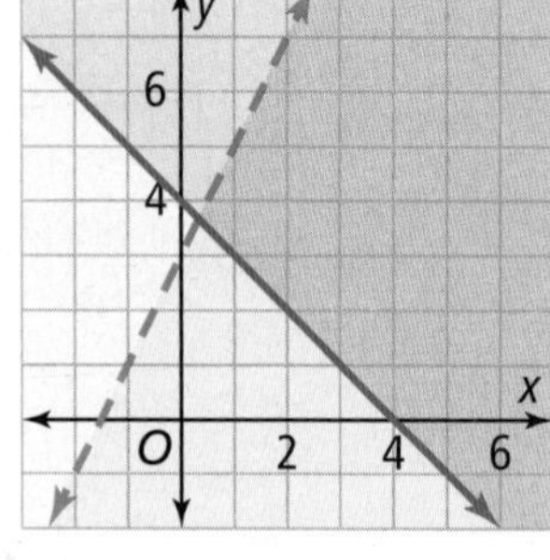

Determine the equation of each line using the slope and *y*-intercept.

The slope of the red boundary line is 2 and it has a *y*-intercept of 3.

The slope of the blue boundary line is −1 and it has a *y*-intercept of 4.

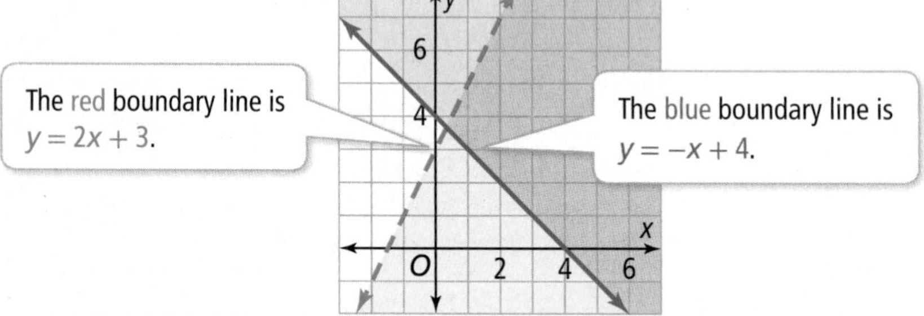

The solutions to the system are below the dashed red line, so one inequality is $y < 2x + 3$.

The solutions to the system are above the solid blue line, so the other inequality is $y \geq -x + 4$.

The graph shows the system of inequalities, $y < 2x + 3$ and $y \geq -x + 4$.

CONTINUED ON THE NEXT PAGE

EXAMPLE 2 CONTINUED

Try It! **2.** What system of inequalities is shown by each graph?

a.

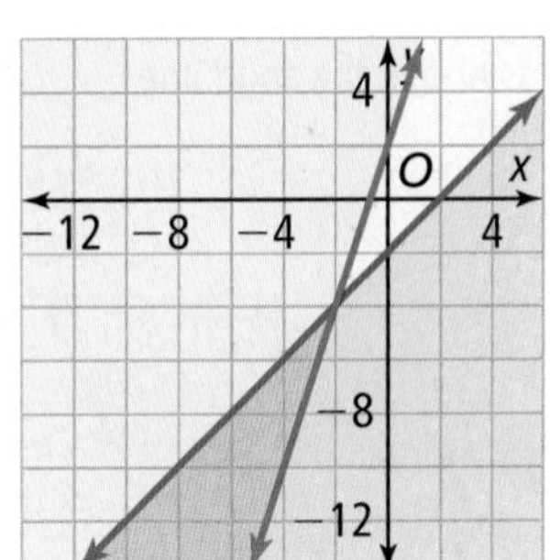

b.

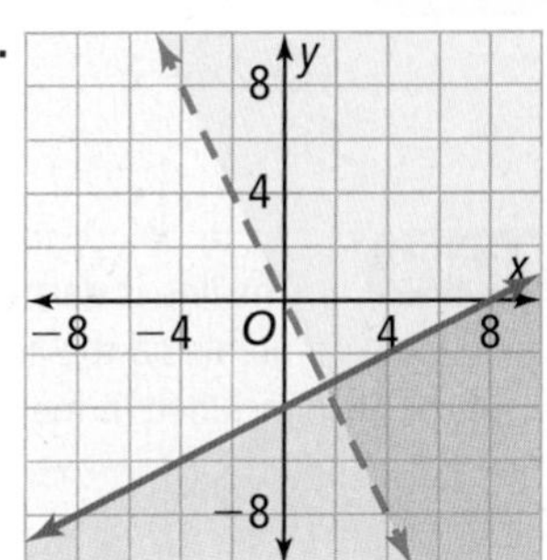

APPLICATION

EXAMPLE 3 Use a System of Inequalities

Malia has \$500 to purchase water bottles and pairs of socks for a fundraiser for her school's cross-country team. She needs to buy a total of at least 200 items without buying too many of just one item. What graph shows the possible numbers of water bottles and pairs of socks that Malia should buy?

Formulate Let x represent the number of water bottles and y represent the number of pairs of socks that Malia buys.

Write a system of inequalities.

$x + y \geq 200$ ········ Malia needs to buy *at least* 200 items.

$2x + 3y \leq 500$ ········ Malia can spend *at most* \$500.

Compute Graph the system of inequalities.

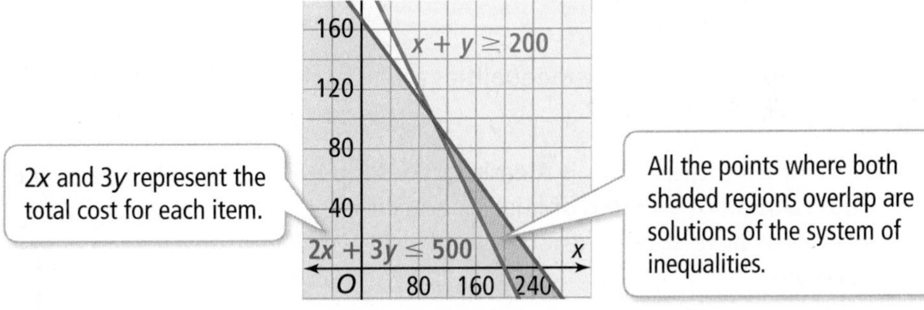

Interpret Malia could buy any combination of numbers of water bottles and pairs of socks represented by points in the overlapping region. However, she should be careful to choose a number of each item close to what she expects to sell. For example, she could buy 250 water bottles and 0 pairs of socks, but a more even distribution of items might be preferable.

Try It! **3.** Use the graph in Example 3 to determine if Malia can buy 75 water bottles and 100 pairs of socks. Explain.

Concept Summary

CONCEPT SUMMARY Systems of Linear Inequalities

ALGEBRA $y < x + 1$ .... All points below the dashed line

$y \geq 2x - 2$ .... All points above the solid line

GRAPH

The line is dashed so the points on the line are not included in the solution.

The solution of the system of linear inequalities is the shaded region.

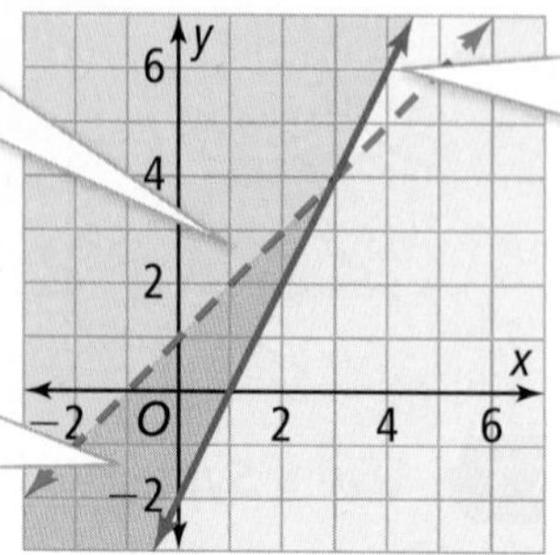

The line is solid so the points on the line may be included in the solution.

Do You UNDERSTAND?

1. ESSENTIAL QUESTION How is the graph of a system of linear inequalities related to the solutions of the system of inequalities?

2. **Error Analysis** A student says that (0, 1) is a solution to the following system of inequalities.
   $y > x$
   $y > 2x + 1$
   She says that (0, 1) is a solution because it is a solution of $y > x$. Explain the error that the student made.

3. **Vocabulary** How many inequalities are in a *system of inequalities*?

4. **Use Appropriate Tools** Is it easier to describe the solution of a system of linear inequalities in words or to show it using a graph? Explain.

Do You KNOW HOW?

Identify the boundary lines for each system of inequalities.

5. $y > -3x + 4$
   $y \leq 8x + 1$

6. $y < -6x$
   $y \geq 10x - 3$

Graph each system of inequalities.

7. $y \leq -3x$
   $y < 2$

8. $y \geq x - 4$
   $y < -x$

9. What system of inequalities is shown by the graph?

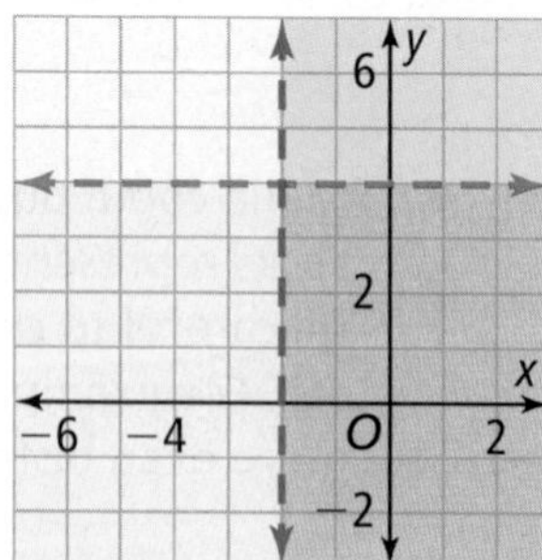

Scan for Multimedia

Practice Tutorial

Additional Exercises Available Online

UNDERSTAND

10. **Look for Relationships** How does a real-world situation that is best described by a system of linear inequalities differ from a real-world situation that is best described by a single linear inequality?

11. **Error Analysis** Describe and correct the error a student made in writing the system of inequalities represented by the graph shown below.

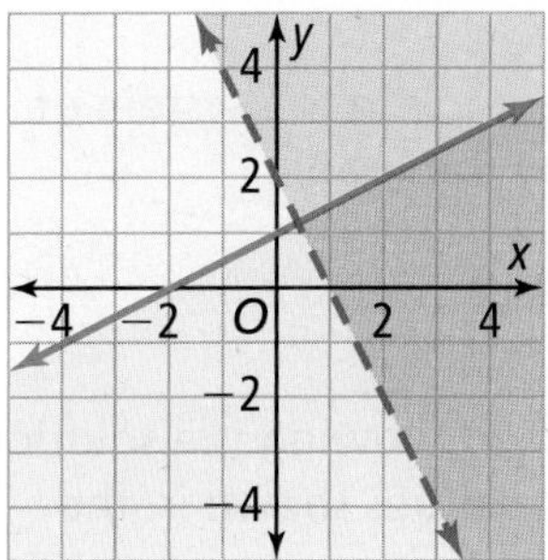

The red boundary line is $y = 0.5x + 1$.
Since the line is solid, use $\leq$ or $\geq$.
The blue boundary line is $y = -2x + 2$.
Since the line is dashed, use $<$ or $>$.

$y \leq 0.5x + 1$
$y < -2x + 2$

12. **Mathematical Connections** How is a system of two linear inequalities in two variables similar to a system of two linear equations in two variables? How is it different?

13. **Reason** In Example 3, the inequality made sense only in the first quadrant. What two inequalities could you add to the system to indicate this? Explain.

14. **Higher Order Thinking** Can you write a system of three inequalities that has no solutions? Explain.

15. **Reason** Could the solutions of a system of inequalities be a rectangular region? If so, give an example.

PRACTICE

Graph each system of inequalities.
SEE EXAMPLES 1 AND 3

16. $y < 2x + 1$
$y \leq -x - 4$

17. $y \leq 3x - 2$
$y > x - 2$

18. $y \geq -\frac{1}{2}x + 1$
$y > x + 3$

19. $y < \frac{1}{3}x$
$y \geq -4x + 1$

20. $2x + 3y < 5$
$y \geq 2x - 3$

21. $x + 4y > 3$
$x - y \leq 2$

22. $y > 0.3x + 2$
$y < -0.2x + 1$

23. $y \leq 0.25x - 4$
$y \geq -x - 3$

24. $y < -2x - 5$
$4x - y < 3$

25. $-6x + 4y \geq 8$
$y < -x - 1$

26. $x > 1$
$y < 2x - 3$
$y > x$

27. $y \leq -3x$
$y > -x - 2$
$y > 2$

What system of inequalities is shown by each graph? SEE EXAMPLES 2 AND 3

28.
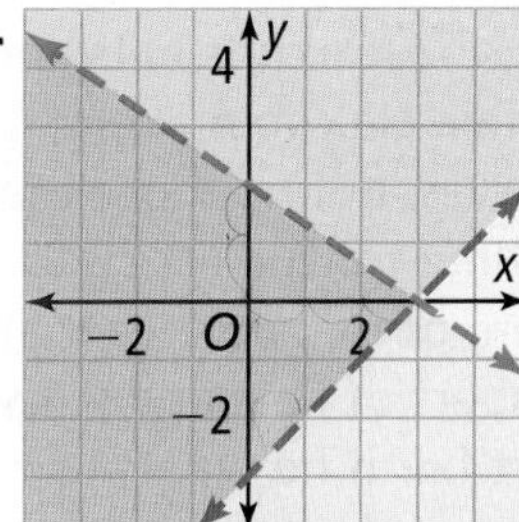

29.
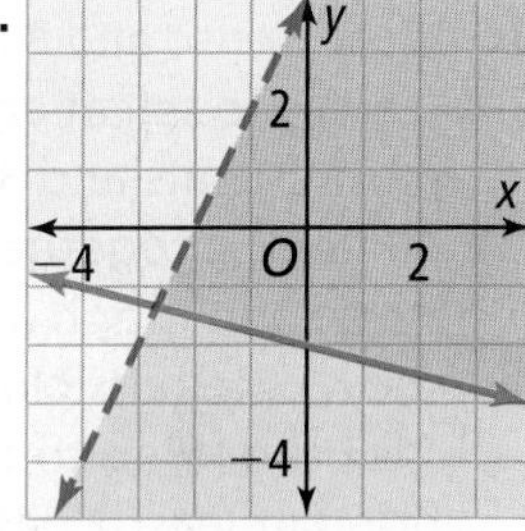

30.
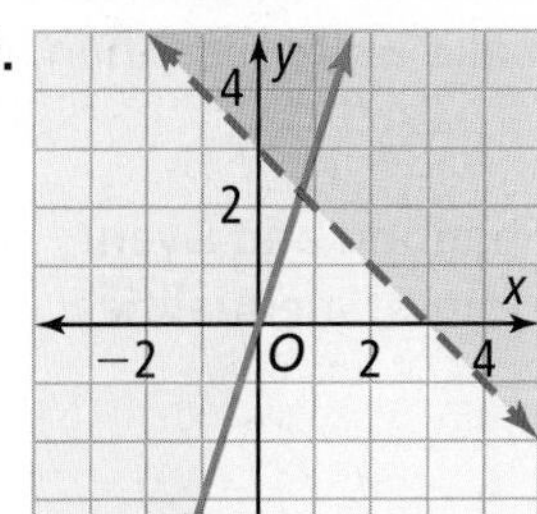

31.
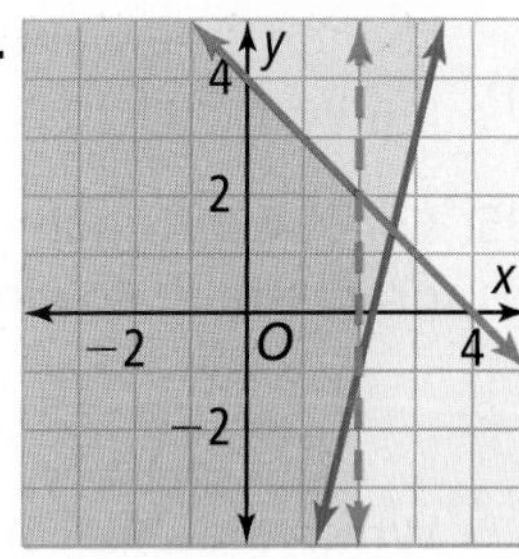

PRACTICE & PROBLEM SOLVING

APPLY

32. **Make Sense and Persevere** A group of at most 10 people wants to purchase a combination of seats in Section A and Section B, but does not want to spend more than \$450. Graph the system of inequalities that represents the possible ticket combinations they could buy. List three possible combinations they could buy.

33. **Model With Mathematics** Kendra earns \$10 per hour babysitting and \$15 per hour providing tech support. Her goal is to save at least \$1,000 by the end of the month while not working more than 80 hours. Write and graph a system of inequalities that shows how many hours Kendra could work at each job to meet her goal. What is the fewest number of hours she could work and still meet her goal?

34. **Make Sense and Persevere** Alex knits hats and scarves to sell at an art fair. He can make at most 20 hats and 30 scarves, but no more than 40 items altogether, in time for the art fair. Write and graph a system of inequalities that shows the possible numbers of hats and scarves Alex can bring to the art fair if he wants to bring at least 25 items. How do the solutions change if he wants to make more hats than scarves? Explain.

35. **Construct Arguments** Shannon and Dyani graph the following system of inequalities.

$y \geq \frac{1}{2}x - 1$

$x - y > 1$

Which graph is correct? Explain.

Shannon's graph

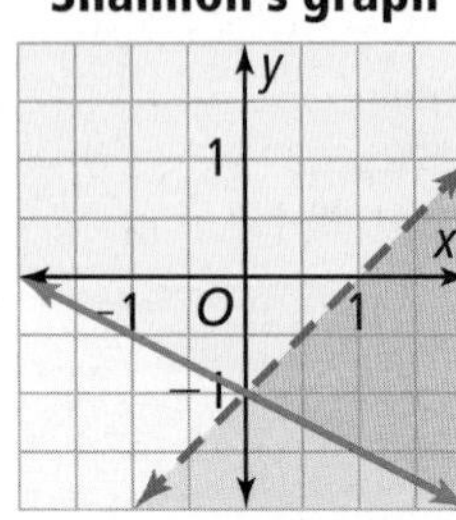

Dyani's graph

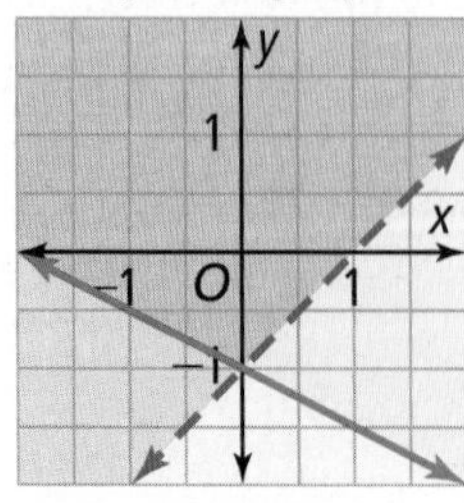

ASSESSMENT PRACTICE

Use the graph to answer Exercises 36 and 37.

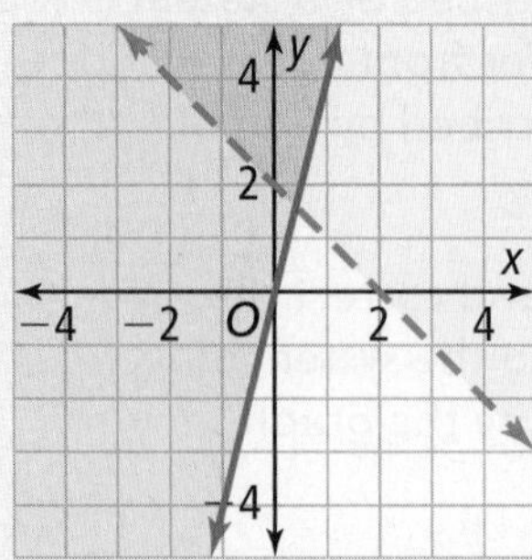

36. Fill in the blanks to complete the system of inequalities shown by the graph.

y ___ $-x +$ ___

y ___ $4x$

37. **SAT/ACT** Which of the following is a solution of the system of inequalities shown in the graph?

Ⓐ (3, 2)
Ⓑ (−3, 2)
Ⓒ (−1, 4)
Ⓓ (1, −4)

38. **Performance Task** A person is planning a weekly workout schedule of cardio and yoga. He has at most 12 hours per week to work out. The amounts of time he wants to spend on cardio and yoga are shown.

Part A Write a system of linear inequalities to represent this situation.

Part B Graph the system of inequalities. Is there a minimum number of hours the person will be doing cardio? Explain.

TOPIC 4

Topic Review

TOPIC ESSENTIAL QUESTION

1. How do you use systems of linear equations and inequalities to model situations and solve problems?

Vocabulary Review

Choose the correct term to complete each sentence.

2. A(n) __________ is made up of two or more inequalities.
3. A(n) __________ is an inequality that is in the same form as a linear equation in two variables, but with an inequality symbol instead of an equal sign.
4. A(n) __________ is an ordered pair that makes all of the inequalities in the system true.
5. The __________ is the set of all ordered pairs that satisfy the inequality.

- linear inequality in two variables
- solution of an inequality in two variables
- solution of a system of linear inequalities
- system of linear inequalities

Concepts & Skills Review

LESSON 4-1 Solving Systems of Equations by Graphing

Quick Review

Systems of equations can have one solution, infinitely many solutions, or no solution. Graphing a system of linear equations can result in either an approximate solution or an exact solution.

Example

What is the solution of the system of equations? Use a graph.

$y = 3x - 1$

$y = -2x + 3$

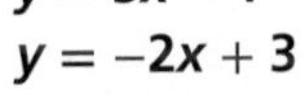

The graph intersects at one point, so the system of linear equations has one solution. Find the point of intersection. The graph intersects at (0.8, 1.4).

Check that the solution works for both equations.

$y = 3x - 1$	$y = -2x + 3$
$1.4 \stackrel{?}{=} 3(0.8) - 1$	$1.4 \stackrel{?}{=} -2(0.8) + 3$
$1.4 = 1.4$ ✓	$1.4 = 1.4$ ✓

The system of equations has one solution at (0.8, 1.4).

Practice & Problem Solving

Approximate the solution of each system of equations by graphing.

6. $y = 5x + 4$
   $y = -3x - 8$

7. $y = -3x - 7$
   $y = 1.5x + 4$

8. **Use Structure** Describe the solution set of the system of equations made by the equation $y = 1.5x + 4.5$ and the graphed line.

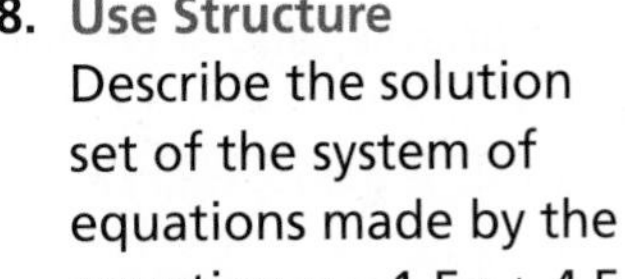

9. **Model With Mathematics** Kiyo is considering two catering companies for a party. A+ Food charges \$35 per person and \$75 to setup. Super Cater charges \$38 per person with no setup fee. Write and solve a system of equations to represent the charges for catering by each company. Which company should Kiyo use if she expects 28 guests?

LESSON 4-2 Solving Systems of Equations by Substitution

Quick Review

To use substitution to solve a system of equations, isolate the variable in one equation and substitute its value into the other equation. Solve for the variable. Then use that value to solve for the other variable.

Example

Solve the system of equations. $y = 3x - 5$, $4x - 2y = 8$

Substitute $3x - 5$ for y and solve for x.

$$4x - 2y = 8$$
$$4x - 2(3x - 5) = 8$$
$$4x - 6x + 10 = 8$$
$$-2x = -2$$
$$x = 1$$

Substitute 1 for x in either equation and solve for y.

$$y = 3x - 5$$
$$= 3(1) - 5$$
$$= -2$$

The solution of the system of equations is $(1, -2)$.

Practice & Problem Solving

Use substitution to solve each system of equations.

10. $y = 5x - 2$
    $3x - 5y = 4$

11. $y = 2x - 3$
    $y = 8 - 2x$

12. $x = 4y - 8$
    $3x - 6y = 12$

13. $y = 2.5x - 8$
    $3x + 5y = 12$

Identify whether each system of equations has infinitely many solutions or no solution.

14. $3y = 3x - 9$
    $y - 2 = x$

15. $3x - 4y = 12$
    $\frac{3}{4}x = y + 3$

16. **Mathematical Connections** A room has a perimeter of 40 feet. The length is 4 less than 2 times the width. What are the dimensions of the room?

17. **Model With Mathematics** Benson has 58 more boxed action figures than collector pins. In total he has 246 collectible items. How many of each type of collectible item does Benson own?

LESSON 4-3 Solving Systems of Equations by Elimination

Quick Review

To use elimination to solve a system of equations, multiply one or both equations by a number so that the coefficient of one variable in both equations is the same or opposite. Then add or subtract to eliminate one variable, and solve for the remaining variable.

Example

Solve the system of equations. $4x - 3y = 12$, $5x - 6y = 18$

Multiply the first equation by -2 and add the two equations to eliminate y and solve for x.

$4x - 3y = 12$ Multiply by -2. → $-8x + 6y = -24$

$5x - 6y = 18$ → $5x - 6y = 18$

$$-3x = -6$$
$$x = 2$$

Substitute 2 for x into either equation and solve for y.

$$5(2) - 6y = 18$$
$$y = -\frac{4}{3}$$

The solution of the system of equations is $\left(2, -\frac{4}{3}\right)$.

Practice & Problem Solving

Solve each system of equations.

18. $2x - y = -2$
    $3x - 2y = 4$

19. $5x - 2y = 10$
    $4x + 3y = -6$

Is each pair of systems equivalent? Explain.

20. $2x - 3y = 14$, $5x - 2y = 8$ and $4x - 6y = 28$, $-15x + 6y = -24$

21. $3x - 4y = -6$, $2x + 5y = 1$ and $6x - 8y = 12$, $6x + 15y = 3$

22. **Generalize** Do you always have to multiply one or both equations to use elimination? Explain.

23. **Model With Mathematics** Carmen and Alicia go to the office supply store to purchase packs of pens and paper. Carmen bought 5 packs of paper and 3 packs of pens for \$36.60. Alicia bought 6 packs of paper and 6 packs of pens for \$53.40. What is the price of one pack of paper and one pack of pens?

LESSON 4-4 Linear Inequalities in Two Variables

Quick Review

A **linear inequality in two variables** is an inequality that is in the same form as a linear equation in two variables but with an inequality symbol instead of an equal sign. A **solution of a linear inequality in two variables** is an ordered pair that satisfies the inequality.

Example

What inequality is shown by the graph?

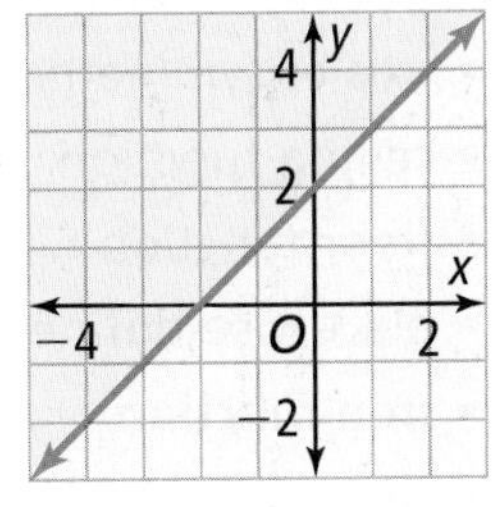

The slope of the line is 1 and its y-intercept is 2. Therefore, the equation of the line is $y = x + 2$. The boundary line is solid, and all values of x and y that make the inequality true lie on the line or above the line. The inequality shown by the graph is $y \geq x + 2$.

Practice & Problem Solving

Use the graph to tell whether each ordered pair is a solution of the inequality $y \geq 2x - 3$.

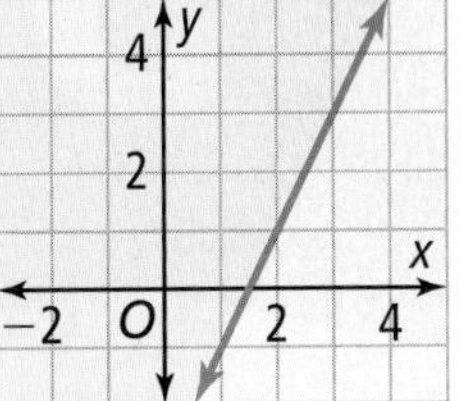

24. (2, 5)

25. (3, −1)

26. (−2, 4)

Graph the inequality in the coordinate plane.

27. $y > 4x - 9$

28. $y \leq 1.5x + 4$

29. **Reason** Write an inequality in two variables for which (2, 5) and (−3, −1) are solutions.

30. **Make Sense and Persevere** Renaldo has a budget of \$500 to buy gift boxes for a party. Large boxes cost \$65 and small boxes cost \$35. Write and graph an inequality that represents the number of each type of gift box that Renaldo can buy. If Renaldo buys 6 small gift boxes, how many large gift boxes can he afford to buy?

LESSON 4-5 Systems of Linear Inequalities

Quick Review

A **system of linear inequalities** is made up of two or more inequalities. The **solutions of a system of linear inequalities** is the set of all ordered pairs that satisfy the inequalities in the system.

Example

What system of inequalities is shown by the graph? Describe the solutions of the system of inequalities.

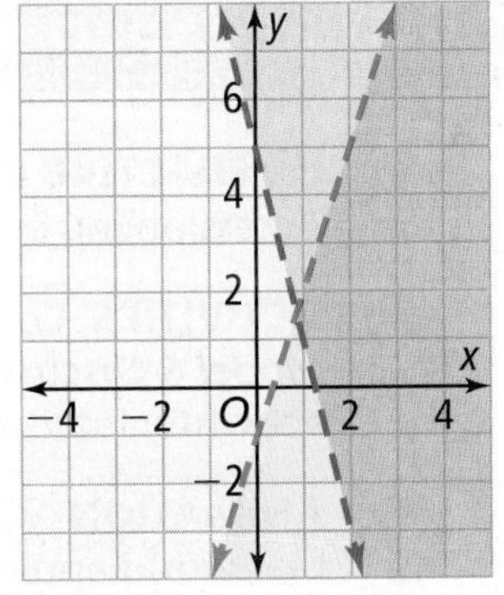

Determine the equation of each line using the slope and y-intercept.

Points below the red dashed line satisfy the inequality $y < 3x - 1$. Points above the blue dashed line satisfy the inequality $y > -4x + 5$.

The solutions to the system lie in the region where the graphs overlap.

Practice & Problem Solving

Graph each system of inequalities.

31. $y < 2x + 3$
$y \leq -3x + 1$

32. $y \geq 4x$
$y < -x - 5$

33. **Generalize** What two inequalities can you add to any system of inequalities to indicate that only answers in the first quadrant make sense?

34. **Model With Mathematics** Olivia makes and sells bracelets and necklaces. She can make up to 60 pieces per week, but she can only make up to 40 bracelets and 40 necklaces. Write and graph a system of inequalities that shows the combination of bracelets and necklaces that she can make if she wants to sell at least 30 items per week. If necklaces sell for \$80 each and bracelets sell for \$5 each, what is the most money she can make in a week? Explain.

TOPIC 5

Piecewise Functions

How do you use piecewise-defined functions to model situations and solve problems?

Topic Overview

Topic Vocabulary

- absolute value function
- axis of symmetry
- ceiling function
- floor function
- piecewise-defined function
- step function
- vertex

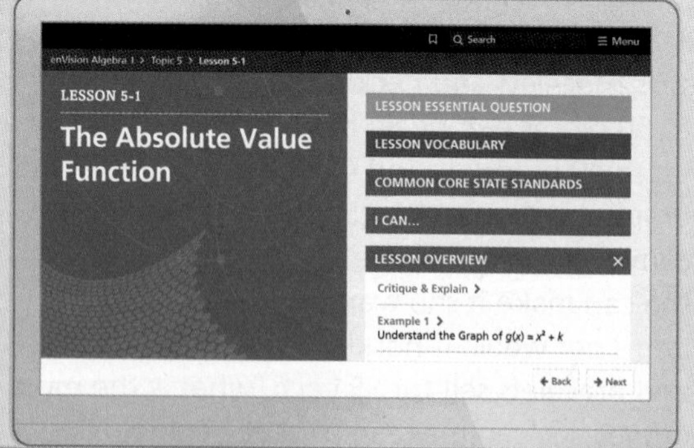

Go online | **PearsonRealize.com**

Digital Experience

INTERACTIVE STUDENT EDITION Access online or offline.

ACTIVITIES Complete ***Explore & Reason, Model & Discuss***, and ***Critique & Explain*** activities. Interact with Examples and Try Its.

ANIMATION View and interact with real-world applications.

PRACTICE Practice what you've learned.

MATHEMATICAL MODELING IN 3 ACTS

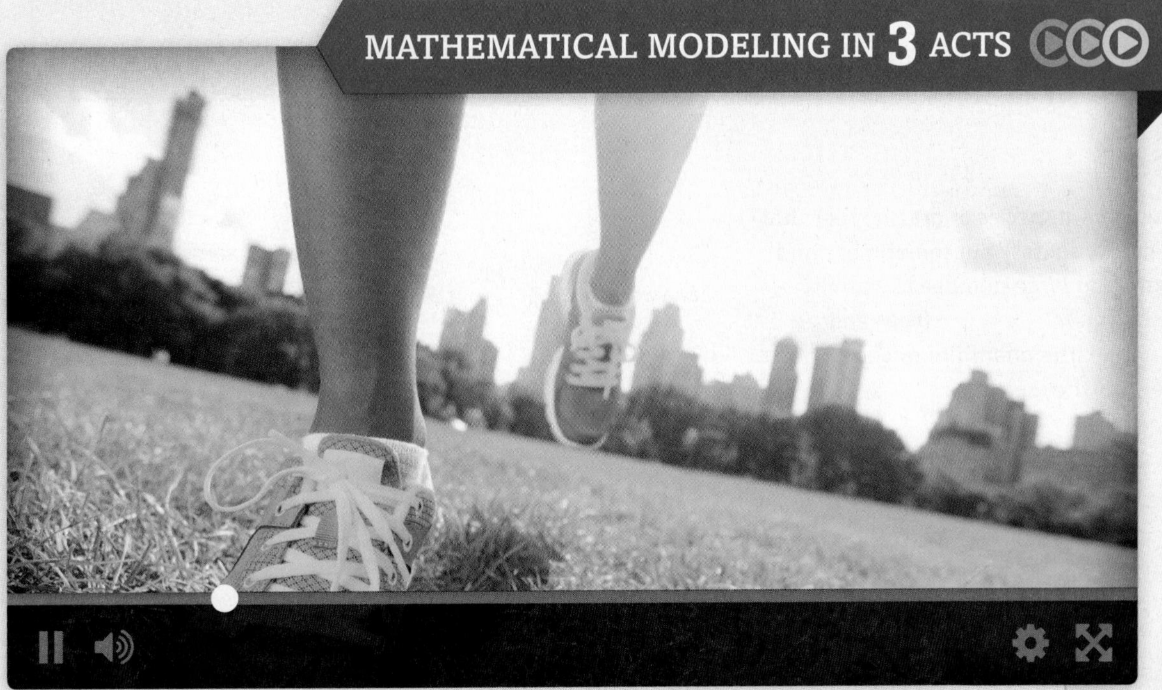

The Mad Runner

People run in many different places: on the soccer field during a game, around the neighborhood, on the basketball court, on the street to catch a bus, in gym class.

Sometimes people run on flat ground and other times they run up or down hills or even up and down stairs. They also run on different surfaces, such as grass, pavement, sand, or a basketball court. Think about this during the Mathematical Modeling in 3 Acts lesson.

TOPIC 5

VIDEOS Watch clips to support ***Mathematical Modeling in 3 Acts Lessons*** and **enVision™ *STEM Projects.***

CONCEPT SUMMARY Review key lesson content through multiple representations.

ASSESSMENT Show what you've learned.

GLOSSARY Read and listen to English and Spanish definitions.

TUTORIALS Get help from ***Virtual Nerd***, right when you need it.

MATH TOOLS Explore math with digital tools and manipulatives.

Did You Know?

Locusts are a species of grasshopper that are mostly solitary but sometimes band together in large numbers. Swarming locusts can fly great distances and consume large quantities of vegetation wherever they settle.

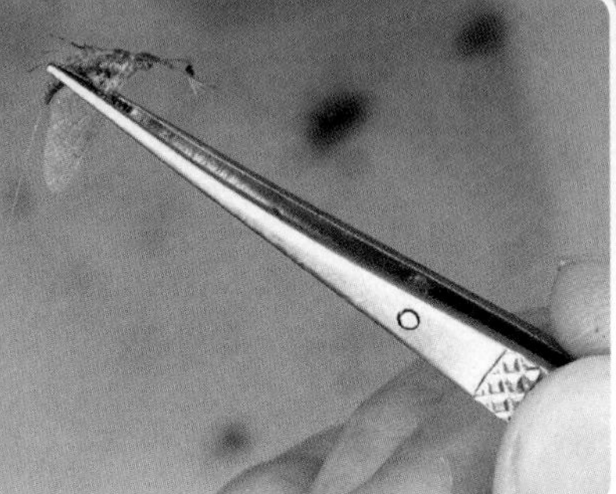

Ecologists study seasonal populations, such as insects, to determine how the population in one year is related to the population in the next. Modeling populations helps scientists manage pest insects.

Over 90% of the animals on Earth are insects.

Rest of animal population

The only place on Earth without insects is the ocean.

One of the largest cicada broods, Brood VI, has a periodic life cycle and spends 17 years underground between outbreaks. The brood is projected to surface in 2034.

Your Task: Predict a Population

You and your classmates will analyze a model for population growth and determine how increases in the rate of reproduction affect an insect population.

5-1 The Absolute Value Function

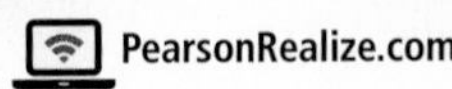

I CAN... analyze functions that include absolute value expressions.

VOCABULARY

- absolute value function
- axis of symmetry
- vertex

EXPLORE & REASON

Groups of students are hiking from mile markers 2, 6 and 8 to meet at the waterfall located at mile marker 5.

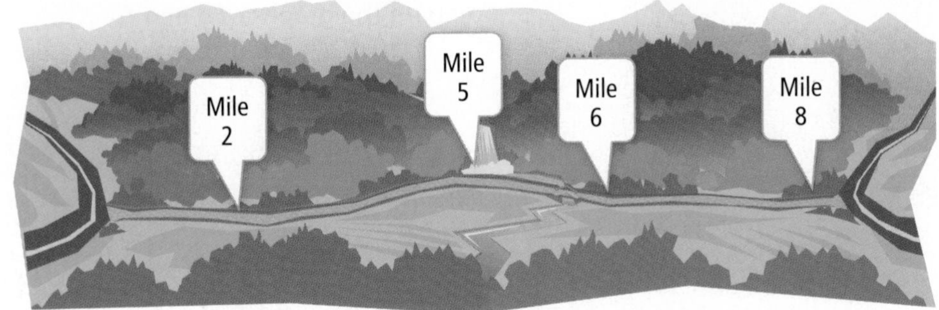

A. How can you use the mile marker to determine the number of miles each group of students needs to hike to the waterfall?

B. **Model With Mathematics** Make a graph that relates the position of each group on the trail to their distance from the waterfall.

C. How would the points in your graph from part B change as the groups of students approach the waterfall?

ESSENTIAL QUESTION

What are the key features of the graph of the absolute value function?

EXAMPLE 1 Graph the Absolute Value Function

What are the features of the graph of $f(x) = |x|$?

Make a table of values and graph the **absolute value function** $f(x) = |x|$.

x	$f(x) = \|x\|$	$(x, f(x))$
−2	2	(−2, 2)
−1	1	(−1, 1)
0	0	(0, 0)
1	1	(1, 1)
2	2	(2, 2)

The *vertex*, (0, 0), is the turning point of the graph.

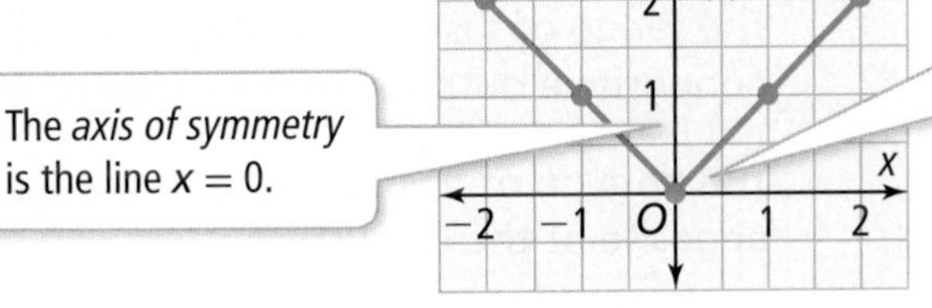

The *axis of symmetry* is the line $x = 0$.

The graph has a **vertex**, where the axis of symmetry intersects the graph. It represents the minimum value in the range.

LOOK FOR RELATIONSHIPS
How does the nature of absolute value contribute to the symmetric appearance of the graph?

The graph has an **axis of symmetry**, which intersects the vertex and divides the graph into two sections, or pieces, that are images of each other under a reflection.

Try It! 1. What are the domain and range of $f(x) = |x|$?

CONCEPTUAL UNDERSTANDING

EXAMPLE 2 Transform the Absolute Value Function

A. How do the domain and range of $g(x) = 2|x|$ compare with the domain and range of $f(x) = |x|$?

Compare the graphs of g and f.

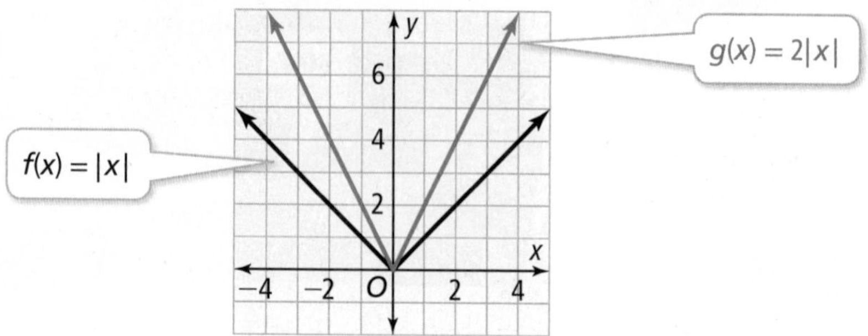

The domain of f and the domain of g are all real numbers.

Because the absolute value expression produces only nonnegative values, the range of f is $y \geq 0$. Multiplying $|x|$ by a positive factor, in this case, 2, yields nonnegative outputs, so the range of g is also $y \geq 0$.

The domain and range of the function g are the same as those of function f.

B. How do the domain and range of $h(x) = -1|x|$ compare with the domain and range of $f(x) = |x|$?

Compare the graphs of h and f.

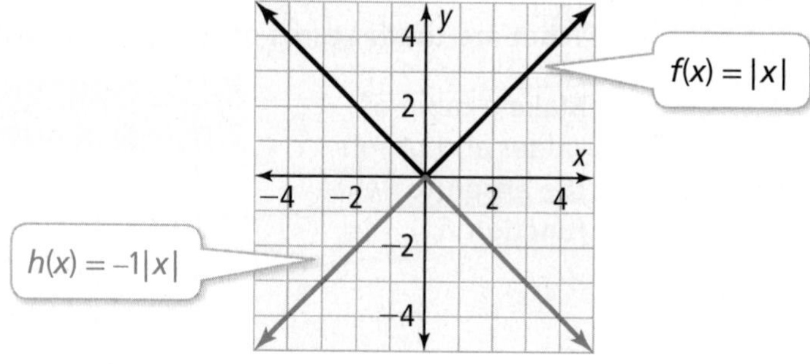

USE APPROPRIATE TOOLS
Why is it helpful to use both a graph and a table to explore the domain and range of functions that involve absolute value expressions?

The domain of f and the domain of h are all real numbers.

The range of f is $y \geq 0$. Multiplying $|x|$ by a negative factor, -1, yields nonpositive outputs, so the range of h is $y \leq 0$.

The domain of h is the same as the domain of f. The range of h is the opposite of the range of f.

Try It! 2. How do the domain and range of each function compare with the domain and range of $f(x) = |x|$?

a. $g(x) = \frac{1}{2}|x|$

b. $h(x) = -2|x|$

Activity

Assess

APPLICATION

EXAMPLE 3 Interpret the Graph of a Function

Jay rides in a boat from his home to his friend's home in a neighboring state. The graph of the function $d(t) = 30\,|t - 1.5|$ shows the distance of the boat in miles from the state line at t hours. Assume the graph shows Jay's entire trip.

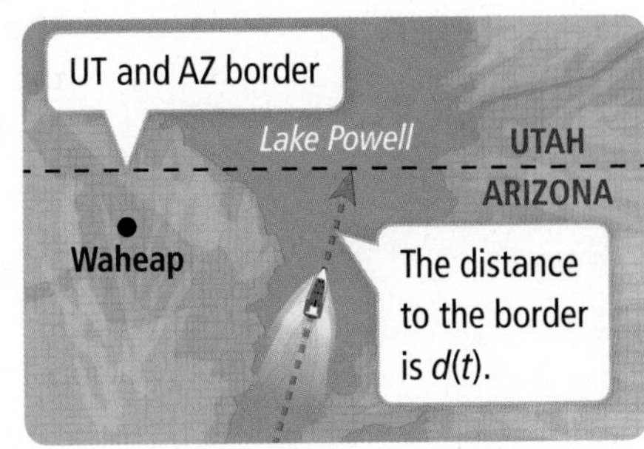

COMMON ERROR
Remember that a graph representing the motion of an object may not be a picture of its path.

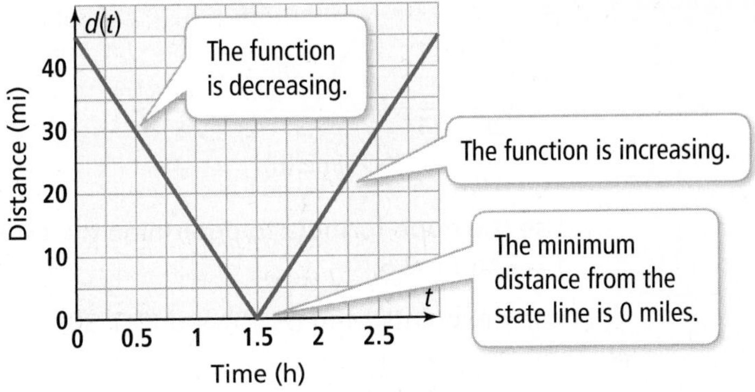

A. How far does Jay travel to visit his friend?

Jay began his trip 45 mi from the state line, traveled towards the state line, which he crossed after an hour and a half. He then traveled away from the state line and was 45 mi from the state line after 3 h. He traveled a total of 90 mi to visit his friend.

B. How does the graph relate to the domain and range of the function?

Since Jay's entire trip is 3 h, the domain of the function is $0 \leq t \leq 3$.

For the section of the domain $0 < t < 1.5$, his distance to the border is decreasing. For $1.5 < t < 3$ his distance from the border is increasing.

The maximum and minimum values on the graph are 45 and 0, so the range of the function is $0 \leq d(t) \leq 45$.

Try It! 3. A cyclist competing in a race rides past a water station. The graph of the function $d(t) = \frac{1}{3}|t - 60|$ shows her distance from the water station at t minutes. Assume the graph represents the entire race. What does the graph tell you about her race?

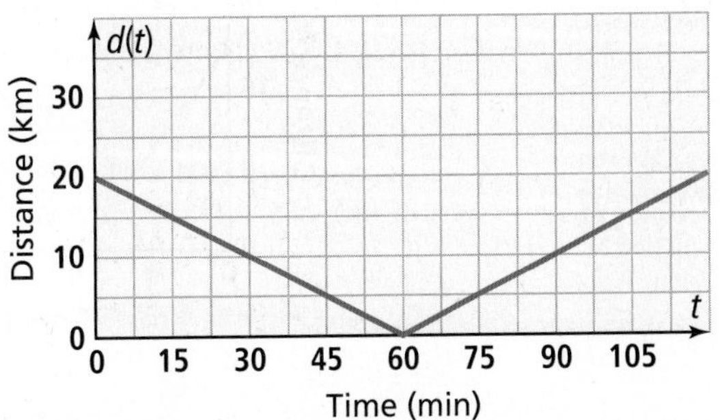

EXAMPLE 4 Determine Rate of Change

The graph shows Jay's boat ride across the state line from Example 3. What is the rate of change over the interval $2 \leq t \leq 2.5$? What does it mean in terms of the situation?

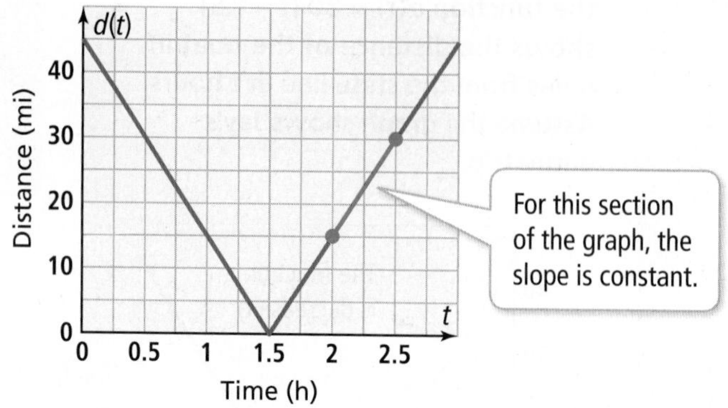

Use the slope formula to determine the rate of change from $t = 2$ to $t = 2.5$.

Use the points from (2, 15) and (2.5, 30).

$$m = \frac{y_2 - y_1}{x_2 - x_1}$$
$$= \frac{30 - 15}{2.5 - 2}$$
$$= \frac{15}{0.5}$$
$$= 30$$

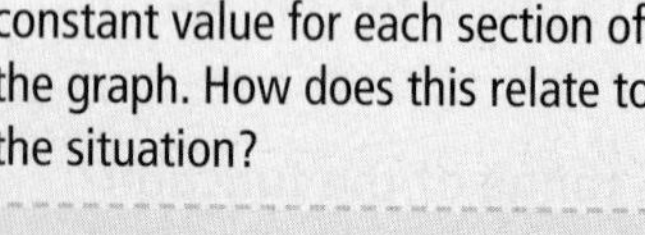

MAKE SENSE AND PERSEVERE
The rate of change is a different constant value for each section of the graph. How does this relate to the situation?

The rate of change over this interval is 30.

The rate of change represents the speed of the boat in miles per hour. Since the rate of change is positive, Jay's distance from the border is increasing. The boat is traveling at 30 mi/h away from the border.

Try It! 4. Kata gets on a moving walkway at the airport. Then, 8 s after she gets on, she taps Lisa, who is standing alongside the walkway. The graph shows Kata's distance from Lisa over time. Calculate the rate of change in her distance from Lisa from 6 s to 8 s, and then from 8 s to 12 s. What do the rates of change mean in terms of Kata's movement?

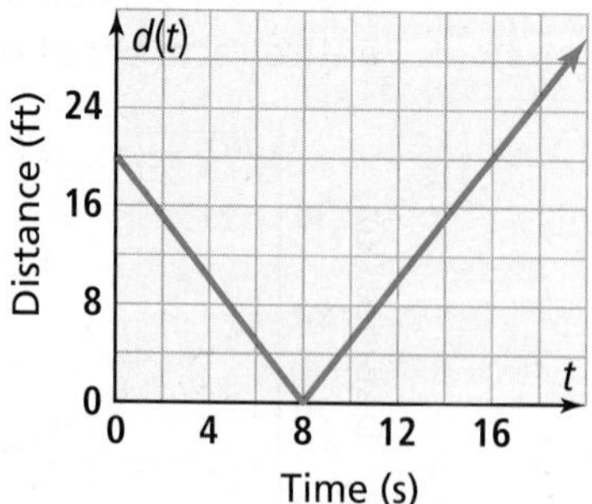

CONCEPT SUMMARY The Absolute Value Function

WORDS The graph of the absolute value function has a vertex, which represents the minimum value of the function. The axis of symmetry intersects the vertex and divides the graph into two sections that are images of each other under a reflection.

ALGEBRA $f(x) = |x|$

GRAPH

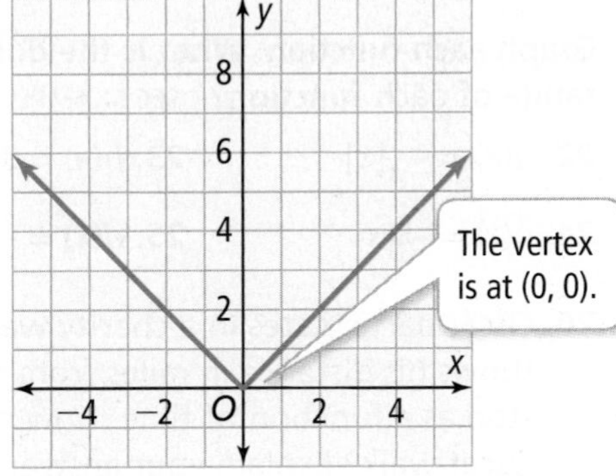

The domain is all real numbers, the range is $y \geq 0$.

Do You UNDERSTAND?

1. **ESSENTIAL QUESTION** What are the key features of the graph of the absolute value function?

2. **Communicate Precisely** How do the domain and range of $g(x) = a|x|$ compare to the domain and range of $f(x) = |x|$ when $0 < a < 1$? Explain.

3. **Make Sense and Persevere** The graph of the function $g(x) = a|x|$ includes the point (1, 16). What is another point on the graph of the function? What is the value of a?

4. **Error Analysis** Janiece says that the vertex of the graph of $g(x) = a|x|$ always represents the minimum value of the function g. Explain her error.

Do You KNOW HOW?

Find the domain and range of each function.

5. $g(x) = 5\,|x|$

6. $h(x) = -2|x|$

Graph each function.

7. $g(x) = 1.5\,|x|$

8. $h(x) = -0.8|x|$

9. What is the rate of change over the interval $15 \leq x \leq 18$?

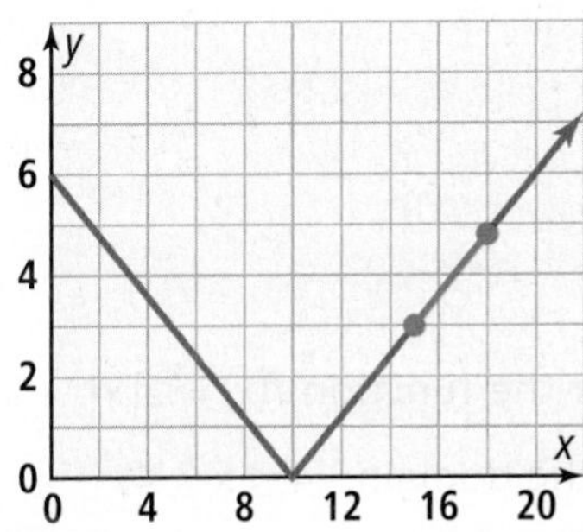

PRACTICE & PROBLEM SOLVING

Scan for Multimedia

Practice Tutorial

Additional Exercises Available Online

UNDERSTAND

10. **Reason** How does changing the sign of the constant a from positive to negative affect the domain and range of $f(x) = a|x|$?

11. **Communicate Precisely** Compare and contrast the graph of $f(x) = |x|$ and the graph of $f(x) = x$. How are they alike? How do they differ?

12. **Error Analysis** Describe and correct the error a student made in determining the relationship between the domain and range of $f(x) = 10|x|$ and $f(x) = |x|$.

> The domain of $f(x) = 10|x|$ is the same as the domain of $f(x) = |x|$. The range of $f(x) = 10|x|$ is 10 times the range of $f(x) = |x|$. ✗

13. **Higher Order Thinking** For which values of a would the graph of $f(x) = a|x|$ form a right angle at the vertex? Explain.

14. **Use Structure** The table shows selected values for the function $g(x) = a|x|$. Copy and complete the table. Write any unknown answers in terms of a and b.

x	$g(x) = a\|x\|$
−4	b
■	a
■	0
1	■
■	b
■	$2b$

15. **Reason** Consider the function $f(x) = 2|x|$.

a. Graph f over the domain $-4 \le x \le 4$.

b. What is the rate of change over the interval $0 \le x \le 4$?

c. How is the rate of change over this interval related to the form of the function?

PRACTICE

Tell whether each point is on the graph of $f(x) = |x|$. If it is, give the coordinates of another point with the same y value. SEE EXAMPLE 1

16. (11, 11)

17. (−2.3, −2.3)

18. (0, 1)

19. (15, −15)

20. (−8, 8)

21. (1, 0)

Graph each function. What is the domain and range of each function? SEE EXAMPLE 2

22. $g(x) = -\frac{1}{4}|x|$

23. $h(x) = 3.5|x|$

24. $p(x) = -5|x|$

25. $d(x) = \frac{1}{3}|x|$

26. Oscar participates in a charity walk. The graph shows his distance in miles from the water stop as a function of time. How many miles did Oscar walk? Explain your answer. SEE EXAMPLE 3

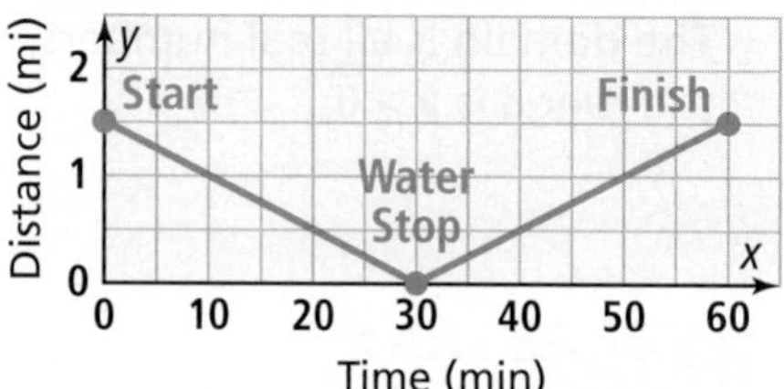

For the graph shown, find the rate of change over the interval. SEE EXAMPLE 4

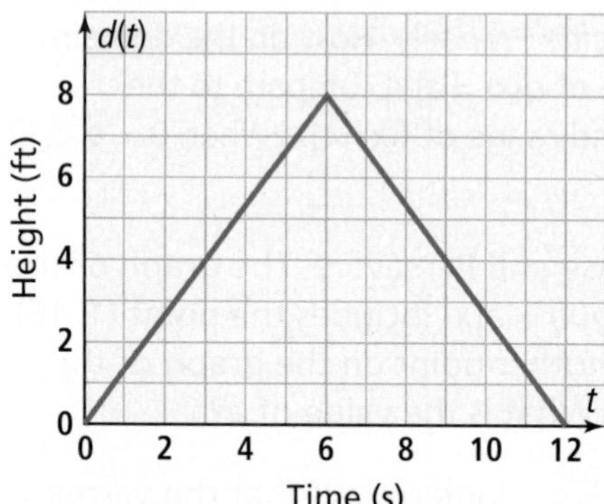

27. $3 \le t \le 6$

28. $7 \le t \le 10$

For each description, write a function in the form $g(x) = a|x|$.

29. vertex at (0, 0); passes through (1, 3)

30. range is $y \le 0$; passes through (−1, −4)

PRACTICE & PROBLEM SOLVING

APPLY

31. Model With Mathematics A game designer is looking for two functions to model the solid lines in the figure she constructed. What functions represent the solid lines?

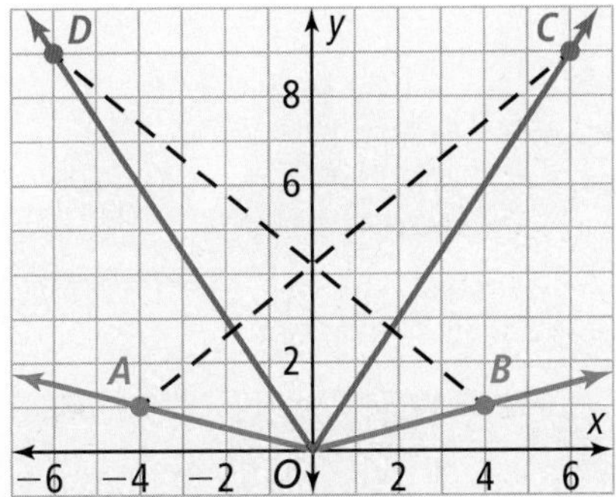

32. Make Sense and Persevere The graph shows the distance between a bicyclist and a sandwich shop along her route. Estimate the rate of change over the highlighted interval. What does the rate mean in terms of the situation?

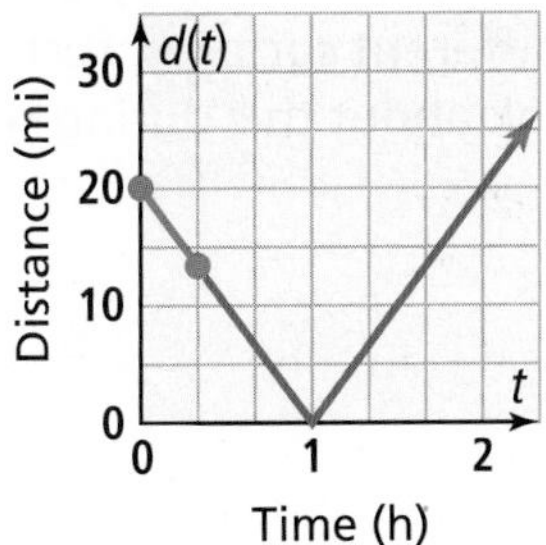

33. Make Sense and Persevere The function $h(x) = -|x| + 34$ models the height of the roof of a house, where x is the horizontal distance from the center of the house. If a raindrop falls from the end of the roof, how far from the center of the base does it land? Explain your solution.

ASSESSMENT PRACTICE

34. The graph of $f(x) = -0.1|x|$ opens ____. The point (____, −10) is on the graph.

35. SAT/ACT For what domain is the range of $y = -x$ and $y = -|x|$ the same?

Ⓐ $\{x \mid x < 0\}$

Ⓑ $\{x \mid x \leq 0\}$

Ⓒ $\{x \mid x > 0\}$

Ⓓ $\{x \mid x \geq 0\}$

Ⓔ all real numbers

36. Performance Task The position of a lizard in a video game is modeled on a coordinate plane. The lizard follows the path shown.

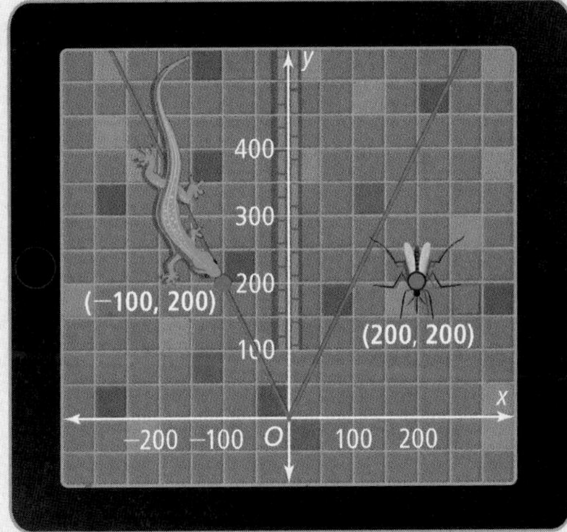

Part A Write a function that includes an absolute value expression for the position of the lizard.

Part B Interpret the graph. Find the vertex and determine the intervals in which the function is increasing, decreasing; and any maximum or minimum values.

Part C Where would the function need to intersect the x-axis so that the lizard can eat the mosquito?

Part D Write a function for which the new vertex that you found in Part C is a solution to the function, and allows the lizard to eat the mosquito.

The Mad Runner

People run in many different places: on the soccer field during a game, around the neighborhood, on the basketball court, on the street to catch a bus, in gym class.

Sometimes people run on flat ground and other times they run up or down hills or even up and down stairs. They also run on different surfaces, such as grass, pavement, sand, or a basketball court. Think about this during the Mathematical Modeling in 3 Acts lesson.

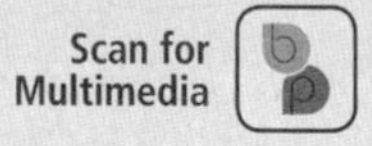

ACT 1 Identify the Problem

1. What is the first question that comes to mind after watching the video?
2. Write down the main question you will answer about what you saw in the video.

ACT 2 Develop a Model

3. Make a graph that represents this situation.

ACT 3 Interpret the Results

4. Did your graph match the actual answer exactly? If not, what might explain the difference?

Activity Assess

5-2 Piecewise-Defined Functions

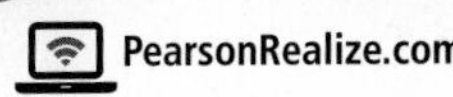

I CAN… graph and apply piecewise-defined functions.

VOCABULARY

- piecewise-defined function

EXPLORE & REASON

In a relay race, each runner carries a baton for an equal distance before handing off the baton to the next runner.

Path of the Baton		
	Time (min)	Total Distance (mi)
Start	0	0
Runner 1	3	0.25
Runner 2	5.75	0.50
Runner 3	9	0.75
Runner 4	11.50	1.00

A. Graph the distance traveled by the baton as a function of time. How is the speed of each runner represented in the graph?

B. Who is the fastest runner?

C. **Communicate Precisely** How is the graph of this function similar to the graph of a linear function? How is it different?

ESSENTIAL QUESTION

What are the key features of piecewise-defined functions?

CONCEPTUAL UNDERSTANDING

EXAMPLE 1 Understand Piecewise-Defined Functions

How is $f(x) = 2|x|$ related to a linear function?

Inspect the graph of the function $f(x) = 2|x|$. The graph has two pieces that meet at the vertex. Each piece is part of a line.

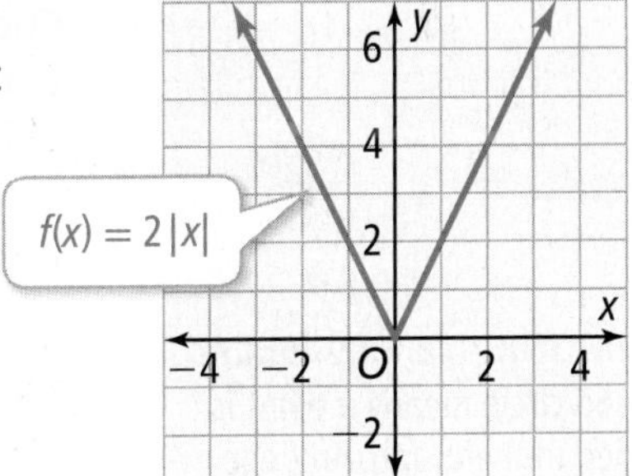

Find the rule for each piece of the function.

When $x \geq 0$, the rule is $f(x) = 2x$.

When $x < 0$, the rule is $f(x) = -2x$.

> **STUDY TIP**
> Recall that $|x| = x$, when $x \geq 0$ and $|x| = -x$ when $x < 0$.

You can write this function in terms of its pieces, each defined for a given domain.

$$f(x) = \begin{cases} 2x, & x \geq 0 \\ -2x, & x < 0 \end{cases}$$

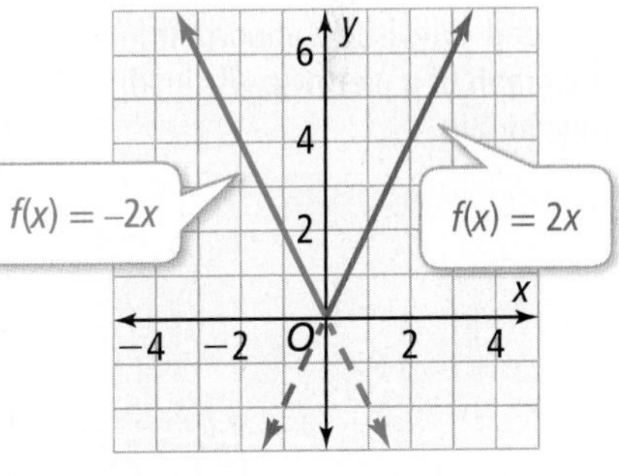

The function f is a *piecewise-defined* function. A **piecewise-defined function** has different rules for different intervals of its domain.

The function $f(x) = 2|x|$ has two pieces over two intervals of the domain. For each interval, the piece is a linear function.

Try It! 1. Express $f(x) = -3|x|$ as a piecewise-defined function.

EXAMPLE 2 Graph a Piecewise-Defined Function

A. What is the graph of $f(x) = \begin{cases} x + 1, & x \le 2 \\ -\frac{3}{2}x + 6, & x > 2 \end{cases}$?

Graph each piece of the function for the given domain.

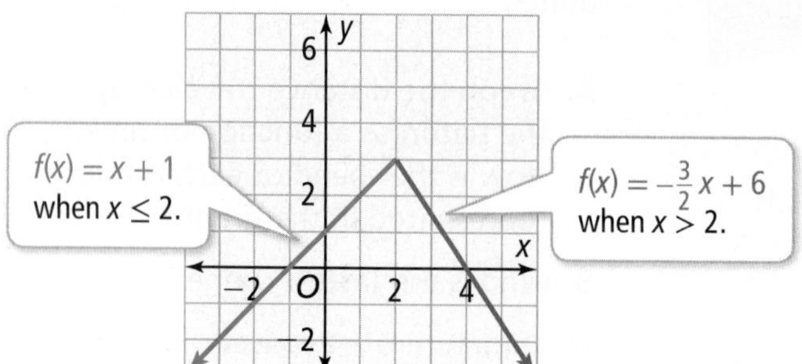

COMMON ERROR
You might assume that the pieces of a piecewise-defined function must connect, but this is not necessarily the case.

B. Over what part of the domain is the function increasing? Decreasing?

The function f is increasing when $x \le 2$ and decreasing when $x > 2$.

Try It! **2.** Graph the following function. $f(x) = \begin{cases} x - 2, & x \le 1 \\ -2x + 3, & x > 1 \end{cases}$

EXAMPLE 3 Analyze the Graph of a Piecewise-Defined Function

Cheyenne's mother is reviewing the monthly water bills from the summer. Each monthly bill includes a graph like the one shown, which reflects the different rates charged for water based on usage.

Several relatives visited Cheyenne's family in July and their water bill more than doubled. Assuming that the water consumption did not double that month, what is a possible explanation for the increase?

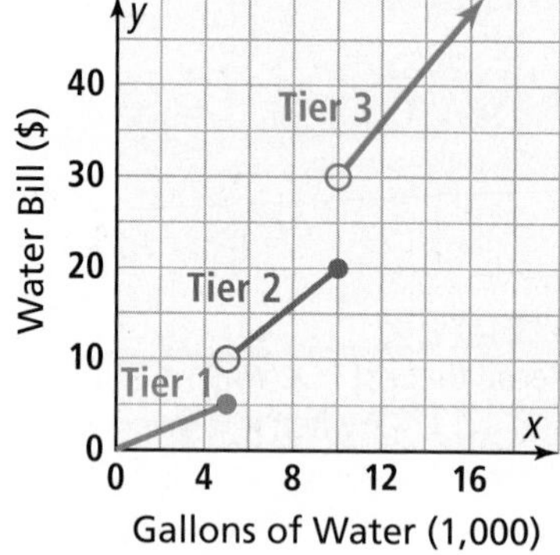

COMMUNICATE PRECISELY
A closed circle means a point is included in the graph. An open circle means the point is not included. Why is this important for the graph of a piecewise-defined function?

The graph shows three tiers of pricing for water consumption: from 0 to 5000 gal, from 5001 to 10,000 gal, and more than 10,000 gal.

The large increase in the bill probably resulted from the usage increasing across one boundary of the domain, from Tier 1 to Tier 2, or Tier 2 to Tier 3.

At the Tier 1–Tier 2 boundary 5,000 gal of usage results in a bill of \$5 while using slightly more water results in a bill of at least \$10.

Try It! **3.** Make a conjecture about why a utility company might charge higher rates for greater levels of water consumption.

EXAMPLE 4 Apply a Piecewise-Defined Function

A gym owner wants to purchase custom wristbands for a marketing promotion. She thinks she will need about 75 bands. Her assistant insists that ordering over 100 wristbands will be less expensive than ordering 75. How can the assistant convince the gym owner?

Formulate Write a rule to represent each price point.

Let x = number of wristbands

Let $f(x)$ = total cost

Number of wristbands	Price ($)	•	Wristbands	+	Shipping ($)
0–50	2.00	•	x	+	20
51–100	1.00	•	x	+	10
more than 100	0.50	•	x		

Write a piecewise-defined function to represent the situation.

$$f(x) = \begin{cases} 2x + 20, & 0 \leq x \leq 50 \\ x + 10, & 50 < x \leq 100 \\ 0.5x, & x > 100 \end{cases}$$

0 to 50 wristbands
51 to 100 wristbands
over 100 wristbands

Compute Evaluate the function for $f(75)$ and $f(101)$.

$$f(75) = 75 + 10 = 85$$

$$f(101) = 0.5(101) = 50.5$$

The cost for 75 wristbands is $85 and the cost for 101 wristbands is $50.50.

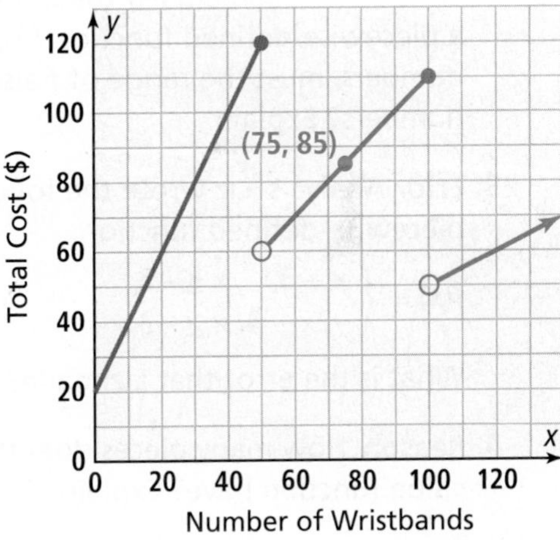

Interpret The gym owner will spend less if she orders more than 100 wristbands.

Try It! **4.** What is the difference in cost between one order of 200 wristbands, two orders of 100 wristbands each, and four orders of 50 wristbands each?

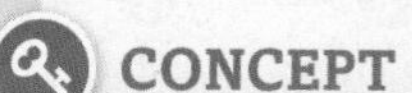

CONCEPT SUMMARY Piecewise-Defined Functions

WORDS Piecewise-defined functions are defined by different rules for different intervals of the domain.

ALGEBRA $f(x) = \begin{cases} -\frac{1}{3}x - 2, & x \leq 3 \\ x + 1, & x > 3 \end{cases}$ The boundary is 3.

GRAPH

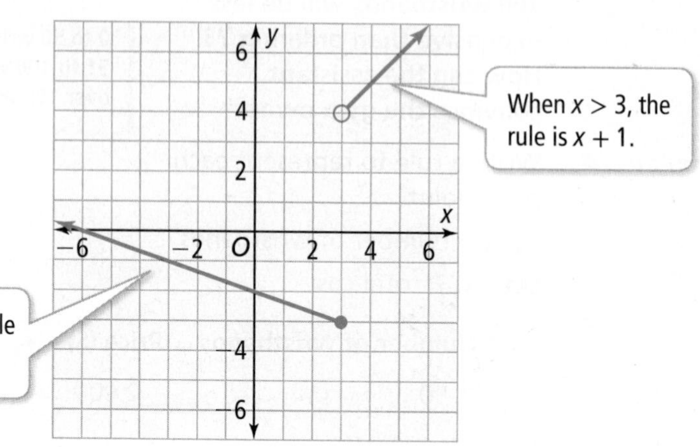

Do You UNDERSTAND?

1. **ESSENTIAL QUESTION** What are the key features of piecewise-defined functions?

2. **Construct Arguments** If the domain of a piecewise-defined function f is all real numbers, must the range of f also be all real numbers? Explain.

3. **Error Analysis** Liz wrote the following piecewise-defined function:

$$f(x) = \begin{cases} x - 3, & x \leq -3 \\ -2x - 4, & x \geq -3 \end{cases}$$

What is the error that Liz made?

4. **Reason** How many pieces does the absolute value function have? Explain.

Do You KNOW HOW?

Express each function as a piecewise-defined function.

5. $f(x) = 5|x|$

6. $f(x) = -2|x|$

Graph each function.

7. $f(x) = \begin{cases} -3x + 1, & x \leq 1 \\ x + 1, & x > 1 \end{cases}$

8. $f(x) = \begin{cases} 2x - 1, & x < 3 \\ -2x + 4, & x \geq 3 \end{cases}$

9. A function f is defined by the rule $-0.5x + 1$ for the domain $x < 1$ and by the rule x for the domain $x \geq 1$. Write the piecewise-defined function f using function notation.

PRACTICE & PROBLEM SOLVING

Scan for Multimedia

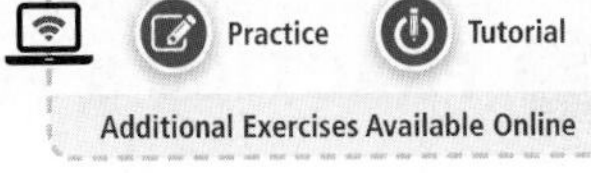

Additional Exercises Available Online

UNDERSTAND

10. Generalize Describe two ways you could express the function $f(x) = |x|$.

11. Look for Relationships How are the pieces of a piecewise-defined function related to the domain? Explain.

12. Error Analysis Describe and correct the error a student made in expressing the function $f(x) = 3|x|$ as a piecewise-defined function.

$f(x) = 3|x|$

$f(x) = \begin{cases} 3x, & x \leq 0 \\ -3x, & x > 0 \end{cases}$ ✗

13. Communicate Precisely A piecewise-defined f is shown. Use function notation to describe the function and determine the x- and y-intercepts.

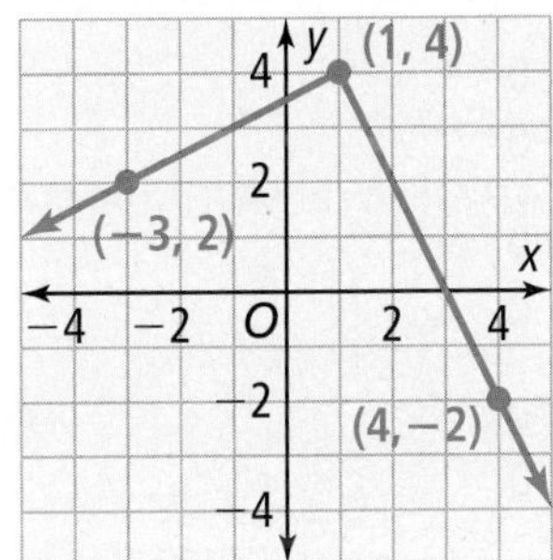

14. Reason A piecewise-defined function is shown.

$$f(x) = \begin{cases} x - 1, & x < n \\ -x + 4, & x \geq n \end{cases}$$

a. If $n = 5$, what is the range of f?

b. Does changing the value of n change the range? Explain.

15. Higher Order Thinking For a given piecewise-defined function, the pieces of the function are defined for intervals of the domain, $x \leq 1$ and $x > 1$.

a. Explain how you could find the y-intercept for the intervals over the intervals $x \leq 1$ and $x > 1$.

b. In general, how could you find the y-intercept for two pieces over the intervals $x \leq n$ and $x > n$?

PRACTICE

Express each absolute value function as a piecewise-defined function. SEE EXAMPLE 1

16. $f(x) = 6|x|$

17. $f(x) = -|x|$

18. $f(x) = \frac{1}{2}|x|$

19. $f(x) = -1.5|x|$

Graph each function. Identify the intervals where the function is increasing, decreasing, or constant. SEE EXAMPLE 2

20. $f(x) = \begin{cases} x + 1, & x < 1 \\ -x - 2, & x \geq 1 \end{cases}$

21. $f(x) = \begin{cases} -\frac{4}{3}x + 4, & x \leq 6 \\ 2x - 8, & x > 6 \end{cases}$

22. $f(x) = \begin{cases} x - 3, & x \leq -2 \\ x, & -2 < x \leq 2 \\ -2x + 2, & x > 2 \end{cases}$

23. A cell phone company charges \$0.10 per text message if a customer sends up to 100 messages per month. The company charges \$0.08 per text if a customer sends between 101–200 messages, and \$0.06 per text if the customer sends between 201–300 messages. Today is the last day of the month. Tamira has sent 200 text messages, is it worth it for her to send 1 more text message? Explain. SEE EXAMPLES 3 AND 4

Write a piecewise-defined function for each graph. SEE EXAMPLE 4

24.

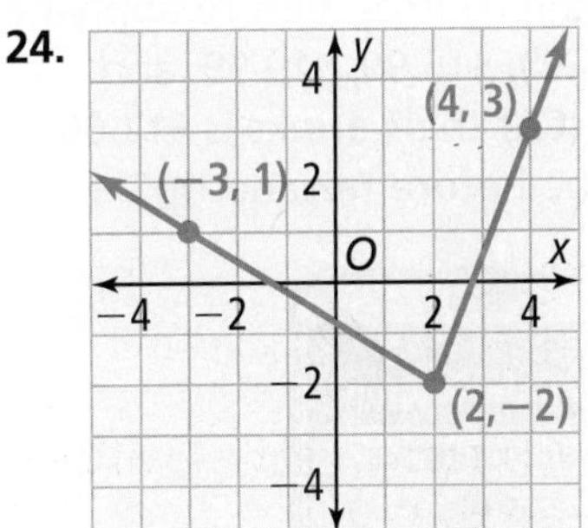

25.

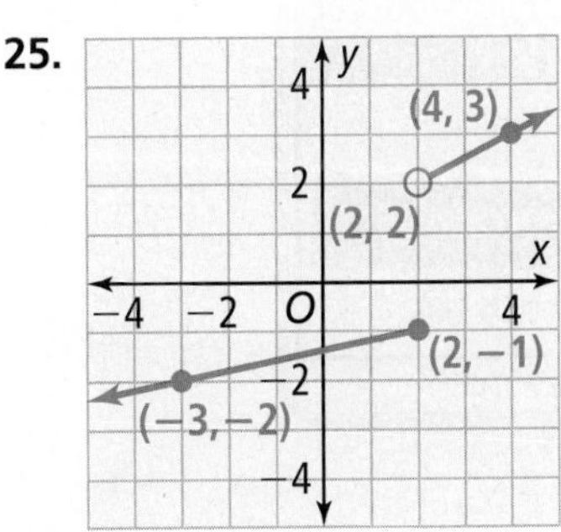

PRACTICE & PROBLEM SOLVING

APPLY

26. Model With Mathematics Selena needs at least 22 subway rides for the month. She has two options for buying subway cards. Write a function that represents the situation. Can she buy more than 22 rides and save money? Explain.

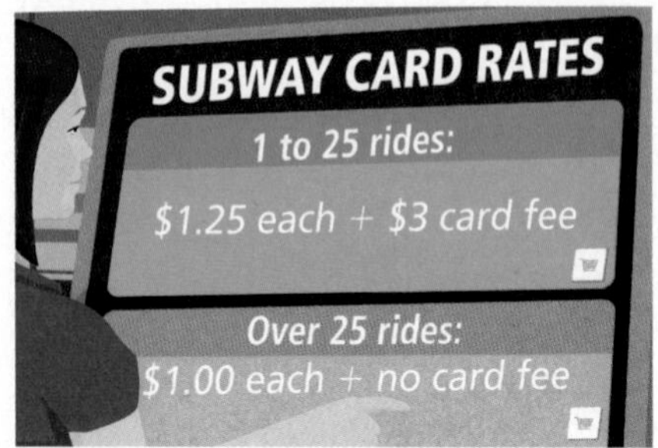

27. Make Sense and Persevere Reagan had \$122 in his savings account. He deposited \$70 each week from his job for the first five weeks of summer. In the sixth week, Reagan got a raise and increased his weekly deposits by \$12.

a. Write a piecewise-defined function to represent his bank balance.

b. Find $f(8)$.

c. What does $f(8) - 122$ mean in terms of the situation?

28. Make Sense and Persevere A group of friends eat at Jae's Cafe. They have an online coupon. The costs of their main courses, before applying the coupon, are \$13.99, \$16.99, \$19.99, and \$21.99. The total cost of their drinks is \$12.00. What will their bill be before tax and tip?

ASSESSMENT PRACTICE

29. The graph of function f is shown.

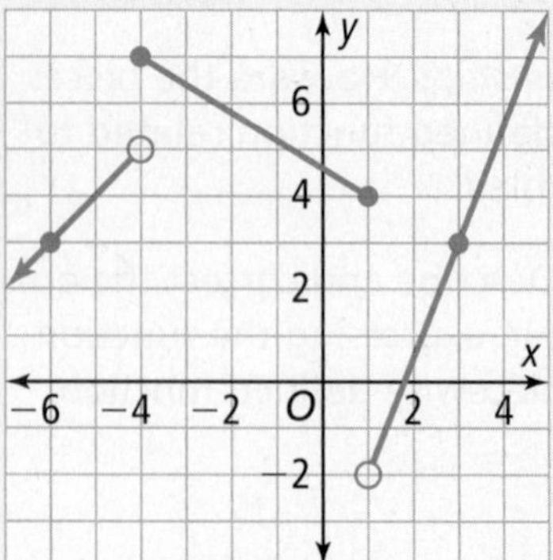

The domain of f is _____. The range of f is _____. There are _____ values in the domain where $f(x) = 4$ and $f(1) =$ _____.

30. SAT/ACT Which function has the same graph as $f(x) = 0.1|x|$?

Ⓐ $f(x) = \begin{cases} 0.1x, & x < 0 \\ -0.1x, & x > 0 \end{cases}$

Ⓑ $f(x) = \begin{cases} 0.1x, & x \le 0 \\ -0.1x, & x > 0 \end{cases}$

Ⓒ $f(x) = \begin{cases} 0.1x, & x > 0 \\ -0.1x, & x < 0 \end{cases}$

Ⓓ $f(x) = \begin{cases} 0.1x, & x \ge 0 \\ -0.1x, & x < 0 \end{cases}$

Ⓔ $f(x) = \begin{cases} -0.1x, & x \ge 0 \\ 0.1x, & x < 0 \end{cases}$

31. Performance Task Sue charges \$15 for the first hour of babysitting and \$10 for each additional hour, with each fraction of an hour counting as a whole hour. The rates that Vic charges for x hours of babysitting are modeled by the function shown.

$$f(x) = \begin{cases} 12.5x, & 0 \le x < 4 \\ 10x, & 4 \le x < 8 \\ 9.5x, & x \ge 8 \end{cases}$$

Part A Who will charge more to babysit for 10 hours? Justify your response.

Part B What is the rate of change for each function over the interval $7 \le x \le 11$?

Part C Which average rate of change is more meaningful? Explain.

Activity Assess

5-3 Step Functions

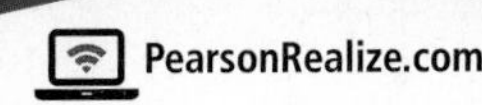

I CAN... graph and apply step functions.

VOCABULARY

- ceiling function
- floor function
- step function

CRITIQUE & EXPLAIN

Students are told there is a function where decimals are the inputs and each decimal is rounded to the nearest whole number to get the output. Beth and Latoya each make a sketch of the graph of the function.

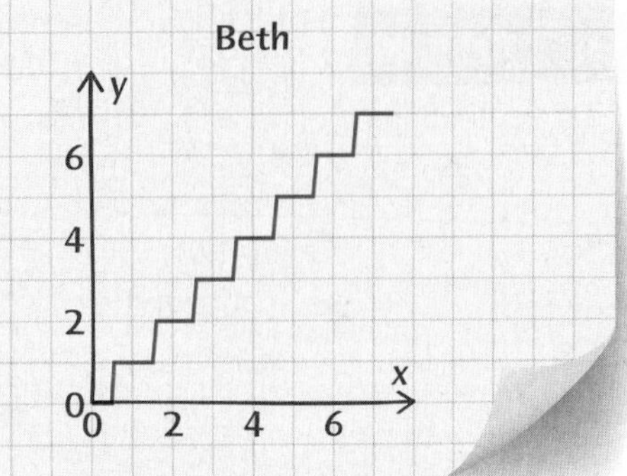

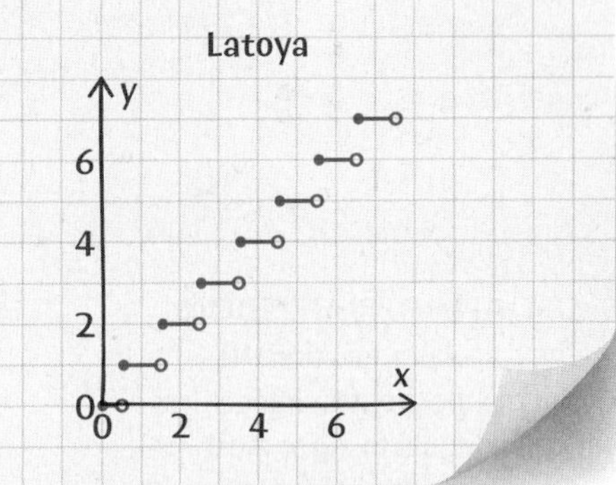

A. **Make Sense and Persevere** What is causing both students to create graphs that look like steps?

B. Which graph do you think is correct? Explain.

C. What does the graph of this function look like? Explain.

ESSENTIAL QUESTION **How are step functions related to piecewise-defined functions?**

CONCEPTUAL UNDERSTANDING

EXAMPLE 1 Understand Step Functions

A. What is the graph of the ceiling function?

A **step function** is a piecewise-defined function that consists of constant pieces. The graph resembles a set of steps.

The **ceiling function** is a kind of step function. It rounds numbers up to the nearest integer. It is notated as $f(x) = \text{ceiling}(x)$ or $f(x) = \lceil x \rceil$.

Make a table of values and graph.

x	$f(x) = \lceil x \rceil$
−2.4	−2
−1.4	−1
−0.5	0
0.7	1
1.8	2
2.1	3
3.1	4

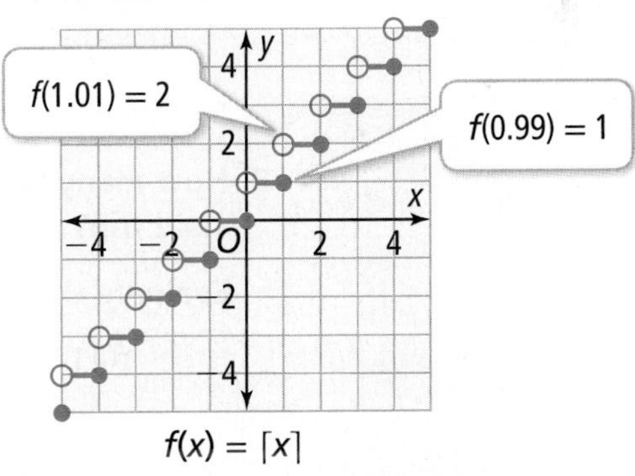

The domain is all real numbers. The range is all integers.

COMMUNICATE PRECISELY
The symbol for ceiling is very similar to other related symbols. What clue can help you remember the meaning of the symbol?

CONTINUED ON THE NEXT PAGE

EXAMPLE 1 CONTINUED

B. What is the graph of the floor function?

The **floor function** is another kind of step function. It rounds numbers down to the nearest integer. It is notated as $f(x) = \text{floor}(x)$ or $f(x) = \lfloor x \rfloor$.

Make a table of values and graph.

x	$f(x) = \lfloor x \rfloor$
−2.4	−3
−1.4	−2
−0.5	−1
0.7	0
1.8	1
2.1	2
3.1	3

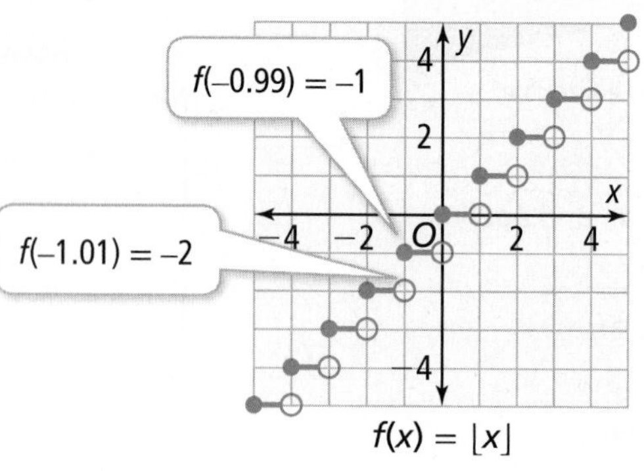

USE APPROPRIATE TOOLS
The calculator function INT returns the greatest integer less than or equal to x. For most calculators, the INT function is the same as floor(x). For others, it is the same only for $x > 0$.

The domain is is all real numbers. The range is all integers.

Try It! 1. Evaluate each function for the given value.

a. $f(x) = \lceil x \rceil$; $x = 2.65$

b. $f(x) = \text{floor}(x)$; $x = 2.19$

APPLICATION

EXAMPLE 2 Use a Step Function to Represent a Real-World Situation

Some students are planning a field trip. If there are 40 students and adults or fewer going on the field trip, they rent vans that hold 15 people. If there are more than 40 students and adults, they rent buses that hold 65 people.

A. What function can you use to represent this situation?

Number of vehicles to rent — Total number of students and adults

$$f(x) = \begin{cases} \left\lceil \frac{x}{15} \right\rceil, & 0 < x \leq 40 \\ \left\lceil \frac{x}{65} \right\rceil, & x > 40 \end{cases}$$

Each van holds 15 people.

Each bus holds 65 people.

B. How many buses are needed if 412 students and adults are going on a field trip?

Evaluate the function for $f(412)$.

$$f(412) = \left\lceil \frac{412}{65} \right\rceil$$
$$= \lceil 6.34 \rceil$$
$$= 7$$

Seven buses are needed if 412 students and adults are going on a field trip.

Try It! 2. The postage for a first-class letter weighing one ounce or less is \$0.47. Each additional ounce is \$0.21. The maximum weight of a first-class letter is $3\frac{1}{2}$ oz. Write a function to represent the situation.

APPLICATION

EXAMPLE 3

Use a Step Function to Solve Problems

Jamal and his brother plan to rent a karaoke machine for a class event. The graph shows the rental costs.

A. How much should they expect to spend if they rent the karaoke machine from 8:00 A.M. until 7:30 P.M.?

Karaoke Machine Rental

Rental Cost ($): 0, 20, 40, 60, 80 (y-axis); Hours Rented: 0, 2, 4, 6, 8 (x-axis)

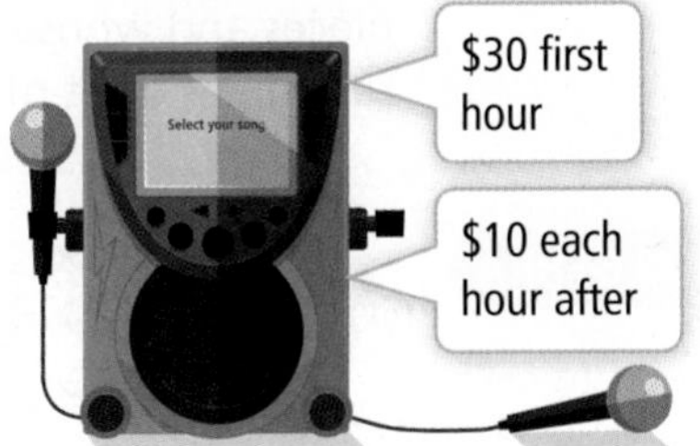

> **COMMON ERROR**
> Even though the graph is not connected, the domain of the function is continuous because it includes all positive real numbers.

Step 1 Write a function to represent the rental costs.

$$f(x) = \begin{cases} 30\lceil x \rceil, & 0 < x \leq 1 \\ 10\lceil x \rceil + 20, & x > 1 \end{cases}$$

$30 for the first hour, or any fraction of an hour

an additional $10 for each hour, or any fraction of an hour after the first hour

Step 2 Determine the duration of the rental.

8:00 A.M. to 7:30 P.M. is 11 h, 30 min or $11\frac{1}{2}$ h.

Step 3 Evaluate the function for $f(11.5)$.

$$\begin{aligned} f(11.5) &= 10\lceil 11.5 \rceil + 20 \\ &= 10(12) + 20 \\ &= 140 \end{aligned}$$

The cost of the rental will be $140.

B. The class event ended early, so Jamal could return the machine by 7:05 P.M. How much money would he save if he returned the machine at 7:05 P.M.?

Jamal would save no money if he returned the machine at 7:05 P.M. He will be charged for the full hour.

Try It! **3.** You rent a karaoke machine at 1 P.M. and plan to return it by 4 P.M. Will you save any money if you return the machine 15 min early? Explain.

CONCEPT SUMMARY Step Functions

	Step Function	Ceiling Function	Floor Function
WORDS	A step function is a piecewise-defined function that consists of constant pieces and whose graph resembles a set of steps.	The least integer function, also called the ceiling function, returns the least integer greater than or equal to x.	The greatest integer function, also called the floor function, returns the greatest integer less than or equal to x.
ALGEBRA	$f(x) = \begin{cases} 4, & 0 < x \leq 2 \\ 8, & 2 < x \leq 5 \\ 12, & 5 < x \leq 8 \end{cases}$	$f(x) = \lceil x \rceil$	$f(x) = \lfloor x \rfloor$
GRAPHS	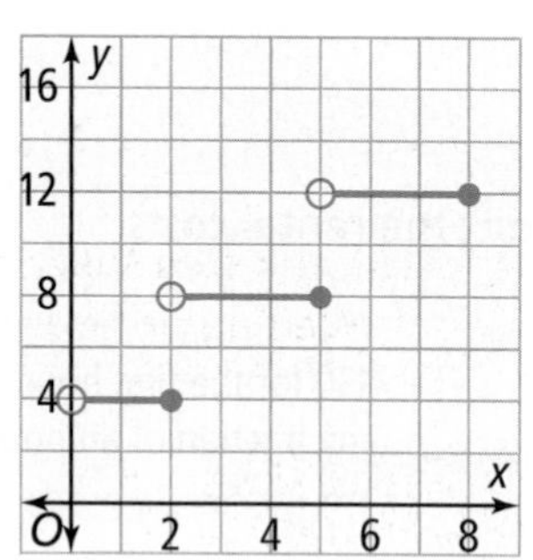	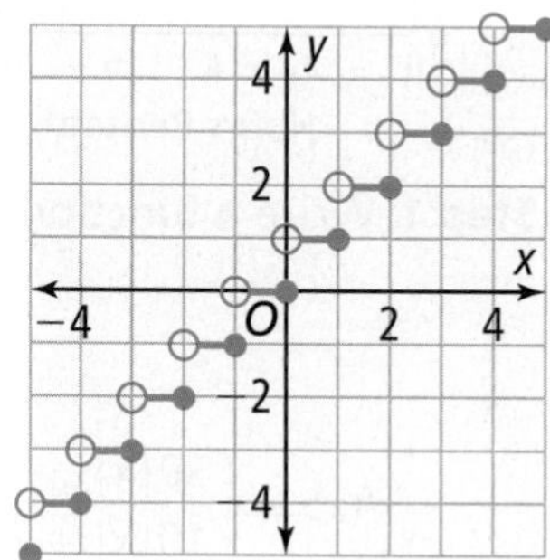	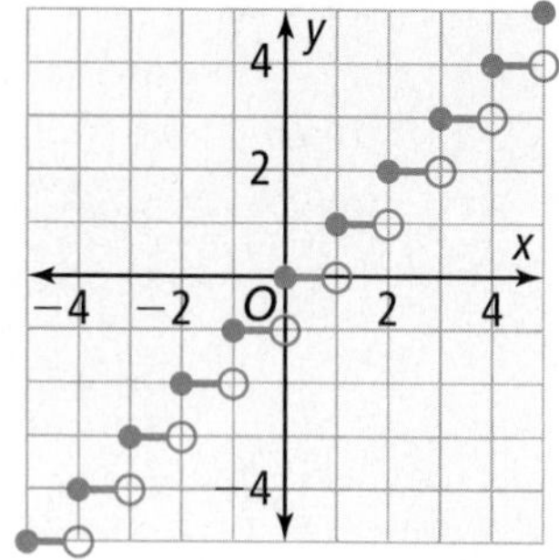

Do You UNDERSTAND?

1. ESSENTIAL QUESTION How are step functions related to piecewise-defined functions?

2. **Vocabulary** How are the *ceiling function* and the *floor function* similar? How are they different?

3. **Error Analysis** Jason defined the following step function.

$$f(x) = \begin{cases} 5, & 0 \leq x \leq 10 \\ 6, & 10 \leq x \leq 20 \\ 7, & 20 \leq x \leq 30 \end{cases}$$

What is the error that Jason made?

4. **Reason** For the function that rounds numbers to the nearest whole number, what are the pieces of the domain for the interval from 0 to 4?

Do You KNOW HOW?

Evaluate the ceiling function for the given value.

5. $f(x) = \lceil x \rceil$; $x = 5.13$

6. $f(x) = \text{ceiling}(x)$; $x = 11.71$

Evaluate the floor function for the given value.

7. $f(x) = \lfloor x \rfloor$; $x = 9.37$

8. $f(x) = \text{floor }(x)$; $x = 5.49$

9. Graph the function f.

x	$f(x)$
$0 < x \leq 1$	4
$1 < x \leq 2$	5
$2 < x \leq 3$	6
$3 < x \leq 4$	7
$4 < x \leq 5$	8
$5 < x \leq 6$	9

PRACTICE & PROBLEM SOLVING

Scan for Multimedia

Practice Tutorial

Additional Exercises Available Online

UNDERSTAND

10. **Communicate Precisely** Many calculators use an INT function which returns the greatest integer less than or equal to x. The graph of **Y1 = INT(X)** is shown. How is this function like the floor function? How is it different?

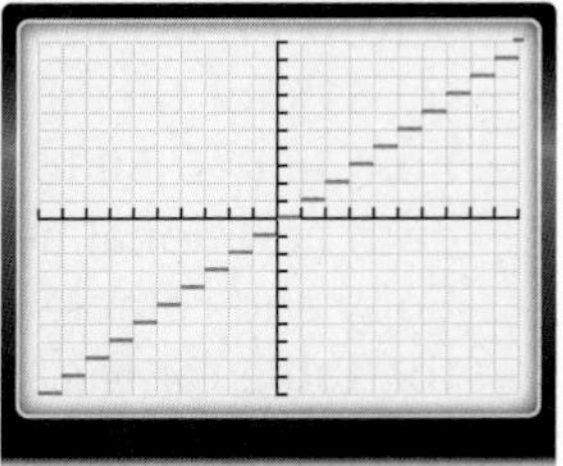

11. **Look for Relationships** How are the pieces of a step function related to the domain of the function? Justify your thinking.

12. **Error Analysis** Kenji wrote a step function to round numbers up to nearest multiple of three. Describe and correct the error he made.

$$f(x) = \begin{cases} 3, 3 < x \leq 6 \\ 6, 6 < x \leq 9 \\ 9, 9 < x \leq 12 \\ 12, 12 < x \leq 15 \end{cases}$$ ✗

13. **Communicate Precisely** Explain how you can use the graph shown below to find the value of the step function for $x = 1$. How is this different from finding the value for $x = 1$ when the graph of a function is a straight line?

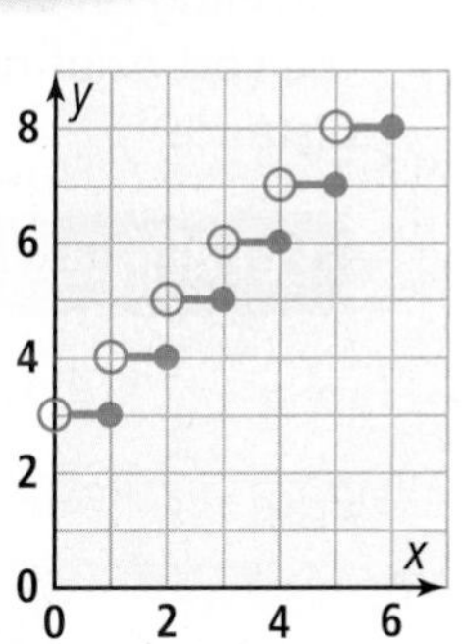

14. **Higher Order Thinking** Results of the **INT** function are shown in the spreadsheet.

a. If $f(x) = \text{INT}(x)$, what is $f(4.6)$, $f(5)$, and $f(-6.5)$?

b. Write $f(x) = \text{INT}(x)$ as a step function for the domain $-4 \leq x \leq 4$.

	A	B
1	−3.1	=INT(A1)
2	−2.4	−3
3	−1.8	−2
4	−0.9	−1
5	0	0
6	0.8	0
7	1.9	1
8	2.8	2

PRACTICE

Evaluate the function for the given value.

SEE EXAMPLE 1

15. $f(x) = \lceil x \rceil;\ x = 0.1$

16. $f(x) = \text{ceiling}(x);\ x = 5.15$

17. $f(x) = \lfloor x \rfloor;\ x = -4.01$

18. $f(x) = \text{ceiling}(x);\ x = 13.20$

19. $f(x) = \lfloor x \rfloor;\ x = 7.06$

20. $f(x) = \text{floor }(x);\ x = 33.7$

21. $f(x) = \text{floor }(x);\ x = 23.2$

22. $f(x) = \lfloor x \rfloor;\ x = -8.4$

For each table, graph the step function and write a rule for f using the ceiling or floor function.

SEE EXAMPLES 2 AND 3

23.

x	$f(x)$
$0 < x \leq 1$	5
$1 < x \leq 2$	6
$2 < x \leq 3$	7
$3 < x \leq 4$	8
$4 < x \leq 5$	9
$5 < x \leq 6$	10

24.

x	$f(x)$
$0 \leq x < 2$	3
$2 \leq x < 4$	4
$4 \leq x < 6$	5
$6 \leq x < 8$	6
$8 \leq x < 10$	7
$10 \leq x < 12$	8

Sketch the graph of each function over the domain $0 < x \leq 10$.

25. The function g returns the greatest integer $g(x)$ that is less than or equal to $x + 2$.

26. The function f returns the least integer $f(x)$ that is greater than $3x$.

PRACTICE & PROBLEM SOLVING

Practice | Tutorial

Mixed Review Available Online

APPLY

27. Mathematical Connections There are 240 seniors in Kathryn's school. Her class is planning a trip, and is taking buses that hold a maximum of 50 passengers. Assume that the trip is optional.

a. Write a step function f that maps the number of students x, to the number of buses needed, $f(x)$.

b. What assumptions do you need to make to write the function?

c. What is the average rate of change of the function over the interval from 40 to 60? From 60 to 80?

d. What do the average rates of change mean in terms of the situation? Explain.

28. Construct Arguments Amit parks his car for 144 h, and Nan parks her car for 145 h. Does Nan pay more? If so, how much more? Make a table and then graph a function to support your answer.

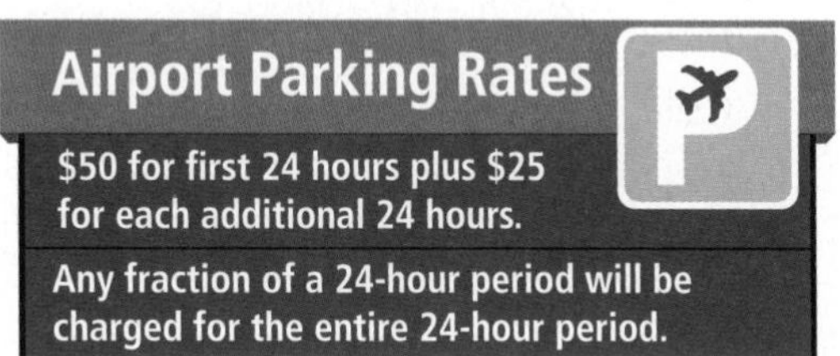

29. Model With Mathematics Mia has $350 in her bank account at the beginning of the school year. Every week she withdraws $50. Two graphs model the situation.

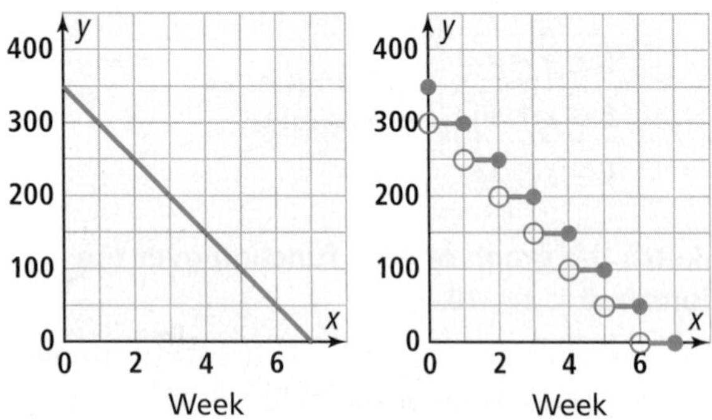

a. Write a function for each graph.

b. How do the graphs and the functions differ in how they represent the situation?

c. What are the advantages and disadvantages of each type of function?

ASSESSMENT PRACTICE

30. A resort rents skis for $15 for the first hour and $7.50 for each additional hour. Copy and complete the table for the step function that models the total cost, in dollars, of renting skis for x hours.

x	$f(x)$
____	15
$1 < x \leq 2$	____
____	____
$3 < x \leq 4$	____
____	45
$5 < x \leq 6$	____

31. SAT/ACT What is the value of $f(2) + f(4) + f(11) + f(12)$ for the function f?

$$f(x) = \begin{cases} 100, & 0 < x \leq 4 \\ 95, & 4 < x \leq 8 \\ 90, & 8 < x \leq 12 \\ 95, & 12 < x \leq 16 \end{cases}$$

Ⓐ 30

Ⓑ 280

Ⓒ 290

Ⓓ 380

Ⓔ 300

32. Performance Task Abdul and his family are traveling on a toll highway. The table shows the cost of using the highway as a function of distance.

Exit Number	Distance (mi)	Toll ($)
1	0	0.00
2	40	1.25
3	75	1.75
4	85	1.90
5	120	2.25
6	150	2.50

Part A Write a step function t to represent the cost of the tolls in terms of distance.

Part B Assume their car averages 30 mi/gal and gasoline costs $3.50/gal. Write a function g to represent the cost of the gas in terms of distance.

Part C Use functions t and g to determine the cost of Abdul's trip if his family leaves the highway at Exit 5.

5-4 Transformations of Piecewise-Defined Functions

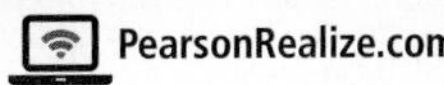

I CAN… graph and analyze transformations of the piecewise-defined functions.

MODEL & DISCUSS

Cleo takes three 1-hour classes at a community college. The graph shows the time she spends in each class.

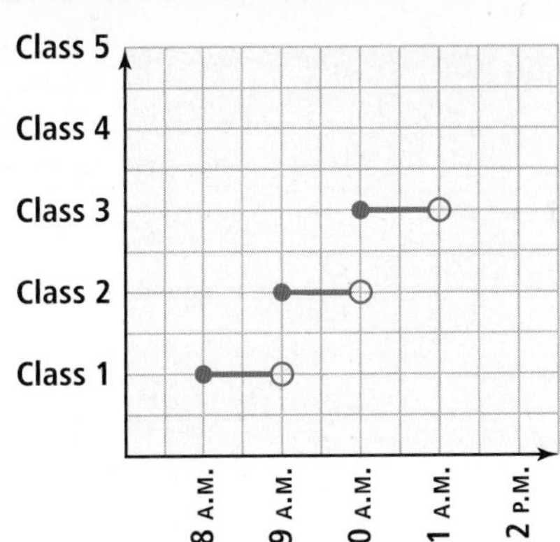

A. Next semester, each class will start an hour later. How will this change the graph?

B. How will the graph change if she takes two 90-minute classes, one starting at 8:30 A.M. and the second at 10:00 A.M.?

C. Construct Arguments Starting in the fall, Cleo will take three classes in a row with the first starting at 7:00 A.M. Cleo says that she can update the graph by moving all three steps one unit to the left. Do you agree? Justify your answer.

ESSENTIAL QUESTION How do the constants affect the graphs of piecewise-defined functions?

APPLICATION

EXAMPLE 1 Translate Step Functions

Uptown Sandwich Shop is increasing the number of bonus points by 2 in the shop's rewards program. How will the total points awarded for a $3.80 item change?

Uptown Sandwich Shop Rewards Program
1 point for each $1 you spend plus 5 bonus points for each visit. No fractional points awarded.

You can represent the two versions of the reward program with step functions. Use the INT function on a graphing calculator to graph the two functions.

> **STUDY TIP**
> Recall that the INT function, which returns the greatest integer less than or equal to x, is another name for the floor function.

	Reward points	=	Dollar part of amount spent	+	Bonus points
Before:	$f(x)$	=	INT(x)	+	5
After:	$g(x)$	=	INT(x)	+	7

(an increase of 2 points)

Enter the functions.

Plot1 Plot2 Plot3
\Y1 = int (X)+5
\Y2 = int (X)+7
\Y3 =
\Y4 =
\Y5 =
\Y6 =
\Y7 =

Graph the functions.

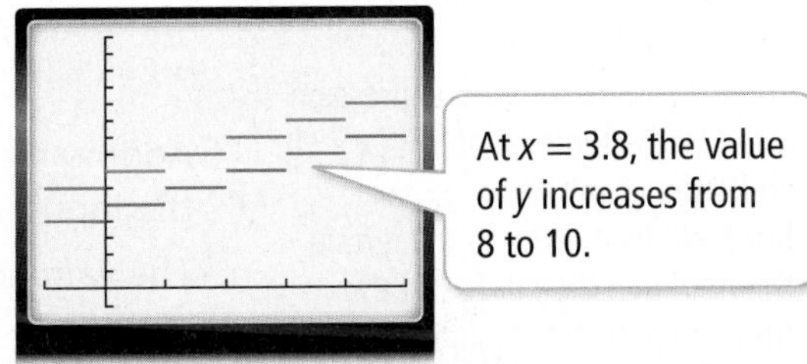

The graph is translated up 2 units. The points for a $3.80 item increase from 8 to 10.

Try It! 1. How will the total points awarded for a $1.25 juice drink change if the bonus points are decreased by 2 points?

EXAMPLE 2 Vertical Translations of the Absolute Value Function

How does adding a constant to the output affect the graph of $f(x) = |x|$?

Compare the graphs of $h(x) = |x| - 4$ and $g(x) = |x| + 2$ with the graph of $f(x) = |x|$.

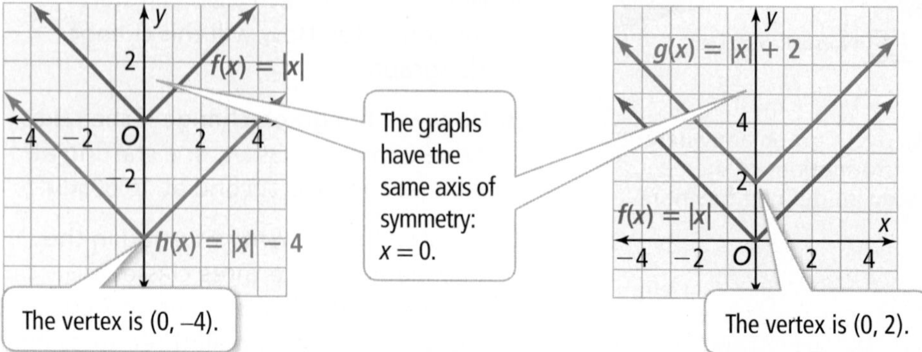

STUDY TIP
Recall that the vertex is the point where the axis of symmetry intersects the graph.

Adding a constant, k, outside of the absolute value bars changes the value of $f(x)$, or the output. It does not change the input. The value of k, in $g(x) = |x| + k$, translates the graph of $f(x) = |x|$ vertically by k units. The axis of symmetry does not change.

Try It! **2.** For each function, identify the vertex and the axis of symmetry.

a. $p(x) = |x| + 3$

b. $g(x) = |x| - 2$

EXAMPLE 3 Horizontal Translations of the Absolute Value Function

How does adding a constant to the input affect the graph of $f(x) = |x|$?

Compare the graph of $g(x) = |x - 4|$ with the graph of $f(x) = |x|$.

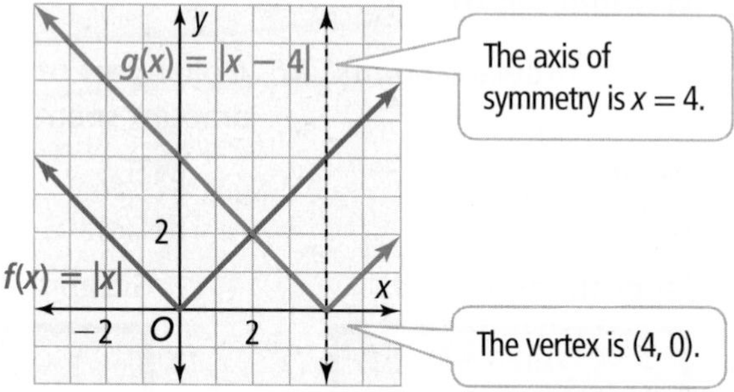

COMMON ERROR
You may think that the expression $x - 4$ in the function $g(x) = |x - 4|$ shifts the graph of $f(x) = |x|$ horizontally 4 units to the left, in the *negative* direction. But the function will shift 4 units to the right because (4, 0) is a solution to the function when $h = 4$.

Adding a constant, h, inside the absolute value bars changes the value of x, the input, as well as the value of $f(x)$, the output.

The value of h, in $g(x) = |x - h|$ translates the graph of $f(x) = |x|$ horizontally by h units. If $h > 0$, the translation is to the right. If $h < 0$, the translation is to the left. Because the input is changed, the translation is horizontal, and the axis of symmetry also shifts.

Try It! **3.** For each function, identify the vertex and the axis of symmetry.

a. $g(x) = |x - 3|$

b. $p(x) = |x + 5|$

CONCEPTUAL UNDERSTANDING

EXAMPLE 4 Understand Vertical and Horizontal Translations

What information do the constants h and k provide about the graph of $g(x) = |x - h| + k$?

Compare the graphs of $g(x) = |x - 4| - 2$ and $g(x) = |x + 5| + 1$ with the graph of $f(x) = |x|$.

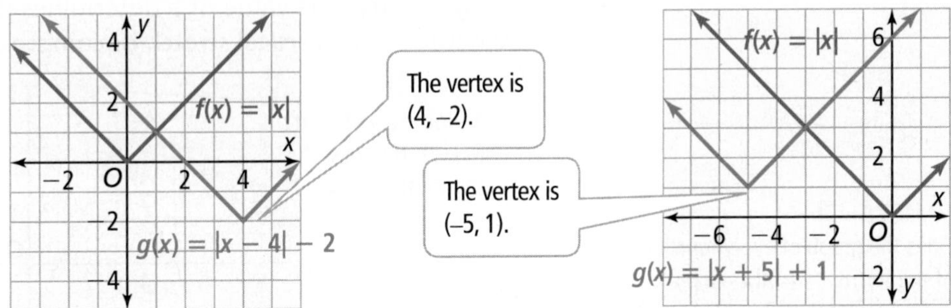

USE STRUCTURE
If the function $g(x) = |x + 5| + 1$, is in the form $g(x) = |x - h| + k$, what are the values of h and k?

The value of h translates the graph horizontally and the value of k translates it vertically. The vertex of the graph $g(x) = |x - h| + k$ is at (h, k).

Try It! 4. Find the vertex of the graph of each function.

a. $g(x) = |x - 1| - 3$

b. $g(x) = |x + 2| + 6$

EXAMPLE 5 Understand Vertical Stretches and Compressions

How does the constant a affect the graph of $g(x) = a|x|$?

Compare the graphs of $g(x) = \frac{1}{2}|x|$ and $g(x) = -4|x|$ with the graph of $f(x) = |x|$.

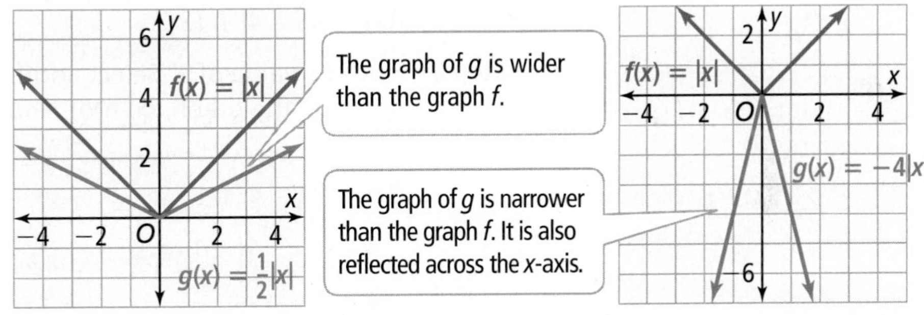

In $g(x) = a|x|$, the constant a multiplies the output of the function $f(x) = |x|$ by a.

- When $0 < |a| < 1$ the graph of $g(x) = a|x|$ is a vertical compression towards the x-axis of the graph of $f(x) = |x|$.
- When $|a| > 1$, the graph of $g(x) = a|x|$ is a vertical stretch away from the x-axis of the graph of $f(x) = |x|$.
- When $a < 0$, the graph of g is reflected across the x-axis.

The value of a stretches or compresses the graph vertically.

Try It! 5. Compare the graph of each function with the graph of $f(x) = |x|$.

a. $g(x) = 3|x|$

b. $g(x) = -\frac{1}{3}|x|$

EXAMPLE 6 Understand Transformations of the Absolute Value Function

A. How do the constants *a*, *h*, and *k* affect the graph of $g(x) = a|x - h| + k$?

Graph $g(x) = -2|x + 3| + 4$.

The values of *h* and *k* determine the location of the vertex and the axis of symmetry. The value of *a* determines the direction of the graph and whether it is a vertical stretch or compression of the graph of $f(x) = |x|$.

GENERALIZE
Does the graph of every function of the form $g(x) = a|x - h| + k$ have a *y*-intercept?

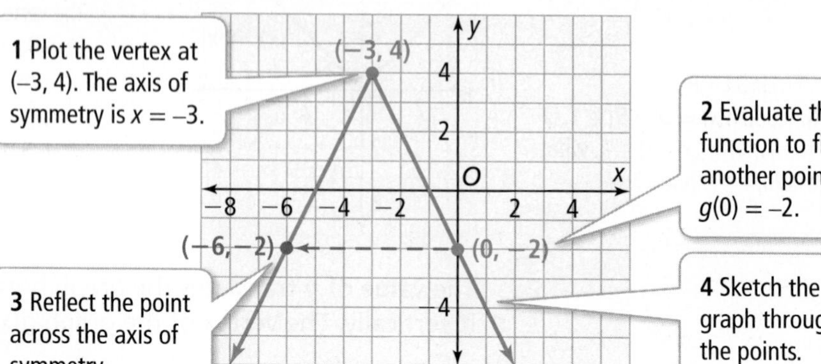

Since $|a| > 1$ and *a* is negative the graph is a vertical stretch of the graph of $f(x) = |x|$ that is reflected across the *x*-axis.

B. How can you use the constants *a*, *h*, and *k* to write a function given its graph?

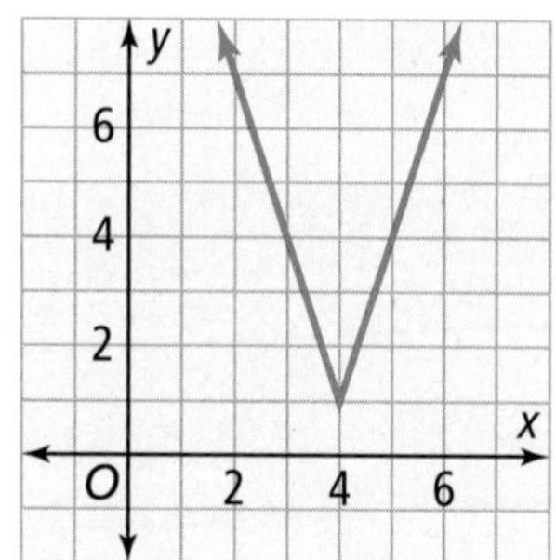

Step 1 Identify the vertex of the graph.

The vertex is (4, 1), so $h = 4$ and $k = 1$.

The function has the form $f(x) = a|x - 4| + 1$.

Step 2 Find the value of *a*. Select another point on the graph, $(x, f(x))$, and solve for *a*.

$f(x) = a|x - 4| + 1$

$4 = a|5 - 4| + 1$

$a = 3$

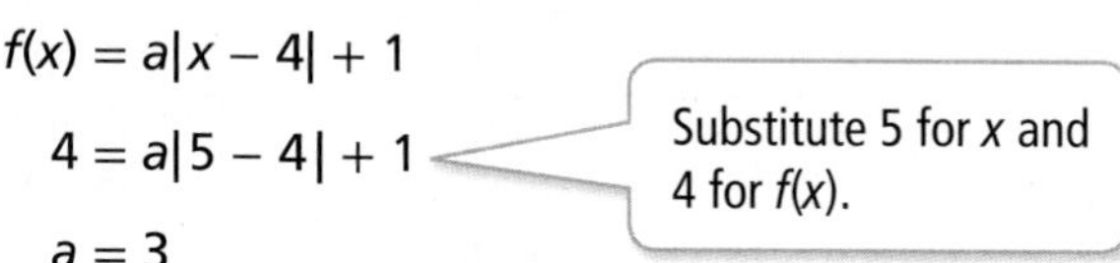

The graph represents the function $f(x) = 3|x - 4| + 1$.

 **Try It!** **6. a.** Write a function for the graph shown.

b. Write the function of the graph after a translation 1 unit right and 4 units up.

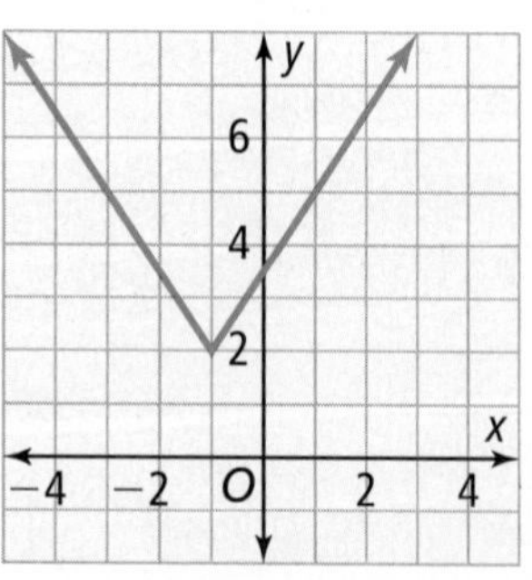

CONCEPT SUMMARY Transformations of the Absolute Value Function

WORDS The graph of $g(x) = a|x - h| + k$ is a transformation of the graph of the absolute value function, $f(x) = |x|$.

- Adding a constant, h, to the input translates the graph of f horizontally.
- Adding a constant, k, to the output translates the graph of f vertically.
- Multiplying the input by a constant, a, greater than 1 results in a vertical stretch of the graph of f.
- Multiplying the input by a constant, a, less than 1 but greater than 0 results in a vertical compression of the graph of f.
- When $a < 0$ the graph of the function is reflected across the x-axis.

ALGEBRA $g(x) = a|x - h| + k$

The vertex of the graph is (h, k).

NUMBERS $g(x) = -2|x + 3| + 4$

The vertex of the graph is $(-3, 4)$.

GRAPH

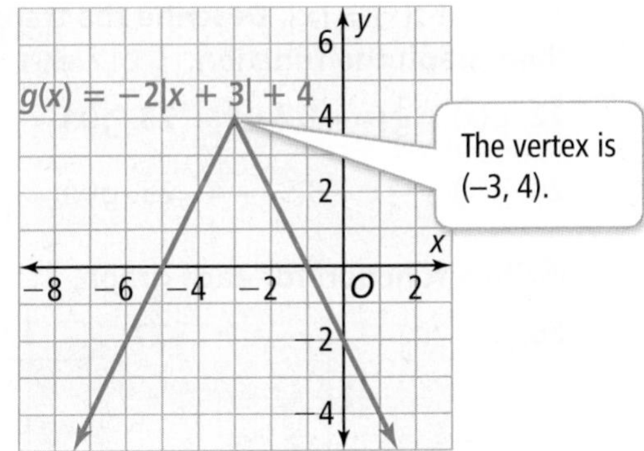

Do You UNDERSTAND?

1. ESSENTIAL QUESTION How do the constants affect the graphs of piecewise-defined functions?

2. **Generalize** How do the constants a, h, and k affect the domain and range of $g(x) = a|x - h| + k$ when $a > 0$?

3. **Error Analysis** Jacy says that $f(x) = 4|x - 1|$ and $f(x) = |4x - 1|$ have the same graph. Is Jacy correct? Explain.

4. **Use Structure** How can you reflect the graph of $f(x) = 3|x + 2| + 1$ across the x-axis?

Do You KNOW HOW?

Find the vertex and graph each function.

5. $f(x) = |x| + 2.5$

6. $f(x) = |x + 2.5|$

7. $f(x) = |x - 2| + 4$

8. $f(x) = -3|x + 1| - 5$

9. Write a function for the graph.

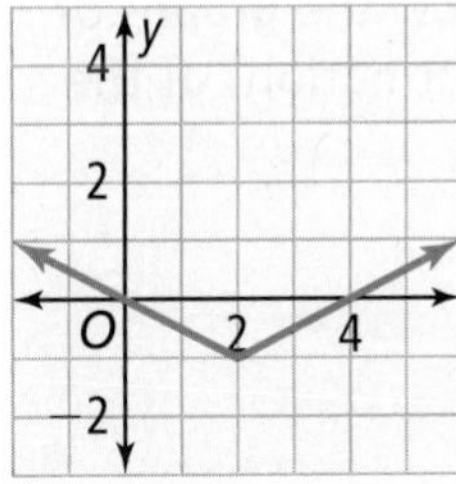

UNDERSTAND

10. Model With Mathematics Give two examples of functions that include an absolute value expression and have a vertex of $(-1, 3)$.

11. Mathematical Connections Consider the function $f(x) = 2|x + 1| - 7$.

a. A linear function containing one branch of the function is $f(x) = 2(x + 1) - 7$. What linear function contains the other branch?

b. For the general function $f(x) = a|x - h| + k$, what are the two linear functions containing the branches?

12. Use Appropriate Tools Explain how you can write a second step function that translates the graph of the step function shown down 6 units.

Plot1 Plot2 Plot3
\Y1 = int (X)+2
\Y2 =
\Y3 =
\Y4 =
\Y5 =
\Y6 =
\Y7 =

13. Error Analysis Describe and correct the errors a student made in describing the graph of the function $f(x) = -0.5|x + 1| + 3$.

> The graph of $y = -0.5|x + 1| + 3$ compresses the graph of $y = |x|$ vertically toward the x-axis, and moves the vertex to $(1, 3)$. ✗

14. Higher Order Thinking Write each function Y1 through Y4. Explain how the graphs of Y2 through Y4 are transformations of the graph of Y1.

Plot1 Plot2 Plot3
\Y1 = abs(X−3)
\Y2 = Y1+4
\Y3 = 2Y1
\Y4 = −Y1
\Y5 =
\Y6 =
\Y7 =

PRACTICE

15. Describe the transformation for the pair of step functions. SEE EXAMPLE 1

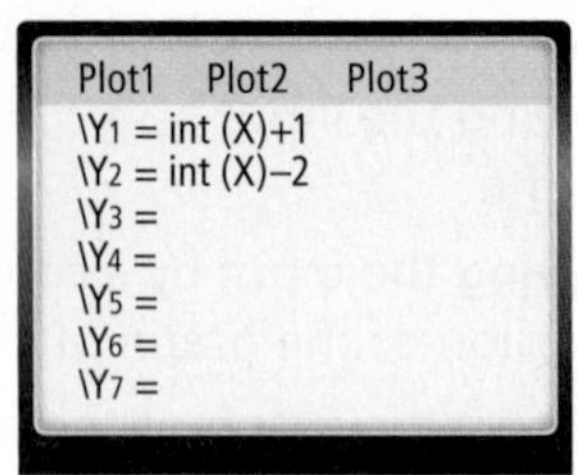

Find the vertex and graph each function.
SEE EXAMPLES 2, 3, AND 4

16. $f(x) = |x| - 2$

17. $f(x) = |x| + 1$

18. $f(x) = |x + 0.5|$

19. $f(x) = |x - 1|$

20. $f(x) = |x + 7| - 2$

21. $f(x) = |x - 0.5| + 0.5$

Compare the graph of each function with the graph of $f(x) = |x|$. Describe the transformation, then graph the function. SEE EXAMPLES 4, 5, AND 6

22. $g(x) = \frac{1}{3}|x + 6| - 1$

23. $g(x) = -4|x - 2| - 1$

24. $g(x) = -|x + 3.5| + 4$

25. $g(x) = \frac{5}{4}|x - 2| + 7$

Write a function for each graph. SEE EXAMPLE 6

26.

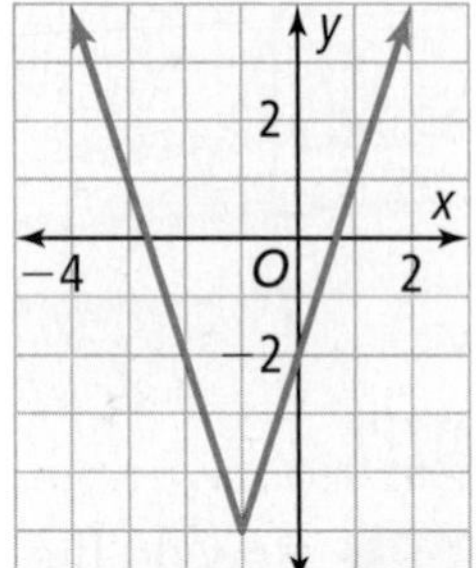

27.

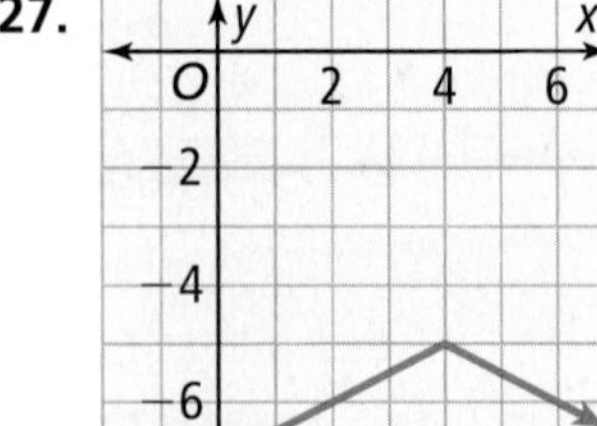

What function g describes the graph of f after the given transformations?

28. $f(x) = |x|$; translated 2 units up and 1 unit right

29. $f(x) = |x| + 1$; translated 3 units down and 2 units left

30. $f(x) = |x|$; reflected across the x-axis and translated 4 units up

31. $f(x) = |x|$; vertically stretched by a factor of 3 and reflected across the x-axis

PRACTICE & PROBLEM SOLVING

APPLY

32. Model With Mathematics The rates for Carolina's dog boarding service are shown. Carolina plans on increasing the rate for the first hour by \$5.

a. Make a graph that shows the step functions for the cost of boarding a dog before and after the rate increase.

b. How much will it cost to board a dog for 4 hours after the rate increase?

33. Model With Mathematics Emma wants to model the sides of a pyramid by using a function that includes an absolute value expression. Emma will place the pyramid on a coordinate grid as shown. What function should she use? For what domain?

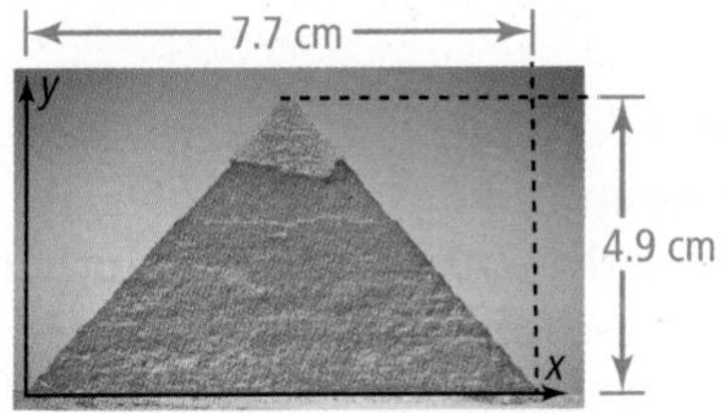

34. Make Sense and Persevere One part of a dog agility course is an obstacle called an A-frame. Assume that the left corner of the A-frame corresponds to the point (0, 0). What function that includes an absolute value expression could you use to model the obstacle? What is the domain of the function? Explain your reasoning.

ASSESSMENT PRACTICE

Fill in the blanks with the correct answer.

35. The graph of $g(x) = -|x + 15| - 7$, is a vertical translation of the graph of the _______ function, $f(x) = |x|$ by _______ units. The graph of g is a horizontal translation of the graph of f by _______ units. The vertex of the graph of g is _______. The y-intercept is _______, and there is/are _______ x-intercept(s).

36. SAT/ACT Which function has the same graph as $f(x) = 4|x - 2| + 2$?

Ⓐ $f(x) = 2|2x - 4| + 2$

Ⓑ $f(x) = 2|2x - 1| + 2$

Ⓒ $f(x) = 2|2x - 1| + 1$

Ⓓ $f(x) = 2|2x - 4| + 1$

Ⓔ none of these

37. Performance Task You are playing a ship trapping game. There are 4 of your opponent's red ships on the screen. You can send out 3 strikes from your blue ships through the red ships' positions to capture them. Each strike sends two lasers that resemble the graph of a function with an absolute value expression.

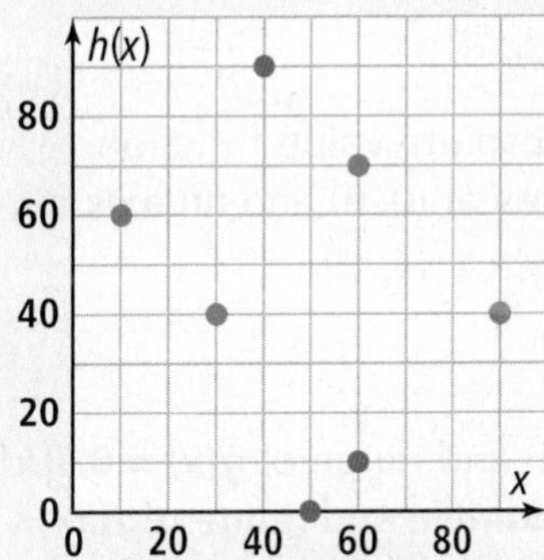

Part A How can symmetry help you find a path to capture two ships?

Part B Write three functions that represent strike paths to capture the ships. Show how each ship is captured by a function.

Part C For your function that captures two ships, can you write a different function from one of your other ships that represent strikes paths to capture these two ships? Explain.

TOPIC 5

Topic Review

TOPIC ESSENTIAL QUESTION

1. How do you use piecewise-defined functions to model situations and solve problems?

Vocabulary Review

Choose the correct term to complete each sentence.

2. The __________ intersects the vertex, and divides the graph into two congruent halves that are images of each other under a reflection.
3. The __________ rounds numbers up to the nearest integer.
4. The __________ has an algebraic expression with absolute value symbols.
5. A(n) __________ has different rules for different intervals of its domain.

- absolute value function
- axis of symmetry
- ceiling function
- floor function
- piecewise-defined function
- step function
- vertex

Concepts & Skills Review

LESSON 5-1 The Absolute Value Function

Quick Review

The graph of the absolute value function, $f(x) = |x|$ has a **vertex** at (0, 0) and an **axis of symmetry** $x = 0$.

Example

How do the domain and range of $g(x) = 0.5|x|$ compare with the domain and range of $f(x) = |x|$?

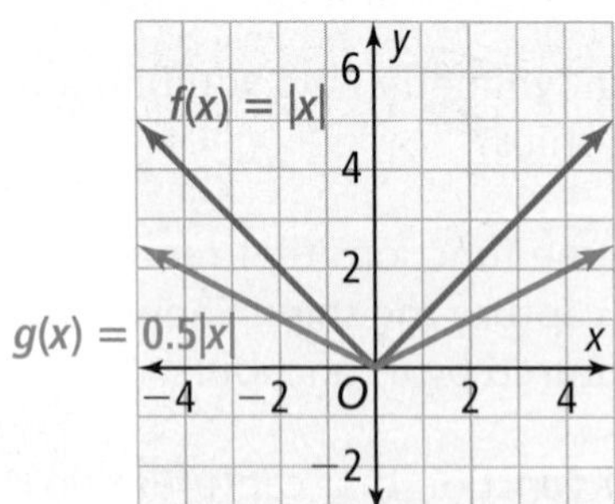

The domain of f and the domain of g are all real numbers. The range of both functions is $y \geq 0$.

Practice & Problem Solving

Tell whether each point is on the graph of $f(x) = |x|$. If it is, give the coordinates of another point with the same y-coordinate.

6. (8, 8)
7. (−5, 5)
8. (−3.5, −3.5)

Graph each function. What is the domain and range of each function?

9. $f(x) = -2.5|x|$
10. $g(x) = \frac{1}{3}|x|$

For each function, find the vertex and tell whether it represents a maximum or minimum value of the function.

11. $g(x) = -6.3|x|$
12. $g(x) = 7|x|$

13. **Look for Relationships** Find the domain, range, and vertex of the graphed function.

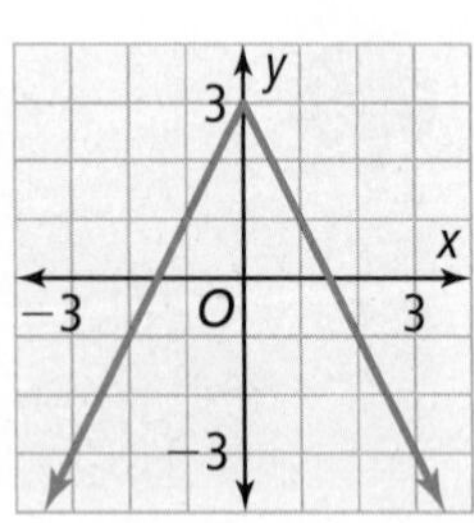

Piecewise-Defined Functions

Quick Review

A **piecewise-defined function** has different rules for different intervals of the domain.

You can express functions of the form $g(x) = a|x|$ as piecewise-defined functions using a pair of linear rules with boundaries on the domain.

Example

What is the graph of $f(x) = \begin{cases} -x - 5, & x < 0 \\ \frac{1}{4}x + 2, & x \geq 0 \end{cases}$**?**

Over what interval of the domain is the function increasing? Decreasing?

Graph each rule of the function for the given interval of the domain.

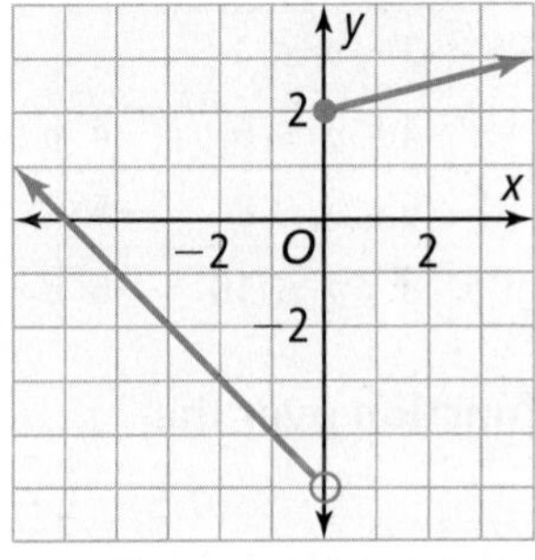

The function is decreasing when $x < 0$.
The function is increasing when $x \geq 0$.

Practice & Problem Solving

Express each function as a piecewise-defined function.

14. $f(x) = 4|x|$

15. $f(x) = -2|x|$

Graph each piecewise-defined function. Identify the intervals over which the function is increasing, decreasing, or constant.

16. $f(x) = \begin{cases} x + 1, & x < -1 \\ \frac{1}{2}x - 2, & -1 \leq x \end{cases}$

17. $f(x) = \begin{cases} -x + 4, & -2 < x \leq 3 \\ x - 5, & 3 < x \end{cases}$

18. Error Analysis Describe and correct the error a student made in expressing the function $f(x) = -5|x|$ as a piecewise-defined function.

$$f(x) = -5|x|,\ f(x) = \begin{cases} -5x, & x < 0 \\ 5x, & x > 0 \end{cases}$$

19. Write a piecewise-defined function that represents the graph.

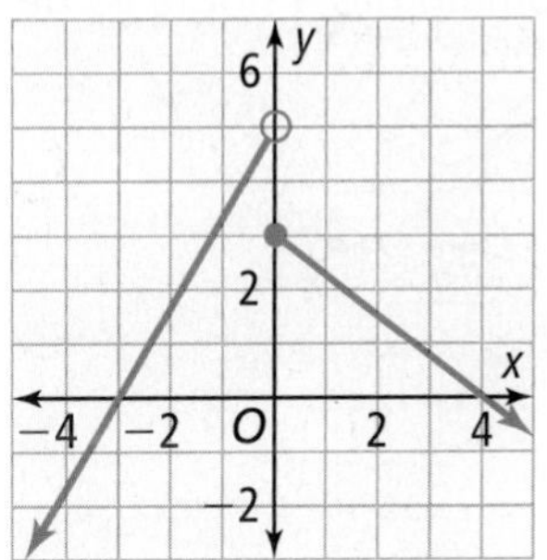

20. Model With Mathematics A jeweler sells rings for \$35 each plus a flat fee of \$5 for shipping for orders up to 10 rings. If customers order more than 10 rings, the cost is \$30 per ring and shipping is free. Write a piecewise function to represent the situation.

Quick Review

Step functions are a type of piecewise-defined function that consists of constant pieces. The constant pieces of the function result in a graph that looks like the steps of a staircase.

The floor and ceiling functions are specific types of step functions. The **ceiling function** rounds numbers up to the nearest integer. The **floor function** rounds numbers down to the nearest integer.

Example

Graph the function *f*. What is the domain and range of the function?

x	$f(x)$
$0 < x \leq 3$	4
$3 < x \leq 6$	6
$6 < x \leq 9$	8
$9 < x \leq 12$	10

Each section of the domain has a single value assigned to it.

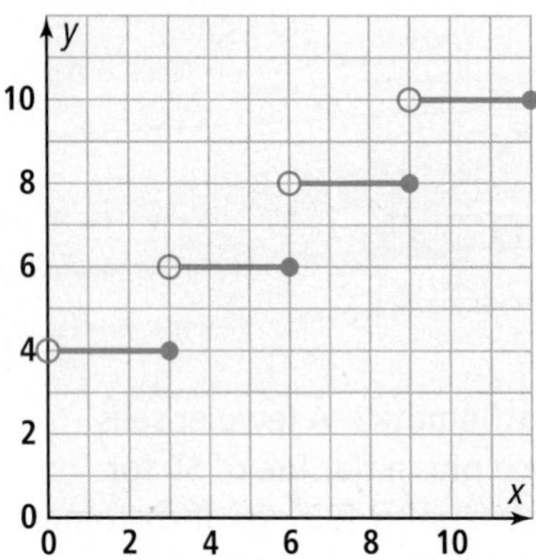

The domain of f is $0 < x \leq 12$. The range is the set values {4, 6, 8, 10}.

Practice & Problem Solving

Evaluate the ceiling function for the given value.

21. $f(x) = \lceil x \rceil$; $x = 7.03$

22. $f(x) = \text{ceiling}(x)$; $x = 2.6$

Evaluate the floor function for the given value.

23. $f(x) = \lfloor x \rfloor$; $x = 6.1$

24. $f(x) = \text{floor}(x)$; $x = 0.08$

For each table, graph the step function and write a rule for *f* using a ceiling or floor function.

25.

x	$f(x)$
$1 < x \leq 2$	7
$2 < x \leq 3$	8
$3 < x \leq 4$	9
$4 < x \leq 5$	10
$5 < x \leq 6$	11

26.

x	$f(x)$
$0 < x \leq 2$	−2
$2 < x \leq 4$	−3
$4 < x \leq 6$	−4
$6 < x \leq 8$	−5
$8 < x \leq 10$	−6

Sketch the graph of each function over the domain $0 < x \leq 10$.

27. The function g returns the greatest integer $g(x)$ less than or equal to $2x$.

28. The function f returns the least integer $f(x)$ greater than $x - 3$.

29. Make Sense and Persevere Egg cartons hold a dozen eggs in each container. Write a step function that represents the number of egg cartons needed as a function of the number of eggs over the domain $0 < x \leq 72$. Is the function a floor or a ceiling function? Explain.

Quick Review

The graph of $g(x) = a|x - h| + k$ is a transformation of the graph of $f(x) = |x|$ when $a \neq 1$, $h \neq 0$, or $k \neq 0$. The vertex of the graph is located at (h, k). The value of h indicates that the graph of g is a horizontal translation of h units of the graph of f. The value of k indicates that the graph of g is a vertical translation of k units of the graph of f.

When $|a| > 1$, the graph of g is a vertical stretch of the graph of f. When $0 \leq |a| \leq 1$, the graph is a vertical compression of the graph of f.

Example

For the function $g(x) = 2|x + 3| - 4$, find the vertex and graph the function. Describe the graph of g as a transformation of the graph of $f(x) = |x|$.

The vertex is located at (h, k), so the vertex of this graph is $(-3, -4)$.

Graph the function.

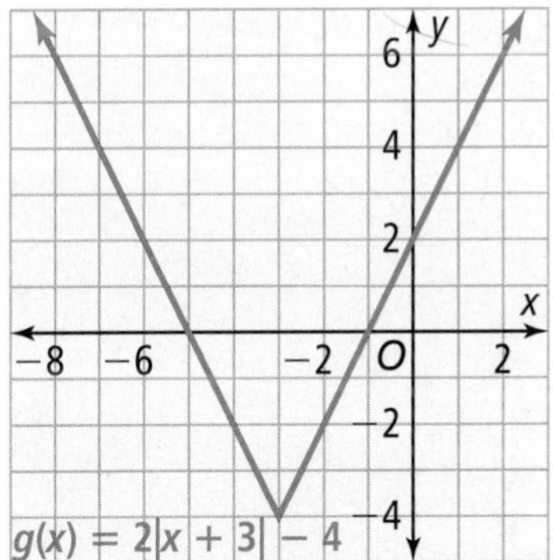

The graph of g is a translation of the graph of f horizontally, 3 units to the left, and vertically 4 units down. It is also a vertical stretch of the graph of f by a factor of 2.

Practice & Problem Solving

Find the vertex and graph each function.

30. $g(x) = |x| + 4$
31. $g(x) = |x - 2|$
32. $g(x) = |x + 1| - 2$
33. $g(x) = |x - 3| + 1$

Compare each function with $f(x) = |x|$. Describe the graph of g as transformation of the graph of f.

34. $g(x) = 2|x + 6| - 1$
35. $g(x) = -|x - 2| - 1$
36. $g(x) = -0.5|x| + 4$
37. $g(x) = \frac{3}{2}|x - 1| + 8$

Write the function that includes absolute value expressions for each graph.

38.

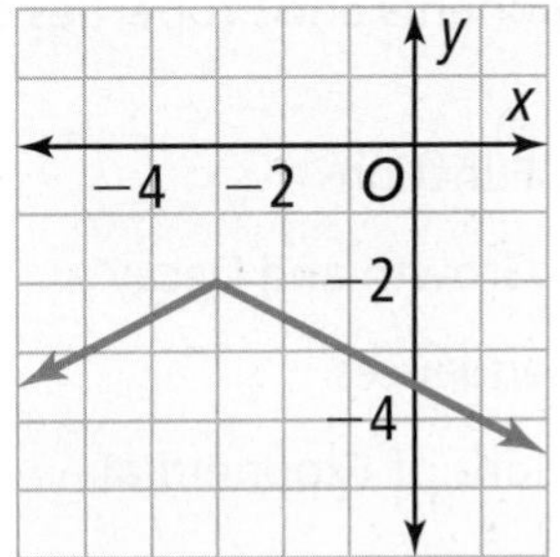

39.

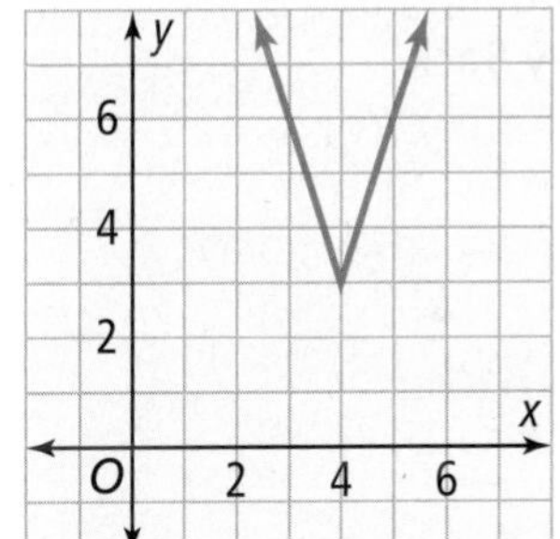

40. **Use Structure** Write two functions that have a vertex of $(2, -1)$.

What function g describes the graph of f after the given transformations?

41. $f(x) = |x| + 3$; translated 1 unit up and 5 units right

42. $f(x) = |x - 1| + 5$; translated 2 units down and 4 units left

43. **Make Sense and Persevere** A traffic cone is 18 in. tall and 12 in. wide. You want to sketch an image of the traffic cone on a coordinate grid with one edge at (0, 0). What function that includes an absolute value expression could represent the traffic cone? What would be the domain of the function? Explain.

Exponents and Exponential Functions

TOPIC ESSENTIAL QUESTION

How do you use exponential functions to model situations and solve problems?

Topic Overview

Topic Vocabulary

- asymptote
- compound interest
- constant ratio
- decay factor
- exponential decay
- exponential function
- exponential growth
- geometric sequence
- growth factor
- rational exponent

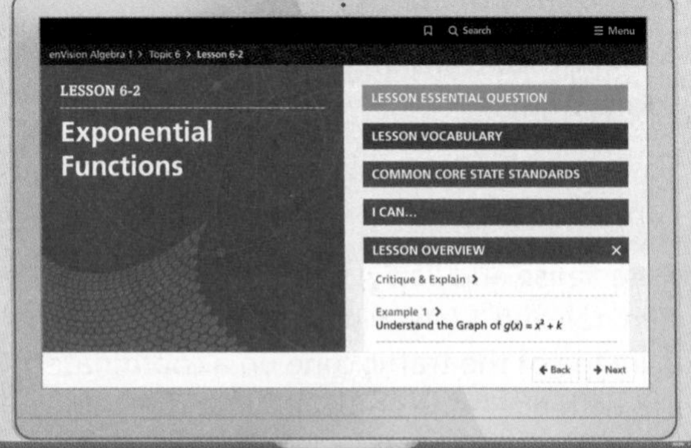

 Go online | **PearsonRealize.com**

Digital Experience

 **INTERACTIVE STUDENT EDITION** Access online or offline.

 **ACTIVITIES** Complete ***Explore & Reason, Model & Discuss***, and ***Critique & Explain*** activities. Interact with Examples and Try Its.

 **ANIMATION** View and interact with real-world applications.

 **PRACTICE** Practice what you've learned.

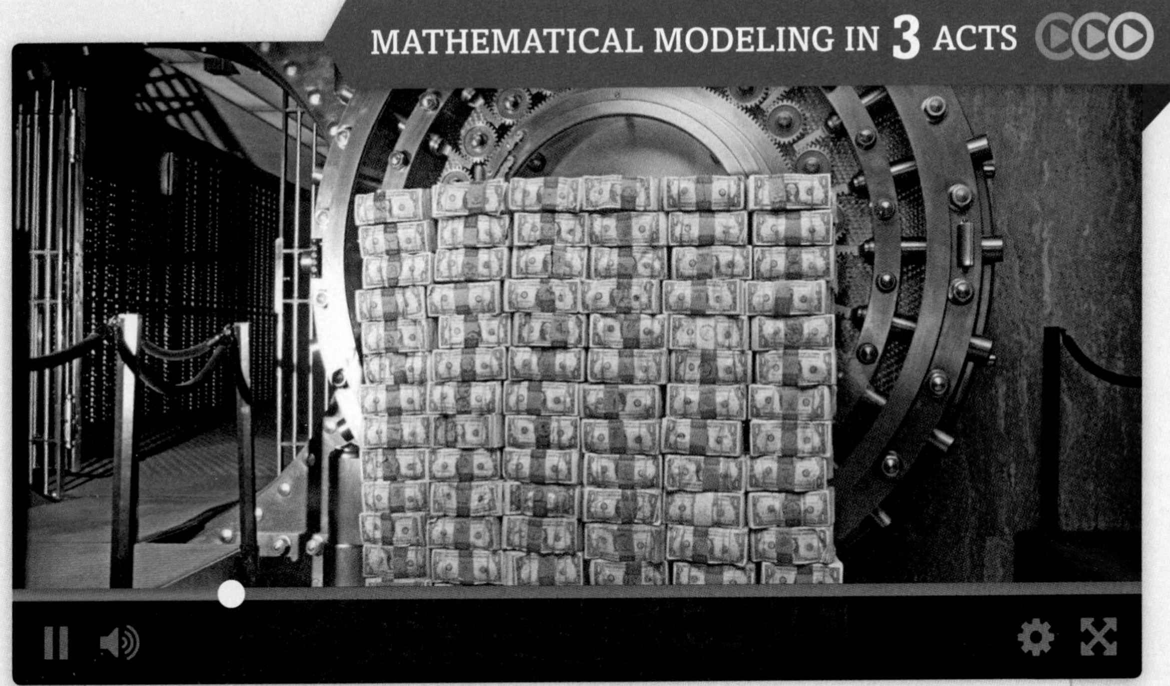

Big Time Pay Back

Most people agree that investing your money is a good idea. Some people might advise you to put money into a bank savings account. Other people might say that you should invest in the stock market. Still others think that buying bonds is the best investment option.

Is a bank savings account a good way to let your money grow? Just how much money can you make from a savings account? In the Mathematical Modeling in 3 Acts lesson, you'll see an intriguing situation about an investment option.

TOPIC 6

VIDEOS Watch clips to support ***Mathematical Modeling in 3 Acts Lessons*** and **enVision™ *STEM Projects.***

CONCEPT SUMMARY Review key lesson content through multiple representations.

ASSESSMENT Show what you've learned.

GLOSSARY Read and listen to English and Spanish definitions.

TUTORIALS Get help from ***Virtual Nerd***, right when you need it.

MATH TOOLS Explore math with digital tools and manipulatives.

Moore's Law predicts advancements in many digital electronics, stating that **growth is exponential.**

Moore's Law, 1965 (projected for 10 years): The number of **transistors in a chip will double approximately every 12 months.**

Moore's Law, amended 1975 (projected for 10 years): The number of **transistors in a chip will double approximately every 24 months.**

If you applied Moore's Law to space travel, a trip to the moon would take one minute.

Corollary to Moore's Law: For a chip of fixed size, the transistors will **decrease in size by 50% every 24 months.**

Transistor

Integrated Circuit

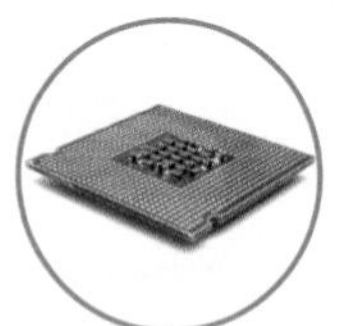

Microprocessor

If cars and transistors shrank at the same rate, **today's cars would be the size of ants.**

Your Task: Predict the Future Using Moore's Law

You and your classmates will predict the features of a cellular phone released 3 years from now, and decide whether or not Moore's Law is sustainable for the next 20 years.

6-1 Rational Exponents and Properties of Exponents

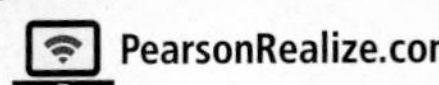

I CAN… use properties of exponents to solve equations with rational exponents.

VOCABULARY

- rational exponent

CRITIQUE & EXPLAIN

Students are asked to write an equivalent expression for 3^{-3}.

Casey and Jacinta each write an expression on the board.

Casey
$3^{-3} = -27$

Jacinta
$3^{-3} = \frac{1}{27}$

A. Who is correct, Casey or Jacinta? Explain.

B. **Reason** What is the most likely error that was made?

ESSENTIAL QUESTION

What are the properties of rational exponents and how are they used to solve problems?

CONCEPTUAL UNDERSTANDING

EXAMPLE 1 Write Radicals Using Rational Exponents

What does $3^{\frac{1}{2}}$ equal?

You can think of exponentiation as repeated multiplication.

$3^2 = 3 \cdot 3$ ········ Multiply 3 by itself 2 times.

$3^3 = 3 \cdot 3 \cdot 3$ ········ Multiply 3 by itself 3 times.

$3^4 = 3 \cdot 3 \cdot 3 \cdot 3$ ········ Multiply 3 by itself 4 times.

etc.

But what does $3^{\frac{1}{2}}$ mean? You cannot multiply 3 by itself $\frac{1}{2}$ times. Since interpreting exponents as repeated multiplication does not work in this case, you have to *define* a new meaning for expressions like $3^{\frac{1}{2}}$.

GENERALIZE
The Power of a Power Property says that $(a^m)^n = a^{mn}$ for all integers m and n.

Whatever the new definition is, you want it to obey the same rules of exponents that you know for integers, such as the Power of a Power Property.

$$\left(3^{\frac{1}{2}}\right)^2 = 3^{\frac{1}{2} \cdot 2} = 3^1 = 3$$

When you square $3^{\frac{1}{2}}$ …

… the result is 3.

You know that a number whose square is 3 is $\sqrt{3}$. So in order to define raising a number to the $\frac{1}{2}$ power in a way that makes sense, define $3^{\frac{1}{2}}$ to be $\sqrt{3}$.

You can define the meaning of other rational exponents in a similar way. If the nth root of a is a real number and m is an integer, then $a^{\frac{1}{n}} = \sqrt[n]{a}$, and $a^{\frac{m}{n}} = \sqrt[n]{a^m} = (\sqrt[n]{a})^m$.

Try It! 1. What does $2^{\frac{1}{3}}$ equal? Explain.

EXAMPLE 2 Use the Product of Powers Property to Solve Equations With Rational Exponents

What is the solution of $\left(3^{\frac{x}{2}}\right)\left(3^{\frac{x}{3}}\right) = 3^9$?

STUDY TIP
To multiply two powers with a common base, keep the common base and add the exponents.

Rewrite the left side of the equation with one exponent.

$$\left(3^{\frac{x}{2}}\right)\left(3^{\frac{x}{3}}\right) = 3^9$$

$$3^{\frac{x}{2}+\frac{x}{3}} = 3^9 \quad \text{Product of Powers Property}$$

$$3^{\frac{3x}{6}+\frac{2x}{6}} = 3^9 \quad \text{Write the exponents with a common denominator.}$$

$$3^{\frac{5x}{6}} = 3^9$$

$$\frac{5x}{6} = 9 \quad \text{The bases are the same, so set the exponents equal.}$$

$$\frac{6}{5}\left(\frac{5x}{6}\right) = \frac{6}{5}(9) \quad \text{Multiply both sides by } \frac{6}{5}.$$

$$x = \frac{54}{5}$$

The solution is $\frac{54}{5}$.

Try It! 2. What is the solution of $\left(2^{\frac{x}{4}}\right)\left(2^{\frac{x}{6}}\right) = 2^3$?

EXAMPLE 3 Use the Power of a Power Property to Solve Equations With Rational Exponents

A. What is the solution of $27^{x-4} = 3^{2x-6}$?

STUDY TIP
To find the power of a power, keep the base and multiply the exponents.

$$27^{x-4} = 3^{2x-6}$$

$$(3^3)^{x-4} = 3^{2x-6} \quad \text{Rewrite 27 with a base of 3.}$$

$$3^{3x-12} = 3^{2x-6} \quad \text{Power of a Power Property}$$

$$3x - 12 = 2x - 6 \quad \text{Write the exponents as an equation.}$$

$$3x - 12 - 3x = 2x - 6 - 3x$$

$$-12 = -x - 6$$

$$-12 + 6 = -x - 6 + 6$$

$$-6 = -x$$

$$6 = x$$

The solution is 6.

B. What is the solution of $\left(\frac{1}{125}\right)^{-\frac{x}{2}} = \left(\frac{1}{25}\right)^{-\frac{x}{3}-2}$?

Step 1 Rewrite the equation so both sides have the same base.

$$\left(\frac{1}{125}\right)^{-\frac{x}{2}} = \left(\frac{1}{25}\right)^{-\frac{x}{3}-2}$$

$$(5^{-3})^{-\frac{x}{2}} = (5^{-2})^{-\frac{x}{3}-2}$$

Rewrite $\frac{1}{125}$ and $\frac{1}{25}$ as powers of 5.

$$5^{\frac{3x}{2}} = 5^{\frac{2x}{3}+4} \quad \text{Power of a Power Property}$$

CONTINUED ON THE NEXT PAGE

EXAMPLE 3 CONTINUED

Step 2 Write the exponents as an equation and solve.

$$\frac{3x}{2} = \frac{2x}{3} + 4$$
$$6\left(\frac{3x}{2}\right) = 6\left(\frac{2x}{3} + 4\right)$$
$$9x = 4x + 24$$
$$9x - 4x = 4x + 24 - 4x$$
$$5x = 24$$
$$\frac{5x}{5} = \frac{24}{5}$$
$$x = 4.8$$

The solution is $x = 4.8$.

COMMON ERROR
Remember to distribute across both terms when multiplying.

Try It! **3.** What is the solution of each equation?

a. $256^{x+2} = 4^{3x+9}$ **b.** $\left(\frac{1}{8}\right)^{\frac{x}{2}-1} = \left(\frac{1}{4}\right)^{\frac{x}{3}}$

APPLICATION

EXAMPLE 4 Use the Power of a Product Property to Solve Equations With Rational Exponents

Adam is setting up for an outdoor concert. He places three square blankets near the band as shown in the picture. What is the area of Blanket C?

Formulate

Area	=	length	•	width
12	=	$8^{\frac{1}{2}}$	•	$x^{\frac{1}{2}}$
Area of the grass rectangle		Side length of Blanket B		Side length of Blanket C

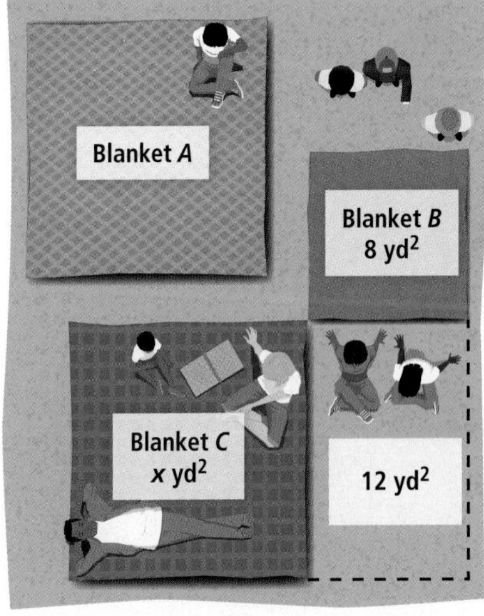

Compute

Solve for x, the area of Blanket C.

$$12 = \left(8^{\frac{1}{2}}\right)\left(x^{\frac{1}{2}}\right)$$
$$12 = (8x)^{\frac{1}{2}}$$

Multiply the bases and keep the exponent.

$$12^2 = \left[(8x)^{\frac{1}{2}}\right]^2$$
$$144 = 8x$$

Square both sides.

$$\frac{144}{8} = \frac{8x}{8}$$
$$18 = x$$

Interpret

The area of Blanket C is 18 yd^2.

Check Compare the product of $\sqrt{18}$ and $\sqrt{8}$ to the rectangular area of 12.

$$(\sqrt{8})(\sqrt{18}) = \left(8^{\frac{1}{2}}\right)\left(18^{\frac{1}{2}}\right)$$
$$= (8 \cdot 18)^{\frac{1}{2}} = 144^{\frac{1}{2}}$$
$$= 12$$

Try It! **4.** When the side length of Blanket A is multiplied by $2^{\frac{1}{2}}$ the result is 6 yards. Find the area of Blanket A.

EXAMPLE 5 Use the Quotient of Powers Property to Solve Equations With Rational Exponents

Terrarium A and Terrarium B are cubes. The side length of Terrarium A is twice the side length of Terrarium B. What is the value of x?

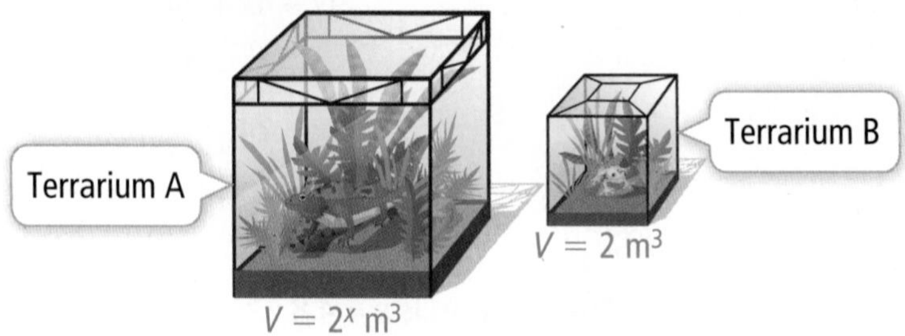

Step 1 Write a proportion using the side lengths.

$$\frac{(2^x)^{\frac{1}{3}}}{2^{\frac{1}{3}}} = 2$$ The ratio of the side lengths is 2.

$$\frac{2^{x \cdot \frac{1}{3}}}{2^{\frac{1}{3}}} = 2$$

Step 2 Use properties of exponents to simplify.

$$\frac{2^{\frac{x}{3}}}{2^{\frac{1}{3}}} = 2$$

$$2^{\frac{x}{3} - \frac{1}{3}} = 2$$ Quotient of Powers Property

$$2^{\frac{x-1}{3}} = 2$$

$$2^{\frac{x-1}{3}} = 2^1$$ Write 2 with an exponent.

STUDY TIP
To divide two powers with the same base, keep the common base and subtract the exponents.

Step 3 Equate the exponents and solve for x.

$$\frac{x-1}{3} = 1$$

$$x - 1 = 3$$

$$x = 4$$

The value of x is 4.

 **Try It!** **5.** What is the value of x if the side length of Terrarium A is four times the side length of Terrarium B?

CONCEPT SUMMARY Rational Exponents and Properties of Exponents

WORDS If the nth root of a is a real number and m is an integer, then

$a^{\frac{1}{n}} = \sqrt[n]{a}$ $\quad$ $a^{\frac{m}{n}} = \sqrt[n]{a^m} = (\sqrt[n]{a})^m$

	Power of a Power	Power of a Product	Product of Powers	Quotient of Powers
ALGEBRA	$(a^m)^n = a^{mn}$	$(ab)^m = a^m \cdot b^m$	$a^m \cdot a^n = a^{m+n}$	$\frac{a^m}{a^n} = a^{m-n}, a \neq 0$
NUMBERS	$\left(256^{\frac{1}{4}}\right)^{\frac{1}{2}} = 256^{\frac{1}{4} \cdot \frac{1}{2}}$ $= 256^{\frac{1}{8}}$ $= 2$	$(4 \times 9)^{\frac{1}{2}} = 4^{\frac{1}{2}} \cdot 9^{\frac{1}{2}}$ $= 2 \cdot 3$ $= 6$	$16^{\frac{1}{4}} \times 16^{\frac{1}{4}} = 16^{\frac{1}{4}+\frac{1}{4}}$ $= 16^{\frac{2}{4}}$ $= 16^{\frac{1}{2}}$ $= 4$	$\frac{8^{\frac{2}{3}}}{8^{\frac{1}{3}}} = 8^{\frac{2}{3}-\frac{1}{3}}$ $= 8^{\frac{1}{3}}$ $= 2$

Do You UNDERSTAND?

1. **ESSENTIAL QUESTION** What are the properties of rational exponents and how are they used to solve problems?

2. **Communicate Precisely** A square has an area of 15 ft^2. What are two ways of expressing its side length?

3. **Look for Relationships** If $3^x = 3^y$, what is the relationship between x and y?

4. **Error Analysis** Corey wrote $\sqrt[3]{4^2}$ as $4^{\frac{3}{2}}$. What error did Corey make?

5. **Reason** When is it useful to have rational exponents instead of radicals?

6. **Vocabulary** How are *rational exponents* different than whole number exponents? How are they the same?

Do You KNOW HOW?

Write each radical using rational exponents.

7. $\sqrt{7}$

8. $\sqrt{15}$

9. $\sqrt[3]{6^4}$

10. $\sqrt[3]{2^3}$

11. $\sqrt[4]{2^4}$

12. $\sqrt{8^3}$

Solve each equation.

13. $\left(2^{\frac{x}{3}}\right)\left(2^{\frac{x}{2}}\right) = 2^5$

14. $\left(4^{\frac{x}{2}}\right)\left(4^{\frac{x}{5}}\right) = 4^8$

15. $64^{x+1} = 4^{x+7}$

16. $16^{(x-3)} = 2^{(x-6)}$

17. $\left(\frac{1}{243}\right)^{-\frac{x}{3}} = \left(\frac{1}{9}\right)^{-\frac{x}{2}+1}$

18. $\left(\frac{1}{36}\right)^{(x-4)} = \left(\frac{1}{216}\right)^{x+1}$

PRACTICE & PROBLEM SOLVING

UNDERSTAND

19. **Make Sense and Persevere** Describe two ways to express the edge length of a cube with a volume shown.

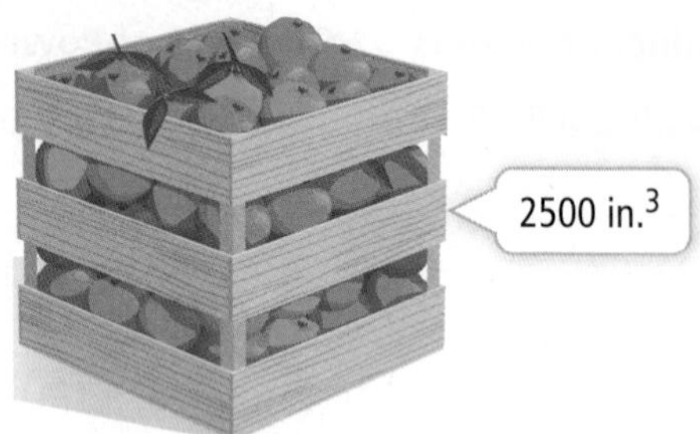

20. **Construct Arguments** Explain why $5^{\frac{4}{3}}$ must be equal to $\sqrt[3]{5^4}$ if the Power of a Power Property holds for rational exponents.

21. **Error Analysis** Describe and correct the error a student made when starting to solve the equation $8^{x+3} = 2^{2x-5}$.

$$8^{x+3} = 2^{2x-5}$$
$$(2^3)^{x+3} = 2^{2x-5}$$
$$2^{3x+3} = 2^{2x-5}$$
$$\vdots$$
✗

22. **Construct Arguments** The Power of a Quotient rule is $\left(\frac{a}{b}\right)^m = \frac{a^m}{b^m}$, $b \neq 0$. Will this rule work with rational exponents if $\frac{a}{b}$ is a positive number? Give an example to support your argument.

23. **Higher Order Thinking** The Zero Exponent Property is $a^0 = 1$, $a \neq 0$.
    a. How could you use properties of exponents to explain why $a^0 = 1$?
    b. How could the Zero Exponent Property be applied when solving equations with rational exponents?

24. **Use Structure** Consider the expression $\sqrt{\sqrt{625}}$.
    a. Write the radical using rational exponents.
    b. Describe two different ways to evaluate the expression.
    c. Simplify the expression from part (b).

PRACTICE

Write each radical using rational exponents. SEE EXAMPLE 1

25. $\sqrt{3}$

26. $\sqrt[3]{7}$

27. $\sqrt[5]{3^2}$

28. $\sqrt[4]{2^{-5}}$

29. $\sqrt[3]{a^2}$

30. $\sqrt{b^a}$

Solve each equation. SEE EXAMPLES 2–5

31. $\left(5^{\frac{x}{3}}\right)\left(5^{\frac{x}{4}}\right) = 5^5$

32. $\left(2^{\frac{x}{2}}\right)\left(4^{\frac{x}{2}}\right) = 2^6$

33. $\left(3^{\frac{x}{2}+1}\right) = \left(3^{-\frac{5x}{2}}\right)$

34. $625^{2x-3} = 25^{3x-2}$

35. $\left(\frac{1}{243}\right)^{-\frac{x}{3}} = \left(\frac{1}{9}\right)^{-\frac{x}{2}+1}$

36. $8^{\frac{-x}{3}} = 4$

37. $49^{\frac{x}{4}-1} = 343^{\frac{x}{3}}$

38. $3 = \left(5^{\frac{1}{2}}\right)\left(x^{\frac{1}{2}}\right)$

39. $2 = \left(4^{\frac{1}{3}}\right)\left(2^{\frac{x}{3}}\right)$

40. $\frac{27^{\frac{1}{4}}}{3^{\frac{x}{4}}} = 1$

41. $5^{-\frac{2}{3}} = \frac{125^{\frac{x}{3}}}{25^{\frac{4}{3}}}$

42. $\frac{6^{\frac{1}{4}}}{36^{-\frac{x}{2}}} = 1$

For each partial solution, identify the property of exponents that is used. SEE EXAMPLES 2–4

43.

$$36^{\frac{x}{3}+3} = 216^{\frac{x}{5}}$$
$$(6^2)^{\frac{x}{3}+3} = (6^3)^{\frac{x}{5}}$$
$$6^{\frac{2x}{3}+6} = 6^{\frac{3x}{5}}$$
$$\vdots$$

44.

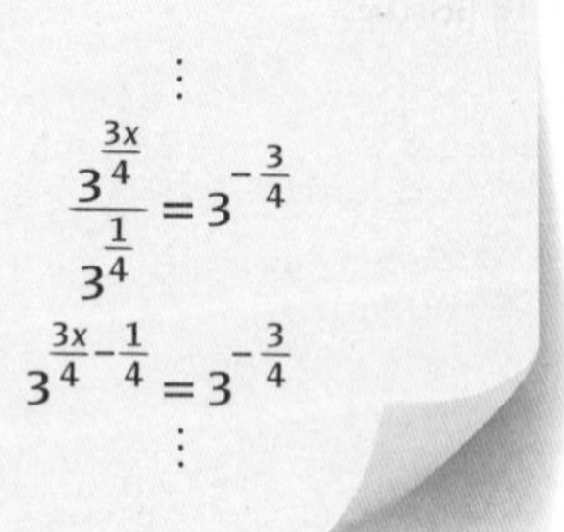

PRACTICE & PROBLEM SOLVING

APPLY

45. Use Appropriate Tools The formula for the volume V of a sphere is $\frac{4}{3}\pi r^3$. What is the radius of the basketball shown?

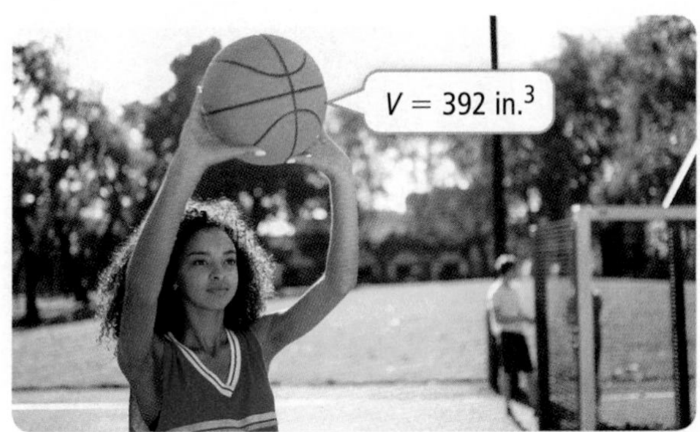

46. Use Structure A singing contest eliminates contestants after each round. To find the number of contestants in the next round, raise the number of contestants in the current round to the power of $\frac{6-n}{7-n}$, where n is the number of the current round. The number of contestants in Round 2 is 243. How many contestants will be in Round 5?

47. Make Sense and Persevere Photos A, B, and C are all square photos. The area of Photo C is the same as a rectangular photo whose length is the side length of Photo A and whose width is the side length of Photo B. Use the properties of rational exponents to write and solve an equation to find the side length of Photo A to two decimal places.

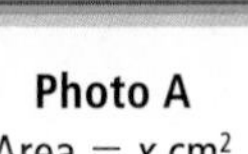

Photo A
Area = x cm²

Photo B
Area = 72 cm²

Photo C
Area = 110 cm²

ASSESSMENT PRACTICE

48. Match each expression with its equivalent expression.

I. $\sqrt[4]{2^5}$	**A.** $2^{\frac{1}{5}}$
II. $\sqrt{5}$	**B.** $2^{\frac{5}{4}}$
III. $\sqrt[5]{2^4}$	**C.** $2^{\frac{4}{5}}$
IV. $\sqrt[5]{2}$	**D.** $5^{\frac{1}{2}}$

49. SAT/ACT What is the value of x in $27^{\frac{x}{2}} = 3^{x-1}$?

Ⓐ -3
Ⓑ -2
Ⓒ $\frac{1}{3}$
Ⓓ 2
Ⓔ 3

50. Performance Task It is possible to write any positive integer as the sum of powers of 2 with whole number exponents. For example, you can write 75 in the following manner.

$$2^0 + 2^1 + 2^3 + 2^6 = 75$$

Part A Use the equation above to write 75 as the sum of powers of 8, using rational exponents. What are possible values for a, b, c and d?

$$8^a + 8^b + 8^c + 8^d = 75$$

Part B How can you modify the equation you wrote in part A to express 75 as sum of powers of 16?

$$16^a + 16^b + 16^c + 16^d = 75$$

Part C Given that a, b, c, and d are rational numbers, for what types of integer values of x is the following equation true? Explain your answer.

$$x^a + x^b + x^c + x^d = 75$$

Activity Assess

6-2 Exponential Functions

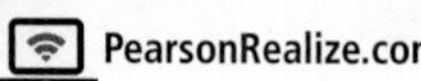

I CAN... describe and graph exponential functions.

VOCABULARY

- asymptote
- constant ratio
- exponential function

EXPLORE & REASON

Use two pieces of $8\frac{1}{2}$ in.-by-11 in. paper. Fold one of the pieces of paper accordion-style for five folds. Fold the other in half for five folds. After each fold, unfold each piece of paper and count the total number of rectangular sections.

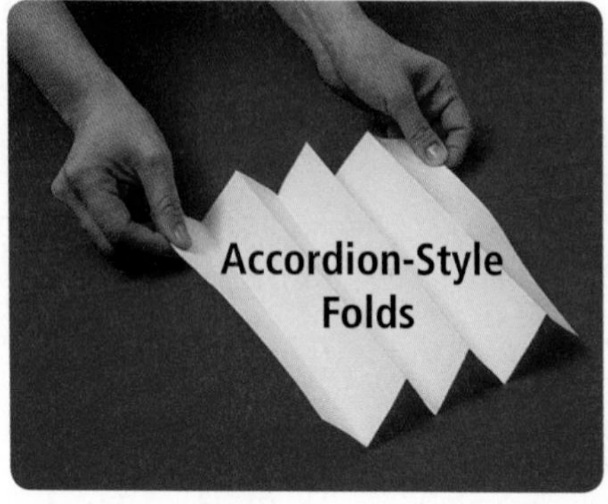

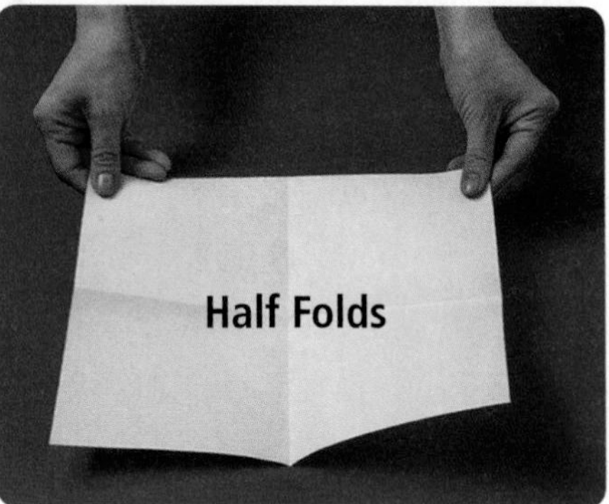

A. Find the pattern relating the number of folds to the number of sections for each folding style. What do you notice?

B. **Make Sense and Persevere** Explain why the two different folded styles of paper produce different results.

ESSENTIAL QUESTION

What are the characteristics of exponential functions?

CONCEPTUAL UNDERSTANDING

EXAMPLE 1 Key Features of $f(x) = 2^x$

A. What does the graph of $f(x) = 2^x$ look like?

The table and graph show $f(x) = 2^x$.

x	$f(x) = 2^x$
−2	$\frac{1}{4}$
−1	$\frac{1}{2}$
0	1
1	2
2	4
3	8

As x-values approach $-\infty$, y-values approach 0.

The y-intercept is 1.

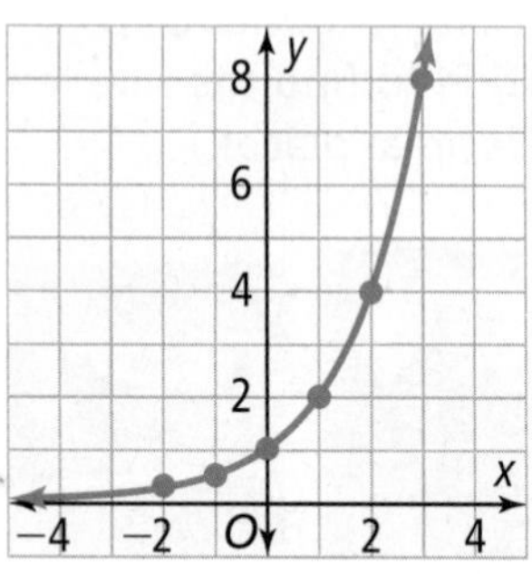

COMMON ERROR
The graph of $f(x) = 2^x$ does not have a y-value of exactly 0, so it does not have an x-intercept.

B. What are the characteristics of the graph of $f(x) = 2^x$?

The graph of $f(x) = 2^x$ is continuous between and beyond the x-values shown, so the domain is all real numbers.

CONTINUED ON THE NEXT PAGE

EXAMPLE 1 CONTINUED

The function gets closer and closer to the x-axis, but never quite reaches it. When a function approaches a line in this manner, the line is called an **asymptote.**

The asymptote of f is $y = 0$. The range is $y > 0$.

Try It! 1. Identify the key features of the function $f(x) = b^x$ for $b = 2$ and $b = \frac{1}{2}$.

APPLICATION

EXAMPLE 2 Graph Exponential Functions

A network administrator uses the function $f(x) = 5^x$ to model the number of computers a virus spreads to after x hours. If there are 1,000 computers on the network, about how many hours will it take for the virus to spread to the entire network?

Step 1 Make a table.

x	$f(x) = 5^x$
0	1
1	5
2	25
3	125
4	625
5	3,125

Step 2 Graph the function.

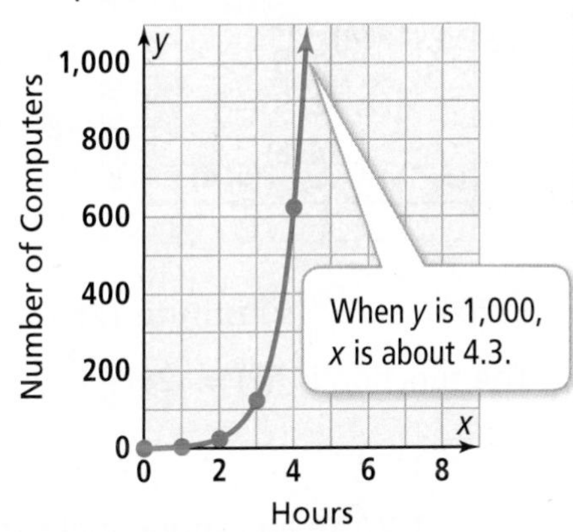

STUDY TIP
When graphing an exponential function, choose a scale for the vertical axis so that the relevant domain is shown.

Step 3 Use a calculator to check if your answer, $5^{4.3} = 1{,}012.91$, is close to 1,000. ✓

$5^{4.3}$ 1012.910373

It will take the virus about 4.3 hours to spread to the entire network.

Try It! 2. How long will it take for the virus to spread to 50,000 computers?

CONCEPT Exponential Function

An **exponential function** is the product of an initial amount and a **constant ratio** raised to a power. Exponential functions are modeled using $f(x) = a \cdot b^x$, where a is a nonzero constant, $b > 0$, and $b \neq 1$.

$$f(x) = a \cdot b^x$$

a is the initial amount. b is the constant ratio.

EXAMPLE 3 Write Exponential Functions

STUDY TIP
Note that exponential functions have constant ratios rather than differences.

A. What is the written form of the function represented by the table?

x	$f(x)$
0	4
1	12
2	36
3	108
4	324

The initial amount is 4.

$12 \div 4 = 3$
$36 \div 12 = 3$
$108 \div 36 = 3$
$324 \div 108 = 3$

The constant ratio is 3.

In $f(x) = a \cdot b^x$, substitute 4 for a and 3 for b.
The function is $f(x) = 4(3)^x$.

B. What is the written form of the function represented by the graph?

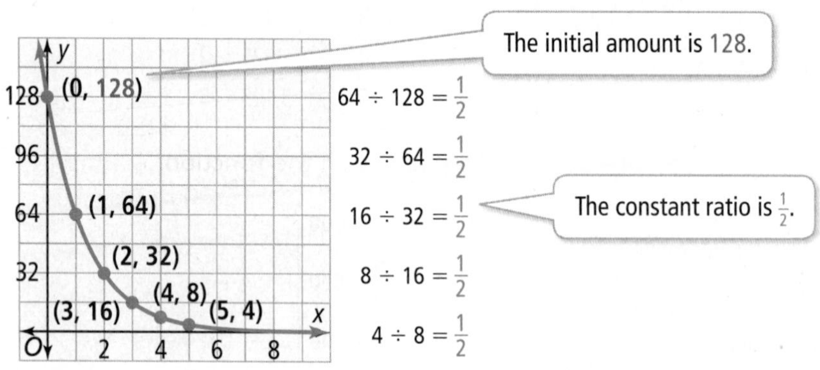

In $f(x) = a \cdot b^x$, substitute 128 for a and $\frac{1}{2}$ for b.
The function is $f(x) = 128\left(\frac{1}{2}\right)^x$.

Try It! 3. Write an exponential function for each set of points.

a. (0, 3), (1, 12), (2, 48), (3, 192), and (4, 768)

b. (0, 2,187), (1, 729), (2, 243), (3, 81), and (4, 27)

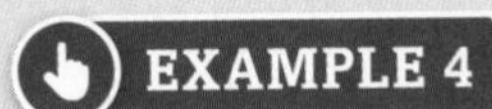

EXAMPLE 4 Compare Linear and Exponential Functions

Talisha is offered two pledge options for donating to a charity. Which option will increase the pledge amount faster over time?

Option A: \$100 for the first week, and each week after that the amount increases by \$25

Week	Payment (\$)
0	100
1	125
2	150
3	175
4	200
5	225

Initial value: 100. Constant increase: +25, +25, +25, +25, +25

Option B: \$1 for the first week, and each week after that the amount triples

Week	Payment (\$)
0	1
1	3
2	9
3	27
4	81
5	243

Initial value: 1. Constant ratio: ×3, ×3, ×3, ×3, ×3

CONSTRUCT ARGUMENTS
Will an exponential model with a base greater than 1 always have a greater rate of change over time? Explain.

Option A is a linear function and increases at a constant rate.

Since the ratio of consecutive terms in Option B is constant, the exponential function will increase faster over time.

Try It! **4.** Identify each function as linear or exponential. Explain.

a. $f(x)$ equals the number of branches at level x in a tree diagram, where at each level each branch extends into 4 branches.

b. $f(x)$ equals the number of boxes in row x of a stack in which each row increases by 2 boxes.

CONCEPT SUMMARY Exponential Functions

Exponential Functions are modeled using $f(x) = a \cdot b^x$, where a is the initial amount and b is the constant ratio.

	$b > 1$	$0 < b < 1$
ALGEBRA	$f(x) = 2(3)^x$	$f(x) = 81\left(\frac{2}{3}\right)^x$

TABLES

x	$f(x)$	
0	2	× 3
1	6	× 3
2	18	× 3
3	54	× 3
4	162	× 3
5	486	

x	$f(x)$	
0	81	× $\frac{2}{3}$
1	54	× $\frac{2}{3}$
2	36	× $\frac{2}{3}$
3	24	× $\frac{2}{3}$
4	16	× $\frac{2}{3}$
5	10.7	

GRAPHS

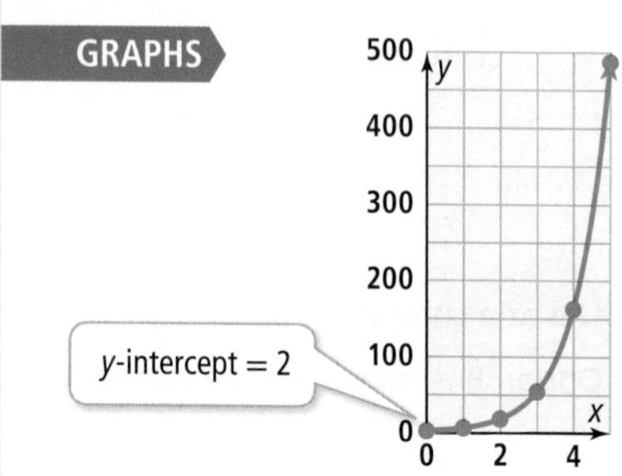

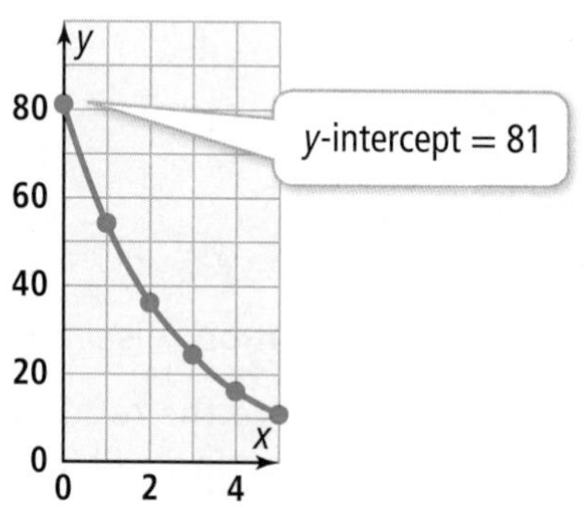

Do You UNDERSTAND?

1. ESSENTIAL QUESTION What are the characteristics of exponential functions?

2. **Look for Relationships** How can you tell whether the graph of a function of form $f(x) = ab^x$ where $a > 0$ will increase or decrease from left to right?

3. **Make Sense and Persevere** Why is $b \neq 1$ a condition for $f(x) = ab^x$?

4. **Error Analysis** Martin says that $f(x) = 2(4)^x$ starts at 4 and has constant ratio of 2. What error did Martin make? Explain.

Do You KNOW HOW?

Graph each function.

5. $f(x) = 3^x$

6. $f(x) = \left(\frac{1}{4}\right)^x$

Write each exponential function.

7.

x	$f(x)$
0	4
1	2
2	1
3	$\frac{1}{2}$
4	$\frac{1}{4}$

8.

x	$f(x)$
0	3
1	6
2	12
3	24
4	48

PRACTICE & PROBLEM SOLVING

Scan for Multimedia   Practice  Tutorial

Additional Exercises Available Online

UNDERSTAND

9. **Make Sense and Persevere** An exponential function of form $f(x) = b^x$ includes the points (2, 16), (3, 64), and (4, 256). What is the value of b?

10. **Reason** Is $y = 0$ the asymptote of all functions of the form $f(x) = ab^x$? Explain your reasoning.

11. **Error Analysis** Describe and correct the error a student made in writing an exponential function.

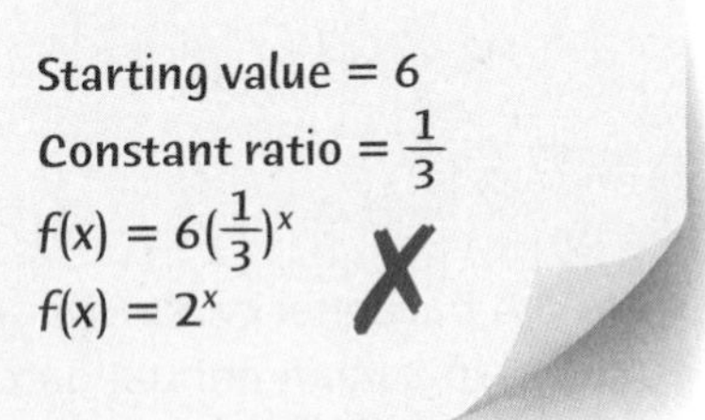

12. **Use Structure** The function $f(x) = 4\left(\frac{1}{2}\right)^x$ is graphed below. Describe how the graph would change for $a > 4$ and $1 < a < 4$.

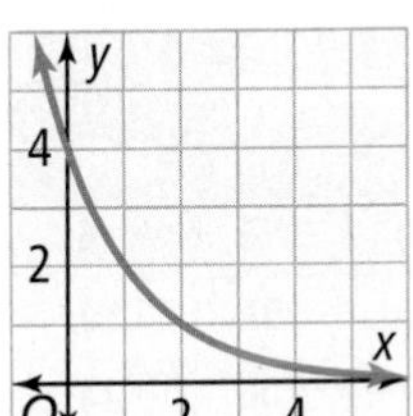

13. **Higher Order Thinking** The exponential function $f(x) = 2^x$ increases as x increases. Do all exponential functions behave this way? Use algebraic reasoning to support your answer.

14. **Use Structure** What happens to the graph of an exponential function when the initial value, a, is less than 0? Explain.

PRACTICE

Identify the key features of each exponential function. SEE EXAMPLE 1

15. $f(x) = 4^x$

16. $f(x) = \left(\frac{1}{3}\right)^x$

Graph each exponential function. SEE EXAMPLE 2

17. $f(x) = 0.5^x$

18. $f(x) = 6^x$

19. $f(x) = 2(3)^x$

20. $f(x) = 4\left(\frac{1}{2}\right)^x$

Write each exponential function. SEE EXAMPLE 3

21.

x	$f(x)$
0	2
1	8
2	32
3	128
4	512

22.

x	$f(x)$
0	4
1	$\frac{4}{3}$
2	$\frac{4}{9}$
3	$\frac{4}{27}$
4	$\frac{4}{81}$

23.

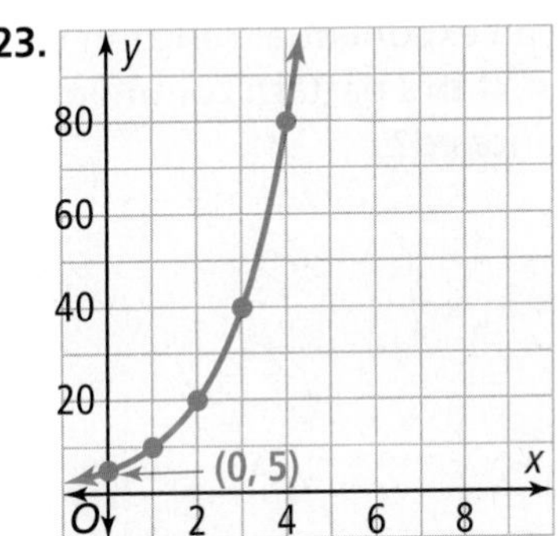

Tell whether each function is linear or exponential. Explain your reasoning. SEE EXAMPLE 4

24.

x	$f(x)$
0	5
1	9
2	13
3	17
4	21

25.

x	$f(x)$
0	216
1	36
2	6
3	1
4	$\frac{1}{6}$

APPLY

26. **Make Sense and Persevere** Write an exponential function to model earthquake intensity as a function of a Richter Scale number. How can you use your function to compare the intensity of the 1811 New Madrid and 1906 San Francisco earthquakes?

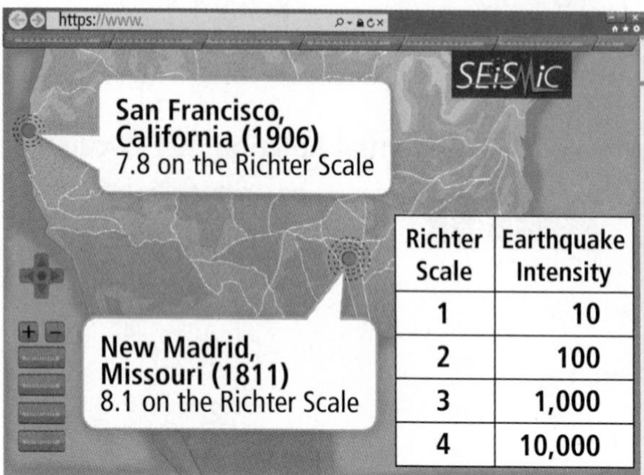

Richter Scale	Earthquake Intensity
1	10
2	100
3	1,000
4	10,000

27. **Model With Mathematics** A television show will be canceled if the estimated number of viewers falls below 2.5 million by Week 10. Use the graph to write an exponential function to model the situation. If this pattern continues, will the show be canceled?

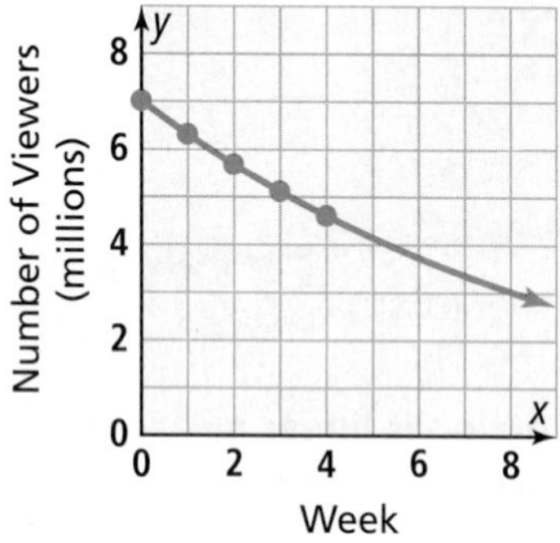

28. **Make Sense and Persevere** The table shows the number of algae cells in pool water samples. A pool will turn green when there are 24 million algae cells or more. Write and graph an exponential function to model the expected number of algae cells as a function of the number of days. If the pattern continues, in how many days will the water turn green?

Day	Number of Algae Cells
0	2000
1	10,000
2	50,000
3	250,000
4	1,250,000

ASSESSMENT PRACTICE

29. Consider the function $f(x) = 3(5)^x$.

The y-intercept is ________.

The asymptote is ________.

The domain is ________.

The range is ________.

30. **SAT/ACT** What is the y-intercept of $f(x) = 8\left(\frac{1}{2}\right)^x$?

Ⓐ 0

Ⓑ $\frac{1}{2}$

Ⓒ 1

Ⓓ 2

Ⓔ 8

31. **Performance Task** A gardener can increase the number of dahlia plants in an annual garden by either buying new bulbs each year or dividing the existing bulbs to create new plants. The table shows the expected number of bulbs for each method.

Year	Buy New Bulbs	Divide Existing Bulbs
0	6	6
1	56	12
2	106	24
3	156	48
4	206	96

Part A For each method, write a function to model the expected number of plants for each year.

Part B Use your functions to find the expected number of plants in 10 years for each method.

Part C How does the expected number of plants in five years compare to the expected number of plants in 15 years? Explain how these patterns could affect the method the gardener decides to use.

6-3 Exponential Growth and Decay

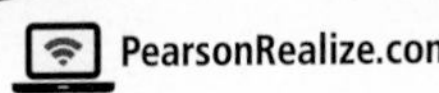

I CAN… use exponential functions to model situations and make predictions.

VOCABULARY

- compound interest
- decay factor
- exponential decay
- exponential growth
- growth factor

EXPLORE & REASON

Cindy is buying a new car and wants to learn how the value of her car will change over time. Insurance actuaries predict the future value of cars using depreciation functions. One such function is applied to the car whose declining value is shown at the right.

Years After Purchase	Value
0 yr	\$10,000
1 yr	\$8,520
2 yr	\$7,213
3 yr	\$6,100
4 yr	\$5,210

A. Describe how the value of the car decreases from year to year.

B. **Model With Mathematics** What kind of function would explain this type of pattern?

C. Given your answer to Part B, what is needed to find the function the actuary is using? Explain.

ESSENTIAL QUESTION

What kinds of situations can be modeled with exponential growth or exponential decay functions?

CONCEPTUAL UNDERSTANDING

EXAMPLE 1 Exponential Growth

The population of Hillville grows at an annual rate of 15%. What will the estimated population of Hillville be in five years?

You can model **exponential growth** with a function $f(x) = a \bullet b^x$, where $a > 0$ and $b > 1$.

$$f(x) = a \bullet b^x$$

$$f(x) = a(1 + r)^x$$

An exponential growth function has a **growth factor** that is equal to 1 plus the growth rate.

Step 1 Write the exponential growth function that models the expected population growth.

Let x = time in years, a = initial amount, and r = growth rate.

$$\begin{aligned} f(x) &= a(1 + r)^x \\ &= 5{,}000(1 + 0.15)^x \\ &= 5{,}000(1.15)^x \end{aligned}$$

The function is $f(x) = 5{,}000(1.15)^x$.

MODEL WITH MATHEMATICS In an exponential growth situation, the change in y is always proportional to the value of y itself; that is, with greater y-values, the function increases more rapidly. What other exponential growth situations can you think of?

CONTINUED ON THE NEXT PAGE

EXAMPLE 1 CONTINUED

Step 2 Find the expected population in 5 years.

$$f(5) = 5{,}000(1.15)^5$$
$$\approx 10{,}056.79$$

In 5 years, the population is expected to be about 10,057.

COMMON ERROR
You may incorrectly record a decimal number when you are finding "how many" people. Remember that the number of people should be a whole number.

Try It! 1. The population of Valleytown is also 5,000, with an annual increase of 1,000. Can the expected population for Valleytown be modeled with an exponential growth function? Explain.

CONCEPT Interest

Interest is calculated in two ways: simple interest and compound interest.

Simple interest is interest paid only on the principal.

Compound interest is interest that is paid both on the principal and on the interest that has already been paid. The compound interest formula is an exponential growth function.

Compound Interest Formula

$$A = P\left(1 + \frac{r}{n}\right)^{nt}$$

A = amount paid
P = principal amount
r = rate of interest
n = number of times per year the interest is compounded
t = time in years

LOOK FOR RELATIONSHIPS
How is the compound interest formula related to $f(x) = a(1 + r)^x$?

The graph below shows \$10 at 5% simple interest and at 5% interest compounded quarterly.

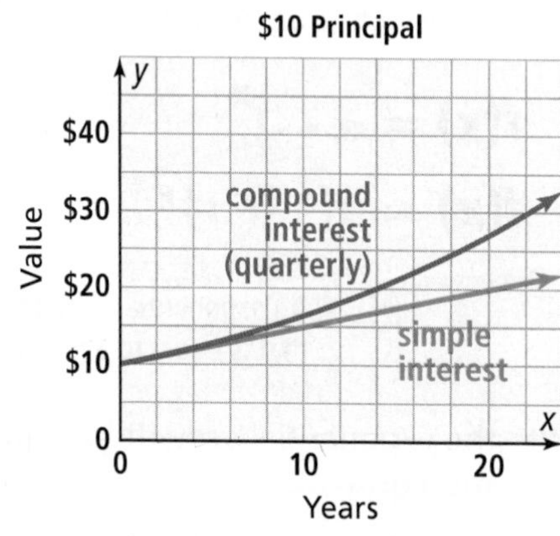

APPLICATION

EXAMPLE 2 Exponential Models of Growth

Kimberly's family invested in a Certificate of Deposit (CD) for her when she was born. The interest is compounded quarterly.

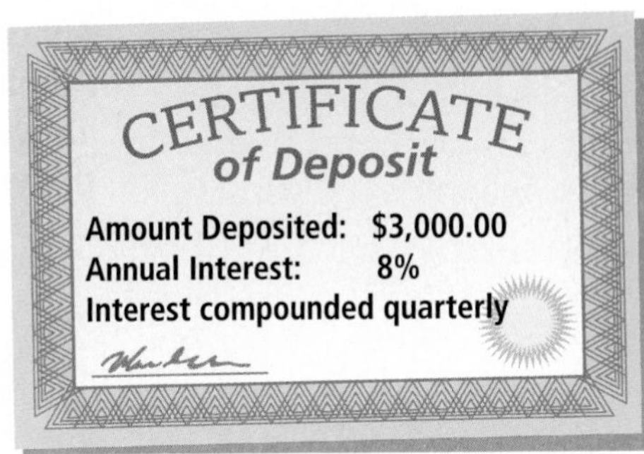

A. What is the value of the CD at the end of five years?

Use the compound interest formula.

$$A = P\left(1 + \frac{r}{n}\right)^{nt}$$

$$= 3{,}000\left(1 + \frac{0.08}{4}\right)^{4t}$$

The principal amount is 3,000. The rate of interest is 8%, or 0.08. The number of times per year the interest is calculated is 4.

$$= 3{,}000(1 + 0.02)^{4t}$$

The 8% interest is paid over 4 periods, so 2% interest is paid each period.

$$= 3{,}000(1.02)^{4t}$$

$$= 3{,}000(1.02)^{4(5)}$$

$$= 4{,}457.84$$

At the end of five years, the value of the CD will be $4,457.84.

USE STRUCTURE
Use the order of operations when entering your numbers on a calculator. How can the omission of parentheses change your answer?

B. Will the value of Kimberly's CD be greater after 15 years if it is compounded annually rather than quarterly?

Compare the exponential function you found in Part A with annual compounding ($n = 1$) over the same 15 years.

REASON
The simple interest formula is $A = P(1 + rt)$. How is simple interest similar to annual compounding? How is it different?

Quarterly:

$$A = 3{,}000(1.02)^{4t}$$

$$= 3{,}000(1.02)^{4\times 15}$$

$$= 3{,}000(1.02)^{60}$$

$$= \$9{,}843.09$$

Annually:

$$A = P\left(1 + \frac{r}{n}\right)^{nt}$$

$$= 3{,}000\left(1 + \frac{0.08}{1}\right)^{1(15)}$$

Since the interest is only compiled once per year, the entire 8% interest is paid one time.

$$= 3{,}000(1.08)^{15}$$

$$= \$9{,}516.51$$

The value of Kimberly's CD will be less if the interest is compounded annually rather than quarterly.

 **Try It!** 2. a. What will be the difference after 15 years if the interest is compounded semiannually rather than quarterly?

b. What will be the difference after 15 years if the interest is compounded monthly rather than quarterly?

Activity Assess

APPLICATION

EXAMPLE 3 Exponential Decay

A video is labeled a fan favorite if it receives at least 1,000 views per day. Amelia posts a video that gets 8,192 views on the first day. The number of views decreases by 25% each day after that. In how many days total will the video stop being a fan favorite?

Number of Days	Views
0	8,192
1	6,144
2	4,608
3	3,456

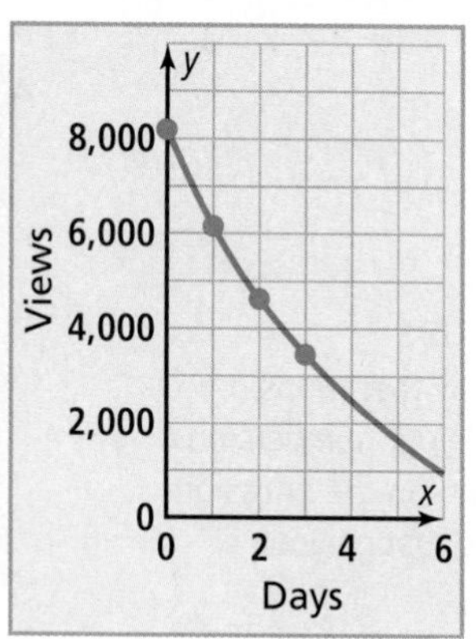

USE STRUCTURE
How does the exponential decay function differ from the exponential growth function?

You can model **exponential decay** with a function of the form $f(x) = a \cdot b^x$, where $a > 0$ and $0 < b < 1$.

The **decay factor** is 1 minus the decay rate.

$$f(x) = a \cdot b^x$$

$$f(x) = a(1 - r)^x$$

r is the decay rate.

Step 1 Model the situation.

Let x = time in years, a = initial amount, and r = decay rate.

$f(x) = a(1 - r)^x$

$= 8{,}192(1 - 0.25)^x$

$= 8{,}192(0.75)^x$

The decay factor is written as a decimal less than 1.

Step 2 Write an equation to find x if $f(x) = 1{,}000$.

$1{,}000 = 8{,}192(0.75)^x$

Step 3 Estimate the solution of the equation using a graphing calculator.

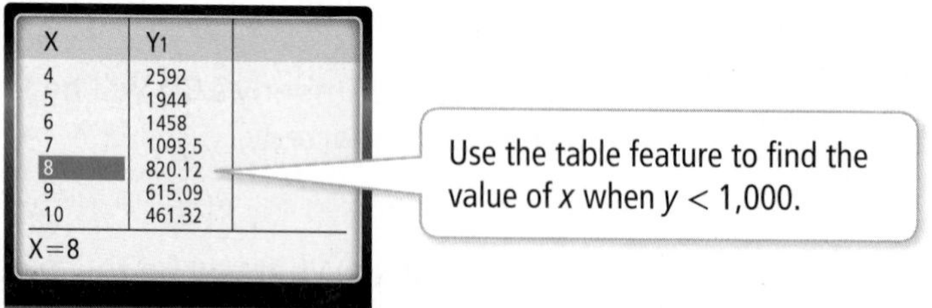

X	Y_1
4	2592
5	1944
6	1458
7	1093.5
8	820.12
9	615.09
10	461.32

X=8

Use the table feature to find the value of x when $y < 1{,}000$.

The video will stop being a fan favorite in 8 days.

Try It! **3.** Suppose the number of views decreases by 20% per day. In how many days will the number of views per day be less than 1,000?

APPLICATION

EXAMPLE 4 Exponential Models of Decay

The number of pika in a region is decreasing. How does the decrease in the pika population for years 1 to 5 compare to the population for years 6 to 10?

Initial population: 144 pikas

Write an exponential decay function to model the situation.

$$f(x) = a(1 - r)^x$$
$$= 144(1 - 0.08)^x$$
$$f(x) = 144(0.92)^x$$

Find the average rate of change for each interval.

Year 1 to Year 5: $1 \leq x \leq 5$

$f(1) \approx 132$ $f(5) \approx 95$

$$\frac{95 - 132}{5 - 1} = \frac{-37}{4} = -9.25$$

Year 6 to Year 10: $6 \leq x \leq 10$

$f(6) \approx 87$ $f(10) \approx 63$

$$\frac{63 - 87}{10 - 6} = \frac{-24}{4} = -6$$

STUDY TIP
Use the slope formula to find the average rate of change between two points:

$$m = \frac{y_2 - y_1}{x_2 - x_1}$$

For years 1 to 5, the pika population decreases by an average of 9.25 pikas per year. For years 6 to 10 the pika population decreases by an average of 6 pikas per year. The average rate of change for the pika population decreases as years increase.

Try It! 4. How would the average rate of change over the same intervals be affected if the population increased at a rate of 8%?

APPLICATION

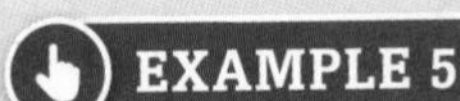

EXAMPLE 5 Exponential Growth and Decay

Rich is comparing the cost of maintaining his car with the depreciating value of the car. When will the cost and value be the same?

Value: starts at $20,000, decreases by 15% per year.

Maintenance cost: $500 the first year, increases by 28% per year.

Formulate Write the exponential functions.

Value of the car: $f(x) = 20(0.85)^x$

Cost of maintenance: $g(x) = 0.5(1.28)^x$

Compute Solve by graphing.

Find the point of intersection: (9, 4.5).

Interpret The value of the car and the cost of maintenance are both about $4,500 at 9 years.

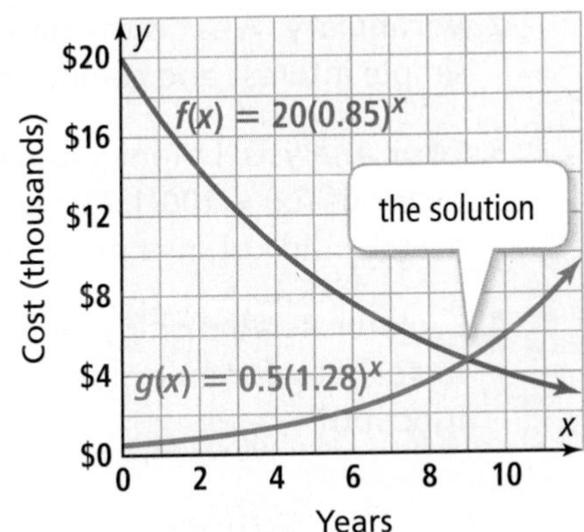

Try It! 5. Explain how to use tables on a graphing calculator to answer this question.

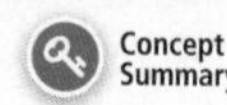

CONCEPT SUMMARY Exponential Growth and Decay

	Exponential Growth	Exponential Decay	Compound Interest
ALGEBRA	$f(x) = a \bullet b^x$ $f(x) = a(1 + r)^x$	$f(x) = a \bullet b^x$ $f(x) = a(1 - r)^x$	$f(x) = a \bullet b^x$ $A = P\left(1 + \frac{r}{n}\right)^{nt}$
NUMBERS	$f(x) = 4(1 + 0.5)^x$	$f(x) = 4(1 - 0.5)^x$	$A = 5\left(1 + \frac{0.12}{2}\right)^{2t}$
WORDS	initial value: 4 growth rate: 50% growth factor: 1.5	initial value: 4 decay rate: 50% decay factor: 0.5	principal: 5 annual interest rate: 12% periods per year: 2
GRAPHS	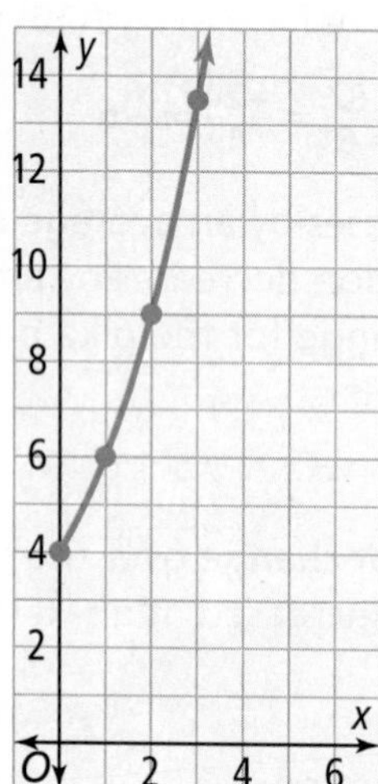	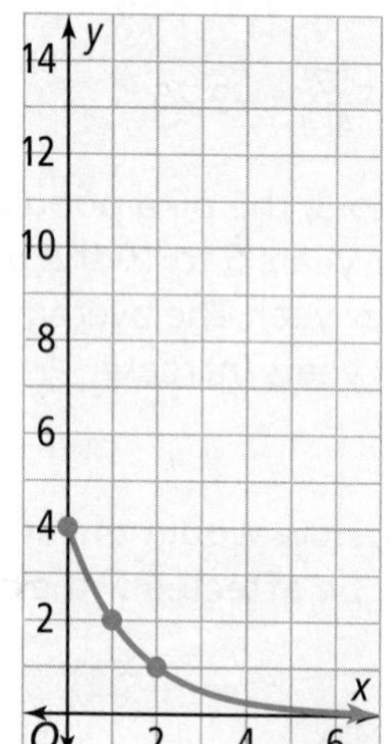	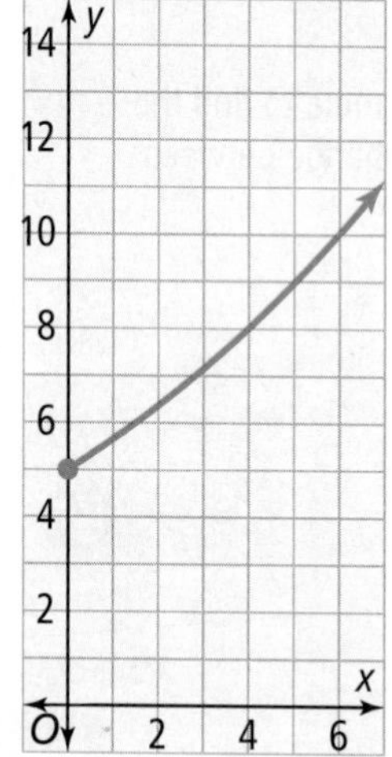

Do You UNDERSTAND?

1. ESSENTIAL QUESTION What kinds of situations can be modeled with exponential growth or exponential decay functions?

2. **Vocabulary** What is the difference between simple interest and *compound interest*?

3. **Error Analysis** LaTanya says that the growth factor of $f(x) = 100(1.25)^x$ is 25%. What mistake did LaTanya make? Explain.

4. **Look for Relationships** Why is the growth factor $1 + r$ for an exponential growth function?

Do You KNOW HOW?

Write an exponential growth or decay function for each situation.

5. initial value of 100 increasing at a rate of 5%

6. initial value of 1,250 increasing at a rate of 25%

7. initial value of 512 decreasing at a rate of 50%

8. initial value of 10,000 decreasing at a rate of 12%

9. What is the difference in the value after 10 years of an initial investment of $2,000 at 5% annual interest when the interest is compounded quarterly rather than annually?

UNDERSTAND

10. **Look for Relationships** How is an exponential growth function of the form $f(x) = a(1 + r)^x$ related to an exponential function of the form $f(x) = a \bullet b^x$?

11. **Generalize** What is the asymptote of the graph of an exponential growth or exponential decay function? Explain your reasoning.

12. **Error Analysis** Describe and correct the error a student made in writing an equation to find the annual value of an investment of \$1,000 at 4% annual interest compounded semiannually.

$$A = 1{,}000(1+0.04)^{4t}$$
$$= 1{,}000(1.04)^{4t}$$

✗

13. **Use Appropriate Tools** Describe how you could use a graphing calculator to estimate the value of x when $f(x) = 8(1.25)^x$ equals 15.

14. **Higher Order Thinking** In Example 2, you used the formula $A = P\left(1 + \frac{r}{n}\right)^{nt}$ to solve problems involving compound interest.

   a. How is the growth factor of a function that models compound interest affected as n increases? Explain.

   b. Copy and complete the table.

n	$A = 3{,}000\left(1 + \frac{0.08}{n}\right)^{5n}$
12	■
365	■
1,000	■
10,000	■
100,000	■

   c. What is the relationship between the value of the function and the change in the growth factor as n increases? Explain.

PRACTICE

Write an exponential growth function to model each situation. SEE EXAMPLE 1

15. initial value: 20
growth factor: 1.25

16. initial value: 100
growth factor: 1.05

Compare each investment to an investment of the same principal at the same rate compounded annually. SEE EXAMPLE 2

17. principal: \$8,000
annual interest: 6%
interest periods: 4
number of years: 20

18. principal: \$10,000
annual interest: 3.5%
interest periods: 2
number of years: 5

Write an exponential decay function to model each situation. Then estimate the value of x for the given value of $f(x)$. SEE EXAMPLE 3

19. initial value: 100
decay factor: 0.95
$f(x) = 60$

20. initial value: 5,000
decay factor: 0.7
$f(x) = 100$

Write an exponential decay function to model each situation. Compare the average rates of change over the given intervals. SEE EXAMPLE 4

21. initial value: 50
decay factor: 0.9
$1 \leq x \leq 4$ and
$5 \leq x \leq 8$

22. initial value: 25
decay factor: 0.8
$2 \leq x \leq 4$ and
$6 \leq x \leq 8$

Write an exponential function to model the data in each table. Identify the growth or decay factor.
SEE EXAMPLES 1–4

23.

x	$f(x)$
0	4
1	2
2	1
3	$\frac{1}{2}$
4	$\frac{1}{4}$

24.

x	$f(x)$
0	100
1	110
2	121
3	133.1
4	146.41

Model each pair of situations with exponential functions f and g. Find the approximate value of x that makes $f(x) = g(x)$. SEE EXAMPLE 5

25. f: initial value of 100 decreasing at a rate of 5%
g: initial value of 20 increasing at a rate of 5%

26. f: initial value of 40 increasing at a rate of 25%
g: initial value of 10,000 decreasing at a rate of 16%

PRACTICE & PROBLEM SOLVING

APPLY

27. Model With Mathematics A plant will become invasive when the number of plants reaches 10,000. Model the situation with an exponential growth function. How many years will it take for the plant to become invasive? Explain how you found the solution.

28. Look for Relationships Joshua invests \$500 at the interest rate shown. Felix invests \$1,000 in an account with the same compounding, but at 6% interest rate. Model each investment with an exponential growth function. Whose money will double first? Explain.

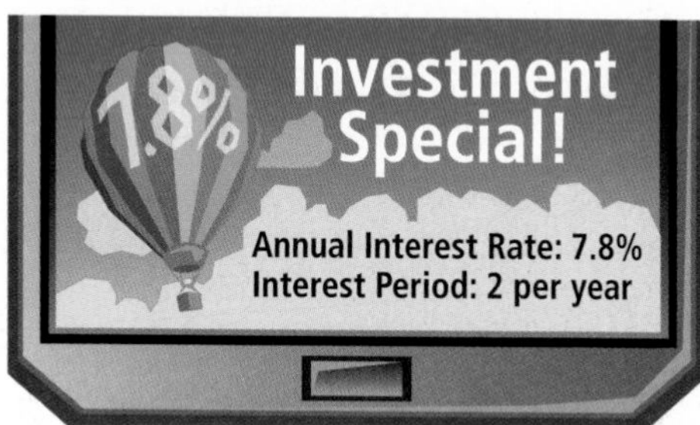

29. Make Sense and Persevere Write and graph exponential functions to model the number of students at School A and at School B as a function of number of years. In about how many years will the number of students at both schools be approximately the same? Explain how you can use a graph to determine the answer.

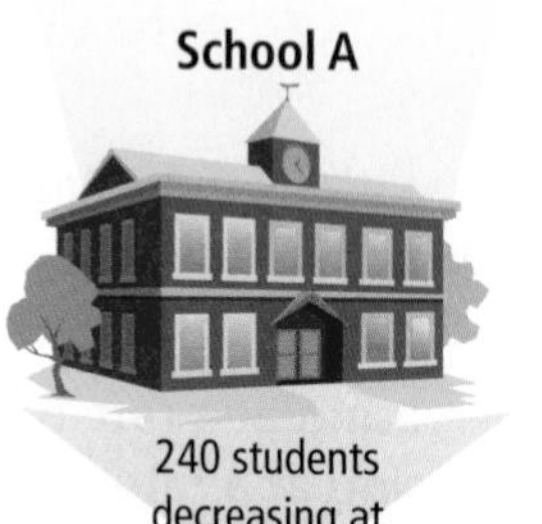

240 students decreasing at an annual rate of 2%

180 students increasing at an annual rate of 3%

ASSESSMENT PRACTICE

30. Classify each function as an exponential growth function or an exponential decay function.

$f(x) = 2(1.02)^x$

$f(x) = 5000(3)^x$

$f(x) = 7500(0.91)^x$

$f(x) = 189(1 - 0.25)^x$

$f(x) = 2485(1 + 0.25)^x$

31. SAT/ACT Which function models the value in x years of an investment at 3% annual interest compounded quarterly?

Ⓐ $150(1 - 0.03)^{4x}$

Ⓑ $150(1 + 0.03)^{4x}$

Ⓒ $150(1 - 0.03)^{x}$

Ⓓ $150(1 + 0.0075)^{4x}$

Ⓔ $150(1 - 0.0075)^{x}$

32. Performance Task Isabel has \$10,000 to invest. She is choosing between the three investment opportunities shown.

Investment	Annual Interest	Number of Interest Periods
A	4%	1
B	4%	4
C	4.2%	1

Part A Write a function for each investment to model its value in x years.

Part B Suppose Isabel only wants to invest her money for five years. Which investment will have the greatest value in five years?

Part C Which investment will make Isabel a millionaire first?

6-4 Geometric Sequences

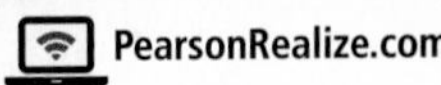
PearsonRealize.com

I CAN… identify and describe geometric sequences.

VOCABULARY
- geometric sequence

Activity Assess

EXPLORE & REASON

A seating plan is being designed for Section 12 of a new stadium.

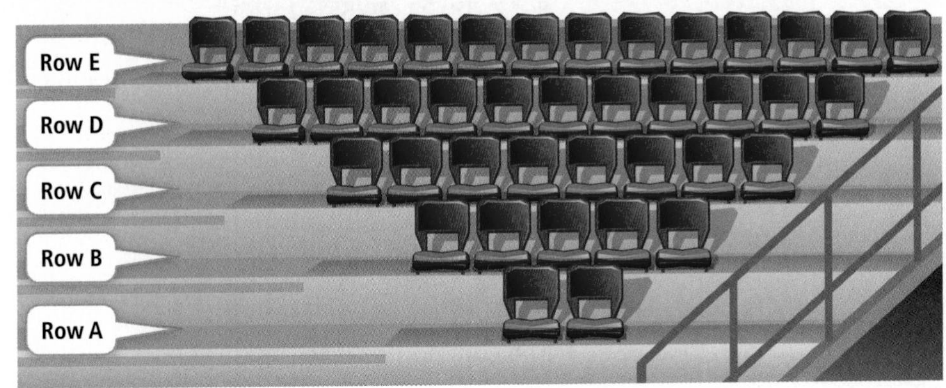

A. Describe the pattern.

B. Write an equation for this pattern.

C. Use Structure Row Z of Section 12 must have at least 75 seats. If the pattern continues, does this seating plan meet that requirement? Justify your answer.

ESSENTIAL QUESTION

How are geometric sequences related to exponential functions?

EXAMPLE 1 Identify Arithmetic and Geometric Sequences

Is each sequence an arithmetic or a geometric sequence?

A **geometric sequence** is a number sequence in which each term after the first term is found by multiplying the previous term by a common ratio.

Look for a common difference or a common ratio between consecutive terms.

> **STUDY TIP**
> The common ratio is the fixed number used to find terms in a geometric sequence. The common ratio cannot be zero.

A. $3, 2, \frac{4}{3}, \frac{8}{9}, \frac{16}{27}, \ldots$

$2 - 3 = -1$ $\quad \frac{4}{3} - 2 = -\frac{2}{3}$

no common difference

$2 \div 3 = \frac{2}{3}$ $\quad \frac{4}{3} \div 2 = \frac{2}{3}$ $\quad \frac{8}{9} \div \frac{4}{3} = \frac{2}{3}$ $\quad \frac{16}{27} \div \frac{8}{9} = \frac{2}{3}$

Divide the second term by the first term in each consecutive pair to find the *common ratio*.

The sequence does not have a common difference, but has a common ratio of $\frac{2}{3}$, so it is a geometric sequence.

B. 3, 4.5, 6, 7.5, 9, …

$4.5 - 3 = 1.5$ $\quad 6 - 4.5 = 1.5$ $\quad 7.5 - 6 = 1.5$ $\quad 9 - 7.5 = 1.5$

There is a common difference.

The sequence has a common difference of 1.5, so it is an arithmetic sequence.

Try It! 1. Is each sequence an arithmetic or a geometric sequence? Explain.

a. 1, 2.2, 4.84, 10.648, 23.4256, … **b.** 1, 75, 149, 223, 297, …

EXAMPLE 2 Write the Recursive Formula For a Sequence

What recursive formula describes the geometric sequence 8, 12, 18, 27, 40.5, ...?

Recursive formula:

$$a_n = r\,(a_{n-1})$$

*n*th term, common ratio, previous term

Find the common ratio.

$$\frac{12}{8} = \frac{18}{12} = \frac{27}{18} = \frac{40.5}{27} = \frac{3}{2}$$

The common ratio is $\frac{3}{2}$.

$a_n = \frac{3}{2}(a_{n-1})$ ········· Substitute $\frac{3}{2}$ for r.

The recursive formula is $a_n = \frac{3}{2}(a_{n-1})$, where the initial condition is $a_1 = 8$.

STUDY TIP

Remember, you used explicit and recursive formulas with arithmetic sequences. In an *explicit definition*, the output for any term depends on the term number. In applying a *recursive definition*, the output is used as the next input.

Try It! **2.** Write the recursive formula for the geometric sequence 3,072, 768, 192, 48, 12, ...

EXAMPLE 3 Use the Explicit Formula

What is the 10th term in the sequence shown in Example 2?

Explicit formula:

$$a_n = a_1(r)^{n-1}$$

*n*th term, first term, common ratio

The first term is 8. The common ratio is $\frac{3}{2}$.

$$a_{10} = 8\left(\frac{3}{2}\right)^9$$
$$= 307.546875$$

The 10th term in the sequence is 307.55 rounded to the nearest hundredth.

Try It! **3.** What is the 12th term of the sequence described?

Initial condition is 3.

Recursive formula is $a_n = 6(a_{n-1})$.

CONCEPTUAL UNDERSTANDING

EXAMPLE 4 Connect Geometric Sequences and Exponential Functions

The number of subscribers to a blog doubles each week.

How can the trend in subscribers be modeled?

The number of subscribers doubles each week, so an exponential function models the situation. The initial number of subscribers is 5, and that number doubles each week.

The trend can also be modeled as a geometric sequence with an initial value of 5 and a common ratio of 2.

$a_n = a_1(r)^{n-1}$

$a_n = 5(2)^{n-1}$ .... Substitute 5 for a_1, 2 for r.

The number of subscribers changes by a constant ratio, so both an exponential function and a geometric sequence can model the situation.

 **Try It!** **4.** How many subscribers will there be in Week 9 if the initial number of subscribers is 10?

APPLICATION

EXAMPLE 5 Apply the Recursive and Explicit Formulas

The number of people attending the annual Town International Food Festival has decreased 20% each year since the first year.

Annual Town International Food Festival
1,250
Attended Last Year!

A. How can the attendance for the first 5 years be modeled?

The attendance is declining at a constant rate of 20%, so a geometric sequence can model the trend.

Find the common ratio. The common ratio is the decay factor here.

$1 - r$

$1 - 0.2 = 0.8$

Write a recursive formula to describe the trend.

$a_n = r(a_{n-1})$

$a_n = 0.8(a_{n-1})$ ········ Substitute 0.8 for r.

The recursive formula is $a_n = 0.8(a_{n-1})$, where the attendance at the first festival is $a_1 = 1{,}250$.

B. If the trend continues, what will the attendance be in 10 years?

Use the explicit formula to find the attendance in year 10.

$a_n = a_1(r)^{n-1}$

$a_{10} = 1{,}250(0.8)^{10-1}$

$a_{10} = 1{,}250(0.8)^9$

Use a calculator to evaluate the expression.

Attendance in 10 years will be about 168 people.

GENERALIZE
How is the form of a geometric sequence related to the types of questions that can be answered efficiently using that form?

Try It! 5. The formula $a_n = 1.5(a_{n-1})$ with an initial value of 40 describes a sequence. Use the explicit formula to determine the 5th term of the sequence.

CONCEPT SUMMARY Explicit and Recursive Formulas

	Explicit formula	Recursive formula
ALGEBRA	$a_n = a_1(r)^{n-1}$ nth term, first term, common ratio **Initial condition:** a_1 is the first term	$a_n = r(a_{n-1})$ nth term, common ratio, previous term
NUMBERS	$a_n = 2(3)^{n-1}$ $a_1 = 2$	$a_n = 3(a_{n-1})$
GRAPH	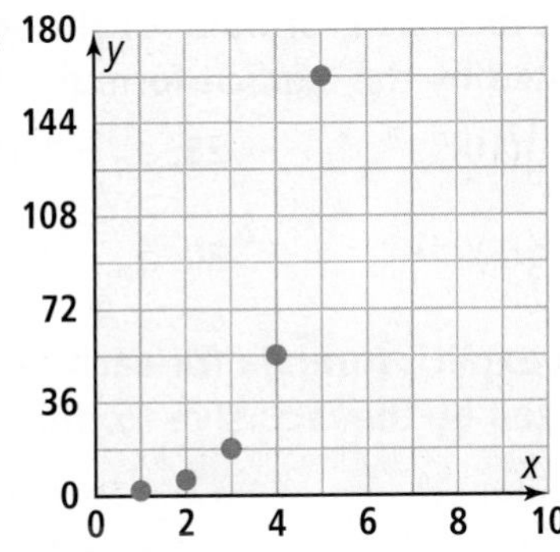	

Do You UNDERSTAND?

1. ESSENTIAL QUESTION How are geometric sequences related to exponential functions?

2. **Vocabulary** How are *geometric sequences* similar to arithmetic sequences? How are they different?

3. **Error Analysis** For a geometric sequence with $a_1 = 3$ and a common ratio r of 1.25, Jamie writes $a_n = 1.25 \cdot (3)^{n-1}$. What mistake did Jamie make?

4. **Generalize** Is a sequence geometric if each term in the sequence is x times greater than the preceding term?

Do You KNOW HOW?

Determine whether the sequence is an arithmetic or a geometric sequence. If it is geometric, what is the common ratio?

5. 30, 6, 1.2, 0.24, 0.048, ...

6. 0.5, 2, 8, 32, 148, ...

Write the recursive formula for each geometric sequence.

7. 640, 160, 40, 10, 2.5, ...

8. 2, 5, 12.5, 31.25, 78.125, ...

9. What is the recursive formula for a sequence with the following explicit formula? $a_n = 1.25 \cdot (3)^{n-1}$

10. A sequence has an initial value of 25 and a common ratio of 1.8. How can you write the sequence as a function?

Scan for Multimedia

Practice Tutorial

Additional Exercises Available Online

UNDERSTAND

11. **Make Sense and Persevere** Explain how to write a formula to describe the sequence 1, 3, 9, 27, 81, 243, ...

12. **Look for Relationships** How are geometric sequences related to exponential growth and decay functions? Explain your reasoning.

13. **Error Analysis** Describe and correct the error a student made when writing a recursive formula from an explicit formula.

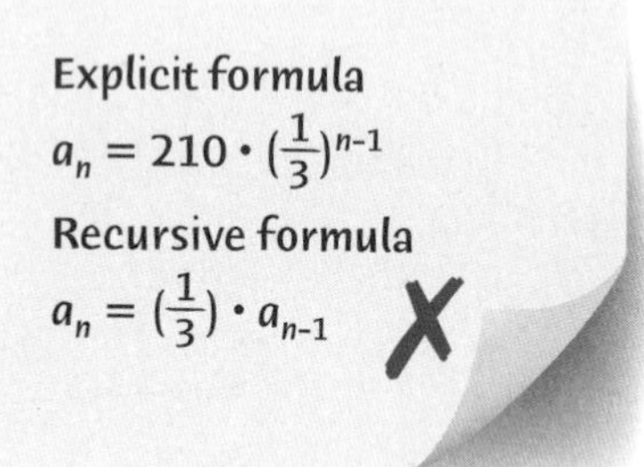

14. **Use Appropriate Tools** Explain how you could use a graphing calculator to determine whether the data in the table represents a geometric sequence.

n	a_n
1	20
2	90
3	405
4	1822.5
5	8201.25

15. **Higher Order Thinking** In Example 5, a geometric sequence is written as a function.

    a. How is the domain of a function related to the numbers in the sequence?

    b. How is the range of the function related to the numbers in the sequence?

16. **Mathematical Connections** A pendulum swings 80 cm on its first swing, 76 cm on its second swing, 72.2 cm on its third swing, and 68.59 cm on its fourth swing.

    a. If the pattern continues, what explicit formula can be used to find the distance of the nth swing?

    b. Use your formula to find the distance of the 10th swing.

PRACTICE

Determine whether the sequence is a geometric sequence. If it is, write the recursive formula.

SEE EXAMPLES 1 AND 2

17. 8, 12, 18, 27, 40.5, ...

18. $3, \frac{3}{2}, \frac{3}{4}, \frac{3}{8}, \frac{3}{16}, \ldots$

19. $\frac{1}{27}, \frac{1}{9}, \frac{1}{3}, 1, 3, \ldots$

20. $\frac{10}{3}, \frac{8}{3}, 2, \frac{4}{3}, \frac{2}{3}, \ldots$

21. 1, 1, 2, 3, 5, ...

22. $2, \frac{8}{3}, \frac{32}{9}, \frac{128}{27}, \frac{512}{81}, \ldots$

23. 1, 1.2, 1.4, 1.6, 1.8, ...

24. $\frac{1}{2}, 2, 8, 32, 128, \ldots$

25. 9, 18, 36, 74, 144, ...

26. $\frac{4}{5}, 4, 20, 100, 500, \ldots$

Write the recursive formula for the sequence represented by the explicit formula. SEE EXAMPLE 3

27. $a_n = \frac{1}{5}(10)^{n-1}$

28. $a_n = 1.1(6)^{n-1}$

29. $a_n = \frac{2}{3}(5)^{n-1}$

30. $a_n = 0.4(8)^{n-1}$

Write an explicit formula for each sequence represented by the recursive formula. SEE EXAMPLE 5

31. $a_n = \frac{4}{5}(a_{n-1})$, $a_1 = 100$

32. $a_n = 8(a_{n-1})$, $a_1 = 1$

33. $a_n = \frac{5}{9}(a_{n-1})$, $a_1 = 10$

34. $a_n = 6(a_{n-1})$, $a_1 = 7$

Write each geometric sequence using function notation.

SEE EXAMPLE 4

35. $a_n = \frac{3}{4}(a_{n-1})$, $a_1 = 20$

36. $a_n = 3(a_{n-1})$, $a_1 = 7$

37. $a_n = 2a_{n-1}$, $a_1 = 4$

38. $a_n = \frac{2}{3}a_{n-1}$, $a_1 = 99$

Write a function to model each geometric sequence in the table.

39.

n	a_n
1	9
2	3
3	1
4	$\frac{1}{3}$
5	$\frac{1}{9}$

40.

n	a_n
1	18
2	54
3	162
4	486
5	1,458

PRACTICE & PROBLEM SOLVING

APPLY

41. Make Sense and Persevere A new optical illusion is posted to the Internet. Write a recursive formula to describe the pattern. Then, write the explicit formula that can be used to find the number of times the optical illusion is shared after eight hours?

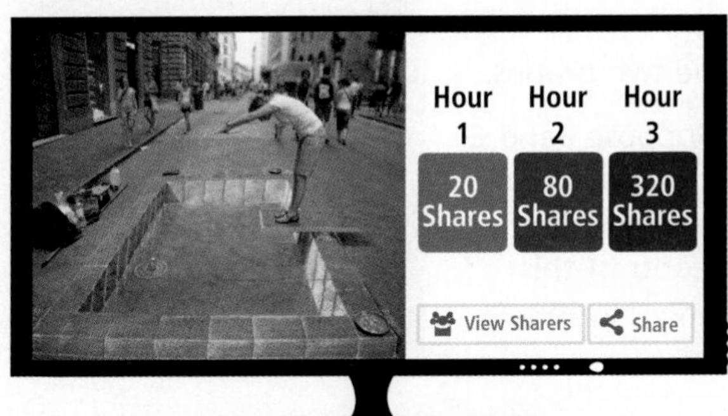

42. Construct Arguments Write the recursive formula for a geometric sequence that models the data in the table. Use the explicit formula to determine whether there will be 1,000 participants by the tenth year of the Annual Clean-Up Day.

Annual Clean-up Day

Year	Participants
1	16
2	24
3	36
4	54
5	81

43. Model With Mathematics The number of bacteria in the sample shown decreases by a factor of $\frac{2}{3}$ every hour. Write a geometric sequence to model the pattern. How many hours will it take for the number of bacteria to decrease below 1,000?

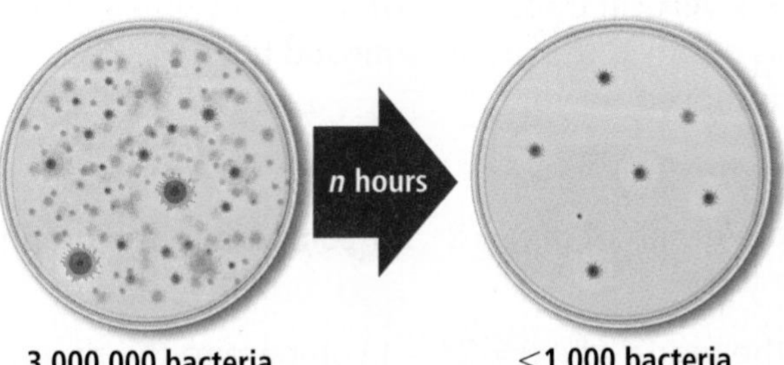

ASSESSMENT PRACTICE

44. Is each sequence shown a geometric sequence? Select *Yes* or *No*.

	Yes	No
6, 18, 30, 42, 54, ...	☐	☐
$2, 3, \frac{9}{2}, \frac{27}{4}, \frac{81}{8}, \ldots$	☐	☐
1024, 256, 64, 16, 4, ...	☐	☐
243, 162, 81, 54, 27, ...	☐	☐

45. SAT/ACT What is the explicit formula for the sequence 360, 180, 90, 45, 22.5, ...?

Ⓐ $a_n = \frac{1}{2}(360)^{n-1}$

Ⓑ $a_n = \frac{1}{2}(a_{n-1})$

Ⓒ $a_n = 360(a_{n-1})$

Ⓓ $a_n = 360\left(\frac{1}{2}\right)^{n-1}$

Ⓔ $a_n = 360 + \frac{1}{2}(a_{n-1})$

46. Performance Task A computer program generates the patterns shown each time the program loops.

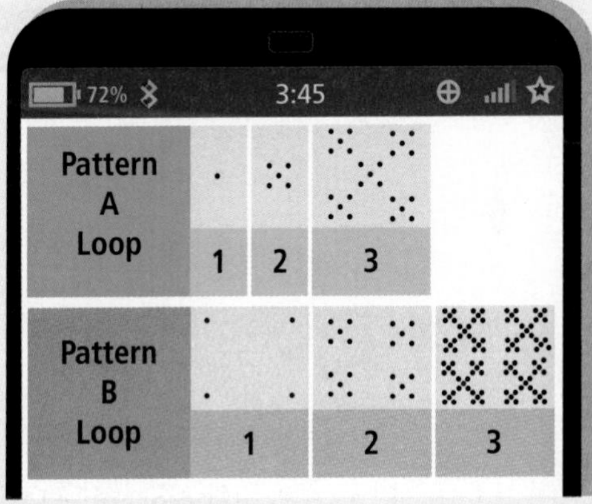

Part A Write the recursive formula for the geometric sequence that models each pattern.

Part B How are the geometric sequences for patterns A and B related?

Part C If pattern B has x dots at loop n, how many dots does pattern A have at loop n? Explain.

6-5 Transformations of Exponential Functions

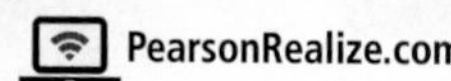

I CAN… perform, analyze, and use transformations of exponential functions.

Activity Assess

MODEL & DISCUSS

A radio station uses the function $f(x) = 100(3)^x$ to model the growth of Band A's fan base.

A. What would the graph of the function look like for Band B with a fan base growing twice as fast as Band A's fan base?

B. Compare and contrast the two graphs.

C. **Look for Relationships** Suppose Band C starts with a fan base of 200 fans that is growing twice as fast as Band A's fan base. Compare and contrast this new function with the previous two functions.

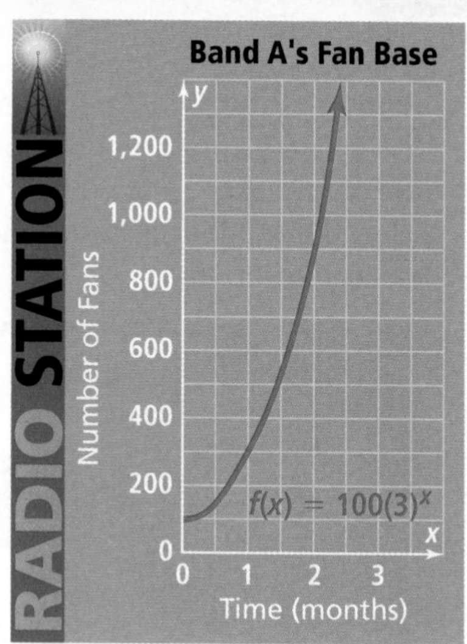

ESSENTIAL QUESTION

How do changes in an exponential function relate to translations of its graph?

CONCEPTUAL UNDERSTANDING

EXAMPLE 1 Vertical Translations of Graphs of Exponential Functions

How does the value of k affect the graph of $f(x) = 2^x + k$?

Compare the graphs of $g(x) = 2^x + 3$ and $j(x) = 2^x - 3$ to the graph of $f(x) = 2^x$.

x	$f(x) = 2^x$	$g(x) = 2^x + 3$	$j(x) = 2^x - 3$
−2	$\frac{1}{4}$	$3\frac{1}{4}$	$-2\frac{3}{4}$
−1	$\frac{1}{2}$	$3\frac{1}{2}$	$-2\frac{1}{2}$
0	1	4	−2
1	2	5	−1
2	4	7	1

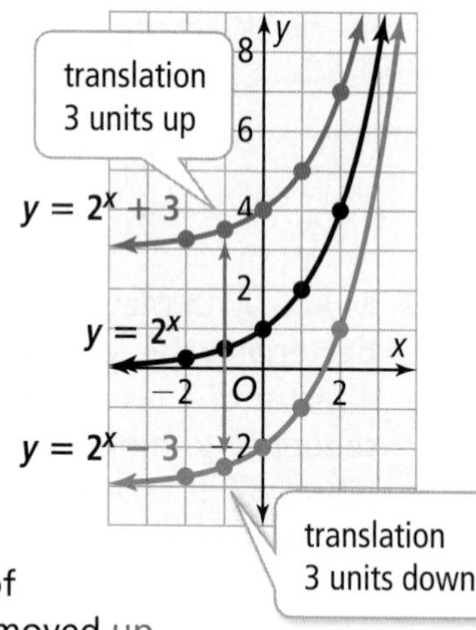

The graph of $f(x) = 2^x + k$ is a vertical translation of the graph of $f(x) = 2^x$. If k is positive, the graph is moved up. If k is negative, the graph is moved down.

Try It! 1. a. How does the graph of $g(x) = 2^x + 1$ compare to the graph of $f(x) = 2^x$?

b. How does the graph of $j(x) = 2^x - 1$ compare to the graph of $f(x) = 2^x$?

EXAMPLE 2 Horizontal Translations of Graphs of Exponential Functions

A. Compare the graph of $g(x) = 2^{x-h}$ with the graph of $f(x) = 2^x$ when $h > 0$. What effect does h have on the graph of g?

Let $h = 5$. Compare the graph of $g(x) = 2^{x-5}$ to the graph of $f(x) = 2^x$.

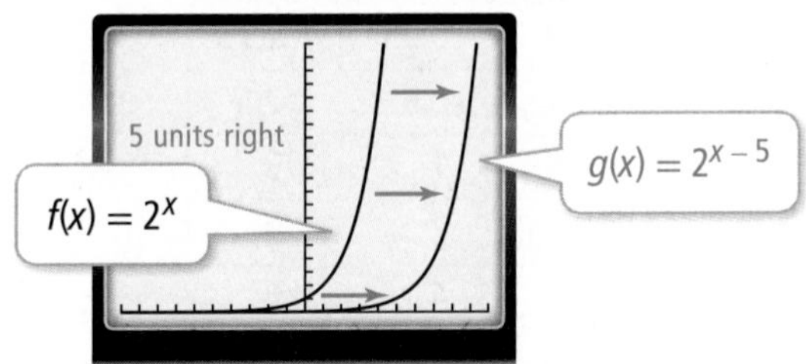

COMMON ERROR
Remember that the graph is translated right when h is positive and left when h is negative. This is the opposite of the effect of subtraction of a positive on a number line.

When $h > 0$, the graph is translated h units to the right. The graph of $g(x)$ is a translation of $f(x)$ to the right by 5 units.

B. Compare the graph of $j(x) = 2^{x-h}$ with the graph of $f(x) = 2^x$ when $h < 0$. What effect does h have on the graph of j?

Let $h = -3$. Compare the graph of $j(x) = 2^{x+3}$ to the graph of $f(x) = 2^x$.

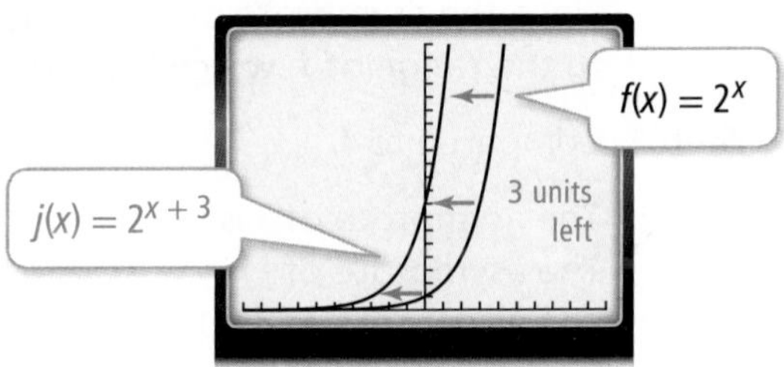

When $h < 0$, the graph is translated h units to the left. The graph of $j(x)$ is a translation of $f(x)$ to the left by 3 units.

Try It! 2. Compare the graph of each function with the graph of $f(x) = 2^x$. What effect does h have on the graph of each?

a. $g(x) = 2^{x+2}$ **b.** $j(x) = 2^{x-2}$

EXAMPLE 3 Compare Two Different Transformations of $f(x) = 2^x$

How can you compare the properties of g, given in the table, to the properties of j, given in the graph? Both functions are translations of f.

USE STRUCTURE
The range of $f(x) = 2^x$ is $f(x) > 0$. How do different transformations of $f(x) = 2^x$ affect the range of the function?

x	$f(x) = 2^x$	$g(x)$
−2	0.25	2.25
−1	0.5	2.5
0	1	3
1	2	4
2	4	6

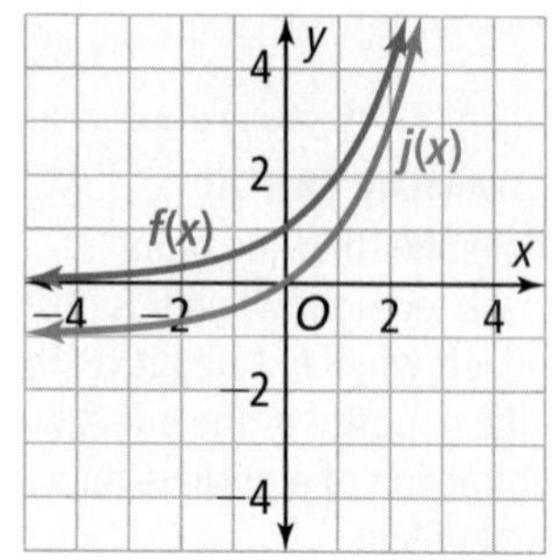

Step 1 Compare g to f.

The y-intercept of the graph of f is 1.
The y-intercept of the graph of g is 3.
The y-values for g are 2 units greater than the corresponding y-values for f. The asymptote of f is $y = 0$. So, the asymptote of g is 2 units greater, $y = 2$.

Since the asymptote of g is $y = 2$, the range of g is $y > 2$, as compared to the range of f, which is $y > 0$.

Step 2 Compare j to f.

The asymptote of f is $y = 0$.
The asymptote of j is $y = -1$.
The asymptote of j is 1 unit less than the asymptote of f.

Since the asymptote of j is $y = -1$, the range of j is $y > -1$, as compared to the range of f, which is $y > 0$.

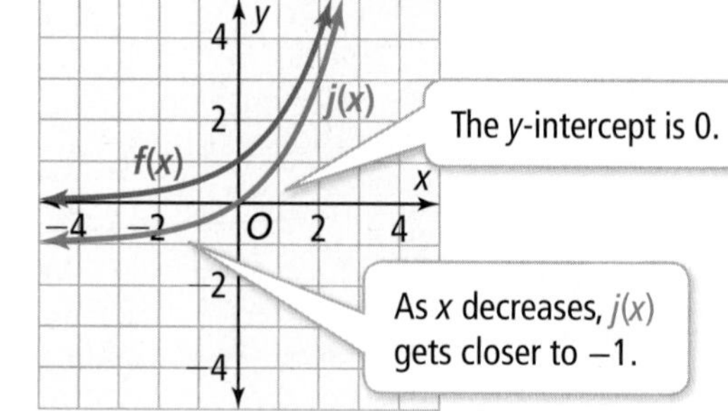

Step 3 Compare g to j.

The graph of g is the graph of f translated 2 units up, while the graph of j is the graph of f translated 1 unit down.

So, the graph of g is the graph of j translated 3 units up. Thus, the asymptote of g is 3 units greater than the asymptote of j and the y-values of g are 3 units greater than the y-values of j.

Try It! **3. a.** The graph of the function b is a vertical translation of the graph of $a(x) = 3^x$, and has a y-intercept of 0. How does the graph of $c(x) = 3^x + 1$ compare to the graph of b?

b. How does the graph of $m(x) = 3^x - 3$ compare to the graph of $p(x) = 3^x + 4$?

CONCEPT SUMMARY Translations of Exponential Functions

	Vertical Translations	Horizontal Translations
ALGEBRA	$f(x) = a^x + k$	$f(x) = a^{(x-h)}$
NUMBERS	$f(x) = 0.5^x$ $g(x) = 0.5^x + 3$ $j(x) = 0.5^x - 3$	$f(x) = 0.5^x$ $g(x) = 0.5^{x+3}$ $j(x) = 0.5^{x-3}$
GRAPHS	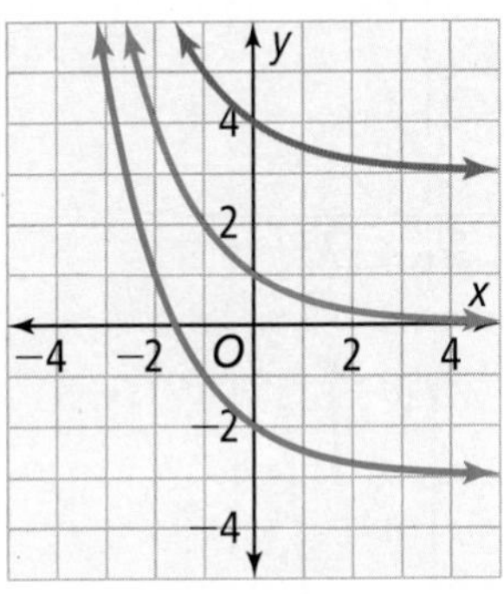	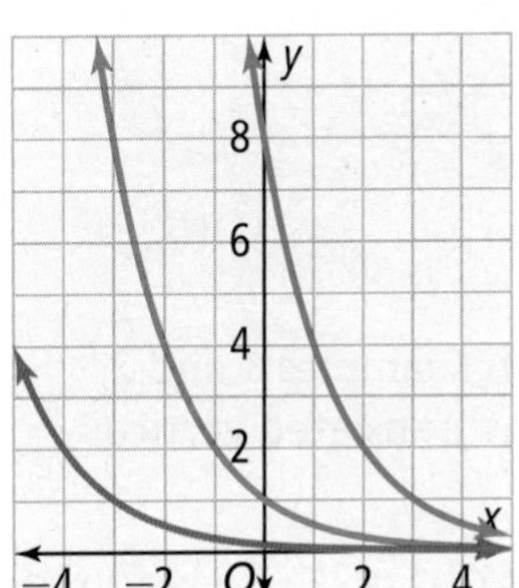

Do You UNDERSTAND?

1. ESSENTIAL QUESTION How do changes in an exponential function relate to translations of its graph?

2. **Communicate Precisely** How is the effect of k on the graph of $a^x + k$ similar to the effect of h on the graph of a^{x-h}? How is it different?

3. **Error Analysis** Tariq graphs $g(x) = 2^x + 6$ by translating the graph of $f(x) = 2^x$ six units right. What mistake did Tariq make?

4. **Reason** As the value of k switches from a positive to a negative number, what is the effect on the graph of $f(x) = 2^x + k$?

5. **Use Structure** The general form of vertical translations of exponential functions is $f(x) = a^x + k$. The general form of horizontal translations of exponential functions is $f(x) = a^{x-h}$. Why do you think one involves addition and one involves subtraction?

Do You KNOW HOW?

Compare the graph of each function to the graph of $f(x) = 2^x$.

6. $g(x) = 2^x + 1$

7. $p(x) = 2^{x-1}$

8. $j(x) = 2^x - 4$

9. $g(x) = 2^{x+1}$

10. Compare the function represented by the graph of $g(x) = 2^x - 3$ to the function represented by the table.

x	$j(x)$
−2	1.25
−1	1.5
0	2
1	3
2	5

Compare the graph of each function to the graph of $f(x) = 0.4^x$.

11. $g(x) = 0.4^{x+1}$

12. $p(x) = 0.4^{x-1}$

13. $j(x) = 0.4^x + 1$

14. $g(x) = 0.4^x - 1$

Scan for Multimedia | Practice | Tutorial

Additional Exercises Available Online

UNDERSTAND

15. **Make Sense and Persevere** Let $f(x) = a^x$. Describe two ways you could identify the value of k in the transformation implied by $g(x) = a^x + k$ from the graphs of f and g.

16. **Error Analysis** Describe and correct the error a student made in analyzing the transformation $g(x) = a^{x-h}$.

> The graph of $g(x) = a^{x-h}$ is the graph of $f(x) = a^x$ translated h units to the left. ✗

17. **Higher Order Thinking** In Examples 1 and 2, the graph of $f(x) = 2^x$ was translated vertically and horizontally.

    a. Compare the graph of $g(x) = 2^{x+3} + 4$ to the graph of $f(x) = 2^x$.

    b. In general, when the graph of an exponential function is translated both vertically and horizontally, what is the effect on the asymptote?

    c. In general, when the graph of an exponential function is translated both vertically and horizontally, what is the effect on the domain and the range?

18. a. **Use Appropriate Tools** Copy and complete the table. Compare the graphs of f and g.

x	$f(x) = 4^{\frac{1}{2}x}$	$g(x) = 4^x$
−2		
−1		
0		
2		
4		

    b. What point do the functions have in common?

    c. Describe the asymptote of each function.

PRACTICE

Compare the graph of each function to the graph of $f(x) = 2^x$. SEE EXAMPLES 1–3

19. $g(x) = 2^x - 6$

20. $p(x) = 2^{x+4}$

21. $g(x) = 2^{x-1}$

22. $j(x) = 2^x + \frac{3}{4}$

Find the value of k or h in each of the graphs.
SEE EXAMPLES 1–3

23. 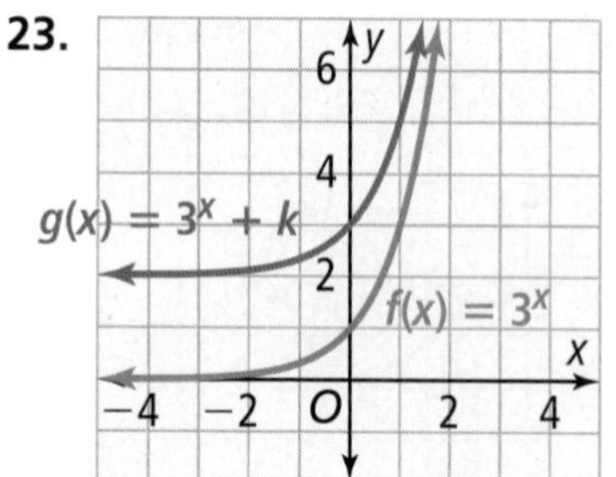

24. 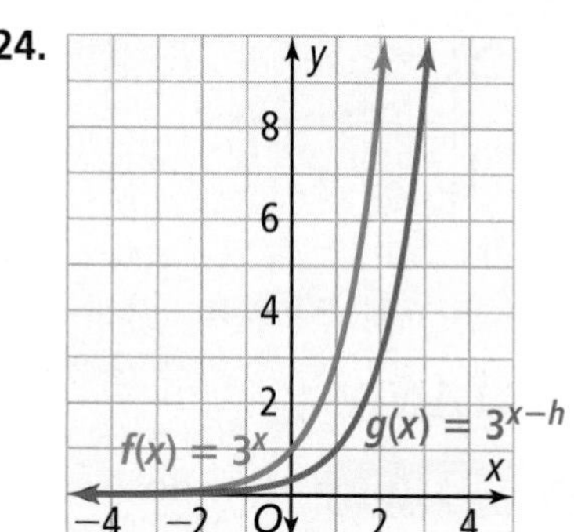

Graph each function and its transformation.
SEE EXAMPLES 1–3

25. $f(x) = 4^x$
    $g(x) = 4^x + k$ for $k = -4$

26. $f(x) = 0.5^x$
    $g(x) = 0.5^{x-h}$ for $h = -5$

Compare the y-intercepts, asymptotes, and ranges for the graphs of f and g. SEE EXAMPLE 3

27. $f(x) = 4^x$

x	$g(x)$
−2	3.0625
−1	3.25
0	4
1	7
2	19

28. 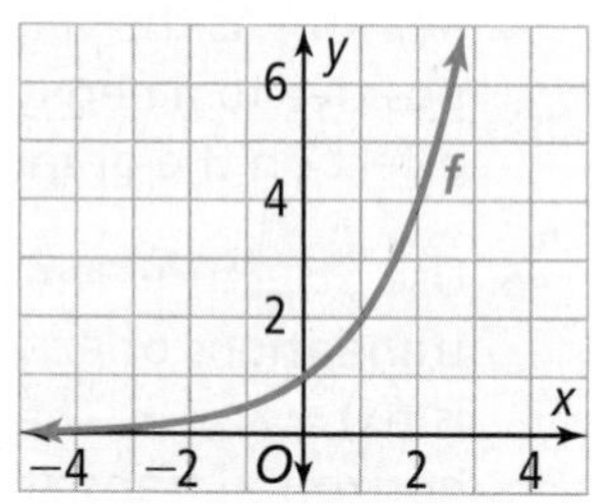

The graph of g is a horizontal translation 3 units to the left of the graph of $f(x) = 2^x$.

Practice Tutorial

Mixed Review Available Online

PRACTICE & PROBLEM SOLVING

APPLY

29. **Reason** How are graphs of $f(x) = 2^{x-h}$ similar and different for positive and negative values of h?

30. **Communicate Precisely** How does the graph of $f(x) = 2^{x+2}$ compare to the graph of $g(x) = 2^x + 2$?

31. Compare the function represented by the graph of $g(x) = 2^{x+0.5}$ to the graph of the function represented by the table.

x	$j(x)$
−2	0.088
−1	0.177
0	0.354
1	0.707
2	1.414

32. **Model With Mathematics** The function in the graph models an online gaming tournament that is expected to start with 400 players, with half of the players being eliminated in each round.

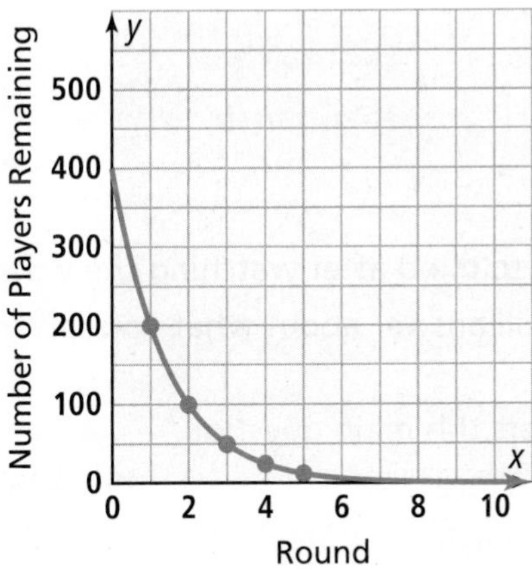

a. Describe how the graph will change if the starting number of players is 600 instead of 400. Explain your reasoning.

b. Describe how the graph will change if the starting number of players is 800 instead of 400?

ASSESSMENT PRACTICE

33. Consider the function $f(x) = 0.5^x$.

a. Graph $f(x)$, $g(x) = 0.5^x + k$ for $k = -1$, and $j(x) = 0.5^{x-h}$ for $h = 1$ in the same coordinate plane.

b. What are the y-intercepts of the graphs of g and j?

34. **SAT/ACT** The graph of g is a translation 4 units to the right of the graph of $f(x) = 5^x$. What is g?

Ⓐ $g(x) = 5^x + 4$

Ⓑ $g(x) = 5^x - 4$

Ⓒ $g(x) = 5^{x+4}$

Ⓓ $g(x) = 5^{x-4}$

Ⓔ $g(x) = 5^{4x}$

35. **Performance Task** Darnell is thinking about investing \$500 in a savings plan. The graph shows how Darnell's \$500 will grow if he invests his money in the plan today.

Part A How will the graph change if Darnell selects the same savings plan, but waits 5 years to invest his \$500?

Part B If Darnell waits 5 years, in approximately how many years will his investment reach \$1,000? Explain your reasoning.

Part C Suppose that instead of \$500, Darnell invests \$1,000 in the savings plan today. Describe how the graph will change. How can you use the transformed graph to estimate how many years will it take for his investment to reach \$7,500?

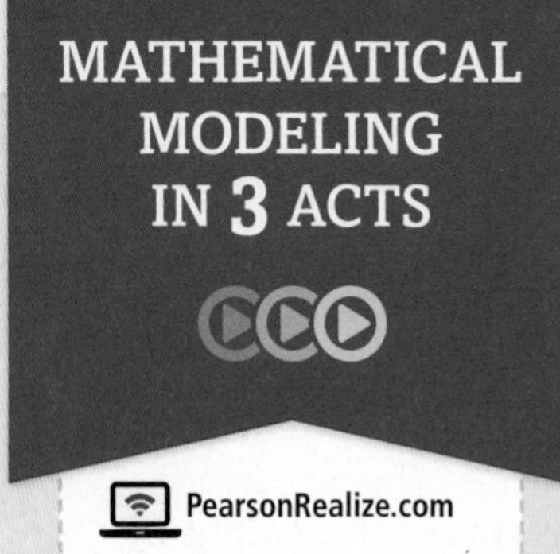

PearsonRealize.com

Big Time Pay Back

Most people agree that investing your money is a good idea. Some people might advise you to put money into a bank savings account. Other people might say that you should invest in the stock market. Still others think that buying bonds is the best investment option.

Is a bank savings account a good way to let your money grow? Just how much money can you make from a savings account? In the Mathematical Modeling in 3 Acts lesson, you'll see an intriguing situation about an investment option.

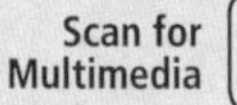

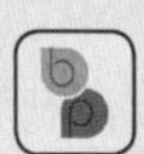

ACT 1 Identify the Problem

1. What is the first question that comes to mind after watching the video?
2. Write down the main question you will answer about what you saw in the video.
3. Make an initial conjecture that answers this main question.
4. Explain how you arrived at your conjecture.
5. Write a number that you know is too small.
6. Write a number that you know is too large.
7. What information will be useful to know to answer the main question? How can you get it? How will you use that information?

ACT 2 Develop a Model

8. Use the math that you have learned in this Topic to refine your conjecture.

ACT 3 Interpret the Results

9. Is your refined conjecture between the highs and lows you set up earlier?
10. Did your refined conjecture match the actual answer exactly? If not, what might explain the difference?

TOPIC 6

Topic Review

TOPIC ESSENTIAL QUESTION

1. How do you use exponential functions to model situations and solve problems?

Vocabulary Review

Choose the correct term to complete each sentence.

2. A population's growth can be modeled by a(n) __________ function of the form $f(x) = a \cdot b^x$, where $a > 0$ and $b > 1$.
3. An exponential function repeatedly multiplies an initial amount by the same positive number, called the __________.
4. A(n) __________ is a number sequence formed by multiplying a term in the sequence by a fixed nonzero number, or a common ratio, to find the next term.
5. __________ is interest that is paid both on the principal and on the interest that has already been paid.
6. As x or y gets larger in absolute value, the graph of the exponential function gets closer to the line called a(n) __________.

- geometric sequence
- constant ratio
- simple interest
- decay factor
- compound interest
- exponential decay
- exponential growth
- exponential function
- asymptote
- growth factor

Concepts & Skills Review

LESSON 6-1 Rational Exponents and Properties of Exponents

Quick Review

If the nth root of a is a real number and m is an integer, then $a^{\frac{1}{n}} = \sqrt[n]{a}$ and $a^{\frac{m}{n}} = (\sqrt[n]{a})^m$.

Power of a Power: $(a^m)^n = a^{mn}$

Power of a Product: $(a \cdot b)^m = a^m b^m$

Product of Powers: $a^m \cdot a^n = a^{m+n}$

Quotient of Powers: $\frac{a^m}{a^n} = a^{m-n}, a \neq 0$

Example

How can you use the Power of a Power Property to solve $64^{x-3} = 16^{2x-1}$?

Rewrite the equation so both expressions have the same base.

$$64^{x-3} = 16^{2x-1}$$
$$(2^6)^{x-3} = (2^4)^{2x-1}$$
$$2^{6x-18} = 2^{8x-4}$$
$$6x - 18 = 8x - 4$$
$$-18 = 2x - 4$$
$$-14 = 2x$$
$$-7 = x$$

The solution is –7.

Practice & Problem Solving

Write each radical using rational exponents.

7. $\sqrt{8}$

8. $\sqrt[3]{12}$

Solve each equation.

9. $\left(6^{\frac{x}{2}}\right)\left(6^{\frac{x}{3}}\right) = 6^6$

10. $36^{4x-1} = 6^{x+2}$

11. **Make Sense and Persevere** Describe two ways to express the edge length of a cube with a volume of 64 cm^3.

12. **Model With Mathematics** Use rational exponents to express the relationship between the dollar values of two prizes in a contest.

Prize	Value
Bicycle	\$256
Luxury vehicle	\$65,536

LESSON 6-2 Exponential Functions

Quick Review

An exponential function is the product of an initial amount and a **constant ratio** raised to a power. Exponential functions are expressed using $f(x) = a \cdot b^x$, where a is a nonzero constant, $b > 0$, and $b \neq 1$.

Example

Find the initial amount and the constant ratio of the exponential function represented by the table.

x	$f(x)$	
0	3	The initial amount is 3.
1	12	$12 \div 3 = 4$
2	48	$48 \div 12 = 4$
3	192	$192 \div 48 = 4$
4	768	$768 \div 192 = 4$

The constant ratio is 4.

In $f(x) = a \cdot b^x$, substitute 3 for a and 4 for b.

The function is $f(x) = 3(4)^x$.

Practice & Problem Solving

Graph each exponential function.

13. $f(x) = 2.5^x$

14. $f(x) = 5(2)^x$

15. Write the exponential function for this table.

x	0	1	2	3
$f(x)$	0.5	1	2	4

16. **Make Sense and Persevere** Write an equation for an exponential function that models the expected number of bacteria as a function of time. Graph the function. If the pattern continues, in which month will the bacteria exceed 45,000,000?

Month	Number of Bacteria
0	2,500
1	7,500
2	22,500
3	67,500
4	202,500

LESSON 6-3 Exponential Growth and Decay

Quick Review

An **exponential growth function** can be written as $f(x) = a(1 + r)^x$. An exponential decay function can be written as $f(x) = a(1 - r)^x$.

Example

Chapter City has a population of 18,000 and grows at an annual rate of 8%. What is the estimated population of Chapter City in 6 years?

Let x = time in years, a = initial amount, and r = growth rate.

$$f(x) = a(1 + r)^x$$
$$= 18{,}000(1 + 0.08)^x$$

The function is $f(x) = 18{,}000(1.08)^x$.

Find the expected population in 6 years.

$f(6) = 18{,}000(1.08)^6 \approx 28{,}563.74$

After 6 years, the population is expected to be about 28,564.

Practice & Problem Solving

17. **Make Sense and Persevere** An exponential function of the form $f(x) = b^x$ includes the points (2, 36), (3, 216), and (4, 1,296). What is the value of b?

Write an exponential growth or decay function to model each situation.

18. initial value: 50, growth factor: 1.15

19. initial value: 200, decay factor: 0.85

Construct Arguments Compare each investment to an investment of the same principal at the same rate compounded annually.

20. principal: $12,000
annual interest: 5%
interest periods: 2
number of years: 10

21. principal: $20,000
annual interest: 2.5%
interest periods: 4
number of years: 15

LESSON 6-4 Geometric Sequences

Quick Review

A **geometric sequence** is a number sequence in which each term after the first term is found by multiplying the previous term by a common ratio.

Explicit formula: $a_n = a_1(r)^{n-1}$

Recursive formula: $a_n = r(a_{n-1})$

Example

What are the explicit and recursive formulas for the geometric sequence 9, 22.5, 56.25, 140.625, 351.5625, ... ?

$\frac{22.5}{9} = \frac{56.25}{22.5} = \frac{140.625}{56.25}$

$= \frac{351.5625}{140.625} = \frac{5}{2}$ ········· Find the common ratio.

The common ratio is $\frac{5}{2}$. The first term is 9.

The explicit formula is $a_n = 9\left(\frac{5}{2}\right)^{n-1}$

The recursive formula is $a_n = \frac{5}{2}(a_{n-1})$, $a_1 = 9$.

Practice & Problem Solving

Determine if the sequence is a geometric sequence. If it is, write the explicit and recursive formulas.

22. $5, \frac{5}{2}, \frac{5}{4}, \frac{5}{8}, \frac{5}{16}, \ldots$

23. 2, 5, 8, 11, 14, ...

24. 8, 16, 32, 64, 128, ...

25. $\frac{1}{5}, \frac{2}{5}, \frac{4}{5}, \frac{8}{5}, \frac{16}{5}, \ldots$

Translate each explicit formula to recursive form.

26. $a_n = 2.2(4)^{n-1}$

27. $a_n = 6(3.5)^{n-1}$

28. Write the explicit and recursive formula for a geometric sequence modeled in the table. Will the number of signatures reach 7,000 by the end of the second week? Explain.

Petition to Turn Parking Lot into Park

Day	Number of Signatures
1	40
2	60
3	90
4	135

LESSON 6-5 Transformations of Exponential Functions

Quick Review

The graph of $g(x) = a^x + k$ is the graph of a^x translated up when $k > 0$ and translated down when $k < 0$.

The graph of $g(x) = a^{x-h}$ is the graph of a^x translated right when $h > 0$ and translated left when $h < 0$.

Example

Compare the graphs of $g(x) = 3^x - 2$ and $f(x) = 3^x$.

x	$f(x)$	$g(x)$
−2	$\frac{1}{9}$	$-\frac{17}{9}$
−1	$\frac{1}{3}$	$-\frac{5}{3}$
0	1	−1
1	3	1
2	9	7

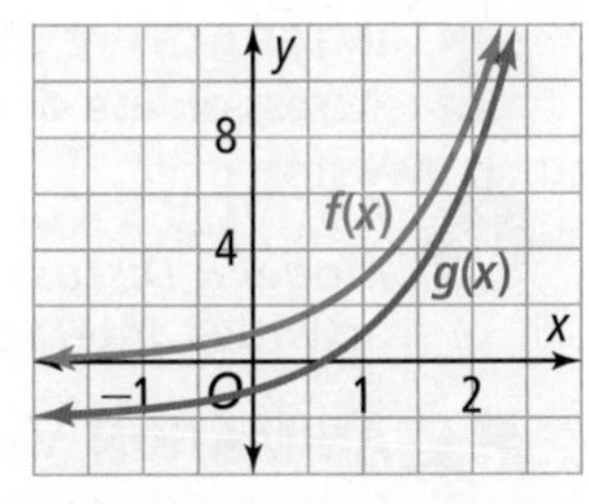

The graph of $g(x)$ is translated 2 units down from the graph of $f(x)$.

Practice & Problem Solving

Compare the graph of each function to the graph of $f(x) = 3^x$.

29. $g(x) = 3^x - 5$

30. $j(x) = 3^x + 10$

31. $g(x) = 3^{x-2}$

32. $j(x) = 3^{x+3}$

Graph each function and its transformation.

33. $f(x) = 1.5^x$, $g(x) = 1.5^x + k$ for $k = 2$

34. $f(x) = 4^x$, $g(x) = 4^x - k$ for $k = 0.5$

Polynomials and Factoring

TOPIC ESSENTIAL QUESTION

How do you work with polynomials to rewrite expressions and solve problems?

Topic Overview

Topic Vocabulary

- Closure Property
- degree of a monomial
- degree of a polynomial
- difference of two squares
- monomial
- perfect-square trinomial
- polynomial
- standard form of a polynomial

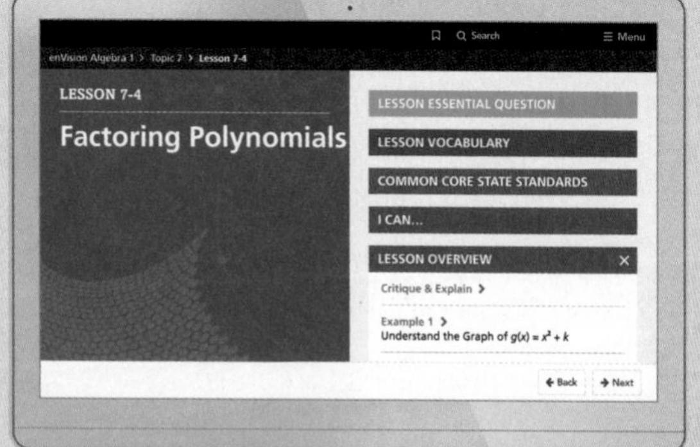

Go online | **PearsonRealize.com**

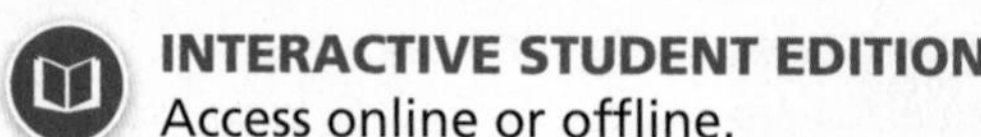
Digital Experience

INTERACTIVE STUDENT EDITION Access online or offline.

ACTIVITIES Complete ***Explore & Reason, Model & Discuss***, and ***Critique & Explain*** activities. Interact with Examples and Try Its.

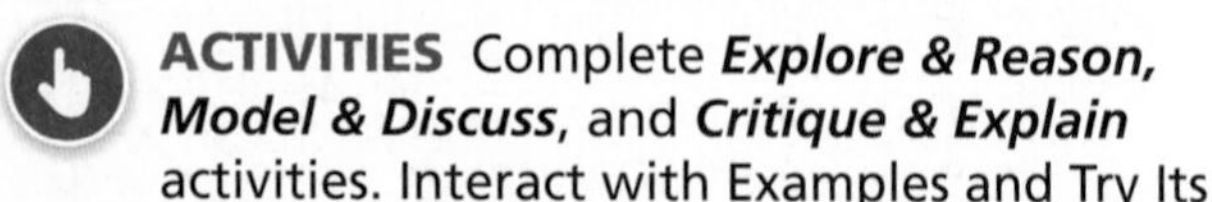
ANIMATION View and interact with real-world applications.

PRACTICE Practice what you've learned.

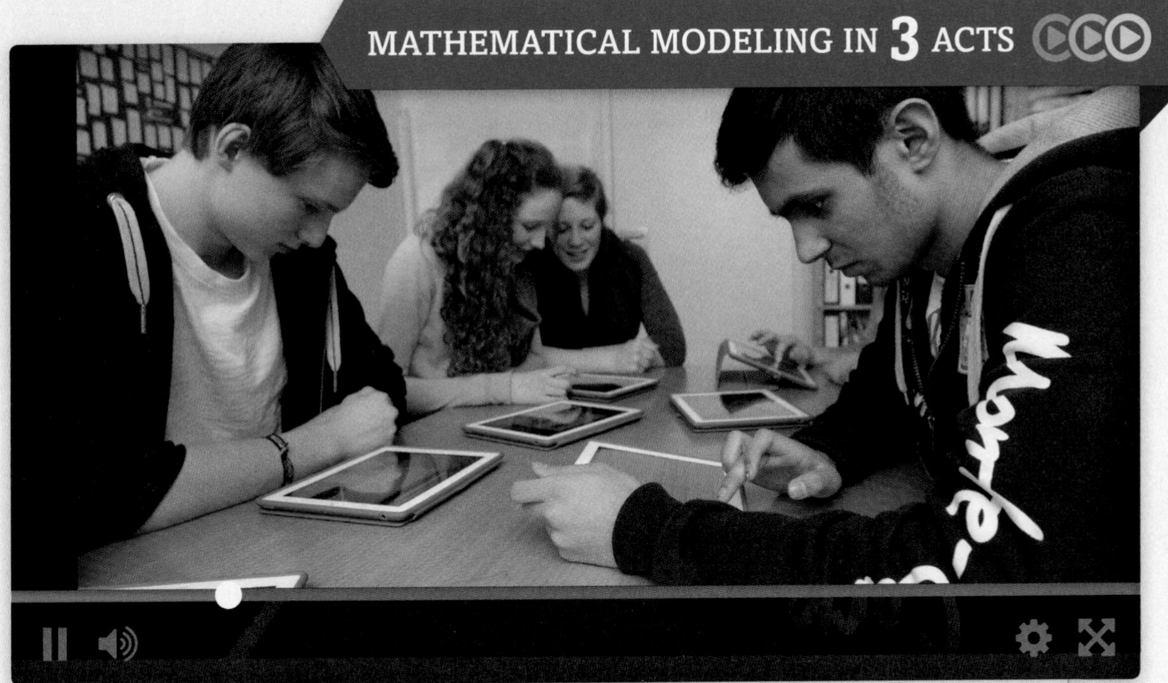

Who's Right?

People often approach a problem in different ways. Sometimes their solutions are the same, but other times different approaches lead to very different, but still valid, solutions.

Suppose you had to solve a system of linear equations. You might solve it by graphing while a classmate might use substitution. Is one way of solving a problem always better than another? Think about this during the Mathematical Modeling in 3 Acts lesson.

TOPIC 7

VIDEOS Watch clips to support ***Mathematical Modeling in 3 Acts Lessons*** and **enVision™ *STEM Projects***.

CONCEPT SUMMARY Review key lesson content through multiple representations.

ASSESSMENT Show what you've learned.

GLOSSARY Read and listen to English and Spanish definitions.

TUTORIALS Get help from ***Virtual Nerd***, right when you need it.

MATH TOOLS Explore math with digital tools and manipulatives.

Did You Know?

Businesses can use functions to estimate their revenue and expenses, and then use that information to set sales targets and prices.

For every **100 new products** introduced each year, only **5 succeed**.

The **biggest advertiser** on TV
COMMUNICATION COMPANIES

The second biggest
CARS

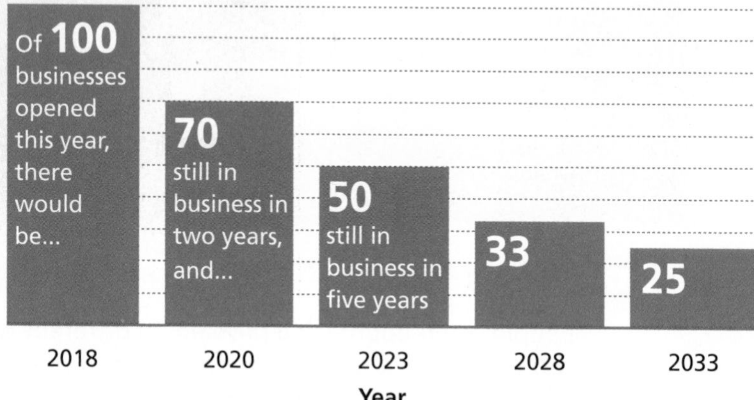

About **543,000 new businesses** are started every month in the United States.

Your Task: Make Business Decisions

You and your classmates will choose a business to model. You will suggest and defend choices for the number of items to make and the price(s) at which to sell them. Then, you will research ways that your decisions could change based on market factors.

7-1 Adding and Subtracting Polynomials

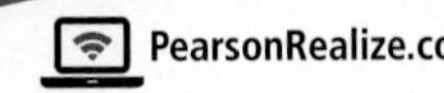

I CAN… combine like terms to simplify polynomials.

VOCABULARY

- Closure Property
- degree of a monomial
- degree of a polynomial
- monomial
- polynomial
- standard form of a polynomial

EXPLORE & REASON

Each year the Student Council conducts a food drive. At the end of the drive, the members report on the items collected.

A. Describe two different ways that the students can sort the items that were collected.

B. Model With Mathematics Write two expressions to represent the number and type of items collected.

C. Share your expression with classmates. How are the expressions similar? How are they different? Why are they different?

ESSENTIAL QUESTION

How does adding or subtracting polynomials compare to adding or subtracting integers?

CONCEPTUAL UNDERSTANDING

EXAMPLE 1 Understand Polynomials

A. Why does a constant have a degree of 0?

A **monomial** is a real number, a variable, or the product of a real number and one or more variables with whole number exponents.

The **degree of a monomial** is the sum of the exponents of the variables of a monomial.

STUDY TIP
Remember to find the sum of the exponents of the variables in each term, not just the greatest exponent of any variable.

$15x^2$ — The variable has an exponent of 2, so the degree is 2.

$\frac{1}{2}x^5y^2$ — The sum of the variable exponents is 7, so the degree is 7.

A constant has no variable. However, any number to the 0 power is 1, so you can multiply a constant by x^0 without changing the value of the constant.

$$7 \longrightarrow 7x^0$$
$$= 7(1)$$
$$= 7$$

The exponent of the variable is 0, so the degree of this monomial is 0.

So, the degree of a constant is 0.

CONTINUED ON THE NEXT PAGE

EXAMPLE 1 CONTINUED

B. Why is $5x^3 - 4$ called a cubic binomial?

A **polynomial** is a monomial or the sum or difference of two or more monomials, called terms.

Polynomials are named according to their degree. The **degree of a polynomial** is the greatest degree of any term of the polynomial.

Polynomial	Degree	Name Based on Degree
7	0	Constant
$4x$	1	Linear
$3x^2 + 2x + 1$	2	Quadratic
$-5x^2y$	3	Cubic
$4x^2y^2 + 5x - 2y + 6$	4	Fourth Degree

Polynomials with a degree greater than 3 are named by their degree—fourth degree, fifth degree, and so on.

Polynomials are also named according to how many terms they have.

Polynomial	Number of Terms	Name Based on Number of Terms
$4x$	1	Monomial
$x + 7$	2	Binomial
$-5x^2y + x^2 + x$	3	Trinomial
$4x^2y^2 + 5x - 2y + 6$	4	Polynomial

Polynomials with more than 3 terms do not have special names.

$5x^3 - 4$ is called a cubic binomial because it has a degree of 3 and two terms.

Try It! 1. Name each polynomial based on its degree and number of terms.

a. $-2xy^2$

b. $6xy - 3x + y$

EXAMPLE 2 Write Polynomials in Standard Form

What is the standard form of the polynomial $7x - 5 - x^3 + 6x^4 - 3x^2$?

The **standard form of a polynomial** is the form of a polynomial in which the terms are written in descending order according to their degree.

LOOK FOR RELATIONSHIPS
Why is writing polynomials in standard form important? How will it be useful?

Rewrite the polynomial in standard form.

$7x - 5 - x^3 + 6x^4 - 3x^2$

$6x^4$ has the greatest degree, 4, so write it first.

$6x^4 - x^3 - 3x^2 + 7x - 5$

The standard form of the polynomial is $6x^4 - x^3 - 3x^2 + 7x - 5$.

Try It! 2. Write each polynomial in standard form.

a. $7 - 3x^3 + 6x^2$

b. $2y - 3 - 8y^2$

EXAMPLE 3 Add and Subtract Monomials

VOCABULARY
Remember, *like terms* are terms with exactly the same variable factors in an expression.

LOOK FOR RELATIONSHIPS
Which terms in a polynomial are like terms? How does combining them change the polynomial?

How can you use the properties of operations to combine like terms and write the expression $4x + 3x^2 + 2x + x^2 + 5$ in standard form?

Use algebra tiles to model the expression.

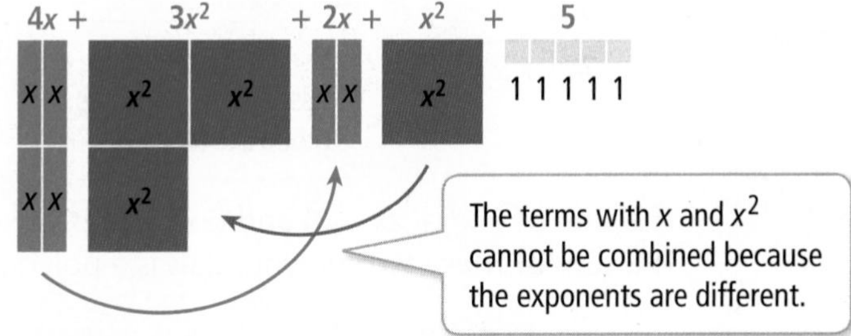

Rearrange the tiles to group like terms together.

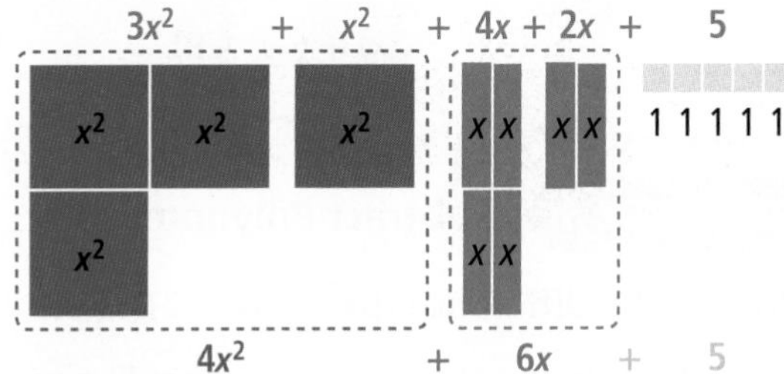

The expression $4x + 3x^2 + 2x + x^2 + 5$ written in standard form is $4x^2 + 6x + 5$.

You can also rewrite the expression in standard form using the properties of operations.

$$4x + 3x^2 + 2x + x^2 + 5$$
$$= (3x^2 + x^2) + (4x + 2x) + 5$$
$$= 4x^2 + 6x + 5$$

You can apply the same properties of operations for real numbers to operations with monomials.

Try It! **3.** Combine like terms and write each expression in standard form.

a. $4x^2 - 3x - x^2 + 3x$ **b.** $7y^3 - 3y + 5y^3 - 2y + 7$

EXAMPLE 4 Add Polynomials

A. How is adding polynomials like adding whole numbers?

Consider the expressions $123 + 405$ and $(x^2 + 2x + 3) + (4x^2 + 5)$.

$$\begin{array}{r} 123 \\ +\,405 \\ \hline 528 \end{array}$$

Only like place values can be added.

Only like terms can be added.

$$\begin{array}{r} x^2 + 2x + 3 \\ +\,4x^2 \qquad\; + 5 \\ \hline 5x^2 + 2x + 8 \end{array}$$

Before you add polynomials, the terms must be aligned with like terms. This is similar to how, before adding whole numbers, the numbers must be aligned according to their place value.

CONTINUED ON THE NEXT PAGE

EXAMPLE 4 CONTINUED

B. What is the sum of $(4x^2 + 2x - 3)$ and $(3x^2 + 6)$?

To add two polynomials, combine like terms.

Method 1: Add vertically.

$$\begin{array}{r} 4x^2 + 2x - 3 \\ +3x^2 \quad\quad + 6 \\ \hline 7x^2 + 2x + 3 \end{array}$$

Align like terms.

Method 2: Add horizontally.

$(4x^2 + 2x - 3) + (3x^2 + 6)$

$= (4x^2 + 3x^2) + (2x) + (-3 + 6)$

$= 7x^2 + 2x + 3$

Use the Commutative and Associative Properties to group like terms.

COMMON ERROR
Be careful to align like terms when adding polynomials vertically.

The sum of $(4x^2 + 2x - 3)$ and $(3x^2 + 6)$ is $7x^2 + 2x + 3$.
The sum of these two polynomials is a polynomial.

Try It! **4.** Simplify. Write each answer in standard form.

a. $(3x^2 + 2x) + (-x + 9)$ **b.** $(-2x^2 + 5x - 7) + (3x + 7)$

EXAMPLE 5 Subtract Polynomials

What is the difference $(6x^2 + 3x - 2) - (3x^2 + 5x - 8)$?

To subtract two polynomials subtract like terms.

Method 1: Subtract vertically by lining up like terms.

Line up like terms. Then subtract.

$$\begin{array}{r} 6x^2 + 3x - 2 \\ \underline{-(3x^2 + 5x - 8)} \end{array} \quad \xrightarrow{\text{Distribute } -1 \text{ to each term.}} \quad \begin{array}{r} 6x^2 + 3x - 2 \\ -3x^2 - 5x + 8 \\ \hline 3x^2 - 2x + 6 \end{array}$$

COMMON ERROR
Remember that subtraction is adding the opposite. Be sure to find the opposite of every term in the second polynomial by distributing –1 to each term.

Method 2: Subtract horizontally.

$(6x^2 + 3x - 2) - (3x^2 + 5x - 8)$

$= 6x^2 + 3x - 2 - 3x^2 - 5x + 8$

Distribute –1 to each term in the subtracted expression.

$= (6x^2 - 3x^2) + (3x - 5x) + (-2 + 8)$

$= 3x^2 - 2x + 6$

Use the Commutative and Associative Properties to combine like terms. Then simplify.

The difference of $(6x^2 + 3x - 2)$ and $(3x^2 + 5x - 8)$ is $3x^2 - 2x + 6$.
The difference of these two polynomials is also a polynomial.

In Examples 4 and 5, the result of adding or subtracting two polynomials is another polynomial. The **Closure Property** states that polynomials are closed under addition or subtraction because the result of these operations is another polynomial.

Try It! **5.** Simplify. Write each answer in standard form.

a. $(3x^2 + 4x + 2) - (-x + 4)$ **b.** $(-5x - 6) - (4x^2 + 6)$

APPLICATION

EXAMPLE 6 Apply Polynomials

An engineer is reviewing the layout of a solar farm. The solar farm shown has 4 small panels, 33 medium panels, and 32 large panels. What is the total area of the farm's solar panels?

USE STRUCTURE
How could you use what you know about polynomial addition to find an expression for the area of each small solar panel?

Write an expression to represent the total area of the solar panels.

Total area = Total area of large panels + Total area of medium panels + Total area of small panels

$= (32x^2 + 384x) + (33x^2 + 272x) + (4x^2 + 24x)$

$= (32x^2 + 33x^2 + 4x^2) + (384x + 272x + 24x)$

$= 69x^2 + 680x$

Use the Commutative and Associative Properties to group like terms. Then add.

The total area of the solar panels is modeled by the expression $69x^2 + 680x$, where x is the width, in meters, of each solar panel.

Try It! **6.** What expression models the difference between the total area of the large solar panels and the total area of the small solar panels?

CONCEPT SUMMARY Adding and Subtracting Polynomials

STANDARD FORM **Standard Form of a Polynomial:** $3x^4 - 3x^2 + 4x - 2$

In standard form the monomial terms are written in descending order according to their degree.

NAMING POLYNOMIALS Polynomials can be named according to the number of terms and their degree.

$12x^3 + 6xy - 5$

There are 3 terms, so it is a trinomial.

The highest degree is 3, so it is cubic.

So $12x^3 + 6xy - 5$ is a cubic trinomial.

POLYNOMIAL OPERATIONS

Adding Polynomials

$(-2x^3 + 4x^2 - 5) + (4x^3 + 2x^2 - x + 8)$

$= (-2x^3 + 4x^3) + (4x^2 + 2x^2) + (-x) + (-5 + 8)$

$= 2x^3 + 6x^2 - x + 3$

Subtracting Polynomials

$(3x^2 - 2x + 4) - (-3x^2 - x + 6)$

$= 3x^2 - 2x + 4 + 3x^2 + x - 6$

$= (3x^2 + 3x^2) + (-2x + x) + (4 - 6)$

$= 6x^2 - x - 2$

Add or subtract like terms just like you add or subtract digits with the same place value.

Do You UNDERSTAND?

1. ESSENTIAL QUESTION How does adding or subtracting polynomials compare to adding or subtracting integers?

2. **Communicate Precisely** How does the definition of the prefixes *mono-*, *bi-*, and *tri-* help when naming polynomials?

3. **Vocabulary** Describe the relationship between the *degree of a monomial* and the *standard form of a polynomial.*

4. **Use Structure** Explain why the sum $x + x$ is equal to $2x$ instead of x^2.

5. **Error Analysis** Rebecca says that all monomials with the same degree are like terms. Explain Rebecca's error.

Do You KNOW HOW?

Name each polynomial based on its degree and number of terms.

6. $\frac{x}{4} + 2$

7. $7x^3 + xy - 4$

Write each polynomial in standard form.

8. $2y - 3 - y^2$

9. $3x^2 - 2x + x^3 + 6$

Simplify each expression.

10. $(x^2 + 2x - 4) + (2x^2 - 5x - 3)$

11. $(3x^2 - 5x - 8) - (-4x^2 - 2x - 1)$

12. A square prism has square sides with area $x^2 + 8x + 16$ and rectangular sides with area $2x^2 + 15x + 28$. What expression represents the surface area of the square prism?

UNDERSTAND

13. Reason How is it possible that the sum of two quadratic trinomials is a linear binomial?

14. Error Analysis Describe and correct the error a student made when naming the polynomial.

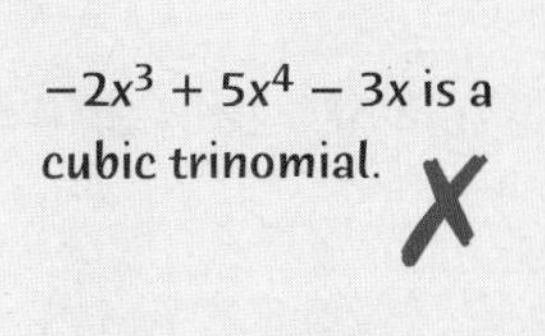

$-2x^3 + 5x^4 - 3x$ is a cubic trinomial. ✗

15. Error Analysis Describe and correct the error a student made when subtracting the polynomials.

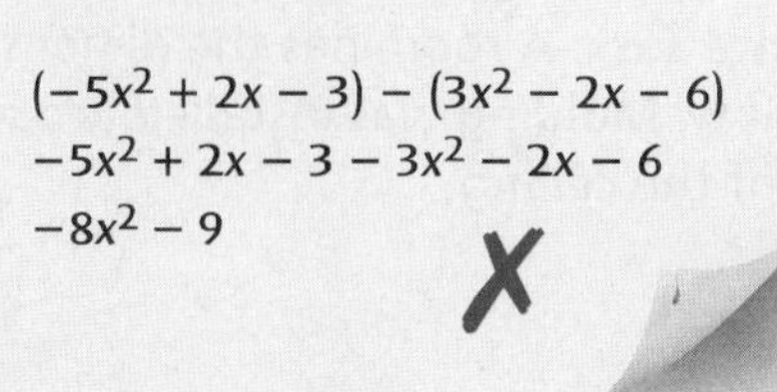

$(-5x^2 + 2x - 3) - (3x^2 - 2x - 6)$
$-5x^2 + 2x - 3 - 3x^2 - 2x - 6$
$-8x^2 - 9$ ✗

16. Reason What is the missing term in the equation?

a. $(\_\_\_ + 7) + (2x - 6) = -4x + 1$

b. $(a^2 + \_\_\_ + 1) - (\_\_\_ + 5a + \_\_\_) = 4a^2 - 2a + 7$

17. Higher Order Thinking Describe each statement as *always, sometimes,* or *never* true.

a. A linear binomial has a degree of 0.

b. A trinomial has a degree of 2.

c. A constant has a degree of 1.

d. A cubic monomial has a degree of 3.

18. Make Sense and Persevere Consider the set of linear binomials $ax + b$, where a and b are positive integers, $a > 0$ and $b > 0$.

a. Does the set have closure for addition? Explain.

b. Does the set have closure for subtraction? Explain.

PRACTICE

Find the degree of each monomial. SEE EXAMPLE 1

19. $\frac{x}{4}$

20. $-7xy$

21. 21

22. $4x^2y$

Name each polynomial based on its degree and number of terms. SEE EXAMPLE 1

23. $17yx^2 + xy - 5$

24. $5x^3 + 2x - 8$

25. $100x^2 + 3$

26. $-9x^4 + 8x^3 - 7x + 1$

Simplify each expression. Write the answer in standard form. SEE EXAMPLES 2 AND 3

27. $3x + 2x^2 - 4x + 3x^2 - 5x$

28. $5 + 8y^2 - 12y^2 + 3y$

29. $3z - 7z^2 - 5z + 5z^2 + 2z^2$

30. $7 - 2x + 3 + 5x + 4x^2$

Add or subtract. Write each answer in standard form. SEE EXAMPLES 4 AND 5

31. $(3b - 8) + (7b + 4)$

32. $(2x^2 - 7x^3 + 8x) + (-8x^3 - 3x^2 + 4)$

33. $(5y^2 - 2y + 1) - (y^2 + y + 3)$

34. $(-7a^4 - a + 4a^2) - (-8a^2 + a - 7a^4)$

35. $(4m^2 - 2m + 4) + (2m^2 + 2m - 5)$

Write an expression to represent each situation. SEE EXAMPLE 6

36. Find the perimeter of the rectangle.

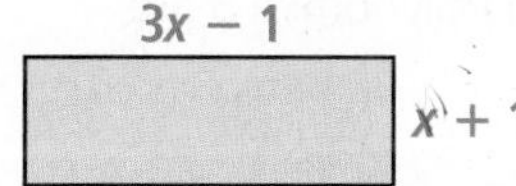

37. A cube has square sides with area $x^2 + 24x + 144$. What expression represents the surface area of the cube?

38. A rectangle has a length of $5x + 2$ in. and a width of $4x + 6$ in. What is the perimeter of the rectangle?

PRACTICE & PROBLEM SOLVING

Practice | Tutorial

Mixed Review Available Online

APPLY

39. Mathematical Connections The perimeters of the two figures are equal.

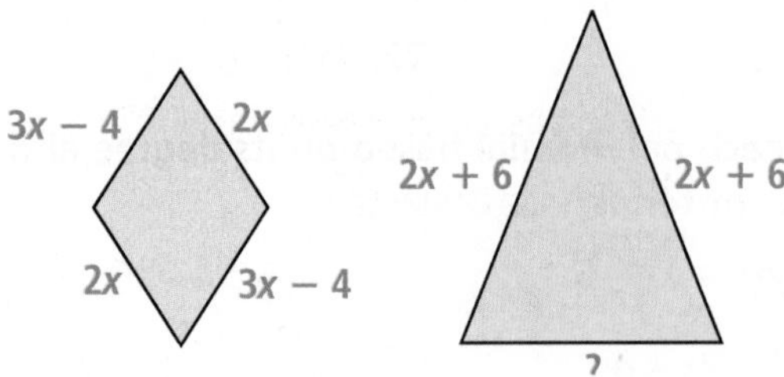

What expression represents the missing side length?

40. Make Sense and Persevere The owners of a house want to knock down the wall between the kitchen and family room.

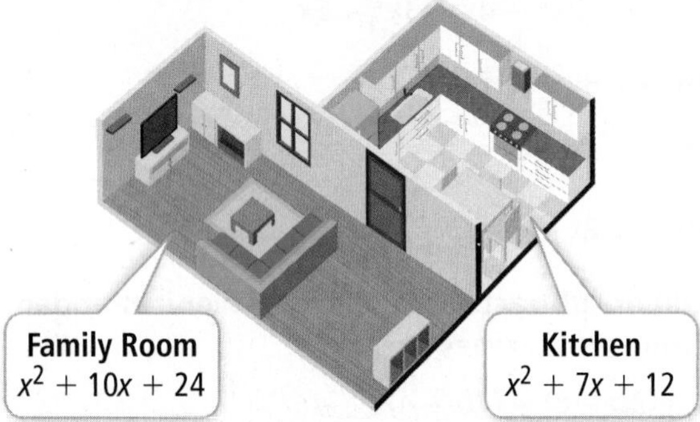

What expression represents the area of the new combined open space?

41. Reason Polynomial A has degree 2; Polynomial B has degree 4. What can you determine about the name and degree of the sum of the polynomials and the difference of the polynomials if

a. Polynomial A is a binomial and Polynomial B is a monomial?

b. Both Polynomial A and Polynomial B are binomials?

42. Model With Mathematics A large indoor market is set up with 4 rows of booths. There are large booths with an area of x^2 sq. units, medium booths with an area of x sq. units, and small booths with an area of 1 sq. unit. In the marketplace, two of the rows contain 7 large booths, 6 medium booths, and 5 small booths each. The other two rows each contain 3 large booths, 5 medium booths, and 10 small booths. What is the total area of the booths in the marketplace?

ASSESSMENT PRACTICE

43. Which expression is equivalent to $(x^2 + 3x - 5) - (4x^2 + 3x - 6)$?

Ⓐ $5x^2 + 6x - 11$

Ⓑ $-3x^4 + 6x^2 + 1$

Ⓒ $-3x^2 + 1$

Ⓓ $-3x^2 + 6x - 11$

44. SAT/ACT What is the sum of $-2x^2 + 3x - 4$ and $3x^2 - 4x + 6$?

Ⓐ $x^4 - x^2 + 2$

Ⓑ $5x^4 + 7x^2 + 10$

Ⓒ 2

Ⓓ $x^2 - x + 2$

Ⓔ $2x^6$

45. Performance Task A room has the dimensions shown below. Molding was installed around the edge of the ceiling.

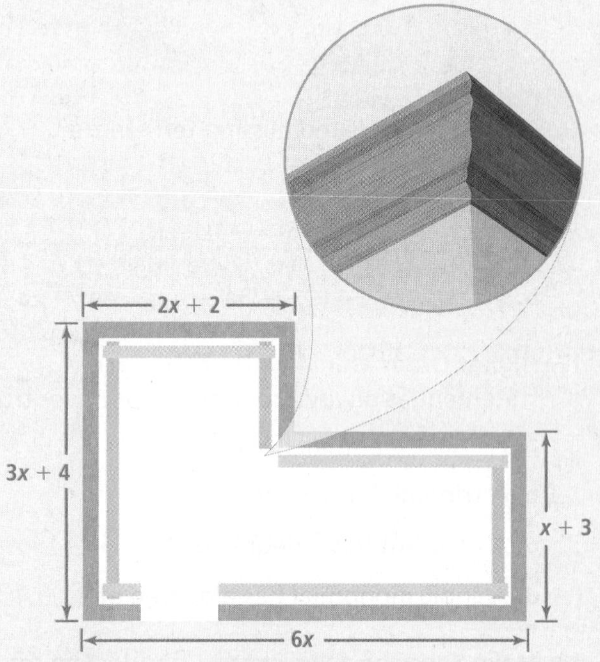

Part A Write an expression to represent the amount of molding needed.

Part B Sam used 80 feet of molding. What is the measurement of each edge of the ceiling?

7-2 Multiplying Polynomials

PearsonRealize.com

I CAN… multiply two polynomials.

MODEL & DISCUSS

Samantha makes the abstract painting shown using vertical and horizontal lines and four colors.

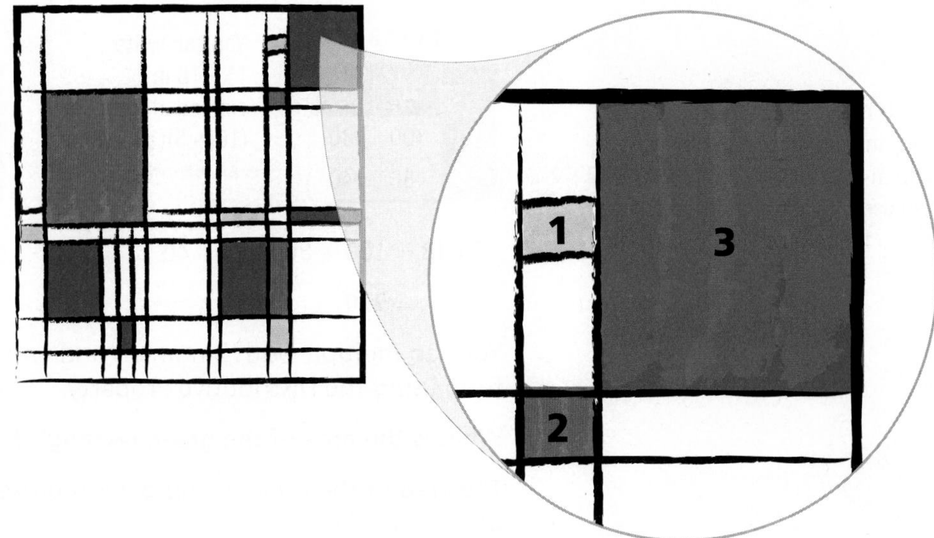

A. How can you use mathematics to describe the areas of Rectangle 1 and Rectangle 2?

B. **Look for Relationships** How can you use mathematics to describe the area of Rectangle 3?

ESSENTIAL QUESTION **How does multiplying polynomials compare to multiplying integers?**

EXAMPLE 1 Multiply a Monomial and a Trinomial

What is the product of $-4x^3$ and $(x^2 + 3x - 4)$?

Use the Distributive Property. The Distributive Property works for polynomials in the same way that it works for real numbers.

$$-4x^3(x^2 + 3x - 4) = -4x^3(x^2) + -4x^3(3x) + -4x^3(-4)$$
$$= -4x^5 - 12x^4 + 16x^3$$

Distribute $-4x^3$ to each term of the trinomial.

The product is $-4x^5 - 12x^4 + 16x^3$.

Notice that the product of these two polynomials is a polynomial.

COMMON ERROR
You may incorrectly state that $-4x^3(x^2)$ is $-4x^6$. Recall that when multiplying terms with exponents, you add the exponents of like bases.

Try It! 1. Find each product.

a. $-2x^2(x^2 + 3x + 4)$

b. $-4x(2x^2 - 3x + 5)$

CONCEPTUAL UNDERSTANDING

EXAMPLE 2 Use a Table to Find the Product of Polynomials

A. How is multiplying binomials like multiplying two-digit numbers?

Multiply the expressions 15 • 18 and $(x + 5)(x + 8)$ using a table.

15 · 18

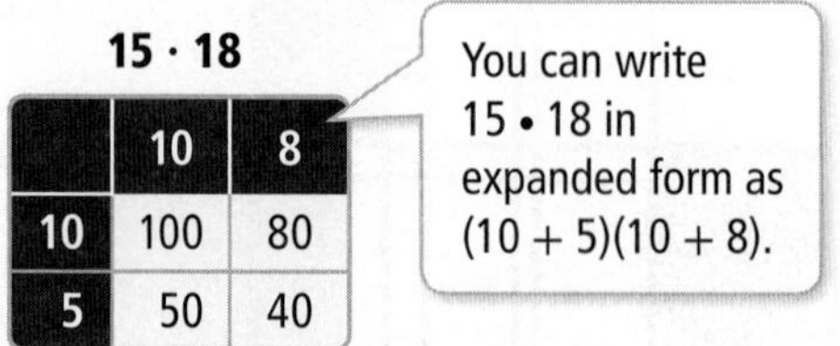

	10	8
10	100	80
5	50	40

$(x + 5)(x + 8)$

	x	8
x	x^2	$8x$
5	$5x$	40

> **STUDY TIP**
> Once the two-digit numbers are written in expanded form, you can also use the Distributive Property to find the product.

$$15 \cdot 18 = 100 + 80 + 50 + 40$$
$$= 270$$

$$(x + 5)(x + 8) = x^2 + 8x + 5x + 40$$
$$= x^2 + 13x + 40$$

You can multiply both binomials and two-digit numbers in expanded form using the Distributive Property.

B. What is the area of the green rectangle?

The area of the green rectangle is represented by the expression $(2x + 1)(x + 3)$.

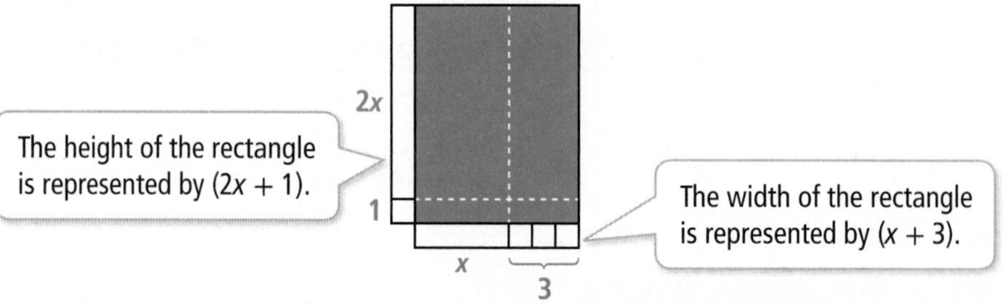

Use a table to find the area of each section of the rectangle.

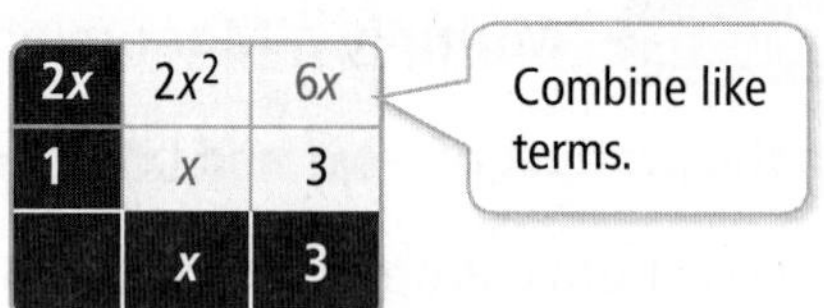

$2x$	$2x^2$	$6x$
1	x	3
	x	3

The area of the green rectangle is $2x^2 + 7x + 3$. Again, the product of these two polynomials is a polynomial.

Try It! 2. Find the area of each green rectangle.

a.

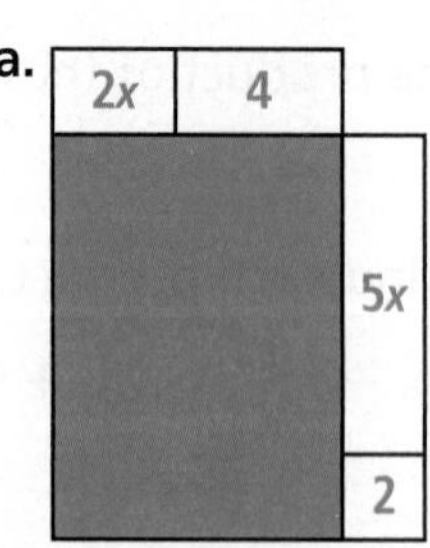

b.

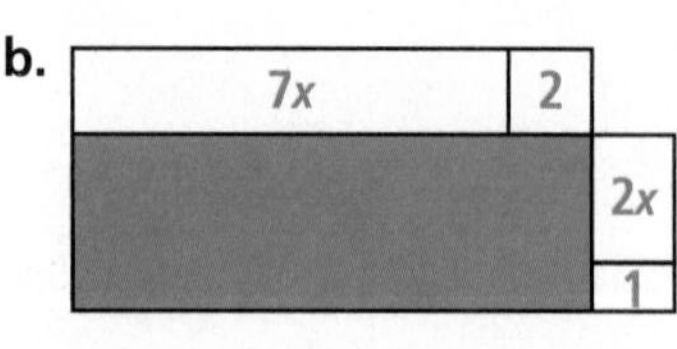

EXAMPLE 3 Multiply Binomials

How can you use the Distributive Property to rewrite $(2x + 4)(x - 5)$ as a polynomial?

Distribute each term in the first binomial to each term in the second binomial.

$(2x + 4)(x - 5) = 2x(x - 5) + 4(x - 5)$ .... Distribute $2x$ and 4 to the second binomial.

$= 2x(x) + 2x(-5) + 4(x) + 4(-5)$ ... Distribute $2x$ and 4 to each term in the second binomial.

$= 2x^2 - 10x + 4x - 20$ .... Multiply.

$= 2x^2 - 6x - 20$ .... Combine like terms.

The product of $(2x + 4)$ and $(x - 5)$ is $2x^2 - 6x - 20$.

Again, the product of these two polynomials is a polynomial.

GENERALIZE
Compare the factors and the final product. What generalizations can you make from this example?

Try It! **3.** Find each product.

a. $(5x - 4)(2x + 1)$

b. $(3x - 5)(2x + 4)$

EXAMPLE 4 Multiply a Trinomial and a Binomial

A. How can you use a table to find the product of $(x^2 + 2x - 1)$ and $(3x + 4)$?

Write the terms for each polynomial in the first row and column of the table. Multiply to find each product.

$3x + 4$ | $x^2 + 2x - 1$

	x^2	$2x$	-1
$3x$	$3x^3$	$6x^2$	$-3x$
4	$4x^2$	$8x$	-4

Combine the like terms.

	x^2	$2x$	-1
$3x$	$3x^3$	$6x^2$	$-3x$
4	$4x^2$	$8x$	-4

$(x^2 + 2x - 1)(3x + 4) = 3x^3 + 6x^2 + 4x^2 + 8x + (-3x) + (-4)$

$= 3x^3 + 10x^2 + 5x - 4$

So $(x^2 + 2x - 1)(3x + 4) = 3x^3 + 10x^2 + 5x - 4$. When you multiply a trinomial by a binomial, the result is six individual products. Using a table is one method you can use to help organize these products.

CONTINUED ON THE NEXT PAGE

Activity Assess

EXAMPLE 4 CONTINUED

B. How is multiplying a trinomial by a binomial like multiplying a three-digit number by a two-digit number?

Consider the products $312 \cdot 24$ and $(3x^2 + x + 2)(2x + 4)$.

Multiply each place of the three-digit number by 4 ones and 2 tens. Then find the sum.

$$\begin{array}{r} 312 \\ \times \quad 24 \\ \hline 1,248 \\ +\ 6,240 \\ \hline 7,488 \end{array}$$

Multiply each term of the trinomial by +4 and 2x. Then combine like terms.

$$\begin{array}{r} 3x^2 + x + 2 \\ \times \qquad 2x + 4 \\ \hline 12x^2 + 4x + 8 \\ +\ 6x^3 + 2x^2 + 4x \qquad \\ \hline 6x^3 + 14x^2 + 8x + 8 \end{array}$$

STUDY TIP
As you multiply, remember to line up like terms so combining them in the last step will be easier.

When multiplying a trinomial by a binomial, you multiply each term of the trinomial by each term of the binomial. This is similar to how, when multiplying a three-digit number by a two-digit number, you multiply by each place value of the two-digit number.

Try It! 4. Find each product.

a. $(2x - 5)(-3x^2 + 4x - 7)$

b. $(-3x^2 + 1)(2x^2 + 3x - 4)$

EXAMPLE 5 Closure and Multiplication

Why is the operation of multiplication closed over the set of polynomials?

For each example in this lesson, you have found the product of two polynomials. In each case the product has also been a polynomial.

Consider the first example: $-4x^3(x^2 + 3x - 4)$.

$$-4x^3(x^2 + 3x - 4) = -4x^3(x^2) + -4x^3(3x) + -4x^3(-4)$$
$$= -4x^5 - 12x^4 + 16x^3$$

x^3, x^2, and x have whole number exponents, so the product will also have whole number exponents.

When you multiply two polynomials, the result is the sum or difference of terms. Each term is a real number coefficient multiplied by a variable raised to a whole number exponent. Each term is a monomial and the sum or difference of monomials is a polynomial. So polynomials are closed under multiplication.

Try It! 5. Why is it important that the product of two polynomials have only whole number exponents?

APPLICATION

EXAMPLE 6 Apply Multiplication of Binomials

A smartphone has a screen that has a width of x and a height that is 1.8 times the width. The outer dimensions of the phone are shown.

Write an expression for the portion of the phone that is not occupied by the screen. Assume that the phone is rectangular.

Formulate Write expressions to represent the area of the screen and the area of the phone.

Area of screen $= x(1.8x)$

Area of phone $= (x + 1)(1.8x + 3)$

Compute Express each area in standard form.

Area of screen $= x(1.8x) = 1.8x^2$

Area of phone $= (x + 1)(1.8x + 3)$

$= x(1.8x + 3) + 1(1.8x + 3)$

$= 1.8x^2 + 3x + 1.8x + 3$

$= 1.8x^2 + 4.8x + 3$

Subtract the area of the screen from the area of the phone.

Non-screen Area = Area of Phone − Area of Screen

$= (1.8x^2 + 4.8x + 3) - 1.8x^2$

$= 4.8x + 3$

Interpret The expression $4.8x + 3$ represents the portion of the phone's surface not occupied by the screen.

Try It! 6. Suppose the height of the phone in Example 6 were 1.9 times the width but all of the other conditions were the same. What expression would represent the area of the phone's surface not occupied by the screen?

CONCEPT SUMMARY Multiplying Polynomials

There are different methods that can be used to multiply polynomials. The methods used for multiplying polynomials are similar to the methods used for multiplying multi-digit numbers.

	Binomial × Binomial	Binomial × Trinomial
ALGEBRA	**Multiply Horizontally** $(x+3)(x-2)$ $= x(x-2) + 3(x-2)$ $= x^2 - 2x + 3x - 6$ $= x^2 + x - 6$	**Multiply Horizontally** $(x+3)(x^2+4x-2)$ $= x(x^2+4x-2) + 3(x^2+4x-2)$ $= x^3 + 4x^2 - 2x + 3x^2 + 12x - 6$ $= x^3 + 7x^2 + 10x - 6$
	Multiply Vertically $x - 2$ $\times\ x + 3$ $3x - 6$ $+\ x^2 - 2x$ $x^2 + x - 6$	**Multiply Vertically** $x^2 + 4x - 2$ $\times\ x + 3$ $3x^2 + 12x - 6$ $+\ x^3 + 4x^2 - 2x$ $x^3 + 7x^2 + 10x - 6$

DIAGRAMS

	x	3
x	x^2	$3x$
-2	$-2x$	-6

$x^2 + x - 6$

	x	3
x^2	x^3	$3x^2$
$4x$	$4x^2$	$12x$
-2	$-2x$	-6

$x^3 + 7x^2 + 10x - 6$

Do You UNDERSTAND?

1. ESSENTIAL QUESTION How does multiplying polynomials compare to multiplying integers?

2. **Use Appropriate Tools** When multiplying two variables, how is using the Distributive Property similar to using a table?

3. **Error Analysis** Mercedes states that when multiplying $4x^3(x^3 + 2x^2 - 3)$ the product is $4x^9 + 8x^6 - 12x^3$. What was Mercedes's error?

4. **Use Structure** When multiplying polynomials, why is the degree of the product different from the degree of the factors?

Do You KNOW HOW?

Find each product.

5. $-2x^3(3x^2 - 4x + 7)$

6. $(2x + 6)(x - 4)$

7. $(x - 2)(3x + 4)$

8. $(5y - 2)(4y^2 + 3y - 1)$

9. $(3x^2 + 2x - 5)(2x - 3)$

10. Find the area of the rectangle.

$2x + 4$

$4x - 2$

UNDERSTAND

11. Make Sense and Persevere The area of a rectangle is given. Identify the missing terms in the length and width.

$(x + \_\_)$

$x^2 + 11x + 28$ $(\_\_ + 4)$

12. Use Structure The table shows the product when multiplying two binomials. What is the relationship between the numbers in the factors and the terms in the product?

Binomials	Products
$(x + 3)(x + 4)$	$x^2 + 7x + 12$
$(x + 2)(x - 5)$	$x^2 - 3x - 10$
$(x - 3)(x - 5)$	$x^2 - 8x + 15$

13. Error Analysis Describe and correct the error a student made when multiplying two binomials.

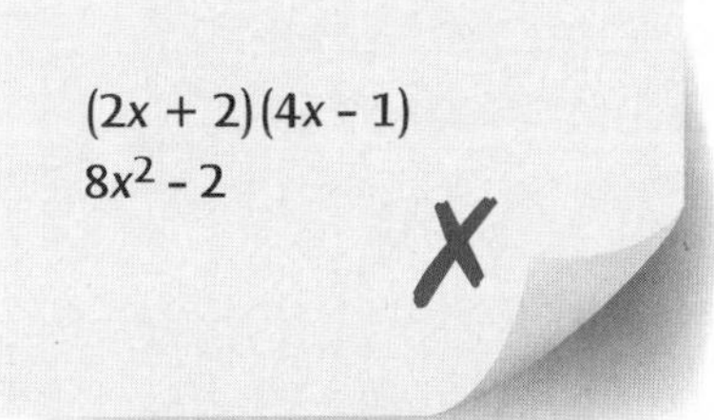

14. Use Appropriate Tools Use a table to find the product of $(3x + 4)(x^2 + 3x - 2)$. How are the like terms in a table arranged?

15. Higher Order Thinking Is it possible for the product of a monomial and trinomial to be a binomial? Explain.

16. Mathematical Connections A triangle has a height of $2x + 6$ and a base length of $x + 4$. What is the area of the triangle?

17. Communicate Precisely Explain how to find the combined volume of the two rectangular prisms described. One has side lengths of $3x$, $2x + 1$, and $x + 3$. The other has side lengths of $5x - 2$, $x + 9$, and 8.

PRACTICE

Find each product. SEE EXAMPLE 1

18. $6x(x^2 - 4x - 3)$

19. $-y(-3y^2 + 2y - 7)$

20. $3x^2(-x^2 + 2x - 4)$

21. $-5x^3(2x^3 - 4x^2 + 2)$

Use a table to find each product. SEE EXAMPLE 2

22. $(x - 6)(3x + 4)$

23. $(2x + 1)(4x + 1)$

Use the Distributive Property to find each product. SEE EXAMPLE 3

24. $(x - 6)(x + 3)$

25. $(3x - 4)(2x + 5)$

26. $(x - 8)(2x + 3)$

Find each product. SEE EXAMPLE 4

27. $(y + 3)(2y^2 - 3y + 4)$

28. $(2x - 7)(3x^2 - 4x + 1)$

29. $(2x^2 - 3x)(-3x^2 + 4x - 2)$

30. $(-2x^2 + 1)(2x^2 - 3x - 7)$

31. $(x^2 + 3x)(3x^2 - 2x + 4)$

32. Find the area of the shaded region.
SEE EXAMPLE 6

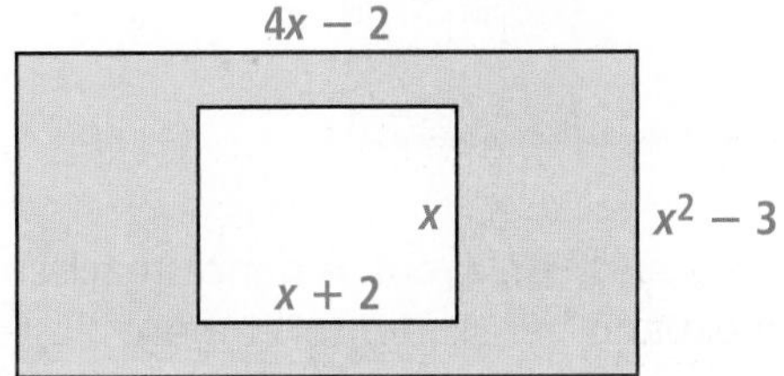

33. A rectangular park is $6x + 2$ ft long and $3x + 7$ ft wide. In the middle of the park is a square turtle pond that is 8 ft wide. What expression represents the area of the park not occupied by the turtle pond? SEE EXAMPLE 6

PRACTICE & PROBLEM SOLVING

APPLY

34. Model With Mathematics The volume of a cube is calculated by multiplying the length, width, and height. What is the volume of this cube?

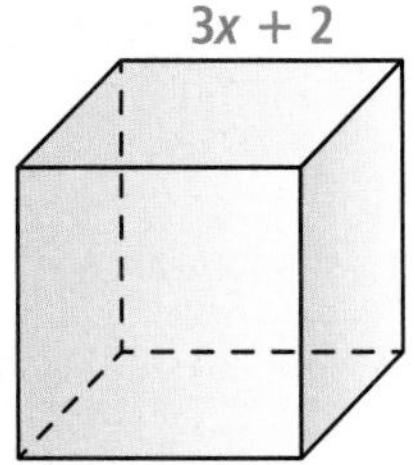

35. Reason The product of the binomial and the trinomial shown is a polynomial with four terms. Change one of the terms of the binomial or the trinomial so the product is also a trinomial.

$(2x + 2)(x^2 + 2x - 4) = 2x^3 + 7x^2 - 2x - 12$

36. Make Sense and Persevere What is the area of the painting shown?

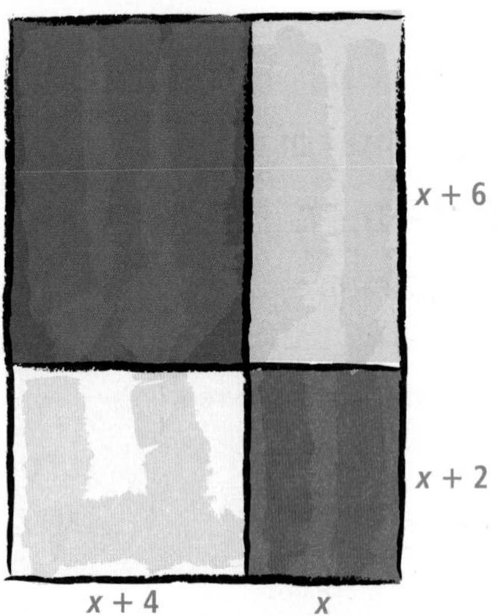

37. Make Sense and Persevere A dance teacher wants to expand her studio to fit more classes. What is the combined area of Studio A and Studio B?

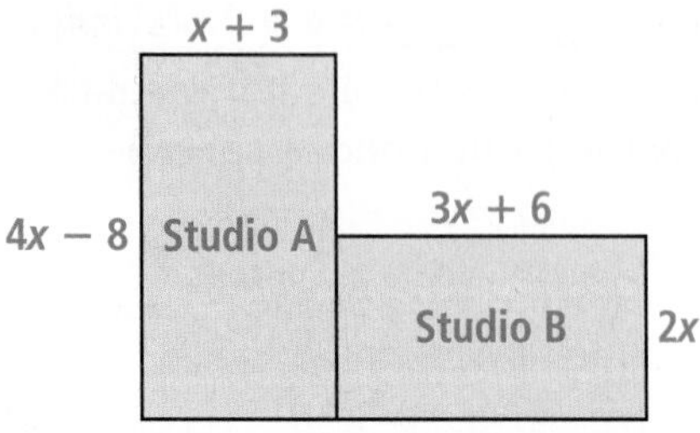

ASSESSMENT PRACTICE

38. Write the expression as a sum of monomials.

$$(x + 4)(2x + 1) - [(x - 5)(x + 3)] + 3x^2$$

39. SAT/ACT What is the product of $-2x + 2$ and $x - 5$?

Ⓐ $-2x^2 - 10$

Ⓑ $-2x^2 + 12x - 10$

Ⓒ $-x - 3$

Ⓓ $-2x^2 - 12x - 10$

40. Performance Task The net of a rectangular box and its dimensions are shown.

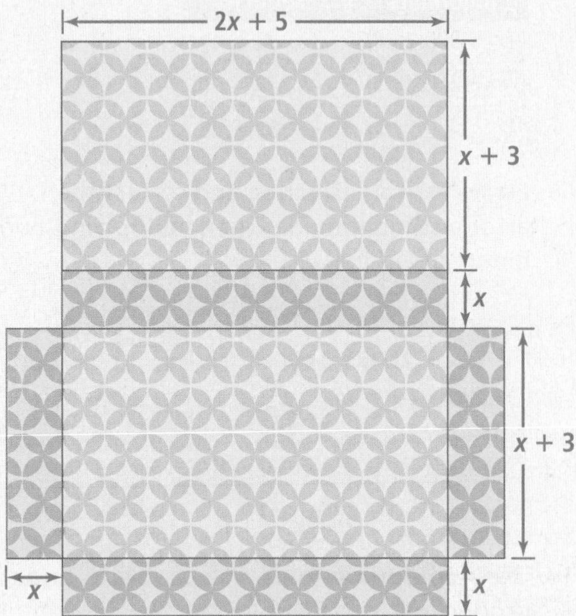

Part A Write an expression for the surface area of the box in terms of x.

Part B Evaluate the polynomial expression you found in Part A. What integer value of x would give the prism a surface area of about 600 cm^2?

7-3 Multiplying Special Cases

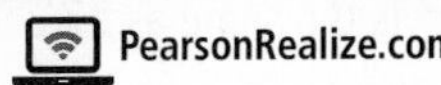

I CAN… use patterns to multiply binomials.

VOCABULARY
- difference of two squares

EXPLORE & REASON

The table gives values for x and y and different expressions.

x	y	$(x-y)(x+y)$	x^2	y^2	(x^2-y^2)
7	4				
6	2				
3	9				

A. Copy and complete the table.

B. Describe any patterns you notice.

C. **Use Structure** Try substituting variable expressions of the form $7p$ and $4q$ for x and y. Does the pattern still hold? Explain.

ESSENTIAL QUESTION

What patterns are there in the product of the square of a binomial and the product of a sum and a difference?

CONCEPTUAL UNDERSTANDING

EXAMPLE 1 Determine the Square of a Binomial

A. Why is $(a+b)^2$ considered a special case when multiplying polynomials?

Use the Distributive Property.

$$\begin{aligned}(a+b)^2 &= (a+b)(a+b)\\ &= a(a+b)+b(a+b)\\ &= a^2+ab+ba+b^2\\ &= a^2+2ab+b^2\end{aligned}$$

first term squared; twice the product of the first and last terms; last term squared

Use a visual model.

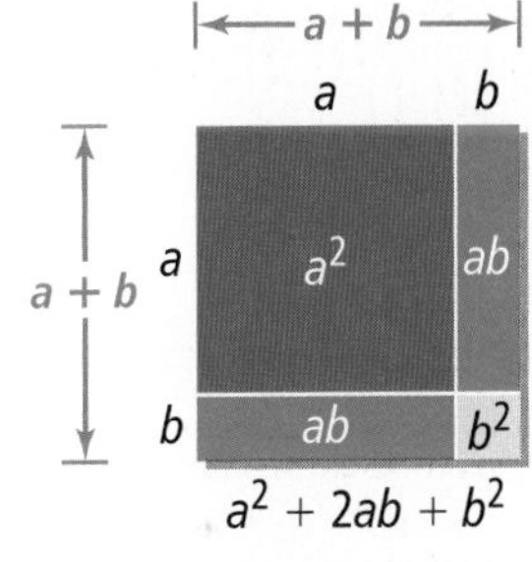

GENERALIZE
When squaring a binomial, think about how you can use the terms in the binomial to quickly determine the product. What generalizations about terms can you make?

The square of a binomial follows the pattern $(a+b)^2 = a^2+2ab+b^2$.

B. What is the product $(5x-3)^2$?

Use the pattern you found in Part A to find the square of a difference.

$(5x-3)^2 = [5x+(-3)]^2$ ····· Rewrite the difference as a sum.

$= (5x)^2 + 2(5x)(-3) + (-3)^2$ ····· Substitute $5x$ and -3 into $a^2+2ab+b^2$.

$= 25x^2 - 30x + 9$ ····· Simplify.

You can write the product $(5x-3)^2$ as $25x^2-30x+9$.

CONTINUED ON THE NEXT PAGE

EXAMPLE 1 CONTINUED

C. How can you use the square of a binomial to find the product 29^2?

Rewrite the product as a difference of two values whose squares you know, such as $(30 - 1)^2$. Then use the pattern for the square of a binomial to find its square.

$$(30 - 1)^2 = (30)^2 + 2(30)(-1) + (-1)^2$$
$$= 900 - 60 + 1$$
$$= 841$$

(30 − 1) is the same as 29. So, $(30 - 1)^2$ is the same as 29^2.

So, $29^2 = 841$. In general, you can use the square of a binomial to find the square of a large number by rewriting the number as the sum or difference of two numbers with known squares.

Try It! **1.** Find each product.

a. $(3x - 4)^2$

b. 71^2

EXAMPLE 2 Find the Product of a Sum and a Difference

A. What is the product $(a + b)(a - b)$?

Use the Distributive Property to find the product.

$$(a + b)(a - b) = a(a - b) + b(a - b)$$
$$= a^2 - ab + ba - b^2$$
$$= a^2 - b^2$$

The middle terms drop out because they are opposites.

first term squared

last term squared

The product of two binomials in the form $(a + b)(a - b)$ is $a^2 - b^2$. The product of the sum and difference of the same two values results in the **difference of two squares**.

B. What is the product $(5x + 7)(5x - 7)$?

Use the pattern you found in Part A.

$$(5x + 7)(5x - 7) = (5x)^2 - (7)^2$$ Substitute $5x$ and 7 into $a^2 - b^2$.

$$= 25x^2 - 49$$ Simplify.

The product of $(5x + 7)(5x - 7)$ is $25x^2 - 49$. It is the difference of two squares, $(5x)^2 - 7^2$.

COMMON ERROR
Remember that the last terms of each binomial are opposites. So, the product of the last terms will always be negative.

CONTINUED ON THE NEXT PAGE

EXAMPLE 2 CONTINUED

C. How can you use the difference of two squares to find the product of 43 and 37?

Rewrite the product as the sum and difference of the same two numbers a and b.

43 and 37 are each 3 units from 40.

$$(40 + 3)(40 - 3) = (40)^2 - (3)^2$$
$$= 1{,}600 - 9$$
$$= 1{,}591$$

$(40 + 3)(40 - 3)$ is of the form $(a + b)(a - b)$, so it is equivalent to the difference of two squares.

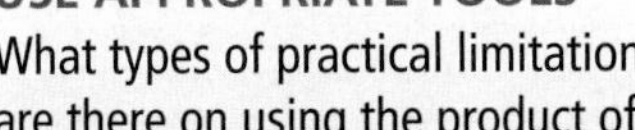

USE APPROPRIATE TOOLS
What types of practical limitations are there on using the product of a sum and difference to find the product of two numbers?

You can use the difference of two squares to mentally find the product of large numbers when the numbers are the same distance from a known square.

Try It! **2.** Find each product.

a. $(2x - 4)(2x + 4)$ **b.** $56 \bullet 44$

APPLICATION

EXAMPLE 3 Apply the Square of a Binomial

A graphic designer is developing images for icons. The square pixelated image is placed inside a border that is 2 pixels wide on all sides. If the area of the border of the image is 176 square pixels, what is the area of the image?

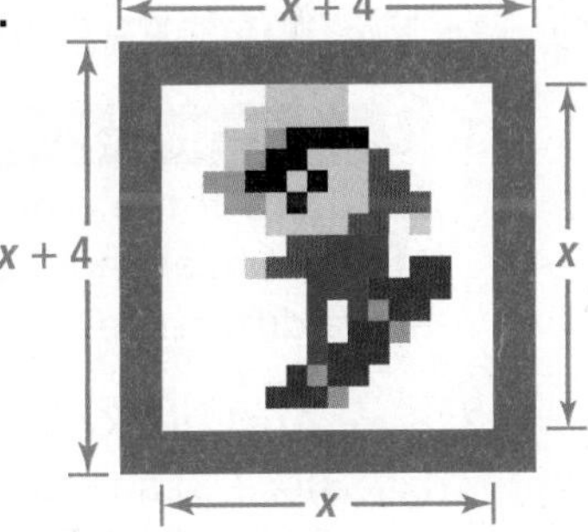

Let x represent the length and width of the image.

Formulate The area of the image and the border is represented by the expression $(x + 4)^2$.

Total area	−	Area of Image	=	Area of Border
$(x + 4)^2$	−	x^2	=	176

Compute

$$(x + 4)^2 - x^2 = 176$$
$$x^2 + 8x + 16 - x^2 = 176$$
$$8x + 16 = 176$$
$$8x = 160$$
$$x = 20$$

Find the product of the squared binomial first.

Interpret The image will be 20 pixels by 20 pixels. The area of the image is $20 \bullet 20$, or 400 square pixels.

Try It! **3.** What is the area of the square image if the area of the border is 704 square pixels and the border is 4 pixels wide?

CONCEPT SUMMARY Multiplying Special Cases

	Square of a Binomial	Product of a Sum and Difference
WORDS	The square of a binomial, $(a + b)^2$, always follows the same pattern: the square of the first term, plus twice the product of the first and last term, plus the square of the last term.	The product of two binomials in the form $(a + b)(a - b)$ results in the difference of two squares.
ALGEBRA	$(a + b)^2 = a^2 + 2ab + b^2$ or $(a - b)^2 = a^2 - 2ab + b^2$	$(a + b)(a - b) = a^2 - b^2$ (difference of two squares)
NUMBERS	$(x + 4)^2 = (x + 4)(x + 4)$ $= x^2 + 4x + 4x + 16$ $= x^2 + 8x + 16$	$(x - 7)(x + 7) = x^2 - 7x + 7x - 49$ $= x^2 - 49$

Do You UNDERSTAND?

1. ESSENTIAL QUESTION What patterns are there in the product of the square of a binomial and the product of a sum and a difference?

2. **Error Analysis** Kennedy multiplies $(x - 3)(x + 3)$ and gets an answer of $x^2 - 6x - 9$. Describe and correct Kennedy's error.

3. **Vocabulary** The product $(x + 6)(x - 6)$ is equivalent to an expression that is called the *difference of two squares*. Explain why the term *difference of two squares* is appropriate.

4. **Use Structure** Explain why the product of two binomials in the form $(a + b)(a - b)$ is a binomial instead of a trinomial.

Do You KNOW HOW?

Write each product in standard form.

5. $(x - 7)^2$

6. $(2x + 5)^2$

7. $(x + 4)(x - 4)$

8. $(3y - 5)(3y + 5)$

Use either the square of a binomial or the difference of two squares to find the area of each rectangle.

9. 54 cm by 54 cm

10. 24 in. by 36 in.

PRACTICE & PROBLEM SOLVING

Additional Exercises Available Online

UNDERSTAND

11. Generalize Find each product.

- $(x + 9)(x + 9)$
- $(x - 7)(x - 7)$
- $(2x - 1)^2$

a. What do all products of the square of a binomial have in common?

b. Will the third term of the square of a binomial always be positive? Explain.

c. What is the relationship between the sign of the binomial and the sign of the second term in the product?

d. What is true about the exponents representing perfect square variables?

12. Look for Relationships Find a value for m or n to make a true statement.

a. $mx^2 - 36 = (3x + 6)(3x - 6)$

b. $(mx + ny)^2 = 4x^2 + 12xy + 9y^2$

13. Error Analysis Describe and correct the error a student made when squaring $(x + 5)$.

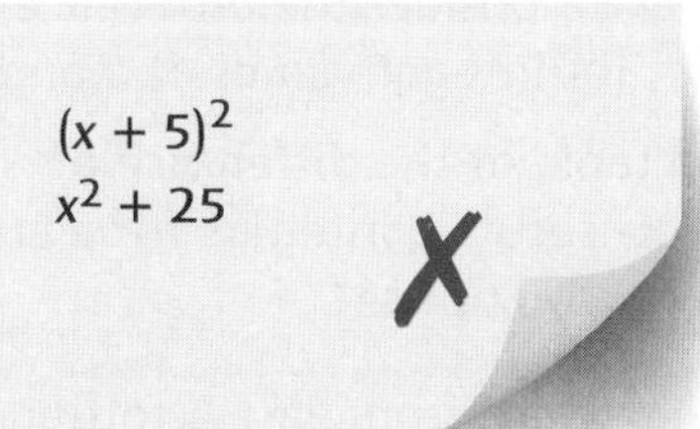

14. Use Structure The expression $96^2 - 95^2$ is a difference of two squares. How can you use the factors $(96 - 95)(96 + 95)$ to make it easier to simplify this expression?

15. Construct Arguments Jacob makes the following conjectures. Is each conjecture correct? Provide arguments to support your answers.

a. The product of any two consecutive even numbers is 1 less than a perfect square.

b. The product of any two consecutive odd numbers is 1 less than a perfect square.

PRACTICE

Write each product in standard form. SEE EXAMPLE 1

16. $(y + 9)(y + 9)$ **17.** $(5x - 3)(5x - 3)$

18. $(a + 11)(a + 11)$ **19.** $(x - 13)(x - 13)$

20. $(p + 15)^2$ **21.** $(3k + 8)^2$

22. $(x - 4y)^2$ **23.** $(2a + 3b)^2$

24. $\left(\frac{2}{5}x + \frac{1}{5}\right)^2$ **25.** $(0.4x + 1.2)^2$

Use the square of a binomial to find each product. SEE EXAMPLE 1

26. 56^2 **27.** 72^2

Write each product in standard form. SEE EXAMPLE 2

28. $(x - 12)(x + 12)$ **29.** $(2x + 5)(2x - 5)$

30. $(3a - 4b)(3a + 4b)$ **31.** $(x^2 - 2y)(x^2 + 2y)$

32. $\left(\frac{1}{4}x - \frac{2}{3}\right)\left(\frac{1}{4}x + \frac{2}{3}\right)$ **33.** $(x + 2.5)(x - 2.5)$

Use the product of sum and difference to find each product. SEE EXAMPLE 2

34. $32 \cdot 28$ **35.** $83 \cdot 97$

36. Consider the figure shown. SEE EXAMPLE 3

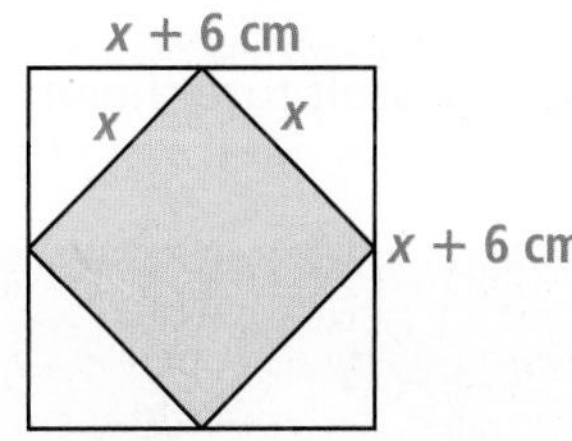

a. What expression represents the total area of the four white triangles?

b. If the length of each side of the shaded square is 12 cm, what is the total area of the four white triangles?

37. What is the area of the shaded region? SEE EXAMPLE 3

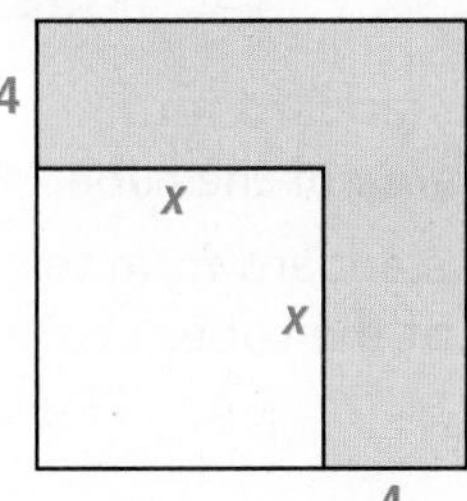

PRACTICE & PROBLEM SOLVING

APPLY

38. Mathematical Connections The radius of the inner circle of a tile pattern shown is x inches. Write a polynomial in standard form to represent the area of the space between the inner and outer circle.

39. Make Sense and Persevere In the figure shown, the darker square is removed.

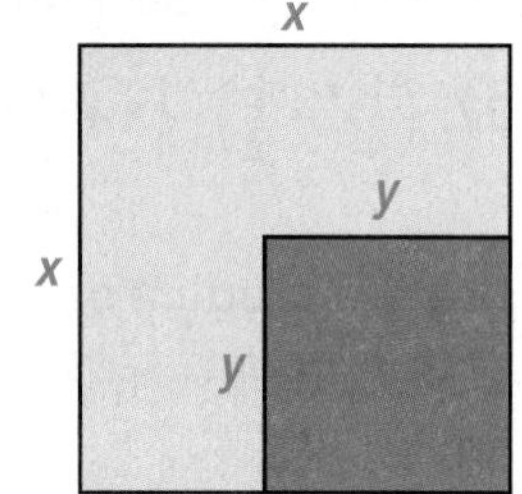

a. Divide the remaining figure into two rectangles. What are the dimensions of each rectangle?

b. What is the area of each rectangle?

c. What is the total area of the remaining figure? How does this figure represent the difference of two squares?

40. Higher Order Thinking The sculpture shown contains a large cube.

a. Write a polynomial in standard form to represent the surface area of the cube.

b. Write a polynomial in standard form to represent the volume of the cube.

ASSESSMENT PRACTICE

41. Consider each expression. Can you use the expression to find the product 53^2? Select *Yes* or *No* in each row.

	Yes	No
$(50 + 3)^2$	❑	❑
$(50 - 3)^2$	❑	❑
$(60 + 7)^2$	❑	❑
$(60 - 7)^2$	❑	❑
$(50 + 3)(50 - 3)$	❑	❑

42. SAT/ACT What is the product of $(3x^2 - 4y)(3x^2 + 4y)$?

Ⓐ $9x^4 - 24x^2y - 16y^2$
Ⓑ $3x^2 - 4y^2$
Ⓒ $9x^4 - 16y^2$
Ⓓ $3x^2 + 14x^2y - 4y$

43. Performance Task Consider the difference of squares $a^2 - b^2$, for integer values of a and b.

Part A Make a table of the difference of squares using consecutive integers for a and b. What pattern do you notice?

Part B Use the pattern from Part A to find pair of consecutive integers that generates a difference of squares of –45.

Part C Make a table of the difference of squares using consecutive even integers for a and b. What pattern do you notice?

Part D Use the pattern from Part C to find a pair of consecutive even integers that generates a difference of squares of –100.

 Activity  Assess

7-4 Factoring Polynomials

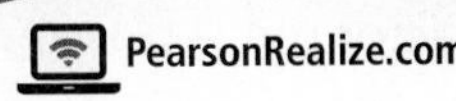

I CAN… factor a polynomial.

MODEL & DISCUSS

A catering company has been asked to design meal boxes for entrees and side dishes.

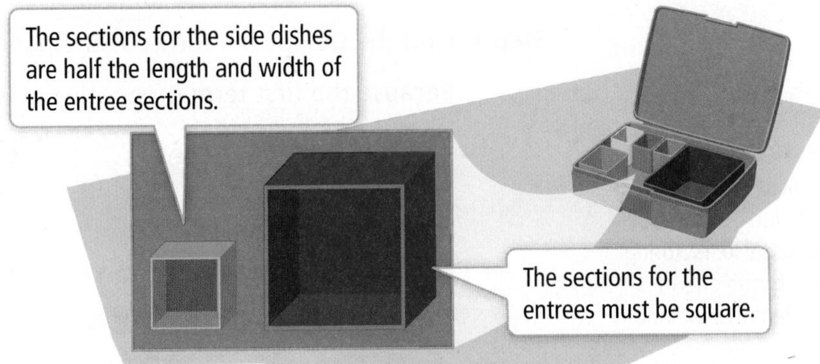

A. Design a meal box that meets each of these requirements:

a. Equal numbers of sections for entrees and side dishes

b. More sections for entrees than for side dishes

c. More sections for side dishes than for entrees

B. Use Structure For each meal box from Part A, write an algebraic expression to model the area of the meal boxes.

ESSENTIAL QUESTION

How is factoring a polynomial similar to factoring integers?

EXAMPLE 1 Find the Greatest Common Factor

What is the greatest common factor (GCF) of the terms of $12x^5 + 8x^4 - 6x^3$?

STUDY TIP
Recall that finding the prime factorization of a number is expressing the number as a product of only prime numbers.

Step 1 Write the prime factorization of the coefficient for each term to determine if there is a greatest common factor other than 1.

12	8	6
$2 \cdot 2 \cdot 3$	$2 \cdot 2 \cdot 2$	$2 \cdot 3$

One instance of 2 is the only common factor of the numbers, so the GCF of the coefficients of this trinomial is 2.

Step 2 Determine the greatest common factor for the variables of each term.

x^5	x^4	x^3
$x \cdot x \cdot x \cdot x \cdot x$	$x \cdot x \cdot x \cdot x$	$x \cdot x \cdot x$

Three instances of x are the only common factors of the terms, so the GCF of the variables is x^3.

The greatest common factor of the terms $12x^5 + 8x^4 - 6x^3$ is $2x^3$.

Try It! 1. Find the GCF of the terms of each polynomial.

a. $15x^2 + 18$

b. $-18y^4 + 6y^3 + 24y^2$

CONCEPTUAL UNDERSTANDING

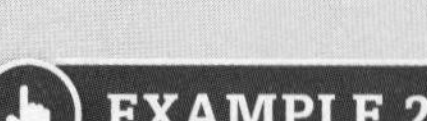

EXAMPLE 2 Factor Out the Greatest Common Factor

Why is it helpful to factor out the GCF from a polynomial?

Consider the polynomial $-12x^3 + 18x^2 - 27x$.

Step 1 Find the GCF of the terms of the polynomial, if there is one.

Because the first term is negative, it is helpful to factor out -1.

$-12x^3$ → $-1 \bullet 2 \bullet 2 \bullet 3 \bullet x \bullet x \bullet x$

$18x^2$ → $-1 \bullet (-2) \bullet 3 \bullet 3 \bullet x \bullet x$

$-27x$ → $-1 \bullet 3 \bullet 3 \bullet 3 \bullet x$

The greatest common factor is $-3x$.

COMMON ERROR
Remember to include the negative sign when factoring out the GCF of negative terms. Also, factoring out a -1 from a positive term generates two negative factors.

Step 2 Factor the GCF out of each term of the polynomial.

$-3x(4x^2 - 6x + 9)$

Factoring out the greatest common factor results in a polynomial with smaller coefficients and/or smaller exponents of the variable(s). This makes it easier to analyze the polynomial or factor it further.

Try It! **2.** Factor out the GCF from each polynomial.

a. $x^3 + 5x^2 - 22x$ **b.** $-16y^6 + 28y^4 - 20y^3$

APPLICATION

EXAMPLE 3 Factor a Polynomial Model

Alani is in charge of marketing for a travel company. She is designing a brochure that will have 6 photos. The photos can be arranged on the page in a number of ways.

There are 2 main square photos which have a length of x in. on each side.

There are 4 narrower photos that are each 1 in. by x in.

A. What is the total area of the photos?

First, find the area of each type of photo.

$$\begin{aligned}\text{Area} &= \text{area of square photos} + \text{area of narrower photos}\\ &= 2(x^2) + 4(1x)\\ &= 2x^2 + 4x\end{aligned}$$

There are 2 square photos, each with an area of x^2 in.^{2}. There are 4 narrower photos, each with an area of $1x$ in.^{2}.

The total area of the photos is $2x^2 + 4x$ in.^{2}.

CONTINUED ON THE NEXT PAGE

EXAMPLE 3 CONTINUED

B. Find a rectangular arrangement for the photos. What factored expression represents the area of the arrangement?

Try placing the photos in one row.

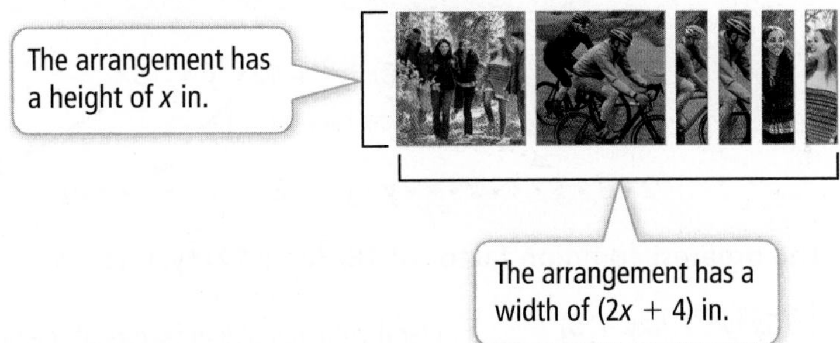

The arrangement has a height of x in.

The arrangement has a width of $(2x + 4)$ in.

The factored form that represents the area of the arrangement is $x(2x + 4)$.

C. Factor out the GCF from the polynomial. What does the GCF represent in this situation?

The GCF of $2x^2$ and $4x$ is $2x$. So you can rewrite the expression as $2x(x + 2)$.

MODEL WITH MATHEMATICS
Think about how to represent this situation mathematically. How is the GCF useful in solving this problem?

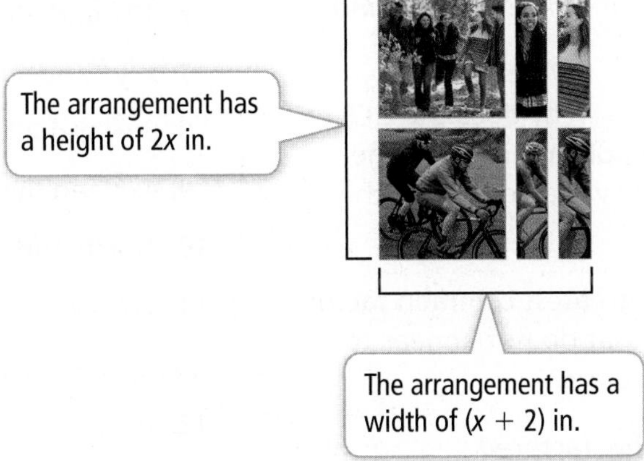

The arrangement has a height of $2x$ in.

The arrangement has a width of $(x + 2)$ in.

The GCF represents the height of one possible arrangement of the photos.

D. Which of these two arrangements is a more practical use of the space on a page of the brochure?

The arrangement based on the GCF is more practical because the arrangement with the photos in one line will likely be too wide for a page.

Try It! 3. Suppose the dimensions of the narrower photos were increased to 2 in. by x in. What expression would represent the new arrangement based on the GCF?

CONCEPT SUMMARY Factoring Polynomials

WORDS Determine if a polynomial can be factored. If the polynomial can be factored, find the greatest common factor of the terms and factor it out.

ALGEBRA

$$18x^3y^2 + 12x^2y + 15x$$

Find the GCF of the terms.

$$2 \cdot 3 \cdot 3 \cdot x \cdot x \cdot x \cdot y \cdot y \qquad 2 \cdot 2 \cdot 3 \cdot x \cdot x \cdot y \qquad 3 \cdot 5 \cdot x$$

The greatest common factor of $18x^3y^2 + 12x^2y + 15x$ is $3x$.

$3x(6x^2y^2 + 4xy + 5)$

Identify the remaining factors of the polynomial after factoring out the GCF, then write it in factored form.

Do You UNDERSTAND?

1. **ESSENTIAL QUESTION** How is factoring a polynomial similar to factoring integers?

2. **Look for Relationships** Why does the GCF of the variables of a polynomial have the *least* exponent of any variable term in the polynomial?

3. **Reason** What is the greatest common factor of two polynomials that do not appear to have any common factors?

4. **Error Analysis** Andrew factored $3x^2y - 6xy^2 + 3xy$ as $3xy(x - 2y)$. Describe and correct his error.

5. **Error Analysis** Wendell says that the greatest common factor of x^6 and x^8 is x^2, since the greatest common factor of 6 and 8 is 2. Is Wendell correct? Explain.

Do You KNOW HOW?

Find the GCF of each pair of monomials.

6. $10x$ and 25
7. x^3y^2 and x^5y
8. $8a^2$ and $28a^5$
9. $4x^3$ and $9y^5$
10. $12a^5b$ and $16a^4b^2$
11. $14x^{10}y^8$ and $15x^6y^9$

Factor out the GCF from each polynomial.

12. $10a^2b + 12ab^2$
13. $-3x^4 + 12x^3 - 21x^2$
14. $15x^3y - 10x^2y^3$
15. $x^{10} + x^9 - x^8$
16. $3x^3y^2 - 9xz^4 + 8y^2z$
17. $100a^7b^5 - 150a^8b^3$

UNDERSTAND

18. **Use Structure** What term and $12x^2y$ have a GCF of $4xy$? Write an expression that shows the monomial factored out of the polynomial.

19. **Look for Relationships** Write a trinomial that has a GCF of $4x^2$.

20. **Error Analysis** Describe and correct the error a student made when factoring $10a^3b - 5a^2b^2 - 15ab$.

$10a^3b - 5a^2b^2 - 15ab$
$5a(2a^2b - ab^2 - 3b)$ ✗

21. **Make Sense and Persevere** Write the difference in factored form.

$(24x^4 - 15x^2 + 6x) - (10x^4 + 5x^2 - 4x)$

22. **Higher Order Thinking** In the expression $ax^2 + b$, the coefficients of a and b are multiples of 2. The coefficients c and d in the expression $cx^2 + d$ are multiples of 3. Will the GCF of $ax^2 + b$ and $cx^2 + d$ *always, sometimes,* or *never* be a multiple of 6? Explain.

23. **Make Sense and Persevere** What is the GCF in the expression $x(x + 5) - 3x(x + 5) + 4(x + 5)$?

24. **Look for Relationships** Find the greatest common factor of the terms $x^{n+1}y^n$ and x^ny^{n-2}, where n is a whole number greater than 2. How can you factor the expression $x^{n+1}y^n + x^ny^{n-2}$?

25. **Mathematical Connections** consider the following set of monomials.

$A = \{2x, 3x, 4x, 5xy, 7x, 9y, 12xy, 13x, 15x\}$

The GCF the elements in subset $B = \{2x, 3x\}$ is x. Create 6 different subsets of A, such the GCFs of the elements are 1, $2x$, 3, $4x$, $5x$, and y.

PRACTICE

Find the GCF of each group of monomials.

SEE EXAMPLE 1

26. $8y^3$ and $28y$

27. $9a^2b^3$, $15ab^2$, and $21a^4b^3$

28. $18m^2$ and 25

29. x^2y^3 and x^3y^5

Factor out the GCF from each polynomial.

SEE EXAMPLE 2

30. $12x^2 - 15x$

31. $-4y^4 + 6y^2 - 14y$

32. $3m^2 - 10m + 4$

33. $24x^3y^2 - 30x^2y^3 + 12x^2y^4$

The areas of the rectangles are given. Use factoring to find expressions for the missing dimensions.

SEE EXAMPLE 3

34.

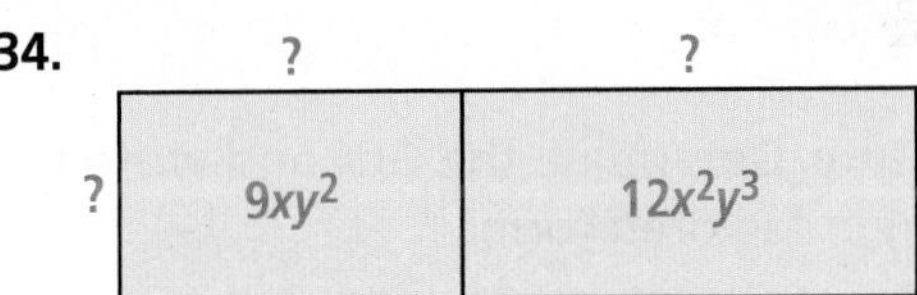

35.

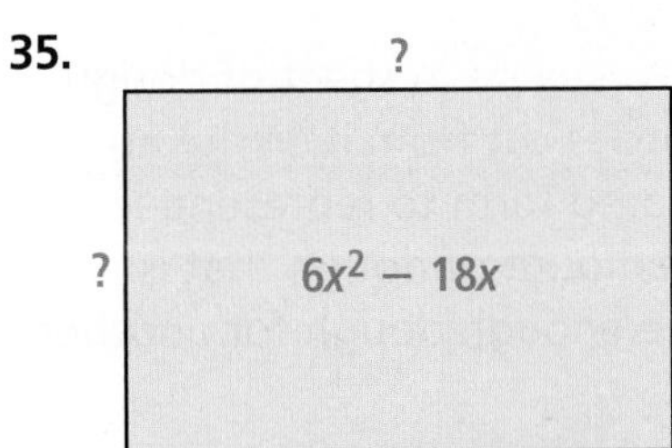

36.

?

? $10a^2b^3 + 15ab^2 + 20a^2b$

37. A farmer wants to plant three rectangular fields so that the widths are the same. The areas of the fields, in square yards, are given by the expressions $12x^2y$, $9xy^2$, and $21xy$. What is the width of the fields if $x = 3$ and $y = 4$?

SEE EXAMPLE 3

PRACTICE & PROBLEM SOLVING

APPLY

38. Model With Mathematics Write an expression in factored form to represent the volume in the canister not occupied by the tennis balls. Assume the canister is cylinder with volume $V = \pi r^2 h$.

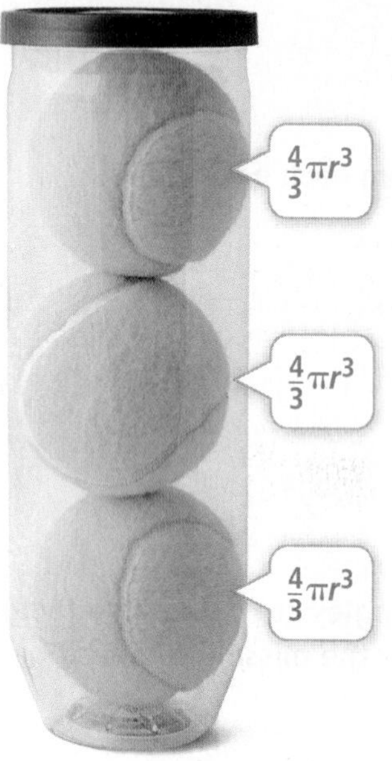

39. Use Structure Determine the GCF and write the expression in factored form.

$(6x^2 + 4x) + (4x^2 - 8x)$

40. Make Sense and Persevere A sheet of dough has six identical circles cut from it. Write an expression in factored form to represent the approximate amount of dough that is remaining. Is there enough dough for another circle?

ASSESSMENT PRACTICE

41. Fill in the blanks to find the factor pairs for $18x^4 + 12x^3 - 24x^2$.

■	$6x^2 + 4x - 8$
$2x$	$■x^{■} + ■x^{■} - ■x$
$x^{■}$	$18x^2 + 12x - 24$
$■x^{■}$	$3x^2 + 2x - 4$

42. SAT/ACT The area of a rectangle is $12x^3 - 18x^2 + 6x$. The width is equal to the GCF. What could the dimensions of the rectangle be?

Ⓐ $6x(2x^2 - 3x)$

Ⓑ $3(4x^3 - 6x^2 + 2x)$

Ⓒ $x(12x^2 - 18x + 6)$

Ⓓ $6x(2x^2 - 3x + 1)$

43. Performance Task Camilla is designing a platform for an athletic awards ceremony. The areas for two of the three faces of a platform are given.

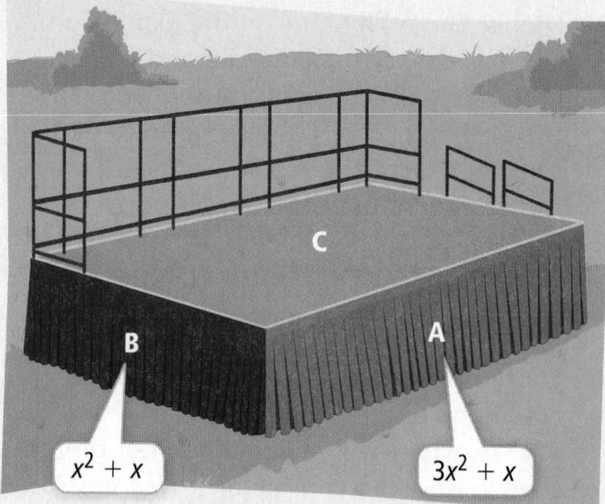

Part A What are the dimensions of each face of the platform?

Part B What is the area of the top of the platform?

Part C What expression represents the surface area of the entire platform, including the bottom?

Part D What expression represents the volume of the platform?

  Activity  Assess

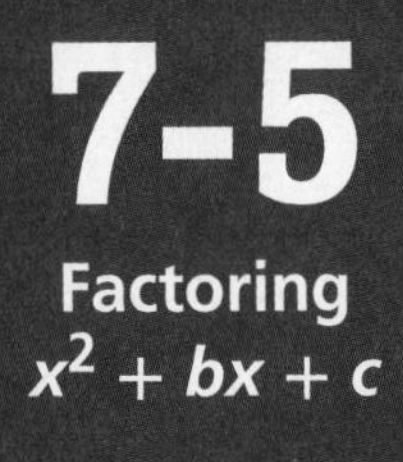

7-5 Factoring $x^2 + bx + c$

PearsonRealize.com

I CAN… factor a quadratic trinomial.

EXPLORE & REASON

Consider the following puzzles.

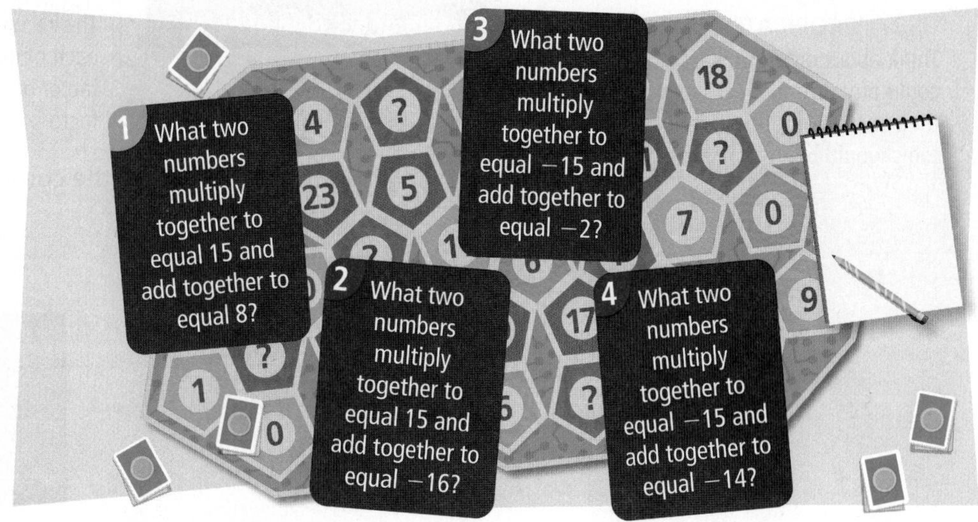

A. Find the solutions to the four puzzles shown.

B. **Look for Relationships** Write a set of four number puzzles of your own that have the same structure as these four. Describe the pattern.

ESSENTIAL QUESTION **How does recognizing patterns in the signs of the terms help you factor polynomials?**

CONCEPTUAL UNDERSTANDING

EXAMPLE 1 Understand Factoring a Trinomial

A. How does factoring a trinomial relate to multiplying binomials?

Consider the binomial product $(x + 2)(x + 3)$ and the trinomial $x^2 + 5x + 6$.

The product of the second terms of the binomials is equal to the last term of the trinomial.

$$(x + 2)(x + 3) = x^2 + 3x + 2x + 6$$
$$= x^2 + 5x + 6$$

The sum of the second terms of the binomials is equal to the coefficient of the second term of the trinomial.

LOOK FOR RELATIONSHIPS
How does factoring a trinomial relate to the Distributive Property?

When factoring a trinomial, you work backward to try to find the related binomial factors whose product equals the trinomial.

You can factor a trinomial of the form $x^2 + bx + c$ as $(x + p)(x + q)$ if $pq = c$ and $p + q = b$.

CONTINUED ON THE NEXT PAGE

EXAMPLE 1 CONTINUED

B. What is the factored form of $x^2 + 5x + 6$?

Identify a factor pair of 6 that has a sum of 5.

USE APPROPRIATE TOOLS
Think about different ways you could organize the factors and their sums. What organizational tools would be useful?

Factors of 6	Sum of Factors
1 and 6	7
2 and 3	5 ✓

The second term of each binomial is a factor of 6. These two factors add to 5.

If you factor using algebra tiles, the correct factor pair will form a rectangle.

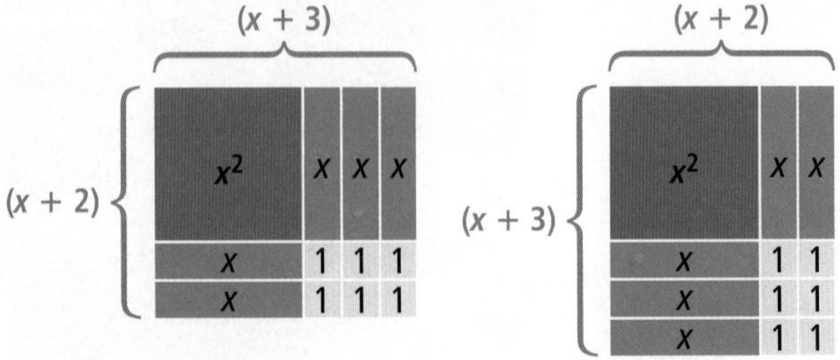

The factored form of $x^2 + 5x + 6$ is $(x + 2)(x + 3)$.

Check $(x + 2)(x + 3) = x^2 + 3x + 2x + 6$

$= x^2 + 5x + 6$ ✓

The first term of each binomial is x, since $x \cdot x = x^2$.

Try It! **1.** Write the factored form of each trinomial.

a. $x^2 + 13x + 36$

b. $x^2 + 11x + 28$

EXAMPLE 2 Factor $x^2 + bx + c$, When $b < 0$ and $c > 0$

What is the factored form of $x^2 - 11x + 18$?

Identify a factor pair of 18 that has a sum of -11.

Because b is negative and c is positive, inspect only negative factors.

Factors of 18	Sum of Factors
−1 and −18	−19
−2 and −9	−11

Even though there are more factor pairs for 18, there is no need to continue once you find the correct sum.

The factored form of $x^2 - 11x + 18$ is $(x - 2)(x - 9)$.

Check $(x - 2)(x - 9) = x^2 - 9x - 2x + 18$

$= x^2 - 11x + 18$ ✓

Try It! **2.** Write the factored form of each trinomial.

a. $x^2 - 8x + 15$

b. $x^2 - 13x + 42$

EXAMPLE 3 Factor $x^2 + bx + c$, When $c < 0$

What is the factored form of $x^2 + 5x - 6$?

Identify a factor pair of −6 that has a sum of 5.

COMMON ERROR
You may think that the pairs of factors 1, −6 and −1, 6 are the same. However, the sums of the two factors are different.

Because c is negative, the factors will have opposite signs.

Factors of −6	Sum of Factors
1 and −6	−5
−1 and 6	5

The factored form of $x^2 + 5x - 6$ is $(x - 1)(x + 6)$.

Try It! 3. Write the factored form of each trinomial.

a. $x^2 - 5x - 14$

b. $x^2 + 6x - 16$

EXAMPLE 4 Factor a Trinomial With Two Variables

A. How does multiplying binomials in two variables relate to factoring trinomials?

Consider the following binomial products.

$$(x + 2y)(x + 4y) = x^2 + 6xy + 8y^2$$
$$(x - 3y)(x + 5y) = x^2 + 2xy - 15y^2$$
$$(x - 7y)(x - 9y) = x^2 - 16xy - 63y^2$$

Each trinomial has the form $x^2 + bxy + cy^2$. Trinomials of this form are factorable when there is a factor pair of c that has a sum of b.

B. What is the factored form of $x^2 + 10xy + 24y^2$?

Identify a factor pair of 24 that has a sum of 10.

Factors of 24	Sum of Factors
3 and 8	11
4 and 6	10

STUDY TIP
When factoring a trinomial with two variables, make sure the factors contain both variables. Check your answer to determine whether you factored correctly.

The factored form of $x^2 + 10xy + 24y^2$ is $(x + 4y)(x + 6y)$.

Check $(x + 4y)(x + 6y) = x^2 + 6xy + 4xy + 24y^2$
$= x^2 + 10xy + 24y^2$ ✓

Try It! 4. Write the factored form of each trinomial.

a. $x^2 + 12xy + 32y^2$

b. $x^2 - 10xy + 21y^2$

APPLICATION

EXAMPLE 5 Apply Factoring Trinomials

Benjamin is designing a new house. The bedroom closet will have one wall that contains a closet system using three different-sized storage units. The number and amount of wall space needed for each of the three types of storage units is shown. What are the dimensions of the largest amount of wall space that will be needed?

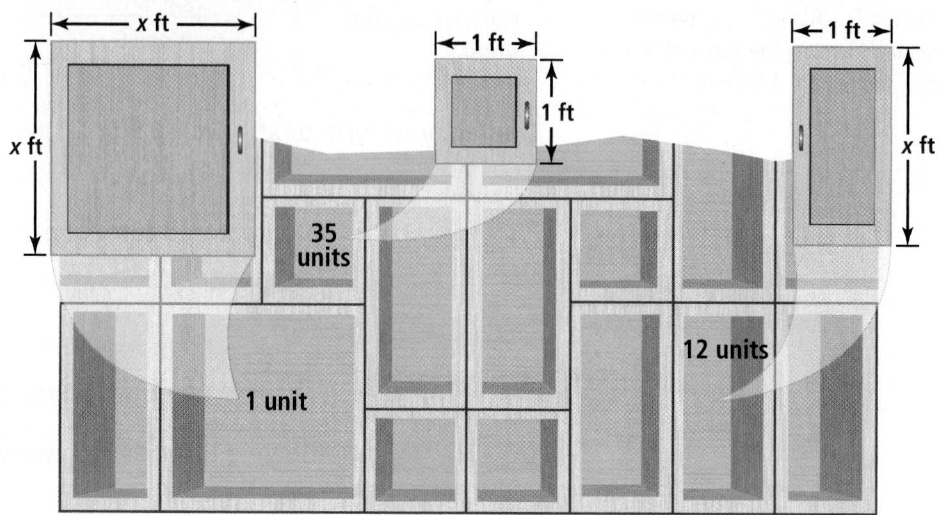

Formulate The largest possible closet storage system will use all of the units. Write an expression that represents the wall area of the closet in terms of the storage units.

$$x^2 + 12x + 35$$

Compute Because the area of a rectangle is the product of the length and width, factor the expression to find binomials that represent the length and width of the closet wall.

Factors of 35	Sum of Factors
1 and 35	36
5 and 7	12

$$x^2 + 12x + 35 = (x + 5)(x + 7)$$

Interpret The dimensions of the largest amount of wall space that will be needed are $(x + 7)$ ft by $(x + 5)$ ft.

Try It! 5. What would be the dimensions of the largest wall area you would need if you used 11 of the 1 ft-by-1 ft units while keeping the other units the same?

CONCEPT SUMMARY Factoring $x^2 + bx + c$

To factor a trinomial of the form $x^2 + bx + c$, find a factor pair of c that has a sum of b. Then use the factors you found to write the binomials that have a product equal to the trinomial.

	***b* and *c* are positive.**	***b* is negative and *c* is positive.**	***c* is negative.**
WORDS	When the values of both b and c are positive, the second terms of the binomials are both positive.	When the value of b is negative and that of c is positive, the second terms of the binomials are both negative.	When the value of c is negative, the second terms of the binomials have opposite signs.
NUMBERS	*b* and *c* are positive. $x^2 + 9x + 14$ $= (x + 2)(x + 7)$	*b* is negative and *c* is positive. $x^2 - 9x + 14$ $= (x - 2)(x - 7)$	*c* is negative. $x^2 - 5x - 14$ $= (x + 2)(x - 7)$

Do You UNDERSTAND?

1. **ESSENTIAL QUESTION** How does recognizing patterns in the signs of the terms help you factor polynomials?

2. **Error Analysis** A student says that since $x^2 - 5x - 6$ has two negative terms, both factors of c will be negative. Explain the error the student made.

3. **Reason** What is the first step to factoring any trinomial? Explain.

4. **Communicate Precisely** To factor a trinomial $x^2 + bx + c$, why do you find the factors of c and not b? Explain.

Do You KNOW HOW?

List the factor pairs of c for each trinomial.

5. $x^2 + 17x + 16$

6. $x^2 + 4x - 21$

For each trinomial, tell whether the factor pairs of c will be both positive, both negative, or opposite signs.

7. $x^2 - 11x + 10$

8. $x^2 + 9x - 10$

9. Copy and complete the table for factoring the trinomial $x^2 - 7x + 12$.

Factors of 12	Sum of Factors
−1 and −12	?
?	−7
−2 and −6	−8

PRACTICE & PROBLEM SOLVING

Scan for Multimedia | Practice | Tutorial | Additional Exercises Available Online

UNDERSTAND

10. **Mathematical Connections** Explain how factoring a trinomial is like factoring a number. Explain how it is different.

11. **Use Appropriate Tools** How can you use algebra tiles to factor a trinomial? How do you determine the binomial factors from an algebra tile model?

12. **Look for Relationships** How are the binomial factors of $x^2 + 7x - 18$ and $x^2 - 7x - 18$ similar? How are they different?

13. **Error Analysis** Describe and correct the error a student made in making a table in order to factor the trinomial $x^2 - 11x - 26$.

Factors	Sum of Factors
−1 and 11	10
1 and −11	−10

The trinomial $x^2 - 11x - 26$ is not factorable because no factors of *b* sum to *c*. ✗

14. **Higher Order Thinking** Given that the trinomial $x^2 + bx + 8$ is factorable as $(x + p)(x + q)$, with *p* and *q* being integers, what are four possible values of *b*?

15. **Reason** What is missing from the last term of the trinomial $x^2 + 5xy + 4$ so that it is factorable as the product of binomials?

16. **Look for Structure** How does the sign of the last term of a trinomial help you know what type of factors you are looking for?

17. **Reason** A rectangle has an area of $x^2 + 7x + 12$ in.^{2}. Use factoring to find possible dimensions of the rectangle. Explain why you can use factoring to find the answer.

PRACTICE

Factor each trinomial represented by the algebra tiles. SEE EXAMPLE 1

18.

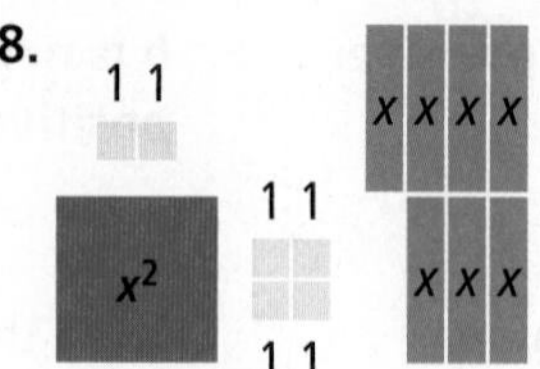

19.

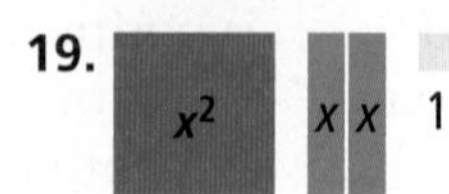

Complete the table to factor each trinomial.
SEE EXAMPLES 1 AND 3

20. $x^2 + 9x + 20$

Factors of *c*	Sum of Factors
?	?
?	9
?	?

21. $x^2 + 9x - 22$

Factors of *c*	Sum of Factors
?	?
?	?
?	9
?	?

Write the factored form of each trinomial.
SEE EXAMPLES 1, 2, 3, 4, AND 5

22. $x^2 + 15x + 44$

23. $x^2 - 11x + 24$

24. $x^2 + 2x - 15$

25. $x^2 - 13x + 30$

26. $x^2 + 9x + 18$

27. $x^2 - 2x - 8$

28. $x^2 + 7xy + 6y^2$

29. $x^2 - 12x + 27$

30. $x^2 + 10x + 16$

31. $x^2 - 16xy + 28y^2$

32. $x^2 - 10xy - 11y^2$

33. $x^2 + 16x + 48$

34. $x^2 - 13x - 48$

35. $x^2 + 15xy + 54y^2$

PRACTICE & PROBLEM SOLVING

APPLY

36. Make Sense and Persevere The volume of a rectangular box is represented by $x^3 + 3x^2 + 2x$. Use factoring to find possible dimensions of the box. How are the dimensions of the box related to one another?

37. Model with Mathematics A lake has a rectangular area roped off where people can swim under a lifeguard's supervision. The swimming section has an area of $x^2 + 3x - 40$ square feet, with the long side parallel to the lake shore.

a. What are possible dimensions of the roped-off area? Use factoring.

b. How much rope is needed for the three sides that are not along the beach? Explain.

c. The rope used to mark the swimming area is 238 ft long. What is x when the total length of rope is 238 ft?

38. Make Sense and Persevere Sarah has a large square piece of foam for an art project. The side lengths of the square are x in. To fit her project, Sarah cuts a section of foam from two of the sides so she now has a rectangle. How much foam does Sarah cut from each of the two sides?

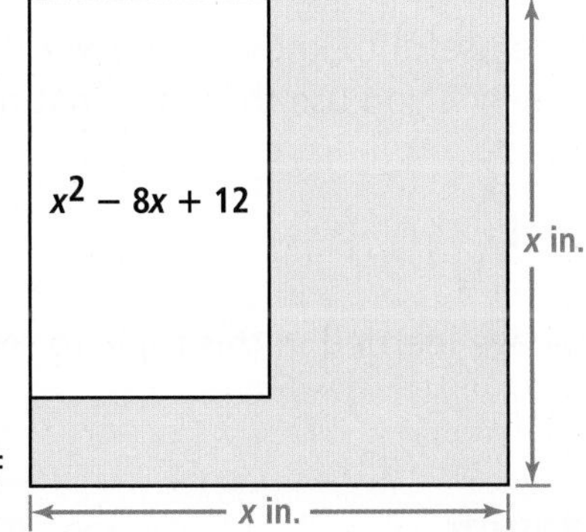

ASSESSMENT PRACTICE

39. Match each trinomial with its factored form.

I. $x^2 + 13x + 30$ — A. $(x - 10)(x + 3)$
II. $x^2 + x - 30$ — B. $(x - 6)(x + 5)$
III. $x^2 - 7x - 30$ — C. $(x - 5)(x + 6)$
IV. $x^2 - x - 30$ — D. $(x + 10)(x + 3)$

40. SAT/ACT What is the factored form of $4x^3 - 24x^2 - 28x$?

Ⓐ $4x(x - 7)(x + 1)$
Ⓑ $4x(x - 1)(x + 7)$
Ⓒ $x(x - 7)(x + 4)$
Ⓓ $x(x - 4)(x + 7)$
Ⓔ $4(x - 7)(x - 1)$

41. Performance Task A city is designing the layout of a new park. The park will be divided into several different areas, including a field, a picnic area, and a recreation area. One design of the park is shown below.

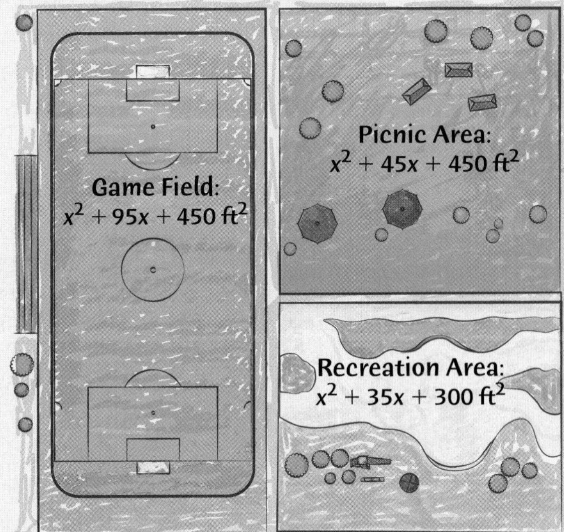

Part A Use factoring to find the dimensions of each of the three areas of the park shown

Part B Describe two different ways to find the total area of the park.

Part C What are the dimensions of the entire park?

Part D Can you find the value of x? Explain.

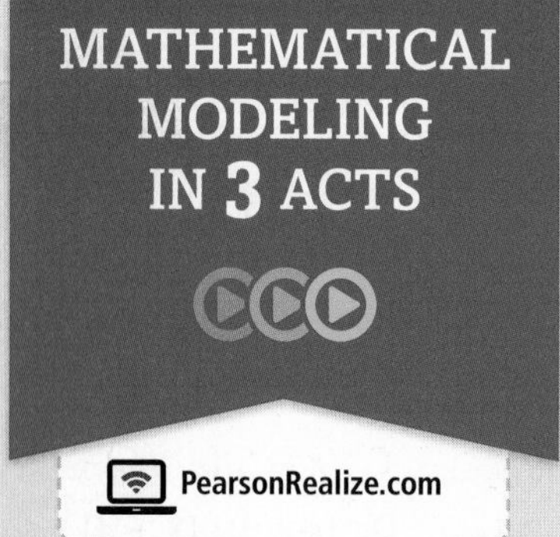

PearsonRealize.com

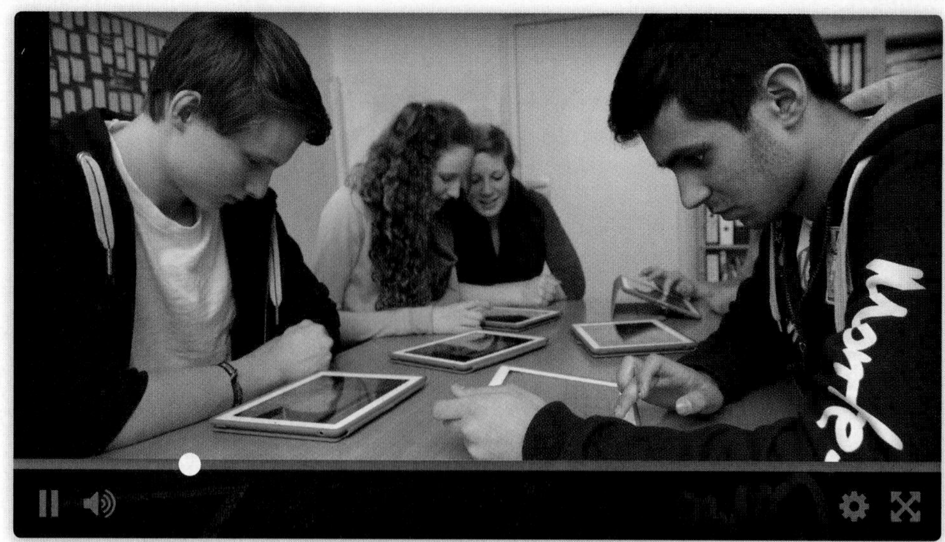

Who's Right?

People often approach a problem in different ways. Sometimes their solutions are the same, but other times different approaches lead to very different, but still valid, solutions.

Suppose you had to solve a system of linear equations. You might solve it by graphing, while a classmate might use substitution. Is one way of solving a problem always better than another? Think about this during the Mathematical Modeling in 3 Acts lesson.

Scan for Multimedia 

ACT 1 Identify the Problem

1. What is the first question that comes to mind after watching the video?
2. Write down the main question you will answer about what you saw in the video.
3. Make an initial conjecture that answers this main question.
4. Explain how you arrived at your conjecture.
5. What information will be useful to know to answer the main question? How can you get it? How will you use that information?

ACT 2 Develop a Model

6. Use the math that you have learned in this topic to refine your conjecture.

ACT 3 Interpret the Results

7. Did your refined conjecture match the actual answer exactly? If not, what might explain the difference?

Activity Assess

7-6 Factoring $ax^2 + bx + c$

PearsonRealize.com

I CAN... factor a quadratic trinomial when $a \neq 1$.

EXPLORE & REASON

A website design company resizes rectangular photos so they fit on the screens of various devices.

A. What expression represents the width of the photo?

B. Write three possible lengths and corresponding widths of the photo by substituting different values for x.

C. Make Sense and Persevere Why would the company use an expression to represent the area? Explain.

ESSENTIAL QUESTION

How is factoring a quadratic trinomial when $a \neq 1$ similar to factoring a quadratic trinomial when $a = 1$?

EXAMPLE 1 Factor Out a Common Factor

What is the factored form of $3x^3 + 15x^2 - 18x$?

Before factoring the trinomial into two binomials, look for any common factors that you can factor out.

$$3x^3 \quad + \quad 15x^2 \quad - \quad 18x$$

$$3 \cdot x \cdot x \cdot x \quad + \quad 3 \cdot 5 \cdot x \cdot x \quad - \quad 2 \cdot 3 \cdot 3 \cdot x$$

There is a common factor of $3x$.

So, $3x^3 + 15x^2 - 18x = 3x(x^2 + 5x - 6)$.

Then factor the resulting trinomial, $x^2 + 5x - 6$.

Because c is negative in the trinomial $x^2 + 5x - 6$, the factors will have opposite signs.

Factors of −6	Sum of Factors
1 and −6	−5
−1 and 6	5

The factored form of $x^2 + 5x - 6$ is $(x - 1)(x + 6)$, so the factored form of $3x^3 + 15x^2 - 18x$ is $3x(x - 1)(x + 6)$.

VOCABULARY
The answer $3x(x - 1)(x + 6)$, is $3x^3 + 15x^2 - 18x$ factored completely. There are other ways you can factor the polynomial, but only one way to factor it completely.

Try It! 1. Factor each trinomial.

a. $5x^2 - 35x + 50$

b. $6x^3 + 30x^2 + 24x$

CONCEPTUAL UNDERSTANDING

EXAMPLE 2 Understand Factoring by Grouping

A. If $ax^2 + bx + c$ is a product of binomials, how are the values of a, b, and c related?

Consider the product $(3x + 4)(2x + 1)$.

$$\begin{aligned}(3x + 4)(2x + 1) &= (3x)(2x) + (3x)(1) + (4)(2x) + (4)(1)\\ &= 6x^2 + 3x + 8x + 4\\ &= 6x^2 + 11x + 4\end{aligned}$$

The product is $6x^2 + 11x + 4$. Notice that $ac = (6)(4)$ or $(3)(2)(4)(1)$, which is the product of all of the coefficients and constants from $(3x + 4)(2x + 1)$.

In the middle step, the coefficients of the x-terms, 3 and 8, add to form $b = 11$. They are composed of pairs of the coefficients and constants from the original product; $3 = (3)(1)$ and $8 = (4)(2)$.

If $ax^2 + bx + c$ is the product of binomials, there is a pair of factors of ac that have a sum of b.

STUDY TIP
To speed up your search, when looking for a factor pair that has a sum of b, you can rule out factor pairs with sums that are obviously far from the target.

B. How can you factor $ax^2 + bx + c$ by grouping?

Consider the trinomial $6x^2 + 11x + 4$, $a = 6$ and $c = 4$, so $ac = 24$.

Find the factor pair of 24 with a sum of 11.

Factors of 24	Sum of Factors
2 and 12	14
3 and 8	11

Rewrite $11x$ as $3x$ and $8x$.

USE STRUCTURE
Common factors are not limited to monomials. Here the common factors are monomials and binomials.

$$\begin{aligned}6x^2 + 11x + 4 &= 6x^2 + 3x + 8x + 4\\ &= (6x^2 + 3x) + (8x + 4) && \text{Group as two binomials.}\\ &= 3x(2x + 1) + 4(2x + 1) && \text{Factor out the GCF of each binomial.}\\ &= (3x + 4)(2x + 1) && \text{Use the Distributive Property.}\end{aligned}$$

The factored form of $6x^2 + 11x + 4$ is $(3x + 4)(2x + 1)$.

Check $(3x + 4)(2x + 1) = 6x^2 + 3x + 8x + 4$
$= 6x^2 + 11x + 4$ ✓

Try It! 2. Factor each trinomial.

a. $10x^2 + 17x + 3$

b. $2x^2 + x - 21$

EXAMPLE 3 Factor a Trinomial Using Substitution

How can you use substitution to help you factor $ax^2 + bx + c$ as the product of two binomials?

Consider the trinomial $3x^2 - 2x - 8$.

STEP 1 Multiply $ax^2 + bx + c$ by a to transform x^2 into $(ax)^2$.

$$3[3x^2 - 2x - 8]$$

$$= 3(3)x^2 - 2(3)x - 8(3)$$

$$= (3x)^2 - 2(3x) - 24$$

Multiply the entire trinomial by 3. The new trinomial is not equivalent to the original. Remember to divide by 3 as a last step.

$ax = 3x$

STEP 2 Replace ax with a single variable. Let $p = ax$.

$$= p^2 - 2p - 24$$

Substitute p for $3x$.

STEP 3 Factor the trinomial.

$$= (p - 6)(p + 4)$$

STEP 4 Substitute ax back into the product. Remember $p = 3x$. Factor out common factors if there are any.

$$= (3x - 6)(3x + 4)$$

$$= 3(x - 2)(3x + 4)$$

Substitute $3x$ for p.

STUDY TIP
Because you multiplied the original expression by a new factor, the answer will not be equivalent unless you divide out the same factor at the end of your computations.

STEP 5 Since you started by multiplying the trinomial by a, you must divide by a to get a product that is equivalent to original trinomial.

$$(x - 2)(3x + 4)$$

This product is equivalent to the original trinomial.

The factored form of $3x^2 - 2x - 8$ is $(x - 2)(3x + 4)$. In general, you can use substitution to help transform $ax^2 + bx + c$ with $a \neq 1$ to a simpler case in which $a = 1$, factor it, and then transform it back to an equivalent factored form.

Try It! 3. Factor each trinomial using substitution.

a. $2x^2 - x - 6$

b. $10x^2 + 3x - 1$

CONCEPT SUMMARY Factoring $ax^2 + bx + c$

	Factor by Grouping	Factor Using Substitution
ALGEBRA	To factor a trinomial of the form $ax^2 + bx + c$, find a factor pair of ac that has a sum of b. Rewrite bx as a sum of those factors. Then factor out the GCFs from the expression twice to factor the original trinomial as the product of two binomials.	To factor a trinomial of the form $ax^2 + bx + c$, multiply the trinomial by a. Rewrite the first two terms using ax. Substitute a single variable for ax. Factor the trinomial. Substitute ax back in for the variable. Divide by a.
NUMBERS	$3x^2 + 22x + 7$ $= 3x^2 + 21x + 1x + 7$ $= 3x(x + 7) + 1(x + 7)$ $= (3x + 1)(x + 7)$	$3x^2 - 20x - 7$ $3[3x^2 - 20x - 7]$ $= (3x)^2 - 20(3x) - 21$ $= p^2 - 20p - 21$ $= (p - 21)(p + 1)$ $= (3x - 21)(3x + 1)$ $= 3(x - 7)(3x + 1)$ $= (x - 7)(3x + 1)$

Do You UNDERSTAND?

1. ESSENTIAL QUESTION How is factoring a quadratic trinomial when $a \neq 1$ similar to factoring a quadratic trinomial when $a = 1$?

2. **Error Analysis** A student says that for $ax^2 + bx + c$ to be factorable, b must equal $a + c$. Explain the error in the student's thinking.

3. **Reason** Suppose you can factor $ax^2 + bx + c$ as $(px + q)(sx + t)$, where p, q, s, and t are integers. If $c = 1$, what do you know about the two binomial factors?

4. **Reason** When factoring $ax^2 + bx + c$ by substitution, why is it acceptable to multiply the polynomial by a to start?

5. **Construct Arguments** Felipe is factoring the expression $2x^2 - x - 28$. He knows $-x$ should be rewritten as $7x$ plus $-8x$, but he is not sure which order to place the terms in the expression. Explain to Felipe why it does not matter what order the terms are in.

Do You KNOW HOW?

List the factor pairs of ac for each trinomial.

6. $2x^2 + 7x + 4$
7. $12x^2 - 5x - 2$

Tell whether the terms of each trinomial share a common factor other than 1. If there is a common factor, identify it.

8. $15x^2 - 10x - 5$
9. $3x^3 - 2x^2 - 1$

Rewrite the x-term in each trinomial to factor by grouping.

10. $35x^2 + 17x + 2$
11. $12x^2 + 20x + 3$

Factor each trinomial to find possible dimensions of each rectangle.

12. $A = 5x^2 + 17x + 6$

13. $A = 6x^2 + 7x - 5$

UNDERSTAND

14. Mathematical Connections How is factoring a common factor out of a trinomial like factoring common factors out of the numerator and denominator of a fraction? How is it different?

15. Make Sense and Persevere What are all possible values of b for which $7x^2 + bx + 3$ is factorable, if the factors have integer coefficients and constants?

16. Look for Relationships Can you factor the trinomial $3x^2 + 5x + 3$ into linear factors with integer coefficients? Explain.

17. Error Analysis Describe and correct the error a student made in factoring $2x^2 + 11x + 15$.

$ac = 2 \times 15 = 30; b = 11$

Factors of 30	Sum of Factors
1×30	$1 + 30 = 31$
2×15	$2 + 15 = 17$
3×10	$3 + 10 = 13$
5×6	$5 + 6 = 11$

$2x^2 + 11x + 15 = (x + 5)(x + 6)$ 

18. Higher Order Thinking Can you factor the trinomial $6x^2 + 7x - 6$ as $(px + q)(sx + t)$, where p, q, s, and t are integers? Explain why or why not.

19. Reason Use factoring to arrange the following algebra tiles first into one rectangle and then into two rectangles of equal size.

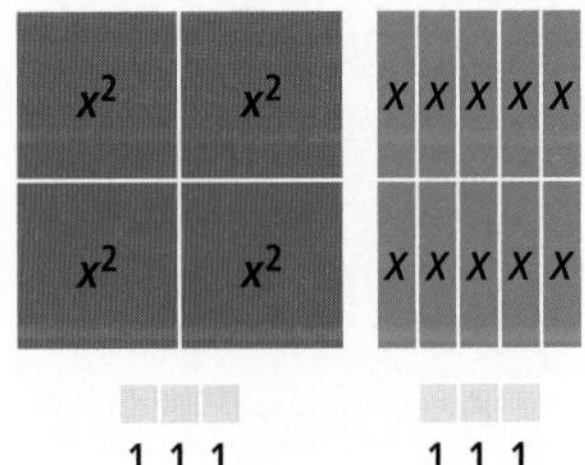

20. Use Structure What is the factored form of $pqx^2 + (mp + qn)x + mn$?

PRACTICE

Factor the trinomial represented by the algebra tiles.

21.

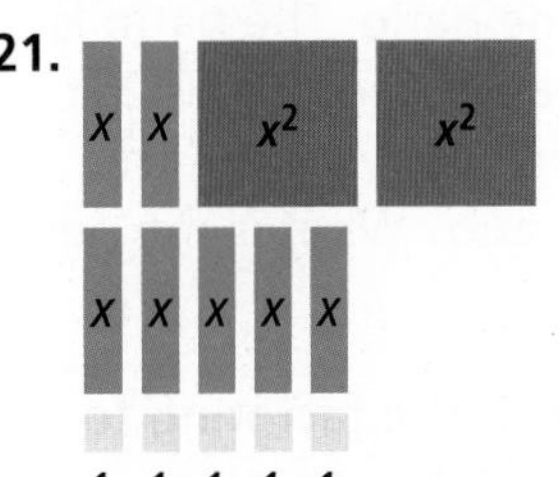

22.

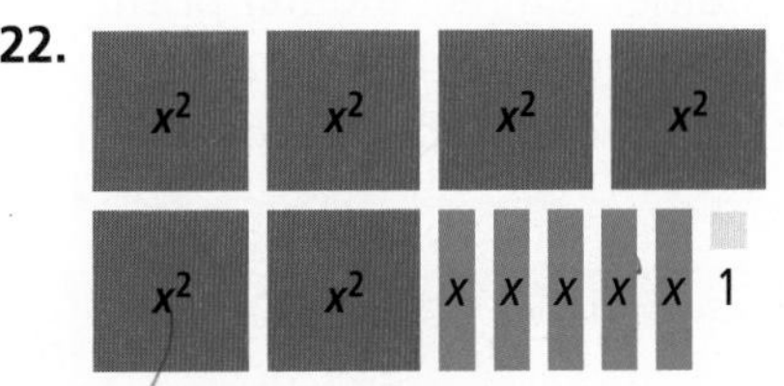

Factor each trinomial. SEE EXAMPLE 1

23. $4x^2 + 16x + 12$

24. $2x^2 - 16x + 30$

25. $3x^2 + 12x - 63$

26. $6x^2 + 12x - 48$

Identify the factor pairs of ac you could use to rewrite b to factor each trinomial by grouping.
SEE EXAMPLE 2

27. $7x^2 + 9x + 2$

28. $6x^2 + 11x - 2$

29. $8x^2 - 2x - 1$

30. $10x^2 + 19x + 6$

31. $15x^2 - 16x - 7$

32. $12x^2 + 11x + 2$

Factor each trinomial completely.
SEE EXAMPLES 1, 2, AND 3

33. $4x^2 + 13x + 3$

34. $6x^2 - 25x - 14$

35. $2x^2 + 7x - 4$

36. $12x^2 + 13x + 3$

37. $6x^3 + 9x^2 + 3x$

38. $8x^2 - 10x - 3$

39. $12x^2 + 16x + 5$

40. $16x^3 + 32x^2 + 12x$

41. $21x^2 - 35x - 14$

42. $16x^2 + 22x - 3$

43. $9x^2 + 46x + 5$

44. $24x^3 - 10x^2 - 4x$

Factor each trinomial completely.

45. $3x^2 + xy - 2y^2$

46. $2x^2 + 9xy + 10y^2$

47. $5x^2 - 4xy - y^2$

48. $2x^2 + 10xy + 12y^2$

Practice | Tutorial
Mixed Review Available Online

PRACTICE & PROBLEM SOLVING

APPLY

49. Reason A rectangular patio has an area of $2x^2 + 13x - 24$ ft^2. Use factoring to find possible dimensions of the patio. The patio is to be enlarged so that each dimension is 2 ft greater than it was originally. What are the new dimensions of the patio? What is the new area of the patio?

50. Make Sense and Persevere Use factoring to find possible dimensions of the container shown. The container is a rectangular prism. What are the dimensions of the container if $x = 3$? What is the volume of the container if $x = 4$?

51. Model With Mathematics A photographer is placing photos in a mat for a gallery show. Each mat she uses is x in. wide on each side. The total area of each photo and mat is shown.

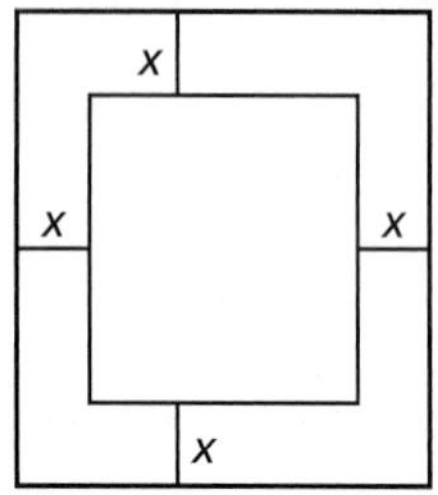

Area $= 4x^2 + 36x + 80$

a. Factor the total area to find possible dimensions of a photo and mat.

b. What are the dimensions of the photos in terms of x?

c. Explain why the photographer might use x to represent the width of the mat.

ASSESSMENT PRACTICE

52. The trinomial $ax^2 + bx + c$ is factorable when factors of _?_ have a sum of _?_.

53. SAT/ACT What is the factored form of $3x^2 - 5x - 12$?

Ⓐ $(x - 4)(3x + 1)$

Ⓑ $(x - 3)(3x + 4)$

Ⓒ $(x + 4)(3x - 9)$

Ⓓ $3(x + 2)(x - 3)$

Ⓔ $3(x - 4)(x + 1)$

54. Performance Task A paint tray has an area of $42x^2 + 135x + 108$ in.^{2}. The square paint compartments that are all the same size and spaced evenly, though the space along the edge of the tray is twice as wide as the space between squares.

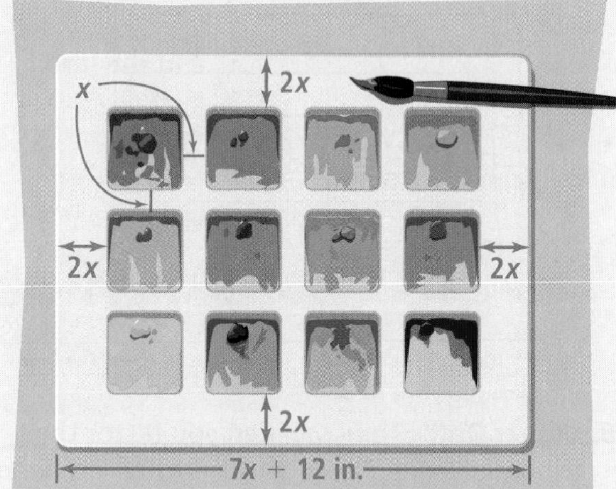

Part A What is the width of the paint tray?

Part B What is the area of each of the paint compartments in the tray?

Part C How wide are the edges of the tray if the width of the paint tray is 45 in.?

Activity Assess

7-7 Factoring Special Cases

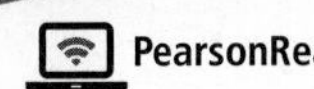
PearsonRealize.com

I CAN… factor special trinomials.

VOCABULARY

- perfect-square trinomial

CRITIQUE & EXPLAIN

Seth and Bailey are given the polynomial $8x^2 + 48x + 72$ to factor.

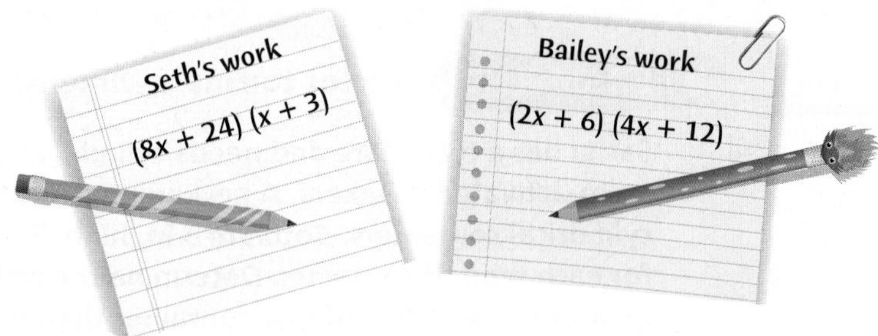

A. Analyze each factored expression to see if both are equivalent to the given polynomial.

B. How can the product of different pairs of expressions be equivalent?

C. **Look for Relationships** Find two other pairs of binomials that are different, but whose products are equal.

ESSENTIAL QUESTION

What special patterns are helpful when factoring a perfect-square trinomial and the difference of two squares?

CONCEPTUAL UNDERSTANDING

EXAMPLE 1 Understand Factoring a Perfect Square

What is the factored form of a perfect-square trinomial?

A **perfect-square trinomial** results when a binomial is squared.

$$(a + b)(a + b) = (a + b)^2 = a^2 + 2ab + b^2$$
$$(a - b)(a - b) = (a - b)^2 = a^2 - 2ab + b^2$$

The first and last terms are perfect squares. The middle term is twice the product of the first and last terms of the binomial.

A. What is the factored form of $x^2 + 14x + 49$?

Write the last term as a perfect square.

$$x^2 + 14x + 49 = x^2 + 14x + 7^2$$
$$= x^2 + 2(7)x + 7^2$$
$$= (x + 7)(x + 7) = (x + 7)^2$$

$2ab = 2(7)x = 14x$, so the trinomial fits the pattern.

B. What is the factored form of $9x^2 - 30x + 25$?

Write the first and last terms as a perfect square.

$$9x^2 - 30x + 25 = (3x)^2 - 30x + 5^2$$
$$= (3x)^2 - 2(3x)(5) + 5^2$$
$$= (3x - 5)(3x - 5) = (3x - 5)^2$$

$2ab = 2(3x)(5) = 30x$, so the trinomial fits the pattern.

COMMON ERROR
Be careful to identify the correct values for a and b when factoring special cases. The value of a can be different from x.

The factored form of a perfect-square trinomial is $(a + b)^2$ when the trinomial fits the pattern $a^2 + 2ab + b^2$, and $(a - b)^2$ when the trinomial fits the pattern $a^2 - 2ab + b^2$.

CONTINUED ON THE NEXT PAGE

EXAMPLE 1 CONTINUED

Try It! 1. Factor each trinomial.

a. $4x^2 + 12x + 9$ b. $x^2 - 8x + 16$

APPLICATION

EXAMPLE 2 Factor to Find a Dimension

Sasha has a tech store and needs cylindrical containers to package her voice-activated speakers. A packaging company makes two different cylindrical containers. Both are 3 in. high. The volume information is given for each type of container. Determine the radius of each cylinder. How much greater is the radius of one container than the other?

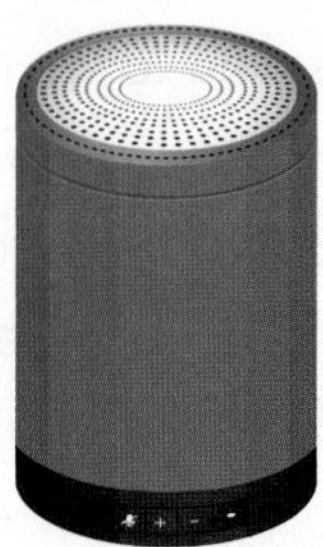

Volume:
$3\pi x^2$ in.^{3}

Volume:
$\pi(3x^2 + 30x + 75)$ in.^{3}

Formulate The formula for the volume of a cylinder is $V = \pi r^2 h$, where r is the radius and h is the height of the cylinder. The height of both containers is 3 in., so both expressions will have 3π in common.

Factor 3 out of the trinomial

$3\pi x^2 = 3\pi(x^2)$ $\pi(3x^2 + 30x + 75) = 3\pi(x^2 + 10x + 25)$

Factor the expressions to identify the radius of each cylinder.

Compute The expression $x^2 = x \cdot x$, so the radius of the first cylinder is x in.

Factor the expression $x^2 + 10x + 25$ to find the radius of the second cylinder.

$$x^2 + 10x + 25 = x^2 + 2(5)x + 5^2$$
$$= (x + 5)^2$$

Rewrite the first and last terms as squares.

The radius of the second cylinder is $(x + 5)$ in.

Find the difference between the radii.

$$(x + 5) - x = 5$$

Interpret The larger cylinder has a radius that is 5 in. greater than the smaller one.

Try It! 2. What is the radius of a cylinder that has a height of 3 in. and a volume of $\pi(27x^2 + 18x + 3)$ in.^{3}?

Activity Assess

EXAMPLE 3 Factor a Difference of Two Squares

How can you factor the difference of squares using a pattern?

Recall that a binomial in the form $a^2 - b^2$ is called the difference of two squares.

$$(a - b)(a + b) = a^2 - ab + ab - b^2 = a^2 - b^2$$

A. What is the factored form of $x^2 - 9$?

Write the last term as a perfect square.

$$x^2 - 9 = x^2 - 3^2$$
$$= (x + 3)(x - 3)$$

$a = x$ and $b = 3$, so the binomial fits the pattern.

REASON
Determine whether the factoring rule for a difference of two squares makes sense by working backward.

B. What is the factored form of $4x^2 - 81$?

Write the first and last terms as perfect squares.

$$4x^2 - 81 = (2x)^2 - 9^2$$
$$= (2x + 9)(2x - 9)$$

$a = 2x$ and $b = 9$, so the binomial fits the pattern.

The difference of two squares is a factoring pattern when one perfect square is subtracted from another. If a binomial follows that pattern, you can factor it as a sum and difference.

Try It! **3.** Factor each expression.

a. $x^2 - 64$

b. $9x^2 - 100$

EXAMPLE 4 Factor Out a Common Factor

What is the factored form of $3x^3y - 12xy^3$?

Factor out a greatest common factor of the terms if there is one. Then factor as the difference of squares.

$3x^3y - 12xy^3 = 3xy(x^2 - 4y^2)$ Factor out the GCF, $3xy$.

$= 3xy[x^2 - (2y)^2]$ Write each term in the brackets as a perfect square.

$= 3xy(x + 2y)(x - 2y)$ Use the difference of squares pattern.

The factored form of $3x^3y - 12xy^3$ is $3xy(x + 2y)(x - 2y)$.

Try It! **4.** Factor each expression completely.

a. $4x^3 + 24x^2 + 36x$

b. $50x^2 - 32y^2$

CONCEPT SUMMARY Factoring Special Cases of Polynomials

	Factoring a Perfect-Square Trinomial	Factoring a Difference of Two Squares
ALGEBRA	$a^2 + 2ab + b^2 = (a + b)^2$ $a^2 - 2ab + b^2 = (a - b)^2$	$a^2 - b^2 = (a + b)(a - b)$
WORDS	Use this pattern when the first and last terms are perfect squares and the middle term is twice the product of the expressions being squared.	Use this pattern when a binomial can be written as a difference of two squares. Both terms must be perfect squares.
NUMBERS	$x^2 + 16x + 64 = x^2 + 2(8)x + 8^2$ $= (x + 8)^2$ $x^2 - 16x + 64 = x^2 - 2(8)x + 8^2$ $= (x - 8)^2$	$x^2 - 36 = x^2 - 6^2$ $= (x + 6)(x - 6)$ $2x^2 - 72 = 2(x^2 - 36)$ $= 2(x^2 - 6^2)$ $= 2(x + 6)(x - 6)$

Do You UNDERSTAND?

1. ESSENTIAL QUESTION What special patterns are helpful when factoring a perfect-square trinomial and the difference of two squares?

2. **Error Analysis** A student says that to factor $x^2 - 4x + 2$, you should use the pattern of a difference of two squares. Explain the error in the student's thinking.

3. **Vocabulary** How is a perfect square trinomial similar to a perfect square number? Is it possible to have a perfect square binomial? Explain.

4. **Communicate Precisely** How is the pattern for factoring a perfect-square trinomial like the pattern for factoring the difference of two squares? How is it different?

5. **Construct Arguments** Why is it important to look for a common factor before factoring a trinomial?

Do You KNOW HOW?

Identify the pattern you can use to factor each expression.

6. $4x^2 - 9$
7. $x^2 + 6x + 9$
8. $9x^2 - 12x + 4$
9. $5x^2 - 30x + 45$
10. $100 - 16y^2$
11. $3x^2 + 30x + 75$

Write the factored form of each expression.

12. $49x^2 - 25$
13. $36x^2 + 48x + 16$
14. $3x^3 - 12x^2 + 12x$
15. $72x^2 - 32$

16. What is the side length of the square shown below?

Area = $x^2 + 22x + 121$

PRACTICE & PROBLEM SOLVING

Scan for Multimedia

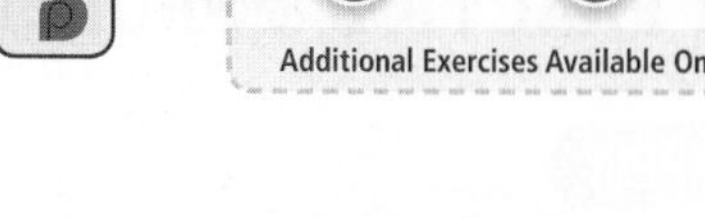

UNDERSTAND

17. **Mathematical Connections** How could you use special factoring patterns to quickly rewrite the difference $50^2 - 45^2$ as a product? Explain.

18. **Reason** Is the expression $x^2 - 50$ factorable? Explain why or why not.

19. **Look for Relationships** What is the completely factored form of the expression $16x^4 - y^4$? Describe the method(s) of factoring you used.

20. **Error Analysis** Describe and correct the error a student made in factoring $x^2 - 36$.

Use the perfect-square trinomial pattern to factor $x^2 - 36$ because both terms are perfect squares.

$x^2 - 36 = (x - 6)(x - 6)$ 

21. **Higher Order Thinking** Use the visual shown as a starting point. Describe how you can use diagrams to show that $a^2 - b^2 = (a + b)(a - b)$.

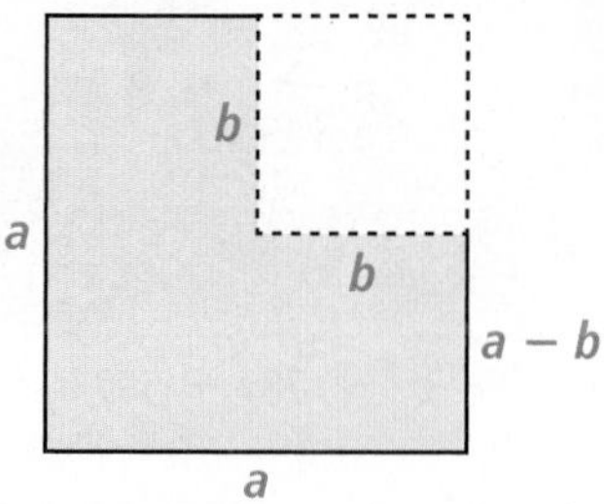

22. **Make Sense and Persevere** Describe the steps you would use to factor the expression $x^4 - 8x^2 + 16$.

23. **Reason** A rectangle has a width that is twice the length. If the area of the rectangle is represented by the expression $18x^2 + 48x + 32$, what expression represents the length of the rectangle? Explain.

24. **Communicate Precisely** How can you determine if a binomial of the form $x^2 - \frac{a}{b}$ is factorable using rational constants?

PRACTICE

Identify the value of *c* that would make the trinomial factorable using the perfect-square pattern. SEE EXAMPLE 1

25. $x^2 + 24x + c$

26. $x^2 - 10x + c$

27. $6x^2 - 36x + c$

28. $3x^2 + 24x + c$

Given the area of each square, factor to find the side length. SEE EXAMPLES 1 AND 2

29. Area $= 36x^2 + 120x + 100$

30. Area $= 144x^2 - 24x + 1$

Factor each expression completely.
SEE EXAMPLES 1, 3, and 4

31. $x^2 + 16x + 64$

32. $x^2 - 25$

33. $x^2 - 18x + 81$

34. $x^2 - 14x + 49$

35. $100x^2 - 36$

36. $16x^2 + 40x + 25$

37. $8x^2 - 32x + 32$

38. $16x^2 - 81y^2$

39. $2x^3 + 32x^2 + 128x$

40. $7x^3y - 63xy^3$

41. $49x^3 - 16xy^2$

42. $121x^2 + 110x + 25$

43. $-3x^3 + 18x^2 - 27x$

44. $64x^2y^2 - 144z^2$

Factor each expression as the product of binomials.

45. $x^2 - \frac{1}{4}$

46. $x^2 - \frac{1}{9}$

47. $p^2 - \frac{49}{100}$

48. $x^2 + x + \frac{1}{4}$

PRACTICE & PROBLEM SOLVING

Practice Tutorial

Mixed Review Available Online

APPLY

49. **Reason** In front of a school are several gardens in rectangular raised beds. For each of the areas of a rectangular garden given, use factoring to find possible dimensions. Could the garden be square? If so, explain why.

    a. $x^2 + 32x + 256$

    b. $x^2 - 4y^2$

    c. $x^2 - 20x + 100$

50. **Make Sense and Persevere** The area of a rectangular rug is $49x^2 - 25y^2$ in.^{2}. Use factoring to find possible dimensions of the rug. How are the side lengths related? What value would you need to subtract from the longer side and add to the shorter side for the rug to be a square?

51. **Model With Mathematics** A furniture company created an L-shaped table by removing part of a square table.

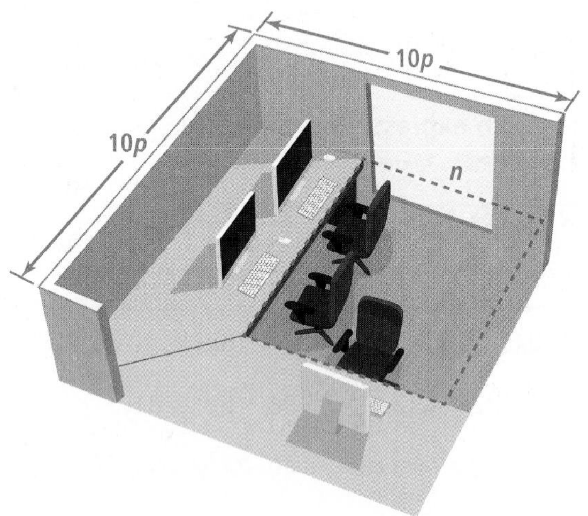

    a. Write an expression that represents the area of the L-shaped table.

    b. What are all the side lengths of the L-shaped table?

    c. The furniture company decides to create another table with the same area, but needs this table to be rectangular. What are the possible dimensions of the rectangular table? Explain.

ASSESSMENT PRACTICE

52. Match each expression with its factored form.

I.	$25m^2 - 9n^2$	A.	$(5m + 3n)^2$
II.	$25m^2 - 30mn + 9n^2$	B.	$(5m - 3n)^2$
III.	$25m^2 - 30mn - 9n^2$	C.	$(5m + 3n)(5m - 3n)$
IV.	$25m^2 + 30mn + 9n^2$	D.	does not factor

53. **SAT/ACT** What is the factored form of $6x^2 - 60x + 150$?

    Ⓐ $6(x - 25)^2$

    Ⓑ $6(x - 5)(x - 10)$

    Ⓒ $6(x - 5)^2$

    Ⓓ $6(x - 5)(x + 5)$

54. **Performance Task** Two pieces of fabric are being used for clothing designs for a fashion show at school Expressions for the areas of the rectangular pieces are shown.

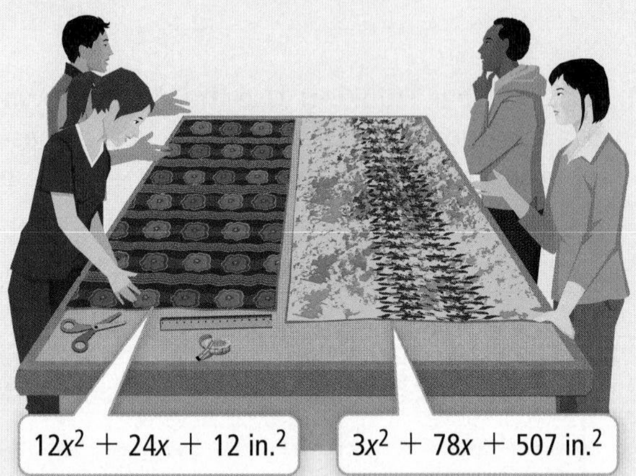

Part A Factor the expressions for the areas completely.

Part B Using the factorings from Part A, write all of the possible dimensions of the pieces of fabric as binomials with integer coefficients.

Part C Assume that the table is about 6 ft long. Using integer values for x, which set of binomials yields to most reasonable dimensions based on the picture?

Part D Using your result from Part C what are the dimensions in inches of the two pieces of fabric?

TOPIC 7

Topic Review

TOPIC ESSENTIAL QUESTION

1. How do you work with polynomials to rewrite expressions and solve problems?

Vocabulary Review

Choose the correct term to complete each sentence.

2. The __________ states that polynomials are closed under addition or subtraction because the result of these operations is another polynomial.
3. A(n) __________ results when a binomial is squared.
4. A(n) __________ is a real number, a variable, or the product of a real number and one or more variables with whole number exponents.
5. The product of two binomials in the form $(a + b)(a - b)$ is $a^2 - b^2$, which is called the __________.
6. The __________ is a an expression in which the terms are written in descending order according to their degree.

- Closure Property
- degree of a monomial
- degree of a polynomial
- difference of two squares
- monomial
- perfect-square trinomial
- polynomial
- standard form of a polynomial

Concepts & Skills Review

LESSON 7-1 Adding and Subtracting Polynomials

Quick Review

A **polynomial** is a monomial or the sum or difference of two or more monomials, called terms. Polynomials are named according to their degree. The **degree of a polynomial** is the greatest degree of any term of the polynomial. The **standard form of a polynomial** is a polynomial in which terms are written in descending order according to their degree.

Example

What is the difference $(5x^2 + 3x - 5) - (2x^2 + 8)$?

$(5x^2 + 3x - 5) - (2x^2 + 8)$

$= 5x^2 + 3x - 5 - 2x^2 - 8$ ······ Apply subtraction to each term in the second expression.

$= (5x^2 - 2x^2) + (3x) + (-5 - 8)$ ······ Use the Commutative and Associative Properties to group like terms.

$= 3x^2 + 3x - 13$ ······ Simplify.

The difference is $3x^2 + 3x - 13$.

Practice & Problem Solving

Name each monomial based on its degree.

7. $2xy$
8. -6
9. $3x^2y$

Add or subtract to simplify each expression. Write your final answer in standard form.

10. $(5x - 1) + (2x - 3)$
11. $(2x^2 - 4x - 1) - (3x^2 + 8x - 4)$
12. $(5b^4 - 2 + 3b^2) + (5b^2 - 4 + 3b^4)$
13. **Reason** What is the missing term in the equation? $(\_\_ + 5) + (3x - 2) = 8x + 3$. Explain.
14. **Make Sense and Persevere** A garden center has $(3x^2 + 12x + 18)$ sq. ft of sod. One week, they receive $(4x^2 + 16x + 60)$ sq. ft of sod, and sell $(2x^2 + 9x + 27)$ sq. ft of sod. What expression represents the area of the remaining sod?

LESSON 7-2 Multiplying Polynomials

Quick Review

Use the Distributive Property to multiply polynomials as you would when multiplying integers numbers. Distribute the first polynomial to each term in the second polynomial.

Example

How can you use the Distributive Property to rewrite $(3x - 5)(4x - 9)$ as a polynomial?

Distribute the first binomial to each term in the second binomial.

$(3x - 5)(4x - 9)$

$= 3x(4x - 9) - 5(4x - 9)$ ········ Distribute $3x$ and -5 to the second binomial.

$= 3x(4x) + 3x(-9) - 5(4x) - 5(-9)$ ········ Distribute $3x$ and -5 to each term in the second binomial.

$= 12x^2 - 27x - 20x + 45$ ········ Multiply.

$= 12x^2 - 47x + 45$ ········ Combine like terms.

The product is $12x^2 - 47x + 45$.

Practice & Problem Solving

Use the Distributive Property to find each product.

15. $(x + 7)(x - 5)$ **16.** $(2x - 5)(3x + 1)$

Use a table to find each product.

17. $(4x - 3y)(5x + y)$ **18.** $(x + 4)(x^2 - 3x - 1)$

19. **Make Sense and Persevere** Identify the missing terms in the quotient and divisor.

$(\_\_\_ + 3)(x + \_\_\_) = x^2 + 11x + 24$

20. **Model With Mathematics** The volume of a cube is calculated by multiplying the length, width and height. What is the volume of this cube in standard form?

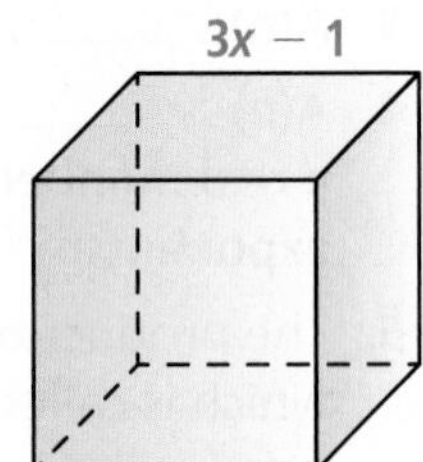

LESSON 7-3 Multiplying Special Cases

Quick Review

The square of a binomial always follows the same pattern, $a^2 + 2ab + b^2$. The product of two binomials in the form $(a + b)(a - b)$ is $a^2 - b^2$. This is called the **difference of two squares**.

Example

What is the product $(4x - 9)(4x + 9)$?

Use the pattern.

$(4x - 9)(4x + 9)$

$= (4x)^2 - (9)^2$ ········ Substitute $4x$ and 9 and for a and b in $a^2 - b^2$.

$= 16x^2 - 81$ ········ Simplify.

The product is $16x^2 - 81$.

Practice & Problem Solving

Write each product in standard form.

21. $(b + 12)(b + 12)$ **22.** $(4x + 1)(4x + 1)$

23. $(6x - 9)(6x + 9)$ **24.** $(3x - 4y)(3x + 4y)$

25. $(1.5x + 2)(1.5x - 2)$ **26.** $(3a - 5b)^2$

27. **Look for Relationships** Find a value for m to make a true statement.

$mx^2 - 64 = (5x + 8)(5x - 8)$

28. **Modeling With Mathematics** Write polynomials in standard form to represent the surface area and volume of the cube.

5x − 2 ft

LESSON 7-4 Factoring Polynomials

Quick Review

To factor a common monomial factor out of a polynomial, first write the prime factorization of the coefficient for each term to determine if there is a greatest common factor other than 1. Then determine the greatest common factor for the variables of each term.

Example

What is the GCF of the terms of $16x^6 - 8x^4 + 4x^3$?

First, write the prime factorization of the coefficients for each term.

$16 = 2 \cdot 2 \cdot 2 \cdot 2$
$8 = 2 \cdot 2 \cdot 2$
$4 = 2 \cdot 2$

Each number has a common coefficient of 4, so the GCF of the coefficients is 4.

Next, determine the GCF of the variables for each term.

$x^6 = x \cdot x \cdot x \cdot x \cdot x \cdot x$
$x^4 = x \cdot x \cdot x \cdot x$
$x^3 = x \cdot x \cdot x$

Each term has the common factor of x^3, so the GCF of the variables is x^3.

The GCF of $16x^6 - 8x^4 + 4x^3$ is $4x^3$.

Practice & Problem Solving

Find the GCF of each group of monomials.

29. $6x^2$, $21x$

30. bc^2, b^3c

31. $14x^2y^2$, $84x^3y^5$, $21xy^3$

32. $24a^2$, 18

Factor out the GCF from each polynomial.

33. $15x^3 - 42x$

34. $6y^5 - 42y^3 + 18y$

35. $12a^3 + 18a^2 - 36a$

36. $49a^5b^3 - 14a^2b^2 + 35ab$

37. **Look for Relationships** Write a trinomial that has a GCF of $3x$.

38. **Use Structure** Determine the GCF and write the expression in factored form.

$(8x^2 - 12x) + (6x^2 - 4x)$

LESSON 7-5 Factoring $x^2 + bx + c$

Quick Review

To factor $x^2 + bx + c$, find the factor pair of c that has a sum of b. Then use those factors to write the binomial factors of the trinomial.

Example

What is the factored form of $x^2 - 9x + 14$?

Identify a factor pair of 14 that has a sum of –9.

Factors of 14	Sum of Factors
–1 and –14	–15
–2 and –7	–9

The factored form of $x^2 - 9x + 14$ is $(x - 2)(x - 7)$.

Practice & Problem Solving

Complete the table to factor the trinomial

39. $x^2 + 7x - 18$

Factors of c	Sum of Factors
■	■
■	■
■	7

Write the factored form of each trinomial.

40. $x^2 + 12x + 32$

41. $x^2 + 3x - 28$

42. $x^2 - 13x - 48$

43. $x^2 + 18xy + 45y^2$

44. **Look for Relationships** How are the binomial factors of $x^2 + 4x - 21$ and $x^2 - 4x - 21$ similar? How are they different?

TOPIC 7 REVIEW

Factoring $ax^2 + bx + c$

Quick Review

To factor a trinomial of the form $ax^2 + bx + c$, find the factor pair of ac that has a sum of b. Then use the factors you found to write the binomials that have a product equal to the trinomial.

Example

What is the factored form of $2x^2 + 9x - 5$?

For the trinomial $2x^2 + 9x - 5$, $a = 2$ and $c = -5$, so $ac = -10$. Find the factor pair of -10 that has a sum of 9.

Factors of −10	Sum of Factors
−2 and 5	3
2 and −5	−3
−1 and 10	9

Since −1 and 10 are the correct factor pair, rewrite $9x$ as $-1x$ and $10x$.

$2x^2 + 9x - 5$

$= 2x^2 + 10x - 1x - 5$ ········ Rewrite.

$= (2x^2 + 10x) + (-1x - 5)$ ···· Group as two binomials.

$= 2x(x + 5) - 1(x + 5)$ ········ Factor out the GCFs.

$= (2x - 1)(x + 5)$ ·············· Distributive Property

The factored form of $2x^2 + 9x - 5$ is $(2x - 1)(x + 5)$.

Practice & Problem Solving

Identify all of the factor pairs of *ac* you could use to rewrite *b* in order to factor each trinomial by grouping.

45. $5x^2 + 9x + 4$

46. $2x^2 + x - 15$

Write the factored form of each trinomial.

47. $3x^2 + 10x + 8$

48. $4x^2 - 3x - 10$

49. $5x^2 + 7x - 6$

50. $6x^2 + 13x + 6$

51. $10x^2 + 3x - 4$

52. $12x^2 + 22x + 6$

53. Make Sense and Persevere What are all the possible values of b for which $3x^2 + bx - 8$ is factorable using only integer coefficients and constants?

54. Reason A parking lot has an area of $2x^2 + 9x - 5$ square meters. Use factoring to find possible dimensions of the parking lot. The parking lot is to be enlarged so that each dimension is 5 meters greater than it was originally. What are the new dimensions of the parking lot? What is the new area of the parking lot?

LESSON 7-7 Factoring Special Cases

Quick Review

A **perfect-square trinomial** results when a binomial is squared.

Factor a perfect-square trinomial:

$a^2 + 2ab + b^2 = (a + b)^2$

$a^2 - 2ab + b^2 = (a - b)^2$

Use these patterns when the first and last terms are perfect squares and the middle term is twice the product of the numbers being squared.

Factor a difference of two squares:

$a^2 - b^2 = (a + b)(a - b)$

Use this pattern when a binomial can be written as a difference of two squares.

Example

What is the factored form of $9x^2 - 121$?

Write the first and last term as a perfect square.

$$
\begin{aligned}
9x^2 - 121 &= (3x)^2 - 11^2 \\
&= (3x - 11)(3x + 11)
\end{aligned}
$$

Practice & Problem Solving

Identify the value of *c* that would make each trinomial factorable using the perfect-square pattern.

55. $x^2 + 16x + c$

56. $2x^2 - 28x + c$

Write the factored form of each expression.

57. $x^2 + 10x + 25$

58. $x^2 - 121$

59. $x^2 - 18x + 81$

60. $9x^2 - 49y^2$

61. $3x^2 + 18x + 27$

62. $4x^2 - 56x + 196$

63. **Reason** Is the expression $3x^2 - 49$ factorable using only integer coefficients and constants? Explain why or why not.

64. **Make Sense and Persevere** The area of a playground is $36x^2 - 16y^2$ square feet. Without removing common factors, factor to find possible dimensions of the playground. How are the side lengths related? What value would you need to subtract from the longer side and add to the shorter side for the playground to be a square?

TOPIC

8

Quadratic Functions

? TOPIC ESSENTIAL QUESTION

How can you use sketches and equations of quadratic functions to model situations and make predictions?

Topic Overview

enVision™ STEM Project:
Make Business Decisions

8-1 Key Features of a Quadratic Function

8-2 Quadratic Functions in Vertex Form

8-3 Quadratic Functions in Standard Form

8-4 Modeling With Quadratic Functions

Mathematical Modeling in 3 Acts:
The Long Shot

8-5 Linear, Exponential, and Quadratic Models

Topic Vocabulary

- parabola
- quadratic parent function
- quadratic regression
- standard form of a quadratic function
- vertex form of a quadratic function
- vertical motion model

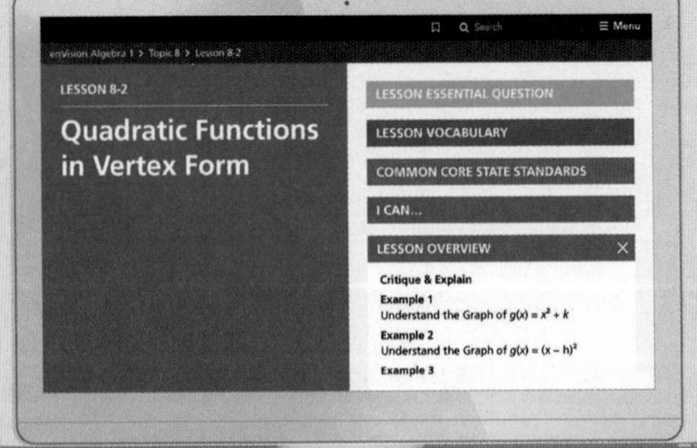

Go online | **PearsonRealize.com**

Digital Experience

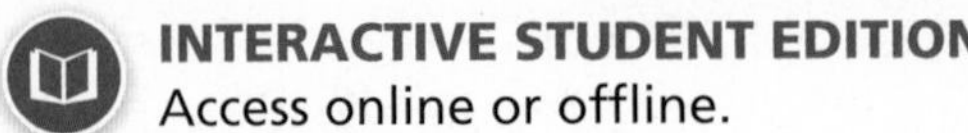
INTERACTIVE STUDENT EDITION Access online or offline.

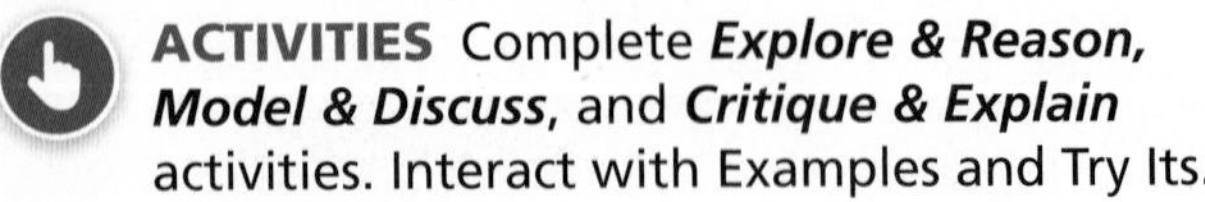
ACTIVITIES Complete ***Explore & Reason, Model & Discuss***, and ***Critique & Explain*** activities. Interact with Examples and Try Its.

ANIMATION View and interact with real-world applications.

PRACTICE Practice what you've learned.

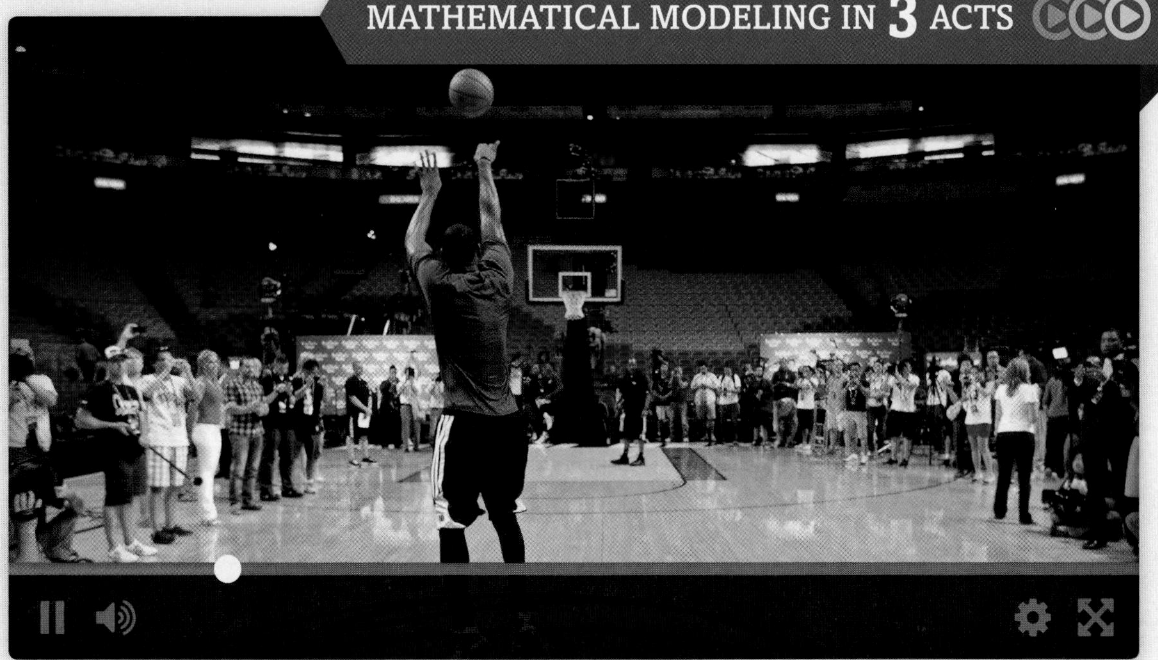

The Long Shot

Have you ever been to a basketball game where they hold contests at halftime? A popular contest is one where the contestant needs to make a basket from half court to win a prize. Contestants often shoot the ball in different ways. They might take a regular basketball shot, a hook shot, or an underhand toss.

What's the best way to shoot the basketball and make a basket? In the Mathematical Modeling in 3 Acts lesson, you decide!

VIDEOS Watch clips to support ***Mathematical Modeling in 3 Acts Lessons*** and **enVision™** ***STEM Projects.***

CONCEPT SUMMARY Review key lesson content through multiple representations.

ASSESSMENT Show what you've learned.

GLOSSARY Read and listen to English and Spanish definitions.

TUTORIALS Get help from *Virtual Nerd*, right when you need it.

MATH TOOLS Explore math with digital tools and manipulatives.

Did You Know?

The goal of a business owner is to maximize profits. Businesses have to consider many things to set the best price for their products.

A typical small business has a net profit margin of around 10%. This means 90% of its revenue is spent on costs, such as rent, labor, and raw materials.

The day after Thanksgiving is known as Black Friday because that is the day many retailers begin to turn a profit for the year. Being "in the black" is an accounting term for "making a profit."

Market equilibrium is when supply = demand.

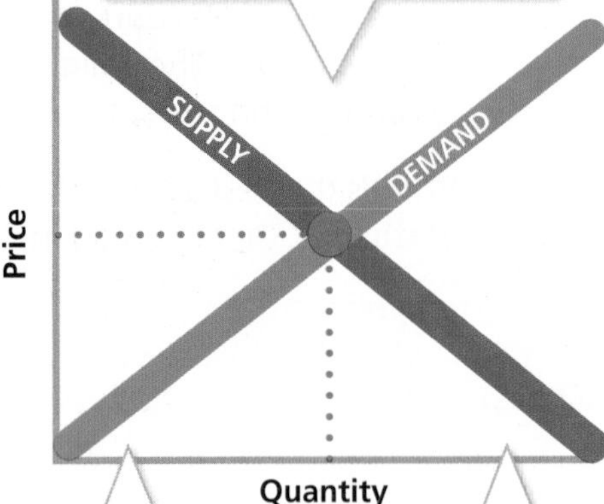

Demand is how much of a product people want to buy. The higher the demand, the higher producers can price the product.

Supply is how much of a product is available. The higher the supply, the lower the price producers can charge.

Your Task: Make Business Decisions

You and your classmates will pick an industry, then suggest and defend your choice of the number of an item to make and the price at which to sell the item.

Activity Assess

8-1 Key Features of a Quadratic Function

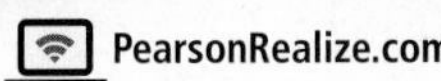

I CAN... identify key features of the graph of the quadratic parent function.

VOCABULARY

- parabola
- quadratic parent function

EXPLORE & REASON

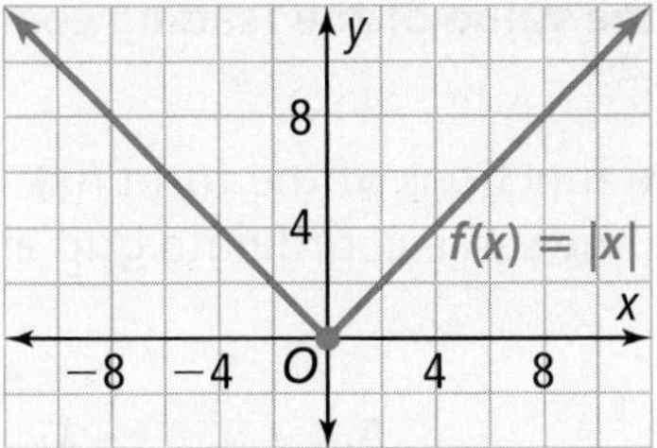

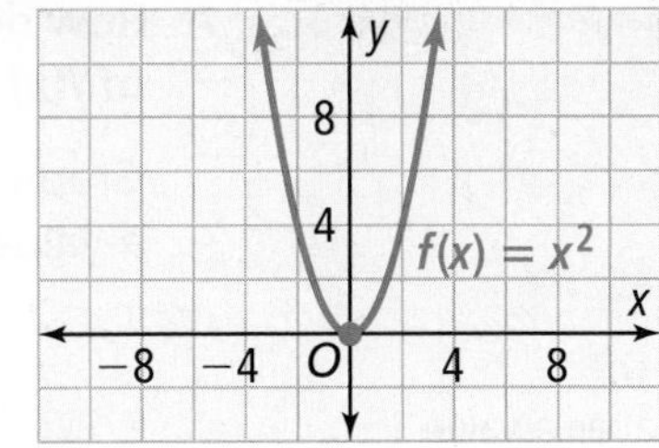

A. Look for Relationships How is the graph of $f(x) = |x|$ similar to the graph of $f(x) = x^2$? How is it different?

B. What do you notice about the axis of symmetry in each graph?

ESSENTIAL QUESTION

What is the quadratic parent function and how can you recognize the key features of its graph?

EXAMPLE 1 Identify a Quadratic Parent Function

What is a quadratic parent function and what are its characteristics?

The **quadratic parent function** is $f(x) = x^2$. It is the simplest function in the quadratic function family. The graph of the function is a curve called a **parabola**.

x	$f(x) = x^2$	(x, y)
−2	4	(−2, 4)
−1	1	(−1, 1)
0	0	(0, 0)
1	1	(1, 1)
2	4	(2, 4)

The vertex is the lowest (or highest) point on the graph of a quadratic function.

The axis of symmetry is $x = 0$.

The parabola opens up.

The vertex is (0, 0). It is the turning point of the graph.

The axis of symmetry intersects the vertex, and divides the parabola in half.

LOOK FOR RELATIONSHIPS
Think about how the features of a quadratic function compare and contrast to those of a linear function.

Try It! 1. When are the values of $f(x)$ positive and when are they negative?

CONCEPTUAL UNDERSTANDING

EXAMPLE 2 Understand the Graph of $f(x) = ax^2$

A. How does the value of the leading coefficient, *a*, affect the graph of $f(x) = ax^2$?

Graph some functions of the form $f(x) = ax^2$ with different positive *a*-values on the same coordinate grid and compare them.

COMMON ERROR
You may think that an *a* value with an absolute value less than 1 would decrease the width of the parabola. However, it increases the width of the parabola.

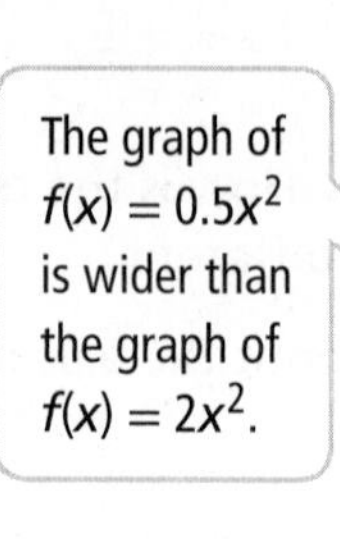

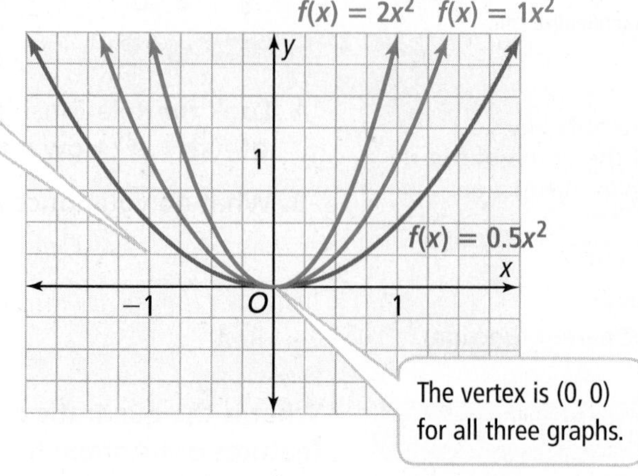

The vertex is (0, 0) for all three graphs.

For $0 < |a| < 1$, the shape of the parabola is wider than the parent function. For $|a| > 1$, the shape of the parabola is narrower than the parent function.

B. How does the sign of *a* affect the graph of $f(x) = ax^2$?

Graph two functions of the form $f(x) = ax^2$ with opposite *a*-values on the same coordinate grid, and compare them.

LOOK FOR RELATIONSHIPS
Consider whether the value of *a* has an effect on the location of the vertex of the graph of $f(x) = ax^2$.

When $a > 0$, the *y*-coordinate of the vertex is the minimum value of the function. When $a < 0$, it is the maximum.

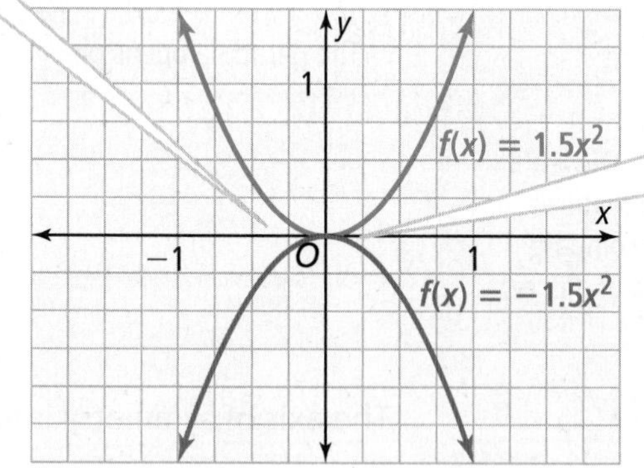

$f(x) = -ax^2$ is a reflection of $f(x) = ax^2$ over the *x*-axis.

When $a > 0$, the parabola opens upward.
When $a < 0$, the parabola opens downward.

 **Try It!** 2. How does the sign of *a* affect the domain and range of $f(x) = ax^2$?

EXAMPLE 3 Interpret Quadratic Functions from Tables

Over what interval is $f(x) = 4x^2$ increasing? Over what interval is it decreasing?

Use the function to make a table of values.

x	$f(x) = 4x^2$	(x, y)
−2	16	(−2, 16)
−1	4	(−1, 4)
0	0	(0, 0)
1	4	(1, 4)
2	16	(2, 16)

The function values are **decreasing**.

The vertex (0, 0) is the turning point of the function, where it changes from decreasing to increasing.

The function values are **increasing**.

STUDY TIP
Remember that since the function has a minimum value, the parabola opens upward. If the function has a maximum value, the parabola opens downward.

The function is decreasing over the interval $x < 0$ and increasing over the interval $x > 0$.

Try It! 3. A function of the form $g(x) = ax^2$ increases over the interval $x < 0$ and decreases over the interval $x > 0$. What is a possible value for a? Explain.

APPLICATION

EXAMPLE 4 Apply Quadratic Functions

The owner of a new dance studio is installing wooden floors in all of the dance rooms. How much should the owner expect to spend on flooring for a square room with 15-ft side lengths?

Write a function that can be used to determine the cost of the flooring.

$c(x) =$ price per ft^2 of flooring • area of dance floor in ft^2

$c(x) = 8.75 \cdot x^2$

Find the value of the function when $x = 15$.

$c(x) = 8.75x^2$

$c(15) = 8.75(15)^2$ .... Substitute 15 for x.

$c(15) = 1{,}968.75$ .... Simplify.

The cost for a new floor for a square dance floor with sides of 15 ft is \$1,968.75.

Try It! 4. By how much will the cost increase if the side length of the dance floor is increased by 2 ft?

EXAMPLE 5 Compare the Rate of Change

A. How do the average rates of change for $f(x) = 0.75x^2$ and $g(x) = 1.5x^2$ over the interval $2 \leq x \leq 4$ compare?

Step 1 Graph the two functions.

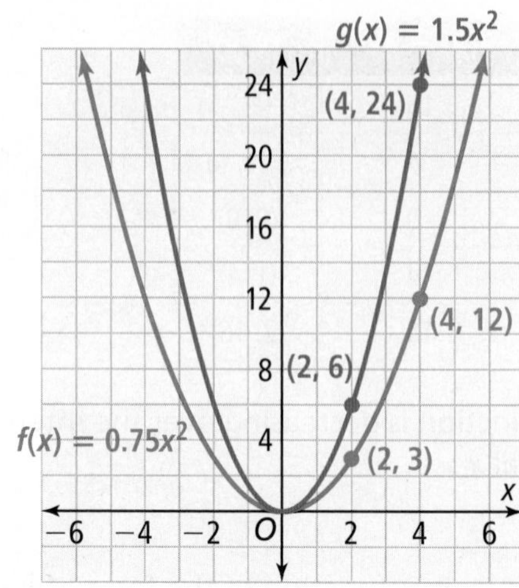

Step 2 Find the value of each function at the endpoints of the interval.

$f(2) = 0.75(2)^2 = 3$

$f(4) = 0.75(4)^2 = 12$

$g(2) = 1.5(2)^2 = 6$

$g(4) = 1.5(4)^2 = 24$

STUDY TIP
Use what you know about finding rates of change for linear functions. Think about the differences for quadratic functions.

Step 3 Find the slope of the line that passes through each pair of points.

$f(x)$: $\frac{12 - 3}{4 - 2} = \frac{9}{2} = 4.5$

$g(x)$: $\frac{24 - 6}{4 - 2} = \frac{18}{2} = 9$

The rate of change for function g is twice the rate of change for function f.

On average, the values of function f increase by 4.5 units and the values of function g increase by 9 units for each unit increase in x over the interval $2 \leq x \leq 4$.

B. How do the rates of change relate to the values of *a* in the functions?

For positive intervals, the greater the value of a, the greater the average rate of change. In this case the ratio of the a-values in the two functions is the same as the ratio of the average rates of change.

Try It! **5.** How do the average rates of change for $f(x) = -0.5x^2$ and $g(x) = -1.5x^2$ over the interval $-5 \leq x \leq -2$ compare?

CONCEPT SUMMARY Features of the Quadratic Function $f(x) = ax^2$

$f(x) = x^2$	$f(x) = ax^2$

GRAPHS

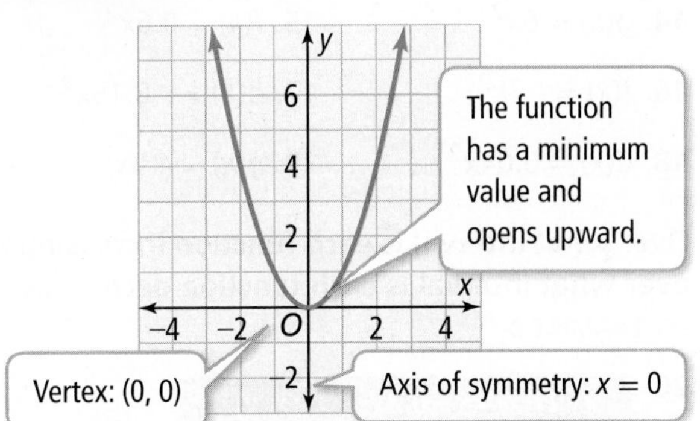

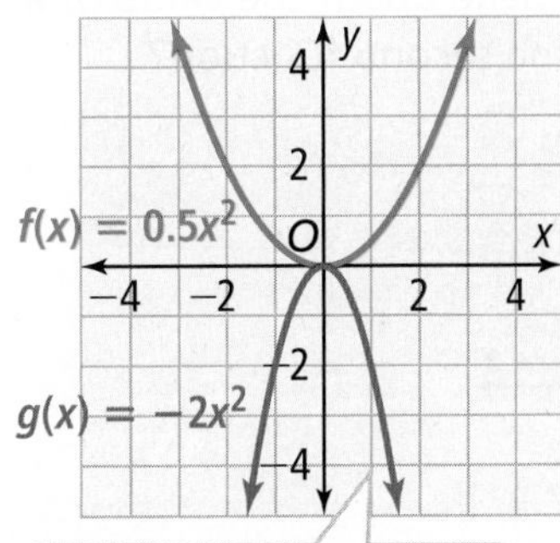

When $a < 0$, the parabola opens downward.

WORDS

The function $f(x) = x^2$ is the same as $f(x) = 1x^2$. It is the quadratic parent function. The function decreases over the interval $x < 0$ and increases over the interval $x > 0$.

When $0 < |a| < 1$, the graph of $f(x) = ax^2$ is wider than the graph of $f(x) = x^2$. When $|a| > 1$, graph of $f(x) = ax^2$ is narrower than the graph of $f(x) = x^2$.

Do You UNDERSTAND?

1. **ESSENTIAL QUESTION** What is the quadratic parent function and how can you recognize the key features of its graph?
2. **Communicate Precisely** How is the graph of $f(x) = ax^2$ similar to the graph of $f(x) = x^2$? How is it different?
3. **Vocabulary** Make a conjecture about why the term *quadratic parent function* includes the word "parent."
4. **Error Analysis** Abby graphed the function $f(x) = -13x^2$ by plotting the point $(-2, 52)$. Explain the error Abby made in her graph.

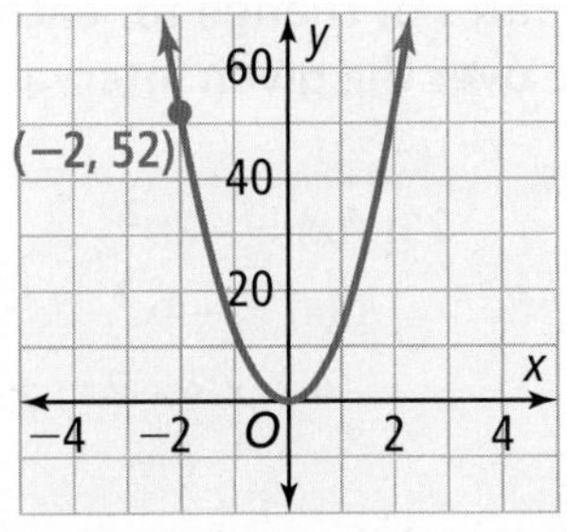

Do You KNOW HOW?

How does the value of a in each function affect its graph when compared to the graph of the quadratic parent function?

5. $g(x) = 4x^2$
6. $h(x) = 0.8x^2$
7. $j(x) = -5x^2$
8. $k(x) = -0.4x^2$
9. Given the function $f(x) = 2.5x^2 + 3$, find the average rate of change over the interval $0 \leq x \leq 4$. What does the average rate of change tell you about the function?

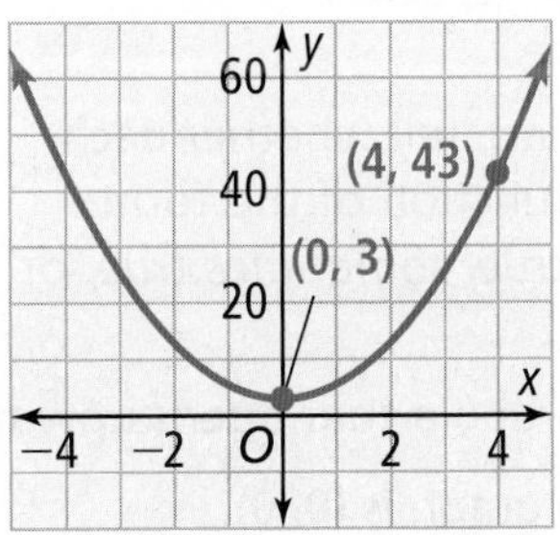

PRACTICE & PROBLEM SOLVING

Scan for Multimedia

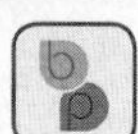

Additional Exercises Available Online

UNDERSTAND

10. Generalize The graph of the parent quadratic function $f(x) = x^2$ and that of a second function of the form $g(x) = ax^2$ are shown. What conclusion can you make about the value of a in the equation of the second function?

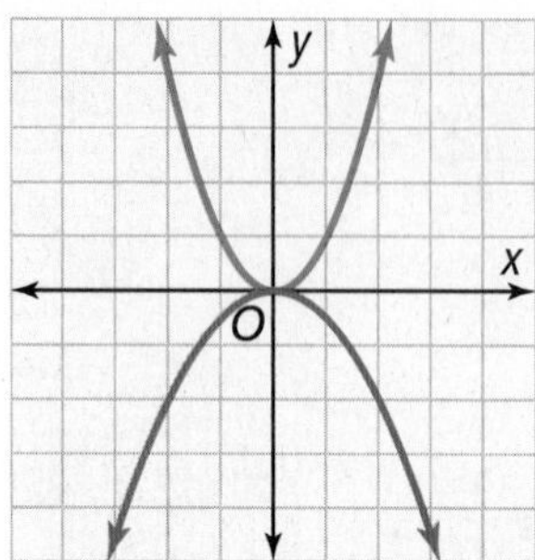

11. Error Analysis Describe and correct the error a student made in finding the average rate of change for $f(x) = 0.5x^2$ over the interval $-4 \le x \le -2$.

Find the slope of the line that passes through (-4, -8) and (-2, -2).

$\frac{-2-(-8)}{-2-(-4)} = \frac{6}{2} = 3$ ✗

12. Use Structure Use the table shown below to describe the intervals over which $f(x) = 15x^2$ is increasing and decreasing.

x	$f(x) = 15x^2$	(x, y)
−2	60	(−2, 60)
−1	15	(−1, 15)
0	0	(0, 0)
1	15	(1, 15)
2	60	(2, 60)

13. Higher Order Thinking Tell whether each statement about a function of the form $f(x) = ax^2$ is *always true, sometimes true*, or *never true*.

a. The graph is a parabola that opens upward.

b. The vertex of the graph is (0, 0).

c. The axis of symmetry of the graph is $x = 0$.

PRACTICE

How does the value of a in each function affect its graph when compared to the graph of the quadratic parent function? SEE EXAMPLES 1 AND 2

14. $g(x) = 6x^2$

15. $f(x) = 0.6x^2$

16. $f(x) = -7x^2$

17. $h(x) = -0.15x^2$

18. $C(x) = 0.04x^2$

19. $g(x) = 4.5x^2$

Over what interval is each function increasing and over what interval is each function decreasing? SEE EXAMPLE 3

20.

x	$f(x) = -0.3x^2$	(x, y)
−2	−1.2	(−2, −1.2)
−1	−0.3	(−1, −0.3)
0	0	(0, 0)
1	−0.3	(1, −0.3)
2	−1.2	(2, −1.2)

21.

x	$f(x) = 13x^2$	(x, y)
−2	52	(−2, 52)
−1	13	(−1, 13)
0	0	(0, 0)
1	13	(1, 13)
2	52	(2, 52)

Write a quadratic function for the area of each figure. Then find the area for the given value of x. SEE EXAMPLE 4

22. $x = 13$

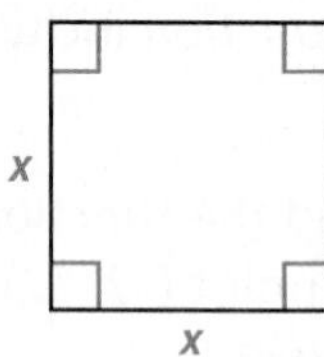

23. $x = 2.5$

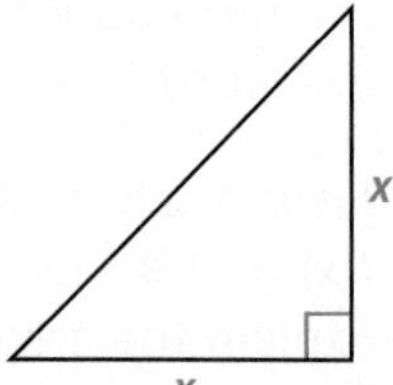

How do the average rates of change for each pair of functions compare over the given interval? SEE EXAMPLE 5

24. $f(x) = 0.1x^2$
$g(x) = 0.3x^2$
$1 \le x \le 4$

25. $f(x) = -2x^2$
$g(x) = -4x^2$
$-4 \le x \le -2$

PRACTICE & PROBLEM SOLVING

APPLY

26. Reason Some students can plant 9 carrots per square foot in the community garden shown. Write a function f that can be used to determine the number of carrots the students can plant. Give a reasonable domain for the function. How many carrots can the students plant in a garden that is square with 4-ft side lengths?

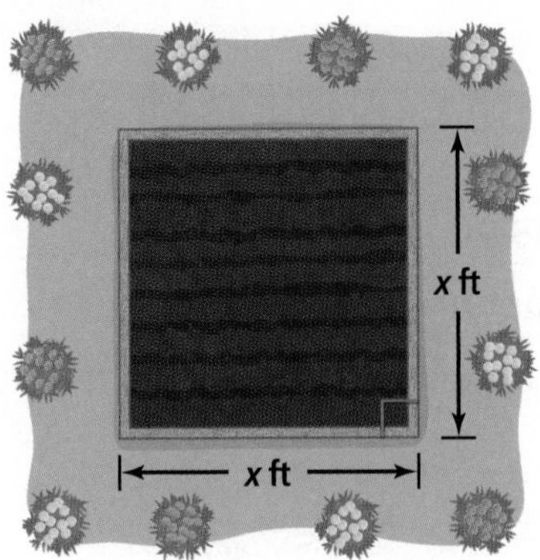

27. Make Sense and Persevere A burrito company uses the function $C(x) = 1.74x^2$ to calculate the number of calories in a tortilla with a diameter of x inches.

a. Find the average rates of change for the function over the intervals $6 < x < 8$ and $9 < x < 11$.

b. Interpret the average rates of change.

c. What does the difference in the average rates of change mean in terms of the situation?

28. Reason An architect uses a computer program to design a skateboard ramp. The function $f(x) = ax^2$ represents the shape of the ramp's cross section. A portion of the design is shown. The scale of each axis is 1 unit per grid line. On the ramp, a person can skateboard from point A through point B and over to a point C. If point C is the same distance above the x-axis as point B, what are its coordinates? Explain.

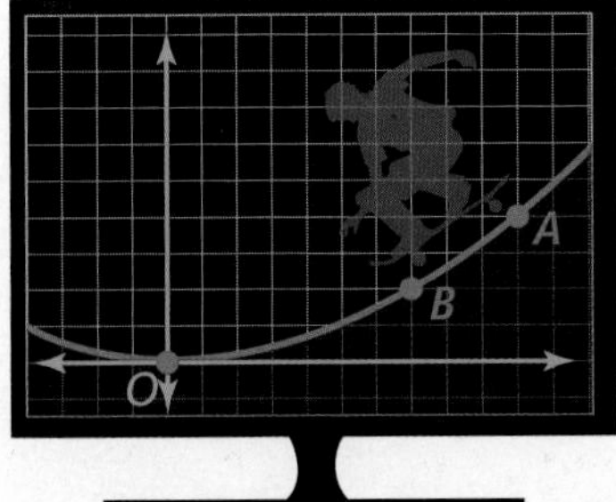

ASSESSMENT PRACTICE

29. The total cost, in dollars, of a square carpet can be determined by using $f(x) = 15x^2$, where x is the side length in yards. Which of the following are true? Select all that apply.

Ⓐ The cost of a carpet increases and then decreases as the side length increases.

Ⓑ The cost of the carpet is \$15 per square yard.

Ⓒ The cost of a carpet with a side length of 3 yd is \$135.

Ⓓ The cost of a carpet with 6-yd sides is twice the cost of a carpet with 3-yd sides.

Ⓔ The cost of a carpet increases at a constant rate as the side length increases.

30. SAT/ACT The graph of $f(x) = ax^2$ opens downward and is narrower than the graph of the quadratic parent function. Which of the following could be the value of a?

Ⓐ −2 Ⓑ −0.5 Ⓒ 0.5 Ⓓ 1 Ⓔ 2

31. Performance Task A manufacturer has two options for making cube-shaped boxes. The cost is calculated by multiplying the surface area of the box by the cost per square inch of the cardboard.

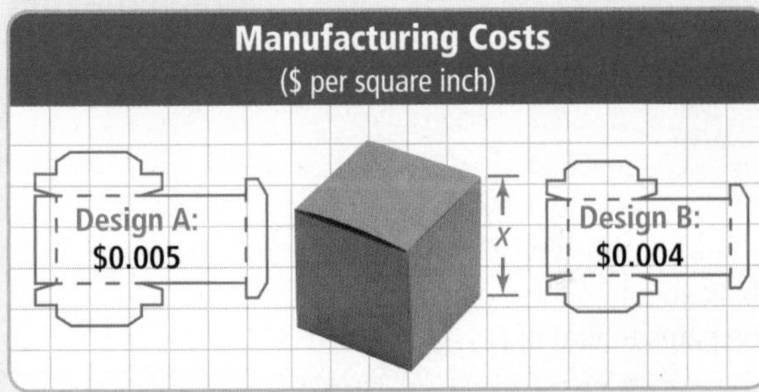

Part A Write a quadratic function of the form $f(x) = ax^2$ for each design that can be used to determine the total cardboard cost for cubes with any side length. Interpret the value of a in each function.

Part B How do the average rates of change for the designs compare for cubes with side lengths greater than 6 in., but less than 8 in.?

Part C Make a conjecture about the packaging costs for each design when the side length of the cube is greater than 36 in. Explain your conjecture.

8-2 Quadratic Functions in Vertex Form

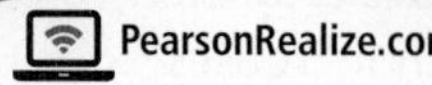

I CAN... graph quadratic functions using the vertex form.

VOCABULARY

- vertex form of a quadratic function

CRITIQUE & EXPLAIN

Allie states that the two graphs shown may look different, but they are actually the same figure. Esteban disagrees, stating that they are different figures because they look different.

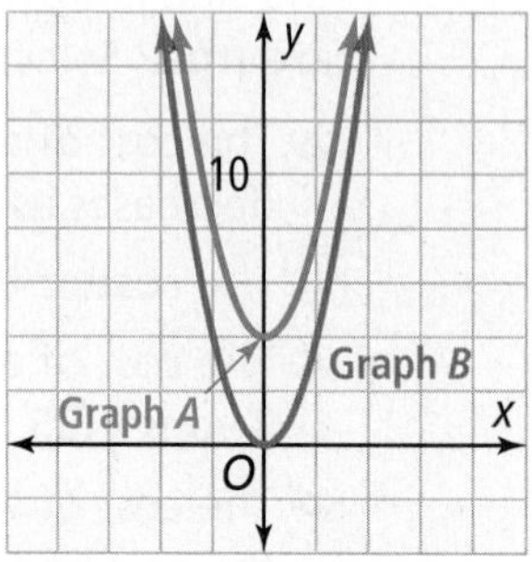

A. Give one mathematical argument to support Esteban's thinking.

B. Give one mathematical argument to support Allie's thinking.

C. Reason Who do you agree with? What argument can you give to justify your reasoning?

ESSENTIAL QUESTION

How can the vertex form of a quadratic function help you sketch the graph of the function?

EXAMPLE 1 Understand the Graph of $g(x) = x^2 + k$

How does the graph of $g(x) = x^2 - 4$ compare to that of $f(x) = x^2$?

Graph the function g and the parent function f.

LOOK FOR RELATIONSHIPS
Think about how the graph of g compares to that of f.

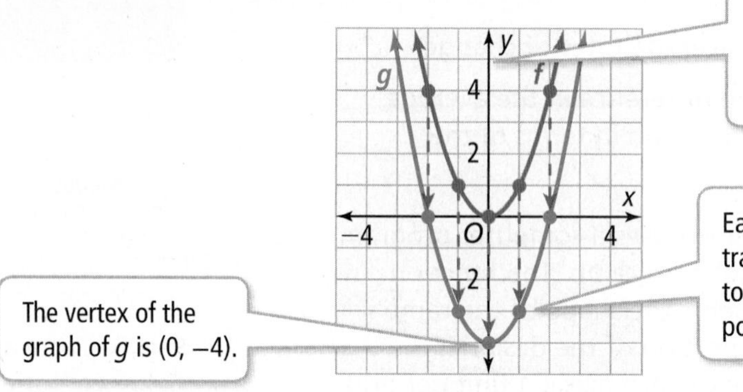

The value of k in $g(x) = x^2 + k$ translates the graph of the parent function f, vertically k units. The vertex of the graph of g is at $(0, k)$, in this case $(0, -4)$. The value of k does not affect the axis of symmetry.

Try It! **1.** How does the graph of each function compare to the graph of $f(x) = x^2$?

a. $h(x) = x^2 + 3$ **b.** $j(x) = x^2 - 2$

EXAMPLE 2 Understand the Graph of $g(x) = (x - h)^2$

How does the graph of $g(x) = (x - 3)^2$ compare to that of $f(x) = x^2$?

Graph the function g and the parent function f.

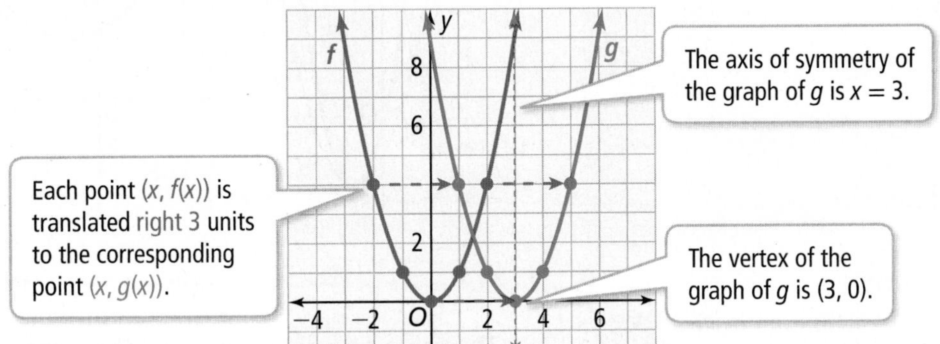

COMMON ERROR
You may think that the graph of $g(x) = (x - 3)^2$ would be a horizontal translation of the graph of $f(x) = x^2$ to the left in the negative direction along the x-axis. However, the translation is to the right in the positive direction.

The value of h in $g(x) = (x - h)^2$ translates the graph of the parent function horizontally h units. The vertex of the graph of g is at $(h, 0)$, in this case (3, 0). The value of h also translated the axis of symmetry horizontally.

Try It! 2. How does the graph of each function compare to the graph of $f(x) = x^2$?

a. $h(x) = (x + 1)^2$ b. $j(x) = (x - 5)^2$

CONCEPTUAL UNDERSTANDING

EXAMPLE 3 Understand the Graph of $f(x) = a(x - h)^2 + k$

A. What information do the values of h and k provide about the graph of $f(x) = (x - h)^2 + k$?

Graph several functions of the form $f(x) = (x - h)^2 + k$. Look at the location of the vertex of each graph.

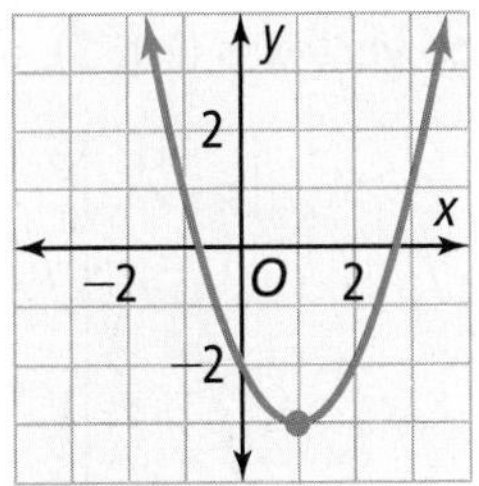

$f(x) = (x - 1)^2 - 3$
vertex: (1, −3)

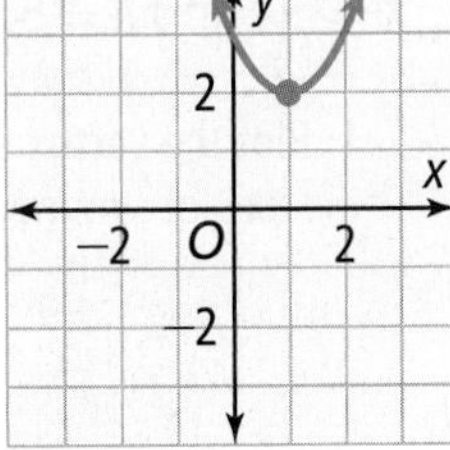

$f(x) = (x - 1)^2 + 2$
vertex: (1, 2)

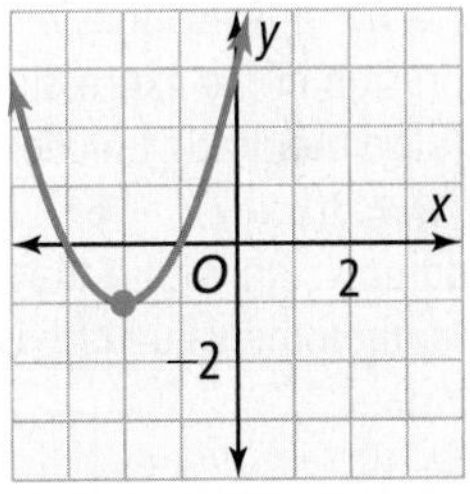

$f(x) = (x + 2)^2 - 1$
vertex: (−2, −1)

USE STRUCTURE
Consider $f(x) = (x - 1)^2 - 3$ to be in the form $f(x) = a(x - h)^2 + k$. What is the a-value of this function?

The values of h and k determine the location of the vertex and the axis of symmetry of the parabola. The vertex of the graph of $f(x) = (x - h)^2 + k$ is at (h, k). The axis of symmetry is $x = h$.

CONTINUED ON THE NEXT PAGE

EXAMPLE 3 CONTINUED

B. How does the value of *a* affect the graph of $f(x) = a(x - h)^2 + k$?

Graph each of the functions shown in part A. Then graph a new function with a different value of *a* to see how it affects the graph.

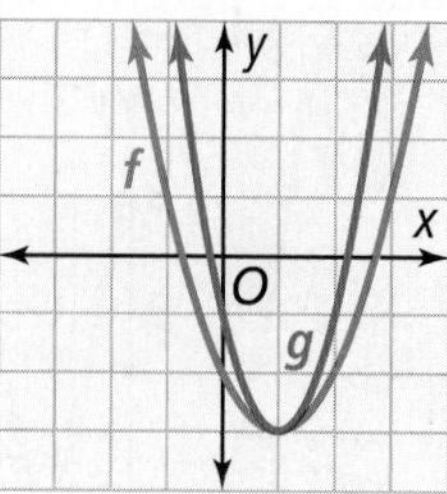

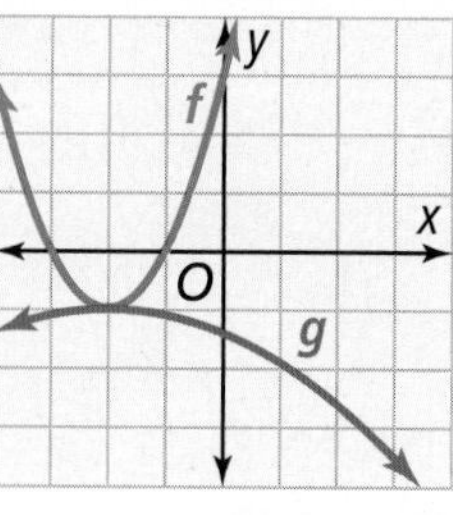

$f(x) = (x - 1)^2 - 3$
$g(x) = 2(x - 1)^2 - 3$

$f(x) = (x - 1)^2 + 2$
$g(x) = 0.25(x - 1)^2 + 2$

$f(x) = (x + 2)^2 - 1$
$g(x) = -0.1(x + 2)^2 - 1$

STUDY TIP
Notice that when $0 < |a| < 1$, the shape of the parabola is wider than the parent function. When $|a| > 1$, the shape of the parabola is narrower than the parent function.

The value of *a* does not affect the location of the vertex. The sign of *a* affects the direction of the parabola. The absolute value of *a* affects the width of the parabola.

The function $f(x) = a(x - h)^2 + k$, where $a \neq 0$ is called the **vertex form of a quadratic function**. The vertex of the graph is (h, k). The graph of $f(x) = a(x - h)^2 + k$ is a translation of the function $f(x) = ax^2$ that is translated *h* units horizontally and *k* units vertically.

Try It! 3. How does the graph of $f(x) = -3(x - 5)^2 + 7$ compare to the graph of the parent function?

EXAMPLE 4 Graph Using Vertex Form

How can you use the vertex form of a quadratic function to sketch the graph of the function?

COMMON ERROR
Recall that vertex form $f(x) = a(x - h)^2 + k$ includes a subtraction sign in the expression "$(x - h)$". If a quadratic function such as $f(x) = 3(x + 7)^2 - 6$ has an addition sign within that expression, then the value of *h* is negative.

Graph $f(x) = -2(x + 1)^2 + 5$.

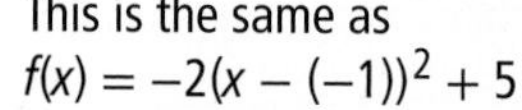

$h = -1$ and $k = 5$, so the vertex is $(-1, 5)$, and the axis of symmetry is $x = -1$.

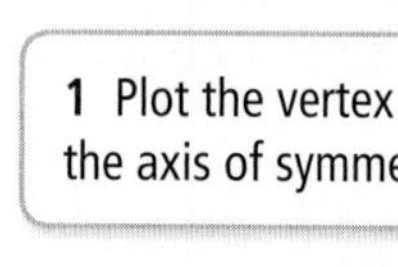

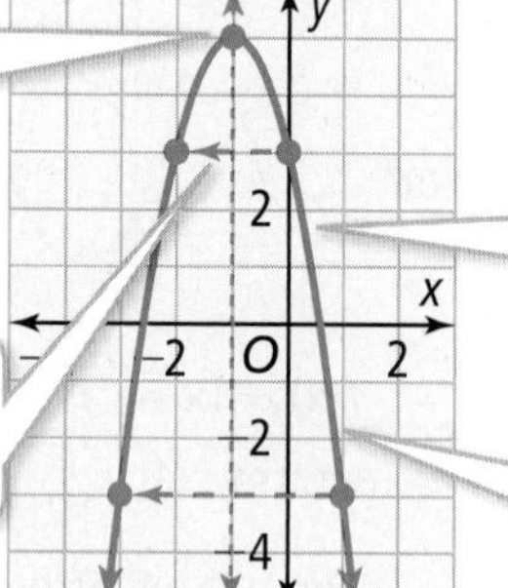

Try It! 4. Find the vertex and axis of symmetry, and sketch the graph of the function.

a. $g(x) = -3(x - 2)^2 + 1$

b. $h(x) = (x + 1)^2 - 4$

APPLICATION

EXAMPLE 5 Use Vertex Form to Solve Problems

Deshawn and Chris are playing soccer. Chris takes a shot on goal. Deshawn is 3 ft in front of the goal and can reach the top of the 8-ft goal when standing directly beneath it. Can he block the shot from his current position without moving or jumping?

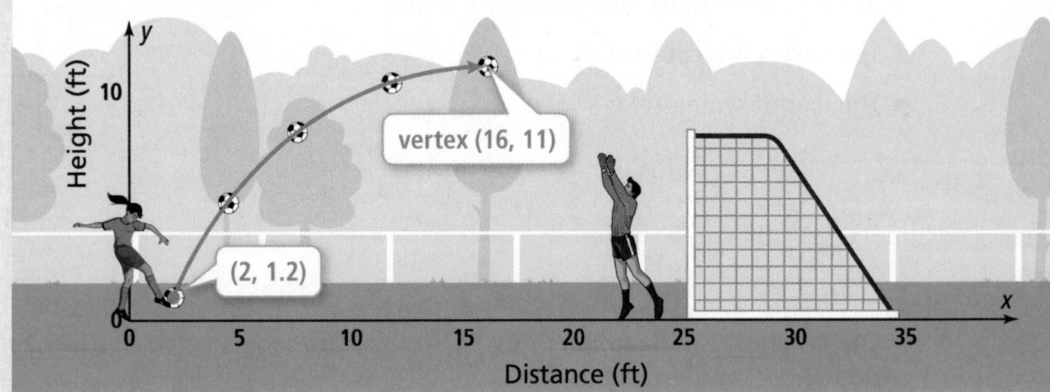

Formulate You can describe the parabolic path of the soccer ball using a quadratic function. The vertex of parabola is given, so write the function in vertex form.

$$f(x) = a(x - h)^2 + k$$

$$f(x) = a(x - 16)^2 + 11$$ Substitute $h = 16$ and $k = 11$.

Compute Use another point on the path of the ball to find the value of a.

The point (2, 1.2) represents the point where Chris's foot makes contact with the ball.

$$1.2 = a(2 - 16)^2 + 11$$ Substitute $x = 2$ and $f(x) = 1.2$.

$$1.2 = 196a + 11$$ Simplify.

$$-9.8 = 196a$$ Simplify.

$$\frac{-9.8}{196} = \frac{196a}{196}$$ Divide each side by 196.

$$a = -0.05$$

$$f(x) = -0.05(x - 16)^2 + 11$$ Substitute $a = -0.05$ into the function.

Use the function to find the altitude of the ball at Deshawn's position.

Deshawn is 3 ft in front of the goal, so his position is 25 ft – 3 ft = 22 ft.

$$f(22) = -0.05(22 - 16)^2 + 11$$ Substitute $x = 22$ into the function.

$$\approx 9.2$$

Interpret When the ball reaches Deshawn it will be about 9.2 ft above the ground, which is above his 8-ft reach.

Deshawn cannot block Chris's shot from his current position without jumping or moving.

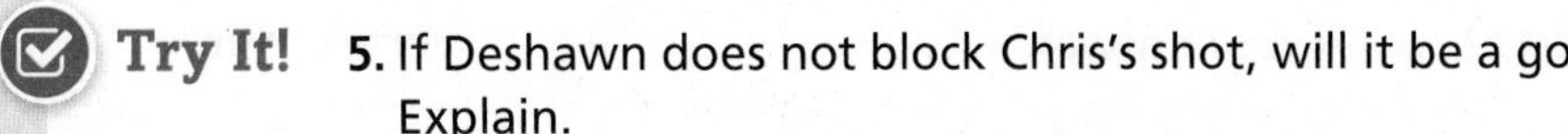

Try It! 5. If Deshawn does not block Chris's shot, will it be a goal? Explain.

CONCEPT SUMMARY Vertex Form of a Quadratic Function

ALGEBRA

$f(x) = a(x - h)^2 + k$

- The graph of f is the graph of $g(x) = ax^2$ translated horizontally h units and vertically k units.
- The vertex is located at (h, k).
- The axis of symmetry is $x = h$.

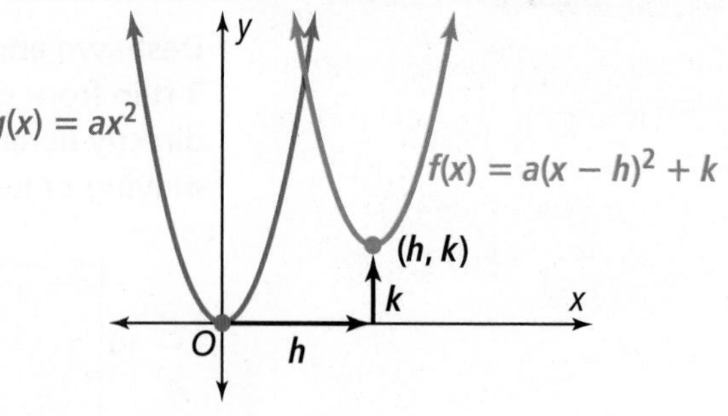

NUMBERS

$f(x) = -2(x - 1)^2 + 3$

- The graph of f is the graph of $g(x) = -2x^2$ translated right 1 unit and up 3 units.
- The vertex is located at (1, 3).
- The axis of symmetry is $x = 1$.

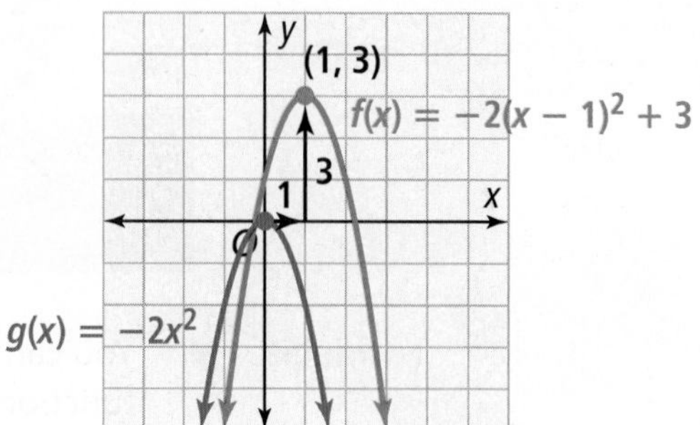

Do You UNDERSTAND?

1. **ESSENTIAL QUESTION** How can the vertex form of a quadratic function help you sketch the graph of the function?

2. **Reason** A table of values for the quadratic function g is shown. Do the graphs of the functions g and $f(x) = 3(x - 1)^2 + 2$ have the same axis of symmetry? Explain.

x	$g(x)$
−4	8
−2	3
0	0
6	3

3. **Use Structure** How are the form and the graph of $f(x) = (x - h)^2 + k$ similar to the form and graph of $f(x) = |x - h| + k$? How are they different?

4. **Error Analysis** Sarah said the vertex of the function $f(x) = (x + 2)^2 + 6$ is (2, 6). Is she correct? Explain your answer.

Do You KNOW HOW?

Graph each function.

5. $g(x) = x^2 + 5$

6. $f(x) = (x - 2)^2$

7. $h(x) = -2(x + 4)^2 + 1$

8. Write a function in vertex form for the parabola shown below.

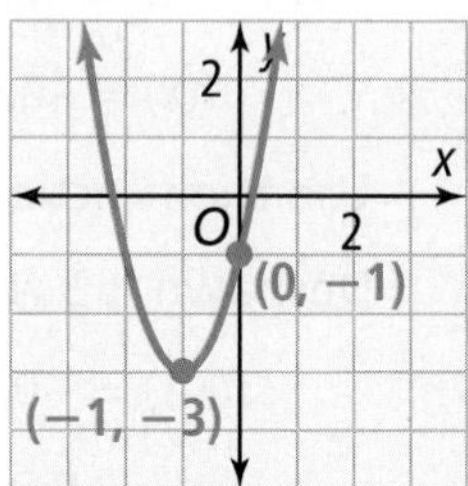

9. The height of a ball thrown into the air is a quadratic function of time. The ball is thrown from a height of 6 ft above the ground. After 1 second, the ball reaches its maximum height of 22 ft above the ground. Write the equation of the function in vertex form.

UNDERSTAND

10. **Make Sense and Persevere** How can you determine the values of h and k from the graph shown? Write the function for the parabola.

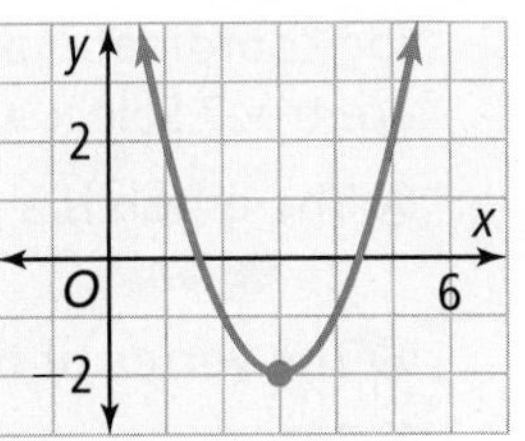

11. **Reason** To graph the function $f(x) = (x - 5)^2 - 8$, a student translates the graph of the quadratic parent function 5 units right and 8 units down. Can a student produce the graph of $f(x) = 2(x + 3)^2 - 5$ by simply translating the quadratic parent function? Explain.

12. **Error Analysis** A student used the steps shown to graph $f(x) = (x - 1)^2 + 6$. Describe and correct the student's error.

1. Plot the vertex at (-1, 6).
2. Graph points at (-2, 15) and (-3, 22).
3. Reflect the points across the axis of symmetry $x = -1$.
4. Connect the points with a parabola. ✗

13. **Mathematical Connections** The graph shown is a translation of the graph of $f(x) = 2x^2$. Write the function for the graph in vertex form.

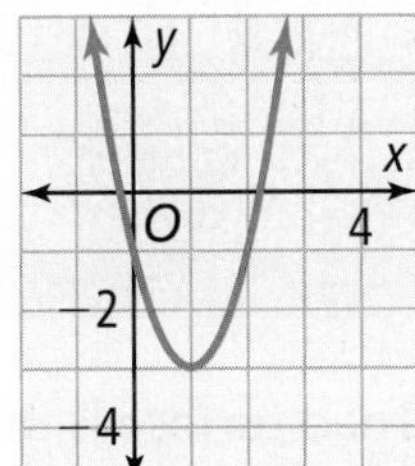

14. **Higher Order Thinking** The graph of h is the graph of $g(x) = (x - 2)^2 + 6$ translated 5 units left and 3 units down.
    a. Describe the graph of h as a translation of the graph of $f(x) = x^2$.
    b. Write the function h in vertex form.

PRACTICE

Identify the vertex and the axis of symmetry for each function. SEE EXAMPLES 1 AND 2

15. $f(x) = x^2 + 2$
16. $f(x) = x^2 - 5$
17. $g(x) = x^2 - 1$
18. $h(x) = x^2 + 0.5$
19. $f(x) = x^2 - 2.25$
20. $f(x) = x^2 + 50$
21. $h(x) = x^2 + 7$
22. $g(x) = (x - 1)^2$
23. $g(x) = (x + 2)^2$
24. $f(x) = (x - 6)^2$
25. $f(x) = (x - 0.5)^2$
26. $g(x) = (x - 4)^2$

Each graph shown is a translation of the graph of $f(x) = x^2$. Write each function in vertex form. SEE EXAMPLE 3

27. 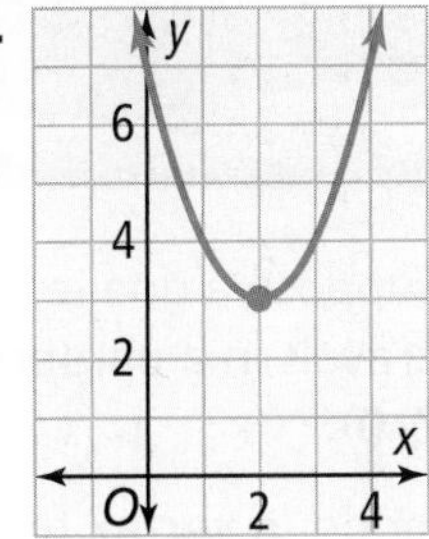

28. 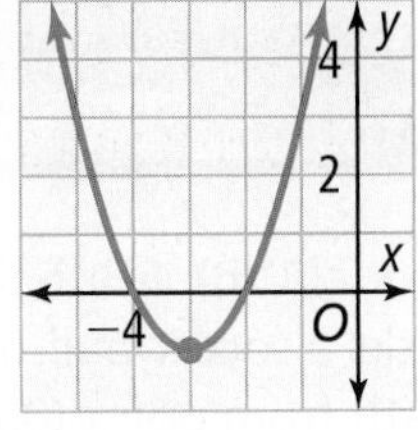

Identify the vertex, axis of symmetry, and direction of the graph of each function. Compare the width of the graph to the width of the graph of $f(x) = x^2$. SEE EXAMPLE 3

29. $f(x) = 2(x + 1)^2 + 4$
30. $g(x) = (x - 3)^2 - 3$
31. $g(x) = -0.75(x - 5)^2 + 6$
32. $h(x) = -3(x + 2)^2 - 5$

Sketch the graph of each function. SEE EXAMPLE 4

33. $f(x) = 2(x - 1)^2 + 4$
34. $g(x) = -2(x - 0.5)^2 + 1$
35. $f(x) = 0.5(x + 2)^2 + 2$
36. $h(x) = -2(x - 2)^2 - 2$

Each graph represents a quadratic function. Write each function in vertex form. SEE EXAMPLE 5

37. 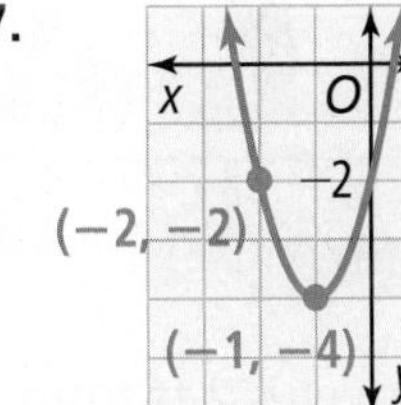

38. 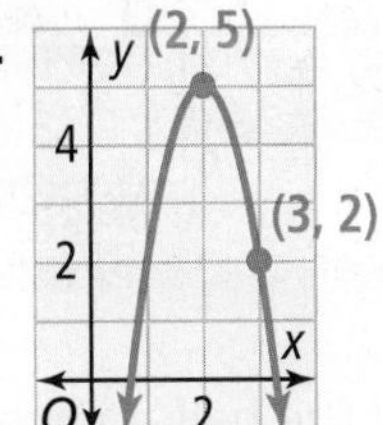

PRACTICE & PROBLEM SOLVING

APPLY

39. **Make Sense and Persevere** A computer game designer uses the function $f(x) = 4(x - 2)^2 + 6$ to model the path of the fish. The horizontal path of the squid intersects the path of the fish. At what other point does the squid's path intersect the path of the fish?

40. **Model With Mathematics** Suppose a goalie kicks a soccer ball. The ball travels in a parabolic path from point (0, 0) to (57, 0).

    a. Consider a quadratic function in vertex form for the path of the ball. Which values can you determine? What values are you unable to determine? Explain.

    b. **Technology** Use a graphing calculator to explore the undetermined values. Find a set of values that generates a realistic graph. Explain how the key features of the graph correspond to the situation.

41. **Construct Arguments** The function $f(x) = -(x - 1)^2 + 8$ models the path of a volleyball. The height of the net is 7 ft 4 in.

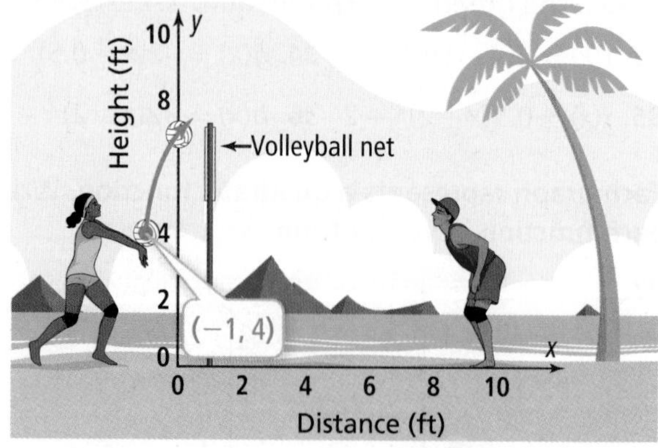

Will the ball go over if the player is 2 ft from the net? 4 ft, from the net? Explain.

ASSESSMENT PRACTICE

42. The function $f(x) = 2(x - 3)^2 + 9$ is graphed in the coordinate plane. Which of the following are true? Select all that apply.

    Ⓐ The graph is a parabola that opens downward.

    Ⓑ The vertex of the graph is (−3, 9).

    Ⓒ The axis of symmetry of the graph is $x = 3$.

    Ⓓ The y-intercept of the graph is 9.

    Ⓔ The minimum of the function is 9.

43. **SAT/ACT** The graph of $g(x) = x^2$ is translated right 2 units and down 10 units. Which of the following is the function of the new graph?

    Ⓐ $f(x) = (x + 2)^2 - 10$

    Ⓑ $f(x) = (x - 2)^2 - 10$

    Ⓒ $f(x) = 2x^2 - 10$

    Ⓓ $f(x) = -2x^2 - 10$

    Ⓔ $f(x) = -2(x - 10)^2$

44. **Performance Task** An engineer is designing a suspension bridge with a center cable. The cable is shaped like a parabola and is attached to stability towers on both ends at the same height. For simplicity she assumes a quadratic function, and uses $f(x) = 0.0006(x - 300)^2 + 6$ to model the cable between the towers.

Part A How high above the road surface is the lowest point of the cable?

Part B How far apart are the two towers? Explain.

8-3

Quadratic Functions in Standard Form

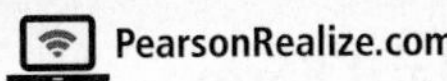
PearsonRealize.com

I CAN… graph quadratic functions using standard form.

VOCABULARY

- standard form of a quadratic function

EXPLORE & REASON

Three functions of the form $f(x) = ax^2 + bx$ are graphed for $a = 2$ and different values of b.

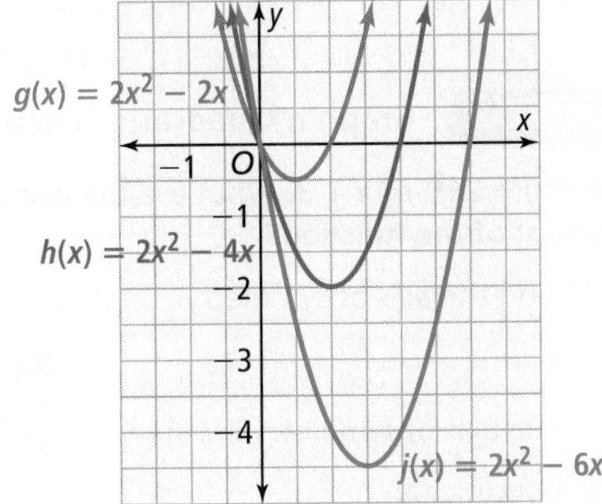

A. What do the graphs have in common? In what ways do they differ?

B. What do you notice about the x-intercepts of each graph? What do you notice about the y-intercepts of each graph?

C. **Look for Relationships** Look at the ratio $\frac{b}{a}$ for each function and compare it to its graph. What do you notice?

? ESSENTIAL QUESTION How is the standard form of a quadratic function different from the vertex form?

CONCEPTUAL UNDERSTANDING

EXAMPLE 1 Relate c to the Graph of $f(x) = ax^2 + bx + c$

What information does c provide about the graph of $f(x) = ax^2 + bx + c$?

Graph several functions of the form $f(x) = ax^2 + bx + c$. Look for a connection between the graphs and the value of c for each function.

GENERALIZE
Consider the graphs of quadratic functions with the same c-values but different a- and b-values from those shown in the example.

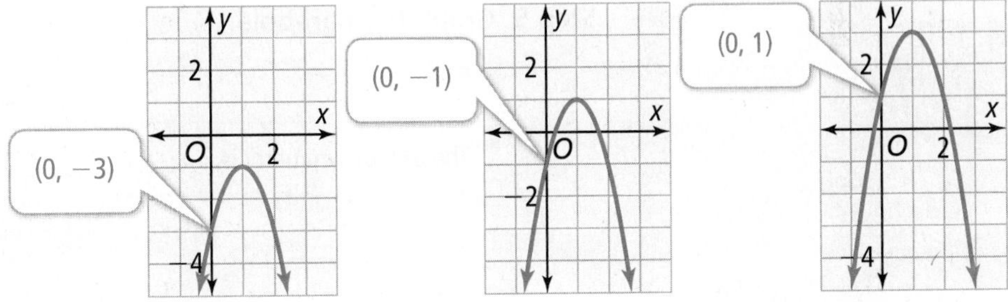

$f(x) = -2x^2 + 4x - 3$ $c = -3$

$f(x) = -2x^2 + 4x - 1$ $c = -1$

$f(x) = -2x^2 + 4x + 1$ $c = 1$

The value of c corresponds to the y-intercept of the graph of $f(x) = ax^2 + bx + c$.

 **Try It!** 1. Evaluate $f(x) = ax^2 + bx + c$ for $x = 0$. How does $f(0)$ relate to the result in Example 1?

CONCEPT Standard Form of a Quadratic Equation

The **standard form of a quadratic function** is $f(x) = ax^2 + bx + c$, where $a \neq 0$. The value c is the y-intercept of the graph. The axis of symmetry of the graph is the line $x = -\frac{b}{2a}$ and the x-coordinate of the vertex is $-\frac{b}{2a}$.

EXAMPLE 2 Graph a Quadratic Function in Standard Form

Graph $f(x) = 2x^2 + 4x + 3$. What are the axis of symmetry, vertex, and y-intercept of the function?

Step 1 Find the axis of symmetry.

$$x = -\frac{b}{2a} = -\frac{4}{2(2)} = -1$$

The x-coordinate of the vertex is also -1.

The axis of symmetry is $x = -1$.

Step 2 Plot the vertex.

Use the x-coordinate of the vertex to find the y-coordinate.

$f(x) = 2x^2 + 4x + 3$

$f(-1) = 2(-1)^2 + 4(-1) + 3$ ········ Substitute -1 for x.

$= 1$ ········ Simplify.

The y-coordinate of the vertex is 1. So, plot the vertex $(-1, 1)$.

USE STRUCTURE
Consider Step 3. Is there a situation where following this procedure would not yield two points on the parabola?

Step 3 Plot the y-intercept and its reflection.

$f(x) = 2x^2 + 4x + 3$ — The value of c is the y-intercept.

Plot $(0, 3)$ and its reflection across the axis of symmetry $(-2, 3)$.

Step 4 Plot another point and its reflection.

Evaluate the function for another x-value. For $x = 1$, $f(1) = 9$. The reflection of $(1, 9)$ across the axis of symmetry is $(-3, 9)$. Plot $(1, 9)$ and $(-3, 9)$.

Step 5 Graph the parabola.

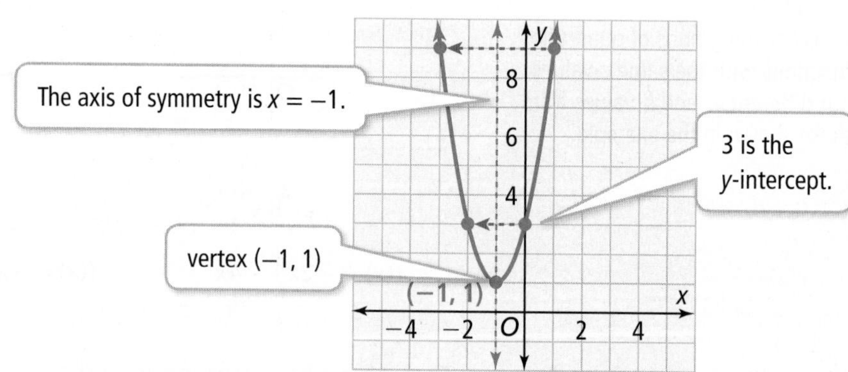

CONTINUED ON THE NEXT PAGE

Try It! **2.** Graph each function. What are the y-intercept, the axis of symmetry, and the vertex of each function?

a. $f(x) = x^2 + 2x + 4$ **b.** $g(x) = -0.75x^2 + 3x - 4$

APPLICATION

EXAMPLE 3 Compare Properties of Quadratic Functions

The trajectory of the water from Fountain A is represented by a function in standard form while the trajectory of the water from Fountain B is represented by a table of values. Compare the vertex of each function. Which trajectory reaches a greater height in feet?

Fountain A:
$f(x) = -x^2 + 2x + 8$

Fountain B:

x	y
−6	5
−5	8
−4	10
−3	8
−2	5

COMMON ERROR
You may incorrectly state that the x-coordinate of the vertex is −1. Remember that the formula is $-\frac{b}{2a}$. Make sure to include the negative in your calculations.

Find the vertex of each function.

Fountain **A**

Find the x-coordinate.

$$-\frac{b}{2a} = -\frac{2}{2(-1)} = 1$$

Find the y-coordinate.

$$f(1) = -(1)^2 + 2(1) + 8 = 9$$

The vertex is (1, 9).

Fountain **B**

Find the vertex.

x	y
−6	5
−5	8
−4	10
−3	8
−2	5

The vertex is (−4, 10).

Fountain **A** reaches a height of 9 ft.

Fountain **B** reaches a height of 10 ft.

The water from Fountain B reaches a greater height.

CONTINUED ON THE NEXT PAGE

Try It! **3.** Compare $f(x) = -0.3x^2 - 0.6x - 0.2$ to function g, shown in the graph. What are the maximum values? Which function has the greater maximum value?

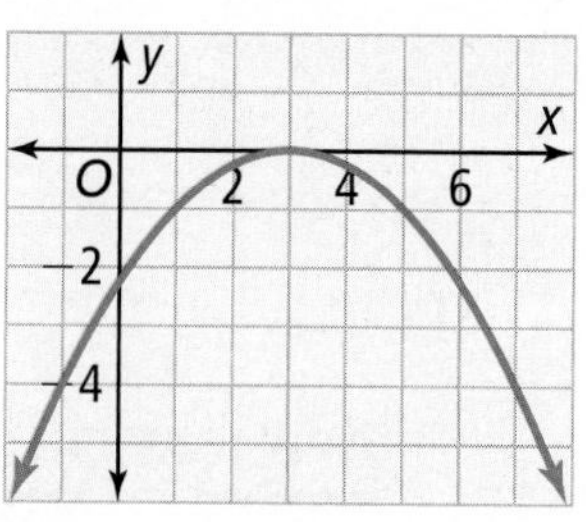

APPLICATION

EXAMPLE 4 Analyze the Structure of Different Forms

Mia tosses a ball to her dog. The function $f(x) = -0.5(x - 2)^2 + 8$ represents the ball's path.

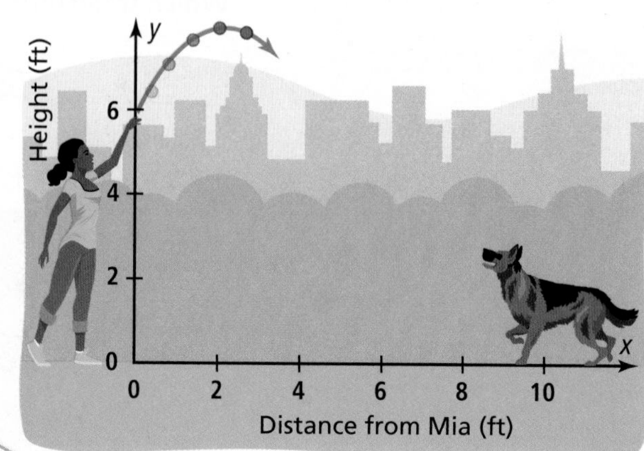

A. What does the vertex form of the function tell you about the situation?

$f(x) = a(x - h)^2 + k$

$\mathbf{f(x) = -0.5(x - 2)^2 + 8}$

$a = -0.5$. Since $a < 0$, the parabola opens downward.

$h = 2$ and $k = 8$, so the vertex is (2, 8).

The vertex form tells you the vertex of the graph of the function, which is (2, 8). The ball reaches a maximum height of 8 ft above the ground, 2 ft away from where Mia releases it.

B. What does the standard form of a function tell you about the situation?

Rewrite the function in standard form.

$f(x) = -0.5(x - 2)^2 + 8$

$= -0.5(x^2 - 4x + 4) + 8$ .... Expand $(x - 2)^2$.

$= -0.5x^2 + 2x + 6$ .... Use the Distributive Property and simplify.

$f(x) = ax^2 + bx + c$

$\mathbf{f(x) = -0.5x^2 + 2x + 6}$

The y-intercept is 6.

The standard form tells you the y-intercept of the graph of the function, which is (0, 6). The ball was 6 ft above the ground when Mia threw it.

MAKE SENSE AND PERSEVERE
Think about the reasonableness of the domain and range when you graph the function. Do both positive and negative values makes sense?

Try It! **4.** Suppose the path of the ball in Example 4 is $f(x) = -0.25(x - 1)^2 + 6.25$. Find the ball's initial and maximum heights.

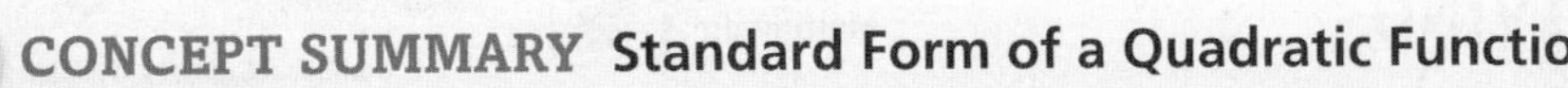

CONCEPT SUMMARY Standard Form of a Quadratic Function

ALGEBRA Standard form: $f(x) = ax^2 + bx + c$, where $a \neq 0$.

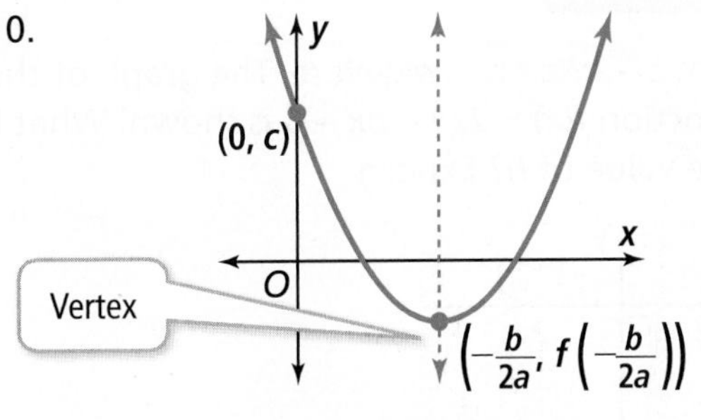

y-intercept: c

Axis of symmetry: $x = -\frac{b}{2a}$

x-coordinate of the vertex: $-\frac{b}{2a}$

y-coordinate of the vertex: $f\left(-\frac{b}{2a}\right)$

Vertex: $\left(-\frac{b}{2a}, f\left(-\frac{b}{2a}\right)\right)$

NUMBERS Standard form: $f(x) = 2x^2 + 8x + 5$.

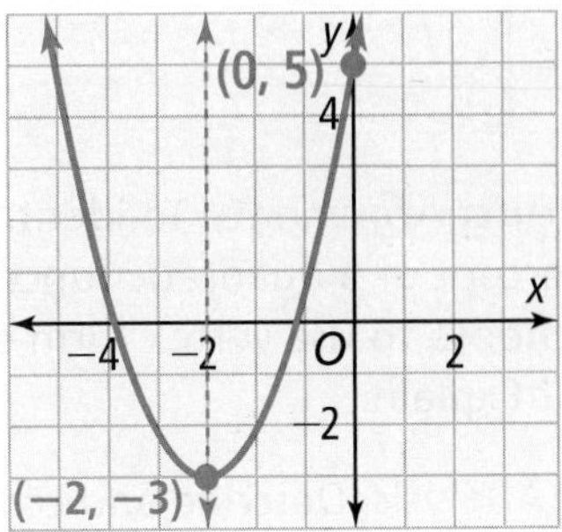

y-intercept: 5

Axis of symmetry: $x = -\frac{8}{2(2)} = -2$

x-coordinate of the vertex: $-\frac{8}{2(2)} = -2$

y-coordinate of the vertex: $f(-2) = -3$

Vertex: $(-2, -3)$

Do You UNDERSTAND?

1. **ESSENTIAL QUESTION** How is the standard form of a quadratic function different from the vertex form?

2. **Communicate Precisely** How are the form and graph of $f(x) = ax^2 + bx + c$ similar to the form and graph of $g(x) = ax^2 + bx$? How are they different?

3. **Vocabulary** How can you write a quadratic function in *standard form,* given its vertex form?

4. **Error Analysis** Sage began graphing $f(x) = -2x^2 + 4x + 9$ by finding the axis of symmetry $x = -1$. Explain the error Sage made.

Do You KNOW HOW?

Graph each function. For each, identify the axis of symmetry, the y-intercept, and the coordinates of the vertex.

5. $f(x) = 2x^2 + 8x - 1$

6. $f(x) = -0.5x^2 + 2x + 3$

7. $f(x) = -3x^2 - 6x - 5$

8. $f(x) = 0.25x^2 - 0.5x - 6$

9. A water balloon is tossed into the air. The function $h(x) = -0.5(x - 4)^2 + 9$ gives the height, in feet, of the balloon from the surface of a pool as a function of the balloon's horizontal distance from where it was first tossed. Will the balloon hit the ceiling 12 ft above the pool? Explain.

PRACTICE & PROBLEM SOLVING

Scan for Multimedia

Practice Tutorial

Additional Exercises Available Online

UNDERSTAND

10. Make Sense and Persevere The graph of the function $f(x) = 2x^2 - bx - 6$ is shown. What is the value of b? Explain.

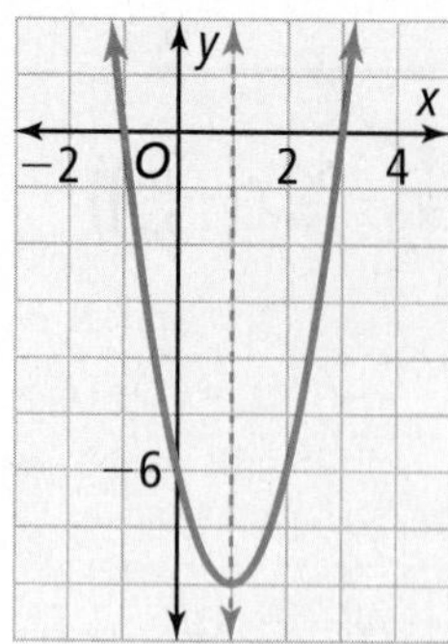

11. Construct Arguments To identify the y-intercept of a quadratic function, would you choose to use vertex form or standard form? Explain.

12. Error Analysis Describe and correct the error a student made when writing the quadratic function $f(x) = 2(x + 3)^2 - 4$ in standard form.

$f(x) = 2(x + 3)^2 - 4$
$f(x) = 2x^2 + 6x + 9 - 4$
$f(x) = 2x^2 + 6x + 5$ ✗

13. Communicate Precisely Estimate the coordinates of the vertex of the graph of $f(x) = 1.25x^2 - 2x - 1$ below. Then explain how to find the exact coordinates.

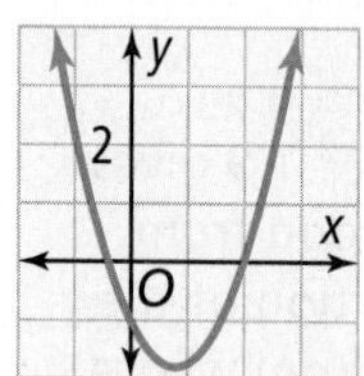

14. Higher Order Thinking Points (2, −1), (−2, 7), (1, −2), (0, −1), and (4, 7) lie on the graph of a quadratic function.

a. What is the axis of symmetry of the graph?

b. What is the vertex?

c. What is the y-intercept?

d. Over what interval does the function increase?

PRACTICE

What is the y-intercept of each function? SEE EXAMPLE 1

15. $f(x) = 2x^2 - 4x - 6$ **16.** $f(x) = 0.3x^2 + 0.6x - 0.7$

17. $f(x) = -2x^2 - 8x - 7$ **18.** $f(x) = 3x^2 + 6x + 5$

19. $f(x) = -x^2 - 2x + 3$ **20.** $f(x) = -0.5x^2 + x + 2$

Find the y-intercept, the axis of symmetry, and the vertex of the graph of each function. SEE EXAMPLE 2

21. $f(x) = 2x^2 + 8x + 2$ **22.** $f(x) = -2x^2 + 4x - 3$

23. $f(x) = 0.4x^2 + 1.6x$ **24.** $f(x) = -x^2 - 2x - 5$

25. $f(x) = 5x^2 + 5x + 12$ **26.** $f(x) = 4x^2 + 12x + 5$

27. $f(x) = x^2 - 6x + 12$ **28.** $f(x) = -2x^2 + 16x + 40$

Compare each function to function f, shown in the table. Which function has a lesser minimum value? Explain. SEE EXAMPLE 3

x	$(x, f(x))$
1	(1, 0)
2	(2, −3)
3	(3, −4)
4	(4, −3)
5	(5, 0)

29. $g(x) = 2x^2 + 8x + 3$ **30.** $h(x) = x^2 + x - 3.5$

Compare each function to function f, shown in the graph below. Which function has a greater maximum value? SEE EXAMPLE 3

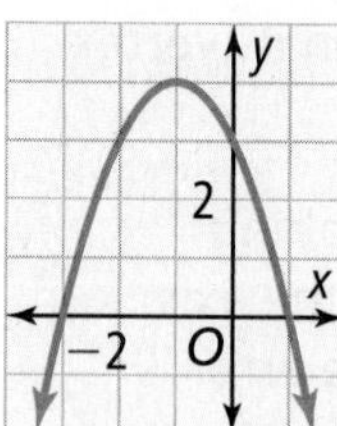

31. $g(x) = -2x^2 - 4x + 3$ **32.** $h(x) = -1.5x^2 - 4.5x + 1$

Write each function in standard form. SEE EXAMPLE 4

33. $f(x) = 4(x + 1)^2 - 3$ **34.** $f(x) = 0.1(x - 2)^2 - 0.1$

35. $f(x) = -2(x - 9)^2 + 15$ **36.** $f(x) = -(x + 3)^2 + 8$

PRACTICE & PROBLEM SOLVING

Practice Tutorial

Mixed Review Available Online

APPLY

37. Use Structure Two balls are tossed up into the air. The function $f(x) = -4.9x^2 + 14.7x + 0.975$ models the path of Ball A. The path of Ball B over time is shown in the table. Which ball reaches a greater height? How much greater? Explain how you can answer without graphing either function.

Time (s)	Height (m)
x	$g(x)$
0	1.975
1	11.775
1.5	13
2	11.775
2.5	1.975

38. Use Structure The position of a ball after it is kicked can be determined by using the function $f(x) = -0.11x^2 + 2.2x + 1$, where y is the height, in feet, above the ground and x is the horizontal distance, in feet, of the ball from the point at which it was kicked. What is the height of the ball when it is kicked? What is the highest point of the ball in the air?

39. Reason A banner is hung for a party. The distance from a point on the bottom edge of the banner to the floor can be determined by using the function $f(x) = 0.25x^2 - x + 9.5$, where x is the distance, in feet, of the point from the left end of the banner. How high above the floor is the lowest point on the bottom edge of the banner? Explain.

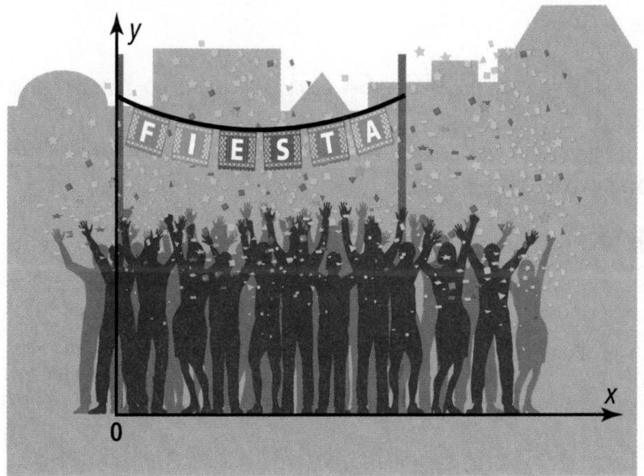

ASSESSMENT PRACTICE

40. An object is launched at 64 ft per second from an elevated platform. The function $f(x) = -16x^2 + 64x + 6$, models its trajectory over time, x. Which of the following are true? Select all that apply.

Ⓐ The height of the platform is 6 ft.

Ⓑ The object reaches its maximum height after 2 seconds.

Ⓒ The maximum height of the object is 70 ft.

Ⓓ The object will be lower than 40 feet at 1 second.

Ⓔ The height of the object increases and then decreases.

41. SAT/ACT What is the maximum value of $f(x) = -4x^2 + 16x + 12$?

Ⓐ 12 Ⓑ 16 Ⓒ 24 Ⓓ 28 Ⓔ 64

42. Performance Task Two models are used to predict monthly revenue for a new sports drink. In each model, x is the number of \$1-price increases from the original \$2 per bottle price.

Model A $f(x) = -12.5x^2 + 75x + 200$

Model B

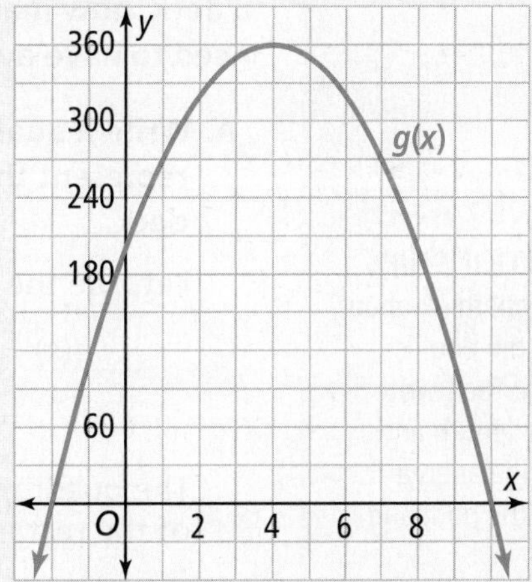

Part A Identify the price you would set for each model to maximize monthly revenue. Explain.

Part B A third model includes the points (9, 605), (8, 600), (10, 600), (7, 585), and (11, 585). What price maximizes revenue according to this model? Explain.

8-4 Modeling With Quadratic Functions

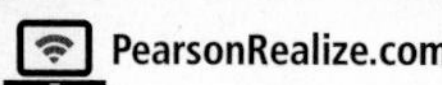

I CAN… use quadratic functions to model real-world situations.

VOCABULARY
- quadratic regression
- vertical motion model

MODEL & DISCUSS

The graphic shows the heights of a supply package dropped from a helicopter hovering above ground.

A. Model With Mathematics Would a linear function be a good model for the data? Explain.

B. Would a quadratic function be a good model for the data? Explain.

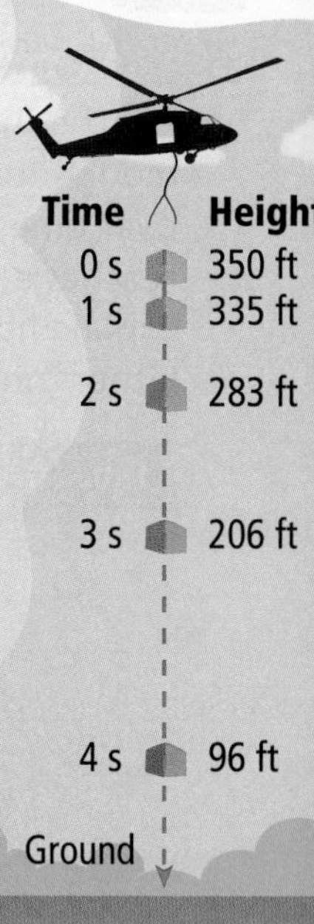

ESSENTIAL QUESTION

What kinds of real-world situations can be modeled by quadratic functions?

APPLICATION

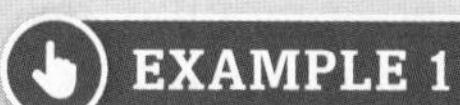

EXAMPLE 1 Use Quadratic Functions to Model Area

A company offers rectangular pool sizes with dimensions as shown. Each pool includes a deck around it. If Carolina wants a 15-ft wide pool with a deck, how many square feet will she need to have available in her yard?

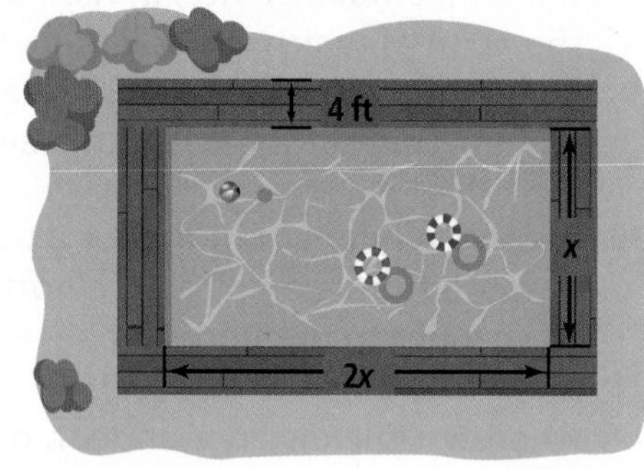

A. Write a quadratic function to represent the area of the pool and deck.

Let x be the width of the pool.

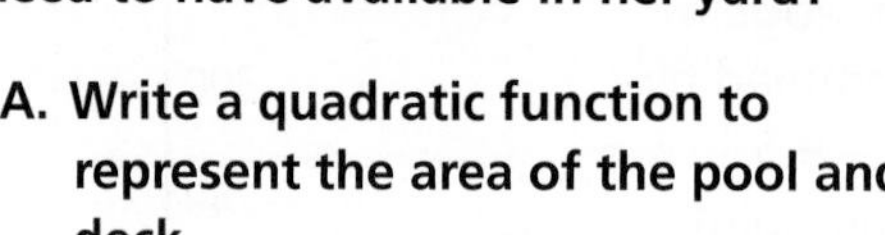

$f(x) = (2x + 8)(x + 8)$ — Area = Length × Width

$= 2x^2 + 24x + 64$

The quadratic function $f(x) = 2x^2 + 24x + 64$ can be used to find the area of the rectangular pool and the deck.

LOOK FOR RELATIONSHIPS
To write the function, think about how the length of the pool is related to its width. Then write expressions for the length and width of the rectangular area that contains both the pool and the deck.

B. Find the area of the pool and the deck.

$f(15) = 2(15)^2 + 24(15) + 64$ — Substitute 15 for x.

$= 874$

Carolina needs 874 ft^2 to build a 15-ft wide pool with deck.

Try It! 1. Suppose the length of the pool in Example 1 is 3 times the width. How does the function that represents the combined area of the pool and the deck change? Explain.

CONCEPT Vertical Motion Model

The equation $h(t) = -16t^2 + v_0t + h_0$ is the **vertical motion model**. The variable h represents the height of an object, in feet, t seconds after it is launched into the air. The term v_0 is the object's initial vertical velocity and h_0 is its initial height.

CONCEPTUAL UNDERSTANDING

EXAMPLE 2 Model Vertical Motion

A diver jumps off a high platform at an initial vertical velocity of 16 ft/s.

A. What quadratic function represents the height *h* of the diver after *t* seconds of the dive?

Use the vertical motion model to write the quadratic function.

$h(t) = -16t^2 + v_0t + h_0$

$h(t) = -16t^2 + 16t + 30$

Initial vertical velocity is 16 ft/s.

height of the platform is 30 ft.

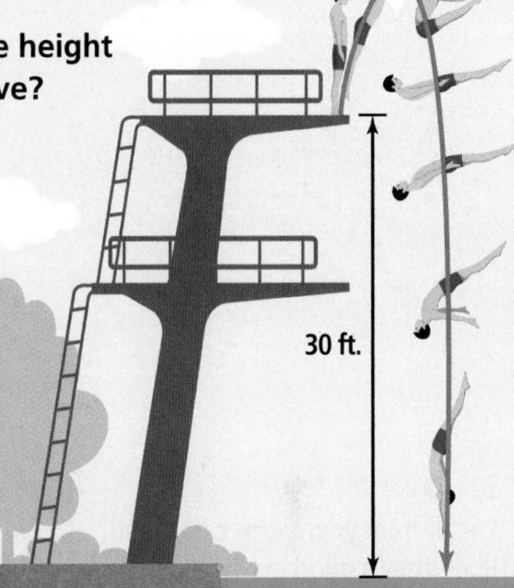

B. How many feet above the platform will the diver be at the highest point of his dive?

Find the maximum value of the graph described by $h(t) = -16t^2 + 16t + 30$.

$t = -\frac{b}{2a}$ — The maximum value is located at t-value of the axis of symmetry.

$t = -\frac{16}{2(-16)}$

$= \frac{1}{2}$

$h\left(\frac{1}{2}\right) = -16\left(\frac{1}{2}\right)^2 + 16\left(\frac{1}{2}\right) + 30$ — Substitute the t-value into the function to find $h(t)$, the y-value of the vertex.

$= 34$

The vertex is $\left(\frac{1}{2}, 34\right)$.

The platform is at a height of 30 ft and the vertex is at 34 ft. So the diver will be about 34 – 30, or 4 feet above the platform.

USE STRUCTURE
What do you notice about the structure of the vertical motion model and the standard form of a quadratic function? How are they similar?

Try It! 2. Find the diver's maximum height above the water if he dives from a 20-ft platform with an initial velocity of 8 ft/s.

APPLICATION

EXAMPLE 3 Assess the Fit of a Function by Analyzing Residuals

Each year, for the past five years, ticket prices for a school play have increased by \$1. The director used the function $f(x) = -7x^2 + 90x + 750$ to represent the relationship between the number of price increases and the average predicted revenue per show, shown in the table. How well does the function represent the actual revenue data?

Step 1 Use the function to find the predicted values for each price increase. Subtract the predicted from the actual revenues to find the residuals.

Ticket Price (\$)	Price Increase x	Actual Revenue (\$)	Predicted Revenue $f(x)$	Residual
5	0	745	750	−5
6	1	846	833	+13
7	2	910	902	+8
8	3	952	957	−5
9	4	1008	988	+10

Step 2 Make a scatterplot of the data and graph the function on the same coordinate grid.

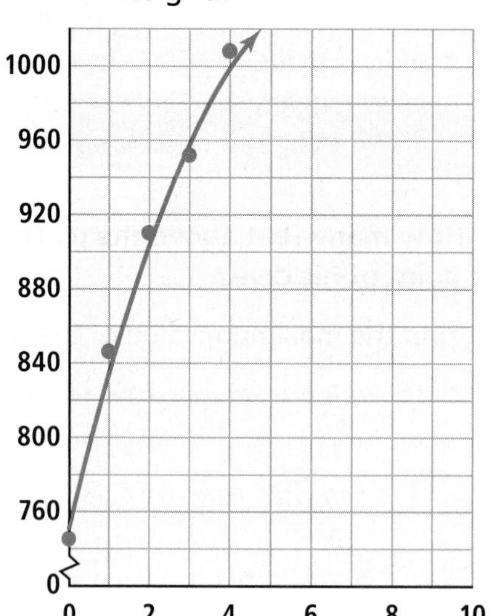

Step 3 Make a residual plot to show the fit of the function to the data.

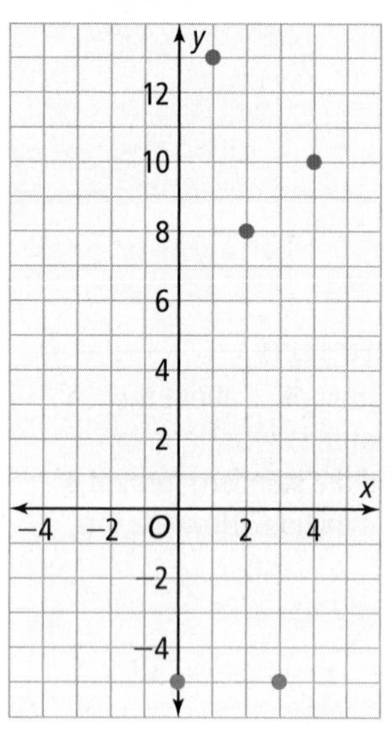

STUDY TIP

Recall from your work with trend lines, that a good model would have roughly equal numbers of positive and negative residuals.

Step 4 Assess the fit of the function using the residual plot.

The residual plot shows both positive and negative residuals, which indicates a generally good model.

Try It! **3.** Make a scatterplot of the data and graph the function $f(x) = -8x^2 + 95x + 745$. Make a residual plot and describe how well the function fits the data.

Price Increase (\$)	0	1	2	3	4
Sales (\$)	730	850	930	951	1010

APPLICATION

EXAMPLE 4 Fit a Quadratic Function to Data

The theater director at the high school wants to find the most accurate quadratic model for ticket sales based on the data in Example 3. How would the revenue be affected if the prices increase one more time?

Quadratic regression is a method used to find the quadratic function that best fits a data set.

STUDY TIP
You may recall that *linear regression* fits a line to the data. For *quadratic regression*, you will fit a parabola to data.

Step 1 Use a graphing calculator. Enter the price increase, *x*, and average revenue, *y*, as lists.

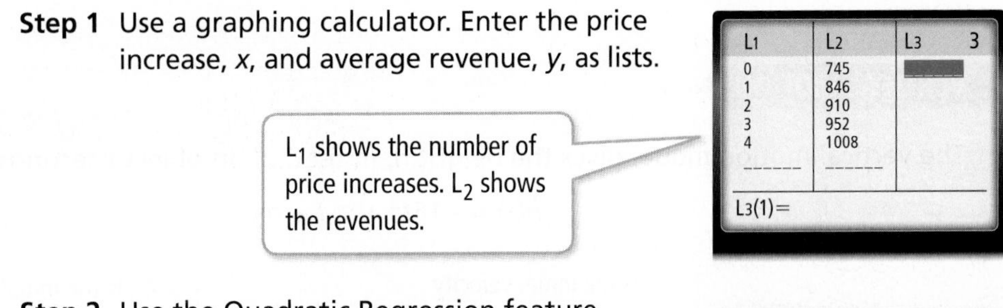

Step 2 Use the Quadratic Regression feature.

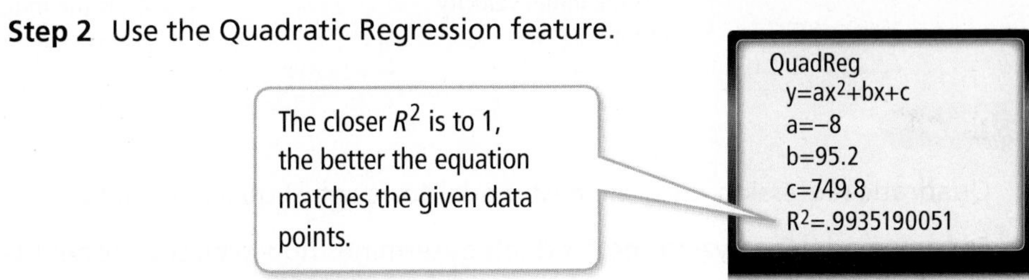

Use the values for *a, b,* and *c* to write an equation for the function.

The function $f(x) = -8x^2 + 95.2x + 749.8$ is a good model of the relationship between the number of \$1 increases and the predicted revenue per show.

Step 3 Graph the data and quadratic regression. Use the Trace function to determine the predicted revenue after the fifth \$1 price increase, so find $f(x)$ when $x = 5$.

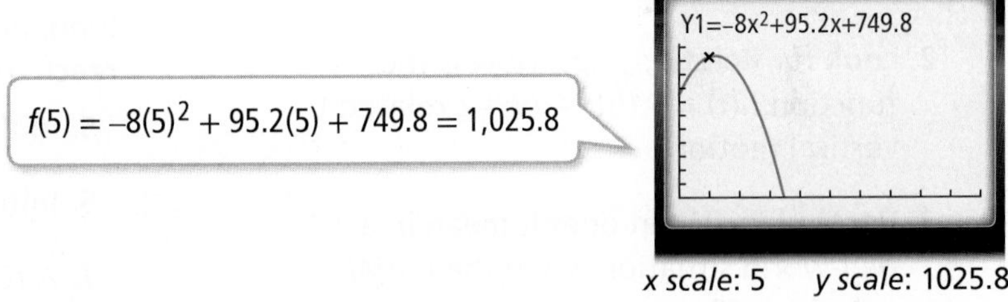

If the price of a ticket increases to \$10, the predicted revenue will be \$1,025.80.

REASON
Since tickets for this year are \$10 each, the predicted value of \$1,025.80 will not be the actual sales. You can reason that the actual sales will be a multiple of \$10.

Try It! 4. Use the model in Example 4 to determine the predicted revenue after the 6th and 7th price increases. What do you notice?

CONCEPT SUMMARY Modeling With Quadratic Functions

AREA

When the length and width of rectangle are each variable expressions, a quadratic function can be used to model the rectangle's area.

$A = (3x + 4)(x - 2)$
$= 3x^2 - 2x - 8$

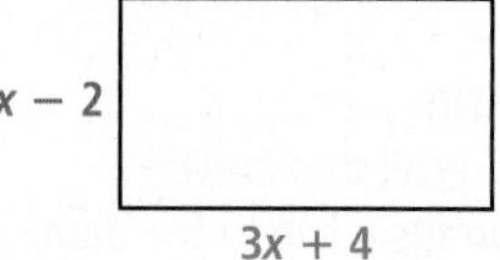

VERTICAL MOTION

The vertical motion model gives the height h, in feet, of an object t seconds after launch.

$$h(t) = -16t^2 + v_0t + h_0$$

v_0 is the initial velocity

h_0 is the initial height

DATA

Quadratic regression finds the best model for a set of quadratic data.

For any model, analyzing the residuals determines how well the model fits the data.

Residual = Data value − Predicted value

Do You UNDERSTAND?

1. ESSENTIAL QUESTION What kinds of real-world situations can be modeled by quadratic functions?

2. **Look for Relationships** How is the function $h(t) = -16t^2 + bt + c$ related to vertical motion?

3. **Vocabulary** What does it mean in a real-world situation when the *initial velocity* is 0?

4. **Error Analysis** Chen uses $h(t) = -16t^2 + 6t + 16$ to determine the height of a ball t seconds after it is thrown at an initial velocity of 16 ft/s from an initial height of 6 ft. Describe the error Chen made.

Do You KNOW HOW?

Write a vertical motion model in the form $h(t) = -16t^2 + v_0t + h_0$ for each situation presented. For each situation, determine how long, in seconds, it takes the thrown object to reach maximum height.

5. Initial velocity: 32 ft/s; initial height: 20 ft

6. Initial velocity: 120 ft/s; initial height: 50 ft

7. A rectangular patio has a length four times its width. It also has a 3-ft wide brick border around it. Write a quadratic function to determine the area of the patio and border.

8. The data are modeled by $f(x) = -2x^2 + 16.3x + 40.7$. What does the graph of the residuals tell you about the fit of the model?

x	y
1	55.0
2	65.3
3	71.6
4	73.9
5	72.2

PRACTICE & PROBLEM SOLVING

Scan for Multimedia   

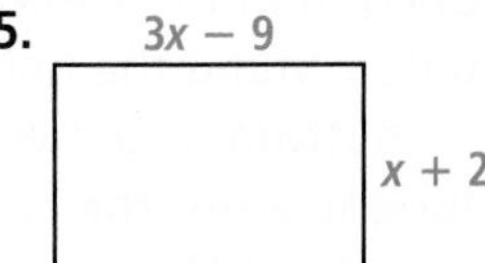

UNDERSTAND

9. **Make Sense and Persevere** For each vertical motion model, identify the maximum height reached by the object and the amount of time for the object to reach the maximum height.

   a. $h(t) = -16t^2 + 200t + 25$

   b. $h(t) = -16t^2 + 36t + 4$

10. **Reason** When a student uses quadratic regression on a graphing calculator to model data, the value of R^2 is 0.2. Make a conjecture about the fit of the model.

11. **Error Analysis** Describe and correct the error a student made when interpreting the graph of the vertical motion model $h(t) = -at^2 + bt + c$.

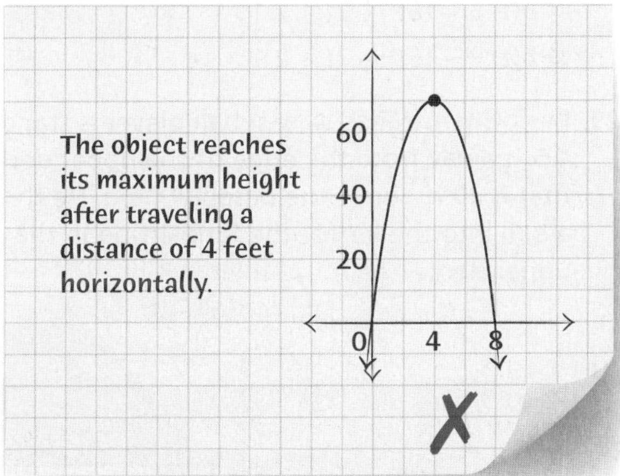

12. **Look for Relationships** In the graph of a vertical motion model shown, how is the initial velocity related to the vertex of the parabola?

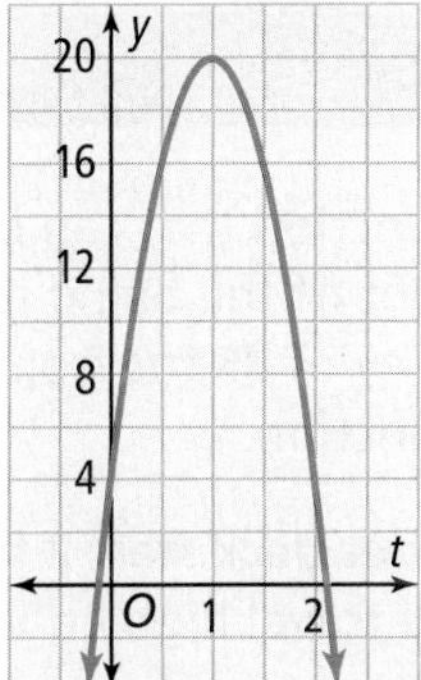

13. **Higher Order Thinking** The function $f(x) = x^2 + 3x - 10$ models the area of a rectangle.

   a. Describe the length and width of the rectangle in terms of x.

   b. What is a reasonable domain and range for the situation? Explain.

PRACTICE

Use a quadratic function to model the area of each rectangle. Graph the function. Evaluate each function for $x = 8$. SEE EXAMPLE 1

14. Rectangle with sides $2x + 4$ and $x + 3$

15. Rectangle with sides $3x - 9$ and $x + 2$

Write a function h to model the vertical motion for each situation, given $h(t) = -16t^2 + v_0t + h_0$. Find the maximum height. SEE EXAMPLE 2

16. initial vertical velocity: 32 ft/s initial height: 75 ft

17. initial vertical velocity: 200 ft/s initial height: 0 ft

18. initial vertical velocity: 50 ft/s initial height: 5 ft

19. initial vertical velocity: 48 ft/s initial height: 6 ft

Make a scatterplot of the data and graph the function on the same coordinate grid. Calculate the residuals and make a residual plot. Describe the fit of the function to the data. SEE EXAMPLE 3

20. $f(x) = 2x^2 - x + 1$

x	y
−2	13
−1	8
0	6
1	9
2	12

21. $f(x) = -x^2 + 3x + 2$

x	y
−2	−6
−1	−1
0	3
1	4
2	3

Use a graphing calculator to find a quadratic regression for each data set. Round values to the nearest ten-thousandth. SEE EXAMPLE 4

22.

x	y
0	15.50
1	11.21
2	8.43
3	5.67
4	3.43

23.

x	y
100	567.3
500	443.2
900	362.3
1,300	312.2
1,700	307.3

APPLY

24. Model With Mathematics A student drops a rock over the edge of the well and hears it splash into water after 3 seconds. Write a function in the form $h(t) = -16t^2 + v_0t + h_0$ to determine the height of the rock above the bottom of the well t seconds after the student drops the rock. What is the distance from the surface of the water to the bottom of the well?

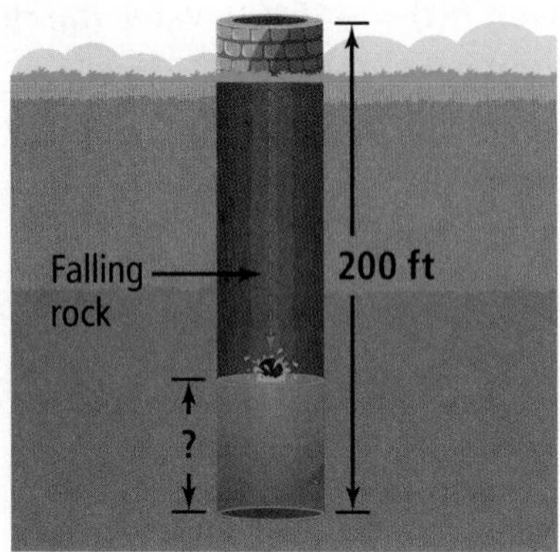

25. Construct Arguments The table below shows profits for a new model of headphones as a function of price x. The manufacturer says the price should be set at \$15 to maximize profits. Do you agree? Justify your answers.

Price ($)	Profit ($ thousands)
16	240
17	223
18	200
19	173
20	140

26. Mathematical Connections Dakota bought 120 ft of wire fencing at \$0.50/ft to enclose a rectangular playground. The playground surface will be covered with mulch at a cost of \$1.25/ft^2. Write a quadratic function that can be used to determine the total cost of fencing and mulch for a playground with side length x. What is the cost if one side is 20 ft?

ASSESSMENT PRACTICE

27. The function $h(t) = -16t^2 + 96t + 10$ models the path of a projectile.

By inspecting the function you can tell that the initial height of the projectile is ________ ft, and the initial velocity is ________ ft/s.

The projectile reaches a maximum height of ________ ft at time ________ s.

28. SAT/ACT A basketball is thrown straight up into the air from a height of 2.1 ft with an initial velocity of 7 ft/s. Which function models the height of the ball after t seconds?

Ⓐ $h(t) = -16t^2 + 2.1t + 7$

Ⓑ $h(t) = -16t^2 - 2.1t + 7$

Ⓒ $h(t) = -16t^2 + 2.1t - 7$

Ⓓ $h(t) = -16t^2 + 7t + 2.1$

Ⓔ $h(t) = -16t^2 - 7t + 2.1$

29. Performance Task A baseball player is standing 1.5 ft away from the edge of the upper deck that is 20 ft above the baseball field. He throws a ball into the air for the fans sitting in the upper deck.

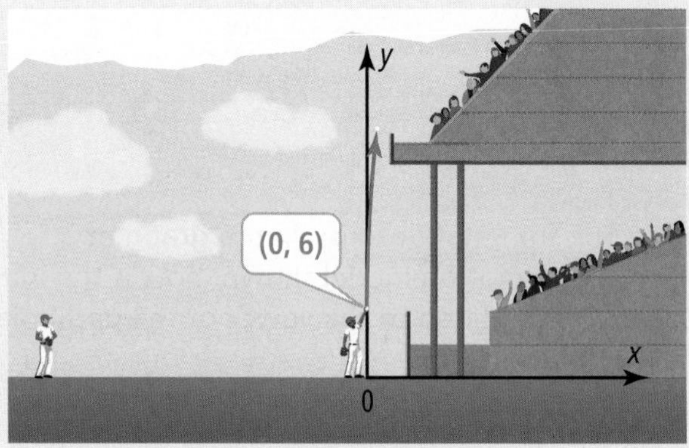

Part A Write a quadratic function that can be used to determine the height of the ball if it is thrown at an initial velocity of 35 ft/s from a height of 6 ft. Graph the function.

Part B The seats for the upper deck start 2 ft from the edge. Will the ball travel high enough to land on the upper deck?

MATHEMATICAL MODELING IN 3 ACTS

PearsonRealize.com

The Long Shot

Have you ever been to a basketball game where they hold contests at halftime? A popular contest is one where the contestant needs to make a basket from half court to win a prize. Contestants often shoot the ball in different ways. They might take a regular basketball shot, a hook shot, or an underhand toss.

What is the best way to shoot the basketball to make a basket? Think about this during this Mathematical Modeling in 3 Acts lesson.

ACT 1 Identify the Problem

1. What is the first question that comes to mind after watching the video?
2. Write down the Main Question you will answer.
3. Make an initial conjecture that answers this Main Question.
4. Explain how you arrived at your conjecture.

ACT 2 Develop a Model

5. Use the math that you have learned in the topic to refine your conjecture.

ACT 3 Interpret the Results

6. Did your refined conjecture match the actual answer exactly? If not, what might explain the difference?

8-5 Linear, Exponential, and Quadratic Models

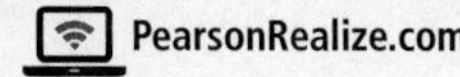

I CAN… determine whether a linear, exponential, or quadratic function best models a data set.

MODEL & DISCUSS

Jacy and Emma use different functions to model the value of a bike x years after it is purchased. Each function models the data in the table.

Jacy's function: $f(x) = -14.20x + 500$

Emma's function: $f(x) = 500(0.85)^x$

Time (yr)	Value ($)
0	500.00
1	485.20
2	472.13
3	461.00
4	452.10

A. Make Sense and Persevere Why did Jacy and Emma not choose a quadratic function to model the data?

B. Whose function do you think is a better model? Explain.

C. Do you agree with this statement? Explain why or why not.

To ensure that you are finding the best model for a table of data, you need to find the values of the functions for the same values of x.

ESSENTIAL QUESTION

How can you determine whether a linear, exponential, or quadratic function best models data?

CONCEPTUAL UNDERSTANDING

EXAMPLE 1 Determine Which Function Type Represents Data

A. How can you determine whether the data in the table can be modeled by a linear function?

First, confirm that the differences in the x-values are constant. Then analyze the *first differences*.

x	y	1st Differences
−2	−1	
−1	1	$1 - (-1) = 2$
0	3	$3 - 1 = 2$
1	5	$5 - 3 = 2$
2	7	$7 - 5 = 2$

(Each x-value increases by +1.)

The differences between consecutive y-values are the first differences.

GENERALIZE
Look at the data in the table. What do you notice about the differences between consecutive y-values?

A linear function best models the data when the first differences are constant.

CONTINUED ON THE NEXT PAGE

EXAMPLE 1 CONTINUED

B. How can you determine whether the data in the table can be modeled by a quadratic function?

Analyze the *second differences*.

x	y	1st Differences
0	3	
1	9	$9 - 3 = 6$
2	19	$19 - 9 = 10$
3	33	$33 - 19 = 14$
4	51	$51 - 33 = 18$

2nd Differences
$10 - 6 = 4$
$14 - 10 = 4$
$18 - 14 = 4$

First differences are not constant. Check the second differences.

The differences between consecutive first differences are called the *second differences*.

A quadratic function best models the data when the second differences are constant.

COMMON ERROR
You may forget to confirm that the differences between the x-values are constant. If differences between the x-values are not constant, then the differences or ratios between the y-values will not be accurate indicators of whether a linear, quadratic, or exponential function best represents the data.

C. How can you determine whether the data in the table can be modeled by an exponential function?

The first differences and second differences are not constant. Find and analyze the ratios of consecutive y-values.

x	y	1st Differences	2nd Differences
0	1		
1	2	$2 - 1 = 1$	
2	4	$4 - 2 = 2$	$2 - 1 = 1$
3	8	$8 - 4 = 4$	$4 - 2 = 2$
4	16	$16 - 8 = 8$	$8 - 4 = 4$

Ratios of y-Values
$\frac{2}{1} = 2$
$\frac{4}{2} = 2$
$\frac{8}{4} = 2$
$\frac{16}{8} = 2$

The first differences and second differences are not constant, so the data do not represent a linear or quadratic function.

The ratios of consecutive y-values are the same.

An exponential function best models the data when the ratios of consecutive y-values are the same.

Try It! 1. Does a linear, quadratic, or exponential function best model the data? Explain.

a.

x	0	1	2	3	4
y	−2	−5	−14	−29	−50

b.

x	−2	−1	0	1	2
y	4	12	36	108	324

  Activity Assess

APPLICATION

EXAMPLE 2 Choose a Function Type for Real-World Data

The owner of a framing store tracks the cost of bubble wrap for packing pictures like the one shown. How can you use the data to estimate the cost of the bubble wrap for a picture with a length of 75 in.?

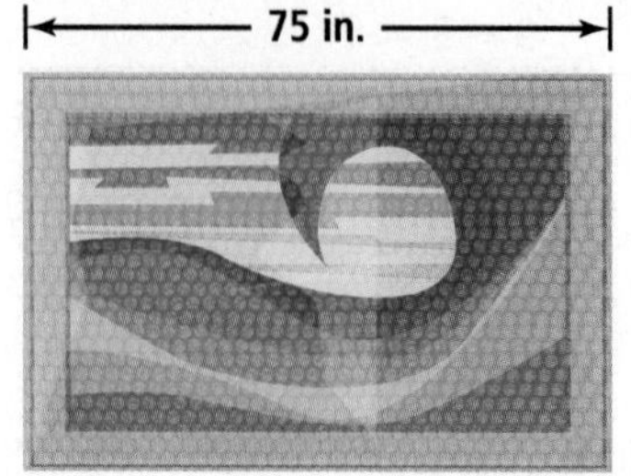

Length (in.)	Bubble Wrap Cost ($)
6	0.10
12	0.31
18	0.62
24	1.04
30	1.57

Step 1 Determine whether a linear, exponential, or quadratic function model best represents the data.

Analyze at the differences or ratios to determine which model best fits the data.

Length (in.) x	Bubble Wrap Cost ($) y	1st Differences	2nd Differences
6	0.10		
12	0.31	$0.31 - 0.10 = 0.21$	
18	0.62	$0.62 - 0.31 = 0.31$	$0.31 - 0.21 = 0.10$
24	1.04	$1.04 - 0.62 = 0.42$	$0.42 - 0.31 = 0.11$
30	1.57	$1.57 - 1.04 = 0.53$	$0.53 - 0.42 = 0.11$

The first differences are not constant.

The second differences are roughly constant.

A quadratic model best represents the data.

Step 2 Write a quadratic function that represents the data.

Use a graphing calculator to find a quadratic regression. Enter the data as lists, and use the quadratic regression feature.

QuadReg
$y=ax^2+bx+c$
a=.001488095
b=.007595238
c=.002
R^2=.9999917607

STUDY TIP
You can find a quadratic regression for any set of data whether it is quadratic or not. Because the R^2 value is so close to 1, the quadratic equation generated by the calculator is a good model for the data.

Step 3 Substitute $x = 75$ into the equation.

Enter function $y = 0.0015x^2 + 0.0076x + 0.002$ and evaluate for $x = 75$.

The cost of bubble wrap for a 75-in. picture is about $9.01.

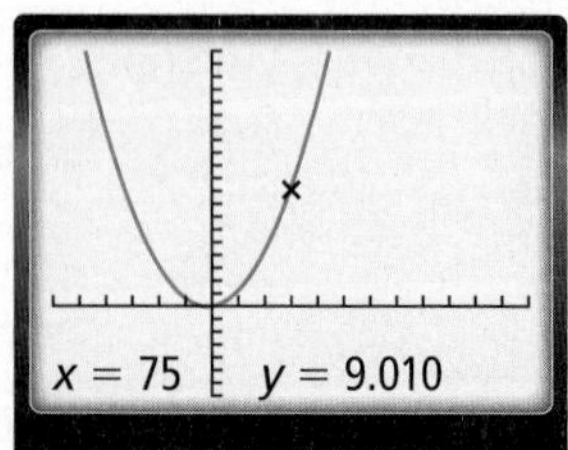

CONTINUED ON THE NEXT PAGE

 **Try It!** **2.** Determine whether a linear, quadratic, or exponential function best models the data. Then, use regression to find the function that models the data.

x	0	1	2	3	4
y	100	89.5	78.9	68.4	57.8

EXAMPLE 3 Compare Linear, Exponential, and Quadratic Growth

The graph shows population models for three cities, based on data over a five-year period. If the populations continue to increase in the same ways, when will the population of City C exceed the populations of the other two cities?

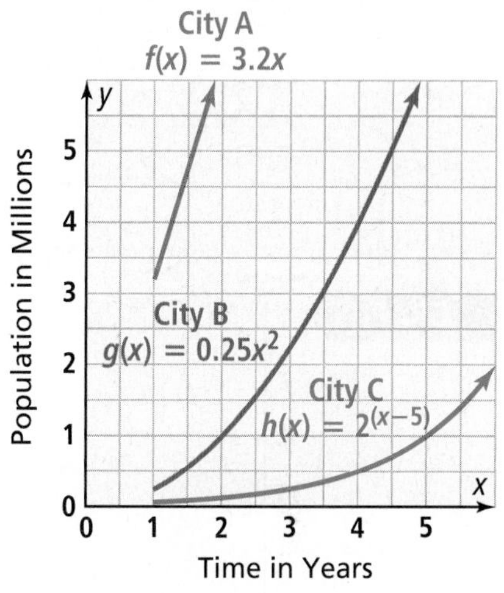

Method 1 Use the table of values.

x	$f(x)$	$g(x)$	$h(x)$
4	12.8	4.0	0.5
5	16.0	6.25	1
6	19.2	9.0	2
7	22.4	12.25	4
8	25.6	16.0	8
9	28.8	20.25	16
10	32.0	25.0	32
11	35.2	30.25	64

The population of City C is greater than those of City A and City B.

Method 2 Use a graphing calculator to determine the points of intersection.

x scale: 10 *y scale*: 32

Use your calculator to find the point where function h exceeds functions f and g.

USE STRUCTURE
Look at the structure of each of the graphs. Notice that a quantity that increases exponentially will eventually exceed a quantity that increases linearly or quadratically.

After 10 years, the population of City C will exceed the populations of City A and City B. It will continue to outgrow the other cities because it is growing exponentially.

 **Try It!** **3.** Compare the functions $f(x) = 3x + 2$, $g(x) = 2x^2 + 3$, and $h(x) = 2^x$. Show that as x increases, $h(x)$ will eventually exceed $f(x)$ and $g(x)$.

CONCEPT SUMMARY Linear, Quadratic, and Exponential Functions

	Linear	Quadratic	Exponential
WORDS	The 1st differences are constant.	The 2nd differences are constant.	The ratios of consecutive y-values are constant.

TABLES

$f(x) = 2x + 3$

x	y	1st Differences
0	3	
1	5	2
2	7	2
3	9	2

$f(x) = 0.25x^2 + 0.5x + 0.25$

		Differences	
x	y	1st	2nd
0	0.25		
1	1.00	0.75	
2	2.25	1.25	0.5
3	4.00	1.75	0.5

$f(x) = 2^{x-3}$

x	y	Ratios
0	0.125	
1	0.25	$\frac{0.25}{0.125} = 2$
2	0.5	$\frac{0.5}{0.25} = 2$
3	1.00	$\frac{1}{0.5} = 2$

GRAPHS

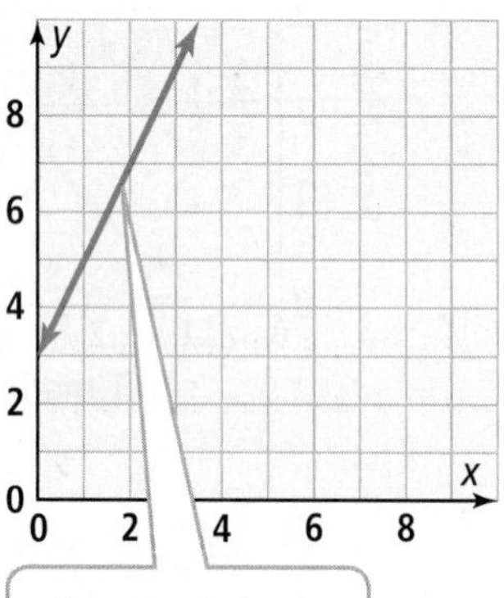

The rate of change is constant.

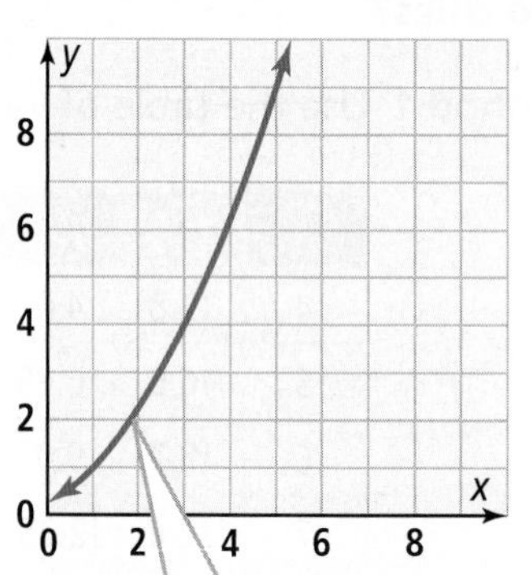

The rate of change in this function increases as the value of x increases.

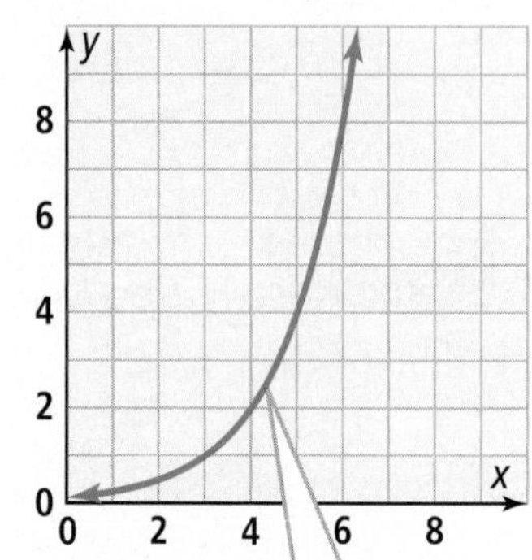

The rate of change in this function increases by equal factors as the value of x increases.

Do You UNDERSTAND?

1. ESSENTIAL QUESTION How can you determine whether a linear, exponential, or quadratic function best models data?

2. **Reason** The average rate of change of a function is less from $x = 1$ to $x = 4$ than from $x = 5$ to $x = 8$. What type of function could it be? Explain.

3. **Error Analysis** Kiyo used a quadratic function to model data with constant first differences. Explain the error Kiyo made.

Do You KNOW HOW?

Determine whether the data are best modeled by a linear, quadratic, or exponential function.

4.

x	0	1	2	3	4
y	−2	1	10	25	46

5.

x	−2	−1	0	1	2
y	2	7	12	17	22

6. A company's profit from a certain product is represented by $P(x) = -5x^2 + 1{,}125x - 5{,}000$, where x is the price of the product. Compare the growth in profits from $x = 120$ to $x = 140$ and from $x = 140$ to $x = 160$. What do you notice?

PRACTICE & PROBLEM SOLVING

Scan for Multimedia

Practice | Tutorial

Additional Exercises Available Online

UNDERSTAND

7. **Communicate Precisely** Create a flow chart to show the process to determine whether a given data set represents a function that is linear, quadratic, exponential, or none of these.

8. **Generalize** Calculate the 2nd differences for data in each table. Use a graphing calculator to find the quadratic regression for each data set. Make a conjecture about the relationship between the a values in the quadratic models and the 2nd differences of the data.

x	y
0	0
1	3
2	12
3	27
4	48

x	y
1	0.5
2	2
3	4.5
4	8
5	12.5

x	y
0	4
1	16
2	36
3	64
4	100

x	y
3	58.5
5	162.5
7	318.5
9	526.5
11	786.5

9. **Error Analysis** What is the error in the student's reasoning below? Describe how to correct the statement.

The data can be modeled with a linear function because the first differences are constant.

x	y
-3	-8
-1	-2
0	4
1	10
3	16

10. **Higher Order Thinking** A savings account has a balance of \$1. Savings Plan A will add \$1,000 to an account each month, and Plan B will double the amount each month.

    a. Which plan is better in the short run? For how long? Explain.

    b. Which plan is better in the long run? Explain.

PRACTICE

Determine whether a linear, quadratic, or exponential function is the best model for the data in each table. SEE EXAMPLE 1

11.

x	y
0	1
1	3
2	9
3	27
4	81

12.

x	y
0	1
1	2
2	7
3	16
4	29

13.

x	y
0	56
1	57
2	50
3	35
4	12

14.

x	y
0	−6
1	−3
2	0
3	3
4	6

Do the data suggest a linear, quadratic, or an exponential function? Use regression to find a model for each data set. SEE EXAMPLE 2

15.

x	0	1	2	3	4
y	−20	−17.5	−15.1	−12.5	−10

16.

x	6	7	8	9	10
y	−19	−12	−7	−4	−3

17. **Use the functions shown.** SEE EXAMPLE 3

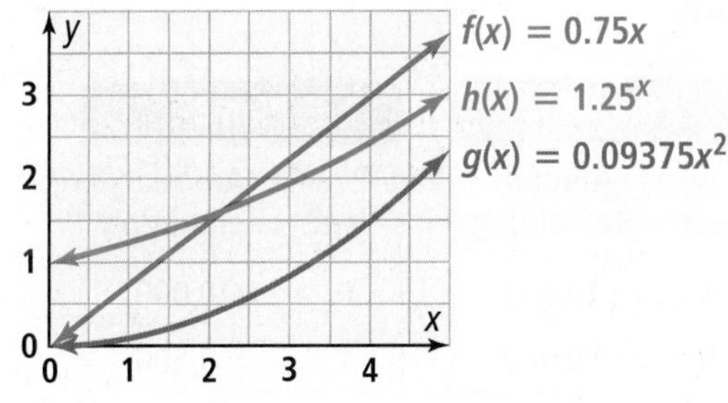

    a. Evaluate each function for $x = 6$, $x = 8$ and $x = 12$.

    b. When will function h exceed function f and function g?

Mixed Review Available Online

PRACTICE & PROBLEM SOLVING

APPLY

18. Model With Mathematics The data in the table show the population of a city for the past five years. A new water plant will be built when the population exceeds 1 million. Will the city need a new water plant in the next ten years? Use a function model to justify your answer.

Year	2016	2017	2018	2019	2020
Population	794,000	803,000	814,000	822,000	830,000

19. Construct Arguments The graphic shows costs for rectangular lots of different widths. Each lot is twice as long as it is wide.

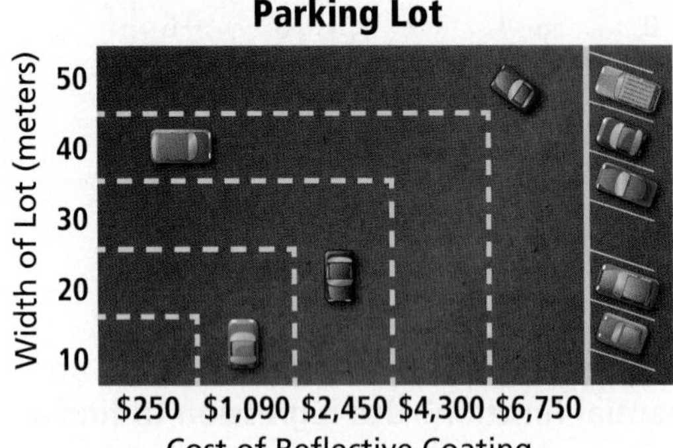

To coat a parking lot 300 m long and 150 m wide, a developer budgeted $20,220, or three times the cost of a lot 50 m wide. Will the budget be sufficient? Justify your answers using a function model.

20. Construct Arguments Carmen is considering two plans to pay off a $10,000 loan. The tables show the amount remaining on the loan after *x* years.

Plan A	
Year	Amount Remaining
0	10,000
1	9,000
2	8,100
3	7,290
4	6,561

Plan B	
Year	Amount Remaining
0	10,000
1	9,500
2	9,000
3	8,500
4	8,000

Which plan should Carmen use to pay off the loan as soon as possible? Justify your answer using a function model.

ASSESSMENT PRACTICE

21. Function f has constant second differences. Which of the following are true? Select all that apply.

Ⓐ The graph of f is a parabola.

Ⓑ The graph of f is a straight line.

Ⓒ The ratios of the y-values increase as x increases.

Ⓓ The function f is an exponential function.

Ⓔ The function f has constant first differences.

22. SAT/ACT At what point will $f(x) = 3^x$ exceed $g(x) = 2x + 5$ and $h(x) = x^2 + 4$?

Ⓐ (1, 7)

Ⓑ (1.8, 7.3)

Ⓒ (2, 9)

Ⓓ (2.4, 9.8)

23. Performance Task Ella wrote three different computer apps to analyze some data. The tables show the time in milliseconds y for each app to analyze data as a function of the number of data items x.

App A	
x	y
4	81
5	243
6	729
7	2,187
8	6,561

App B	
x	y
4	4,042
5	5,040
6	6,038
7	7,036
8	8,034

App C	
x	y
4	4,400
5	5,375
6	6,550
7	7,925
8	9,500

Part A Use regression on a graphing calculator to find a function that models each data set. Explain your choice of model.

Part B Make a conjecture about which app will require the most time as the number of data items gets very large. How could you support your conjecture?

TOPIC 8

Topic Review

TOPIC ESSENTIAL QUESTION

1. How can you use sketches and equations of quadratic functions to model situations and make predictions?

Vocabulary Review

Choose the correct term to complete each sentence.

2. The graph of a quadratic function is a(n) ________.
3. The function $f(x) = x^2$ is called the ________.
4. To model the height of an object launched into the air t seconds after it is launched, you can use the ________.
5. The ________ is $f(x) = ax^2 + bx + c$.
6. A(n) ________ is a method used to find a quadratic function that best fits a data set.

- parabola
- quadratic parent function
- quadratic regression
- standard form of a quadratic function
- vertex form of a quadratic function
- vertical motion model

Concepts & Skills Review

LESSON 8-1 Key Features of Quadratic Functions

Quick Review

The graph of $f(x) = ax^2$ is a **parabola** with **vertex** (0, 0) and **axis of symmetry** $x = 0$. When $a > 0$, the parabola opens upward and the function has a minimum at the vertex. When $a < 0$, the parabola opens downward and the function has a maximum at the vertex.

Example

Compare the graph of $g(x) = -0.2x^2$ with the graph of $f(x) = x^2$.

The graph of g opens downward and is wider than the graph of f. For both graphs, the axis of symmetry is $x = 0$ and the vertex is (0, 0).

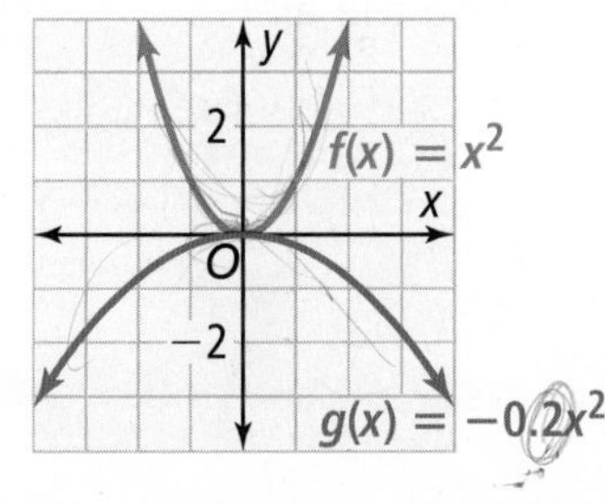

Practice and Problem Solving

Compare the graph of each function with the graph of $f(x) = x^2$.

7. $g(x) = 1.5x^2$
8. $h(x) = -9x^2$
9. **Communicate Precisely** Explain how you can you tell whether a function of the form $f(x) = ax^2$ has a minimum or a maximum value and what that value is.
10. **Model With Mathematics** Artificial turf costs \$15/sq ft to install, and sod costs \$0.15/sq ft to install. Write a quadratic function that represents the cost of installing artificial turf on a square plot with a side length of x feet, and a second quadratic function that represents the cost of installing sod on the same plot. How do the graphs of the two functions differ?

TOPIC 8 REVIEW

LESSON 8-2 Quadratic Functions in Vertex Form

Quick Review

The **vertex form of a quadratic function** is $f(x) = a(x - h)^2 + k$. The vertex of the graph is at (h, k) and the axis of symmetry is $x = h$.

Example

Graph the function $f(x) = (x + 1)^2 - 1$.

The vertex is $(-1, -1)$ and the axis of symmetry is $x = -1$.

Use the points $(0, 0)$ and $(1, 3)$ to find two other points. Reflect each point across the axis of symmetry.

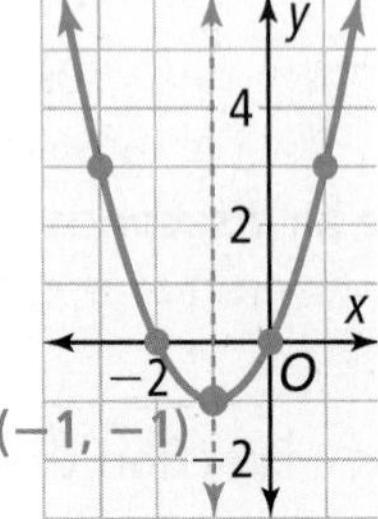

Practice and Problem Solving

11. Look for Relationships Graph the functions below. How are the graphs alike? How are the graphs different from each other?

$$f(x) = -5(x - 3)^2 + 2$$
$$g(x) = -2(x - 3)^2 + 2$$

Identify the vertex and axis of symmetry of the graph of each function.

12. $g(x) = (x + 8)^2 + 1$ **13.** $h(x) = (x - 5)^2 - 2$

14. An astronaut on the moon throws a moon rock into the air. The rock's height, in meters, above the moon's surface x seconds after it is thrown can be determined by the function $h(x) = -1.6(x - 2.5)^2 + 15$. What is the maximum height of the rock above the moon's surface? How many seconds after being thrown does the rock reach this height?

LESSON 8-3 Quadratic Functions in Standard Form

Quick Review

The standard form of a quadratic function is $f(x) = ax^2 + bx + c$, where $a \neq 0$. The y-intercept is c and the axis of symmetry, which is also the x-coordinate of the vertex, is $x = -\frac{b}{2a}$.

Example

Graph the function $f(x) = 3x^2 - 6x + 2$.

The y-intercept is 2.

Find the axis of symmetry.

$$x = -\frac{b}{2a} = -\frac{-6}{2(3)} = 1$$

Find the y-coordinate of the vertex.

$$f(1) = 3(1)^2 - 6(1) + 2 = -1$$

Plot the vertex $(1, -1)$ and identify the axis of symmetry.

Plot the y-intercept $(0, 2)$. Reflect that point across the axis of symmetry.

Practice and Problem Solving

Identify the y-intercept, axis of symmetry, and vertex of the graph of each function.

15. $g(x) = -x^2 + 4x + 5$ **16.** $h(x) = -3x^2 + 7x + 1$

17. When given a function in standard form, how can you determine if the parabola has a minimum or maximum value?

18. Graph the function $f(x) = -3x^2 + 12x + 5$.

19. Reason A ball is tossed into the air. The function $f(x) = -16x^2 + 4x + 5$ represents the height in feet of the ball x seconds after it is thrown. At what height was the ball tossed into the air?

LESSON 8-4 Modeling With Quadratic Functions

Quick Review

Quadratic functions can model situations. For example, the vertical motion model is a quadratic function.

Example

Alberto launches an emergency flare at an initial velocity of 64 ft/s from an initial height of 6 ft. The flare must reach a height of 100 ft to be seen by a rescue team. Is Alberto's launch successful?

Substitute 64 for v_0 and 6 for h_0 in the vertical motion model.

$$h(t) = -16t^2 + 64t + 6$$

Find the vertex $(t, h(t))$.

$$t = -\frac{b}{2a} = -\frac{64}{2(-16)} = 2$$

$$h(2) = -16(2)^2 + 64(2) + 6 = 70$$

The vertex is (2, 70).

The flare will reach a maximum height of 70 ft, so Alberto's launch is not successful.

Practice and Problem Solving

Write a function h to model the vertical motion for each situation, given $h(t) = -16t^2 + v_0t + h_0$. Find the maximum height.

20. initial velocity: 54 ft/s
    initial height: 7 ft
21. initial velocity: 18 ft/s
    initial height: 9 ft

Write a quadratic function to represent the area of each rectangle. Graph the function. Interpret the vertex and intercepts. Identify a reasonable domain and range.

22. Rectangle with sides $x + 5$ and $2x - 1$

23. Rectangle with sides $2x - 3$ and $x + 1$

24. **Make Sense and Persevere** Given a vertical motion model, how can you identify the amount of time an object is in the air before it reaches the ground?

LESSON 8-5 Linear, Exponential, and Quadratic Models

Quick Review

To determine which function best models a data set, analyze the differences and ratios between consecutive y-values when the differences in consecutive x-values are constant.

Example

Determine whether the function below is linear, quadratic, or exponential.

x	y	1st Diff.	2nd Diff.	Ratios
0	1			
1	3	2		3
2	9	6	4	3
3	27	18	12	3

Since the ratio between the y-values is constant, the function is exponential.

Practice and Problem Solving

25. **Make Sense and Persevere** What is the first step in determining whether a table shows a linear, quadratic, or exponential function?

Determine whether the data in the tables represent a linear, quadratic, or exponential function.

26.

x	0	1	2	3	4
y	3	7	19	39	67

27.

x	−2	0	2	4	6
y	−20	−6	8	22	36

TOPIC 9

Solving Quadratic Equations

? TOPIC ESSENTIAL QUESTION

How do you use quadratic equations to model situations and solve problems?

Topic Overview

enVision™ STEM Project:
Designing a T-Shirt Launcher

9-1 Solving Quadratic Equations Using Graphs and Tables

9-2 Solving Quadratic Equations by Factoring

9-3 Rewriting Radical Expressions

9-4 Solving Quadratic Equations Using Square Roots

9-5 Completing the Square

9-6 The Quadratic Formula and the Discriminant

Mathematical Modeling in 3 Acts:
Unwrapping Change

9-7 Solving Systems of Linear and Quadratic Equations

Topic Vocabulary

- completing the square
- discriminant
- linear-quadratic system
- Product Property of Square Roots
- quadratic equation
- quadratic formula
- root
- standard form of a quadratic equation
- Zero-Product Property
- zeros of a function

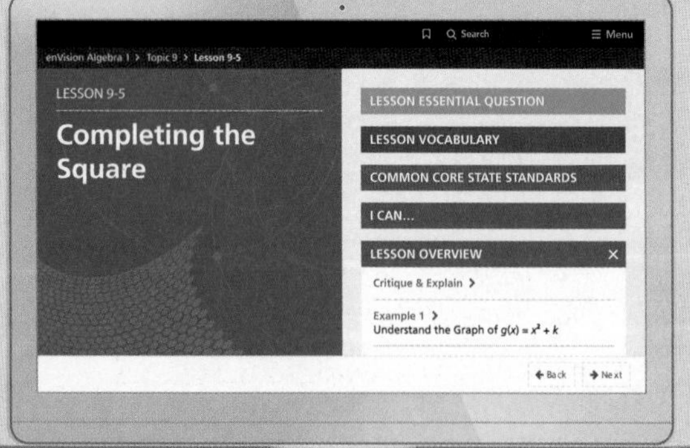

Go online | **PearsonRealize.com**

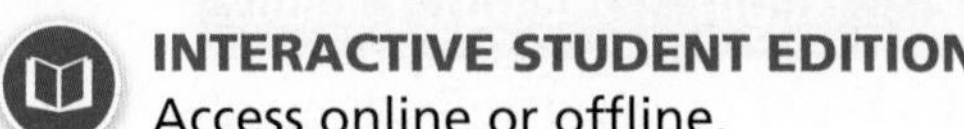

Digital Experience

INTERACTIVE STUDENT EDITION Access online or offline.

ACTIVITIES Complete ***Explore & Reason, Model & Discuss***, and ***Critique & Explain*** activities. Interact with Examples and Try Its.

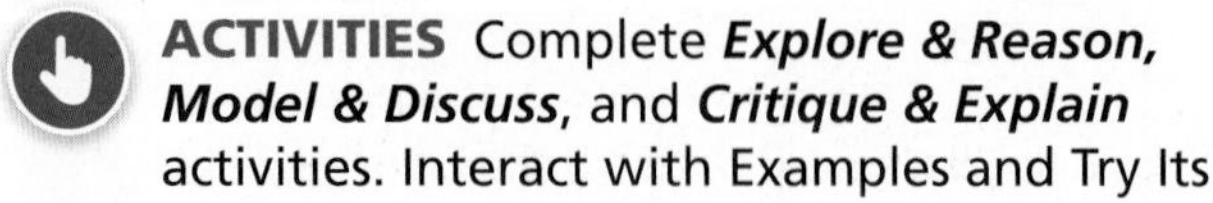

ANIMATION View and interact with real-world applications.

PRACTICE Practice what you've learned.

Unwrapping Change

When you arrange a group of objects in different ways, it seems like the space they take up has changed. But, the number of objects didn't change!

We use coin wrappers to store coins in an efficient way. How much more efficient is it than the alternative? Think about this during the Mathematical Modeling in 3 Acts lesson.

TOPIC 9

VIDEOS Watch clips to support ***Mathematical Modeling in 3 Acts Lessons*** and **enVision™** ***STEM Projects.***

CONCEPT SUMMARY Review key lesson content through multiple representations.

ASSESSMENT Show what you've learned.

GLOSSARY Read and listen to English and Spanish definitions.

TUTORIALS Get help from ***Virtual Nerd***, right when you need it.

MATH TOOLS Explore math with digital tools and manipulatives.

Did You Know?

Objects launched or thrown into the air follow a **parabolic path**. The force of gravity and the horizontal and vertical velocities determine a quadratic function for an object's path.

Gravity

Earth: 9.8 m/s^2

Mars 3.7 m/s^2

Moon 1.6 m/s^2

The **weaker the gravity, the higher an object will fly** and the longer it will remain airborn.

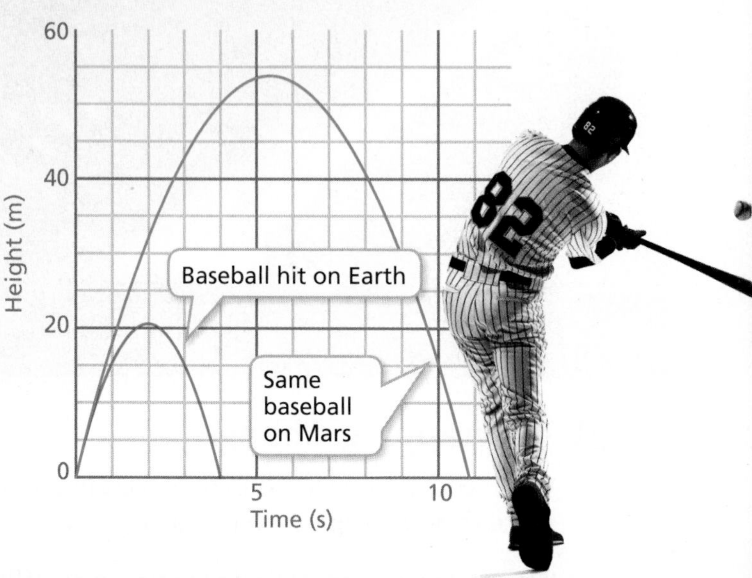

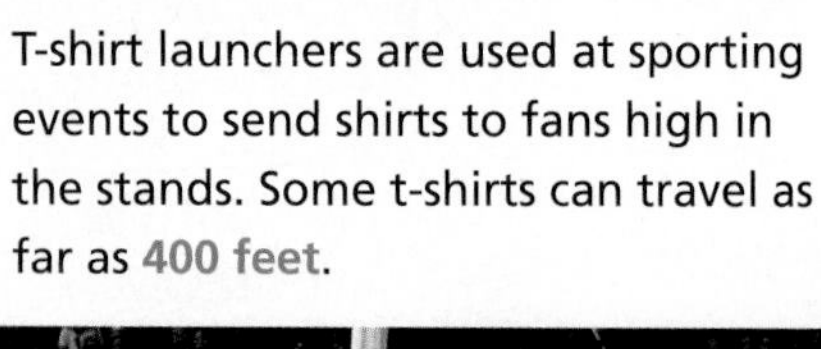

T-shirt launchers are used at sporting events to send shirts to fans high in the stands. Some t-shirts can travel as far as **400 feet**.

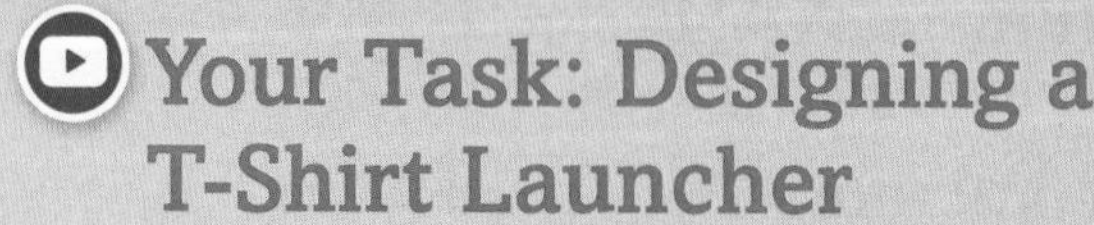

Your Task: Designing a T-Shirt Launcher

You and your classmates will design a t-shirt launcher and determine possible heights and distances on Earth and other planets.

9-1 Solving Quadratic Equations Using Graphs and Tables

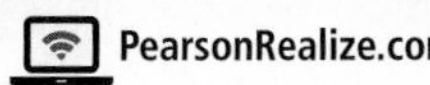
PearsonRealize.com

I CAN… use graphs and tables to find solutions of quadratic equations.

VOCABULARY

- quadratic equation
- zeros of a function

EXPLORE & REASON

The path of a golf ball hit from the ground resembles the shape of a parabola.

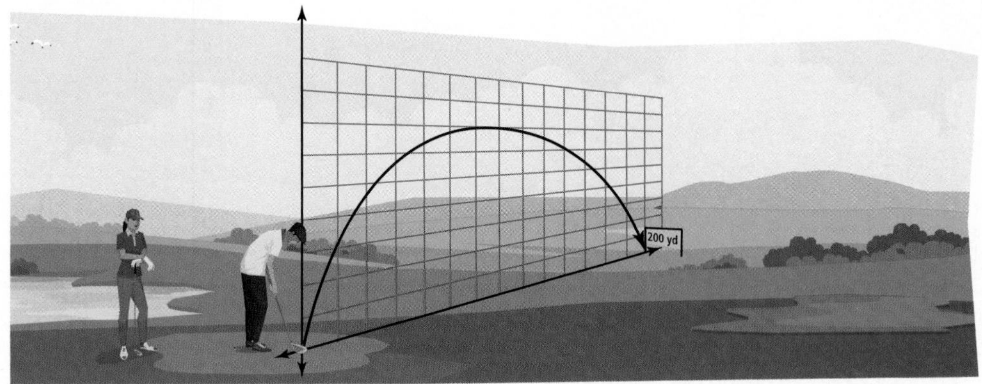

A. What point represents the golf ball before it is hit off the ground?

B. What point represents the golf ball when it lands on the ground?

C. **Look for Relationships** Explain how the points in Part A and B are related to the ball's distance from the ground.

ESSENTIAL QUESTION

How can graphs and tables help you solve quadratic equations?

CONCEPTUAL UNDERSTANDING

EXAMPLE 1 Recognize Solutions of Quadratic Equations

Why are the *x*-intercepts of the graph of a quadratic function important to the solution of a related equation?

A. Find the solutions of the quadratic equation $x^2 - 16 = 0$.

A **quadratic equation** is an equation of the second degree. The related function of a quadratic equation with 0 on one side is the quadratic expression given on the other side.

CONSTRUCT ARGUMENTS
Think about the connection between the graph of the function and the solutions to the quadratic equation. What evidence can you give that the *x*-intercept is the solution of the quadratic equation?

Graph the related function, $f(x) = x^2 - 16$.

The solutions of a quadratic equation are the value or values that make the equation true.

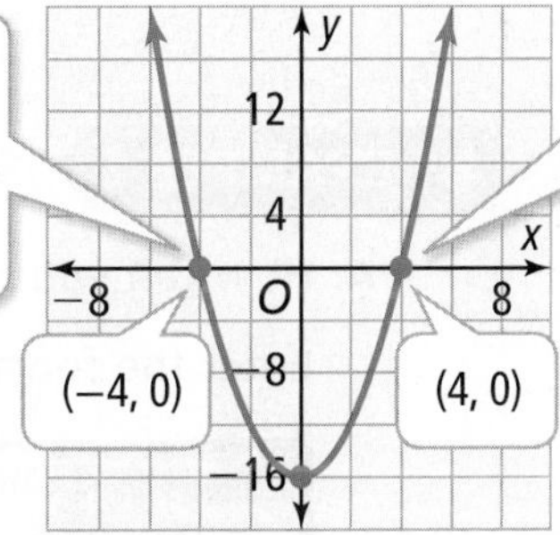

The *x*-intercepts of *f* occur where $x^2 - 16 = 0$ and represent the solutions of the equation.

The graph of the function has two *x*-intercepts, so the equation has two real solutions. The solutions of the equation $x^2 - 16 = 0$ are $x = -4$ and $x = 4$. Solutions to an equation of the form $f(x) = 0$, are called the **zeros of a function.** The zeros of a function correspond to the *x*-intercepts of the function.

CONTINUED ON THE NEXT PAGE

EXAMPLE 1 CONTINUED

B. Find the solutions of $x^2 - 14x + 49 = 0$.

Graph the related function $f(x) = x^2 - 14x + 49$.

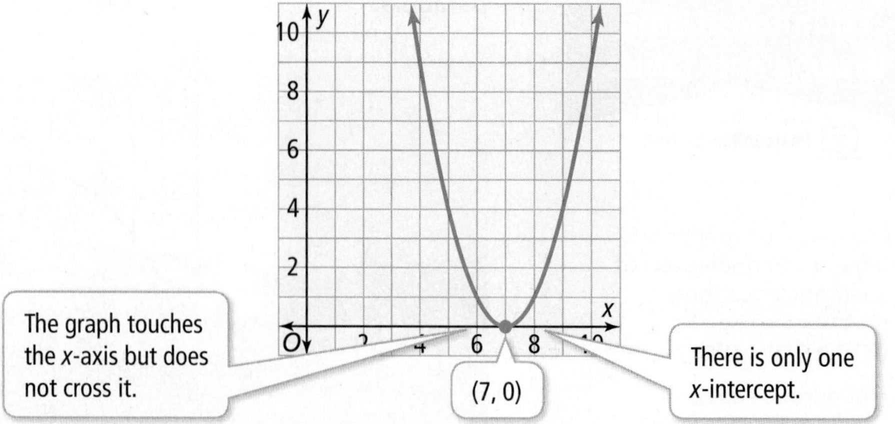

The graph of the function has only one x-intercept, so the equation has only one real solution, $x = 7$.

C. Find the solutions of $x^2 + 3x + 7 = 0$.

Graph the related function $f(x) = x^2 + 3x + 7$.

STUDY TIP
A quadratic equation can have 0, 1, or 2 real solutions.

The graph of the function has no x-intercepts, so the equation has no real solutions.

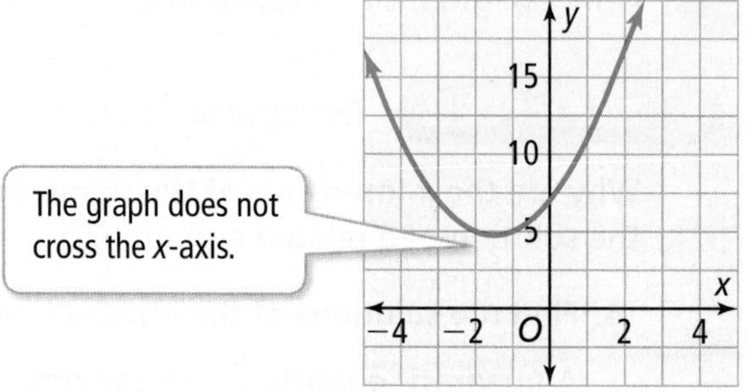

Try It! **1.** What are the solutions of each equation?

a. $x^2 - 36 = 0$

b. $x^2 + 6x + 9 = 0$

EXAMPLE 2 Solve Quadratic Equations Using Tables

A. How can you use a table to find the solutions of $x^2 - 7x + 6 = 0$?

Enter the function $y = x^2 - 7x + 6$ into a graphing calculator.

LOOK FOR RELATIONSHIPS
How would the solutions of this quadratic equation appear in a graph?

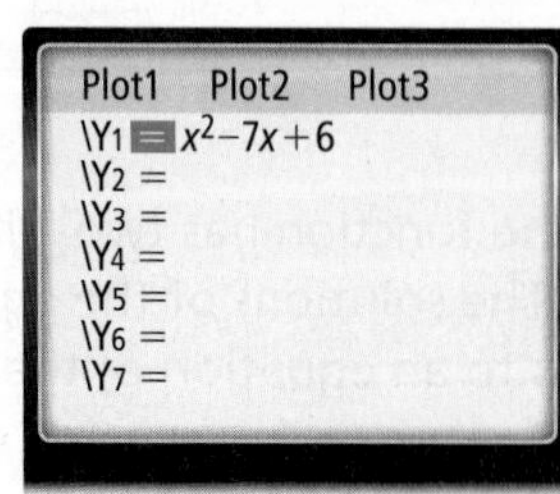

X	Y1
1	0
2	−4
3	−6
4	−6
5	−4
6	0

X=1

Use the table to identify the values of x when $y = 0$.

There are two real solutions, $x = 1$ and $x = 6$.

CONTINUED ON THE NEXT PAGE

EXAMPLE 2 CONTINUED

B. How can you use a table to estimate the solutions of $3x^2 + 5x - 2 = 0$?

> **USE APPROPRIATE TOOLS**
> The solution may not always appear in a table when $y = 0$. Would a graph be more useful in finding the solution for this quadratic equation?

Enter the function $y = 3x^2 + 5x - 2$ into a graphing calculator.

The table shows one solution, $x = -2$.

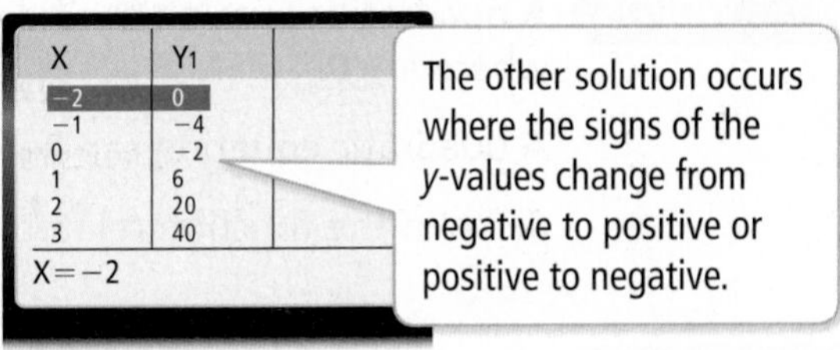

X	Y1
−2	0
−1	−4
0	−2
1	6
2	20
3	40

X=−2

Refine the table settings to find the other solution of the equation. Change the table settings to show steps of 0.25.

The other solution is between 0.25 and 0.5.

Using a table has limitations. When the corresponding x-values for $y = 0$ are not shown in the table, you can estimate the solution.

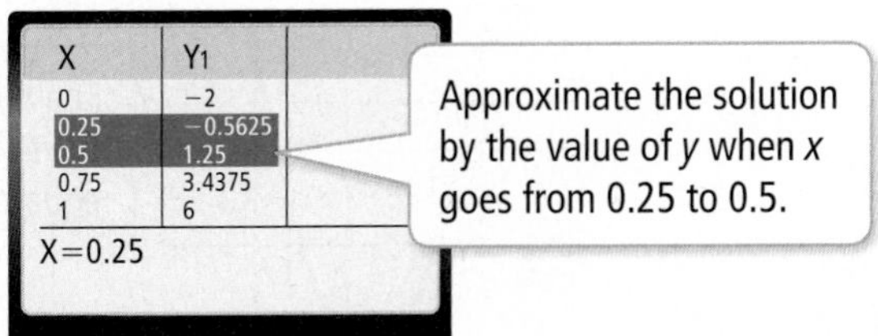

X	Y1
0	−2
0.25	−0.5625
0.5	1.25
0.75	3.4375
1	6

X=0.25

 **Try It!** **2.** Find the solutions for $4x^2 + 3x - 7 = 0$ using a table. If approximating, give the answer to the nearest tenth.

APPLICATION

EXAMPLE 3 Use Approximate Solutions

Anastasia hits her golf ball off the tee. The height of the golf ball is modeled by the function $f(x) = -5x^2 + 25x + 1$, where x is the number of seconds after the golf ball is hit. How long is the golf ball in the air?

Graph $f(x) = -5x^2 + 25x + 1$ to find when $y = 0$.

The graph of the function shows the x-intercept at 5.04. This means the golf ball was in the air about 5 seconds before it hit the ground.

> **CONSTRUCT ARGUMENTS**
> What are the benefits of using a graph to approximate a solution? When is a table more useful than a graph?

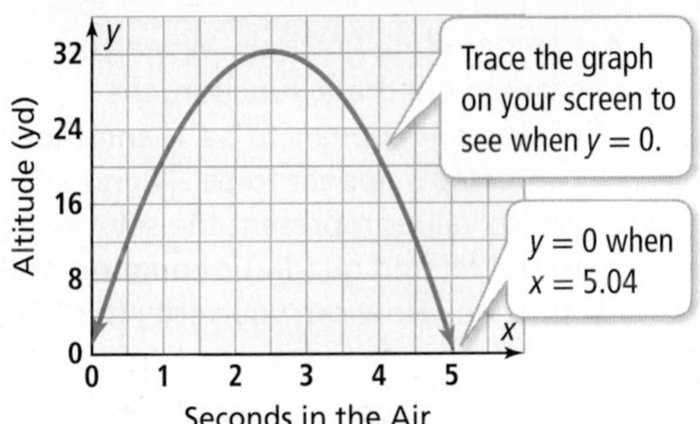

 **Try It!** **3.** At the next tee, a golf ball was hit and modeled by $-16x^2 + 11x + 6 = 0$. When will the golf ball hit the ground?

CONCEPT SUMMARY Solving Quadratic Equations Using Graphs and Tables

WORDS A quadratic equation can be written in standard form $ax^2 + bx + c = 0$, where $a \neq 0$.

A quadratic equation can have 0, 1, or 2 real solutions.

Zeros of the function related to a quadratic equation are the solutions of the equation.

ALGEBRA $x^2 + 5x + 4 = 0$ The solutions are $x = -4$ and $x = -1$.

GRAPH $f(x) = x^2 + 5x + 4$

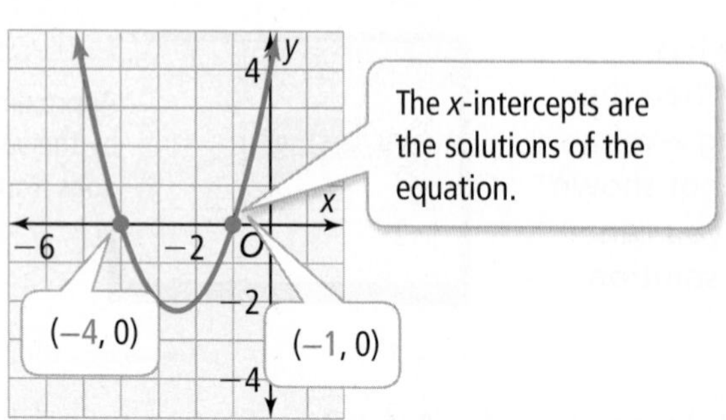

TABLE

x	y
−5	4
−4	0
−3	−2
−2	−2
−1	0

The solutions are the x-values when the y-values are 0.

Do You UNDERSTAND?

1. **ESSENTIAL QUESTION** How can graphs and tables help you solve quadratic equations?

2. **Reason** In a table that shows no exact solutions, how do you know if there are any solutions? How can you find an approximate solution?

3. **Error Analysis** Eli says that the solutions to $x^2 + 100 = 0$ are −10 and 10 because 10^2 is 100. What is the error that Eli made? Explain.

4. **Communicate Precisely** When you graph a quadratic function, the y-intercept appears to be 1, and the x-intercepts appear to be −4 and 2.5. Which values represent the solution(s) to the related quadratic equation of the function? How can you verify this? Explain.

Do You KNOW HOW?

Use each graph to find the solution of the equation.

5. $-x^2 + 2x - 1 = 0$

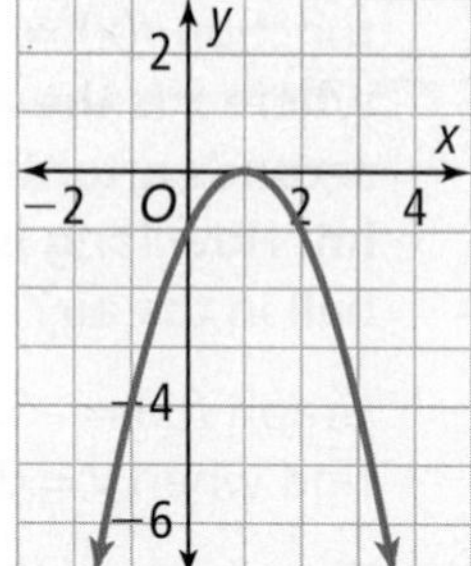

6. $x^2 + x - 6 = 0$

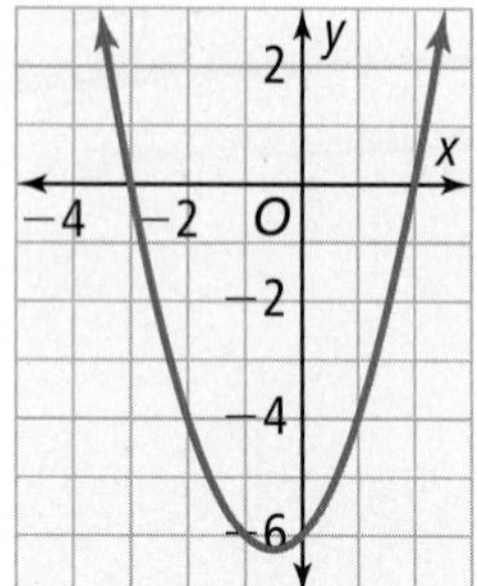

Solve each quadratic equation by graphing the related function.

7. $x^2 - 2x - 3 = 0$

8. $x^2 + x + 1 = 0$

Find the solutions of each equation using a table. Round approximate solutions to the nearest tenth.

9. $x^2 + 3x - 4 = 0$

10. $3x^2 - 2x + 1 = 0$

11. What are the solutions of $-5x^2 + 10x + 2 = 0$? Round approximate solutions to the nearest tenth.

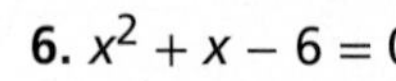

PRACTICE & PROBLEM SOLVING

Scan for Multimedia 

Practice Tutorial

Additional Exercises Available Online

UNDERSTAND

12. **Communicate Precisely** Consider the quadratic equation $x^2 + 2x - 24 = 0$.

    a. How could you solve the equation using a graph? Explain.

    b. How could you solve the equation using a table? Explain.

13. **Generalize** For an equation of the form $ax^2 + bx + c = 0$, where the graph crosses the y-axis once and does not intersect the x-axis. Describe the solution(s) of the equation.

14. **Error Analysis** Describe and correct the error a student made in stating the number of solutions of a quadratic equation. Explain.

    A quadratic equation has either two solutions or no solution. ✗

15. **Higher Order Thinking** Infinitely many quadratic equations of the form $ax^2 + bx + c = 0$ can have the same two solutions. Sketch the graphs of two quadratic functions on the same grid to show how this could be true.

16. **Communicate Precisely** How many zeros does the function shown have? Explain.

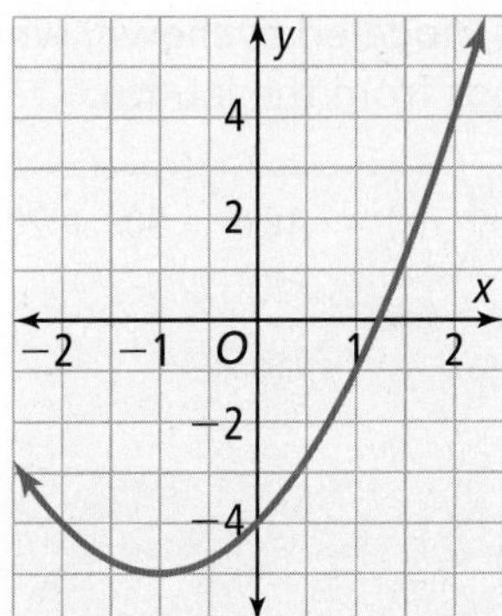

17. **Mathematical Connections** If a quadratic function has a maximum value that is greater than 0, how many zeros does the function have? Explain.

PRACTICE

Use each graph to find the solution of the related equation. SEE EXAMPLE 1

18. $x^2 - 2x + 2 = 0$

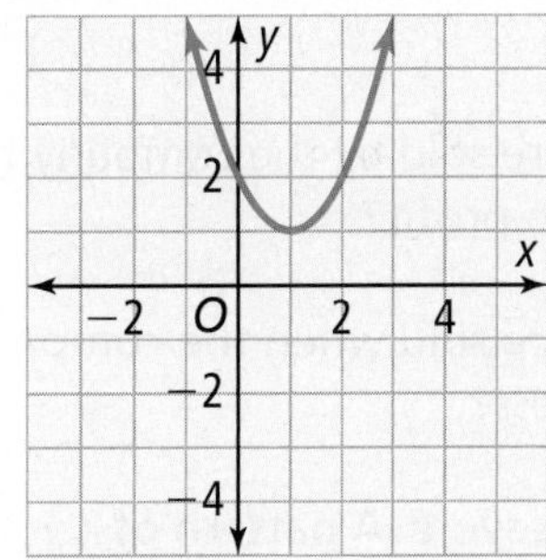

19. $-x^2 - x + 6 = 0$

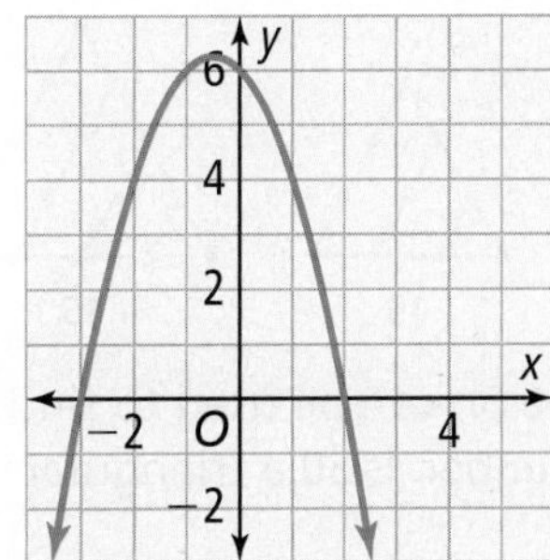

Solve each quadratic equation by graphing the related function. Round approximate solutions to the nearest tenth. SEE EXAMPLES 1 AND 3

20. $x^2 - 121 = 0$
21. $x^2 - 4x + 4 = 0$
22. $x^2 + 3x + 7 = 0$
23. $x^2 - 5x = 0$
24. $-x^2 + 6x + 7 = 0$
25. $-x^2 + 8x - 7 = 0$
26. $x^2 - 2 = 0$
27. $2x^2 - 11x + 12 = 0$
28. $-3x^2 + 5x + 7 = 0$
29. $-16x^2 + 70 = 0$

Find the solutions for each equation using a table. Round approximate solutions to the nearest tenth. SEE EXAMPLE 2

30. $x^2 - 16 = 0$
31. $x^2 + 8x + 16 = 0$
32. $x^2 + 3x + 1 = 0$
33. $x^2 + 4x + 6 = 0$

PRACTICE & PROBLEM SOLVING

APPLY

34. Model With Mathematics A small company shows the profits from their business with the function $P(x) = -0.01x^2 + 60x + 500$, where x is the number of units they sell and P is the profit in dollars.

a. How many units are sold by the company to earn the maximum profit?

b. How many units are sold when the company starts showing a loss?

35. Make Sense and Persevere A pattern of triangular numbers is shown. The first is 1, the second is 3, the third is 6, and so on.

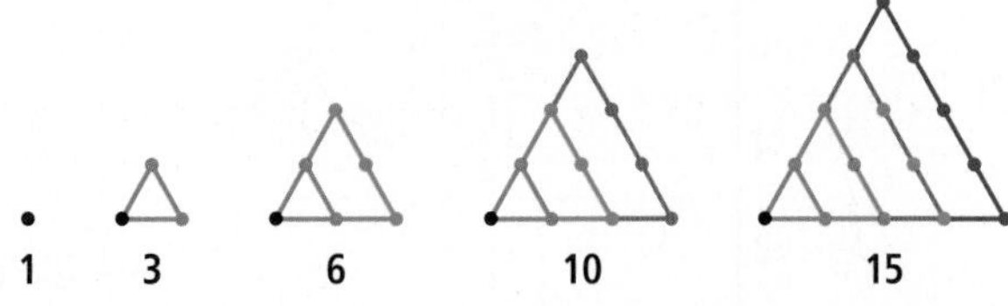

The formula $0.5n^2 + 0.5n$ can be used to find the nth triangular number. Is 50 a triangular number? Explain.

36. Make Sense and Persevere The equation $-16x^2 + 10x + 15 = 0$ represents the height, in feet, of a flotation device above the water after x seconds. The linear term represents the initial velocity. The constant term represents the initial height.

a. If the initial velocity is 0, when should the flotation device land in the water?

b. If the initial height is 0, when does the flotation device land in the water?

ASSESSMENT PRACTICE

37. Does each quadratic equation have two solutions? Select *Yes* or *No*.

	Yes	No
$0 = 2x^2 + 1$	❑	❑
$0 = 2x^2 + 5x + 1$	❑	❑
$0 = 2x^2 + 5x$	❑	❑
$0 = 4x^2 - 4x + 1$	❑	❑
$0 = 4x^2 - 4x - 1$	❑	❑

38. SAT/ACT What are the solutions of $x^2 + 2x - 15 = 0$ using the graph shown?

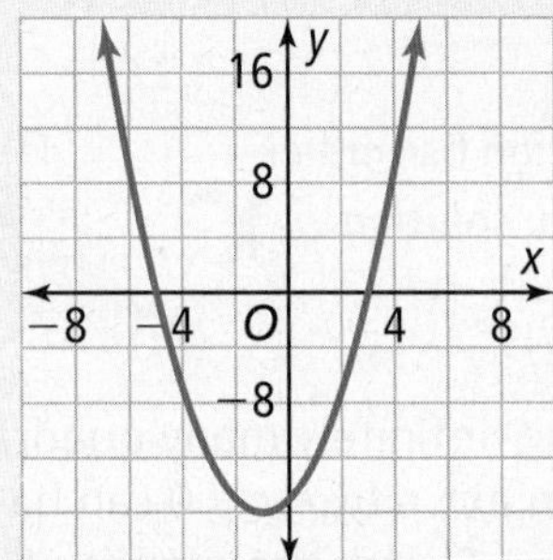

Ⓐ −3, 3
Ⓑ −5, 3
Ⓒ −8, 5
Ⓓ −16, 0

39. Performance Task A human catapult is used to launch a person into a lake. The height, in feet, of the person is modeled as shown, where x is the time in seconds from the launch.

Part A What equation can you use to find when the person touches the lake? Find the solution.

Part B Are your solutions the same for the equation and problem? Why or why not?

Part C What is the greatest height reached?

9-2 Solving Quadratic Equations by Factoring

PearsonRealize.com

I CAN... find the solution of a quadratic equation by factoring.

VOCABULARY

- standard form of a quadratic equation
- Zero-Product Property

Activity Assess

MODEL & DISCUSS

An artist has started a mosaic tile design on a wall. She needs to cover the entire wall.

A. Write expressions to represent the length of the wall and width of the wall.

B. Use Structure What expression represents the area of the entire wall? Explain.

C. How can you determine the area of the part of the wall that the artist has not yet covered?

ESSENTIAL QUESTION

How does factoring help you solve quadratic equations?

EXAMPLE 1 Use the Zero-Product Property

How can you find the solution of the equation $(x - 9)(5x + 2) = 0$?

The **Zero-Product Property** states that for all real numbers a and b, if $ab = 0$, then either $a = 0$ or $b = 0$.

Set each factor of the equation equal to zero to find the solution.

$(x - 9) = 0$ or $(5x + 2) = 0$

$x = 9$ $\qquad$ $x = -\frac{2}{5}$

Either $(x - 9)$ or $(5x + 2)$ is equal to 0 according to the Zero-Product Property.

LOOK FOR RELATIONSHIPS
Think about solving this equation using a table and graph. How would the solutions appear in a table? In a graph?

Check each solution.

Substitute 9 for x.

$$(9 - 9)(5(9) + 2) = 0$$
$$(0)(47) = 0$$
$$0 = 0 \checkmark$$

Substitute $-\frac{2}{5}$ for x.

$$\left(-\frac{2}{5} - 9\right)\left(5\left(-\frac{2}{5}\right) + 2\right) = 0$$
$$\left(-9\frac{2}{5}\right)(0) = 0$$
$$0 = 0 \checkmark$$

The solutions of $(x - 9)(5x + 2) = 0$ are $x = 9$ and $x = -\frac{2}{5}$.

Try It! **1.** Solve each equation.

a. $(2x - 1)(x + 3) = 0$  **b.** $(2x + 3)(3x - 1) = 0$

CONCEPTUAL UNDERSTANDING

EXAMPLE 2 Solve by Factoring

How can you use factoring to solve $x^2 + 9x = -20$?

The **standard form of a quadratic equation** is $ax^2 + bx + c = 0$, where $a \neq 0$.

Step 1 Write the equation in standard form.

$x^2 + 9x = -20$

$x^2 + 9x + 20 = 0$

When solving a quadratic equation by factoring, always begin by writing the equation in standard form.

Step 2 Make a table to find the set of factors to solve $x^2 + 9x + 20 = 0$. The set of factors that have a product of 20 and a sum of 9 can be used to solve the equation.

Factors of 20	Sum of Factors
1, 20	21
2, 10	12
4, 5	9

The factors 4 and 5 have a product of **20** and a sum of **9.**

STUDY TIP
If you can factor the standard form of the equation then you can find the solution.

Step 3 Rewrite the standard form of the equation in factored form.

$(x + 4)(x + 5) = 0$

Step 4 Use the Zero-Product Property to solve the equation.

$(x + 4) = 0$ or $(x + 5) = 0$

$x = -4$ $\quad$ $x = -5$

The solutions of $x^2 + 9x + 20 = 0$ are $x = -4$ and $x = -5$.

 **Try It!** **2.** Solve each equation by factoring.

a. $x^2 + 16x + 64 = 0$ **b.** $x^2 - 12x = 64$

APPLICATION

EXAMPLE 3 Use Factoring to Solve a Real-World Problem

A museum vault has an outer steel wall with a uniform width of x. The area of the museum vault ceiling and the outer steel wall is 1,664 ft^2. What is the width of the outer steel wall?

20 ft, 40 ft, x

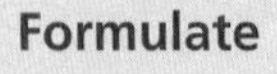

Formulate Write an equation to represent the area of the vault.

$(2x + 20)(2x + 40) = 1{,}664$

length × width = area

Compute Use the Distributive Property. Write the equation in standard form.

$(2x + 20)(2x + 40) = 1{,}664$

$4x^2 + 120x - 864 = 0$

$\frac{4x^2}{4} + \frac{120x}{4} - \frac{864}{4} = \frac{0}{4}$

Divide each term by 4 to simplify the equation.

$x^2 + 30x - 216 = 0$

$(x - 6)(x + 36) = 0$

CONTINUED ON THE NEXT PAGE

EXAMPLE 3 CONTINUED

Interpret The solutions of the equation are $x = 6$ and $x = -36$.

The length of the wall cannot be negative. Therefore −36 cannot be a solution. The width of the wall is 6 ft.

Check the solution.

Substitute 6 for x in the original equation.

$$[2(6) + 20]\ [2(6) + 40] = 1{,}664$$

$$(32)(52) = 1{,}664\ \checkmark$$

Try It! **3.** A picture inside a frame has an area of 375 cm^2.

What is the width of the frame?

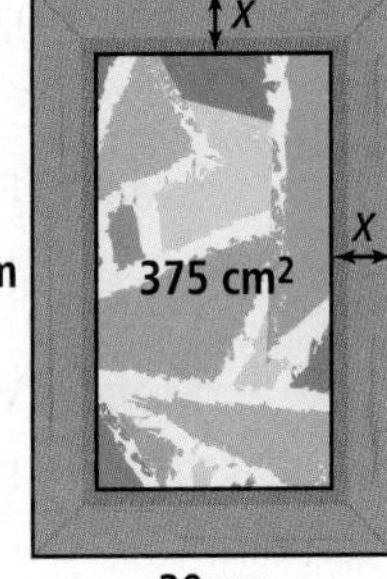

EXAMPLE 4 Use Factored Form to Graph a Quadratic Function

How can you use factoring to graph the function $f(x) = x^2 - 2x - 8$?

Step 1 Factor the related quadratic equation.

$x^2 - 2x - 8 = 0$

$(x + 2)(x - 4) = 0$

Step 2 Determine the solutions of the equation.

$(x + 2) = 0$ or $(x - 4) = 0$

$x = -2$ $x = 4$

Step 3 Find the coordinates of the vertex. Find the average of the x-intercepts 4 and −2.

$$\frac{4 + (-2)}{2} = 1$$

The x-coordinate of the vertex is 1.

Find the y-coordinate of the vertex.

$f(x) = (1)^2 - 2(1) - 8 = -9$

Substitute the x-coordinate in the quadratic function.

The vertex is (1, −9).

STUDY TIP
A parabola is symmetrical so the vertex is halfway between the two x-intercepts.

Step 4 Plot the vertex and the x-intercepts.

Use the vertex and x-intercepts to sketch the graph.

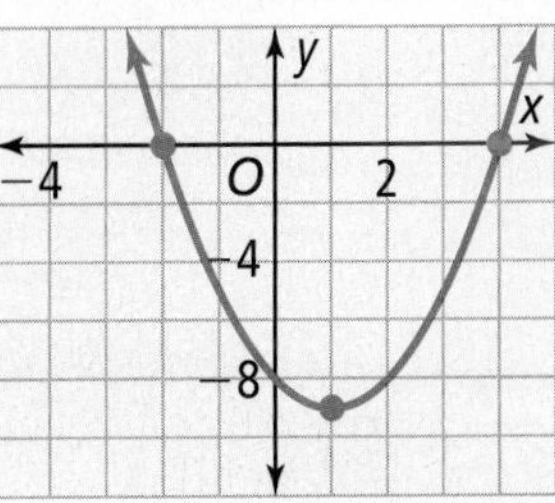

Try It! **4.** Use factoring to graph the function $f(x) = 2x^2 + 5x - 3$.

EXAMPLE 5 Write the Factored Form of a Quadratic Function

How can you write the factored form of the quadratic function related to a graph?

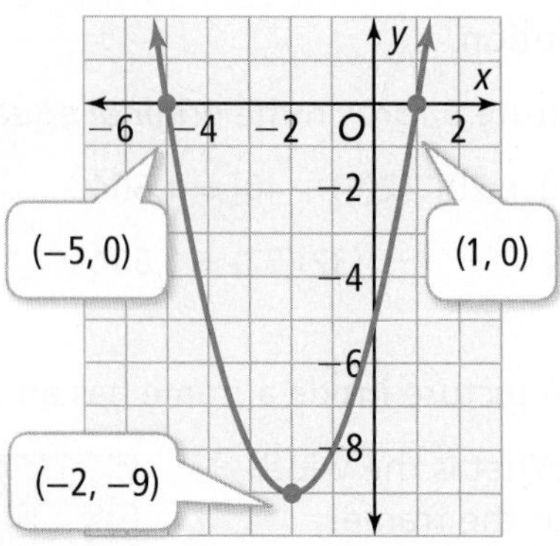

Step 1 Find the x-intercepts.

The x-intercepts are −5 and 1.

Step 2 Write a quadratic equation in factored form.

Use the x-intercepts, which are also the solutions of the quadratic equation, as the factors.

$$a(x - p)(x - q) = 0$$

$$a[x - (-5)]\ [x - (1)] = 0$$

$$a(x + 5)(x - 1) = 0$$

Substitute the x-intercepts for p and q.

STUDY TIP

There are an infinite number of parabolas that pass through (−5, 0) and (1, 0). You will need to determine the value of a to find the one parabola that also passes through (−2, −9).

Step 3 Write the function in factored form.

Use a third point to solve for a.

$$f(x) = a(x + 5)(x - 1)$$

$$-9 = a(-2 + 5)(-2 - 1)$$

$$a = 1$$

Use the vertex. Substitute −2 for x and −9 for $f(x)$.

The factored form of the quadratic function is $f(x) = 1(x + 5)(x - 1)$ or $f(x) = (x + 5)(x - 1)$.

Try It! **5.** What is the factored form of the function?

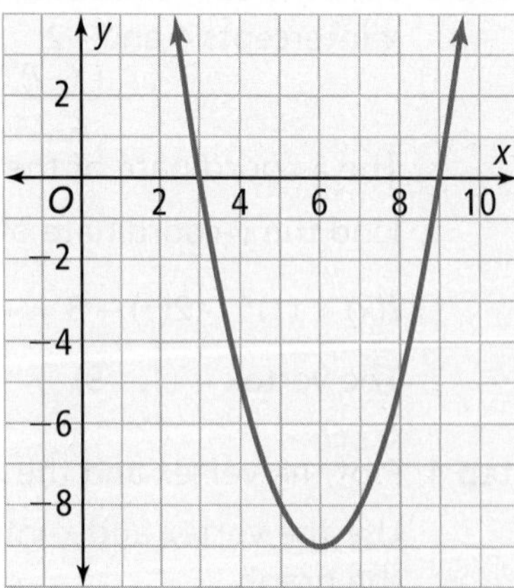

Concept Summary Assess

CONCEPT SUMMARY Solving Quadratic Equations by Factoring

WORDS The **Zero-Product Property** states that for all real numbers a and b, if $ab = 0$, then either $a = 0$ or $b = 0$. You can apply the Zero-Product Property to a factored quadratic equation to help you find the x-intercepts of the graph of the related function.

ALGEBRA $x^2 + 2x - 3 = 5$

$$x^2 + 2x - 8 = 0$$

Write the equation in standard form and factor.

$$(x + 4)(x - 2) = 0$$

$$(x + 4) = 0 \quad \text{or} \quad (x - 2) = 0$$

$$x = -4 \qquad\qquad x = 2$$

The solutions of the quadratic equation are $x = -4$ and $x = 2$.

GRAPH 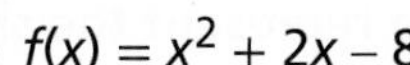 $f(x) = x^2 + 2x - 8$

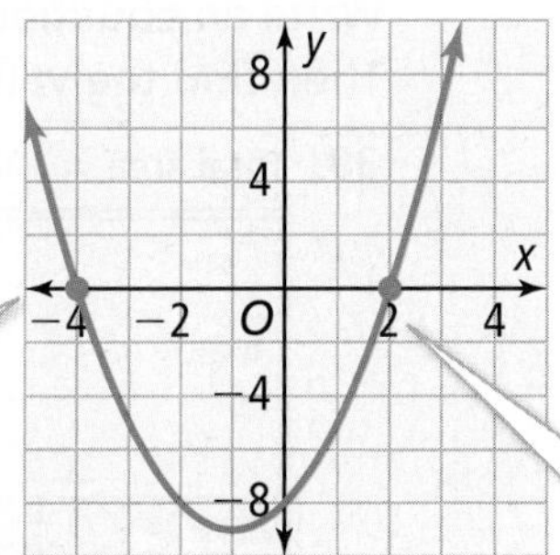

The x-intercepts are −4 and 2.

The x-intercepts of the graph correspond to the zeros of the function.

Do You UNDERSTAND?

1. **ESSENTIAL QUESTION** How does factoring help you solve quadratic equations?

2. **Use Structure** Compare the solutions of $2x^2 + 5x - 7 = 0$ and $4x^2 + 10x - 14 = 0$. What do you notice? Explain.

3. **Vocabulary** What is the *Zero-Product Property*? When can you use it to solve a quadratic equation? Explain.

4. **Generalize** If a perfect-square trinomial has a value of 0, how many solutions does the equation have? Explain.

Do You KNOW HOW?

Solve each equation.

5. $(x - 10)(x + 20) = 0$
6. $(3x + 4)(x - 4) = 0$

Solve each equation by factoring.

7. $x^2 + 18x + 32 = 0$
8. $x^2 - 4x - 21 = 0$

Solve each equation.

9. $x^2 + 2x = -1$
10. $x^2 - 8x = 9$
11. $2x^2 + x = 15$
12. $5x^2 - 19x = -18$

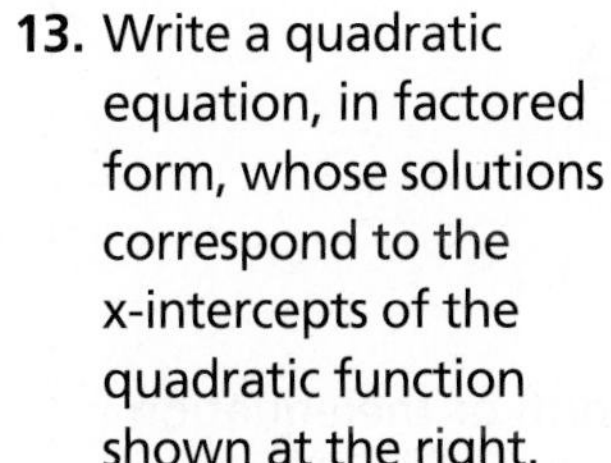

13. Write a quadratic equation, in factored form, whose solutions correspond to the x-intercepts of the quadratic function shown at the right.

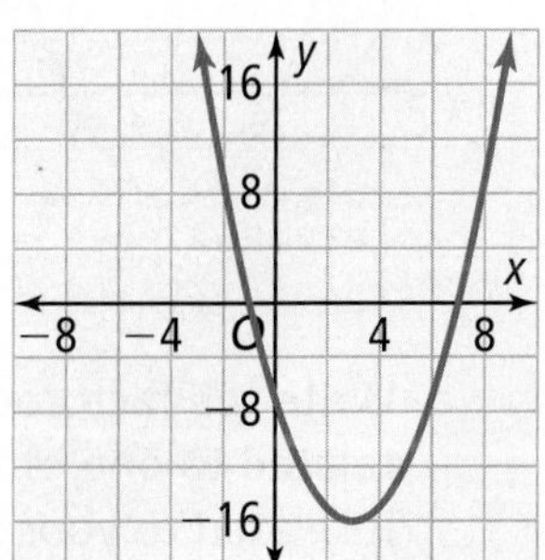

14. Factor the equation $x^2 - 6x + 5 = 0$. Find the coordinates of the vertex of the related function, and graph the function $y = x^2 - 6x + 5$.

PRACTICE & PROBLEM SOLVING

Scan for Multimedia

Practice Tutorial

Additional Exercises Available Online

UNDERSTAND

15. **Reason** One solution of a quadratic equation is 8. What do you know about the quadratic equation? What are two ways you would know if a quadratic equation could have this solution?

16. **Communicate Precisely** Write a quadratic equation for each condition below. Explain your reasoning.

    a. The equation has solutions that are opposites.

    b. The equation has one solution.

17. **Error Analysis** Describe and correct the error a student made in factoring.

$$x^2 + 2x - 3 = 5$$
$$(x - 1)(x + 3) = 5$$
$$x - 1 = 5 \text{ or } x + 3 = 5$$
$$x = 6 \text{ or } x = 2$$

✗

18. **Make Sense and Persevere** Explain how you would factor $2x^2 + 8x + 6 = 0$.

19. **Higher Order Thinking** Both parabolas are graphs of quadratic functions.

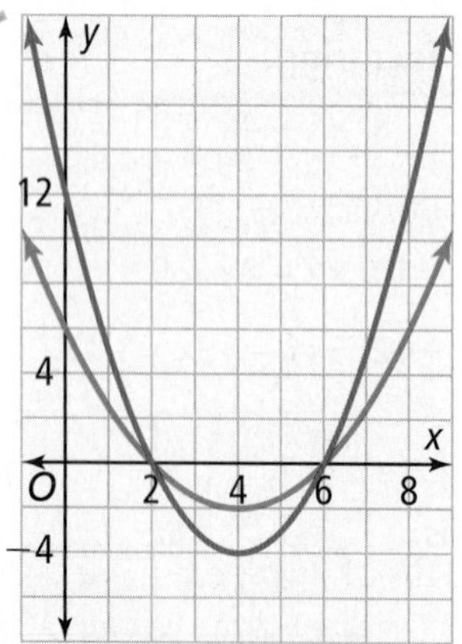

a. Write the factored form of the equation related to one of the functions. Which curve is related to your function?

b. Use a constant factor to find the equation related to the other function.

c. What relationship do you see between the two functions? How are these reflected in the constant?

PRACTICE

Solve each equation. SEE EXAMPLE 1

20. $(x - 5)(x + 2) = 0$

21. $(2x - 5)(7x + 2) = 0$

22. $3(x + 2)(x - 2) = 0$

23. $(3x - 8)^2 = 0$

Solve each equation by factoring.
SEE EXAMPLES 2 AND 3

24. $x^2 + 2x + 1 = 0$

25. $x^2 - 5x - 14 = 0$

26. $x^2 + 7x = 0$

27. $2x^2 - 5x + 2 = 0$

28. $2x^2 + 3x = 5$

29. $5x^2 + 16x = -3$

Write an equation to represent the shaded area. Then find the value of *x*. SEE EXAMPLE 3

30. Total area = 198 cm^2

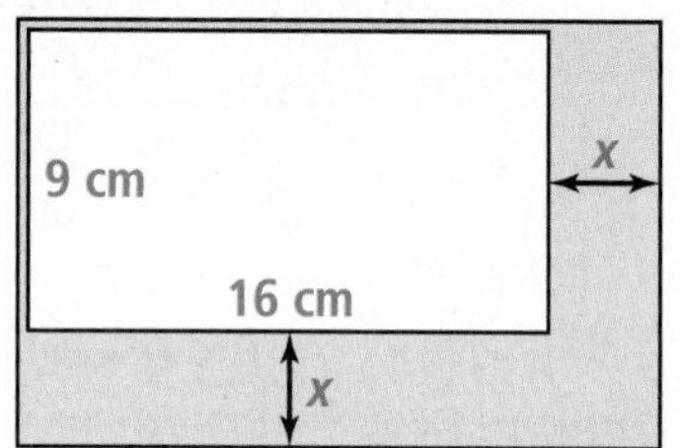

31.

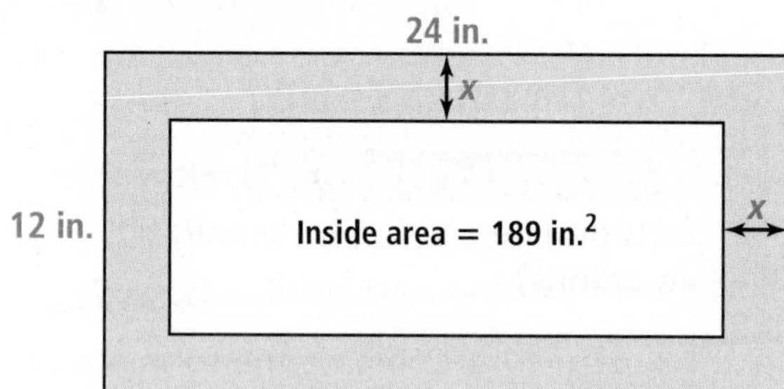

Factor, find the coordinates of the vertex of the related function, then graph. SEE EXAMPLE 4

32. $x^2 - 2x - 63 = 0$

33. $x^2 + 16x + 63 = 0$

Write the factored form for the quadratic function. SEE EXAMPLE 5

34.

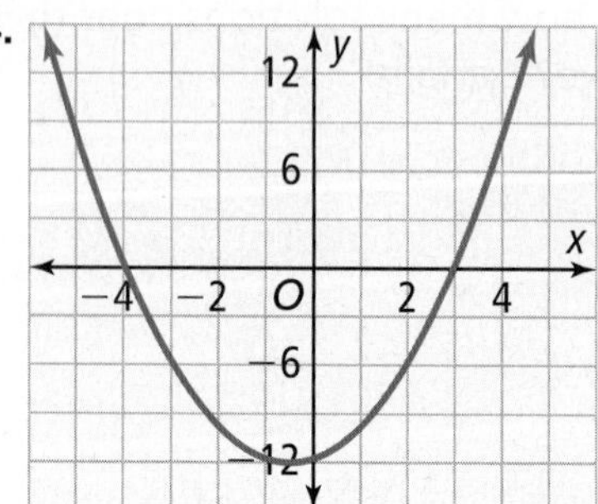

Mixed Review Available Online

PRACTICE & PROBLEM SOLVING

APPLY

35. Mathematical Connections A streamer is launched 3 s after a fuse is lit and lands 8 s after it is lit.

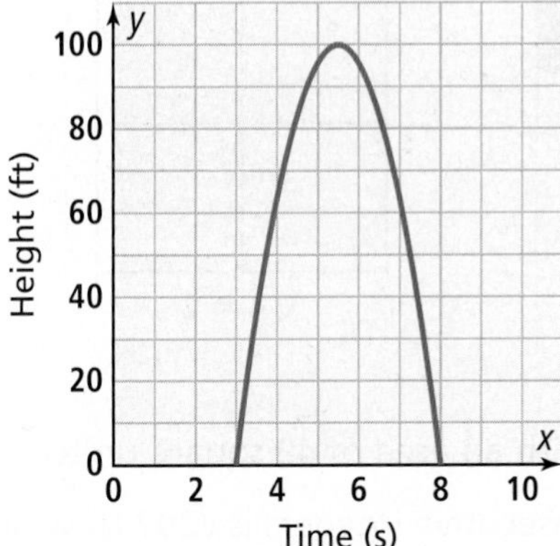

a. What is a quadratic equation in factored form that models the situation?

b. What is the vertex of the function related to your equation? How does this compare with the vertex of the graph?

c. What can you multiply your factored form by to get the function for the graph? Explain your answer.

36. Use Structure A 15 ft long cable is connected from a hook to the top of a pole that has an unknown height. The distance from the hook to the base of the pole is 3 ft shorter than the height of the pole.

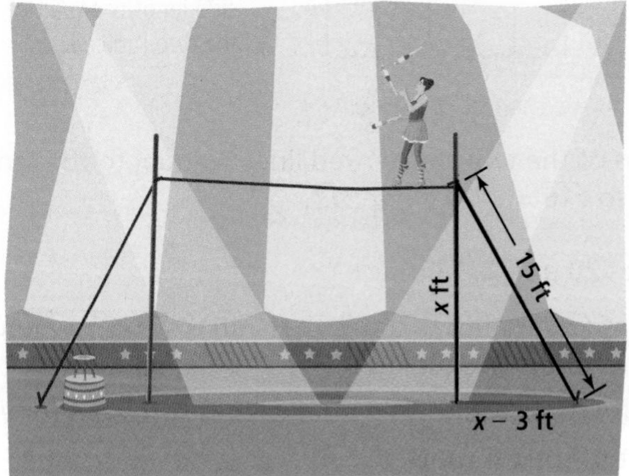

a. What can you use to find the height of the pole?

b. Write and solve a quadratic equation to find the height of the pole.

c. How far is the hook from the base of the pole?

ASSESSMENT PRACTICE

37. Match each equation with one or more factors of its standard form.

I. $x^2 + 6x = -8$	A. $2x - 3$
II. $2x^2 + x = 6$	B. $x + 4$
III. $x^2 + 2x = 8$	C. $x - 4$
IV. $2x^2 + 5x = 12$	D. $x + 2$
V. $2x^2 - 11x = -12$	E. $x - 2$

38. SAT/ACT A quadratic equation of the form $x^2 + bx + c = 0$ has a solution of -2. Its related function has a vertex at (2.5, −20.25). What is the other solution to the equation?

Ⓐ −11
Ⓑ −4.5
Ⓒ 0.5
Ⓓ 7
Ⓔ 9

39. Performance Task An engineer is designing a water fountain that starts 1 ft off of the edge of a 10 ft wide pool. The water from the fountain needs to project into the center of the pool. The path of the water from the fountain is in the shape of a parabola.

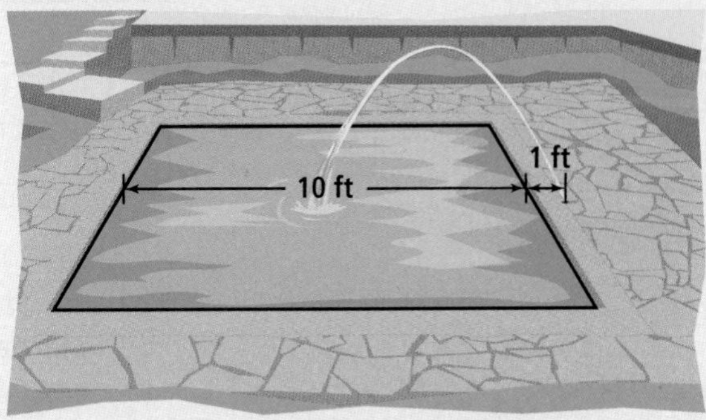

Part A Let the the point (1, 0) be the location of the starting point of the water. Write a quadratic equation to model the path of the water.

Part B What is the maximum height of the water? Use your equation from Part A.

Part C What is the equation for the path of the water if the maximum height of the water must be 4 ft?

9-3 Rewriting Radical Expressions

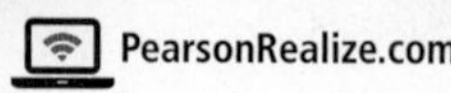

I CAN... write equivalent radical expressions.

VOCABULARY

- Product Property of Square Roots

Activity Assess

EXPLORE & REASON

The table shows the relationship between the area of a square, the side length of the square, and the square root of the area. A square with an area of 4 and a side length of 2 is shown at the right.

Area of Square (square units)	$s = \sqrt{\text{area}}$	Side Length, s (units)
1	$s = \sqrt{1}$	1
4	$s = \sqrt{4}$	2
9	$s = \sqrt{9}$	3
16	$s = \sqrt{16}$	4
25	$s = \sqrt{25}$	5

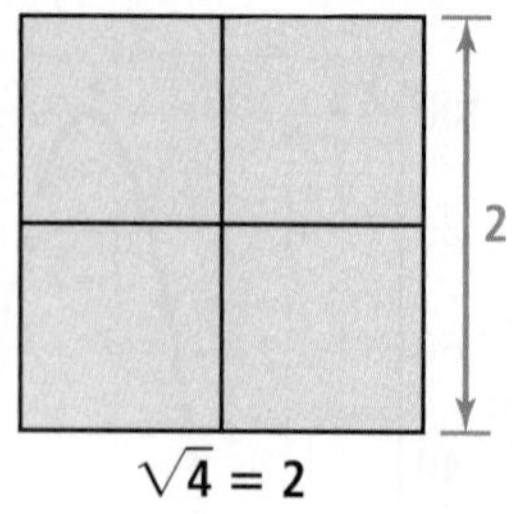

A. What is the side length of a square with an area of 49 square units?

B. **Use Structure** Between what two consecutive integers is $\sqrt{20}$? How do you know?

C. Think of three squares that have a side length between 3 and 4. What is the area of each square?

ESSENTIAL QUESTION How does rewriting radicals in different forms help you communicate your answers?

CONCEPTUAL UNDERSTANDING

EXAMPLE 1 Use Properties to Rewrite Radical Expressions

A. How can you visually show $\sqrt{16}$ is equivalent to $2\sqrt{4}$?

STUDY TIP
Recall that the square root is a number you multiply by itself to get the radicand.

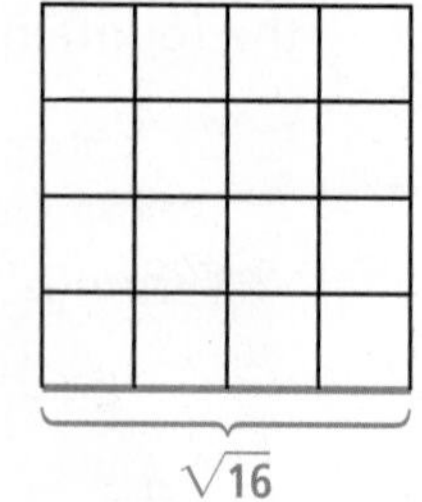

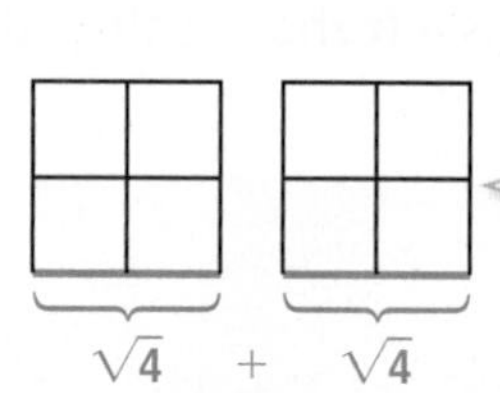

Draw squares using grid paper that have side lengths equal to the two radicals.

The sum of the lengths of the two smaller red lines is equal to the length of the larger red line, so $\sqrt{16} = \sqrt{4} + \sqrt{4}$ or $2\sqrt{4}$.

B. How can you compare $\sqrt{20}$ and $2\sqrt{5}$?

The **Product Property of Square Roots** states that $\sqrt{ab} = \sqrt{a} \cdot \sqrt{b}$ when both a and b are greater than or equal to 0.

Use properties of square roots to show an equivalent expression for $\sqrt{20}$.

Write $\sqrt{20}$ as a product of square roots.

$$\sqrt{20} = \sqrt{4} \cdot \sqrt{5}$$
$$= \sqrt{2 \cdot 2} \cdot \sqrt{5}$$
$$= 2\sqrt{5}$$

A perfect square factor of 20 is 4.

The radical expression $\sqrt{20}$ is equivalent to $2\sqrt{5}$.

CONTINUED ON THE NEXT PAGE

EXAMPLE 1 CONTINUED

 **Try It!** 1. Compare each pair of radical expressions.

a. $\sqrt{36}$ and $3\sqrt{6}$

b. $6\sqrt{2}$ and $\sqrt{72}$

EXAMPLE 2 Write Equivalent Radical Expressions

What is an equivalent expression for $\sqrt{63}$?

$$\sqrt{63} = \sqrt{9 \cdot 7}$$
$$= \sqrt{3 \cdot 3} \cdot \sqrt{7}$$
$$= 3\sqrt{7}$$

Write a factorization of 63 using as many perfect squares as possible. Note that 9 is a perfect square.

The expression $\sqrt{63}$ is equivalent to $3\sqrt{7}$.

Try It! 2. Rewrite each expression to remove perfect square factors other than 1 in the radicand.

a. $\sqrt{44}$

b. $3\sqrt{27}$

EXAMPLE 3 Write Equivalent Radical Expressions With Variables

What is an equivalent expression for $\sqrt{63x^9}$?

Rewrite the expressions to remove perfect square factors in the radicand.

$$\sqrt{63x^9} = \sqrt{9 \cdot 7 \cdot x^9}$$
$$= \sqrt{9 \cdot 7 \cdot x^4 \cdot x^4 \cdot x}$$
$$= \sqrt{3 \cdot 3} \cdot \sqrt{7} \cdot \sqrt{x^4 \cdot x^4} \cdot \sqrt{x}$$
$$= 3x^4\sqrt{7x}$$

Rewrite x^9 as $x^4 \cdot x^4 \cdot x$ to show the perfect square factors.

USE STRUCTURE
Think about the exponents of variables in terms that are perfect squares. How does the exponent of a variable determine when there is a perfect square factor of the expression?

The expression $\sqrt{63x^9}$ is equivalent to $3x^4\sqrt{7x}$.

Try It! 3. Rewrite each expression to remove perfect square factors other than 1 in the radicand.

a. $\sqrt{25x^3}$

b. $5\sqrt{4x^{17}}$

EXAMPLE 4 Multiply Radical Expressions

How can you write an expression for the product of $3\sqrt{5x} \cdot 2\sqrt{15x^3}$ without any perfect square factors in the radicand?

Find the product.

STUDY TIP
When rewriting the product under the radicand, it is easier to find perfect squares by replacing each number with its factors. Instead of writing $5 \cdot 15$ as 75, write the factors, $5 \cdot 3 \cdot 5$.

$$3\sqrt{5x} \cdot 2\sqrt{15x^3}$$
$$= 3 \cdot 2\sqrt{5x \cdot 15x^3}$$

Use the Product Property of Square Roots to multiply the radicands.

$$= 6\sqrt{5 \cdot 3 \cdot 5 \cdot x^4}$$
$$= 6 \cdot \sqrt{5 \cdot 5} \cdot \sqrt{3} \cdot \sqrt{x^2 \cdot x^2}$$

Rewrite to show the perfect-square factors.

$$= 6 \cdot 5 \cdot x^2 \cdot \sqrt{3}$$
$$= 30x^2\sqrt{3}$$

The expression $3\sqrt{5x} \cdot 2\sqrt{15x^3}$ is equivalent to $30x^2\sqrt{3}$.

Try It! 4. Write an expression for each product without perfect square factors in the radicand.

a. $\frac{1}{2}\sqrt{21x^3} \cdot 4\sqrt{7x^2}$ b. $2\sqrt{12x^9} \cdot \sqrt{18x^5}$

APPLICATION

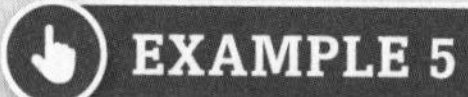

EXAMPLE 5 Write a Radical Expression

A light fixture in an ice cream shop is in the shape of an ice cream cone and the cone has a height that is 7 times the radius. The expression for the slant height is $\sqrt{r^2 + h^2}$, where r is the radius and h is the height of the cone. The slant height should be no longer than 24 in. to fit on the wall. What is the slant height of the cone with the radius shown?

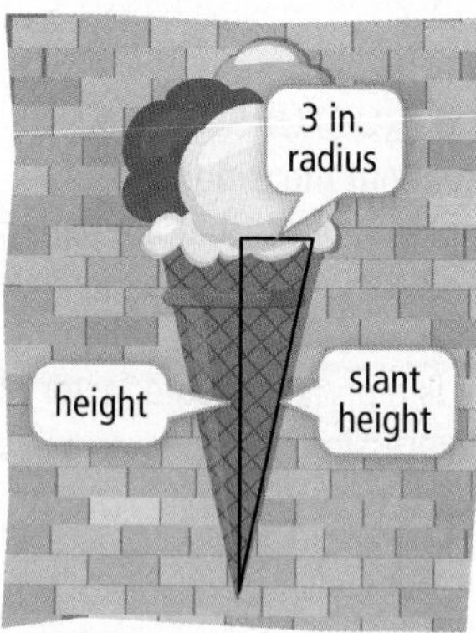

Formulate Let r = radius and $7r$ = height.

$$\sqrt{r^2 + h^2} = \sqrt{r^2 + (7r)^2}$$

Substitute the values into the slant height expression

Compute

$$= \sqrt{r^2 + 49r^2}$$
$$= \sqrt{50r^2}$$
$$= \sqrt{5 \cdot 5 \cdot 2 \cdot r^2}$$
$$= 5r\sqrt{2}$$

Interpret To determine the slant height of the cone, evaluate the expression for $r = 3$.

$$5 \cdot 3\sqrt{2} \approx 21.2$$

The slant height is about 21 in. so it will fit on the wall.

Try It! 5. Another cone has a slant height s that is 5 times the radius. What is the simplified expression for the height in terms of the radius?

CONCEPT SUMMARY Rewriting Radical Expressions

WORDS A radical expression is written in the simplest form when there are no perfect square factors other than 1 in the radicand.

ALGEBRA Product Property of Square Roots

$\sqrt{ab} = \sqrt{a} \cdot \sqrt{b}$ when $a \geq 0$ and $b \geq 0$

NUMBERS

$$\sqrt{63} = \sqrt{9 \cdot 7} = \sqrt{3 \cdot 3 \cdot 7} = 3\sqrt{7}$$

Use the same properties when there are variables under the radical.

$$\sqrt{28x^3} = \sqrt{4 \cdot 7 \cdot x^2 \cdot x} = \sqrt{2 \cdot 2 \cdot 7 \cdot x \cdot x \cdot x} = 2x\sqrt{7x}$$

$$4\sqrt{3} \cdot 6\sqrt{6} = 4 \cdot 6\sqrt{3 \cdot 6} = 24\sqrt{3 \cdot 3 \cdot 2} = 24 \cdot 3\sqrt{2} = 72\sqrt{2}$$

$$5\sqrt{3x^2} \cdot 2\sqrt{6x} = 5 \cdot 2\sqrt{3 \cdot 6 \cdot x^2 \cdot x} = 10\sqrt{3 \cdot 3 \cdot 2 \cdot x^2 \cdot x} = 10 \cdot 3 \cdot x\sqrt{2x} = 30x\sqrt{2x}$$

Do You UNDERSTAND?

1. ESSENTIAL QUESTION How does rewriting radicals in different forms help you communicate your answer?

2. **Vocabulary** State the *Product Property of Square Roots* in your own words.

3. **Communicate Precisely** Write an expression for $\sqrt{32}$ without any perfect square factors in the radicand. Explain your steps.

4. **Error Analysis** Rikki says that the product $\sqrt{3x^3} \cdot \sqrt{x}$ is $3x^2$. Explain Rikki's error and write the correct product.

5. **Construct Arguments** Is $\sqrt{45}$ in simplest form? Explain.

6. **Make Sense and Persevere** Describe how you would simplify an expression so that there are no perfect square factors in the radicand.

Do You KNOW HOW?

Factor each radicand using the Product Property of Square Roots.

7. $\sqrt{80}$
8. $\sqrt{x^7}$
9. $\sqrt{40x^4}$
10. $\sqrt{11x^5}$
11. $\sqrt{200}$
12. $8\sqrt{8}$

Write an expression for each product without a perfect square factor other than 1 in the radicand.

13. $4\sqrt{3x^3} \cdot 3\sqrt{2x^2}$

14. $x\sqrt{2x^5} \cdot 2x\sqrt{8x}$

15. $\sqrt{7x} \cdot 3\sqrt{10x^7}$

Compare each pair of radical expressions by writing each expression as a product of square roots in simplest form.

16. $\sqrt{72}$ and $2\sqrt{50}$

17. $5\sqrt{28}$ and $\sqrt{119}$

Write each expression so there are no perfect square factors other than 1 in the radicand.

18. $\sqrt{100x^8}$

19. $4x^2y\sqrt{2x^4y^6}$

PRACTICE & PROBLEM SOLVING

Scan for Multimedia

Practice | Tutorial

Additional Exercises Available Online

UNDERSTAND

20. **Use Structure** For $\sqrt{x^n}$, consider rewriting this expression without a perfect square factor in the radicand for even and odd values of n, where n is a positive integer.

    a. What is the expression when n is even?

    b. What is the expression when n is odd?

21. **Error Analysis** Describe and correct the error a student made in multiplying $2\sqrt{7x^2}$ by $2\sqrt{14x^3}$.

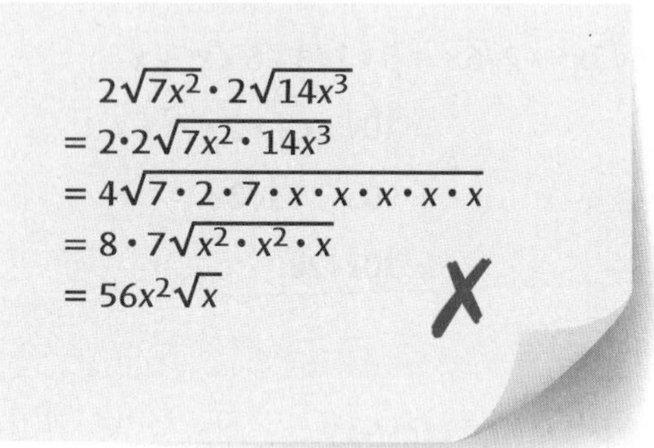

22. **Use Structure** Find $\sqrt{591x^{15}y^3} \cdot \sqrt{591x^{15}y^3}$ without calculating or simplifying.

23. **Communicate Precisely** Why do the multiplication properties of exponents apply to radicals? Explain.

24. **Make Sense and Persevere** How many perfect squares are under each radical?

Radical	Perfect squares
$\sqrt{8}$	
$\sqrt{18}$	
$\sqrt{32x^6}$	
$\sqrt{50x}$	
$\sqrt{72}$	

25. **Higher Order Thinking** Can you use the Product Property of Square Roots to find equivalent expressions for each radical? Explain.

    a. $\sqrt[3]{24x^8}$

    b. $\sqrt[4]{3^9x^{13}}$

PRACTICE

Compare each pair of radical expressions.
SEE EXAMPLE 1

26. $6\sqrt{3}$ and $\sqrt{108}$

27. $2\sqrt{21}$ and $4\sqrt{5}$

28. $40\sqrt{42}$ and $42\sqrt{40}$

29. $\frac{1}{2}\sqrt{120}$ and $\sqrt{30}$

30. $\sqrt{68}$ and $2\sqrt{18}$

31. $\sqrt{96}$ and $3\sqrt{15}$

Write each expression so the radicand has no perfect squares other than 1. SEE EXAMPLES 2 AND 3

32. $\sqrt{210}$

33. $\sqrt{250}$

34. $\sqrt{108}$

35. $2\sqrt{21}$

36. $\sqrt{98x^8}$

37. $\sqrt{200x^3}$

38. $\sqrt{32x^4y^3}$

39. $4x\sqrt{\frac{1}{4}x^6}$

Write each expression so the radicand has no perfect squares other than 1. SEE EXAMPLE 4

40. $\sqrt{12x} \cdot \sqrt{3x}$

41. $\sqrt{2x^9} \cdot \sqrt{26x^6}$

42. $\sqrt{27m} \cdot \sqrt{6m^{20}}$

43. $\sqrt{2x^3} \cdot \sqrt{25x^2y}$

44. $\sqrt{9x^9} \cdot \sqrt{18x^3}$

45. $\sqrt{32x} \cdot \sqrt{72x^{18}}$

Write an expression in simplest form for the missing side length. Then find the side lengths of each triangle to the nearest tenth when $x = 15$.
SEE EXAMPLE 5

46.

2x ft

?

6x ft

47.

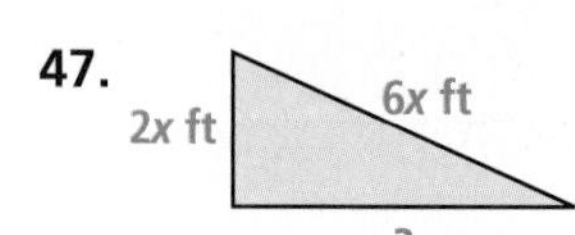

Practice Tutorial

Mixed Review Available Online

PRACTICE & PROBLEM SOLVING

APPLY

48. Use Structure The time it takes a planet to revolve around the sun in Earth years can be modeled by $t = \sqrt{d^3}$, where d is the average distance from the sun in astronomical units (AU).

a. Write an equivalent equation for the function.

b. How long does it take Saturn, pictured above, to orbit the sun? Show that both expressions give the same value.

49. Model With Mathematics A baseball "diamond" is a square that measures 90 ft on each side.

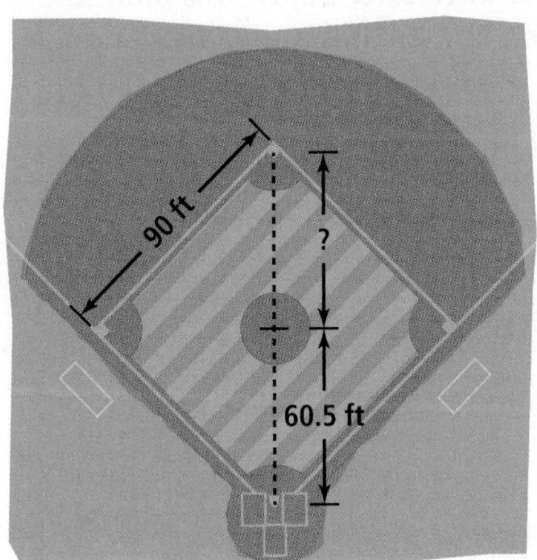

a. Write an expression for the distance from 2nd base to home plate in feet. What is this distance to the nearest tenth?

b. The pitcher standing on the pitcher's mound is about to throw to home plate but turns around and throws to 2nd base. How much farther is the throw? Explain.

50. Model With Mathematics A framed television has a ratio of width to height of about 1.732 : 1.

a. For a television with a height of h inches, what is an equivalent expression for the length of the diagonal? Justify your answer.

b. Write an expression for the perimeter.

ASSESSMENT PRACTICE

51. Copy and complete the table. Find the product of each row and column without a perfect square factor in the radicand and enter it in the appropriate cell.

	$\sqrt{48}$	$5x\sqrt{6x^3}$
$\sqrt{12}$	■	■
$2x\sqrt{6x}$	■	■
$4x^2\sqrt{2x^5}$	■	■

52. SAT/ACT A car skidded s ft when traveling on a damp paved road. The expression $r = \sqrt{18s}$ is an estimate of the car's rate of speed in ft/s.

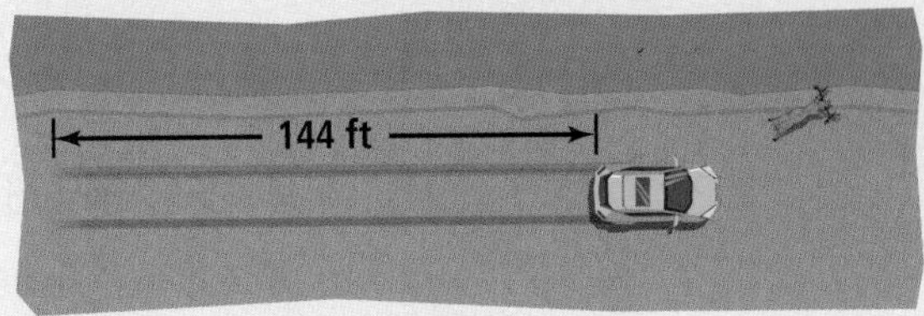

Which expression represents the speed of the car in feet per second?

Ⓐ $24\sqrt{6}$
Ⓑ $12\sqrt{6}$
Ⓒ $36\sqrt{2}$
Ⓓ $24\sqrt{3}$
Ⓔ $48\sqrt{2}$

53. Performance Task Copy the figure. Center it on a large piece of paper so you can expand it.

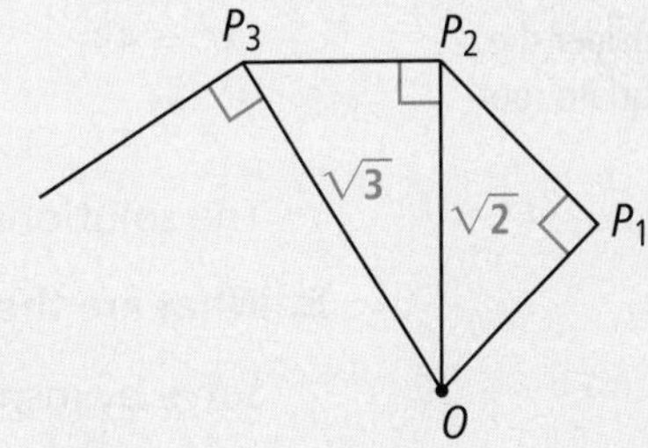

Part A Use the pattern to complete the triangle on the left. Label the side lengths.

Part B Continue using the pattern to add triangles while labeling side lengths.

Part C Are equivalent expressions of the square roots appropriate? Explain your reasoning.

9-4 Solving Quadratic Equations Using Square Roots

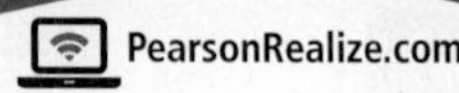

I CAN… solve quadratic equations by taking square roots.

EXPLORE & REASON

A developer is building three square recreation areas on a parcel of land. He has not decided what to do with the enclosed triangular area in the center.

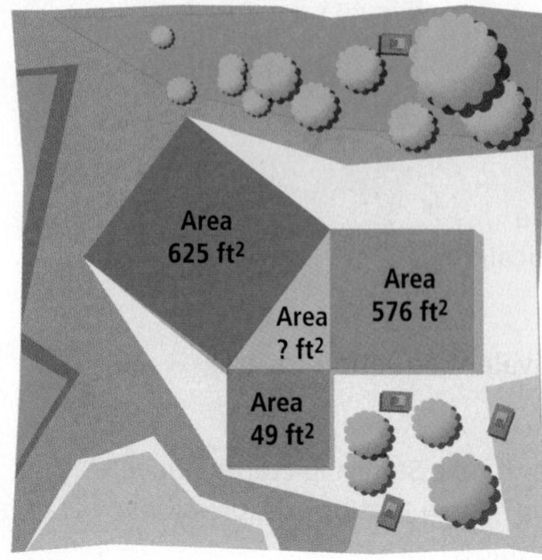

A. How can you determine the side lengths of the enclosed triangle?

B. What relationships do you notice among the areas of the squares?

C. **Look for Relationships** How can the developer adjust this plan so that each recreation area covers less area but still has a similar triangular section in the middle? Explain.

ESSENTIAL QUESTION How can square roots be used to solve quadratic equations?

EXAMPLE 1 Solve Equations of the Form $x^2 = a$

A. What are the solutions of the equation $x^2 = 49$?

Solve by inspection.

$$x^2 = 49$$

$$x = \pm 7$$

Remember that 49 is the square of 7 and −7.

The solutions of the equation are 7 and −7.

B. What are the solutions of the equation $x^2 = -121$?

Solve by inspection.

$$x^2 = -121$$

$$\sqrt{x^2} = \sqrt{-121}$$

There is no real number that can be multiplied by itself to produce a negative number. A negative radicand indicates that there is no real solution to an equation of the form $x = \sqrt{a}$.

STUDY TIP
When taking a square root to solve an equation, always consider the positive and negative square root solutions.

 **Try It!** 1. Solve each equation by inspection.

a. $x^2 = 169$

b. $x^2 = -16$

EXAMPLE 2 Solve Equations of the Form $ax^2 = c$

A. What are the solutions of the equation $7x^2 = 112$?

Isolate the variable using properties of equality.

$$7x^2 = 112$$
$$\frac{7x^2}{7} = \frac{112}{7}$$
$$x^2 = 16$$
$$\sqrt{x^2} = \sqrt{16}$$
$$x = \pm 4$$

16 is a perfect square.

B. What are the solutions of the equation $-3x^2 = -24$?

Isolate the variable using properties of equality.

$$-3x^2 = -24$$
$$\frac{-3x^2}{-3} = \frac{-24}{-3}$$
$$x^2 = 8$$
$$x = \pm\sqrt{8}$$

Take the square root of both sides to solve for x.

REASON
You could rewrite $\pm\sqrt{8}$ as $\pm 2\sqrt{2}$. What is the advantage of using $\pm\sqrt{8}$? What would be the advantage of using $\pm 2\sqrt{2}$?

Try It! 2. What are the solutions for each equation? If the solution is not a perfect square, state what two integers the solution is between.

a. $5x^2 = 125$

b. $-\frac{1}{2}x^2 = -36$

CONCEPTUAL UNDERSTANDING

EXAMPLE 3 Solve Equations of the Form $ax^2 + b = c$

How can you solve the quadratic equation $3x^2 - 5 = 22$?

Rewrite the equation in the form $x^2 = a$.

$$3x^2 - 5 = 22$$
$$3x^2 = 27$$
$$x^2 = 9 \quad \text{Write in the form } x^2 = a\text{, where } a \text{ is a real number.}$$
$$\sqrt{x^2} = \sqrt{9} \quad \text{Take the square root of each side of the equation.}$$
$$x = \pm 3$$

LOOK FOR RELATIONSHIPS
Compare the steps to solve a quadratic equation to those of solving a linear equation. How are the steps similar? How are they different?

You can use the properties of equality to write the equation $3x^2 - 5 = 22$ in the form $x^2 = a$. Since a is a perfect square there are two integer answers. The solutions of this quadratic equation are -3 and 3.

Try It! 3. Solve the quadratic equations.

a. $-5x^2 - 19 = 144$

b. $3x^2 + 17 = 209$

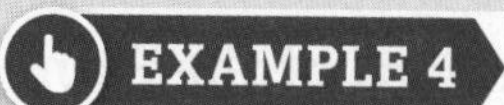

APPLICATION

EXAMPLE 4 Determine a Reasonable Solution

A cell phone tower has a guy-wire for support as shown. The height of the tower and the distance from the tower to where the guy-wire is secured on the ground are the same distance. What is the height of the tower?

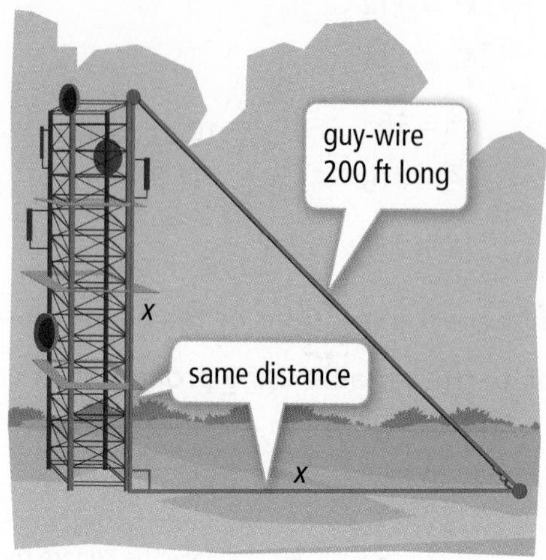

Formulate Write an equation that relates the lengths of the sides of the triangle formed by the guy-wire, the tower, and the distance on the ground from the tower to where the guy-wire is secured.

Let x represent the height of the tower and the distance on the ground.

$$x^2 + x^2 = 200^2$$

Use x in the Pythagorean Theorem for the side lengths since the two lengths are the same.

Compute Solve the equation for x.

$$x^2 + x^2 = 200^2$$
$$2x^2 = 40{,}000$$
$$x^2 = 20{,}000$$
$$\sqrt{x^2} = \sqrt{20{,}000}$$
$$x = \sqrt{2 \cdot 100 \cdot 100}$$
$$x = \pm 100\sqrt{2}$$

Rewrite 20,000 using 100 as a factor.

Interpret The height of the tower must be positive, so the solution is $100\sqrt{2} \approx 141$.

The height of the cell phone tower is approximately 141 ft.

Try It! 4. Find the distance from the base of the tower to the midpoint of the guy-wire.

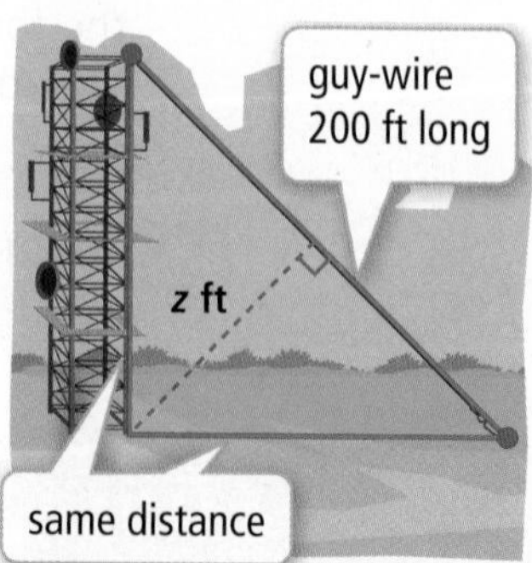

CONCEPT SUMMARY Solving Quadratic Equations Using Square Roots

WORDS To solve a quadratic equation using square roots, isolate the variable, and take the square root of both sides of the equation.

NUMBERS

$x^2 = 25$

$x = \pm 5$

Solve by inspection. Remember that 25 is the square of 5 and −5.

$5x^2 - 8 = 12$

$5x^2 = 20$

$x^2 = 4$

$\sqrt{x^2} = \sqrt{4}$

$x = \pm 2$

Use ± to indicate there are two solutions, one positive and one negative.

$2x^2 + 9 = 1$

$2x^2 = -8$

$x^2 = -4$

$\sqrt{x^2} = \sqrt{-4}$

$x = \sqrt{-4}$

No solution

A negative radicand has no solution.

Do You UNDERSTAND?

1. **ESSENTIAL QUESTION** How can square roots be used to solve quadratic equations?

2. **Construct Arguments** How many solutions does $ax^2 = c$ have if a and c have different signs? Explain.

3. **Reason** How do you decide when to use the ± symbol when solving a quadratic equation?

4. **Error Analysis** Trey solved $2x^2 = 98$ and said that the solution in 7. Is he correct? Why or why not?

5. **Communicate Precisely** How is solving an equation in the form $ax^2 = c$ similar to solving an equation in the form $ax^2 + b = c$? How are they different?

Do You KNOW HOW?

Solve each equation by inspection.

6. $x^2 = 400$

7. $x^2 = -25$

Solve each equation.

8. $3x^2 = 400$

9. $-15x^2 = -90$

10. $2x^2 + 7 = 31$

11. $2x^2 - 7 = 38$

12. $-4x^2 - 1 = 48$

13. $-4x^2 + 50 = 1$

14. $3x^2 + 2x^2 = 150$

15. $3x^2 + 18 = 5x^2$

Solve for x.

16.

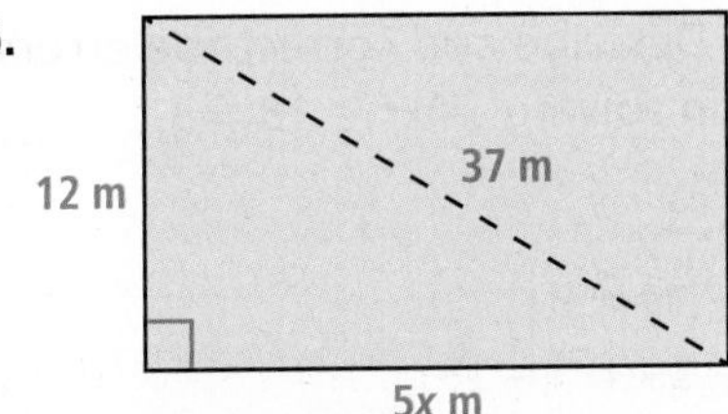

17.

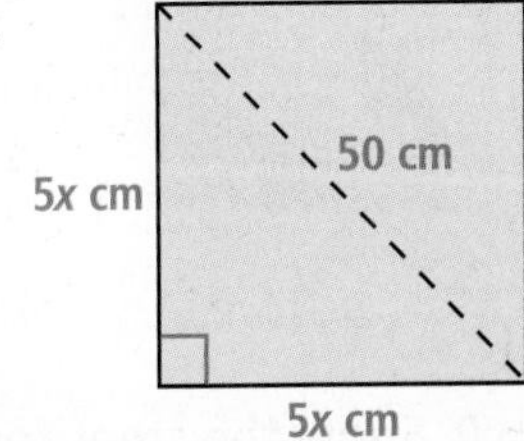

PRACTICE & PROBLEM SOLVING

UNDERSTAND

18. **Make Sense and Persevere** Where will the parabola intersect the line? What equation did you solve to find the intersection?

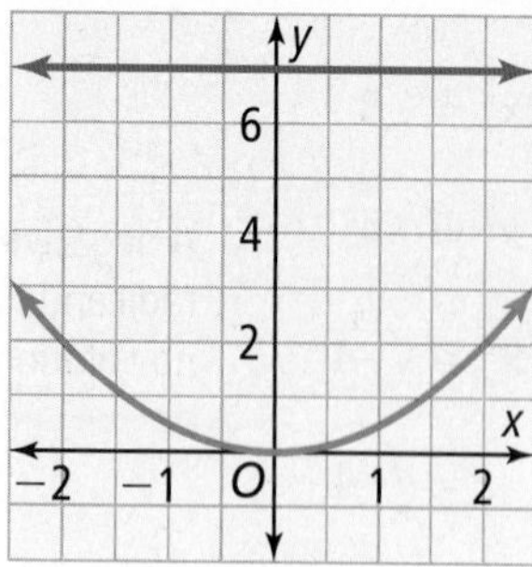

19. **Use Appropriate Tools** When solving an equation of the form $ax^2 + b = c$, what does the error message indicate? What situation may cause this error?

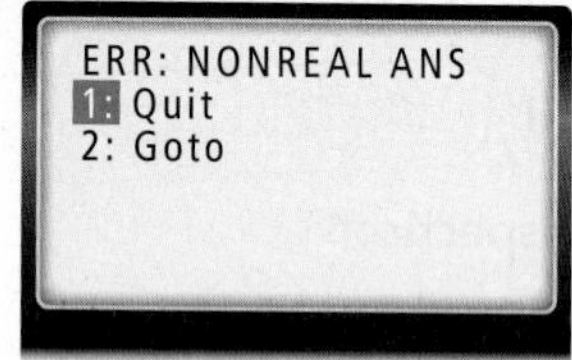

20. **Communicate Precisely** When does solving a quadratic equation of the form $ax^2 = c$ yield the given result?

    a. a rational solution

    b. an irrational solution

    c. one solution

    d. no solutions

21. **Error Analysis** Describe and correct the errors a student made in solving $-4x^2 + 19 = 3$.

$$-4x^2 + 19 = 3$$
$$-4x^2 + 19 - 19 = 3 - 19$$
$$-4x^2 = -16$$
$$-2x = -4$$
$$x = 2$$

✗

22. **Higher Order Thinking**

    a. Solve $(x - 5)^2 - 100 = 0$. Show the steps for your solution.

    b. Explain how you could solve an equation of the form $(x - d)^2 - c = 0$ for x.

PRACTICE

Solve each equation by inspection. SEE EXAMPLE 1

23. $x^2 = 256$

24. $x^2 = 144$

25. $x^2 = -20$

26. $x^2 = -27$

27. $x^2 = 91$

28. $x^2 = 0.25$

Solve each equation. SEE EXAMPLE 2

29. $12x^2 = 300$

30. $-x^2 = 0$

31. $0.1x^2 = 100$

32. $227x^2 = 1{,}816$

33. $-36x^2 = -36$

34. $-16x^2 = 200$

Solve each equation. SEE EXAMPLE 3

35. $x^2 + 65 = 90$

36. $x^2 - 65 = 90$

37. $3x^2 + 8 = 56$

38. $3x^2 - 8 = 56$

39. $\frac{4x^2 + 10}{2} = 5$

40. $\frac{8x^2 - 40}{4} = 470$

Solve each equation. Approximate irrational solutions to the nearest hundredth. SEE EXAMPLE 4

41. $6x^2 + 2x^2 = 80$

42. $6x^2 + (2x)^2 = 80$

Solve for x. Then find the side lengths of each triangle to the nearest tenth. SEE EXAMPLE 4

43.

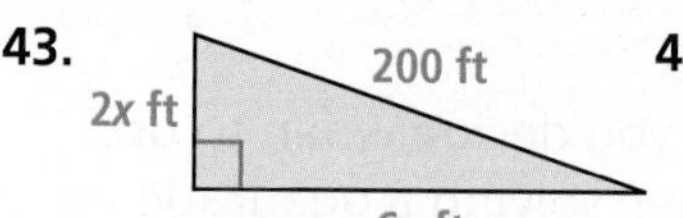

44.

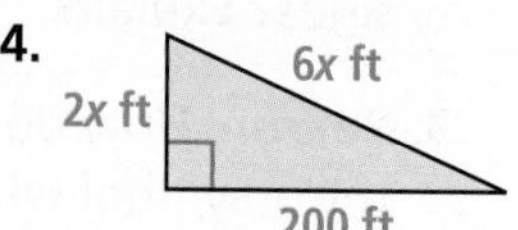

45. Use two methods to solve $x^2 - 900 = 0$. Explain.

46. At a certain time of day, the sun shines on a large flagpole causing a shadow that is twice as long as the flagpole is tall. What is the height of the flagpole to the nearest tenth of a foot?

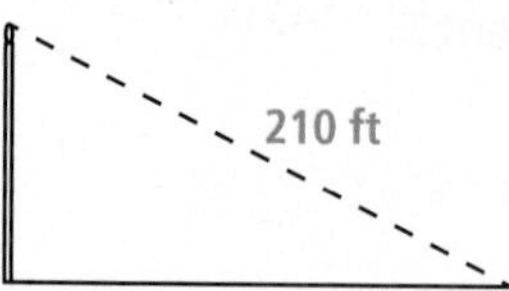

PRACTICE & PROBLEM SOLVING

APPLY

47. A test weight is dropped from the top of a fire department training tower onto a net three feet off of the ground. Use $-16t^2$ for the change in height per second.

a. Write an equation to determine the time it takes for the test weight to drop on to the net.

b. How long does it take before the test weight is caught by the net? Explain.

48. **Make Sense and Persevere** Calculate the distance in miles between the two points shown on the map.

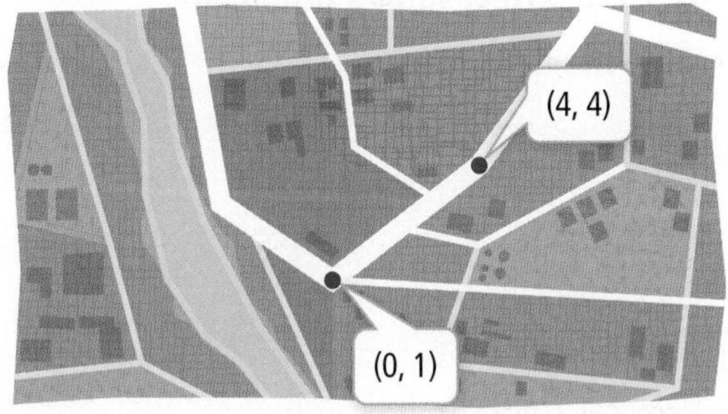

49. **Make Sense and Persevere** The evacuation slide from an aircraft is shown. If the slide is 73 feet long, what is its height at the top in feet?

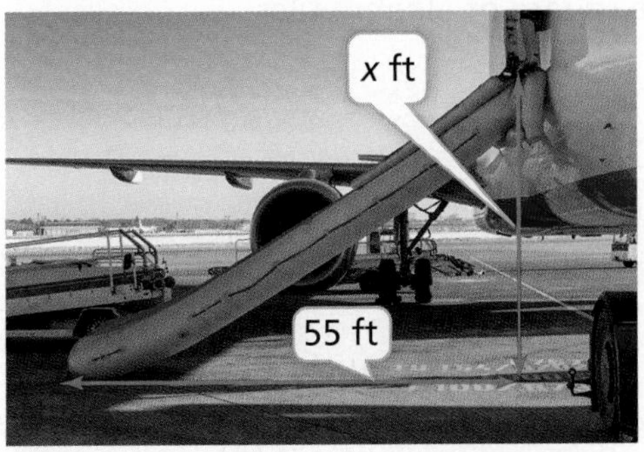

ASSESSMENT PRACTICE

50. Fill in the solutions of $2{,}900 - 5x^2 = 840$.

+ ______ and − ______

51. **SAT/ACT** A park has an area of 280 m^2. A rectangular region with a length three times its width will be added to give the park a total area of 435 m^2. Which equation can be solved to find the width of the region?

Ⓐ $x + 3x + 280 = 435$

Ⓑ $(x \cdot 3x) + 280 = 435$

Ⓒ $(x^2 + 3x) + 280 = 435$

Ⓓ $x^2 + (3x)^2 + 280 = 435$

52. **Performance Task** A CEO flies to three different company locations. The flight times for two of her legs are shown.

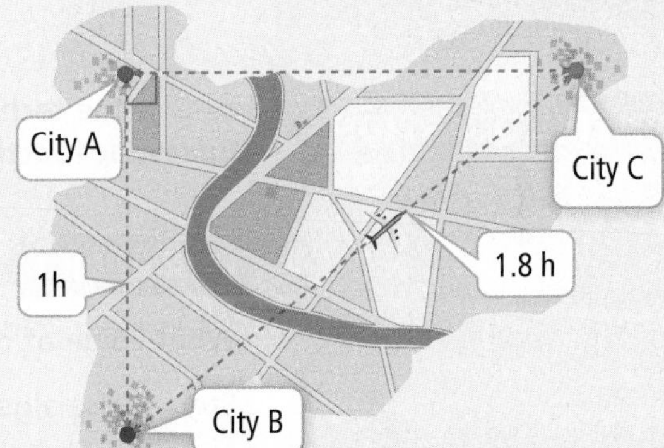

Part A The plane travels at an average speed of 120 mph. Find the distance between City A and City B and the distance between City B and City C.

Part B Write and solve a quadratic equation that can be used to find the distance between City A and City C.

Part C How long will the flight between City C and City A last?

9-5 Completing the Square

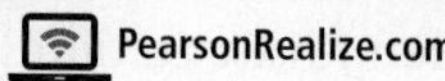

PearsonRealize.com

I CAN... use completing the square to solve quadratic equations.

VOCABULARY

- completing the square

CRITIQUE & EXPLAIN

Enrique and Nadeem used different methods to solve the equation $x^2 - 6x + 9 = 16$.

Enrique

$x^2 - 6x + 9 = 16$
$x^2 - 6x - 7 = 0$
$(x - 7)(x + 1) = 0$
$x - 7 = 0$ OR $x + 1 = 0$
$x = 7$ OR $x = -1$
The solutions are 7 and -1.

Nadeem

$x^2 - 6x + 9 = 16$
$(x - 3)^2 = 16$
$x - 3 = \pm 4$
$x - 3 = 4$ OR $x - 3 = -4$
$x = 7$ OR $x = -1$
The solutions are 7 and -1.

A. Critique Enrique's work. If his method is valid, explain the reasoning he used. If his method is not valid, explain why not.

B. Critique Nadeem's work. If his method is valid, explain the reasoning he used. If his method is not valid, explain why not.

C. Use Structure Can you use either Enrique's or Nadeem's method to solve the equation $x^2 + 10x + 25 = 3$? Explain.

ESSENTIAL QUESTION

How is the technique of completing the square helpful for analyzing quadratic functions?

EXAMPLE 1 Complete the Square

What value of c makes $x^2 + 6x + c$ a perfect-square trinomial?

Step 1 Use algebra tiles to model the trinomial.

$x^2 + 6x$

Rearrange the tiles.

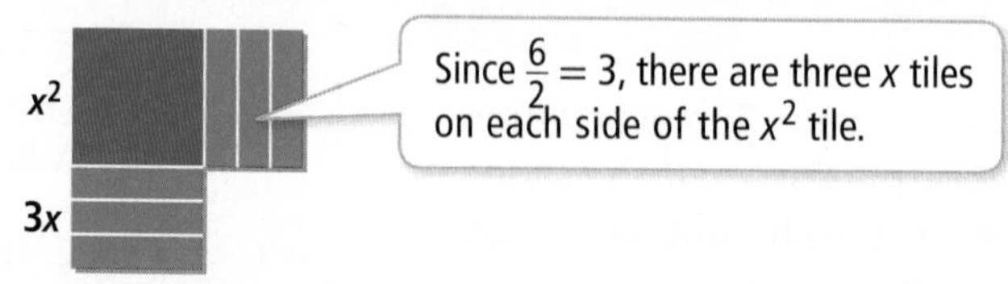

USE STRUCTURE
How would the algebra tiles be rearranged if the coefficient of x were 12?

Step 2 Add 1-tiles to complete the square of algebra tiles.

$x^2 + 6x + 9$

x^2 $3x$ $3x$

Since $\frac{6}{2} = 3$ and $3^2 = 9$, there are nine 1-tiles.

REASON
In the equation $x^2 + 6x + c$, consider the possible values for c. Can c have a negative value in a perfect-square trinomial?

Notice that the number of 1-tiles added to the square, 9, is equal to the square of half of the coefficient of x, or $\left(\frac{b}{2}\right)^2$.

CONTINUED ON THE NEXT PAGE

COMMON ERROR
Make sure you include the sign of the x-term when finding the value that completes the square.

EXAMPLE 1 CONTINUED

Step 3 Write $x^2 + 6x + 9$ as a binomial squared.

$$x^2 + 6x + 9 = (x + 3)^2$$

The constant term, 3, of the binomial is half the coefficient, 6, of the x-term.

The value of c that makes $x^2 + 6x + c$ a perfect-square trinomial is 9.

The process of adding $\left(\frac{b}{2}\right)^2$ to $x^2 + bx$ to form a perfect-square trinomial is called **completing the square.** Completing the square is useful when a quadratic expression is not factorable and can be used with any quadratic expression.

 **Try It!** 1. What value of c completes the square?

a. $x^2 + 12x + c$ **b.** $x^2 + 8x + c$

EXAMPLE 2 Solve $x^2 + bx + c = 0$

How can you find the solutions of $x^2 - 14x + 16 = 0$?

Step 1 Write the equation in the form $ax^2 + bx = d$.

$$x^2 - 14x + 16 = 0$$
$$x^2 - 14x = -16$$

Step 2 Complete the square.

$$x^2 - 14x + 49 = -16 + 49$$
$$x^2 - 14x + 49 = 33$$

Use $\left(\frac{14}{2}\right)^2 = 49$ and add 49 to each side.

Step 3 Write the trinomial as a binomial squared.

$$x^2 - 14x + 49 = (x - 7)^2 = 33$$

Step 4 Solve for x.

$$x - 7 = \pm\sqrt{33}$$
$$x = 7 \pm \sqrt{33}$$

The solutions are $x = 7 + \sqrt{33}$ and $x = 7 - \sqrt{33}$.

 **Try It!** 2. What are the solutions of each quadratic equation? Solve by completing the square.

a. $x^2 + 10x - 9 = 0$ **b.** $x^2 - 8x - 6 = 0$

APPLICATION

EXAMPLE 3 Complete the Square When $a \neq 1$ Initially

The hedge maze has a 2-yard wide walkway around it. What are the dimensions of the maze?

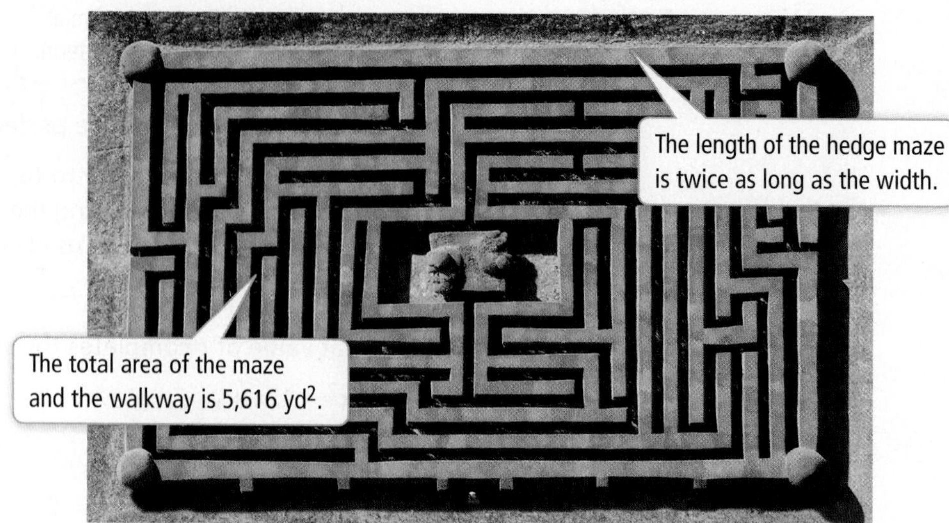

Formulate Let x be the width of the maze. So, $(x + 4)$ is the width of the maze and walkway, and $(2x + 4)$ is the length of the maze and walkway.

$$\text{length} \times \text{width} = \text{area}$$

$$(2x + 4) \times (x + 4) = 5{,}616$$

Compute

$$(2x + 4)(x + 4) = 5{,}616$$

$$2x^2 + 12x + 16 = 5{,}616$$

Use completing the square since the quadratic is not factorable.

$$2x^2 + 12x = 5{,}600$$

$$x^2 + 6x = 2{,}800$$

Put the equation in the form $x^2 + bx = d$ by dividing each side by 2.

$$x^2 + 6x + 9 = 2{,}800 + 9$$

Add: $\left(\frac{6}{2}\right)^2 = 9$ to each side.

$$(x + 3)^2 = 2{,}809$$

$$x + 3 = \pm\sqrt{2{,}809}$$

$$x = -3 + \sqrt{2{,}809} \quad \text{or} \quad x = -3 - \sqrt{2{,}809}$$

$$= -3 + 53 \qquad = -3 - 53$$

$$= 50 \qquad = -56$$

Interpret The negative solution does not make sense in this situation, so $x = 50$.

The width of the maze is 50 yd. and the length of the maze is 100 yd. With the walkway, the total width is 54 yd, and the total length is 104 yd.

Try It! 3. A maze and walkway with the same total area of 5,616 square yards has a walkway that is one yard wide. What are the dimensions of this maze?

CONCEPTUAL UNDERSTANDING

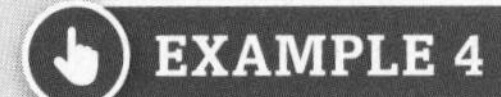

EXAMPLE 4 Use Completing the Square to Write a Quadratic Function In Vertex Form

How can you use completing the square to rewrite the quadratic function $y = x^2 - 8x + 11$ in vertex form?

Recall that the vertex form of a quadratic function is $y = a(x - h)^2 + k$, where (h, k) is the vertex. Completing the square is useful in order to identify $(x - h)^2$.

$$y = x^2 - 8x + 11$$

$$y - 11 = x^2 - 8x \quad \text{Isolate } x^2 + bx.$$

$$y - 11 + 16 = x^2 - 8x + 16 \quad \text{Complete the square.}$$

$$y + 5 = (x - 4)^2$$

$$y = (x - 4)^2 - 5$$

The vertex form of the quadratic function is $y = (x - 4)^2 - 5$.

Try It! **4.** What is the vertex form of each function?

a. $y = x^2 - 2x + 3$

b. $y = x^2 + 6x + 25$

APPLICATION

EXAMPLE 5 Write Vertex Form When $a \neq 1$

Astronauts train for flying in zero gravity using a special plane that flies in parabolic arcs. The graph shown approximates the altitude a, in meters, of a plane in relation to the time t, in seconds during a training session.

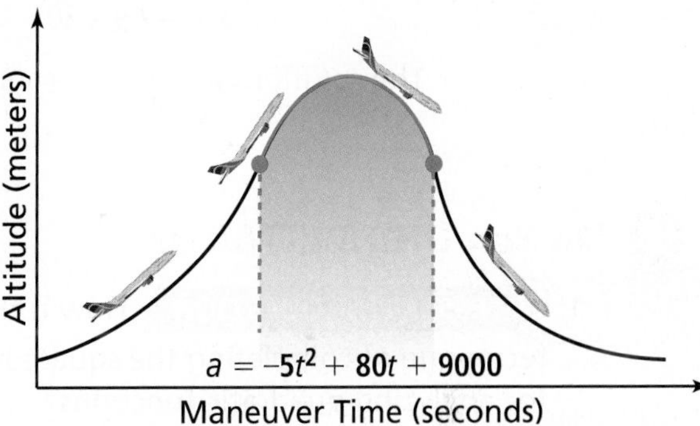

What is the maximum altitude reached by the plane? At what time does the plane reach its maximum altitude?

$$a = -5t^2 + 80t + 9{,}000$$

$$a - 9{,}000 = -5t^2 + 80t$$

$$a - 9{,}000 = -5(t^2 - 16t)$$

Factor out −5 so the expression in parentheses has the form $t^2 + bt$.

$$a - 9{,}000 - 5(64) = -5(t^2 - 16t + 64)$$

Add $\left(-\frac{16}{2}\right)^2 = 64$ to complete the square.

$$a - 9{,}320 = -5(t - 8)^2$$

$$a = -5(t - 8)^2 + 9{,}320$$

COMMON ERROR

When you complete the square inside the parentheses on the right side, add the product of −5(64) to the other side of the equation.

The vertex is (8, 9,320). The maximum altitude of the plane is 9,320 m. That altitude is reached after 8 s.

Try It! **5.** Find the minimum value of the function $y = 7x^2 + 168x + 105$.

CONCEPT SUMMARY Completing the Square

WORDS To complete the square, add the square of half of the coefficient of x to both sides of a quadratic equation.

Completing the square is useful for changing $ax^2 + bx + c$ to the form $a(x - h)^2 + k$.

ALGEBRA $x^2 + bx \rightarrow x^2 + bx + \left(\frac{b}{2}\right)^2$

$= \left(x + \frac{b}{2}\right)^2$

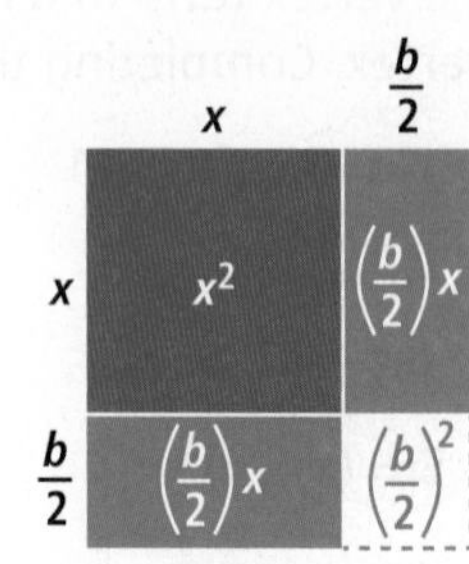

NUMBERS To complete the square for $x^2 + 14x + 19 = 0$, first subtract 19 from both sides, and then add $\left(\frac{14}{2}\right)^2 = 49$ to both sides.

$$x^2 + 14x = -19$$
$$x^2 + 14x + 49 = -19 + 49$$
$$(x + 7)^2 = 30$$
$$x + 7 = \pm\sqrt{30}$$
$$x = -7 \pm \sqrt{30}$$

The solutions are $x = -7 + \sqrt{30}$ and $x = -7 - \sqrt{30}$.

Do You UNDERSTAND?

1. **ESSENTIAL QUESTION** How is the technique of completing the square helpful for analyzing quadratic functions?

2. **Vocabulary** Why does it make sense to describe adding 25 to $x^2 + 10x$ as *completing the square*?

3. **Error Analysis** A student began solving $x^2 + 8x = 5$ by writing $x^2 + 8x + 16 = 5$. Explain the error the student made.

4. **Communicate Precisely** How is changing a quadratic function from standard form to vertex form like solving a quadratic equation by completing the square? How is it different?

5. **Look for Relationships** Why is it necessary for the coefficient of x^2 to be 1 before completing the square?

Do You KNOW HOW?

Find the value of c that makes each expression a perfect-square trinomial.

6. $x^2 + 26x + c$

7. $x^2 + 2x + c$

8. $x^2 + 18x + c$

Solve each equation.

9. $x^2 + 8x = -1$

10. $2x^2 - 24x - 4 = 0$

11. $x^2 - 4x = 7$

Write each function in vertex form.

12. $y = x^2 + 4x - 5$

13. $y = 5x^2 - 10x + 7$

14. $y = x^2 + 8x - 15$

PRACTICE & PROBLEM SOLVING

UNDERSTAND

15. Use Structure What value of c completes the square for each area model below? Represent the area model as a perfect-square trinomial and as a binomial squared.

a.

	x	4
x	x^2	$4x$
4	$4x$	c

b.

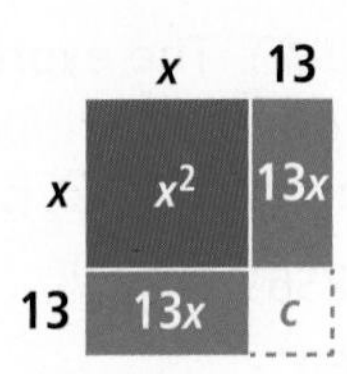

16. Construct Arguments To solve the equation $x^2 - 7x - 9 = 0$, would you use graphing, factoring, or completing the square if you want exact solutions? Explain.

17. Error Analysis Describe and correct the error a student made in writing the quadratic function $y = 2x^2 + 12x + 1$ in vertex form.

$$y = 2x^2 + 12x + 1$$
$$y = 2(x^2 + 6x) + 1$$
$$y + 9 = 2(x^2 + 6x + 9) + 1$$
$$y + 9 = 2(x + 3)^2 + 1$$
$$y = 2(x + 3)^2 - 8$$

✗

18. Reason Find the solution to the equation $x^2 + 4x = -12$. Explain your reasoning.

19. Mathematical Connections Use the graph of $f(x) = x^2 - 2x - 1$ to estimate the solutions of $f(x) = 5$. Then find the exact solutions.

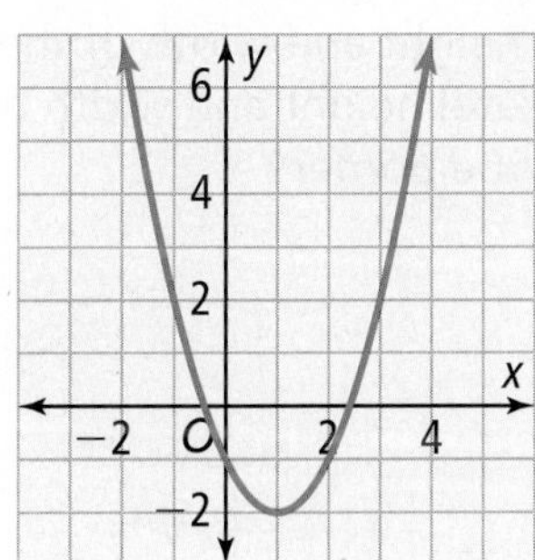

PRACTICE

Find the value of c that makes each expression a perfect-square trinomial. Write each expression as a binomial squared. SEE EXAMPLE 1

20. $x^2 + 16x + c$

21. $x^2 + 22x + c$

22. $p^2 - 30p + c$

23. $k^2 - 5k + c$

24. $g^2 + 17g + c$

25. $q^2 - 48q + c$

Solve each equation by completing the square. SEE EXAMPLES 2 AND 3

26. $x^2 + 6x = 144$

27. $x^2 - 4x = 30$

28. $m^2 + 16m = -59$

29. $x^2 - 2x - 35 = 0$

30. $5n^2 - 3n - 15 = 0$

31. $4w^2 + 12w - 44 = 0$

32. $3r^2 + 18r = 21$

33. $2v^2 - 10v - 20 = 8$

Find the value of x. If necessary, round to the nearest hundredth. SEE EXAMPLE 3

34. Area of triangle = 8

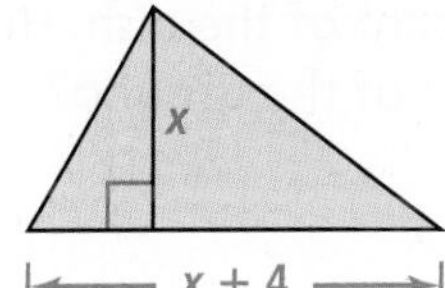

35. Area of rectangle = 50

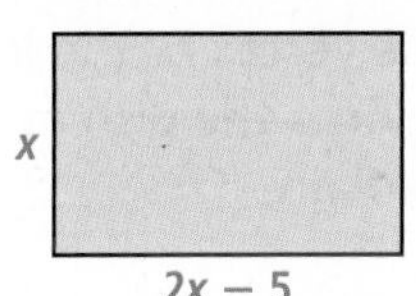

Write each function in vertex form, and identify the vertex. SEE EXAMPLES 4 AND 5

36. $y = x^2 + 4x - 3$

37. $y = x^2 + 12x + 27$

38. $y = x^2 - 6x + 12$

39. $y = x^2 - 14x - 1$

40. $y = 3x^2 - 6x - 2$

41. $y = 2x^2 - 20x + 35$

42. $y = -x^2 - 8x - 7$

43. $y = -4x^2 + 16x + 5$

Write each function in vertex form. Tell whether each graph could represent the function.

44. $y = x^2 + 6x + 3$

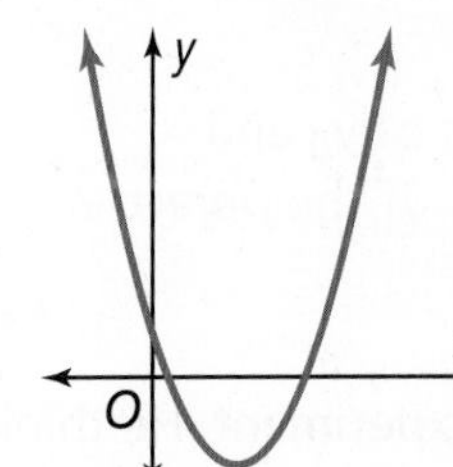

45. $f(x) = -x^2 - 10x - 21$

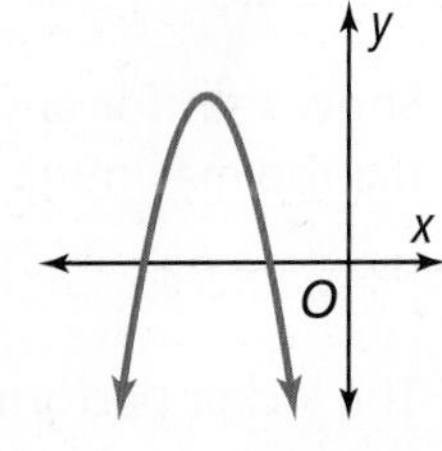

PRACTICE & PROBLEM SOLVING

APPLY

46. **Model With Mathematics** You are designing a square banner for a school assembly. You want the banner to be gold with vertical purple bars as shown. You have enough material to make the area of the rectangular gold section 36 ft^2. What are the dimensions of the banner?

47. **Reason** The profile of a satellite dish is shaped like a parabola. The bottom of the dish can be modeled by the function shown, where x and $f(x)$ are measured in meters. Use the vertex form of the quadratic function to determine the vertex or the lowest point of the dish. How wide is the dish at 18 m off of the ground? Explain.

48. **Higher Order Thinking** The kicker on a football team uses the function, $h = -16t^2 + v_0t + h_0$, to model the height of a football being kicked into the air.

    a. Show that for any values of v_0 and h_0, the maximum height of the object is $\frac{(v_0)^2}{64} + h_0$.

    b. The kicker performs an experiment. He thinks if he can double the initial upward velocity of the football kicked from the ground, the maximum height will also double. Is the kicker correct? If not, how does the maximum height change? Explain.

ASSESSMENT PRACTICE

49. A rectangle is 8 cm longer than it is wide. Its area is 250 cm^2. The width of the rectangle is about ________. The rectangle's perimeter is about ________.

50. **SAT/ACT** The expressions $f(x) = x^2 + 12x + c$ and $g(x) = x^2 - 20x + d$ are perfect-square trinomials. What is the value of $f(0) - g(0)$?

    Ⓐ −256

    Ⓑ −64

    Ⓒ 0

    Ⓓ 32

51. **Performance Task** An electronics manufacturer designs a smartphone with an aspect ratio (the ratio of the screen's height h to its width w) of 16 : 9.

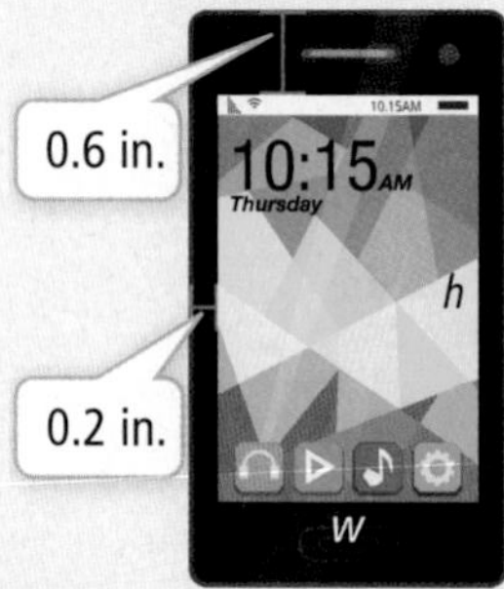

Part A Write the width in terms of h. What is the area of the phone, including the border, in terms of h?

Part B The total area of the screen and border is about 21.48 in.^{2}. What is the value of h?

Part C What are the height and width of the screen? What is the total height and width of the phone including the border?

Activity Assess

9-6 The Quadratic Formula and the Discriminant

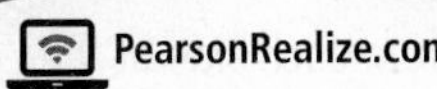

PearsonRealize.com

I CAN... use the quadratic formula to solve quadratic equations.

VOCABULARY

- discriminant
- quadratic formula
- root

EXPLORE & REASON

Three quadratic equations are shown on the whiteboard.

$x^2 - 6x + 12 = 0$

$x^2 - 6x + 9 = 0$

$x^2 - 6x - 5 = 0$

A. How many real solutions are there for each of the quadratic equations shown? Explain your answer.

B. Use Appropriate Tools Use your graphing calculator to graph the related function for each equation. What are the function equations for each graph's reflection over the *x*-axis? Explain how you found the function equations.

C. What do you notice about the graphs that have zero *x*-intercepts? One *x*-intercept? Two *x*-intercepts?

ESSENTIAL QUESTION

When should you use the quadratic formula to solve equations?

EXAMPLE 1 Derive the Quadratic Formula

How can you use completing the square to create a general formula that solves every quadratic equation?

Step 1 Complete the square for the quadratic equation $ax^2 + bx + c = 0$, $a \neq 0$.

$$ax^2 + bx + c = 0$$

$$ax^2 + bx = -c$$ Isolate $ax^2 + bx$.

$$x^2 + \frac{b}{a}x = -\frac{c}{a}$$ Divide by a. Note that a cannot be 0.

$$x^2 + \frac{b}{a}x + \left(\frac{b}{2a}\right)^2 = -\frac{c}{a} + \left(\frac{b}{2a}\right)^2$$

$$\left(x + \frac{b}{2a}\right)^2 = -\frac{c}{a} + \frac{b^2}{4a^2}$$

$$\left(x + \frac{b}{2a}\right)^2 = \left(\frac{4a}{4a}\right)\left(-\frac{c}{a}\right) + \frac{b^2}{4a^2}$$ Multiply $-\frac{c}{a}$ by $\frac{4a}{4a}$ to get like denominators.

$$\left(x + \frac{b}{2a}\right)^2 = -\frac{4ac}{4a^2} + \frac{b^2}{4a^2}$$

$$\left(x + \frac{b}{2a}\right)^2 = \frac{b^2}{4a^2} - \frac{4ac}{4a^2}$$

$$\left(x + \frac{b}{2a}\right)^2 = \frac{b^2 - 4ac}{4a^2}$$

STUDY TIP
Recall that in order to complete the square of a quadratic equation you need to take half of the coefficient of the linear term and square it.

CONTINUED ON THE NEXT PAGE

EXAMPLE 1 CONTINUED

Step 2 Solve for x.

$$\left(x + \frac{b}{2a}\right)^2 = \frac{b^2 - 4ac}{4a^2}$$

COMMUNICATE PRECISELY
The $\pm$ sign is used to show there is a positive and negative solution to the equation.

$$\left(x + \frac{b}{2a}\right) = \pm\sqrt{\frac{b^2 - 4ac}{4a^2}}$$

Take the square root of each side of the equation.

$$x = \pm\sqrt{\frac{b^2 - 4ac}{4a^2}} - \frac{b}{2a}$$

Subtract $\frac{b}{2a}$ from each side of the equation.

$$x = \frac{\pm\sqrt{b^2 - 4ac}}{2a} - \frac{b}{2a}$$

$$x = \frac{-b \pm\sqrt{b^2 - 4ac}}{2a}$$

The **quadratic formula** gives solutions of quadratic equations in the form $ax^2 + bx + c = 0$ for real values of a, b, and c. The quadratic formula is a useful method to find the solutions of any quadratic equations.

Try It! 1. What is the maximum number of solutions the quadratic formula can give? Explain.

EXAMPLE 2 Use the Quadratic Formula

How can you use the quadratic formula to find the solutions of $x^2 - 7 = 4x$?

Write the equation in standard form and identify a, b, and c.

$$x^2 - 4x - 7 = 0$$

$a = 1, b = -4, c = -7$

$$x = \frac{-b \pm \sqrt{b^2 - 4ac}}{2a}$$

COMMON ERROR
You might get the sign of $-b$ wrong if you forget to use parentheses when substituting negative values for b.

$$x = \frac{-(-4) \pm \sqrt{(-4)^2 - 4(1)(-7)}}{2(1)}$$

Substitute the values for a, b, and c into the quadratic formula.

$$x = \frac{4 \pm \sqrt{44}}{2}$$

$$x = \frac{4 + \sqrt{44}}{2} \approx 5.32 \text{ and } x = \frac{4 - \sqrt{44}}{2} \approx -1.32$$

The solutions of $x^2 - 7 = 4x$ are $x \approx 5.32$ and $x \approx -1.32$.

Graphing the equation helps verify that the solutions found using the quadratic formula are correct.

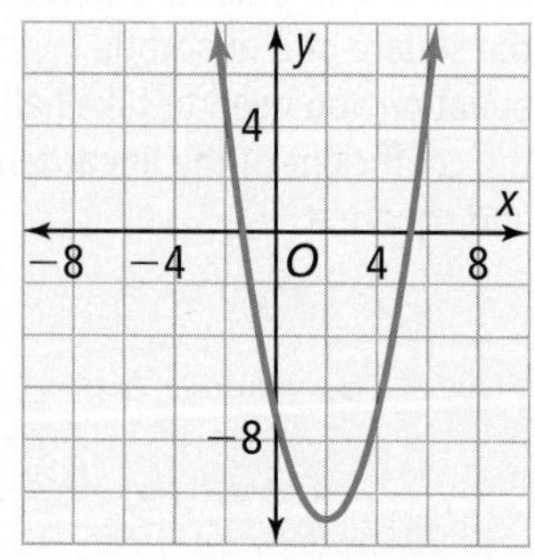

Try It! 2. Find the solutions of each equation using the quadratic formula.

a. $21 - 4x = x^2$

b. $x^2 - 2x = 24$

APPLICATION

EXAMPLE 3 Find Approximate Solutions

The function shown represents the height of a frog *x* seconds after it jumps off a rock. How many seconds is the frog in the air before it lands on the ground?

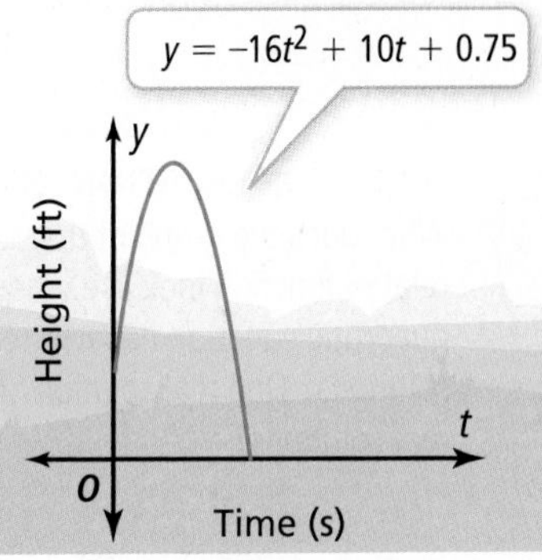

Formulate Write a related quadratic equation with $y = 0$ to find when the frog lands on the ground. Although the path of the frog's jump is a parabolic curve, you are being asked to find the time of the jump and not the distance of the jump. The function representing the time of the jump is also parabolic, but the parabola is not the same.

$$-16t^2 + 10t + 0.75 = 0$$

Find the values of *a*, *b*, and *c* in the equation.
$a = -16$, $b = 10$, $c = 0.75$

Compute Substitute the values of *a*, *b*, and *c* into the quadratic formula.

$$t = \frac{-(10) \pm \sqrt{(10)^2 - 4(-16)(0.75)}}{2(-16)}$$

$$= \frac{-10 \pm \sqrt{148}}{-32}$$

$$= \frac{-10 \pm 12.17}{-32}$$

$$t = \frac{-10 + 12.17}{-32} = -\frac{2.17}{32} \approx -0.068 \text{ and}$$

$$t = \frac{-10 - 12.17}{-32} = \frac{-22.17}{-32} \approx 0.693$$

Interpret The negative value for *t* is not a realistic answer in this situation because time is positive.

The frog is in the air about 0.7 s before it lands on the ground.

Try It! **3.** The height of another frog over time is modeled by the function $y = -16t^2 + 10t + 0.3$. How many seconds is this frog in the air before landing on the ground? Round your answer to the nearest hundredth.

CONCEPTUAL UNDERSTANDING

EXAMPLE 4 Understand and Use the Discriminant

How can you determine the number of solutions of a quadratic equation without solving it?

In the quadratic formula $x = \frac{-b \pm \sqrt{b^2 - 4ac}}{2a}$, the **discriminant** is the expression $b^2 - 4ac$. The discriminant indicates the number of real solutions of the equation. The solutions of a quadratic equation are also called its **roots**. Roots are the input values for which the related function is zero.

If $b^2 - 4ac > 0$, there are two real solutions.

If $b^2 - 4ac = 0$, there is one real solution.

If $b^2 - 4ac < 0$, there are no real solutions.

LOOK FOR RELATIONSHIPS
What does the graph of the related function look like when a quadratic equation has two real solutions? One real solution? No real solutions?

A. Find the number of solutions for $x^2 - 4x + 3 = 0$.

$x^2 - 4x + 3 = 0$

$(-4)^2 - 4(1)(3) = 4$

The discriminant is > 0, so there are two real roots.

$y = x^2 - 4x + 3$

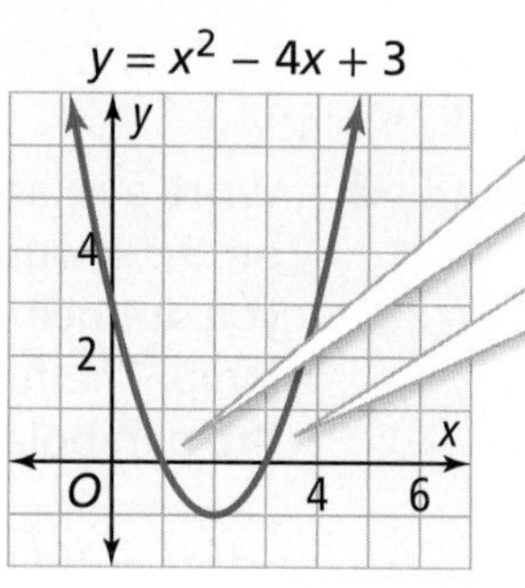

The graph of the related function intersects the x-axis at two points.

B. Find the solutions for $-x^2 + 4x - 4 = 0$.

$-x^2 + 4x - 4 = 0$

$(4)^2 - 4(-1)(-4) = 0$

The discriminant is 0, so there is one real root.

$y = -x^2 + 4x - 4$

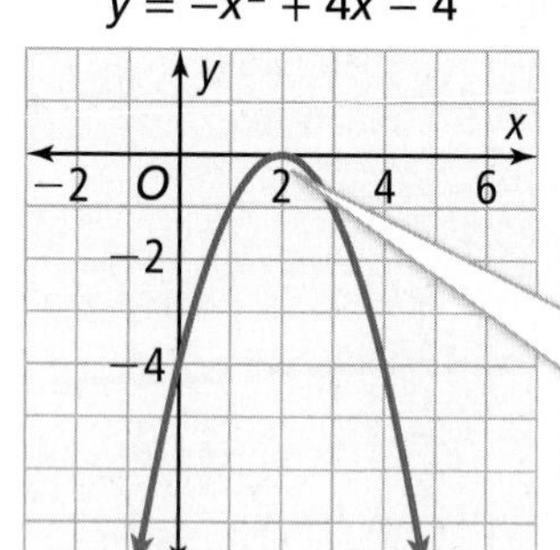

The graph of the related function intersects the x-axis at one point.

C. Find the solutions for $x^2 - 4x + 5 = 0$.

$x^2 - 4x + 5 = 0$

$(-4)^2 - 4(1)(5) = -4$

The discriminant is < 0, so there are no real roots.

$y = x^2 - 4x + 5$

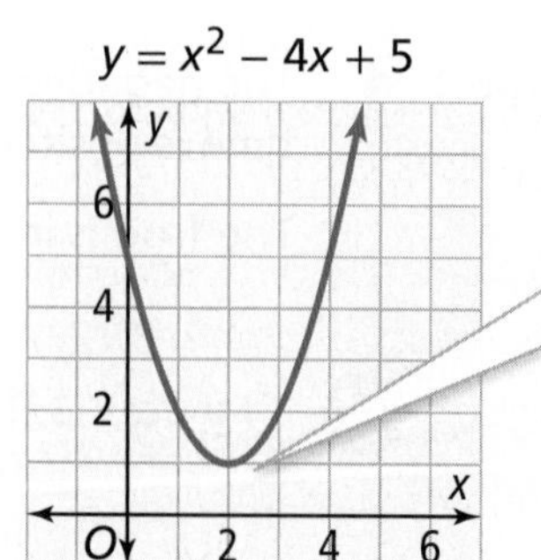

The graph of the related function does not intersect the x-axis.

Try It! 4. Use the discriminant to find the number of roots of each equation.

a. $x^2 - 10x + 25 = 0$

b. $-x^2 - 6x - 10 = 0$

CONCEPT SUMMARY Using the Quadratic Formula

	Equation	Quadratic Formula	Discriminant
ALGEBRA	$ax^2 + bx + c = 0$	$x = \frac{-b \pm \sqrt{b^2 - 4ac}}{2a}$	$b^2 - 4ac$
NUMBERS	$2x^2 - 3x - 1 = 0$	$x = \frac{-(-3) \pm \sqrt{(-3)^2 - 4(2)(-1)}}{2(2)}$ $x = \frac{3 + \sqrt{17}}{4} \approx 1.78$ and $x = \frac{3 - \sqrt{17}}{4} \approx -0.28$	$(-3)^2 - 4(2)(-1) = 17$ $17 > 0$, two real solutions
	Related Function		
GRAPH	$y = 2x^2 - 3x - 1$ 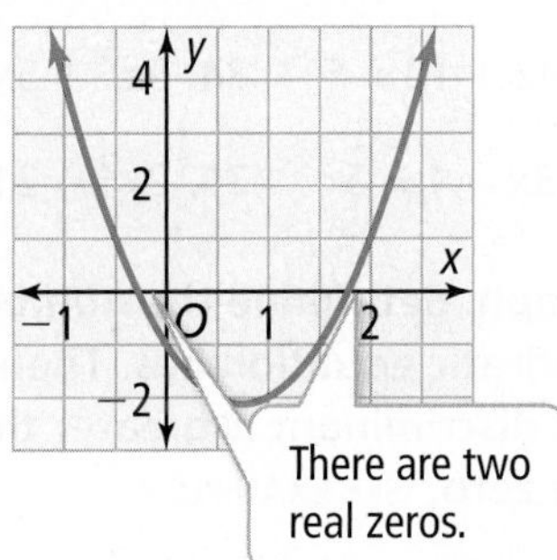		The discriminant of the related equation is > 0.

Do You UNDERSTAND?

1. ESSENTIAL QUESTION When should you use the quadratic formula to solve equations?

2. **Reason** What value of b^2 is needed for there to be exactly one real solution of a quadratic equation? Explain.

3. **Vocabulary** How are the *roots* of a quadratic equation related to its *discriminant*?

4. **Error Analysis** A student says that the quadratic formula cannot be used to solve $-23x^2 + 5 = 0$. Explain the error the student made.

5. **Reason** When is completing the square better than using the quadratic formula?

Do You KNOW HOW?

Identify *a*, *b*, and *c* in each of the quadratic equations.

6. $4x^2 + 2x - 1 = 0$

7. $-x^2 + 31x + 7 = 0$

8. $2x^2 - 10x - 3 = 0$

9. $x^2 + x - 1 = 0$

Given the discriminant of a quadratic equation, determine the number of real solutions.

10. 8

11. −3

12. 0

13. 1

PRACTICE & PROBLEM SOLVING

Scan for Multimedia

Practice | Tutorial

Additional Exercises Available Online

UNDERSTAND

14. Mathematical Connections Why does a quadratic equation have to be in standard form before applying the quadratic formula to find solutions?

15. Error Analysis Describe and correct the error a student made in solving $3x^2 + 9x - 4 = 0$.

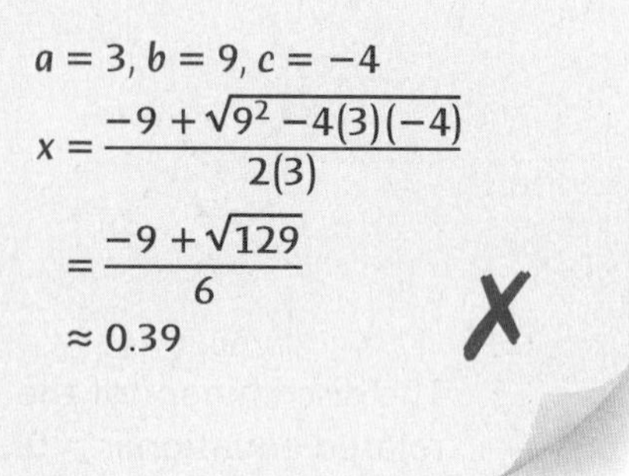

16. Reason Which method would you use to solve each equation? Explain.

a. $x^2 + 9x = 0$

b. $11x^2 - 4 = 0$

c. $7x^2 + 11x - 6 = 0$

17. Use Structure The graph of a quadratic function is shown below. Describe how you could change the graph so that the discriminant of the new related quadratic equation is positive.

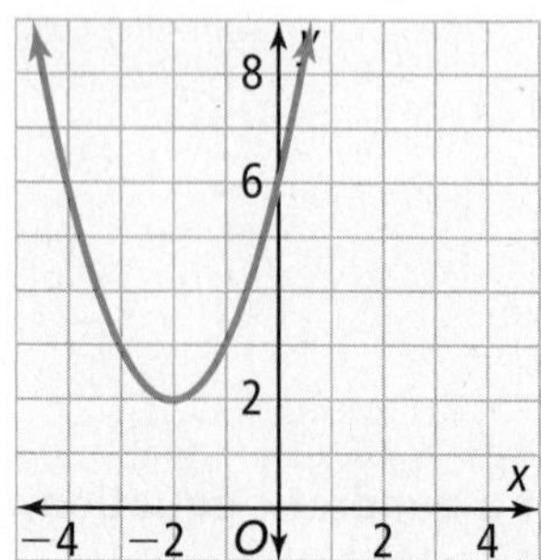

18. Higher Order Thinking Use the quadratic formula to prove the axis of symmetry can be found using $-\frac{b}{2a}$. What does the discriminant of a quadratic equation tell you about the vertex of the graph of the related function?

PRACTICE

Solve each equation using the quadratic formula. Round to the nearest hundredth.
SEE EXAMPLES 1, 2, AND 3

19. $-2x^2 + 12x - 5 = 0$

20. $x^2 + 19x - 7 = 0$

21. $3x^2 + 18x - 27 = 0$

22. $-7x^2 + 2x + 1 = 0$

23. $2x^2 + 9x + 7 = 0$

24. $-x^2 + 9x + 5 = -3$

25. $4x^2 + 17x - 5 = 4$

26. $5x^2 + 10x + 7 = 2$

27. $-6x^2 + 5x - 2 = -11$

28. $-2x^2 + 4x + 9 = -3$

Use the discriminant to determine the real roots for each equation. SEE EXAMPLE 4

29. $3x^2 - 9x - 16 = 0$

30. $-4x^2 + 7x - 11 = 0$

31. $2x^2 - 6x + 3 = 0$

32. $5x^2 - 20x + 20 = 0$

33. $7x^2 - 14x + 12 = 5$

34. $9x^2 + 5x - 2 = -4$

35. $-8x^2 - 3x - 1 = 5$

36. $2x^2 - 21x - 7 = 4$

For each graph, determine the number of roots the related quadratic equation has. Then determine whether its discriminant is greater than, equal to, or less than zero. SEE EXAMPLE 4

37.

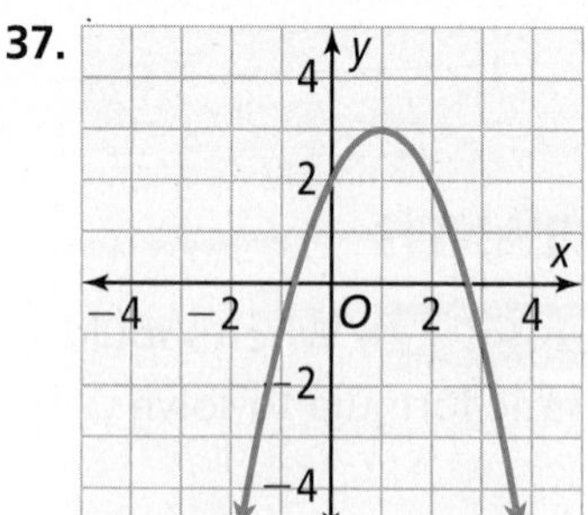

38.

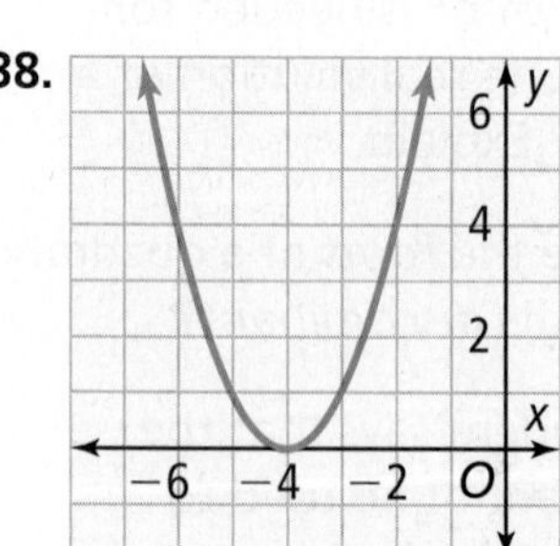

PRACTICE & PROBLEM SOLVING

APPLY

39. Reason A quadratic function can be used to model the height y of an object that is thrown over time x. What are the values of the discriminant of the related equation of the function $f(x) = -16t^2 + 35t + 5$, which models a ball being thrown into the air?

40. Model With Mathematics The function $f(x) = -16x^2 + 64x + 5$ models the height y, in feet, of a watermelon from a watermelon launcher after x seconds.

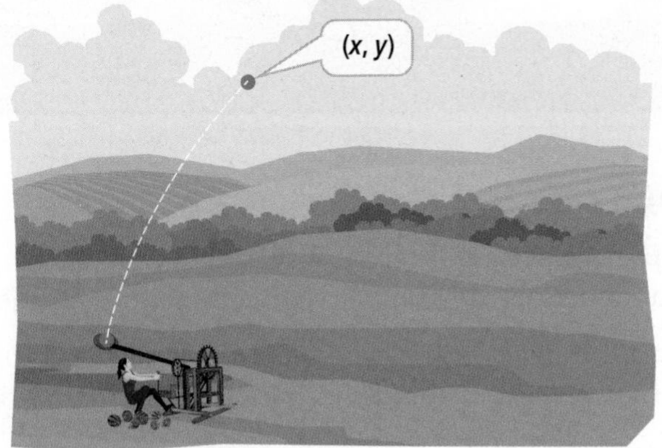

a. Write a quadratic equation that can be used to determine when the watermelon reaches 20 ft.

b. Use the discriminant to predict the number of solutions to the equation from part (a).

c. What are the approximate solutions of the equation you wrote in part a?

41. Make Sense and Persevere The student council is raising money for school dances by selling spirit T-shirts. The function $R = -5n^2 + 85n + 1{,}000$ models the revenue R in dollars they expect per increase of n dollars over the original price of each T-shirt. The goal is $1,250.

a. Write a quadratic equation to find the dollar increase n in price needed to meet this goal.

b. Solve the equation using the quadratic formula. What price(s) will result in the student council meeting their goal?

ASSESSMENT PRACTICE

42. A quadratic equation has no real solutions. Choose *Yes* or *No* to tell whether each is a possible value of the discriminant.

	Yes	No
–4	❑	❑
–2	❑	❑
0	❑	❑
2	❑	❑
4	❑	❑

43. SAT/ACT What is the discriminant of $x^2 - x - 3 = 0$?

Ⓐ –11
Ⓑ 0
Ⓒ 11
Ⓓ 13
Ⓔ –13

44. Performance Task A skier made 2 jumps that were recorded by her coach. A function that models the height y, in meters, at x seconds for each jump is shown.

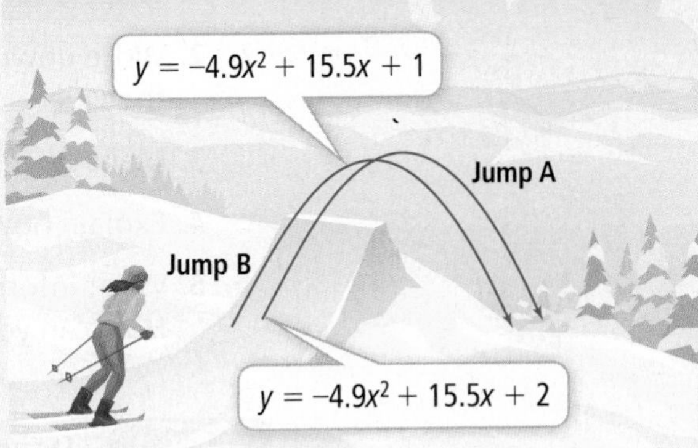

Part A Predict which jump kept the skier in the air for the greatest number of seconds.

Part B Use the quadratic formula to find how long the skier was in the air during Jump A.

Part C Use the quadratic formula to find how long the skier was in the air during Jump B.

Part D Do your results support your prediction? Explain.

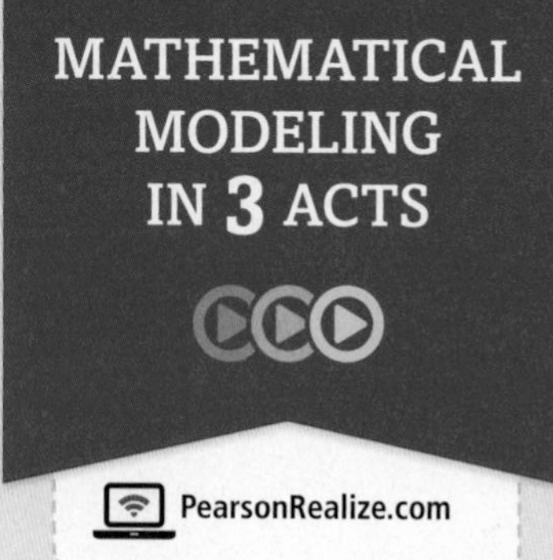

Unwrapping Change

When you arrange a group of objects in different ways, it seems like the space they take up has changed. But, the number of objects didn't change!

We use coin wrappers to store coins in an efficient way. How much more efficient is it than the alternative? Think about this during the Mathematical Modeling in 3 Acts lesson.

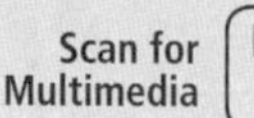

ACT 1 Identify the Problem

1. What is the first question that comes to mind after watching the video?
2. Write down the main question you will answer about what you saw in the video.
3. Make an initial conjecture that answers this main question.
4. Explain how you arrived at your conjecture.
5. What information will be useful to know to answer the main question? How can you get it? How will you use that information?

ACT 2 Develop a Model

6. Use the math that you have learned in this Topic to refine your conjecture.

ACT 3 Interpret the Results

7. Did your refined conjecture match the actual answer exactly? If not, what might explain the difference?

9-7 Solving Systems of Linear and Quadratic Equations

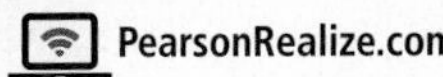

PearsonRealize.com

I CAN… solve a system with linear and quadratic equations.

VOCABULARY

- linear-quadratic system

MODEL & DISCUSS

An architect is designing an archway for a building that has a 9 ft ceiling. She is working with the constraints shown at the right.

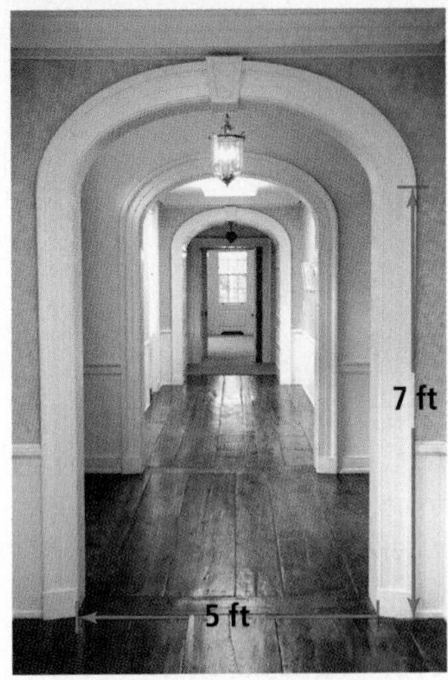

A. Find a quadratic model for the arches if the highest point of the arch touches the ceiling.

B. Use Structure Describe how to change the model so that the highest point of the arch does not touch the ceiling.

ESSENTIAL QUESTION

How is solving linear-quadratic systems of equations similar to and different from solving systems of linear equations?

CONCEPTUAL UNDERSTANDING

EXAMPLE 1 Understand Linear-Quadratic Systems of Equations

Why are the solutions of a linear-quadratic system of equations related to the solutions of a quadratic equation?

A **linear-quadratic system** of equations includes a linear equation and a quadratic equation and is represented on a graph by their corresponding line and parabola.

$y = mx + b$

$y = ax^2 + bx + c$

The graphs below of a line and three parabolas show that a line can intersect a parabola at 0, 1, or 2 points. The solutions are where the parabola and the purple line of each system intersect.

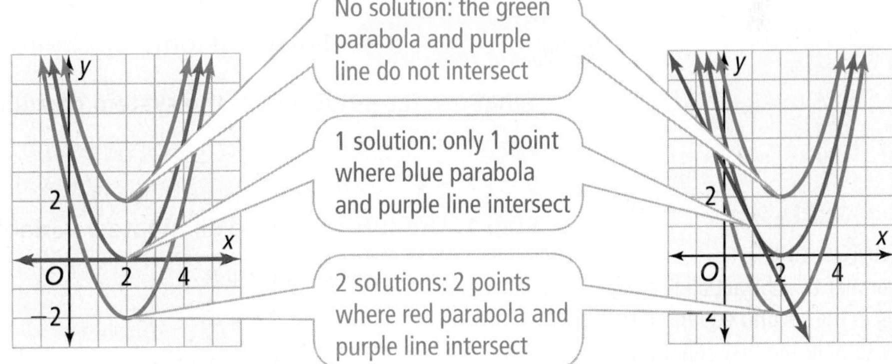

REASON
A line can intersect a parabola a maximum of two times because setting a quadratic equation equal to a linear equation results in a quadratic equation.

A linear-quadratic system of equations, just like a quadratic equation, can have 0, 1, or 2 real solutions.

Try It! **1.** How many solutions does the system of equations at the right have? Explain.

$y = x$

$y = x^2$

EXAMPLE 2 Solve a Linear-Quadratic Equation by Graphing

How can you use graphs to find the solutions of the equation $5 - x^2 = x + 3$?

Set each side of the equation $5 - x^2 = x + 3$ equal to y, and write the equations as a linear-quadratic system of equations.

$$y = 5 - x^2$$
$$y = x + 3$$

Graph the equations in the system on the same coordinate plane.

USE APPROPRIATE TOOLS
A graphing calculator can be used to calculate intersection points when the equations are defined in its function editor.

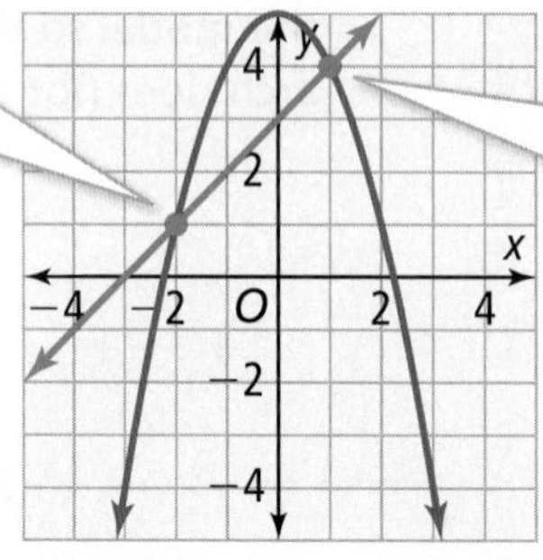

The solutions of the system appear to be (1, 4) and (−2, 1) where the two graphs intersect.

Check that each x-value is a solution of the equation $5 - x^2 = x + 3$.

$5 - (1)^2 = (1) + 3$ $\qquad$ $5 - (-2)^2 = (-2) + 3$

$4 = 4$ ✓ $\qquad$ $1 = 1$ ✓

The solutions of the equation are $x = 1$ and $x = -2$.

Try It! 2. What are the solutions of each of the equations? Rewrite each as a system of equations, and graph to solve.

a. $x^2 + 1 = x + 3$ $\qquad$ b. $5 - 0.5x^2 = -0.5x + 2$

EXAMPLE 3 Solve Systems of Equations Using Elimination

What are the solutions of the system of equations below?

$$y = x^2 - 6x + 8$$
$$y = 2x - 4$$

Step 1 Use subtraction to eliminate a variable in the system of equations.

COMMON ERROR
Remember to subtract all like terms in the second equation from a like term in the first equation.

$$\begin{array}{r} y = x^2 - 6x + 8 \\ -(y = \quad\;\; 2x - 4) \\ \hline 0 = x^2 - 8x + 12 \end{array}$$

Subtract the linear equation from the quadratic equation to eliminate the y-variable. Line up like terms.

Solve the resulting equation by factoring.

$$(x - 6)(x - 2) = 0$$

$x - 6 = 0$ $\quad$ or $\quad$ $x - 2 = 0$

$x = 6$ $\qquad$ $x = 2$

CONTINUED ON THE NEXT PAGE

EXAMPLE 1 CONTINUED

Step 2 Substitute $x = 6$ and $x = 2$ in $y = 2x - 4$, and determine the corresponding values of y.

$y = 2(6) - 4$ $\qquad$ $y = 2(2) - 4$

$y = 12 - 4$ $\qquad$ $y = 4 - 4$

$y = 8$ $\qquad$ $y = 0$

Use the linear equation $y = 2x - 4$ to solve for y since it requires fewer steps.

The solutions of the system of equations are (6, 8) and (2, 0).

Try It! 3. Use elimination to solve each system of equations.

a. $y = -x + 4$
$y = x^2 - 2$

b. $y = -x^2 + 4x + 2$
$y = 2 - x$

APPLICATION

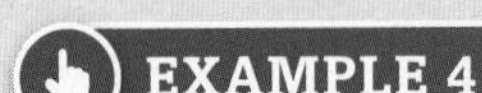

EXAMPLE 4 Solve Systems Using Substitution

A phone company launches the sale of two phones in the same week. The phone on the right is an upgraded version of the other phone. During what week are the sales projected to be the same for both phones, in thousands? What will the weekly sales of each phone be for that week?

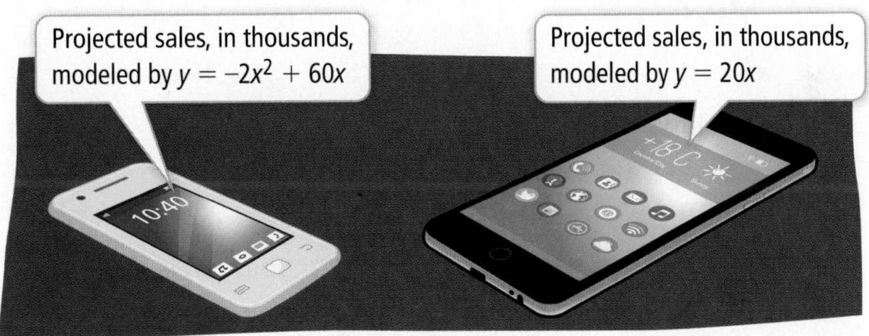

Formulate Model the projected sales by writing a system of equations. Let x represent the number of weeks since the launch.

$y = 20x$

$y = -2x^2 + 60x$

Compute Solve the system of equations using substitution.

$20x = -2x^2 + 60x$ — Substitute $20x$ for y in the second equation.

$0 = -2x^2 + 40x$

$0 = -2x(x - 20)$ — Factor the binomial, then set each factor equal to 0 and solve.

$-2x = 0$ $\qquad$ $x - 20 = 0$

$x = 0$ $\qquad$ $x = 20$

$y = 20(20)$ $\qquad$ $y = -2(20)^2 + 60(20)$

$y = 400$ $\qquad$ $y = 400$ — Projected sale of 400,000 for both phones.

Interpret The models project that both phones will have weekly sales of 400,000 phones at 20 weeks after the launch.

CONTINUED ON THE NEXT PAGE

Try It! 4. Could you have used elimination or graphing to solve this linear-quadratic system of equations? Explain.

CONCEPT SUMMARY Solving Linear-Quadratic Systems of Equations

WORDS A system of equations composed of a linear equation and a quadratic equation has 0, 1, or 2 solutions. The system of equations can be solved using elimination, substitution, or graphing.

$y = mx + b$

$y = ax^2 + bx + c$

	Elimination	Substitution	Graphing
ALGEBRA	$y = x^2 + x$ $y = x - 1$ $y = x^2 + x$ $-y = -x + 1$ $0 = x^2 + 1$ $x^2 = -1$ No solution	$y = -2x + 3$ $y = -x^2 + 2$ $-2x + 3 = -x^2 + 2$ $x^2 - 2x + 1 = 0$ $(x - 1)^2 = 0$ $x - 1 = 0$ $x = 1$ $y = -2(1) + 3 = 1$ Solution is (1, 1)	$y = \frac{1}{2}x + 1$ $y = -x^2 - 8x - 14$ 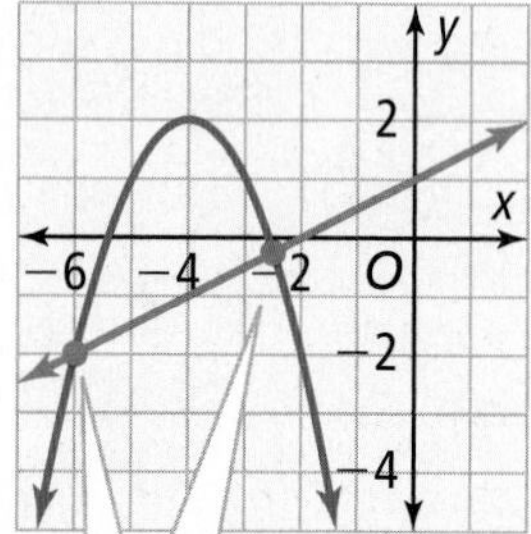 The solutions are where the line and parabola intersect at (−6, −2) and (−2.5, −0.25).

Do You UNDERSTAND?

1. **ESSENTIAL QUESTION** How is solving linear-quadratic systems of equations similar to and different from solving systems of linear equations?

2. **Error Analysis** A student claims that a linear-quadratic system of equations has three solutions. Explain the error the student made.

3. **Vocabulary** What are the characteristics of a *linear-quadratic system* of equations?

4. **Reason** What system of equations could you use to solve the equation $x^2 - 3 = 7$? Explain.

Do You KNOW HOW?

Rewrite each equation as a system of equations.

5. $3 = x^2 + 2x$

6. $x = x^2 - 5$

7. $2x^2 - 5 = x + 7$

8. $x^2 - 2x + 3 = x + 4$

Find the solution of each system of equations.

9. $\begin{cases} y = x^2 + 3x + 1 \\ y = -x + 1 \end{cases}$

10. $\begin{cases} y = x^2 + 1 \\ y = -2x \end{cases}$

11.

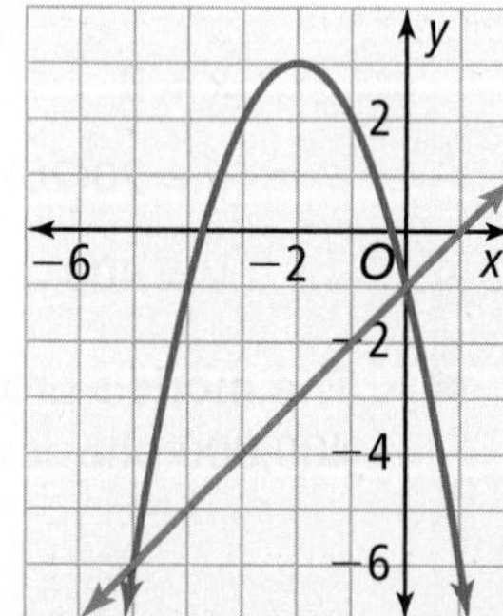

UNDERSTAND

12. **Mathematical Connections** How is the graph of a linear-quadratic system of equations different from the graph of a linear system of equations? How are the graphs similar?

13. **Look for Relationships** What does the graph of the system of equations tell you about its solution?
$y = 3x^2 - 4x + 2$
$y = 8x - 10$

14. **Higher Order Thinking** Given the equation $y = x^2 + 3x + 2$, write an equation for a line that intersects the parabola the given number of times.
   a. 0
   b. 1
   c. 2

15. **Error Analysis** Describe and correct the error a student made in solving the system of equations.
$y = 2x^2 + 3$
$y = 3x + 1$

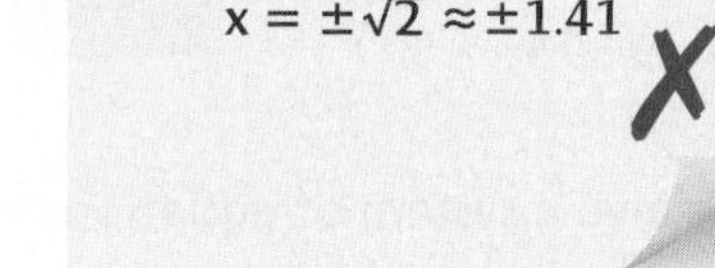

16. **Use Appropriate Tools** How do you select the appropriate method for solving a linear-quadratic system? Describe when you would use graphing, elimination, and substitution.

17. **Use Structure** Write the linear-quadratic system of equations that is represented by the graph.

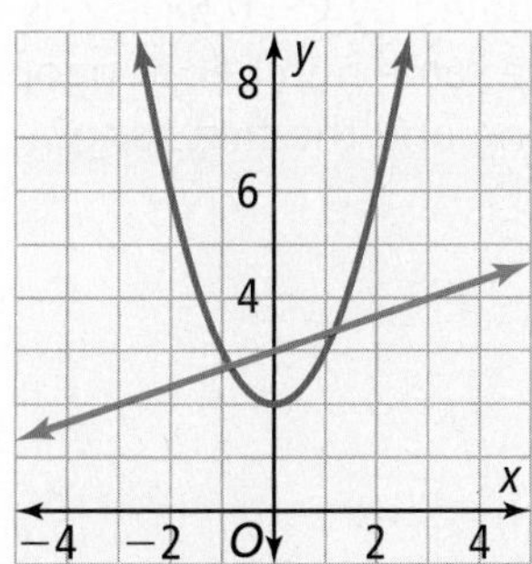

PRACTICE

Rewrite each equation as a system of equations, and then use a graph to solve. SEE EXAMPLES 1 AND 2

18. $\frac{1}{3}x^2 + 2 = -x + 8$

19. $2x^2 - 3x = -2x + 1$

20. $5x^2 = 3x - 7$

21. $x^2 - 2x = 2x - 4$

Rewrite each equation as a system of equations and graph to solve. SEE EXAMPLE 2

22. $x^2 - 4 = x + 2$

23. $-2x + 4 = -0.5x^2 + 4$

Find the solution of each system of equations. SEE EXAMPLES 1–4

24. $y = x^2 + 3x - 2$
$y = 2x$

25. $y = -4x^2 + x + 1$
$y = -7x + 1$

26. $y = 0.5x^2 - 8x + 13$
$y = x - 3$

27. $y = 7x^2 + 12$
$y = 14x + 5$

28. $y = -x^2 - 2x + 9$
$y = 3x + 20$

29. $y = -5x^2 + 6x - 3$
$y = -4x - 3$

30. $y = 0.75x^2 + 4x - 5$
$y = 4x - 5$

31. $y = -2x^2 + 6x + 7$
$y = 13 - 2x$

32. A ropes course facility offers two types of courses, a low ropes course and a high ropes course. The price of a high ropes adventure is five times as much as a low ropes adventure. Eight members of the high school adventure club choose to participate in the low ropes course, and 15 members choose the high ropes course. The total cost is $1,411. What is the price of each type of ropes course adventure?

PRACTICE & PROBLEM SOLVING

Practice | Tutorial

Mixed Review Available Online

APPLY

33. **Make Sense and Persevere** An equation that models the height of an object dropped from the top of a building is $y = -16x^2 + 30$ where x is time in sec. Another equation $y = 14$ models the path of a bird flying in the air. Write a system of equations and then solve to find how many seconds the object is in the air before it crosses the bird's path.

34. **Reason** A car accelerates after being completely stopped at a stop sign and enters the highway. The distance the car has traveled in miles after x minutes is represented by $y = 0.5x^2$. A truck is traveling in the same direction at a constant speed so that its distance in miles from the same stop sign after x minutes is represented by $y = x + 4$. After how many minutes will the car pass the truck? Explain.

35. **Model With Mathematics** At the beginning of a month, the number of people rock climbing increases and then decreases by the end of the month. The number of people zip-lining steadily increases throughout the same month. The models show the number of people y for each type of activity based on the number of days x since the beginning of the month.

a. Write a system of equations that represents this situation.

b. On what day or days were the same number of people rock climbing and zip-lining?

c. How many people were participating in each activity on that day or days?

ASSESSMENT PRACTICE

36. What is the solution of the system of equations?

$y = x^2 - 5x - 8$

$y = -2x - 4$

37. **SAT/ACT** What is the solution of the system of equations?

$y = 6x^2 + 3x - 11$

$y = 3x - 5$

Ⓐ (1, −2), (−1, −8)
Ⓑ (1, −1)
Ⓒ (−2, 1), (−8, −1)
Ⓓ (−1, −8)

38. **Performance Task** A music streaming service tracks the number of times songs are played. Two different songs are released on the same day. The functions model the number of times y, in thousands, each song is played x days following their release.

Part A Write and solve a system of equations to find the number of days since the release when both songs are played the same number of times.

Part B How many solutions are there? Explain.

Part C A third song is released on the same day as the other two. The number of times this song is played is modeled by $y = 0.5x + 2$. Is there a day when the same number of people listen to the third song and the first song? Explain.

TOPIC 9

Topic Review

TOPIC ESSENTIAL QUESTION

1. How do you use quadratic equations to model situations and solve problems?

Vocabulary Review

Choose the correct term to complete each sentence.

2. The __________ is $ax^2 + bx + c = 0$, where $a \neq 0$.
3. The process of adding $\left(\frac{b}{2}\right)^2$ to $x^2 + bx$ to form a perfect-square trinomial is called __________.
4. The x-intercepts of the graph of the function are also called the __________.
5. The __________ states that $\sqrt{ab} = \sqrt{a} \cdot \sqrt{b}$, where both a and b are greater than or equal to 0.
6. The __________ states that for all real numbers a and b, if $ab = 0$, then either $a = 0$ or $b = 0$.

- completing the square
- discriminant
- Product Property of Square Roots
- quadratic equation
- quadratic formula
- standard form of a quadratic equation
- Zero-Product Property
- zeros of a function

Concepts & Skills Review

LESSON 9-1 Solving Quadratic Equations Using Graphs and Tables

Quick Review

A **quadratic equation** is an equation of the second degree. A quadratic equation can have 0, 1 or 2 solutions, which are known as the **zeros of the related function**.

Example

Find the solutions of $0 = x^2 + x - 2$.

The x-intercepts of the related function are −2, and 1, so the equation has two real solutions.

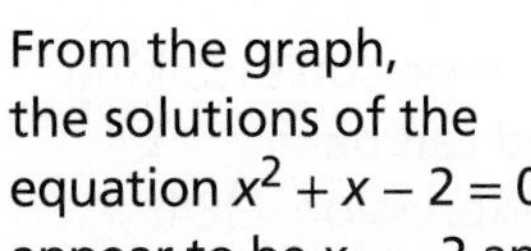

From the graph, the solutions of the equation $x^2 + x - 2 = 0$ appear to be $x = -2$ and $x = 1$.

It is important to verify those solutions by substituting into the equation.

$(-2)^2 + (-2) - 2 = 0$ $\quad$ $1^2 + 1 - 2 = 0$

$0 = 0$ $\quad$ $0 = 0$

Practice & Problem Solving

Solve each quadratic equation by graphing.

7. $x^2 - 16 = 0$
8. $x^2 - 6x + 9 = 0$
9. $x^2 + 2x + 8 = 0$
10. $2x^2 - 11x + 5 = 0$

Find the solutions for each equation using a table. Round to the nearest tenth.

11. $x^2 - 64 = 0$
12. $x^2 - 6x - 16 = 0$
13. **Model With Mathematics** A video game company uses the profit model $P(x) = -x^2 + 14x - 39$, where x is the number of video games sold, in thousands, and $P(x)$ is the profit earned in millions of dollars. How many video games would the company have to sell to earn a maximum profit? How many video games would the company have to sell to not show a profit?

TOPIC 9 REVIEW

LESSON 9-2 Solving Quadratic Equations by Factoring

Quick Review

The **standard form of a quadratic equation** is $ax^2 + bx + c = 0$, where $a \neq 0$. The **Zero-Product Property** states that for all real numbers *a* and *b*, if $ab = 0$, then either $a = 0$ or $b = 0$. The solutions of a quadratic equation can often be determined by factoring.

Example

How can you use factoring to solve $x^2 + 4x = 12$?

First write the equation in standard form.

$x^2 + 4x - 12 = 0$

Then, rewrite the standard form of the equation in factored form.

$(x - 2)(x + 6) = 0$

Use the Zero-Product Property. Set each factor equal to zero and solve.

$x - 2 = 0$ or $x + 6 = 0$

$x = 2$ $\quad$ $x = -6$

The solutions of $x^2 + 4x - 12 = 0$ are $x = 2$ and $x = -6$.

Practice & Problem Solving

Solve each equation by factoring.

14. $x^2 + 6x + 9 = 0$

15. $x^2 - 3x - 10 = 0$

16. $x^2 - 12x = 0$

17. $2x^2 - 7x - 15 = 0$

Factor, find the coordinates of the vertex of the related function, and then graph it.

18. $x^2 - 12x + 20 = 0$

19. $x^2 - 8x + 15 = 0$

20. **Error Analysis** Describe and correct the error a student made in factoring.

$$2x^2 - 8x + 8 = 0$$
$$2(x^2 - 4x + 4) = 0$$
$$2(x - 2)(x - 2) = 0$$
$$x = -2$$

LESSON 9-3 Rewriting Radical Expressions

Quick Review

A radical expression in simplest form has no perfect square factors other than 1 in the radicand. The **Product Property of Square Roots** states that $\sqrt{ab} = \sqrt{a} \cdot \sqrt{b}$, when $a \geq 0$ and $b \geq 0$.

Example

Write an expression for $5\sqrt{3x} \cdot 2\sqrt{12x^3}$ without any perfect squares in the radicand.

$5\sqrt{3x} \cdot 2\sqrt{12x^3}$ .... Multiply the constants, and use the Product Property of Square Roots to multiply the radicands.

$= 5 \cdot 2\sqrt{3x \cdot 12x^3}$

$= 10\sqrt{36x^4}$ .... Simplify.

$= 10 \cdot 6 \cdot x^2$ .... Simplify.

$= 60x^2$

The expression $5\sqrt{3x} \cdot 2\sqrt{12x^3}$ is equivalent to $60x^2$.

Practice & Problem Solving

Write an equivalent expression without a perfect square factor in the radicand.

21. $\sqrt{420}$

22. $4\sqrt{84}$

23. $\sqrt{35x} \cdot \sqrt{21x}$

24. $\sqrt{32x^5} \cdot \sqrt{24x^7}$

Compare each pair of radical expressions.

25. $2x^2\sqrt{21x}$ and $\sqrt{84x^5}$

26. $3xy\sqrt{15xy^2}$ and $\sqrt{135x^4y^3}$

27. **Model With Mathematics** A person's walking speed in inches per second can be approximated using the expression $\sqrt{384\ell}$, where ℓ is the length of a person's leg in inches. Write the expression in simplified form. What is the walking speed of a person with a leg length of 31 in.

LESSON 9-4 Solving Quadratic Equations Using Square Roots

Quick Review

To solve a quadratic equation using square roots, isolate the variable and find the square root of both sides of the equation.

Example

Use the properties of equality to solve the quadratic equation $4x^2 - 7 = 57$.

Rewrite the equation in the form $x^2 = a$.

$4x^2 - 7 = 57$

$4x^2 = 64$ ······ Rewrite using the form $x^2 = a$, where a is a real number.

$x^2 = 16$

$\sqrt{x^2} = \sqrt{16}$ ······ Take the square root of each side of the equation.

$x = \pm 4$

Since 16 is perfect square, there are two integer answers. The solutions of the quadratic equation $4x^2 - 7 = 57$ are $x = -4$ and $x = 4$.

Practice & Problem Solving

Solve each equation by inspection.

28. $x^2 = 289$
29. $x^2 = -36$
30. $x^2 = 155$
31. $x^2 = 0.64$

Solve each equation.

32. $5x^2 = 320$
33. $x^2 - 42 = 358$
34. $4x^2 - 18 = 82$
35. **Higher Order Thinking** Solve $(x - 4)^2 - 81 = 0$. Explain the steps in your solution.
36. **Communicate Precisely** Use the equation $d = \sqrt{(12 - 5)^2 + (8 - 3)^2}$ to calculate the distance between the points (3, 5) and (8, 12). What is the distance?

LESSON 9-5 Completing the Square

Quick Review

The process of adding $\left(\frac{b}{2}\right)^2$ to $x^2 + bx$ to form a perfect-square trinomial is called **completing the square**. This is useful for changing $ax^2 + bx + c$ to the form $a(x - h)^2 + k$.

Example

Find the solutions of $x^2 - 16x + 12 = 0$.

First, write the equation in the form $ax^2 + bx = d$.

$x^2 - 16x = -12$

Complete the square.

$b = -16$, so $\left(\frac{-16}{2}\right)^2 = 64$

$x^2 - 16x + 64 = -12 + 64$

$x^2 - 16x + 64 = 52$

Write the trinomial as a binomial squared.

$(x - 8)^2 = 52$

Solve for x.

$x - 8 = \sqrt{52}$

$x = 8 \pm 2\sqrt{13}$

$x = 8 + 2\sqrt{13}$ and $x = 8 - 2\sqrt{13}$.

Practice & Problem Solving

Find the value of c that makes each expression a perfect-square trinomial. Then write the expression as a binomial squared.

37. $x^2 + 18x + c$
38. $x^2 - 6x + c$
39. $x^2 - 15x + c$
40. $x^2 + 24x + c$

Solve each equation by completing the square.

41. $x^2 + 18x = 24$
42. $x^2 - 10x = 46$
43. $x^2 + 22x = -39$
44. $3x^2 + 42x + 45 = 0$
45. **Construct Arguments** To solve the equation $x^2 - 9x - 15 = 0$, would you use graphing, factoring, or completing the square if you want exact solutions? Explain.

The Quadratic Formula and the Discriminant

Quick Review

The **quadratic formula**, $x = \frac{-b \pm \sqrt{b^2 - 4ac}}{2a}$, gives solutions of quadratic equations in the form $ax^2 + bx + c = 0$ for real values of a, b, and c where $a \neq 0$. The quadratic formula is a useful method to find the solutions of quadratic equations that are not factorable.

The **discriminant** is the expression $b^2 - 4ac$, which indicates the number of solutions of the equation. The solutions of a quadratic equation are also called its **roots**, which are the input values when the related function's output value is zero.

If $b^2 - 4ac > 0$, there are 2 real solutions.

If $b^2 - 4ac = 0$, there is 1 real solution.

If $b^2 - 4ac < 0$, there are no real solutions.

Example

Use the quadratic formula to find the solutions of $x^2 - 9 = 5x$.

Write the equation in standard form $ax^2 + bx + c = 0$ and identify a, b and c.

$x^2 - 5x - 9 = 0$

$a = 1,\ b = -5,\ c = -9$

$$x = \frac{-b \pm \sqrt{b^2 - 4ac}}{2a}$$

$$= \frac{-5 \pm \sqrt{(-5)^2 - 4(1)(-9)}}{2(1)}$$

$$= \frac{5 \pm \sqrt{61}}{2}$$

$$x = \frac{5 + \sqrt{61}}{2} \approx 6.41 \text{ and}$$

$$= \frac{5 - \sqrt{61}}{2} \approx -1.41$$

The approximate solutions of $x^2 - 9 = 5x$ are $x \approx 6.41$ and $x \approx -1.41$.

Practice & Problem Solving

Solve each equation using the quadratic formula.

46. $2x^2 + 3x - 5 = 0$

47. $-5x^2 + 4x + 12 = 0$

48. $3x^2 + 6x - 1 = 4$

49. $4x^2 + 12x + 6 = 0$

Use the discriminant to determine the number of real solutions for each equation.

50. $3x^2 - 8x + 2 = 0$

51. $-4x^2 - 6x - 1 = 0$

52. $7x^2 + 14x + 7 = 0$

53. $2x^2 + 5x + 3 = -5$

54. **Error Analysis** Describe and correct the error a student made in solving $3x^2 - 5x - 8 = 0$.

$a = 3,\ b = -5,\ c = 8$

$$x = \frac{-5 \pm \sqrt{(-5)^2 - 4(3)(8)}}{2(3)}$$

$$= \frac{-5 \pm \sqrt{-71}}{6}$$

There are no real solutions.

55. **Reason** The function $f(x) = -5x^2 + 20x + 55$ models the height of a ball x seconds after it is thrown into the air. What are the possible solutions to the related equation? Explain.

Solving Systems of Linear and Quadratic Equations

Quick Review

A **linear-quadratic system** of equations includes a linear equation and a quadratic equation. The graph of the system of equations is a line and a parabola.

$y = mx + b$

$y = ax^2 + bx + c$

You can solve a linear-quadratic system of equations by graphing, elimination, or substitution.

Example

What are the solutions of the system of equations?

$\mathbf{y = x^2 - 5x + 4}$

$\mathbf{y = x - 4}$

Graph the equations in the system on the same coordinate plane.

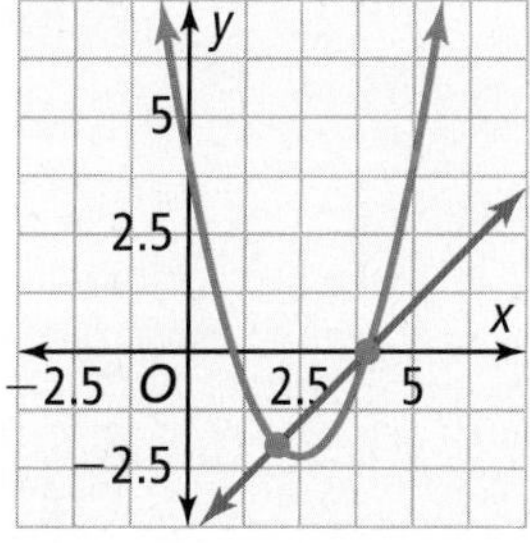

The solutions are where the parabola and the line intersect, which appear be at the points (2, −2) and (4, 0).

Check that the ordered pairs are solutions of the equations $y = x^2 - 5x + 4$ and $y = x - 4$.

$-2 = (2)^2 - 5(2) + 4$ $\qquad$ $0 = 4 - 4$

$-2 = 4 - 10 + 4$ $\qquad$ $0 = 0$

$-2 = -2$ $\qquad$ and

and $\qquad$ $-2 = 2 - 4$

$0 = (4)^2 - 5(4) + 4$ $\qquad$ $-2 = -2$

$0 = 16 - 20 + 4$

$0 = 0$

The solutions of the system are (2, −2) and (4, 0).

Practice & Problem Solving

Rewrite each equation as a system of equations, and then use a graph to solve.

56. $4x^2 = 2x - 5$

57. $2x^2 + 3x = 2x + 1$

58. $x^2 - 6x = 2x - 16$

59. $0.5x^2 + 4x = -12 - 1.5x$

Find the solution(s) of each system of equations.

60. $y = x^2 + 6x + 9$
$y = 3x$

61. $y = x^2 + 8x + 30$
$y = 5 - 2x$

62. $y = 3x^2 + 2x + 1$
$y = 2x + 1$

63. $y = 2x^2 + 5x - 30$
$y = 2x + 5$

64. **Make Sense and Persevere** Write an equation for a line that does not intersect the graph of the equation $y = x^2 + 6x + 9$.

65. **Reason** A theater company uses the revenue function $R(x) = -50x^2 + 250x$, where x is the ticket price in dollars. The cost function of the production is $C(x) = 450 - 50x$. What ticket price is needed for the theater to break even?

TOPIC

10

Working With Functions

? TOPIC ESSENTIAL QUESTION

What are some operations on functions that you can use to create models and solve problems?

Topic Overview

Topic Vocabulary

- cube root function
- inverse of a function
- square root function

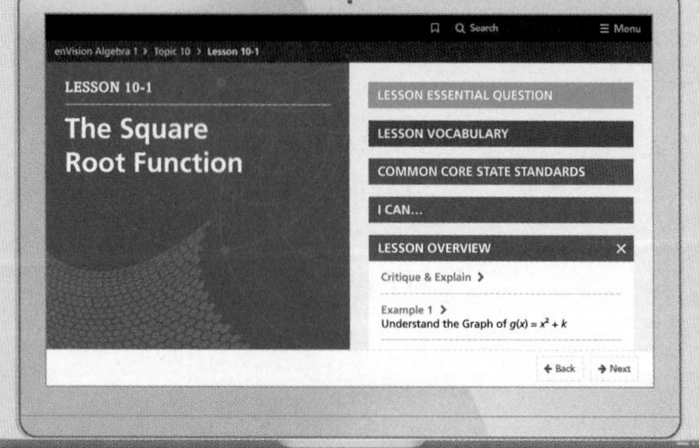

Digital Experience

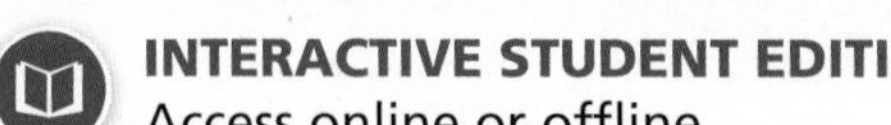

INTERACTIVE STUDENT EDITION Access online or offline.

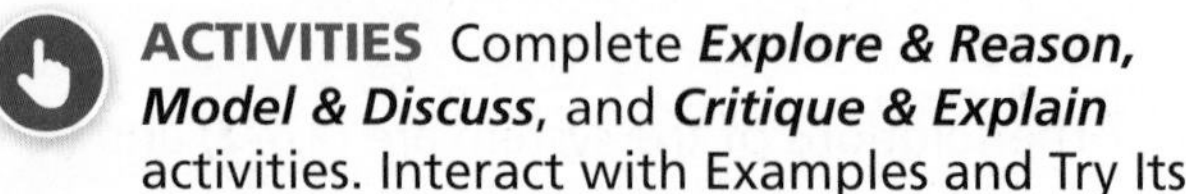

ACTIVITIES Complete ***Explore & Reason, Model & Discuss***, and ***Critique & Explain*** activities. Interact with Examples and Try Its.

ANIMATION View and interact with real-world applications.

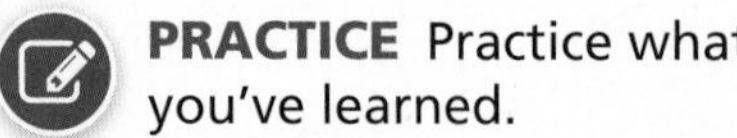

PRACTICE Practice what you've learned.

Go online | **PearsonRealize.com**

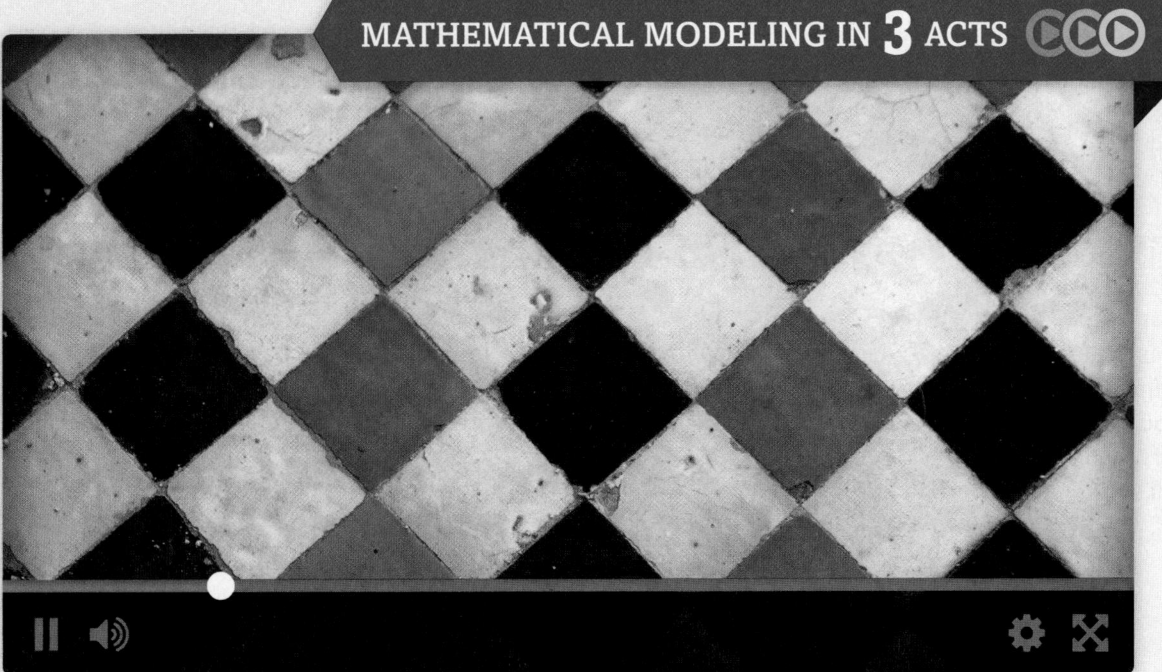

Edgy Tiles

For more than 3,000 years, people have glazed ceramics and other materials to make decorative tile patterns. Tiles used to be used only in important buildings or by the very rich, but now you can find tiles in almost any house.

Before you start tiling a wall, floor, or other surface, it's important to plan out how your design will look. Think about this during the Mathematical Modeling in 3 Acts lesson.

VIDEOS Watch clips to support ***Mathematical Modeling in 3 Acts Lessons*** and **enVision™ *STEM Projects*.**

CONCEPT SUMMARY Review key lesson content through multiple representations.

ASSESSMENT Show what you've learned.

GLOSSARY Read and listen to English and Spanish definitions.

TUTORIALS Get help from ***Virtual Nerd***, right when you need it.

MATH TOOLS Explore math with digital tools and manipulatives.

Did You Know?

Standing up, the average **person** takes up **2 square feet** of space.

Population density (number of people per square mile) of Manhattan: **70,517**

Land Area

Earth: 196.9 million mi^2

United States: 3.535 million mi^2

Population

Earth: 7.648 billion people

United States: 325 million people

San Francisco

Chicago

New York

The cities of San Francisco, Chicago, and New York all have **population density greater than 10,000.**

For the Chicago Cubs World Series parade and rally on November 4, 2016, an estimated **5 million people** lined the streets of Chicago, Illinois.

Your Task: Program a Square Root Algorithm

Sports arenas and open spaces are designed to hold great numbers of people. You and your classmates will design a square building to hold a given number of people.

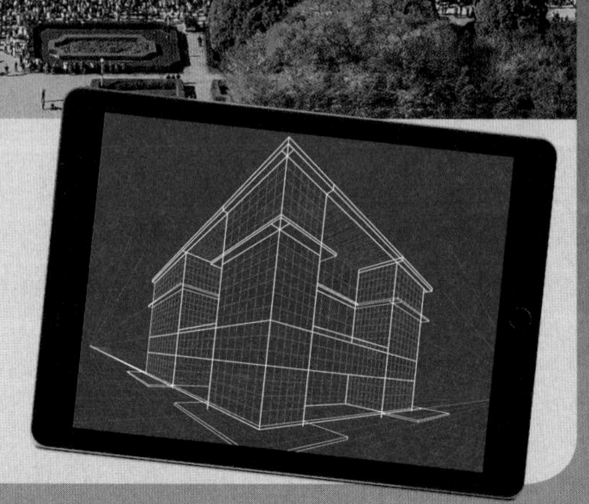

10-1 The Square Root Function

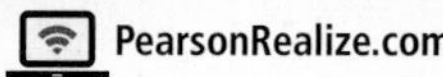
PearsonRealize.com

I CAN… describe the key features of the square root function.

VOCABULARY

- square root function

EXPLORE & REASON

One of the strangest mysteries archaeology was discovered in Diquís Delta of Costa Rica. Hu of sphere-shaped stones wer found.

A. The formula for the sur of a sphere is $SA = 4\pi r$ is the surface area of in terms of the circur the great circle?

B. The circumferences circles of spheres r from about 6 cm to 6 m. Ma graph that represents circumference as a

C. Look for Relationships What similarities and differences about the graph from Part B and the graph of a quadratic function?

ESSENTIAL QUESTION

What key features are shared among the square root function and translations of the square function.

CONCEPTUAL UNDERSTANDING

EXAMPLE 1 Key Features of the Square Root Function

What are the key features of $f(x) = \sqrt{x}$?

The function $f(x) = \sqrt{x}$ is the **square root function**.

Make a table and graph the function.

x	$f(x) = \sqrt{x}$
0	0
1	1
4	2
9	3
16	4

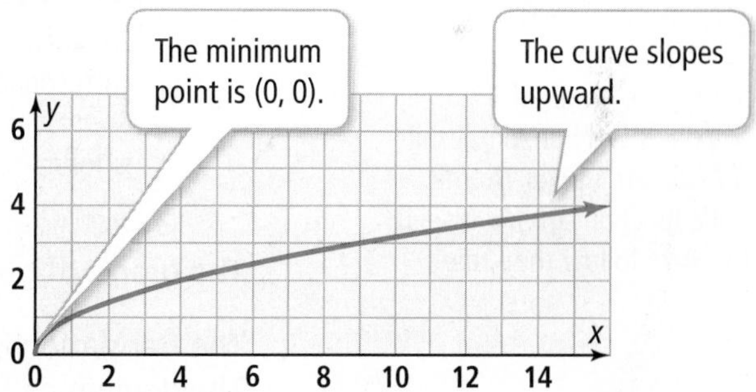

COMMON ERROR
Recall that $\sqrt{x}$ is equal to the *positive* square root of x.

The domain is restricted to $x \geq 0$, because only nonnegative numbers have a real square root. Since the square root of a number cannot be negative, the range is $f(x) \geq 0$.

For $f(x) = \sqrt{x}$, the x- and y-intercepts of the graph of the function are both 0. The graph is increasing for all values in the domain of f.

Try It! 1. Graph each function. What are the intercepts, domain, and range of the function?

a. $p(x) = -\sqrt{x}$

b. $q(x) = \sqrt{\frac{x}{10}}$

EXAMPLE 2 Translations of the Square Root Function

A. How does the graph of $g(x) = \sqrt{x} + 3$ compare to the graph of $f(x) = \sqrt{x}$?

Graph each function.

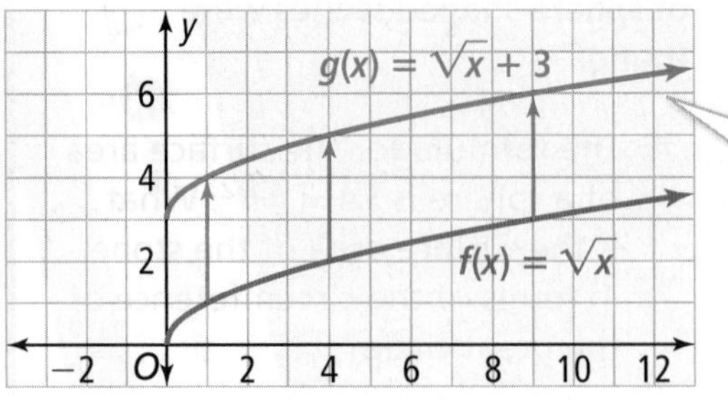

For each x-value, the corresponding y-value is 3 units greater for g than it is for f.

The graph of $g(x) = \sqrt{x} + 3$ is a vertical translation of $f(x) = \sqrt{x}$.

The translation is a result of adding a constant to the output of a function. The domain for both functions is $x \geq 0$. The range for function f is $y \geq 0$, so the range for function g is $y \geq 3$.

B. How does the graph of $g(x) = \sqrt{x + 3}$ compare to the graph of $f(x) = \sqrt{x}$?

Graph each function.

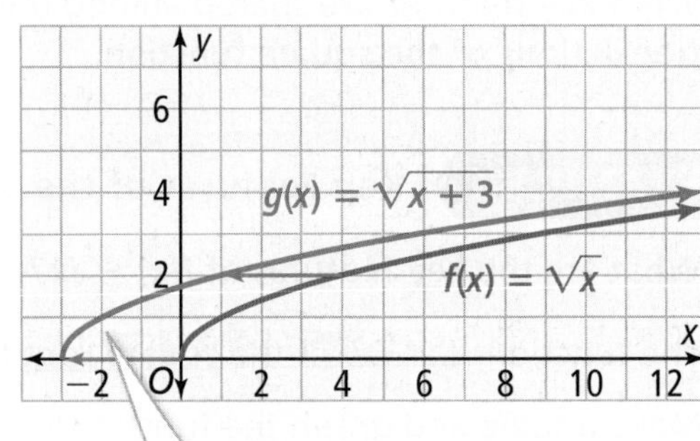

For each y-value, the corresponding x-value is 3 units less for g than it is for f.

USE STRUCTURE
Notice that the graph of $g(x) = \sqrt{x + 3}$ is a horizontal shift of $f(x) = \sqrt{x}$ left 3 units. Do the quadratic functions $g(x) = (x + 3)^2$ and $f(x) = x^2$ follow the same pattern?

The graph of $g(x) = \sqrt{x + 3}$ is a horizontal translation of $f(x) = \sqrt{x}$.

The translation is the result of adding a constant to the input of a function. The domain of f is $x \geq 0$, and the domain of g is $x \geq -3$. The range for both functions is $y \geq 0$.

Try It! 2. How does each graph compare to the graph of $f(x) = \sqrt{x}$?

a. $g(x) = \sqrt{x} - 4$

b. $p(x) = \sqrt{x - 10}$

EXAMPLE 3 Rate of Change of the Square Root Function

For the function $f(x) = \sqrt{x}$, how does the average rate of change from $x = 0$ to $x = 0.3$ compare to the average rate of change from $x = 0.3$ to $x = 0.6$?

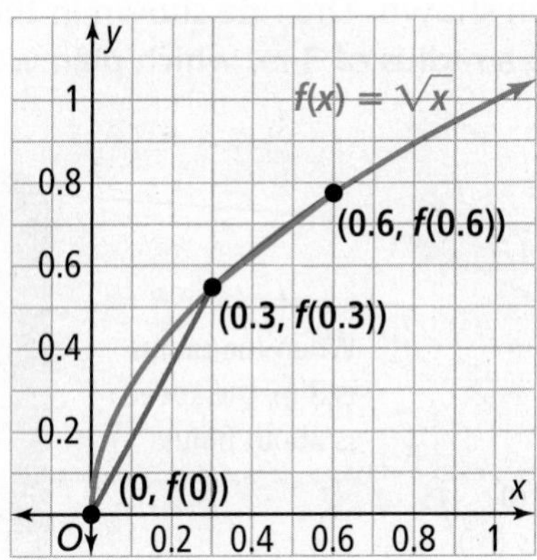

Step 1 Evaluate the function for the x–values that correspond to the endpoints of each interval.

$$f(0) = \sqrt{0}$$
$$= 0$$
$$f(0.3) = \sqrt{0.3}$$
$$\approx 0.548$$
$$f(0.6) = \sqrt{0.6}$$
$$\approx 0.775$$

Step 2 Find the average rate of change over each interval.

From $x = 0$ to $x = 0.3$:

$$\frac{f(0.3) - f(0)}{0.3 - 0} \approx \frac{0.548 - 0}{0.3 - 0}$$
$$= \frac{0.548}{0.3}$$
$$\approx 1.83$$

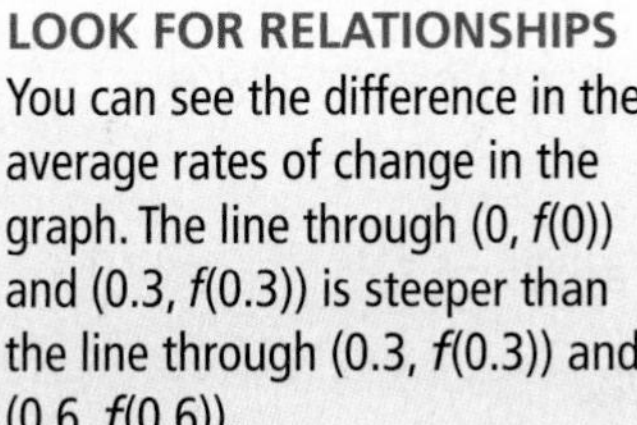

LOOK FOR RELATIONSHIPS
You can see the difference in the average rates of change in the graph. The line through (0, $f(0)$) and (0.3, $f(0.3)$) is steeper than the line through (0.3, $f(0.3)$) and (0.6, $f(0.6)$).

From $x = 0.3$ to $x = 0.6$:

$$\frac{f(0.6) - f(0.3)}{0.6 - 0.3} \approx \frac{0.775 - 0.548}{0.6 - 0.3}$$
$$= \frac{0.227}{0.3}$$
$$\approx 0.757$$

The average rate of change over the interval $0 \le x \le 0.3$ is greater than the average rate of change over the interval $0.3 \le x \le 0.6$.

Try It! 3. For the function $h(x) = \sqrt{2x}$, find $h(8)$, $h(10)$, and $h(12)$. Then find the average rate of change of the function over each interval.

a. $8 \le x \le 10$

b. $10 \le x \le 12$

APPLICATION

EXAMPLE 4 Compare Functions

Two plans are being considered to determine the speed of a theme park ride with a circular wall that spins. Plan A is represented by the function with the graph shown. The ride shown in the photo is an example of Plan B. If the ride has a radius of 3 m, which plan would result in a greater speed for the ride?

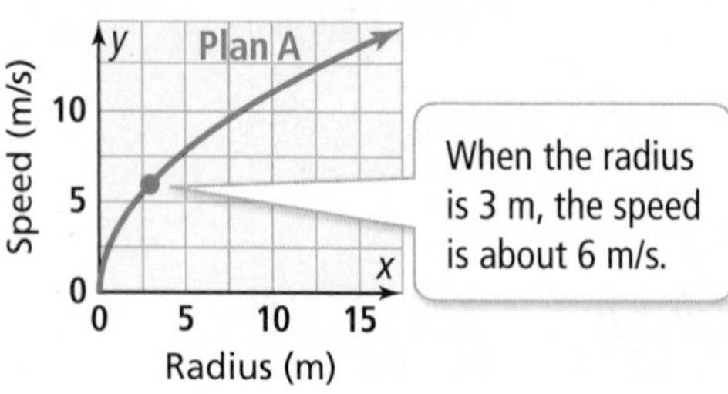

Plan B is represented by the function $f(r) = 5\sqrt{r}$, where r is the radius of the ride, and $f(r)$ is the speed.

USE APPROPRIATE TOOLS
How could you determine the radius in meters for both plans given a corresponding speed of 7.5 m/s?

Compare the plans.

Plan A

The graph of Plan A shows that the corresponding speed at a radius of 3 meters is about 6 m/s.

OR

Plan B

Evaluate $f(r) = 5\sqrt{r}$ for $r = 3$.

$$f(3) = 5\sqrt{(3)}$$
$$\approx 8.7$$

The ride using Plan B has a speed of about 8.7 m/s when the radius is 3 m.

With a radius of 3 m, the speed of the ride using Plan A is 6 m/s, and the speed of the ride using Plan B is about 8.7 m/s.

So, the ride using Plan B has a greater speed for a radius of 3 m.

Try It! **4.** To the nearest thousandth, evaluate each function for the given value of the variable.

a. $v(x) = \frac{\sqrt{x}}{10}$; $x = 17$

b. $w(x) = \sqrt{\frac{x}{10}}$; $x = 17$

CONCEPT SUMMARY Translations of the Square Root Function

ALGEBRA $g(x) = \sqrt{x-h} + k$

- domain: $x \geq h$
- range: $y \geq k$
- minimum point: (h, k)

NUMBERS $g(x) = \sqrt{x-2} + 4$

- domain: $x \geq 2$
- range: $y \geq 4$
- minimum point: (2, 4)

GRAPH

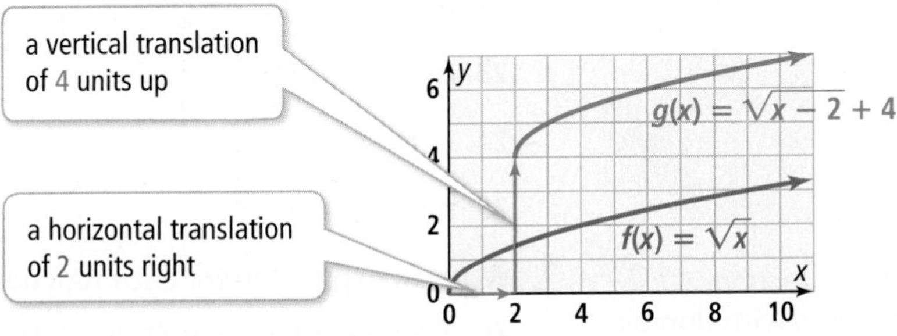

Do You UNDERSTAND?

1. **ESSENTIAL QUESTION** What key features are shared among the square root function and translations of the square function.

2. **Use Structure** Explain why each function is, or is not, a translation of the square root function $f(x) = \sqrt{x}$.

   a. $h(x) = 2\sqrt{x+1}$

   b. $g(x) = \sqrt{x+2} - 3$

3. **Error Analysis** A student identified (6, 12) and (9, 27) as points on the graph of the function $f(x) = \sqrt{3x}$. What error did the student make?

4. **Reason** What is the domain of $f(x) = \sqrt{x+3}$?

Do You KNOW HOW?

How does the graph of each function compare to the graph of $f(x) = \sqrt{x}$?

5. $g(x) = \sqrt{x} - 2$

6. $h(x) = \sqrt{x-5}$

7. $p(x) = 5 + \sqrt{x}$

8. $q(x) = \sqrt{7+x}$

For the given function, find the average rate of change to the nearest hundredth over the given interval.

9. $f(x) = \sqrt{x+7}$; $2 \leq x \leq 10$

10. $g(x) = \sqrt{x+7}$; $-3 \leq x \leq 5$

11. $h(x) = \sqrt{2x}$; $0 \leq x \leq 10$

UNDERSTAND

12. Use Appropriate Tools Use a graphing calculator to graph $f(x) = -\sqrt{x+7}$. Describe the domain and range of the function.

13. Error Analysis Describe and correct the error a student made when comparing the graph of $g(x) = \sqrt{x+3}$ to the graph of $f(x) = \sqrt{x}$.

1. The expression under the radical in $g(x)$ is $x + 3$.
2. $x + 3$ is to the right of x, so the graph of g is a translation of the graph of f by 3 units to the right.

14. Higher Order Thinking Write a function involving a square root expression with domain $x \geq \frac{7}{2}$ and range $y \leq 2$.

15. Mathematical Connections Consider the two functions $f(x) = \sqrt{x}$ and $g(x) = -\sqrt{x}$.

a. What is the average rate of change for each function from $x = 4$ to $x = 9$?

b. How are the two values in part (a) related to each other?

c. Suppose the average rate of change for $f(x)$ between two values of x is 0.32. What is the rate of change for $g(x)$ between the same two values of x?

16. Use Structure For a function of the form $f(x) = a\sqrt{x-h} + k$, why are some real numbers excluded from the domain and the range?

17. Communicate Precisely Explain the steps of each calculation.

a. Find $f(10)$ if $f(x) = \frac{\sqrt{2x}}{7}$.

b. Find $f(10)$ if $f(x) = \sqrt{\frac{2x}{7}}$.

PRACTICE

Find the *x*- and *y*-intercepts of each function. If there is no intercept, write *Does not exist.*
SEE EXAMPLE 1

18. $f(x) = \sqrt{x} - 2$

19. $g(x) = \sqrt{x-9}$

20. $h(x) = \sqrt{x+9}$

21. $k(x) = \sqrt{x+4} - 9$

How does each graph compare to the graph of $f(x) = \sqrt{x}$? SEE EXAMPLE 2

22. $q(x) = \sqrt{x} + 11$

23. $r(x) = \sqrt{x+11}$

24. $s(x) = \sqrt{x-2} + 5$

25. $t(x) = \sqrt{x+3} - 6$

Write an expression for each function. SEE EXAMPLE 2

26. a translation by 6 units up of $f(x) = \sqrt{x}$.

27. a translation by $\frac{1}{2}$ unit to the right of $f(x) = \sqrt{x}$.

28. a translation by 2 units down and 1 unit to the left of $f(x) = \sqrt{x}$.

Find the value of the given function at each end of the range of values of the variable. Then calculate the average rate of change of the function between the two values of the variable.
SEE EXAMPLES 3 AND 4

29. $p(x) = \sqrt{15x}$; $0.01 \leq x \leq 1.01$

30. $q(x) = \sqrt{x+11}$; $-3 \leq x \leq 0$

31. $r(x) = \sqrt{2x-7}$; $5 \leq x \leq 10$

32. $t(x) = \sqrt{\frac{x-4}{2}}$; $4 \leq x \leq 8$

Describe the domain and range for each function. SEE EXAMPLE 1

33. Function p from Exercise 29

34. Function q from Exercise 30

35. Function r from Exercise 31

36. function t from Exercise 32

PRACTICE & PROBLEM SOLVING

APPLY

37. Model With Mathematics A teacher adjusts the grades of an exam using a curve. If a student's raw score on a test is x, the score based on the curve is given by the function $c(x) = 10\sqrt{x}$.

Five students received raw scores of 49, 42, 55, and 72. What are their scores according to the curve?

38. Make Sense and Persevere A group of campers leave Camp 2 and hike x miles along the path to Camp 3. The distance d between the group of campers and Camp 1 is given by $d(x) = \sqrt{x^2 + 1}$.

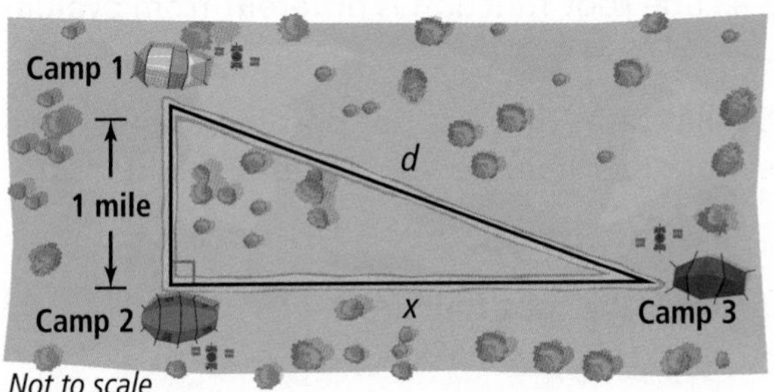

Not to scale

a. Use the function to find the distance d of the campers when $x = 1, 10, 15, 18.5, 25$, and 50.

b. When the campers have hiked 5 miles from Camp 2, their distance from Camp 1 is $\sqrt{5^2 + 1} = \sqrt{26} \approx 5.1$ miles. How much farther do they need to hike until they double their distance from Camp 1? Show your work.

39. Communicate Precisely The distance to the horizon is a function of height above sea level. If the height h above sea level is measured in feet and the distance d to the horizon is measured in miles, then $d(h) \approx 1.22\sqrt{h}$.

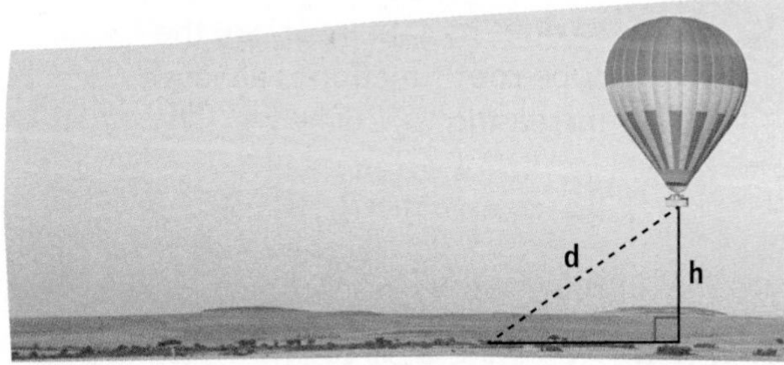

On a hot-air balloon ride, a passenger looks out from 54 ft above sea level. What is the distance from the passenger to the horizon?

ASSESSMENT PRACTICE

40. Which of the following functions are vertical translations of $f(x) = \sqrt{x}$? Select all that apply.

Ⓐ $g(x) = \sqrt{x} - 4$

Ⓑ $h(x) = 3 + \sqrt{x}$

Ⓒ $k(x) = \sqrt{-5 + x}$

Ⓓ $m(x) = \sqrt{5x}$

Ⓔ $n(x) = -7 + \sqrt{x}$

41. SAT/ACT For the square root function $p(x) = \sqrt{x}$, the average rate of change between $x = 13$ and $x = a$ is 0.155. What is the value of a?

Ⓐ −4

Ⓑ 0

Ⓒ 5

Ⓓ 8

Ⓔ 11

42. Performance Task The relationship between the surface area A and the diameter D of each glass sphere can be described using the equation shown.

PART A Find the average rate of change in the diameter for surface areas between 20 in.^{2} and 10 in.^{2}.

PART B Find the average rate of change in the diameter when the surface area decreases from 16 in.^{2} to 14 in.^{2}.

PART C Find the average rate of change in D when A increases from 14.9 to 15.1 in.^{2}, and find the average rate of change in D when A increases from 14.99 to 15.01 in.^{2}.

PART D Describe a pattern in parts A, B, and C.

Activity Assess

10-2 The Cube Root Function

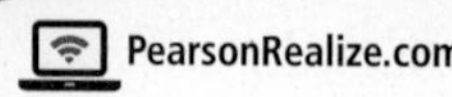
PearsonRealize.com

I CAN… identify the key features of the cube root function.

VOCABULARY

- cube root function

CRITIQUE & EXPLAIN

Emilia wrote several radical expressions on the whiteboard.

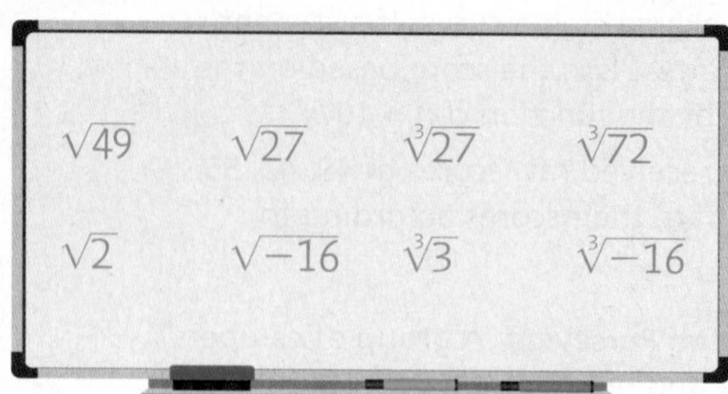

A. Evaluate each expression, and explain how to plot each value on a real number line.

B. Explain how evaluating a cube root function is different from evaluating a square root function.

C. **Construct Arguments** Emilia states that it is not possible to plot either $\sqrt{-16}$ or $\sqrt[3]{-16}$ on the real number line. Do you agree? Explain.

ESSENTIAL QUESTION

What are the key features of the cube root function?

CONCEPTUAL UNDERSTANDING

EXAMPLE 1 Key Features of the Cube Root Function

A. What are the key features of $f(x) = \sqrt[3]{x}$?

The function $f(x) = \sqrt[3]{x}$ is the **cube root function**.

Make a table of values.

x	−8	−1	0	1	8
$f(x)$	−2	−1	0	1	2

$(-2)^3 = -8$, so $\sqrt[3]{-8} = -2$.

Since $x^3 = 0$ only when $x = 0$, the origin is the only point where the graph of $f(x) = \sqrt[3]{x}$ intercepts both the x- and y-axes.

LOOK FOR STRUCTURE
How does the cube root affect the domain and range of the function?

Now graph the function.

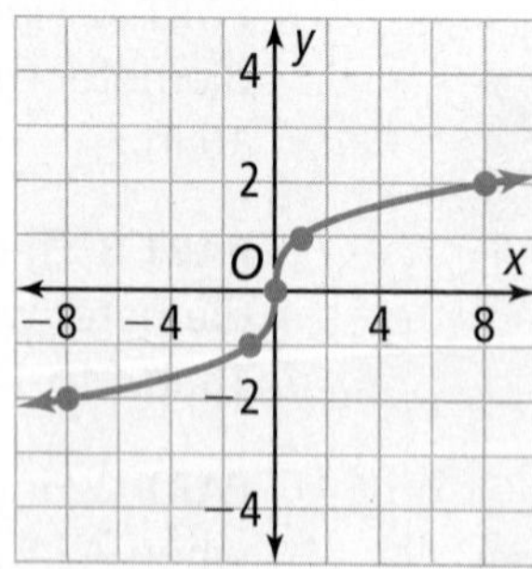

As the value of x increases, so does its cube root. So, the cube root function is always increasing.

There are no restrictions on the x- or y-values, so the domain and range are all real numbers.

CONTINUED ON THE NEXT PAGE

EXAMPLE 1 CONTINUED

B. What are the maximum and minimum values for $f(x) = \sqrt[3]{x}$ over the interval $-8 \leq x \leq 8$?

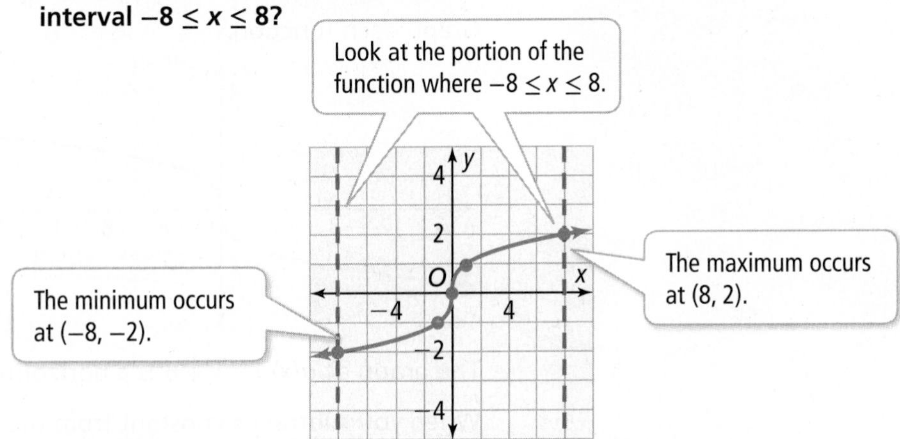

GENERALIZE
Will this strategy—using the end points of the domain to find the maximum and minimum values of a cube root function—work for all functions?

The maximum value for $f(x) = \sqrt[3]{x}$ when $-8 \leq x \leq 8$ is 2, and the minimum value is −2.

Since the function is always increasing, the maximum and minimum values of the function occur at the endpoints of the given interval.

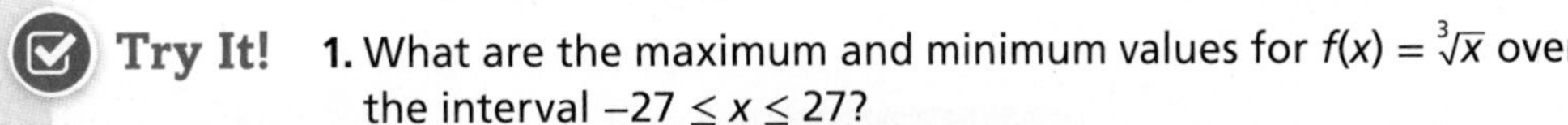

Try It! 1. What are the maximum and minimum values for $f(x) = \sqrt[3]{x}$ over the interval $-27 \leq x \leq 27$?

EXAMPLE 2 Translations of the Cube Root Function

A. How does the graph of $g(x) = \sqrt[3]{x} + 4$ compare to the graph of $f(x) = \sqrt[3]{x}$?

Graph each function.

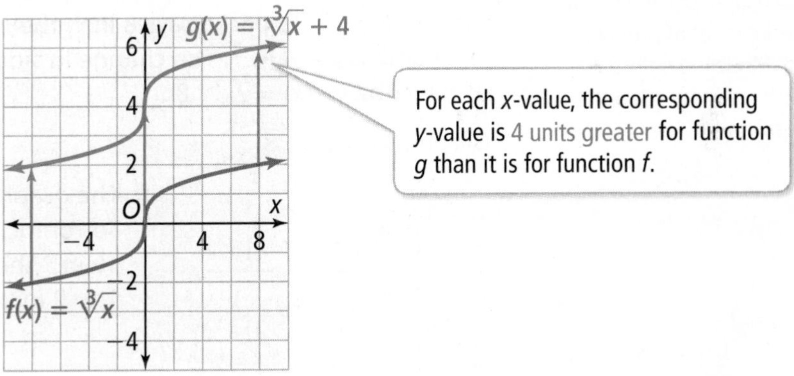

The graph of $g(x) = \sqrt[3]{x} + 4$ is a vertical translation of the graph of $f(x) = \sqrt[3]{x}$.

As with other functions you have studied, when you add a constant to the output of the cube root function $f(x) = \sqrt[3]{x}$, the graph of the resulting function, $g(x) = \sqrt[3]{x} + k$, is a vertical translation of the graph of f. The domain and the range for both functions are all real numbers.

CONTINUED ON THE NEXT PAGE

EXAMPLE 2 CONTINUED

B. How does the graph of $g(x) = \sqrt[3]{x+6}$ compare to the graph of $f(x) = \sqrt[3]{x}$?

Graph each function.

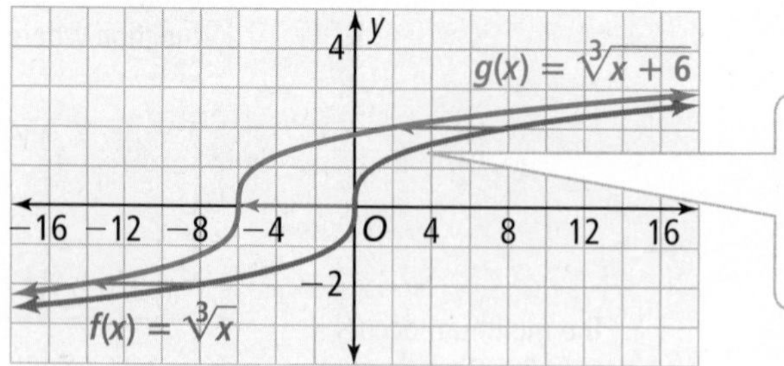

For each y-value, the corresponding x-value is 6 units less for function g than it is for function f.

The graph of $g(x) = \sqrt[3]{x+6}$ is a horizontal translation of $f(x) = \sqrt[3]{x}$.

When you subtract a constant from the input of the cube root function $f(x) = \sqrt[3]{x}$, the graph of the resulting function, $g(x) = \sqrt[3]{x-h}$, is a horizontal translation of the graph of f. The domain and the range for both functions are all real numbers.

Try It! 2. Compare the graph of each function to the graph of $f(x) = \sqrt[3]{x}$.

a. $g(x) = \sqrt[3]{x} - 2$

b. $p(x) = \sqrt[3]{x+1}$

APPLICATION

EXAMPLE 3 Model a Problem Using the Cube Root Function

Creative Clays is increasing the package size for its art clay. Designers are considering different sizes. Assume that the new package will be a cube with volume x in.^{3}. For what increases in volume would the side length increase between 1 in. and 2 in.?

Each orginal clay cube contains 8 in.^{3} of clay.

MODEL WITH MATHEMATICS
Mathematics has many industrial and commercial applications, such as the development of product packaging. Modeling before production begins can prevent expensive mistakes.

Since the volume of the new package is x in.^{3} and the volume of old package is 8 in.^{3}, the increase in volume is $x - 8$ in.^{3}. The change in side length of the cube is $f(x) = \sqrt[3]{x-8}$.

Graph $f(x) = \sqrt[3]{x-8}$.

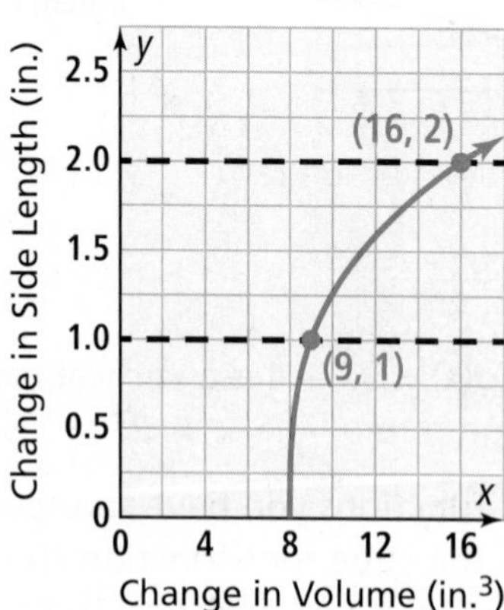

The graph shows that $f(9) = 1$ and $f(16) = 2$. So for increases in volume between 9 and 16 in.^{3} the side length would increase by 1 to 2 in.

Try It! 3. A cube has a volume of 10 cm^3. A larger cube has a volume of x cm^3. Consider the function $f(x) = \sqrt[3]{x-10}$. What do the values $f(14)$ and $f(19)$ represent?

EXAMPLE 4 Compare Rates of Change of a Function

For the function $f(x) = \sqrt[3]{x-1}$, how does the average rate of change from $x = 1$ to $x = 5$ compare to the average rate of change from $x = 5$ to $x = 9$?

Step 1 Evaluate the function for the *x*-values that correspond to the endpoints of each interval.

Interval: $1 \leq x \leq 5$

$f(1) = \sqrt[3]{1-1} = 0$ $\quad f(5) = \sqrt[3]{5-1} \approx 1.59$

Interval: $5 \leq x \leq 9$

$f(5) = \sqrt[3]{5-1} \approx 1.59$ $\quad f(9) = \sqrt[3]{9-1} = 2$

Step 2 Find the average rate of change over each interval.

$$\frac{f(5) - f(1)}{5-1} \approx \frac{1.59 - 0}{5-1} \approx 0.40$$

$$\frac{f(9) - f(5)}{9-5} \approx \frac{2 - 1.59}{9-5} \approx 0.10$$

The average rate of change of the function $f(x) = \sqrt[3]{x-1}$ appears to decrease when $x \geq 1$ and as the *x*-values corresponding to the endpoints of the interval increase. This is consistent with the curve becoming less steep when $x \geq 1$ and *x* increases.

Try It! 4. Compare the average rates of change for $f(x) = 2\sqrt[3]{x-3}$ over the intervals $-12 \leq x \leq -8$ and $-4 \leq x \leq 0$.

EXAMPLE 5 Compare Rates of Change of Two Functions

The graph and table represent translations of the cube root function $f(x) = \sqrt[3]{x}$. Values in the table are rounded to the nearest hundredth. Which function has a greater average rate of change over the interval $2 \leq x \leq 4$?

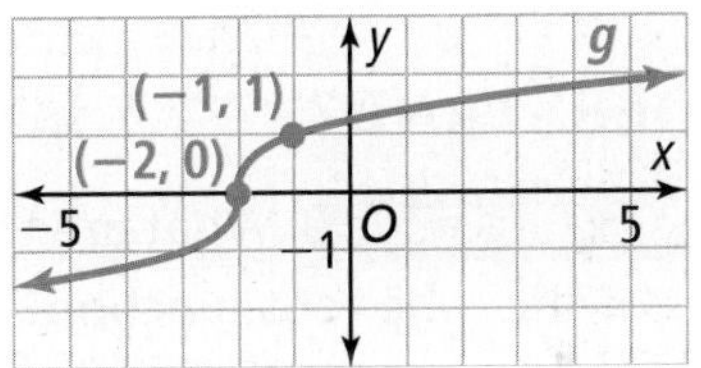

x	h(x)
0	1.22
1	2.22
2	2.48
3	2.66
4	2.81

COMMON ERROR
You may be tempted to express calculated values to a higher precision. This is misleading with estimated data. For reasonable comparisons, express both values in the same level of precision.

The function *g* is *f* translated to the left 2 units, so $g(x) = \sqrt[3]{x+2}$. Use this function to find the average rate of change in the interval $2 \leq x \leq 4$.

$$\frac{g(4) - g(2)}{4-2} \approx \frac{1.82 - 1.59}{4-2} = 0.115$$

To find the average rate of change for $h(x)$, use the values in the table directly.

$$\frac{h(4) - h(2)}{4-2} \approx \frac{2.81 - 2.48}{4-2} = 0.165$$

The average rate of change of $h(x)$ is greater than the average rate of change of $g(x)$ on the interval $2 \leq x \leq 4$.

CONTINUED ON THE NEXT PAGE

Try It! **5.** Which function has the greater average rate of change over the interval $-5 \leq x \leq 0$: the translation of $f(x) = \sqrt[3]{x}$ to the right 1 unit and up 2 units, or the function $r(x) = \sqrt[3]{x} + 3$?

CONCEPT SUMMARY The Cube Root Function $f(x) = \sqrt[3]{x}$.

GRAPH

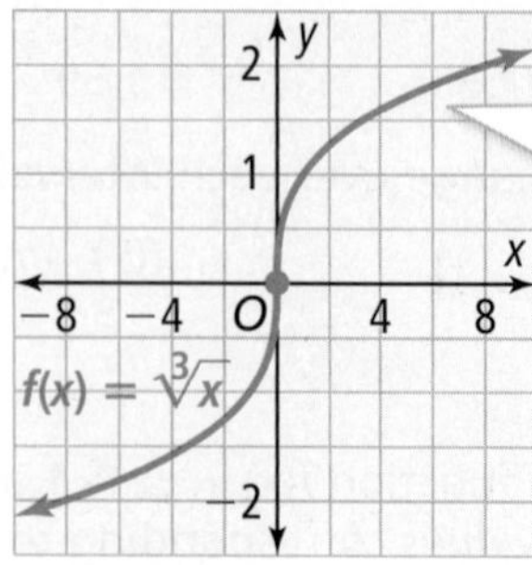

KEY FEATURES

- ***x*-intercept** 0
- ***y*-intercept** 0
- **domain** all real numbers
- **range** all real numbers

Do You UNDERSTAND?

1. ESSENTIAL QUESTION What are the key features of the cube root function?

2. Error Analysis Timothy uses his calculator to investigate the domain and range of $f(x) = \sqrt[3]{x}$. He estimates the range as $-2 \leq y \leq 2$. What is the error that Timothy made?

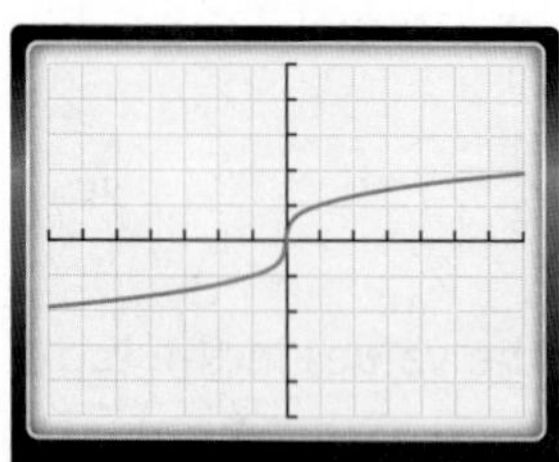

3. Look for Relationships Explain how the graph of $f(x) = \sqrt[3]{x}$ is related to the graph of $g(x) = -\sqrt[3]{x}$.

Do You KNOW HOW?

4. Identify the domain and range of $s(x) = \sqrt[3]{3x}$.

5. Describe how the graph of $g(x) = \sqrt[3]{x} - 3$ is related to the graph of $f(x) = \sqrt[3]{x}$.

6. Find the maximum and minimum values of $f(x) = \sqrt[3]{x - 1}$ for $-2 \leq x \leq 9$.

7. Calculate the average rate of change of $g(x) = \sqrt[3]{x} + 3$ for $4 \leq x \leq 7$.

8. Describe how the graph of $g(x) = \sqrt[3]{x - 4}$ is related to the graph of $f(x) = \sqrt{x}$.

PRACTICE & PROBLEM SOLVING

Scan for Multimedia

Practice Tutorial

Additional Exercises Available Online

UNDERSTAND

9. **Reason** Explain why the x- and y-intercepts of $f(x) = \sqrt[3]{x}$ are the same.

10. **Look for Relationships** Compare the average rates of change for $f(x) = \sqrt[3]{x}$ and $f(x) = \sqrt[3]{x} + 5$ for $0 \leq x \leq 4$.

11. **Error Analysis** Hugo calculated that the average rate of change of $f(x) = \sqrt[3]{3x}$ for $0 \leq x \leq 5$ is 1.026. Explain the error that Hugo made.

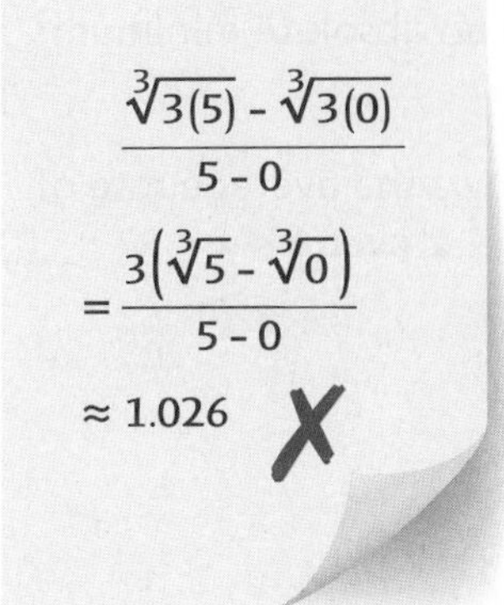

$$\frac{\sqrt[3]{3(5)} - \sqrt[3]{3(0)}}{5-0}$$
$$= \frac{3(\sqrt[3]{5} - \sqrt[3]{0})}{5-0}$$
$$\approx 1.026$$

12. **Use Appropriate Tools** Find the average rate of change of $f(x) = \sqrt[3]{x}$ for $0 \leq x \leq 4$. Use the symmetry of the function to predict its average rate of change for $-4 \leq x \leq 0$.

13. **Reason** Which gives a better approximation of the rate of change of $f(x) = \sqrt[3]{x}$ near $x = 1$: the average rate of change for $-1 \leq x \leq 3$ or for $\frac{1}{2} \leq x \leq \frac{3}{2}$? Explain your reasoning.

14. **Higher Order Thinking** Consider the function $f(x) = x^3$. How can you find two different intervals that have the same average rate of change? Explain how you can generalize your statement.

15. **Use Structure** For each condition, describe a translation or pair of translations of $f(x) = \sqrt[3]{x}$ that results in the graph of function g.

    a. The y-intercept of the graph of g is -2.

    b. The graph of g passes through the point $(3, 5)$.

    c. The x-intercept of the graph of g is -1.

PRACTICE

For each function, identify domain, range, and intercepts. SEE EXAMPLE 1

16. $f(x) = \sqrt[3]{x - 3}$
17. $f(x) = \sqrt[3]{2x}$
18. $f(x) = \sqrt[3]{x} - 1$
19. $f(x) = \sqrt[3]{x + 2}$

Describe translations that transform the graph of $f(x) = \sqrt[3]{x}$ into the graph of the given function. SEE EXAMPLE 2

20. $g(x) = \sqrt[3]{x - 3}$
21. $p(x) = \sqrt[3]{x} + 2$
22. $p(x) = \sqrt[3]{x} - 10$
23. $q(x) = \sqrt[3]{x + 7}$
24. $j(x) = \sqrt[3]{x + 4} - 8$
25. $k(x) = \sqrt[3]{\frac{1}{2} + x} - \frac{3}{4}$

Graph each function. Use the graph to estimate the values of x that satisfy each condition. SEE EXAMPLE 3

26. $f(x) = \sqrt[3]{x}$; $1 \leq f(x) \leq 2$

27. $g(x) = \sqrt[3]{x - 2}$; $1 \leq g(x) \leq 2$

28. $p(x) = \sqrt[3]{x - 1} + 3$; $2 \leq p(x) \leq 5$

Calculate the average rate of change for each function over the given interval. SEE EXAMPLE 4

29. $f(x) = \sqrt[3]{x}$ for $3 \leq x \leq 10$

30. $g(x) = \sqrt[3]{x} + 2$ for $-4 \leq x \leq 0$

31. $p(x) = \sqrt[3]{4x + 5}$ for $-1 \leq x \leq 1$

Let $f(x) = \sqrt[3]{x}$. The function g is shown in the graph. For each function, use <, >, or = to complete each of the statements. SEE EXAMPLE 5

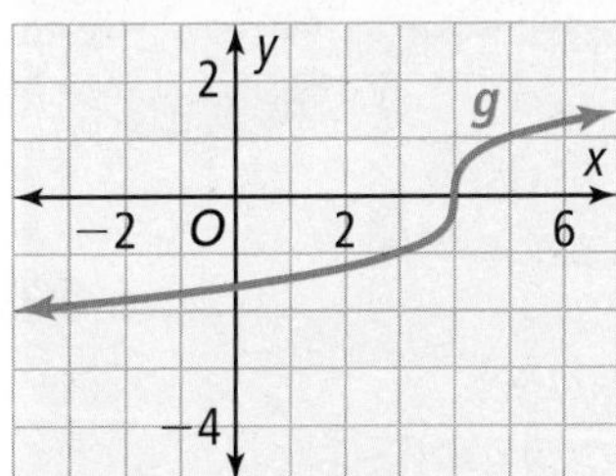

32. $f(3)$ ____ $g(3)$

33. x-intercept of f ______ x-intercept of g

34. y-intercept of f ______ y-intercept of g

PRACTICE & PROBLEM SOLVING

APPLY

35. **Model With Mathematics** Tamika's Auto Sales opened recently. Weekly sales are shown in the table.

Week	1	2	3	4	5	6
Cars Sold	9	13	14	15	17	18

Plot the sales on a graph and write a cube root function that approximately models the sales. Explain what the features of the cube root function mean for the dealer's sales in the long run.

36. **Communicate Precisely** Max Wax Company packages colored wax to make homemade candles in cube-shaped containers. The production line needs to plan sizes of the containers based on the associated costs. Write a cube root function that tells the side lengths of the container, x, in inches for a given cost, C.

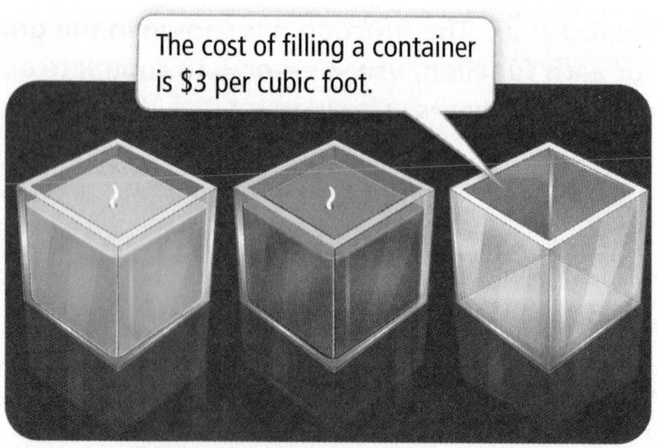

37. **Mathematical Connections** A cube has the same volume as a box that is 4 ft 5 in. long, 3 ft 2 in. wide, and 4 ft 3 in. deep.

a. Write an expression that models the length of one side of the cube.

b. Find the side length of the cube.

c. Does the cube or the box have a greater surface area? How much greater?

ASSESSMENT PRACTICE

38. Analyze the key features of $g(x) = \sqrt[3]{x - 8} + 4$. Which of the following are true? Select all that apply.

Ⓐ The domain of g is $x \geq 8$.

Ⓑ The range of g is the set of all real numbers.

Ⓒ As x approaches infinity, $g(x)$ approaches infinity.

Ⓓ The graph of g is a translation of the graph of $f(x) = \sqrt[3]{x}$ left 8 units and up 4 units.

Ⓔ The function has an absolute minimum at $x = 8$.

39. **SAT/ACT** Which shows the average rate of change of $f(x) = \sqrt[3]{x} - 2$ over $1 \leq x \leq 4$?

Ⓐ 0.47

Ⓑ 0.20

Ⓒ −0.20

Ⓓ −0.47

Ⓔ −1.53

40. **Performance Task** Paul is filling spherical water balloons for an experiment. It is important that each balloon holds exactly the same volume of water, but Paul does not have a good instrument for measuring capacity.

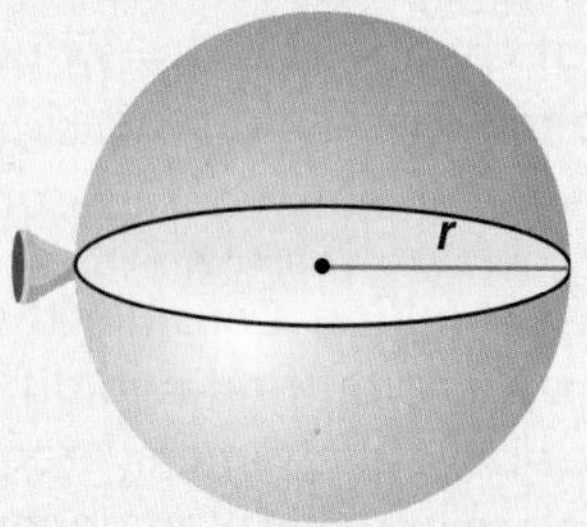

Part A Write a cube root function that allows Paul to predict the radius associated with a given volume using $V = \frac{4}{3}\pi r^3$.

Part B Describe a reasonable domain and range.

Part C If each balloon should have a volume of 72 in.^{3}, what radius should the balloon have?

10-3 Analyzing Functions Graphically

PearsonRealize.com

I CAN… identify the common features of a function when given an equation or graph.

Activity Assess

MODEL & DISCUSS

Each table represents part of a function.

x	$f(x)$
−2	1
−1	4
0	5
1	4
2	1

x	$g(x)$
−2	20
−1	10
0	5
1	2.5
2	1.25

x	$h(x)$
−2	11
−1	8
0	5
1	2
2	−1

x	$j(x)$
−2	2
−1	1
0	0
1	1
2	2

x	$k(x)$
−2	21
−1	11
0	5
1	3
2	5

A. Plot the points of each function on a graph. Describe what you know about each function.

B. Look for Relationships Which functions are related? Explain your reasoning.

ESSENTIAL QUESTION

What can you learn about a function by analyzing its graph?

EXAMPLE 1 Analyze Domain and Range

The graphs of three functions are shown. What are their domains and ranges?

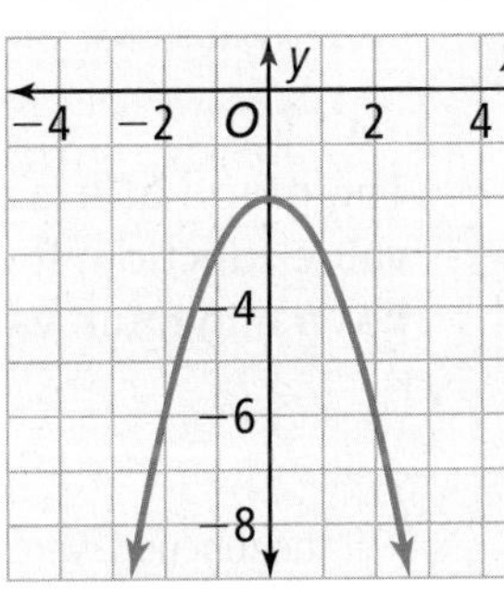

$g(x) = -x^2 - 2$

Domain: all real numbers

Range: $y \leq -2$

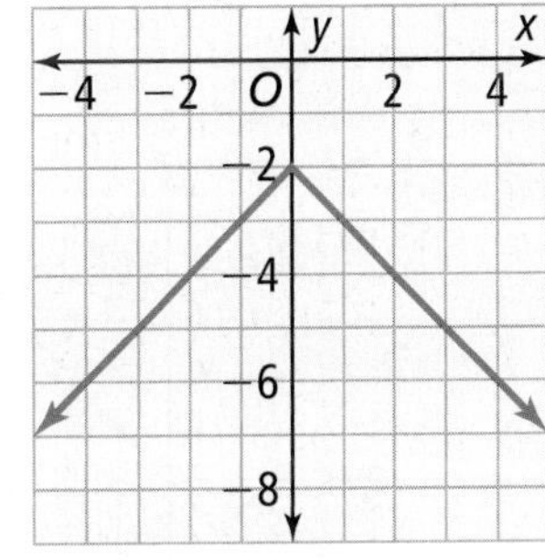

$h(x) = -|x| - 2$

Domain: all real numbers

Range: $y \leq -2$

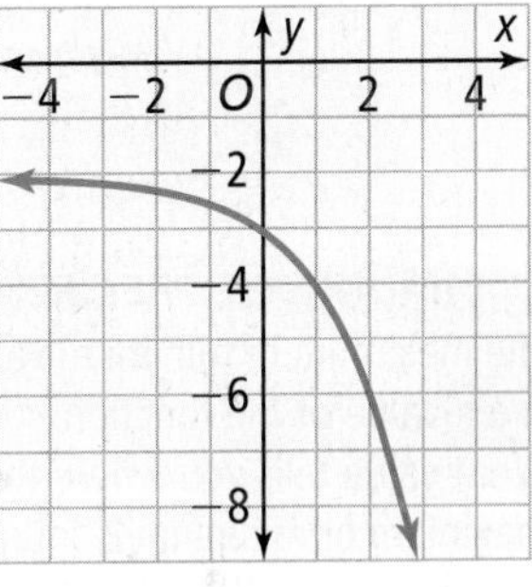

$j(x) = -2^x - 2$

Domain: all real numbers

Range: $y < -2$

To find the range of f, note that $x^2 \geq 0$ for all x. Therefore $-x^2 \leq 0$, and $-x^2 - 2 \leq -2$ for all x. So the range of f is $y \leq -2$.

You can find the ranges of h and j in a similar way. The range of h is $y \leq -2$. The range of j is $y < -2$.

COMMON ERROR
Remember to extend the function, beyond the edges of the sketch when the domain is all real numbers. The graph of j, for example, continues down and to the right out of view as x increases.

Try It! **1.** Explain how you can determine the ranges of h and j from the expressions that define them.

EXAMPLE 2 Analyze Maximum and Minimum Values

Which of these functions has a maximum value and/or a minimum value?

$f(x) = 2x - 3$ **$g(x) = -\left(\frac{1}{2}\right)^x + 4$** **$h(x) = |x + 1| + 2$**

Consider the graphs of a linear function, an exponential function, and a translation of the absolute value function.

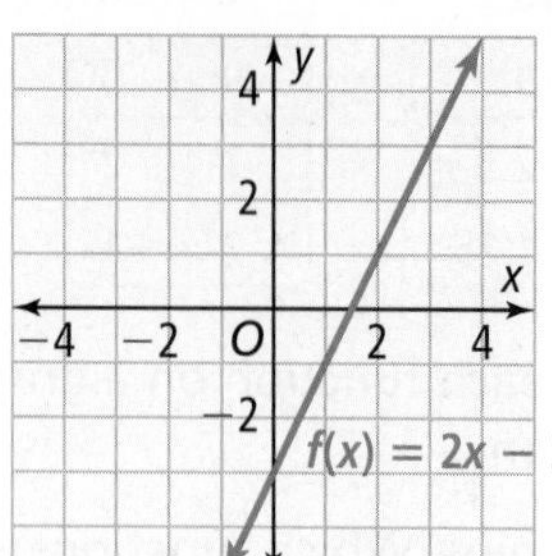

The graph of the linear function f increases at a constant rate. There is no maximum or minimum value.

As the x-value increases the y-value approaches 4, but it never reaches 4.

The graph of the function g is a translation of an exponential function. It is bounded above by the asymptote $y = 4$ which means that $g(x) < 4$. However it has no maximum because it is always increasing.

The function g also has no minimum. As x decreases, $g(x)$ decreases.

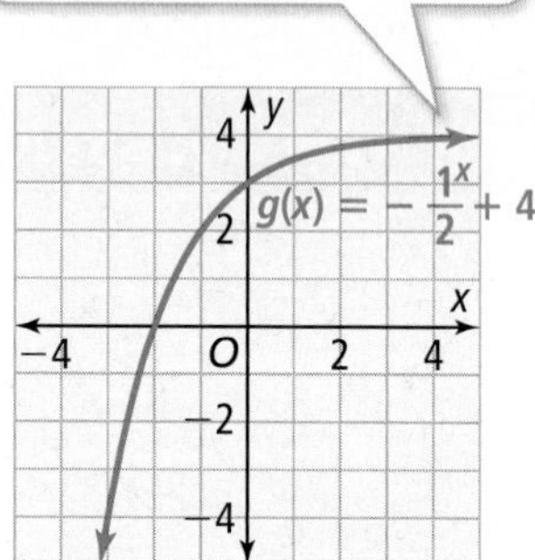

COMMUNICATE PRECISELY
The maximum or minimum value is a y-value of the function. What value tells you *where* the maximum or minimum is found?

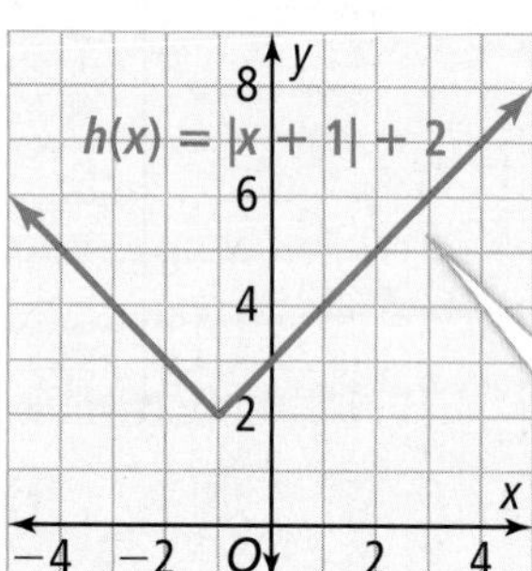

The graph of h is a translation of the absolute value function. It opens upward so the function has a minimum value of 2 at the vertex $(-1, 2)$.

If the function were instead $h(x) = -|x + 1| + 2$, the absolute value function would open down. It would then have a maximum value instead of a minimum value.

Try It! **2.** Does each function have a maximum value and/or a minimum value? Sketch the graph of each function to help you.

a. $f(x) = x^2 - 3x + 1$

b. $g(x) = 2\sqrt{x + 1}$

c. $h(x) = \sqrt[3]{8(x - 1)} + 5$

CONCEPTUAL UNDERSTANDING

EXAMPLE 3 Understand Axes of Symmetry

Which of the functions shown has an axis of symmetry?

STUDY TIP

If you fold a sketch of the graph along the axis of symmetry, the parts of the graph on either side of the axis of symmetry will coincide.

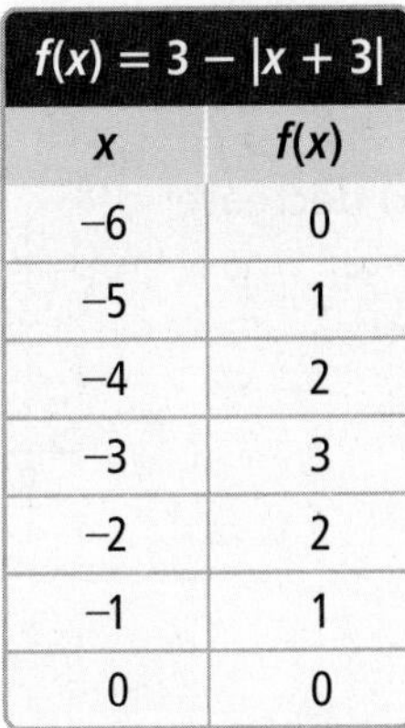

$f(x) = 3 - \lvert x + 3 \rvert$	
x	$f(x)$
−6	0
−5	1
−4	2
−3	3
−2	2
−1	1
0	0

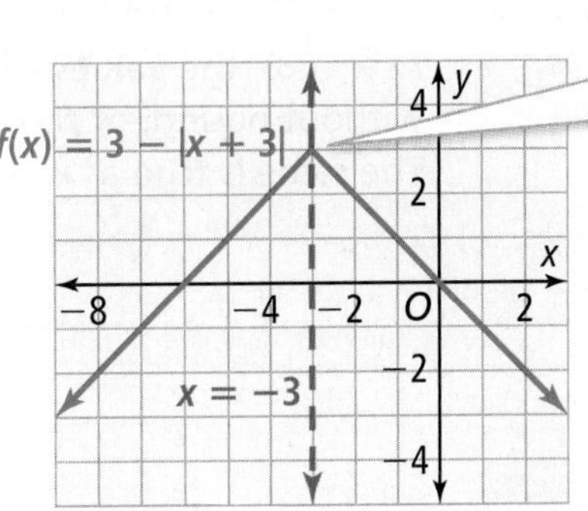

Translations of the absolute value function always have an axis of symmetry passing through the vertex.

$g(x) = (x - 2)^2$	
x	$g(x)$
−1	9
0	4
1	1
2	0
3	1
4	4
5	9

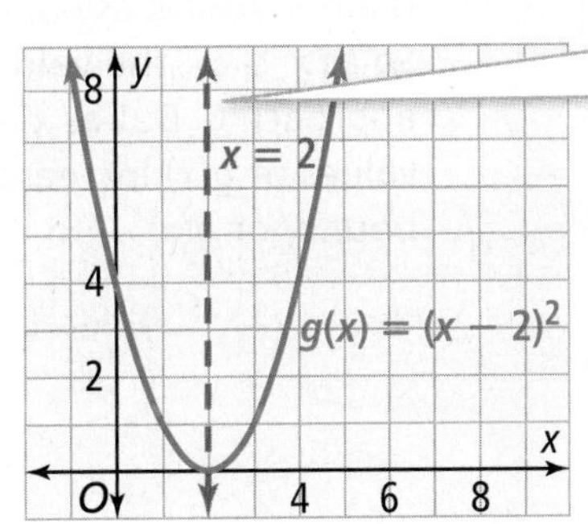

Quadratic functions always have a vertical axis of symmetry.

$h(x) = \sqrt{x - 4}$	
x	$h(x)$
4	0
5	1
8	2
13	3
20	4
29	5
40	6

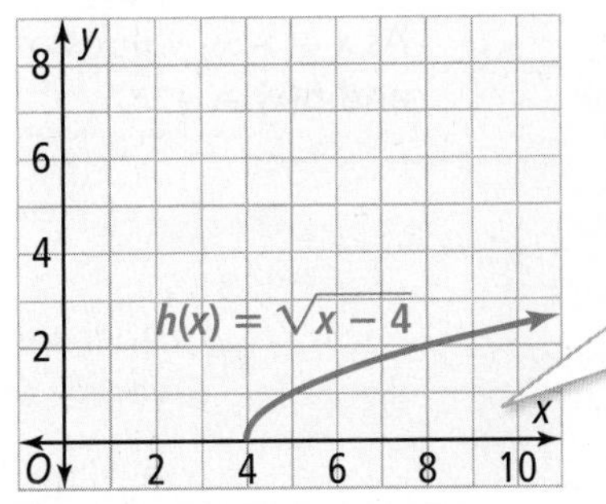

This function does not have an axis of symmetry. There is no way to fold the graph so that one side aligns with the other.

Quadratic functions and translations of the absolute value function have an axis of symmetry.

Try It! 3. Does each function have an axis of symmetry? Sketch graphs to help you.

a. $g(x) = 2^x$ b. $h(x) = \sqrt[3]{x + 4}$

EXAMPLE 4 Analyze End Behaviors of Graphs

What is the end behavior of each function?

> **LOOK FOR RELATIONSHIPS**
> You can determine end behavior of polynomial functions, such as a quadratic function, by looking at the leading term. The end behavior of $g(x) = ax^2$ is the same as the end behavior of $f(x) = ax^2 + bx + c$ when $a \neq 0$.

End behavior describes what happens to the ends of the graph of a function as x approaches infinity or negative infinity (written as $x \to \infty$ and $x \to -\infty$).

As $x \to \infty$, the values of $f(x)$ decrease without bound, or $f(x) \to -\infty$. The same is true as $x \to -\infty$.

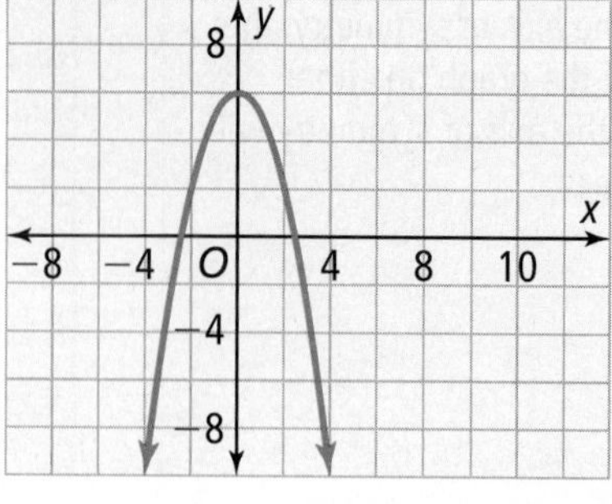

$f(x) = -x^2 + 6$

For this exponential function, there is a horizontal asymptote at $y = 0$. So as $x \to \infty$, the values of $g(x)$ approach 0. But as $x \to -\infty$, the values of $g(x)$ increase without bound, or $g(x) \to \infty$.

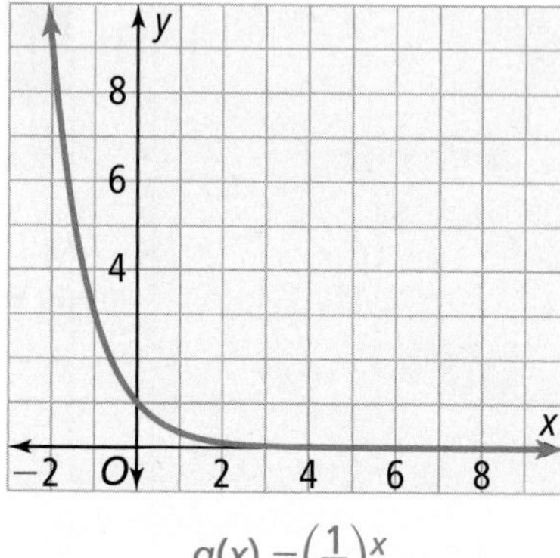

$g(x) = \left(\frac{1}{3}\right)^x$

As $x \to \infty$, the values of $h(x)$ grow less and less steeply, but they do not approach any asymptote, so $h(x) \to \infty$. As $x \to -\infty$, values of $h(x)$ decrease, and $h(x) \to -\infty$.

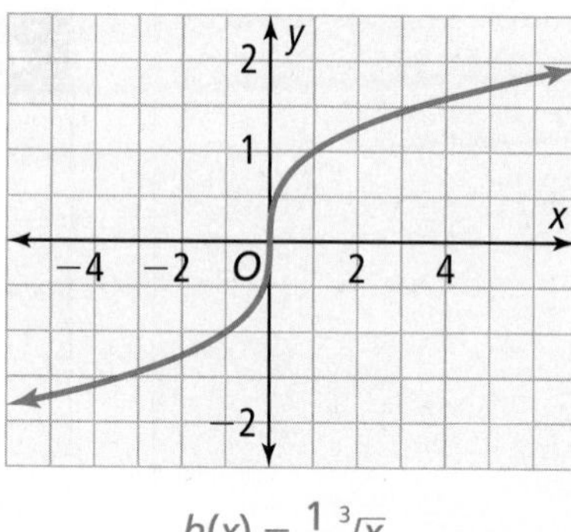

$h(x) = \frac{1}{2}\sqrt[3]{x}$

 **Try It!** **4.** Compare the end behaviors of the functions.

$f(x) = 2^{x+2}$ $\quad$ $g(x) = \left(\frac{1}{3}\right)^x + 4$ $\quad$ $h(x) = x^2 - 2x + 1$

Concept Summary

Assess

CONCEPT SUMMARY Common Features of Functions

	WORDS	GRAPHS
Domain and Range	The domain of f is the set of all real numbers. The range of f is the set of all real number less than or equal to 6.	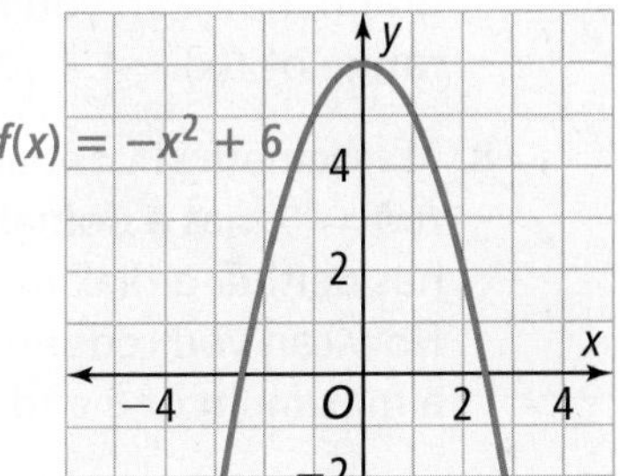
Maximum and Minimum Values	g has no maximum value. The minimum value of g is 0, for $x = -3$.	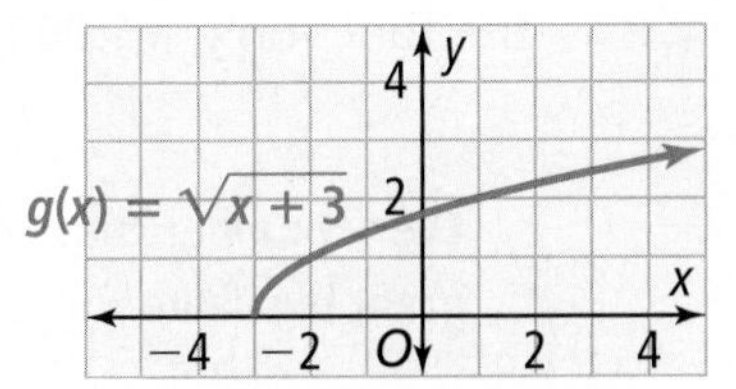
Axis of Symmetry	A vertical line that divides a function into mirror images is an axis of symmetry. The line $x = 2$ is an axis of symmetry for h.	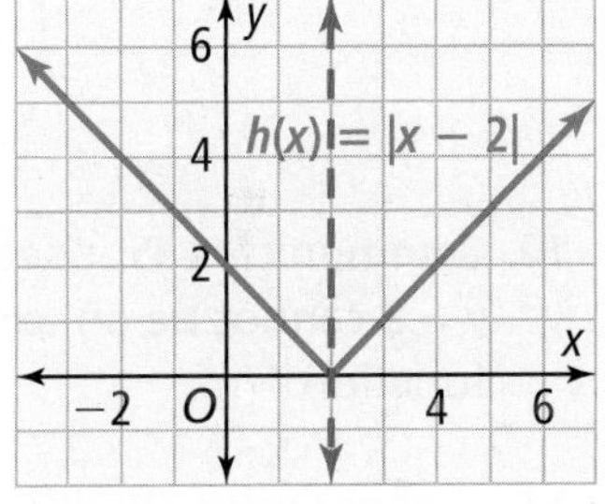
End Behavior	End behavior describes what happens to the ends of the graph. As $x \to \infty$, $k(x) \to \infty$. As $x \to -\infty$, $k(x) \to -2$.	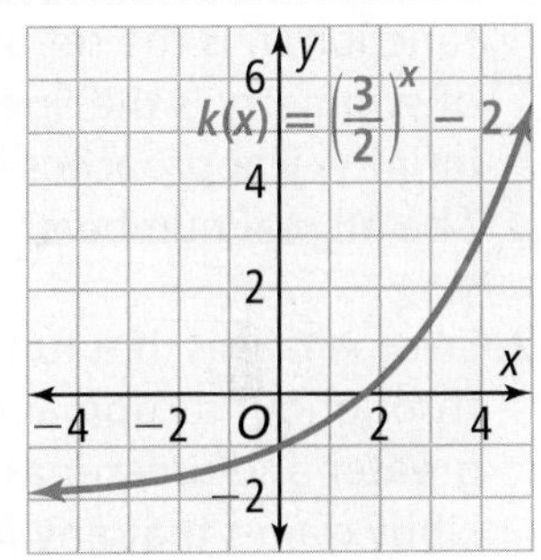

Do You UNDERSTAND?

1. ESSENTIAL QUESTION What can you learn about a function by analyzing its graph?

2. **Error Analysis** Kona states that the maximum value of $f(x) = -2^x$ is 0. Explain Kona's error.

3. **Look for Relationships** How are behaviors of quadratic functions like those of the absolute value function?

Do You KNOW HOW?

For each function identify the domain and range, state the maximum and minimum values, identify the axis of symmetry, if it exists, and describe the end behavior.

4. $f(x) = \sqrt{x - 5}$

5. $g(x) = x^2 + 2x + 1$

6. $h(x) = 2 - |x + 6|$

PRACTICE & PROBLEM SOLVING

Scan for Multimedia

Practice Tutorial

Additional Exercises Available Online

UNDERSTAND

7. **Look for Relationships** Without sketching the graph, how can you identify the domain and range of $f(x) = 4 - \sqrt{2x - 5}$?

8. **Mathematical Connections** The function $f(x) = \sqrt[3]{x}$ has a domain of all real numbers and has neither a maximum nor a minimum value. How can you redefine the domain so that f has a maximum of 8 and a minimum of -8?

9. **Error Analysis** Describe and correct the error a student made in describing the end behavior of the function $y = 1{,}000{,}000 - x^2$.

Every number that I enter for x gives a great big value for y, so as $x \to \infty$, $y \to \infty$.

10. **Communicate Precisely** Explain why the line $y = 3$ cannot be an axis of symmetry for a function.

11. **Higher Order Thinking** The domain of a function, f, is the set of all real numbers. Its axis of symmetry is the line $x = 4$. As x approaches infinity, y approaches infinity. Can the range of f be all real numbers? Explain your reasoning.

12. **Error Analysis** If a function is increasing throughout its domain, the y-values are greater and greater as x approaches infinity. Libby claims that any function that has all real numbers as its domain and is increasing everywhere must have all real numbers as its range as well. Is Libby correct? Explain why or why not.

13. **Use Structure** For what values of a and b would the graph of f have an axis of symmetry?

$$f(x) = \begin{cases} a\sqrt[3]{x}, & x \le b \\ \sqrt[3]{x}, & x > b \end{cases}$$

PRACTICE

Sketch the graph of each function and identify its domain and range. SEE EXAMPLE 1

14. $f(x) = x^2 - 2$

15. $f(x) = \sqrt{x - 3}$

16. $f(x) = 5^x$

17. $f(x) = 3 - |x - 4|$

Use the graph of each function to help you identify its maximum and minimum values, if they exist. SEE EXAMPLE 2

18. $f(x) = 3 - x^2$

19. $f(x) = \sqrt[3]{x}$

20. $f(x) = -2^x$

21. $f(x) = 5|x| - 8$

State the equation of the axis of symmetry for each function, if it exists. SEE EXAMPLE 3

22.

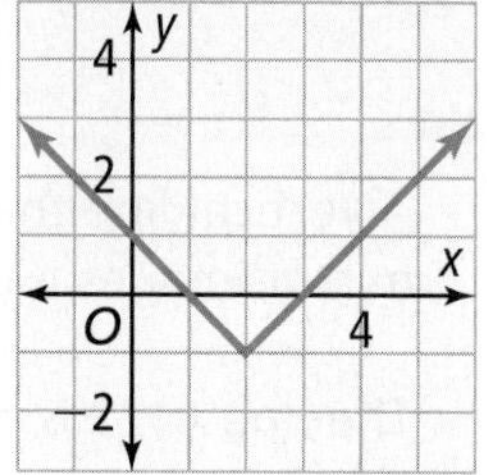

23.

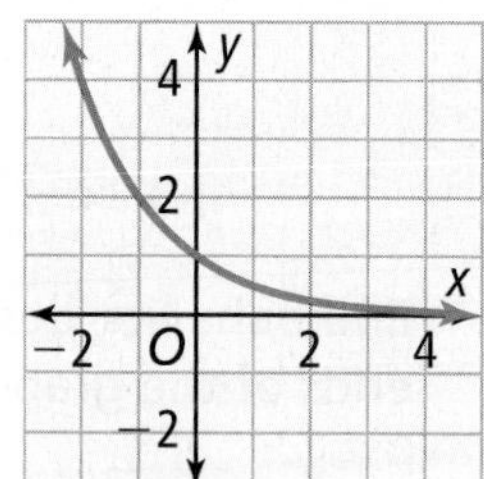

24.

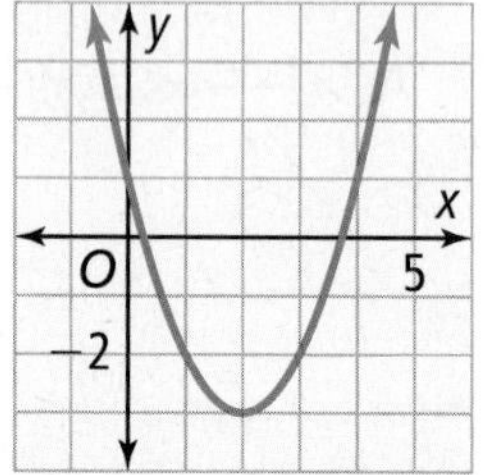

Describe the end behavior of each function. SEE EXAMPLE 4

25. $f(x) = 1 - 3x$

26. $f(x) = x^2 + 2$

27. $f(x) = -7^x$

28. $f(x) = |x + 2| - 8$

29. $f(x) = -3(x + 4)^2$

30. $f(x) = \sqrt{x} - 5$

PRACTICE & PROBLEM SOLVING

APPLY

31. Model With Mathematics The average high temperatures for four different cities, Anchorage, AK, Kansas City, MO, Miami, FL, and New York, NY, have been used to create the graph. Use information about maximum and minimum values to complete the legend for the graph. Explain your reasoning.

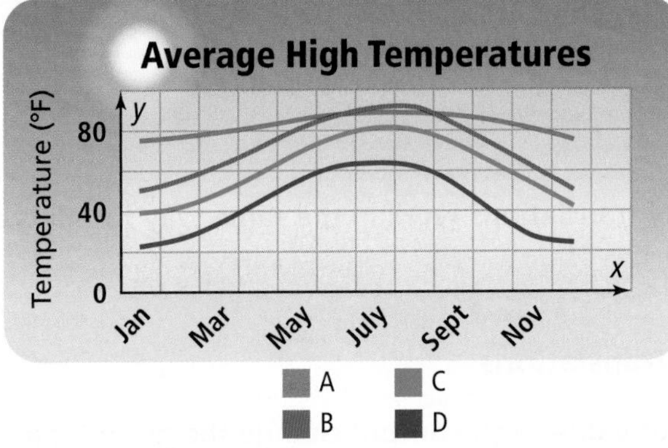

A C
B D

32. Make Sense and Persevere A marketing company is designing a new package for a box of cereal. They have determined that the function $C(x) = 4.5x^2$ models the cost of a box with side lengths as shown (measured in inches). Identify a reasonable domain and range for the function.

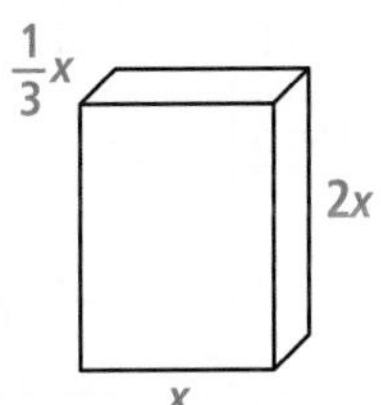

33. Model With Mathematics Yumiko is an animator. She uses computer-generated imagery (CGI) to create scenes for a movie. The shapes and features she uses are defined by functions. Which features of functions will be useful for Yumiko, and how can she use them in her work?

ASSESSMENT PRACTICE

34. Analyze the behavior of $f(x) = x^2 - 2x + 5$. Which of the following are true? Select all that apply.

Ⓐ As x approaches infinity, y approaches infinity.

Ⓑ As x approaches negative infinity, y approaches negative infinity.

Ⓒ f has an axis of symmetry at $x = 1$.

Ⓓ The domain of f is the set of all real numbers.

Ⓔ The maximum value of f is 4, for $x = 1$.

35. SAT/ACT Which function has an axis of symmetry at $x = 1$ and a maximum value of 3?

Ⓐ $y = 1 - |x - 3|$

Ⓑ $y = |x - 1| + 3$

Ⓒ $y = |x + 1| - 3$

Ⓓ $y = 3 - |x - 1|$

Ⓔ $y = |x - 3| + 1$

36. Performance Task Jack started a small business recently, and he has been tracking his monthly profits, summarized in the table below.

Jan	$3	May	$100
Feb	$10	June	$180
Mar	$25	July	$415
Apr	$40	Aug	$795

Part A Create a graph to show Jack's profits over time. Determine the type of function that will best model Jack's profits based on data collected so far.

Part B Evaluate features of the function that will be relevant to Jack's business. Explain what those features mean in this context.

Part C Write an equation that models the growth of Jack's business. Use your function to predict Jack's profits for August of the following year. Is your prediction reasonable? Explain why or why not.

10-4 Translations of Functions

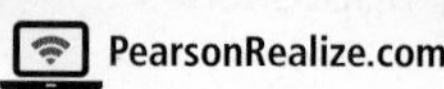

I CAN… graph and analyze transformations of functions.

CRITIQUE & EXPLAIN

The figure shows $f(x) = \sqrt{x}$ and $g(x) = \sqrt[3]{x}$. Venetta says that vertical translations will work in the same way for these functions as they do for quadratic and exponential functions. Tonya disagrees.

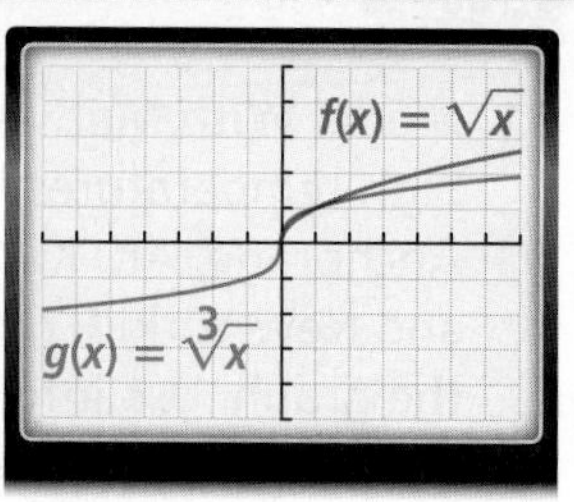

A. For $f(x) + c$ and $g(x) + c$, what translation do you expect when c is positive? When c is negative?

B. Generalize Which student is correct? Explain your answer.

ESSENTIAL QUESTION

Do horizontal and vertical translations work in the same way for all types of functions?

EXAMPLE 1 Vertical Translations

How does adding a constant value to the output change the graph of a function?

Consider how the value of the constant changes the graph of each function shown.

You can write this operation as $g(x) = f(x) + k$. This means that for a value of x, g takes the output of f and adds the constant k.

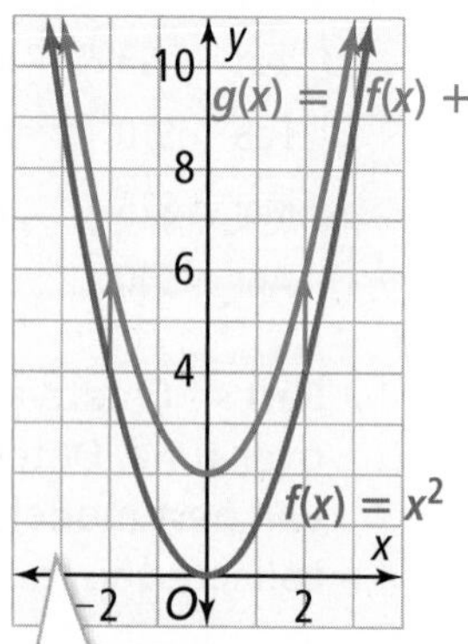

The graph of g is a translation of f up 2 units.

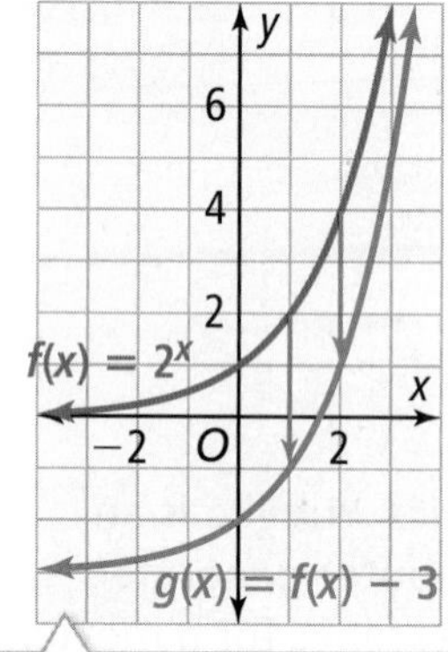

The graph of g is a translation of f down 3 units.

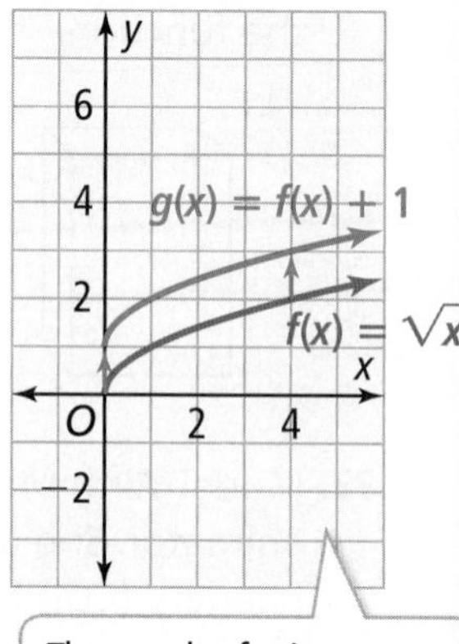

The graph of g is a translation of f up 1 unit.

LOOK FOR RELATIONSHIPS
Adding a negative constant k to a function decreases the function value by k, so it moves the graph down k units.

Adding a positive constant translates the graph up, while adding a negative constant translates the graph down.

Try It! 1. For each function $g(x) = f(x) + k$, how does the value of k affect the graph of function f?

a. $g(x) = f(x) + 7$

b. $g(x) = f(x) - 9$

EXAMPLE 2 Analyze Horizontal Translations

How does subtracting a constant from the input change the graph of a function?

Consider how the value of the constant changes the graph of each function shown.

You can write this operation generally as $g(x) = f(x - h)$. This means that g takes the input of f and subtracts the constant h before applying function f.

To see what happens to the graph when you subtract a constant from the input, consider what inputs for g you would need to get the same output as f for a given input x.

For example, if $g(x) = f(x + 2)$, you would need an input x_1 that is 2 units *less* than x for $g(x_1) = f(x)$. So the graph of g is the graph of f shifted 2 units to the *left*.

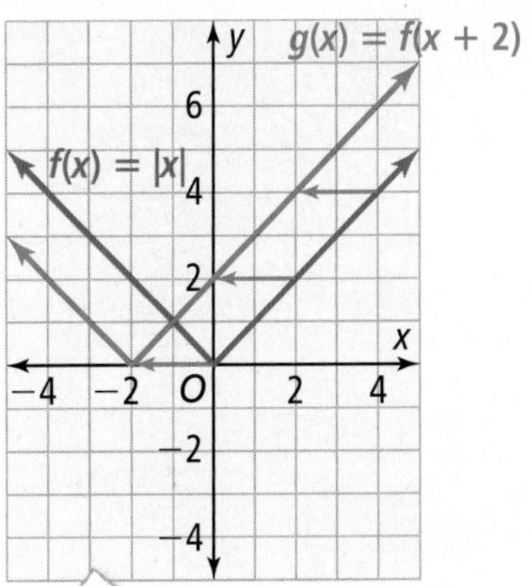

The graph of g is a translation of f left 2 units.

COMMON ERROR
The expression $x + 2$ in the function $f(x + 2)$ shifts the graph of $f(x)$ horizontally in the *negative* direction, not the positive direction. You can think of this as $f(x - (-2))$, so the constant is negative.

You can use the same reasoning to see how the graph changes for any function.

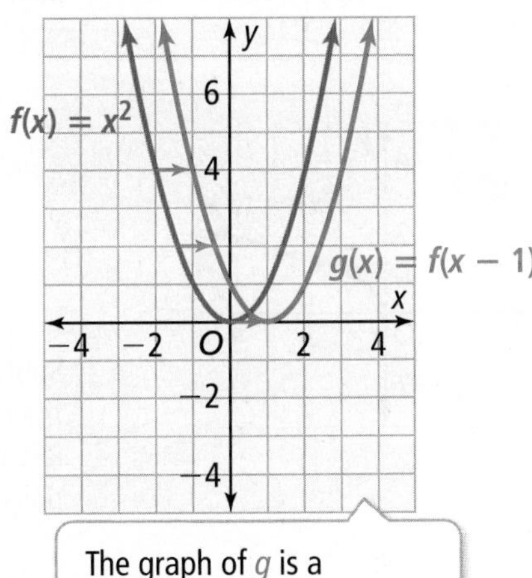

The graph of g is a translation of f right 1 unit.

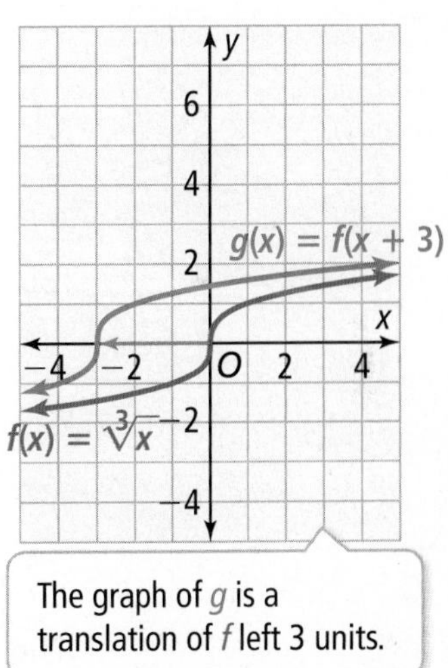

The graph of g is a translation of f left 3 units.

Subtracting a positive constant from x translates the graph to the right, while subtracting a negative constant from x translates the graph to the left.

Try It! 2. For each function $g(x) = f(x - h)$, how does the value of h affect the graph of function f?

a. $g(x) = f(x - 8)$

b. $g(x) = f(x + 7)$

CONCEPTUAL UNDERSTANDING

EXAMPLE 3 Combine Translations

How does subtracting a constant value from the input and adding a constant value to the output change the graph of a function?

Graph $g(x) = f(x + 4) - 1$ for various types of functions f.

In the form $g(x) = f(x - h) + k$, $g(x) = f(x - (-4)) + (-1)$, so $h = -4$ and $k = -1$.

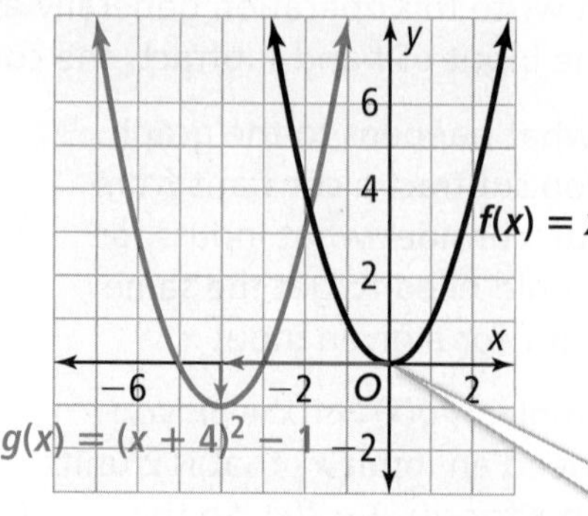

Subtracting −4 from x translates the vertex 4 units left. Adding −1 translates the vertex 1 unit down.

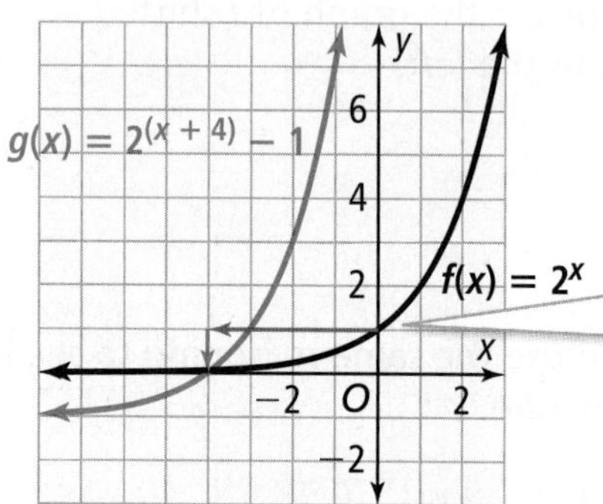

Subtracting −4 from x translates the reference point 4 units left. Adding −1 translates the point 1 unit down.

REASON
For function graphs without a vertex, consider what points you can use as a reference points when you translate.

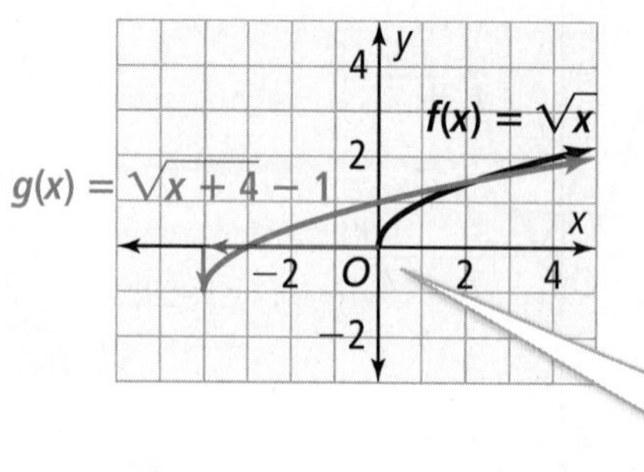

Subtracting −4 from x translates the reference point 4 units left. Adding −1 translates the point 1 unit down.

The combination of translations represented by $g(x) = f(x + 4) - 1$ affects the graph of these functions the same way. All points of graph f are translated left 4 units and down 1 unit.

The combined horizontal and vertical translations are independent of each other. Although they can be applied in either order, the horizontal one is applied first. Given $g(x) = f(x - h) + k$, the graph of function g is the graph of function f translated h units horizontally, then translated k units vertically.

Try It! 3. Graph f and $g(x) = f(x - 2) + 3$.

a. $f(x) = x^2$ b. $f(x) = 2^x$ c. $f(x) = \sqrt{x}$

CONCEPT SUMMARY Translations of Functions

WORDS

Changes to the output translate the graph vertically.

$k > 0$: shifts $|k|$ units up

$k < 0$: shifts $|k|$ units down

Changes to the input translate the graph horizontally.

$h > 0$: shifts $|h|$ units right

$h < 0$: shifts $|h|$ units left

ALGEBRA

$g(x) = f(x) + k$ — translates k units vertically

$g(x) = f(x - h)$ — translates h units horizontally

$g(x) = f(x - h) + k$ — translates h units horizontally and k units vertically

NUMBERS

$g(x) = f(x) - 2$ — translates 2 units down

$g(x) = f(x + 3)$ — translates 3 units left

$g(x) = f(x + 3) - 2$ — translates 3 units left and 2 units down

GRAPHS

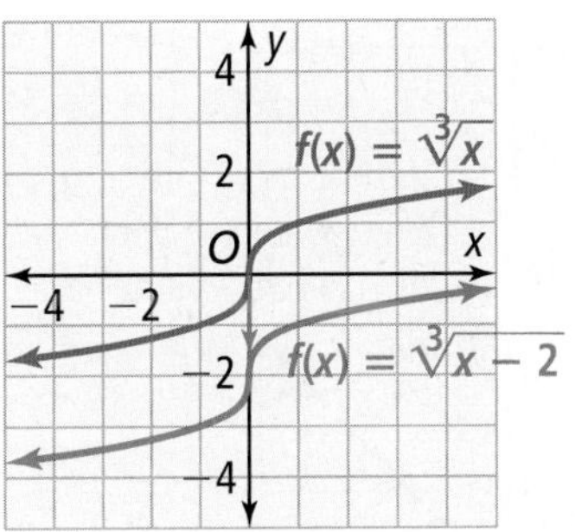

y
4
$f(x) = \sqrt[3]{x+3}$
2
O
x
−4 −2 2 4
$f(x) = \sqrt[3]{x}$
−2
−4

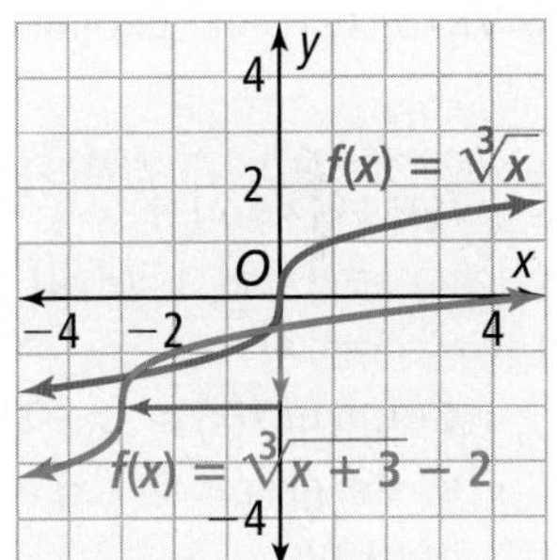

Do You UNDERSTAND?

1. **ESSENTIAL QUESTION** Do horizontal and vertical translations work in the same way for all types of functions?

2. **Use Structure** How can translations help you sketch the graph of $f(x) = x^2 + 8x + 16$?

3. **Error Analysis** Ashton says that $f(x) = \sqrt{x - 3}$ has domain $x \geq -3$. Is Ashton correct? Explain your reasoning.

4. **Construct Arguments** Explain why adding a number to the output of a function shifts its graph vertically.

Do You KNOW HOW?

Sketch the graph of each function.

5. $f(x) = |x| + 4$
6. $f(x) = (x - 2)^3$
7. $f(x) = \sqrt{x + 2}$
8. $f(x) = 3^x - 5$
9. $f(x) = (x - 1)^2 - 2$
10. $f(x) = \sqrt{x + 4} + 3$
11. What is the equation of the graph?

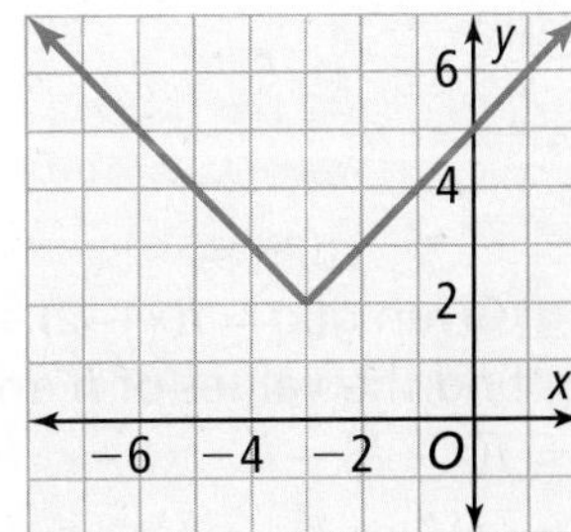

PRACTICE & PROBLEM SOLVING

Scan for Multimedia

Practice | Tutorial

Additional Exercises Available Online

UNDERSTAND

12. **Reason** How does the graph of $f(x) = 5$ change for $g(x) = f(x - h) + k$, where h and k are constants?

13. **Use Structure** The graph of $g(x) = f(x - 2) + 1$ is shown. Sketch the graph of f.

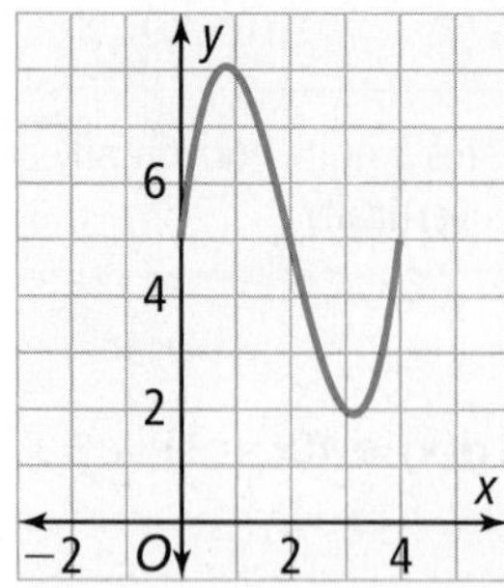

14. **Error Analysis** Victor is asked to explain how the graph of $g(x) = |x - 2| + 2$ relates to the graph of $f(x) = |x|$. His work is shown below. Is Victor correct? Explain why or why not.

$f(x) = |x - 2| + 2$
$= |x| + (-2 + 2)$
$= |x|$
Graph of $f(x) = |x - 2| + 2$ is the same as the graph of $f(x) = |x|$, with vertex at (0, 0).

✗

15. **Use Structure** Describe a combination of translations to apply to the floor function, $f(x) = \lfloor x \rfloor$, that leaves its graph appearing unchanged. Write the new equation.

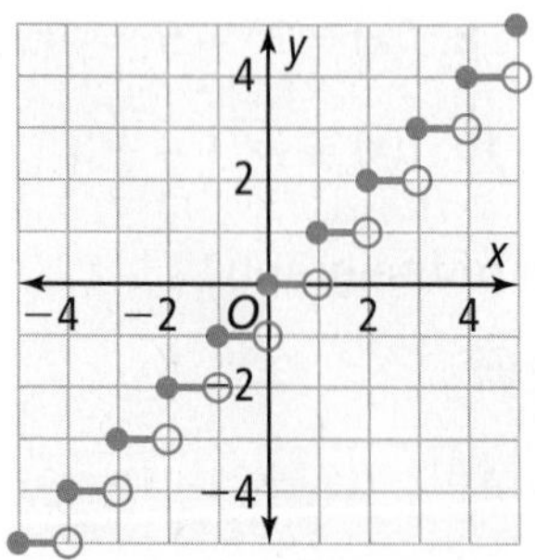

16. **Higher Order Thinking** Given $g(x) = f(x - 2) + 4$ and $j(x) = g(x + 5) - 3$, find the values of h and k in the equation $j(x) = f(x - h) + k$.

PRACTICE

Sketch the graph of each function.
SEE EXAMPLES 1 AND 2

17. $g(x) = |x| + 6$

18. $g(x) = x^2 - 3$

19. $g(x) = \frac{1}{3}x + 2$

20. $g(x) = \sqrt{x} - 8$

21. $g(x) = (x - 2)^2$

22. $g(x) = |x + 4|$

23. $g(x) = \sqrt{x + 3}$

24. $g(x) = \sqrt[3]{x - 5}$

Each graph is a translation of the given function. Write the function for the graph. SEE EXAMPLE 2

25. $f(x) = x^2$

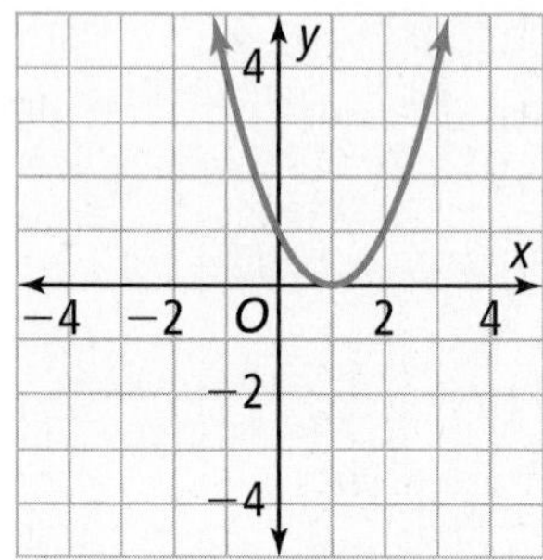

26. $f(x) = \sqrt[3]{x}$

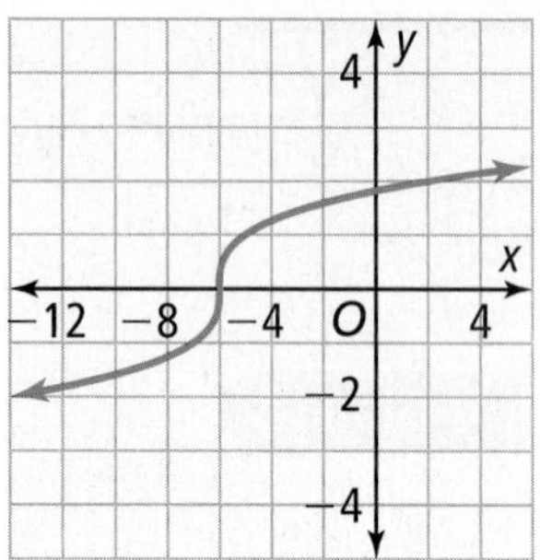

27. $f(x) = |x|$

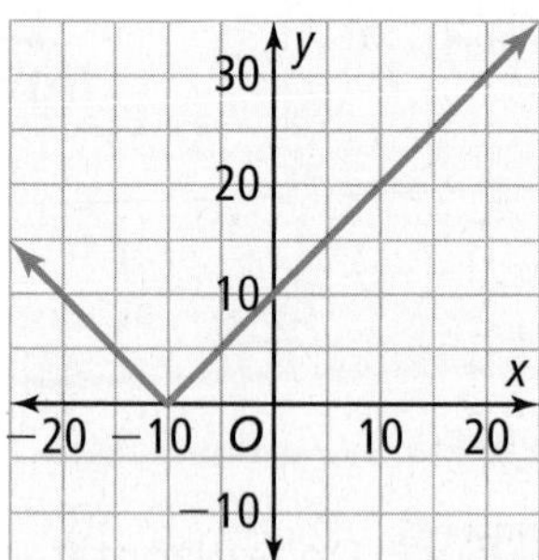

28. $f(x) = \sqrt{x}$

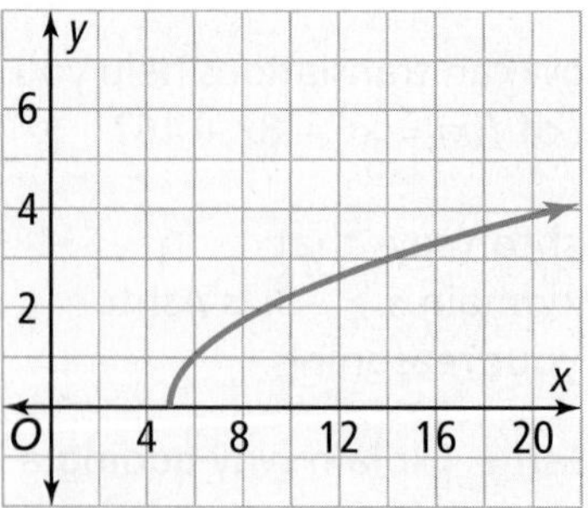

Sketch the graph of each function. SEE EXAMPLE 3

29. $g(x) = 2^{x+4} - 7$

30. $g(x) = |x + 4.3| - 2.7$

PRACTICE & PROBLEM SOLVING

APPLY

31. Make Sense and Persevere The height, *h*, in meters of a Saturn V rocket *t* seconds after launch is modeled by the graph shown. Note that the graph is not the actual path of the rocket. A launch is delayed by 60 seconds by a technical problem. Describe the effect on *h*(*t*) as a translation. Sketch the graph of the height of the rocket *t* seconds from the original launch time.

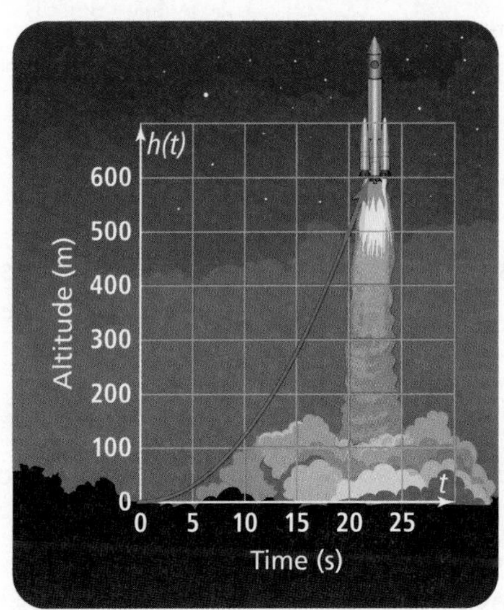

32. Mathematical Connections The costs for a new publishing company can be classified as fixed costs, such as rent and insurance, or variable costs, such as materials and labor. Fixed costs are constant, while variable costs change as the number of items produced changes. The graph shows the weekly variable costs based on the number of books produced.

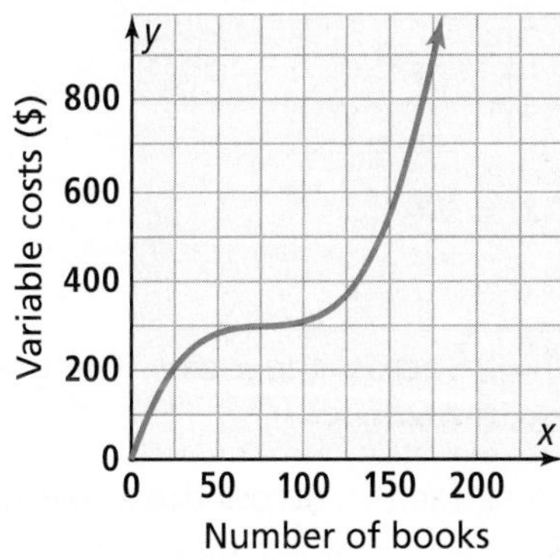

a. If weekly fixed costs are \$300, sketch a graph showing total expenses for the week.

b. Find the total cost of producing 75 books in a week.

ASSESSMENT PRACTICE

33. Which is true about the graph of the function $f(x) = (x - 2)^2 - 3$? Select all that apply.

Ⓐ It is a parabola that opens upward.

Ⓑ It is a parabola that opens downward.

Ⓒ The vertex is (2, −3).

Ⓓ The vertex is (−2, −3).

Ⓔ The vertex is (2, 3).

34. SAT/ACT How is the function $f(x) = \sqrt{x}$ translated to obtain the graph of $g(x) = \sqrt{x + 5} + 6$?

Ⓐ Shift $f(x) = \sqrt{x}$ up 5 units and right 6 units.

Ⓑ Shift $f(x) = \sqrt{x}$ right 5 units and down 6 units.

Ⓒ Shift $f(x) = \sqrt{x}$ left 5 units and up 6 units.

Ⓓ Shift $f(x) = \sqrt{x}$ left 5 units and down 6 units.

Ⓔ Shift $f(x) = \sqrt{x}$ down 5 units and left 6 units.

35. Performance Task In a computer football game, you are attempting to kick a field goal. Every kick in the game can be modeled by a horizontal translation of the function shown. Assume the translations are to the nearest tenth of a yard. The goal post is 10 yards behind the goal line.

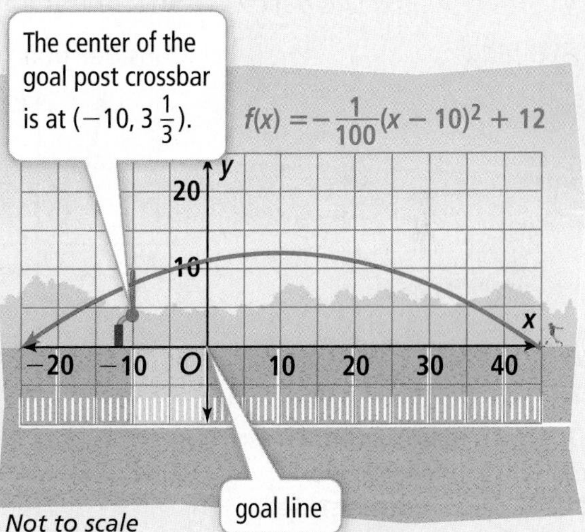

Part A How far from the goal line is the football placed in the figure shown?

Part B What is the maximum distance from the goal line the football can be placed for the kick to clear the crossbar?

Part C Write the function for the kick in Part B.

Activity Assess

10-5 Compressions and Stretches of Functions

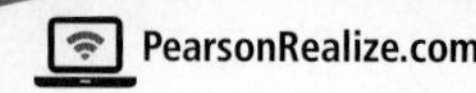
PearsonRealize.com

I CAN… change functions to compress or stretch their graphs.

EXPLORE & REASON

The graphs of three quadratic functions g, h, and j all have a vertex of (0, 0). Additional points that lie on the graph of each function are shown.

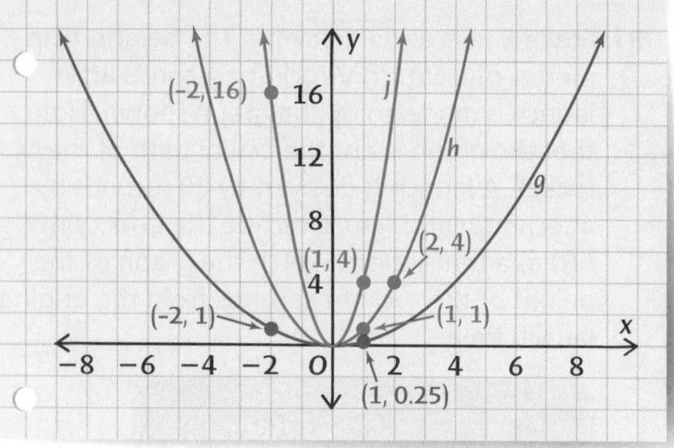

A. Write a quadratic function for each parabola.

B. **Communicate Precisely** How are these functions similar? How are they different?

C. Using your knowledge of compressions and stretches of other functions and your answers to parts A and B, describe how how to write a vertical stretch or compression of $f(x) = \sqrt{x}$.

ESSENTIAL QUESTION

What change to a function will result in a vertical or horizontal stretch or compression of its graph?

EXAMPLE 1 Analyze Reflections Across the x-Axis

How does multiplying the output by −1 change the graph of a function?

Consider $g(x) = -1f(x)$ for $f(x) = x^2$ and for $f(x) = \sqrt[3]{x}$.

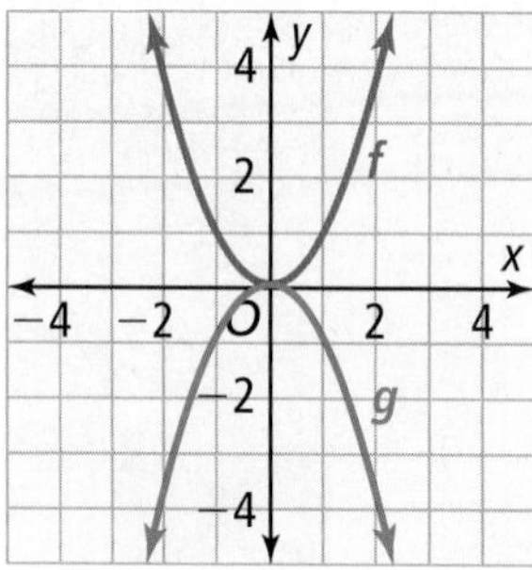

$f(x) = x^2$

$g(x) = -x^2$

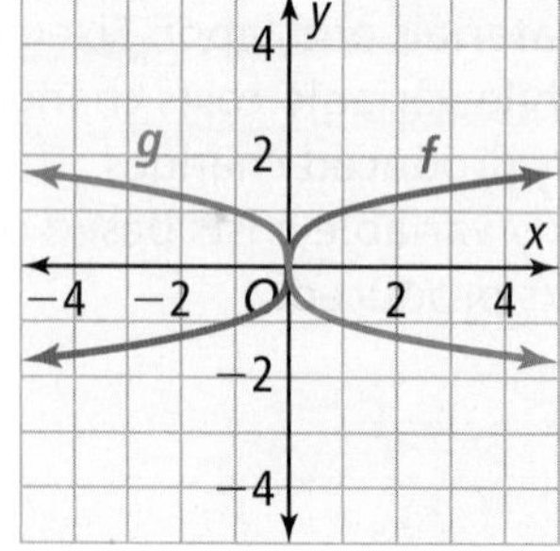

$f(x) = \sqrt[3]{x}$

$g(x) = -\sqrt[3]{x}$

The graph of $g(x) = -x^2$ is a reflection of $f(x) = x^2$ across the x-axis. The graph of $g(x) = -\sqrt[3]{x}$ is a reflection of $f(x) = \sqrt[3]{x}$ across the x-axis.

In general, if $g(x) = -1f(x)$, the graph of g is a reflection across the x-axis of the graph of f.

LOOK FOR RELATIONSHIPS
Recall the transformations of other functions you have studied. How does the graph of a linear function change when the output is multiplied by −1?

Try It! 1. Write a function with a graph that is the reflection of the graph of f across the x-axis.

a. $f(x) = x$

b. $f(x) = \sqrt{x}$

EXAMPLE 2 Analyze Vertical Stretches of Graphs

How does multiplying the output by a constant with an absolute value greater than 1 change the graph of a function?

Consider $g(x) = kf(x)$ for $|k| > 1$ when $f(x) = x^2$ and when $f(x) = \sqrt[3]{x}$.

$f(x) = x^2$ $g(x) = 2x^2$

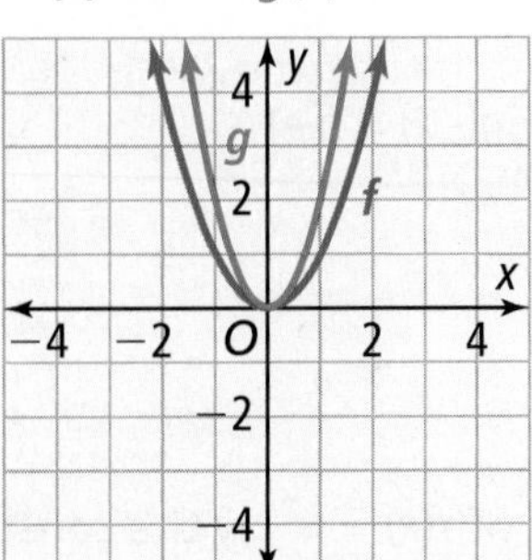

$f(x) = \sqrt[3]{x}$ $g(x) = 4\sqrt[3]{x}$

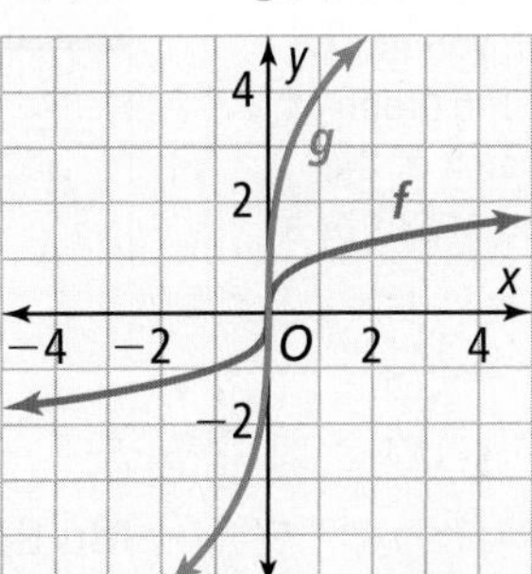

REASON
Think about how the *y*-values of the function change for the same input values when the output is multiplied by a constant greater than 1.

The graph of $g(x) = 2x^2$ is a vertical stretch of $f(x) = x^2$ away from the *x*-axis. The graph of $g(x) = 4\sqrt[3]{x}$ is a vertical stretch of $f(x) = \sqrt[3]{x}$ away from the *x*-axis.

In general, if $g(x) = kf(x)$ for $|k| > 1$, the graph of *g* is a vertical stretch away from the *x*-axis of the graph of *f*.

Try It! 2. Write a function with a graph that is a vertical stretch of the graph of *f*, away from the *x*-axis.

a. $f(x) = x$ **b.** $f(x) = \sqrt{x}$

EXAMPLE 3 Analyze Vertical Compressions of Graphs

How does multiplying the output by a constant with an absolute value between 0 and 1 change the graph of a function?

Consider $g(x) = kf(x)$ for $0 < |k| < 1$ when $f(x) = |x + 1|$ and when $f(x) = x^2$.

$f(x) = |x + 1|$ $g(x) = \frac{1}{2}|x + 1|$

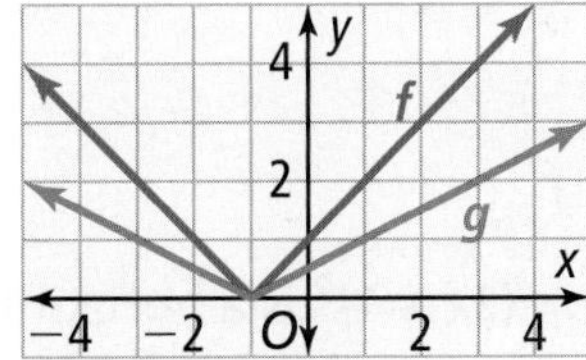

$f(x) = x^2$ $g(x) = \frac{1}{2}x^2$

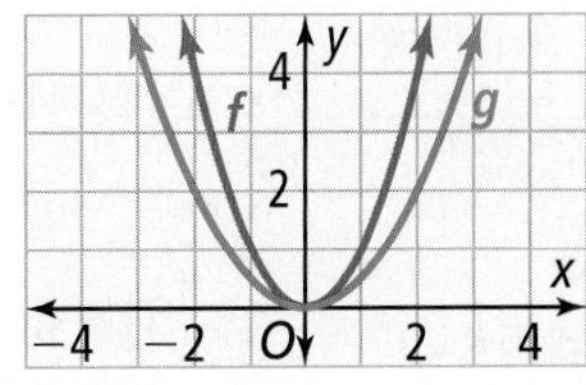

The graph of $g(x) = \frac{1}{2}|x + 1|$ is a vertical compression of $f(x) = |x + 1|$ toward the *x*-axis. The graph of $g(x) = \frac{1}{2}x^2$ is a vertical compression of $f(x) = x^2$ toward the *x*-axis.

In general, if $g(x) = kf(x)$ for $0 < |k| < 1$, the graph of *g* is a vertical compression toward the *x*-axis of the graph of *f*.

Try It! 3. Write a function with a graph that is a vertical compression of the graph of *f*, toward the *x*-axis.

a. $f(x) = \sqrt{x}$ **b.** $f(x) = |x|$

CONCEPTUAL UNDERSTANDING

EXAMPLE 4 Analyze Horizontal Stretches of Graphs

Why does multiplying the input of the function stretch the graph horizontally?

Consider $g(x) = f(kx)$ for $0 < k < 1$ when $f(x) = x^2$.

x	$f(x)$	$g(x)$
–2	4	1
–1	1	0.25
0	0	0
1	1	0.25
2	4	1

$g(-2) = f(-1)$

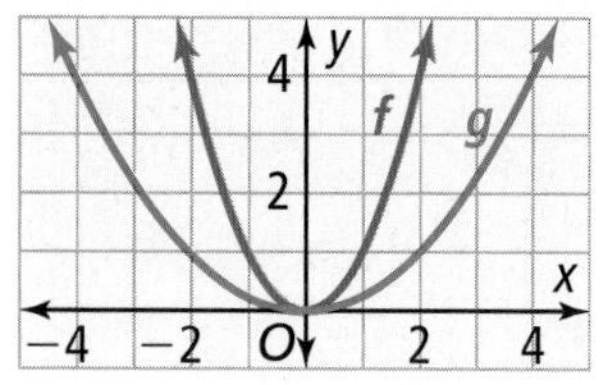

$f(x) = x^2$ $\quad g(x) = \left(\frac{1}{2}x\right)^2$

LOOK FOR RELATIONSHIPS
To get the same *y*-values from function *g* as from *f*, you must double the input *x*. The graph of *g* is a horizontal stretch of the graph of *f* away from *y*-axis by a scale factor of 2.

Multiplying the input of $f(x) = x^2$ by the constant $\frac{1}{2}$ yields $g(x) = \left(\frac{1}{2}x\right)^2$. To get *y*-values from function *g* that are equal to those from function *f* you need to input *x*-values into *g* that are farther away from the *y*-axis than the *x*-values you input into *f*. So the graph of *g* is a horizontal stretch away from the *y*-axis of the graph of *f*.

Try It! 4. Why is $g(x) = 0.2x + 2$ a horizontal stretch of $f(x) = x + 2$?

EXAMPLE 5 Analyze Horizontal Compressions of Graphs

How does multiplying the input by a constant with an absolute value greater than 1 change the graph of a function?

Consider $g(x) = f(kx)$ for $|k| > 1$ when $f(x) = x^2 + 2$ and when $f(x) = |x + 1|$.

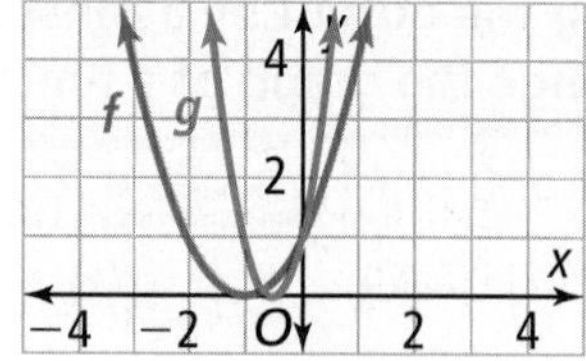

$f(x) = (x + 1)^2$

$g(x) = (2x + 1)^2$

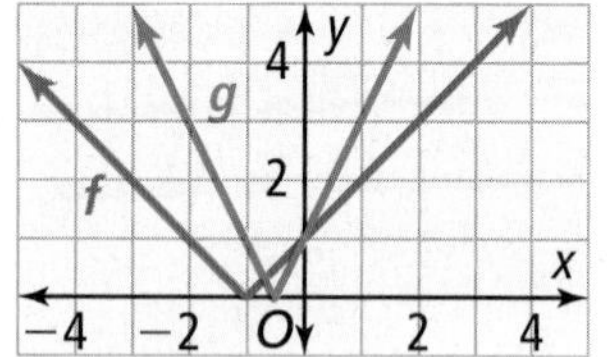

$f(x) = |x + 1|$

$g(x) = |2x + 1|$

The graph of $g(x) = (2x + 1)^2$ is a horizontal compression of $f(x) = (x + 1)^2$ toward the *y*-axis. The graph of $g(x) = |2x + 1|$ is a horizontal compression of $f(x) = |x + 1|$ toward the *y*-axis.

In general, when $g(x) = f(kx)$ for $|k| > 1$, the graph of *g* is a horizontal compression toward the *y*-axis of the graph of *f*.

COMMON ERROR
You might think that as *k* increases the graph of the function $f(kx)$ would stretch horizontally. Instead, it compresses the graph horizontally as *k* increases.

Try It! 5. Write a function with a graph that is a horizontal compression of the graph of *f*, toward the *y*-axis.

a. $f(x) = \sqrt[3]{x}$ $\qquad$ b. $f(x) = x^2$

CONCEPT SUMMARY Stretches and Compressions of Functions

	Vertical Stretch or Compression	Horizontal Stretch or Compression
WORDS	$g(x) = kf(x)$ stretches or compresses the graph of f vertically by a factor of k	$g(x) = f(kx)$ stretches or compresses the graph of f horizontally by a factor of k
ALGEBRA	$f(x) = \sqrt{x}$ $g(x) = 3\sqrt{x}$	$f(x) = x^2$ $g(x) = (0.6x)^2$
GRAPHS	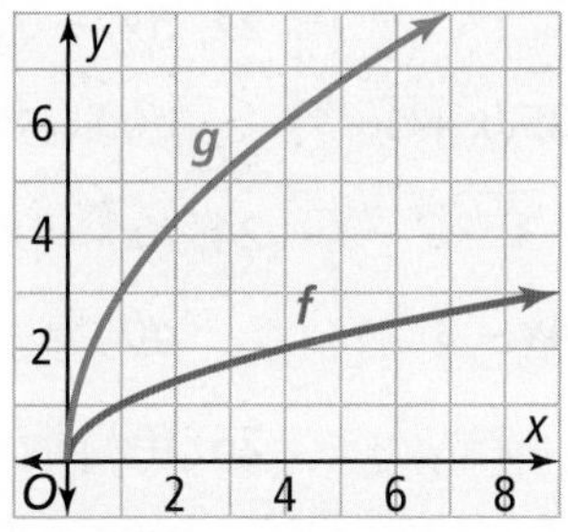	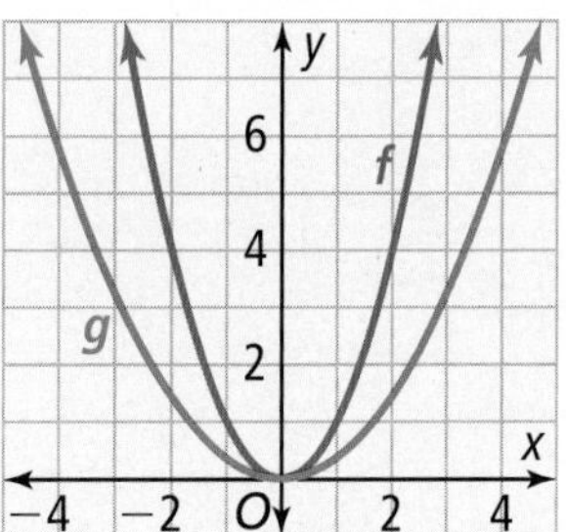

Do You UNDERSTAND?

1. ESSENTIAL QUESTION What change to a function will result in a vertical or horizontal stretch or compression of its graph?

2. **Error Analysis** A student says that the graph of the function $g(x) = 0.4f(x)$ is a horizontal compression of the function f. Explain the error the student made.

3. **Communicate Precisely** Compare and contrast a vertical stretch and a horizontal stretch.

4. **Reason** Given the function f and the constant k, write the general form for a horizontal stretch of the function. Make sure to include any constraints on k.

Do You KNOW HOW?

Tell whether the graph of g is a reflection across the x-axis of the graph of f.

5. $f(x) = 4x + 5$
   $g(x) = -4x - 5$

6. $f(x) = -3x^2 + 7$
   $g(x) = 3x^2 + 7$

Given $k = 8$, describe how the graph of each function relates to f.

7. $g(x) = f(kx)$

8. $g(x) = kf(x)$

9. Identify whether a horizontal stretch or compression was used to produce the graph of g given the graph of f shown below.

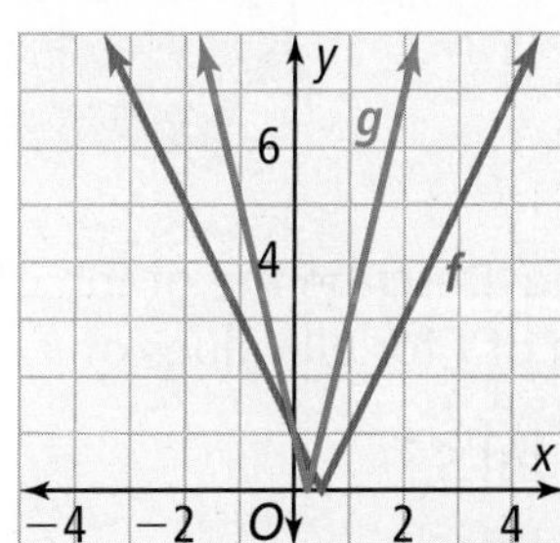

Scan for Multimedia | Practice | Tutorial | Additional Exercises Available Online

UNDERSTAND

10. Mathematical Connections Is the slope m of a line $y = mx + b$ related to vertical and horizontal compressions and stretches of the graph of the line? Explain.

11. Look for Relationships Graph $f(x) = \sqrt{x}$ and $g(x) = \sqrt{2x}$. Explain why you can consider the function g to be either a vertical stretch of f or a horizontal compression of f.

12. Make Sense and Persevere Two graphs of two quadratic functions $f(x)$ and $g(x) = f(kx)$ are shown below. What is the approximate value of k?

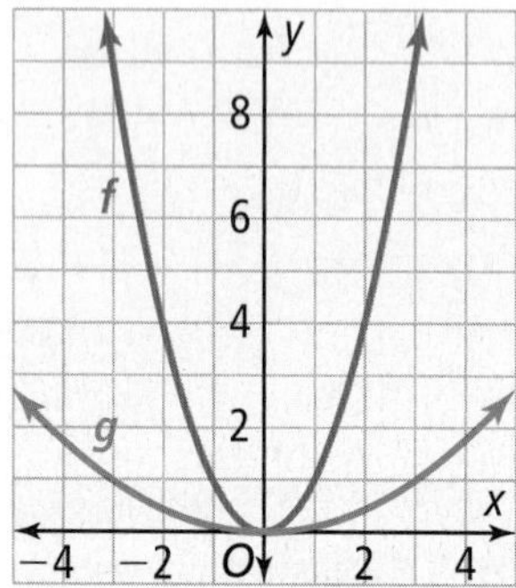

13. Error Analysis Describe and correct the error a student made in describing the relationship between the graphs of the two functions.

$f(x) = x^2 + 1$

$g(x) = (4x)^2 + 1$

Because the input of f is being multiplied by a constant to get g, the graph of g is the graph of f being horizontally stretched or compressed The constant is 4, which is greater than 1, so it is a horizontal stretch.

✗

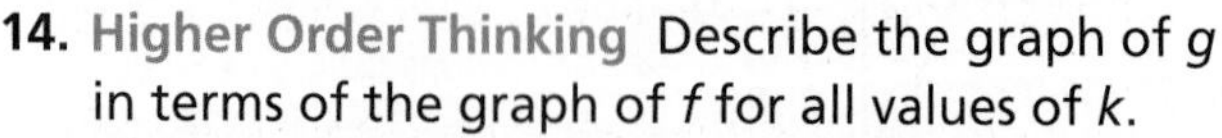

14. Higher Order Thinking Describe the graph of g in terms of the graph of f for all values of k.

a. $g(x) = kf(x)$ for $0 < |k| < 1$

b. $g(x) = kf(x)$ for $1 < |k|$

c. $g(x) = f(kx)$ for $0 < |k| < 1$

PRACTICE

Write a function with a graph that is the reflection of the graph of f across the x-axis. SEE EXAMPLE 1

15. $f(x) = x^2 - 3$

16. $f(x) = |2x + 5|$

17. $f(x) = -\sqrt{2x}$

18. $f(x) = -x + 4$

For each pair, tell whether the graph of g is a vertical or horizontal compression or stretch of the graph of f. SEE EXAMPLES 2, 3, 4 AND 5

19. $f(x) = |x + 3|$
$g(x) = 2|x + 3|$

20. $f(x) = x^2 - 4$
$g(x) = (0.5x)^2 - 4$

21. $f(x) = \sqrt{x + 1}$
$g(x) = 0.25\sqrt{x + 1}$

22. $f(x) = \sqrt[3]{x - 1}$
$g(x) = \sqrt[3]{2x - 1}$

23. $f(x) = x - 3$
$g(x) = 0.4x - 3$

24. $f(x) = |x - 2|$
$g(x) = \frac{2}{3}|x - 2|$

25. $f(x) = x^2 + 2$
$g(x) = 6x^2 + 12$

26. $f(x) = \sqrt{x}$
$g(x) = \sqrt{7x}$

For each graph, identify the transformation applied to f that results in g, and identify the value of k.

27.

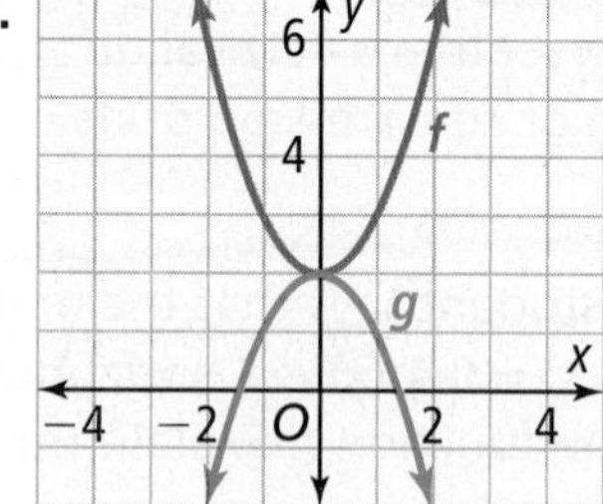

28.

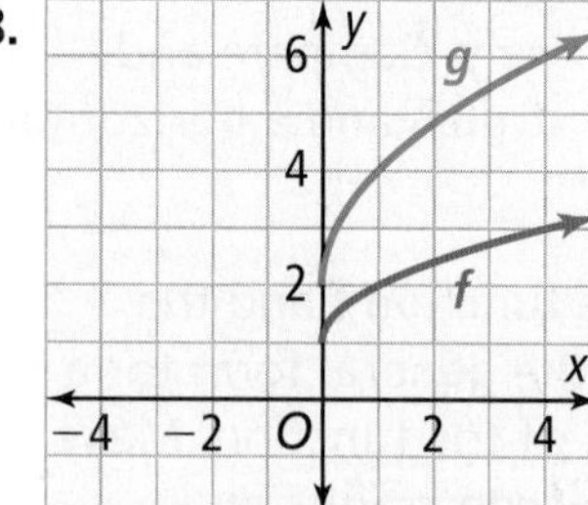

29. The graph of g is a reflection of the graph of $f(x) = \sqrt{x}$ across the x-axis and a vertical stretch of that graph by a factor of 3. Write the function g.

PRACTICE & PROBLEM SOLVING

APPLY

30. Make Sense and Persevere A company's logo is modeled by the function $f(x) = -|x| + 2$. For a new design, the company wants the logo to be narrower. What are two ways the function f could be altered so that the graph of the new function gives a narrower logo? Explain.

31. Reason The area A of a square is given by $A = s^2$, where s is a side length of the square.

a. Graph the function $A = s^2$ on a grid. How does the graph change when you double the side length of the square? Describe the changes in terms of stretches and compressions.

b. Write a function that gives the side length of a square in terms of its area.

c. Graph your function from part (b).

d. How does this graph change when you double the side length of the square? Describe the changes in terms of stretches and compressions.

32. Model With Mathematics The speed of a wave in the ocean in meters per second can be determined using the function $f(x) = 3.13\sqrt{x}$, where x represents the depth in meters of the water under the wave.

a. Graph the function.

b. Identify the domain and range.

c. How fast are the waves in the figure moving over the water?

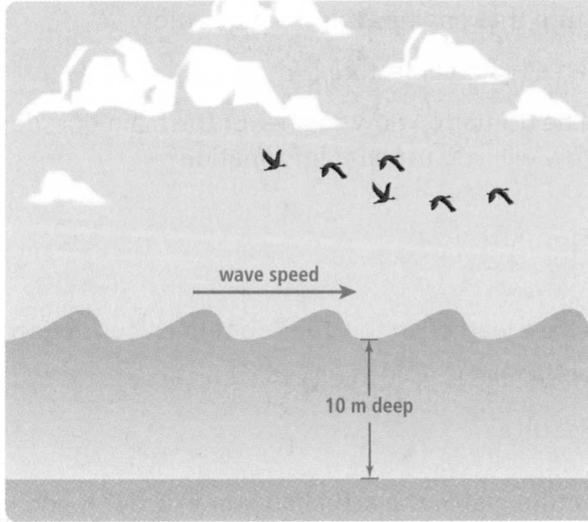

ASSESSMENT PRACTICE

33. What is a function rule for g such that the graph of g is a reflection across the x-axis of the graph of $f(x) = |2x + 5|$?

34. SAT/ACT Which function has a graph that is a vertical stretch of the graph of $f(x) = 4x^2 - 1$?

Ⓐ $g(x) = 6(4x^2 - 1)$

Ⓑ $g(x) = 0.6(4x^2 - 1)$

Ⓒ $g(x) = 4(6x)^2 - 1$

Ⓓ $g(x) = -(4x^2 - 1)$

35. Performance Task The period, in seconds, of a pendulum's swing on Earth is given by the function $f(x) = 2\pi\sqrt{\frac{x}{9.8}}$, where x is the length of the pendulum in meters. On the moon, the equation that gives the period of the pendulum is $g(x) = 2\pi\sqrt{\frac{x}{1.6}}$.

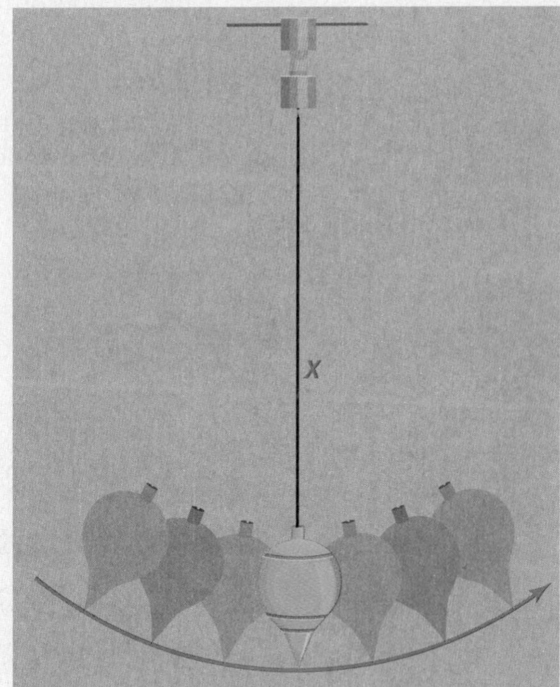

Part A Graph both functions on the same grid.

Part B Write the moon function in terms of $f(x)$.

Part C If $g(x) = kf(x)$, what does the value of k tell you about how a pendulum swings on the moon as compared to on Earth?

Part D Describe how the graph of g differs from the graph of f in terms of stretches and compressions.

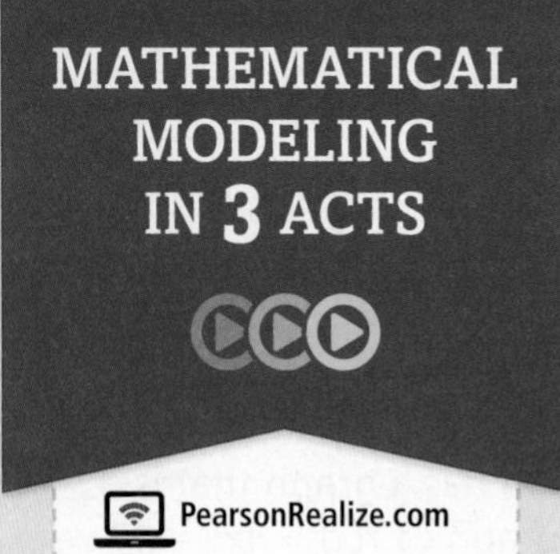

PearsonRealize.com

Video

Edgy Tiles

For more than 3,000 years, people have glazed ceramics and other materials to make decorative tile patterns. Tiles used to be used only in important buildings or by the very rich, but now you can find tiles in almost any house.

Before you start tiling a wall, floor, or other surface, it's important to plan out how your design will look. Think about this during the Mathematical Modeling in 3 Acts lesson.

ACT 1 Identify the Problem

1. What is the first question that comes to mind after watching the video?
2. Write down the main question you will answer about what you saw in the video.
3. Make an initial conjecture that answers this main question.
4. Explain how you arrived at your conjecture.
5. What information will be useful to know to answer the main question? How can you get it? How will you use that information?

ACT 2 Develop a Model

6. Use the math that you have learned in this Topic to refine your conjecture.

ACT 3 Interpret the Results

7. Did your refined conjecture match the actual answer exactly? If not, what might explain the difference?

10-6 Operations With Functions

PearsonRealize.com

I CAN… add, subtract, and multiply functions.

EXPLORE & REASON

The graphs of $f(x) = x^2$ and $g(x) = x^2 + 3$ are shown.

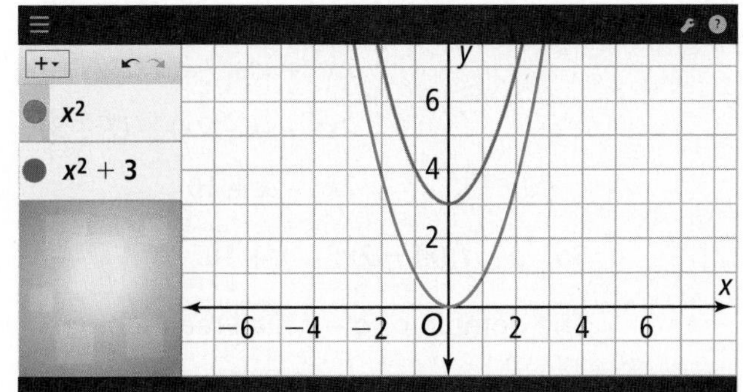

A. Compare the domain and range of each function.

B. Graph another function of the form $f(x) = x^2 + c$ using a different constant added to x^2.

C. **Look for Relationships** Does changing a function by adding a constant alter the domain of the function? Does changing a function by adding a constant alter the range of the function? Explain.

ESSENTIAL QUESTION

How can you extend addition, subtraction, and multiplication from numbers to functions?

CONCEPTUAL UNDERSTANDING

EXAMPLE 1 Add and Subtract Functions

A. If $f(x) = 2x - 3$ and $g(x) = 2x^2 + x + 7$, what is $f + g$? How do the domain and range of $f + g$ compare with the domains and ranges of f and g?

Just as you can add numbers, expressions, and polynomials, you can also add functions. The sum of two functions f and g is another function called $f + g$. The function $f + g$ is defined as $(f + g)(x) = f(x) + g(x)$.

STUDY TIP
In $f + g$, the plus sign indicates the addition of functions. In $f(x) + g(x)$, the plus sign indicates the addition of numbers.

$$f(x) + g(x) = (2x - 3) + (2x^2 + x + 7)$$
$$= 2x^2 + (2x + x) + (-3 + 7)$$
$$= 2x^2 + 3x + 4$$

When adding polynomials, you add the like terms.

So, $(f + g)(x) = 2x^2 + 3x + 4$.

Notice that f is a linear function and g and $f + g$ are quadratic functions. The domains of f, g, and $f + g$ are the same: all real numbers. The range of f is all real numbers. You can find the range of the quadratic functions graphically or algebraically. The range of g is $y \geq 6.875$ and the range of $f + g$ is $y \geq 2.875$.

In general, the domain and range of the combined functions may be different from the domain and range of the original functions. If a value is not in the domain of one of the functions, it is not in the domain of the sum or difference of the original functions either.

CONTINUED ON THE NEXT PAGE

EXAMPLE 1 CONTINUED

B. If $f(x) = 2x - 3$ and $g(x) = 2x^2 + x + 7$, what is $g - f$?

The difference of two functions $g - f$ is defined as $(g - f)(x) = g(x) - f(x)$.

$$\begin{aligned} g(x) - f(x) &= (2x^2 + x + 7) - (2x - 3) \\ &= 2x^2 + x + 7 - 2x + 3 \\ &= 2x^2 + (x - 2x) + (7 + 3) \\ &= 2x^2 - x + 10 \end{aligned}$$

COMMON ERROR
Recall that when subtracting a polynomial, every term in that polynomial must be subtracted.

So, $(g - f)(x) = 2x^2 - x + 10$.

The domain of $g - f$ is all real numbers, and the range is $y \geq 9.875$.

Try It! **1.** If $f(x) = 15x^2 - 8x + 4$ and $g(x) = 11x + 6$, what is $f - g$?

EXAMPLE 2 Multiply Functions

A. What is the product of the two functions $f(x) = 9x + 20$ and $g(x) = x + 5$?

The product of two functions $f \cdot g$ is defined as $(f \cdot g)(x) = f(x) \cdot g(x)$.

$$\begin{aligned} f(x) \cdot g(x) &= (9x + 20)(x + 5) \\ &= 9x(x) + 9x(5) + 20(x) + 20(5) \\ &= 9x^2 + 45x + 20x + 100 \\ &= 9x^2 + 65x + 100 \end{aligned}$$

USE STRUCTURE
Think about the properties you could use to simplify the product of the two functions.

So, $(f \cdot g)(x) = 9x^2 + 65x + 100$.

B. Are the domain and range of functions f and g the same as the domain and range of $f \cdot g$?

Since f and g are both linear functions, the domain and range for both functions are all real numbers.

The product of f and g is a quadratic function, the domain is all real numbers, but the range is limited.

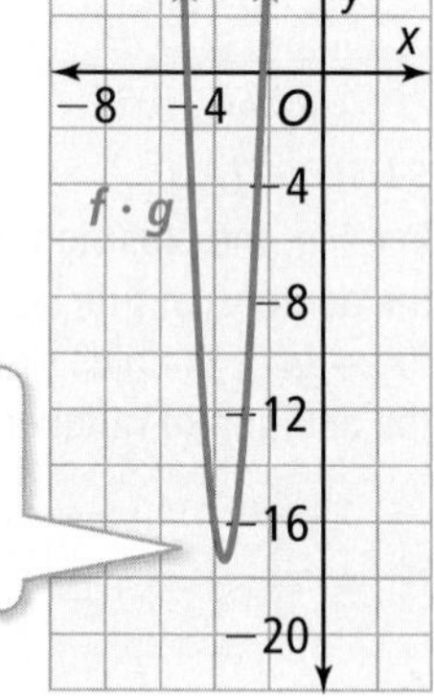

The vertex is at (−3.6, −17.4), and the graph opens up, so the range is $y \geq -17.4$.

The domain of $f \cdot g$ is the same as the domain of f and g, but the range is different.

Try It! **2.** Find the product of f and g. What are the domain and the range of the product?

a. $f(x) = \sqrt{x}$
$g(x) = 2x - 1$

b. $f(x) = 3x^2 + 4$
$g(x) = 2^x$

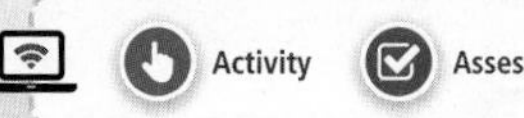

APPLICATION

EXAMPLE 3 Apply Function Operations

A cylinder has a height that is twice its radius. The cylinder is sealed at the top and bottom to form a container. Find a function for the total surface area of the container. What dimensions would yield a total surface area of about 120 ft^2?

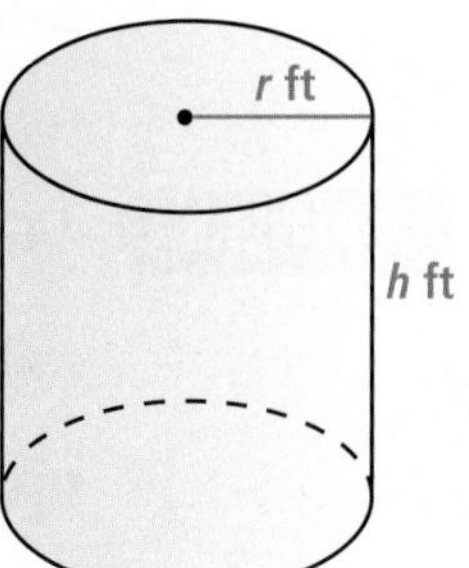

Formulate Write a function for the surface area of the top and bottom of the cylinder.

$f(r) = 2 \cdot \text{area of the base}$

$= 2\pi r^2$

Write a function for the lateral surface area of the cylinder. Recall that the lateral surface is the curved surface of the cylinder. Unrolled, it would form a rectangle.

$g(r) = \text{height} \cdot \text{circumference}$

$= h \cdot 2\pi r$

$= 2r \cdot 2\pi r$ — The height is twice the radius.

$= 4\pi r^2$

Compute The total surface area is the sum of the area of the bases and the lateral surface area. Find $f + g$.

$f(r) + g(r) = 2\pi r^2 + 4\pi r^2$

$= 6\pi r^2$

Graph $(f + g)(r) = 6\pi r^2$ to find the value of r that corresponds to a total surface area of 120 ft^2.

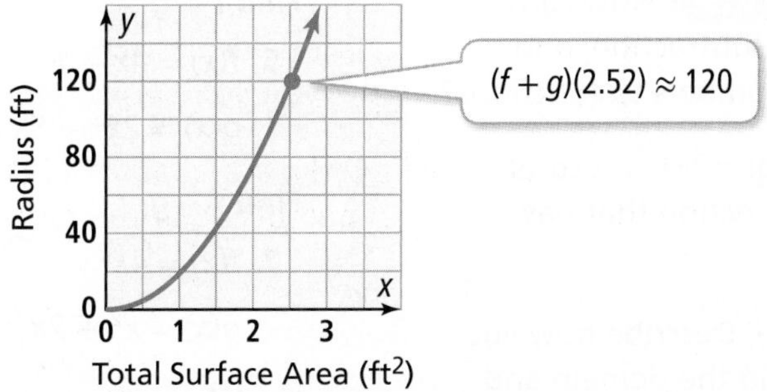

Interpret When the radius is 2.52 ft, the total surface area of the cylinder is about 120 ft^2. The height of the cylinder would be twice the radius, or 5.04 ft.

Try It! 3. Suppose the cylinder in Example 3 is not sealed, so the total surface area includes only the area of the bottom and the lateral surface area. What dimensions would yield a total surface area of about 120 ft^2?

CONCEPT SUMMARY Function Operations

	Adding Functions	Subtracting Functions	Multiplying Functions
ALGEBRA	$f + g$	$f - g$	$f \cdot g$
	$f(x) = x^2 + 3$	$f(x) = 3^x$	$f(x) = x + 1$
	$g(x) = 2^x$	$g(x) = x + 2$	$g(x) = x - 4$
	$f(x) + g(x) = (x^2 + 3) + (2^x)$	$f(x) - g(x) = (3^x) - (x + 2)$	$f(x) \cdot g(x) = (x + 1)(x - 4)$
			$= x^2 - 4x + x - 4$
	$(f + g)(x) = x^2 + 3 + 2^x$	$(f - g)(x) = 3^x - x - 2$	$(f \cdot g)(x) = x^2 - 3x - 4$
GRAPHS	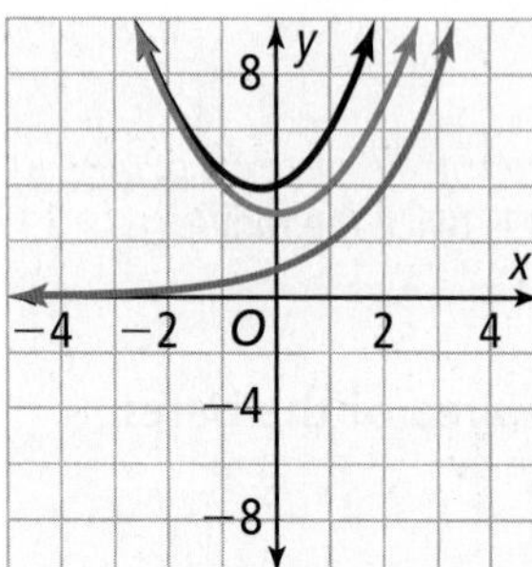	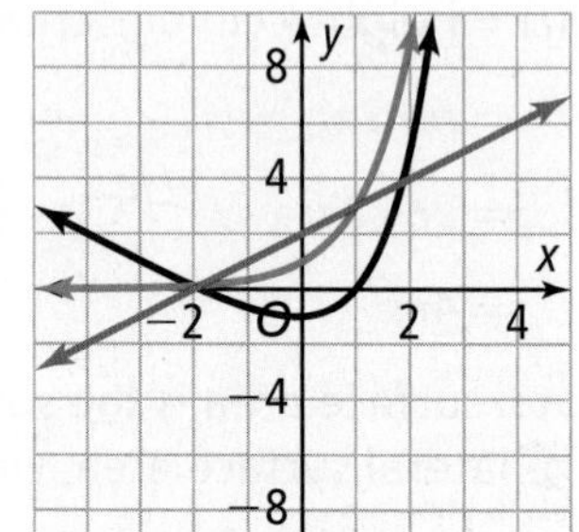	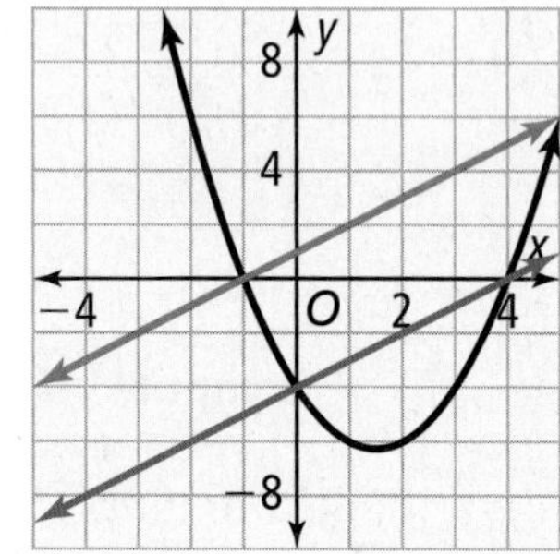

Do You UNDERSTAND?

1. ESSENTIAL QUESTION How can you extend addition, subtraction, and multiplication from numbers to functions?

2. **Use Structure** What property is useful when subtracting a function that has multiple terms?

3. **Use Appropriate Tools** Describe how you can use a graph to find the domain and range of two combined functions.

4. **Error Analysis** A student claimed that the functions $f(x) = \sqrt{x}$ and $g(x) = 2x - 5$ cannot be combined because there are no like terms. Explain the error the student made.

Do You KNOW HOW?

Find $f + g$.

5. $f(x) = 4x + 1$
   $g(x) = 2x^2 - 5x$

6. $f(x) = x^2$
   $g(x) = 3^x$

Find $f - g$.

7. $f(x) = 4x^2$
   $g(x) = x^2 + 2x + 7$

8. $f(x) = 6x + 5$
   $g(x) = \sqrt{2x}$

Find $f \cdot g$.

9. $f(x) = 3x^2 - 2$
   $g(x) = x^2 - 4x$

10. $f(x) = 6x$
    $g(x) = 8^x$

Go Online | PearsonRealize.com

PRACTICE & PROBLEM SOLVING

UNDERSTAND

11. Mathematical Connections How is adding functions like adding polynomials? How is it different?

12. Look for Relationships Write two functions that, when combined by adding, have a different domain than at least one of the original functions.

13. Make Sense and Persevere Given the graphs of f and g, sketch the graphs of $f + g$ and $f \bullet g$.

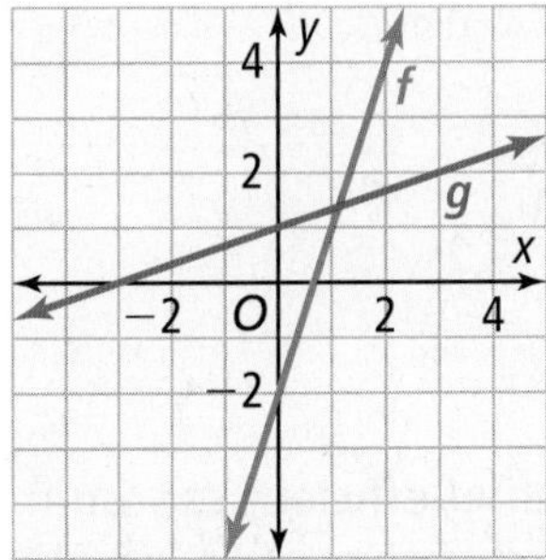

14. Error Analysis Describe and correct the error a student made in multiplying the two functions, $f(x) = x^3 + 3x^2 + 1$ and $g(x) = 2x - 1$.

$$(x^3 + 3x^2 + 1)(2x - 1)$$
$$= x^3(2x) + 3x^2(2x) + 2x$$
$$= 2x^4 + 6x^3 + 2x$$

✗

15. Higher Order Thinking What two functions could you multiply to create the function shown in the graph? How do the domain and range of each of the functions compare to the domain and range of the graphed function?

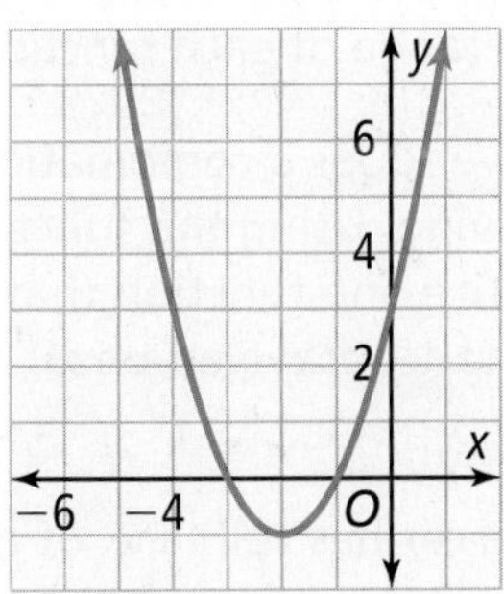

PRACTICE

Find $f + g$. SEE EXAMPLE 1

16. $f(x) = 6x^3 + 7x$

$g(x) = x^2 - 3x + 2$

17. $f(x) = 3\sqrt{x}$

$g(x) = -2x + 4$

Find $f - g$. SEE EXAMPLE 1

18. $f(x) = 2x^3 + 2x^2 - 3$

$g(x) = 8x + 15$

19. $f(x) = 7^x$

$g(x) = 5x^2 - 2x - 4$

Find $f \bullet g$. SEE EXAMPLE 2

20. $f(x) = 9x - 2$

$g(x) = x^2 + 4x - 7$

21. $f(x) = 3x^2 + 8x + 2$

$g(x) = -6x + 1$

22. $f(x) = 3^x$

$g(x) = 5x^2 - 2$

23. $f(x) = \sqrt{5x}$

$g(x) = 7x + 2$

Given the graphs of f and g, graph $f + g$. Compare the domain and range of $f + g$ to the domains and ranges of f and g.

24.

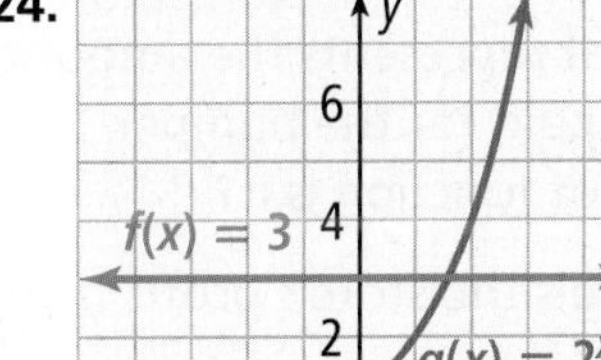
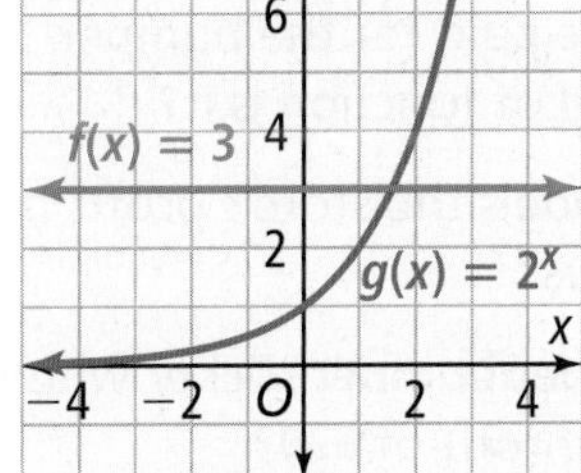

25.

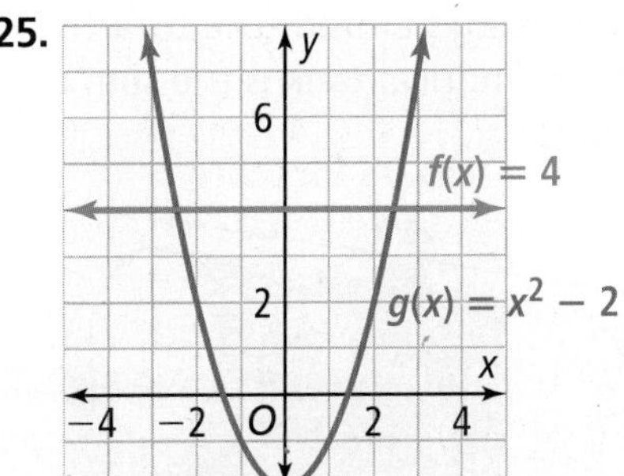

26. A florist charges \$10 for delivery plus an additional \$2 per mile from the flower shop. The florist pays the delivery driver \$0.50 per mile and \$5 for gas per delivery. If x is the number of miles a delivery location is from the flower shop, what expression models the amount of money the florist earns for each delivery? SEE EXAMPLE 3

Practice | Tutorial
Mixed Review Available Online

PRACTICE & PROBLEM SOLVING

APPLY

27. **Make Sense and Persevere** A laser tag center charges \$50 to set up a party, and \$75 per hour. The center pays its employees that work the party a total of \$36 per hour.

  a. Write a function f that represents the amount of revenue from a party that runs for x hours.

  b. Write a function g that represents the expenses for a party that runs for x hours.

  c. Write a combined function that represents the amount of profit the laser tag center makes on a party that runs x hours.

28. **Reason** A store is selling bumper stickers in support of a local sports team. The function $h(x) = -20x^2 + 80x + 240$ models the revenue, in dollars, the store expects to make by increasing the price of a bumper sticker x dollars over the original price of \$2. The store paid a total of \$200 for the bumper stickers.

  a. Write a function that represents the amount of money the store paid for the bumper stickers. What kind of function is it?

  b. What function models the store's profit from the bumper stickers?

  c. What is the price per bumper sticker when the store makes a profit of \$20?

29. **Model With Mathematics** The surface of a cylindrical tank is being painted. The total surface area of a cylindrical tank is the sum of two area functions.

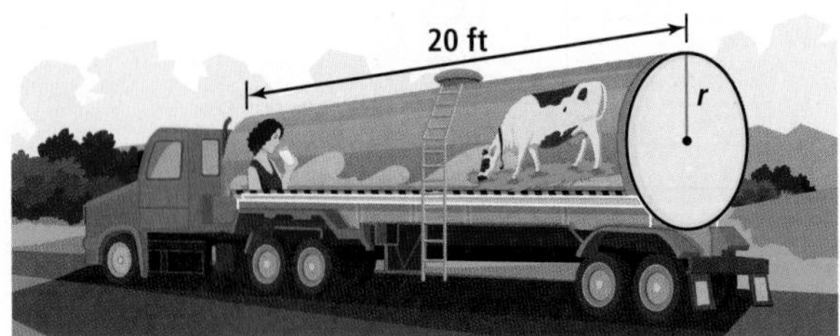

  a. Write a function that gives the total area of the two circular ends as a function of radius.

  b. Write a function that gives the lateral surface area of the cylinder as a function of radius.

  c. Combine the functions from parts (a) and (b) to get the total surface area of the cylinder as a function of radius.

ASSESSMENT PRACTICE

30. Given the functions $f(x) = x + 8$ and $g(x) = x^2 - 9$, which of the following are true statements about $f - g$? Select all that apply.

  Ⓐ It is a linear function.
  Ⓑ It is a quadratic function.
  Ⓒ The domain is all real numbers.
  Ⓓ The range is all real numbers.
  Ⓔ The range is $y \geq 17$.

31. **SAT/ACT** The function h is the sum of the functions $f(x) = 3x + 5$ and $g(x) = 2x^2 - 6x - 2$. Which represents h?

  Ⓐ $h(x) = 5x^2 - x - 2$
  Ⓑ $h(x) = 2x^2 - 3x + 3$
  Ⓒ $h(x) = 2x^2 + 9x + 7$
  Ⓓ $h(x) = -3x + 3$

32. **Performance Task** A fuel-efficient car can travel 6 miles further per gallon than average while driving on the highway, and about 4 miles less than average while in the city.

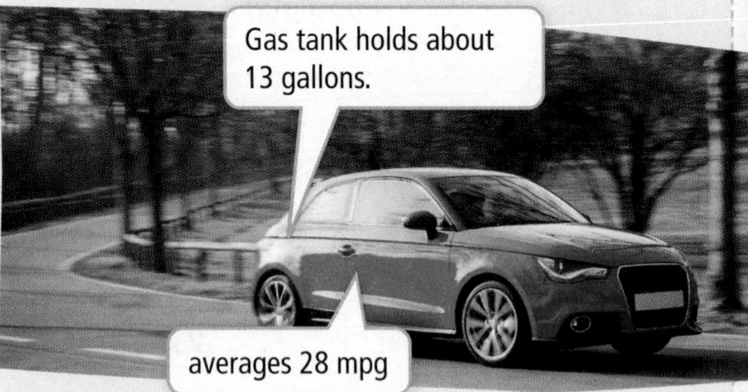

Part A Write two functions to determine the distance the driver could travel in the city or on the highway, using x gallons of gasoline.

Part B Assuming that the car has full tank of gas, what is the domain and range of each function?

Part C Suppose the driver does a combination of city and highway driving. Using the functions you found in Part A, write one function that could represent the distance traveled on x gallons of gasoline.

Part D Assume that the car has full tank of gas, what is the domain and range of the function you found in Part C?

Activity Assess

10-7 Inverse Functions

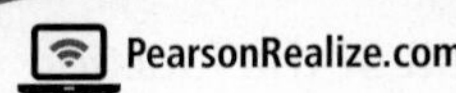

PearsonRealize.com

I CAN… use inverse functions to solve problems.

VOCABULARY

- inverse of a function

EXPLORE & REASON

The tables of data show food orders for different parties.

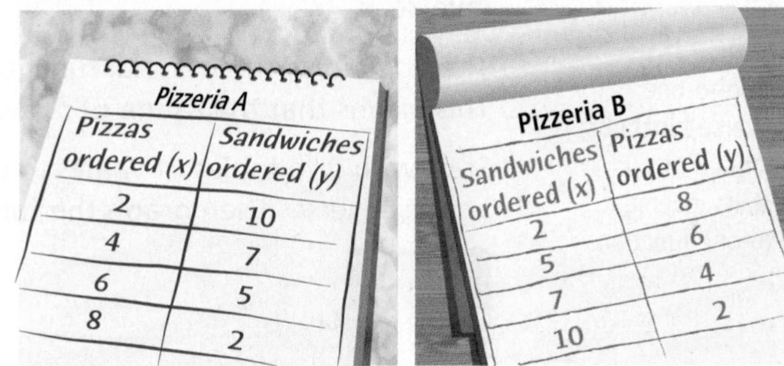

A. Graph the data points shown in the tables. Use a different color for each data set.

B. Look for Relationships What observations can you make about the graphs of the data in the two tables?

C. What similarities and differences do you notice about the data?

? ESSENTIAL QUESTION How can you use inverse functions to help solve problems?

CONCEPTUAL UNDERSTANDING

EXAMPLE 1 Understand Inverse Functions

What is the inverse of the function $f(x) = 2x + 6$?

The **inverse of a function** reverses the order of the outputs and inputs of a function. The inverse of a function f is usually written as f^{-1} (read "f inverse"). If $f(x) = y$, then $f^{-1}(y) = x$ for all x in the domain of f and all y in the range of f. A function f has an inverse function f^{-1} if and only if the original function f is one-to-one. The function f is also the inverse of f^{-1}.

VOCABULARY
Remember, a *one-to-one function* is a function for which each item in the range corresponds to exactly one item in the domain.

Make tables for the function and its inverse.

f	
x	y
0	6
1	8
2	10
3	12

Switch the x-values and the y-values to find the inverse.

f^{-1}	
x	y
6	0
8	1
10	2
12	3

The data in the table for the inverse function are linear. Write an equation for the inverse function.

$$m = \frac{1-0}{8-6} = \frac{1}{2}$$

Identify the slope and then use point-slope form.

$$y - y_1 = m(x - x_1)$$
$$y - 0 = \frac{1}{2}(x - 6)$$
$$y = \frac{1}{2}x - 3$$

The inverse of the function is $f^{-1}(x) = \frac{1}{2}x - 3$.

Try It! 1. How is the slope of f^{-1} related to the slope of f?

EXAMPLE 2 Graph Inverse Functions

What is the graph of $f(x) = x^2$ for $x \geq 0$? What is the graph of its inverse, f^{-1}?

COMMON ERROR
Recall that only one-to-one functions have inverse functions. By limiting the domain of $f(x) = x^2$ to $x \geq 0$, its inverse becomes a one-to-one function.

The domain of the original function f is restricted to nonnegative values. This means that the range of f^{-1} will be restricted to nonnegative values.

Start with two tables of values to show points on the graph of the function and its inverse. Then graph the functions.

f

x	y
0	0
1	1
2	4
3	9

Switch the x-values and the y-values to find points on the graph of the inverse.

f^{-1}

x	y
0	0
1	1
4	2
9	3

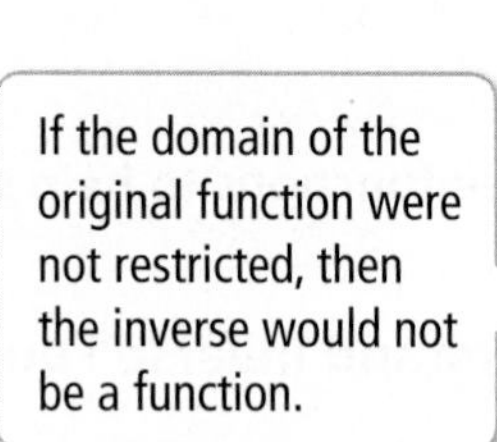

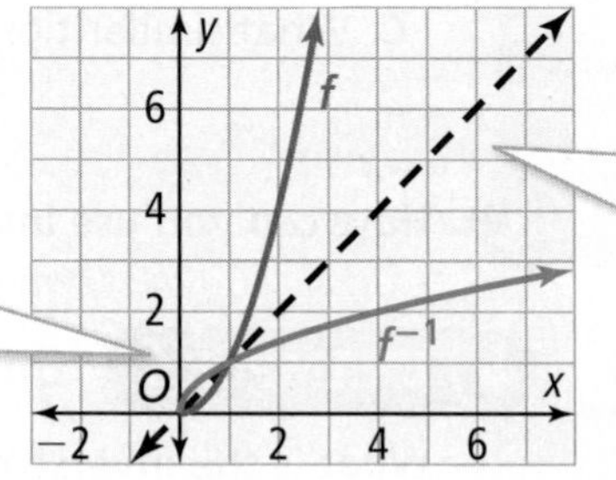

Notice that if the grid were folded along the line of the equation $y = x$, the original function and its inverse would coincide.

The graph of the inverse of a function is a reflection of the graph of the original function across the line representing the equation $y = x$.

Try It! **2.** Graph each function and its inverse.

a. $f(x) = 3x - 2$

b. $f(x) = 2x^2, x \geq 0$

EXAMPLE 3 Find the Inverse of a Function Algebraically

How can you find the inverse function of $f(x) = 2x + 6$ algebraically?

Write the original function as an equation.

$$y = 2x + 6$$

$$x = 2y + 6$$

$$x - 6 = 2y$$

$$\frac{1}{2}x - 3 = y$$

Switch x and y to switch domain and range. Then solve for y.

The inverse function of $f(x) = 2x + 6$ is $f^{-1}(x) = \frac{1}{2}x - 3$.

LOOK FOR RELATIONSHIPS
What are the similarities and differences between the processes for finding the inverse of a function algebraically and by using a table?

Try It! **3.** Find the inverse of each function.

a. $f(x) = 3x^2, x \geq 0$

b. $f(x) = x - 7$

APPLICATION

EXAMPLE 4 Interpret Inverse Functions

Keenan plans to fly 1,097 miles from Miami to New York City to help assemble a dinosaur exhibit at a museum. He wants to use the miles he earns from his credit card purchases to pay for his flight. How much will Keenan need to spend in order to earn enough miles for the flight from Miami to New York City?

Formulate Find the function f that represents the balance of Keenan's airline miles.

miles balance = mile per dollar spent • amount spent + bonus miles

$$f(x) = 0.1 \cdot x + 500$$

Since Keenan earns 1 mile for every $10 he spends, he earns 0.1 mile for every $1 that he spends.

Find the inverse of the function.

$$y = 0.1x + 500$$
$$x = 0.1y + 500$$
$$x - 500 = 0.1y$$
$$10(x - 500) = (0.1y)10$$
$$10x - 5{,}000 = y$$

Reverse the variables and solve for y to find the inverse function.

The inverse function is $f^{-1}(x) = 10x - 5{,}000$. The inverse function represents the amount Keenan spends, $f^{-1}(x)$, to earn x miles.

Compute Substitute 1,097 for x.

$$f^{-1}(1{,}097) = 10(1{,}097) - 5{,}000$$
$$= 10{,}970 - 5{,}000$$
$$= 5{,}970$$

Interpret Keenan needs to spend $5,970 to earn enough miles for his trip.

Try It! **4.** Suppose the credit card company changes the program so Keenan earns 1 mile for every $8 he spends. How would that change the amount of money Keenan needs to spend to earn the miles for his trip?

CONCEPT SUMMARY Finding the Inverse of a Function

TABLES Switch the x-values and y-values in the table.

x	y
1	7
2	11
3	15

→

x	y
7	1
11	2
15	3

GRAPH Reflect the graph across the line represented by the equation $y = x$. If needed, restrict the domain of the original function so its inverse will also be a function.

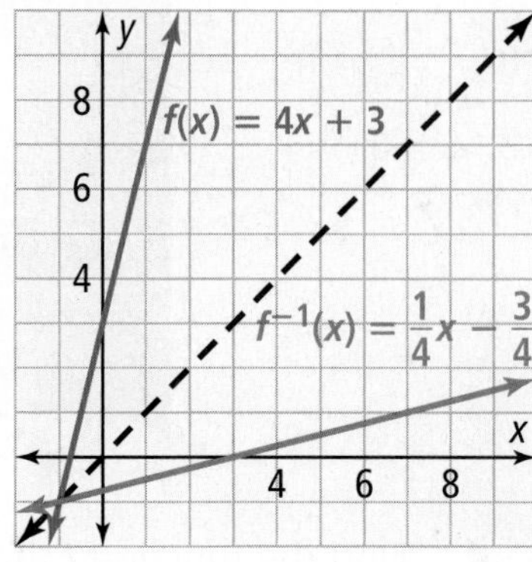

ALGEBRA When the function is written as an equation, in terms of x and y, switch the variables and solve for y.

$y = 4x + 3$

$$x = 4y + 3$$
$$x - 3 = 4y$$
$$\frac{x-3}{4} = y$$
$$y = \frac{1}{4}x - \frac{3}{4}$$

Do You UNDERSTAND?

1. **ESSENTIAL QUESTION** How can you use inverse functions to help solve problems?

2. **Error Analysis** A student claims that the graph of the inverse of a function is a reflection across the x-axis of the graph of the original function. Explain the error the student made.

3. **Vocabulary** Does every function have an inverse function? Explain.

4. **Reason** If the graph of a function crosses the x-axis twice, does the function have an inverse function? Explain.

Do You KNOW HOW?

Copy and complete each table of values for the function. Then make a table of values for the inverse of the function.

5. $y = -2x + 3$

x	y
0	■
1	■
2	■
3	■

6. $y = 8x$

x	y
0	■
1	■
2	■
3	■

Write the inverse of each function.

7. $f(x) = 2x + 11$

8. $f(x) = \sqrt{x}$

PRACTICE & PROBLEM SOLVING

UNDERSTAND

9. Mathematical Connections How is the inverse of a function similar to inverse operations? How is it different? Explain.

10. Error Analysis Describe and correct the error a student made finding the inverse of $f(x) = -x + 4$.

$y = -x + 4$
$-x = y + 4$
$-x - 4 = y$
The inverse of the function is
$f^{-1}(x) = -x - 4$.

11. Reason Does each function have an inverse function? If so, write the inverse function. If not, explain how you could restrict the domain so that function *f* does have an inverse function.

a. $f(x) = 5x$

b. $f(x) = 5x^2$

c. $f(x) = |5x|$

12. Construct Arguments Can a relation that is not a function have a function as its inverse? Give an example to support your answer.

13. Use Structure What is the inverse of the function graphed below? Describe how you found your answer.

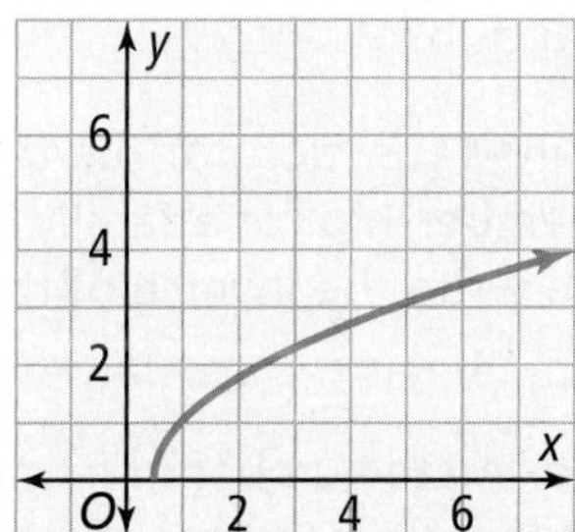

14. Higher Order Thinking What is the inverse of $f(x) = -x$? Use a graph of the function to support your answer.

PRACTICE

For each table, create a table of values for the inverse function. SEE EXAMPLE 1

15.

x	y
0	11
1	15
2	19
3	23

16.

x	y
0	3
1	4
2	7
3	12

Graph each function and its inverse. SEE EXAMPLE 2

17. $f(x) = -\frac{1}{3}x + 2$

18. $f(x) = \frac{3}{4}x - 1$

19. $f(x) = 0.25x^2, x \geq 0$

20. $f(x) = \sqrt{3x}$

Tell whether the functions *f* and *g* are inverses or not. SEE EXAMPLE 2

21.

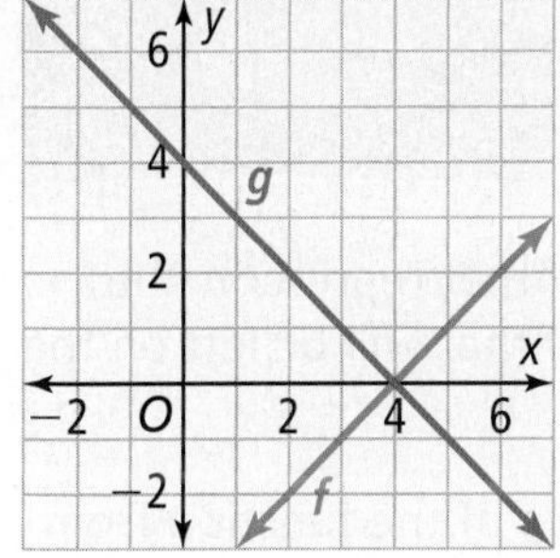

22.

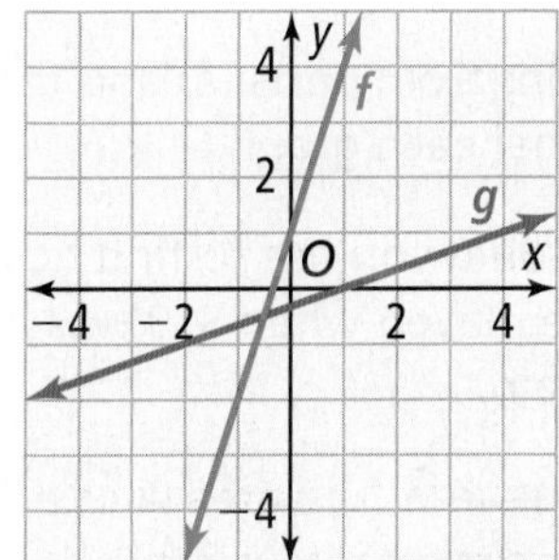

Find the inverse of each function. SEE EXAMPLE 3

23. $f(x) = -5x - 11$

24. $f(x) = 0.7x + 4$

25. $f(x) = 7x + 12$

26. $f(x) = 9x^2, x \geq 0$

27. $f(x) = x^2 + 7, x \geq 0$

28. $f(x) = \sqrt{4x + 1}$

29. Camilla has \$100 in her savings account. She will put 25% of her salary in her account every time she gets paid at work. Camilla wants to save \$1,250 to go on vacation this summer. Write and evaluate the inverse function to find the amount of money Camilla must earn at work to reach her savings goal. SEE EXAMPLE 4

PRACTICE & PROBLEM SOLVING

Practice Tutorial

Mixed Review Available Online

APPLY

30. **Reason** The perimeter P of a square is given by the equation $P = 4s$, where s is a side length of the square. What is the inverse of $P = 4s$? What type of question could you answer by using the inverse function?

31. **Model With Mathematics** A raffle has a \$50 gift card to a miniature golf course as a prize.

a. Write a function f that represents the amount of money that will be left on the gift card after x games.

b. What is the inverse of the function from part (a)?

c. Graph the functions from parts (a) and (b) on the same grid. Label each graph.

d. Which function would you use to find how many games were played when \$10 was left on the card? Explain.

32. **Make Sense and Persevere** The area A of a circle in terms of the circle's radius r is $A = \pi r^2$.

a. Explain the restrictions on the domain of the function $A = \pi r^2$ and the inverse function in this context.

b. Write the inverse function of $A = \pi r^2$.

c. Use the inverse function you wrote in part (b) to find the radius of a circle that has an area of 50.25 in.^{2}. Round your answer to the nearest inch.

ASSESSMENT PRACTICE

33. Match each function with its inverse.

I. $f(x) = 4x - 8$	A. $f(x)^{-1} = \frac{1}{2}\sqrt{x}$
II. $f(x) = 0.25x - 2$	B. $f(x)^{-1} = 0.25x + 2$
III. $f(x) = 4x^2, x \geq 0$	C. $f(x)^{-1} = 4x + 8$
IV. $f(x) = 2x^2, x \geq 0$	D. $f(x)^{-1} = \sqrt{\frac{1}{2}x}$

34. **SAT/ACT** What is the inverse of the function $f(x) = -\sqrt{2x}$?

Ⓐ $f(x)^{-1} = 0.5x^2, x \geq 0$
Ⓑ $f(x)^{-1} = 0.5x^2, x \leq 0$
Ⓒ $f(x)^{-1} = 0.5x^2$
Ⓓ $f(x)^{-1} = -0.5x^2$

35. **Performance Task** A health club advertises a new family membership plan, as shown in the advertisement.

Part A Write two functions, one that gives the total cost of a membership for the first member and one that gives the total cost for each additional member. Write each function, y, in terms of the number of months, x, a member belongs to the health club.

Part B Write a combined function for the total cost on the family membership for a family of three members. Then write the inverse of the function.

Part C Find the approximate number of months that a family of three will be members of the health club if they spend a total of \$1,380.

TOPIC 10

Topic Review

TOPIC ESSENTIAL QUESTION

1. What are some operations on functions that you can use to create models and solve problems?

Vocabulary Review

Choose the correct term to complete each sentence.

2. The __________ is the function $f(x) = \sqrt[3]{x}$.
3. A(n) __________ reverses the inputs and outputs of a function.
4. The __________ is the function $f(x) = \sqrt{x}$.

- square root function
- inverse of a function
- cube root function

Concepts & Skills Review

LESSON 10-1 The Square Root Function

Quick Review

The **square root function** is $f(x) = \sqrt{x}$.

Example

How does the graph of $g(x) = \sqrt{x-4}$ compare to the graph of $f(x) = \sqrt{x}$?

Graph each function.

For each *y*-value, the corresponding *x*-value is 4 units more for function *g* than it is for function *f*.

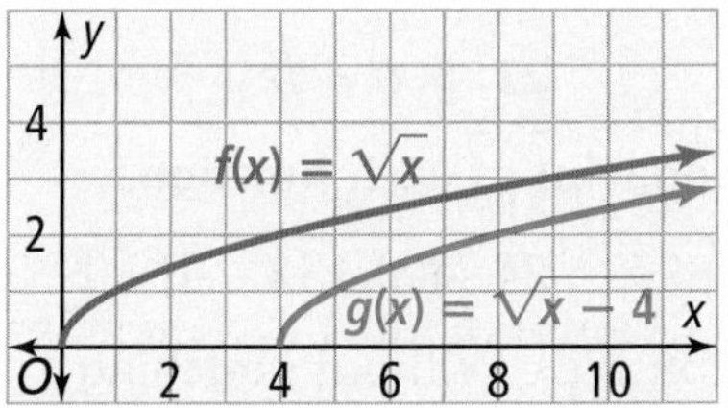

The graph of $g(x) = \sqrt{x-4}$ is a horizontal translation of $f(x) = \sqrt{x}$ 4 units to the right. The domain for function *f* is $x \geq 0$, and the domain for function *g* is $x \geq 4$. The range for both functions is the same, $y \geq 0$.

Practice & Problem Solving

How does each graph compare to the graph of $f(x) = \sqrt{x}$?

5. $g(x) = \sqrt{x} + 4$
6. $g(x) = \sqrt{x-8}$
7. $g(x) = \sqrt{x-1} - 5$
8. $g(x) = \sqrt{x+2} - 8$

Write an expression that represents each function.

9. $g(x)$, which is a translation 5 units down of $f(x) = \sqrt{x}$
10. $h(x)$, which is a translation 2 units left of $f(x) = \sqrt{x}$
11. **Use Appropriate Tools** Use a graphing calculator to graph $f(x) = -\sqrt{x-3}$. Describe the domain and range of the function.
12. **Communicate Precisely** The maximum speed of a sailboat is measured in knots and is estimated using the equation $s(\ell) = 1.34\sqrt{\ell}$, where ℓ is the length of the sailboat in feet. What is the approximate speed of a sailboat that has a length of 45 ft?

TOPIC 10 REVIEW

LESSON 10-2 The Cube Root Function

Quick Review

The **cube root function** is $f(x) = \sqrt[3]{x}$.

Example

For the function $f(x) = \sqrt[3]{x+2}$, how does the average rate of change from $2 \le x \le 4$ compare to the average rate of change from $6 \le x \le 8$?

Evaluate the function for each x-value.

Interval: $2 \le x \le 4$

$f(2) = \sqrt[3]{2+2} \approx 1.59$ $\quad$ $f(4) = \sqrt[3]{4+2} \approx 1.82$

Interval: $6 \le x \le 8$

$f(6) = \sqrt[3]{6+2} = 2$ $\quad$ $f(8) = \sqrt[3]{8+2} \approx 2.15$

Find the average rate of change over each interval.

From $2 \le x \le 4$: $\quad$ From $6 \le x \le 8$:

$\frac{1.82 - 1.59}{4 - 2} \approx 0.12$ $\quad$ $\frac{2.15 - 2}{8 - 6} \approx 0.08$

The average rate of change of the function $f(x) = \sqrt[3]{x+2}$ decreases as the x-values of the interval increase.

Practice and Problem Solving

Describe translations that transform the graph of $f(x) = \sqrt[3]{x}$ into the graph of the given function.

13. $g(x) = \sqrt[3]{x+5}$
14. $h(x) = \sqrt[3]{x} + 4$
15. $j(x) = \sqrt[3]{x-1} + 2$
16. $p(x) = \sqrt[3]{x+1.5} - 2.5$

Calculate the average rate of change for each function over the given interval.

17. $f(x) = \sqrt[3]{x}$ for $5 \le x \le 9$
18. $g(x) = \sqrt[3]{x+6}$ for $-3 \le x \le 0$
19. **Look for Relationships** Compare the average rates of change for $f(x) = \sqrt[3]{x}$ and $g(x) = \sqrt[3]{x-3}$ for $-2 \le x \le 2$.
20. **Communicate Precisely** A fish store needs more cube-shaped fish tanks for its display shelves. Each fish requires 1 ft^3 of water, and it costs \$5 per ft^3 for the tanks. Write a cube root function that gives the side lengths of the container x in inches for a given cost C.

LESSON 10-3 Analyzing Functions Graphically

Quick Review

If you know the algebraic structure of a function, you can often use its graph to determine key features of the function.

Example

For the function $f(x) = \sqrt{x-5}$, identify the domain and range, maximum and minimum values, and axis of symmetry, and describe the end behavior.

First graph the function.

The domain is $x \ge 5$, and the range is $y \ge 0$.

The minimum is 0 when $x = 5$.

There is no axis of symmetry.

As $x \to \infty$, $f(x) \to \infty$, and as $x \to 5$, $f(x) \to 0$.

Practice & Problem Solving

Sketch the graph of each function and identify its domain and range.

21. $f(x) = x^2 + 6$
22. $g(x) = \sqrt{x+5}$

Describe the end behavior of each function.

23. $j(x) = -5^x$
24. $d(x) = |x - 4| - 2$
25. **Look for Relationships** Without sketching the graph, how can you identify the end behavior of $f(x) = x^2 - 5x + 8$?
26. **Model With Mathematics** The height of a ball thrown from the top of a building is modeled by $h(t) = -16t^2 + 48t + 80$, where $h(t)$ is the height of the ball in feet after t seconds. The height of another ball hit by a bat on a small hill is modeled by $g(t) = -16t^2 + 98t + 20$. Give the maximum values and the axes of symmetry for both functions.

LESSON 10-4 Translations of Functions

Quick Review

The graph of $g(x) = f(x) + k$ is the graph of f shifted up $|k|$ units when $k > 0$ or translated down $|k|$ units when $k < 0$.

The graph of $g(x) = f(x - h)$ is the graph of f shifted right $|h|$ units when $h > 0$ or translated left $|h|$ units when $h < 0$.

Example

Given $f(x) = 3^x$, how does the graph of g compare with the graph of f if $g(x) = f(x) + 4$?

Graph both equations.

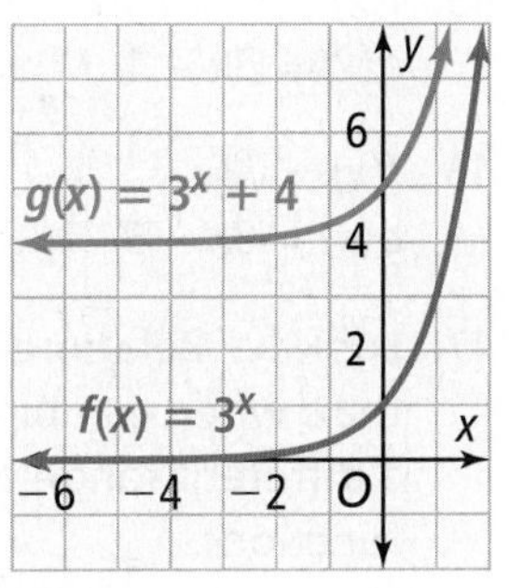

The graph of g translates the graph of f 4 units up.

Practice & Problem Solving

Sketch the graph of each function.

27. $g(x) = |x - 3|$

28. $g(x) = x^2 + 5$

29. The graph shown is a translation of the function $f(x) = x^2$. Write the function for the graph.

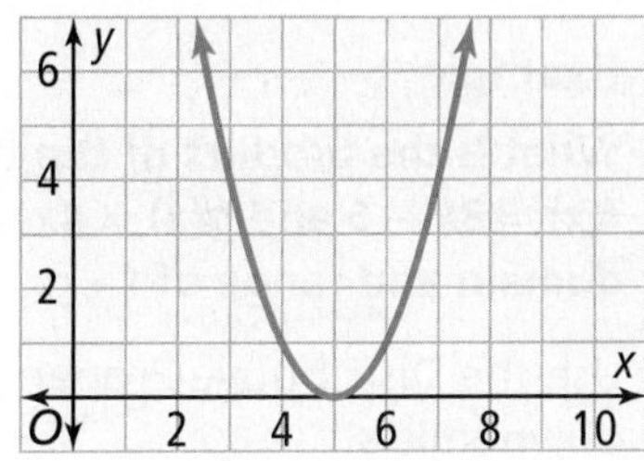

30. **Reason** Given $f(x) = -3$ and $g(x) = f(x - h) + k$, describe how the constants h and k affect the graph of g.

LESSON 10-5 Compressions and Stretches of Functions

Quick Review

The graph of $g(x) = kf(x)$ is the graph of f stretched away from the x-axis when $|k| > 1$ and compressed toward the x-axis when $0 < |k| < 1$.

The graph of $g(x) = f(kx)$ is the graph of f stretched away from the y-axis when $0 < |k| < 1$ and compressed toward the y-axis when $|k| > 1$.

Example

Given $f(x) = \sqrt[3]{x + 2}$, how does the graph of g compare with the graph of f if $g(x) = 2f(x)$?

Graph both functions.

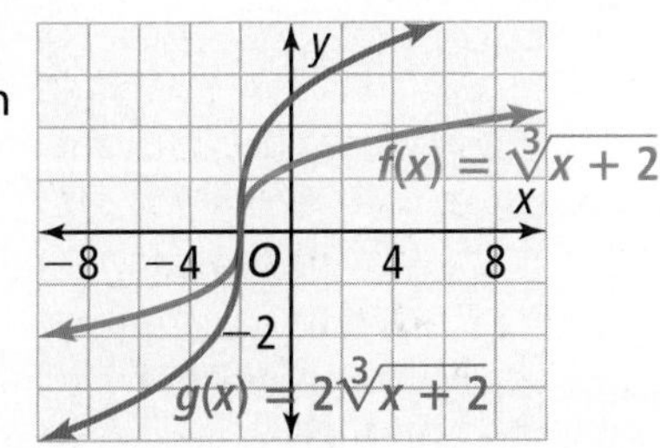

The graph of g stretches the graph of f vertically away from the x-axis by a factor of 2.

Practice & Problem Solving

Write a function with a graph that is the reflection of the graph of f across the x-axis.

31. $f(x) = x^2 + 5$

32. $f(x) = |2x - 1|$

For each pair, tell whether the graph of g is a vertical or horizontal compression or stretch of the graph of f.

33. $f(x) = |2x - 5|$
 $g(x) = 2|2x - 5|$

34. $f(x) = x^2 + 9$
 $g(x) = 0.25x^2 + 9$

35. $f(x) = \sqrt{x - 4}$
 $g(x) = \sqrt{4x - 4}$

36. $f(x) = 2x - 9$
 $g(x) = 6x - 27$

37. **Look for Relationships** Graph $f(x) = |x - 3|$ and $g(x) = 3|x - 3|$. Is the graph of g a vertical stretch or a horizontal compression of the graph of f? Explain.

38. **Make Sense and Persevere** A T-shirt designer uses the function $f(x) = x^2 - 3$ to sew parabolas on his clothing. What are two ways the function could be altered to make the parabolas wider? Explain.

TOPIC 10 REVIEW

LESSON 10-6 Operations With Functions

Quick Review

You can add, subtract, and multiply functions to form new functions.

Example

What is the product of the two functions $f(x) = 3x - 5$ and $g(x) = 4x - 1$? Determine the domain and range of $f \cdot g$.

Use the Distributive Property when multiplying polynomials.

$$f(x) \cdot g(x) = (3x - 5) \cdot (4x - 1)$$
$$= 3x(4x) + 3x(-1) + (-5)(4x) + (-5)(-1)$$
$$= 12x^2 - 3x - 20x + 5$$
$$(f \cdot g)(x) = 12x^2 - 23x + 5$$

The domain and range of the original functions are all real numbers. The domain of $f \cdot g$ is all real numbers. The range of $f \cdot g$ is all real numbers greater than or equal to approximately −6.02.

Practice & Problem Solving

Find $f + g$.

39. $f(x) = 3x^2 + 5x$
 $g(x) = 2x - 8$

40. $f(x) = 3x^2 - 5x + 1$
 $g(x) = x^2 - 8x - 3$

41. $f(x) = \sqrt{2x}$
 $g(x) = 4 - x$

42. $f(x) = 4^x - 1$
 $g(x) = 2x^2 + 5x - 3$

Find $f \cdot g$.

43. $f(x) = 5x^2 + 2x$
 $g(x) = 3x - 1$

44. $f(x) = x^2 + 2x - 5$
 $g(x) = x - 4$

45. $f(x) = \sqrt{3x}$
 $g(x) = 6x - 5$

46. $f(x) = 2^x$
 $g(x) = 4x^2 - 3x - 8$

47. **Look for Relationships** Write two functions that, when combined by multiplying, have a different range than at least one of the functions.

48. **Make Sense and Persevere** A clothing company has determined that the revenue function for selling x thousands of hats is $R(x) = -5x^2 + 23x$. The cost function for producing those hats is $C(x) = 2x + 9$. Write a combined function that represents the profit for selling x thousands of hats, and determine the clothing company's profit from selling 3,000 hats.

Inverse Functions

Quick Review

The **inverse of a function** reverses the inputs and outputs of a function. A function f has an inverse function f^{-1} only if the original function f is one-to-one.

To graph the inverse of a function, switch the x- and y-values in the table, or reflect the graph across the line $y = x$. To create an inverse equation, switch the variables and solve for y.

Example

What is the inverse function of $f(x) = 3x - 8$?

Write the original function as an equation

$y = 3x - 8$

$x = 3y - 8$ .... Switch x and y and solve for y.

$x + 8 = 3y - 8 + 8$ .... Add 8 to both sides.

$x + 8 = 3y$ .... Simplify.

$\frac{x+8}{3} = \frac{3y}{3}$ .... Divide both sides by 3.

$\frac{x+8}{3} = y$ .... Simplify.

The inverse function of $f(x) = 3x - 8$ is $f^{-1}(x) = \frac{x+8}{3}$.

Practice & Problem Solving

For each table, create a table of values for the inverse function.

49.

x	y
0	3
1	5
2	8
3	11

50.

x	y
0	2
1	4
2	8
3	16

Find the inverse of each function.

51. $f(x) = 4x - 7$

52. $f(x) = 3x^2 - 8, x \geq 0$

53. $f(x) = \sqrt{2x - 3}$

54. $f(x) = 5 + 2x$

55. Error Analysis Describe and correct the error a student made finding the inverse of $f(x) = 2x^2 + 3$.

$y = 2x^2 + 3$

$x = 2y^2 + 3$

$x + 3 = 2y^2$

$\frac{x+3}{2} = y^2$

$\sqrt{\frac{x+3}{2}} = y$

The inverse of the function is $f^{-1}(x) = \sqrt{\frac{x+3}{2}}$.

56. Reason The surface area A of a cube is given by the equation $A = 6s^2$, where s is the side length of the cube. What is the inverse of $A = 6s^2$? What type of question could you answer by using the inverse function?

Statistics

TOPIC ESSENTIAL QUESTION

How do you use statistics to model situations and solve problems?

Topic Overview

Topic Vocabulary

- conditional relative frequency
- joint frequency
- joint relative frequency
- marginal frequency
- marginal relative frequency
- normal distribution
- standard deviation
- variance

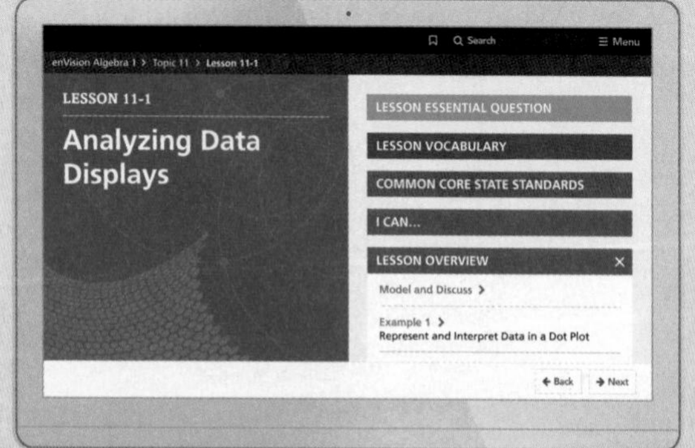

Go online | **PearsonRealize.com**

Digital Experience

INTERACTIVE STUDENT EDITION Access online or offline.

ACTIVITIES Complete ***Explore & Reason, Model & Discuss***, and ***Critique & Explain*** activities. Interact with Examples and Try Its.

ANIMATION View and interact with real-world applications.

PRACTICE Practice what you've learned.

Text Message

Text messages used be just that: text only. Now you can send multimedia messages (or MMS) with emojis, images, audio, and videos. Did you know Finland was the first country to offer text messaging to phone customers?

Some people send and receive so many texts that they use textspeak to make typing faster. RU 1 of them? You will see one person keep track of his text messages in this Modeling Mathematics in 3 Acts lesson.

VIDEOS Watch clips to support ***Mathematical Modeling in 3 Acts Lessons*** and **enVision™** ***STEM Projects.***

CONCEPT SUMMARY Review key lesson content through multiple representations.

ASSESSMENT Show what you've learned.

GLOSSARY Read and listen to English and Spanish definitions.

TUTORIALS Get help from ***Virtual Nerd***, right when you need it.

MATH TOOLS Explore math with digital tools and manipulatives.

Did You Know?

The average energy consumption in U.S. households is many times greater than countries in the rest of the world.

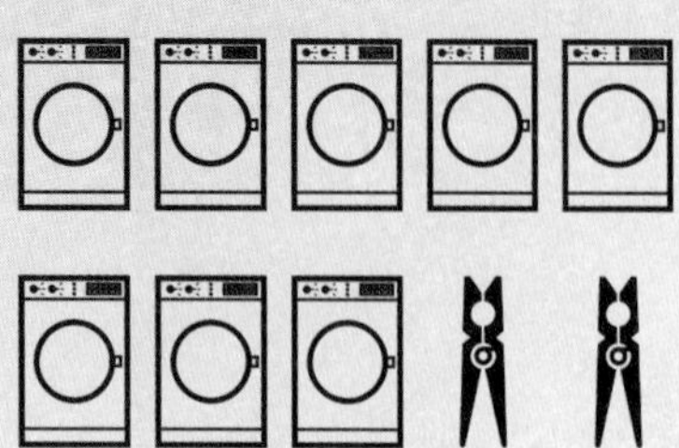

Total Annual Energy Consumption for Select Countries (in million tons of oil equivalent)

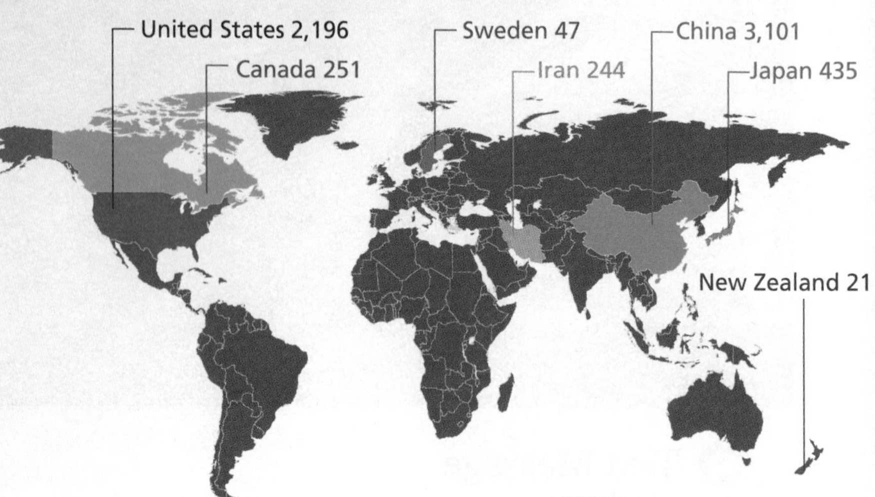

About 80% of American homes have a clothes dryer, which uses around 12% of the home's electricity to dry about 300 loads of laundry each year.

In the United States, petroleum, natural gas, and coal have provided most of the energy for more than 100 years.

About 86% of the world's energy is supplied by fossil fuels.

In 2013, winds generated almost 3% of the world's electricity. World-wide, wind-generated power grows at a rate of about 17% per year.

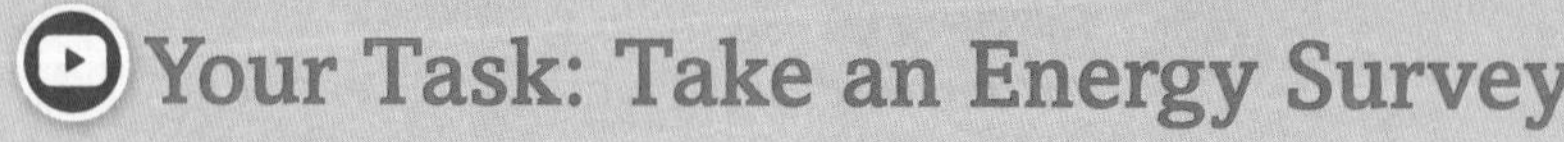

Your Task: Take an Energy Survey

You and your classmates will develop a survey, and then gather and analyze data looking for ways to reduce energy consumption.

11-1 Analyzing Data Displays

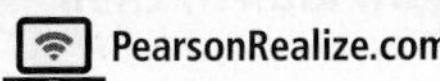

I CAN… organize and understand data using dot plots, histograms, and box plots.

Activity | Assess

MODEL & DISCUSS

MARKET RESEARCHERS WANTED!

A clothing company is designing a new line of shirts. Look around your classroom and collect data about the color of top worn by each student. If a student's top has multiple colors, choose the most prevalent one.

A. Explain why you chose to organize the data the way that you did.

B. How do you think the company could use these data?

C. **Use Appropriate Tools** How would you display these data in a presentation?

ESSENTIAL QUESTION

What information about data sets can you get from different data displays?

APPLICATION

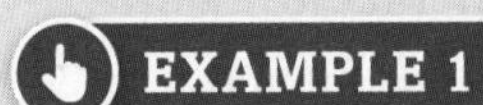

EXAMPLE 1 Represent and Interpret Data in a Dot Plot

Manuel plans to buy a new car with the gas mileage shown. To determine if the gas mileage of this car is good, he gathers data on the estimated city driving fuel efficiency, in miles per gallon, of several other cars. How does the fuel efficiency of the car he wants to buy compare to the fuel efficiency of the other cars he researched?

25	45	26	35	31	26	30	28
29	26	28	26	27	27	28	28

CONSTRUCT ARGUMENTS Why is a dot plot a good way to show individual values? What kind of data do other types of displays show?

Manuel wants to compare individual values, so a dot plot is a good way to show that information.

Create a dot plot of the data by first drawing a number line that represents the range of the data. Plot each value from the table as a dot above the number line.

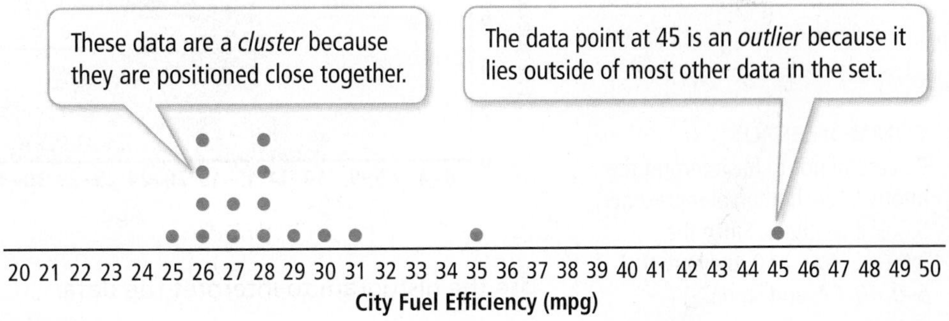

These data are a *cluster* because they are positioned close together.

The data point at 45 is an *outlier* because it lies outside of most other data in the set.

20 21 22 23 24 25 26 27 28 29 30 31 32 33 34 35 36 37 38 39 40 41 42 43 44 45 46 47 48 49 50

City Fuel Efficiency (mpg)

Use the dot plot to interpret the data.

The dot plot shows that most of the values are clustered between 25 and 28.

The car Manuel plans to buy has about the same city fuel efficiency as comparable cars.

Try It! **1.** What might account for the outlier?

EXAMPLE 2 Represent and Interpret Data in a Histogram

A marketing team is about to launch a campaign for a new product that is targeted at adults aged 25–34 years. The team is researching the age range of viewers of a certain TV show to decide whether to advertise during the show. The data show the ages of a random sample of 30 viewers of the show. Based on the findings, should the marketing team launch their campaign during this particular show?

14	21	22	17	24	20	26	15	20	22	14	24	26	15	17
21	32	30	16	31	25	25	19	16	21	37	17	20	15	16

Histograms are often used to represent data over ranges of numbers.

To create a histogram, first decide on an appropriate interval for the data.

Create a frequency table to organize the data.

Age Range	Frequency
0–4	
5–9	
10–14	II
15–19	~~IIII~~ ~~IIII~~
20–24	~~IIII~~ ~~IIII~~
25–29	IIII
30–34	III
35–39	I
40–44	

Remember that the intervals must be consistent.

Use the frequency table to create a histogram.

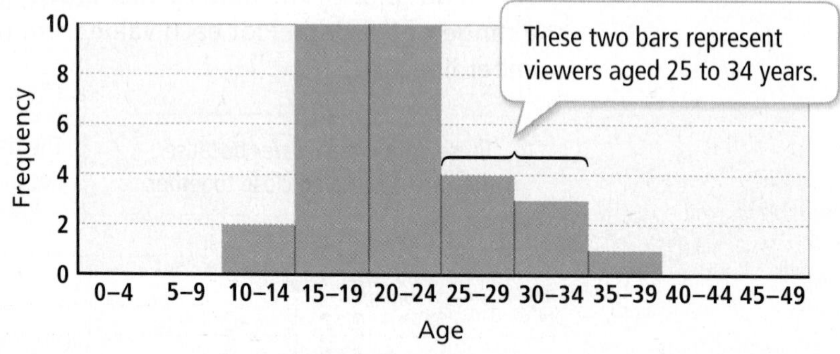

COMMON ERROR
Be careful not to misinterpret the intervals. Each interval represents 5 possible values. Since the intervals start at 0, they are 0–4, 5–9, 10–14, and so on.

Use the histogram to interpret the data.

The histogram reveals that fewer than 25% of the viewers are between the ages of 25 and 35.

Based on this information, the marketing team should not launch their campaign during this particular show.

Try It! 2. What age group would be a good match for products advertised on this TV show? Explain.

EXAMPLE 3 Represent and Interpret Data in a Box Plot

Students at a local high school organized a fundraiser for charity. Kaitlyn, the student council president, announces that more than half of the students raised over $50 each. The amounts of money raised by a random sample of 24 students is shown. Do the data support Kaitlyn's claim?

$59	$42	$25	$38	$45	$54	$68	$32
$26	$54	$50	$45	$42	$48	$50	$25
$45	$36	$55	$27	$31	$32	$49	$54

Kaitlyn's claim is about the distribution of values, so a box plot will reveal the information needed.

A *box plot* shows the distribution of data using a 5-number summary.

The *minimum* value is the least value in the set.

The *maximum* value is the greatest value in the set.

The *median* is the middle value in the set when the numbers are arranged from least to greatest.

The *first quartile* is the middle number between the minimum value and the median. The *third quartile* is the middle number between the median and the maximum value.

List the data from least to greatest to identify each of these values.

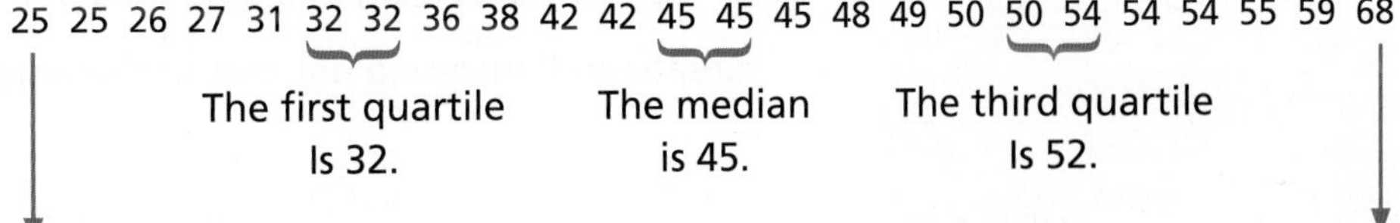

Create a box plot of the data.

> **VOCABULARY**
> The interquartile range, *IQR*, represents the range of the middle 50% of the data. Subtract the Q_1 value from the Q_3 value to find the IQR. In this example the IQR is 52 – 32, or 20.

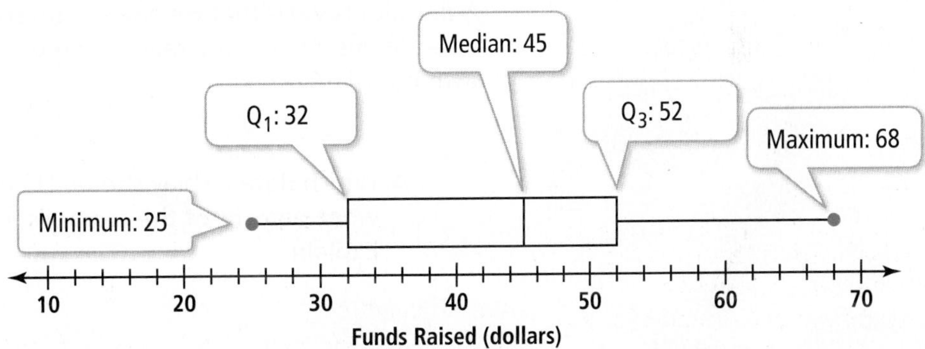

Use the box plot to interpret the data. The box plot shows that, based on the sample, the median amount of money collected was $45. Since half of this population collected $45 or less, the data do not support Kaitlyn's claim.

Try It! 3. Suppose Kaitlyn wants to make the statement that 25% of the students raised over a certain amount. What is that amount? Explain.

CONCEPTUAL UNDERSTANDING

EXAMPLE 4 Choose a Data Display

Helena's dance team scores 68 points at a competition. The scores for all of the teams that competed are shown.

66	89	81	75
90	79	82	68
80	82	65	80
81	66	81	83

A. Helena wants to know what place her team finished. Should Helena use a dot plot, histogram, or box plot to display the data?

Compare the features of the three types of data displays.

- A dot plot has dots for each value in the data. It shows clusters of data and outliers.
- A histogram groups values in a data set into ranges or intervals. Individual values are not displayed but trends are observable.
- A box plot shows center and spread of a data set. A box plot does not show individual data but summarizes the data using 5 key pieces of information.

Helena is interested in displaying individual scores. A dot plot will display the data in a way that is most helpful to Helena.

CONSTRUCT ARGUMENTS
What would be a good display choice if Helena wanted to compare her team's score with the median?

B. What place did Helena's team finish in the competition?

Create and analyze a dot plot of the data.

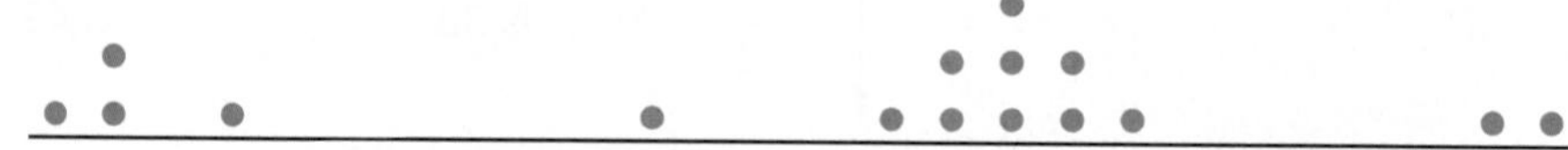

A dot plot reveals that Helena's team score was low compared to the other teams. Only three teams scored lower, so Helena's team placed 13th out of 16.

Try It! 4. Which data display should Helena use if she wants to know what percent of the teams scored higher than her team? Explain.

CONCEPT SUMMARY Data Displays

	Dot Plots	Histograms	Box Plots
WORDS	Dot plots display each data value from a set of data. They show clusters, gaps, and outliers in a data set.	Histograms do not show individual values, but show clearly the shape of the data. The data are organized into intervals. The bars show the frequency, or number of times, that the data within that interval occur.	Box plots show the center (median) and spread of a distribution. Box plots provide the following information about a data set: minimum, maximum, and median values, and the first and third quartile.
GRAPHS			

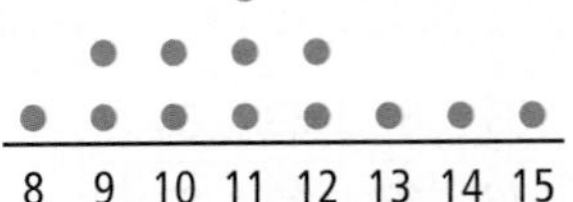

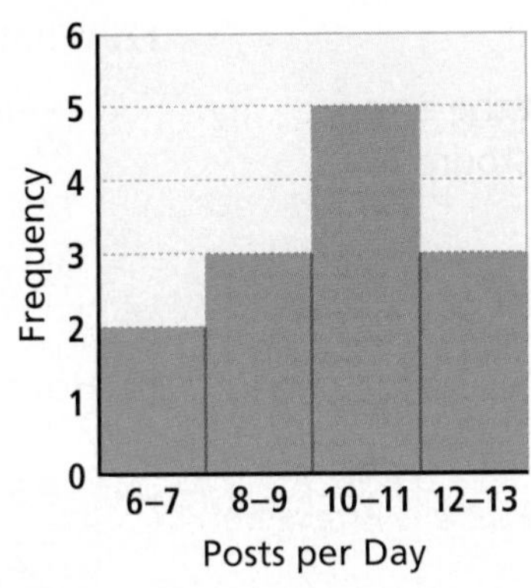

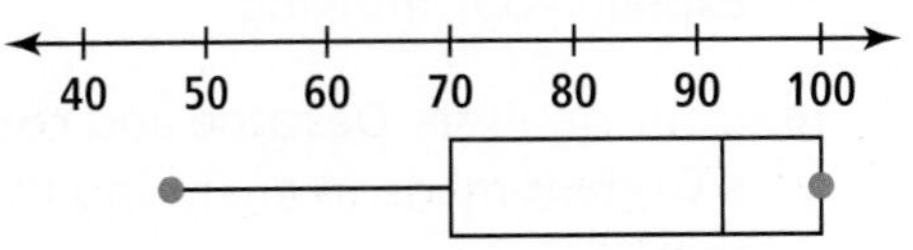

Do You UNDERSTAND?

1. ESSENTIAL QUESTION What information about data sets can you get from different data displays?

2. **Communicate Precisely** How is a dot plot different from a box plot? How are they similar?

3. **Use Appropriate Tools** If you want to see data values grouped in intervals, which data display should you choose? Explain.

4. **Error Analysis** Taylor says you can determine the mean of a data set from its box plot. Is Taylor correct? Explain your reasoning.

5. **Use Structure** Can you determine the minimum and maximum values of a data set simply by looking at its dot plot? Histogram? Box plot? Explain.

Do You KNOW HOW?

Use the data set shown for exercises 6–11.

7	5	8	15	4
9	10	1	12	8
13	7	11	8	10

6. Make a dot plot for the data. What information does the display reveal about the data set?

7. Make a histogram for the data. What information does the display reveal about the data set?

8. Make a box plot for the data. What information does the display reveal about the data set?

Identify the most appropriate data display to answer each question about the data set. Justify your response.

9. What is the median of the data set?

10. How many data values are greater than 7?

11. How many values fall in the interval 10 to 12?

UNDERSTAND

12. **Reason** A data set is represented by the box plot shown. Between which two values would the middle 50% of the data be found? Explain.

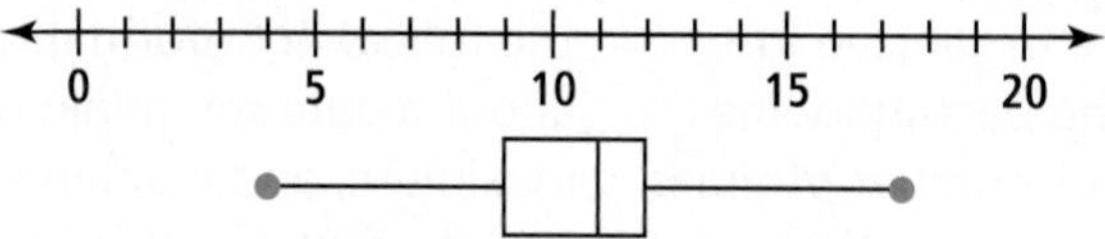

13. **Generalize** Write a scenario for which a dot plot would be the best display for a data set. Explain your thinking.

14. **Error Analysis** Describe and correct the errors a student made in analyzing the histogram shown.

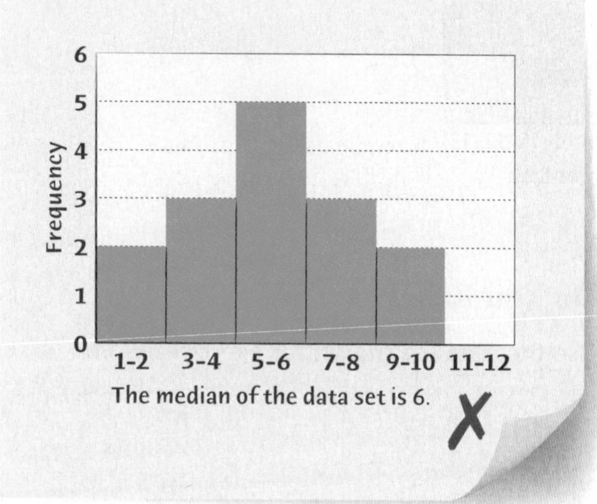

15. **Higher Order Thinking** The box plot represents a data set with 12 values. The minimum, first quartile, median, third quartile, and maximum values are 6, 8, 10, 12, and 14, respectively.

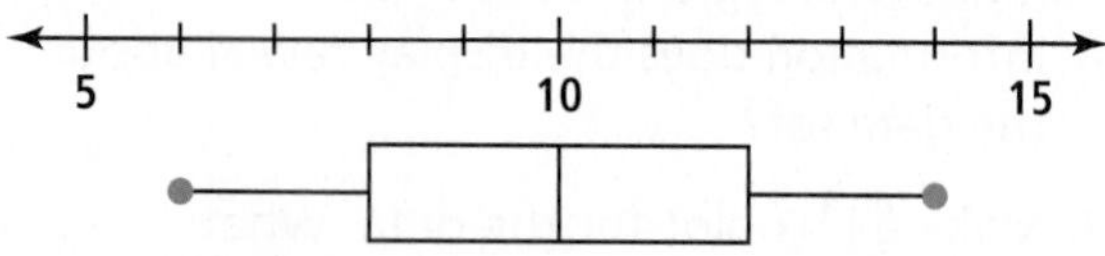

a. Is it possible to create a dot plot for the data set using just the box plot and the values given? Explain.

b. Is it possible to create a histogram using just the box plot and the values given? Explain.

PRACTICE

For each data set, create the data display that best reveals the answer to the question. Explain your reasoning. SEE EXAMPLES 1–4

16. What is the median value of the data set?

40	47	43	35
42	32	40	47
49	46	50	42
48	43	34	45

17. What is the frequency of the data value 83?

85	81	83	84	83	80
84	86	76	83	82	83
82	82	84	89	85	83

18. How many data values are between 7 and 9?

9.6	5.5	8.4	9.1	6.7
7.2	11.5	9.2	5.2	7.6
11.1	6.1	7.2	14.8	12.5
8.4	10.5	10.2	8.4	13.5

Choose whether a dot plot, histogram, or box plot is the most appropriate data display to answer each question about a data set. Explain.
SEE EXAMPLE 4

19. How many data values are greater than any given value in the data set?

20. What are the frequencies for each interval of 5 points?

21. 25% of the data values are less than which value?

Consider the data set represented by the dot plot. Create a different data display that better reveals the answer to each question. SEE EXAMPLES 1–4

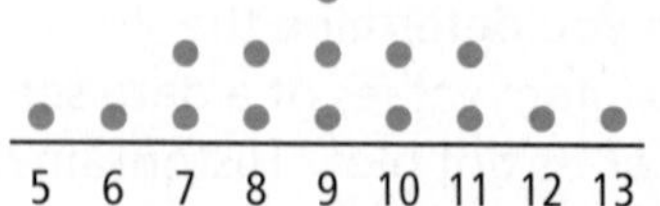

22. How many data values are in the interval between 8 and 10 inclusive?

23. What is the first quartile of the data set?

Practice Tutorial

Mixed Review Available Online

PRACTICE & PROBLEM SOLVING

APPLY

24. Model With Mathematics Isabel knits scarves and sells them online. The table shows the prices of the scarves she sold last month. At what prices were the middle 50% of the scarves sold? Create a data display that will reveal the answer.

Prices of Scarves ($)				
35	32	60	80	36
90	45	76	96	92
100	120	60	38	75
36	36	100	100	100
95	58	100	85	40

25. Make Sense and Persevere Lucy usually pays between \$0.40 and \$0.60 per ounce for her favorite shampoo. She gathers prices of the same shampoo at different stores near her home. Prices are shown in dollars in the table. Create a data display that allows Lucy to easily compare the price she is paying to the other prices. How does the price she is currently paying compare?

Shampoo Pricing Comparison				
0.55	0.95	0.29	0.65	0.39
0.99	0.42	1.10	0.99	0.75
0.65	0.99	0.34	0.85	0.99
0.95	0.75	0.95	0.50	0.75

26. Use Structure Aaron scores 82 points at his karate tournament. He wants to compare his score to the others in the competition to see how many competitors scored higher than he did. The table shows all scores for the competition. What type of data display is appropriate to answer his question? Create the data display and analyze Aaron's performance.

Karate Scores					
78	66	82	86	72	70
74	86	30	80	89	80
82	68	100	84	84	42
86	82	80	94	78	82

ASSESSMENT PRACTICE

27. Consider a box plot. Does a box plot display the features of a data set listed below? Select Yes or No.

	Yes	No
Median of the data set	❑	❑
Individual values in the data set	❑	❑
Outliers	❑	❑
Minimum of the data set	❑	❑

28. SAT/ACT From which display(s) can the median of a data set be determined?

Ⓐ Dot plot only

Ⓑ Box plot only

Ⓒ Dot plot and box plot

Ⓓ Histogram and box plot

Ⓔ Dot plot, histogram, and box plot

29. Performance Task A group of students use a stopwatch to record times for a 100-yard dash. Tell whether each student should choose a dot plot, a histogram, or a box plot to display the data. Explain your reasoning. Then create the display.

12.5	13.5	14.1	12.8	13.4
14.0	11.5	14.2	13.9	14.4
13.3	14.5	13.2	13.6	12.0
14.5	13.5	14.4	14.1	13.9

Part A Neil wants a data display that clearly shows the shape of the data distribution.

Part B Yuki wants a display that shows the spread of data above and below the median.

Part C Thato wants a display that groups the data by intervals.

Part D Edwin wants a display that he could use to find the mean of the data set.

11-2 Comparing Data Sets

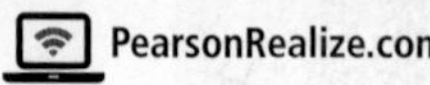

I CAN... use measures of center and spread to compare data sets.

CRITIQUE & EXPLAIN

The prices of paintings sold at two galleries in the last month are shown. Stacy and Diego both have a painting they want to sell.

- **Stacy wants Gallery I to sell her painting because it has the highest sales price.**
- **Diego wants Gallery II to sell his painting because it has the most consistent sales prices.**

A. Do you agree with Stacy or Diego? Explain your reasoning.

B. Reason What reason(s) could there be for the differences in sales prices between the two galleries and for the outlier in Gallery I?

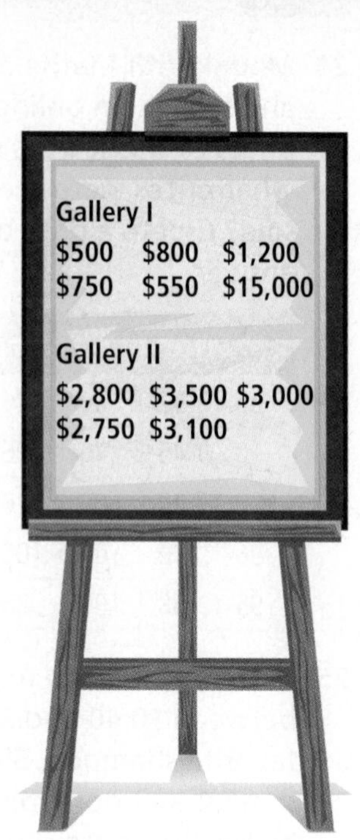

ESSENTIAL QUESTION

How can you use measures of center and spread to compare data sets?

EXAMPLE 1 Compare Data Sets Displayed in Dot Plots

Sawyer has narrowed his car search down to two different types of cars. To make an informed decision, he gathers data on estimated highway fuel efficiency (mpg) of the two different types of cars. The dot plots show the data for each type.

Type 1

Dot plot, Highway Fuel Efficiency (mpg), axis 30 to 55: 33: 2 dots; 34: 3; 35: 3; 36: 3; 37: 2; 38: 2; 41: 1.

Type 2

Dot plot, Highway Fuel Efficiency (mpg), axis 30 to 55: 35: 1 dot; 36: 1; 37: 2; 38: 2; 39: 2; 40: 2; 41: 1; 42: 1; 43: 1; 44: 2; 51: 1.

VOCABULARY
An *outlier* is a data value that is very different from the others. In the data set for Type 2, 51 appears to be an outlier.

A. If highway fuel efficiency is the most important feature to Sawyer, which type of car should Sawyer purchase?

The data displays suggest that Type 2 cars have better highway fuel efficiency. The data for Type 1 car are clustered from 33 to 38 and the data for Type 2 cars are clustered from 35 to 44.

Based on this data display, Sawyer should purchase a car in the Type 2 category.

CONTINUED ON THE NEXT PAGE

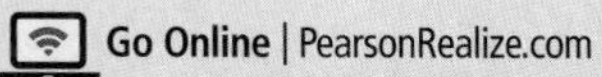

EXAMPLE 1 CONTINUED

B. Sawyer wants more information about the fuel efficiency of each type of car, so he calculates the mean and the mean absolute deviation (MAD) of the two data sets. How can these measures help him make a more informed decision?

STUDY TIP
Remember that the mean absolute deviation (MAD) is a measure of variability that describes how much the data values are spread out from the mean of the data set.

Mean Fuel Efficiency

Type 1 Cars: 35.75 mpg
Type 2 Cars: 40.25 mpg

The mean fuel efficiency of Type 2 cars is greater than the mean fuel efficiency of Type 1 cars.

Sawyer also wants to consider how much his data vary to determine reliability. The mean absolute deviation (MAD) is the mean of the differences between each value in a data set and the mean of the data set. The MAD helps you determine how much data vary within a particular data set.

To calculate mean absolute deviation, calculate the absolute value of the difference between each data point and the mean. Then find the mean of those differences.

MAD for Type 1 Cars (mean: 35.75)

$|33 - 35.75| = 2.75$
$|34 - 35.75| = 1.75$
$|35 - 35.75| = 0.75$
$|36 - 35.75| = 0.25$
$|37 - 35.75| = 1.25$
$|38 - 35.75| = 2.25$
$|41 - 35.75| = 5.25$

Multiply each difference by the number of times it appears in the data set.

$2.75(2) + 1.75(3) + 0.75(3) + 0.25(3) + 1.25(2) + 2.25(2) + 5.25 = 26$

The sum of all of the differences between the data points and the mean is 26. Divide that by the number of data points to find the MAD.

$26 \div 16 \approx 1.63$

The MAD of Type 1 cars is about 1.63.

Use a similar process to find the MAD of Type 2 cars. The MAD of Type 2 cars is about 2.94.

So, while the mean fuel efficiency for Type 2 cars is greater than for Type 1 cars, there is more variation with Type 2 cars. This could mean that the expected fuel efficiency is less reliable for Type 2 cars.

Try It! **1.** How does the outlier in the second data set affect the mean and the MAD?

EXAMPLE 2 Compare Data Sets Displayed in Box Plots

Kaitlyn and Philip go to neighboring high schools, and both are sponsoring charity fundraisers. Kaitlyn claims that students at her school are raising more for charity than the students at Philip's school. The amounts raised by a random sample of 30 students at each school are shown in the box plots below. Do the data support Kaitlyn's claim?

Kaitlyn's High School

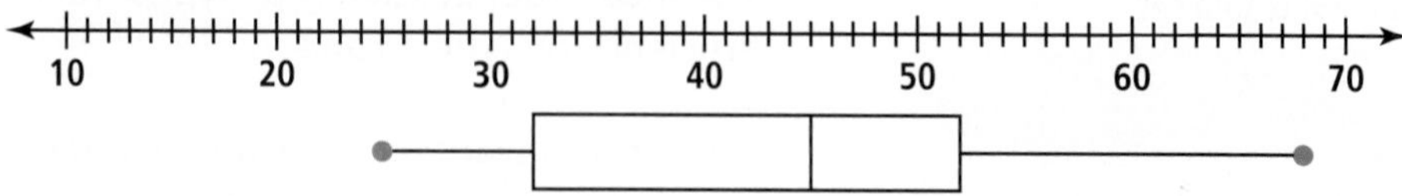

Philip's High School

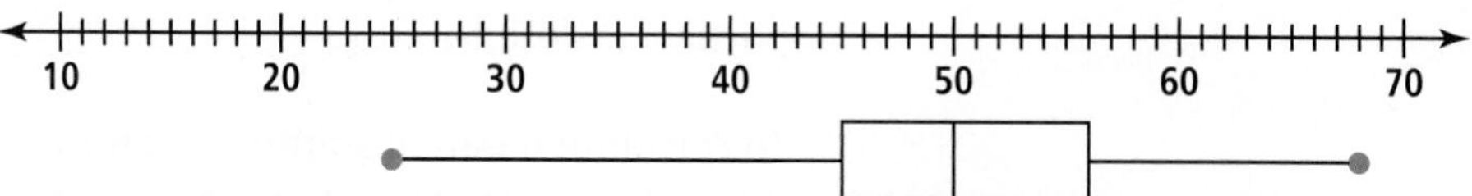

Analyze the distribution of values in each data set.

	Kaitlyn's High School	Philip's High School
Minimum Value	25	25
Maximum Value	68	68
First Quartile	32	45
Median	45	50
Third Quartile	52	56
Interquartile Range (IQR)	20	11

USE STRUCTURE
Recall that the interquartile range (IQR) is the difference of the third and first quartiles and represents the spread of the middle 50% of the data values. How does the structure of a box plot represent the IQR?

While the minimum and maximum amount of money raised at each school was the same, the spread of data points between the minimum and maximum values varies.

- The sample data show that 50% of the students at Kaitlyn's school raised between \$32 and \$52. At Philip's school, 50% of the students in the sample raised between \$45 and \$56.
- Based on the data, 50% of the students at Kaitlyn's school raised \$45 or more; At Philip's school, 50% raised \$50 or more.

The data do not support Kaitlyn's claim. Instead, they suggest that individual students at Philip's school raised more money than individual students at Kaitlyn's school.

 **Try It!** **2.** How does the IQR compare to the range for each school?

APPLICATION

EXAMPLE 3 Compare Data Sets Displayed in Histograms

A marketing team compares the ages of a random sample of 30 viewers of two popular new shows to decide which product to advertise during each show. During which show should the marketing team advertise a product that is targeted at adults aged 20–29?

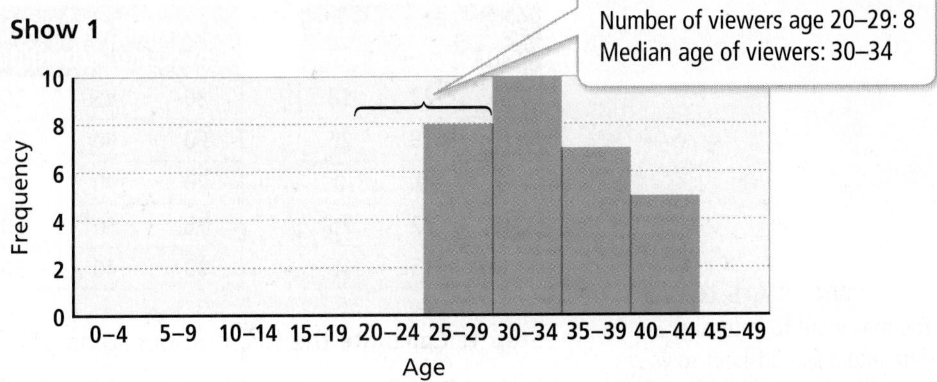

COMMON ERROR
When comparing histograms of data sets, be sure the intervals of the histogram are the same.

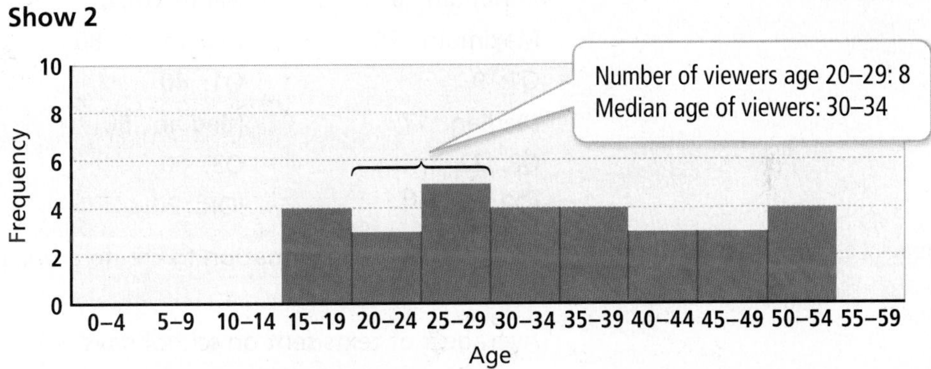

From the data displays, you can make several observations about the data collected by the marketing team.

- Of the 30 viewers in the sample, each show has 8 viewers between the ages of 20 and 29.
- Show 1 has no viewers between the ages of 20 and 24.
- Show 2 has viewers in each subsection of the target range; 20–24 and 25-29.
- Show 2 also has viewers in the age brackets just above and just below the target range, who are potential customers.

Based on this sample, the marketing team should advertise during Show 2 because that show has broader appeal.

 **Try It!** 3. If the marketing team wants to advertise a product that is targeted at adults 25–34, during which show should they advertise? Explain.

CONCEPTUAL UNDERSTANDING

EXAMPLE 4 Make Observations With Data Displays

Nadia collected data from 15 classmates about the number of text messages they send on school days and the number of text messages they send on non-school days. Nadia organized her data in the tables below. How can you use a box plot to compare the data that she collected?

Average # of texts sent on school days		
14	23	18
17	19	26
4	9	0
19	22	25
8	15	16

Average # of texts sent on non-school days		
80	45	50
50	60	75
20	40	0
75	50	60
30	40	50

USE APPROPRIATE TOOLS
You may want to enter the data into a spreadsheet so you can easily sort and perform calculations.

Step 1: Calculate the five-number summary for each set of data.

School Day Texts
Minimum: 0
Maximum: 26
Q1: 9
Median: 17
Q3: 22
IQR: 13

Non-School Day Texts
Minimum: 0
Maximum: 80
Q1: 40
Median: 50
Q3: 60
IQR: 20

Step 2: Use the information to create a box plot to represent each set of data.

Average # of texts sent on school days

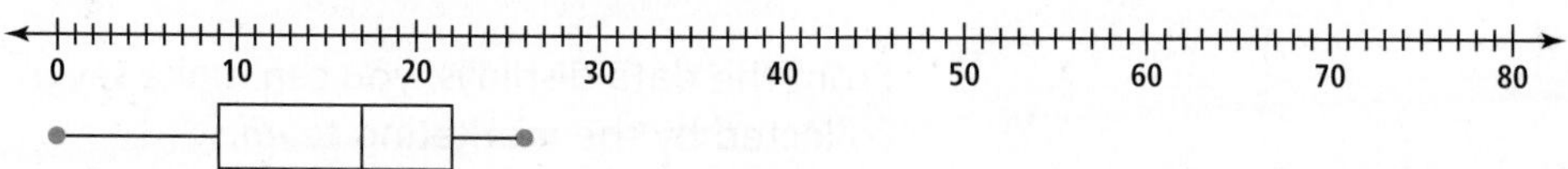

Average # of texts sent on non-school days

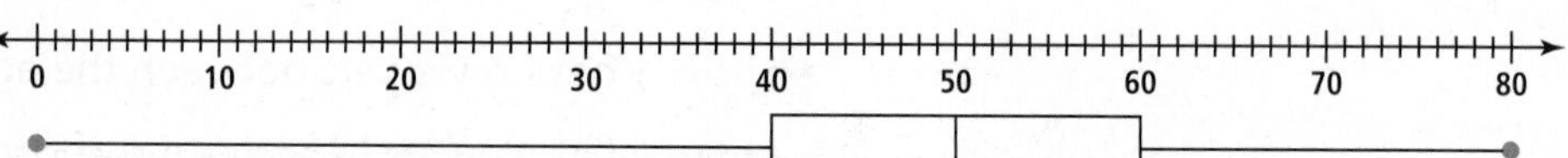

Step 3: Use the data displays to make observations about the data sets.

- Students send far more texts on non-school days than on school days.
- There is more variation in the number of texts sent on non-school days than on school days.
- One person does not send any texts on non-school days. This represents an outlier because it is far from the other data values.

 **Try It!** **4. a.** Provide a possible explanation for each of the observations that was made.

b. Make 2 more observations about the data that Nadia collected.

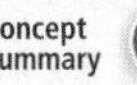

CONCEPT SUMMARY Comparing Data Sets

You can compare data sets using statistical measures of center and measures of variability or spread.

DOT PLOTS Dot plots show how a particular data point fits in with the rest of the data.

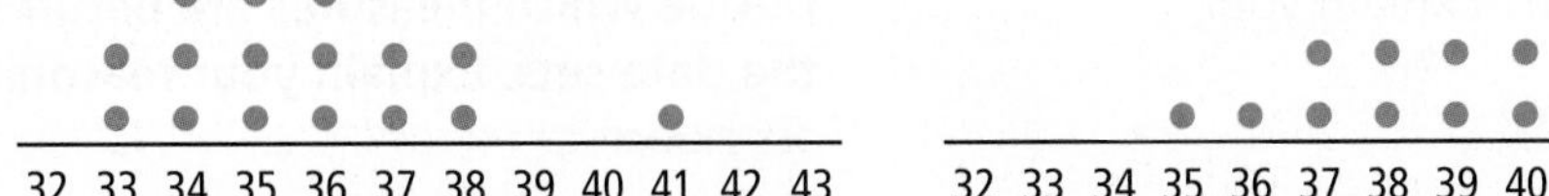

For a more specific measure of variance, find the mean absolute deviation.

BOX PLOTS Box plots show the minimum, maximum, and measures of center of the data.

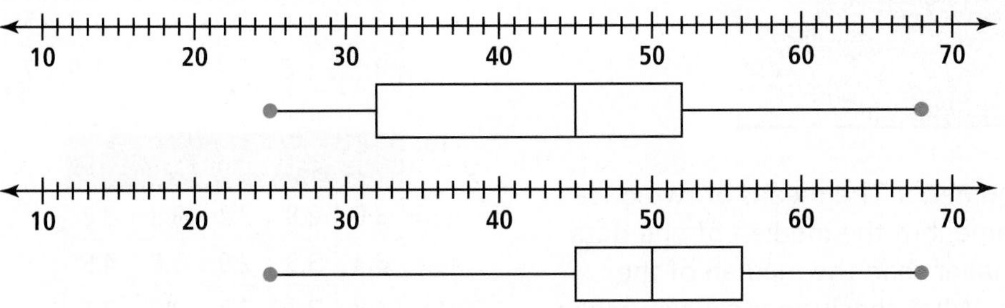

HISTOGRAMS Histograms allow you to easily compare data ranges.

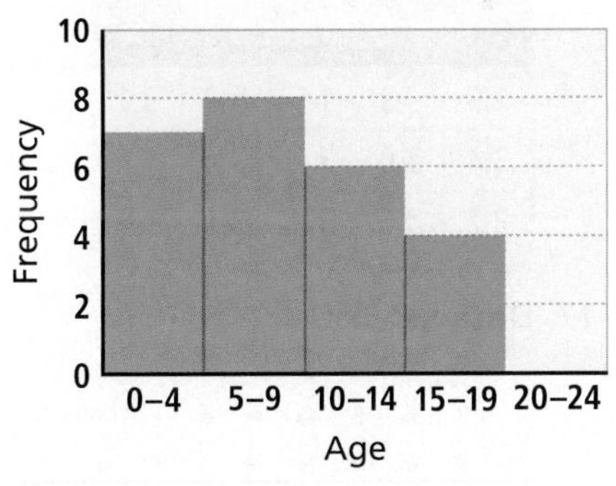

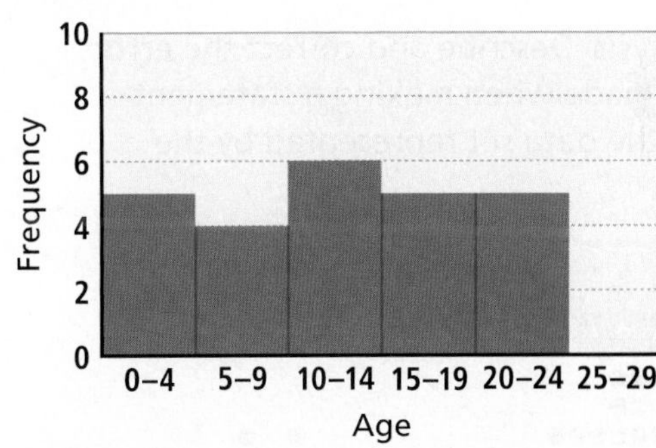

Do You UNDERSTAND?

1. **ESSENTIAL QUESTION** How can you use measures of center and spread to compare data sets?

2. **Communicate Precisely** How are the MAD and the IQR similar? How are they different?

3. **Reason** When comparing two sets of data, it is common to look at the means. Why might the MAD be a useful piece of information to compare in addition to the mean?

4. **Error Analysis** Val says that if the minimum and maximum values of two data sets are the same, the median will be the same. Is Val correct? Explain.

Do You KNOW HOW?

Use the two data sets.

Data Set A				
86	87	98	85	90
94	89	83	76	84
83	90	87	87	86

Data Set B				
80	89	70	75	87
88	75	87	89	81
84	87	88	81	87

5. How do the means compare?

6. How do the MADs compare?

7. How do the medians compare?

8. How do the IQRs compare?

9. Which measures of center and spread are better for comparing data sets A and B? Explain.

PRACTICE & PROBLEM SOLVING

Scan for Multimedia | Practice | Tutorial

Additional Exercises Available Online

UNDERSTAND

10. **Reason** The mean of the data set represented by the histogram is 12. What is a reasonable estimate for the median? Explain your reasoning.

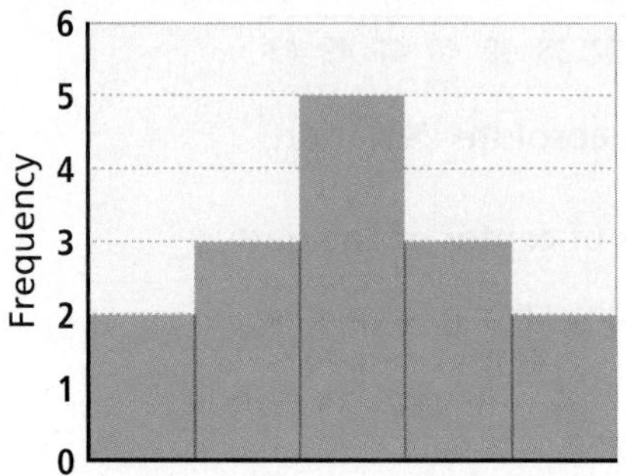

11. **Construct Arguments** The means of two data sets are the same, but the median of one data set is much smaller than the median of the other data set. What conclusions can you make about the sets from this information?

12. **Error Analysis** Describe and correct the errors a student made when making a statement based on the data set represented by the dot plot.

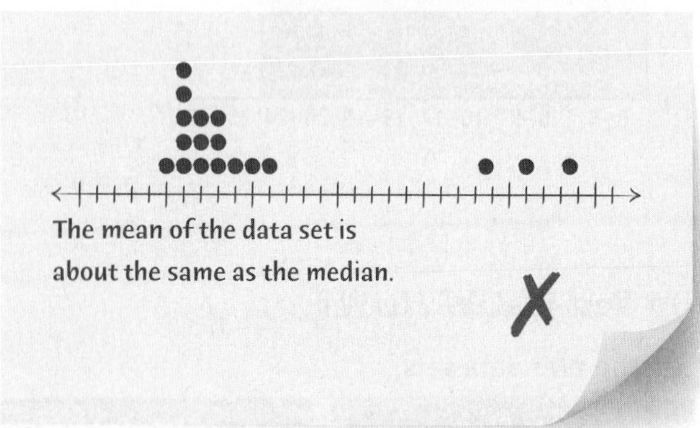

13. **Communicate Precisely** How are the IQR and the range of a data set similar in terms of comparing data sets? How are they different?

14. **Higher Order Thinking** Two data sets each have a median of 10. The first data set has an IQR of 22 and the second data set has an IQR of 8.

 a. What conclusions can you make about the data sets? Explain.

 b. Is it possible to also make a prediction about the MADs from the information given? Explain.

PRACTICE

For each pair of data sets, compare the means and the MADs, and then the medians and the IQRs. Decide which measures are better for comparing the data sets. Explain your reasoning.

SEE EXAMPLES 1–4

15.

Data Set A			
5	6	5	4
5	4	5	6
6	5	4	5
4	5	6	5

Data Set B			
5	9	2	5
6	1	5	8
3	5	5	4
5	7	4	6

16.

Data Set A				
3.0	2.8	3.2	3.3	3.2
3.4	3.3	2.9	3.0	4.5
4.8	3.1	3.2	4.9	3.1

Data Set B				
1.9	3.3	1.5	3.2	3.1
3.4	3.0	3.2	3.4	1.6
3.2	3.6	3.5	3.1	3.3

17. **Data Set A**

70 71 72 73 74 75 76 77 78 79 80 81 82 83 84 85

Data Set B

70 71 72 73 74 75 76 77 78 79 80 81 82 83 84 85

18. A researcher claims that students tend to have more apps on their smart phones than adults. Do the data support the researcher's claim? Explain. SEE EXAMPLE 2

Number of Apps

10 15 20 25 30 35 40

Students' phones

Adults' phones

PRACTICE & PROBLEM SOLVING

APPLY

19. Model With Mathematics The mean score on last year's math final exam was 82, with MAD of 3.5 points. Scores for this year's exam are shown in the table. How do the scores for the two years compare?

Math Final Exam Scores				
85	82	88	84	85
84	86	70	95	86
99	71	85	92	79
88	85	91	82	85
86	75	84	78	100

20. Make Sense and Persevere The points of each player on Parker's basketball team for the season are shown in the table. The points of an opposing team are represented by the box plot. How does Parker's team compare?

Points per Player				
35	32	60	80	36
90	45	76	96	92
100	120	60	38	75

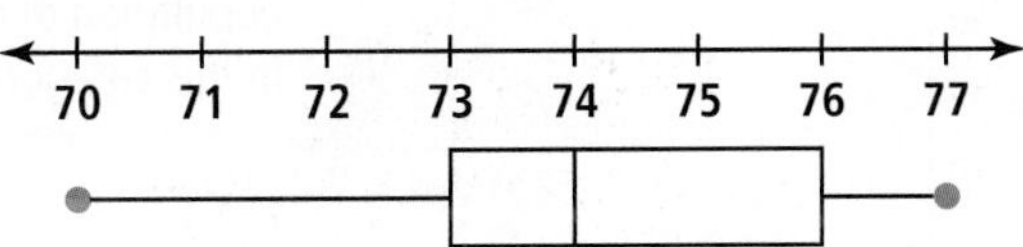

21. Use Structure The label on the cereal box says the weight is 12 ounces. The dot plots show weights of two random samples of 16 boxes packaged on two different machines. How can you compare the data sets to see if there is a problem with one of the machines?

Machine A

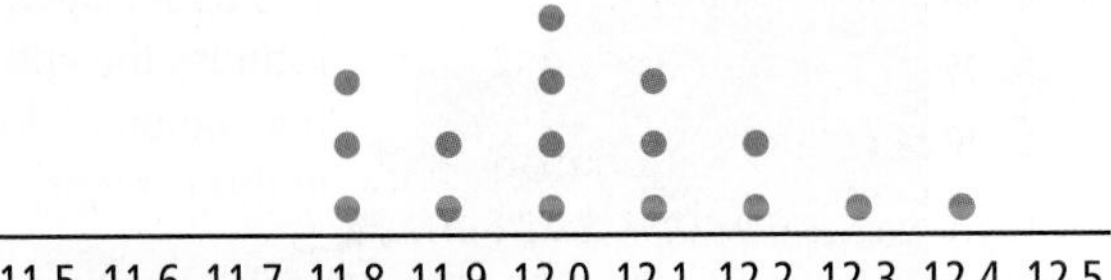

Machine B

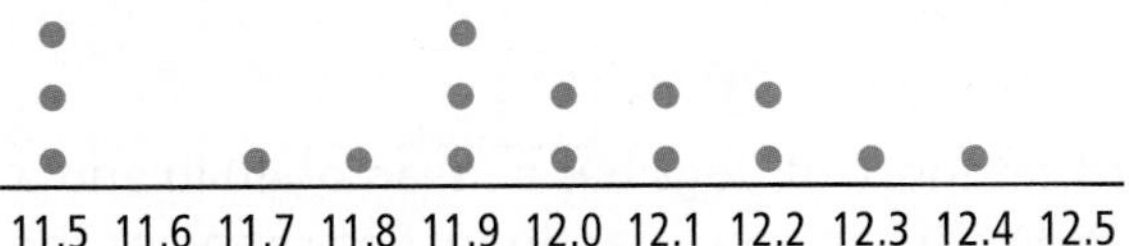

ASSESSMENT PRACTICE

22. The table shows the number of minutes Dylan and Kyle spent on their homework each night over the past 5 nights.

Dylan	Kyle
45	30
40	35
80	50
60	70
20	30

Based on this data, which of the following statements are true? Select all that apply.

Ⓐ The median of Kyle's data is greater than the median of Dylan's data.

Ⓑ On average, Dylan spends more time on homework than Kyle.

Ⓒ The mean is greater than the median in both groups.

Ⓓ The IQR of the data is greater for Kyle.

23. SAT/ACT The histograms that correspond to two data sets look identical. What conclusion can you make about the data sets.

Ⓐ The data points in each set are the same.

Ⓑ The mean of each of the data sets is the same.

Ⓒ The median of each of the data sets is the same.

Ⓓ none of these

24. Performance Task A consumer group tested battery life times for two different smart phones. Results are shown in the tables below.

Phone A				
10.0	14.2	12.0	15.1	16.0
14.0	0.9	14.2	9.5	15.0
14.2	15.0	9.5	12.5	14.2
13.0	15.0	14.2	11.0	9.0

Phone B				
12.5	13.0	14.0	13.5	15.0
14.0	14.0	12.0	15.0	12.8
12.8	15.0	13.0	15.2	16.0
14.0	13.6	14.2	13.8	15.1

Part A Find the mean and MAD for each data set.

Part B Find the median and IQR for each data set.

Part C Create data displays that will allow you to compare the two data sets.

Part D Which cell phone battery is likely to last longer? Explain your reasoning.

11-3 Interpreting the Shapes of Data Displays

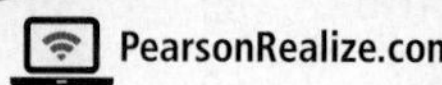

I CAN… interpret shapes of data displays representing different types of data distributions.

Activity Assess

EXPLORE & REASON

A meteorologist looks at measures of center to summarize the last 10 days of actual high temperatures.

A. Find the median, mean, and mode of the data.

B. Which of the three measures of center seems to be the most accurate in describing the data? Explain.

C. Communicate Precisely How can you describe the data?

ESSENTIAL QUESTION How does the shape of a data set help you understand the data?

CONCEPTUAL UNDERSTANDING

EXAMPLE 1 Interpret the Shape of a Distribution

The histograms show the weights of all of the dogs entered in two different categories in a dog show. Consider each data set. What inferences can you make based on the shape of the data?

The histogram is *symmetric* and shows the data are evenly distributed around the center.

The mean and median of the data are equal or almost equal.

Based on the data, you can infer that most of the dogs in this category weigh between 30 and 59 pounds.

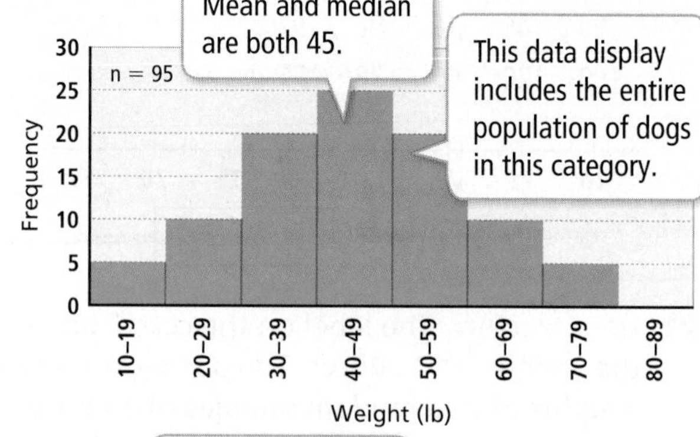

The histogram shows the data are *skewed right*. The mean is greater than the median.

Based on the data, you can infer that most of the dogs in this category weigh less than 30 pounds.

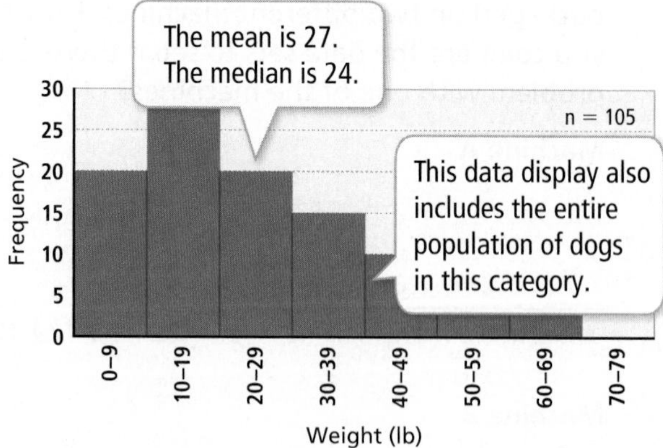

GENERALIZE
The mean includes all the values in the data set for its calculation. Should the mean always be used to make an inference when the data are evenly distributed?

Try It! 1. Suppose a third category of dogs has a mean of 40 lb and a median of 32 lb. What can you infer about the shape of the histogram for the dogs in this category?

APPLICATION

EXAMPLE 2 Interpret the Shape of a Skewed Data Display

Customers of a bagel shop complained that some bagels weigh less than the amount on the label. A quality control manager randomly sampled 30 bagels and weighed them. Based on this sample, is a change in the process for making bagels warranted?

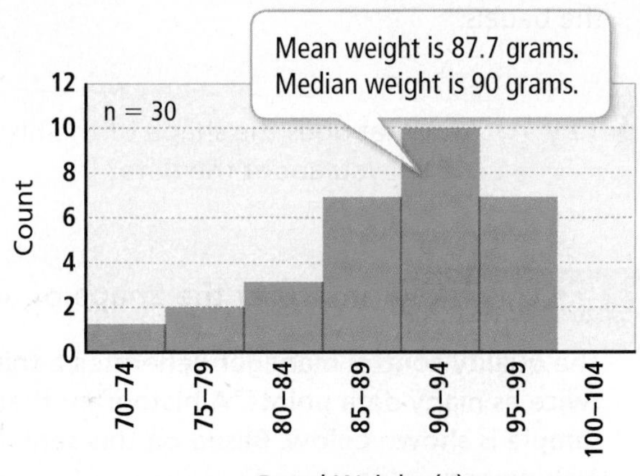

COMMON ERROR
You may think that a conclusion can be made based on this sample. However, because the sample size is small, it is difficult to ensure that the sample is representative of the entire population.

The shape of the data display is skewed left. That is common when the mean of a data set is less than the median of a data set.

Because the mean of the sample is less than the advertised weight, the quality control manager wants to recommend some changes to the production process. However, because the sample consists of only 30 bagels, the manager decides to generate another random sample.

Try It! **2.** How do skewed data affect the mean in this context?

EXAMPLE 3 Compare Shapes of Skewed Data Displays

The manager generates a second random sample of 30 bagels. Is a change in the process for making bagels warranted based on this sample? How does this sample compare to the previous sample?

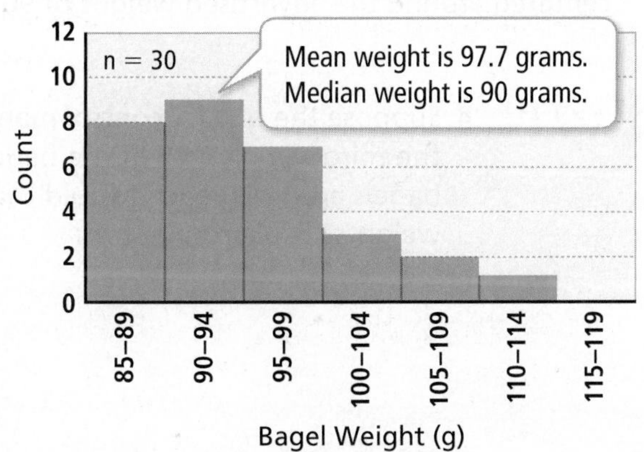

CONTINUED ON THE NEXT PAGE

EXAMPLE 3 CONTINUED

The shape of this data display is skewed right. This often occurs when the mean of the data is greater than the median of the data. In this example, the mean is greater than the advertised weight and greater than the mean weight from the first sample.

Based only on this sample, the manager could recommend changes. However, because this sample gives opposite results from the first sample, the manager now has conflicting findings about the mean weights of the bagels.

Try It! 3. What does the shape of the histogram for the second sample tell you about the data?

EXAMPLE 4 Interpret the Shape of a Symmetric Data Display

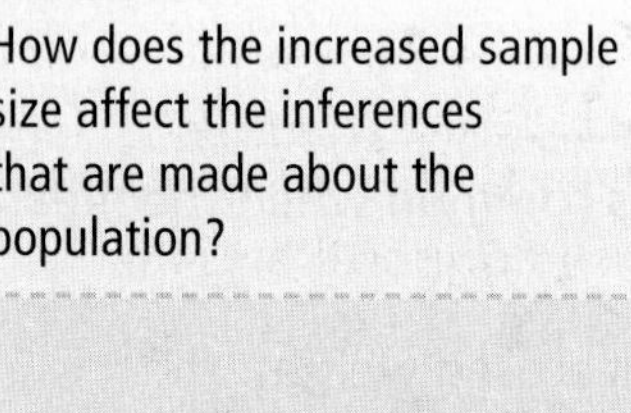

The quality control manager generates a third random sample that contains twice as many data points. A histogram that represents this third, larger sample is shown below. Based on this sample, is a change in the process for making bagels warranted?

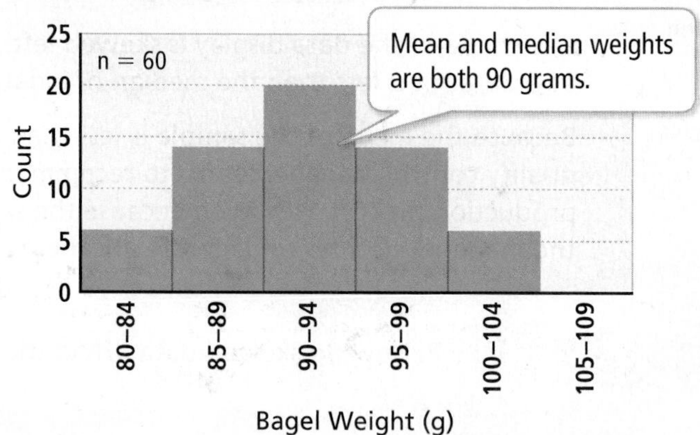

The data points are symmetrically distributed around the center. In this sample, the mean and median weights are the same.

Based on this larger sample, the quality control manager determines that the process of making bagels does not need to change because the data are centered around the advertised weight of 90 grams.

Try It! 4. Suppose the quality control manager adds another 10 bagels to the third sample. If 5 of the bagels are 78 g each, and 5 of the bagels are 106 g each, would that affect the mean and median weights? Explain.

CONCEPTUAL UNDERSTANDING

EXAMPLE 5 Comparing the Shapes of Data Sets

Jennifer is considering job offers from three different school districts. The histograms show the salary ranges for similar positions in each school district. What do the shapes of the data tell Jennifer about the teacher salaries in each district?

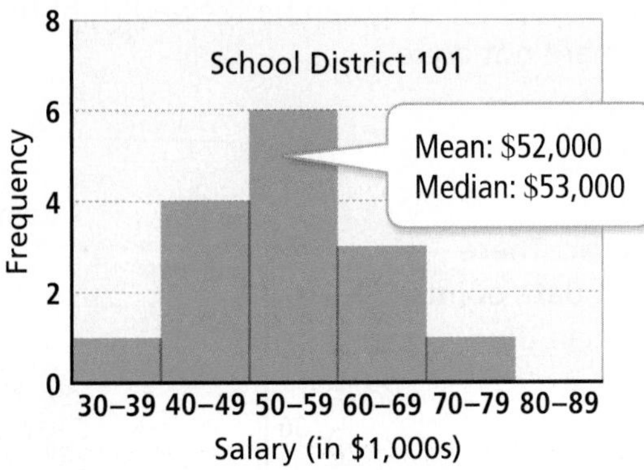

The data from teachers with similar positions in School District 101 have salaries that center around the mean. This indicates that the salaries of the teachers are fairly evenly distributed.

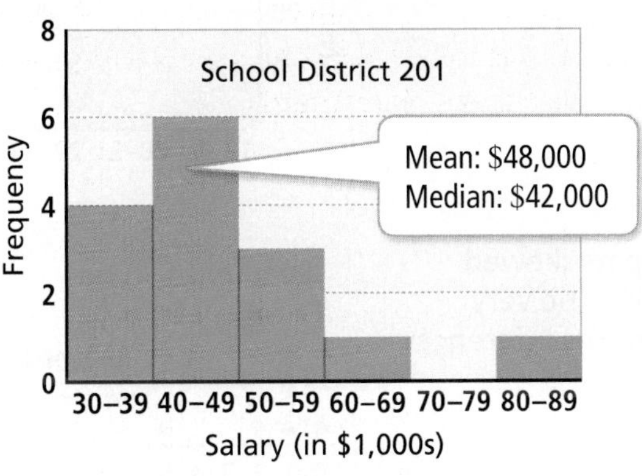

The data from teachers in School District 201 is skewed right. Most of the teachers in that district have salaries that are lower than the mean. This indicates that there are only a few teachers that make a higher salary.

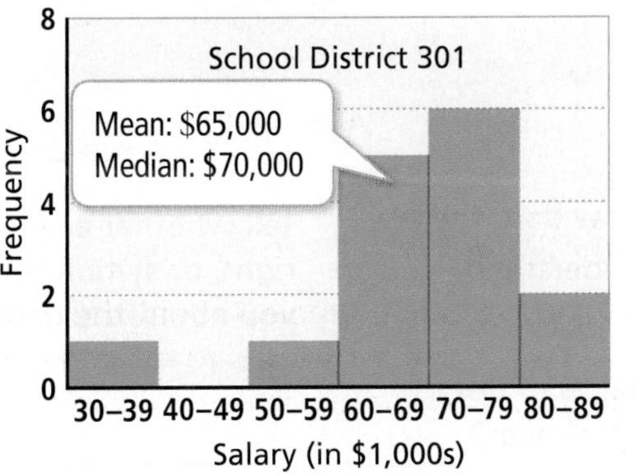

The data from teachers in School District 301 is skewed left. Most of the teachers with similar positions have salaries that are higher than the mean.This indicates that there are more teachers that make a higher salary.

COMMON ERROR
When data displays are "skewed right," the "tail" of the graph goes toward the right. When data displays are "skewed left," the tail goes to the left.

If Jennifer's starting salary is the same at each school district, she should strongly consider School District 101 or School District 301. Based on the data represented here, these districts have more potential for Jennifer to advance her salary.

Try It! 5. Suppose a fourth school district offers Jennifer a job. School District 401 has a mean salary of $57,000 and a median salary of $49,000. Should Jennifer consider accepting the job offer with School District 401? Explain.

CONCEPT SUMMARY Interpreting the Shapes of Data Displays

WORDS The shape of a data display reveals a lot about the data set.

In a **symmetric** data display, the data points are evenly spread on either side of the center. The mean is equal (or approximately equal) to the median.

In a **skewed** data display, the data points are unevenly spread on either side of the center (median). A data display can be skewed right or skewed left. The mean and median are not equal.

GRAPHS This data set is symmetric. There are a similar number of data points greater than and less than the mean.

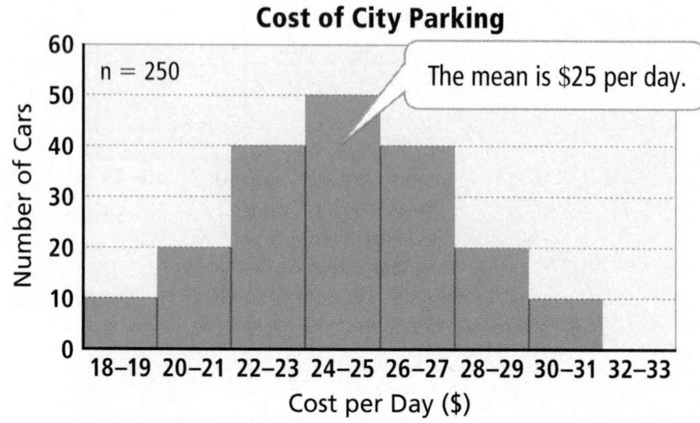

One family with 5 pets skewed the data to the right. The very small sample size makes inferences unreliable.

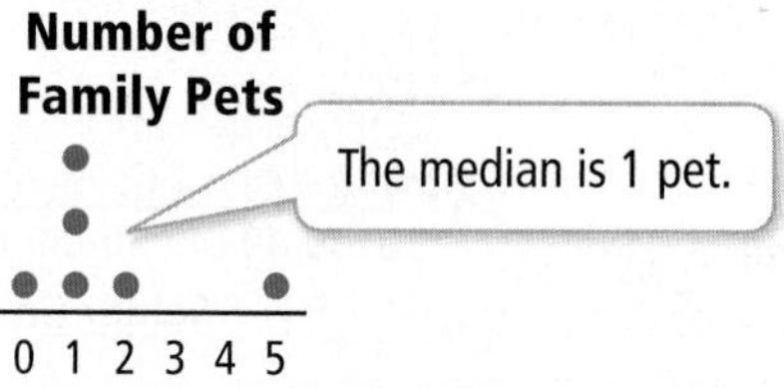

Do You UNDERSTAND?

1. **ESSENTIAL QUESTION** How does the shape of a data set help you understand the data?

2. **Use Structure** How are the shapes of dot plots, histograms, and box plots similar? How are they different?

3. **Error Analysis** Nicholas says that the display for a skewed data distribution is symmetrical about the mean. Is Nicholas correct? Explain your reasoning.

Do You KNOW HOW?

Tell whether each display is skewed left, skewed right, or symmetric. Interpret what the display tells you about the data set.

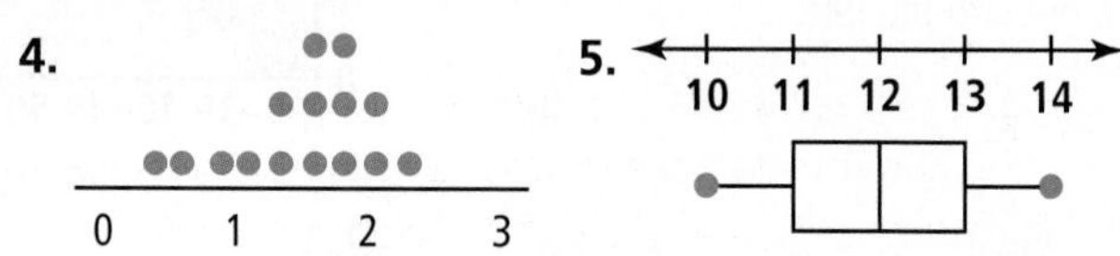

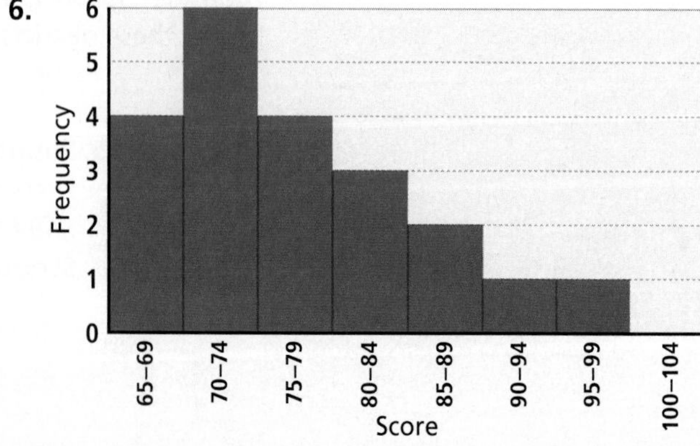

PRACTICE & PROBLEM SOLVING

Scan for Multimedia

Practice | Tutorial

Additional Exercises Available Online

UNDERSTAND

7. **Construct Arguments** A student in your class does not understand why the mean is less than the median when a data display is skewed left. How can you explain this relationship to the student?

8. **Look for Relationships** Two data sets have the same median. If one data set is skewed right and the other is skewed left, how are the means of the two data sets related?

9. **Error Analysis** Describe and correct the error(s) a student made in interpreting the shape of a box plot.

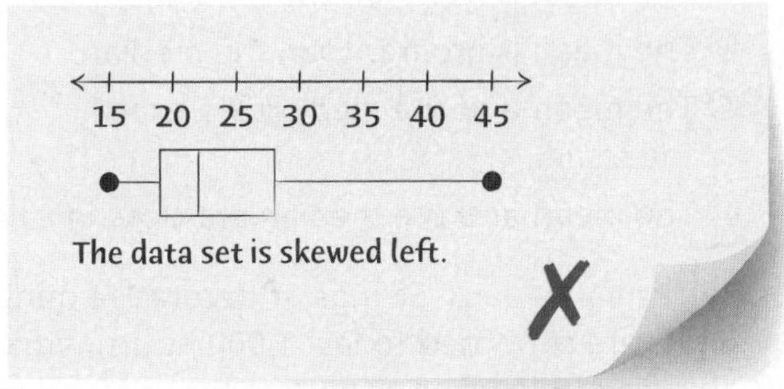

10. **Reason** Two data sets both have a mean of 10. The first set has a MAD of 1.5, and the second has a MAD of 3. How are the shapes of the data displays similar? How are they different?

11. **Higher Order Thinking** Data display A is symmetric with a mean of 50 and a MAD of 5. Data display B is symmetric with a mean of 75 and a MAD of 5.

    a. How are the data displays similar? How are they different?

    b. If the shapes of the displays are not identical, how could values in data set B be changed so that the displays are exactly the same?

12. **Make Sense and Persevere** The data represent the average number of hours 12 students spend on homework each night. Create two different data sets that could be represented by the display.

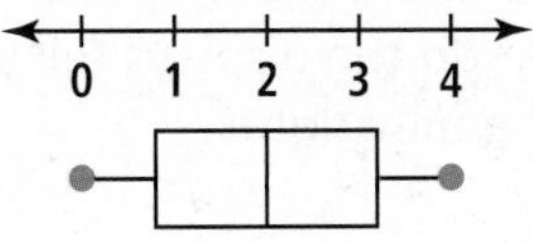

PRACTICE

Compare each pair of data displays. Tell whether each display is skewed left, skewed right, or symmetric. SEE EXAMPLES 1–3

13. Data Set A

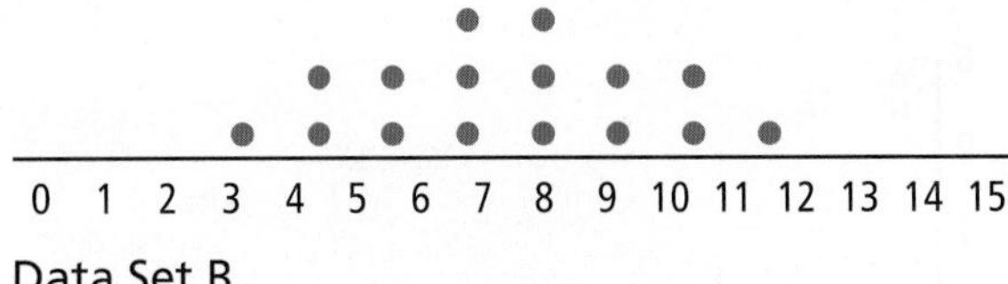

Data Set B

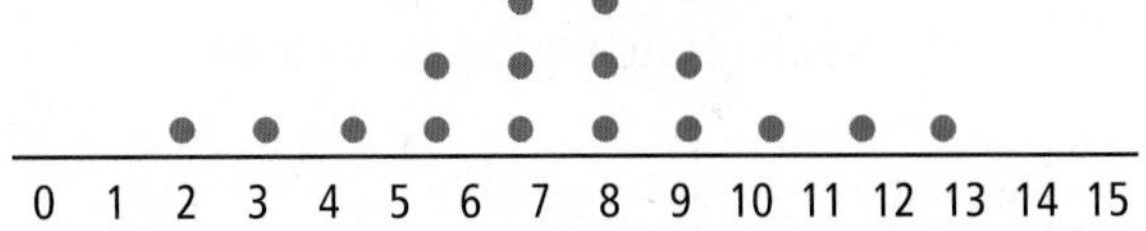

14. Data Set A

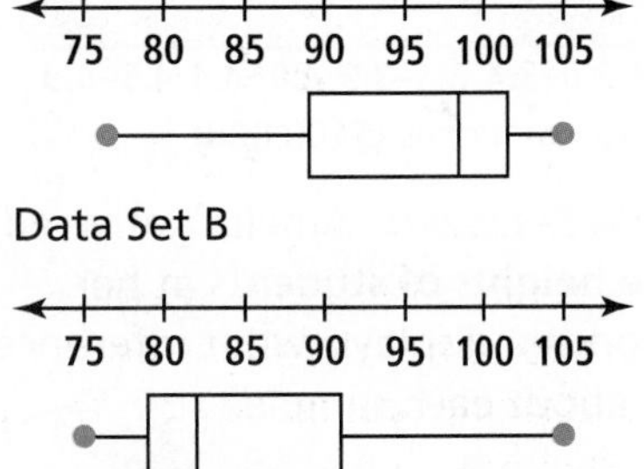

Interpret the shape of each display for the given context and make an inference based on a measure of center. SEE EXAMPLES 4 AND 5

15. The data represent amounts raised by students for a charity.

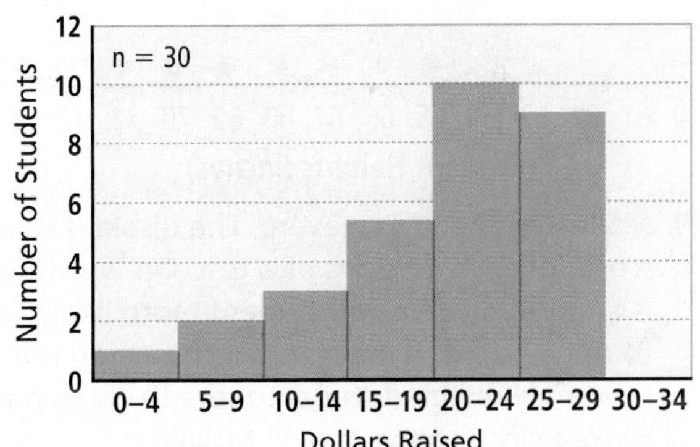

16. The data represent thousands of points scored in a video game tournament.

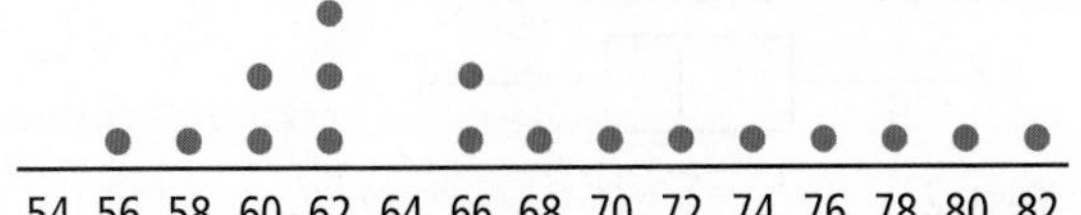

PRACTICE & PROBLEM SOLVING

Practice Tutorial

Mixed Review Available Online

APPLY

17. **Mathematical Connections** The displays represent house prices in a town over two consecutive years. What do the displays tell you about the change in house prices in the two years?

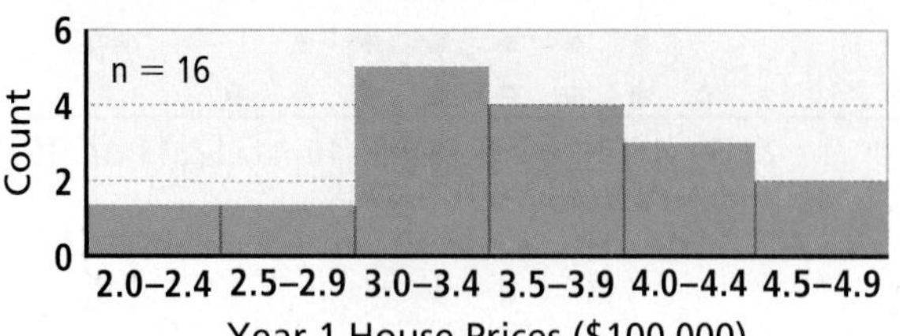

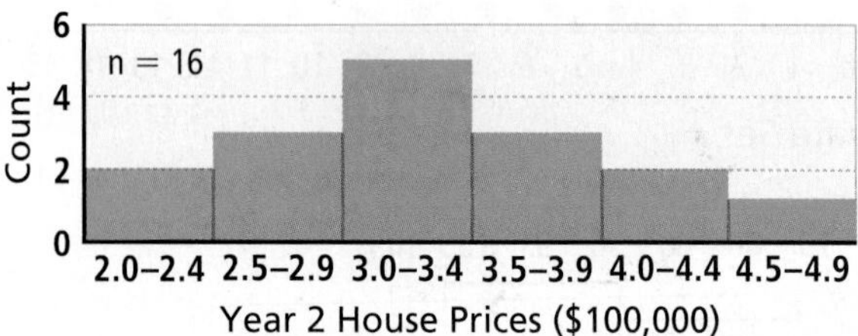

18. **Make Sense and Persevere** Amelia gathered data about the heights of students at her school. Based on the displays, what inferences can you make about each sample?

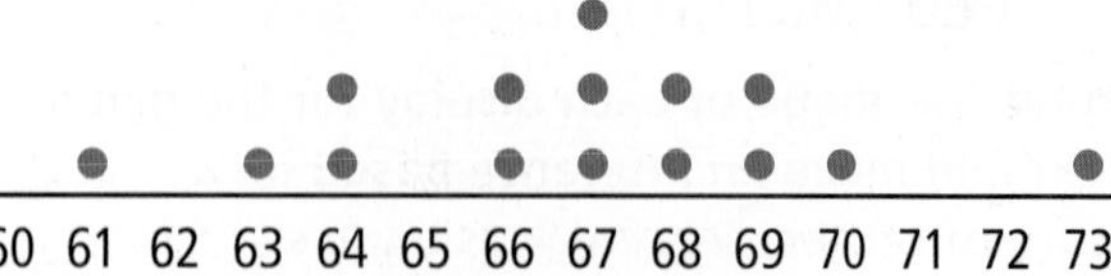

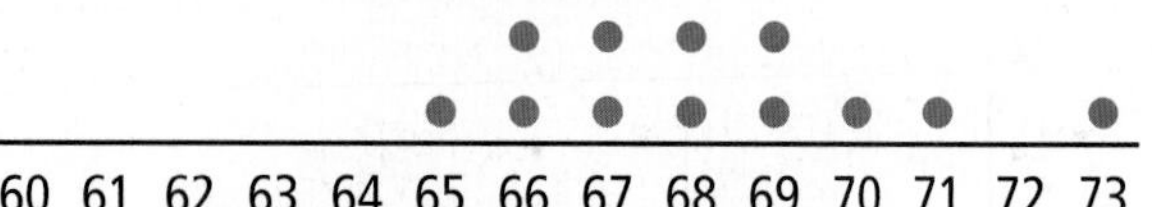

19. **Make Sense and Persevere** The displays show scores on two versions of a test. On which test is a randomly selected student more likely to get a higher score? On which version is a randomly selected student more likely to have a score close to the mean? Explain.

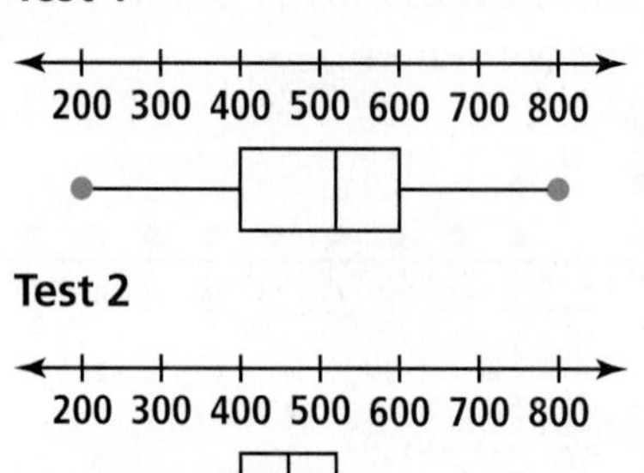

ASSESSMENT PRACTICE

20. A data display is symmetrical about the data value 10. Select all that apply.

Ⓐ The mean is about 10.

Ⓑ The median is about 10.

Ⓒ The mean must be greater than the median.

Ⓓ The median must be greater than the mean.

Ⓔ The majority of data values in the data set are greater than 10.

21. **SAT/ACT** The shape of a data set is relatively symmetrical. What does that indicate about the measures of center?

Ⓐ The mean is less than the median.

Ⓑ The mean is greater than the median.

Ⓒ The mean and the median are exactly the same.

Ⓓ The mean and the median are close in value.

22. **Performance Task** Strings of decorative mini lights are supposed to last 1,000 hours, with an acceptable error of plus or minus 50 hours. Data from two quality control tests are given.

Mini Lights Lifespan

TEST 1				
975	1,025	950	950	975
1,050	925	1,050	1,025	1,050
1,000	1,075	975	950	1,025

TEST 2				
975	1,000	1,025	1,000	1,000
1,025	1,000	950	975	1,025
1,000	975	1,050	1,000	1,000

Part A Find the mean, MAD, median, and IQR for each data set.

Part B Select the type of data display that you think will best allow you to compare the data sets. Explain your reasoning. Create the data displays.

Part C Interpret and compare the shapes of the data displays. What do the displays tell you about the quality of the mini lights?

11-4 Standard Deviation

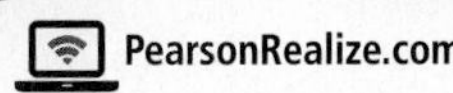

I CAN… quantify and analyze the spread of data.

VOCABULARY

- normal distribution
- standard deviation
- variance

MODEL & DISCUSS

A meteorologist compares the high temperatures for two cities during the past 10 days.

A. Create a data display for each city's high temperatures.

B. Use Structure What does the shape of each data display indicate about the data set and the measures of center?

ESSENTIAL QUESTION

Why does the way in which data are spread out matter?

EXAMPLE 1 Interpret the Variability of a Data Set

The makers of a certain brand of light bulbs claim that the average life of the bulb is 1,200 hours. The life spans, in hours, of a sample of Brand A light bulbs are shown. How close to the claim were the light bulbs in this sample?

1,150	1,231	1,305	1,080	1,125	1,295	1,127	1,184	1,099	1,123
1,204	1,345	1,173	1,126	1,220	1,245	1,283	1,225	1,185	1,275

A. What type of data display will provide the best view of the data?

The numbers in the data set span a large range of numbers. To understand how these numbers relate to the claimed mean, create a histogram.

USE STRUCTURE
How does the shape of the distribution help you identify the mean?

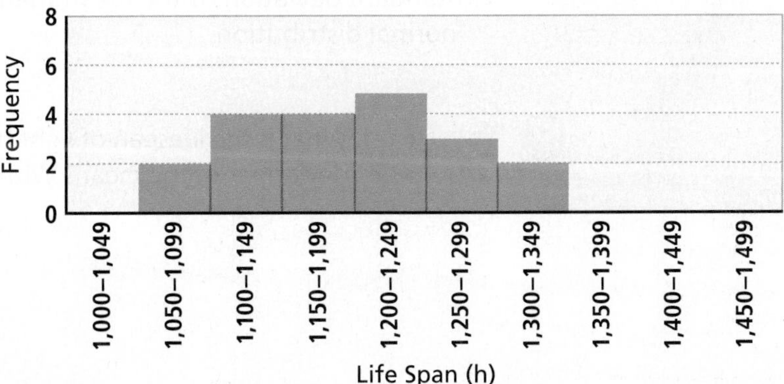

CONTINUED ON THE NEXT PAGE

EXAMPLE 1 CONTINUED

B. What does the display reveal about the data?

The data forms a bell-shaped curve. Data that is in this shape is said to have a **normal distribution**.

LOOK FOR RELATIONSHIPS
Most data values in a normally distributed set are clustered around the mean. The farther from the mean, the fewer data values there are.

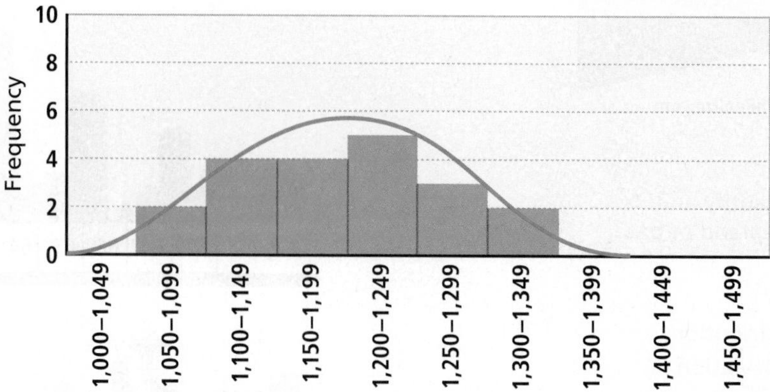

When data are normally distributed, the most useful measure of spread is the **standard deviation**. Standard deviation is a measure that shows how data vary, or deviate, from the mean.

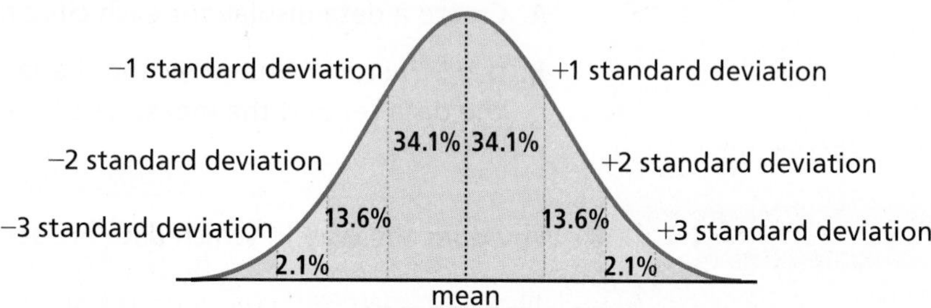

In a normal distribution,

- About 68% of data fall within one standard deviation of the mean.
- About 95% of data fall within two standard deviations of the mean.
- About 99.7% of data fall within three standard deviations of the mean.

The standard deviation for this sample of lightbulbs is 75.5 hours.

The mean of this data set is 1,200. Light bulbs with a life span between 1,124.5 hours and 1,275.5 hours lie within one standard deviation of the mean. In a large sample drawn randomly among such light bulbs, we would always expect about 68% of the life spans to be within one standard deviation of the mean thanks to the predictive power of the normal distribution.

 **Try It!** **1.** What is the lifespan of light bulbs that are within 2 standard deviations of the mean? Within 3 standard deviations of the mean?

CONCEPTUAL UNDERSTANDING

EXAMPLE 2 Calculate the Standard Deviation of a Sample

The table shows the number of cars sold by an auto sales associate over an eight-week period. How much variability do the data show?

18	25	18	10	17	15	18	15

You can find the variability by solving for the standard deviation for a sample, using the formula $s = \sqrt{\frac{\sum(x - \overline{x})^2}{n - 1}}$. To calculate it, follow these steps.

Step 1 Find the mean of the data by finding the sum of the data points and dividing by 8. The notation $\overline{x}$ is used to indicate the mean.

$\overline{x} = 17$

Step 2 Find the difference between each data value, x, and the mean, $\overline{x}$. Then square each difference.

COMMON ERROR
Remember to square the differences between each data value and the mean. Otherwise, the sum of the differences will be zero.

x	18	25	18	10	17	15	18	15
$\overline{x}$	17	17	17	17	17	17	17	17
$x - \overline{x}$	1	8	1	−7	0	−2	1	−2
$(x - \overline{x})^2$	1	64	1	49	0	4	1	4

Step 3 Find the variance.

The **variance** of a total population, often noted σ^2, is the mean of the squares of the differences between each data value and the mean. When finding the variance of a sample, often noted s^2, dividing by n provides too small an estimate of the variance of the population. This is because data points from the sample are likely to cluster more closely around the sample mean than the population mean. If you divide by $n - 1$ instead of n, you get a slightly bigger number that is closer to the true population variance.

$$s^2 = \frac{1 + 64 + 1 + 49 + 0 + 4 + 1 + 4}{7}$$

$$s^2 \approx 17.71$$

In this sample, $n = 8$ so we divide by $n - 1$, or 7.

Step 4 Take the square root of the variance to find the standard deviation, s.

$$s \approx \sqrt{17.71}$$

$$s \approx 4.21$$

Since only whole cars can be sold, it makes sense to round the standard deviation to 4.

The standard deviation is about 4 cars and the mean is about 17 cars, so there is some variability in the data. The sales associate will sell between 13 and 21 cars about 68% of the time because those values are one standard deviation from the mean.

Try It! 2. The table shows the number of cars sold by the auto sales associate over the next eight-week period. How much variability do the data show?

12	14	29	10	17	16	18	16

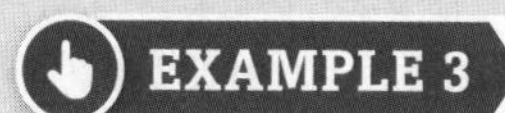

EXAMPLE 3 Find Standard Deviation of a Population

The table displays the number of points scored by a football team during each of their regular season games.

24	13	10	21	18	3
27	18	20	14	7	27

A. What are the mean and standard deviation for this data set?

Find the mean of the data by finding the sum and dividing by 16.

$\bar{x} \approx 16.8$

Find the variance. Use n as the denominator because the data represent the full population.

$$\sigma^2 = \frac{\sum(x - \bar{x})^2}{n}$$

$$\sigma^2 \approx \frac{51.36 + 14.69 + 46.69 + 17.36 + 1.36 + 191.36 + 103.36 + 1.36 + 10.03 + 8.03 + 96.69 + 103.36}{12}$$

$\sigma^2 \approx 53.8$

In this example, divide by n because you are working with the entire population of games.

STUDY TIP
Use the Greek letter σ (sigma) for standard deviation when working with *populations.* Use s when working with *samples.*

Find the standard deviation by taking the square root of the variance.

$\sigma \approx \sqrt{53.8}$

$\sigma \approx 7.3$

The mean number of points that the team scored was about 17. The standard deviation is about 7.3. This means that the team scored between about 10 and 25 points in about 68 percent of their games.

B. The team played in two post-season games, scoring 7 points in one and 14 points in the other. How do these games affect the overall mean and standard deviation of the number of points scored all season?

Use graphing technology to find the mean and standard deviation.

L1	L2	L3 1
24		
13		
10		
21		
18		
3		
27		

L1(1)=24

Enter all 14 scores as a list in the graphing calculator.

Use the STAT menu, to find the mean and standard deviation.

When the team includes their post-season games, the mean number of points scored decreases to about 15.9. The standard deviation remains about 7.3.

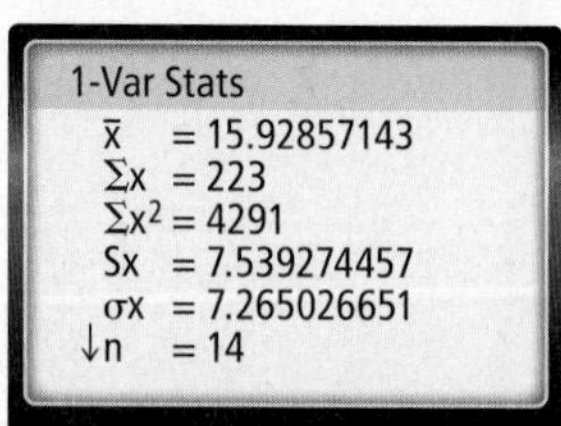

 **Try It!** 3. What was the range of points that the team scored in 95% of their regular season games?

APPLICATION

EXAMPLE 4 Compare Data Sets Using Standard Deviation

The histograms show the life spans of a sample of light bulbs from 2 companies. The first shows a sample from Brand A and the second from Brand B. The red lines indicate the mean and each standard deviation from the mean. Compare the distributions of life spans for the two light bulb brands.

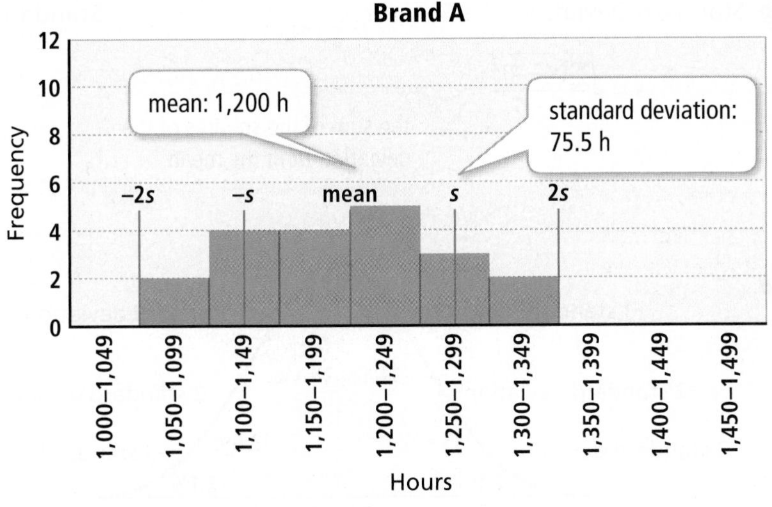

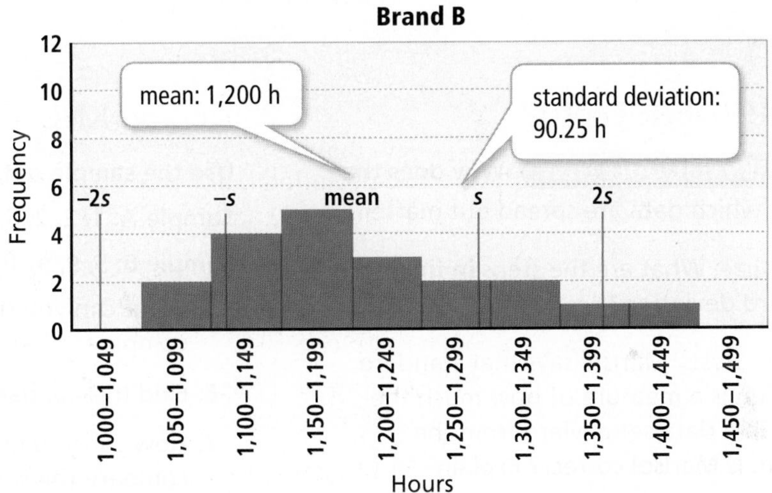

Both brands of light bulbs have an average life of about 1,200 hours.

The standard deviation for the data set for Brand A is less than the standard deviation for Brand B. This suggests that Brand A light bulbs show less variability in their life spans.

Since their light bulbs are more consistently closer to the mean, Brand A light bulbs are more predictable in their life spans than Brand B.

USE STRUCTURE
How does the shape of each graph help you compare the standard deviations?

Try It! **4.** Compare Brand C, with mean 1,250 hours and standard deviation 83 hours, to Brands A and B.

CONCEPT SUMMARY Standard Deviation

WORDS Standard deviation is a measure of spread, or variability. It indicates by how much the values in a data set deviate from the mean. It is the square root of the variance. The variance is the average of the squared deviations from the mean. When data are normally distributed (in a bell curve), the mean and the standard deviation describe the data set completely.

ALGEBRA Standard Deviation of a Sample

$$s = \sqrt{\frac{\sum(x - \bar{x})^2}{n - 1}}$$

the sum of the squares of the deviation from the mean

Standard Deviation of a Population

$$s = \sqrt{\frac{\sum(x - \bar{x})^2}{n}}$$

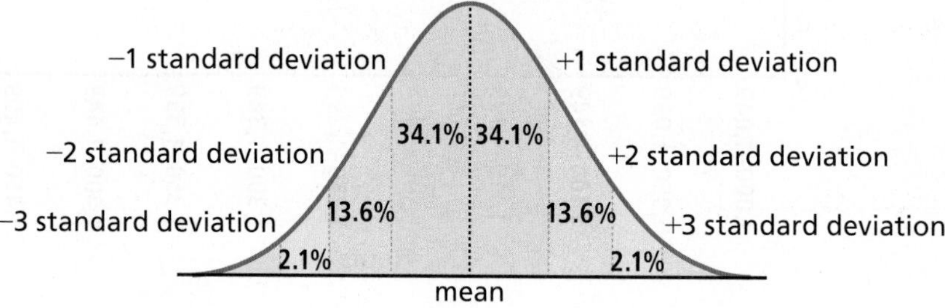

Do You UNDERSTAND?

1. ESSENTIAL QUESTION Why does the way in which data are spread out matter?

2. **Generalize** What are the steps in finding standard deviation?

3. **Error Analysis** Marisol says that standard deviation is a measure of how much the values in a data set deviate from the median. Is Marisol correct? Explain.

4. **Use Structure** If you add 10 to every data value in a set, what happens to the mean, range, and standard deviation. Why?

Do You KNOW HOW?

Use the sample data for Exercises 5–7.

Sample A: 1, 2, 2, 5, 5, 5, 6, 6

Sample B: 5, 9, 9, 10, 10, 10, 11, 11

5. What can you determine by using range to compare the spread of the two samples?

6. Find the standard deviation for each sample.

7. How can you use standard deviation to compare the spread of each sample?

8. Based on the histogram, what data values are within one standard deviation of the mean?

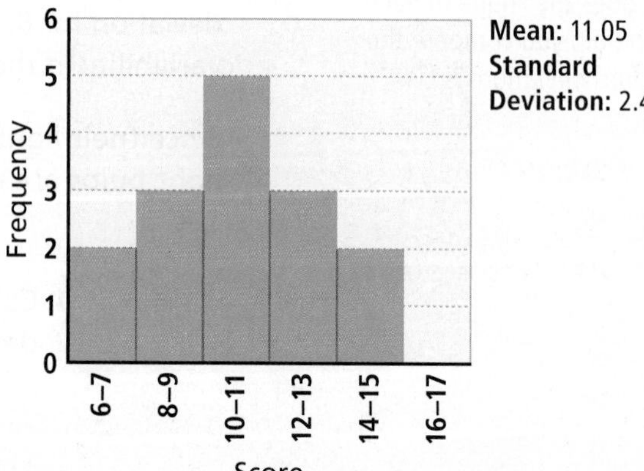

PRACTICE & PROBLEM SOLVING

Scan for Multimedia

Practice | Tutorial

Additional Exercises Available Online

UNDERSTAND

9. Generalize Two data sets have the same number of values. The first data set has a mean of 7.2 and a standard deviation of 1.25. The second data set has a mean of 7.2 and a standard deviation of 2.5.

a. How can you tell which data set is more spread out?

b. How is the shape of a histogram for the first data set different from the shape of a histogram for the second data set?

10. Error Analysis Describe and correct the errors a student made in calculating the standard deviation of a data set.

$$\sigma^2 = \frac{(-4) + 2 + (-1) + (-3) + 5 + 1}{6} = \frac{0}{6} = 0$$

$$\sigma = \sqrt{0} = 0$$

✗

11. Use Appropriate Tools The screen shows statistics for a data set that has been entered into a graphing calculator. Does 8.7 fall within 2 standard deviations of the mean of the data set? Explain.

1-Var Stats
$\bar{x}$ = 13.14035088
Σx = 2247
Σx^2 = 32883
Sx = 4.443522436
σx = 4.43051063
↓n = 171

12. Higher Order Thinking A data set has data one standard deviation below the mean at 76.2 and data one standard deviation above the mean at 105.4.

a. What is the mean of the data set?

b. What is the standard deviation of the data set?

c. What end values of the data are two standard deviations from the mean?

PRACTICE

Find and use the mean and the standard deviation to compare the variability of each pair of sample data sets. SEE EXAMPLES 1, 2, AND 4

13. Data Set A: 6, 9, 1, 2, 3, 4, 4, 5

Data Set B: 10, 5, 5, 2, 3, 7, 4, 8

14.

Data Set A	Data Set B
21.25	41.50
42.25	29.25
2.00	39.75
40.50	40.00
19.75	38.25
57.75	51.25
39.25	42.00
78.75	31.00
38.50	37.75
62.25	49.00

15. Find and use the mean and standard deviation to compare the variability of the populations represented in the dot plots. SEE EXAMPLES 3–4

Data Set A

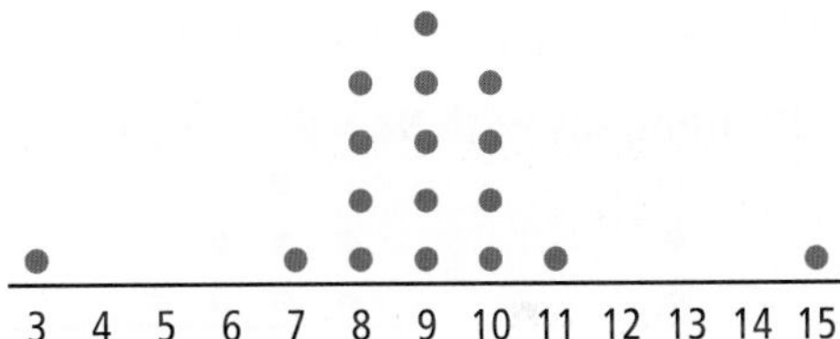

Data Set B

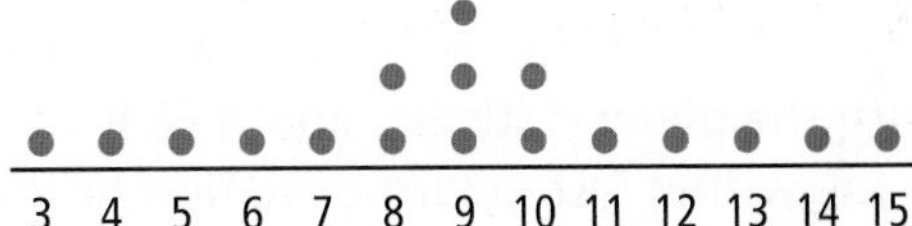

Data values in normally distributed data sets A and B are integers from 0 to 30 inclusive. Identify the range of values that satisfies each description.
SEE EXAMPLE 2

Data Set A: mean: 12; standard deviation: 2

Data Set B: mean: 18; standard deviation: 3

16. All data values within 2 standard deviations from the mean of data set A

17. All data values more than 2 standard deviations from the mean of data set A

18. All data values within 1 standard deviation of the mean of data set B

PRACTICE & PROBLEM SOLVING

Practice Tutorial

Mixed Review Available Online

APPLY

19. Make Sense and Persevere The data display shows the number of runners with finishing times under 7 hours for all marathons run in a given year. How could you estimate the number of runners who had finishing times less than 2 standard deviations below the mean?

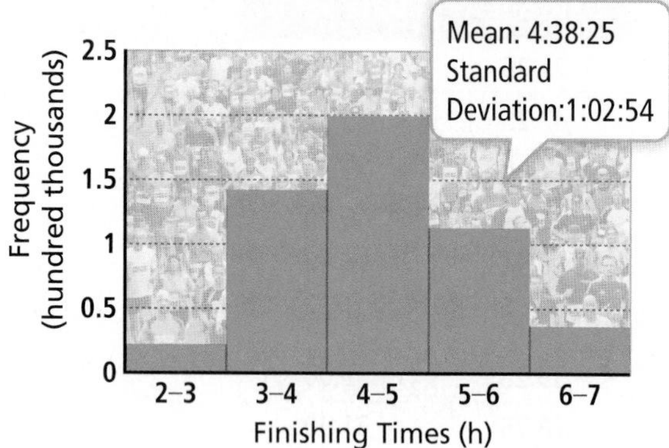

20. Make Sense and Persevere Last year, twelve hydrangea bushes had a mean of 14 blooms each, with a standard deviation of 2. The dot plot shows the number of blooms on the same bushes this year after a new plant food is used. What conclusions can you draw about the use of the new plant food and the number of blooms?

Hydrangeas with New Plant Food

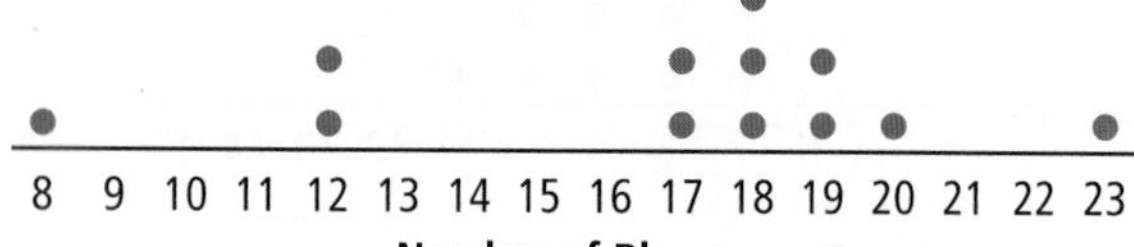

21. Make Sense and Persevere On a standardized test with the given statistics, about 68% of the scores fall within 1 standard deviation of the mean and about 95% of the scores fall within two standard deviations of the mean.

Mean Score: 450 **Standard Deviation:** 125

Total Number of Test Takers: 78,000

What is your score if you can say that you scored above the middle 95% of the people who took the test? How many test takers can say that?

ASSESSMENT PRACTICE

22. Consider a data set with a mean of 5.72 and a standard deviation of 1.55. Are the numbers within one standard deviation of the mean? Select *Yes* or *No*.

	Yes	No
7.51	❑	❑
4.18	❑	❑
4.16	❑	❑
10.00	❑	❑

23. SAT/ACT The variance for a data set with 8 items is 144. What is the standard deviation?

Ⓐ 4

Ⓑ 8

Ⓒ 12

Ⓓ none of these

24. Performance Task The table shows the top ten average driving distances in 2015 for male and female professional golfers. The mean for men is 310.9 yards, and the mean for women is 267.2 yards.

Men Average Drive(yd)	Women Average Drive(yd)
317.7	274.4
315.2	269.4
313.7	269.2
311.6	267.6
309.9	267.1
309.8	266.2
309.0	265.3
308.2	265.1
307.7	264.0
306.1	263.0

Part A Find the range for each data set. What do the ranges tell you about gender and average driving distance?

Part B Calculate the standard deviation for each sample. How can you use standard deviation to better understand the relationship between gender and average driving distance?

Part C How would histograms for the top ten men's and women's average driving distances be similar? How would they be different?

11-5 Two-Way Frequency Tables

PearsonRealize.com

I CAN… organize data in two-way frequency tables and use them to make inferences.

VOCABULARY
- conditional relative frequency
- joint frequency
- joint relative frequency
- marginal frequency
- marginal relative frequency

EXPLORE & REASON

Baseball teams at a high school and a college play at the same stadium. Results for every game last season are given for both teams. There were no ties.

Baseball Season Results at Mountain View Stadium

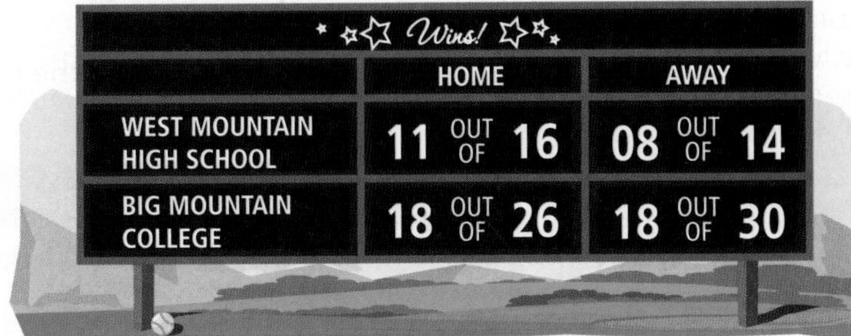

A. How could you organize the data in table form?

B. Look for Relationships How would you analyze the data to determine whether the data support the claim that the team that plays at home is more likely to win?

ESSENTIAL QUESTION

How can you use two-way frequency tables to analyze data?

APPLICATION

EXAMPLE 1 Interpret a Two-Way Frequency Table

Owners of a major food chain are planning to add a vegetarian item to its menu. Customers were asked to choose one of two vegetarian items. The results are shown in the table. What trends do the results suggest?

A joint frequency is at the joint of a column and a row.

	Veggie Burger	Veggie Pizza	Totals
Male	50	40	90
Female	60	75	135
Totals	110	115	225

A marginal frequency is at the margin, or edge of a column or row.

STUDY TIP
A two-way frequency table can show possible relationships between two sets of categorical data.

Joint frequencies indicate the frequency of a single option for one category; for example, the frequency of males choosing a veggie burger.

Marginal frequencies indicate the total frequency for each option or category, such as the total frequency of female respondents.

The joint frequencies suggest that male customers prefer veggie burgers over veggie pizzas, and female customers prefer veggie pizzas over veggie burgers.

The marginal frequencies suggest that all of the respondents showed only a slight preference for veggie pizza over a veggie burger. They also indicate that more females than males were surveyed.

Try It! 1. What do the marginal frequencies tell you about the number of male and female respondents?

 Activity  Assess

APPLICATION

EXAMPLE 2 Interpret a Two-Way Relative Frequency Table

What do the survey results reveal about male and female customer preferences for veggie burgers?

COMMON ERROR
Divide each frequency by the total count, found in the bottom right corner of the two-way frequency table. Express relative frequency as a fraction, decimal, or percent.

Joint relative frequency is the ratio, or percent, of the joint frequency to the total.

Marginal relative frequency is the ratio, or percent, of the marginal frequency to the total.

	Veggie Burger	Veggie Pizza	Totals
Male	$\frac{50}{225} \approx 22\%$	$\frac{40}{225} \approx 18\%$	$\frac{90}{225} = 40\%$
Female	$\frac{60}{225} \approx 27\%$	$\frac{75}{225} \approx 33\%$	$\frac{135}{225} = 60\%$
Totals	$\frac{110}{225} \approx 49\%$	$\frac{115}{225} \approx 51\%$	$\frac{225}{225} = 100\%$

Of the customers surveyed, about 22% were males who selected veggie burgers and about 27% were females who selected veggie burgers. So, a greater percent of females than males selected veggie burgers.

 **Try It!** 2. How can you tell whether a greater percent of customers surveyed selected veggie burger or veggie pizza?

CONCEPTUAL UNDERSTANDING

EXAMPLE 3 Calculate Conditional Relative Frequency

Using data from Examples 1 and 2, a marketing team concludes that females prefer veggie burgers more than men do. Do the survey results support this conclusion?

Conditional relative frequency is the ratio of the joint frequency and the related marginal frequency.

Calculating the conditional relative frequency for each row will adjust for differences in the number of male and female customers surveyed.

CONSTRUCT ARGUMENTS
What do the conditional relative frequencies tell you about associations between gender and menu item choice?

	Veggie Burger	Veggie Pizza	Totals
Male	$\frac{50}{90} \approx 56\%$	$\frac{40}{90} \approx 44\%$	$\frac{90}{90} = 100\%$
Female	$\frac{60}{135} \approx 44\%$	$\frac{75}{135} \approx 56\%$	$\frac{135}{135} = 100\%$

Conditional relative frequency $= \frac{\text{joint frequency}}{\text{marginal frequency}}$

The results do not support this conclusion. The conditional relative frequencies show that while about 56% of the males surveyed prefer veggie burgers, only about 44% of the females prefer veggie burgers.

 **Try It!** 3. What conclusion could the marketing team make about male and female preferences for veggie pizza? Justify your answer.

EXAMPLE 4 Interpret Conditional Relative Frequency

The marketing team also concludes that there is a greater variation between the percent of men and women who like veggie pizza than there is for those who prefer veggie burgers. Do the survey results support this conclusion?

USE STRUCTURE
The conditional relative frequencies calculated for rows are not the same as those calculated for columns. How are the questions you can answer looking at the table in Example 3 different from the questions you can answer looking at the table in Example 4?

Calculating the conditional relative frequency for each column allows you to analyze male and female preferences within each food choice category.

The conclusion is supported by the survey results. Conditional relative frequencies show that of the customers who prefer veggie pizza, 65% are female and only 35% are male. Of those who prefer veggie burgers, 55% are female and 45% are male.

	Veggie Burger	Veggie Pizza
Male	$\frac{50}{110} \approx 45\%$	$\frac{40}{115} \approx 35\%$
Female	$\frac{60}{110} \approx 55\%$	$\frac{75}{115} \approx 65\%$
Totals	$\frac{110}{110} = 100\%$	$\frac{115}{115} = 100\%$

Try It! **4.** What conclusion could you draw if the percentages for male and female customers were the same across the rows in this table?

EXAMPLE 5 Interpret Data Frequencies

A random sample of spectators entering a stadium were asked whether they were cheering for the Bears or the Tigers in a championship game. The sample was categorized according to gender and team.

	Cheering for Bears	Cheering for Tigers	Total
Male	72	65	137
Female	49	44	93
Totals	121	109	230

A. What does the joint relative frequency $\frac{65}{230}$ represent in this context?

Joint relative frequency is the ratio of the joint frequency to the total.

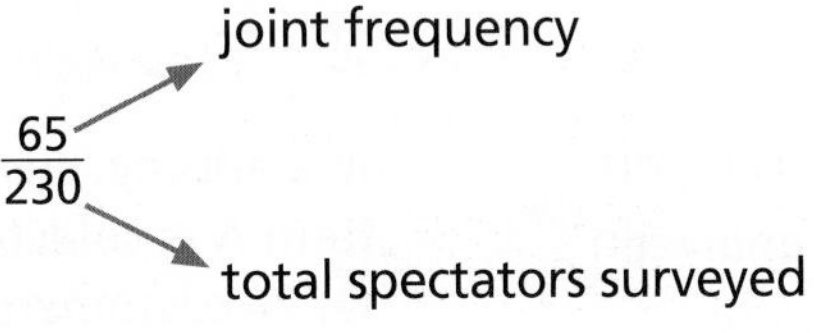

Find the joint frequency 65 in the table. You can see that 65 males cheered for the Tigers, so $\frac{65}{230}$ represents the ratio of male Tigers fans to the total number of people surveyed.

B. What does the conditional relative frequency $\frac{49}{93}$ represent in this context?

Conditional relative frequency is the ratio of the joint frequency to the related marginal frequency.

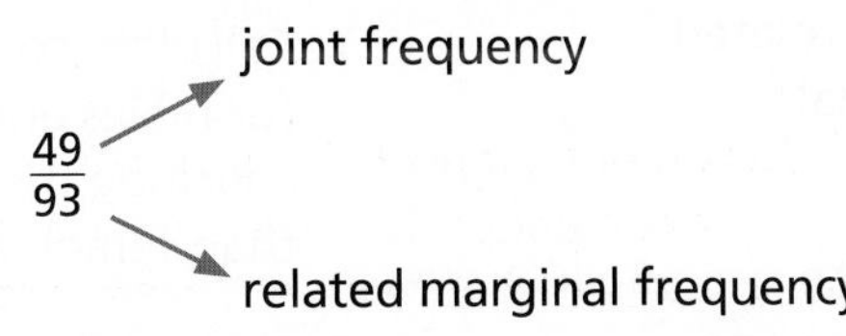

The number $\frac{49}{93}$ represents the ratio of female Bears fans to the number of females surveyed.

Try It! **5.** What does the conditional relative frequency $\frac{72}{137}$ represent in this context?

Concept Summary | Assess

CONCEPT SUMMARY Two-Way Frequency Tables

WORDS Two-way frequency tables show relationships between two sets of categorical data. Entries can be frequency counts or relative frequencies. Entries in the body of the table are **joint frequencies** (counts) or **joint relative frequencies** (ratios). Entries in the totals column or row are **marginal frequencies** or **marginal relative frequencies**.

Conditional relative frequencies show the frequency of responses for a given condition, or the ratio of the joint frequencies to the corresponding marginal frequency.

TABLES

Movie Time Preferences

	Afternoon	Evening	Totals
Student	$\frac{90}{200} = 45\%$	$\frac{50}{200} = 25\%$	$\frac{140}{200} = 70\%$
Adult	$\frac{20}{200} = 10\%$	$\frac{40}{200} = 20\%$	$\frac{60}{200} = 30\%$
Totals	$\frac{110}{200} = 55\%$	$\frac{90}{200} = 45\%$	$\frac{200}{200} = 100\%$

20 of the 200 respondents, or 10%, were adults who prefer the afternoon show.

70% of the respondents were students.

Conditional Relative Frequency

	Afternoon	Evening	Totals
Student	$\frac{90}{140} \approx 64\%$	$\frac{50}{140} \approx 36\%$	$\frac{140}{140} = 100\%$
Adult	$\frac{20}{60} \approx 33\%$	$\frac{40}{60} \approx 67\%$	$\frac{60}{60} = 100\%$

Of all of the adult respondents, 33% prefer afternoon shows.

Conditional Relative Frequency

	Afternoon	Evening
Student	$\frac{90}{110} \approx 82\%$	$\frac{50}{90} \approx 56\%$
Adult	$\frac{20}{110} \approx 18\%$	$\frac{40}{90} \approx 44\%$
Totals	$\frac{110}{110} = 100\%$	$\frac{90}{90} = 100\%$

Of all of the respondents that prefer evening shows, 44% were adults.

Do You UNDERSTAND?

1. ESSENTIAL QUESTION How can you use two-way frequency tables to analyze data?

2. **Communicate Precisely** How are joint frequencies and marginal frequencies similar? How are they different?

3. **Look for Relationships** How are conditional relative frequencies related to joint frequencies and marginal frequencies?

4. **Error Analysis** Zhang says that the marginal relative frequency for a given variable is 10. Could Zhang be correct? Explain your reasoning.

Do You KNOW HOW?

In a survey, customers select Item A or Item B. Item A is selected by 20 males and 10 females. Of 20 customers who select Item B, five are males.

5. Make a two-way frequency table to organize the data.

6. Make a two-way relative frequency table to organize the data.

7. Calculate conditional relative frequencies for males and females. Is it reasonable to conclude that males prefer Item A more than females do?

8. Calculate conditional relative frequencies for Item A and Item B. Is it reasonable to conclude that a customer who prefers Item B is more likely to be a female than a male?

Go Online | PearsonRealize.com

UNDERSTAND

9. **Reason** An equal number of juniors and seniors were surveyed about whether they prefer lunch item A or B. Is it reasonable to infer from the table that more juniors prefer lunch item B while more seniors prefer lunch item A? Explain.

	Item A	Item B	Totals
Junior	0.1	0.4	0.5
Senior	0.3	0.2	0.5
Totals	0.6	0.4	1.0

10. **Error Analysis** Describe and correct the errors a student made when making a generalization based on a two-way frequency table.

Which subject do you prefer?			
	Math	Language Arts	Totals
Male	45	45	90
Female	30	30	60
Totals	75	75	150

Male students prefer math more than female students do. 

11. **Look for Relationships** In a two-way relative frequency table, how are joint relative frequencies and marginal relative frequencies related?

12. **Higher Order Thinking** Students are surveyed to see how long they studied for a test.
    - 10% of the students who studied 3 hours or more failed the test.
    - 40% of the students who studied less than 3 hours passed the test.
    - 2 students who studied 3 hours or more failed the test.
    - 4 students who studied less than 3 hours passed the test.

    a. Make a two-way frequency table that shows the association between hours spent studying and passing the test.

    b. Does the association appear to be significant? Explain.

PRACTICE

In a survey, music club members select their preference between Song A or Song B. Song A is selected by 30 teens and 10 adults. Of 20 members who select Song B, five are teens. SEE EXAMPLES 1–4

Make a two-way frequency table to organize the data.

13. Is it reasonable to say that more people surveyed prefer Song A? Explain.

14. Is it reasonable to say that more adults than teens participated in the survey? Explain.

Calculate conditional relative frequencies.

15. Is it reasonable to say that teens prefer Song A more than adults do? Explain.

16. Is a member who prefers Song B significantly more likely to be an adult than a teen? Explain.

In the two-way frequency table, frequencies are shown on the top of each cell in blue, and relative frequencies are shown at the bottom in red. Most of the frequencies are missing. SEE EXAMPLES 1–5

High School Graduate?	Choice A	Choice B	Totals
Yes	16 0.08	___ ___	___ 0.56
No	___ ___	24 ___	___ ___
Totals	___ ___	___ ___	___ ___

17. Complete the table.

18. Calculate conditional relative frequencies for yes and no.

19. Calculate conditional relative frequencies for Choices A and B.

20. Is a high school graduate more likely to prefer Choice A or B? Explain.

21. Is someone who prefers Choice A more likely to be a high school graduate than not? Explain.

22. What does the joint relative frequency $\frac{64}{200}$ represent in this context?

23. What does the conditional relative frequency $\frac{96}{120}$ represent in this context?

PRACTICE & PROBLEM SOLVING

Practice | Tutorial

Mixed Review Available Online

APPLY

24. Construct Arguments Is there a significant association between income and whether or not a voter supports the referendum? Justify your answer.

Do you support the referendum?			
Income	Yes	No	Totals
≤ $100,000	80	20	100
> $100,000	40	10	50
Totals	120	30	150

25. Make Sense and Persevere A gardener is only satisfied when a hydrangea bush has at least 14 blooms. How can you organize the data shown in the dot plots into two-way frequency tables to make inferences about the new plant food and the number of blooms?

Hydrangeas Without New Plant Food

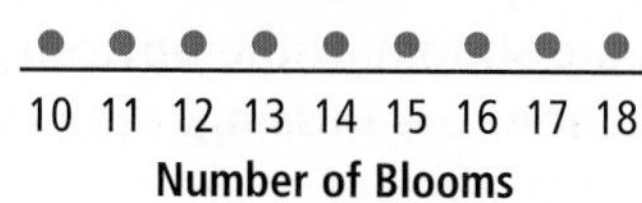

Hydrangeas with New Plant Food

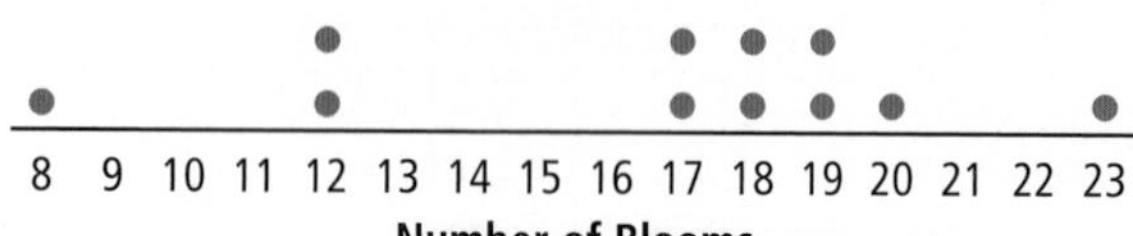

26. Construct Arguments Based on the survey data below, a marketing team for an airline concludes that someone between 18 and 24 years of age is more likely never to have flown on a commercial airliner than someone 25 years or older. Do you agree with this conclusion? Justify your answer.

Terminal

Have you ever flown on a commercial airline?			
	Yes	No	Totals
18–24 yrs	198	81	279
25+ yrs	2,539	448	2,987
Totals	2,737	529	3,266

ASSESSMENT PRACTICE

27. Consider a two-way frequency table. Select all that apply.

Ⓐ The sum of all joint frequencies equals the total frequency.

Ⓑ The sum of all marginal frequencies equals the total frequency.

Ⓒ The sum of all marginal frequencies in a row equals the total frequency.

Ⓓ The sum of all joint frequencies in a column equals the marginal frequency at the bottom of the column.

Ⓔ A relative frequency is the ratio of a joint frequency and a marginal frequency.

28. SAT/ACT In a two-way frequency table, the joint frequency in a cell is 8 and the marginal frequency in the same row is 32. What is the conditional relative frequency for the cell?

Ⓐ 0.12

Ⓑ 0.20

Ⓒ 0.25

Ⓓ 0.40

Ⓔ 0.50

29. Performance Task A high school offers a prep course for students who are taking a retest for a college entrance exam.

- Of 25 students who took the prep course, 20 scored at least 50 points higher on the retest than on the original exam.
- Overall, 100 students took the retest and 50 students scored at least 50 points higher on the retest than on the original exam.

Part A Create a two-way frequency table to organize the data.

Part B Funding for the prep course may be cut because more students scored at least 50 points higher on the retest without taking the prep course. Do you agree with this decision? If not, how could you use a two-way frequency table to construct an argument to keep the funding?

MATHEMATICAL MODELING IN 3 ACTS

PearsonRealize.com

Video

Text Message

Text messages used be just that: text only. Now you can send multimedia messages (or MMS) with emojis, images, audio, and videos. Did you know Finland was the first country to offer text messaging to phone customers?

Some people send and receive so many texts that they use textspeak to make typing faster. RU 1 of them? You will see one person keep track of his text messages in this Modeling Mathematics in 3 Acts lesson.

Scan for Multimedia

ACT 1 Identify the Problem

1. What is the first question that comes to mind after watching the video?
2. Write down the main question you will answer about what you saw in the video.
3. Make an initial conjecture that answers this main question.
4. Explain how you arrived at your conjecture.
5. What information will be useful to know to answer the main question? How can you get it? How will you use that information?

ACT 2 Develop a Model

6. Use the math that you have learned in this Topic to refine your conjecture.

ACT 3 Interpret the Results

7. Is your refined conjecture between the highs and lows you set up earlier?
8. Did your refined conjecture match the actual answer exactly? If not, what might explain the difference?

TOPIC 11

Topic Review

? TOPIC ESSENTIAL QUESTION

1. How do you use statistics to model situations and solve problems?

Vocabulary Review

Choose the correct term to complete each sentence.

2. __________ is a measure of spread that reflects how the data vary from the mean.
3. __________ indicate the frequency of a single option for one category.
4. A(n) __________ is a data distribution that forms a bell-shaped curve.
5. __________ is the ratio of the joint frequency and the related marginal frequency.

- conditional relative frequency
- joint frequencies
- normal distribution
- standard deviation
- joint relative frequency

Concepts & Skills Review

LESSON 11-1 Analyzing Data Displays

Quick Review

Dot plots show counts of values within data sets. **Histograms** show the distribution of values within a data set in ranges or intervals. **Box plots** show the center and spread of a distribution using a five-number summary.

Example

The table below shows a class's math test scores. Create a histogram of the data.

83	92	56	63	80	91	78	59
75	79	62	85	81	90	82	74
60	95	88	82	77	74	68	82

Break the scores into intervals of 10.

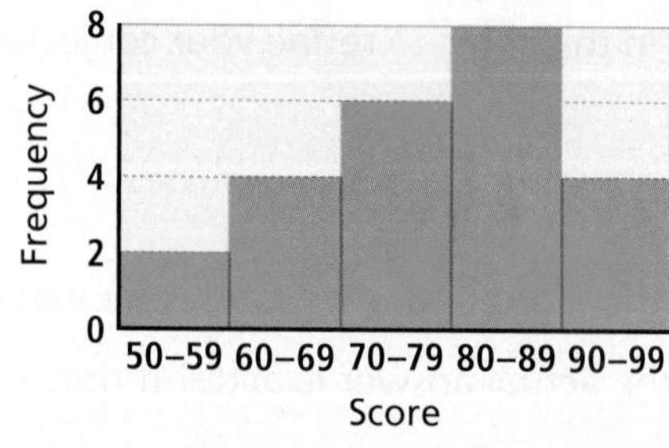

Practice & Problem Solving

6. **Generalize** In what situations would a box plot be the best display for a data set?

7. In what situations would a dot plot be the best display for a data set?

For the data set below, create the data display that best reveals the answer to the question. Explain your reasoning.

8. What is the frequency of the data value 35?

30	33	35	39
37	35	31	36
39	30	35	35

Choose the most appropriate data display to answer each question about a data set. Explain.

9. What are the frequencies for each interval of 2 points?

10. How many data values are less than any given value in the data set?

LESSON 11-2 Comparing Data Sets

Quick Review

You can compare data sets using statistical measures of center and measures of spread. The shape of the data in data displays indicates the relationship between measures of center. The mean absolute deviation (MAD) describes how much the data values vary from the mean of a data set. It is the mean of the absolute deviations.

Example

Micah would like to purchase a new golf club. He gathers data on the average driving distance (in yards) of two different types of clubs. The dot plots show the data for each type.

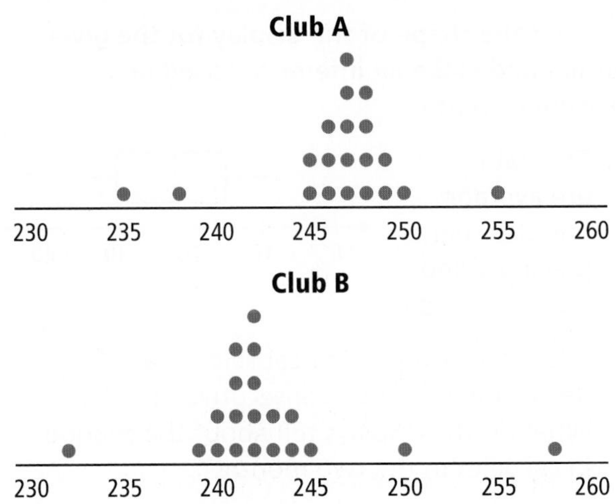

If Micah is most interested in increasing his driving distance, which golf club should he purchase?

The data show that Club A has better driving distance. Most of the dots in the data display for Club A golf clubs are clustered from 245 to 250 yd, and the dots in the data display for Club B golf clubs are clustered from 239 to 245 yd. Therefore, Micah should purchase Club A.

Practice & Problem Solving

11. **Construct Arguments** If the mean is greater than the median for a given data set, what does that indicate about the data?

12. For the given data sets, compare the means and the MADs, and then the medians and the IQRs. Decide which measures are better for comparing the data sets. Explain your reasoning.

Data Set A			
3	8	7	5
7	1	4	9
5	4	2	6
4	1	4	3

Data Set B			
4	6	2	5
3	7	8	6
8	2	9	3
6	2	8	6

13. **Model With Mathematics** Last year's school basketball team had a mean average score of 78 with a mean absolute deviation of 4.5 points. The scores for this year's team are shown in the table. How do the scores for the two years compare?

83	65	90	88	75	82
68	78	80	82	94	73
78	85	80	81	74	88

Quick Review

When the shape of a data display is **symmetric**, the data values are evenly spread on either side of the center. The mean is close to the median. When the shape of a data display is **skewed**, the data display is skewed right or skewed left. The mean and median are not equal.

Example

The histogram shows the heights of players on a football team. The mean height is 59 in. What inferences can you make about the shape of the data?

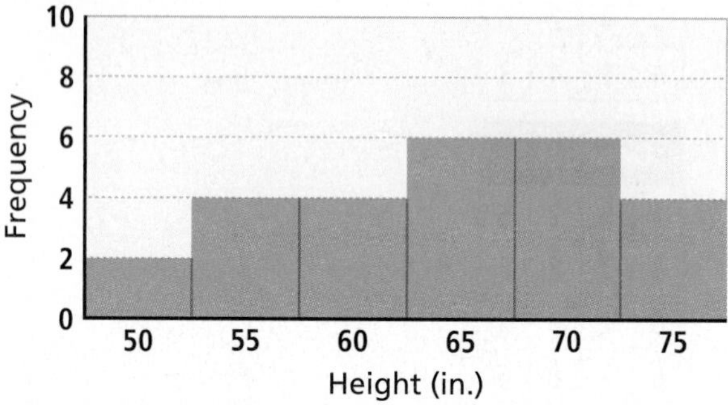

The histogram shows the data are skewed to the left. The mean is less than the median.

Based on the data, you can infer that most of the players are taller than 59 in.

Practice & Problem Solving

14. Look for Relationships One data set has a median that is less than the mean, while a second data set has a median that is greater than the mean. What does this mean for the graph of the data sets?

Tell whether each display is skewed left, skewed right or symmetric.

15. **16.**

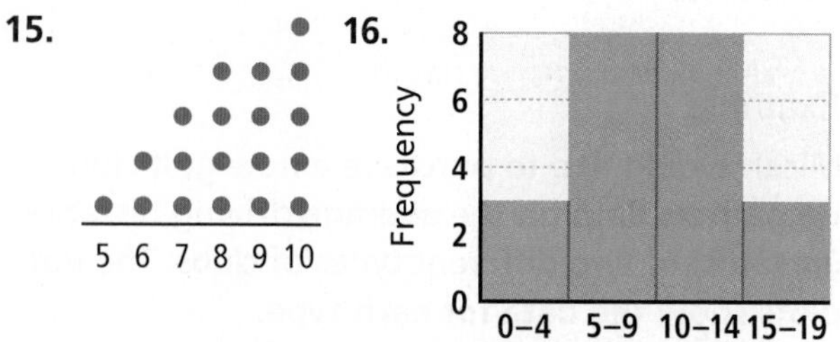

Interpret the shape of the display for the given context and make an inference based on a measure of center.

17. The data are average minutes spent playing video games each day.

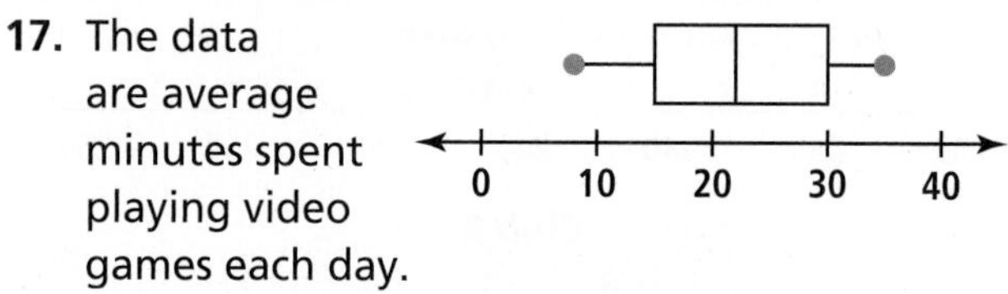

18. The displays represent car sales at a dealership over two consecutive months. What do the displays tell about the change in car sales in the two months?

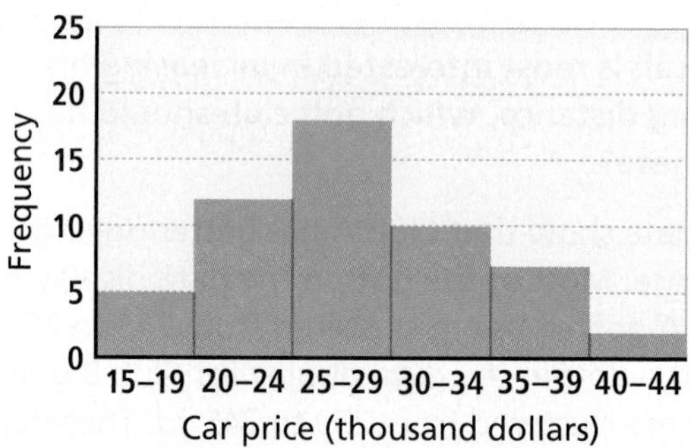

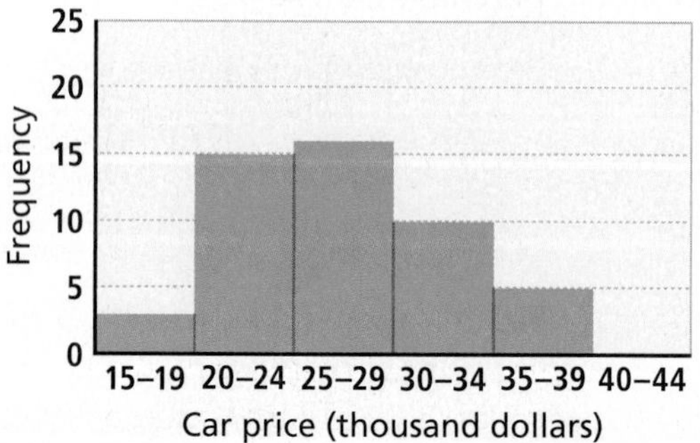

LESSON 11-4 Standard Deviation

Quick Review

Standard deviation indicates by how much the values in a data set deviate from the mean. It is the square root of the **variance**, the mean of the squared deviations from the mean.

Example

The table shows the number of hot dogs sold per day by a street vendor over a two-week period. How much variability do the sample data show?

40	28	18	36	52	41	29
24	30	27	51	34	42	35

Mean: $\bar{x} \approx 35$; variance: $s^2 \approx 95.41$; standard deviation: $s \approx 9.77$

The standard deviation is relatively large, so the data show quite a bit of variability. Typically, the vendor sells between 25 and 45 hot dogs per day.

Practice & Problem Solving

19. **Reason** The mean of a data set is 50.5 and the standard deviation is about 9.6. Does 70.5 fall within 2 standard deviations of the mean of the data set? Explain.

Find and use the mean and the standard deviation to compare the variability of the data sets.

20. **Sample A:** 15, 12, 8, 18, 16, 13, 14, 10; **Sample B:** 16, 19, 11, 9, 8, 10, 15, 11

21. **Make Sense and Persevere** A normally distributed sample of bank accounts shows a mean of \$22,000 and a standard deviation of \$1,275. How much money would be in an account that contains more than the middle 95% of the accounts? How many accounts would meet that requirement?

LESSON 11-5 Two-Way Frequency Tables

Quick Review

Two-way frequency tables show relationships between two sets of categorical data. **Joint frequencies** indicate the frequency of one category. **Marginal frequencies** indicate the total frequency for each category.

Example

A teacher asked her students to choose between the museum or the zoo for a class trip. The results are shown in the table. What trends do the results suggest?

	Museum	Zoo	Totals
Male	5	7	12
Female	12	6	18
Totals	17	13	30

The joint frequencies suggest that males prefer the zoo and females prefer the museum. The marginal frequencies suggest that all respondents showed a slight preference for going to the museum.

Practice & Problem Solving

In a survey, TV viewers can choose between two movies. 40 men and 10 women choose the action movie that is featured. Of the 30 people who chose the comedy, 20 are women and 10 are men.

22. Make a two-way frequency table to organize the data. Is it reasonable to say that more people surveyed prefer action movies? Explain.

23. **Construct Arguments** According to the data below, is there a significant association between age and a person's news source? Justify your answer.

Where do you get most of your news?			
Age	**TV**	**Internet**	**Totals**
≤ 30	50	80	130
> 30	30	40	70
Totals	80	120	200

Visual Glossary

English	Spanish

A

Absolute value function $f(x) = |x|$

Función de valor absoluto $f(x) = |x|$

Example

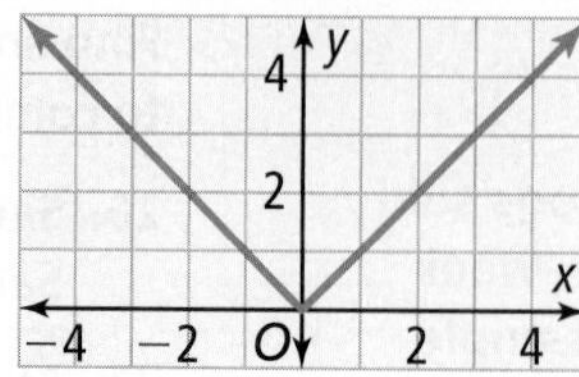

Arithmetic sequence A number sequence formed by adding a fixed number to each previous term to find the next term. The fixed number is called the *common difference*.

Progresión aritmética En una progresión aritmética la diferencia entre términos consecutivos es un número constante. El número constante se llama la diferencia común.

Example 4, 7, 10, 13, … is an arithmetic sequence with a common difference of 3.

Asymptote A line that the graph of a function gets closer to as x or y gets larger in absolute value.

Asíntota Línea recta a la que la gráfica de una función se acerca indefinidamente, mientras el valor absoluto de x o y aumenta.

Example

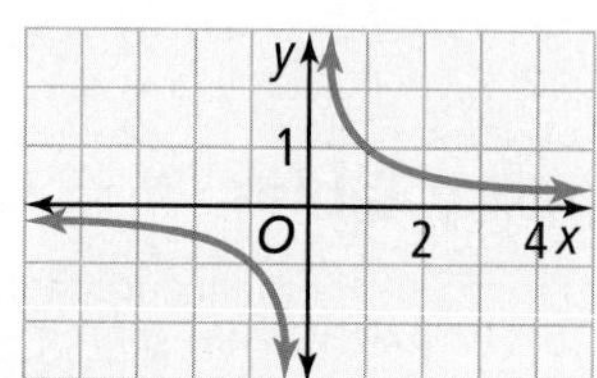

The y-axis is a vertical asymptote for $y = \frac{1}{x}$. The x-axis is a horizontal asymptote for $y = \frac{1}{x}$.

Axis of symmetry The line that intersects the vertex, and divides the graph into two congruent halves that are reflections of each other.

Eje de simetría El eje de simetría es la línea que corta el vértice y divide la gráfica en dos mitades congruentes que son reflexiones una de la otra.

Example

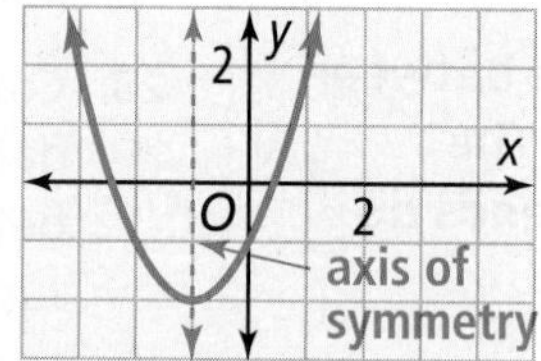

C

Causation When a change in one quantity causes a change in a second quantity. A correlation between quantities does not always imply causation.

Causalidad Cuando un cambio en una cantidad causa un cambio en una segunda cantidad. Una correlación entre las cantidades no implica siempre la causalidad.

Ceiling function A function that rounds numbers up to the nearest integer.

Función techo Función que redondea los números hacia arriba al entero más cercano.

English	Spanish

Closure property A set of numbers is closed under an operation when the result of the operation is also part of the same set of numbers.

Propiedad de cerradura Un conjunto de números está cerrado bajo una operación cuando el resultado de la operación también forma parte del mismo conjunto de números.

Example The set of integers is closed under addition because the sum of two integers is always an integer.

Common difference The difference between consecutive terms of an arithmetic sequence.

Diferencia común La diferencia común es la diferencia entre los términos consecutivos de una progresión aritmética.

Example The common difference is 3 in the arithmetic sequence 4, 7, 10, 13, …

Completing the square The process of adding $\left(\frac{b}{2}\right)^2$ to $x^2 + bx$ to form a perfect-square trinomial.

Completar el cuadrado El proceso de sumar $\left(\frac{b}{2}\right)^2$ a $x^2 + bx$ para formar un trinomio cuadrado perfecto.

Example $x^2 + 6x - 7 = 9$ is rewritten as $(x + 3)^2 = 25$ by completing the square.

Compound inequalities Two inequalities that are joined by *and* or *or*.

Desigualdades compuestas Dos desigualdades que están enlazadas por medio de una *y* o una *o*.

Examples $5 < x$ and $x < 10$
$14 < x$ or $x \leq -3$

Compound interest Interest paid on both the principal and the interest that has already been paid.

Interés compuesto Interés calculado tanto sobre el capital como sobre los intereses ya pagados.

Example For an initial deposit of \$1,000 at a 6% interest rate with interest compounded quarterly, the function $y = 1000\left(\frac{0.06}{4}\right)^{4x}$ gives the account balance y after x years.

Conditional relative frequency The ratio of the joint frequency and the related marginal frequency.

Frecuencia relativa condicional La razón de la frecuencia conjunta y la frecuencia marginal relacionada.

Example

	Afternoon	Evening	Totals
Student	$\frac{90}{140} = 64\%$	$\frac{50}{140} = 36\%$	$\frac{140}{140} = 100\%$
Adult	$\frac{20}{60} = 33\%$	$\frac{40}{60} = 67\%$	$\frac{60}{60} = 100\%$

Constant ratio The number that an exponential function repeatedly multiplies an initial amount by.

Razón constante El número por el que una función exponencial multiplica repetidamente a una cantidad inicial.

Example In an exponential function of the form $f(x) = ab^x$, b is the constant ratio.

VISUAL GLOSSARY

English / Spanish

Continuous A graph that is unbroken.

Continua Una gráfica continua es una gráfica ininterrumpida.

Example

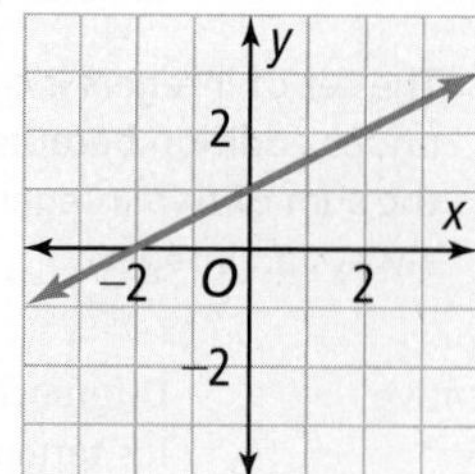

Correlation coefficient A number from −1 to 1 that tells you how closely the equation of the line of best fit models the data. It is represented by the variable, r.

Coeficiente de correlación Número de −1 a 1 que indica con cuánta exactitud la línea de mejor encaje representa los datos. Se representa con la variable r.

Example

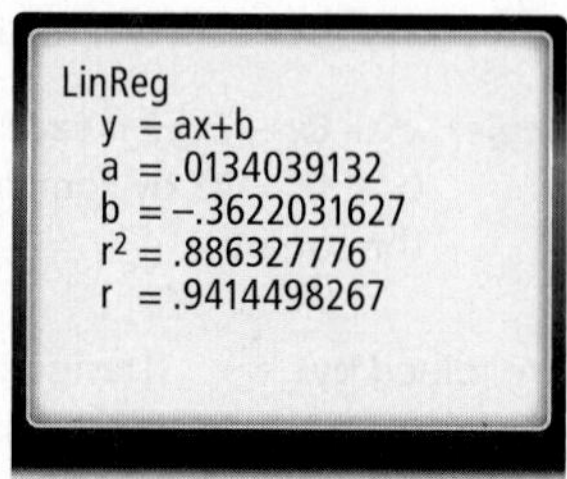

The correlation coefficient is approximately 0.94.

Cube root function $f(x) = \sqrt[3]{x}$

Función de raíz cúbica $f(x) = \sqrt[3]{x}$

Example

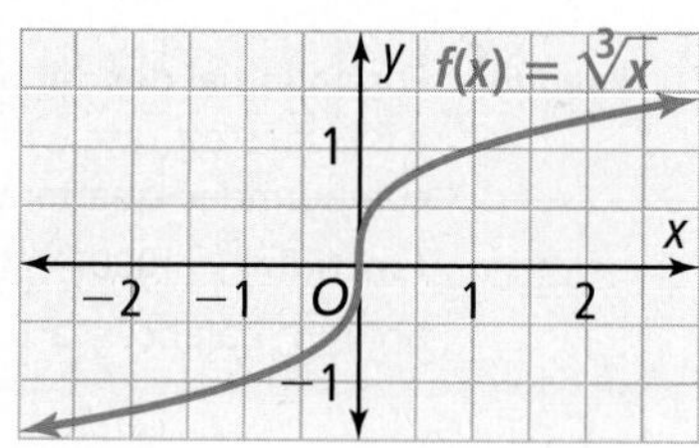

D

Decay factor 1 minus the decay rate in an exponential function when $0 < b < 1$.

Factor de decremento 1 menos la tasa de decremento en una función exponencial si $0 < b < 1$.

Example The decay factor of the function $y = 5(0.3)^x$ is 0.3.

Degree of a monomial The sum of the exponents of the variables of a monomial.

Grado de un monomio La suma de los exponentes de las variables de un monomio.

Example $-4x^3y^2$ is a monomial of degree 5.

Degree of a polynomial The highest degree of any term of the polynomial.

Grado de un polinomio El grado de un polinomio es el grado mayor de cualquier término del polinomio.

Example The polynomial $P(x) = x^6 + 2x^3 - 3$ has degree 6.

English — Spanish

Difference of two squares A difference of two squares is an expression of the form $a^2 - b^2$. It can be factored as $(a + b)(a - b)$.

Diferencia de dos cuadrados La diferencia de dos cuadrados es una expresión de la forma $a^2 - b^2$. Se puede factorizar como $(a + b)(a - b)$.

Examples $25a^2 - 4 = (5a + 2)(5a - 2)$
$m^6 - 1 = (m^3 + 1)(m^3 - 1)$

Discrete A graph composed of isolated points.

Discreta Una gráfica discreta es compuesta de puntos aislados.

Example

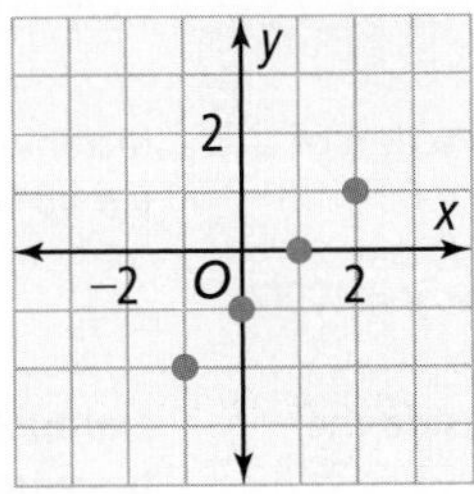

Discriminant The discriminant of a quadratic equation of the form $ax^2 + bx + c = 0$ is $b^2 - 4ac$. The value of the discriminant determines the number of solutions of the equation.

Discriminante El discriminante de una ecuación cuadrática $ax^2 + bx + c = 0$ es $b^2 - 4ac$. El valor del discriminante determina el número de soluciones de la ecuación.

Example The discriminant of $2x^2 + 9x - 2 = 0$ is 97.

Domain (of a relation or function) The possible values for the input of a relation or function.

Dominio (de una relación o función) Posibles valores de entrada de una relación o función.

Example In the function $f(x) = x + 22$, the domain is all real numbers.

E

Elements (of a set) Members of a set.

Elementos Partes integrantes de un conjunto.

Example Cats and dogs are elements of the set of mammals.

Explicit formula An explicit formula expresses the *n*th term of a sequence in terms of *n*.

Fórmula explícita Una fórmula explícita expresa el *n*-ésimo término de una progresión en función de *n*.

Example Let $a_n = 2n + 5$ for positive integers *n*. If $n = 7$, then $a_7 = 2(7) + 5 = 19$.

Exponential decay A situation modeled with a function of the form $y = ab^x$, where $a > 0$ and $0 < b < 1$.

Decremento exponencial Para $a > 0$ y $0 < b < 1$, la función $y = ab^x$ representa el decremento exponencial.

Example $y = 5(0.1)^x$

English	Spanish

Exponential function The function $f(x) = b^x$, where $b > 0$ and $b \neq 1$.

Función exponencial La función $f(x) = b^x$, donde $b > 0$ y $b \neq 1$.

Example

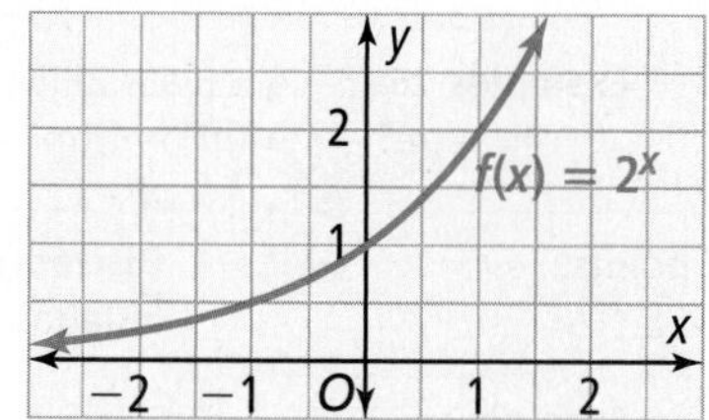

Exponential growth A situation modeled with a function of the form $y = ab^x$, where $a > 0$ and $b > 1$.

Incremento exponencial Para $a > 0$ y $b > 1$, la función $y = ab^x$ representa el incremento exponencial.

Example $y = 100(2)^x$

Extrapolation The process of predicting a value outside the range of known values.

Extrapolación Proceso que se usa para predecir un valor por fuera del ámbito de los valores dados.

F

Family of functions A group of functions that use the same common operation in their equation forms.

Familia de funciones Un grupo de funciones que usan la misma operación común en su forma de ecuación.

Example $f(x) = 3x + 7$ and $f(x) = \frac{2}{3}x - 9$ are members of the linear family of functions.

Floor function The floor function rounds numbers down to the nearest integer.

Función piso La función piso redondea los números hacia abajo al entero más cercano.

Formula An equation that states a relationship among quantities.

Fórmula Ecuación que establece una relación entre cantidades.

Example The formula for the volume V of a cylinder is $V = \pi r^2 h$, where r is the radius of the cylinder and h is its height.

Function A relation in which each element of the domain corresponds with exactly one element in the range.

Función Una relación en la cual cada elemento del dominio se corresponde con exactamente un elemento del rango.

Example Earned income is a function of the number of hours worked. If you earn \$4.50/h, then your income is expressed by the function $f(h) = 4.5h$.

Function notation A method for writing variables as a function of other variables.

Notación de una función Un método para escribir variables como una función de otras variables.

Example $f(x) = 3x - 8$ is in function notation.

English | Spanish

Geometric sequence A number sequence formed by multiplying a term in a sequence by a fixed number to find the next term.

Progresión geométrica Tipo de sucesión numérica formada al multiplicar un término de la secuencia por un número constante, para hallar el siguiente término.

Example 9, 3, 1, $\frac{1}{3}$, ... is an example of a geometric sequence.

Growth factor 1 plus the growth rate in an exponential function when $b > 1$.

Factor incremental 1 más la tasa de incremento en una función exponencial si $b > 1$.

Example The growth factor of $y = 7(1.3)^x$ is 1.3.

Identity An equation that is true for every value.

Identidad Una ecuación que es verdadera para todos los valores.

Example $5 - 14x = 5\left(1 - \frac{14}{5}x\right)$ is an identity because it is true for any value of x.

Interpolation The process of estimating a value between two known quantities.

Interpolación Proceso que se usa para estimar el valor entre dos cantidades dadas.

Inverse function If function f pairs a value b with a, then its inverse, denoted f^{-1}, pairs the value a with b. If f^{-1} is also a function, then f and f^{-1} are inverse functions.

Funcion inversa Si la función f empareja un valor b con a, entonces su inversa, cuya notación es f^{-1}, empareja el valor a con b. Si f^{-1} también es una función, entonces f y f^{-1} son funciones inversas.

Example If $f(x) = x + 3$, then $f^{-1}(x) = x - 3$.

Joint frequency The frequency of a single option for one category.

Frecuencia conjunta La frecuencia de una única opción por categoría.

Example

	Afternoon	Evening	Totals
Student	90	50	140
Adult	20	40	60
Totals	110	90	200

90, 50, 20, and 40 are joint frequencies.

Joint relative frequency The ratio, or percent, of the joint frequency to the total.

Frecuencia relativa conjunta La razón, o porcentaje, de la frecuencia conjunta al total.

Example

	Afternoon	Evening	Totals
Student	$\frac{90}{200} = 45\%$	$\frac{50}{200} = 25\%$	$\frac{140}{200} = 70\%$
Adult	$\frac{20}{200} = 10\%$	$\frac{40}{200} = 20\%$	$\frac{60}{200} = 30\%$
Totals	$\frac{110}{200} = 55\%$	$\frac{90}{200} = 45\%$	$\frac{200}{200} = 100\%$

45%, 25%, 10%, and 20% are joint relative frequencies.

VISUAL GLOSSARY

English | Spanish

Linear function A function whose graph is a line is a linear function. You can represent a linear function with a linear equation.

Función lineal Una función cuya gráfica es una recta es una función lineal. La función lineal se representa con una ecuación lineal.

Example

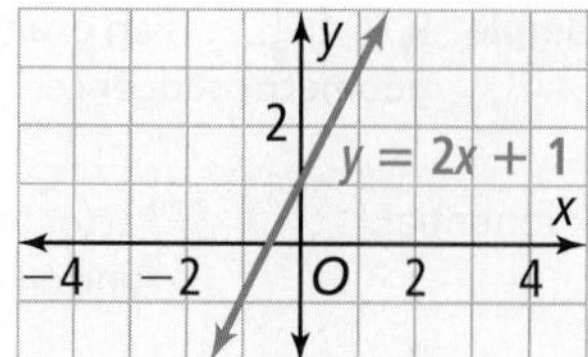

Linear inequality in two variables An inequality in two variables whose graph is a region of the coordinate plane that is bounded by a line. Each point in the region is a solution of the inequality.

Desigualdad lineal con dos variables Una desigualdad lineal es una desigualdad de dos variables cuya gráfica es una región del plano de coordenadas delimitado por una recta. Cada punto de la región es una solución de la desigualdad.

Example

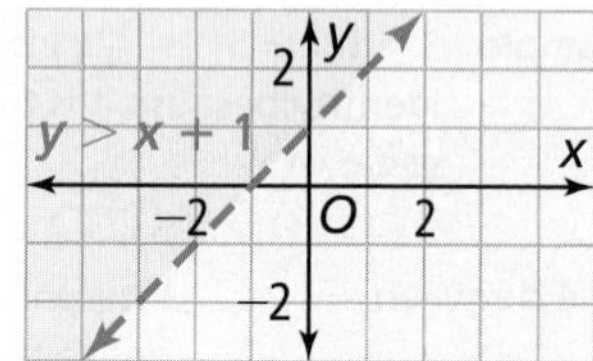

Linear-quadratic system A system of equations that includes a linear equation and a quadratic equation and is represented on a graph by the corresponding line and parabola.

Sistema cuadrático lineal Un sistema de ecuaciones que incluye una ecuación lineal y una ecuación cuadrática y se representa en una gráfica con su línea y su parábola correspondientes.

Example

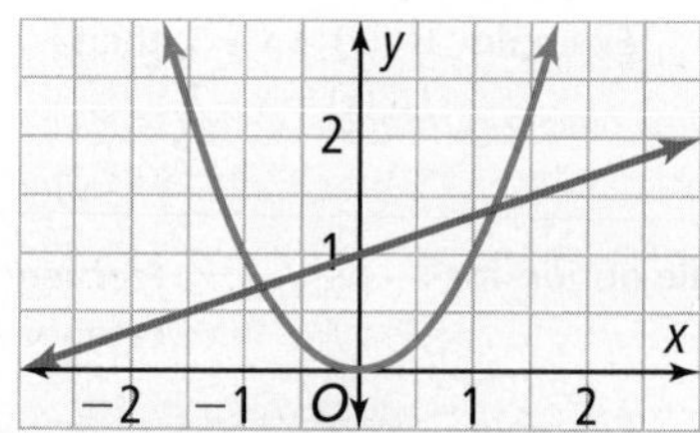

Linear regression A method used to calculate the line of best fit.

Regresión lineal Método que se utiliza para calcular la línea de mejor ajuste.

Line of best fit The most accurate trend line on a scatter plot showing the relationship between two sets of data.

Recta de mayor aproximación La línea de tendencia en un diagrama de puntos que más se acerca a los puntos que representan la relación entre dos conjuntos de datos.

Example

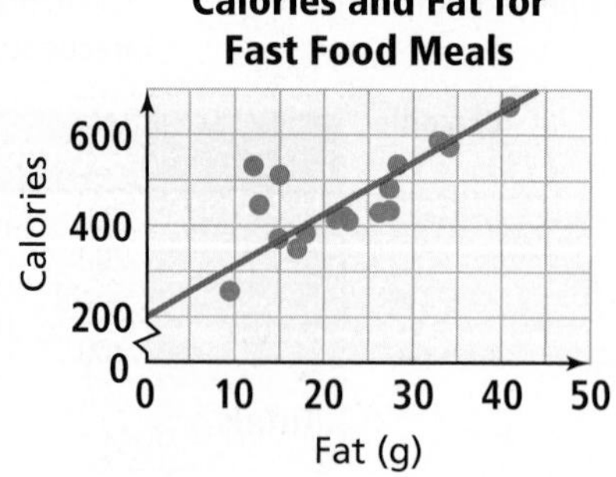

English | Spanish

Literal equation An equation expressed in variables.

Ecuación literal Ecuación que se expresa con variables.

Example $4x + 2y = 18$ is a literal equation.

M

Marginal frequency The total frequency for each option or category.

Frecuencia marginal La frecuencia total para cada opción o categoría.

Example

	Afternoon	Evening	Totals
Student	90	50	140
Adult	20	40	60
Totals	110	90	200

140, 60, 110, and 90 are marginal frequencies.

Marginal relative frequency The ratio, or percent, of the marginal frequency to the total.

Frecuencia relativa marginal La razón, o porcentaje, de la frecuencia marginal al total.

Example

	Afternoon	Evening	Totals
Student	$\frac{90}{200} = 45\%$	$\frac{50}{200} = 25\%$	$\frac{140}{200} = 70\%$
Adult	$\frac{20}{200} = 10\%$	$\frac{40}{200} = 20\%$	$\frac{60}{200} = 30\%$
Totals	$\frac{110}{200} = 55\%$	$\frac{90}{200} = 45\%$	$\frac{200}{200} = 100\%$

70%, 30%, 55%, and 45% are marginal relative frequencies.

Monomial A real number, a variable, or a product of a real number and one or more variables with whole-number exponents.

Monomio Número real, variable o el producto de un número real y una o más variables con números enteros como exponentes.

Example 9, n, and $-5xy^2$ are examples of monomials.

N

Negative association When y-values tend to decrease as x-values increase, the two data sets have a negative association.

Asociación negativa Cuando los valores de y tienden a disminuir a medida que los valores de x aumentan, los dos conjuntos de datos tienen una asociación negativa.

Example

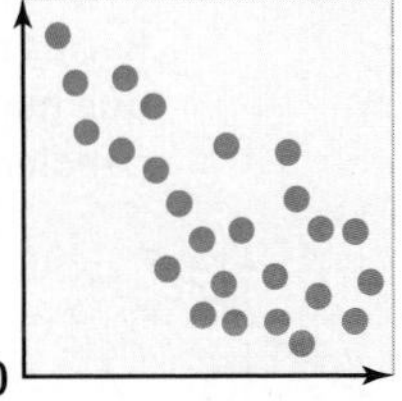

Negative correlation When data with a negative association are modeled with a line, there is a negative correlation.

Correlación negativa Cuando los datos que tienen una asociación negativa se representan con una línea, hay una correlación negativa.

Example

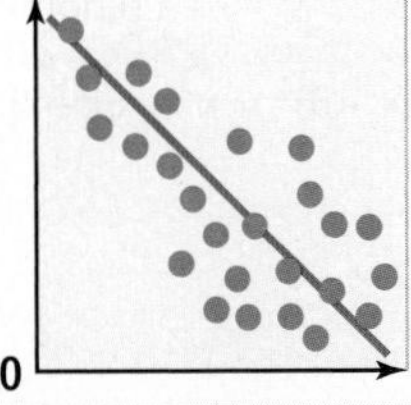

VISUAL GLOSSARY

English	Spanish

No association When there is no general relationship between x-values and y-values, the two data sets have no association.

Sin asociación Cuando no existe ninguna relación general entre los valores de x y los valores de y, los dos conjuntos de datos no tienen ninguna asociación.

Example

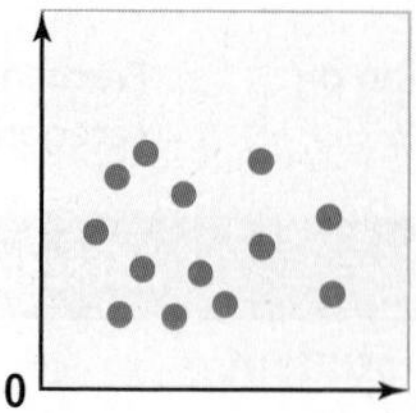

Normal distribution A normal distribution shows data that vary randomly from the mean in the pattern of a bell-shaped curve.

Distribución normal Una distribución normal muestra, con una curva en forma de campana, datos que varían alcatoriamento respecto de la media.

Example

Distribution of Test Scores

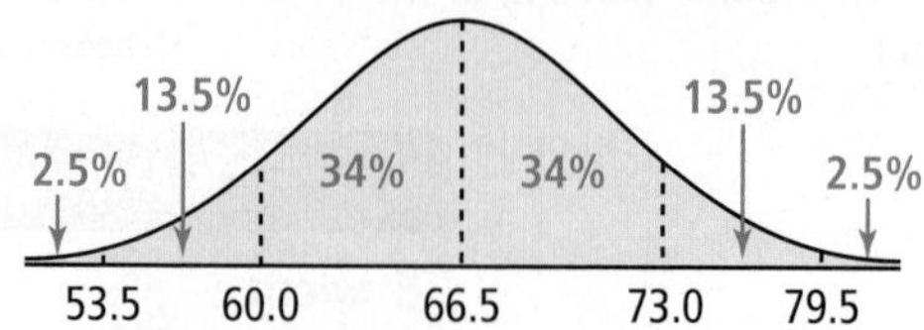

In a class of 200 students, the scores on a test were normally distributed. The mean score was 66.5 and the standard deviation was 6.5. The number of students who scored greater than 73 percent was about 13.5% + 2.5% of those who took the test.
16% of 200 = 32
About 32 students scored 73 or higher on the test.

P

Parabola The graph of a quadratic function.

Parábola La gráfica de una función cuadrática.

Example

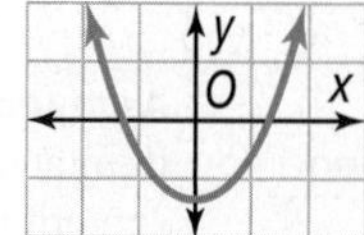

Parallel lines Two lines in the same plane that never intersect. Parallel lines have the same slope.

Rectas paralelas Dos rectas situadas en el mismo plano que nunca se cortan. Las rectas paralelas tienen la misma pendiente.

Example

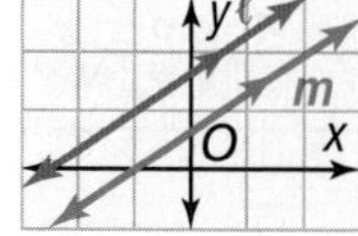

Perfect-square trinomial Any trinomial of the form $a^2 + 2ab + b^2$ or $a^2 - 2ab + b^2$. It is the result when a binomial is squared.

Trinomio cuadrado perfecto Todo trinomio de la forma $a^2 + 2ab + b^2$ ó $a^2 - 2ab + b^2$. Es el resultado cuando un binomio se eleva al cuadrado.

Example $(x + 3)^2 = x^2 + 6x + 9$

English	Spanish

Perpendicular lines Lines that intersect to form right angles. Two lines are perpendicular if the product of their slopes is –1.

Rectas perpendiculares Rectas que forman ángulos rectos en su intersección. Dos rectas son perpendiculares si el producto de sus pendientes es –1.

Example

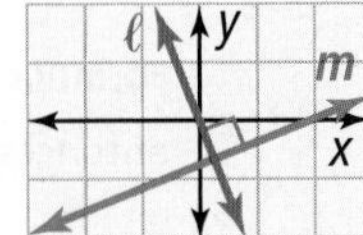

Piecewise-defined function A piecewise-defined function has different rules for different parts of its domain.

Función definida por fragmentos Una función definida por fragmentos tiene reglas diferentes para diferentes partes de su dominio.

Point-slope form A linear equation of a nonvertical line written as $y - y_1 = m(x - x_1)$. The line passes through the point (x_1, y_1) with slope m.

Forma punto-pendiente La ecuación lineal de una recta no vertical que pasa por el punto (x_1, y_1) con pendiente m está dada por $y - y_1 = m(x - x_1)$.

Example An equation with a slope of $-\frac{1}{2}$ passing through (2, –1) would be written $y + 1 = -\frac{1}{2}(x - 2)$ in point-slope form.

Polynomial A monomial or the sum or difference of two or more monomials.

Polinomio Un monomio o la suma o diferencia de dos o más monomios.

Example $2x^2$, $3x + 7$, 28, and $-7x^3 - 2x^2 + 9$ are all polynomials.

Positive association When y-values tend to increase as x-values increase, the two data sets have a positive association.

Asociación positiva Cuando los valores de y tienden a aumentar a medida que los valores de x aumentan, los dos conjuntos de datos tienen una asociación positiva.

Example

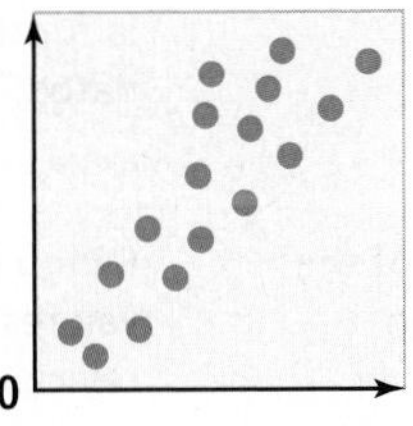

Positive correlation When data with a positive association are modeled with a line, there is a positive correlation.

Correlación positiva Cuando los datos que tienen una asociación positiva se representan con una línea, hay una correlación positiva.

Example

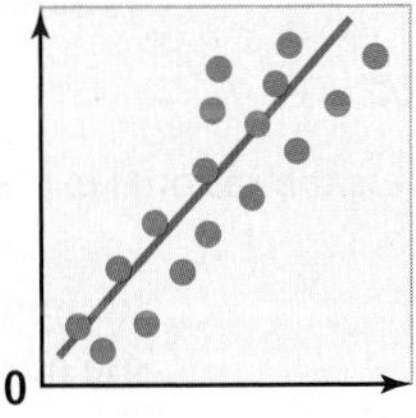

Product Property of Square Roots $\sqrt{ab} = \sqrt{a} \cdot \sqrt{b}$, when both a and b are greater than or equal to 0.

Propiedad del producto de las raíces cuadradas $\sqrt{ab} = \sqrt{a} \cdot \sqrt{b}$, cuando tanto a como b son mayores que o iguales a 0.

Example $\sqrt{16 \cdot 25} = \sqrt{16} \cdot \sqrt{25}$

English | Spanish

Quadratic equation An equation of the second degree.

Ecuación cuadrática Una ecuación de segundo grado.

Example $4x^2 + 9x - 5 = 0$

Quadratic formula If $ax^2 + bx + c = 0$ and $a \neq 0$, then $x = \frac{-b \pm \sqrt{b^2 - 4ac}}{2a}$.

Fórmula cuadrática Si $ax^2 + bx + c = 0$ y $a \neq 0$, entonces $x = \frac{-b \pm \sqrt{b^2 - 4ac}}{2a}$.

Example $2x^2 + 10x + 12 = 0$

$$x = \frac{-b \pm \sqrt{b^2 - 4ac}}{2a}$$

$$x = \frac{-10 \pm \sqrt{10^2 - 4(2)(12)}}{2(2)}$$

$$x = \frac{-10 \pm \sqrt{4}}{4}$$

$$x = \frac{-10 + 2}{4} \text{ or } \frac{-10 - 2}{4}$$

$$x = -2 \text{ or } -3$$

Quadratic function A function of the form $y = ax^2 + bx + c$, where $a \neq 0$. The graph of a quadratic function is a parabola, a U-shaped curve that opens up or down.

Función cuadrática La función $y = ax^2 + bx + c$, en la que $a \neq 0$. La gráfica de una función cuadrática es una parábola, o curva en forma de U que se abre hacia arriba o hacia abajo.

Example $y = 5x^2 - 2x + 1$ is a quadratic function.

Quadratic parent function The simplest quadratic function $f(x) = x^2$ or $y = x^2$.

Función cuadrática madre La función cuadrática más simple $f(x) = x^2$ ó $y = x^2$.

Example $y = x^2$ is the parent function for the family of quadratic equations of the form $y = ax^2 + bx + c$.

Quadratic regression A method used to find the quadratic function that best fits a data set.

Regresión cuadrática Método que se utiliza para hallar la función cuadrática que se ajusta mejor a un conjunto de datos.

Range (of a relation or function) The possible values of the output, or dependent variable, of a relation or function.

Rango (de una relación o función) El conjunto de todos los valores posibles de la salida, o variable dependiente, de una relación o función.

Example In the function $y = |x|$, the range is the set of all nonnegative numbers.

Rational exponent Another way to express radicals.

Exponente racional Otra forma de expresar los radicales.

Example $\sqrt[3]{x} = x^{\frac{1}{3}}$

$\frac{1}{3}$ is the rational exponent.

Reciprocal The reciprocal of a number is 1 divided by that number.

Recíproco El recíproco de un número es 1 dividido entre ese número.

Example $\frac{2}{5}$ and $\frac{5}{2}$ are reciprocals because $1 \div \frac{2}{5} = \frac{5}{2}$.

English | Spanish

Recursive formula A recursive formula defines the terms in a sequence by relating each term to the ones before it. It is composed of an initial value and a rule for generating the sequence.

Fórmula recursiva Una fórmula recursiva define los términos de una secuencia al relacionar cada término con los términos que lo anteceden. Está compuesta por un valor inicial y una regla para generar la secuencia.

Example Let $a_n = 2.5a_{n-1} + 3a_{n-2}$.
If $a_5 = 3$ and $a_4 = 7.5$, then
$a_6 = 2.5(3) + 3(7.5) = 30$.

Relation Any set of ordered pairs.

Relación Cualquier conjunto de pares ordenados.

Example {(0, 0), (2, 3), (2, − 7)} is a relation.

Residual The difference between the *y*-value of a data point and the corresponding *y*-value of a model for the data set.

Residuo La diferencia entre el valor de *y* de un punto y el valor de *y* correspondiente a ese punto en el modelo del conjunto de datos.

Root The input values for which the related function is zero.

Ráiz Los valores de entrada para los cuales la función relacionada es cero.

S

Sequence An ordered list of numbers that often forms a pattern.

Progresión Lista ordenada de números que muchas veces forma un patrón.

Example −4, 5, 14, 23 is a sequence.

Set A well-defined collection of elements.

Conjunto Un grupo bien definido de elementos.

Example The set of integers:
{. . . , −3, −2, −1, 0, 1, 2, 3, . . .}

Simple interest Interest paid only on the principal.

Interés simple Intéres basado en el capital solamente.

Example The interest on $1,000 at 6% for 5 years is $1,000(0.06)5 = $300.

Slope-intercept form The slope-intercept form of a linear equation is $y = mx + b$, where m is the slope of the line and b is the *y*-intercept.

Forma pendiente-intercepto La forma pendiente-intercepto es la ecuación lineal $y = mx + b$, en la que m es la pendiente de la recta y b es el punto de intersección de esa recta con el eje *y*.

Example $y = 8x - 2$

Solution of an inequality in two variables Any ordered pair that makes the inequality true.

Solución de una desigualdad con dos variables Cualquier par ordenado que haga verdadera la desigualdad.

Example Each ordered pair in the yellow area and on the solid red line is a solution of $3x - 5y \leq 10$.

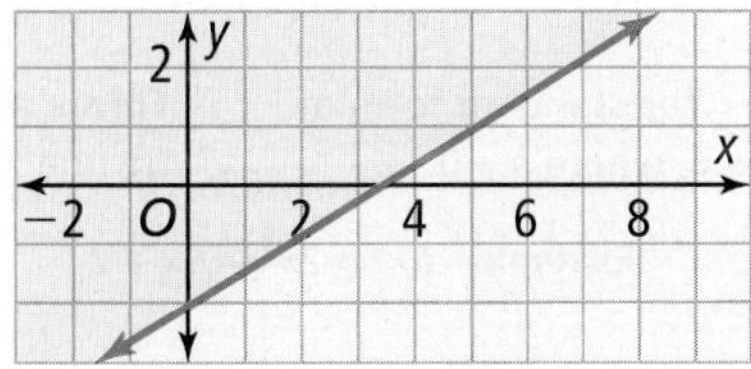

English | Spanish

Solution of a system of linear inequalities Any ordered pair that makes all of the inequalities in the system true.

Solución de un sistema de desigualdades lineales Todo par ordenado que hace verdaderas todas las desigualdades del sistema.

Example

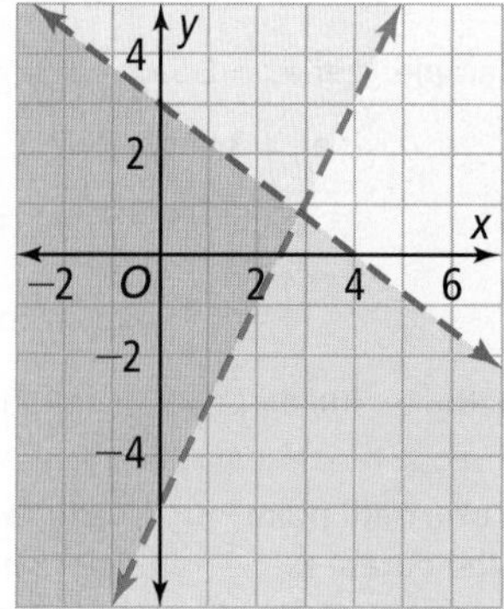

The shaded green area shows the solution of the system $\begin{matrix} y > 2x - 5 \\ 3x + 4y < 12 \end{matrix}$.

Square root function A function that contains the independent variable in the radicand.

Función de raíz cuadrada Una función que contiene la variable independiente en el radicando.

Example $y = \sqrt{2x}$ is a square root function.

Standard deviation A measure of how data varies, or deviates, from the mean.

Desviación típica Medida de cómo los datos varían, o se desvían, de la media.

Example Use the following formula to find the standard deviation.

$$\sigma = \sqrt{\frac{\Sigma(x - \bar{x})^2}{n}}$$

Standard form of a linear equation The standard form of a linear equation is $Ax + By = C$, where A, B, and C are real numbers and A and B are not both zero.

Forma normal de una ecuación lineal La forma normal de una ecuación lineal es $Ax + By = C$, donde A, B y C son números reales, y donde A y B no son iguales a cero.

Example $6x - y = 12$

Standard form of a polynomial The form of a polynomial that places the terms in descending order by degree.

Forma normal de un polinomio Cuando el grado de los términos de un polinomio disminuye de izquierda a derecha, está en forma normal, o en orden descendente.

Example $15x^3 + x^2 + 3x + 9$

Standard form of a quadratic equation The standard form of a quadratic equation is $ax^2 + bx + c = 0$, where $a \neq 0$.

Forma normal de una ecuación cuadrática Cuando una ecuación cuadrática se expresa de forma $ax^2 + bx + c = 0$.

Example $-x^2 + 2x - 9 = 0$

Standard form of a quadratic function The standard form of a quadratic function is $f(x) = ax^2 + bx + C$, where $a \neq 0$.

Forma normal de una función cuadrática La forma normal de una función cuadrática es $f(x) = ax^2 + bx + C$, donde $a \neq 0$.

Example $f(x) = 2x^2 - 5x + 2$

Step-function A step-function pairs every number in an interval with a single value. The graph of a step function can look like the steps of a staircase.

Función escalón Una función escalón empareja cada número de un intervalo con un solo valor. La gráfica de una función escalón se puede parecer a los peldaños de una escalera.

English | Spanish

Subset A subset of a set consists of elements from the given set.

Subconjunto Un subconjunto de un conjunto consiste en elementos del conjunto dado.

Example If $B = \{1, 2, 3, 4, 5, 6, 7\}$ and $A = \{1, 2, 5\}$, then A is a subset of B.

System of linear inequalities Two or more linear inequalities using the same variables.

Sistema de desigualdades lineales Dos o más desigualdades lineales que usen las mismas variables.

Example $y \leq x + 11$
$y < 5x$

T

Term of a sequence A term of a sequence is any number in a sequence.

Término de una progresión Un término de una secuencia es cualquier número de una secuencia.

Example −4 is the first term of the sequence −4, 5, 14, 23.

Transformation A transformation of a function maps each point of its graph to a new location.

Transformación Una transformación de una función desplaza cada punto de su gráfica a una ubicación nueva.

Example Transformations can be translations, rotations, reflections, or dilations.

Translation A transformation that shifts the graph of a function the same distance horizontally, vertically, or both.

Translación Proceso de mover una gráfica horizontalmente, verticalmente o en ambos sentidos.

Example

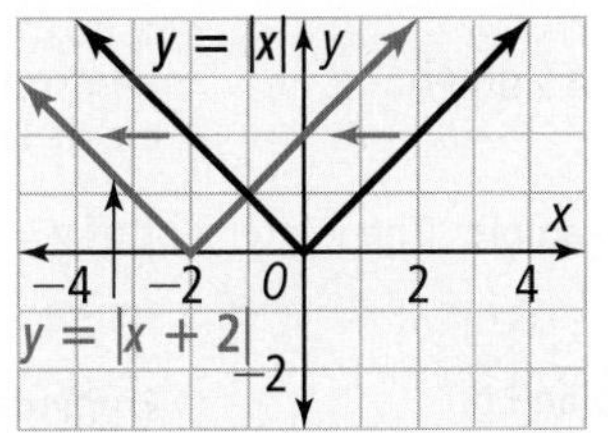

$y = |x + 2|$ is a translation of $y = |x|$.

Trend line A line that models the data in a scatter plot by showing the general direction of the data.

Línea de tendencia Una línea que representa los datos en un diagrama de puntos y muestra la dirección general de los datos.

Example

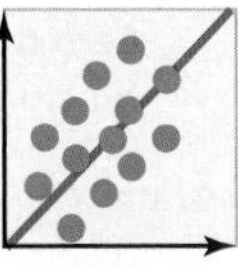

Positive

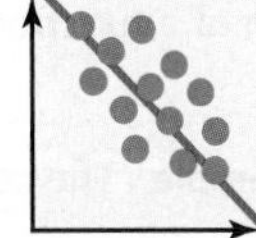

Negative

V

Variance The mean of the squares of the difference between each data value and the mean.

Varianza La media de los cuadrados de la diferencia entre cada valor de los datos y la media.

Example

x	18	25	18	10	17	15	18	15
$\overline{x}$	17	17	17	17	17	17	17	17
$x - \overline{x}$	1	8	1	−7	0	−2	1	−2
$(x - \overline{x})^2$	1	64	1	49	0	4	1	4

The variance is $s^2 = \frac{1 + 64 + 1 + 49 + 0 + 4 + 1 + 4}{7}$.

English	Spanish

Vertex The highest or lowest point on the graph of a function.

Vértice El punto más alto o más bajo de la gráfica de una función.

Example

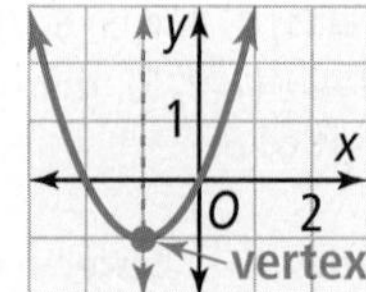

Vertex form of a quadratic function The function $f(x) = a(x - h)^2 + k$, where $a \neq 0$. The vertex of the graph is at (h, k).

Forma canónica de una función cuadrática La función $f(x) = a(x - h)^2 + k$, donde $a \neq 0$. El vértice de la gráfica está en (h, k).

Example If the vertex form of a function is $f(x) = 5(x + 3)^2 + 7$, the vertex of the graph is $(-3, 7)$.

Vertical motion model The vertical motion model is the quadratic function $h(t) = -16t^2 + v_0t + h_0$. The variable h represents the height of an object, in feet, t seconds after it is launched into the air. The term v_0 is the object's initial velocity and h_0 is its initial height.

Modelo de movimiento vertical El modelo de movimiento vertical es la función cuadrática $h(t) = -16t^2 + v_0t + h_0$. La variable h representa la altura en pies de un objeto t segundos después de lanzarlo al aire. El término v_0 es la velocidad inicial del objeto y h_0 es su altura inicial.

Example If an object is launched from a height of 10 ft with an initial velocity of 8 ft/s, then the equation of the object's height over time is $h(t) = -16t^2 + 8t + 10$.

Y

y-intercept The y-coordinate of a point where a graph crosses the y-axis.

Intercepto en y Coordenada y por donde la gráfica cruza el eje de las y.

Example The y-intercept of $y = 5x + 2$ is 2.

Z

Zero-Product Property For all real numbers a and b, if $ab = 0$, then $a = 0$ or $b = 0$.

Propiedad del producto cero Para todos los números reales a y b, si $ab = 0$, entonces $a = 0$ ó $b = 0$.

Example $x(x + 3) = 0$

$x = 0$ or $x + 3 = 0$

$x = 0$ or $x = -3$

Zero of a function An x-intercept of the graph of a function.

Cero de una función Intercepto x de la gráfica de una función.

Example The zeros of $y = x^2 - 4$ are ± 2.

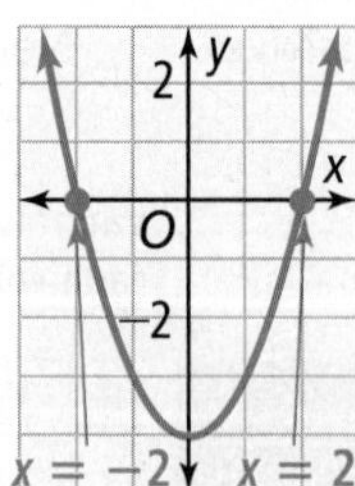

Index

E

F

G

H

I

J

L

M

INDEX

T

V

W

X

Y

Z

Acknowledgments

Photographs

Cover:
CVR Ociacia/Shutterstock;

Topic 01:
003 Ut/crissy pascual/zuma press,inc./Alamy Stock Photo; **026** Bonetta/iStock/Getty Images; **032L** Neirfy/Fotolia; **032R** Smspsy/Fotolia; **039L** Photosindia Batch5/PhotosIndia.com LLC/ Alamy Stock Photo; **039R** Photosindia Collection/Getty Images; **043** Maridav/Fotolia;

Topic 02:
055 FStop Images GmbH/Alamy Stock Photo; **068** Pbpvision/Alamy Stock Photo; **082** Mariusz Szczygiel/Fotolia;

Topic 03:
087 Mike Kemp/Rubberball/Getty Images; **097** Tracy King/Fotolia; **098** Matousekfoto/Fotolia; **099** Mevans/E+/Getty Images; **102** Foryouinf/iStock/Getty Images; **112** Vadim Petrakov/ Shutterstock/Asset Library; **117** Photolife2016/Fotolia; **125** Bogdan Wankowicz/Shutterstock/ Asset Library;

Topic 04:
141 Jeff Greenberg/PhotoEdit; **151B** Oliver Gerhard/Alamy Stock Photo; **151T** Juliaphoto/ Fotolia; **153** Travis Manley/Fotolia; **154L** F9photos/Fotolia; **154R** Alexander Fediachov/ Shutterstock; **161** Kravka/Shutterstock; **164** Jenny Thompson/Fotolia;

Topic 05:
181 Maridav/Fotolia; **209T** Hamdan/Shutterstock; **209B** Natallia Vintsik/Fotolia;

Topic 06:
215 Tomas del amo/Alamy Stock Photo; **222L** Gareth Boden/Pearson Education Ltd.; **222R** Gareth Boden/Pearson Education Ltd.; **223T** Dmussman/Shutterstock; **223B** Cultura Creative/ Alamy Stock Photo; **224L** Pearson Education, Inc.; **224R** Pearson Education, Inc.; **231** Luminis/ Fotolia; **235** Moosehenderson/Fotolia; **238** Tom Gilks/Alamy Stock Photo; **245** Grant Faint/ Photographer's Choice/Getty Images;

Topic 07:
259 Agencja Fotograficzna Caro/Alamy Stock Photo; **265** Paul White/UK Industries/Alamy Stock Photo; **273** Gunter Marx/BI/Alamy Stock Photo; **282T** Vittorio Valletta/Agf Srl/ Alamy Stock Photo; **282B** Asiapics/Alamy Stock Photo; **284** Monkey Business/Fotolia; **285** Redsnapper/Alamy Stock Photo; **288** Design56/123RF; **297** Brian Kinney/Shutterstock; **302** Jose Luis Stephens/Alamy Stock Photo

Topic 08:
315 Larry w. Smith/epa/Newscom; **321** Larry w. Smith/epa/Newscom; **323** Studio Source/Alamy Stock Photo; **333** Wdg Photo/Shutterstock;

Topic 09:
383 Mario Hagen/Shutterstock; **386** Floresco Productions/Cultura RM/Alamy Stock Photo;

Topic 10:
413 Marco Diaz Segura/Shutterstock; **416** Joern Sackermann/Alamy Stock Photo; **419** Jason Edwards/National Geographic/Getty Images; **419** Efrain Padro/Alamy Stock Photo; **422** Double Photo Studio/Shutterstock; **433** DariosStudio/Alamy Stock Photo; **445** Konstantin Trubavin/123RF; **449** Frederic Cirou/PhotoAlto/Alamy Stock Photo; **452L** Apopium/Fotolia; **452R** Marc Xavier/Fotolia; **455** Erick Nguyen/Alamy Stock Photo; **458** World Foto/Alamy Stock Photo;

Acknowledgments

Topic 11:
490T MaxyM/Shutterstock; **490B** Kanonsky/Fotolia;

STEM

STEM Andrew Orlemann/Shutterstock; STEM Alexander Y/Shutterstock; STEM Andrii Gorulko/Shutterstock; STEM Aksonov/E+/Getty Images; STEM Andrew Orlemann/Shutterstock; STEM Samuel Borges Photography/Shutterstock; STEM Noppawan09/Shutterstock; STEM Michael Simons/123RF; STEM Aleksandar Mijatovic/Shutterstock; STEM Halfpoint/Shutterstock; STEM Pixelyuk/Shutterstock; STEM Diyanadimitrova/Fotolia; STEM Gyuszko-Photo/Shutterstock; STEM Zstockphotos/123RF; STEM RTimages/Alamy Stock Photo; STEM Dikobraziy/Shutterstock; STEM Gst/Shutterstock; STEM Bjoern Wylezich/Shutterstock; STEM Bjoern Wylezich/Shutterstock; STEM Bjoern Wylezich/Shutterstock; STEM Igor Filonenko/Alamy Stock Photo; STEM Air Images/Shutterstock; STEM Sasa Prudkov/Shutterstock; STEM SATJA2506/Shutterstock; STEM Spline_x/Shutterstock; STEM Svitlana-ua/Shutterstock; STEM Piotr Malczyk/Alamy Stock Photo; STEM M. Unal Ozmen/Shutterstock; STEM Konstantin Gushcha/Shutterstock; STEM Zocchi Roberto/Shutterstock; STEM Roger Bacon/Reuters/Alamy Stock Photo; STEM Maksimilian/Shutterstock; STEM Robert/Fotolia; STEM Clarence Holmes Wildlife/Alamy Stock Photo; STEM Bjoern Wylezich/Shutterstock; STEM Bjoern Wylezich/Shutterstock; STEM Bjoern Wylezich/Shutterstock; STEM Bjoern Wylezich/Shutterstock; STEM Bjoern Wylezich/Shutterstock; STEM Aina Zimnika/Fotolia; STEM Jultud/Fotolia; STEM Arrows/Fotolia; STEM Andrey Armyagov/Shutterstock; STEM 1r1ska/Shutterstock; STEM Robuart/Shutterstock; STEM Pedro Alexandre Teixeira/Shutterstock; STEM Veronchick84/Shutterstock; STEM Sean Pavone/Shutterstock; STEM Bjoern Wylezich/Shutterstock;